The University of Chicago School Mathematics Project

Transition Mathematics

Teacher's Edition

Authors

Zalman Usiskin

and

James Flanders
Cathy Hynes
Lydia Polonsky
Susan Porter
Steven Viktora

About the Cover
If a person runs at a constant speed, then the graph of the
ordered pairs (time, distance) is a line. This example combines algebra
and geometry with applied arithmetic–
a major theme of this book.

ScottForesman
Editorial Offices: Glenview, Illinois   Regional Offices: Sunnyvale, California •
Tucker, Georgia • Glenview, Illinois • Oakland, New Jersey • Dallas, Texas

Acknowledgments

Authors

Zalman Usiskin
Professor of Education, The University of Chicago

James Flanders
UCSMP

Cathy Hynes
Mathematics Teacher, The University of Chicago Laboratory Schools

Lydia Polonsky
UCSMP

Susan Porter
Mathematics Teacher, Evanston Township H.S., Evanston, Illinois

Steven S. Viktora
Chairman, Mathematics Department, New Trier H.S., Winnetka, IL

UCSMP Production and Evaluation:

Series Editors: Zalman Usiskin, Sharon L. Senk

Managing Editor: Natalie Jakucyn

Technical Coordinator: Susan Chang

Evaluation Component Directors: Larry Hedges, Susan Stodolsky

Director of the Field Trial Evaluation: Kathryn Sloane

Director of the Nationwide Evaluation: Sandra Mathison

Assistant to the Directors: Penelope Flores

Teacher's Edition Additional Author: Sharon Mallo
Lake Park H.S. East, Roselle, Illinois

Editorial Development and Design

ScottForesman staff, Paragraphics Inc., PROVIZION

We wish to acknowledge the generous support of the **Amoco Foundation** in helping to make it possible for these materials to be developed and tested, and the additional support of the **Carnegie Corporation of New York** in the nationwide field-testing of these materials.

ISBN: 0-673-33406-6

CONTENTS   Teacher's Edition

The complete Contents for the Student Edition begins on page *vi*.

Note:
The **Professional Sourcebook** is located at the back of the Teacher's Edition.

UCSMP Helps You Update Your Curriculum and Better Prepare Your Students!

As reports from national commissions have shown, students currently are not learning enough mathematics, and the curriculum has not kept pace with changes in mathematics and its applications.

In response to these problems, UCSMP has developed a complete program for grades 7-12 that upgrades the school mathematics experience for the average student. The usual four-year high-school mathematics content—and much more—is spread out over six years. The result is that students learn more mathematics and they are better prepared for the variety of mathematics they will encounter in their future mathematics courses and in life.

In addition, UCSMP helps students view their study of mathematics as worthwhile, as full of interesting information, as related to almost every endeavor. With applications as a hallmark of all UCSMP materials, students no longer ask, "How does this topic apply to the world I know?"

For a complete description of the series, see pages **T19-T52** at the back of the **Teacher's Edition.**

In short, UCSMP...

Prepares students to use mathematics effectively in today's world.

Promotes independent thinking and learning.

Helps students improve their performance.

Provides the practical support you need.

"I believe that by the end of this year my 7th graders will know more math than any kids I have taught so far, in any class. I think they probably know more right now than most of my pre-algebra kids have in the past."

Mary Nelson, teacher, Jason Lee School, Vancouver, WA

Imagine using a text that has been developed as part of a coherent 7-12 curriculum design, one that has been tested on a large scale *before* publication, and most important, has bolstered students' mathematical abilities, which is reflected in test scores. Read on to find out how UCSMP has done that, and more.

For a detailed discussion of the development and testing of **Transition Mathematics,** see pages **T46-T50.**

Years of field-testing and use have brought impressive results. Experience these results in the new 1992 Edition!

UNIQUE DEVELOPMENT   This book was developed at the University of Chicago with funds provided by the Amoco Foundation and the Carnegie Corporation of New York.

PLANNING   Initial planning was done with input from professors, classroom teachers, school administrators, and district and state supervisors of mathematics, along with the recommendations by national commissions and international studies. In particular, the UCSMP secondary curriculum is the first full mathematics curriculum to implement the recommendations of the NCTM Standards committees.

AUTHORSHIP   Authors were chosen for expertise in the relevant areas of school mathematics and for classroom experience. Dr. Zalman Usiskin, Professor of Education at the University of Chicago, is the director of UCSMP and coordinated the writing of these materials.

FIELD-TESTING AND EVALUATION   Pilot testing began with teaching and revising based on firsthand experience by the initial team of authors. Then, evaluation was made from local studies, and the materials were revised again. Further evaluation and revisions were based on national studies. The **Scott, Foresman 1992 Edition** includes the further enhancements of updated data, additional teacher notes, a Transition Mathematics Teacher Kit with Manipulative Activities Sourcebook, a Transition Mathematics Manipulative Kit, and a Transition Mathematics Quiz and Test Writer.

The Perfect Transition from Arithmetic to Algebra and Geometry

Transition Mathematics is designed to attract and keep students in mathematics —not to weed them out. It consolidates the arithmetic of the previous grades and at the same time prepares students for algebra and geometry.

Consistent organization leads to mastery

The following features are built into every lesson, providing a consistent path for learning.

Lesson Introduction

gets students reading mathematics on a daily basis. Provided are key concepts, relevant vocabulary, and meaningful examples for students to read and discuss. Topics are placed in real-world settings so students know why they are studying them.

LESSON

8-1

Bar Graphs

According to the preliminary figures of the 1990 U.S. Census, about 3.5 million people of Asian or Pacific Islander ancestry were living in the U.S. in 1990. This number includes 806,000 Chinese; 775,000 Filipinos; 701,000 Japanese; 355,000 Koreans; 262,000 Vietnamese; 260,000 Pacific Islanders; and 170,000 of other nationalities.

The preceding paragraph shows numerical information in **prose** writing. Prose allows a person to insert opinions and extra information. It is the usual way you are taught to write.

Numbers in paragraphs are not always easy to follow. Many people prefer to see numbers displayed. One common display is the **bar graph**.

Example 1 Display the above numerical information in a bar graph.

Solution Step 1: Every bar graph is based on a number line. Draw a number line with a *uniform scale*. A uniform scale is one where numbers that are equally spaced differ by the same amount. Below, the *interval* of the scale is 100,000 people. This interval is chosen so that all of the numbers will fit on the graph.

Step 2: Graph each of the numbers.

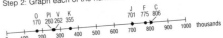

Step 3: Draw a segment from 0 to each number. Each segment is a *bar* of the bar graph. Then raise each bar above the number line.

336

Four Kinds of Questions

provide a variety of contexts, encouraging students to think about each problem.

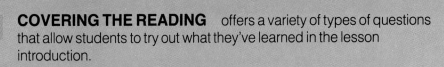

COVERING THE READING offers a variety of types of questions that allow students to try out what they've learned in the lesson introduction.

APPLYING THE MATHEMATICS offers real-world and other applications of the lesson concepts.

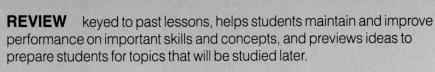

REVIEW keyed to past lessons, helps students maintain and improve performance on important skills and concepts, and previews ideas to prepare students for topics that will be studied later.

EXPLORATION extends the lesson content, offering an interesting variety of applications, generalizations, and extensions, including open-ended experiments, research, and much more.

Questions

Covering the Reading

In 1–3, **a.** write the decimal in English and **b.** convert the decimal to a fraction.

1. 8.27   **2.** 630.5   **3.** 0.001

4. The probability of a single birth being a boy is about .52. Convert this number to a percent.

In 5 and 6, convert to a percent.

5. 0.724   **6.** 8

7. 3.14 is an approximation to π. Convert this number to a fraction.

8. Write 2.35 as a fraction in lowest terms.

9. About 1/4 of all families with two children are likely to have two girls. What percent of families is this?

10. The cost of living in 1988 was about $3\frac{1}{3}$ times what it was in 1970. What percent is this?

Applying the Mathematics

11. Write 4.2/1.04 as a fraction in lowest terms.

12. Ariel put 6.5 gallons of gasoline in a 12-gallon gas tank. So the tank is 6.5/12 full. What simple fraction of the tank is this?

13. A money market account at a local bank pays 6.75% interest. What fraction is this?

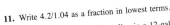

In 14–17, complete the table. Put fractions in lowest terms.

	Fraction	Decimal	Percent
	1/2	0.5	50%
14.	?	?	9.8%
15.	?	3.2	?
16.	5/16	?	?
17.	?	0.27	?

Review

18. Find twelve percent of ten thousand. *(Lessons 1-1, 2-6)*

19. Would you prefer to buy something at 30% off or 1/3 off? *(Lesson 2-6)*

In 20–22, calculate. *(Lessons 2-1, 2-2, 2-6)*

20. $1918.37 \times 10,000$ **21.** 14% of 231   **22.** 3^5

In 23 and 24, give the word name for the decimal. *(Lesson 2-1)*

23. One followed by nine zeros

24. One followed by fifteen zeros

25. Order from smallest to largest: .011, 1/10, 1/100. *(Lessons 1-2, 1-8)*

In 26–28, rewrite the number in scientific notation. *(Lesson 2-3)*

26. 3,320,000 square miles, the approximate area of the Sahara desert

27. 27,878,400 square feet, the number of square feet in a square mile

28. 525,600 minutes, the number of minutes in a 365-day year

29. Leslie used 30% of her $5.00 allowance to buy a magazine. How much did the magazine cost? *(Lesson 2-6)*

In 30–32, write the numbers as decimals. *(Lessons 1-1, 2-2, 2-5)*

30. fifty-million fifty

31. 2.4×10^5

32. 3200%

Exploration

33. Examine this sequence of numbers.
```
0.5
0.2 5
0.1 2 5
0.0 6 2 5
0.0 3 1 2 5
0.0 1 5 6 2 5
0.0 0 7 8 1 2 5
0.0 0 3 9 0 6 2 5
0.0 0 1 9 5 3 1 2 5
```
a. Find a pattern and describe it in words.
b. What is the next number in the sequence?

Prepares Students to Use Mathematics Effectively in Today's World

"If I wrote a textbook, this is what I'd write, because it makes kids know what they're going to use the mathematics for." **Joseph Georgeson,** Bayside Middle School, Glendale, WI

Real-World Applications

Students study each mathematical idea in depth through applications and practical problems, providing opportunities to develop skills and to understand the importance of mathematics in everyday life.

Wider Scope

Transition Mathematics presents the history of major ideas and recent developments in mathematics and applications, which both teachers and students really like. In addition, ideas from geometry and preparation for algebra are integrated with arithmetic.

Lesson integrating Applied Arithmetic

LESSON

1-5

Negative Numbers

On every item a store sells, the store can make money, money, or break even. Here are some of the possibiliti

In English	In mathematics
make $3	3
make $2	2
make $1	1
break even	0
lose $1	-1
lose $1.50	-1.5
lose $2	-2
lose $3	-3

The numbers along the number line describe the situ using words. Higher numbers on the line are larger profits. T site of m -1.50, ar gative nu

- sign

d, but no su temper bowlir alled p 12 and e can

Lesson integrating Pre-Geometry

(bottom) Lesson integrating Pre-Algebra

LESSON

8-3

Graphing Equations

In a triangle, the sum of the measures of all three ar In a *right triangle*, one angle has measure 90°. So th of the other two angles must add to 90°. Suppose the angle measures are x and y. Seven pairs of possible x and y are in the table below. The ordered pairs are below the table.

x	y
10	80
20	70
35	55
52	38
45	45
80	10
62.8	27.2

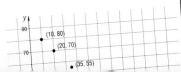

LESSON

7-4

Solving x - a = b

The equation $x - 59 = 12$ is an equation of the form $x - a = b$. To solve this equation just convert the subtraction to addition using the Add-Opp Property. Then solve the resulting equation as you did in Chapter 5.

Example 1 Solve $x - 59 = 12$.

Solution Convert to addition
$$x + -59 = 12$$
Add 59 to both sides. $\quad x + -59 + 59 = 12 + 59$
$$x + 0 = 71$$
Simplify. $\quad x = 71$

Check Substitute 71 for x in the original sentence. Does $71 - 59 = 12$? Yes. So 71 is the solution.

LESSON

2-3

Scientific Notation for Large Numbers

Light travels at a speed of about 186,281.7 miles per second. Since there are 60 seconds in a minute, light travels $60 \times 186{,}281.7$ miles per minute. This works out to 11,176,902 miles per minute. (You should check this on your calculator.) To find out how far light travels in an hour, you must multiply by 60 again.

$$60 \times 11{,}176{,}902 = 670{,}614{,}120 \text{ miles}$$

There are now three possible things your calculator will do.
1. It may display all 9 digits.

    `670614120.`

2. It may display an error message. The number is too big. The E tells you there is an error and the calculator will refuse to do anything until you clear the number.

    `E 6.7061412`   `6.7061412 E`   `ERROR`

3. It may display the number in **scientific notation.** The display usually looks

    `6.7061412 08`   `6.7061  8`   `6.7061 ×10 08`

Scientific notation is the way that scientific calculators display very large and very small numbers. The display usually looks like one of those shown here. Each of these stands for the number 6.7061412×10^8 or a rounded value of that number. The user is expected to know that the 8 (or 08) stands for 10^8. To convert the number into decimal notation, move the decimal point 8 places to the right. (The display at the right contains $\times$ 10 and is clearest.)

If you multiply this number by 24, scientific calculators will give you the scientific notation for 16,094,738,880.

    `1.60947 10`

Review

In 30–32, suppose it costs 30¢ for the first minute and 18¢ for each additional minute on a long-distance phone call. Then $c = .30 + .18(m - 1)$, where c is the total cost and m is the number of minutes talked. *(Lesson 4-8)*

30. Calculate c when $m = 6$.

31. What will it cost to talk for 10 minutes?

32. *Multiple choice* For $2.10, how long can you talk?
(a) 7 minutes   (b) 9 minutes
(c) 10 minutes   (d) 11 minutes

33. Give three instances of this pattern: There are $6n$ legs on n insects. *(Lesson 4-2)*

34. Three instances of a general pattern are given. Describe the pattern using two variables. *(Lesson 4-2)*
$$\frac{31.4}{2} \cdot \frac{2}{31.4} = 1 \qquad \frac{7}{8} \cdot \frac{8}{7} = 1 \qquad \frac{100}{11} \cdot \frac{11}{100} = 1$$

In 35 and 36, evaluate when $a = 3$, $b = 5$, and $c = 7$. *(Lessons 4-5, 4-7)*

35. $3(c + 10b - a^2)$ **36.** $a[a + b(b + c)]$

Exploration

37. Scientific calculators often store more digits than they display.
  a. Key in π. Record what you got. Then multiply by 100,000. Now subtract 314,159. Your calculator now displays some digits after those it displayed for π. What are these digits?
  b. Key in $\frac{1}{17}$. Record what you get. Then multiply by 100,000. Now subtract 5882. Compare this result with what you recorded. What extra digits for $\frac{1}{17}$ were stored in the calculator?
  c. Use a similar process to find the digits your calculator stores when you calculate $\frac{1}{13}$.
  d. What is the repetend for $\frac{1}{13}$?

38. Run this program with values of N that you pick.

```
10  PRINT "VALUE OF N"
15  INPUT N
20  IF N >= 8 THEN PRINT "TOO BIG"
25  IF N <= 6 THEN PRINT "TOO SMALL"
30  IF N <> 7 THEN PRINT "NOT CORRECT"
35  IF N = 7 THEN PRINT "JUST RIGHT"
40  END
```

  a. What is the meaning of $>=$ in this program?
  b. What is the meaning of $<=$ in this program?
  c. What is the meaning of $<>$ in this program?

T9

Develops Independent Thinking and Learning

"The other books don't help you much. It's more the teacher, and with this book I use now, I get help from the reading and from the teacher."

Transition Mathematics student, Edison Junior High School, Wheaton, IL

Reading

GREAT FOR STUDENTS Well-written explanations and examples enable students to successfully apply what they've read and also serve as a great reference tool, encouraging students to look for answers on their own. The reading also helps to motivate students by connecting mathematics to their world, which makes it more interesting to them.

GREAT FOR TEACHERS Because students can read and understand the text, you have the freedom to teach in a variety of ways. Instead of merely explaining every day what the text says, you can concentrate on developing further examples and explanations tailored to your students' needs.

Problem Solving

Every lesson contains a variety of problem-solving questions applying the mathematics. Students learn about the selection of problem-solving strategies to encourage efficient methods. In addition, requiring students to read helps develop thinkers who are more critical and aware.

CHAPTER 6

Problem-Solving Strategies

- **6-1:** Being a Good Problem Solver
- **6-2:** Read Carefully
- **6-3:** Draw a Picture
- **6-4:** Trial and Error
- **6-5:** Make a Table
- **6-6:** Work with a Special Case
- **6-7:** Try Simpler Numbers

240

LESSON

6-1

Being a Good Problem Solver

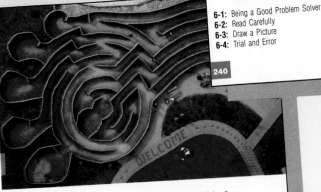

In Chapter 5, you learned how to solve any equation of the form $a + x = b$ for x. The method was to add $-a$ to each side and then simplify. This method is an example of an algorithm. An **algorithm** is a sequence of steps that leads to a desired result.

Not all algorithms are short. The algorithm called *long division* can involve many steps.

$$34\overline{)25.50} \atop \begin{array}{r} .75 \\ \underline{23\ 8} \\ 1\ 70 \end{array}$$

Chapter Review

The main objectives for the chapter are organized into sections corresponding to the four main types of understanding this book promotes: Skills, Properties, Uses, and Representations. Thus, the Chapter Review extends the multi-dimensional approach to understanding, offering a broader perspective that helps students put everything in place.

SKILLS include simple and complicated procedures for getting answers. The emphasis is on *how* to carry out algorithms.

PROPERTIES cover the mathematical justifications for procedures and other theory. To fully understand ideas, students must answer the common question, "But *why* does it work that way?"

USES include real-world applications of the mathematics. To effectively apply what they learn, students must know *when* different models or techniques are relevant.

REPRESENTATIONS provide concrete ways to conceptualize what it is that is being studied. Visual images, such as graphs and diagrams, are included here.

All these views have validity, and together they contribute to the deep understanding of mathematics that students need to have, in order to be independent thinkers and learners.

Chapter Review

Questions on SPUR Objectives

SPUR stands for **S**kills, **P**roperties, **U**ses, and **R**epresentations. The Chapter Review questions are grouped according to the SPUR Objectives for this chapter.

SKILLS deal with the procedures used to get answers.

■ **Objective A:** *Understand the methods followed by good problem solvers. (Lesson 6-1)*

1. *Multiple-choice* Which advice should be followed to become a better problem solver?
   (a) Check work by answering the question the same way you did it.
   (b) Be flexible.
   (c) Skip over words you don't understand as long as you can write an equation.
   (d) none of (a) through (c)

2. If you can apply an algorithm to a problem, then the problem becomes an ?.

3. After Nancy multiplies 1487×309 on her calculator, what would be a good way to check her answer?

■ **Objective B:** *Determine solutions to sentences by trial and error. (Lesson 6-4)*

4. Which integer between 10 and 20 is a solution to $3x + 15 = 66$?

5. *Multiple choice* Which number is *not* a solution to $n^2 \geq n$?
   (a) 0   (b) 0.5   (c) 1   (d) 2

6. Choose one number from each row so that the sum of the numbers is 255.

88	84	9
69	79	76
108	104	102

7. What number between 1000 and 1050 has 37 as a factor?

PROPERTIES deal with the principles behind the mathematics.

■ **Objective C:** *Determine whether a number is prime or composite. (Lesson 6-2)*

8. Is 49 prime or composite? Explain your answer.

9. Is 47 prime or composite? Explain your answer.

10. List all composite numbers n with $20 < n < 30$.

11. List all prime numbers between 30 and 40.

■ **Objective D:** *Find the meaning of unknown words. (Lesson 6-2)*

12. What is a tetrahedron?

13. What is a perfect number?

■ **Objective E:** *Make a table to find patterns and make generalizations. (Lesson 6-5)*

14. Mandy is saving to buy a present for her parents' anniversary. She has $10 now and adds $5 a week.
   a. How much will she save in 12 weeks?
   b. How much will she save in w weeks?

15. Consider 2, 4, 8, 16, 32, ... (the powers of 2). Make a table listing all the factors of these numbers. How many factors does 256 have?

■ **Objective F:** *Work with a special case to determine whether a pattern is true. (Lesson 6-6)*

16. Is there any n-gon with $n+2$ diagonals?

17. To divide a decimal by 1 million, you can move the decimal point ? places to the ?.

■ **Objective G:** *Use special cases to determine that a property is false or to give evidence that it is true. (Lesson 6-6)*

18. Let $a = 5$ and $b = -4$ to test whether $2a + b = a + (b + a)$. Is the property false or do you have more evidence that it is true?

19. Show that $5x + 5y$ is not always equal to $10xy$ by choosing a special case.

USES deal with applications of mathematics in real situations.

■ **Objective H:** *Use simpler numbers to answer a question requiring only one operation. (Lesson 6-7)*

20. If you fly 430 miles in 2.5 hours, how fast have you gone?

21. If you buy 7.3 gallons of gas at a cost of $1.19 per gallon, what is your total cost (to the penny)?

■ **Objective I:** *Use drawings to solve real problems. (Lesson 6-3)*

22. Nine teams are to play each other in a tournament. How many games are needed?

23. Five hockey teams are to play each other two times in a season. How many games are needed?

24. Bill is older than Becky. Becky is younger than Bob. Bob is older than Barbara. Barbara is older than Bill. Who is second oldest?

25. Interstate 25 runs north and south through Wyoming and Colorado. Denver is 70 miles from Colorado Springs and 112 miles from Pueblo. Cheyenne is 171 miles from Colorado Springs and 101 miles from Denver. Pueblo is 42 miles from Colorado Springs. Cheyenne is north of Denver. Which of these four cities, all on Interstate 25, is farthest south?

REPRESENTATIONS deal with pictures, graphs or objects that illustrate concepts.

■ **Objective J:** *Draw a diagram to find the number of diagonals in a polygon. (Lesson 6-3)*

26. How many diagonals does a hexagon have?

27. How many diagonals does a decagon have?

■ **Objective K:** *Draw a diagram to aid in solving geometric problems. (Lesson 6-3)*

28. All the diagonals of a pentagon are drawn. Into how many sections is the interior divided?

29. In polygon *ABCDEFGHI* all diagonals from *A* are drawn. How many triangles are formed?

Helps Students Improve Their Performance

"Thank you for writing this book. I am starting to understand math and getting better grades."

Transition Mathematics student, Golden Ring Middle School, Baltimore, MD

Strategies for increasing skills are combined in a unique fashion—and there is evidence that the result is a remarkable improvement in student achievement.

DAILY REVIEW reinforces skills learned in the chapter and combines and maintains skills from earlier chapters.

The **SUMMARY** gives an overview of the entire chapter and helps students consider the material as a whole.

The **VOCABULARY** section provides a checklist of terms, symbols, and properties students must know. Students can refer to the lesson or to the Glossary for additional help.

T12

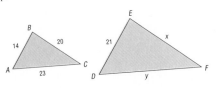

Review

In 18 and 19, triangles ABC and DEF are similar with corresponding sides parallel. (*Lesson 11-8*)

18. Find x.

19. Find y.

20. If 30% of a number is 51, what is 40% of that same number? (*Lessons 2-6, 10-3*)

21. If $x = -4$ and $y = -2$, what is $-3x$ divided by $2y$? (*Lessons 4-4, 10-5, 11-3*)

22. What is 14% of 200? (*Lesson 2-6*)

CHAPTER 5

Summary

A large variety of situations lead to addition. These situations are of two types: putting-together or slide. Some situations can be interpreted as either of these types.

In a putting-together situation, a count or measure x is put together with a count or measure y. If x and y have the same units and there is no overlap, the result has count or measure $x + y$. When the lengths of the sides of a polygon are put together, the result is the perimeter of the polygon. In a putting-together situation, x and y must be positive or zero.

In slide situations, a slide x is followed by a slide y. The result is a slide $x + y$. In slide situations, there may be changes forward or back, up or down, in or out, clockwise or counterclockwise. One direction is positive, the other negative. So in a slide situation, x and y can be positive, zero, or negative.

From these situations, you can see many properties of addition. Zero is the additive identity. Every number has an opposite or additive inverse. Addition is both commutative and associative.

Suppose you know one addend a and the sum b and would like to find the other addend. Then you are trying to find x in an equation $x + a = b$. This sentence can be solved using the Addition Property of Equality and the other properties of addition.

Vocabulary

You should be able to give a general description and a specific example of each of the following ideas.

Lesson 5-1
Putting-together Model for Addition
addend
Lesson 5-2
common denominator
Lesson 5-3
Slide Model for Addition
$\pm$ or $+/-$
Lesson 5-4
additive identity
Additive Identity Property of Zero
additive inverse
Property of Opposites, Op-op Property
Lesson 5-5
absolute value, | |
Lesson 5-6
revolution, full turn, quarter turn
clockwise, counterclockwise
magnitude of turn
Fundamental Property of Turns

Lesson 5-7
Commutative Property of Addition
Associative Property of Addition
Lesson 5-8
Addition Property of Equality
situation of the form $x + a = b$
Lesson 5-9
line segment, segment, $\overline{AB}$
$\overleftrightarrow{AB}$
polygon, side, vertex (vertices), angle of polygon
quadrilateral, pentagon, hexagon, ..., n-gon
diagonal of a polygon
convex polygon
Lesson 5-10
perimeter
AB

Unique Tools for Mastery

PROGRESS SELF-TEST provides the opportunity for feedback and correction—before students are tested formally. The Student Edition contains full solutions to questions on this test to enhance accurate self-evaluation.

CHAPTER REVIEW arranges questions according to the four dimensions of understanding—Skills, Properties, Uses, and Representations—to help students master those concepts that have not yet been mastered. Questions are keyed to objectives and lessons for easy reference.

The **QUIZZES** and **CHAPTER TESTS** in the Teacher's Resource File offer further help to assess mastery. There is at least one quiz per chapter. The regular chapter test comes in parallel Forms A and B and covers all objectives. For each chapter, there is also a Chapter Test in Cumulative Form. You choose the test format which best suits your needs!

TRANSITION MATHEMATICS QUIZ AND TEST WRITER provides computer-generated quizzes and tests for additional assessment flexibility.

CHAPTER 5

Progress Self-Test

Take this test as you would take a test in class. Then check your work with the solutions in the Selected Answers section in the back of the book.

In 1–7, simplify.

1. $3 + {}^-10$
2. $^-460 + {}^-250$
3. $^-9.8 + {}^-(^-1)$
4. $x + y + {}^-x + 4$
5. $|{}^-8|$
6. $|{}^-2| + |1| + |0|$
7. $^-6 + 42 + {}^-11 + 16 + {}^-12$
8. Evaluate $|{}^-A + 8|$ when $A = {}^-3$.

In 9–11, solve.

9. $x + 43 = 31$
10. $^-25 + y = 12$
11. $8 = {}^-2 + z + {}^-5$

In 12–15, write as a single fraction in lowest terms.

12. $\frac{53}{12} + \frac{11}{12}$
13. $\frac{5}{x} + \frac{10}{x}$
14. $\frac{17}{9} + \frac{8}{3}$
15. $\frac{1}{4} + \frac{3}{8} + \frac{2}{16}$

In 16 and 17, consider the equation $50 = W + {}^-20$.

16. To solve this equation, what number should you add to both sides?
17. What property enables you to add the same number to both sides of an equation?
18. $(2 + 3) + 4 = 2 + (3 + 4)$ is an instance of what property?
19. Give an instance of the Addition Property of Zero.
20. A polygon with 6 sides is called a __?__.
21. A pentagon has two sides of length 3 cm and three sides of length 4 cm. What is its perimeter?
22. *Multiple choice* If L and K are points, which symbol stands for a number?
 (a) LK (b) $\overline{LK}$ (c) $\overleftrightarrow{LK}$ (d) $\overrightarrow{LK}$

23. Ms. A's class has m students. Mr. [ ] has n students. Together there are 5[ ] in the classes. How are m, n, and S[ ]

In 24 and 25, Sally was 20 points behin[ ] she is 150 points ahead. Let c be the ch[ ] Sally's status.
24. What equation can be solved to find [ ]
25. Solve that equation.

In 26 and 27, use the figure below. A is[ ]
26. If $MA = 16$ and $AP = 8$, what is M[ ]

M[ ]————————A

27. If $MA = 2.3$ and $MP = 3$, what is [ ]
28. Picture the addition problem $^-3 + 2$[ ] number line and give the sum.
29. An iron bar is 3 cm longer than 5 m[ ] meters, how long is the bar?
30. Is $^-5.498765432101 + 5.49876543$[ ] positive, negative, or zero?

In 31 and 32, use the figure below. Ass[ ] small angles with vertex O have the sam[ ]
31. What is m∠VOW?
32. If you are standing at O facing U a[ ] to X, what is the magnitude of your [ ]

[figure with rays labeled V, W, O, U, X, Y]

33. What is the result when a 50° clock[ ] is followed by a 250° counterclockw[ ]
34. *Multiple choice* Which is not a sid[ ] polygon *WXYZ*? (a) $\overline{WX}$ (b) $\overline{WY}$ (c)[ ] (d) Each of (a), (b), (c) is a side.

CHAPTER 5

Chapter Review

Questions on **SPUR** Objectives

SPUR stands for **S**kills, **P**roperties, **U**ses, and **R**epresentations. The Chapter Review questions are grouped according to the SPUR Objectives for this chapter.

SKILLS deal with the procedures used to get answers.

■ **Objective A:** *Add any numbers written as decimals or fractions.* (Lessons 5-2, 5-3, 5-5)

In 1–9, add.

1. $^-16 + 4$
2. $^-7 + {}^-8 + {}^-9$
3. $7 + {}^-2.4 + 5$
4. $^-31 + 32$
5. $6/11 + 5/11$
6. $\frac{12}{17} + \frac{^-12}{17}$
7. $6 + \frac{^-8}{9}$
8. $2/3$ and $6/7$
9. $1/2$, $1/3$, and $1/4$
10. Write $\frac{40}{c} + \frac{^-10}{c}$ as a single fraction.

■ **Objective B:** *Calculate absolute value.* (Lesson 5-5)

11. $|{}^-12| = ?$
12. $|4| = ?$
13. $|0| + |3| + |{}^-5| = ?$
14. $^-|7| + |4| = ?$

■ **Objective C:** *Apply properties of addition to simplify expressions.* (Lesson 5-4)

15. $^-(^-(^-17)) = ?$
16. $^-(^-4) + 3 = ?$
17. $^-40 + 0 = ?$
18. $(86 + {}^-14) + ({}^-86 + 14) = ?$
19. $^-(^-(0 + \frac{2}{3})) = ?$
20. $11/4 + y + {}^-11/4 = ?$
21. When $a = {}^-42$, then $^-a + 6 = ?$
22. If $b = 2$, then $b + {}^-b = ?$

■ **Objective D:** *Solve equations of the form $x + a = b$.* (Lesson 5-8)

23. Solve $x + {}^-32 = {}^-12$.
24. Solve $6.3 = t + 2.9$.
25. Solve $\frac{10}{3} + y = \frac{1}{3}$.
26. Solve $0 + a = 4 + 1$.
27. Solve $3 + c + {}^-5 = 36$.
28. Solve $^-8 = 14 + (d + {}^-6)$.
29. Solve for x: $x + y = 180$.
30. Solve for c: $a + b + c = p$.

■ **Objective E:** *Find the perimeter of a polygon.* (Lesson 5-10)

31. What is the perimeter of a square in which one side has length 3?
32. If $x = 23$, what is the perimeter of the polygon *ABCDE*?

[figure of polygon ABCDE with sides labeled: A to B = x, B to C = 7, A 12, E 18, D 20, C]

33. Measure the sides of polygon *GHIJ* to find its perimeter to the nearest centimeter.

[figure of rectangle GHIJ]

34. An octagon has 3 sides of length 5 and 4 sides of length 6. What is its perimeter?
35. For polygon *ABCDE* in Question 32, if the perimeter is 82, what equation can be solved to find x?

Provides the Practical Support You Need

Continual involvement of teachers and instructional supervisors—in planning, writing, rewriting, and evaluating—has made this program convenient and adaptable to your needs.

Before each chapter you'll find the following:

DAILY PACING CHART shows you at a glance two alternate ways to pace the chapter.

TESTING OPTIONS list the chapter quizzes and tests for ease of planning.

OBJECTIVES are letter-coded and keyed to Progress Self-Test, Chapter Review, Lesson Masters, and Chapter Tests, showing a direct correspondence between what is taught and what is tested.

CHAPTER 2 ■ LARGE AND SMALL NUMBERS

DAILY PACING CHART ■ CHAPTER 2

Students in the Full Course should complete the entire text by the end of the year. Students in the Minimal Course spend more time when there are quizzes and more time on the Chapter Review. Therefore, these students may not complete all of the chapters in the text.

DAY	MINIMAL COURSE	FULL COURSE
1	2-1	2-1
2	2-2	2-2
3	2-3	2-3
4	Quiz (TRF); Start 2-4.	Quiz (TRF); 2-4
5	Finish 2-4.	2-5
6	2-5	2-6
7	2-6	2-7
8	2-7	Quiz (TRF); 2-8
9	Quiz (TRF); Start 2-8.	2-9
10	Finish 2-8.	Progress Self-Test
11	2-9	Chapter Review
12	Progress Self-Test	Chapter Test (TRF)
13	Chapter Review	
14	Chapter Review	
15	Chapter Test (TRF)	

TESTING OPTIONS

■ Quiz on Lessons 2-1 Through 2-3   ■ Chapter 2 Test, Form A   ■ Chapter 2 Test, Cumulative Form
■ Quiz on Lessons 2-4 Through 2-7   ■ Chapter 2 Test, Form B

A Quiz and Test Writer is available for generating additional questions, additional quizzes, or additional forms of the Chapter Test.

PROVIDING FOR INDIVIDUAL DIFFERENCES

The student text is written for the average student. The program, however, can be adapted for both less capable and more capable students.

A blackline master (in the Teacher's Resource File) is provided for each lesson for those students who need more practice. The Teacher's Edition frequently provides an Error Analysis feature to provide additional instructional strategies.

For students who require additional challenge, Extension activities are regularly provided in the Teacher's Edition.

OBJECTIVES ■ CHAPTER 2

Students should master the chapter objectives by the time they complete the chapter. To ensure objective mastery, there is continual review built into each set of lesson questions. After students complete the chapter lessons, they assess their mastery on the Progress Self-Test. Then they do the Chapter Review and pay special attention to those questions that match the objectives missed on the Progress Self-Test. Students can get extra practice on these objectives by using the master for each lesson in the Teacher's Resource File.

OBJECTIVES FOR CHAPTER 2 (Organized into the SPUR categories—Skills, Properties, Uses, and Representations)	Progress Self-Test Questions	Chapter Review Questions	Teacher's Resource File	
			Lesson Master*	Chapter Test Forms A and B
SKILLS				
A: Multiply by 10, 100, 1000,...	1	1–4	2-1	1
B: Change word names for numbers to decimals.	3	5, 6	2-1, 2-8	4, 6, 23
C: Convert powers to decimals.		7, 8	2-2	3, 18, 19, 20, 21
D: Give decimals and English word names for positive and negative integer powers of 10.	27	9–14	2-2, 2-8	11, 12, 13
E: Multiply by 0.1, 0.01, 0.001, ..., and $\frac{1}{10}$, $\frac{1}{100}$, $\frac{1}{1000}$....	4, 5	15–18	2-4	2
F: Multiply by powers of ten.	6, 7, 8	19–22	2-2, 2-8	5, 7
G: Convert large and small numbers into scientific notation.	15, 16	23–26	2-3, 2-9	14, 15, 16, 23
H: Convert percents to decimals.	9, 20	27–30	2-5	31–40
I: Know common fraction and percent equivalents.	22	31–34	2-5	31–40
J: Find percents of numbers.	2	35–38	2-6	10
K: Convert terminating decimals to fractions or percents.	21	39–44	2-7	22, 31–40
PROPERTIES				
L: Know and apply the Substitution Principle.	28	45–48	2-6	9
M: Identify numbers as being written in scientific notation.	26	49, 50	2-3, 2-9	30
USES				
N: Find percents of quantities in real situations.	23, 24, 25	51–53	2-6	25, 28, 29
O: Translate actual quantities into and out of scientific notation.	29	54, 55	2-3, 2-9	17
REPRESENTATIONS				
P: Indicate key sequences and displays on a calculator for large and small numbers.	12, 13, 17, 18	56–63	2-3, 2-9	8, 24

*The Lesson Masters are numbered to match the lessons.

52A

52

OVERVIEW anticipates and addresses your needs for the upcoming chapter.

PERSPECTIVES a unique feature, provides the rationale for the inclusion of topics or approaches, provides mathematical background, and makes connections within UCSMP materials. This is interesting information you'll really use!

Professional Sourcebook for UCSMP

Also at your fingertips is a wealth of information that includes valuable background material on topics ranging from research to review. See pages **T19-T52** at the back of the **Teacher's Edition.**

OVERVIEW ■ CHAPTER 2

Four notations are introduced in Chapter 2: exponential notation; scientific notation with positive exponents; percent; and scientific notation with negative exponents. The first two notations are common ways of representing large numbers; the latter two are used for small numbers. (For example, though 50% looks large, it is just another name for $\frac{1}{2}$.) The chapter title refers to the large and small numbers commonly represented by these notations.

The chapter could also be entitled "The Decimal System and

Powers of 10." All the notations are based on the relationship between the decimal system and the number 10. Powers of 10 are instrumental in scientific notation, and the symbol % means to multiply by $\frac{1}{100}$, or 10^{-2}.

Although the content is standard, you may be surprised at the early introduction of percent and negative exponents. Percent is introduced here because the interpretation of the % symbol is very important, and we want to give students virtually the entire year to work with it. Only some types of percent prob-

lems are given in this chapter. Other types are introduced in later chapters.

PERSPECTIVES ■ CHAPTER 2

The Perspectives provide the rationale for the inclusion of topics or approaches, provide mathematical background, and make connections within UCSMP.

2-1
MULTIPLYING BY 10
This is the key lesson in Chapter 2. Two important ideas are introduced here. First, if you know how to multiply by 10, then you can figure out how to multiply by 100, 1000, 10,000, and so on. For example, using 10 as a factor twice (10 × 10) is the same as multiplying by 100, or using 10 as a factor three times is the same as multiplying by 1000.

This rule is extended three times in the chapter. In Lesson 2-2, it is related to positive powers of 10. In Lesson 2-4, it is reversed and related to multiplication by $\frac{1}{10}$, $\frac{1}{100}$, and so on. In Lesson 2-8, the connection is made with negative powers.

The second important idea in this lesson is the use of word names such as *thousand* or *million* as names for numbers to be multiplied. In print, one sees a word name like *43 million* more often than one sees the pure decimal 43,000,000. The introductory cartoon for Chapter 2 shows a debt limit of *1.2 trillion*, which means

"1.2 times a trillion." Thus, for dealing with numbers in the real world, the ability to translate back and forth from word names to decimals is crucial. This idea will also be extended in later lessons.

2-2
POWERS
The operation that is implicit in 3^2 is called *powering* or *exponentiation*. The number 3 in the expression 3^2 is the base; the number 2, the exponent. The result (9) is the power. We prefer the term *powering* because it conveys the idea of the result of the operation.

There are two important ideas in this lesson; the skill of powering and the use of the scientific calculator. First, if the exponent is a positive integer, the relationship of powering to repeated multiplication can be used to change a number from exponential notation (say 4^5) to decimal notation (1024). (The idea of repeated multiplication, already stressed in Lesson 2-1, is a

familiar one.) Without a calculator, however, the repeated multiplication calculations are usually tedious, and only small integer exponents and bases can be considered.

Second, it is not always necessary to resort to repeated multiplication to change from exponential notation to decimal notation. A calculator with an x^y key can calculate powers directly. And of course, because of the relationship between the powers of 10 and the number of zeros, it is easy to calculate very large powers of 10 even without using a calculator.

2-3
SCIENTIFIC NOTATION FOR LARGE NUMBERS
Scientific notation is introduced early because students using scientific calculators must be able to interpret answers displayed in scientific notation. Also, the use of calculators in class gives teachers the freedom to use real data. Such numbers might otherwise lead to tedious hand calculation; with a

calculator there is no difficulty. Real data tend to be more interesting and show students where math is useful, and the result is often a large number displayed in scientific notation.

2-4
MULTIPLYING BY $\frac{1}{10}$ OR .1
For many students, the relationship between positive and negative integer powers of 10 is clearer when demonstrated with decimals. That is, students more readily understand the connection between 1000 and $\frac{1}{1000}$ than between 1000 and .001. And for some students, it is easier to see that $\frac{1}{10} \times \frac{1}{10} = \frac{1}{100}$ than .1 × .1 = .01. Indeed, the hardest part of this lesson may be to learn the fraction equivalents for .1, .01, .001, and so on.

Probably the simplest way to learn the fraction equivalents is to recall the place values to the right of the decimal point: tenth, hundredth, thousandth, and so on. Furthermore, just as the decimal point moves three places to the right, for example, when you multiply by 1000, it moves three places to the left when you multiply by $\frac{1}{1000}$ or .001.

A particularly important skill to learn in this lesson is how to multiply by $\frac{1}{100}$ or .01. That skill will be needed for the percent work in the next lesson.

2-5
PERCENT
The approach used for percent is simple. This lesson treats the word *percent* as a word name, like *million* or *thousandth*. Percent is another name for *hundredths*; that is, 3 percent = 3 hundredths, 100% = 100 hundredths = 1, and so on. Thus, multiplying by .01 or $\frac{1}{100}$ for 1% is no different than multiplying by 1,000,000 for 1 million, as was done in Lesson 2-1.

Students must learn decimal and fraction equivalents for the most

common percents. Those shown on the number lines on page 71 are a minimum. Both this lesson and the next give practice with the equivalents.

2-6
PERCENT OF A QUANTITY
This lesson gives practice in finding percents and shows their utility. Finding percents of numbers, an important skill, will be reinforced many times in succeeding lessons and by the end of the year should be second nature.

The Substitution Principle is the first property to be named. Later, this principle will be applied in the substitution of numbers for variables and in the solution of equations.

To some students, the Substitution Principle seems so obvious that it should not need stating. But this principle makes *percent of* problems almost automatic. It also encourages students to write out the steps of a problem and should be emphasized for that reason.

2-7
FRACTIONS, DECIMALS, AND PERCENTS
Students converted simple fractions to decimals in Lesson 1-8 and changed percents to decimals in Lesson 2-5. In this lesson, students reverse the process and change terminating decimals to fractions and percents. The more difficult task of converting repeating decimals to simple fractions is covered in Lesson 12-2.

Converting, changing, and *simplifying* are different words for the same idea: rewriting. Reasons for rewriting are as follows:
(1) *Situational constraints.* It may be necessary to perform a computation, and the algorithm or the available calculator requires that the number be in a certain form.
(2) *Clarity.* A particular number may be easier to understand in a

given notation. For instance, in **Example 3**, it is easier to understand $\frac{7}{14}$ than $\frac{25}{52}$.
(3) *Facility.* It may be easier to work with a number in one notation than in another. For instance, it is often easier to multiply fractions than decimals: $\frac{3}{4} \times \frac{7}{8}$, rather than 0.75 × 0.875.
(4) *Consistency.* When available data are given in different notations, it may be necessary to put all data in one form to compare or describe them.

The goal of this lesson is to teach *flexibility.* A student should be able to write a number as a fraction, a decimal, or a percent, depending on the situation.

2-8
MORE POWERS OF 10
Negative exponents are introduced early in the course for several reasons. First, this material reinforces concepts from previous lessons of this chapter, specifically the work with powers of 10 and scientific notation, and serves as the logical completion of these discussions. Second, as noted earlier, scientific calculators display numbers very near zero in scientific notation with negative exponents, and it is important for students to be able to deal with these numbers. Third, by going so quickly to negative exponents, it becomes less likely that students misinterpret powering as multiplication.

2-9
SCIENTIFIC NOTATION FOR SMALL NUMBERS
In this lesson, students use negative powers of 10 to write small numbers in scientific notation. This task is easier if students understand how to multiply by negative powers of 10 (Lesson 2-8). At the same time, the concepts in this lesson may help students master the material covered in Lesson 2-8. This lesson also extends the use of the calculator.

Super Teaching Support

"My students like the book! I like the book! Thank you!!"

Kathryn Shank, teacher, Irvine High School, Irvine, CA

1 **RESOURCES** save you time by coordinating all of the ancillaries to the lesson.

2 **OBJECTIVES** are letter-coded for easy reference.

3 **TEACHING NOTES** provide everything you need, suggestions for discussing the examples, calculator tips, mental math and estimation suggestions, dialogue to generate higher-order thinking, and more.

4 **READING** provides comprehension tips and strategies.

5 **ALTERNATE APPROACH/USING MANIPULATIVES** provide suggestions for students to use concrete materials.

6 **ADDITIONAL EXAMPLES** provide parallel examples to those in the text for added flexibility.

7 **ERROR ANALYSIS** pinpoints typical student errors and provides remediation strategies for correcting the errors.

8 **NOTES ON QUESTIONS** highlight important aspects of questions and provide helpful suggestions to enhance learning.

9 **MAKING CONNECTIONS** helps you connect present content and ideas to material covered in an earlier or later lesson, chapter, or text.

10 The **LESSON MASTER** is pictured where you need it for your convenience.

11 **SMALL GROUP WORK** shows how students may work together in a cooperative way.

12 **MORE PRACTICE** lists the Lesson Master for additional practice of the lesson skills and concepts.

13 **EXTENSION** offers high-interest activities for all students, as well as enrichment activities for students needing additional challenge. These well-liked activities provide ideas for technology, estimation, mental math, careers, and additional applications.

14 **EVALUATION** tells what you need to know about the quizzes and tests. It also provides **Alternative Assessment** suggestions to encourage different evaluation formats, such as oral presentation and cooperative learning.

LESSON 5-5

1 **RESOURCES**
- Lesson Master 5-5
- Visual for Teaching Aid 26: **Questions 45** and **46**
- Two-Color Counters (from *Transition Mathematics Manipulative Kit*)
- Overhead Two-Color Counters (from *Transition Mathematics Teacher Kit*)
- *Manipulative Activities Sourcebook*, Activity 6

2 **OBJECTIVES**

A Add any numbers written as decimals or fractions.
B Calculate absolute value.

3 **TEACHING NOTES**

Absolute value is so easy to calculate that many students do not realize what they are doing. As a result, absolute values involving variables can be very confusing. It is very helpful to split the idea of absolute value into two parts: when the number is not negative; and when the number is negative.

4 **Reading** You may wish to have students read this lesson aloud in class. Ask students to explain absolute value in their own words after they read the explanation in the text. Do *not* let students say, "The absolute value is the number without its sign." Repeatedly stress that the absolute value of a negative number is the *opposite* of that number.

Alternate Approach/ Using Manipulatives

Allow students to use two-color counters to add positive and negative numbers. You may wish to relate the use of the counters to football. Suggest that one color represents a gain of one yard and the other color represents a loss of one yard. Ask what the net change in position would be if a team gained one yard and then lost one yard. (0) Have students conclude that a pair of counters—one of each color—represents zero.

To add 7 and -4, students would use 7 positive counters and 4 negative counters. After pairing the positive and negative counters, 3 positive counters are left. Hence, 7 + -4 = 3. Repeat the procedure for other examples, and then allow students to work in groups to make up and solve their own addition problems.

6

ADDITIONAL EXAMPLES

1. Simplify.

a. $|\frac{3}{4}|$ $\frac{3}{4}$

b. $|-.5|$ .5

c. $|2| + |-3|$ 5

2. Find each sum.

a. $8 + -10$ -2

b. $\frac{1}{2} + -\frac{3}{4}$ $-\frac{1}{4}$

c. $-.5 + -.05$ -.55

7

Error Analysis Students often have difficulty adding a positive and a negative number as in Additional Examples 2a and 2b. Suggest that students think about how they would represent the addition with arrows on the number line. Students may want to construct a number line from -10 to 10 and use it when completing addition problems with sums between -10 and 10. Instead of drawing the arrows, some students may benefit from tracing arrows with their fingers.

8

NOTES ON QUESTIONS

Question 39: You might ask students if they found this question easier to evaluate with mixed numbers or with fractions.

9

Making Connections for Question 42: Angle measure is reviewed in preparation for the work with turns in the next lesson.

10

NAME _____

11 **NOTES ON QUESTIONS**

Small Group Work for Questions 45 and 46:

Suggest that students count squares in some sort of order, for example, by size. In that way, they can keep track of the squares they have counted and perhaps find a pattern to make the counting easier. Have the groups compare strategies or patterns they have found.

FOLLOW-UP

12 **MORE PRACTICE**

For more questions on SPUR Objectives, use *Lesson Master 5-5*, shown on page 209.

13 **EXTENSION**

Have students discuss how using the commutative and associative properties of addition can simplify the computations.

1. $-75 + 36 + 75$ (36)
2. $97 + -86 + -97$ (-86)
3. $-7 + -68 + -3$ (-78)
4. $132 + -4 + -6$ (122)

(**1.** and **2.** have two addends with a sum of zero. **3.** and **4.** have addends with a sum of -10.)

14 **EVALUATION**
Alternative Assessment

Tell the students to imagine that they have to explain how to add a positive number and a negative number to a friend who knows about positive and negative numbers but does not know how to add them. Ask the students to use real-life situations in their explanations. Have each student write a brief description of his or her explanation and the corresponding problem.

Components Designed for Ease of Teaching

Student Edition
full color

Teacher's Edition
annotated and with margin notes

Teacher's Resource File
About 600 blackline masters, organized into five sections, to cover your every classroom need!

Quiz and Test Masters
Quizzes (at least one per chapter)
Chapter Tests, Forms A and B (parallel forms)
Chapter Tests, Cumulative Form
Comprehensive Tests (four per text, including Final Exam, primarily multiple choice)

Lesson Masters
(one or two per lesson)

Computer Masters

Answer Masters
(provide answers for questions in student text; oversized type to enable display in class, allowing students to grade their own work)

Teaching Aid Masters
(patterns for manipulatives; masters for overhead transparencies; forms, charts, and graphs from the PE; coordinate grids; and more)

Additional Ancillaries

Solution Manual
Computer Software
Visual Aids
Transition Mathematics Quiz and Test Writer

Transition Mathematics Teacher Kit

1 Geometry template

Manipulative Activities Sourcebook

Overhead materials

Transition Mathematics Manipulative Kit

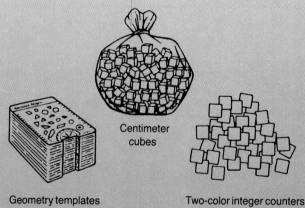

Centimeter cubes

Geometry templates

Two-color integer counters

UCSMP
SCOTT, FORESMAN

The University of Chicago School Mathematics Project

Transition Mathematics

Authors

Zalman Usiskin

and

James Flanders
Cathy Hynes
Lydia Polonsky
Susan Porter
Steven Viktora

About the Cover
If a person runs at a constant speed, then the graph of the
ordered pairs (time, distance) is a line. This example combines algebra
and geometry with applied arithmetic–
a major theme of this book.

ScottForesman
Editorial Offices: Glenview, Illinois   Regional Offices: Sunnyvale, California •
Tucker, Georgia • Glenview, Illinois • Oakland, New Jersey • Dallas, Texas

ACKNOWLEDGMENTS

For permission to reproduce indicated information on the following pages, acknowledgment is made to:
3 Decimal notation table, from a *History of Mathematical Notations* by Florian Cajori, © 1928, Open Court Publishing Company. **73** Information for graph on New Car Sales, from *Automotive News*, September 24, 1990. **241** Quote from *How to Solve It*, by George Polya, © 1973, Princeton University Press. **352** Indoor greenery graph, from *USA Today*, © 1984. **366** Ups & downs of travel cost bar graph, from *USA Today*, © 1984. **377** U.S. oil imports graph, American Petroleum Institute, Washington, D.C.

Extant Materials Unless otherwise acknowledged, all photos are the property of Scott, Foresman and Company. Page positions are as follows: (T)top, (C)center, (B)bottom, (L)left, (R)right, (INS)inset.

4 Jim Whitmer **5** Lee Boltin **7T** Michele & Tom Grimm/After-Image **7B** Reprinted with permission from MATHEMATICS AND HUMOR, copyright 1978 by the National Council of Teachers of Mathematics **8** Focus on Sports **12** Focus on Sports **13** Brent Jones **18** Chuck O'Rear/Woodfin Camp & Associates **23** NASA **25** David Carriere/After-Image **26** Grace Moore/Taurus Photos, Inc. **28** Wolfgang Kaehler **33** Bob Daemmrich **40** C. W. Schwartz/ANIMALS ANIMALS **51** Thomas Braise/After-Image **52** Dan McCoy/Rainbow **53** Reprinted by permission: Tribune Media Services **54** David Malin/Anglo-Australian Telescope Board **55** Roger Ressmeyer **56** David Carriere/After-Image **57** Jessica Anne Ehlers/Bruce Coleman Inc. **61** Mitchell B. Reibel/Sportschrome, Inc. **62** Eric Meola/The Image Bank **70** Jim Anderson/Woodfin Camp & Associates **74** Spencer Grant/Taurus Photos, Inc. **75** Alan Oddie/PhotoEdit **78** Jonathan T. Wright/Bruce Coleman Inc. **79** Everett C. Johnson/After-Image **80** Courtesy Elizabeth Dupee **82** E. R. Degginger/Bruce Coleman Inc. **86** Courtesy Park, Davis & Co. **87** Topham from The Image Works **88** Alec Duncan/Taurus Photos, Inc. **90** D. Mason/West Stock **92** Robert P. Carr/Bruce Coleman Inc. **94** Lee Boltin **96** Alan Becker/The Image Bank **98** Courtesy U.S. Capitol Historical Society, National Geographic Photography, George F. Mobley **100** Mike Douglas/The Image Works **101T** The Granger Collection, New York **101B** Bill Gallery/Stock Boston **105** Spencer W. Jones/Bruce Coleman Inc. **106** Reprinted with special permission of King Features Syndicate, Inc. **108** David R. Frazier Photolibrary **113** David R. Frazier Photolibrary **115** Grant V. Faint/The Image Bank **117** Jonathan T. Wright/Bruce Coleman Inc. **122** Milt & Joan Mann/Cameramann International, Ltd. **124** Vince Streano/After-Image **125** David Madison/Bruce Coleman Inc. **126** Teri Gilman/After-Image **129** Thomas Zimmermann/FPG **132** David R. Frazier Photolibrary **137** National Portrait Gallery, London **138** Stacy Pick/Stock Boston **138INS(C)** The Granger Collection, New York **138INS(R)** The Bettmann Archive **140** Enrico Ferorelli/Dot Picture Agency **142** Steve Solum/Bruce Coleman Inc. **144** Official U.S. Navy Photograph **145T** John Madere/The Image Bank **146** The Granger Collection **149** Bob Daemmrich/The Image Works **150** Michael Heron/Woodfin Camp & Associates **153** Milt & Joan Mann/Cameramann International, Ltd. **154** Milt & Joan Mann/Cameramann International, Ltd. **156** Jeffry W. Myers/Stock Boston **157** Frank Oberle/After-Image **158** Walter Chandoha **162** Alfred Pasieka/Taurus Photos, Inc. **163** Milt & Joan Mann/Cameramann International, Ltd. **166** Audrey Ross/Bruce Coleman Inc. **170** David Madison **178** Don and Pat Valenti **185** Gilbert Grant/Photo Researchers **186** David R. Frazier Photolibrary **188** Ron Thomas/FPG **190** Gabe Palmer/After-Image **191** James W. Kay/After-Image **192** G. Newman Haynes/The Image Works **193** Brent Jones **196** Jim Whitmer **198** Walter Chandoha **201** Alan Carey/The Image Works **205** Adolf Schmidecker/FPG **206** David W. Hamilton/The Image Bank **211** Joseph Nettis/Photo Researchers **212** Robert Frerck/After-Image **214** Matt Bradley/Bruce Coleman Inc. **219** Milt & Joan Mann/Cameramann International, Ltd. **224** Dan Guravich/Photo Researchers **226** Harald Sund/The Image Bank **228** Peter Gridley/FPG **230** Milt & Joan Mann/Cameramann International, Ltd. **232** Baron Wolman/After-Image **233** David Falconer/After-Image **238** Georg Gerster/COMSTOCK INC. **239** Carl Roessler/Bruce Coleman Inc. **240-241** Courtesy Hallmark, Inc. **241T** Copyright 1987, Newsday, Inc. Reprinted by permission. **242** Georg Gerster/COMSTOCK INC. **244** Stanford University **245** Bryan F. Peterson/The Stock Market **246** Dennis Hallinan/FPG **249** Kevin Ho-

ran/Stock Boston **253** Larry Reynolds **254** Cezus/FPG **257** Mark Antman/The Image Works **267** Alan Becker/The Image Bank **268** Walter Chandoha **275** Bob Martin/ALLSPORT **278** Pete Turner/The Image Bank **278INS** Mike Mitchell/After-Image **282** Peter Gridley/FPG **283L** G. & M. Kohier/FPG **283R** Charles Gatewood/The Image Works **285** David Madison **287T** David Madison/Bruce Coleman Inc. **290** Kevin Horan/Stock Boston **292** D. Sucsy/FPG **293** Sullivan Rogers/Bruce Coleman Inc. **294** The Bettmann Archive **295** G. A. Belluche, Jr./FPG **296** Carl Roessler/FPG **298** David R. Frazier Photolibrary **299** Bob Daemmrich **301** Library of Congress **302** Travelpix/FPG **303** Lawrence Migdale **306** FPG **307** Joanna McCarthy/The Image Bank **312** HERMAN © 1984 Universal Press Syndicate. Reprinted with permission. All Rights Reserved. **318** Coco McCoy/Rainbow **321** Paul H. Henning/Third Coast **322** Reprinted by permission: Tribune Media Services **332** Dennis Hallinan/FPG **333** David R. Frazier Photolibrary **334** David R. Frazier Photolibrary **336** Lawrence Migdale **337** Clyde H. Smith/FPG **339** Library of Congress **340** R. Laird/FPG **341** Brent Jones **348** David Madison **354** Brent Jones **356** John S. Flannery/Bruce Coleman Inc. **357** Travelpix/FPG **361B** © 1988 M. C. Escher Heirs/Cordon Art-Baarn-Holland. Photograph from the Collection of C. V. S. Roosevelt, Washington, D.C. **361T** Mel Digiacomo/The Image Bank **363** P. Pearson/Click/Chicago/Tony Stone **367** Frithfoto/Bruce Coleman Inc. **369L** Lynn M. Stone/Bruce Coleman Inc. **369R** Bruce Coleman Inc. **372** Jeff Foott/Bruce Coleman Inc. **373** © 1988 M. C. Escher Heirs/Cordon Art-Baarn-Holland. **374T** © 1988 M. C. Escher Heirs/Cordon Art-Baarn-Holland. **382** David J. Maenza/The Image Bank **384** Ames Research Center/NASA **393** Rick Browne/Stock Boston **398** Grant Heilman Photography **399** James H. Carmichael/Bruce Coleman Inc. **400** David Madison/Bruce Coleman Inc. **407** Charles Feil/After-Image **408** Terry G. Murphy/ANIMALS ANIMALS **412** Bob Daemmrich **413(all)** Des & Jen Bartlett/Bruce Coleman Inc. **416** Timothy O'Keefe/Bruce Coleman Inc. **417** Kevin Galvin/Bruce Coleman Inc. **418** Teri Gilman/After-Image **421** Adolf Schmidecker/FPG **423** John Coletti/Stock Boston **426** Isaac Geib/Grant Heilman Photography **429L** Daemmrich/Stock Boston **429R** David R. Frazier Photolibrary **430** Bob Daemmrich/The Image Works **432** Owen Franken/Stock Boston **433** E. R. Degginger/Earth Scenes **434** Manfred Kage/Peter Arnold, Inc. **436** The Erik Hildes-Heim Collection/Smithsonian Institution **439** Jeffrey Sylvester/FPG **443** David Carriere/After-Image **445** Mike Mitchell/After-Image **448** David R. Frazier Photolibrary **450** David Lissy/The Picture Cube **453** Janeart Ltd./The Image Bank **457** David Madison/Bruce Coleman Inc. **458** Chad Slattery/After-Image **463** Cameron Davidson/Bruce Coleman Inc. **468** James W. Kay/Bruce Coleman Inc. **471** Grant Heilman Photography **477T** Tom Edwards/ANIMALS ANIMALS **479** Don and Pat Valenti **484** Henley & Savage/After-Image **485** David R. Frazier Photolibrary **486** Brent Jones **487** Joachim Messerschmidt/Bruce Coleman Inc. **488** D. & J. McClurg/Bruce Coleman Inc. **489** Focus On Sports **491** Hans Reinhard/Bruce Coleman Inc. **492** S. L. Craig, Jr./Bruce Coleman Inc. **495** Chad Slattery/After-Image **497** Bryan Peterson/West Stock **499** Norman Myers/Bruce Coleman Inc. **506** Bob Daemmrich **508** Bob Daemmrich/The Image Works **509** Bob Daemmrich/The Image Works **511** Kunsthistorisches Museum, Vienna/The Bridgeman Art Library from Art Resource, NY **514** Myrleen Ferguson/PhotoEdit **515** Eunice Harris/The Picture Cube **516** David R. Frazier Photolibrary **522** Franz Kraus/The Picture Cube **523** David R. Frazier Photolibrary **524** Don and Pat Valenti **528** Ken Kaminsky/The Picture Cube **529** Kevin Syms/David R. Frazier Photolibrary **530** Gill C. Kenny/The Image Bank **535** Frank Oberle/Bruce Coleman Inc. **537** David H. Wells/The Image Works **546** John Eastcott/Yva Momatiuk/The Image Works **553** David R. Frazier Photolibrary **555** Gabe Palmer/After-Image **556** David R. Frazier Photolibrary **560** Harry Hartman/Bruce Coleman Inc. **563** Jonathan L. Barkan/The Picture Cube **565** Willie L. Hill, Jr./Stock Boston **566** Kandinsky, Composition VIII, No. 260; July 1923; Collection, Solomon R. Guggenheim Museum, New York. Photo: David Heald. **568** Tim Heneghan/West Stock **569** Walter Chandoha **573** George Dillon/Stock Boston **575** Hirmer Fotoarchiv, Munich **577** Mike Mazzaschi/Stock Boston **578** Norman Owen Tomalin/Bruce Coleman, Inc. **581** Frank Siteman/The Picture Cube **584** Jon Feingersh/Stock Boston **587** Bob Burch/West Stock **588** Cezus/FPG **589** Robert Fried/Stock Boston **593** Jeff Persons/Stock Boston **594** Owen Franken/Stock Boston **597** David Madison/Bruce Coleman Inc. **598** Glenn Short/Bruce Coleman Inc. **599** *Portraits and Lives of Illustrious Men* by Andre Thevet, Keruert et Chaudiere, Paris, 1584 **600** Jon Riley/After-Image **602** Derek Fell **605** D. Dietrich/FPG **607** Will & Deni McIntyre/Aperture Photobank **609** Don Mason/West Stock **610** NASA **611** Rene Sheret/After-Image **612** GEOPIC (TM)/Earth Satellite Corporation **614** Jeff Albertson/Stock Boston **617** Joel W. Rogers/Alaska Photo

It takes many people to put together a project of this kind and we cannot thank them all by name. We wish particularly to acknowledge James Schultz and Glenda Lappan of the UCSMP Advisory Board, who commented on early versions of the manuscript; Carol Siegel, who coordinated the use of these materials in schools; Edgar Arredondo, Janine Crawley, Maryann Kannappan, and Mary Lappan of our technical staff.

We wish to acknowledge and give thanks to the following teachers who taught preliminary versions of *Transition Mathematics*, participated in the pilot or formative research, and contributed many ideas to help improve this book:

Chris Coley
Parkside Community Academy
Chicago, Illinois

Alice Ekstrom
Lively Junior High School
Elk Grove, Illinois

Pat Finegan
Glenbrook South High School
Glenview, Illinois

Jonelle Glass
McClure Junior High School
Western Springs, Illinois

Rose Gunn
Grove Junior High School
Elk Grove, Illinois

Wilhelm Lilly
Kenwood Academy
Chicago Public Schools

Sharon Mallo
Mead Junior High School
Elk Grove Village, Illinois

Doc Mutchmore
Glenbrook South High School
Glenview, Illinois

Candace Schultz
Wheaton-Warrenville Middle School
Wheaton, Illinois

We also wish to acknowledge the following schools which used an earlier version of *Transition Mathematics* in a nationwide study and whose comments, suggestions, and performance guided the changes made for this version.

Powell Junior High School
Littleton, Colorado

16th St. Middle School
St. Petersburg, Florida

Walt Disney Magnet School
Gale Academy
Hubbard High School
Von Steuben High School
Chicago, Illinois

Hillcrest High School
Country Club Hills, Illinois

Friendship Junior High School
Des Plaines, Illinois

Bremen High School
Midlothian, Illinois

Holmes Junior High School
Mt. Prospect, Illinois

Sundling Junior High School
Winston Park Junior High School
Palatine, Illinois

Adams Junior High School
Schaumburg, Illinois

Edison Junior High School
Wheaton, Illinois

Golden Ring Middle School
Sparrows Point High School
Baltimore, Maryland

Walled Lake Central High School
Walled Lake, Michigan

Columbia High School
Columbia, Mississippi

Oak Grove High School
Hattiesburg, Mississippi

Roosevelt Middle School
Taylor Middle School
Albuquerque, New Mexico

Gamble Middle School
Schwab Middle School
Cincinnati, Ohio

Tuckahoe Middle School
Richmond, Virginia

Jason Lee School
Shumway Junior High School
Vancouver, Washington

We wish to acknowledge the hundreds of other schools and thousands of other students who have used earlier versions of these materials.

UCSMP Transition Mathematics

The University of Chicago School Mathematics Project (UCSMP) is a long-term project designed to improve school mathematics in grades K-12. UCSMP began in 1983 with a 6-year grant from the Amoco Foundation. Additional funding has come from the Ford Motor Company, the Carnegie Corporation of New York, the National Science Foundation, the General Electric Foundation, GTE, and Citicorp.

The project is centered in the Departments of Education and Mathematics of the University of Chicago, and has the following components and directors:

Resources	Izaak Wirszup, Professor Emeritus of Mathematics
Primary Materials	Max Bell, Professor of Education
Elementary Teacher Development	Sheila Sconiers, Research Associate in Education
Secondary	Sharon L. Senk, Associate Professor of Mathematics Michigan State University
	Zalman Usiskin, Professor of Education
Evaluation	Larry Hedges, Professor of Education
	Susan Stodolsky, Professor of Education

From 1983-1987, the director of UCSMP was Paul Sally, Professor of Mathematics. Since 1987, the director has been Zalman Usiskin.

The text *Transition Mathematics* was developed by the Secondary Component (grades 7-12) of the project, and constitutes the first year in a six-year mathematics curriculum devised by that component. As texts in this curriculum completed their multi-stage testing cycle, they were published by Scott Foresman. A list of the six texts follows.

Transition Mathematics
Algebra
Geometry
Advanced Algebra
Functions, Statistics, and Trigonometry
Precalculus and Discrete Mathematics

A first draft of *Transition Mathematics* was written and piloted during the 1983-84 school year. After a major revision, a field trial edition was used in twelve schools in 1984-85. A second revision was given a comprehensive nationwide test during 1985-86. Results are available by writing UCSMP. A hardcover project edition incorporated changes based on results of testing and comments from many students and teachers. The Scott Foresman edition is based on improvements suggested by the authors, editors, and some of the many teacher and student users of earlier editions.

Comments about these materials are welcomed. Address queries to Mathematics Product Manager, ScottForesman, 1900 East Lake Avenue, Glenview, Illinois 60025, or to UCSMP, The University of Chicago, 5835 S. Kimbark, Chicago, IL 60637.

This book is designed for the course immediately preceding first-year algebra. Its content and questions have been carefully sequenced to provide a smooth path from arithmetic to algebra, and from the visual world and arithmetic to geometry. It is for this reason that this book is entitled *Transition Mathematics*.

Transition Mathematics differs from other books for this course in six major ways. First, it has **wider scope**, including substantial amounts of geometry integrated with the arithmetic and algebra that is customary. This is to correct the present situation in which many students who finish algebra find themselves without enough prior knowledge to succeed in geometry. Also, some students never get as far as geometry yet need to be able to deal with measurements and the geometry of objects.

Second, **reading and problem solving** are emphasized throughout. The lessons are written for students and each contains questions covering that reading. They must learn to read mathematics in order to become able to use mathematics outside of school. Our testing shows students can and should be expected to read. Every lesson also contains problem-solving questions applying the mathematics. Like skills, problem solving must be practiced; when practiced it becomes far less difficult. Some problem-solving techniques are so important that at times they (rather than the problems) should be the focus of instruction; consequently, an entire chapter is devoted to these techniques.

Third, there is a **reality orientation** towards both the selection of content and the approaches allowed the student in working out problems. Being able to do arithmetic is of little ultimate use to an individual unless he or she can apply that content. Each arithmetic operation is studied in detail for its applications to real-world problems. Real-life situations motivate ideas and provide additional settings for practice.

Fourth, fitting the reality orientation, students are expected to use current **technology**. Calculators are assumed throughout this book because virtually all individuals who use mathematics today find it helpful to have them. Scientific calculators are recommended because they use an order of operations closer to that found in algebra and have numerous keys that are helpful in understanding concepts at this level. Computer exercises show how the computer can be used as a helpful tool in doing mathematics.

Fifth, **four dimensions of understanding** are emphasized: skill in carrying out various algorithms; developing and using mathematical properties and relationships; applying mathematics in realistic situations; and representing or picturing mathematical concepts. We call this the SPUR approach: **S**kills, **P**roperties, **U**ses, **R**epresentations. On occasion, a fifth dimension of understanding, the historical dimension, is discussed.

Sixth, the **instructional format** is designed to maximize the acquisition of both skills and concepts. The book is organized around lessons meant to take one day to cover. Ideas introduced in a lesson are reinforced through "Review" questions in the immediately succeeding lessons. This daily review feature allows students several nights to learn and practice important concepts and skills. The lessons themselves are sequenced into carefully constructed chapters. At the end of each chapter, a carefully focused Progress Self-Test and a Chapter Review, each keyed to objectives in all the dimensions of understanding, are then used to solidify performance of skills and concepts from the chapter so that they may be applied later with confidence. Finally, to increase retention, important ideas are reviewed in "Review" questions of later chapters.

CONTENTS

Welcome to *Transition Mathematics*. We hope you enjoy this book; it was written for you. Its goals are to solidify the arithmetic you already know and to prepare you for algebra and geometry.

You need to have some tools to do any mathematics. The most basic tools are paper, pencils, and erasers (everyone makes mistakes sometimes). For this book, you will also need the following drawing equipment:

ruler (to draw and measure along lines, with both centimeter and inch markings)
compass (to draw circles)
protractor (to draw and measure angles)

It is best if both the ruler and protractor are transparent plastic.

You will also need a scientific calculator in many places in this book, beginning in Chapter 1. Scientific calculators differ widely in the range of keys they have. If you are going to buy or borrow a calculator, it should have the following keys: x^y or y^x (powering), $\sqrt{x}$ (for square root), $x!$ (factorial), $\pm$ or $+/-$ (for negative numbers), π (pi), and $1/x$ (reciprocals), and it should write very large or very small numbers in scientific notation. We recommend a *solar-powered* calculator so that you do not have to worry about batteries, though some calculators have batteries which can last for many years and work in dim light. A good calculator can last for many years.

There is another important goal of this book: to assist you to become able to learn mathematics on your own, so that you will be able to deal with the mathematics you see in newspapers, magazines, on television, on any job, and in school. The authors, who are all experienced teachers, offer the following advice.

1. You can watch basketball hundreds of times on television. Still, to learn how to play basketball, you must have a ball in your hand and actually dribble, shoot, and pass it.

   Mathematics is no different. You cannot learn much mathematics just by watching other people do it. You must participate. Some teachers have a slogan:

   Mathematics is not a spectator sport.

2. You are expected to read each lesson. Read slowly, and keep a pencil with you as you check the mathematics that is done in the book. Use the Glossary or a dictionary to find the meaning of a word you do not understand.

3. If you cannot answer a question immediately, don't give up! Read the lesson again; read the question again. Look for examples. If you can, go away from the problem and come back to it a little later. Do not be afraid to ask questions and to talk to others when you do not understand something. You are expected to learn many things by reading, but school is designed so that you do not have to learn everything by yourself.

We hope you join the many thousands of students who have enjoyed this book. We wish you much success.

CHAPTER 1 ■ DECIMAL NOTATION

DAILY PACING CHART ■ CHAPTER 1

Students in the Full Course should complete the entire text by the end of the year. Students in the Minimal Course spend more time when there are quizzes and more time on the Chapter Review. Therefore, these students may not complete all of the chapters in the text.

For more information on pacing, see *General Teaching Suggestions: Pace* on page T35 of the Teacher's Edition. Quizzes and tests are provided in the Teacher's Resource File (TRF).

DAY	MINIMAL COURSE	FULL COURSE
1	1-1	1-1
2	1-2	1-2
3	1-3	1-3
4	1-4	1-4
5	Quiz (TRF); Start 1-5.	Quiz (TRF); 1-5
6	Finish 1-5.	1-6
7	1-6	1-7
8	1-7	Quiz (TRF); 1-8
9	Quiz (TRF); Start 1-8.	1-9
10	Finish 1-8.	1-10
11	1-9	Progress Self-Test
12	1-10	Chapter Review
13	Progress Self-Test	Chapter Test (TRF)
14	Chapter Review	
15	Chapter Review	
16	Chapter Test (TRF)	

TESTING OPTIONS
■ Quiz on Lessons 1-1 Through 1-4　■ Chapter 1 Test, Form A
■ Quiz on Lessons 1-5 Through 1-7　■ Chapter 1 Test, Form B
A Quiz and Test Writer is available for generating additional questions, additional quizzes, or additional forms of the Chapter Test.

PROVIDING FOR INDIVIDUAL DIFFERENCES
The student text is written for the *average* student. The program, however, can be adapted for both less capable and more capable students.

A blackline master (in the Teacher's Resource File) is provided for each lesson for those students who need more practice. The Teacher's Edition frequently provides Error Analysis and Alternate Approach features to provide additional instructional strategies.

For students who require additional challenge, Extension activities are regularly provided in the Teacher's Edition.

OBJECTIVES ■ CHAPTER 1

After students complete the chapter lessons, they assess their mastery on the Progress Self-Test. Then they do the Chapter Review and pay special attention to those questions that match the objectives missed on the Progress Self-Test. Students can get extra practice on these objectives by using the master for each lesson in the Teacher's Resource File.

OBJECTIVES FOR CHAPTER 1 (Organized into the SPUR categories—Skills, Properties, Uses, and Representations)	Progress Self-Test Questions	Chapter Review Questions	Teacher's Resource File Lesson Master*	Chapter Test Forms A and B
SKILLS				
A: Translate back and forth from English into the decimal system.	1, 2, 5, 6	1–6	1-1, 1-2	1, 2, 3, 4, 5, 7
B: Order decimals and fractions.	7, 8, 30	7–13	1-2, 1-5, 1-8, 1-9	6, 27, 31
C: Give a number that is between two decimals.	14, 15	14–17	1-2, 1-5	38
D: Round any decimal up or down or to the nearest value of a decimal place.	9, 10	18–24	1-3, 1-4	10, 11, 12
E: Estimate answers to arithmetic questions to the nearest integer.	22	25, 26	1-4	21
F: Use a calculator to perform arithmetic operations.	24	27–29	1-7	37
G: Convert simple fractions and mixed numbers to decimals.	4	30–33	1-8, 1-9	23, 24, 25, 26, 30
H: Know by memory the common decimals and fractions between 0 and 1.	3, 19	34–40	1-8	28
PROPERTIES				
I: Use the < and > symbols correctly between numbers.	16, 17, 18	41–43	1-6	16, 19
J: Correctly use the raised bar symbol for repeating decimals.	25	44, 45	1-8	29
K: Use the equal fractions property to rewrite fractions.	31, 32, 33	46–48	1-10	34, 35, 36
USES				
L: Round to estimate a given number in a real situation.	21	49–51	1-3, 1-4	9, 13, 39
M: Give situations where estimates are preferred over exact values.	28	52, 53	1-3	41
N: Correctly interpret situations with two directions as positive, negative, or corresponding to zero.	11	54–56	1-5, 1-6	14, 15
REPRESENTATIONS				
O: Graph a decimal on a number line.	26, 27	57–59	1-2, 1-5	32, 33
P: Read a number line.	12, 13	60–63	1-2	8, 17, 18
Q: Indicate key sequences for doing an arithmetic problem on a calculator.	23	64, 65	1-7, 1-8	20, 22
HISTORY (Note: This chapter has an additional category for History)				
R: Give people and rough dates for the development of key ideas in arithmetic.	34	66, 67	1-1, 1-2, 1-8	40

*The Lesson Masters are numbered to match the lessons.

OVERVIEW ■ CHAPTER 1

Chapter 1 may strike you as a rather unusual first chapter for a book at this level. There is no computation with decimals, fractions, or whole numbers. There is an all-important reason for delaying computation: it makes very little sense for students to compute if they do not know what the numbers they are using could represent.

Whereas this chapter deals with writing and ordering decimals, Chapter 2 goes into the relationships between decimals and the number 10. Do not fear if students do not have everything down pat by the time they leave this chapter; there is an entire second chapter in which these ideas get applied immediately.

Calculators are needed throughout this book, and it is assumed students have calculators for all

tests. Calculators first appear in Lesson 1-7. This gives the student time to get one. If a student has to buy a calculator, make sure that it is a *scientific calculator*.

For use with these materials, a calculator must have the four operations, scientific notation, parentheses, and powers. It is easier, but not necessary, when all the students have the same model. Advise the students to bring the instructions for the calculator to class.

We assume that students have whole number computation well in hand before beginning this book. If your students do not, this is not a suitable book for them. On the other hand, computation with decimals, percents, fractions, integers, scientific notation, powers, and roots is integrated throughout the

book; students sometimes use calculators, sometimes not. We have observed that students differ in how often they want to use their calculators.

Throughout this book, it is important to focus on reading for comprehension. Because many students are not used to reading a mathematics text, we have provided specific suggestions in each lesson in Chapter 1 (and occasionally thereafter) for helping students adjust to this expectation. You may wish to use these ideas or develop your own.

Before beginning this chapter, make certain that the students have read the section entitled "To the Student" so that they know what materials they are expected to have.

PERSPECTIVES ■ CHAPTER 1

The Perspectives provide the rationale for the inclusion of topics or approaches, provide mathematical background, and make connections within UCSMP.

1-1

DECIMALS FOR WHOLE NUMBERS

There are two equally important goals in this lesson: providing an introduction to the decimal system and initiating the student in reading mathematics.

The discussion of decimals includes some history as well as place value. Some students are surprised that the word *decimal* is used with whole numbers, but this term can refer to any numbers in a base-ten number system.

1-2

DECIMALS FOR NUMBERS BETWEEN WHOLE NUMBERS

Since many students have learned to measure length by counting spaces, they think that measuring is just a special kind of counting.

Actually, counting is a special kind of measuring. The key difference is in the units. A measure unit can be split up. Even money, which is a measure, can be split up into units smaller than cents. (How many Italian lira are there to a penny? Have students look in a newspaper.)

Simon Stevin's argument for his new "decimal fractions" (digits to the right of the ones digit, discussed on page 9) was that some of the same addition, subtraction, multiplication, and division algorithms could be used on these numbers as on whole numbers. By the way, Stevin did not use a decimal point. The decimal point was first used in 1657 by William Oughtred, an English mathematician, who also invented the × sign for multiplication. (See the opener for Chapter 4, page 138.)

In some books, the style is to place a 0 before *every* decimal between 0 and 1. For example, 0.5 would be written for .5. This approach, however, does not correspond to the representations of decimals in the real world. Often decimals are written without zeros; for instance, a team that wins 3 of 4 games is listed as having a winning percentage of .750, not 0.750. To help develop flexibility, this text uses both forms.

It is very important that students learn to order decimals. They will get more practice in the next two lessons, which are devoted to rounding.

1-3

ESTIMATING BY ROUNDING UP OR DOWN

Students often learn to estimate by being asked to estimate the answer to a problem like 39×51. However, because students know how to get the exact value in such problems, they think there is little reason to estimate.

As a result, many students do not consider estimation as important as exact computation. Such a view is too narrow, and the first paragraph of this lesson points out five types of situations in which estimates are preferred over exact values.

Rounding up and rounding down are both common types of rounding. You would probably round up in estimating how many algebra books to have on hand for next year's students but round down in estimating how much you weigh. Once students can round up and down, it is easier to understand rounding to the nearest.

1-4

ESTIMATING BY ROUNDING TO THE NEAREST

The students' experience with rounding up and rounding down should help them understand rounding to the nearest. This lesson also reinforces the importance of place value and order.

When experienced users need to round up half the time and down the other half, they use a variety of strategies. One is to round so that the digit preceding the rounding is even. Thus, 7.45 would round down to 7.4; 7.55 would round up to 7.6. Another strategy is to alternate rounding up and rounding down, but only when the "critical digit" is 5.

1-5

NEGATIVE NUMBERS

Negative numbers are not difficult for students to grasp. Everyone is familiar with temperature. In this

lesson, we give many other examples to take advantage of student intuition gained from experience. The number line is also helpful; it provides the kind of understanding we call "representation."

1-6

SYMBOLS FOR INEQUALITY

All of the work on ordering in the previous lessons has prepared the students for the introduction of the inequality symbols in this lesson. You may have been wishing you had these symbols even earlier; the best time for introducing new symbols is when a need has already presented itself.

In a curriculum currently used in Hungary, the symbols for $<$ and $>$ are introduced on the first day of first grade. The students are told that the symbol opens up to the larger number.

1-7

KNOWING YOUR CALCULATOR

Most students can use calculators to add, subtract, multiply, and divide, but do not know much else about them.

This lesson develops a language for discussing calculator use for the rest of the year. Phrases like *key sequence* will be helpful, particularly in Chapter 4 when discussing order of operations. Special keys will be used in Chapter 2. Some calculators may require second function keys for π, and those calculators will use second function keys for many other purposes, too.

1-8

DECIMALS FOR SIMPLE FRACTIONS

Lesson 1-8 covers much material, and you may wish to spend an extra day on it. However, the next lesson further develops the same ideas, so there are two days on the topic regardless.

The changing of fractions to decimals and the graphing of fractions on the number line help develop

the concept of the *fraction as representing a single number*. Many students spend years of work with fractions before they are taught that $\frac{a}{b}$ means dividing a by b. They think of a fraction as two numbers and, as a result, cannot order fractions or rename a fraction as a decimal.

To convert a fraction to a decimal on a calculator that does fractions, first enter the fraction (press the numerator, a fraction key, then the denominator), and then press either $\boxed{=}$ or $\boxed{F \rightarrow D}$.

1-9

DECIMALS FOR MIXED NUMBERS

This is a rather easy lesson. The introduction of only one new idea, converting a mixed number to a decimal, allows time to review the many ideas from Lesson 1-8.

Some calculators that do simple fractions can deal with mixed numbers as well. Of course, there is a limit to the number of digits that can be entered.

1-10

EQUAL FRACTIONS

We do not speak of "reducing" fractions because the fraction $\frac{2}{3}$ has the same value as $\frac{6}{9}$. That is, though the numerator and denominator are smaller, $\frac{2}{3}$ is not smaller than $\frac{6}{9}$. Many people feel the phrase "reducing" conveys an incorrect impression. However, the phrase "in lowest terms" is universal, and we recommend its use.

Although it is possible to find the prime factorizations of the numerator and denominator to simplify a fraction, the drawbacks of this strategy are suggested by the fact that few adults use it. Most adults find just one number that is a factor of both the numerator and denominator, and divide both by it. Then they work with the simpler fraction. After some practice, students learn to divide the numerator and denominator by the largest common factor they can readily identify.

CHAPTER 1

We recommend 13 to 16 days for this chapter: 10 to 12 days on the lessons, 1 day for the Progress Self-Test, 1 or 2 days for the Chapter Review, and 1 day for the exam. (See the Daily Pacing Chart on page 2A.) If you spend more than 16 days on this chapter, you are moving too slowly. Keep in mind that each lesson includes Review questions to help students firm up content studied previously.

Decimal Notation

2

The chart below shows how the ten **digits**

| 0 | 1 | 2 | 3 | 4 | 5 | 6 | 7 | 8 | 9 |

have developed over the years. Notice that the Greeks and Romans did not write numbers the way we do. Instead they used the letters of their alphabets. The Romans used fewer letters than the Greeks. For larger numbers, the Romans used L for fifty, C for one hundred, D for five hundred, and M for one thousand. From about 100 B.C. until about 1400 A.D., Europeans most often wrote numbers using Roman numerals.

In the years 600–900 A.D., the Hindus developed the decimal system. The **decimal system** is the system in which *any* whole number can be written with just ten symbols. The Arabs wrote about this system. Europeans did not learn about it until 1202 A.D., when Leonardo of Pisa, an Italian mathematician also known as Fibonacci, translated an Arabic manuscript into Latin.

The Development of Arabic Numerals

Greeks	α	β	γ	δ	ε	ζ	η	θ	ι
Romans	I	II	III	IV	V	VI	VII	VIII	IX
976 A.D.	I	?	?	?	V	?	7	8	9
10th century	T	ω	Ͷ	P	Ψ	O	V	Ȝ	S
1077 A.D.	?	?	?	?	?	?	?	8	2
11th century	I	?	Ԑ	B	Ч	?	?	8	σ
11th century	I	?	Ʒ	?	Ч	?	?	8	9
12th century	I	?	?	?	?	?	V	?	?
1200 A.D.	I	?	?	?	9	?	?	8	?
15th century	I	?	?	?	9	P	?	?	?
1490 A.D.	O	?	2	3	?	?	6	?	8	?
1522 A.D.	o	I	?	3	4	5	6	7	8	9

CHAPTER 1 Decimal Notation   3

USING PAGES 2 AND 3
Point out the history of our symbols shown on these pages. Many of the symbols we use today developed relatively recently.

Actually, decimals are even more recent than this information suggests. In the 1500s and 1600s there were still many people who calculated with Roman numerals, and the notation to the right of the decimal point was developed only in the late 1600s. The superiority of decimals over fractions and Roman numerals was not universally recognized until the 1700s. The metric system did not enter the picture until the late 1700s. Not until the 1800s did the concept of "real number" develop as we know it today.

RESOURCES
■ Lesson Master 1-1
▣ Visual for Teaching Aid 1:
Use the Place Value Chart
to reinforce the main ideas
of the lesson.
*The Teaching Aids are avail-
able both as blackline masters and as overhead visuals.*

OBJECTIVES

*Letter codes refer to the
SPUR Objectives on page
2B.*
A Translate back and forth
from English into decimal
whole numbers.
R Give peoples and rough
dates for the development
of key ideas in arithmetic.

LESSON

1-1

Decimals for Whole Numbers

In the decimal system, the smallest ten **whole numbers** need only one digit. Today we write them as 0, 1, 2, 3, 4, 5, 6, 7, 8, and 9. But look again at the chart on page 3. Notice that the symbols we use today did not all appear until the late 1400s.

Two digits are needed to write the next ninety whole numbers as decimals.

| 10 | 11 | 12 | . . . | 19 | 20 | 21 | . . . | 99 |

Notice that we call the whole numbers *decimals* even though there are no decimal points.

The next nine hundred whole numbers can be written with three digits.

| 100 | 101 | 102 | . . . | 200 | 201 | . . . | 999 |

By using more digits, very large numbers can be written. The census estimate of the U.S. population at the end of 1989, was 248239010 people. To make this easier to read, groups of digits are separated by commas.

In decimal notation:
2 4 8 , 2 3 9 , 0 1 0

In English words:
Two hundred forty-eight million, two hundred thirty-nine thousand, ten.

Notice that decimal notation is shorter than English words.

4

Each digit in a decimal has a **place value.** Here are the place values for the nine digits of the number that represents the U.S. population.

2 4 8 , 2 3 9 , 0 1 0

hundred millions
ten millions
millions
hundred thousands
ten thousands
thousands
hundreds
tens
ones

The U.S. population is an example of a **count.** The most basic use of numbers is as counts. For every count there is a **counting unit.** Counts are always whole numbers, never fractions between whole numbers. Here are some examples.

Phrase	Count	Counting unit
0 eight-legged insects	0	eight-legged insects
28 letters in "antidisestablishmentarianism"	28	letters
U.S. population of 248,239,010	248,239,010	people

Questions

Covering the Reading

1. What letter did the Greeks use to denote the number one? α

2. How did the Romans denote the number two? II

3. What letter did the Romans use to stand for the number of fingers on one normal human hand? V

4. What letter did the Romans use to stand for the number of fingers on two hands? X

5. What people invented the decimal system? the Hindus

6. When was the decimal system invented? 600–900 A.D.

7. Name the smallest whole number. zero

8. Who was Fibonacci, what did he do that relates to the decimal system, and when did he do it? See margin.

9. About when did all the symbols for the numbers zero through nine appear as we know them? the late 1400s

LESSON 1-1 Decimals for Whole Numbers 5

TEACHING NOTES

Reading Encourage students to read the chart on page 3 and the history in the text carefully, going back and forth from chart to text, re-reading definitions, and memorizing the place values.

To help students develop comprehension skills, you can have them read the lesson aloud. Then, ask for the main ideas and list them on the board. The list should include digits, decimal system, whole numbers, place value and names of places, count, and counting unit. You can also have students suggest questions for class discussion. For more information on reading skills, see *General Teaching Suggestions: Reading* on page T37 of the Teacher's Edition.

Making Connections
Stress the names of the decimal places up to hundred million. The names beyond hundred million are introduced in Lesson 2-1.

ADDITIONAL ANSWERS
8. He was an Italian mathematician who translated Arabic mathematics documents into Latin in A.D. 1202. The documents contained decimal arithmetic.

In 10–12, written in the decimal system, how many whole numbers have

10. one digit?   10

11. two digits?   90

12. three digits?   900

In 13–18, consider the number 568,249. Name the digit in each place.

13. thousands   8   **14.** ones   9

15. hundreds   2   **16.** tens   4

17. ten thousands   6   **18.** hundred thousands   5

19. A number is written as a decimal. Must there be a decimal point?
No

20. Name one advantage of writing numbers as decimals rather than using English words.   Numbers as decimals are shorter.

21. A count is always what kind of number?   whole number

22. Name something for which the count is between one million and one billion.   Sample: U.S. population

23. Consider the U.S. population in 1989.
   a. Name the count.   the count is 248,239,010
   b. Name the counting unit.   people

Applying the Mathematics

24. Give an example of a count that is larger than the 1989 U.S. population.   Sample: 1980 world population

25. Consider the number of stars on a U.S. flag.
   a. Name the count.   50
   b. Name the counting unit.   stars

26. The book of the Old Testament called Numbers gets its name because it begins with a census of the adult males of the tribes of Israel. The ancients did not have our numerals. So they wrote out the population in words. ''. . . of the tribe of Reuben, were forty and six thousand and five hundred.'' Write this number as a decimal.   46,500

27. Federal aid is often given on the basis of population: the greater the population, the greater the aid. According to these 1980 Census data,

   a. which of the four metropolitan areas would get the most aid?

   b. which of the four metropolitan areas would get the least aid?

Salinas-Monterey, California	290,444	
Appleton-Oshkosh, Wisconsin	291,325	most
McAllen-Edinburg, Texas	283,229	least
Pensacola, Florida	289,782	

Monterey, California

28. Tell why the counts in Question 27 are estimates, even on the day they were made.   See margin.

In 29–31, write as a decimal.

29. 6 hundred million   600,000,000

30. ten thousand   10,000

31. five hundred six   506

32. In decimal notation, what is the smallest five-digit whole number?
   10,000

33. In decimal notation, write the number that is one less than ten thousand.   9999

Exploration

34. In Europe, the decimal numeral for seven is sometimes written as shown in the cartoon. Why is this done?
   to distinguish it from the numeral for 1.

HE'S NEVER BEEN THE SAME SINCE RETURNING FROM EUROPE!

7777   7

FOLLOW-UP

MORE PRACTICE
For more questions on SPUR Objectives, use *Lesson Master 1-1*, shown below.

28. It is impossible to get an exact count.

NAME _____

LESSON MASTER 1-1
QUESTIONS ON **SPUR** OBJECTIVES

■ **SKILLS** *Objective A (See pages 49–51 for objectives.)*

1. Consider the number 502,139,846.
What digit is in each place?

a. ten millions	0
b. ones	6
c. hundred thousands	1
d. ten thousands	3

In 2–6, write each as a decimal.

2. ten thousand forty-three	10,043
3. one hundred twenty-five thousand	125,000
4. six thousand four	6,004
5. two hundred three million	203,000,000
6. forty-two thousand seven hundred	42,700

In 7–9, give a word name for each.

7. 6024   six thousand twenty-four

8. 30,100,063   thirty million, one hundred thousand
             sixty-three

9. 600,200   six hundred thousand, two hundred

■ **HISTORY** *Objective R*

10. *Multiple choice* Which group of people invented the decimal system?
(a) Europeans   (b) Greeks
(c) Hindus   (d) Romans   c

Transition Mathematics © Scott, Foresman and Company   1

7

LESSON

1-2

Decimals for Numbers Between Whole Numbers

Measuring is as common and important a use of numbers as counting. A **unit of measure** can always be split into smaller parts. This makes measures different from counts.

For instance, you can split up measures of time. Suppose someone runs 200 meters and is timed in between 21 and 22 seconds. This time **interval** is pictured on the **number line** below. The marks on the number line are called *tick marks*. The interval on this number line is one second, the distance between two tick marks.

To get more accuracy, blow up the number line between 21 and 22. Then split that interval into ten parts. The interval on the new number line is **one tenth** of a second. The location of the dot shows that the time we are graphing is between 21.8 and 21.9 seconds.

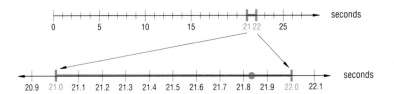

In early 1984, a U.S. women's record in the 200-meter dash was set by Evelyn Ashford. Her time of 21.83 is what is being graphed. To graph 21.83, split the interval between 21.8 and 21.9 into ten parts. The interval on the new number line is one **one-hundredth** of a second.

8

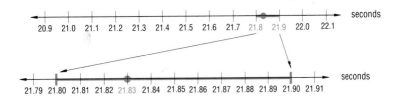

In 21.83, the digit 8 is in the **tenths place.** The digit 3 is in the **hundredths place.** For more accuracy, still more places to the right of the decimal can be used. For instance, here is the famous number pi, written π. The number π is the circumference of (distance around) a circle whose diameter is 1.

$$\pi = 3.1415926\ldots$$

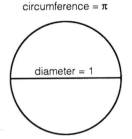

circumference = π

diameter = 1

3 . 1 4 1 5 9 2 6 ...

tenths
hundredths
thousandths
ten-thousandths
hundred-thousandths
millionths
ten-millionths
etc.

The names of the places to the right of the decimal point are similar to the names of the places to the left. Think of the ones place and the decimal point as the center. Then there is perfect balance of names to the right and to the left.

Today's uses often require many decimal places. Some instruments need to be accurate to within millionths of an inch. (That's much less than the thickness of this page.) Computers work at speeds often measured in billionths of a second.

Decimal places were first extended to the right by Simon Stevin, a Flemish mathematician, in 1585. Before then, fractions were used. Decimals are now more common than fractions for measurements. One reason is that they are easier to put in order and compare.

LESSON 1-2   9

Reading   A good strategy is to read aloud and discuss the lesson through **Example 1.** Stress the difference between a count and a measure, and carefully go over place value to the right of the decimal point. Then students can study **Example 2** and its solutions themselves. Give them plenty of time to do this carefully.

Use Evelyn Ashford's track record on page 8 to discuss the idea that no measurement is exact. There is always the possibility that the measure could be made more accurate by including more places to the right of the decimal. The issue of what degree of accuracy is reasonable leads to the concept of estimating by rounding up or down, which is discussed in Lesson 1-3.

1. A board measures 3.182 meters. Show an interval on each number line containing the measure.

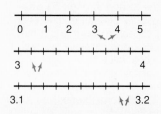

Error Analysis Students may try to graph 3.182 on each number line. Be sure to emphasize the meaning of the word *interval*.

2. Which is larger?
a. 5 or 4.99
5
b. .007 or .06
.06
c. .0025 or .002
.0025

Example 1   Which is larger, 3.01 or 2.999?

Solution   Align the decimal points. "Align" means to put one above the other.

          3.01
          2.999

Start at the left of each number. 3 is larger than 2, so 3.01 is larger.

Example 2   Which is the largest?   0.0073   0.007294   0.00078

Solution 1   Again, align the decimal points.

          0.0073
          0.007294
          0.00078

The bottom number is smallest because it has 0 thousandths while the others have 7 thousandths. To find which of the first two is larger, compare the ten thousandths place. The 3 is larger than the 2, so the top number is largest.

Solution 2   Some people like to rewrite all the numbers to show the same number of decimal places. Adding zeros to the right of a number does not affect its value. ($5 is the same as $5.00.)

          0.007300
          0.007294
          0.000780

Now it is easy to tell that the top number is largest.

In Example 2, a zero appears to the left of the decimal point of each number. This is often done to make it easier to order numbers. It also draws attention to the decimal point and corresponds to the display on most calculators. Notice that two different solutions are given to answer the question of Example 2. When there is more than one way of getting the answer to a question, you should try to learn all the ways.

Some of the questions for this lesson are review. Review questions are very important. You should seek help from friends or your teacher if you cannot do them. The lesson numbers in parentheses following review questions tell where the idea of the question is explained.

10

In 1–4, consider the number 21.83.

1. Between what two consecutive whole numbers is this number?
21 and 22

2. What digit is in the tenths place? 8

3. What digit is in the hundredths place? 3

4. What special event does 21.83 seconds measure?
Evelyn Ashford's time in the 200-meter dash

In 5–10, consider the number 654,987.123456789. What digit is in each place?

5. thousandths 3   **6.** tenths 1

7. hundredths 2   **8.** ten thousandths 4

9. millionths 6   **10.** hundred thousandths 5

11. What digit is in the millionths place of π? 2

12. Name a kind of measurement that can require accuracy to billionths. Sample: computer speed.

13. Who invented the idea of extending decimal places to the right, and when? Simon Stevin, 1585

14. Name one advantage of decimals over fractions.
Sample: easier to order and compare

In 15–18, tell which of the three given numbers is largest and which is smallest.

15. 0.033, 0.015, 0.024
0.033; 0.015

16. 6.783, .6783, 67.83
67.83; .6783

17. 0.98, 0.8, 0.9
0.98; 0.8

18. 4.398, 4.4, 4.4001
4.4001; 4.398

19. a. What is the name of the number that is the circumference of a circle with diameter 1? pi or π
    b. Give the first five decimal places of this number. ("Decimal places" refer to places to the *right* of the decimal point.)
14159

In 20–25, use the number line drawn here. The tick marks are equally spaced. Which letter (if any) corresponds to the given number?

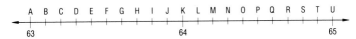

20. 63.4 E   **21.** 64.0 K   **22.** 64.3 N

23. 64.8 S   **24.** 64.80 S   **25.** 64.08
none; between K and L

26. What is the difference between a count and a measure?
Measures can be split; counts cannot.

LESSON 1-2 Decimals for Numbers Between Whole Numbers   **11**

Here are examples showing decimals translated into English.

3.5	three and five tenths
3.54	three and fifty-four hundredths
3.549	three and five hundred forty-nine thousandths

In 27–30, use the above examples to help translate the given number into English.   See margin.

27. 5.9   **28.** 324.66   **29.** 0.024   **30.** 1.414

31. In the decimal for one thousandth, how many zeros are between the decimal point and the one?   2

32. To find a number between 8.2 and 8.3, write them as 8.20 and 8.30. Then any decimal beginning with 8.21, 8.22, and so on up to 8.29 is between them. Use this idea to find a number between 44.6 and 44.7.   Samples: 44.61, 44.69

33. A store sells 5 pairs of socks for $16. Mel wants 1 pair and divides 16 by 5, using a calculator. The calculator shows 3.2. What should Mel pay? $3.20

34. In 1988, Florence Griffith-Joyner (pictured below) set a women's world record of 10.49 seconds in the 100-meter dash. If this record was lowered by a tenth of a second, what would the new record be?   10.39 sec

In 35 and 36, order the numbers from smallest to largest.

35. three thousandths   middle
four thousandths   largest
three millionths   smallest

36. sixty-five thousandths   smallest
sixty-five thousand   largest
sixty five   middle

37. In the 1988 Olympics Florence Griffith-Joyner ran 200 meters in 21.34 seconds. Is this faster or slower than the 1984 time of Evelyn Ashford?   faster

12

In 38 and 39, write as a decimal. *(Lesson 1-1)*

38. four hundred million   400,000,000

39. thirty-one thousand sixty-eight   31,068

40. Consider the number 587,402,139. What number is in each place? *(Lesson 1-1)*
  a. thousands   2   **b.** hundred thousands   4
  c. ten millions   8   **d.** ones   9

41. Based on population, which area will get the most federal aid? *(Lesson 1-1)*
  Kansas City, Missouri-Kansas (population 1,575,000)
  Seattle, Washington (1,862,000)
  Miami-Hialeah, Florida (1,814,000)
  Denver, Colorado (1,640,000)
  Seattle, Washington

42. Written as a decimal, the number one million is a 1 followed by how many zeros? *(Lesson 1-1)*   6

43. In ''76 trombones,'' name the count and the counting unit. *(Lesson 1-1)*   76; trombones

44. a. What is the largest number of places to the right of the decimal point that your calculator will display?   Answers will vary.
   b. If your calculator has a key for π, what does it display when you press that key?   Samples: 3.1415927, 3.141592653

FOLLOW-UP

MORE PRACTICE
For more questions on SPUR Objectives, use *Lesson Master 1-2,* shown below.

EXTENSION
Computer *Computer Master 1,* provided in the Teacher's Resource File, corresponds to the number line activities of this lesson. For more general information on computer skills, see *General Teaching Suggestions: Computers* on pages T42–T43 of the Teacher's Edition.

NAME _____

LESSON **MASTER   1–2**
QUESTIONS ON SPUR OBJECTIVES

■ SKILLS   *Objective A (See pages 49–51 for objectives.)*
1. Write three and twenty thousandths as a decimal.   3.020
2. Write six hundred and four hundredths as a decimal.   600.04
3. Write 0.025 in words.   twenty-five thousandths
4. Write 3.7 in words.   three and seven tenths

■ SKILLS   *Objective B*
5. Order from smallest to largest: 0, .023, .23, 2.3
   0.   2.3   .23   .023
6. Which is largest: one tenth, one thousandth, one millionth, or one billionth?   one tenth

■ SKILLS   *Objective C*
In 7 and 8, write a number that is between the two given decimals.
7. 3.99 and 4   sample: 3.995
8. 0.62 and 0.63   sample: 0.621

■ REPRESENTATIONS   *Objective P*
In 9 and 10, use this number line.
12   13   14   15
9. What is the unit?   0.1
10. What number is graphed?   13.4

In 11 and 12, use this number line.
8   10   12   14
11. What is the unit?   0.2
12. What number is graphed?   10.8

2   Transition Mathematics © Scott, Foresman and Company

13

LESSON 1-3

RESOURCES
■ Lesson Master 1-3

TEACHING NOTES

This is a good lesson for students to read on their own; the discussion is based on real situations and is not too technical. Also, most students have probably had some experience with rounding. Some teachers prefer to cover Lessons 1-3 and 1-4 in a single day. If these are done together, do the Covering the Reading questions orally and assign all the other questions.

Reading To focus attention on reading skills, ask students to make a list of the main ideas from the lesson and also to be ready to explain the examples. If students have read carefully, they should have identified the following key points: reasons for estimating; rounding up, down, and to the nearest; and truncating.

1-3

Estimating by Rounding Up or Rounding Down

In many types of situations, an **estimate** may be preferred over an exact value.

1. An exact value may *not be worth the trouble* it would take to get it.
   Example: About 3500 people attended the half time concert.

2. An estimate is often *easier to work with* than the exact value.
   Example: Instead of multiplying $169.95, let's use $170.

3. It may be *safer* to use an estimate than to try to use an exact value.
   Example: The trip will cost at least $1800, so we will budget $2000 to play it safe.

4. An exact *value may change* from time to time, forcing an estimate.
   Example: I estimate that the coin will land heads 5 times in 10 tosses.

5. Predictions of the future or notions about the past usually are estimates, since *exact values may be impossible to obtain*.
   Example: One estimate of the world population in the year 2000 is 7 billion.

The most common method of estimating is **rounding.** There are three kinds of rounding: **rounding up, rounding down,** and rounding to the nearest. Here are some examples of rounding up and rounding down. (In Lesson 1-4, rounding to the nearest is discussed.) Rounding is almost always done with a particular decimal place in mind.

14

Example 1   A certain type of label is sold in packages of 100. If you need 1325 labels, how many labels must you buy?

Solution   You must buy more labels than you need. So you need to round *up* to the next 100. Since 1325 is between 1300 and 1400, round up to 1400.

Example 2   A store sells six cans of orange juice for $1.39. You want one can. So you divide 1.39 by 6 to get the cost. Your calculator shows 0.2316666. What will you probably have to pay for the can?

Solution   The store will probably round *up* to the next penny. Pennies are hundredths of dollars, so look at the hundredths place in 0.2316666. The hundredths place is 3. That means that 0.2316666 is between 0.23 and 0.24. You will probably have to pay $0.24, which is 24¢.

Example 3   Some calculators round *down*, or **truncate,** all long decimals to the preceding millionth (the sixth decimal place). What will such a calculator show for π = 3.1415926535...?

Solution   The sixth decimal place is 2. The calculator will show 3.141592.

Questions

Covering the Reading

1. Give an example of a situation where an estimate should be preferred over an exact value.
   Sample: number attending an outdoor concert
2. Name five reasons why estimates are often preferred over exact values.   See margin.

3. The most common way of estimating is by __?__.   rounding

4. Name three types of rounding.   up, down, to the nearest

5. A certain type of label is sold in packages of 100. If you need 1721 labels, how many labels must you buy?   1800

6. Some special pencils are sold in packages of 10. A teacher needs one pencil for each student in a class of 32. How many pencils must be bought?   at least 40

LESSON 1-3   Estimating by Rounding Up or Rounding Down   15

Questions 17-20: These suggest situations where rounding up and rounding down might be used.

Question 30: This is the first Exploration question requiring the use of another book. Looking up answers in resource books demonstrates clearly that mathematics is not confined to math textbooks and math class.

10. It is cut off or rounded down to a particular decimal place.

30. to cut off a part of

7. A store sells three cans of soup for $1. You want one can. So you divide $1.00 by 3 to get the cost. Your calculator shows 0.333333. How much will you probably have to pay for the can? 34¢

8. A store sells a dozen eggs for $1.09. You want a half dozen. To find out how much you will pay, you divide $1.09 by 2 on your calculator. The calculator shows 0.545. How much will you have to pay? 55¢

9. If a calculator rounds down to the preceding millionth, what will it show for 0.0123456? 0.012345

Applying the Mathematics

10. When a decimal is truncated, what happens to it? See margin.

11. Suppose a calculator rounds down to the preceding hundred-millionth (the eighth decimal place). What will it show for 0.97531246809? 0.97531246

12. Round $1795 **a.** up to the next ten dollars, and **b.** down to the preceding ten dollars. a. $1800; b. $1790

13. Round 5280, the number of feet in a mile, **a.** up to the next 1000, and **b.** down to the preceding 1000. a. 6000; b.5000

14. Round 30.48, the number of centimeters in a foot, as follows: **a.** up to the next tenth. 30.5 **b.** down to the preceding tenth. 30.4

15. Round $30.48 as follows:
a. up to the next ten dollars. $40
b. down to the preceding ten dollars. $30

16. Round 1.609344, the number of kilometers in a mile, **a.** up to the next thousandth, and **b.** down to the preceding thousandth. a. 1.610; b. 1.609

In 17–20, tell whether a high or a low estimate would be preferred.

17. You are estimating how large a birthday cake to order for a party. high

18. You estimate how much money you should take on a trip. high

19. You estimate how much weight an elevator can carry without being overloaded. low

20. You estimate how many minutes it will take to do your math homework. high

Review

In 21 and 22, order the numbers from smallest to largest. *(Lesson 1-2)*

21. 5.1, 5.01, 5.001   5.001, 5.01, 5.1

22. .29, 0.3, .07   .07, .29, 0.3

23. Which number does not equal 0.86? *(Lesson 1-2)*
0.860   .86   .086   .086

In 24 and 25, find a number that is between the two given numbers. *(Lesson 1-2)*

24. 5.8 and 5.9
Samples: 5.81, 5.89

25. 5.9 and 6
Samples: 5.91, 5.99

In 26 and 27, use this number line. *(Lesson 1-2)*

```
     Z  Y  X  W  V  U  T  S  R  Q  P  O  N  M  L  K  J  I
   ←————————————————————————————————————————————————————
            2              3              4
```

26. What is the interval on the number line?   0.2

27. Which letter on the number line corresponds to the given number?
a. 3.0 Q **b.** 2.8 R **c.** 1.4 Y

28. Write this number as a decimal: four million, thirty thousand.
(Lesson 1-1)   4,030,000

Exploration

29. The men's world record in the mile (as of October, 1990) was set by the British runner, Steve Cram, in 1985. It is usually written as 3:46.32. Translate the number 3:46.32 into English.
three minutes, forty-six and thirty-two hundredths seconds

30. What is a dictionary definition of the word *truncate*?
See margin.

31. On this and other computer questions in this book, it is possible that your computer will not act as other computers. If you get a strange message or no response, ask your teacher for help.
  a. Put your computer in programming mode, and type ?INT(4.57). The ? is short for PRINT. You could also type PRINT INT(4.57). Now press the RETURN key. What does the computer print?   4
  b. Try part **a** with the following: ?INT(115.68), ?INT(789), ?INT(30000.12345), and ?INT(.995). Based on what the computer prints, what does INT() do to the number inside the parentheses?   rounds down to the nearest integer

FOLLOW-UP

MORE PRACTICE
For more questions on SPUR Objectives, use *Lesson Master 1-3*, shown below.

EXTENSION
Although students do not need calculators until Lesson 1-7, Lessons 1-2 and 1-3 refer to calculators. If students have them, the class could experiment to find out whether their calculators truncate or round up in certain circumstances. Ask students to devise a single problem that will help them make this determination. (A problem such as 2÷3 will work.)
  For more information on calculators, see *General Teaching Suggestions: Calculators* on page T40 of the Teacher's Edition.

NAME _____

LESSON **MASTER   1–3**
QUESTIONS ON **SPUR** OBJECTIVES

■**SKILLS** *Objective D (See pages 49–51 for objectives.)*

1. Round 234.37 down to the preceding tenth. 234.3
2. Round 7.6247 up to the next hundredth. 7.63
3. Round .8977 up to the next hundredth. .90
4. Round 8,700,657 down to the preceding million. 8,000,000
5. Round 7376 down to the preceding ten. 7370
6. Round 785.63 up to the next tenth. 785.7
7. If your calculator truncates after six decimal places, what will it display for 0.37373737373737 . . . ? 0.373737
8. Joe's calculator truncates after eight decimal places. What will his calculator display for 0.3333333337? 0.33333333

■**USES** *Objective L*

9. Susan is to bring 250 paper cups to a neighborhood party. The cups are sold in packages of 48. How many packages will she need to buy? 6 packages

10. The store sells a pound of butter (four sticks) for $1.99. You buy only one stick. After dividing, your calculator shows 0.4975. What will you pay? $0.50 or 50¢

■**USES** *Objective M*

11. Give a situation where a *high*, rather than a low estimate is needed. sample: when estimating the cost of a trip

12. Rick put 295 miles on the family car during the month of June. When discussing the matter with his father, Rick made the statement, "That's only about 75 miles a week, Dad!" Was Rick's estimate high or low? high

Transition Mathematics © Scott, Foresman and Company   **3**

LESSON 1-4

RESOURCES
■ Lesson Master 1-4
■ Quiz on Lessons 1-1
   Through 1-4

OBJECTIVES

Letter codes refer to the SPUR Objectives on page 2B.

D Round any decimal to the nearest value of a decimal place.

E Estimate answers to arithmetic questions to the nearest integer.

L Round to estimate a given number in a real situation.

TEACHING NOTES

Reading Here is the perfect opportunity to send students home to read the lesson by themselves and do all the questions. On the next day, give students an opportunity to ask questions about the reading. Go over the assigned questions, asking for answers and explanations.

In **Example 3,** students should be able to estimate $10.49 as $10.50.

One skill not covered here but which you might wish to discuss is *reasonableness*. The average jet speed of 597.31 in Additional Example 1 would almost always be rounded to 600 mph.

LESSON

1-4

Estimating by Rounding to the Nearest

Lasers, like the one above, travel at the speed of light.

If 38 is rounded *up* to the next ten, the result is 40. If 38 is rounded *down* to the preceding ten, the result is 30. The number 40 is nearer to 38 than 30, so 40 is a better estimate of 38. When 38 is rounded to 40, we say that 38 has been **rounded to the nearest** 10.

■ ■ ■ ■ ■ ■ ■ ■

Example 1 The speed of light is nearly 186,281.7 miles per second. Round this quantity to the nearest
  a. mile per second
  b. ten miles per second
  c. hundred miles per second
  d. thousand miles per second
  e. ten thousand miles per second.

Solutions
  a. 186,281.7 is between 186,281 and 186,282. Because .7 is greater than .5, the number 186,281.7 is nearer to 186,282.
  b. 186,281.7 is between 186,280 and 186,290. Because 81.7 is closer to 80 than to 90, the rounded value is nearer 186,280.
  c. 186,281.7 is between 186,200 and 186,300 and is closer to 186,300.
  d. The answer is 186,000.
  e. The answer is 190,000.

The more accuracy that is needed, the closer one would want to be to the original value.

■ ■ ■ ■ ■ ■ ■ ■

Example 2 To calculate interest at 8.237%, the number 0.08237 may be used as a multiplier. Round this number to the nearest **a.** tenth, **b.** hundredth, **c.** thousandth, and **d.** ten thousandth.

18

Solutions
a. 0.08237 is between 0.0 and 0.1. It is nearer to 0.1, so that's the answer.
b. 0.08237 is between 0.08 and 0.09 and is nearer to 0.08.
c. 0.08237 is between 0.082 and 0.083 and is closer to 0.082.
d. 0.08237 is between 0.0823 and 0.0824 and is nearer to 0.0824.

■ ■ ■ ■ ■ ■ ■■■

Example 3 Paula must multiply $10.49 by 7 to find the cost of seven tapes. She rounds $10.49 to the nearest ten cents, $10.50, to estimate.

Actual cost: $10.49   Paula's estimate: $10.50
                  × 7   × 7
               ———   ———
               $73.43 $73.50

In Example 3, Paula can get a quick estimate by rounding $10.49 to the nearest dollar, $10. She can then estimate the cost in her head.

If the digit to the right of the place to be rounded to is a 5, there may be a choice in rounding. For instance, to round $10.50 to the nearest dollar, either $10 or $11 can be a correct answer. When there are many numbers with 5s to be rounded, it makes sense to round up half the time and round down the other half of the time.

Questions

Covering the Reading

1. Round 43 as follows: **a.** up to the next ten, **b.** down to the preceding ten, and **c.** to the nearest ten.   a. 50; b. 40; c. 40

2. Round 0.547 as follows: **a.** up to the next hundredth, **b.** down to the preceding hundredth, and **c.** to the nearest hundredth.
a. 0.55; b. 0.54; c. 0.55

3. Round 88.8888 to the nearest **a.** hundredth, **b.** tenth, **c.** one, **d.** ten, and **e.** hundred.   a. 88.89; b. 88.9; c. 89; d. 90; e. 100

4. To estimate the cost of 4 records at $4.69 each, you might round $4.69 to the nearest ten cents. What do you get for the rounded value? $4.70

LESSON 1-4   Estimating by Rounding to the Nearest   **19**

ADDITIONAL EXAMPLES
1. On an overseas flight, a jet averaged 597.31 miles per hour. Round this quantity to the nearest:
a. tenth of a mile per hour
597.3
b. mile per hour
597
c. ten miles per hour
600
d. hundred miles per hour
600

2. The fraction $\frac{1}{7}$ is about equal to .142857. Round to the nearest:
a. hundred-thousandth
.14286
b. hundredth
.14
c. tenth
.1
d. whole number
0

3. *Multiple choice* Which equals 5.96 × 43? (No calculators allowed.) (a) 2.5628 (b) 25.628 (c) 256.28 (d) 2562.8
(c)

Question 3: In situations other than those involving money, students often have questions about leaving terminal zeros to the right of the decimal point. They have to satisfy the number of places called for in the question. For example, 88.898 rounded to the nearest hundredth is 88.90, not 88.900.

Error Analysis for Question 27: *Dozen* is a number name, just like *hundred*. Many students will view it as a unit, but it is not.

Question 30: Students may write 3.8 because they rounded 3.775 to the nearest tenth. Refer students to the definition of *truncate* on page 15.

Question 32: This requires students to judge whether information is or is not useful in a problem. It exemplifies the important skill of *solving problems with unnecessary information*.

ADDITIONAL ANSWERS
8. when the first digit to the right of the place to be rounded to is a 5 and there are no other digits to the right

23. samples: 3.21, 3.39

24. samples: 6.291, 6.299

25. There are none. These numbers are equal.

5. To estimate the cost of 4 records at $4.69 each, you might round $4.69 to the nearest dollar. What is your rounded value?   **$5.00**

6. Estimate the cost of 6 shirts at $19.95 each by rounding to the nearest dollar and then multiplying.   **$120**

7. Round the speed of light to the nearest hundred thousand miles per second.   **200,000 miles per second**

8. When is there a choice in rounding to the nearest?   **See margin.**

9. The number 0.0525 is used in some calculations of interest on savings. Round this number to the nearest thousandth.
0.053 or 0.052

10. When there are many numbers ending in 5 to be rounded, what is the sensible thing to do?
round up half the time, down the other half

Applying the Mathematics

11. The U.S. Internal Revenue Service allows taxpayers to round all amounts to the nearest dollar. But half dollars must be rounded up. In figuring income tax, to what value can you round each amount?
a. $89.46   **$89**   b. $165.50   **$166**
c. $100.91   **$101**   d. $5324.28   **$5324**

12. Round 2.54, the number of centimeters in an inch, to the nearest tenth.   **2.5**

13. Round 328.35, the average consumer price index in December, 1986, to the nearest whole number.   **328**

14. Round 3.666666 to the nearest **a.** tenth, **b.** hundredth, **c.** thousandth, and **d.** ten-thousandth.
a. 3.7; b. 3.67; c. 3.667; d. 3.6667

15. Round 12.5300 to the nearest hundredth.   **12.53**

16. You buy items costing $4.99, $6.99, and $8.99 in a store.
a. Add these numbers.   **$20.97**
b. How close would you be if you rounded each given number to the nearest dollar and then added?   **$21, only 3¢ off**

17. Consider the addition problem 2.898765489 + 8.1898989898.
  a. Estimate the answer by rounding both numbers to the nearest whole number and adding the estimates.   11
  b. How could you get a better estimate?
  by rounding to the nearest tenth or hundredth, for example

In 18–21, what is the answer rounded to the nearest whole number? (Hint: You should be able to do these mentally.)

18. 6 × $3.99 $24

19. $11.95 divided by 2 $6

20. 920.9994 − 0.0003992   921

21. 2.0123456789 + 3.0123456789   5

22. A number is rounded to the nearest hundred. The resulting estimate is 9,600.
  a. What is the smallest value the original number might have had?   9550
  b. What is the largest value the original number might have had?   9649

Review

In 23–25, find a number that is between the two given numbers. *(Lesson 1-2)*   See margin.

23. 3.2 and 3.4   **24.** 6.3 and 6.29   **25.** 14.23 and 14.230

26. Write one thousand, five hundred six and three tenths as a decimal. *(Lesson 1-2)*   1506.3

27. John bought a dozen eggs. In "a dozen eggs," what is the count and what is the counting unit? (Watch out!) *(Lesson 1-1)*   12; eggs

28. If a calculator shows that you should pay $1.534 for something, what will a store probably charge you? *(Lesson 1-3)* $1.54

29. Round 1.008 as follows: **a.** up to the next hundredth, and **b.** down to the preceding hundredth. *(Lesson 1-3)*   a. 1.01; b. 1.00

30. Truncate 3.775 to one decimal place. *(Lesson 1-3)*   3.7

31. The number ten million consists of a one followed by how many zeros? *(Lesson 1-1)*   7

Exploration

32. a. Find the number that satisfies all of these conditions.
    Condition 1: When rounded up to the next hundred, the number becomes 600.
    Condition 2: When rounded down to the preceding ten, the number becomes 570.
    Condition 3: When rounded to the nearest ten, the number is increased by 4.
    Condition 4: The number is a whole number.   576
  b. Are any of the conditions not needed?   1 and 4

FOLLOW-UP

MORE PRACTICE
For more questions on SPUR Objectives, use *Lesson Master 1-4*, shown below.

EVALUATION
A quiz covering Lessons 1-1 through 1-4 is provided in the Teacher's Resource File on page 1.

NAME _____

LESSON **MASTER   1–4**
QUESTIONS ON **SPUR** OBJECTIVES

■**SKILLS**   *Objective D (See pages 49–51 for objectives.)*

1. Round 10.61 to the nearest tenth.   10.6
2. Round 49.7 to the nearest whole number.   50
3. Round 534,789 to the nearest thousand.   535,000
4. Round 67.343 to the nearest hundredth.   67.34
5. *Multiple choice* The number 12.3 has already been rounded to the nearest tenth. Which of the following could not have been the original number?
(a) 12.30   (b) 12.34
(c) 12.35   (d) 12.40   d
6. Round 7.0007 up to the next hundredth.   7.01
7. Round 60,776 down to the preceding ten.   60,770

■**SKILLS**   *Objective E*

8. When estimating 74.60237 − 70.003 to the nearest whole number,
   a. what subtraction should you use?   75 − 70
   b. what estimate do you get?   5
9. When estimating 9 × 7.93 to the nearest whole number,
   a. what multiplication should you use?   9 × 8
   b. what estimate do you get?   72

■**USES**   *Objective L*

10. If a bill of $14.93 is to be split among three diners, about how much should each person pay? $15 ÷ 3 = $5
11. According to recent statistics, the total enrollment in elementary and secondary day schools in the United States is 39,513,379 students. Round this number to the nearest hundred thousand.   39,500,000

4   *Transition Mathematics © Scott, Foresman and Company*

OBJECTIVES

*Letter codes refer to the
SPUR Objectives on page
2B.*
B Order decimals.
C Give a number that is between two decimals.
N Correctly interpret situations with two directions as
positive, negative, or corresponding to zero.
O Graph a decimal on a
number line.

LESSON

1-5

Negative Numbers

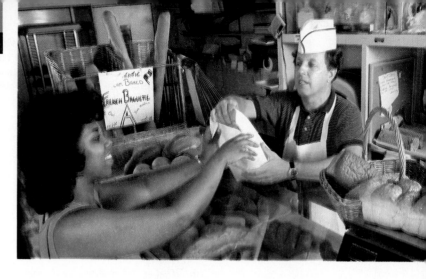

On every item a store sells, the store can make money, lose money, or break even. Here are some of the possibilities.

In English	In mathematics
make $3	3
make $2	2
make $1	1
break even	0
lose $1	-1
lose $1.50	-1.5
lose $2	-2
lose $3	-3

The numbers along the number line describe the situation without using words. Higher numbers on the line are larger and mean more profits. Lower numbers mean lower profits. The ⁻ (nega-tive) sign stands for **opposite of.** The opposite of making $1.50 is losing $1.50. So the opposite of 1.50 is -1.50, and vice versa. The numbers with the ⁻ sign are called **negative numbers.**

There are three common ways in which the ⁻ sign for negatives is said out loud.

-3: negative 3   correct
-3: opposite of 3   correct
-3: minus 3   very commonly used, but can be confus-
                    ing, since there is no subtraction here.

Most people know negative numbers from temperatures. But they are found in many other situations. On TV bowling, -12 means "behind by 12 pins." The symbol +12, called **positive** 12, means "ahead by 12 pins." The numbers 12 and +12 are identi-cal. (In this book we use +12 as little as we can. The + sign can get confused with addition.)

22

On a horizontal number line, negative numbers are almost always placed at the left. The numbers identified on the number line drawn here are the **integers**. The **positive integers** are the numbers 1, 2, 3, …. The positive integers are sometimes called the **natural numbers.** The **negative integers** are -1, -2, -3, …. *Zero* is an integer but is neither positive nor negative.

negative numbers   positive numbers

Negative numbers can be used when a situation has two opposite directions. Either direction may be picked as positive. The other is then negative. Zero stands for the starting point. The table below gives some situations that often use negative numbers.

Situation	Negative	Zero	Positive
savings account	withdrawal	no change	deposit
time	before	now	after
games	behind	even	ahead
business	loss	break even	profit
elevation	below sea level	sea level	above sea level

Example 1

The shore of the Dead Sea in Israel, the lowest land on Earth, is 1286 feet below sea level. This can be represented by -1286 feet.

Example 2

Suppose time is measured in seconds. Then 4.3 seconds before the launch of a space shuttle is given by -4.3 seconds. Rounded to the nearest second, that is -4 seconds. One *minute* after the launch is 60 seconds. The time of launch is 0 seconds.

LESSON 1-5 Negative Numbers   23

Reading Emphasize the correct ways of reading –3 (negative 3 or opposite of 3). Students often say *minus 3* because that is commonly used outside math class, even though it is misleading.

Call attention to the structure of the chart on page 23 so that students realize they must read it across rather than down. For example, ask students to use the chart to give specific examples of the use of positive and negative numbers in games.

Number lines help students understand the visual representation of negative numbers. Stress that negative numbers appear to the left on a horizontal number line and down on a vertical one.

One discussion topic students like is other real-world examples of opposites: batteries, a magnet, a compass, football gains and losses, above and below par in golf, stock market gains and losses, and so on.

ADDITIONAL EXAMPLES
1. In golf, a score used as a standard is called *par*. Name an integer that represents each of the following scores at the 1988 U.S. Open Golf Tournament.
a. Curtis Strange and Nick Faldo at six under par
–6
b. Ben Crenshaw at even par
0
c. Bill Mayfair at three over par
+3
2. Write a number to represent the depth of the Marianas Trench, the deepest part of the Pacific Ocean. It is 36,198 feet below sea level.
–36,198

Covering the Reading

1. Translate -4 into English in two different ways.
   negative four, opposite of four
2. You withdraw $25 from a savings account. Is this transaction considered positive, or is it considered negative?   negative
3. Next to a bowler's name on TV is the number -8. Is the bowler ahead or behind?   behind
4. On a horizontal number line, negative numbers are usually to the __?__ of positive numbers.   left
5. On a vertical number line, negative numbers are usually __?__ positive numbers.   below
6. Graph -7, -3, -9.6, 0, and 2 on a horizontal number line.
   See margin.
7. Graph a profit of $4, a loss of $7, breaking even, and a profit of $10 on a vertical number line.   See margin.

In 8–10, three words or phrases relating to a situation are given. Which would usually be considered positive? which negative? which zero?   8.–10. See margin.

8. Football: losing yardage, gaining yardage, no gain

9. Time: tomorrow, today, yesterday

10. Stock market: no change, gain, loss

11. What numbers are the integers?   ...,-3, -2, -1, 0, 1, 2, 3, ...

12. Which of the following numbers is not an integer? 5   0   -5   .5
    .5
13. Another name for *positive integer* is __?__.   natural number

14. Give an example of an integer that is neither positive nor negative.   0

15. Give an example of a negative number that is not an integer.
    Samples: -1.5, -π, -2.36

Applying the Mathematics

16. Suppose time is measured in days and 0 stands for today.
    a. What number stands for yesterday?   -1
    b. What number stands for tomorrow?   1
    c. What number stands for the day before yesterday?   -2
    d. What number stands for the day after tomorrow?   2

17. You guess how many points your school's basketball team will score in its next game. What number could stand for:
    a. a guess 3 points too high?   3
    b. a guess ten points too low?   -10
    c. a perfect guess?   0

24

In 18–21, use the number line drawn here. Which letter corresponds to the given number?

A B C D E F G H I J K L M N O P Q R S T U
-10   -9   -8

18. -9.1 *J*   **19.** -8.4 *Q*   **20.** -9.0 *K*   **21.** -10.1
none

22. Pick the two numbers that are equal: -43.3, -43.03, -43.30, 43.3
-43.3 and -43.30

23. Which numbers are not natural numbers? -1 0 $\frac{1}{2}$ 1 2
-1, 0, $\frac{1}{2}$

In 24–27, round to the nearest integer.

24. -1.75 *-2*   **25.** -3.9 *-4*   **26.** -43.06 *-43* **27.** -0.53 *-1*

Review

28. Order from smallest to largest: 439   349   394   493. *(Lesson 1-1)*
349, 394, 439, 493

29. Order from smallest to largest: 5.67   5.067   5.607   5.60.
(Lesson 1-2)   5.067, 5.60, 5.607, 5.67

30. Write as a decimal: four hundred sixty-two thousand and one tenth. *(Lesson 1-2)*   462,000.1

31. What number is in the thousands place of 24,680.13579?
(Lesson 1-2)   4

32. What number is in the thousandths place of 24,680.13579?
(Lesson 1-2)   5

33. Round $28.47 as follows: **a.** up to the next dollar, **b.** down to the preceding dollar, and **c.** to the nearest dollar. *(Lessons 1-3, 1-4)*
a. $29; b. $28; c. $28

34. Suppose the points are equally spaced on the number line drawn here. If *E* is 1 and *L* is 2, what number corresponds to *C*? *(Lesson 1-2)*
1.2

D   E   C   I   M   A   L

Exploration

35. Use an almanac to find the place in the United States with the lowest elevation. What number represents this elevation?
Death Valley; about -282 feet

36. Find an example of negative numbers that is not given in this lesson.   samples: east positive, west negative; clockwise positive, counterclockwise negative; under budget positive, over budget negative

FOLLOW-UP

MORE PRACTICE
For more questions on SPUR Objectives, use *Lesson Master 1-5*, shown below.

EVALUATION
Alternative Assessment
Have students respond to these true-false statements:
1. All numbers are either positive or negative.
F

2. On a horizontal number line, -8 is to the left of -7.
T

3. On a vertical number line, -5 is below -6.
F

4. Every positive integer has a negative opposite.
T

5. Zero is not an integer.
F

NAME _____

LESSON **MASTER   1-5**
QUESTIONS ON **SPUR** OBJECTIVES

■SKILLS   *Objective B (See pages 49–51 for objectives.)*
In 1 and 2, identify the largest and the smallest number in each group.

1. -0.003; -0.030; 0.003; 0.030
largest ____0.030____   smallest ____-0.030____

2. -5; -4.98; 4.981; 5
largest ____5____   smallest ____-5____

In 3 and 4, order from smallest to largest.

3. -9 0 -8 9   ____-9, -8, 0, 9____

4. -7.47 -7.474 -7.46   ____-7.474, -7.47, -7.46____

■SKILLS   *Objective C*
In 5 and 6, give a number that is between the two given decimals.

5. -4 and -5   sample: -4.4

6. -1.5 and -1.75   sample: -1.6

■USES   *Objective N*

7. A business loss of $30,000 corresponds to what number?   -30,000

8. During a space shuttle launch, what number would represent:

a. 6 seconds after the launch   6

b. 2 seconds before the launch   -2

c. the exact time of the launch   0

■REPRESENTATIONS   *Objective O*

9. Graph the numbers 0, -2, -3, and 2 on the number line below.

10. Graph the numbers 4, 3.8, 3, and 2.5 on the number line below.

5

OBJECTIVES

Letter codes refer to the SPUR Objectives on page 2B.

I Use the < and > symbols correctly between numbers.

N Correctly interpret situations with two directions as positive, negative, or corresponding to zero.

TEACHING NOTES

Reading After students have read Lesson 1-6 on their own, you might ask them for a summary of the important points. Such a synopsis should include the two Cautions on page 27, as well as notes about the inequality symbols.

To preserve clarity, mathematicians usually do not use more than one type of inequality symbol in the same sentence.

If you expect students to have their own calculators, remind them that scientific calculators are needed for the next lesson.

LESSON

1-6

Symbols for Inequality

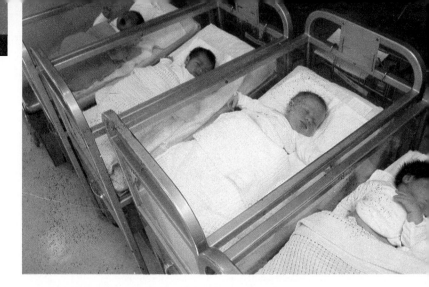

Counts are frequently compared. For instance, in 1960 there were about 4,097,000 births in the United States. In 1980 there were about 3,612,000 births. To indicate that there were fewer births in 1980 we write

$$3,612,000 < 4,097,000$$

The symbol < means **is less than.** The symbol > means **is greater than,** so we could also write

$$4,097,000 > 3,612,000$$

The symbols < and > are examples of **inequality symbols.** These symbols always point to the smaller number. Comparison of populations is useful in knowing whether more schools or hospitals should be built, or how many people could buy a particular item, or watch a television program.

Measures can also be compared. You probably have compared your height and weight to those of other people. Mario is 5'6" tall. Setsuko is 4'10" tall. You can conclude:

Mario is taller than Setsuko.
$$5'6" > 4'10"$$
Setsuko is shorter than Mario.
$$4'10" < 5'6"$$

Numbers can be compared, whether they are positive, negative, or zero. For instance, a temperature of 0°C is colder than one of 4°C. In symbols,

$$0 < 4.$$

A temperature of -7°C is colder than either of these temperatures.

$$-7 < 0$$
$$-7 < 4$$

26

Numbers on a number line are easy to compare. Smaller numbers are usually to the *left* of, or *below* larger numbers. The numbers -7, 0, and 4 are graphed on the vertical and the horizontal number lines below.

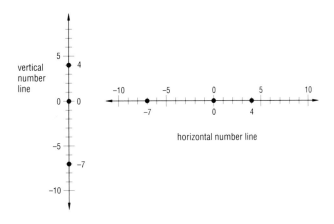

When numbers are in order, inequalities can be combined. For the number lines pictured here, you could write either -7 < 0 < 4 or 4 > 0 > -7.

Caution: Even though 10 is greater than 5, -10 is less than -5. In symbols, -10 < -5. This is because -10 could mean a lower temperature or bigger loss than -5.

Caution: Do not use > and < in the same sentence. For instance, do not write 5 > 3 < 4.

Questions

Covering the Reading

1. Give an example of an occasion when it would be useful to compare counts.
   Samples: comparing numbers of births, comparing heights
2. What is the meaning of the symbol <?   is less than

3. What is the meaning of the symbol >?   is greater than

In 4–7, rewrite the sentence using inequality symbols.

4. -5 is less than -3.   -5 < -3

5. 6 is greater than -12.   6 > -12

6. 4'11" is shorter than 5'.   4'11" < 5'

7. 0 is between -2 and 2. (Use two symbols.)   -2 < 0 < 2, or 2 > 0 > -2

LESSON 1-6   Symbols for Inequality   27

ADDITIONAL EXAMPLES
1. The higher score wins the game. If Tony scores -6 and Laura scores -10, who is the winner?
Tony

Error Analysis Students may mistake -10 for the higher score. Tell students to think of -10 as a bigger loss than -6 and, therefore, the lesser number.

2. Write the numbers 3.4, -34, and -3.4 in order using inequality symbols.
**-34 < -3.4 < 3.4 or
3.4 > -3.4 > -34**

In 8–10, write a sentence with the same meaning, using the other inequality symbol.

8. $2 < 2.1$ $2.1 > 2$

9. $18 > 0$ $0 < 18$

10. $0.43 < 0.432 < 0.44$ $0.44 > 0.432 > 0.43$

In 11–13, translate into English words.   See margin.

11. $-3 < 3$ **12.** $17 > -1.5$ **13.** $-4 < -3 < -2$

In 14–16, translate into mathematics, using a $>$ or $<$ sign.

14. A temperature of −6°F is colder than a temperature of 15°F.
$-6°F < 15°F$

15. The wrestler Andre the Giant, whose height is 7′4″, is taller than the basketball player David Robinson, whose height is 7′1″.
$7′4″ > 7′1″$

16. That school has 125 ninth-graders and 119 tenth-graders. There are more ninth-graders. $125 > 119$

17. On a horizontal number line, larger numbers are to the __?__ of smaller numbers.   right

18. On a vertical number line, larger numbers are __?__ smaller numbers.   above

Applying the Mathematics

In 19 and 20, translate into mathematics.

19. A profit of $8000 is better than a loss of $2000. $\$8000 > -\$2000$

20. An elevation 300 ft below sea level is higher than an elevation 400 ft below sea level.   -300 ft > -400 ft

In 21–26, choose the correct symbol: $<$, $=$, or $>$.

21. .305 __?__ .3046   >   **22.** .0008 __?__ 0.008   <

23. 6.01 __?__ 6.000001   >   **24.** -14 __?__ -14.5   >

25. -99.5 __?__ 9.95   <   **26.** -3.20 __?__ -3.2   =

In 27 and 28, put the three numbers into one sentence with two inequality symbols.   See margin.

27. 62.1, 6.21, 0.621   **28.** -4.1, -41, and 4.1

29. The thermometer pictured below shows Joanne's body temperature on three consecutive days of a cold. Put the three numbers into one sentence connected by inequality symbols.
99.2 < 99.8 < 100.4 or 100.4 > 99.8 > 99.2

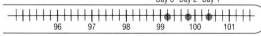

28

30. Consider the number 8249.0351. Name the digit in each place. *(Lesson 1-2)*

  a. thousands   8   **b.** thousandths   5

  c. hundreds   2   **d.** hundredths   3

31. Order 0.07243, 0.07249, and 0.0782 from smallest to largest. *(Lesson 1-2)*   0.07243, 0.07249, 0.0782

32. Name all the whole numbers less than 5. *(Lesson 1-1)*   0, 1, 2, 3, 4

33. Name all the integers between -4 and 3. *(Lesson 1-5)*
-3, -2, -1, 0, 1, 2

34. Suppose time is measured in years and 0 stands for this year. What number stands for:

  a. next year?   1   **b.** last year?   -1

  c. 2010?   21 (in 1989)   **d.** 1925? *(Lesson 1-5)*   -64 (in 1989)

In 35 and 36, estimate each sum to the nearest whole number. *(Lesson 1-4)*

35. 70.0392 + 6.98234   77   **36.** $14.95 + $2.99 + $7.89 $26

37. Round 6.28318... (the number that is 2 times π) to the nearest thousandth. *(Lesson 1-4)*   6.283

38. Write twenty-two and ninety-five hundredths in decimal notation. (This was the winning time in seconds in the 1982 World Rubik's Cube competition.) *(Lesson 1-2)*   22.95

39. The inequality signs < and > were first used by Thomas Harriot, an English mathematician, in 1631. Find out something else about this person.   Sample: Harriot was sent by Sir Walter Raleigh in 1585 to survey and map what is now called North Carolina.

LESSON 1-6   Symbols for Inequality   **29**

FOLLOW-UP

MORE PRACTICE
For more questions on SPUR Objectives, use *Lesson Master 1-6*, shown below.

EXTENSION
Ask students to graph the numbers −5, 6, and −3 on both a vertical and a horizontal number line. Then have students write two sentences about the numbers, one using < symbols and the other with > symbols.

NAME _____

LESSON **MASTER 1-6**
QUESTIONS ON **SPUR** OBJECTIVES

■ **PROPERTIES** *Objective I (See pages 49–51 for objectives.)*
In 1–8, use the <, >, or = symbol correctly in each blank.

1. .603 __<__ .6034   2. -10 __<__ 10

3. -10 __>__ -12   4. 0 __>__ -5

5. 0.0009 __<__ 0.009   6. 99.9 __>__ -100.5

7. -6 __>__ -6.4   8. 7.5 __=__ 7.50

9. *Multiple choice* Which inequality correctly compares the numbers?
(a) 11 > 7 < 9
(b) 7 < 11 > 9
(c) 7 < 9 < 11   c

10. *Multiple choice* Which inequality correctly compares the numbers?
(a) -10 < -5 < -3
(b) -3 > -10 < -5
(c) -10 > -5 > -3   a

In 11 and 12, write the three numbers as one sentence with two inequality symbols.

11. 7.2, 7.25, 7.02   7.02 < 7.2 < 7.25, or
                 7.25 > 7.2 > 7.02

12. -35.4, -354, -305.4   -354 < -305.4 < -35.4 or
                 -35.4 > -305.4 > -354

■ **USES** *Objective N*
In 13–15, write a mathematical sentence, using a > or < sign.

13. A profit of $2500 is better than a loss of $3000.
          2500 > -3000

14. Three games behind the Mets is worse than two games ahead of the Mets.
          -3 < 2

15. A temperature of 0° is higher than one of 3° below zero.
          0 > -3

6   *Transition Mathematics ©, Scott, Foresman and Company*

RESOURCES
- Lesson Master 1-7
- Quiz on Lessons 1-5 Through 1-7

OBJECTIVES

Letter codes refer to the SPUR Objectives on page 2B.

F Use a calculator to perform arithmetic operations.

Q Indicate key sequences for doing an arithmetic problem on a calculator.

TEACHING NOTES

Reading To emphasize that a calculator's usefulness depends on the user, you may want to read this lesson aloud in class as students follow along with their calculators. You can illustrate the importance of key sequences and the proper use of calculator results.

If you distribute calculators each day, develop a routine that takes *no* class time to pass them out or to collect them. If students are expected to bring their own calculators, some may forget. If you do not have calculators for such students, explain your policy regarding the sharing of calculators.

LESSON

1-7

Knowing Your Calculator

Calculators make it easy to do arithmetic quickly and accurately. But they cannot help unless you know how and why to use them. Different calculators may give different answers even when the same buttons are pushed. With this book it is best if you have a **scientific calculator.** (On page 1, there is a description of this kind of calculator.) You should have a calculator with you as you read this lesson.

When a calculator turns on, 0 or 0. will appear in the **display.** We show this as $\boxed{\text{0.}}$

As you press keys (this is called **entering** or **keying in**), the display changes. For instance, here is how to do the addition problem $2 + 5$ on a calculator.

	Display shows
Press 2.	$\boxed{\text{2.}}$
Now press +.	$\boxed{\text{2.}}$
Next press 5.	$\boxed{\text{5.}}$
Now press =.	$\boxed{\text{7.}}$

The set of instructions in the left column above is called the **key sequence** for this problem. We write the key sequence for this problem using boxes for everything pressed but the numbers.

$$2 \quad \boxed{+} \quad 5 \quad \boxed{=}$$

Sometimes we put in the display values underneath the last key pressed.

Key sequence: $\quad 2 \quad \boxed{+} \quad 5 \quad \boxed{=}$

Display: $\quad \boxed{\text{2.}} \ \boxed{\text{2.}} \ \boxed{\text{5.}} \ \boxed{\text{7.}}$

30

The next key sequence is for the calculation of 85 + 9 × 2.

Key sequence: 85 $+$ 9 $\times$ 2 $=$

Display: | 85. | | 85. | | 9. | | 9. | | 2. | | 103. |

If your calculator first added 85 and 9, and then multiplied by 2, it gave you the answer 188. If you got 188, your calculator is probably not a scientific calculator.

Calculators also differ in the way they round decimals to the right of a decimal point. This usually does not make much of a difference, but you should know what your calculator does. To check your calculator, try this experiment.

This book's calculator symbol for division is $\div$.
Key in 2 $\div$ 3 $=$.

The actual answer to 2 divided by 3 is 0.666666666666666..., where the digit 6 repeats forever. No calculator can list all the digits. So the calculator must be programmed to round. (Calculators *are* computers; each key triggers a program.) If the last digit your calculator displays is a 7, your calculator rounds up. If the last digit your calculator displays is a 6, your calculator truncates.

All scientific calculators have a way to enter negative numbers. This is done by a key that looks like +/- or ±. For example, 7 ± keys in -7.

Most scientific calculators have a way of entering the number π. If you have a π key, simply press it. However, on some calculators, you must press two keys to display π. If there is a small π written next to a key, two keys are probably needed. In this case, press inv, 2nd or F before pressing the key with the π next to it.

Questions

Covering the Reading

1. What is a key sequence?   See margin.

2. *True or false*   If you follow the same key sequence on two different calculators, you will always get the same answer.
   False

3. Do the following key sequence on your calculator. Write down what is in the display after each key is pressed.   See margin.
   Key sequence: 8 $+$ 7.2 $\times$ 10 $=$
   Display:

1. What key sequence would be used to calculate each answer?

a. 2)3.5
3.5 $\div$ 2 $=$
b. 87 + 43 − 10
87 $+$ 43 $-$ 10 $=$
c. −6 x −4.5
6 ± X 4.5 ± $=$

2. What problem is represented by this key sequence?
4.2 $-$ .5 X 3 $=$
sample: 4.2 minus the product of .5 and 3 is what number?

3. In Additional Example 2, which would a calculator do first, the subtraction or the multiplication?
Scientific calculators follow the rules for order of operation. Nonscientific calculators compute answers as the numbers are input.

ADDITIONAL ANSWERS
1. a set of instructions for entering numbers and operations into a calculator

3. On a scientific calculator, the blanks will be filled in with: 8, 8, 7.2, 7.2, 10, 80. On a non-scientific calculator, the blanks will be filled in with 8, 8, 7.2, 15.2, 10, 152.

NOTES ON QUESTIONS
Question 7: The final digit in the display may not signal the correct number of decimal places if the calculator rounds to the nearest.

Question 29: Make certain that each student sees an error message. Explain that 5 ÷ 0 is impossible, because no number times 0 equals 5. (If no error message is given, get rid of that calculator.)

5. If the calculator displays 3.1415926 or 3.141592653, it truncates. If it displays 3.1415927 or 3.141592654, it rounds to the nearest. If it displays 3.14159265, you can't tell.

30. a. Division by zero error; **b.** Division by zero error; **c.** Any number divided by zero.

4. What is the key sequence for the problem 15 − 27? $15\,\boxed{-}\,27\,\boxed{=}$

5. Display π on your calculator. Compare your value with the value of π given in Lesson 1-2. Does your calculator truncate, or does it round to the nearest? See margin.

6. What number does the key sequence 87 $\boxed{\pm}$ yield? -87

7. How many decimal places does your calculator display? Perform the following key sequence to find out.

    13717421 $\boxed{\div}$ 333 $\boxed{\div}$ 333667 $\boxed{=}$

On many calculators, the number of decimal places equals the last digit in the display.

Applying the Mathematics

In 8–12, do the arithmetic problem on your calculator.

8. 3.5625 × 512   1824

9. 0.9 + 0.99 + 0.999   2.889

10. 6 × π 18.849555

11. -412 divided by -2   206

12. 8.3 × 5.1 − 3.71   38.62

13. What is the largest number in decimal notation that your calculator can display? Samples: 99,999,999 or 9,999,999,999

14. What is the smallest positive number in decimal notation that your calculator can display? Samples: 0.0000001 or 0.000000001

15. What is the smallest negative number in decimal notation that your calculator can display?
Samples: -99,999,999 or -9,999,999,999

16. Which is larger, $\pi \times \pi$ or 10?   10

17. All calculators have a way of allowing you to correct a mistake in an entry. You press a key to replace one entry with another. On your calculator, what is this key called? $\boxed{C}$, $\boxed{CE}$, or $\boxed{CE/C}$

18. All calculators have a way of starting from scratch with a new calculation. How is this done on your calculator?
$\boxed{C}$, $\boxed{AC}$, or $\boxed{C}\,\boxed{C}$

32

19. a. Order -1, -2, and -1.5 from smallest to largest.   -2, -1.5, -1
   b. Write the numbers in part **a** on one line with inequality signs between them. *(Lesson 1-6)*   -2 < -1.5 < -1 or -1 > -1.5 > -2

20. a. Order from largest to smallest: .3, .33, .303. *(Lesson 1-2)*
   b. Write the three numbers in part **a** on one line with inequality signs between them. *(Lesson 1-6)*
   a) .33, .303, .3; b) .33 > .303 > .3 or .3 < .303 < .33

21. Place the correct sign <, =, or > in the sentence:
   -4 __?__ -10. *(Lesson 1-6)*   >

22. You run a race in 53.7 seconds. Someone beats you by two tenths of a second. What was that person's time? *(Lesson 1-2)*
   53.5 seconds

23. You run a race in 53.7 seconds. Round your time to the nearest second. *(Lesson 1-4)*   **54 seconds**

24. Estimate 896.5555555555 + 7.96113 to the nearest hundred. *(Lesson 1-4)*   **900**

25. Find a number between -4.632 and -4.631. *(Lesson 1-2)*
   Sample: -4.6319

26. Translate into English: 3,412,670. *(Lesson 1-1)*
   three million, four hundred twelve thousand, six hundred seventy

27. Three hundred thousand is written as a three followed by how many zeros? *(Lesson 1-1)*   **5**

28. What number is three less than three hundred thousand? *(Lesson 1-1)*
   299,997

29. Key in 5 ÷ 0 = on your calculator.
   a. What is displayed?   **an error message**
   b. What does the display mean?   **an error**
   c. Why did this happen?   **Division by zero is impossible.**

30. a. Put your computer in programming mode, and type ?78/0. Now press the RETURN key. What does the computer print?
   b. Try the same with ?0/0. What happens?
   c. What other things that you might type in will give the same result?   **See margin.**

FOLLOW-UP

MORE PRACTICE
For more questions on SPUR Objectives, use *Lesson Master 1-7*, shown below.

EXTENSION
You may want to ask students why 0 ÷ 0 gives the same error message as **Question 29**. Explain that $\frac{0}{0}$ could be any number, because any number multiplied by 0 equals 0. Thus, 0 ÷ 0 is undefined.

Small Group Work
Pairs of students can play the game *Wipe Out* on their calculators. The idea is to change a nonzero digit in a number to 0 by subtracting a single number. For example, to wipe out the 7 in 5.0976, subtract .007.

EVALUATION
A quiz covering Lessons 1-5 through 1-7 is provided in the Teacher's Resource File on page 2.

NAME _____

LESSON MASTER 1-7
QUESTIONS ON SPUR OBJECTIVES

■**SKILLS** *Objective F (See pages 49–51 for objectives.)*
In 1–7, use your calculator.

1. 4.7 ÷ .7	6.7142857
2. π ÷ 10	0.31415926
3. 6.3 × 8.2 + 7.4	59.06
4. -500 ÷ -5	100
5. 216 + 24 ÷ 4	222
6. -3 + -4 + 6	-1
7. 9.89 × 6.7 − 10.63 × 2	45.003

■**REPRESENTATIONS** *Objective Q*

8. What does the ± key do?
   changes the sign of the displayed number

In 9–11, write the key sequence for each problem.

9. 216 + 24 ÷ 4	216 + 24 ÷ 4 =
10. π divided by 10	π ÷ 10 =
11. -5 + -6	5 ± + 6 ± =

12. When keying in 6.5 × 7.5, you enter 9.5 instead of 7.5 by mistake. How do you clear your entry of 9.5 without clearing the entire problem?
   Press CE, the clear entry key.

13. Key in 0 ÷ 12. What is displayed?   **0**

14. Key in 12 ÷ 0. What is displayed?   **Error or E**

15. Explain the display in Question 14.
   Division by zero is not defined, so the calculator gives an error.

7

RESOURCES
■ Lesson Master 1-8
▤ Visual for Teaching Aid 6:
  Use to reinforce common
  decimal and fraction equiv-
  alents.
▤ Visual for Teaching Aid 7:
  Use with the Alternate Ap-
  proach.
■ Ruler or Geometry Tem-
  plate (*Transition Mathemat-
  ics Manipulative Kit*)

OBJECTIVES

*Letter codes refer to the
SPUR objectives on page
2B.*
B Order decimals and fractions.
G Convert simple fractions to
  decimals.
H Know by memory the common decimals and frac-
  tions between 0 and 1.
J Correctly use the raised
  bar symbol for repeating
  decimals.
Q Indicate key sequences for
  doing an arithmetic problem on a calculator.
R Give places of origin and
  rough dates for key ideas
  in the development of fraction notation.

LESSON

1-8

Decimals for Simple Fractions

A symbol of the form $\frac{a}{b}$ or a/b is a **fraction** with a **numerator** a and **denominator** b. The fraction bar — or slash / indicates division.

$$\frac{a}{b} = a/b = a \div b$$

In the language of division, the number a is the **dividend,** b is the **divisor,** and $\frac{a}{b}$ is the **quotient.** In $\frac{2}{3}$, 2 is the numerator or dividend, and 3 is the denominator or divisor. The fraction itself is the quotient, the result of dividing 2 by 3.

The fraction bar was first used by the Arabs and later by Fibonacci, but it was not widely used until the 1500s. A curved slash, $a\!\int\!b,$ was first used by the Mexican Manuel Antonio Valdes in 1784. In the 1800s this developed into the slash in a/b.

A **simple fraction** is a fraction with an integer in its numerator and a nonzero integer in its denominator. (Zero cannot be in the denominator of a fraction.) Here are some simple fractions. Notice that the opposite of a simple fraction is a simple fraction.

$$\frac{3}{4} \qquad 3/4 \qquad \frac{-72}{-8} \qquad \frac{3}{11} \qquad -\frac{3}{11} \qquad \frac{0}{135} \qquad \frac{-4}{180}$$

Fractions are very useful because they are related to division. But fractions are harder to order, round, add, and subtract than decimals. So it often helps to find a decimal that equals a given fraction. This is easy to do, particularly with a calculator.

▪ ▪ ▪ ▪ ▪ ▪ ▪ ▪

Example 1   Find the decimal equal to $\frac{7}{4}$.

Solution   Key in: 7 ÷ 4 = . The calculator displays the exact answer, 1.75.

34

....■■■

Example 2   Find a decimal equal to $-\frac{3}{5}$.

Solution   Find the decimal equivalent of $\frac{3}{5}$ first, then take the opposite. Key in: 3 $\div$ 5 $=$ $\pm$. The calculator displays -0.6.

....■■■

Example 3   Find the decimal equal to 3/11.

Solution   Key in: 3 $\div$ 11 $=$. What the calculator shows depends on the way it rounds and the number of decimal places it displays. You might see 0.27272727 or 0.2727273 or 0.2727272, or something like this with fewer or more decimal places. This suggests that the 27 repeats again and again. That is the case.

$$3/11 = 0.27272727272727272727272727272727...,$$

where the 27 repeats forever. For practical purposes an abbreviation is needed. It has become the custom to write

$$3/11 = 0.\overline{27}.$$

The bar over the 27 indicates that the 27 repeats forever. The digits under the bar are the **repetend** of this **infinite repeating decimal.**

Long division can verify that a decimal repeats. Here we again work out 3/11, this time using long division.

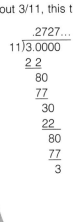

```
      .2727...
11)3.0000
    2 2
      80
      77
      30
      22
      80
      77
       3
```

Notice that the remainders, after subtraction, alternate between 8 and 3. This shows that the digits in the quotient repeat forever.

LESSON 1-8   Decimals for Simple Fractions   35

Reading   To help students read for details, have them read the text up to **Example 1.** Ask questions about the reading, emphasizing the main ideas. Then discuss the important concept illustrated by every example. Check if students can duplicate each division on their calculators. Not only does this discussion reinforce critical issues, it also helps students see how to study examples to get information on their own.

**Alternate Approach/
Using Manipulatives**
To help students remember the fraction-decimal equivalents on page 36, have students make their own number line from 0 to 1. Provide each student with a piece of typing paper. Have students draw and label a number line with 10 inches of space between 0 and 1.

Students can then fold the paper to locate and make a tick mark at 1/2. Students are to continue folding, marking tick marks, and labeling points to show fourths and eighths. Have students fold the paper again and use a different color to make tick marks for thirds and sixths. Finally students should mark fifths and tenths in a third color (a ruler may be needed to locate these points).

Students can then work in pairs and take turns pointing to a tick on the number line and naming it as a fraction and as a decimal.

Making Connections
There is no need to work on operations with fractions here. These are studied in lessons 5-2 (addition), 7-3 (subtraction), 9-8 (multiplication), and 11-2 (division).

ADDITIONAL EXAMPLES
Find the decimal equal to
each fraction.

1. $\frac{9}{25}$
.36

2. $-\frac{3}{2}$
−1.5

3. $\frac{5}{12}$
.41$\overline{6}$

4. $\frac{15}{13}$
1.$\overline{153846}$

5. $\frac{135}{15}$
9

**Error Analysis for
Additional Example 4**
Calculators that round up
may display 1.1538462; other
calculators may display
1.1538461. Do not expect the
students to show the repetend.

■ ■ ■ ■ ■ ■ ■■

Example 4 Find the decimal equal to $\frac{87}{70}$.

Solution Key in: 87 $\div$ 70 $=$.
The author's calculator displays 1.242857142.

That is all you are expected to do at this time. You cannot tell
from this whether or not the decimal repeats. Actually it does, with
the six-digit repetend 428571.

$$\frac{87}{70} = 1.2\overline{428571}$$

All simple fractions are equal to ending or repeating decimals. It
takes experience to know when the decimal repeats. It will help
you throughout this book if you know the decimals for some of
the more common simple fractions between 0 and 1.

Fourths and Eighths	Thirds and Sixths	Fifths and Tenths
$\frac{1}{8} = 0.125$	$\frac{1}{6} = 0.1\overline{6}$	$\frac{1}{10} = 0.1$
$\frac{1}{4} = \frac{2}{8} = 0.25$	$\frac{1}{3} = \frac{2}{6} = 0.\overline{3}$	$\frac{1}{5} = \frac{2}{10} = 0.2$
$\frac{3}{8} = 0.375$	$\frac{3}{6} = 0.5$	$\frac{3}{10} = 0.3$
$\frac{2}{4} = \frac{4}{8} = 0.5$	$\frac{2}{3} = \frac{4}{6} = 0.\overline{6}$	$\frac{2}{5} = \frac{4}{10} = 0.4$
$\frac{5}{8} = 0.625$	$\frac{5}{6} = 0.8\overline{3}$	$\frac{5}{10} = 0.5$
$\frac{3}{4} = \frac{6}{8} = 0.75$		$\frac{3}{5} = \frac{6}{10} = 0.6$
$\frac{7}{8} = 0.875$		$\frac{7}{10} = 0.7$
		$\frac{4}{5} = \frac{8}{10} = 0.8$
		$\frac{9}{10} = 0.9$

Some fractions are whole numbers in disguise.

■ ■ ■ ■ ■ ■ ■ ■■

Example 5 Find the decimal equal to $\frac{91}{13}$.

Solution Key in 91 $\div$ 13 $=$.
The calculator displays ⌈   7.⌉

In Example 5, we say that 91 is **evenly divisible** by 13. Sometimes we merely say that 91 is **divisible** by 13. The number 13
is called a **factor** of 91. The other factors of 91 are 1, 7, and 91.

36

Covering the Reading

1. Consider the fraction $\frac{15}{8}$.
   a. What is its numerator? 15
   b. What is its denominator? 8
   c. What is the sign for division? —
   d. Does it equal 15/8 or 8/15? 15/8
   e. Does it equal 8 ÷ 15? No
   f. Does it equal 15 ÷ 8? Yes
   g. What is the divisor? 8
   h. What is the dividend? 15
   i. Find the decimal equal to it. 1.875

2. Before the 1500s, who used the fraction bar? The Arabs

3. Who first developed a slash symbol for fractions, and when?
   Manuel Antonio Valdes, 1784

4. Which of the following are simple fractions? a, b, and e
   a. $\frac{15}{8}$ b. $\frac{-7}{1}$ c. $\frac{3 \cdot 5}{2 \cdot 3}$ d. $6\frac{2}{3}$ e. -5/6

5. Why is it helpful to be able to find a decimal for a fraction?
   Decimals are easier to order, round, add, and subtract

In 6–10, find the decimal for each fraction.

6. 3/20 .15   7. 23/20 1.15   8. -23/20 -1.15

9. 4/7 .5714286   10. 1/27 $.\overline{037}$

11. In $86.\overline{27}$, what is the repetend? 27

12. In $0.398\overline{8}$, what is the repetend? 8

In 13–15, write the first ten decimal places.
13. $9.8\overline{7}$ 9.8777777777

14. $0.\overline{142857}$ 0.1428571428

15. $-5.\overline{4}$ -5.4444444444

16. If you do not know the decimals for these fractions, you should learn them now. Try to find each decimal without looking at the preceding page.
   a. $\frac{1}{10}$ .1   b. $\frac{2}{10}$ .2   c. $\frac{3}{10}$ .3   d. $\frac{4}{10}$ .4   e. $\frac{5}{10}$ .5

   f. $\frac{6}{10}$ .6   g. $\frac{7}{10}$ .7   h. $\frac{8}{10}$ .8   i. $\frac{9}{10}$ .9   j. $\frac{1}{5}$ .2

   k. $\frac{2}{5}$ .4   l. $\frac{3}{5}$ .6   m. $\frac{4}{5}$ .8   n. $\frac{1}{2}$ .5   o. $\frac{1}{4}$ .25

   p. $\frac{3}{4}$ .75   q. $\frac{3}{8}$ .375   r. $\frac{5}{8}$ .625   s. $\frac{7}{8}$ .875   t. $\frac{1}{3}$ $.\overline{3}$

   u. $\frac{2}{3}$ $.\overline{6}$ v. $\frac{4}{6}$ $.\overline{6}$ w. $\frac{1}{6}$ $.1\overline{6}$ x. $\frac{5}{6}$ $.8\overline{3}$

NOTES ON QUESTIONS
Question 1: Go over this carefully, since it is designed to cover the basic concepts and vocabulary relating fractions to division.

Questions 9, 14, 37: In these questions, the calculator display does not show all digits of the answer. Students learn that a calculator cannot do their thinking for them. This is a crucial part of the lesson.

Question 12: Emphasize that the bar is placed only above the repetend.

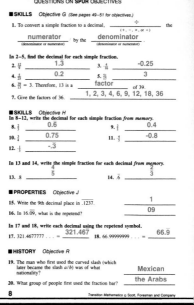

NAME _____

LESSON **MASTER 1–8**
QUESTIONS ON **SPUR** OBJECTIVES

■ SKILLS *Objective G (See pages 49–51 for objectives.)*

1. To convert a simple fraction to a decimal, _____ the
   (+, −, ×, or ÷)
   $\frac{\text{numerator}}{\text{(denominator or numerator)}}$ by the $\frac{\text{denominator}}{\text{(denominator or numerator)}}$

In 2–5, find the decimal for each simple fraction.
2. $\frac{12}{9}$ $1.\overline{3}$ 3. $\frac{-4}{16}$ -0.25
4. $\frac{2}{9}$ 0.2   5. $\frac{21}{7}$ 3
6. $\frac{39}{13}$ = 3. Therefore, 13 is a ____factor____ of 39.
7. Give the factors of 36. 1, 2, 3, 4, 6, 9, 12, 18, 36

■ SKILLS *Objective H*
In 8–12, write the decimal for each simple fraction *from memory.*
8. $\frac{3}{5}$ 0.6   9. $\frac{2}{5}$ 0.4
10. $\frac{3}{4}$ 0.75   11. $\frac{-4}{5}$ -0.8
12. $\frac{-1}{3}$ $-.\overline{3}$

In 13 and 14, write the simple fraction for each decimal *from memory.*
13. .8 $\frac{4}{5}$ 14. $.\overline{6}$ $\frac{2}{3}$

■ PROPERTIES *Objective J*
15. Write the 9th decimal place in $.\overline{1237}$. 1
16. In $16.\overline{09}$, what is the repetend? 09

In 17 and 18, write each decimal using the repetend symbol.
17. 321.4677777 . . . = $321.46\overline{7}$ 18. 66.99999999 . . . = $66.\overline{9}$

■ HISTORY *Objective R*
19. The man who first used the curved slash (which later became the slash a/b) was of what nationality? Mexican
20. What group of people first used the fraction bar? the Arabs

8   Transition Mathematics © Scott, Foresman and Company

In 17–22, give a simple fraction for each decimal. Try to find each fraction without looking at page 36.

17. 0.4 $\frac{2}{5}$ or $\frac{4}{10}$ **18.** .25 $\frac{1}{4}$ **19.** $.\overline{3}$ $\frac{1}{3}$

20. 0.60 $\frac{3}{5}$ or $\frac{6}{10}$ **21.** 0.7 $\frac{7}{10}$ **22.** $.\overline{666}$ $\frac{2}{3}$

23. 92/23 = 4. So we say that 23 is a __?__ of 92.   factor

24. The factors of 12 are 1, 2, 3, 6, 12 and what other number?   4

25. Give the factors of 30.   1, 2, 3, 5, 6, 10, 15, 30

Applying the Mathematics

26. Carpenters often measure in sixteenths of an inch.
  a. Change 3/16″ to a decimal.   .1875 in.
  b. Is 3/16″ shorter or longer than 1/5″?   shorter

27. Rewrite 1/14 as a decimal rounded to the nearest thousandth.   .071

28. Order 3/10, 1/3, and 0.33 from smallest to largest. $\frac{3}{10}$, .33, $\frac{1}{3}$

29. Order $\frac{2}{9}$, $\frac{2}{11}$, and $\frac{2}{7}$ from smallest to largest. $\frac{2}{11}$, $\frac{2}{9}$, $\frac{2}{7}$

Review

30. Find a number between 0.036 and 0.0359. *(Lesson 1-2)*
   Samples: 0.03591 or 0.03599

31. Which is larger, 34.000791 or 34.0079? *(Lesson 1-2)*   34.0079

32. Translate into mathematics: In football, a loss of 2 yards is better than a loss of 3 yards. *(Lesson 1-6)*   -2 > -3

33. What temperature is shown by this thermometer? *(Lesson 1-2)*   99.6°

34. Round 9.8978675645 to the nearest ten-thousandth. *(Lesson 1-4)*
   9.8979

Exploration

35. **a.** Find the decimals for 1/9, 2/9, 3/9, 4/9, 5/9, 6/9, 7/9, and 8/9.
  b. Based on the pattern you find, what fraction should equal $.\overline{9}$?
  c. Is the cartoon true?   a. $.\overline{1}$, $.\overline{2}$, $.\overline{3}$, $.\overline{4}$, $.\overline{5}$, $.\overline{6}$, $.\overline{7}$, $.\overline{8}$; b. 9/9; c. Yes, $.\overline{9}$ = 1.0

36. **a.** Write down the decimals for $\frac{1}{2}$, $\frac{1}{3}$, $\frac{1}{4}$, $\frac{1}{5}$, and $\frac{1}{6}$.
  b. Find the decimals for $\frac{1}{7}$, $\frac{1}{8}$, $\frac{1}{9}$, $\frac{1}{10}$, $\frac{1}{11}$, and $\frac{1}{12}$.
  c. If you keep going, to what number are these decimals getting closer and closer?
   a. .5, $.\overline{3}$, .25, .2, $.1\overline{6}$; b. $.\overline{142857}$, .125, $.\overline{1}$, .1, $.\overline{09}$, $.08\overline{3}$; c. 0

37. Explore the decimals for all simple fractions between 0 and 1 whose denominator is 7. Use your results to give the first twelve decimal places for each of these fractions.   See margin.

LESSON 1-9

Decimals for Mixed Numbers

The number $2\frac{3}{4}$ consists of an integer and a fraction. It is called a **mixed number** (though more accurately it should be called a mixed numeral). This mixed number is the sum of the integer 2 and the fraction $\frac{3}{4}$. Only the plus sign is missing.

Mixed numbers are common in measurement. The blue line segment below is about $2\frac{3}{4}$ inches long. (Is it obvious to you that $2\frac{3}{4}$ is between 2 and 3?)

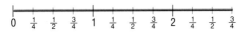

The way we have shown the fractions suggests how the decimal for a mixed number can be found. First calculate the decimal for the simple fraction. Then add that decimal to the integer.

■ ■ ■ ■ ■ ■ ■ ■

Example   Express $2\frac{3}{4}$ in decimal notation.

Solution 1   Remember or calculate: $\frac{3}{4} = 0.75$

Now add. $2\frac{3}{4} = 2 + \frac{3}{4} = 2 + 0.75 = 2.75$

Solution 2   On a scientific calculator, you can key in 2 ⊞ 3 ⊡ 4 ⊟. On simpler calculators, the division must be done first, then the 2 must be added.

Solution 3   Fourths are quarters. Two and three-fourths is like two dollars and three quarters. Two dollars and three quarters is $2.75, which includes the correct decimal.

LESSON 1-9

RESOURCES
■ Master 1-9
▣ Visual for Teaching Aid 4: Use the number lines with the Extension activity.
■ *Manipulative Activities Sourcebook*, Activity 1

OBJECTIVES

Letter codes refer to the SPUR Objectives on page 2B.
B Order decimals and fractions.
G Convert mixed numbers to decimals.

TEACHING NOTES

Reading   Students should read this lesson on their own. When they have finished the reading, you may have them suggest questions based on the lesson content.

Making Connections
During a discussion of the lesson, you might ask why a nonscientific calculator would display 1.25 for Solution 2 in the **Example**. This anticipates work on order of operations in Chapter 4.

ADDITIONAL EXAMPLES
1. Express $3\frac{3}{10}$ in decimal notation.
3.3

2. Express $4\frac{5}{9}$ in decimal notation.
$4.\overline{5}$

Questions

1. Consider the mixed number $10\frac{3}{4}$.
   a. Between what two integers is this number?   **10 and 11**
   b. Identify the integer part of this mixed number.   **10**
   c. Rewrite this number in decimal notation.   **10.75**
   d. Graph this number on a number line.   **See margin.**

2. Repeat Question 1 for the number $4\frac{2}{3}$.   **See margin.**

3. What is it about the mixed number of Question 1 that enables a person to think about it in terms of money?   **See margin.**

In 4–7, change each mixed number to a decimal. (The fraction parts are ones you should know, so try to do these without a calculator.)

4. $2\frac{1}{2}$ **2.5**   5. $7\frac{2}{5}$ **7.4**   6. $1\frac{3}{10}$ **1.3**   7. $17\frac{5}{6}$ **17.83**

In 8–11, change each mixed number to a decimal.

8. $5\frac{1}{8}$ **5.125**   9. $12\frac{3}{16}$ **12.1875**   10. $4\frac{1}{11}$ **4.$\overline{09}$**   11. $20\frac{8}{15}$ **20.53**

12. To find the decimal for a negative mixed number, first calculate the decimal for the corresponding positive mixed number. Then put in the negative sign. Use this idea to find a decimal for the number $-1\frac{4}{5}$.   **-1.8**

13. A stock goes up $4\frac{1}{4}$ dollars a share. What is this in dollars and cents? (Most stock prices are measured in eighths.)   **$4.25**

14. A stock goes down $1\frac{7}{8}$. What is this in dollars and cents?   **-$1.875**

15. Order from the smallest to largest: $2\frac{3}{5}$; $3\frac{2}{5}$; $5\frac{2}{3}$.   **$2\frac{3}{5}$, $3\frac{2}{5}$, $5\frac{2}{3}$**

16. Mouse A is $2\frac{3}{10}$ inches long. Mouse B is $2\frac{1}{4}$ inches long. Which mouse is longer?   **A**

17. Round $12\frac{8}{15}$ to the nearest thousandth.   **12.533**

18. The Preakness, a famous horse race, is $1\frac{3}{16}$ miles long. Convert this length to a length in decimals.   **1.1875 miles**

19. A shelf is measured to be $35\frac{11}{32}$ inches long. Is this shorter or longer than $35\frac{1}{3}$ inches?   **longer**

40

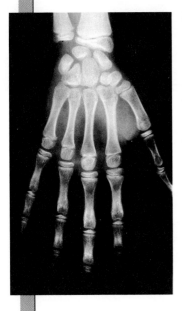

20. Give the decimal for each number. *(Lesson 1-8)*
a. $\frac{1}{6}$ .1$\overline{6}$ **b.** $\frac{2}{6}$.$\overline{3}$ **c.** $\frac{3}{6}$ .5 **d.** $\frac{4}{6}$.$\overline{6}$ **e.** $\frac{5}{6}$ .8$\overline{3}$
f. $\frac{1}{8}$ .125 **g.** $\frac{2}{8}$ .25 **h.** $\frac{3}{8}$ .375 **i.** $\frac{4}{8}$ .5 **j.** $\frac{5}{8}$ .625

21. Consider the number 215,386.945706. Name the digit in the ten thousands place. *(Lesson 1-2)* 1

22. Consider the following sentences. Each human hand has 27 small bones. Together the hands have over 1/4 of the 206 bones in the whole body. *(Lesson 1-1)*
a. Name the counts. 27 and 206
b. Name the counting units. small bones, bones

23. In decimal notation, write the integer that is one less than one million. *(Lesson 1-1)* 999,999

24. Name one advantage of decimals over fractions. *(Lesson 1-8)*
Sample: easier to order
25. a. Which is larger, -4.3 or -4.4? -4.3
b. Find a number between -4.3 and -4.4. *(Lesson 1-5)*
Samples: -4.31 and -4.39
26. Find a number between 2 and 2.1. *(Lesson 1-2)*
Samples: 2.01 and 2.09
27. Estimate 16.432893542050 + 83.5633344441 to the nearest integer. *(Lesson 1-4)* 100

28. Translate into English: 0 > -6. *(Lesson 1-6)*
Zero is greater than negative six.
29. Order -9.99, 9.99, and 9 using the inequality symbol <.
(Lesson 1-6)
-9.99 < 9 < 9.99
30. *True or false* 5 = 5.0 *(Lesson 1-6)* True

31. What digit is in the eleventh decimal place in 7.8$\overline{142}$? *(Lesson 1-8)*
4

In 32 and 33, find all the factors of the number. *(Lesson 1-8)*

32. 36 **33.** 39
1, 2, 3, 4, 6, 9, 12, 18, 36 1, 3, 13, 39

34. Examine a stock market page from a daily newspaper. Approximately how many mixed numbers are there on the page?
Answers will vary.
35. How many decimal places does your computer show when it does computation?
a. Type ?3/4 and press RETURN. What does the computer print, 0.75 or .75? Answers may vary.
b. Type ?2/3 and press RETURN. How many decimal places does the computer print? Does the computer round to the nearest, or does it round down? Answers may vary.
c. Instruct the computer to print decimals for $\frac{1}{7}$ and $\frac{8}{7}$. For which number does the computer show more decimal places?
Usually $\frac{1}{7}$ shows more places.

FOLLOW-UP

MORE PRACTICE
For more questions on SPUR Objectives, use *Lesson Master 1-9*, shown below.

EXTENSION
You may wish to have students convert negative mixed numbers to decimals. For example, ask students to express $-2\frac{3}{4}$ as a decimal. Some students may think that $-2\frac{3}{4} = -2 + \frac{3}{4} = -2 + .75 = -1.25$. Explain that one first expresses $2\frac{3}{4}$ as a decimal and then affixes the opposite sign. Thus, because $2\frac{3}{4} = 2.75$, $-2\frac{3}{4} = -2.75$. Then have students locate $-2\frac{3}{4}$ on a number line. Have them locate other negative mixed numbers as well.

LESSON MASTER 1-9
QUESTIONS ON SPUR OBJECTIVES

■SKILLS *Objective B (See pages 49–51 for objectives.)*
1. Order the following numbers from smallest to largest: $\frac{4}{5}, \frac{2}{3}, \frac{4}{5}$.
3 2 4
5' 3' 5
2. Order the following numbers from smallest to largest: $\frac{2}{3}$, .6, and .667.
.6, $\frac{2}{3}$, .667
3. Consider the numbers $\frac{1}{4}, \frac{3}{5}, \frac{1}{6}, \frac{9}{10}$.
a. Which is the largest? $\frac{9}{10}$
b. Which is the smallest? $\frac{1}{6}$

■SKILLS *Objective G*
In 4–11, write each mixed number as a decimal.
4. $3\frac{1}{2}$ 3.5 5. $-6\frac{3}{5}$ -6.6
6. $4\frac{3}{17}$ 4.18 7. $11\frac{3}{16}$ 11.1875
8. $-1\frac{1}{8}$ -1.125 9. $-7\frac{1}{5}$ -7.2
10. $12\frac{5}{6}$ 12.83 11. $19\frac{3}{4}$ 19.75
12. Round $3\frac{7}{11}$ to the nearest thousandth. 3.636
13. Rewrite $3\frac{5}{12}$ as a decimal. 3.416
14. Round your answer to Question 12 to the nearest hundredth. 3.64

In 15–18, write each decimal as a simple fraction.
15. .$\overline{3}$ $\frac{1}{3}$ 16. 4.125 $4\frac{1}{8}$
17. .25 $\frac{1}{4}$ 18. 3.6 $3\frac{3}{5}$

Transition Mathematics © Scott, Foresman and Company 9

LESSON
1-10

Equal Fractions

Jane was practicing with her calculator. She discovered that when she changed $\frac{3}{4}$, $\frac{6}{8}$, and $\frac{12}{16}$ to decimals, she got 0.75 each time. This shows that

$$\frac{3}{4} = \frac{6}{8} = \frac{12}{16}.$$

These are examples of **equal fractions.** It is easy to find other fractions equal to a given fraction. Just pick a number and multiply the numerator and denominator by that number.

Example 1 Find two other fractions equal to $\frac{2}{3}$.

Solution Multiply the numerator and denominator by 2.
$$\frac{2 \times 2}{3 \times 2} = \frac{4}{6}$$

Check Division shows that $\frac{4}{6} = 0.\overline{6}$ and $\frac{2}{3} = 0.\overline{6}$. So $\frac{4}{6} = \frac{2}{3}$.

To find a second fraction equal to $\frac{2}{3}$, pick another number to multiply by. We use 10.
$$\frac{2 \times 10}{3 \times 10} = \frac{20}{30}$$

Check $\frac{20}{30} = 0.\overline{6}$ also, so $\frac{2}{3} = \frac{20}{30}$.

Consider the fraction 6/15. Suppose we divide its numerator and denominator by 3. This gives the fraction 2/5.

$$\frac{6}{15} \quad \begin{matrix} \text{Divide 6 by 3.} \\ \text{Divide 15 by 3.} \end{matrix} \quad \frac{6/3}{15/3} = \frac{2}{5}$$

Now 6/15 = 0.4 and 2/5 = 0.4. So dividing numerator and denominator by 3 yields an equal fraction. This is true in general.

42

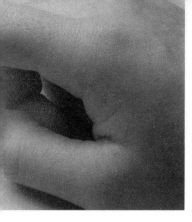

Equal Fractions Property:

If the numerator and denominator of a fraction are both multiplied (or divided) by the same nonzero number, then the resulting fraction is equal to the original one.

Of the many fractions equal to 6/15, the one with the smallest whole numbers is 2/5. We say that 6/15, written in **lowest terms,** equals 2/5. To write a fraction in lowest terms, look for a factor of both the numerator and denominator.

Example 2 Write 20/35 in lowest terms.

Solution 5 is a factor of both 20 and 35. It is the largest whole number that divides both 20 and 35. Divide both numerator and denominator by 5.

$$\frac{20}{35} = \frac{20/5}{35/5} = \frac{4}{7}$$

Check You should verify that 4/7 and 20/35 equal the same decimal.

There are many ways to simplify a fraction. All correct ways lead to the same answer.

Example 3 Simplify $\frac{60}{24}$. (To simplify means to write in lowest terms.)

Solution 1 Vince saw that 4 is a factor of both 60 and 24. Here is his work.

$$\frac{60}{24} = \frac{60/4}{24/4} = \frac{15}{6}$$

Since 3 is a factor of both 15 and 6, $\frac{15}{6}$ is not in lowest terms. Vince needed a second step.

$$\frac{15}{6} = \frac{15/3}{6/3} = \frac{5}{2}$$

$\frac{5}{2}$ is in lowest terms. So $\frac{60}{24} = \frac{5}{2}$.

Reading Before students begin this lesson, ask them to define the terms *numerator, denominator,* and *factor.* Then, depending on your students' abilities and preferences, the reading can be done aloud or silently. You should discuss each example, especially the solutions in **Example 3**, before you assign the questions.

Making Connections
The Equal Fractions Property is based on the Multiplicative Identity Property, namely, that multiplying or dividing by 1 does not change the value of a number. Because the Multiplicative Identity Property is not explained until Chapter 9, it is not mentioned in this lesson. If you decide to discuss this property here, you may also want to show that you *cannot* add or subtract the same number in the numerator and denominator without changing the value of the fraction.

ADDITIONAL EXAMPLES
1. Find two other fractions equal to $\frac{5}{6}$. Check by converting each to a decimal.
sample: $\frac{5}{6} = \frac{10}{12} = \frac{15}{18} = .8\overline{3}$

2. Rewrite in lowest terms.
a. $\frac{30}{45}$
$\frac{2}{3}$

b. $\frac{42}{24}$
$\frac{7}{4}$

3. a. What are the factors of both the numerator and the denominator of $\frac{72}{48}$?
1, 2, 3, 4, 6, 8, 12, 24
b. Which factor will simplify the fraction most quickly? 24

NOTES ON QUESTIONS
Questions 14 and 15:
You might wish to discuss
the representations in these
questions, since they may
clarify the idea of equal fractions for some students.

Question 33: Discuss the
four divisibility tests. If a calculator is being used, it is not
necessary to engage in much
further discussion of this
topic. Divisibility in most situations can be easily checked
by dividing on the calculator.

Solution 2   Heather knew that 3 is a factor of both 60 and 24.
Here is her work.

$$\frac{60}{24} = \frac{60/3}{24/3} = \frac{20}{8}$$

Now she saw that 2 is a factor of 20 and 8.

$$\frac{20}{8} = \frac{20/2}{8/2} = \frac{10}{4}$$

Dividing numerator and denominator again by 2, she got the
same answer Vince got.

Solution 3   Karen did more in her head than either Vince or
Heather. She thought: the factors of 24 are

$$1 \quad 2 \quad 3 \quad 4 \quad 6 \quad 8 \quad 12 \quad 24.$$

Of these, 24 is not a factor of 60, but 12 is. So 12 is the **greatest
common factor** of 24 and 60. Then she divided the numerator and
denominator by this number. Here is Karen's work.

$$\frac{60}{24} = \frac{60/12}{24/12} = \frac{5}{2}$$

Questions

Covering the reading

1. *Multiple choice*   Which of the following is not equal to $\frac{3}{4}$?   b

   (a) $\frac{6}{8}$ (b) $\frac{8}{12}$ (c) 0.75   (d) All of (a) to (c) are equal.

2. The letter P corresponds to the point at 7/2 on the number line
   below. Find two other fractions equal to 7/2.   Samples: $\frac{14}{4}, \frac{21}{6}$, and $\frac{28}{8}$

In 3 and 4, which fraction, if any, is not equal to the others?

3. $\frac{24}{36}$ $\frac{48}{72}$ $\frac{4.8}{7.2}$ $\frac{24 \text{ million}}{36 \text{ million}}$ All are equal.

4. $\frac{8}{12}$ $\frac{3}{4}$ $\frac{15}{20}$ $\frac{30,000}{40,000}$ $\frac{8}{12}$

5. Find a fraction equal to 21/12 that has a bigger numerator.   Sample: $\frac{42}{24}$

6. How can you tell when a fraction is in lowest terms?   See margin.

44

7. **a.** Write the factors of 48. 1, 2, 3, 4, 6, 8, 12, 16, 24, 48
   b. Write the factors of 60. 1, 2, 3, 4, 5, 6, 10, 12, 15, 20, 30, 60
   c. Name all common factors of 48 and 60. 1, 2, 3, 4, 6, 12
   d. Name the greatest common factor of 48 and 60. 12
   e. Write $\frac{48}{60}$ in lowest terms. $\frac{4}{5}$

In 8–11, **a.** name a common factor of the numerator and denominator, and **b.** rewrite in lowest terms.

8. $\frac{21}{12}$ a. 3; b. $\frac{7}{4}$ 9. $\frac{15}{20}$ a. 5; b. $\frac{3}{4}$

10. $\frac{180}{16}$ a. Sample: 4; b. $\frac{45}{4}$ 11. $\frac{240}{72}$ a. Sample: 12; b. $\frac{10}{3}$

Applying the Mathematics

In 12 and 13, find mixed numbers equal to the given numbers.

12. $11\frac{5}{12}$ Sample: $11\frac{10}{24}$ 13. $37\frac{3}{7}$ Sample: $37\frac{6}{14}$

14. What equality of fractions is pictured below? $\frac{2}{8} = \frac{1}{4}$

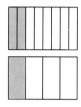

15. Use the idea of Question 14 to picture the equality $\frac{6}{9} = \frac{2}{3}$.
    See margin.
16. As you know, $13/1 = 13$. Find three other fractions equal to 13.
    Samples: 26/2, 39/3, 52/4
17. Find a fraction equal to 8 that has 3 in its denominator. $\frac{24}{3}$

In 18 and 19, write the number as a fraction in lowest terms.

18. fourteen eighths $\frac{7}{4}$ 19. seventy-five hundredths $\frac{3}{4}$

Review

In 20–22, round *up* to the nearest hundredth. *(Lessons 1-3, 1-8, 1-9)*

20. $4\frac{2}{17}$ 4.12   21. 0.00785 0.01   22. 43/50 .86

23. Find three different numbers between 0 and -1. *(Lesson 1-5)*
    Samples: $-\frac{1}{2}$, -.2, -.05
24. Which is larger, $\frac{9}{16}$ or $\frac{4}{7}$? *(Lesson 1-8)* $\frac{4}{7}$

In 25–27, estimate to the nearest tenth. *(Lessons 1-4, 1-7)*

25. four thousand sixty-two times three thousandths 12.2

26. $\pi \times$ -567.34 -1782.4

27. $18 + 1.8 - 0.18$ 19.6

LESSON 1-10 Equal Fractions **45**

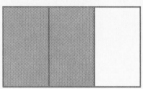

MORE PRACTICE
For more questions on SPUR
Objectives, use *Lesson Mas-
ter 1-10,* shown on page 45.

EXTENSION
Ask students to find fractions
equal to $\frac{3}{4}$ in which neither
the numerator nor the de-
nominator is an integer (for
example, $\frac{2.1}{2.8}$). Or, ask them
to find fractions equal to $\frac{3}{4}$ in
which both the numerator
and the denominator are
fractions (for example, $\frac{3}{5}$
divided by $\frac{4}{5}$).

28. Write $5\frac{13}{16}$ as a decimal. *(Lesson 1-9)*   5.8125

29. Try to find a decimal for each fraction without using a calculator
or looking it up. *(Lesson 1-8)*
   a. 4/10 .4   **b.** 5/8 .625   **c.** 3/4 .75   **d.** 1/3 $.\overline{3}$ **e.** 5/6 $.8\overline{3}$

In 30 and 31, give the factors of the number. *(Lesson 1-8)*

30. 24   1, 2, 3, 4, 6, 8, 12, 24   **31.** 51.   1, 3, 17, 51

32. *True or false*   Sixteen and twenty are both factors of eighty.
   (Lesson 1-8)   True

Exploration

33. To rewrite fractions in lowest terms, you usually must find factors
of the numbers in the numerator and denominator. There are easy
ways to tell whether 2, 3, 5, and 9 are factors of numbers.
   a. What about the digits of an integer tells you whether 2 is a
   factor of it?   if and only if the ones digit is even
   b. What about the digits of an integer tells you whether 5 is a
   factor of it?   if and only if the ones digit is 0 or 5
   c. 3 is a factor of an integer exactly when the sum of the digits of
   the integer is divisible by 3. Which of the following numbers
   is *not* divisible by 3?   321   2856   198   4444   4444
   d. 9 is a factor of an integer exactly when the sum of the digits of
   the integer is divisible by 9. Which of the following numbers
   is *not* divisible by 9?   198   44442   267   87561   267
   e. Find a 5-digit number that is divisible by 5 and 9, but not by 2.
   Samples: 49,995 and 83,115

Summary

Today by far the most common way of writing numbers is in the decimal system. In this chapter, decimals are used for whole numbers, for numbers between whole numbers, for negative numbers, for fractions, and for mixed numbers.

Decimals are easy to order. This makes it easy to estimate them. We estimated decimals by rounding up, rounding down, and rounding to the nearest decimal place. Decimals are also easy to graph on a number line. All calculators represent numbers as decimals. So, if you can write numbers as decimals, then you can make the calculator work for you. By changing fractions to decimals, they can be ordered and you can tell whether two fractions are equal.

SUMMARY

The Summary gives an overview of the entire chapter and provides an opportunity for students to consider the material as a whole. Thus, the Summary can be used to help students relate and unify the concepts presented in the chapter.

Vocabulary

You should be able to give a general description and a specific example of each of the following ideas.

VOCABULARY

Terms, symbols, and properties are listed by lesson to provide a checklist of concepts a student must know. Emphasize to students that they should read the vocabulary list carefully before starting the Progress Self-Test. If students do not understand the meaning of a term, they should refer back to the indicated lesson.

Definitions or descriptions of all terms in the vocabulary list may be found in the Glossary of the student text.

Lesson 1-1
digit
decimal system, decimal notation
whole number
ones place, tens place, hundreds place,
    thousands place, and so on
count, counting unit

Lesson 1-2
measure, unit of measure, interval
number line
tenths place, hundredths place, thousandths place,
    and so on

Lesson 1-3
estimate
rounding up, rounding down
truncate

Lesson 1-4
rounding to the nearest

Lesson 1-5
negative number, opposite
integer, positive integer, negative integer
natural number

Lesson 1-6
inequality symbols
< (is less than), > (is greater than)

Lesson 1-7
scientific calculator
display ⬭
enter, key in, key sequence
± or +/−
inv, 2nd, F

Lesson 1-8
fraction, simple fraction
numerator, denominator
dividend, divisor, quotient
infinite repeating decimal, repetend
evenly divisible, divisible, factor

Lesson 1-9
mixed number, mixed numeral

Lesson 1-10
equal fractions
Equal Fractions Property
lowest terms
greatest common factor

Progress Self-Test

For the development of mathematical competence, feedback and correction, along with the opportunity to practice, are necessary. The Progress Self-Test provides the opportunity for feedback and correction; the Chapter Review provides additional opportunities for practice.

We cannot overemphasize the importance of these end-of-chapter materials. It is at this point that the material "gels" for many students, allowing them to solidify skills and understanding. In general, student performance should be markedly improved after these pages.

USING THE PROGRESS SELF-TEST
Assign the Progress Self-Test as a one-night assignment. Worked-out *solutions* for all questions are in the Selected Answers section of the student book. Encourage students to take the Progress Self-Test honestly, grade themselves, and then be prepared to discuss the test in class.

Advise students to pay special attention to those Chapter Review questions (pages 49–51) which correspond to questions missed on the Progress Self-Test. The chart in the student text keys the Progress Self-Test questions to the lettered SPUR Objectives in the Chapter Review. It also keys the questions to the corresponding lessons where the material is covered.

See Additional Answers on page T53 for answers not shown below.

Take this test as you would take a test in class. You will need a calculator. Then check your work with the solutions in the Selected Answers section in the back of the book.

In 1–4, write as a decimal.
1. seven hundred thousand 700,000
2. forty-five and six tenths 45.6
3. $\frac{1}{4}$ 0.25
4. $15\frac{13}{16}$ 15.8125
5. What number is in the hundredths place of 1234.5678? 6
6. Write 0.003 in English. three thousandths
7. Consider the four numbers .6, .66, .$\overline{6}$, and .606. Which is largest? .$\overline{6}$
8. Consider the four numbers $\frac{1}{2}$, $\frac{2}{5}$, $\frac{1}{3}$, $\frac{3}{10}$. Which is smallest? $\frac{3}{10}$
9. Round 98.76 down to the preceding tenth. 98.7
10. Round 98.76 to the nearest integer. 99
11. Translate into mathematics: An elevation 80 ft. below sea level is higher than an elevation 100 ft. below sea level.
    -80 ft > -100 ft

In 12 and 13, use the number line pictured.

12. Which letter corresponds to the position of $\frac{1}{2}$? M
13. Which letter corresponds to the position of -1.25? F

14. Give a number between 16.5 and 16.6.
15. Give a number between -2.39 and -2.391
    Samples: -2.3909 and -2.3901

In 16–18, which symbol, <, =, or >, goes between the numbers?
16. 0.45 __?__ 0.4500000001 <
17. -9.24 __?__ -9.240 =
18. -4 __?__ -5 >

19. What fraction equals 0.6? $\frac{3}{5}$
20. Give an example of a number that is not an integer. Samples: 4.3, $-\frac{1}{2}$, π
21. A store sells grapes on sale at 69¢ a pound. You need a quarter pound. So you divide by 4 on your calculator. The display shows $\boxed{0.1725}$. What will you have to pay? 18¢
22. Estimate 3.012012012 + 9.0888888888888 to the nearest integer. 12
23. Indicate the key sequence for doing 3.456 × 2.345 on a calculator.
24. Use your calculator to estimate 6 x π to the nearest integer. 19
25. What is the repetend of the repeating decimal 4.5677777777…? 7
26. Graph the numbers 7, 7.7, and 8 on the same number line.
27. Graph these temperatures on the same vertical number line: 5°, -4°, 0°.
28. Give a situation where an estimate must be used because an exact value cannot be obtained.
29. Write a sentence containing a count and a counting unit. Underline the count once and the counting unit twice.
30. Which is largest? one tenth, one millionth, one billionth, one thousandth one tenth
31. Find all the factors of 18. 1, 2, 3, 6, 9, 18
32. Find a fraction equal to 6 with a 5 in the denominator. $\frac{30}{5}$
33. Rewrite 12/21 in lowest terms. 4/7
34. *Multiple choice* When was the decimal system developed? (b)
    (a) between 2000 B.C. and 1000 B.C.
    (b) between 1 A.D. and 1000 A.D.
    (c) between 1000 B.C. and 1 B.C.
    (d) between 1000 A.D. and today

14. sample: 16.51
23. 3.456 × 2.345 =
28. sample: the number of people watching a parade

48

Chapter Review

Questions on **SPUR** Objectives

See margin for answers not shown below.

SPUR stands for **S**kills, **P**roperties, **U**ses, and **R**epresentations.
The Chapter Review questions are grouped according to the
SPUR Objectives for this chapter.

SKILLS deal with the procedures used to get answers.

■ **Objective A:** *Translate back and forth from English into the decimal system.*
(Lessons 1-1, 1-2)

1. Write four thousand three as a decimal. **4003**

2. Write seventy-five hundredths as a decimal. **0.75**

3. Write one hundred twenty million as a decimal. **120,000,000**

4. Write three and six thousandths as a decimal. **3.006**

5. Translate 500,400 into English.

6. Translate 0.001 into English.
one thousandth

■ **Objective B:** *Order decimals and fractions.*
(Lessons 1-2, 1-5, 1-8, 1-9)

7. Which of these numbers is largest, which smallest? **largest: 400,000,001; smallest: 0.4**

   400,000,000   400,000,001
   .40000000000001   0.4

8. Order from smallest to largest:
   0   -0.2   0.2   0.19

9. Order from smallest to largest:
   -586.36   -586.363   -586.34

10. Order $\frac{1}{7}$, $\frac{1}{11}$, and $\frac{1}{9}$ from smallest to largest.

11. Order $\frac{2}{3}$, $\frac{6}{10}$, and 0.66 from smallest to largest. $\frac{6}{10}$, 0.66, $\frac{2}{3}$

12. Order from smallest to largest: $3\frac{1}{3}$, $2\frac{2}{3}$, $4\frac{1}{6}$

13. Order from smallest to largest:
    5.3, 5.$\overline{3}$, 4.33 **4.33, 5.3, 5.$\overline{3}$**

5. five hundred thousand, four hundred
8. -0.2, 0, 0.19, 0.2
9. -586.363, -586.36, -586.34
10. $\frac{1}{11}$, $\frac{1}{9}$, $\frac{1}{7}$
12. $2\frac{2}{3}$, $3\frac{1}{3}$, $4\frac{1}{6}$

■ **Objective C:** *Give a number that is between two decimals.* *(Lessons 1-2, 1-5)*

Samples:

14. Give a number between 73 and 73.1. **73.01**

15. Give a number between -1 and -2. **-1.9**

16. Give a number between 6.99 and 7. **6.991**

17. Give a number between 3.40 and 3.$\overline{40}$. **3.401**

■ **Objective D:** *Round any decimal up or down or to the nearest value of a decimal place.*
(Lessons 1-3, 1-4)

18. Round 345.76 down to the preceding tenth. **345.7**

19. Round 5.8346 up to the next hundredth. **5.84**

20. Round 39 down to the preceding ten. **30**

21. After six decimal places, Joan's calculator truncates. What will her calculator display for 0.59595959595959…? **0.595959**

22. Round 34,498 to the nearest thousand. **34,000**

23. Round 6.81 to the nearest tenth. **6.8**

24. Round 5.55 to the nearest integer. **6**

■ **Objective E:** *Estimate answers to arithmetic calculations to the nearest integer.* *(Lesson 1-4)*

25. Estimate 58.9995320003 + 2.86574309 to the nearest integer. **62**

26. Estimate 6 × 7.99 to the nearest integer. **48**

CHAPTER REVIEW

The main objectives for the chapter are organized in the Chapter Review under the four types of understanding this book promotes—Skills, Properties, Uses, and Representations:

Skills include simple and complicated procedures for getting answers; at higher levels they include the study of algorithms.

Properties cover the mathematical justifications for procedures and other theories; at higher levels they include proofs.

Uses include real-world applications of the mathematics; at higher levels they include modeling.

Representations include graphs and diagrams; at higher levels they include the invention of new objects or metaphors to discuss the mathematics.

To the *lay person*, basic understanding of mathematics is generally found in Skills. The *mathematician* prefers to think of understanding in terms of Properties. The *engineer* often tests understanding by the ability to Use mathematics. The *psychologist* often views "true" understanding as being achieved through Representations or metaphors. The SPUR framework conveys the authors' views that all of these views have validity, and that together they contribute to the deep understanding of mathematics we want students to have.

Whereas end-of-chapter material may be considered optional in some texts, in *Transition Mathematics*, we have selected these objectives and questions with the expectation that they will be covered. Students should be able to answer these questions with about 85% accuracy after studying the chapter.

You may assign these questions over a single night to help students prepare for a test the next day, or you may assign the questions over a two-day period.

If you work the questions over two days, then we recommend assigning the *evens* for homework the first night so that students get feedback in class the next day, then assigning the *odds* the night before the test.

Objective F: *Use a calculator to perform arithmetic operations. (Lesson 1-7)*

27. Find 35.68×123.4. **4402.912**

28. Find $555 + 5.55 + .555 + 0.50$. **561.605**

29. Find $73 - \pi$ to the nearest ten-thousandth. **69.8584**

Objective G: *Convert simple fractions and mixed numbers to decimals. (Lessons 1-8, 1-9)*

30. Give the decimal for $\frac{11}{5}$. **2.2**

31. Give the decimal for $-16/3$. **-5.$\overline{3}$**

32. Change $6\frac{4}{7}$ to a decimal. **6.$\overline{571428}$**

33. Change $5\frac{1}{4}$ to a decimal. **5.25**

Objective H: *Know by memory the common decimals and fractions between 0 and 1. (Lesson 1-8)*

34. Give the decimal for $\frac{3}{4}$. **.75**

35. Give the decimal for $\frac{2}{3}$. **.$\overline{6}$**

36. Give the decimal for 1/5. **.2**

37. Give the decimal for 1/6. **.1$\overline{6}$**

38. Give a simple fraction for .8. **$\frac{4}{5}$**

39. Give a simple fraction for .$\overline{3}$. **$\frac{1}{3}$**

40. Give a simple fraction for 0.25. **$\frac{1}{4}$**

PROPERTIES deal with the principles behind the mathematics.

Objective I: *Use the $<$ and $>$ symbols correctly between numbers. (Lesson 1-6)*

41. Choose the correct symbol $<$, $=$, or $>$: $2.0 \underline{\ ?\ } 0.2$ **>**

42. Choose the correct symbol $<$, $=$, or $>$: $0.1 \underline{\ ?\ } 0.\overline{1}$ **<**

43. Write the numbers $\frac{2}{3}$, .6, and .667 on one line with the correct symbols between them. **.6 $< \frac{2}{3} <$ .667 or .667 $> \frac{2}{3} >$ .6**

Objective J: *Correctly use the raised bar symbol for repeating decimals. (Lesson 1-8)*

44. Give the 13th decimal place in .$\overline{1428}$. **1**

45. Write the repeating decimal $468.5686868\ldots$ using the repetend symbol. **468.5$\overline{68}$**

Objective K: *Use the Equal Fractions Property to rewrite fractions. (Lesson 1-10)*

46. Find another fraction equal to $\frac{2}{7}$. **Sample: $\frac{4}{14}$**

47. Find the factors of 42. **1, 2, 3, 6, 7, 14, 21, 42**

48. Rewrite $\frac{80}{60}$ in lowest terms. **$\frac{4}{3}$**

USES deal with applications of mathematics in real situations.

Objective L: *Round to estimate a given number in a real situation. (Lessons 1-3, 1-4)*

49. A sign gives a city's population as 29,451. Round the population to the nearest thousand. **29,000**

50. To quickly estimate the cost of 5 records at $8.95 each, what rounding should you do? **Round $8.95 to $9.**

51. A store sells 6 granola bars for $2.99. You want 1 bar. Dividing on your calculator gives 0.498333. What will the bar cost you? **50¢**

■ **Objective M:** *Give situations where estimates are preferred over exact values. (Lesson 1-3)*

52. Give a situation where an estimate would be used for a safety reason.

53. Name a reason other than safety for needing an estimate.

■ **Objective N:** *Correctly interpret situations with two directions as positive, negative, or corresponding to zero. (Lessons 1-5, 1-6)*

54. 350 feet below sea level corresponds to what number?   -350

55. Translate into mathematics: A loss of $75,000 is worse than a gain of $10,000.
   -75,000 < 10,000

56. An auto mechanic estimates how much it will cost to fix your car. What number could stand for: **a.** an estimate $25 too low? **b.** an estimate $40 too high? **c.** an estimate equal to the cost?
a. -25; b. 40; c. 0

REPRESENTATIONS deal with pictures, graphs, or objects that illustrate concepts.

■ **Objective O:** *Graph a decimal on a number line. (Lessons 1-2, 1-5).*

57. Graph the numbers 0, 2, and -3 on the same number line.

58. Graph 6, 6.4, and 7 on the same number line.

59. Represent on the same vertical number line: -3°, 1°, and -5°.

■ **Objective P:** *Read a number line. (Lessons 1-2, 1-5)*

In 60 and 61, use this number line.

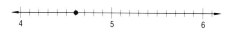

60. What is its unit?   tenths

61. The dot is the graph of what number?   4.6

In 62 and 63, use this number line.

62. What is its unit?   fifths

63. The dot corresponds to what number? $7\frac{1}{5}$

■ **Objective Q:** *Indicate key sequences for doing an arithmetic problem on a calculator. (Lessons 1-7, 1-8)*

64. What is the key sequence for entering -5?   5

65. Give the key sequence for converting $\frac{77}{8.2}$ to a decimal.   77

HISTORY

■ **Objective R:** *Give peoples and rough dates for key ideas in the development of arithmetic. (Lessons 1-1, 1-2, 1-8)*

66. What people invented the decimal system?
the Hindus

67. *Multiple choice* Our symbols for 0,1,2,3,4,5,6,7,8, and 9 did not all appear until about what date?
(a) 2000 B.C.   (b) 1000 A.D.
(c) 1400 A.D.   (d) 1900 A.D.   (c)

EVALUATION
Two tests, Chapter 1 Test, Form A and Chapter 1 Test, Form B, are provided in the Teacher's Resource File. For information on grading, see *General Teaching Suggestions: Grading* on page T44 of the Teacher's Edition.

ASSIGNMENT RECOMMENDATION
We strongly recommend that you assign Lesson 2-1, both reading and some questions, for homework the evening of the test. It gives students work to do after they have completed the test and keeps the class moving. If you do not do this, you may cover one less *chapter* over the course of the year.

ADDITIONAL ANSWERS
52. sample: estimate maximum occupancy of a restaurant

53. sample: An estimate might be easier to work with than an exact amount.

57.

-4 -3 -2 -1 0 1 2 3 4 5

58.
6   6.4   7

59.
5
3
1
-1
-3
-5
-7

CHAPTER 2 ■ LARGE AND SMALL NUMBERS

DAILY PACING CHART ■ CHAPTER 2

Students in the Full Course should complete the entire text by the end of the year. Students in the Minimal Course spend more time when there are quizzes and more time on the Chapter Review. Therefore, these students may not complete all of the chapters in the text.

DAY	MINIMAL COURSE	FULL COURSE
1	2-1	2-1
2	2-2	2-2
3	2-3	2-3
4	Quiz (TRF); Start 2-4.	Quiz (TRF); 2-4
5	Finish 2-4.	2-5
6	2-5	2-6
7	2-6	2-7
8	2-7	Quiz (TRF); 2-8
9	Quiz (TRF); Start 2-8.	2-9
10	Finish 2-8.	Progress Self-Test
11	2-9	Chapter Review
12	Progress Self-Test	Chapter Test (TRF)
13	Chapter Review	
14	Chapter Review	
15	Chapter Test (TRF)	

TESTING OPTIONS
■ Quiz on Lessons 2-1 Through 2-3   ■ Chapter 2 Test, Form A   ■ Chapter 2 Test, Cumulative Form
■ Quiz on Lessons 2-4 Through 2-7   ■ Chapter 2 Test, Form B

A Quiz and Test Writer is available for generating additional questions, additional quizzes, or additional forms of the Chapter Test.

PROVIDING FOR INDIVIDUAL DIFFERENCES

The student text is written for the *average* student. The program, however, can be adapted for both less capable and more capable students.

A blackline master (in the Teacher's Resource File) is provided for each lesson for those students who need more practice. The Teacher's Edition frequently provides an Error Analysis feature to provide additional instructional strategies.

For students who require additional challenge, Extension activities are regularly provided in the Teacher's Edition.

OBJECTIVES ■ CHAPTER 2

Students should master the chapter objectives by the time they complete the chapter. To ensure objective mastery, there is continual review built into each set of lesson questions. After students complete the chapter lessons, they assess their mastery on the Progress Self-Test. Then they do the Chapter Review and pay special attention to those questions that match the objectives missed on the Progress Self-Test. Students can get extra practice on these objectives by using the master for each lesson in the Teacher's Resource File.

OBJECTIVES FOR CHAPTER 2 (Organized into the SPUR categories—Skills, Properties, Uses, and Representations)	Progress Self-Test Questions	Chapter Review Questions	Teacher's Resource File	
			Lesson Master*	Chapter Test Forms A and B
SKILLS				
A: Multiply by 10, 100, 1000,...	1	1–4	2-1	1
B: Change word names for numbers to decimals.	3	5, 6	2-1, 2-8	4, 6, 23
C: Convert powers to decimals.	10, 14, 19	7, 8	2-2	3, 18, 19, 20, 21, 26
D: Give decimals and English word names for positive and negative integer powers of 10.	27	9–14	2-2, 2-8	11, 12, 13
E: Multiply by 0.1, 0.01, 0.001, ..., and $\frac{1}{10}$, $\frac{1}{100}$, $\frac{1}{1000}$....	4, 5	15–18	2-4	2
F: Multiply by powers of ten.	6, 7, 8	19–22	2-2, 2-8	5, 7
G: Convert large and small numbers into scientific notation.	15, 16	23–26	2-3, 2-9	14, 15, 16, 27
H: Convert percents to decimals.	9, 20	27–30	2-5	31–40
I: Know common fraction and percent equivalents.	22	31–34	2-5	31–40
J: Find percents of numbers.	2	35–38	2-6	10
K: Convert terminating decimals to fractions or percents.	21	39–44	2-7	22, 31–40
PROPERTIES				
L: Know and apply the Substitution Principle.	28	45–48	2-6	9
M: Identify numbers as being written in scientific notation.	26	49, 50	2-3, 2-9	30
USES				
N: Find percents of quantities in real situations.	23, 24, 25	51–53	2-6	25, 28, 29
O: Translate actual quantities into and out of scientific notation.	29	54, 55	2-3, 2-9	17
REPRESENTATIONS				
P: Indicate key sequences and displays on a calculator for large and small numbers.	12, 13, 17, 18	56–63	2-3, 2-9	8, 24

The Lesson Masters are numbered to match the lessons.

52B

OVERVIEW ■ CHAPTER 2

Four notations are introduced in Chapter 2: exponential notation; scientific notation with positive exponents; percent; and scientific notation with negative exponents. The first two notations are common ways of representing large numbers; the latter two are used for small numbers. (For example, though 50% looks large, it is just another name for $\frac{1}{2}$.) The chapter title refers to the large and small numbers commonly represented by these notations.

The chapter could also be entitled "The Decimal System and Powers of 10." All the notations are based on the relationship between the decimal system and the number 10. Powers of 10 are instrumental in scientific notation, and the symbol % means to multiply by $\frac{1}{100}$, or 10^{-2}.

Although the content is standard, you may be surprised at the early introduction of percent and negative exponents. Percent is introduced here because the interpretation of the % symbol is very important, and we want to give students virtually the entire year to work with it. Only some types of percent prob-

lems are given in this chapter. Other types are introduced in later chapters.

Student use of scientific calculators (which we encourage) persuaded us to introduce both positive and negative powers of 10 in this chapter. Students need to be able to interpret what is on their calculators in order to use them most effectively, and some scientific calculators switch into scientific notation for any positive number less than .01.

PERSPECTIVES ■ CHAPTER 2

The Perspectives provide the rationale for the inclusion of topics or approaches, provide mathematical background, and make connections within UCSMP.

2-1

MULTIPLYING BY 10

This is the key lesson in Chapter 2. Two important ideas are introduced here. First, if you know how to multiply by 10, then you can figure out how to multiply by 100, 1000, 10,000, and so on. For example, using 10 as a factor twice (10 x 10) is the same as multiplying by 100, or using 10 as a factor three times is the same as multiplying by 1000.

This rule is extended three times in the chapter. In Lesson 2-2, it is related to positive powers of 10. In Lesson 2-4, it is reversed and related to multiplication by $\frac{1}{10}$, $\frac{1}{100}$, and so on. In Lesson 2-8, the connection is made with negative powers.

The second important idea in this lesson is the use of word names such as *thousand* or *million* as names for numbers to be multiplied. In print, one sees a word name like *43 million* more often than one sees the pure decimal *43,000,000*. The introductory cartoon for Chapter 2 shows a debt limit of *1.2 trillion*, which means

"1.2 times a trillion." Thus, for dealing with numbers in the real world, the ability to translate back and forth from word names to decimals is crucial. This idea will also be extended in later lessons.

2-2

POWERS

The operation that is implicit in 3^2 is called *powering* or *exponentiation*. The number 3 in the expression 3^2 is the base; the number 2, the exponent. The result (9) is the power. We prefer the term *powering* because it conveys the idea of the result of the operation.

There are two important ideas in this lesson; the skill of powering and the use of the scientific calculator. First, if the exponent is a positive integer, the relationship of powering to repeated multiplication can be used to change a number from exponential notation (say 4^5) to decimal notation (1024). (The idea of repeated multiplication, already stressed in Lesson 2-1, is a

familiar one.) Without a calculator, however, the repeated multiplication calculations are usually tedious, and only small integer exponents and bases can be considered.

Second, it is not always necessary to resort to repeated multiplication to change from exponential notation to decimal notation. A calculator with an x^y key can calculate powers directly. And of course, because of the relationship between the powers of 10 and the number of zeros, it is easy to calculate very large powers of 10 even without using a calculator.

2-3

SCIENTIFIC NOTATION FOR LARGE NUMBERS

Scientific notation is introduced early because students using scientific calculators must be able to interpret answers displayed in scientific notation. Also, the use of calculators in class gives teachers the freedom to use real data. Such numbers might otherwise lead to tedious hand calculation; with a calculator there is no difficulty. Real data tend to be more interesting and show students where math is useful, and the result is often a large number displayed in scientific notation.

2-4

MULTIPLYING BY $\frac{1}{10}$ OR .1

For many students, the relationship between positive and negative integer powers of 10 is clearer when demonstrated with fractions than with decimals. That is, students more readily understand the connection between 1000 and $\frac{1}{1000}$ than between 1000 and .001. And for some students, it is easier to see that $\frac{1}{10} \times \frac{1}{10} = \frac{1}{100}$ than $.1 \times .1 = .01$. Indeed, the hardest part of this lesson may be to learn the fraction equivalents for .1, .01, .001, and so on.

Probably the simplest way to learn the fraction equivalents is to recall the place values to the right of the decimal point: tenth, hundredth, thousandth, and so on. Furthermore, just as the decimal point moves three places to the right, for example, when you multiply by 1000, it moves three places to the left when you multiply by $\frac{1}{1000}$ or .001.

A particularly important skill to learn in this lesson is how to multiply by $\frac{1}{100}$ or .01. That skill will be needed for the percent work in the next lesson.

2-5

PERCENT

The approach used for percent is simple. This lesson treats the word *percent* as a word name, like *million* or *thousandth*. Percent is another name for *hundredths*; that is, 3 percent = 3 hundredths, 100% = 100 hundredths = 1, and so on. Thus, multiplying by .01 or $\frac{1}{100}$ for 1% is no different than multiplying by 1,000,000 for 1 million, as was done in Lesson 2-1.

Students must learn decimal and fraction equivalents for the most common percents. Those shown on the number lines on page 71 are a minimum. Both this lesson and the next give practice with the equivalents.

2-6

PERCENT OF A QUANTITY

This lesson gives practice in finding percents and shows their utility. Finding percents of numbers, an important skill, will be reinforced many times in succeeding lessons and by the end of the year should be second nature.

The Substitution Principle is the first property to be named. Later, this principle will be applied in the substitution of numbers for variables and in the solution of equations.

To some students, the Substitution Principle seems so obvious that it should not need stating. But this principle makes *percent of* problems almost automatic. It also encourages students to write out the steps of a problem and should be emphasized for that reason.

2-7

FRACTIONS, DECIMALS, AND PERCENTS

Students converted simple fractions to decimals in Lesson 1-8 and changed percents to decimals in Lesson 2-5. In this lesson, students reverse the process and change terminating decimals to fractions and percents. The more difficult task of converting repeating decimals to simple fractions is covered in Lesson 12-2.

Converting, changing, and *simplifying* are different words for the same idea: rewriting. Reasons for rewriting are as follows:

(1) *Situational constraints*. It may be necessary to perform a computation, and the algorithm or the available calculator requires that the number be in a certain form.

(2) *Clarity*. A particular number may be easier to understand in a

given notation. For instance, in **Example 3**, it is easier to understand $\frac{1}{14}$ than $\frac{2.5}{35}$.

(3) *Facility*. It may be easier to work with a number in one notation than in another. For instance, it is often easier to multiply fractions than decimals: $\frac{3}{4} \times \frac{7}{8}$, rather than 0.75×0.875.

(4) *Consistency*. When available data are given in different notations, it may be necessary to put all data in one form to compare or describe them.

The goal of this lesson is to teach *flexibility*. A student should be able to write a number as a fraction, a decimal, or a percent, depending on the situation.

2-8

MORE POWERS OF 10

Negative exponents are introduced early in the course for several reasons. First, this material reinforces concepts from previous lessons of this chapter, specifically the work with powers of 10 and scientific notation, and serves as the logical completion of these discussions. Second, as noted earlier, scientific calculators display numbers very near zero in scientific notation with negative exponents, and it is important for students to be able to deal with these numbers. Third, by going so quickly to negative exponents, it becomes less likely that students misinterpret powering as multiplication.

2-9

SCIENTIFIC NOTATION FOR SMALL NUMBERS

In this lesson, students use negative powers of 10 to write small numbers in scientific notation. This task is easier if students understand how to multiply by negative powers of 10 (Lesson 2-8). At the same time, the concepts in this lesson may help students master the material covered in Lesson 2-8. This lesson also extends the use of the calculator.

New notations are often hard for students to learn, since both a new concept and unfamiliar symbols must be mastered. Though many students will have seen powers and percent before, they may be unsure of their ability to deal with these topics. A student who has seen none of the notations will probably have an especially difficult time. With such students, you may want to move at the slower pace suggested in the Pacing Chart on page 52A. The added review, evaluation and the somewhat slower pace will help them over the rough spots. Thus, we estimate 12 to 15 days for this chapter: 9 to 11 days on the lessons, 1 day for the Progress Self-Test, 1 or 2 days for the Chapter Review, and 1 day for the exam.

CHAPTER 2

Large and Small Numbers

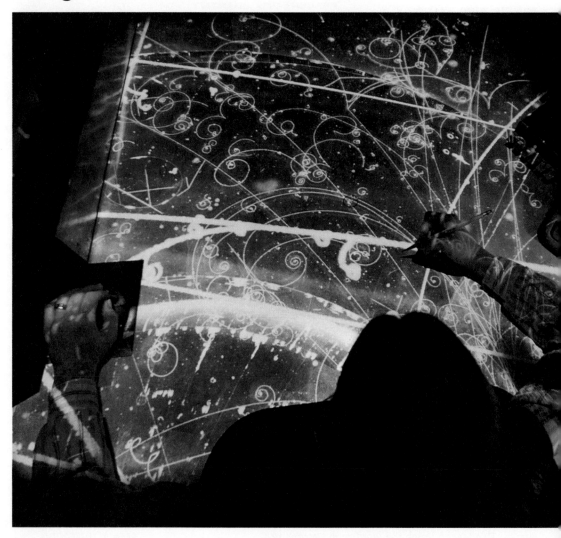

52

Decimal and fraction notations work well for most numbers in everyday use. But a trillion is a large number, which as a decimal is 1,000,000,000,000. With so many digits, this decimal is difficult to work with. So there are other notations that make things easier. One of these other notations is in the newspaper headline in the cartoon.

In this chapter, you will study notations that are particularly useful for work with large and small numbers.

"BY THE WAY, WHAT COMES AFTER A TRILLION?"

The photograph shows the tracks of tiny atomic particles traveling through liquid helium. The mass of an atomic particle is a very small number usually written in scientific notation.

USING PAGES 52 AND 53
Discuss the cartoon on page 53. Students will probably be surprised at the length of the number *1 trillion* when written as a decimal.

Many people cannot really appreciate the size of large numbers. You might mention, for example, that if a million inches were lined up end to end, they would measure almost 16 miles. A million miles is about 40 times around the earth at the equator. If you wanted to count to 1 million and were able to count one number per second without stopping, you would be counting for almost 12 days. If your heart beats 70 times a minute, it would take 10 days to beat 1 million times.

Some students may be interested in extending these illustrations to the size of 1 billion or 1 trillion.

RESOURCES
■ Lesson Master 2-1
▣ Visual for Teaching Aid 8:
World Population. Use with
Questions 29–32.

OBJECTIVES

A Multiply by 10, 100, 1000, and so on.
B Change word names for numbers to decimals.

TEACHING NOTES

Reading After students have read this lesson independently, ask what clues on the printed page helped them locate the main ideas. Discuss the boxed rule, the centered items, and the use of italics or boldface.

Encourage students to memorize the word names for large numbers. They will be used throughout the course and appear frequently in real world situations.

The **Example** illustrates a skill often ignored in math class but frequently required outside it. You might ask students why they think the media use the word form of large numbers instead of the decimal form. (Possible answers: for clarity or to save space.)

54

LESSON

2-1

Multiplying by 10

Consider the whole number 25,794. The 4 is in the ones place. The 9 is in the tens place (so it stands for 90). The 7 is in the hundreds place (so it stands for 700). The 5 is in the thousands place (so it stands for 5000). And the 2 is in the ten-thousands place (so it stands for 20,000). In this way, each place value is ten times the value of the place to its right. This makes it easy to multiply the number by 10. Here is the result when 25,794 is multiplied by 10. Notice that after multiplying, zero is in the ones place.

$$2\,5{,}7\,9\,4$$
$$2\,5{,}7\,9\,4 \times 1\,0 = 2\,5\,7{,}9\,4\,0$$

There is another way to think about this. Write 25,794 with a decimal point and a zero following it. (Remember that you can always insert a decimal point followed by zeros to the right of a whole number without changing its value. For example, $5 = $5.00)

$$2\,5{,}7\,9\,4\,.\,0$$
$$2\,5{,}7\,9\,4.0 \times 1\,0 = 2\,5\,7{,}9\,4\,0\,.$$

To multiply a number in decimal notation by 10, move the decimal point one place to the right.

For example, $62.58 \times 10 = 625.8$ and $.0034 \times 10 = .034$.

This simple idea is very powerful. Suppose you want to multiply a number by 100. Since $100 = 10 \times 10$, multiplying by 100 is like multiplying by 10 and then multiplying by 10 again. So move the decimal point *two* places to the right. For example, $59.072 \times 100 = 5907.2$.

The same idea can be extended to multiply by 1000, 10,000, and so on.

$$10 \times 47.3 = 473.$$
$$100 \times 47.3 = 4730.$$
$$1000 \times 47.3 = 47{,}300.$$
$$10{,}000 \times 47.3 = 473{,}000.$$

So, if you want to multiply by the decimal 1 followed by some zeros (10, 100, 1000, . . .), move the decimal point as many places to the right as there are zeros.

As you know, the numbers 10, 100, 1000, and so on have the short *word names* ten, hundred, thousand. Here are some other numbers that have short word names.

Decimal	Word name
1,000,000	million
1,000,000,000	billion
1,000,000,000,000	trillion
1,000,000,000,000,000	quadrillion
1,000,000,000,000,000,000	quintillion

Now look at the cartoon on page 53. The newsboy is holding up a newspaper mentioning a debt limit of 1.2 trillion dollars. The phrase 1.2 trillion means 1.2 *times* a trillion. Since a trillion has 12 zeros, move the decimal point 12 places to the right.

$$1.2 \text{ trillion} = 1.2 \times 1{,}000{,}000{,}000{,}000$$
$$= 1{,}200{,}000{,}000{,}000$$

Notice how much shorter and clearer 1.2 trillion is than 1,200,000,000,000. For these reasons, it is common to use word names for large numbers in sentences and charts.

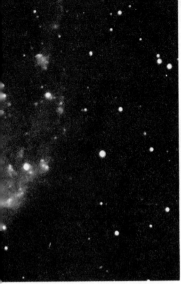

The distance from Earth to a galaxy of stars such as this spiral galaxy is measured in terms of light-years. One light-year is equal to about ten trillion kilometers.

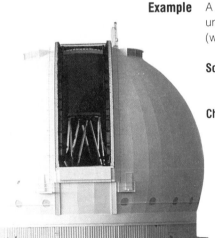

Example A newspaper report in 1990 listed 6.963 million people as unemployed in August. Write this number in decimal notation (without words).

Solution 6.963 million = 6.963 × 1,000,000
= 6,963,000

Check This is easy to check. You would expect 6.963 million to be between 6 million and 7 million.

Questions

Covering the Reading

1. In the number 81,345, the place value of the digit 1 is __?__ times the place value of the digit 3. **10**

In 2–5, multiply each number by 10.

2. 634 **6340**   **3.** 2.4 **24**   **4.** 0.08 **0.8**   **5.** 47.21 **472.1**

6. Give a general rule for multiplying a decimal by 10. **See margin.**

7. Give a general rule for multiplying a decimal by 100. **See margin.**

In 8–11, multiply each number by 100.

8. 113 **11,300**   **9.** .05 **5**   **10.** 7755.2 **775,520**   **11.** 6.301 **630.1**

12. Give a general rule for multiplying a decimal by 1000.
See margin.
13. Give a general rule for multiplying a decimal by 10,000.
See margin.

In 14–17, calculate.

14. $1.43 \times 10,000$ **14,300**   **15.** 32×1000 **32,000**

16. 1000×46.314 **46,314**   **17.** $0.095 \times 10,000$ **950**

In 18–23, give the word name for the decimal 1 followed by:

18. 3 zeros
one thousand
19. 6 zeros
one million
20. 9 zeros
one billion
21. 12 zeros
one trillion
22. 15 zeros
one quadrillion
23. 18 zeros
one quintillion

The quotes in 24–26 are from the *Chicago Sun–Times* of August 28, 1988. Write the underlined numbers in decimal notation.

24. "Estimates of the winter wheat crop have been increased to 2.02 billion bushels." **2,020,000,000**

25. "There are 1.35 million dollars in scholarships and grants that go unused each year because parents and students don't know that they exist." **1,350,000**

26. "Last year some 88 million people shopped by mail or phone … sales for the year range from $22.2 billion to $33.6 billion."
88,000,000; $22,200,000,000; $33,600,000,000

Applying the Mathematics

27. How can rounding be used to help you check your answer to Question 16? **See margin.**

28. 98.765 times what number equals 98,765? **1000**

56

In 29–32, use this graph to estimate the world population for the given year to the nearest tenth of a billion. Write this number in decimal notation.

29. 1950   **30.** 1965   **31.** 1980   **32.** 1990
See margin

World Population in billions of people

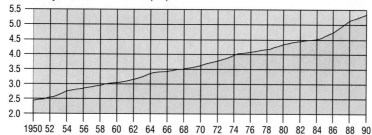

In 33–35, write the number as it might appear in a magazine or newspaper.

33. 230,000,000 people
230 million

34. $15,600,000 in the budget
$15.6 million

35. 26,500,000,000,000 miles to the nearest star   26.5 trillion

36. What is the answer to the question in the cartoon on page 53?
quadrillion

Review

37. The letters are equally spaced on the number line above. *(Lessons 1-2, 1-8)*
   a. What number corresponds to *F*?   0.5
   b. What number corresponds to *B*?   0.1
   c. What letter corresponds to $\frac{3}{5}$?   G

38. Change to decimals: *(Lesson 1-8)*
   a. $\frac{1}{8}$ 0.125   **b.** $\frac{1}{10}$ 0.1   **c.** $\frac{1}{50}$ 0.02   **d.** $\frac{1}{100}$ 0.01

39. Round 2.6494 *down* to thousandths. *(Lesson 1-3)*   2.649

40. Translate into mathematics: Negative ten is less than nine.
   (Lessons 1-5, 1-6)   -10 < 9

Exploration

41. Locate, in a newspaper or magazine, at least two numbers written with a decimal followed by a word name (like those in the example in this lesson). Copy the complete sentences that contain the numbers.   Answers will vary.

42. In England, the word *billion* does not always mean the number 1 followed by 9 zeros. What number does the word *billion* often represent in England?   1,000,000,000,000

RESOURCES
■ Lesson Master 2-2
▣ Visual for Teaching Aid 9:
   Powers of Ten
▣ Visual for Teaching Aid 10:
   Powers of Two
■ *Manipulative Activities
   Sourcebook*, Activity 2

OBJECTIVES

C Convert powers to decimals.
D Give decimals and English word names for positive integer powers of 10.
F Multiply by powers of 10.

TEACHING NOTES

Reading There is a lot for students to digest in this lesson. The terms *base, exponent,* and *power* may be new. Students will learn how to compute positive powers, and will begin to appreciate the ease of taking powers of 10. Also, they should begin to realize that powering often gives surprisingly large results. Thus, this may be an appropriate lesson for a co-operative effort, reading aloud and starting the questions together in class. The vocabulary, calculations, and large answers will seem less intimidating if students can work as a group.

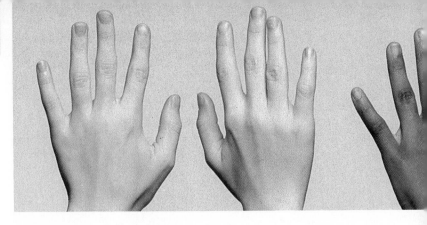

LESSON

2-2

Powers

In Lesson 2-1, you multiplied by 100. This was explained as multiplying by 10, followed by multiplying by 10. This repeated multiplication is so common that there is a shorthand for it. We write

$$10^2$$

(say "10 to the 2nd **power**") to mean 10×10, or 100. In 10^2, the number 10 is called the **base.** The number 2 is called the **exponent.** Similarly, 10^3 (say "10 to the 3rd power") means $10 \times 10 \times 10$, or 1000, and 10^4 (say "10 to the 4th power") means $10 \times 10 \times 10 \times 10$, or 10,000. In this book, only integers will be used as exponents.

There can be powers of any number.

> 3 to the 2nd power $= 3^2 = 3 \times 3 = 9$
> 8 to the 3rd power $= 8^3 = 8 \times 8 \times 8 = 512$
> 1.3 to the 5th power $= 1.3^5 = 1.3 \times 1.3 \times 1.3 \times 1.3 \times 1.3$
> $\qquad = 3.71293$
> 1 to the 7th power $= 1^7 = 1 \times 1 \times 1 \times 1 \times 1 \times 1 \times 1 = 1$

It is useful to know some powers of small numbers without having to calculate them every time. Here are the smallest positive integer powers of 2: $2^2 = 4$, $2^3 = 8$, $2^4 = 16$, $2^5 = 32$, $2^6 = 64$, $2^7 = 128$, $2^8 = 256$, $2^9 = 512$, and $2^{10} = 1024$. If you do not know the powers of 2, you have to calculate them. But the powers of 10 are very special in the decimal system. You can calculate them in your head.

Above we found that $10^2 = 100$, $10^3 = 1000$, and $10^4 = 10,000$. The next power, 10^5, is found by multiplying 10,000 by 10. It is 100,000. So, when written as decimals, 10^2 is a 1 followed by 2 zeros, 10^3 is a 1 followed by 3 zeros, and so on. Then 10^{12} is a 1 followed by 12 zeros. So 10^{12} is another way of writing one trillion.

You have now studied three different ways of representing the place values in the decimal system.

58

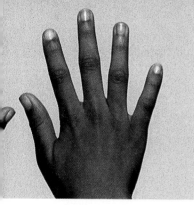

Historically we use 10 as a base because we have ten fingers.

Power of 10	Word name	Written as decimal
10^1	ten	10
10^2	hundred	100
10^3	thousand	1000
10^6	million	1,000,000
10^9	billion	1,000,000,000
10^{12}	trillion	1,000,000,000,000
10^{15}	quadrillion	1,000,000,000,000,000
10^{18}	quintillion	1,000,000,000,000,000,000

You already know a quick way to multiply by 10, 100, 1000, and so on. It is just as quick to multiply by these numbers when they are written as powers.

$$53 \times 10^5 = 53 \times 100,000 = 5,300,000$$
$$2.38 \times 10^4 = 2.38 \times 10,000 = 23,800.$$

The decimal point moves to the right one place for each power of 10.

To multiply by a positive integer power of 10:

Move the decimal point to the right the same number of places as the value of the exponent.

Powers of small numbers can be quite large. $9^8 = 43,046,721$. Only powers of 10 and a few powers of small numbers are easy to calculate by hand. Usually it is quicker and more accurate to use a calculator. A scientific calculator has a special key labeled $\boxed{x^y}$ or $\boxed{y^x}$, the powering key. (If this label is in small print above or below a key, you will need to press $\boxed{\text{inv}}$ or $\boxed{\text{2nd}}$ or $\boxed{\text{F}}$ before pressing the powering key.) For example, to evaluate 5^7:

Key sequence: 5 $\boxed{y^x}$ 7 $\boxed{=}$

Display: $\boxed{5.}$ $\boxed{5.}$ $\boxed{7.}$ $\boxed{78125.}$

$$5^7 = 78,125.$$

Note: Whether the key is labeled $\boxed{x^y}$ or $\boxed{y^x}$, the base is entered before the exponent.

Questions

Covering the Reading

1. Consider 4^6. **a.** Name the base. **b.** Name the exponent. **c.** This number is _?_ to the _?_th _?_.   a. 4; b. 6; c. 4, 6, power

2. Calculate 3^2, 3^3, 3^4, 3^5, and 3^6.   9; 27; 81; 243; 729

3. Give the values of 2^2, 2^3, 2^4, 2^5, and 2^6.   4; 8; 16; 32; 64

LESSON 2-2 Powers   59

4. Calculate 7^6.   5. Calculate 2^{20} and 20^2.   6. Calculate 1^{984}.
117,649   1,048,576; 400   1

7. Calculate 1.08^3. (This kind of calculation is found in money matters.) 1.259712

8. In decimal notation, 10^7 is a 1 followed by __?__ zeros. seven

9. Write 10^6 in two ways: **a.** as a decimal, and **b.** as a word name.
   a. 1,000,000; b. one million

10. Write one thousand in two ways:
    a. as a decimal, and **b.** as a power of 10.   a. 1000; b. 10^3

11. Write as a power of 10. **a.** million; **b.** billion; **c.** trillion.
    a. 10^6; b. 10^9; c. 10^{12}

12. According to the table in this lesson, 10 to the first power equals what number? 10

13. Write 5×10^2 as a decimal. 500

14. Write 3.7×10^4 as a decimal. 37,000

15. What is the general rule for multiplying by a positive integer power of 10? See margin.

16. If you multiply by 10 to the first power, you should move the decimal point how many places to the right? one

17. **a.** Give the next number in this pattern of powers: 256, 64, 16, __?__. 4
    b. What powers of what number are given in part **a**?
    $4^4, 4^3, 4^2,$ ____ or
    $2^8, 2^6, 2^4,$ ____.

Applying the Mathematics

18. What is the number that is 1 less than 10^3? 999

19. Which is larger, 2^3 or 3^2? 3^2

20. The table in this lesson skips from 10^3 to 10^6. Fill in the two rows that are missing. See margin.

21. Ten million is the __?__ power of 10. seventh

22. *Multiple choice* $3^{10} - 2^{10}$ is between
    (a) 1 and 100. (b) 100 and 10,000. (c) 10,000 and 1,000,000. c

23. **a.** Enter the key sequence 3 $\boxed{\times}$ 2 $\boxed{y^x}$ 5 $\boxed{=}$ on your calculator. What number results? 96 or 7776
    b. Some calculators do the multiplication first, then take the power. Other calculators take the power first, then multiply. What did your calculator do first? See margin.

24. *True or false* $2^{10} > 10^3$. True

25. In the early 1980s, a puzzle known as Rubik's Cube was popular. The object in this puzzle is to rearrange a cube to its original position. There are 43,252,003,274,489,856,000 possible positions. Write this number in English. (This shows how much easier decimal notation is than English words.) See margin.

60

26. A census report of August 30, 1988 said the world had grown by 1.8 billion people since 1960. Write 1.8 billion as a decimal. *(Lesson 2-1)* **1,800,000,000**

27. You buy 3 records at $6.95 each. What multiplication should you do to estimate the cost to the nearest dollar? *(Lesson 1-4)* **3 × 7**

28. Give the positive or negative decimal suggested by each situation.
a. Walter Payton ran for thirteen yards on the first play of the game. **13**

b. The deepest lake in the world, Lake Baykal in Siberia, has a point that is fourteen hundred eighty-five meters below sea level. **-1485**
c. Absolute zero is four hundred fifty-nine and sixty-seven hundredths degrees Fahrenheit below zero. *(Lesson 1-5)*. **-459.67**

29. What number results from this key sequence? *(Lesson 1-7)*
8 $\div$ 9 $\div$ 4 $\times$ 200 $=$ **44.$\overline{4}$**

30. What digit is in the thousandths place when $\frac{15}{7}$ is rewritten as a decimal? *(Lessons 1-2, 1-8)* **2**

31. Multiply mentally: **a.** 100 × 10,000; **b.** 180 × 10,000; **c.** 20 × 400. *(Lesson 2-1)* **a. 1,000,000; b. 1,800,000; c. 8000**

32. A *googol* is one of the largest numbers that has a name. Look in a dictionary or other reference book to find out something about this number. **10^{100}, or 1 followed by 100 zeros**

33. On computers, to calculate 3^5, you need to type a symbol, usually, either ^ or ** between the 3 and the 5. Test your computer.
a. What do you have to type in order to get the computer to calculate 3^5? (Remember: You need to type ? or a similar command so that the computer will know you want to see the calculation.) **Answers may vary.**
b. Use the computer to calculate 6^7. Compare the answer to the one given on your calculator. **279936; it is the same.**

FOLLOW-UP

MORE PRACTICE
For more questions on SPUR Objectives, use *Lesson Master 2-2*, shown below.

EXTENSION
You may want to point out that the word name *hundred million*, which stands for 100,000,000, is also the power of 10 found by multiplying *hundred* by *million* ($10^2 \times 10^6$), resulting in 10^8. Students could be given further examples to try to develop the property $x^a \cdot x^b = x^{a+b}$.

NAME _____

LESSON **MASTER 2-2**
QUESTIONS ON **SPUR** OBJECTIVES

■SKILLS *Objective C (See pages 93–95 for objectives.)*

1. Convert 5^4 to a decimal. **625**

2. Write a key sequence for converting 4^5 to a decimal. **sample: 4 $\boxed{x^y}$ 5**

What is the display? **1024**

3. Which is larger: 4^5 or 5^4? **4^5**

■SKILLS *Objective D*

4. Calculate 1^{127}. **1**

5. How do you read 12^8? **12 to the 8 th power**

6. Ten billion is ten to which power? **10**

In 7 and 8, write each as a decimal.

7. $10^4 =$ **10,000**   **8.** $10^8 =$ **100,000,000**

9. Write 10^{12} in words. **one trillion**

10. Write the power of 10 for billion. **9**

■SKILLS *Objective F*

11. What is the general rule for multiplying by a positive power of 10? **Move the decimal point to the right as many times as the power of 10.**

In 12–15, write each product as a decimal.

12. $9 \times 10^3 =$ **9000**

13. $8.3 \times 10^5 =$ **830,000**

14. $80 \times 10^6 =$ **80,000,000**

15. $0.125 \times 10^8 =$ **12,500,000**

12   *Transition Mathematics ©, Scott, Foresman and Company*

■ LESSON 2-3

RESOURCES
■ Lesson Master 2-3
■ Computer Master 3
■ Quiz on Lessons 2-1
  Through 2-3

OBJECTIVES

G Convert large numbers
  into scientific notation.
M Identify numbers as being
  written in scientific
  notation.
O Translate actual quantities
  into and out of scientific
  notation.
P Indicate key sequences
  and displays on a calculator for large numbers.

LESSON

2-3

Scientific Notation for Large Numbers

Light travels at a speed of about 186,281.7 miles per second. Since there are 60 seconds in a minute, light travels $60 \times 186{,}281.7$ miles per minute. This works out to 11,176,902 miles per minute. (You should check this on your calculator.) To find out how far light travels in an hour, you must multiply by 60 again.

$$60 \times 11{,}176{,}902 = 670{,}614{,}120 \text{ miles}$$

There are now three possible things your calculator will do.
1. It may display all 9 digits.

$$\boxed{670614120.}$$

2. It may display an error message. The number is too big. The E tells you there is an error and the calculator will refuse to do anything until you clear the number.

$$\boxed{\text{E } 6.7061412} \quad \boxed{6.7061412 \text{ E}} \quad \boxed{\text{ERROR}}$$

3. It may display the number in **scientific notation.**

$$\boxed{6.7061412 \ 08} \quad \boxed{6.7061 \quad 8} \quad \boxed{6.7061 \ \times 10 \ \ 08}$$

Scientific notation is the way that scientific calculators display very large and very small numbers. The display usually looks like one of those shown here. Each of these stands for the number 6.7061412×10^8 or a rounded value of that number. The user is expected to know that the 8 (or 08) stands for 10^8. So to convert the number into decimal notation, move the decimal point 8 places to the right. (The display at the right above contains $\times 10$ and is clearest.)

If you multiply this number by 24, scientific calculators will give you the scientific notation for 16,094,738,880.

$$\boxed{1.60947 \quad 10}$$

62

This is the number of miles light travels in a day. The calculator will round the decimal to a fixed number of places. So 16,094,738,880 is approximately 1.60947×10^{10}.

> In scientific notation, an integer power of 10 is multiplied by a number greater than or equal to 1 and less than 10.

Here are some numbers written as decimals and in scientific notation.

Decimal notation	Scientific notation
340.67	3.4067×10^2
2,380,000,000	2.38×10^9
60 trillion	6×10^{13}

Here is how to convert decimals into scientific notation.

Example 1   The distance from Earth to the Sun is about 150,000,000 km. Write this number in scientific notation.

Solution   First, move the decimal point to get a number between 1 and 10. In this case, the number is 1.5 and this tells you the answer will look like this:

$$1.5 \times 10^{exponent}$$

The exponent of 10 is the number of places you must move the decimal in 1.5 to the *right* in order to get 150,000,000. You must move it 8 places, so the answer is

$$1.5 \times 10^8.$$

Example 2   The population of the world passed 5.3 billion in 1990. This number is 5,300,000,000 and has too many digits for most calculators. Write it in scientific notation so that it can be entered into a calculator and used.

Solution   Since 1 billion = 10^9, 5.3 billion = 5.3×10^9.
So the number is 5.3×10^9 in scientific notation.

Reading   Emphasize the *form* of scientific notation. After reading the definition in the box on page 63, you may want to stress that there are three parts to the notation: a number from 1 to 10 but less than 10, a multiplication sign, and a power of ten.

Read **Example 1** slowly. Discuss the solution, stressing how the decimal number is renamed in scientific notation. Continue with **Example 2**, which uses the word name *billion*. Have students key in 5.3×10^9 on their calculators (**Example 3**). You may wish to ask a student to demonstrate **Example 4**.

Check how the students' calculators display scientific notation. Be certain that all students understand when an answer is in that notation.

■ ■ ■ ■ ■ ■ ■ ■

Example 3   Enter 5.3 billion on your calculator.

Solution   First write 5.3 billion in scientific notation. This is done in Example 2. From the answer to Example 2, key in

5.3 [EE] 9 or 5.3 [exp] 9.

■ ■ ■ ■ ■ ■ ■ ■

Example 4   Write 45678 in scientific notation.

Solution   Ask yourself: 45,678 equals 4.5678 times what power of 10? The answer to the question is 4. So
$$45678 = 4.5678 \times 10^4.$$

Like calculators, computers use scientific notation for large numbers. Some computer printers cannot write exponents as numbers above the line. So the number 5.1 billion may be written as 5.1 E 9. In this case the E means "exponent of 10" and does not mean that an error has been made.

Questions

Covering the Reading

1. 2.6×10^{13} miles is the approximate distance to the nearest star (other than the Sun), Alpha Centauri. Write this number as a decimal.
26,000,000,000,000 mi

2. 1.6×10^5 kg is the approximate weight of the largest blue whale ever measured. Write this number as a decimal.   160,000 kg

3. In scientific notation, a number greater than or equal to __?__ and less than __?__ is multiplied by an integer __?__ of 10.
1, 10, power

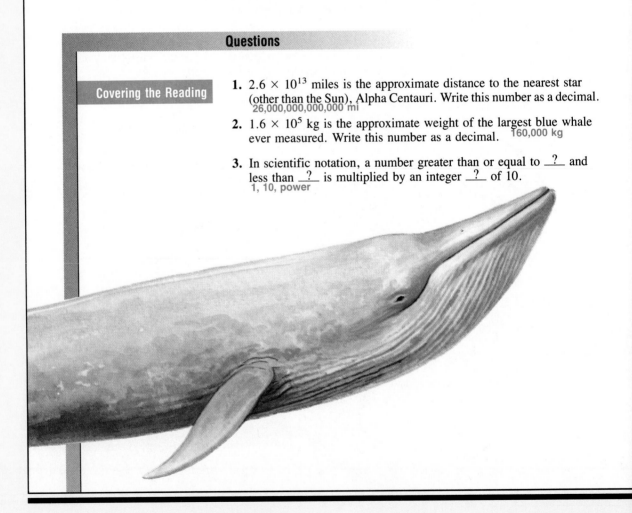

In 4–11, rewrite the number in scientific notation.

4. 800 8×10^2

5. 804 8.04×10^2

6. 3,500,000 square miles, the approximate land area of the U.S.
3.5×10^6

7. 5,880,000,000,000,000,000,000 tons, the approximate mass of Earth. 5.88×10^{21}

8. 59.22 million people, the number of passengers handled by Chicago's O'Hare Airport in 1989.
5.922×10^7

9. 1.2 trillion dollars, a ceiling (1985) on the national debt. (Recall the cartoon on page 53.) $\$1.2 \times 10^{12}$

10. 63.21 6.321×10^1

11. 765.4 7.654×10^2

12. What key sequence can you use to display 6.75×10^{11} on your calculator?   6.75 [EE] 11 or 6.75 [exp] 11

In 13–15, what does your calculator display for each number? Answers may vary.

13. 49×10^{14}

14. 60 trillion

15. 3,800,000,000,000

| 4.9   15 |

| 6.   13 |

| 3.8   12 |

16. The number of miles light travels in a day is given in this lesson. How many miles does light travel in a 365-day year?
5.8746×10^{12}

17. How many seconds are there in a 365-day year?   31,536,000

18. a. Using scientific notation, what is the largest number you can display on your calculator? **b.** What is the smallest number you can display? (Hint: The smallest number is negative.)   See margin.

19. Which is larger, 1×10^{10} or 9×10^9? 1×10^{10}

20. Calculate the first, second, and third powers of 8. *(Lesson 2-2)*
8, 64, 512

In 21 and 22, calculate mentally. *(Lesson 2-1)*

21. $0.0006 \times 10,000$ 6

22. 523×100 52,300

23. Arrange from smallest to largest: $14\frac{3}{5}$, 14.6, $14.\overline{61}$, $14.\overline{6}$.
(Lessons 1-8, 1-9) $14\frac{3}{5} = 14.6, 14.\overline{61}, 14.\overline{6}$

24. Name a fraction whose decimal is 0.9. *(Lesson 1-8)*   Samples: $\frac{9}{10}, \frac{90}{100}$

25. On this number line, what letter corresponds to each number? *(Lessons 1-2, 1-8)*
a. $\frac{3}{5}$ Q   **b.** $-\frac{3}{5}$ E   **c.** .8   S   **d.** -.8   C

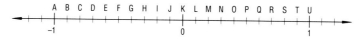

LESSON 2-3   Scientific Notation for Large Numbers   **65**

26. Batting "averages" in baseball are calculated by dividing the number of hits by the number of at-bats and usually rounding to the nearest thousandth. In 1970, Alex Johnson and Carl Yastrzemski had the top two batting averages in the American League. *(Lesson 1-4)*
    a. Johnson had 202 hits in 614 at-bats. What was his average?
    b. Yastrzemski had 186 hits in 566 at-bats. What was his average?
    c. Who was the batting champion?
       a. 0.329; b. 0.329; c. Johnson, since 0.3290 > 0.3286.

27. Write 10^9 **a.** as a decimal, and **b.** using a word name. *(Lesson 2-2)*
    a. 1,000,000,000; b. one billion

Exploration

28. The decimal for 1/17 repeats after 16 digits. Calculators do not display this many digits. However, it is still possible to find all the digits in the repetend.
    a. Find the first six places of the decimals for 2/17, 3/17, and so on up to 16/17.   See margin.
    b. Each of these decimals contains 6 consecutive digits of the 16-digit repetend. Use this information to work out the entire repetend.   .0588235294117647
    c. Did you need to get the decimals to all 16 fractions to work this out?   No, only up through 10/17

29. Kathleen entered 531×10^{20} on her calculator using the key sequence

    531   [EE]   20.

    [531]   [531   00]   [531   20]

    Then she pressed [=].
    a. What is now displayed? **b.** What has happened?   a. [5.31   22]
    b. The number has been converted to scientific notation.

30. a. Type ?2*3 on your computer and press RETURN. What does the computer print? What is the computer doing?   6; multiplying 2 × 3
    b. Increase the number of zeros in the 2 or 3 of part **a** by one, so that you have either ?20*3 or ?2*30. What does the computer print this time?   60
    c. Continue increasing the number of zeros until the computer is forced to print an answer in its form of scientific notation. How does your computer write numbers in scientific notation?
    d. What is the largest number your computer will itself print that is not in scientific notation?
       c. Sample: 6E + 09 for 6 · 10⁹   d. Sample: 99,999,999

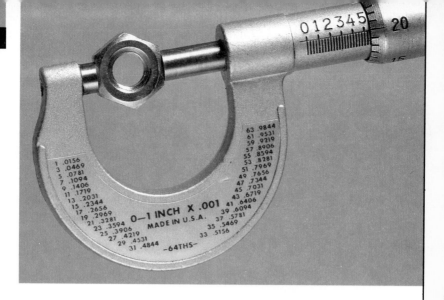

LESSON 2-4

Multiplying by $\frac{1}{10}$ or .1

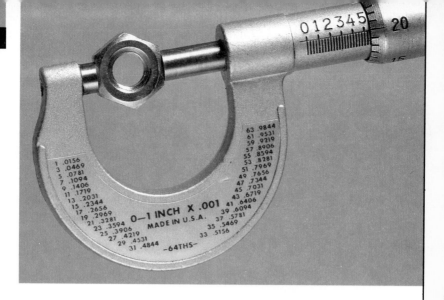

LESSON 2-4

RESOURCES
■Lesson Master 2-4

OBJECTIVE

E Multiply by 0.1, 0.01, 0.001, and so on and by $\frac{1}{10}$, $\frac{1}{100}$, $\frac{1}{1000}$, and so on.

TEACHING NOTES

You may want to use a pattern to introduce multiplication by powers of 10. Write two columns on the board:

23 million	230 million
430.5	4305
0.894	8.94

Have the students discover the two related patterns: (1) the numbers in the right column are 10 times the corresponding numbers in the left column; and (2) the numbers in the left column are one-tenth the corresponding numbers in the right column. Then, write a new number in each column and ask for the corresponding number in the other column.

Change the pattern by making one number 100 times the other. Then, repeat the procedure for 100 and $\frac{1}{100}$. The important concept is that multiplication by $\frac{1}{x}$ undoes multiplication by x.

The numbers 10, 100, 1000, and so on, get larger and larger. By contrast, the numbers 1/10, 1/100, and 1/1000 get smaller and smaller. This can be seen by looking at the decimals for them.

$$\frac{1}{10} \quad = .1 \quad = \text{one tenth}$$

$$\frac{1}{100} \quad = .01 \quad = \text{one hundredth}$$

$$\frac{1}{1000} \quad = .001 \quad = \text{one thousandth}$$

$$\frac{1}{10,000} = .0001 = \text{one ten-thousandth}$$

and so on.

To multiply a decimal by 10, remember that you can move the decimal point one place to the *right*. Multiplication by 1/10 undoes multiplication by 10. So, to multiply by 1/10, you can move the decimal point one place to the *left*.

$$\frac{1}{10} \times 15.283 = 1.5283$$

You can estimate to check. A tenth of $15 is $1.50.

Multiplying by 1/100 is equivalent to multiplying by 1/10 and then multiplying by 1/10 again. So, to multiply by 1/100, move the decimal point *two* places to the *left*.

$$\frac{1}{100} \times 15.283 = 0.15283$$

The pattern continues. Multiplication by 1/1000 is equivalent to multiplying by 1/10 three times. So move the decimal point three places to the left.

$$\frac{1}{1000} \times 15.283 = 0.015283$$

On a calculator, you might want to use decimals instead of fractions. Of course the same pattern holds.

$$.1 \times 12345 = 1234.5$$
$$.01 \times 12345 = 123.45$$
$$.001 \times 12345 = 12.345$$
$$.0001 \times 12345 = 1.2345$$
and so on.

You may wish to check these multiplications on your calculator.

Questions

Covering the Reading

In 1–4, write as a decimal.

1. one tenth   .1

2. 1/100   .01

3. one thousandth   .001

4. 1/10,000   .0001

In 5–8, give a general rule for multiplying a decimal by the given number.   **See margin.**

5. .1

6. 1/10

7. .01

8. 1/10,000

In 9–18, write the answer as a decimal.

9. $\frac{1}{10} \times 46$ 4.6

10. $46 \times \frac{1}{10}$ 4.6

11. $.1 \times 46$ 4.6

12. $46 \times .1$ 4.6

13. $\frac{1}{100} \times 6$ .06

14. $\frac{1}{100} \times 5.93$ .0593

15. 0.01×770 7.7

16. $.001 \times .03$ .00003

17. $\frac{1}{10,000} \times 52$ .0052

18. $250,000 \times .0001$ 25

19. Multiplying by 1/100 is like multiplying by 1/10 and then multiplying by __?__.   1/10

20. To multiply by 1/1000 using a calculator, what decimal should you use?   .001

Applying the Mathematics

21. The number 15.283 is multiplied by 1/10, 1/100, and 1/1000 in this lesson. Continue that pattern for three more multiplications. **See margin.**

22. The number 12345 is multiplied by .1, .01, .001, and .0001 in this lesson. Give the next multiplication in this pattern.
$12345 \times .00001 = .12345$

23. Give an example showing that multiplication by 1/10 undoes multiplication by 10.   Sample: $7 \times 10 = 70$ and $70 \times .1 = 7$

24. By what number can you multiply 46.381 to get 0.46381?   .01

68

25. Betty weighs 87.5 pounds. She weighed about a tenth of that at birth. To the nearest pound, what did she weigh at birth? **9 lb**

26. Multiply $\frac{1}{10^3}$ by 43.87. **.04387**

27. Write the three underlined numbers as decimals. *(Lessons 1-1, 1-9)* The number of students enrolled in grades 9−12 grew from <u>nine million six hundred ninety thousand</u> in 1960 to <u>fourteen million six hundred seventy thousand</u> in 1980. An estimate for 1990 is <u>twelve and a half million</u>. **9,690,000; 14,670,000; 12,500,000**

28. Write the underlined numbers of Question 27 in scientific notation. *(Lesson 2-3)* 9.69×10^6; 1.467×10^7; 1.25×10^7

29. Consider the number $59\frac{5}{11}$. *(Lessons 1-4, 1-9)*
    a. Between what two integers is this number? **59 and 60**
    b. Rewrite this number as a decimal. $59.\overline{45}$
    c. Round this decimal to the nearest millionth. **59.454545**

30. a. Order the numbers -1.4, -14, and 0.14 from smallest to largest. *(Lesson 1-5)*.
    b. Put them in a sentence with two inequality symbols in it. *(Lesson 1-6)*
    c. Graph them on the same number line. *(Lesson 1-2)*
    See margin.

31. As of 1990, the best-selling record album of all time worldwide was Michael Jackson's *Thriller*, which had sold over 41.5 million copies. Write this number in scientific notation. *(Lesson 2-3)* 4.15×10^7

32. Which is larger, 8×3 or 8^3? *(Lesson 2-2)* 8^3

33. Change each fraction to a decimal: **a.** 1/5; **b.** 1/2; **c.** 3/5; **d.** 5/6 *(Lesson 1-8)* a. .2; b. .5; c. .6; d. $.8\overline{3}$

34. Write one quintillion **a.** as a decimal, and **b.** as a power of ten. *(Lesson 2-2)* a. 1,000,000,000,000,000,000; b. 10^{18}

35. In the previous lessons, the largest power of 10 named has been quintillion. But there are larger powers of 10 with names. Look up the given word in a dictionary. (You may need a large dictionary.) Write the number as a decimal and as a power of 10.
    a. sextillion **b.** octillion **c.** nonillion **d.** decillion **See margin.**

36. Use your answer to Question 35. Write six octillionths as a decimal. .00000 00000 00000 00000 00000 06

NOTES ON QUESTIONS
Question 24: Students frequently have trouble with the wording in this question. Discuss what is meant, and help them convert the question into the easier form: ___ × 46.381 = .46381.

Question 35: You may want to provide a dictionary with the required terms for classroom reference.

FOLLOW-UP

MORE PRACTICE
For more questions on SPUR Objectives, use *Lesson Master 2-4*, shown below.

EXTENSION
Ask the students to formulate rules for dividing by 10, 100, and 1000. (Students will recognize that multiplication by $\frac{1}{x}$ is the same as division by x.)

NAME _____

LESSON **MASTER 2-4**
QUESTIONS ON **SPUR** OBJECTIVES

■**SKILLS** *Objective E (See pages 93–95 for objectives.)*

In 1–6, complete each sentence.

1. Multiplying by $\frac{1}{1000}$ is equivalent to first multiplying by $\frac{1}{10}$ or .1, then multiplying by $\frac{1}{10}$ or .1 again, and then multiplying by $\frac{1}{10}$ or .1 once again.

2. Multiplication by .01 "undoes" multiplication by ___**100**___.

3. To multiply by $\frac{1}{10,000}$, you should move the decimal point ___**4**___ places to the ___**left**___.

4. To multiply by .0001, you should move the decimal point ___**4**___ places to the ___**left**___.

5. By what number should you multiply 72.693 to get .72693? $\frac{1}{100}$ or .01

6. By what number should you multiply 0.6 to get 60? ___**100**___

In 7–12, write each product as a decimal.

7. $2.7 \times .01 =$ ___.027___

8. $71 \times \frac{1}{1000} =$ ___.071___

9. $17.621 \times .1 =$ ___1.7621___

10. $\frac{1}{10} \times 34 =$ ___.34___

11. $\frac{1}{10,000} \times 8.5 =$ ___.00085___

12. $9 \times .0000001 =$ ___.00000009___

14

Transition Mathematics © Scott, Foresman and Compa

69

OBJECTIVES

H Convert percents to decimals.
I Know common fraction and percent equivalents.

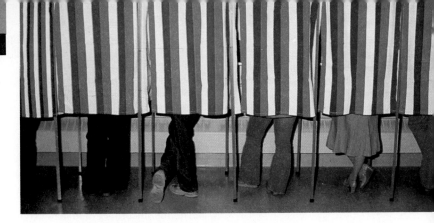

LESSON

2-5

Percent

The symbol % is read **percent.** The percent symbol is very common. Here are four examples of its use.

All items in the sale are 20% off.

Only 73% of the registered voters voted in the election.

That savings account gives a $5\frac{1}{4}$% interest rate.

A baby weighs about 200% more at the age of one year than it does at birth.

The percent sign % means hundredths. So to change a percent to a decimal, just multiply the number in front of the percent sign by $\frac{1}{100}$. Since $\frac{1}{100} = .01$, you can multiply instead by .01 if you wish. The examples use the above percents.

Example 1 Rewrite 20% as a decimal.

Solution $20\% = 20 \times \frac{1}{100} = .20 = .2$
Recall that $.2 = \frac{1}{5}$. So $20\% = \frac{1}{5}$ too.
20% off is the same as $\frac{1}{5}$ off.

Example 2 Rewrite 73% as a decimal.

Solution $73\% = 73 \times .01 = .73$
Here we multiplied by .01.
Multiplying by $\frac{1}{100}$ would give the same answer.
Use whichever is easier for you.

70

Example 3 Rewrite $5\frac{1}{4}\%$ as a decimal.

Solution First change the fraction to a decimal.
$5\frac{1}{4}\% = 5.25\%$
Now multiply by .01 instead of using the % sign.
$= 5.25 \times .01 = 0.0525$
The number 0.0525 is the number you can multiply by to determine the amount of interest in this kind of savings account.

Example 4 Rewrite 200% as a decimal.

Solution $200\% = 200 \times \frac{1}{100} = 2$
Percents of increase (or decrease) use tricky language. A baby that weighs 200% more than it did at birth has increased 2 times its weight. So its final weight is 3 times what it weighed at birth—the original weight *plus* the increase.

In Example 1, 20% was seen to equal the commonly found simple fraction $\frac{1}{5}$. Other percents equal common fractions. Some of these are graphed on the number line below. You should learn these.

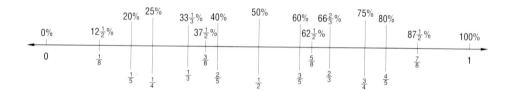

In Example 4, 200% was found to equal the integer 2. 100% = 1. Here is another number line with some other percents indicated on it.

The idea of percent is old. The word *percent* comes from the Latin words *per centum*, meaning "through 100." (Sometimes it is useful to think of percent as "out of 100.") The symbol for percent is much newer. In 1650 the symbol $\frac{o}{o}$ was used. People have used the symbol % only in the last 100 years. Many writers still write "per cent" as two words. (Either one word or two words is correct.)

LESSON 2-5 Percent   71

TEACHING NOTES

Percent is such a pervasive concept that it is important for students to get off to a good start here. Call attention to the idea that *percent* (%) is a word name like *thousand* or *million*, which is used with numbers. Point out that just as 5 thousand can be written $5 \times 1000 = 5000$, or 9 million can be written $9 \times 1,000,000 = 9,000,000$, the symbol % means $\frac{1}{100}$. Thus, an expression such as 25% can be written $25 \times \frac{1}{100} = \frac{25}{100} = \frac{1}{4}$ or $25 \times .01 = .25$

After discussing the examples, you might wish to do **Questions 5, 9, 13, 17, 21,** and **27** in class before assigning the entire set. If more practice is needed, do **Questions 8, 12, 16, 20, 24,** and **28**.

ADDITIONAL EXAMPLES
1. Change to a decimal.
a. 12.5%
.125
b. $5\frac{1}{3}\%$
.053
c. 1000%
10

2. Give a fraction (in lowest terms) or integer equivalent for each percent.
a. 75%
$\frac{3}{4}$
b. $33\frac{1}{3}\%$
$\frac{1}{3}$
c. 350%
$\frac{7}{2}$

NOTES ON QUESTIONS
Questions 15 and 16, 22 and 23: Students may need help converting fractions of a percent. One way to approach this issue is to begin with the decimal equivalent of 1% (.01). Then note that $\frac{1}{2}$% must be half of that; half of .010 is .005. This approach will help students recognize that the decimal equivalent for a fraction of a percent usually begins in the thousandths place or, in some cases, to the right of the thousandths place.

Question 44: Ask each student to find at least one of the specified rates. You may want to bring the appropriate section(s) of a newspaper to class, explain where the information is available, and discuss why it is important.

Questions

Covering the Reading

1. The symbol % is read __?__.   **percent**

2. The symbol % means __?__.   **hundredths**

3. To change a % to a decimal, __?__ the number in front of the % symbol by __?__.   **multiply; .01**

4. Give a sentence using the % symbol that might be in a store ad.
   Sample: save 25% on our clearance sale.

In 5–16, change to a decimal.

5. 80% .8   6. 50% .5   7. 5% .05

8. 2% .02   9. 1.5% .015   10. 5.75% .0575

11. 300% 3   12. 150% 1.5   13. 105% 1.05

14. 10.6% .106   15. $8\frac{1}{2}$% .085   16. $8\frac{1}{3}$% .08$\overline{3}$

In 17–24, change to a decimal and to a simple fraction.

17. 25% .25; $\frac{1}{4}$ 18. 75% .75; $\frac{3}{4}$

19. 20% .2; $\frac{1}{5}$ 20. 10% .1; $\frac{1}{10}$

21. $33\frac{1}{3}$% .$\overline{3}$; $\frac{1}{3}$ 22. $66\frac{2}{3}$% .$\overline{6}$; $\frac{2}{3}$

23. $87\frac{1}{2}$% .875; $\frac{7}{8}$ 24. 40% .4; $\frac{2}{5}$

25. According to the number line in the lesson, which is larger, 2/3 or 5/8?   **2/3**

26. What is a typical interest rate on a savings account?   **Sample: $5\frac{1}{4}$%**

In 27–30, change to a decimal and to a percent.

27. 1/2 .5; 50%   28. 3/5 .6; 60%

29. 7/8 .875; $87\frac{1}{2}$%   30. 3/10 .3; 30%

31. About how old is the symbol %?   **about 100 years**

Applying the Mathematics

In 32 and 33, rewrite each underlined number as either a fraction or a decimal.

32. The teachers wanted a 7% raise and the school board offered 4%.
    7/100 or .07; 1/25 or .04

33. In 1983, the president of Brazil's central bank said, "We cannot live with 150% inflation." Yet in 1988, inflation was 680%.
    $\frac{3}{2}$, $1\frac{1}{2}$, or 1.5; $\frac{34}{5}$, $6\frac{4}{5}$, or 6.8

34. *Multiple choice*   0.3 =
    (a) 300%   (b) 30%   (c) 3%   (d) 0.3%   **b**

35. *Multiple choice*   0.$\overline{3}$ is closest to
    (a) 333%   (b) 33%   (c) 3%   (d) .3%   **b**

72

36. Between what two integers is 250%? (Hint: Change 250% to a decimal.)   2 and 3

37. Between what two integers is 5.625%   0 and 1

38. Change 0.1% to a decimal and to a fraction.   .001; $\frac{1}{1000}$

39. Convert 1/25 to a percent by first changing it to a decimal.   .04 = 4%

40. According to the graph below:
  a. Which automaker had the biggest percent increase in sales?
  b. Which automaker had the biggest percent decrease in sales?
  a. Honda   b. Hyundai

New Car Sales in percent change, 1989-1990

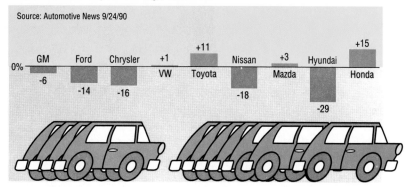

Source: Automotive News 9/24/90

  c. Which automaker had an increase, but the smallest percent increase in sales?   VW
  d. Which automakers were the closest to each other in percent change of sales?   VW and Mazda; Ford, Chrysler, and Nissan
  e. What percent would indicate no change in sales?   0%

Review

41. Multiply 2.3 by:
  a. 1000; **b.** 10; **c.** 10^4; **d.** 1/100; **e.** 0.0001. *(Lessons 2-1, 2-2, 2-4)*
  a. 2300; b. 23; c. 23,000; d. .023; e. .00023
42. Write 72,400,000 in scientific notation. *(Lesson 2-3)* 7.24×10^7

43. Which number is smallest: 9×10^4, 8.2×10^5, or 3.01×10^9?
(Lesson 2-3) 9×10^4

Exploration

44. Money rates are often given as percents. Find the following rates by looking in a daily newspaper or weekly magazine.
  a. the prime interest rate charged by banks to good credit risks
  b. a local mortgage rate on a new home purchase
  c. the interest rate on an account at a local savings institution
  Answers will vary.

LESSON 2-5 Percent   **73**

FOLLOW-UP

MORE PRACTICE
For more questions on SPUR Objectives, use *Lesson Master 2-5*, shown below.

EXTENSION
Divide the class into teams of about five students, and have each team choose one person to announce answers. Name a percent and ask for both its decimal and fraction equivalents. Team A has the first chance to answer. If Team A answers incorrectly, Team B has a chance to answer the same question. Play then moves to Team C, and so on. After each team has had one chance, play begins again with Team A. A team gets a point for each correct two-part answer. A team loses a point for any wrong information in the answer.

NAME _____

LESSON **MASTER**   **2-5**
QUESTIONS ON SPUR OBJECTIVES

■**SKILLS** *Objectives H and I (See pages 93-95 for objectives.)*
In 1-10, complete the chart. Be sure fractions are in lowest terms.

	Percent	Decimal	Fraction
	20%	.2	$\frac{1}{5}$
1.	75%	.75	$\frac{3}{4}$
2.	6.3%	.063	$\frac{63}{1000}$
3.	14.5%	.145	$\frac{29}{200}$
4.	7.2%	.072	$\frac{9}{125}$
5.	300%	3.0	3
6.	25%	.25	$\frac{1}{4}$
7.	37.5%	.375	$\frac{3}{8}$
8.	80%	.80	$\frac{4}{5}$
9.	90%	.90	$\frac{9}{10}$
10.	75%	.75	$\frac{3}{4}$

11. What fraction equals 20%? $\frac{1}{5}$

12. 15% is equivalent to what fraction? $\frac{3}{20}$

13. Write 16% as a decimal.   .16

14. Write $\frac{5}{8}$ as a percent.   62.5%

15. Write $8\frac{1}{3}\%$ as a decimal.   .083

Transition Mathematics © Scott, Foresman and Company   **15**

73

OBJECTIVES

J Find percents of numbers.
L Know and apply the Substitution Principle.
N Find percents of quantities in real situations.

LESSON

2-6

Percent of a Quantity

You have learned to convert percents and fractions to decimals. You have learned to put some decimals in scientific notation. The purpose of all this rewriting is to give you *flexibility*. Sometimes it's easier to use fractions. Sometimes decimals are easier. Sometimes percent or scientific notation is needed.

But why does all of this work? Why can you use .01 in place of $\frac{1}{100}$, or 3×10^6 instead of 3 million, or 0.4 instead of $\frac{2}{5}$ or 40%? The reason is due to a general idea called the **Substitution Principle.**

Substitution Principle

If two numbers are equal, then one can be substituted for the other in any computation without changing the results of the computation.

The Substitution Principle is used in many places. Here it is used to find percents of. The phrase "percent of" is a signal to multiply.

Example 1 Suppose 30% of (thirty percent of) the 2000 students in a high school are freshmen. How many students is this?

Solution   30% of 2000 students
Change "of" to "times."   = 30% × 2000 students
Now use the Substitution Principle,
rewriting 30% as .3   = .3 × 2000 students
                               = 600 students

74

■ ■ ■ ■ ■ ■ ■

Example 2 Suppose 100% of the 2000 students live within the school district. How many students is this?

Solution   100% of 2000 students

Change "of" to "times."   = 100% × 2000 students
Now use the Substitution Principle,
rewriting 100% as 1.   = 1 × 2000 students
                                               = 2000 students

So *all* of the students live in the school district.

From Example 2, you can see that "100% of" means "all of." Since 0% = 0, 0% of the students is 0 × 2000 students. So "0% of" means "none of." You know that 50% is equal to $\frac{1}{2}$. So "50% of" means "half of."

Percents are commonly used, and you must be able to work with them.

■ ■ ■ ■ ■ ■ ■

Example 3 To save money for college, parents put $1500 in a savings certificate that earns 8.25% interest yearly. How much will this certificate earn the first year?

Solution 8.25% of $1500 is the amount of interest. Calculate as follows.

                                               8.25% of $1500
                                             = 8.25% × $1500
Change 8.25% to a decimal.   = 0.0825 × $1500
                                             = $123.75, the amount earned.

Notice that the steps are the same in Examples 1, 2, and 3. Only the numbers are more complicated in Example 3. With a calculator, you do not have to worry about complicated numbers.

75

Example 4 A sofa sells for $569.95. It is put on sale at 20% off. How much will you save if you buy the sofa during the sale? What will the sale price be?

Solution You save 20% of $569.95.

$$20\% \times \$569.95$$
$$= .2 \times \$569.95$$
$$= \$113.99$$

Subtraction tells you what the sale price will be.

$569.95	original price
− 113.99	amount saved
$455.96	sale price

Without a calculator, you might choose to estimate the answer to Example 4. Estimate $569.95 as $570. Because $570 is so close to the actual price, the estimate should be very accurate.

$$20\% \text{ of } \$570$$
$$= 20\% \times \$570$$
$$= .2 \times \$570$$
$$= \$114, \text{ only one penny off the actual amount saved!}$$

This estimate also checks the calculation in Example 4.

Questions

Covering the Reading

1. Why is it useful to have many ways of writing numbers?
   to give flexibility
2. State the Substitution Principle. **See margin.**

3. *True or false?* (Hint: Recall that $20\% = \frac{1}{5}$ and $30\% = \frac{3}{10}$.)
   a. You can substitute $\frac{1}{5}$ for 20% in *any* computation and the answer will not be affected. **True**
   b. $20\% + 30\% = \frac{1}{5} + \frac{3}{10}$ **True**
   c. $20\% \times \$6000 = \frac{1}{5} \times \$6000$ **True**

4. **a.** In calculating 30% of 2000, when is the Substitution Principle used? **when 30% is rewritten as .3**
   b. Calculate 30% of 2000. **600**

5. Match each percent at left with the correct phrase at right.
100% of	none of	0%
50% of	all of	100%
0% of	half of	50%

In 6–9, calculate.

6. 50% of 6000 **3000**   7. 100% of 12 **12**

8. 0% of 50 **0**   9. 150% of 30 **45**

76

10. A sofa sells for $899.
    a. To estimate how much the sofa would cost at 30% off, what value can be used in place of $899? **$900**
    b. Estimate the price at a "30% off" sale. **$630**

11. Estimate how much you can save if a $10.95 record is put on sale at 25% off. **$2.75**

Applying the Mathematics

In 12 and 13, what does each remark mean? **See margin.**

12. "We are with you 100%!"   13. "Let's split it 50-50."

In 14 and 15, take the U.S. population to be about 250,000,000.

14. In your head, figure out what 10% of the U.S. population is. Use this to figure out **a.** 20%, **b.** 30%, **c.** 40%, and **d.** 50% of the population. **See margin.**

15. The U.S. population is now increasing at the rate of about 1.6% a year. How many people is this? **4,000,000 people**

16. In Bakersfield, California, it rains on about 10% of the days in a year. About how many days is this? **36 or 37 days**

17. In store A you see a $600 stereo at 25% off. In store B the same stereo normally costs $575 and is on sale at 20% off. Which store has the lower sale price? **store A**

18. Team E wins 48% of its games. Does team E win or lose more often? **lose**

19. Should you prefer to buy something at half price or at 40% off? **half price**

20. Which is larger, 250% of 10, or 300% of 8? **250% of 10**

21. An interest penalty is charged on credit card purchases if you do not pay on time. Suppose you have $1000 in overdue bills. If the penalty is 1.5% per month, how much interest will you have to pay? **$15**

22. The population of Los Angeles, California, was about 100,000 in 1900 and increased 1800% from 1900 to 1950. How many people is that increase? **1,800,000 people**

LESSON 2-6   Percent of a Quantity   77

NOTES ON QUESTIONS
Question 10b: Students will probably do this problem in two steps. They will find the amount of discount and then subtract that amount from the usual price. In a later discussion of uses of multiplication, students will be encouraged to do this problem in one step by multiplying the usual price by 70%.

Question 14: Ask why it is easy to take 10% of a number (10% = .1; to multiply by .1, move the decimal point one place to the left). Then ask how taking 10% can help to find 20%, 30%, and so on, of a number. (For example, 20% = 2 × 10%.)

Question 16: This provides another opportunity to discuss giving an answer in reasonable form. The exact answer is 36.5, but half a day makes no sense in response to the question asked. Students should round up or down to the nearest integer.

NAME _____

LESSON **MASTER   2-6**
QUESTIONS ON **SPUR** OBJECTIVES

■**SKILLS**   *Objective J (See pages 93–95 for objectives.)*

1. What is 0% of 53? **0**
2. Calculate 27.5% of 1000. **275**
3. What is 200% of 190? **380**
4. Find 15% of 400. **60**

■**PROPERTIES**   *Objective L*

5. Name two numbers that could be substituted for 43%.
   samples: .43 and $\frac{43}{100}$

6. Name a decimal and a percent that could be substituted for $\frac{4}{25}$.
   samples: .16 and 16%

7. According to the Substitution Principle, $\frac{3}{5} \cdot \frac{1}{4} =$
   60 % + **25** %.

8. How is the Substitution Principle used in calculating 40% of 800?
   Change 40% to $\frac{40}{100}$; $\frac{40}{100}$ (800) = 320.

■**USES**   *Objective N*

9. An interest penalty is charged on credit card purchases if one does not pay on time. Suppose Jo has $2100 in overdue bills. If the penalty is 1.4% per month, how much will she have to pay in interest penalty charges the first month? **$29.40**

10. A 5-speed bicycle priced at $109 is on sale at 15% off. What is the sale price? **$92.65**

11. How much is a 15% tip on a meal that costs $7.92? **$1.19**

12. If a $150 bike is on sale at one store for 20% off and at another for 25% off, how much more would you save by going to the second store? **$7.50**

16   Transition Mathematics © Scott, Foresman and Company

MORE PRACTICE
For more questions on SPUR
Objectives, use *Lesson Mas-
ter 2-6,* shown on page 77.

EXTENSION
Using Manipulatives
Allow students to use two-
color counters to solve
problems like the following:

•You have 3 red counters
and 1 yellow counter. What
percent of the counters are
red? How many red counters
must you add so that you
have 80% red counters?
(75% red; add 1)

•You have 2 red counters
and 2 yellow counters. What
percent of the counters are
yellow? How many yellow
counters must you add so
that you have 25% red counters? (50% yellow; add 4)

•You start with 4 red counters
and 3 yellow counters. This
time you can add both red
and yellow counters. In how
many different ways can you
add counters so that you
have 60% yellow counters?
(An infinite number of ways
are possible. Sample: add 4
red and 9 yellow)

EVALUATION
Alternative Assessment
In **Question 30,** students are
asked to write their own percent problem based on real
data. Choose a few of these
and present them to the
class for solution. Discuss
with the students situations in
real life where percent of a
quantity is used.

Review

23. The highest mountain in the world is Mt. Everest in the
    Himalayas. Its peak is about 29,028 feet above sea level and is on
    the Tibet-Nepal border. *(Lessons 1-4, 1-5)*
    a. Should you call its height 29,028 feet, or -29,028 feet? 29,028 ft
    b. Round the height to the nearest 100 feet. 29,000 ft
    c. Round the height to the nearest 1000 feet. 29,000 ft
    d. Round the height to the nearest 10,000 feet. 30,000 ft

24. Write in decimal notation. *(Lessons 1-1, 1-9, 2-2)*
    a. three billion four hundred thousand 3,000,400,000
    b. 5^4 625
    c. 8.3 million 8,300,000
    d. 2.56×10^8 256,000,000
    e. $4\frac{4}{5}$ 4.8

25. Give the value of $\pi/4$ truncated to ten-thousandths. *(Lessons 1-2, 1-3)*
    .7853

26. Multiply 56 by: **a.** 1 **b.** .1 **c.** .01 **d.** .001. *(Lesson 2-4)*
    a. 56; b. 5.6; c. .56; d. .056

27. Change to a percent: **a.** 1/4 **b.** 1/3 **c.** 5/4 *(Lesson 2-5)*
    a. 25%; b. $33\frac{1}{3}$%; c. 125%

28. Write as a power of 10: **a.** quadrillion **b.** ten thousand. *(Lesson 2-2)*
    a. 10^{15}; b. 10^4

29. Write $\frac{48}{100}$ in lowest terms. *(Lesson 1-10)* $\frac{12}{25}$

Exploration

30. a. Find a use of percent in a newspaper or magazine.
    b. Make up a question about the information you have found.
    c. Answer the question you have made up.
    Answers will vary.

78

2-7

Fractions, Decimals, and Percents

RESOURCES
■ Lesson Master 2-7
■ Quiz on Lessons 2-4
Through 2-7

OBJECTIVE

K Convert terminating decimals to fractions or percents.

Every fraction can be converted to a decimal. So can every percent. It is also easy to convert the other way, from decimals into fractions, or decimals into percent.

If a **terminating** (ending) **decimal** has only a few decimal places, just read the decimal in English and write the fraction.

Example 1 Convert 4.53 to a fraction.

Solution Read "four and fifty-three hundredths." That tells you $4.53 = 4\frac{53}{100}$.

Suppose the decimal cannot be easily read. First write it as a fraction over 1. Then multiply numerator and denominator by a power of 10 large enough to get rid of the decimal point in the numerator. This is an application of the Equal Fractions Property.

Example 2 Write 0.036 as a fraction in lowest terms.

Solution Write 0.036 as $\frac{0.036}{1}$.

Multiply numerator and denominator by 1000 to get $\frac{36}{1000}$. To write $\frac{36}{1000}$ in lowest terms, notice that 4 is a factor of both the numerator and denominator. Divide each by 4.

$$0.036 = \frac{36}{1000} = \frac{9}{250}$$

Check Convert $\frac{9}{250}$ to a decimal using a calculator. You should get 0.036.

Using the idea from Example 2, you can convert a fraction with decimals in it to a simple fraction.

LESSON 2-7 Fractions, Decimals, and Percents **79**

Reading After students look over the examples on their own, ask volunteers to explain each example carefully. Students must get accustomed to considering each step in a problem *critically*.

Point out that a fraction with a decimal in the numerator or denominator, the type in **Example 3**, occurs often in applications. **Example 4** exemplifies rewriting for the purpose of facility; that is, the rewriting is necessary to calculate what a worker earns.

ADDITIONAL EXAMPLES
1. Convert 3.027 to a fraction.
$3\frac{27}{1000}$ or $\frac{3027}{1000}$

2. Write .45 as a fraction in lowest terms.
$\frac{9}{20}$

3. Find a fraction equal to $\frac{5.2}{9.36}$ that has integers in both its numerator and its denominator.
$\frac{5}{9}$

4. A newborn baby typically triples his or her weight in the first year. What percent of the original weight is the weight after 1 year?
300%

5. A shirt is reduced by $\frac{1}{3}$. What is the percent savings?
$33\frac{1}{3}\%$

Example 3 Find a fraction equal to $\frac{2.5}{35}$ that has integers in its numerator and denominator.

Solution Multiply the numerator and denominator by 10. This moves the decimal point one place to the right in both the numerator and denominator.

$$\frac{2.5}{35} = \frac{25}{350}$$

Since 25 is a factor of 25 and 350, we get $\frac{2.5}{35} = \frac{1}{14}$.

Now consider percents. Remember that to convert a percent to a decimal, just move the decimal point two places to the left. For example, 53% = 0.53, 1800% = 18, and 6.25% = 0.0625.

To convert decimals to percents, just reverse the procedure. Move the decimal point two places to the right. Here are a few examples.

$$0.46 = 46\%$$
$$3 = 300\%$$
$$0.0007 = 0.07\%$$

To convert fractions to percents, convert them to decimals first. Then convert the decimals to percents.

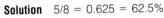

Example 4 A worker receives time-and-a-half for overtime. What percent of a person's pay is this?

Solution Time-and-a-half = $1\frac{1}{2}$ = 1.50 = 150%

Example 5 A photographer reduces the dimensions of photos to 5/8 their original size. A final dimension is what percent of a corresponding original dimension?

Solution 5/8 = 0.625 = 62.5%

Covering the Reading

In 1–3, **a.** write the decimal in English and **b.** convert the decimal to a fraction. **See margin.**

1. 8.27

2. 630.5

3. 0.001

4. The probability of a single birth being a boy is about .52. Convert this number to a percent. **52%**

In 5 and 6, convert to a percent.

5. 0.724 **72.4%**

6. 8 **800%**

7. 3.14 is an approximation to π. Convert this number to a fraction. $3\frac{7}{50}$ or $\frac{157}{50}$

8. Write 2.35 as a fraction in lowest terms. $2\frac{7}{20}$

9. About 1/4 of all families with two children are likely to have two girls. What percent of families is this? **25%**

10. The cost of living in 1988 was about $3\frac{1}{3}$ times what it was in 1970. What percent is this? $333\frac{1}{3}\%$

Applying the Mathematics

11. Write 4.2/1.04 as a fraction in lowest terms. $\frac{105}{26}$

12. Ariel put 6.5 gallons of gasoline in a 12-gallon gas tank. So the tank is 6.5/12 full. What simple fraction of the tank is this? $\frac{13}{24}$

13. A money market account at a local bank pays 6.75% interest. What fraction is this? $\frac{27}{400}$

In 14–17, complete the table. Put fractions in lowest terms.

Fraction	Decimal	Percent
1/2	0.5	50%
14. $\underline{?}\ \frac{49}{500}$	$\underline{?}$ .098	9.8%
15. $\underline{?}\ 3\frac{1}{5}$	3.2	$\underline{?}$ 320%
16. 5/16	$\underline{?}$ .3125	$\underline{?}$ 31.25%
17. $\underline{?}\ \frac{27}{100}$	0.27	$\underline{?}$ 27%

81

MORE PRACTICE
For more questions on SPUR Objectives, use *Lesson Master 2-7*, shown on page 81.

EVALUATION
A quiz covering Lessons 2-4 through 2-7 is provided in the Teacher's Resource File on page 10.

Review

18. Find twelve percent of ten thousand. *(Lessons 1-1, 2-6)* **1200**

19. Would you prefer to buy something at 30% off or 1/3 off? *(Lesson 2-6)* **1/3 off**

In 20–22, calculate. *(Lessons 2-1, 2-2, 2-6)*

20. $1918.37 \times 10,000$
19,183,700

21. 14% of 231
32.34

22. 3^5
243

In 23 and 24, give the word name for the decimal. *(Lesson 2-1)*

23. One followed by nine zeros   **one billion**

24. One followed by fifteen zeros   **one quadrillion**

25. Order from smallest to largest: .011, 1/10, 1/100. *(Lessons 1-2, 1-8)*
1/100, .011, 1/10

In 26–28, rewrite the number in scientific notation. *(Lesson 2-3)*

26. 3,320,000 square miles, the approximate area of the Sahara desert
3.32×10^6

27. 27,878,400 square feet, the number of square feet in a square mile
2.78784×10^7

28. 525,600 minutes, the number of minutes in a 365-day year
5.256×10^5

29. Leslie used 30% of her $5.00 allowance to buy a magazine. How much did the magazine cost? *(Lesson 2-6)*   **$1.50**

In 30–32, write the numbers as decimals. *(Lessons 1-1, 2-2, 2-5)*

30. fifty-million fifty   **50,000,050**

31. 2.4×10^5 **240,000**

32. 3200%   **32**

Exploration

33. Examine this sequence of numbers.
0.5
0.2 5
0.1 2 5
0.0 6 2 5
0.0 3 1 2 5
0.0 1 5 6 2 5
0.0 0 7 8 1 2 5
0.0 0 3 9 0 6 2 5
0.0 0 1 9 5 3 1 2 5
  a. Find a pattern and describe it in words.
  b. What is the next number in the sequence?
    a. Each number is .5 times the one above.; b. 0.00097 65625

2-8

More Powers of 10

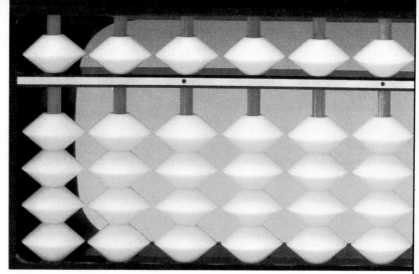

Different versions of this Japanese abacus are still used in some countries for computation. Its operation is based on the powers of 10.

RESOURCES
■ Lesson Master 2-8
▣ Visual for Teaching Aid 12: Use to examine both the positive and negative powers of 10.

OBJECTIVES

B Change word names for small numbers to decimals.
D Give decimals and English word names for negative integer powers of 10.
F Multiply by negative integer powers of 10.

TEACHING NOTES

Point out the symmetry of the positive and negative powers in the patterns on page 84. If students have a difficult time with the zero power, construct a table of powers of a number other than 10 to point out that the zero power of any number is equal to 1. For example:

2^4	16
2^3	8
2^2	4
2^1	2
2^0	?

Ask students to describe the pattern in the right-hand column. (Each number is $\frac{1}{2}$ the number immediately above it.) To continue the pattern, replace the question mark by 1. You can extend both columns to consider negative powers of 2.

A number that is written with an exponent, like 4^3 or 10^9, is said to be in **exponential form.** Exponential form is a short way of writing some large numbers. For example, $2^{20} = 1048576$. The decimal 1,048,576 is longer than the exponential form 2^{20} for the same number. Powers of 10 such as 100, 1000, and 10,000 are easily written in exponential form as 10^2, 10^3, and 10^4. Thus exponential form makes it possible to rewrite *large* numbers in the shorter scientific notation. Now we consider how to use exponential form to write *small* numbers.

Examine this pattern closely. The numbers in each row going across are equal. Guess what should be the next entry going down in each column.

$$10^6 = 1,000,000 = \text{million}$$
$$10^5 = 100,000 \ \ = \text{hundred thousand}$$
$$10^4 = 10,000 \ \ \ = \text{ten thousand}$$
$$10^3 = 1,000 \ \ \ \ \ = \text{thousand}$$
$$10^2 = 100 \ \ \ \ \ \ \ = \text{hundred}$$
$$10^1 = 10 \ \ \ \ \ \ \ \ \ = \text{ten}$$

In the left column, the exponents decrease by 1, so the next entry should be 10^0. In the middle column, each number is 1/10 the number above it. So the next number should be 1/10 of 10, which is 1. The right column gives the place values. Next to the tens place is the ones place. Here is the next row.

$$10^0 = 1 \ \ \ \ \ \ \ \ \ = \text{one}$$

Thus *10 to the zero power is equal to 1.* This is a fact that surprises many people. Check it on your calculator. Also check the zero power of other numbers on your calculator.

If the pattern is continued, negative exponents appear in the left column. This is exactly what is needed in order to represent small numbers.

$$10^{-1} = 0.1 \qquad = \text{one tenth} \qquad = \tfrac{1}{10}$$
$$10^{-2} = 0.01 \qquad = \text{one hundredth} \qquad = \tfrac{1}{100}$$
$$10^{-3} = 0.001 \qquad = \text{one thousandth} \qquad = \tfrac{1}{1000}$$
$$10^{-4} = 0.0001 \qquad = \text{one ten-thousandth} \qquad = \tfrac{1}{10,000}$$
$$10^{-5} = 0.00001 = \text{one hundred-thousandth} = \tfrac{1}{100,000}$$
$$\text{and so on.}$$

The names of the negative powers of 10 follow closely those for the positive powers.

$10^1 = \text{ten}$	$10^{-1} = \text{one tenth}$
$10^2 = \text{one hundred}$	$10^{-2} = \text{one hundredth}$
$10^3 = \text{one thousand}$	$10^{-3} = \text{one thousandth}$
$10^6 = \text{one million}$	$10^{-6} = \text{one millionth}$
$10^9 = \text{one billion}$	$10^{-9} = \text{one billionth}$
$10^{12} = \text{one trillion}$	$10^{-12} = \text{one trillionth}$
$10^{15} = \text{one quadrillion}$	$10^{-15} = \text{one quadrillionth}$
$10^{18} = \text{one quintillion}$	$10^{-18} = \text{one quintillionth}$

Recall that to multiply a decimal by 0.1 or $\tfrac{1}{10}$, just move the decimal point one unit to the left. Since $10^{-1} = 0.1$, the substitution principle tells us that again, to multiply by 10^{-1}, just move the decimal point one unit to the left.

$$829.43 \times 10^{-1} = 82.943$$

To multiply a decimal by 0.01 or 1/100, you know you only have to move the decimal point two units to the left. Since $10^{-2} = 0.01$, the same goes for multiplying by 10^{-2}.

$$829.43 \times 10^{-2} = 8.2943$$

Do you see the simple pattern?

To multiply by a negative integer power of 10:

Move the decimal point to the left as many places as indicated by the exponent.

Example 1   Write 72×10^{-5} as a decimal.

Solution   To multiply by 10^{-5}, move the decimal point five places to the left. So $72 \times 10^{-5} = 72.0 \times 10^{-5} = .00072$.

84

Example 2 Write 6 trillionths as a decimal.

Solution 6 trillionths = 6×10^{-12} = 0.00000 00000 06.
(When a decimal has many digits, we put spaces between groups of five digits to make it easier to count the digits.)

NOTES ON QUESTIONS
Question 5: This reinforces the fact that $10^0 = 1$. Although the reason "because the calculator says so" is not mathematically valid, seeing the display result does help convince students who are still confusing powering with multiplication and want 10^0 to equal 0.

ADDITIONAL ANSWERS
3. a. hundred thousands;
b. ten thousands;
c. thousands;
d. hundreds;
e. tens

18. Move the decimal point to the left as many places as indicated by the exponent.

Questions

Covering the Reading

1. Which one of these numbers is written in exponential form? 7^3
   2/3   million 2×10^6 7^3 1.45

2. Write $10 \times 10 \times 10 \times 10$ in exponential form. 10^4

3. Give the place value name for these powers.
   a. 10^5 **b.** 10^4 **c.** 10^3 **d.** 10^2 **e.** 10^1
   See margin.

4. Continue the pattern of Question 3 to give the place value name for:
   a. 10^0 **b.** 10^{-1}
   ones   tenths

5. Press these keys on your calculator. 10 $\boxed{y^x}$ 0 $\boxed{=}$
   What have you calculated and what is the result? $10^0 = 1$

6. Write as a decimal. **a.** 10^{-2} .01 **b.** 10^{-3} .001

7. Tell whether the number is positive, negative, or equal to zero.
   a. 10^0 **b.** 10^{-1}
   positive   positive

8. 10^7 = ten million. What is a word name for 10^{-7}?
   one ten-millionth

In 9–11, write as a power of 10.

9. one thousandth   **10.** one millionth   **11.** one trillionth
   10^{-3} 10^{-6} 10^{-12}

In 12–17, write as a decimal.

12. 3×10^{-2} .03   **13.** 3.45×10^{-4} .000345

14. 41.3×10^0 41.3   **15.** four thousandths .004

16. sixty billionths   **17.** five millionths
    .00000 0060   .000005

18. What is the general rule for multiplying by a negative power of 10? See margin.

Applying the Mathematics

19. *Multiple choice* Which number does not equal the others? f
    (a) 1%   (b) .01   (c) 1/100   (d) 10^{-2}
    (e) one hundredth   (f) All of (a) through (e) are equal.

20. 64 can be written in exponential form because $4^3 = 64$.
    Write in exponential form.
    a. 81   **b.** 144 12^2 **c.** 32 2^5
    3^4 or 9^2

LESSON 2-8 More Powers of 10   85

NAME _____

LESSON **MASTER 2–8**
QUESTIONS ON **SPUR** OBJECTIVES

■**SKILLS** *Objective B* (See pages 93–95 for objectives.)
In 1–3, write each as a decimal.

1. 9 millionths	0.000009
2. 4.7 ten-thousandths	0.00047
3. 54 billionths	0.000000054

■**SKILLS** *Objective D*
In 4–8, complete the chart. Write the missing decimals and word names.

	Power of Ten	Decimal	Word Name
4.	10^{-2}	.01	one hundredth
5.	10^{-12}	.000000000001	one trillionth
6.	10^{-5}	.00001	one hundred-thousandth
7.	10^{-3}	.001	one thousandth
8.	10^{-6}	.000001	one millionth

■**SKILLS** *Objective F*
In 9–12, write each product in decimal notation.

9. 7.45×10^{-3} =	.00745
10. 53×10^{-10} =	.0000000053
11. 9.12×10^0 =	9.12
12. 75×10^5 =	7,500,000

13. An angstrom is a unit used to measure the length of light waves. One angstrom is equal to 10^{-8} mm. How many millimeters are 53,500.5 angstroms?
0.000535005 mm

14. The electron volt and the kilowatt-hour are two units used in energy conversions. One electron volt is equivalent to $4.45 \cdot 10^{-26}$ kilowatt-hours. To what decimal number is one electron volt equivalent?
.0000000000000000000000000445 kilowatt-hours

18   Transition Mathematics © Scott, Foresman and Company

NOTES ON QUESTIONS

Question 22c: The pattern exemplified by this question deserves special mention. Here, of course, the generalization $x^n \times x^{-n} = 1$ is valid. Discuss what evidence you should have to make a generalization and caution students about jumping to conclusions. Point out that a generalization must be true for an entire class of facts, not just two, as in this case.

Question 24: Students will probably answer by changing 1.2×10^{-8} to .000000012, then moving the decimal point 5 places to the right to get .0012 meter. You might ask if anyone thought of a way to do the calculation directly by adding the exponents.

FOLLOW-UP

MORE PRACTICE
For more questions on SPUR Objectives, use *Lesson Master 2-8*, shown on page 85.

EXTENSION
With some students, you may want to work toward the generalization $a^{-b} = \frac{1}{a^b}$, stated either with words or with variables.

22. c. When ten to a power is multiplied by ten to the opposite of the power, the product is 1.

21. Write 10×10^{-7} as a decimal.   .000001

22. **a.** Calculate $10^4 \times 10^{-4}$.   1
    b. What is a hundred times one one-hundredth?   1
    c. Make a general conclusion from parts **a** and **b**.   See margin.

23. Arrange from smallest to largest: $1, 10^{-5}, 0, 10^2$. $0, 10^{-5}, 1, 10^2$

24. An electron microscope can magnify an object 10^5 times. The length of a poliomyelitis virus is 1.2×10^{-8} meter. Multiply this length by 10^5 to find how many meters long the virus would appear to be when viewed through this microscope.   .0012 m

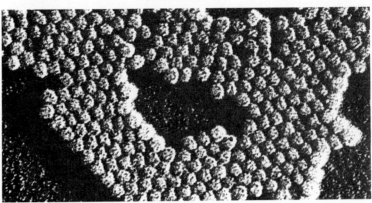

Poliomyelitis virus under magnification

Review

In 25 and 26, change the decimal to **a.** a fraction and **b.** a percent. *(Lesson 2-7)*

25. 12.45   a. $12\frac{45}{100}$ or $12\frac{9}{20}$; b. 1245%

26. 0.1875   a. $\frac{1875}{10,000}$ or $\frac{3}{16}$; b. 18.75%

27. In store C you see a $50 tape marked 30% off. In store D you can buy this tape for $35. Which store gives the better buy? *(Lesson 2-6)*   The price is the same.

28. It rains or snows on about 42% of the days of the year in Seattle, Washington. About how many days per year is this? *(Lesson 2-6)*   153

29. Change 30%:
    a. to a decimal   .3 **b.** to a simple fraction *(Lesson 2-5)* $\frac{3}{10}$

30. 512 is what power of 2? *(Lesson 2-2)*   ninth

31. 93,000,000 miles is the approximate distance from Earth to the Sun. Write this number in scientific notation. *(Lesson 2-3)* 9.3×10^7

Exploration

32. Large computers are able to do computations in nanoseconds. Look in a dictionary for the meaning of *nanosecond*.   one billionth of a second

2-9

Scientific Notation for Small Numbers

Compartments in the outer shell of this dirigible were filled with hydrogen so that it would float in the heavier air.

RESOURCES
- Lesson Master 2-9
- Visual for Teaching Aid 12: Positive and Negative Powers of 10.

OBJECTIVES

G Convert small numbers into scientific notation.

M Identify numbers as being written in scientific notation.

O Translate actual quantities into and out of scientific notation.

P Indicate key sequences and displays on a calculator for small numbers.

The mass of one atom of hydrogen, the lightest element, has been found to be

.00000 00000 00000 00000 00016 75 gram.

(By comparison, a piece of notebook paper weighs more than a gram!) A number this small is quite difficult to read and compute with, in decimal notation. To help you with the reading, we have put a space after every fifth digit of the decimal. But the number can be written in scientific notation. In scientific notation such numbers are easier to deal with.

> A small number written in scientific notation is a number greater than or equal to 1 and less than 10, multiplied by a negative integer power of 10.

For instance, 1.91×10^{-5} is a small number written in scientific notation. The same ideas are involved in putting small numbers into scientific notation as were used with large numbers.

Example 1 Write the mass of one atom of hydrogen, given above, in scientific notation.

Solution First place the decimal point between the 1 and the 6. This gives you 1.675, a number between 1 and 10. Now find the power of 10 by counting the number of places you must move the decimal to the *left* to change 1.675 into .00000 00000 00000 00000 00016 75. (The movement to the left is in the negative direction and signals the negative exponent.) The move is 24 places to the left. So the mass, in scientific notation, is

$$1.675 \times 10^{-24} \text{ grams.}$$

LESSON 2-9 *Scientific Notation for Small Numbers* **87**

TEACHING NOTES

Write the following pattern on the board:

1230	1.23×10^3
123	1.23×10^2
12.3	1.23×10^1
1.23	?
.123	?
.0123	?
.00123	?

Ask students what should replace the question marks to continue the pattern (1.23×10^0, 1.23×10^{-1}, 1.23×10^{-2}, 1.23×10^{-3}). Then use multiplication with the zero power and the negative powers of 10 to confirm that the products are equal to the numbers at left.

Relate the numbers in the right-hand column of the pattern to scientific notation, reviewing the parts to the notation: a number between 1 and 10, a times sign, and a power of 10. Finally, carefully examine the examples with the students, especially **Examples 1** and **3**.

ADDITIONAL EXAMPLES

1. An electronic charge measures about .00000 00004 803 electrostatic units. Write this in scientific notation.
4.803×10^{-10}

2. The volume of a water molecule is about 3×10^{-23} cubic meters. Write this as a decimal.
.00000 00000 00000 00000 003

3. Enter 0.00000 00000 0012 into a calculator.
1.2 [EE] 13 [±]

ADDITIONAL ANSWERS

4. 1.675 [EE] 24 [±]

Example 2 Change 3.97×10^{-8} to a decimal.

Solution Recall that, to multiply by 10^{-8}, move the decimal point 8 places to the left.
$$3.97 \times 10^{-8} = 0.00000\ 00397$$

Example 3 Enter 0.00000 00000 6993 into a calculator.

Solution This decimal is too long to fit on the display. So convert into scientific notation. Starting at 6.993, you must move the decimal point 11 places to the left to get the given number. So $0.00000\ 00000\ 6993 = 6.993 \times 10^{-11}$. To enter that number on your calculator, use the key sequence
$$6.993 \ [EE] \ 11 \ [±].$$

Questions

Covering the Reading

1. A small number in scientific notation is a number greater than or equal to __?__ and less than __?__ multiplied by a __?__ power of __?__. **one; ten; negative integer; ten**

2. Why are small numbers often written in scientific notation? **They are easier to deal with.**

3. Give an example of a small quantity that is usually written in scientific notation. **Sample: masses of atomic particles**

4. Write a key sequence that will display 1.675×10^{-24} on your calculator. **See margin.**

5. What number in scientific notation is given by this key sequence?
$$6.008 \ [EE] \ 5 \ [±] \quad 6.008 \times 10^{-5}$$

In 6–8, rewrite the number in scientific notation.

6. 0.00008052 second, the time needed for TV signals to travel 15 miles **8.052×10^{-5}**

7. 0.28 second, a time needed for sound to travel the length of a football field. **2.8×10^{-1}**

8. 0.00000 00000 00000 00000 0396 gram, the weight of one atom of uranium. **3.96×10^{-22}**

9. Suppose a decimal is multiplied by a negative power of 10. Should its decimal point be moved to the right or to the left? **left**

In 10–12, rewrite the numbers as decimals.

10. 1×10^{-8} centimeter, the angstrom (a unit of measure)
.00000 001 cm

11. 2×10^{-7} meter, the length of the longest known virus
.00000 02 m

12. 2.82×10^{-11} centimeter, the radius of an electron
.00000 00000 282 cm

13. Using your calculator, find the first six places of the decimal for 1/102.   .009803

14. Write the number in *decimal* notation given by the key sequence
4.675 [EE] 7 [±].   .00000 04675

15. Change $\dfrac{3 \times 10^{-8}}{6 \times 10^{-7}}$ to a decimal.   .05

In 16 and 17, choose one of the symbols $<$, $=$, or $>$.

16. 5.37×10^{-5} __?__ 5.37×10^{-4} $<$

17. 49×10^{-9} __?__ 4.9×10^{-8} $=$

18. Write 4,500,000,000 in scientific notation. *(Lesson 2-3)* 4.5×10^9

19. Write as a power of 10.
a. one million 10^6 **b.** one millionth *(Lesson 2-8)* 10^{-6}

20. Calculate 5 to the 7th power. *(Lesson 2-2)*   78,125

21. The Skunks baseball team lost 60% of its games. Did the team win or lose more often? *(Lesson 2-6)*   The team lost more often.

22. a. What fraction is equal to 75%?   3/4 **b.** What is 75% of 400?
(Lessons 2-5, 2-6)   300

In 23–25, write as a decimal. *(Lessons 1-9, 2-5)*

23. 3%   .03   **24.** $-19\frac{7}{10}$ -19.7   **25.** 150%   1.5

26. Between what two integers is 3.4% ? (Watch out!) *(Lesson 2-5)*
0 and 1

27. Newspaper columnist Georgie Anne Geyer once wrote about receiving a tax bill for $0.01. The payment was due June 30, 1984.
a. If Ms. Geyer did not pay her bill by June 30th, she would have to pay a penalty of 10% of her bill. How much is this?
(Lesson 2-6) $.001
b. Also, if she paid late, she would have had to pay an additional interest penalty of 1% of her bill. How much is this? *(Lesson 2-6)*
c. What would be the exact total she owed if she paid the bill late? $.0111
d. Round your answer to part **c** to the nearest penny. *(Lesson 1-4)*
b. $.0001; d. $.01

NOTES ON QUESTIONS
**Error Analysis For
Questions 6–8, 10–12:**
A common mistake in converting scientific notation with negative exponents to a decimal, and vice versa, is to match zeros to the exponent. For example, 2×10^{-6} incorrectly becomes .0000002. Stress that the exponent describes movement of the decimal point, which, in this case, does not translate into the number of zeros.

Question 15:   You might ask students whether the answer should be more or less than 1 and why. (Because $6 \times 10^{-7} > 3 \times 10^{-8}$, the denominator is bigger and the answer is less than one). Many students may think that the 3 and 6 determine the size of this fraction; the size actually depends more on the exponents.

---

28. The narrowest street in the world is in Great Britain. It has a width of $19\frac{5}{16}$ inches. *(Lessons 1-9, 1-8)*
    a. Between what two whole number widths does this width lie?
    b. If you are 19.3 inches wide, could you walk down this street?
    a. 19 and 20; b. yes

In 29 and 30, tell whether a high or a low estimate would be preferred.

29. An airline estimates how much baggage an airplane can carry without being overloaded. *(Lesson 1-3)*   low

30. A caterer estimates how much food to prepare for a graduation party. *(Lesson 1-3)*   high

31. Order from smallest to largest: -.6, -.66, -.666, -.656, -2/3. *(Lessons 1-5, 1-8)* $-\frac{2}{3}$, -.666, -.66, -.656, -.6

32. Change 76.23 to:
    a. a percent   7623% **b.** a fraction *(Lesson 2-7)* $76\frac{23}{100}$

Exploration

33. **a.** On your calculator, what is the smallest positive number that can be displayed? 1×10^{-99} Answers may vary.
    b. What is the largest negative number that can be displayed? -1×10^{-99} Answers may vary.

34. **a.** Type ?0.25*0.3 on your computer and press RETURN. What does the computer print? What is the computer doing?
    b. Put a zero before the 2 or 3 of part **a**, so that you have either ?0.025*0.3 or ?0.25*0.03. What does the computer print this time?
    c. Continue increasing the number of zeros until the computer is forced to print an answer in its form of scientific notation. How does your computer write small numbers in scientific notation?
    d. What is the smallest positive number your computer will itself print that is not in scientific notation?   See margin.

90

Summary

In Chapter 1, you learned three advantages of the decimal system. (1) All of the most common numbers can be written as decimals. (2) Decimals are easy to order. (3) Decimals are used by calculators to represent numbers. In this chapter, another advantage is discussed. (4) Large and small numbers can easily be written as decimals.

The decimal system is based on the number 10. So when numbers are written as decimals, it is easy to multiply by powers of 10. The numbers 10, 100, 1000, ... (or 10^1, 10^2, 10^3, ...) are positive integer powers of 10. The numbers 1/10, 1/100, 1/1000, ... or their decimal equivalents 0.1, 0.01, 0.001, ... (or 10^{-1}, 10^{-2}, 10^{-3}, ...) are negative integer powers of 10. The number one is the zero power of 10.

Percent means multiply by 1/100, so decimals can easily be converted to %. Percents are usually small numbers. To find a percent of a number, multiply the percent by that number. Percents, decimals and fractions are all used often and sometimes interchangeably. So it is useful to be able to convert from one form into another.

Large and small numbers are also often written in exponential form. Scientific notation combines exponential form with decimal notation. It is a standard way used all over the world to express very large or very small numbers.

Vocabulary

You should be able to give a general description and a specific example of each of the following ideas.

Lesson 2-1
million, billion, trillion, and so on

Lesson 2-2
base, exponent, power
$\boxed{x^y}$, $\boxed{y^x}$, x^y

Lesson 2-3
scientific notation for large numbers
 $\boxed{EE}$, $\boxed{exp}$

Lesson 2-5
percent, %

Lesson 2-6
Substitution Principle

Lesson 2-7
terminating decimal

Lesson 2-8
exponential form
millionth, billionth, trillionth, and so on

Lesson 2-9
scientific notation for small numbers

Progress Self-Test

Take this test as you would take a test in class. Then check your work with the solutions in the Selected Answers section in the back of the book.

In 1–10, write as a single decimal.
1. $100,000,000 \times 23.51864$ **2,351,864,000**
2. 34% of 600 **204**
3. 32 billionths **.00000 0032**
4. 824.59×0.00001 **.0082459**
5. $\frac{1}{1000} \times 77$ **.077**
6. 3456.8910×10^5 **345,689,100**
7. 2.816×10^{-3} **.002816**
8. 10^{-7} **.00000 01**
9. 8% **.08**
10. 6^3 **216**

In 11–14, consider 125^6. **base; exponent**
11. 125 is called the __?__ and 6 the __?__.
12. What key sequence can you use to calculate this on your calculator? **125 $\boxed{y^x}$ 6 $\boxed{=}$**
13. What is the resulting display? **See margin.**
14. Give a decimal estimate for 125^6. **3,814,700,000,000**

In 15 and 16, write in scientific notation.
15. 21,070,000,000 **2.107×10^{10}**
16. 0.00000 008 **8×10^{-8}**

In 17 and 18, write the key sequence necessary to enter the number on your calculator.
17. 4.5×10^{13} **4.5 $\boxed{EE}$ 13**
18. 0.00000 01234 56 **1.23456 $\boxed{EE}$ 7 $\boxed{\pm}$**
19. Order from smallest to largest: 4^4 5^3 3^5
20. Between what two integers is 40%? **0 and 1**
21. Rewrite 4.73 as
    a. a simple fraction **$\frac{473}{100}$**
    b. a percent **473%**
22. As a fraction, $33\frac{1}{3}\% = $ __?__. **$\frac{1}{3}$**

19. See margin

23. A recent survey of 150 chefs reported that 30% of the chefs thought broccoli is the top vegetable. How many chefs is this? **45**

24. A stereo system is on sale at 25% off. If the regular price is $699, to the nearest dollar what is the sale price? **$524**
25. Julio correctly answered 80% of the items on a 20-item test. How many did he miss? **4**
26. Why is this number not in scientific notation: 22.4×10^3? **22.4 is not between 1 and 10**
27. What power of 10 equals one million? **sixth**
28. According to the Substitution Principle, $\frac{3}{5} - \frac{1}{10} = $ __?__$\% - $ __?__$\%$. **60, 10**
29. It is estimated that a swarm of 250 billion locusts descended on the Red Sea in 1889. Write this number in scientific notation. **2.5×10^{11}**

Chapter Review

Questions on SPUR Objectives

RESOURCES
- Chapter 2 Test, Form A
- Chapter 2 Test, Form B
- Chapter 2 Test, Cumulative Form

SPUR stands for **S**kills, **P**roperties, **U**ses, and **R**epresentations. The Chapter Review questions are grouped according to the SPUR Objectives for this chapter.

SKILLS deal with the procedures used to get answers.

Objective A: *Multiply by 10, 100, 1000, ...*
(Lesson 2-1)

1. $32 \times 10,000 = $ _?_ **320,000**
2. $100 \times 7.5 = $ _?_ **750**
3. $1,000,000 \times 0.025 = $ _?_ **25,000**
4. What number is 3.5 multiplied by to get 3500? **1000**

Objective B: *Change word names for numbers to decimals. (Lessons 2-1, 2-8)*

5. Write the June, 1984, trade deficit of $10 billion as a decimal. **$10,000,000,000**
6. Write 4.6 millionths as a decimal. **.0000046**

Objective C: *Convert powers to decimals.*
(Lesson 2-2)

7. Convert 4^3 to a decimal. **64**
8. Convert 12^8 to a decimal. **About 429,980,000**

Objective D: *Give decimals and English word names for positive and negative integer powers of 10. (Lessons 2-2, 2-8)*

9. $10^5 = $ _?_ **100,000**
10. In English, 10^9 is _?_. **one billion**
11. $10^{-4} = $ _?_ **.0001**
12. In English, 10^{-2} is _?_. **one hundredth**
13. One trillion is what power of ten? **twelfth**
14. 0.0001 is what power of ten? **negative fourth**

Objective E: *Multiply by 0.1, 0.01, 0.001, ..., and 1/10, 1/100, 1/1000, ... (Lesson 2-4)*

15. $2.73 \times 0.00000\ 001 = $ _?_ **.00000 00273**
16. $495 \times 0.1 = $ _?_ **49.5**

17. $75 \times \frac{1}{1000} = $ _?_ **.075**
18. $2.1 \times \frac{1}{100} = $ _?_ **.021**

Objective F: *Multiply by powers of 10.*
(Lessons 2-2, 2-8)

19. $3 \times 10^7 = $ _?_ **30,000,000**
20. $0.42 \times 10^5 = $ _?_ **42,000**
21. $7.34 \times 10^0 = $ _?_ **7.34**
22. $68.3 \times 10^{-4} = $ _?_ **.00683**

Objective G: *Convert large and small numbers into scientific notation. (Lessons 2-3, 2-9)*

23. Write 480,000 in scientific notation.
24. Write 9,000,000,000,000,000 in scientific notation. **9×10^{15}**
25. Write 0.00013 in scientific notation.
26. Write 0.7 in scientific notation. **7×10^{-1}**
23. 4.8×10^5; 25. 1.3×10^{-4}

Objective H: *Convert percents to decimals.*
(Lesson 2-5)

27. Write 15% as a decimal. **.15**
28. Write 5.25% as a decimal. **.0525**
29. Write 9% as a decimal. **.09**
30. Write 200% as a decimal. **2**

Objective I: *Know common fraction and percent equivalents. (Lesson 2-5)*

31. Change 1/2 to a percent. **50%**
32. Change 4/5 to a percent. **80%**
33. What fraction equals 30%? **$\frac{3}{10}$**
34. What fraction equals $66\frac{2}{3}$%? **$\frac{2}{3}$**

CHAPTER REVIEW

The main objectives for the chapter are organized here into sections corresponding to the four main types of understanding this book promotes: Skills, Properties, Uses, and Representations.

USING THE CHAPTER REVIEW
Whereas end-of-chapter material may be considered optional in some texts, in *Transition Mathematics* we have selected these objectives and questions with the expectation that they will be covered. Students should be able to answer these questions with about 85% accuracy after studying the chapter.

You may assign these questions over a single night to help students prepare for a test the next day, or you may assign the questions over a two-day period.

If you work the questions over two days, then we recommend assigning the *evens* for homework the first night so that students get feedback in class the next day, then assigning the *odds* the night before the test so students can use the answers provided in the book.

■ **Objective J:** *Find percents of numbers.* (Lesson 2-6)

35. What is 50% of 150?   75
36. What is 3% of 3?   .09
37. What is 100% of 6.2?   6.2
38. What is 7.8% of 3500?   273

■ **Objective K:** *Convert terminating decimals to fractions or percents.* (Lesson 2-7)

39. Find a simple fraction equal to 5.7.
40. Find the simple fraction in lowest terms equal to 0.892. $\frac{223}{250}$
41. Convert 0.86 to percent.   86%
42. Convert 3.2 to percent.   320%
43. Convert $\frac{3}{7}$ to percent.   about 42.9%
44. Convert $\frac{11}{8}$ to percent.   137.5%
39. Sample: $\frac{57}{10}$

PROPERTIES deal with the principles behind the mathematics.

■ **Objective L:** *Know and apply the Substitution Principle.* (Lesson 2-6)

45. State the Substitution Principle.   See margin.
46. How is the Substitution Principle used in evaluating 75% of 40?   See margin.
47. Name two numbers that could be substituted for 50%.   .5 and $\frac{1}{2}$
48. According to the Substitution Principle, $\frac{1}{2} + \frac{1}{4} = \underline{\ ?\ }\% + \underline{\ ?\ }\%$.   50; 25

■ **Objective M:** *Identify numbers as being written in scientific notation.* (Lessons 2-3, 2-9)

49. Why is 23×10^4 not in scientific notation?   23 is not between 1 and 10.
50. In scientific notation, a number greater than or equal to $\underline{\ ?\ }$ and less than $\underline{\ ?\ }$ is multiplied by an $\underline{\ ?\ }$ power of 10.
1, 10, integer

USES deal with applications of mathematics in real situations.

■ **Objective N:** *Find percents of quantities in real situations.* (Lesson 2-6)

51. At a "40%-off" sale, what will you pay for $26.50 slacks? $15.90
52. George Bush received about 53.9% of the votes cast in the 1988 presidential election. About 89,000,000 votes were cast. About how many votes did Bush get?   47,970,000
53. The value of a one-carat colorless flawless diamond reached $64,000 in 1980. By October of 1990, the price had dropped 61% of its former value. What was the value in 1990?
about $25,000

■ **Objective O:** *Translate actual quantities into and out of scientific notation.* (Lessons 2-3, 2-9)

54. The number of non-human living things on Earth is estimated at 3×10^{33}. Write this number as a decimal.   3,000,000,000,000,000,000,000,000,000,000,000

55. A piece of paper is about 0.005 inches thick. What is that in scientific notation?
5×10^{-3}

94

REPRESENTATIONS deal with picture, graphs, or objects that illustrate concepts.

Objective P: *Indicate key sequences and displays on a calculator for large and small numbers.*
(Lessons 2-3, 2-9)

56. What key sequence will enter 32 billion on your calculator? **3.2** [EE] **10**

57. What key sequence will enter one trillionth on your calculator? **1** [EE] **12** [±]

58. What key sequence will enter 2^{45} on your calculator? **2** [yˣ] **45**

59. What does your calculator display for the number of Question 58? (*3.5184 13*)

60. If a calculator displays (*4.73   08*), what decimal is being shown? **473,000,000**

61. Estimate 1357975×24681086 using a calculator. **3.3516 × 10¹³**

62. Estimate $.0025 \times .00004567$ using a calculator. **1.1418 × 10⁻⁷**

63. What key sequence will enter 3×10^{21} on your calculator? **3** [EE] **21**

CHAPTER 3  MEASUREMENT

DAILY PACING CHART ■ CHAPTER 3

Students in the Full Course should complete the entire text by the end of the year. Students in the Minimal Course spend more time when there are quizzes and more time on the Chapter Review. Therefore, these students may not complete all of the chapters in the text.

DAY	MINIMAL COURSE	FULL COURSE
1	3-1	3-1
2	3-2	3-2
3	3-3	3-3
4	Quiz (TRF); Start 3-4.	Quiz (TRF); 3-4
5	Finish 3-4.	3-5
6	3-5	3-6
7	3-6	Quiz (TRF); 3-7
8	Quiz (TRF); Start 3-7.	3-8
9	Finish 3-7.	Progress Self-Test
10	3-8	Chapter Review
11	Progress Self-Test	Chapter Test (TRF)
12	Chapter Review	Comprehensive Test (TRF)
13	Chapter Review	
14	Chapter Test (TRF)	
15	Comprehensive Test (TRF)	

TESTING OPTIONS

- ■ Quiz for Lessons 3-1 Through 3-3
- ■ Quiz for Lessons 3-4 Through 3-6
- ■ Chapter 3 Test, Form A
- ■ Chapter 3 Test, Form B
- ■ Chapter 3 Test, Cumulative Form
- ■ Comprehensive Test, Chapters 1-3

A Quiz and Test Writer is available for generating additional questions, additional quizzes, or additional forms of the Chapter Test.

PROVIDING FOR INDIVIDUAL DIFFERENCES

The student text is written for the *average* student. The program, however, can be adapted for both less capable and more capable students.

A blackline master (in the Teacher's Resource File) is provided for each lesson for those students who need more practice. The Teacher's Edition frequently provides Error Analysis and Alternate Approach features to provide additional instructional strategies.

For students who require additional challenge, Extension activities are regularly provided in the Teacher's Edition.

OBJECTIVES ■ CHAPTER 3

After students complete the chapter lessons, they assess their mastery on the Progress Self-Test. Then they do the Chapter Review and pay special attention to those questions that match the objectives missed on the Progress Self-Test. Students can get extra practice on these objectives by using the master for each lesson in the Teacher's Resource File.

OBJECTIVES FOR CHAPTER 3 (Organized into the SPUR categories—Skills, Properties, Uses, and Representations)	Progress Self-Test Questions	Chapter Review Questions	Teacher's Resource File	
			Lesson Master*	Chapter Test Forms A and B
SKILLS				
A: Measure lengths to the nearest inch, half inch, quarter inch, or eighth of an inch, or to the nearest centimeter or tenth of a centimeter.	1	1–4	3-1	12, 13
B: Measure an angle to the nearest degree using a protractor.	12, 13	5–7	3-5	19
C: Distinguish between acute, right, and obtuse angles by sight.	15	8–10	3-6	20, 24
D: Find the area of a square, given the length of one side.	17	11–13	3-7	14
E: Find the volume of a cube, given the length of one side.	21	14, 15	3-8	25
PROPERTIES				
F: Know the relationships in the U.S. system within units of length, weight and capacity.	6	16–18	3-2	10, 11
G: Know the relationships in the metric system within units of length, weight, and capacity.	7, 19	19–21	3-3, 3-8	4, 8, 9
H: Know the relationships between important units in the metric and U.S. systems of measurement.	3, 24	22–25	3-4	15, 17
I: State and apply the Estimation Principle.	23	26, 27	3-4	30, 34
USES				
J: Give appropriate units for measuring mass, length, and capacity in the U.S. or metric system of measurement.	4	28–31	3-2, 3-3	5, 6, 7
K: Convert within the U.S. system of measurement.	5	32–35	3-2	18, 26, 28, 29
L: Convert within the metric system.	8, 9	36–39	3-3	27
M: Convert between the U.S. and metric systems.	10, 11	40–43	3-4	16, 31
N: Identify and measure angles in pictures.	20	44, 45	3-5, 3-6	22, 23, 33
O: Find areas of squares or volumes of cubes in real contexts.	22	46, 47	3-7, 3-8	35
REPRESENTATIONS				
P: Draw a line segment of a given length.	2	48–50	3-1	32
Q: Draw an angle with a given measure.	16	51–53	3-5	21
HISTORY (Note: This chapter has an additional category for History.)				
R: Give countries and approximate dates of origin of current measuring ideas.	25	54–56	3-1, 3-3, 3-5	1, 2, 3

*The Lesson Masters are numbered to match the lessons.

OVERVIEW ■ CHAPTER 3

We have included an entire chapter on measurement at this point for several reasons. First, quantities are used throughout this book. (We use the word *quantity* to indicate the combination of a number and a count or measure unit; 25 *books* and 7.62 *kilograms* are quantities.) Moreover, measurement often involves computing with fractions and decimals, and most students need practice with numbers other than whole numbers. Also, the metric system, one of the main topics in this chapter, is based on powers of 10 and reinforces the work with powers of 10 in Chapter 2. The calculations of both area and volume are also connected with powers (the second and third powers respectively). And finally, after a month on arithmetic, some geometry is a nice break.

Students will need a ruler and a protractor for this chapter. The clear plastic ones are best. If the students buy these, you may want to make specific suggestions about what to get so your students will have similar equipment.

PERSPECTIVES ■ CHAPTER 3

The Perspectives provide the rationale for the inclusion of topics or approaches, provide mathematical background, and make connections within UCSMP.

3-1

MEASURING LENGTH

Students often think that mathematics has always existed in its present form. Once aware of its invention and development, students can gain perspective and realize that mathematics is still growing and changing.

Many students like the description of when, why, and how measures were standardized, and the introductory paragraphs in the lesson can make for lively class discussion.

The references to Thomas Jefferson, the Constitution, and our attachment to England provide an opportunity to relate mathematics and social studies. The beliefs of Thomas Jefferson with respect to weights and measures directly affected the adoption of systems we still use today. At a White House dinner honoring Nobel prize winners in April 1962, President Kennedy said, "I think this is the most extraordinary collection of talent, of human knowledge, that has ever been gathered together at the White House, with the possible exception of when Thomas Jefferson dined alone."

Among Jefferson's many professions were those of surveyor and architect, two vocations requiring accurate measurements. Jefferson saw the advantage of a measuring system based on 10 and tried unsuccessfully to get the new republic to adopt it. However, he was successful in two respects. First, partly as a result of Jefferson's efforts, our money system is based on 10 and was the first system to be so based. Second, Jefferson's thinking also influenced the Constitutional requirement that gave Congress the power to establish a system of weights and measures. This was a revolutionary idea at the time.

3-2

THE CUSTOMARY SYSTEM OF MEASUREMENT

Although we often think of the U.S. system of measurement as a part of our English heritage, the system of measurement used in the United States today never corresponded exactly to that used in England. Most units, however, were the same, and until the 1960s our system was called the English system of measurement. England has officially converted to the metric system, and we are now the only major industrialized country that uses a system other than the metric system.

In the 1970s, it appeared as if the United States were going to convert quickly to the metric system. Standards were set in some states, and books were written "100% metric." Many students learned the metric system but not the customary system in use in the United States. This practice turned out to be shortsighted. Today in England and Canada, many things are still measured in their customary units. In the United States, it will be some time before carpentry and many other trades change to the metric system. Measurements in the machine tool industry, a basic industry in applying standards of measurement, are still almost always made in the units of the U.S. system. Therefore, in this book both systems are used almost equally.

3-3

THE METRIC SYSTEM OF MEASUREMENT

Much information about the metric system is summarized and extended in the chart on page 109. The only units used consistently in this book are those in boldface type described under the chart: kilometer, kilogram, meter, gram, centimeter, liter, millimeter, milligram, and milliliter.

The gram is technically a measure of mass, not weight, but

throughout the world in everyday usage, it is a measure of both (because, for practical purposes, mass and weight are proportional on the surface of Earth). Mass is the amount of substance in an object; weight is a force, the amount of gravity acting on an object, times its mass. The difference between mass and weight is easy to describe in the space age. Astronauts have the same mass whether on Earth or in space. In space, because less gravity is acting on them, they weigh much less than on Earth.

3-4
CONVERTING BETWEEN SYSTEMS

There are three principal reasons for this lesson on conversion between the U.S. and the metric systems. First, as long as the United States keeps two systems, people are going to have to know how to convert from one to the other. Second, because students are inundated with the U.S. system, conversion helps them conceptualize the metric system. Third, traditional measures exist even in countries that have been metric for some time (barrels to measure oil, or picas to measure type size), and practice in conversions that are not exact would be a useful skill even if we had only one official system. We recommend thinking metric when using metric units, thinking U.S. when using U.S. units, and occasionally thinking about the relationships between them.

Even though the Estimation Principle is, theoretically, a principle of continuity and can be described in technical terms, it is easy to understand in this lesson and should be consciously related to its analogue, the Substitution Principle. We use the symbol $\approx$ for *is approximately equal to*. Some books use an equal sign with a dot above it ($\doteq$) as the symbol.

Conversions of length from the U.S. system to the metric system can be exact because 1 inch = 2.54 cm (exactly). Officially, at the U.S. Bureau of Standards, the inch is defined in terms of the centimeter, and thus in terms of the meter. Because 1 inch = 2.54 cm, we can divide both sides by 2.54, and 1 cm = $\frac{1}{2.54}$ in. = 0.39370078... in. Thus, to convert exactly from centimeters to inches, multiply by $\frac{100}{254}$ or $\frac{50}{127}$.

3-5
MEASURING ANGLES

Everyone knows angles are important when studying geometry in class. But angles have many uses in the real world as well. Questions in this lesson demonstrate how angles can be used to indicate differences in direction. In Chapter 5, we will find that angles and turns are closely related. The shape of a protractor also reminds us that angles and circular arcs are related.

3-6
KINDS OF ANGLES

This is a short, relatively easy lesson. It is designed to give some extra time for practice with angle measures, introduced in Lesson 3-5, and for further work with measure units. It also teaches another way of choosing the correct measure from the two scales on most protractors. If an angle is seen to be obtuse and the choices on the protractor are 62° or 118°, the measure must be 118°.

3-7
MEASURING AREA

This lesson is intended primarily to introduce the concept and units of area. Strictly speaking, despite the lesson title, area is usually not *measured*; it is calculated.

The formula $A = lw$ for the area of a rectangle is used in Lesson 4-6 as the first example of a formula. In Chapter 9, that formula is studied as one of the basic uses of multiplication. Toward the end of the book, other area formulas are considered. Thus, the idea of area runs through many chapters.

3-8
MEASURING VOLUME

The purpose of this lesson is to introduce the idea of volume and the units for measuring volume. Until the Middle Ages, the only application known for powers was for calculating areas and volumes. When someone wrote the equivalent of 3^2 or 15^3, they were likely to be thinking of a square or a cube, thus giving rise to the words *squared* and *cubed* for the second and third powers, respectively.

The relationship between volume and weight of water demonstrates how much easier to use the metric system is than the U.S. system. In the U.S. system, a gallon is defined to be exactly 231 cubic inches. A pint is exactly 28.875 cubic inches. A gallon of water weighs approximately 8.3 pounds. In the metric system, a liter is exactly 1000 cubic centimeters. A milliliter is exactly 1 cubic centimeter. A liter of water weighs 1 kilogram at 4°C.

We recommend 11 to 14 days for this chapter: 8 to 10 days on the lessons, 1 day to review the Progress Self-Test, 1 to 2 days on the Chapter Review, and 1 day for the Chapter Test. In addition, a comprehensive test covering Chapters 1–3 is provided for use as a quarter exam.

Some teachers may wish to spend a few more days on actual physical measurement of lengths, angles, and areas. However, we suggest no more than 16 class days; there is much more to do in later chapters.

Measurement

The first units of length were based on the human body. Some of these units are shown on the photograph on the opposite page. For instance, a "hand" was the width of a person's palm. So the size of a hand differed from place to place. These rough units were sufficient for most purposes. But for accurate building, more accurate units were needed. So units began to be *standardized*.

According to tradition, the *yard* originally was the distance from the tip of the nose of King Henry I of England (who reigned from 1100 to 1135) to the tips of his fingers. The *foot* is supposedly based on the foot of Charlemagne (who ruled France and neighboring areas from 768 to 814).

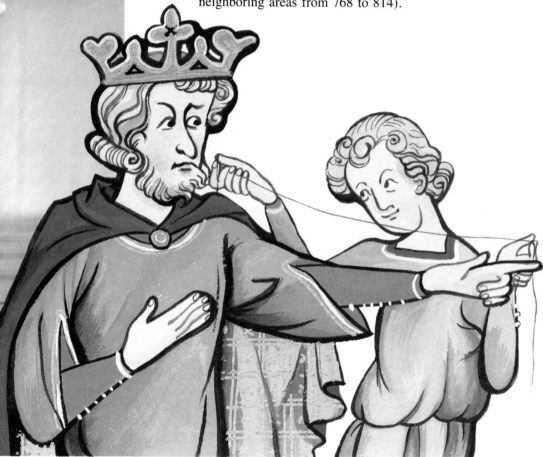

Use the photograph to point out that many of the first measuring units were based on the lengths of body parts. You may want to mention other early measures of length. For example, the pace was the distance of a stride—which was measured from the spot where a heel lifted off the ground to the spot where the same heel touched the ground. Soldiers in the Roman Empire measured distances by counting paces. The pace was equal to 5 feet, which meant that 1000 paces was 5000 feet, or close to our mile. In fact, the Romans used the word *mille* for 1000. This word may be the origin of the unit we call the mile.

CHAPTER 3 Measurement 97

LESSON 3-1

RESOURCES
■ Lesson Master 3-1
▣ Visual for Teaching Aid 13: Measuring Length.
■ Ruler or Geometry Template (*Transition Mathematics Manipulative Kit*)

OBJECTIVES

A Measure lengths to the nearest inch, half inch, quarter inch, or eighth of an inch, or to the nearest centimeter or tenth of a centimeter.

P Draw a line segment of a given length.

R Give countries and approximate dates of origin of the customary and metric systems of measurement.

3-1

Measuring Length

Around the year 1600, scientific experimentation began and more accurate measurement was necessary. Scientists from different countries needed to be able to communicate with each other about their work. With the manufacturing of lenses and clocks, accurate measurement was needed outside of science. About 1760, the industrial revolution began. Hand tools were replaced by power-driven machines. Accurate consistent measurement was needed everywhere.

The writers of the U.S. Constitution in 1787 recognized the need for standardized units. One article in the Constitution reads:

> *The Congress shall have power ... to fix the standard of weights and measures.*

In 1790, Thomas Jefferson proposed to Congress a measuring system based on the number 10. This would closely relate the measuring system to the decimal system. Five years later the metric system, based on the number 10, was established in France. We could have been the first country with this system. But we were emotionally tied to England, at that time an enemy of France. So we adopted the English system of measurement instead. Not until 1866 did the metric system become legal in the United States.

At first the metric system was used mainly in science. But as years go by, it is used in more and more fields and in more and more countries. Even England now has converted to the metric system. The old "English system" or "British Imperial system" has evolved into the **U.S. system** or the **customary system of measurement.** Today in the U.S. we measure in both the metric and U.S. systems.

98

In all systems of measurement, units of length are basic. For the metric system, the base unit of length is the meter. A **centimeter** is $\frac{1}{100}$ or .01 of a meter. For the U.S. system, the base of unit of length is the **inch.**

one inch   one centimeter

The ruler pictured below has centimeters on the top and inches on the bottom.

On the ruler, each centimeter is divided into 10 parts. (Each part is a millimeter.) So it is easy to measure in centimeters. The three segments drawn below have lengths of about 6, 6.3, and 7 centimeters.

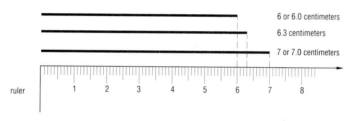

6 or 6.0 centimeters

6.3 centimeters

7 or 7.0 centimeters

ruler

On rulers, inches are usually divided into halves, fourths, and eighths. Look at the part of the ruler drawn below. The longest tick marks between the inches are for half inches. The next longest are for fourths not already marked as $\frac{2}{4}$, $\frac{4}{4}$, and so on. The shortest are for eighths not already marked as $\frac{2}{8}$, $\frac{4}{8}$, and so on. The segments drawn here have lengths of about 1, $1\frac{1}{2}$, $1\frac{3}{4}$, and $1\frac{5}{8}$ inches.

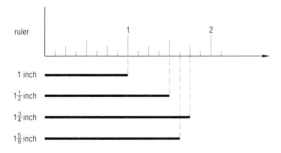

ruler

1 inch

$1\frac{1}{2}$ inch

$1\frac{3}{4}$ inch

$1\frac{5}{8}$ inch

LESSON 3-1   Measuring Length   **99**

Look at the segment that is $1\frac{3}{4}$ inches long. You can see that its length is between 1 and 2 inches. The $\frac{3}{4}$ is not so easily seen. It comes as follows. There are 8 intervals between 1 inch and 2 inches. So each interval equals $\frac{1}{8}$ of an inch. The segment extends to the 6th tick mark. That is $\frac{6}{8}$ of an inch past 1 inch. So its length is $1\frac{6}{8}$ inches. Reduced to lowest terms, this is $1\frac{3}{4}$ inches.

When you measure, you may have a choice of unit. Units can be divided to give you greater accuracy in your measurement. For instance, lengths are often measured in sixteenths or thirty-seconds of an inch. In industry lengths may be measured to hundredths or thousandths or even smaller parts of an inch. Whatever unit you work with, you are rounding to the nearest. Whatever you choose as your rounding unit (tenth of a centimeter, for example) indicates how accurate your measurement is.

Example 1 Find the length of this small paper clip **a.** to the nearest centimeter, and **b.** to the nearest tenth of a centimeter.

Solution

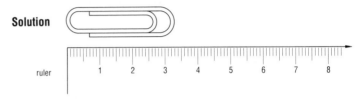

a. 3 centimeters, to the nearest centimeter
b. 3.3 centimeters, to the nearest tenth of a centimeter

Example 2 Find the height of this photograph **a.** to the nearest $\frac{1}{2}$ inch, **b.** to the nearest $\frac{1}{4}$ inch, and **c.** to the nearest $\frac{1}{8}$ inch.

Solution   a. 2 in., **b.** $2\frac{1}{4}$ in., **c.** $2\frac{1}{8}$ in.

Covering the Reading

1. The first units of length were based on   ? .
   lengths of parts of the human body
2. The heights of horses are sometimes measured in hands. What was the way that the length called a hand was originally determined?   width of a person's palm

3. The yard originally was the distance from the   ?   to the   ?   of what king of England?
   tip of nose; tips of fingers; King Henry I
4. Whose foot is said to have been the foot from which today's foot originated?   Charlemagne's

5. Why did units become standardized?   See margin.

6. About when did accurate lengths become needed everywhere?
   1760

In 7–10, *true* or *false*?

7. Thomas Jefferson wanted the U.S. to adopt the English system of measurement.   False

8. The metric system was established in 1795.   True

9. The metric system became legal in the U.S. over 100 years ago.
   True
10. Congress has the power to set standards for measurement in the U.S.   True

11. The English system of measurement now is called by other names. What are those names and why was the name changed?
    See margin.
12. The base unit of length in the metric system is the   ? .
    meter

Charlemagne

These provide measuring
practice. You can give extra
practice measuring length by
having students check each
other's answers for **Questions 20 and 22.**

**Error Analysis for
Questions 21** and **22**
Some students may not understand the words *vertical*
and *horizontal*. Review the
meaning of those terms. You
might relate *horizontal* to the
meaning of *horizon*.

**23. If two numbers are
equal, one may be substituted for the other in any
computation without
changing the results of the
computation.**

**32. a. a size of type, $\frac{1}{6}$ in.
high;**
**b. length used to measure
cloth, 45 in.;**
**c. $\frac{1}{100}$ of a surveyor's
chain, 7.92 in.;**
d. 66 ft, used in surveying

In 13–15, use this ruler to find the length of the segment. Write the
length in lowest terms.

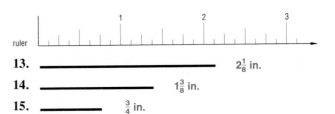

ruler

13. _____ $2\frac{1}{8}$ in.

14. _____ $1\frac{3}{8}$ in.

15. _____ $\frac{3}{4}$ in.

In 16–18, measure the length of each segment:
    a. to the nearest tenth of a centimeter.
    b. to the nearest eighth of an inch.

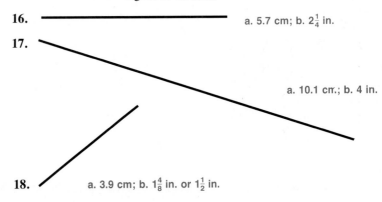

16. _____ a. 5.7 cm; b. $2\frac{1}{4}$ in.

17.

a. 10.1 cm.; b. 4 in.

18. a. 3.9 cm; b. $1\frac{4}{8}$ in. or $1\frac{1}{2}$ in.

Applying the Mathematics

19. Measure the length and the width of this page to the nearest tenth
    of a centimeter.   25.3 cm and 19.7 cm

20. Measure your height:
    a. to the nearest inch.
    b. to the nearest centimeter.   Answers will vary.

21. Draw a vertical segment with length 3.5 inches.
    Check students' segments.
22. Draw a horizontal segment with length 12.4 centimeters.
    Check students' segments.

Review

23. What is the Substitution Principle? *(Lesson 2-6)*   See margin.

24. Use the number line drawn here. The letters refer to points that
    are equally spaced. *(Lesson 1-2)*

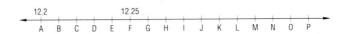

12.2   12.25
A B C D E F G H I J K L M N O P

    a. What number corresponds to *E*?   12.24
    b. What number corresponds to *N*?   12.33
    c. What letter corresponds to 12.3?   K
    d. 12.213 is between which two points?   B and C

102

25. Some people believe that if a sports team or individual appears on the cover of *Sports Illustrated*, then the team or individual becomes jinxed and will suffer a decline in performance. Researchers at the University of Southern California examined 271 covers. They found that 57.6% of the cover subjects improved in performance.

    a. Did more cover subjects improve or decline in performance? *(Lesson 2-5)*   **improve**

    b. How many of the 271 cover subjects improved in performance? *(Lesson 2-6)*   **156**

26. Which is larger—5 to the 6th power, or 6 to the 5th power? *(Lesson 2-2)* 5^6

27. Write 28.2 million (the number of clerks and salesworkers thought in 1988 to be needed in 1995) as a decimal. *(Lesson 2-1)*
28,200,000

In 28 and 29, find equal fractions with 5 in the denominator.
(Lesson 1-10)

28. 16 $\frac{80}{5}$ **29.** $\frac{35}{25}$ $\frac{7}{5}$

30. $\frac{1}{3}$ is how many percent? *(Lesson 2-5)* $33\frac{1}{3}\%$

31. *Multiple choice* Estimate $35.17 - 6.2$. *(Lesson 1-4)*   **(a)**
    (a) 28.97   (b) 34.55   (c) 3.455   (d) 29.15

Exploration

32. There are many units of length that have specialized uses. Find out something about each of these specialized units of length.
    a. pica **b.** ell **c.** link **d.** chain   **See margin.**

33. *Your* "inch" is the length of your thumb, from the tip to the joint in the middle. How close is your inch to an actual inch?
  Answers will vary.

34. Look at the picture that opens this chapter. Find out what the lengths of **a.** a fathom, and **b.** a cubit, are today.
  a. 6 ft; b. approximately 18 in. or 45.72 cm

MORE PRACTICE
For more questions on SPUR Objectives, use *Lesson Master 3-1*, shown below.

EXTENSION
This lesson mentions Thomas Jefferson's proposal for a measuring system based on the number 10. Students may want to do research on Jefferson's beliefs about weights and measures. Ask the students to consider Jefferson's many professions (for example, surveyor and architect) and the role those vocations may have played in his beliefs.

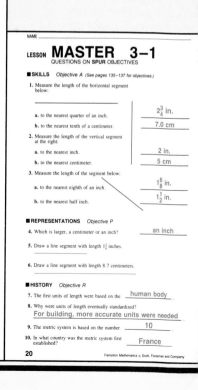

RESOURCES
■ Lesson Master 3-2
▣ Visual for Teaching Aid 14: Use to reinforce the relationships among customary units.

OBJECTIVES

F Know the relationships in the U.S. system within units of length, weight, and capacity.
J Give appropriate units for measuring mass, length, and capacity in the U.S. system of measurement.
K Convert within the U.S. system of measurement.

TEACHING NOTES

Examples 1 and **2** demonstrate an effective teaching principle. Students can do a problem like **Example 1** in their heads, but it is written out to show the use of the Substitution Principle. **Example 2** is identical in form, except that it uses more complicated numbers; most students cannot do such an example in their heads. Using the strategy of **Example 1** as a model makes **Example 2** easier.

Making Connections
There is another reason for having **Examples 1** and **2.** They get students to look at both sides of an equation. This kind of thinking will be used later in solving equations.

Students should memorize the conversions in the chart on page 104.

LESSON

3-2

The Customary System of Measurement

In the customary, or U.S., system of measurement, there are many units. Few people know all of them. So people refer to tables to check relationships between unfamiliar units. Still, because some units are so often used, you should know some relationships by heart.

Common units in the customary system of measurement

For length:	12 inches = 1 foot (ft)
	3 feet = 1 yard (yd)
	5280 feet = 1 mile (mi)
For weight:	16 ounces = 1 pound (lb)
	2000 pounds = 1 short ton
For capacity (liquid or dry volume):	2 pints = 1 quart (qt)
	4 quarts = 1 gallon (gal)

The abbreviation for inch is *in.* (with the period). The abbreviation for ounce is *oz* without a period. Except for the inch, it is now recommended that periods not be used in abbreviations for units of measure. (Periods get confused with decimals.)

The above relationships make it possible to convert from one unit to another.

■ ■ ■ ■ ■ ■ ■ ■

Example 1 Convert 3 gallons to quarts.

Solution Use the Substitution Principle.
Since   1 gallon = 4 quarts,
3×1 gallon $= 3 \times 4$ quarts
$= 12$ quarts.

104

Example 2   How many feet are in 1.7 miles?

Solution   Since

$$1 \text{ mi} = 5280 \text{ ft},$$
$$1.7 \times 1 \text{ mi} = 1.7 \times 5280 \text{ ft}$$
$$= 8976 \text{ feet}.$$

Questions

Covering the Reading

In 1–3, consider the customary system of measurement.

1. Name four units of length.   **inch, foot, yard, mile**

2. Name three units in which a volume of milk could be measured.
pint, quart, gallon

3. Name three units of weight.   **ounce, pound, short ton**

In 4–10, copy and complete each relationship.

4. 1 ft = __?__ in.   **12**   　　**5.** 1 gallon = __?__ quarts   **4**

6. 1 yd = __?__ ft   **3**   　　**7.** 1 quart = __?__ pints   **2**

8. 1 mi = __?__ ft   **5280**   　　**9.** 1 lb = __?__ oz   **16**

10. 1 short ton = __?__ pounds   **2000**

In 11–15, convert:

11. 0.62 mi to feet   **3273.6 ft**

12. 4 yards to feet   **12 ft**

13. 7 tons to pounds   **14,000 lb**

14. 2.2 pounds (the approximate number of pounds in a kilogram) to ounces   **35.2 oz**

15. 8.3 gallons to quarts   **33.2 quarts**

Applying the Mathematics

16. In some cities, a block is $\frac{1}{8}$ mile long. Convert this to feet.   **660 ft**

17. In the U.S. system, a *rod* is defined as 5.5 yards. How many feet are in a rod?   **16.5 ft**

18. In Great Britain, one *gross ton* = 2240 pounds. The longest passenger liner ever built, the *Norway*, weighs about 70,200 gross tons. How many pounds is this?   **157,248,000 lb**

19. How many feet are in 440 yards, a common distance in many school running events?   **1320 ft**

20. How many inches are in 1 mile?   **63,360 in.**

21. You have a 1-pint measuring vessel. How many times would you have to use it to fill a 10-gallon tank?   **80**

LESSON 3-2   The Customary System of Measurement   **105**

22. Name an appropriate unit for measuring each thing.
  a. the distance around a city block   yard or mile
  b. the weight of an elephant   short ton or pound
  c. the amount of gas in a car gas tank   gallon

23. Refer to the cartoon below. What should the chief cook tell Zero?
  See margin.

24. Measure this segment **a.** to the nearest $\frac{1}{8}$ of an inch, and **b.** to the nearest centimeter. *(Lesson 3-1)* **a.** $3\frac{3}{8}$ in.; **b.** 9 cm

---

25. Measure the length of a dollar bill **a.** to the nearest inch, **b.** to the nearest fourth of an inch, and **c.** to the nearest eighth of an inch. *(Lesson 3-1)* **a.** 6 in.; **b.** $6\frac{1}{4}$ in.; **c.** $6\frac{2}{8}$ in. or $6\frac{1}{4}$ in.

26. Write in scientific notation. *(Lessons 2-3, 2-9)*
   a. 118,865,000 the estimated population of Nigeria in 1990
   b. 0.013837 in., the length of 1 point in typesetting
   a. 1.18865×10^{8}; **b.** 1.3837×10^{-2}

27. Calculate. *(Lessons 2-1, 2-4)*
   a. 0.052×100 5.2   **b.** $3.446 \times .0001$ .0003446
   c. $15.36 \times .1$ 1.536   **d.** $640 \times 10,000$ 6,400,000

28. 0% of the 500 students in a school are traveling to a game by bus. How many students is this? *(Lesson 2-6)* 0

29. All systems of measurement in common use in the world today have the same units for time.
   1 hour = 60 minutes, 1 minute = 60 seconds.
   a. How many seconds are in an hour? 3600
   b. How many seconds are in a day? 86,400
   c. How many seconds are in a year? 31,536,000 (365-day year)
   d. How many minutes are in a year? 525,600
   e. If your heart beats 70 times a minute, how many times does it beat in a year? 36,792,000
   f. If a heart beats 70 times a minute, how many times will it beat in 78 years, the average lifetime of a woman in the U.S.? 2.8698×10^{9}

30. An old song goes, "I love you, a bushel and a peck, a bushel and a peck and a hug around your neck, a hug around your neck and a barrel and a heap, a barrel and a heap and I'm talking in my sleep about you …" Three units of capacity of fruits and grains are in the words to the song. What are they and how are they related? See margin.

LESSON 3-2 The Customary System of Measurement **107**

FOLLOW-UP

MORE PRACTICE
For more practice on SPUR Objectives, use *Lesson Master 3-2*, shown below.

EVALUATION
Alternative Assessment
Write the following and similar units on the board: 5 ft, 5 yd, 2 mi, 3 lb, 6 tons, 10 qt, 12 gal. Then point to a unit on the board and ask each student a question requiring conversion: "How many inches (feet, ounces, and so on)?" If a student makes a mistake, ask him or her to refer to the book to name the conversion factor, then calculate the answer.

NAME _____

LESSON

3-3

The Metric System of Measurement

The U.S. system of measurement has three major weaknesses. First, the many units have names that do not help you know how the units are related. Second, the units are multiples of each other in no consistent manner. To see this, look again at the list of relationships in Lesson 3-2. You see the numbers 12, 3, 5280, 16, 2000, 2, and 4. No two are alike. Third, in the decimal system these numbers are not so easy to work with as powers of 10 such as 100, 1000, 10,000, or .1, .01, and .001.

Other older measurement systems had the same weaknesses. So in the late 1700s a movement arose to design a better measurement system. The system devised is called **the international or metric system of measurement.** It is based on the decimal system and is by far the most widely used system of measurement in the world.

In the metric system, prefixes have fixed meanings related to place values in the decimal system. The table on page 109 identifies many of the prefixes. The three most common are kilo-, centi-, and milli-.

kilo-	means 1000
centi-	means $\frac{1}{100}$, or .01
milli-	means $\frac{1}{1000}$, or .001

The basic unit of length is the **meter.** Other units of length are multiples of the meter. (See the table for descriptions of these units.)

1 kilometer = 1 km = 1000 meters
1 centimeter = 1 cm = $\frac{1}{100}$, or .01 meter
1 millimeter = 1 mm = $\frac{1}{1000}$, or .001 meter

108

Units of mass are multiples of the **gram.** In everyday usage, the gram is also used to measure weight.

$$1 \text{ kilogram} = 1 \text{ kg} = 1000 \text{ grams}$$
$$1 \text{ milligram} = 1 \text{ mg} = \tfrac{1}{1000}, \text{ or } .001 \text{ gram}$$

The **liter** and milliliter are used to measure capacity or volume. Soft drinks today are often sold in 2-liter bottles. Smaller amounts are measured in milliliters.

$$1 \text{ milliliter} = 1 \text{ mL} = \tfrac{1}{1000}, \text{ or } .001 \text{ liter}$$

All conversions within the metric system can be done without a calculator because the multiples are powers of 10.

The International or Metric System of Measurement

Table of Prefixes

place value	thousands	hundreds	tens	ones	tenths	hundredths	thousandths
power of 10	10^3	10^2	10^1	10^0	10^{-1}	10^{-2}	10^{-3}
unit of length	kilometer	hectometer	dekameter	meter	decimeter	centimeter	millimeter
unit of mass	kilogram	hectogram	dekagram	gram	decigram	centigram	milligram
unit of capacity	kiloliter	hectoliter	dekaliter	liter	deciliter	centiliter	milliliter

Some other Prefixes:

place value	trillions	billions	millions	millionths	billionths	trillionths
power of 10	10^{12}	10^9	10^6	10^{-6}	10^{-9}	10^{-12}
prefix	tera-	giga-	mega-	micro-	nano-	pico-

Some common units:

Length:
kilometer (km) - used for distances between towns and cities. 1 km ≈ 0.62 mi
meter (m) - used for measuring rooms, heights, and fabrics. A doorknob is about 1 m high.
centimeter (cm) - used for measuring small items.The diameter of an aspirin tablet is about 1 cm.
millimeter (mm) - used for measuring very small items. The thickness of a dime is about 1 mm.

Mass:
kilogram (kg) - used for measuring meat and body weight. A quart of milk weighs about 1 kg.
gram (g) - used for measuring very light items. An aspirin weighs about 1 g.
milligram (mg) - used in measuring vitamin content in food. A speck of sawdust weighs about 1 mg.

Capacity:
liter (L) - used for measuring milk and other liquids.1 liter ≈ 1.06 qt.
milliliter (mL) - used for measuring small amounts such as perfume. 1 teaspoon ≈ 5 mL

LESSON 3-3   The Metric System of Measurement   109

Example 1 How many meters are in 3.46 kilometers?

Solution 3.46 kilometers = 3.46 × 1 km
= 3.46 × 1000 m   *Substitution Principle*
= 3460 m

Example 2 Change 89 milligrams to grams.

Solution 89 milligrams = 89 × 1 mg
= 89 ×.001 g
= 0.089 g

Many of the questions refer to the table on page 109. You should study it before reading the questions.

Questions

Covering the Reading

1. Name two weaknesses of the U.S. system of measurement.
   See margin.
2. Another name for the metric system is __?__.
   the international system
3. Name three common units of length in the metric system.
   Samples: meter, cm, km, mm
4. Name three common units of mass in the metric system.
   Samples: gram, kilogram, milligram
5. Name two common units of capacity in the metric system.
   liter; milliliter

In 6–8, give the meaning of the prefix.

6. kilo- 1000   7. milli- .001 or $\frac{1}{1000}$ 8. centi- .01 or $\frac{1}{100}$

In 9–11, give the abbreviation for each unit.

9. centimeter cm   10. kilogram kg   11. milliliter mL

In 12–17, convert.

12. 90 cm to meters .9 m   13. 345 mL to liters .345 L

14. 5 kg to grams 5000 g   15. 10 km to meters 10,000 m

16. 48 mm to meters .048 m 17. 60 mg to grams .060 g

18. Name something weighing approximately
    a. 1 kg, **b.** 1 g, **c.** 1 mg. See margin.

19. Name something about as long as: **a.** 1 m; **b.** 1 km; **c.** 1 mm.
    See margin.
20. Name something with about as much liquid in it as a liter.
    Sample: a quart of milk.

In 21–23, give the power of 10 associated with each prefix.

21. centi- 10^{-2} 22. milli- 10^{-3} 23. kilo- 10^{3}

110

In 24–26, choose the one best answer.

24. A high-school freshman might weigh: **(c)**
(a) 50 g (b) 50 mg (c) 50 kg (d) 500 g

25. A high-school freshman might be how tall? **(b)**
(a) .7 m (b) 1.7 m (c) 2.2 m (d) 5.6 m

26. A common dimension of camera film is: **(d)**
(a) 35 km (b) 35 cm (c) 35 m (d) 35 mm

Applying the Mathematics

27. Should most students be able to walk one kilometer in an hour?
yes

28. The atomic bomb that exploded on Hiroshima had a force equivalent to 20 kilotons of TNT. How many tons is this? **20,000 tons**

29. The most powerful bomb ever exploded (by the Soviet Union in a test in 1961) had a force of 57 megatons of TNT. How many tons is this? **57,000,000 tons**

30. A millisecond is how many seconds? $\frac{1}{1000}$ **or .001 second**

31. The United States was the first country in the world (1786) to have a money system based on decimals. In our system:
$$1 \text{ dollar} = 100 \text{ cents}$$
or equivalently, 1 cent = $\frac{1}{100}$, or .01, dollar.
a. Convert 56¢ to dollars. **$.56**
b. Convert $13.49 to cents. **1349¢**
c. On September 17, 1983, UPI reported that a truck loaded with 7.6 million new pennies overturned on Interstate 80 in the mountains north of Sacramento, California. How many dollars is that? **$76,000**

LESSON 3-3 The Metric System of Measurement **111**

NOTES ON QUESTIONS
Questions 24–27:
These require students to have some idea of approximate sizes of metric measures. If additional examples are needed, refer the students to the examples supplied with the chart on page 109, and also to everyday items such as a meter stick, milk cartons, juice cans, or the weight of foods found on many food packages.

NAME _____

LESSON **MASTER 3-3**
QUESTIONS ON **SPUR** OBJECTIVES

■ **PROPERTIES** *Objective G (See pages 135–137 for objectives.)*
1. What does the prefix *kilo-* mean? **1000**
2. 1 mL = **$\frac{1}{1000}$** liter.
3. The basic unit of length in the metric system is the **meter** .
4. 1 kg = **1000** grams 5. 1 **centimeter** = $\frac{1}{100}$ meter

In 6–9, complete the following chart.

	Place Value	Thousands	Hundreds	Tens	Ones	Tenths	Hundredths	Thousandths
6.	Power of 10	10^3	10^2	10	10^0	10^{-1}	10^{-2}	10^{-3}
7.	Unit of length	kilo-meter	hectometer	deka-meter	meter	decimeter	centi-meter	milli-meter
8.	Unit of mass	kilo-gram	hecto-gram	dekagram	gram	deci-gram	centigram	milli-gram
9.	Unit of capacity	kiloliter	hecto-liter	deka-liter	liter	deci-liter	centi-liter	milliliter

■ **USES** *Objective J*
10. Give an appropriate unit in the metric system for measuring the length of a surfboard. **meter**
11. Give an appropriate unit in the metric system for measuring the amount of perfume in a bottle. **milliliter**

■ **USES** *Objective L*
12. 9 m = **900** cm
13. 92.634 km = **92,634** m

■ **HISTORY** *Objective R*
14. Another name for the metric system is the **international system**

22   *Transition Mathematics © Scott, Foresman and Company*

Review

32. Write $\frac{2}{1000}$ cm, the diameter of a cloud droplet, as a decimal. *(Lesson 1-8)* .002 cm

33. Order from smallest to largest: 10^{-4}, 0, $\frac{1}{100}$. *(Lessons 2-4, 2-8)* 0, 10^{-4}, $\frac{1}{100}$

34. Order from smallest to largest: 5^2, 2^5, 10^1 *(Lesson 2-2)* 10^1, 5^2, 2^5

35. Complete each with the correct symbol $<$, $=$, or $>$. *(Lessons 1-6, 3-2)*
    a. $2\frac{1}{2}$ pints __?__ 4 quarts $<$
    b. $3\frac{1}{2}$ feet __?__ 2 yards $<$
    c. 2850 feet __?__ 1 mile $<$
    d. 1 lb __?__ 16 oz $=$

36. Which measurement is more accurate, one made to the nearest $\frac{1}{16}$ of an inch, or one made to the nearest $\frac{1}{10}$ of an inch? *(Lessons 1-8, 3-1)* nearest $\frac{1}{16}$

37. Measure the segment at the left to the nearest 0.1 cm *(Lesson 3-1)*
    1.7 cm

38. In a recent survey, 85% of teenagers responding owned bicycles, 80% owned cameras, 72% had designer clothes, and 52% owned TV sets. If there are 30 students in a class that is representative of all teenagers who responded, how many would you expect to own: a. bicycles; b. cameras; c. designer clothes? (2-6)
    a. 25 or 26; b. 24; c. 22

Exploration

39. Almost every country in the world today has a decimal money system. Given is a relationship between monetary units. Name a country in which these units are used. See margin.
    a. 1 franc = 100 centimes
    b. 1 centavo = 100 pesos
    c. 1 kopeck = 100 rubles
    d. 1 yuan = 100 fen
    e. 1 dinar = 1000 fils
    f. 1 rupee = 100 paise
    g. 1 cedi = 100 pesewas

40. The computer program below instructs a computer to convert a length in miles to one in feet. The line numbers 10, 20, and so on at left must be typed. The computer executes the program in the order of the line numbers, which can be any positive integers.
    a. Type in the following.

```
NEW
10      PRINT "WHAT IS LENGTH IN MILES?"
20      INPUT NMILES
30      NFEET = 5280*NMILES
40      PRINT "THE NUMBER OF FEET IS " NFEET
50      END
```

    To see what you have typed, LIST and press RETURN. You can change one line by typing it over. You need not type the entire program again.
    b. To run your program, type RUN and press RETURN. The computer will execute line 10 and ask you to input a number. Input 5 and press RETURN. The computer will then execute the rest of the program. What does the computer print?
    c. Run the program a few times, with values of your own choosing. Write down the values you input and the answers the computer gives.
    b. THE NUMBER OF FEET IS 26400; c. Answers will vary.

3-4

Converting Between Systems

LESSON 3-4

RESOURCES
- Lesson Master 3-4
- Visual for Teaching Aid 16: Use with **Questions 12–15.**
- Ruler or Geometry Template (*Transition Mathematics Manipulative Kit*)

OBJECTIVES

H Know the relationships between important units in the metric and U.S. systems of measurement.
I State and apply the Estimation Principle.
M Convert between the U.S. and metric systems.

TEACHING NOTES

Making Connections
Some students are puzzled by the Estimation Principle and want to use the Substitution Principle of the previous lessons. You might ask students to name situations where they would use the Estimation Principle (sample: add up estimated costs of individual items for a party to get total estimated cost of a party). Point out how the exact conversions (within each system and the conversion between inches and centimeters) are different from approximately equal conversions. Explain the use of the = and ≈ symbols.

Alternate Approach/ Using Manipulatives
Have students measure the same item, such as the length of the room, both in inches and in centimeters. They can then compare the results with the conversions on page 113.

Because using the metric system is so easy, country after country in the world has adopted it. In the United States, science, medicine, and photography are almost all metric. Carpentry and other building trades usually use the U.S. system. The trend is to use metric units more often as time goes by. Some automobiles are manufactured with parts that conform to metric units. Others use customary units. Auto mechanics need tools for each system.

With two systems in use today, it is occasionally necessary to change from units in one system to units in another. This change is called *converting between systems*. Converting between systems is like converting within one system. However, the numbers are more complicated.

There are five conversions you should know. One of these is exact.

1 inch = 2.54 centimeters (exactly)

This conversion is exact because the inch is now officially based on the centimeter. The other four conversions are approximate, so we use the sign ≈. This sign means **is approximately equal to.**

1 meter ≈ 39.37 inches
1 kilometer ≈ 0.62 miles
1 kilogram ≈ 2.2 pounds
1 liter ≈ 1.06 quarts

Because these conversions are not equal, you cannot use the Substitution Principle. However, there is an **Estimation Principle** that serves the same purpose.

Estimation Principle:

If two numbers are nearly equal, then when one is substituted for the other in a computation, the results of the computations will be nearly equal.

Example 1 Convert 50 kilograms into pounds.

Solution 50 kilograms = 50 × 1 kilogram
≈ 50 × 2.2 pounds   Estimation Principle
≈ 110 pounds   (Substitute 2.2 pounds for 1 kilogram.)

Example 2 How many centimeters are in 1 foot?

Solution On page 113, there is no direct conversion given from feet to centimeters. But there is a conversion from inches to centimeters. So change feet to inches. Then convert.
1 foot = 12 inches
= 12 × 1 inch
= 12 × 2.54 centimeters   Substitution Principle
= 30.48 centimeters   (Substitute 2.54 cm for 1 inch.)

In Example 2, the Estimation Principle is not needed because the conversion from inches to centimeters is exact.

Questions

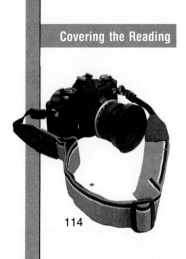

Covering the Reading

1. Name two professions in which a person in the U.S. would use the metric system more than the U.S. system.
   Sample: scientist, nurse, photographer
2. Name two professions in which a person in the U.S. would use U.S. units more than metric units.   Sample: carpenters, plumbers

3. What does the sign ≈ mean?   is approximately equal to

4. What metric unit is a little larger than two pounds?   kilogram

5. What U.S. unit is most like a liter?   quart

6. One relationship between the U.S. and metric system is exact. What relationship is it?   1 in. = 2.54 cm

114

In 7–10, give a relationship between:

7. kilograms and pounds
2.2 lb ≈ 1 kg

8. meters and inches
39.37 in. ≈ 1 m

9. liters and quarts
1.06 qt ≈ 1 L

10. kilometers and miles
.62 mi ≈ 1 km

11. a. State the estimation principle. **b.** Give an example of its use.
See margin

In 12–15, convert.

12. 6 meters to inches
about 236.2 in.

13. 1.8 liters to quarts
about 1.9 qt

14. 0.45 kilograms to pounds
about 1 lb

15. 5 inches to centimeters
12.7 cm

Applying the Mathematics

In 16–20, which is larger?

16. a pound or a kilogram
kilogram

17. a quart or a liter   liter

18. a meter or a yard   meter

19. a centimeter or an inch   inch

20. a kilometer or a mile   mile

21. a. Write $\frac{5}{16}$ as a decimal. **b.** A person needs a drill bit with a diameter of approximately $\frac{5}{16}$ in. If a bit with a metric measure must be used, what diameter is needed?   a. .3125; b. 8 mm

22. An adult human brain weighs about 1.5 kg. Convert this to ounces.
52.8 oz

23. The St. Gotthard Tunnel in Switzerland is the longest car tunnel in the world. Its length is 16.4 km. How many miles is this?
about 10.2 mi

24. $\frac{4}{9}$ is a little less than a half. $\frac{7}{13}$ is a little more than a half. So a reasonable estimate for $\frac{4}{9} + \frac{7}{13}$ is __?__.   1

In 25 and 26, use the Estimation Principle to estimate each result to the nearest integer.

25. $\frac{19}{20} + \frac{19}{18}$ 2

26. $\frac{1}{1000} + \frac{1}{100}$ 0

LESSON 3-4   Converting Between Systems   **115**

EVALUATION
Alternative Assessment
Write the four columns below
on the board.

1 inch		0.62	cm
1 meter	=	1.06	in.
1 kilometer	≈	2.2	lb
1 kilogram		2.54	mi
1 liter		39.37	qt

Call on different students to
choose one item from each
column to state each conversion. For example, 1 kilogram
≈ 2.2 lb.

Review

27. How many inches are in a yard? *(Lesson 3-2)*   36 in.

28. A bucket holds 8 gallons. How many quarts will it hold?
    (Lesson 3-2)   32 qt

29. A 5-lb bag of cat food has how many ounces of food in it?
    (Lesson 3-2)   80 oz

30. How many grams are in 4 kilograms? *(Lesson 3-3)*   4000 g

31. Measure this segment to the nearest millimeter. *(Lessons 3-1,3-3)*
    80 mm

32. One centimeter is what percent of a meter? *(Lessons 2-7,3-3)*   1%

33. What is 50% of 50? *(Lesson 2-6)*   25

34. Convert 0.136 to a fraction in lowest terms. *(Lesson 2-7)* $\frac{17}{125}$

Exploration

35. On every cereal box, the amount of protein per serving is listed.
    a. Find a cereal box and how much protein per serving is listed.
    b. Is this amount given in U.S. units, metric units, or both?
    c. Is the weight of the box given in U.S. units, metric units, or
       both?
       Answers will vary.

36. Examine the computer program in Question 40 of Lesson 3-3.
    Modify that program so that it converts a length in inches to a
    length in centimeters. Run your program a few times with values
    of your own choosing.   Sample:

```
10      PRINT "WHAT IS LENGTH IN INCHES?"
20      INPUT NINCHES
30      NCM = 2.54 * NINCHES
40      PRINT "THE NUMBER OF CM IS "NCM
50      END
```

116

OBJECTIVES

B Measure an angle to the nearest degree using a protractor.
N Identify and measure angles in pictures.
Q Draw an angle with a given measure.
R Give countries of origin and approximate dates of our system for measuring angles.

LESSON

3-5

Measuring Angles

Think of rays of light coming from the sun. Each **ray** has the same starting point, called its **endpoint.** Each ray goes forever in a particular direction. Only a part of any ray can be drawn.

Identified below are rays SB and SA, written $\overrightarrow{SB}$ and $\overrightarrow{SA}$. Two other rays are not identified.

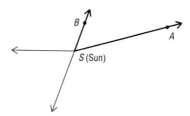

The union of two rays with the same endpoint is an **angle.** The rays are the **sides of the angle.** The endpoint is the **vertex of the angle.** The sides of an angle go on forever; you can draw only part of them.

$\angle$ is the symbol for angle. This symbol was first used by William Oughtred in 1657.

The angle above may be written as $\angle S$, $\angle ASB$, or $\angle BSA$. When three letters are used, the middle letter is the vertex. If an angle shares its vertex with any other angle, you must use three letters to name it. For instance, in the first drawing above, you should not name any angle $\angle S$. Which angle you meant would not be clear.

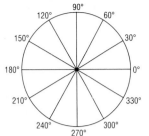

Over 2500 years ago, the Babylonians wrote numbers in a system based on the number 60. So they measured with units based on 60. Even today we use Babylonian ideas to measure time. That is why there are 60 minutes in an hour and 60 seconds in a minute. We also use Babylonian ideas in measuring angles.

The Babylonians divided a circle into 360 equally spaced units, which we call **degrees.** (The number $360 = 6 \times 60$ and is an estimate of the number of days in a year.)

An instrument that looks like half of the circle at left is the **protractor.** The protractor is the most common instrument used for measuring angles. Many protractors look like the one drawn below. Because protractors cover only half of a circle, the degree measures on the outside go only from 0° to 180°.

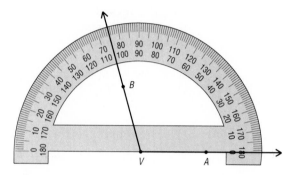

Every protractor has a segment connecting the 0° mark on one side to the 180° mark on the other. This segment is on the *base line* of the protractor. The middle point of this segment is called the *center* of the protractor. In the drawings above and on page 119 this point is named *V*. *V* is usually marked by a hole, an arrow, or a + sign. There are almost always two curved scales on the outside of the protractor. One goes from 0° to 180°. The other goes from 180° to 0°.

To measure an angle with a protractor:

(1) Put the center of the protractor on the vertex of the angle.

(2) Turn the protractor so that one side of the angle is on the base line and the other side of the angle is beneath the curved scales.

(3) The measure of the angle is one of the two numbers crossed by the other side of the angle. Which of the two numbers? The first side of the angle crossed one of the scales at 0°. Pick the number on that scale.

118

On page 118, the measure of angle *AVB* is 105°. We write m∠*AVB* = 105°. Below, m∠*CVD* = 55°.

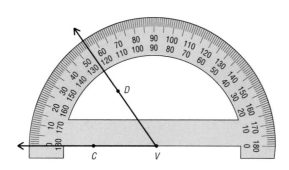

ADDITIONAL EXAMPLES
Draw several angles on the board, and ask students to estimate the measure of each angle. The estimates can be checked with a large demonstration protractor.

NOTES ON QUESTIONS
Question 6: This asks students to name the base line of the protractor. Since there has been no formal discussion of lines or their proper symbols, accept anything that indicates the student has the right idea.

Questions

Covering the Reading

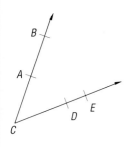

In 1–3, use the angle at left.

1. Name the sides. $\vec{CB}$ (or $\vec{CA}$) and $\vec{CD}$ (or $\vec{CE}$)

2. Name the vertex.   C

3. Which of the following are correct names for the angle?
 (a) ∠*ACE*   (b) ∠*C*   (c) ∠*ECA*   (d) ∠*CBD*
 (e) ∠*ECB*   (f) ∠*DBC*   (g) ∠*ACD*   (h) ∠*ACB*
 (a), (b), (c), (e), and (g)

4. Why did the Babylonians measure with units based on 60?
 Their number system was based on 60.

5. Name two things measured today using ideas of the Babylonians.
 time and angles

In 6–9, use the drawing.

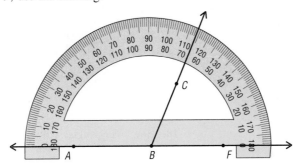

6. Name the base line of this protractor. $\overleftrightarrow{AB}$ (or $\overleftrightarrow{AF}$ or $\overleftrightarrow{BF}$)

7. What point is at the center of this protractor?   B

8. What is the measure of ∠*ABC*?   114°

9. What is the measure of ∠*CBF*?   66°

10. m∠*AVB* stands for the ___?___ of ___?___ *AVB*.   measure; angle

LESSON 3-5   Measuring Angles   **119**

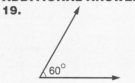
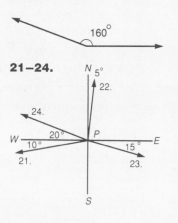

In 11–14, use a protractor. Measure the angle to the nearest degree. (You may have to copy the angles and extend their sides.)

11. 151°

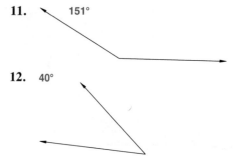

12. 40°

13. 90°   **14.** 75°

15. Who first used the symbol ∠ for an angle and when was this done?   **William Oughtred, 1657**

16. Point X is on $\overrightarrow{UV}$ drawn here. *True* or *false*: $\overrightarrow{UX}$ is the same ray as $\overrightarrow{UV}$.   **True**

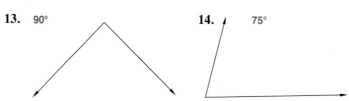

17. Which angle below has the largest angle measure, ∠*JGI*, ∠*IGH*, or ∠*JGH*?   **∠JGH**

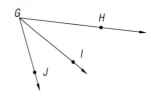

18. How many angles with vertex E are drawn below? (Be careful. Many students' answers are too low.)   **6**

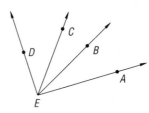

120

120

19. Draw a 60° angle.   **20.** Draw a 160° angle.   **See margin.**
     See margin.

In 21–24, copy the drawing at right, but make your drawing larger. Using your protractor, draw the ray with endpoint P in the given direction.   **See margin.**

21. A tornado is seen 10° South of West.

22. A UFO is seen 5° East of North.

23. A whale is sighted 15° South of East.

24. A tanker is observed 20° North of West.

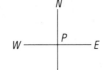

Review

25. While driving through Canada, Kirsten saw the sign below. About how many miles away was Toronto? *(Lesson 3-4)*   **93 mi**

Toronto
150 km

26. Convert 12 liters into quarts. *(Lesson 3-4)*   **about 12.72 qt**

27. Convert 82 mm to meters. *(Lesson 3-3)*   **.082 m**

28. In the metric system, the amount of water in a bathtub could be measured in ___?___. *(Lesson 3-3)*   **liters**

29. In the U.S. system, the amount of water in a bathtub could be measured in ___?___. *(Lesson 3-2)*   **quarts or gallons**

30. Write 41.6 million in scientific notation. *(Lesson 2-3)* 4.16×10^7

31. Roy found that 51 out of 68 people he polled liked the posters he made. Rewrite $\frac{51}{68}$ as a fraction in lowest terms. *(Lesson 1-10)* $\frac{3}{4}$

Exploration

32. Angles are not always measured in degrees. Two other units for measuring angles are the grad and the radian. Find out something about at least one of these units.
   A radian is about 57.3°; a grad is exactly 0.9°.

Kinds of Angles

Angles can be classified by their measures. If the measure of an angle is 90°, the angle is called a **right angle.** Some right angles are drawn below. The sides of this page form right angles at the corners. Many streets intersect at right angles.

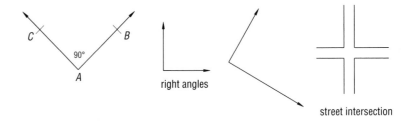

right angles

street intersection

Rays, segments, or lines that form right angles are called **perpendicular.** Above, $\overrightarrow{AC}$ is perpendicular to $\overrightarrow{AB}$. The streets drawn above are also perpendicular. Each long side of this page is perpendicular to each short side.

If the measure of an angle is between 0° and 90°, the angle is called an **acute angle.** An **obtuse angle** is an angle whose measure is between 90° and 180°. Most of the time you can tell whether an angle is acute or obtuse just by looking. If you are unsure, you can measure.

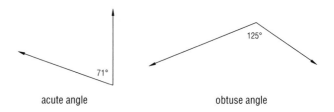

acute angle

obtuse angle

122

A **triangle** gets its name because it contains parts of three angles. The triangle *PQR* drawn here has angles *P, Q,* and *R*. Angle *P* is obtuse while angles *Q* and *R* are acute. △*AOK* below (△ is the symbol for triangle) is called a **right triangle** because one of its angles is a right angle.

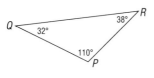

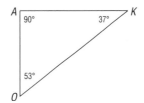

Questions

Covering the Reading

In 1–5, give a definition for the phrase. **See margin.**

1. acute angle   2. obtuse angle

3. right angle   4. right triangle

5. perpendicular lines

In 6–9, an angle has the given measure. Is it acute, right, or obtuse?

6. 40° **acute**   7. 9° **acute**   8. 140° **obtuse**   9. 90° **right**

In 10–13, without measuring, tell whether the angle looks acute, right, or obtuse.

10. **right**   11. **acute**   12. **obtuse**   13. **obtuse**

14. *Multiple choice*   Which triangle looks like a right triangle? **(c)**

(a)   (b)   (c)   (d)

15. In which choice of Question 14 do two segments seem to be perpendicular? **(c)**

TEACHING NOTES

Making Connections
The definition of *perpendicular* uses the words *segments* and *lines*, terms which require only an intuitive understanding here. As long as the notion of *perpendicular* is clear, do not worry about distinctions between lines and segments until Lesson 5-9.

Make certain that students see examples of perpendicular lines that are not horizontal-vertical. (An example is suggested by angle *A* on page 122.) Many students think that *perpendicular* means *vertical*. They may get this idea from such sentences as "the tree is perpendicular to the ground," because in that context, the sentence means the same as "the tree is vertical."

ADDITIONAL EXAMPLES
Refer to **Questions 11–14** on page 120 in Lesson 3-5. Have students classify each angle as an acute, an obtuse, or a right angle.

ADDITIONAL ANSWERS
1. an angle whose measure is between 0° and 90°

2. an angle whose measure is between 90° and 180°

3. an angle whose measure is 90°

4. a triangle with a right angle

5. two lines that form right angles

123

Question 22d: Many students forget the hour hand moves halfway between 6 and 7.

Question 23b: This addresses the confusion of *perpendicular* and *vertical* mentioned in the Teaching Notes. The perpendicular line drawn in the exercise is *not* vertical.

Making Connections for Question 32: This suggests that the measure of the smaller angle between two intersecting two-way streets is a measure of the safety of the intersection. The smaller the angle, the less safe the intersection is. For this reason, most planners try to have streets intersect at right angles. This idea is covered in more detail in Lesson 7-7.

18. samples: angle of ceiling with wall, angle at corner

19. a. right; **b.** 90°

20. a. obtuse; **b.** 134°

21. a. acute; **b.** 60°

30. a. a sharp, severe case of appendicitis; **b.** An acute angle forms a sharp point.

31. a. slow in understanding, dull; **b.** An obtuse angle is dull in that it does not come to a sharp point.

In 16 and 17, use the figure. **a.** Tell whether the angle is acute or obtuse. **b.** Give the measure of the angle.

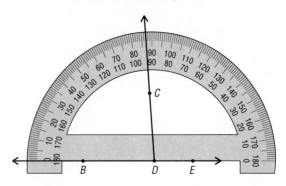

16. ∠CDE   a. obtuse; b. 93°   **17.** ∠CDB   a. acute; b. 87°

Applying the Mathematics

18. Find two examples of right angles different from those mentioned in this lesson.   See margin.

In 19–21, the picture is a closeup of the markings on a giraffe. **a.** Tell whether the angle is acute, right, or obtuse. **b.** Measure the angle.
See margin.

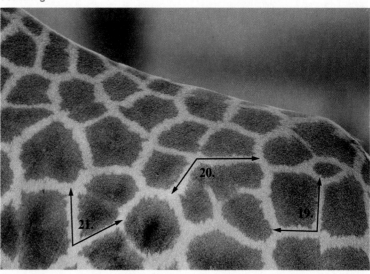

22. Name the type of angle and give the measure of the angle formed by the minute and hour hands of a watch at:
a. 1:00 **b.** 4:00 **c.** 9:00 **d.** 6:30 (Be careful!)
a. acute, 30°; b. obtuse, 120°; c. right, 90°; d. acute, 15°

23. Copy the line. Then draw a line perpendicular to the given line.
a.   **b.**   Check students' drawings.

124

24. Find the measures of the three angles of △*XYZ*. (Hint: Copy the triangle and extend the lines of the sides before measuring.)

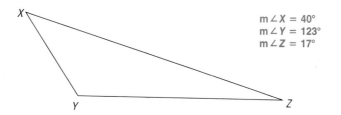

m ∠ *X* = 40°
m ∠ *Y* = 123°
m ∠ *Z* = 17°

Review

25. Tungsten wire four ten-thousandths of an inch in diameter is used to make filaments for light bulbs. *(Lessons 1-8, 2-9)*
  a. Write this number as a decimal.   *.0004 in.*
  b. Write this number in scientific notation. 4×10^{-4} in.

26. According to one survey, teenage boys spend an average of 32% of their allowance on food. Teenage girls spend 26% on the average. If a boy and girl each receive $20, how much more does the boy spend on food? *(Lesson 2-6)*
  $1.20

27. Measure the longest side of triangle *XYZ* above: **a.** to the nearest $\frac{1}{2}$ inch, **b.** to the nearest $\frac{1}{4}$ inch. *(Lesson 3-1)*   a. $3\frac{1}{2}$ in.; b. $3\frac{1}{4}$ in.

28. Complete each statement by using a reasonable metric unit.
  a. In one day we rode 40 _____ on our bikes. *(Lesson 3-3)*   km
  b. A cup can hold about 0.24 _____ of water.   liter
  c. The meat she ate weighed 350 _____.   g

29. Use <, =, or > to complete each relationship. *(Lessons 1-6, 3-3, 3-4)*
  a. 2 meters _____ 1 yard >   **b.** 1 kg _____ 10,000 g <
  c. 1 kg _____ $4\frac{2}{3}$ lb <   **d.** 2 liter _____ 1 gal <
  e. 2 in. _____ 5.08 cm =   **f.** 1000 mm _____ 1 m =

Exploration

30. A person has acute appendicitis.
  a. What does this mean?
  b. Does this use of the word "acute" have any relation to the idea of acute angle?   See margin.

31. a. Look up the meaning of the word "obtuse" in the dictionary. What non-mathematical meaning does this word have?
  b. Is the non-mathematical meaning related to the idea of obtuse angle?   See margin.

32. a. Name a street intersection near your home or school in which the streets do not intersect at right angles.
  b. Approximately what are the measures of the angles formed by the streets?
  c. These kinds of intersections are usually not as safe as right-angle intersections. Is anything done at the intersection you name, to increase its safety?   Answers will vary.

LESSON 3-6 Kinds of Angles **125**

FOLLOW-UP

MORE PRACTICE
For more practice on SPUR Objectives, use *Lesson Master 3-6*, shown below.

EXTENSION
Ask students to count the number of right angles in the closeup for **Questions 19–21.** (We count at least 5 and have no explanation for why there are so many.) Ask the students to draw other patterns for measuring angles.

EVALUATION
A quiz covering Lessons 3-4 through 3-6 is provided in the Teacher's Resource File on page 18.

NAME _____

LESSON **MASTER 3-6**
QUESTIONS ON **SPUR** OBJECTIVES

■**SKILLS** *Objective C (See pages 135–137 for objectives.)*
In 1–3, write >, <, or = in the space provided.

1. The measure of a right angle ____=____ 90°.
2. The measure of an obtuse angle ____>____ 90°.
3. The measure of an acute angle ____<____ 90°.

In 4–7, does the measure describe an acute, an obtuse, or a right angle?
4. 30° ___acute___   5. 90° ___right___
6. 175° ___obtuse___   7. 95° ___obtuse___

In 8–11, determine whether the angle looks acute, right, or obtuse.

8. ___right___

9. ∠*S* ___acute___
10. ∠*K* ___obtuse___
11. ∠*M* ___acute___

12. Draw a line perpendicular to the line below.

26   Transition Mathematics © Scott, Foresman and Company

LESSON 3-7

RESOURCES
■ Lesson Master 3-7
■ Scissors
■ Model of square (such as a floor tile)
■ *Manipulative Activities Sourcebook,* Activity 3

OBJECTIVES

D Find the area of a square, given the length of one side.

O Find areas of squares in real contexts.

TEACHING NOTES

Making Connections
Perimeter is treated in Chapter 5 with addition. The distinction between perimeter and area is specifically discussed in Chapter 9, but you could begin with Figures A and B on page 127. Figure A has an area of 2 cm² and a perimeter of 6 cm. (Notice that, in the pupil's book, these figures are actual size.) Figure B, a rectangle with length 4 cm and width 0.5 cm, has an area of 2 cm² which can be found by cutting the rectangle into 2 equal parts and pasting. However, its perimeter is 9 cm, quite a bit longer than that of Figure A.

Using Manipulatives
You may wish to allow students to actually do the cutting and pasting as you discuss this lesson.

LESSON

3-7

Measuring Area

Area measures the space inside a two-dimensional (flat) figure. You can think of area as measuring how much is shaded within the figures drawn here.

Regardless of how a figure is shaped, it is customary to measure its area in square units. Recall that a **square** is a four-sided figure with four right angles and four sides of equal length. The common units for measuring area are squares with sides of unit length.

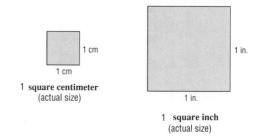

1 **square centimeter**
(actual size)

1 **square inch**
(actual size)

A **square kilometer** is a square with each side having a length of one kilometer.

126

Notice how different area is from length. Each of these figures has shaded area equal to 2 square centimeters. But the lengths of their sides are quite different.

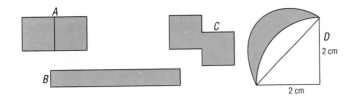

There are three ways to find areas of figures. One way is to count. This will work in Figure A. Another way is to cut and rearrange parts of figures. This will work in figures B and C. But if a figure is complicated, like the shaded part of D, formulas are needed. The simplest formula is that for the area of a square.

Each side has length 5 units.
Counting shows that there are 25 square units.

Each side has length 5.5 units.
Counting shows 25 whole square units,
10 half squares (which equal 5 whole squares)
and an extra quarter square.
This totals 30.25 square units.

Notice that $5^2 = 25$ and $5.5^2 = 30.25$.

> The area of a square equals the second power of the length of one of its sides.

For this reason, 5 to the second power, 5^2, is often read "5 squared." Also, for this reason, we write square inches as in.^{2}, square centimeters as cm^2, and square kilometers as km^2.

Example Find the area of a city block 220 yards on a side.

Solution Area = (220 yd)^2
= 220 yd × 220 yd
= 48,400 square yards
= 48,400 yd^2

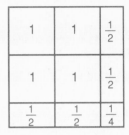

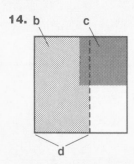
Questions

1. What does area measure in a figure? **the space inside**

2. Suppose length is measured in centimeters. Area will most likely be measured in what units? **square centimeters**

3. What is a square? **a four-sided figure with four sides of equal length and four right angles**

4. Which of the following seem to picture squares? **(b) and (d)**

(a)   (b)   (c)   (d)

5. Give an example of a square you might find outside a mathematics class. **Sample: a caution sign on a street**

6. A square is a _____-dimensional figure. **two**

7. Name three ways to find the area of a figure. **See margin.**

In 8–10, the length of a side of a square is given. Find the area of the square. Be sure to include the correct unit.

8.  **4 cm²**   9.  75 feet **5625 ft²**   10. 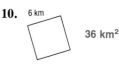 6 km **36 km²**

11. Find the area of a square that is 1.5 inches on a side. **2.25 in.²**

12. 40^2 may be read "40 to the second power" or "40 _?_." **squared**

13. The area of the figure drawn below at the left is how many square inches? **6 in.²**

1 sq in. (not to scale)

14. **a.** Make an accurate drawing of 1 square in. **See margin.**
    b. Shade 0.5 sq in.
    c. On another drawing, shade $\frac{1}{4}$ sq in.
    d. On still another drawing, shade 0.6 sq in.

15. Remember there are 3 feet in a yard.
    a. Picture a square yard and split it up into square feet.
    b. How many square feet are in a square yard?
    a. Check students' drawing. b. 9 ft²

16. A baseball diamond is really square in shape. The distance from home to first is 90 feet. What is the area of the square? **8100 ft²**

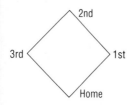

128

17. The area of a room would most likely be measured in what unit of measure: **a.** in the metric system? **b.** in the U.S. system?
a. m²; b. ft²

An acre is a unit equal to 43,560 square feet. Use this fact in Questions 18 and 19.

18. How many square feet are in 10 acres? **435,600 ft²**

19. How many square feet are in a half-acre lot? **21,780 ft²**

Review

20. Complete the statement with < or >. 13.26 __?__ 13 $\frac{4}{13}$. *(Lessons 1-6, 1-9)* **<**

21. Round 2^{30} to the nearest million. *(Lessons 1-4, 2-2)* **1,074,000,000**

22. Which is larger, 0 or 10^0? *(Lesson 2-8)* **10^0**

23. A school has 600 students. *(Lesson 2-6)*
    a. Ten percent of the students is how many students? **60**
    b. Use your answer in **a.** to find 20%, 40%, and 70% of the student body without doing another percent calculation.
    120; 240; 420

24. Measure the length of this printed line (from the M in "Measure" to the " sign in "Measure") to the nearest half centimeter. *(Lesson 3-1)* **10.5 cm**

25. The length of the U.S. Grand Prix race is 322.6 kilometers. About how long is this in miles? *(Lesson 3-4)* **about 200 mi**

26. Sixty kilograms is about how many pounds? *(Lesson 3-4)* **132 lb**

27. Sixty kilograms is about how many grams? *(Lesson 3-3)* **60,000 g**

28. Measure this angle to the nearest degree. *(Lesson 3-5)* **9°**

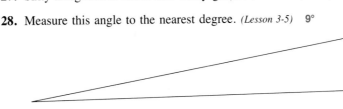

29. An angle has measure 19°. Is it acute, right, or obtuse? *(Lesson 3-6)*
acute

Exploration

30. Before exponents appeared as raised decimal numbers, some people wrote them as Roman numerals on the same line as the base. In this notation, 2 to the fifth power would be 2V. Modern exponent symbols first appeared in 1637 in a book by René Descartes. Find out something else about this famous mathematician and philosopher. **See margin.**

31. Most scientific calculators have a ⬚x²⬚ key. (On some calculators you must press ⬚inv⬚ or ⬚F⬚ before pressing this key.) Explore what this key does. **It squares the number entered.**

FOLLOW-UP

MORE PRACTICE
For more practice on SPUR Objectives, use *Lesson Master 3-7*, shown below.

EVALUATION
Alternative Assessment
Ask the students to name situations in which they or their families might use or have used the concept of area. Ask if they think it is important to know about area, and why.

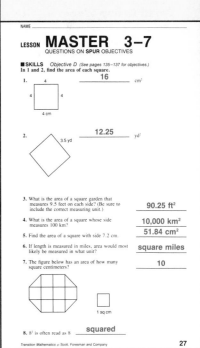

NAME _____

LESSON **MASTER 3-7**
QUESTIONS ON **SPUR** OBJECTIVES

■ **SKILLS** *Objective D (See pages 135–137 for objectives.)*
In 1 and 2, find the area of each square.
1. **16** cm²
4 cm

2. **12.25** yd²
3.5 yd

3. What is the area of a square garden that measures 9.5 feet on each side? (Be sure to include the correct measuring unit.) **90.25 ft²**

4. What is the area of a square whose side measures 100 km? **10,000 km²**

5. Find the area of a square with side 7.2 cm. **51.84 cm²**

6. If length is measured in miles, area would most likely be measured in what unit? **square miles**

7. The figure below has an area of how many square centimeters? **10**

1 sq cm

8. 8² is often read as 8 **squared**

Transition Mathematics © Scott, Foresman and Company

27

OBJECTIVES

E Find the volume of a cube, given the length of one side.
G Know the relationship between length and capacity in the metric system.
O Find volumes of cubes in real contexts.

TEACHING NOTES

Small Group Work
There is no substitute for stacking cubes in all sorts of ways to demonstrate how the same volume can be distributed in different ways. If you have a Rubik's cube, think of it as a cube with a side length of 3 units. Students can take it apart to show the equivalent of 27 cubic units.

Reading As with area, there is a difference between 10 cubic feet and a 10-foot cube. The former is a volume; the latter is a solid whose volume is 1000 cubic feet. Stress to the students that they must read ft^3 or m^3 carefully.

Measuring Volume

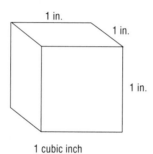

1 cubic inch

1 cubic centimeter

Volume measures space inside a three-dimensional or solid figure. Think of volume as measuring the amount a box, jar, or other container can hold. Or think of volume as telling you how much material is in something that is solid. Whatever the shape of a figure, its volume is usually measured in **cubic units.** A **cube** is a figure with six faces, each face being a square. Sugar cubes, number cubes, and dice are examples. The most common units for measuring volume are cubes with edges of unit length.

In a **cubic meter,** each edge has length 1 meter.
Each face is a square with area 1 square meter.

Volume can be calculated by counting cubes, by cutting and pasting cubic units together, or with the help of formulas. At left is a cube with edges of length 2 units. The picture is partially transparent and shows that 8 unit cubes make up the bigger cube.

Notice that volume is quite different from area. If the outside surface of the cube at left is covered by plastic squares, the amount of plastic is found by adding areas. The volume, however, tells how much sand can be poured into the cube.

There are two layers. The top layer has 2×2 or 4 cubes. So does the bottom layer. In all there are $2 \times 2 \times 2$ or 2^3, or 8 cubes. In general:

> The volume of a cube equals the third power of the length of one of its edges.

For this reason, 2^3, 2 to the third power, is often read "2 cubed." Also, for this reason, we write cubic inches as in.^{3}, cubic centimeters as cm^3, cubic meters as m^3, and so on.

You have already learned that the liter is a metric unit of capacity. Capacity is another word for volume. So the **liter** is a unit of volume. It is defined as the volume of a cube that is 10 centimeters on each side.

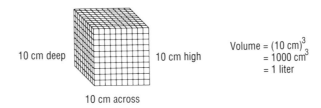

10 cm deep   10 cm high

$$\text{Volume} = (10 \text{ cm})^3$$
$$= 1000 \text{ cm}^3$$
$$= 1 \text{ liter}$$

10 cm across

Soft drinks are often sold in 2-liter bottles. These have a volume of 2000 cm^3.

Questions

Covering the Reading

1. What does volume measure in a 3-dimensional figure?
   the space inside
2. Suppose length is measured in meters. Volume will most likely be measured in what unit?   **cubic meters**

3. What is a cube?   **a figure with 6 square faces**

4. Give an example of a cube you might find outside a math class.
   Sample: sugar cube
5. A cube is a __?__-dimensional figure.   **3**

6. Name three ways to find the volume of a figure.   **See margin.**

7. What does the volume of a cube equal?
   the length of an edge cubed
8. Draw a cube.   **See margin.**

In 9–11, find the volume of a cube with an edge of the given length. Use the correct unit in your answer.

9. 4 inches   **64 in.^{3}**   10. 40 cm   **64,000 cm^3**   11. 7 yards   **343 yd^3**

12. A liter is defined as the volume of a cube with an edge of length __?__.   **10 cm**

13. How many cubic centimeters equal one liter?   **1000 cm^3**

14. A 2-liter bottle has a volume of __?__ cubic centimeters.   **2000**

NOTES ON QUESTIONS
Question 8: Students often do not know how to draw a cube. You may want to show them the method shown below.

ADDITIONAL ANSWERS
6. counting cubes, cutting and pasting cubic units together, using formulas

8. Check students' drawings; see note above.

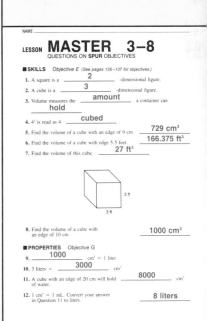

Applying the Mathematics

15. a. Find the volume of a cube with edge 3.25 feet. 34.328125 ft³
b. The correct answer to part **a** is in millionths of a cubic foot. This is too precise for many uses. Round the answer to the nearest hundredth for a more realistic measure. 34.33 ft³

16. Remember that there are 12 inches in a foot. You may want to draw a picture to help with these questions.
a. How many square inches are there in a square foot? 144 in.²
b. How many cubic inches are there in a cubic foot? 1728 in.³

17. Calculate six cubed plus five squared. 241

18. Arrange from smallest to largest: 1 liter, 89 cubic centimeters, and the volume of a cube with edge 9 cm. **See margin.**

You have learned that the liter (a unit of capacity) and the centimeter (a unit of length) are related. In the metric system, these two units are also related to the mass of water. Specifically,

1 cm³ of water equals 1 mL of water and weighs 1 gram.

In 19 and 20, use the above information.

19. How much does a liter of water weigh? 1 kg

20. Suppose an aquarium is a cube 50 cm on a side.
a. How much water will it hold? 125,000 mL
b. How much will the water weigh in kilograms? 125 kg
c. How much will the water weigh in pounds? 275 lb

Review

21. In the first 6 months of 1990, *TV Guide* sold 411,763,664 copies, the most of any magazine. *(Lessons 1-4, 2-3)*
a. Round this number to the nearest hundred thousand.
b. Estimate how many copies would be sold over the entire year.
c. Write your estimate in scientific notation. 8.24 × 10⁸
   a. 411,800,000   b. 824,000,000

22. *Multiple choice* A 10-year-old boy who weighs 75 kg is likely to be: (c)
(a) underweight. (b) about the right weight. (c) overweight.
(Lesson 3-3)

23. Write 3.4 × 10⁻⁴ as **a.** a decimal **b.** a fraction in lowest terms.
(Lessons 2-7, 2-8) a. .00034; b. $\frac{17}{50,000}$

24. Which is not an integer: -4, $\frac{8}{4}$, 5², 0, or $\frac{1}{2}$?
(Lessons 1-5, 1-8, 2-2) $\frac{1}{2}$

25. Give the area of the square drawn at left. *(Lesson 3-7)* 100 cm²

10 cm

26. 10³ meters is how many kilometers? *(Lessons 2-2, 3-3)* 1 km

Exploration

27. You receive a letter from your long-lost aunt and uncle in Japan. They invite you to see their villa, which covers an area of 250 hectares. Is this a lot of land? **See margin.**

132

Summary

The most common uses of numbers are as counts or measures. In this chapter, measures of length, area, volume or capacity, angle measure, and mass or weight are discussed.

There are two systems of measurement in use today in the United States. One is the metric system. Two basic units in the metric system are the meter for length and the kilogram for mass. The other system is called the U.S. or customary system. It uses inches, feet, and so on, for length; ounces, pound, and so on, for weight; and pints, quarts, gallons, and so on for capacity. The metric system is generally easier to work with because its units are related to each other by powers of 10; so it is closely related to the decimal system.

Units for area are usually squares based on units of length. Units for volume are usually cubes based on units of length. The degree, the common unit for angle measure, is based on splitting the circle. It is used in both the metric system and the U.S. system. Angles can be classified by their measure.

Vocabulary

You should be able to give a general description and a specific example of each of the following ideas.

Lesson 3-1
centimeter, inch

Lesson 3-2
foot (ft), yard (yd), mile (mi), inch (in.)
ounce (oz), pound (lb), short ton
pint, quart (qt), gallon (gal)

Lesson 3-3
international or metric system of measurement
milli-, centi-, kilo-
meter (m)
gram (g)
liter (L)

Lesson 3-4
is approximately equal to ($\approx$)
Estimation Principle

Lesson 3-5
ray, $\overrightarrow{AB}$, endpoint of ray, vertex of an angle
angle, sides of an angle, $\angle ABC$, $m\angle ABC$
degree (°)
protractor

Lesson 3-6
right angle, acute angle, obtuse angle
perpendicular
right triangle

Lesson 3-7
area
square, square units
in.^{2}, cm^2, km^2, and so on

Lesson 3-8
volume
cube, cubic units
in.^{3}, cm^3, m^3, and so on

SUMMARY

The Summary gives an overview of the entire chapter and provides an opportunity for students to consider the material as a whole. Thus, the Summary can be used to help students relate the concepts presented in the chapter.

VOCABULARY

Terms, symbols, and properties are listed by lesson to provide a checklist of concepts a student must know. Emphasize to students that they should read the vocabulary list carefully before starting the Progress Self-Test. If students do not understand the meaning of a term, they should refer back to the indicated lesson.

Definitions or descriptions of all terms in the vocabulary list may be found in the Glossary of the student text.

Progress Self-Test

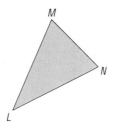

Take this test as you would take a test in class. You will need a protractor, a ruler, and a calculator. Then check your work with the solutions in the Selected Answers section in the back of the book.

1. Measure this segment to the nearest eighth of an inch. $2\frac{5}{8}$ in.

2. **Check students' segments.**

2. Draw a segment with length 6.4 centimeters.

3. Give the exact relationship between inches and centimeters. **2.54 cm = 1 in.**

4. Name the appropriate metric unit for measuring the weight or mass of a person. **kg**

5. How many feet are there in $\frac{3}{4}$ of a mile? **3960 ft**

6. How many quarts are there in 1 gallon? **4 qt**

7. A kiloton is how many tons? **1000 tons**

8. 1103 mg = __?__ g. **1.103 g**

9. 5 centimeters = __?__ meters. **.05m**

10. 3.2 meters ≈ __?__ inches. **125.98 in.**

11. 4 kilometers ≈ __?__ miles. **2.48 mi**

12. Measure angle C to the nearest degree. **135°**

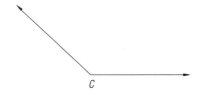

13. Measure $\angle MNL$ to the nearest degree. **76°**

14. An acute angle has measure between __?__ and __?__ degrees. **0; 90**

15. An angle has measure 90°. Is this angle right, acute, or obtuse? **right**

16. Draw an angle with a measure of 123°.

17. Find the area of square with side 4.5 inches.

18. If the side of a square is measured in cm, the area will probably be measured in __?__.

19. How are liters and cubic centimeters related?

20. Which angles of the triangle below seem to be acute, which right, which obtuse?

B and C; none; A

21. Give the volume of the cube drawn below. **125 cm³**

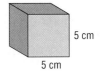

5 cm

5 cm

22. A rug is in the shape of a square 6 feet on a side. How many square yards are in the rug?

23. To convert kilograms to pounds, what estimate can be used? **1 kg ≈ 2.2 lb**

24. Which is larger, 10 quarts or 9 liters? **10 qt**

25. The U.S. system is derived from a measuring system from what country? **England**

16. See margin.
17. 20.25 in.²
18. cm²
19. 1000 cm³ = 1 L
22. 4 yd²

Chapter Review

Questions on **SPUR** Objectives

SPUR stands for **S**kills, **P**roperties, **U**ses, and **R**epresentations.
The Chapter Review questions are grouped according to the
SPUR Objectives for this chapter.

SKILLS deals with the procedures used to get answers.

Objective A: *Measure lengths to the nearest inch, half inch, quarter inch, or eighth of an inch, or to the nearest centimeter or tenth of a centimeter. (Lesson 3-1)*

1. Measure the length of this horizontal segment to the nearest quarter inch.   **2 in.**

    _____

2. Measure the length of the above segment to the nearest tenth of a centimeter. **4.9 cm**

3. Measure the length of the segment below to the nearest centimeter.   **7 cm**

4. Measure the length of the segment below to the nearest eighth of an inch. $2\frac{5}{8}$ **in.**

Objective B: *Measure an angle to the nearest degree using a protractor. (Lesson 3-5)*

5. Measure angle B below.   **63°**
6. Measure angle C below.   **157°**
7. Measure ∠ADC below.   **36°**

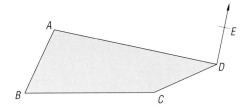

Objective C: *Distinguish between acute, right, and obtuse angles by sight. (Lesson 3-6)*

Use the figure under Objective B.

8. Which angles seem to be acute?   ∠**B, and** ∠**ADC**
9. Does ∠CDE seem to be obtuse, acute, or right?   **obtuse**
10. Name all angles that seem to be right angles.   ∠**ADE**

Objective D: *Find the area of a square, given the length of one side. (Lesson 3-7)*

11. Find the area of the square below.   **4 cm²**
12. Find the area of a square with side 6.5 in.   **42.25 in.²**

2 cm

13. If length is measured in meters, area is most easily measured in what unit?   **m²**

Objective E: *Find the volume of a cube, given the length of one side. (Lesson 3-8)*

14. Find the volume of a cube with one side of length 4 mm.   **64 mm³**
15. To the nearest integer, find the volume of a cube with edge of length 3.75 in.   **53 in.³**

RESOURCES
- Chapter 3 Test, Form A
- Chapter 3 Test, Form B
- Chapter 3 Test, Cumulative Form
- Comprehensive Test, Chapters 1–3

CHAPTER REVIEW

The main objectives for the chapter are organized into sections corresponding to the four main types of understanding this book promotes: Skills, Properties, Uses, and Representations.

PROPERTIES deal with the principles behind the mathematics.

■ **Objective F:** *Know the relationships in the U.S. system within units of length, weight, and capacity. (Lesson 3-2)*

16. Give a relationship between pints and quarts.   **2 pt = 1 qt**

17. How many ounces are in 1 pound?   **16 oz**

18. How are feet and miles related?
5280 ft = 1 mi

■ **Objective G:** *Know the relationships in the metric system within units of length, weight, and capacity. (Lessons 3-3, 3-8)*

19. What is the meaning of the prefix milli-?

20. How are centimeters and liters related?

21. 1 kilogram = _?_ grams.   **1000**
19. .001 or $\frac{1}{1000}$; 20. 1000 cm³ = 1 L

■ **Objective H:** *Know the relationships between important units in the metric and U.S. systems of measurement. (Lesson 3-4)*

22. Give an approximate relationship between pounds and kilograms.   **2.2 lb ≈ 1 kg**

23. How are centimeters and inches related?

24. Which is larger, a mile or a kilometer?   m

25. Which is larger, a meter or a yard?   mete
23. 2.54 cm = 1 in.

■ **Objective I:** *State and apply the Estimation Principle. (Lesson 3-4)*

26. State the Estimation Principle.   See margi

27. To convert liters to quarts, what estimate can be used?   **1 L ≈ 1.06 qt**

USES deal with applications of mathematics in real situations.

■ **Objective J:** *Give appropriate units for measuring mass, length, and capacity in the U.S. or metric system of measurement. (Lessons 3-2, 3-3)*

28. Give an appropriate unit in each system for measuring the distance from New York to London, England.   **mi, km**

29. Give an appropriate unit in the metric system for measuring the length of your foot.

30. Give an appropriate unit in the metric system for measuring the weight of a postage stamp.   **mg**

31. Give an appropriate unit in the U.S. system for measuring the capacity of a fish tank.   **gal**
29. cm

■ **Objective K:** *Convert within the U.S. system of measurement. (Lesson 3-2)*

32. How many inches are in 2.5 yards?   **90 in.**

33. Convert 7.3 gallons to quarts.   **29.2 qt**

34. How many pounds are there in 3 short tons?   **6000 lb**

35. How many feet are in 660 yards?   **1980 ft**

■ **Objective L:** *Convert within the metric system. (Lesson 3-3)*

36. Convert 200 cm to meters.   **2 m**

37. Convert 5 km to meters.   **5000 m**

38. Convert 265 ml to liters.   **.265 L**

39. Convert 60 mg to g.   **.06 g**

■ **Objective M:** *Convert between the U.S. and metric systems. (Lesson 3-4)*

40. How many centimeters are in 2 feet?   60.9

41. In a guide book the distance between Paris and London is given as 872 km. How many miles is this?   **about 540.64 mi**

42. How many quarts are in 6.8 liters?   **7.208 ≈**

43. Convert 100 kg to pounds.   **about 220 lb**

Objective N: *Identify and measure angles in pictures.* (Lessons 3-5, 3-6)

44. Measure ∠ADC to the nearest degree.   70°

45. Name an obtuse angle in this drawing.
∠ABC, ∠BEA, ∠BCD, ∠DEC

n van Eyck, *Portrait*
a Man in a Red Turban

■ **Objective O:** *Find areas of squares or volumes of cubes in real contexts.* (Lessons 3-7, 3-8)

46. A square table has a side of length 2.5 feet. Will a square tablecloth with an area of 6 square feet cover the table?   no

47. How much paint can be put into a cubic container 12 cm on a side?   1728 cm³

EPRESENTATIONS deal with pictures, graphs, or objects that illustrate concepts.

Objective P: *Draw a line segment of a given length.* (Lesson 3-1)   See margin.

48. Draw a line segment with length 3.5 cm.

49. Draw a line segment with length $2\frac{1}{4}$ inches.

50. Draw a vertical line segment with length 4.375 inches.

■ **Objective Q:** *Draw an angle with a given measure.* (Lesson 3-5)   See margin.

51. Draw an angle with a measure of 90°, in which neither side lies on a horizontal line.

52. Draw an angle with a measure of 37°.

53. Draw an angle with a measure of 145°.

STORY

Objective R: *Give countries and approximate dates of origin of current measuring ideas.* (Lessons 3-1, 3-3, 3-5)

54. When and where did the metric system originate?   France, 1790s

55. How was the length of a yard first determined?   See margin.

56. Our system for measuring angles is based on measuring done by what people?   Babylonians

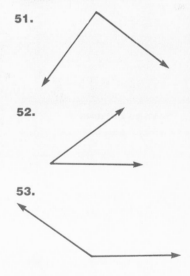

CHAPTER 4 ■ USES OF VARIABLES

DAILY PACING CHART ■ CHAPTER 4

Students in the Full Course should complete the entire text by the end of the year. Students in the Minimal Course spend more time when there are quizzes and more time on the Chapter Review. Therefore, these students may not complete all of the chapters in the text.

DAY	MINIMAL COURSE	FULL COURSE
1	4-1	4-1
2	4-2	4-2
3	4-3	4-3
4	4-4	4-4
5	Quiz (TRF); Start 4-5.	Quiz (TRF); 4-5
6	Finish 4-5.	4-6
7	4-6	4-7
8	4-7	Quiz (TRF); 4-8
9	Quiz (TRF); Start 4-8.	4-9
10	Finish 4-8.	Progress Self-Test
11	4-9	Chapter Review
12	Progress Self-Test	Chapter Test (TRF)
13	Chapter Review	
14	Chapter Review	
15	Chapter Test (TRF)	

TESTING OPTIONS

■ Quiz for Lessons 4-1 Through 4-4   ■ Chapter 4 Test, Form A   ■ Chapter 4 Test, Cumulative Form
■ Quiz for Lessons 4-5 Through 4-7   ■ Chapter 4 Test, Form B

A Quiz and Test Writer is available for generating additional questions, additional quizzes, or additional forms of the Chapter Test.

PROVIDING FOR INDIVIDUAL DIFFERENCES

The student text is written for the *average* student. The program, however, can be adapted for both less capable and more capable students.

A blackline master (in the Teacher's Resource File) is provided for each lesson for those students who need more practice. The Teacher's Edition frequently provides an Error Analysis feature to provide additional instructional strategies.

For students who require additional challenge, Extension activities are regularly provided in the Teacher's Edition.

OBJECTIVES ■ CHAPTER 4

After students complete the chapter lessons, they assess their mastery on the Progress Self-Test. Then they do the Chapter Review and pay special attention to those questions that match the objectives missed on the Progress Self-Test. Students can get extra practice on these objectives by using the master for each lesson in the Teacher's Resource File.

OBJECTIVES FOR CHAPTER 4 (Organized into the SPUR categories—Skills, Properties, Uses, and Representations)	Progress Self-Test Questions	Chapter Review Questions	Teacher's Resource File	
			Lesson Master*	Chapter Test Forms A and B
SKILLS				
A: Use order of operations to evaluate numerical expressions.	1, 3, 4, 5	1–6	4-1, 4-7	11, 12
B: Evaluate numerical expressions containing grouping symbols.	2	7–14	4-5, 4-7	13
C: Evaluate algebraic expressions given the values of all variables.	6, 7, 8, 27	15–24	4-4, 4-5, 4-7	15, 16, 17
D: Choose the correct solution or solutions to an open sentence.	9	25, 26	4-8, 4-9	24
E: Mentally find solutions to equations involving simple arithmetic.	24, 25	27–30	4-8	23
F: Know the correct order of operations.	21	31–34	4-1, 4-5, 4-7	14, 18
PROPERTIES				
G: Given instances of a pattern, write a description of the pattern using variables.	10, 11	35–37	4-2	25
H: Give instances of a pattern described with variables.	30, 31	38–40	4-2	19
USES				
I: Given instances of a real-world pattern, write a description of the pattern using variables.	12	41, 42	4-2	20
J: Write a numerical expression for an English expression involving arithmetic operations.	15, 16	43–46	4-3	26
K: Write an algebraic expression for an English expression involving arithmetic operations.	17, 18	47–50	4-3	5, 6, 7, 8, 9, 10
L: Calculate the value of a variable, given the values of other variables in a formula.	13, 14, 20	51–54	4-6	1, 2, 21
REPRESENTATIONS				
M: Graph the solutions to any inequality of the form $x < a$ and similar inequalities and identify such graphs.	28	55–59	4-9	3
N: Graph the solutions to any inequality of the form $a < x < b$ and similar inequalities and identify such graphs.	29	60–62	4-9	22
HISTORY (Note: This chapter has an additional category for History.)				
O: Give rough dates and names of people for key ideas in arithmetic and algebraic notation.	22	63, 64	4-1, 4-2	4

*The Lesson Masters are numbered to match the lessons.

138B

OVERVIEW ■ CHAPTER 4

Algebra is generally thought of as using letters to represent numbers. In this sense, Chapter 4 begins our study of algebra. However, in earlier grades students probably have been introduced to many ideas that lead naturally to algebra. For instance, they may have had to fill in blanks in sentences like $4 + \_\_\_ = 7$; this is simply the algebra problem $4 + x = 7$ in a different form. Students may have seen formulas for the area of a rectangle or square. They may have seen properties described with variables; one common example is the Commutative Property of Addition: $a + b = b + a$.

This chapter could also be entitled "Notation," since its two major ideas both relate to the ways in which things are written down. The first major concept, order of operations, is found in Lessons 4-1, 4-5, and 4-7. The second important topic is the variable. Three uses of the variable are presented: to describe patterns (Lesson 4-2); in formulas (Lesson 4-6); and as unknowns (Lessons 4-8 and 4-9). The other lessons introduce two important skills with variables: translating from English to variables (4-3) and evaluating expressions (4-4).

Although this chapter introduces many new concepts, everything except order of operations and evaluation skills recurs in lessons in later chapters. Students will have a great deal of practice with formulas, they will solve many sentences, and they will do lots of pattern finding and translating. Chapter 4 serves primarily as an introduction.

PERSPECTIVES ■ CHAPTER 4

The Perspectives provide the rationale for the inclusion of topics or approaches, provide mathematical background, and make connections within UCSMP.

4-1

ORDER OF OPERATIONS

One of the reasons for requiring scientific calculators is that they follow the same order of operations as required in algebra. For example, to evaluate $2 + 3n$ on a scientific calculator when $n = 7$, if one enters the numbers and operations in order from left to right, the value 23 will appear. In contrast, on most four-function nonscientific calculators, the value 35 is the result. Scientific calculators use, and thereby reinforce, the order of operations found in algebra. Emphasize this point. You might also wish to note that computers use the same order of operations as do scientific calculators.

The priority of parentheses in order of operations is introduced in Lesson 4-5. A summary of the rules for order of operations is given in Lesson 4-7.

4-2

DESCRIBING PATTERNS WITH VARIABLES

This is a very important lesson since it is the first transition from arithmetic to algebra—via patterns. We have found that for about half the students, the descriptions of patterns using variables are easy and quite natural. For the other half, even the simplest examples give trouble. These students have difficulty with abstract thinking and need to build up skills in that area to be successful in algebra.

Students should become accustomed to seeing *any* letter used as a variable. However, the letters a, b, c, d or m, n or x, y, z are used most often.

Of course, many patterns are properties that have names, for example, the Commutative Property of Addition on page 146. However, these properties do not need to be discussed now. They will be studied in later chapters, at which time their names will be introduced.

4-3

TRANSLATING EXPRESSIONS

This lesson presents variables in a second way: as translations of English expressions involving arithmetic operations. *Transition Mathematics* works on this skill continually, so do not be concerned if students cannot do all of the translations immediately. There are many phrases used for operations, and it takes time—even for good students—to become accustomed to all of them.

We retain the raised dot (·) for multiplication between a number and a variable in this lesson. In the next lesson, we note that the raised dot can be (and almost always is) deleted.

The statement, "Find the difference between a and b," is ambiguous. It could mean $a - b$, $b - a$, or $|a - b|$. Similarly, the statement, "Find the quotient of 5 and 40," is ambiguous. Does it mean $\frac{40}{5}$ or $\frac{5}{40}$? Many would say the quotient of 5 and 40 is 8, implicitly assuming that the larger is divided by the smaller. Others would say $\frac{5}{40}$, dividing the first by the second. We try to avoid such statements. When they appear, allow all reasonable answers.

4-4

EVALUATING ALGEBRAIC EXPRESSIONS

An important development in this lesson is the elimination of the symbol for multiplication in algebraic expressions. The multiplication symbol, x, can look like the variable *x,* and the · can look like a decimal point. Although a numerical expression requiring multiplication needs a symbol (so 2 x 3 can be differentiated from 23), this is not a problem with variables. Therefore, $6 \cdot t$ becomes $6t$.

Also, the algebraic expression $3x + 2y$ is basically an addition problem involving two products, $3x$ and $2y$. By leaving out the multiplication symbols, the expression looks more like two terms with multiplication occurring before the addition. Not only can this arrangement help students deal with algebraic terms correctly, but it also may be one of the reasons that multiplication occurs before addition in the standard order of operations.

4-5

PARENTHESES

Grouping symbols are needed because many expressions must be written on *one* line in order to be entered into the computer or calculator. Thus, the use of grouping symbols is a traditional skill that has increased in importance with the coming of technology.

In Lesson 4-7, brackets [ ] are introduced as grouping symbols with the same meaning as parentheses. Using brackets is fine for paper and pencil work, but calculators and many computer languages do not accept brackets. The student needs to be able to use either parentheses or brackets.

4-6

FORMULAS

In this lesson, students begin working with formulas. We use formulas that have a geometric representation to illustrate their immediate utility, stressing the need for consistency in units. (Not only is this essential in applications, but it also points up the fact that a formula, like a calculator, does not always do all the work for you.) Finally, we discuss how letters are chosen for formulas and that the same letter in upper case and lower case often stands for different things.

4-7

GROUPING SYMBOLS

At one time, it was common to use braces { } as grouping symbols. However, since braces are used to denote sets, it is confusing to use them as grouping symbols, too. In addition, computer languages do not accept braces as grouping symbols.

The fraction bar is called a *vinculum* (see chart on page 139) and is a grouping symbol that is still in common use. In Europe, the square root of xy may be written $\sqrt{} \, (xy)$. However, in the United States we use the vinculum above the xy instead of the parentheses ($\sqrt{xy}$). We think of it as part of our square root symbol.

In this book, we sometimes underline an expression to emphasize that it should be thought of as a single number. For example, we might write that $\underline{a - b}$ is the result when b is taken away from a. That underline can be thought of as a vinculum.

4-8

OPEN SENTENCES

Variables have the feeling of *knowns* when they appear in patterns or formulas, and for this reason are not threatening. Though students have had experience with variables in patterns and formulas, the use of variables as *unknowns* is what first comes to mind when algebra is discussed. We purposely have left this use to the end of the chapter, because we feel that the idea of *unknown* conveys a mysteriousness about variables that we wish to avoid.

The purpose of this lesson is only to introduce the idea of *unknowns*. The questions are designed to give a nonthreatening view of finding *unknowns*. Do *not* work on ways to solve sentences at this point. Many later lessons are devoted to sentence solving.

4-9

INEQUALITIES

The goals in this lesson are to introduce the idea of solving an inequality and the idea of graphing all solutions. We do not ask students to graph the solutions to *equations* in one variable—it is too much work for too little payoff.

Solving inequalities presents difficulties for many students. They are so accustomed to having one answer to mathematical questions that they cannot fathom how something such as $y < 2$ can have so many solutions.

138D

CHAPTER 4

Uses of Variables

138

Descartes

Ask the students to write the following as you dictate:
   Choose a number.
   Add 3.
   Double.
   Subtract 4.
   Divide by 2.
   Subtract the original number.

Point out that though the students may have selected different numbers, they all got the same answer (1), and they probably wrote the directions on their papers using symbols. People often use symbols such as numbers and pictures to convey messages.

Discuss the chart on page 139. Explain that the operations were done with words and other symbols before these symbols in the chart were developed. You may wish to point out that new symbols for powering and multiplication were created for use with the computer. Stress that new symbols for operations could still be introduced.

You might ask what else was going on in the world at the time these symbols were invented. (For instance, 1489 is three years before Columbus made his first voyage to the New World; 1784 is eight years after the Declaration of Independence.)

Some number patterns are difficult to describe in words. To make things easier, mathematicians invent symbols and define new words. The table below shows some of the more important symbols of arithmetic.

Operation	Symbol	Name for symbol	Inventor of symbol (Year)	Name for result
addition	$+$	plus	Johann Widman (1498)	sum
subtraction	$-$	minus	Johann Widman (1498)	difference
multiplication	$\times$	times	William Oughtred (1631)	product
	•	dot	Gottfried Leibniz (1698)	product
	$*$	asterisk		product
division	$-$ as in $\frac{2}{3}$	bar or vinculum	al-Hassar (1050)	fraction
	$\overline{)}$	into	Michael Stifel (1544)	quotient
	$\div$	divided by	Johann Rahn (1659)	quotient
	: as in 2:3	colon	Gottfried Leibniz (1684)	ratio
	/ as in 2/3	slash	Manuel A. Valdes (1784)	fraction
powering	3 as in 2^3	exponent	René Descartes (1637)	power
	↑ as in 2 ↑ 3	up arrow	?	power
	$**$ as in $2**3$	double asterisk	?	power

Used in arithmetic and on calculators: $+$ $-$ $\times$ $\div$ exponent
Used in algebra: $+$ $-$ •   bar   exponent
Used in computer languages: $+$ $-$ $*$ / $**$ or ↑ or ^ (not listed above)
$\overline{)}$ is used only in long division;   : is used for ratios and instead of $\div$ in some countries

OBJECTIVES

A Use order of operations to evaluate numerical expressions.
F Know the correct order of operations.
O Give rough dates and names of people for key ideas in arithmetic and algebra notation.

TEACHING NOTES

There are several points to consider when teaching order of operations. First, make students aware that it is possible to get different answers to the same question if there is no agreement about what to do first. To emphasize this point, have students evaluate $36 \div 3 + 1$. Then discuss the different answers students obtain.
$[(36 \div 3) + 1 = 13;$
$36 \div (3 + 1) = 9]$

Be sure to emphasize that in expressions involving only addition and subtraction, neither operation has priority. Rather, you do the one which comes first as you work from left to right. The same holds true for expressions involving only multiplication and division. Stress that students must memorize the rules in the box on page 141.

LESSON

4-1

Order of Operations

Names or symbols for numbers and operations make up **numerical expressions.** The **value** of a numerical expression is found by working out the arithmetic. Working out the arithmetic is called **evaluating the expression.** For example, the seven expressions here all have the same value, 2.

$$2, \quad 5 - 3, \quad \tfrac{20}{10}, \quad 5 \times 2 - 8, \quad 2^1, \quad 347.8 - 345.8, \quad 10^0 + 10^0$$

On page 139 is a table of symbols for the operations of arithmetic and algebra. Although there are many symbols, each symbol has a precise meaning. This is important, because the meaning of a numerical expression should be the same for everybody.

But recall Lesson 1-7, where you were asked to evaluate $85 + 9 \times 2$ on your calculator. You keyed in:

$$85 \boxed{+} 9 \boxed{\times} 2 \boxed{=}.$$

If you have a scientific calculator, the calculator multiplied first and displayed 103 as the value. A nonscientific calculator will probably add first; it will wind up with 188.

That can be confusing. Here is another confusing situation. Suppose you have $25, spend $10, and then spend $4. You will wind up with

$$25 - 10 - 4 \text{ dollars.}$$

The situation tells you that the value of this expression is $11. But someone else evaluating $25 - 10 - 4$ might first subtract the 4 from the 10. This would leave $25 - 6$, or $19.

Calculating powers can also be confusing. Consider the expression 2×3^4. Some people might do the multiplication first, getting 6^4, which equals 1296. Others might first calculate the 4th power of 3, getting 2×81, which equals 162. These values aren't even close to each other.

140

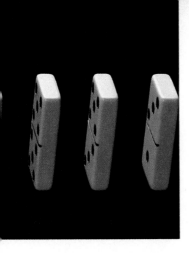

To avoid confusion, rules are needed. These rules tell the order in which operations should be done. These rules have been developed only in this century, but they are now used worldwide.

Order of Operations:

1. Calculate all powers in order, from left to right.
2. Then do multiplications or divisions in order, from left to right.
3. Then do additions or subtractions in order, from left to right.

Example 1 Evaluate $3 + 4 \times 5$.

Solution Multiply before adding. $3 + 4 \times 5 = 3 + 20 = 23$.

Example 2 Evaluate $8 \times 12 - 3 \times 12$.

Solution Do *both* multiplications before the subtraction. Work from left to right.

$$\begin{aligned} & 8 \times 12 - 3 \times 12 \\ = \ & 96 \ - \ 36 \\ = \ & \quad 60 \end{aligned}$$

Example 3 Evaluate $100 \div 20 \times 2$.

Solution Multiplications and divisions have equal priority. So work from left to right. This means do the division first.

$$\begin{aligned} & 100 \div 20 \times 2 \\ = \ & \quad 5 \quad \times 2 \\ = \ & \qquad 10 \end{aligned}$$

Alternate Approach/ Small Group Work
Have students work in pairs or small groups. Provide each group with one non-scientific calculator and one scientific calculator. Have students complete each of the following exercises twice— once with each calculator. Encourage each group to record what key sequence was used and the answer for each exercise.

a. $3 + 4 \times 5$

b. $6 - 2 \div 2$

c. $5 \times 3 - 1$

d. $18 + 12 \div 3$

e. $3 + 7 - 3$

f. $15 \times 9 \div 3$

Ask students if the answer was the same, no matter which calculator was used. (This will depend upon which key sequences were used and which calculators follow the algebraic order of operations.) Ask students if the answers to any of the exercises were the same. (Yes, **c.**, **e.**, and **f.** should have the same answer without regard to which calculator was used.)

Have students invent their own examples. Then allow groups of students to make conjectures about why or why not the same answers were obtained. (Most scientific calculators follow the algebraic order of operations, while arithmetic calculators do not.)

Example 4 Which value is correct for the expression 2×3^4 discussed on page 140?

Solution Calculate the power before doing the multiplication.
$$2 \times 3^4$$
$$= 2 \times 81$$
$$= 162$$

In 3×10^6, the rules for order of operations say to calculate the power first. This is exactly what you would do in scientific notation. So scientific notation follows these rules.

You should check whether your calculator follows all the rules for order of operations. The following example combines three operations and provides a good test of your calculator.

Example 5 Evaluate $10 + 3 \times 4^2$.

Solution First evaluate the power. $10 + 3 \times 4^2 = 10 + 3 \times 16$
Now multiply. $= 10 +\ \ \ 48$
Now add. $= 58$

Questions

Covering the Reading

1. $13.004 - 3.976$ is an example of a __?__ expression.   **numerical**

2. What is the value of the expression in Question 1? **9.028**

3. Finding the value of an expression is called __?__ the expression.
evaluating

4. Why is there a need to have rules for order of operations?
See margin.

In 5–8, an expression contains only the two given operations. Which one should you perform first?

5. division and addition **division**

6. a power and subtraction **power**

7. multiplication and division **whichever is to the left**

8. addition and subtraction **whichever is to the left**

In 9–14, evaluate each expression.

9. $55 - 4 \times 7$ **27**

10. $6 + .03 \times 10$ **6.3**

11. $200 \div 10 \div 2$ **10**

12. $1 \div 9 + 1 \div 7$ **$\overline{.253968}$ ... or $\frac{16}{63}$**

13. $1000 - 3 \times 17^2$ **133**

14. $4^2 + 8^3$ **528**

142

In 15–22, the table on the first page of this chapter will help you.

15. Name three symbols that are used for multiplication, and tell where each is used most often.   **See margin.**

16. Translate "three divided by nine" into symbols in 5 different ways.   **3 ÷ 9, 3/9, $\frac{3}{9}$, 3:9, 9)3̄**

17. How many years ago were the symbols we use for addition and multiplication invented?   **See margin.**

18. When you add, what is the result called?   **sum**

19. When you subtract, what is the result called?   **difference**

20. When you multiply, what is the result called?   **product**

21. When you divide, what is the result called?   **quotient**

22. Why do mathematicians invent symbols?
to make things easier to understand

Applying the Mathematics

23. Calculate the sum of 11 and 4.2.   **15.2**

24. Calculate the product of 6 and 0.3.   **1.8**

25. Calculate 2 divided by 4.   **0.5**

26. Calculate the difference when 0.87 is subtracted from 500.
499.13

In 27–30, each expression is written in a computer language. Evaluate.

27. 2 * 3 + 8   **14**   28. 120 − 3 * 4/4   **117**

29. 200/2 * 10 − 4   **996**   30. 17 + 16 * 3 ↑ 2   **161**

31. *Multiple Choice* Which is largest?   **(c)**
   (a) the sum of .1 and .2
   (b) the product of .1 and .2
   (c) .1 divided by .2
   (d) the second power of .1

32. Find two numbers whose sum is less than their product.
Sample: 2 and 3

33. In which expression below does order of operations make *no* difference?   **87 + 12 − 3**

   87 − 12 + 3   87 + 12 − 3

15. × **is used in arithmetic and on calculators;** · **is used in algebra;** * **is used in some computer languages.**

17. + **about 500 years ago;** × **about 350 years ago;** · **about 300 years ago**

34. Does the angle below appear to be acute, right, or obtuse? *(Lesson 3-6)* **obtuse**

35. Measure the angle to the nearest degree. *(Lesson 3-5)* **115°**

36. Draw a line segment whose length is 14.3 cm. *(Lesson 3-1)*
Check students' segments.

37. Write 0.00000 00000 06543 in scientific notation. *(Lesson 2-9)*
6.543×10^{-12}

38. Some insurance companies give a discount of 15% on homeowner's or renter's insurance if smoke detectors are installed. Suppose you need 3 smoke detectors at $14.99 each. If the insurance bill is $250 a year, will you save money by installing smoke detectors? (They should be installed whether or not you save money.) *(Lesson 2-6)* **You will save money after the first year.**

39. Find the volume of a cube with an edge of length 5 inches. *(Lesson 3-8)* **125 cubic inches**

40. Mathematics is a worldwide language. Mathematicians from different countries usually use the same symbols. Name some symbols outside mathematics that are used throughout the world.
See margin.

41. What is, or was, Esperanto? **See margin.**

42. a. Ask a computer to evaluate the expressions of Questions 27–30 on page 143. (Hint: For Question 27, you should type ?2*3 + 8 and press RETURN.)

b. Does your computer follow the rules for order of operations stated in this lesson? If not, what rules does it seem to follow?
a. Outputs will be 14, 117, 996, 161. b. Yes.

LESSON 4-2

RESOURCES
■ Lesson Master 4-2
▣ Visual for Teaching Aid 20: Describing Patterns with Variables

OBJECTIVES

G Given instances of a pattern, write a description of the pattern using variables.
H Give instances of a pattern described with variables.
I Given instances of a real-world pattern, write a description of the pattern using variables.
O Give rough dates and names of people for key ideas in algebra notation.

A **pattern** is a general idea for which there are many examples. An example of a pattern is called an **instance**. Here are three instances of a pattern with percent.

$$5\% = 5 \times .01$$
$$43.2\% = 43.2 \times .01$$
$$78\% = 78 \times .01$$

In Lesson 2–6, this pattern was described using English words:

The percent sign % means to multiply the number in front of it by $\frac{1}{100}$.

But there is a simpler way to describe this pattern.

$$n\% = n \cdot .01$$

The letter n is called a **variable.** *A variable is a symbol that can stand for any one of a set of numbers or other objects.* Here n can stand for any number. Variables are usually letters. Using $\times$ for multiplication would be confused with using the letter X. So the raised dot $\cdot$ is used instead.

Descriptions with variables have two major advantages over descriptions using words. They look like the instances. Also, they are shorter than the verbal descriptions.

Here are three instances of another pattern.

$$\frac{3}{3} = 1 \qquad \frac{657.2}{657.2} = 1 \qquad \frac{2/5}{2/5} = 1$$

A description using words for the pattern is: If a number is divided by itself, the quotient is equal to one. Another description is: If the numerator and denominator of a fraction are the same number, the value of the fraction is 1. The description with variables is shorter and looks like the instances.

$$\frac{t}{t} = 1$$

We could have used any other letter or symbol in place of t.

TEACHING NOTES

Reading You may wish to have students read this lesson aloud in class. As they do so, stop at each pattern. Ask the students to describe the pattern in their own words before they read the explanation in the text or examine the description with variables.

Suggest that students who find describing patterns difficult determine the elements that stay the same in all instances. Then have them note the numbers that change from one instance to another to determine what happens within one instance. Finally, have students describe the pattern with variables and check the description against the instances given.

1. Give three instances of each pattern.
a. $p + p = 2p$
sample: $3 + 3 = 2 \cdot 3$
b. d tripods have $3 \cdot d$ legs
sample: 5 tripods have $3 \cdot 5$ legs

2. Give the pattern describing these instances. Your pattern should use one variable.
a. $5 + 2 > 5$
$8 + 2 > 8$
$\frac{3}{4} + 2 > \frac{3}{4}$
$a + 2 > a$

b. The area of a square with a side of 4 inches is 4×4 squares inches. The area of a square with a side of .5 inches is $.5 \times .5$ square inches. The area of a square with a side of $2\frac{1}{2}$ inches is $2\frac{1}{2} \times 2\frac{1}{2}$ square inches.
The area of a square with a side of s inches is $s \cdot s$ square inches.

NOTES ON QUESTIONS
Error Analysis for Question 16: Students who write $5 \cdot a = 3 \cdot b + 2 \cdot c$ have seen a pattern but have missed a commonality. Urge students who make this error to read and follow directions carefully. In this case, the directions indicate that only one variable is needed.

Question 17: Notice that we do not calculate the $3 \cdot 100$ or $3 \cdot 5$ because that would disguise the pattern. In the real world, however, such operations would be performed, and the pattern would be more difficult to describe.

ADDITIONAL ANSWERS
1. a symbol that can stand for any one of a set of numbers or other objects

Some patterns need more than one variable to be described. Here is a pattern that requires two different variables. You've seen this pattern before.

$$1.43 + 2.9 = 2.9 + 1.43$$
$$12 + 37 = 37 + 12$$
$$\tfrac{8}{3} + \tfrac{7}{5} = \tfrac{7}{5} + \tfrac{8}{3}$$

Description using variables:
$$a + b = b + a$$

A correct description of a pattern must work for *all* instances. This pattern works for all numbers. It works whether you use decimals or fractions. It is so important that it has a special name you may already know: the commutative property of addition. You will study this property in the next chapter.

Patterns with words can also be described with variables. Here are four instances of a pattern.

> One person has 2 eyes.
> Two people have four eyes in all.
> Three people have 6 eyes in all.
> Four people have 8 eyes in all.

To describe this pattern with variables, rewrite the instances in a convenient way.

> 1 person has $2 \cdot 1$ eyes.
> 2 people have $2 \cdot 2$ eyes in all.
> 3 people have $2 \cdot 3$ eyes in all.
> 4 people have $2 \cdot 4$ eyes in all.

Now a description is easy. It will look like the instances. Let p be any natural number.

> p people have $2 \cdot p$ eyes in all.

Elementary algebra is the study of variables and the operations of arithmetic with variables. Algebra is generally considered to have begun in 1591. In that year, François Viète (Fraw swah Vee yet), a French mathematician, first used variables to describe patterns. Viète's work quickly led to a great deal more mathematics being invented. Within 100 years, the ideas behind almost all of algebra and calculus has been discovered. (Notice how many symbols in the chart opening this chapter were invented in the 1600s.) For this reason, Viète is sometimes called the ''father of algebra.''

146

Covering the Reading

1. What is a variable?   See margin.

2. What use of variables is explained in this lesson?
Variables can help describe patterns.

3. Name two advantages of using variables to describe patterns.
They look like the instances. They are shorter.

In 4–7, give three instances of the pattern being described by variables.

4. $x/x = 1$

5. $n\% = n \cdot .01$ See margin.

6. p people have $2 \cdot p$ eyes.   **7.** $x + y = y + x$

8. Who was the first person to use variables to describe patterns?
François Viète

9. What does elementary algebra study?   Variables and the operations of arithmetic with them.

10. Who is sometimes called the "father of algebra"?   François Viète

11. *Multiple Choice*   Algebra was developed about how many years ago?
(a) 100   (b) 200   (c) 400   (d) 1700   (c)

Applying the Mathematics

In 12–14, give three instances of each pattern.

12. $12 + y = 5 + y + 7$ See margin.

13. $6 \cdot a + 13 \cdot a = 19 \cdot a$ See margin.

14. If your book is d days overdue, your fine will be $20 + d \cdot 5$ cents.
See margin.

In 15–17, three instances of a general pattern are given. Describe the pattern using variables. Only one variable is needed for each description.

15. $10 \cdot 0 = 0$
$8.9 \cdot 0 = 0$
$\frac{15}{5} \cdot 0 = 0$ $a \cdot 0 = 0$

16. $5 \cdot 40 = 3 \cdot 40 + 2 \cdot 40$
$5 \cdot \frac{3}{8} = 3 \cdot \frac{3}{8} + 2 \cdot \frac{3}{8}$
$5 \cdot 0.2995 = 3 \cdot 0.2995 + 2 \cdot 0.2995$
$5 \cdot n = 3 \cdot n + 2 \cdot n$

17. In 3 years, we expect $3 \cdot 100$ more students and $3 \cdot 5$ more teachers.
In 4 years, we expect $4 \cdot 100$ more students and $4 \cdot 5$ more teachers.
In 1 year, we expect 100 more students and 5 more teachers.
See margin.

---

4. sample: $\frac{3}{3} = 1$; $\frac{7.2}{7.2} = 1$;
$\frac{5}{5} = 1$

5. sample: 5% = 5 × .01;
1.2% = 1.2 × .01;
300% = 300 × .01

6. sample: 3 people have
2 · 3 eyes; 5 people have
2 · 5 eyes; 165 people have
2 · 165 eyes

7. sample: 3 + 4 = 4 + 3;
$\frac{1}{2} + \frac{3}{4} = \frac{3}{4} + \frac{1}{2}$;
0.8 + 6 = 6 + 0.8

12. sample: 12 + 3 = 5 + 3
+ 7; 12 + 0 = 5 + 0 + 7;
12 + 8.8 = 5 + 8.8 + 7

13. sample: 6 · 4 + 13 · 4 =
19 · 4; 6 · 9.7 + 13 · 9.7 =
19 · 9.7; 6 · 100 + 13 · 100 =
19 · 100

14. sample: For 8 days
overdue, your fine will be
20 + 8 · 5 cents; for 2 days
overdue, your fine will be
20 + 2 · 5 cents; for 365
days overdue, your fine will
be 20 + 365 · 5 cents.

17. In n years we expect
$n \cdot 100$ more students and
$n \cdot 5$ more teachers.

18. Give three instances of the pattern $a \cdot b = b \cdot a$.   **See margin.**

19. Three instances of a pattern are given. Describe the pattern using two variables.

$$\frac{1}{3} + \frac{5}{3} = \frac{1+5}{3} \qquad \frac{a}{3} + \frac{b}{3} = \frac{a+b}{3}$$

$$\frac{11}{3} + \frac{46}{3} = \frac{11+46}{3}$$

$$\frac{0}{3} + \frac{7}{3} = \frac{0+7}{3}$$

20. Li noticed that $3 + .5$ is not an integer, $4 + .5$ is not an integer, and $7.8 + .5$ is not an integer.
a. Describe a general pattern of these three instances.
b. Find an instance where the general pattern is not true.
c. Explain why the pattern is not always true.   **See margin.**

Review

In 21–26, evaluate. *(Lessons 2-2, 2-5, 4-1)*

21. $25\% \times 60 + 40$ **55**

22. $7 \times 2 \times 8 - 7 \times 2$ **98**

23. $60 + 40 \div 4 + 4$ **74**

24. $12.5 - 11.5 \div 5$ **10.2**

25. $12 - 3^2$ **3**

26. $170 - 5^3$ **45**

In 27 and 28, translate into mathematical symbols. Then evaluate. *(Lessons 1-2, 4-1)*

27. fifty divided by one ten-thousandth   **50/.0001; 500,000**

28. the product of five hundred and five hundredths   **500 · .05; 25**

29. 300 centimeters is how many meters? *(Lesson 3-3)*   **3 meters**

Exploration

30. Show that the pattern $x^2 > x$ is false by finding an instance that is not true.   **Sample: $0.1^2 < 0.1$**

In 31–34, for each sequence of numbers: **a.** Find a pattern. **b.** Describe the pattern you have found in words or with variables. **c.** Write the next term according to your pattern.   **See below.**

31. 6, 12, 18, 24, 30, …

32. 1, 4, 9, 16, 25, …

33. 5, 6, 9, 10, 13, 14, …

34. $\frac{1}{3}, \frac{8}{3}, \frac{27}{3}, \frac{64}{3}, \frac{125}{3}, \ldots$

Samples for 31–34 follow:
31. b. Add 6 to each number to get the next number. c. 36
32. b. Square the natural numbers to get the numbers. c. 36
33. b. Alternately add 1 and 3 to get the next number. c. 17
34. b. Take the cube of each natural number, then divide by 3. c. $\frac{216}{3}$

148

4-3

Translating Expressions

Translation from one language to another is an important communication skill.

RESOURCES
■Lesson Master 4-3

OBJECTIVES

J Write a numerical expression for an English expression involving arithmetic operations.

K Write an algebraic expression for an English expression involving arithmetic operations.

Recall from Lesson 4-1 that $4 + 52$, $9 - 6 \cdot 7$, and $\frac{1}{6}$ are examples of numerical expressions. If an expression contains a variable alone or with number and operation symbols, it is called an **algebraic expression.** Here are some algebraic expressions.

$$t \qquad 3 \cdot a^2 \qquad \frac{z + 400.3}{5} \qquad m - n + m$$

The value of an algebraic expression depends on what is substituted for the variables.

You know how to translate English into numerical expressions.

English expression	numerical expression
the sum of three and five	$3 + 5$
the product of two tenths and fifty	$.2 \times 50$

In the same way, English expressions can be translated into algebraic expressions.

English expression	algebraic expression
the sum of a number and five	$n + 5$
the product of length and width	$\ell \cdot w$

However, many English expressions can translate into the same algebraic expression. The following chart shows some common English expressions and their translations. Notice that in subtraction you must be careful about the order of the numbers.

English expression	algebraic expression
a number *plus* five the *sum* of a number and 5 a number *increased* by five five *more than* a number *add* five to a number	$a + 5$ or $5 + a$

a number *minus* eight
subtract 8 from a number
8 *less than* a number
a number *decreased by* 8

$\Rightarrow \quad h - 8$

eight *minus* a number
subtract a number from 8
8 *less* a number
8 *decreased by* a number

$\Rightarrow \quad 8 - n$

Example 1 A person's annual salary is S. It is increased by $700. What is the new salary?

Solution $S + \$700$

Often you have a choice of what letter to use for a number. We used the letter S in Example 1 because the word "salary" begins with that letter.

Example 2 Esther is five years younger than her sister Ann. If Ann's age is A, what expression stands for Esther's age?

Solution Esther's age is five less than Ann's.
Five less than A is $A - 5$.

Here are some English expressions for multiplication and division. In division as in subtraction, you must be careful about the order of the numbers.

English expression	**algebraic expression**
two *times* a number the *product* of two and a number *twice* a number	$\Rightarrow \quad 2 \cdot m$ or $m \cdot 2$
six *divided by* a number a number *into* six	$\Rightarrow \quad \dfrac{6}{u}$
a number *divided by* six six *into* a number	$\Rightarrow \quad \dfrac{u}{6}$

150

Some English expressions combine operations.

■ ■ ■ ■ ■ ■ ■ ■ ■■

Example 3   Translate "five times a number, increased by 3."

> **Solution**   Let n stand for the number.
> Five times n is $5 \cdot n$.
> $5 \cdot n$ increased by 3 is $5 \cdot n + 3$, or $3 + 5 \cdot n$.

In Example 3, suppose there were no comma after the word "number." The expression "five times a number increased by 3" would then be ambiguous. *Ambiguous* means the expression has more than one possible meaning. We would not know whether to increase by 3 or to multiply by 5 first.

One of the most important abilities to have in mathematics is the ability to translate from English into mathematics. In this book, in every chapter, you will work at increasing that ability.

Questions

Covering the Reading

1. What is the difference between a numerical expression and an algebraic expression?   See margin.

In 2–11, let n stand for the number. Then translate the English into an algebraic expression.

2. twice the number $2 \cdot n$

3. three more than the number $n + 3$ or $3 + n$

4. the number multiplied by four $n \cdot 4$ or $4 \cdot n$

5. the number less five $n - 5$

6. six less the number $6 - n$

7. seven less than the number $n - 7$

8. eight into the number $n/8$

9. the number divided by nine $n/9$

10. the number increased by ten $n + 10$

11. eleven decreased by the number $11 - n$

12. What is the meaning of the word "ambiguous"?
having more than one meaning

13. Give an example of an English expression that is ambiguous.
See margin.

ADDITIONAL EXAMPLES
Translate the English into a numerical or algebraic expression.
1. the new weight of a person who weighed p pounds and then gained three-and-a-half pounds $p + 3.5$

2. the temperature if it was d degrees and dropped ten degrees $d - 10$

3. a number n divided into one hundred $\frac{100}{n}$

4. three times five, plus two $3 \times 5 + 2$

5. eight more than five squared $5^2 + 8$

NOTES ON QUESTIONS
Questions 6, 7, and 23:
These deal with the distinction among *less, less than,* and *is less than.* Many students need practice differentiating these terms.

ADDITIONAL ANSWERS
1. A numerical expression contains only numbers and operation symbols; an algebraic expression contains a variable or variables as well.

13. sample: five times a number increased by six

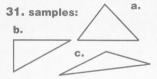
In 14 and 15, give three possible English expressions for the algebraic expression.

14. $x + 10$ See margin.   **15.** $2 - y$ See margin.

16. Translate "a number times six, decreased by five" into an algebraic expression. $6 \cdot n - 5$

17. Tell why "fourteen less five plus three" is ambiguous.   See margin.

In working with a number between 0 and 1, the word "of" is often a signal to multiply. In 18–19, translate into a variable expression. Use t to stand for the number.

18. half of the number $\frac{1}{2} \cdot t$

19. 6% of the number $6\% \cdot t$ or $.06 \cdot t$

20. Write two algebraic expressions for "a number times itself" using two different operations. $t \cdot t, t^2$

21. A person's salary is currently C dollars a week. Write an expression for the new salary if:
  a. the person gets a raise of $50 a week. $C + 50$
  b. the salary is lowered by $12 a week. $C - 12$
  c. the salary is tripled. $C \cdot 3$

22. "Trebled" means "multiplied by three."
  a. What does "quintupled" mean?
  b. What is a word for "multiplying by four"?
  a. multiplied by five; b. quadrupled

The price of a home trebled in 20 years.

23. Translate the following different ideas into mathematics.
  a. Six is less than a number. $6 < n$
  b. six less than a number $n - 6$
  c. six less a number $6 - n$

24. Why is the "quotient of 2 and 4" an ambiguous phrase?
It could mean $\frac{2}{4}$ or $\frac{4}{2}$.

152

25. Measure this segment to the nearest eighth of an inch. *(Lesson 3-1)*
$2\frac{1}{2}$ or $2\frac{4}{8}$ inches

26. Give three instances of this pattern. *(Lesson 4-2)*
$7 \cdot x - 6 \cdot x = x$ See margin.

27. Three instances of a general pattern are given. Describe the pattern using one variable. *(Lesson 4-2)*
1 million/1 = 1 million
$10^2/1 = 10^2$
$8.3/1 = 8.3$ $a/1 = a$

28. Three instances of a general pattern are given. Describe the pattern using two variables. *(Lesson 4-2)*
$4 + 5 + 12 - 5 = 4 + 12$
$\frac{1}{2} + 5 + \frac{1}{3} - 5 = \frac{1}{2} + \frac{1}{3}$
$1.7 + 5 + 6 - 5 = 1.7 + 6$
$a + 5 + b - 5 = a + b$

29. It is about 1110 km by air from Paris to Rome. In miles, how far is it? *(Lesson 3-4)*   about 688.2 miles

30. The USSR won about 21% of the 138 medals awarded at the 1988 Winter Olympic Games. This was the most medals awarded to one country during those games. How many medals did the USSR win? *(Lesson 2-6)*   29 medals

31. a. Draw a triangle with three acute angles.
b. Draw a triangle with a right angle.
c. Draw a triangle with an obtuse angle. *(Lesson 3-6)*   See margin.

32. Find the volume of a cubical box with 10-foot sides. *(Lesson 3-8)*
1000 cubic feet

33. Write 10^{-5} as **a.** a decimal and **b.** a percent. *(Lessons 2-7, 2-8)*
a. .00001; b. .001%

In 34–37, for each sequence of numbers: **a.** Find a pattern. **b.** Describe the pattern you have found in words or with variables. **c.** Write the next term according to your pattern.   See below.

34. 2, 5, 8, 11, 14, . . .   **35.** 1, 3, 6, 10, 15, 21, . . .

36. 1, 1, 2, 3, 5, 8, 13, . . . **37.** 4, 7, 13, 25, 49, . . .

Samples for 34–37 follow:
34. b. Add 3 to each number to get the next number. c. 17
35. b. Add 2, then 3, then 4, and so on. c. 28
36. b. Add the previous two numbers to get the next. c. 21
37. b. Add 3, then 6, then 12, doubling what you add each time. c. 97

FOLLOW-UP

MORE PRACTICE
For more questions on SPUR Objectives, use *Lesson Master 4-3*, shown below.

EXTENSION
The numbers in the sequence in Question 36 are often called the Fibonacci numbers. Have students find out something about Fibonacci, the sequence, and the rabbit problem associated with the sequence.

EVALUATION
Alternative Assessment
Write four algebraic expressions on the board, one for each basic operation with the same number, for example:
$m + 2$; $m - 2$; $2 \cdot m$; $\frac{m}{2}$.
As the students consider each algebraic expression in turn, ask for as many English expressions as possible that would be appropriate for it.

NAME _____

LESSON **MASTER 4-3**
QUESTIONS ON SPUR OBJECTIVES

■**USES** *Objective J (See Chapter Review, pages 183–185, for objectives.)*
In 1–8, translate into mathematical symbols.

1. the sum of twenty-nine and twelve	$29 + 12$
2. forty less than three thousand five hundred	$3500 - 40$
3. thirty less twenty-five	$30 - 25$
4. the product of nine and thirty, increased by five	$9 \cdot 30 + 5$
5. the quotient of forty-five, divided by nine	$\frac{45}{9}$
6. sixteen more than the product of twenty and three	$16 + 20 \cdot 3$
7. three minus three thousandths	$3 - .003$
8. eight ten-thousandths plus six ten-thousandths	$.0008 + .0006$

■**USES** *Objective K*
In 9–15, translate into algebra. Let the number be n.

9. A number is greater than seventy-two.	$n > 72$
10. seventy-two divided by a number, decreased by nine	$\frac{72}{n} - 9$
11. A number is increased by one third.	$n + \frac{1}{3}$
12. Thirty-two is less than the product of twelve and a number.	$32 < 12 \cdot n$
13. twice a number into twenty-four	$\frac{24}{2n}$
14. a number times three decreased by four	$n \cdot (3 - 4)$ or $n \cdot 3 - 4$
15. twice a number plus the same number	$2n + n$

Transition Mathematics ⊙ Scott, Foresman and Company

LESSON

4-4

Evaluating Algebraic Expressions

A library charges 20¢ if a book is not returned on time. Added to the fine is 5¢ for each day overdue. Now let n be the number of days overdue. Then the fine is

$$20 + 5 \cdot n \text{ cents.}$$

The fine can now be calculated for *any number* of days overdue. For a book 13 days overdue, just replace n by 13. The fine is

$$20 + 5 \cdot 13 \text{ cents,}$$

which computes to 85¢.

We say that 13 days is the **value of the variable** n. We can write $n = 13$. The quantity 85¢ is the **value of the expression.** We have evaluated the expression by letting $n = 13$ and finding the value of the resulting expression.

Example	Expression	Value of variable	Value of expression
1	$25 - 3 \cdot n$	2	$25 - 3 \cdot 2 = 19$
2	$25 - 3 \cdot n$	8	$25 - 3 \cdot 8 = 1$
3	$x - 9$	500	$500 - 9 = 491$
4	$x - 9$	9.243	$9.243 - 9 = 0.243$
5	$y^4 + 5$	30	$30^4 + 5 = 810,000 + 5$ $= 810,005$
6	$36 - 2^p$	3	$36 - 2^3 = 36 - 8 = 28$

154

We have been using a dot to stand for multiplication. When one of the numbers being multiplied is a variable, the dot is usually not used.

With · for multiplication	Without ·
$6 \cdot t$	$6t$
$25 - 3 \cdot n$	$25 - 3n$
$4 \cdot A + 5 \cdot B$	$4A + 5B$

The rules for order of operations apply even when the multiplication symbol is absent.

Example

	Expression	Value of variable	Value of expression
7	$6y$	4	$6 \cdot 4 = 24$
8	$20 + 5n$	60	$20 + 5 \cdot 60 = 320$
9	πr^2	5	$\pi \cdot 5^2 = \pi \cdot 25$ $\approx 3.14 \cdot 25$ ≈ 78.5
10	$4A + 3B$	$A = 10, B = 7$	$4 \cdot 10 + 3 \cdot 7 = 61$

In Example 10 the expression contains more than one variable. So you need a value for each variable to get a numerical value for the expression.

TEACHING NOTES

Reading Because the main idea of this lesson is conveyed almost exclusively through examples, you may want to review with your students how to study examples. For instance, you might ask a student to read **Example 6** aloud. Then ask the class, "Why was this example given?" (It reinforces the point that powers are done before subtractions.) Finally, go over the evaluation of the expression in the last column, asking questions about the computation.

ADDITIONAL EXAMPLES
Evaluate the expression for the given value of the variable.
1. $12 - 2 \cdot m$, for $m = 1.5$ **9**

2. $25g + g$, for $g = 3$ **78**

3. $3r^4$, for $r = 2$ **48**

4. $5x^2 + 3x$, for $x = 6$ **198**
5. $85 - 10p$, for $p = \frac{1}{2}$ **80**
6. $6a + 5b$, for $a = 2$, $b = 1$ **17**
7. $3c - \frac{1}{2}d$, for $c = \frac{1}{2}$, $d = 3$ **0**
8. $25 + 3y$, for $y = \frac{1}{3}$ **26**

Questions

Covering the Reading

1. *Multiple choice* If $n = 3$, then $5 \cdot n =$ **(c)**
   (a) 53   (b) 8   (c) 15   (d) none of these

In 2–5, consider the expression $5 \cdot n$ from Question 1. Identify the:

2. variable   *n*

3. value of the variable   3

4. expression $5 \cdot n$

5. value of the expression   15

6. What is the more usual way for writing $5 \cdot n$?   *5n*

7. Do the rules for order of operations apply to variables?   yes

LESSON 4-4 Evaluating Algebraic Expressions   **155**

In 8–10, suppose that a book is n days overdue and the fine is $20 + 5n$ cents. Calculate the fine for a book that is:

8. 1 day overdue 25¢　　　　**9.** 6 days overdue 50¢

10. 20 days overdue $1.20

11. Which example of this lesson calculates the fine for a book that is 60 days overdue? **example 8**

In 12–15, evaluate each expression when d is 5.

12. $d + d$ 10　　　　　　　**13.** $88 - 4d$ 68

14. $2 + 3d$ 17　　　　　　　**15.** $d\%$ 5%

In 16–19, give the value of each expression when $m = 5$ and $x = 9$.

16. $4m + 7x$ 83　　　　　　**17.** $2mx$ 90

18. $1.6x + m^3$ 139.4　　　　**19.** πx^2 exactly 81π, about 254.469

Applying the Mathematics

20. Let A be an age between 1 and 7 years. A boy of age A weighs, on the average, about $17 + 5A$ pounds.
　　a. What is the average weight for 6-year-old boys? **47 lb**
　　b. What is the average weight for 2-year-old boys? **27 lb**
　　c. For each additional year of age, by how much does the average weight change? **5 lb**

21. Suppose x is 100 and y is 25.
　　a. Evaluate $xy - yx$. **0**
　　b. Will the answer to part **a** change if the values of x and y are changed? Why or why not? **See margin.**

22. **a.** Evaluate $2v + 1$ when v is 1, 2, 3, 4, and 5. **3, 5, 7, 9, 11**
　　b. Your answers to part **a** should form a pattern. Describe the pattern in English. **See margin.**

In 23–25, **a.** translate into an algebraic expression. **b.** Evaluate that expression when the number has the value 10.

23. eight less than five times a number a. $5n - 8$; b. 42

24. the product of a number and 4, increased by nine a. $4n + 9$; b. 49

25. the third power of a number a. n^3; b. 1000

Review

In 26 and 27, three instances of a pattern are given. Describe the pattern using one variable. *(Lesson 4-2)*

26.　　$5 + 0 = 5$
　　　　$43.0 + 0 = 43.0$
　　　　$1/2 + 0 = 1/2$
　　　　$a + 0 = a$

27.　$1 \times 60\% = 60\%$
　　　$1 \times 2 = 2$
　　　$1 \times 1 = 1$
　　　$1 \times b = b$

156

28. Four horses have 4 · 4 legs, 2 · 4 ears, and 4 tails. *(Lesson 4-2)*
   a. Six horses have 4 · 6 legs, 2 · __?__ ears, and __?__ tails.   **6, 6**
   b. Eleven horses have __?__ legs, __?__ ears, and __?__ tails.
   c. *h* horses have __?__ legs, __?__ ears, and __?__ tails.   **4h, 2h, h**
      b. 4 · 11, 2 · 11; 11

29. *Multiple choice*   Which is largest? *(Lesson 4-3)*   **(a)**
   (a) the sum of 10 and 1   (b) the product of 10 and 1
   (c) 10 divided by 1   (d) 10 to the first power

30. What is the metric prefix meaning $\frac{1}{1000}$? *(Lesson 3-3)*   **milli-**

31. Which two of these refer to the same numbers? *(Lessons 1-1, 1-5)*
   (a) the whole numbers   (b) the natural numbers   **(b) and (d)**
   (c) the integers   (d) the positive integers

32. Convert $\frac{2.4}{10.24}$ into a simple fraction in lowest terms. *(Lesson 2-7)*
   $\frac{15}{64}$

Exploration

33. A library decides to charge *m* cents for an overdue book and *A* more cents for every day the book is overdue. What will be the fine for a book that is *d* days overdue?   **m + A · d**

34. Computers can evaluate algebraic expressions. Here is a program that evaluates a particular expression.

```
10   PRINT "GIVE VALUE OF YOUR VARIABLE"
20   INPUT X
30   V = 30 * X − 12
40   PRINT "VALUE OF EXPRESSION IS", V
50   END
```

   a. What expression does the above program evaluate?   **30X − 12**
   b. What value does the computer give if you input 3.5 for X?   **93**
   c. Modify the program so that it evaluates the expression
      $25X + X^4$ and test your program when X = 1, X = 2, and
      X = 17. What values do you get?   **26; 66; 83,946**

FOLLOW-UP

MORE PRACTICE
For more questions on SPUR Objectives, use *Lesson Master 4-4*, shown below.

EVALUATION
A quiz covering Lessons 4-1 through 4-4 is provided in the Teacher's Resource File on page 31.

NAME _____

LESSON **MASTER   4–4**
QUESTIONS ON SPUR OBJECTIVES

■**SKILLS**   *Objective C (See Chapter Review, pages 183–185, for objectives.)*
In 1–10, evaluate each expression if *a* = 9, *c* = 2, *t* = 11, and *u* = 0.

1. $t + a^4 =$ **6572**   2. $5c^2 - c + 6 =$ **24**
3. $3t - 4 + u =$ **29**   4. $12 - c^2 \cdot 5 =$ **10**
5. $6a + c + 3t + 2u =$ **89**   6. $17 + \frac{a^3}{3} =$ **260**
7. $9c^2 =$ **36**   8. $5a + 2t =$ **67**
9. $4 + ac + 3 =$ **10**   10. $ut^{10} =$ **0**

In 11–14, let *x* = 10 and *y* = 3. Evaluate each expression.

11. $3x + y =$ **33**   12. $4x^3 =$ **4000**
13. $yx - xy =$ **0**   14. $\frac{1}{2}x + \frac{1}{2}y =$ **6½**

In 15–19, a. translate into an algebraic expression. b. Evaluate that expression when the number has the value 8.

15. a number squared
   a. n^2 b. **64**
16. the product of a number and nine, increased by five.
   a. **9n + 5**   b. **77**
17. two more than the quotient of 4 divided by a number
   a. **4 ÷ n + 2**   b. **2½**
18. the product of five and the square of a number
   a. **5n²**   b. **320**
19. the sum of 16.4, and a number less twenty
   a. **16.4 + (n − 20)**   b. **4.4**

32   *Transition Mathematics* © Scott, Foresman and Company

LESSON

4-5

Parentheses

*These chicks are working from inside their shells to free themselves.
This is akin to what is done when working with parentheses.*

Consider the expression $3 + 4 \cdot 5$. By order of operations, the
multiplication will be done first.

$$3 + 4 \cdot 5$$
$$= 3 + 20$$
$$= 23$$

But what if you want to do the addition first? Then you can use
parentheses.

Parentheses have priority.

$$(3 + 4) \cdot 5$$
$$= (7) \cdot 5$$
$$= 35$$

Parentheses around a single number can always be dropped.
$(7) = 7$. Many students and teachers find it useful to write the
steps of calculations vertically as we have in the examples below.
This helps them avoid errors and makes their work easy to follow.

■ ▪ ▪ ▪ ▪ ▪ ▪ ▪ ■

Example 1   Simplify $7 + 9 \cdot (2 + 3)$.

Solution   Work inside parentheses first.
$$= 7 + 9 \cdot (5)$$
$$= 7 + 9 \cdot 5$$
Now the usual order of operations applies.
$$= 7 + 45$$
$$= 52$$

158

■ ■ ■ ■ ■ ■ ■
Example 2   Evaluate $36 - (17 - n)$ when $n = 4$.

Solution First substitute 4 for n. $36 - (17 - 4)$
Work inside parentheses. $= 36 - (13)$
Drop the parentheses. $= 36 - 13$
                           $= 23$

Parentheses even have priority over taking powers.

■ ■ ■ ■ ■ ■ ■ ■
Example 3   Evaluate $6 + 5 \cdot (4x)^3$ when $x = 2$.

Solution First substitute 2 for x. $6 + 5 \cdot (4 \cdot 2)^3$
Work inside parentheses. $= 6 + 5 \cdot (8)^3$
Powering comes next. $= 6 + 5 \cdot 512$
Multiplication comes next. $= 6 + 2560$
Addition comes last. $= 2566$

The dot for multiplication is usually deleted with parentheses. For the expression of Example 3, it is more common to see $6 + 5(4x)^3$. The 5 next to the parentheses signals multiplication.

■ ■ ■ ■ ■ ■ ■ ■
Example 4   Evaluate $(y + 15)(11 - 2y)$ when $y = 3$.

Solution 1 Substitute 3 for y. $(3 + 15)(11 - 2 \cdot 3)$
Work inside each ( ), following the usual order of operations.
$$= (18)(11 - 6)$$
No operation sign between)(means multiplication.
$$= 18 \cdot 5$$
$$= 90$$

Most scientific calculators have parentheses keys ⟨ and ⟩. To use these keys, just enter the parentheses where they appear in the problem. But remember the hidden multiplications. Here is Example 4, done with a calculator.

Solution 2 Key in: ⟨ 3 + 15 ⟩ × ⟨ 11 − 2 × 3 ⟩ =
The problem without calculators is not very difficult. The calculator solution requires many keystrokes. So unless the numbers are quite complicated, most people prefer not to use a calculator for this kind of problem.

TEACHING NOTES

Reading This is a good lesson for students to read on their own. The tricky details, such as using parentheses with exponents and calculators, are covered clearly in the examples. If students study the examples step-by-step as instructed, the new ideas should be reasonably clear. The rest of the material is a further review of order of operations and variables.

Error Analysis If students repeatedly make mistakes when evaluating expressions, suggest that they write out the steps in order-of-operation problems. Writing out steps forces students to think about the proper order and eliminates many careless mistakes. The solutions should follow the pattern established in the examples in the text.

It is possible to have parentheses inside parentheses. These are called **nested parentheses.** With nested parentheses, work inside the innermost parentheses first.

Example 5   Simplify $300 - (40 + .6(30 - 8))$

Solution $= 300 - (40 + .6(22))$ Work the inside ( ) first.
$= 300 - (40 + 13.2)$ Multiply before adding.
$= 300 - (53.2)$ Work the remaining ( ).
$= 246.8$ $(53.2) = 53.2$

Some calculators enable you to nest parentheses; some do not. You should explore your calculator to see what it allows.

Questions

Covering the Reading

1. What is one reason for using parentheses?
to change order of operations

In 2–5, *true or false*?

2. $5 + 4 \times 3 = (5 + 4) \times 3$ **3.** $5 + 4 \times 3 = 5 + (4 \times 3)$
false   true

4. $5(3) = 15$ true   **5.** $2 + (4) = 8$ false

6. *Multiple Choice*   In evaluating an expression with parentheses: (c)
(a) First do additions or subtractions, from left to right.
(b) First do multiplications or divisions, from left to right.
(c) First work inside parentheses.
(d) First do exponents.
(e) Work from left to right regardless of the operation.

In 7–11, evaluate.

7. $4 + 3(7 + 9)$ 52   **8.** $(12)(3 + 4)$ 84

9. $10 + 20 \div (2 + 3 \cdot 6)$ **10.** $40 - (30 - 5)$ 15
11
11. $(6 + 6)(6 - 6)$ 0

12. Multiplication occurs twice in the expression $2(5 + 4n)$. What are these places?   See margin.

13. Suppose $n = 8$. Write the key sequence that will evaluate $2(5 + 4n)$ on your calculator.   See margin.

In 14–17, $a = 2$, $b = 3$, and $c = 5$. Evaluate each expression.

14. $0.30(c - b)$ 0.6   **15.** $(a + b)(7a + 2b)$ 100

16. $(a + 100b) - (7a - 2b)$ **17.** $20a + 5(c - 3)$ 50
294

160

160

18. What are nested parentheses?   parentheses inside parentheses

19. a. To simplify $1000 - (100 - (10 - 1))$, what should you do first? $10 - 1$
   b. Simplify $1000 - (100 - (10 - 1))$.   909

20. Evaluate $2(x + 12) - 3$ when $x = 8$.   37

21. Evaluate $3 + x(2 + x(1 + x))$ when $x = 5$.   163

Applying the Mathematics

In 22 and 23, when $n = 3$, do the two expressions have the same value?

22. $4(n + 2)$ and $4n + 8$ yes

23. $33 - 7n$ and $(33 - 7)n$ no

In 24 and 25, let a be 10 and b be 31. Which expression has the larger value?

24. $b - (a - 2)$ or $b - a - 2$ $b - (a - 2)$

25. $a + 4(b + 3)$ or $(a + 4)b + 3$ $(a + 4)b + 3$

26. *Multiple Choice*   Begin with a number n. Add 5 to it. Multiply the sum by 4. What number results?
   (a) $n + 5 \cdot 4$
   (b) $4(n + 5)$
   (c) $n + 5 + n \cdot 4$
   (d) $n + 5 + (n + 5)4$ (b)

27. *Multiple Choice*   Begin with a number t. Multiply it by 3. Add 2 to the product. What number results?
   (a) $5t$ (b) $3 + 2t$ (c) $3(t + 2)$ (d) $3t + 2$ (d)

28. Three instances of a pattern are given. Describe the general pattern using three variables.
$$11(3 + 2) = 11 \cdot 3 + 11 \cdot 2$$
$$5(12 + 19.3) = 5 \cdot 12 + 5 \cdot 19.3$$
$$2(0 + 6) = 2 \cdot 0 + 2 \cdot 6 \qquad a(b + c) = ab + ac$$

29. Evaluate $2(3 + n(n + 1) + 5)$ when $n = 14$.   436

In 30 and 31, insert parentheses to make the sentence true.

30. $16 - 15 - 9 = 10$ $16 - (15 - 9) = 10$

31. $16 - 8 - 4 - 2 = 14$ $16 - (8 - 4 - 2) = 14$

Review

32. In many places in the Midwest, a township is a square 6 miles on a side. What is the area of a township? *(Lesson 3-7)*   36 square miles

In 33 and 34, consider the expression $6T + E + 3F + 2S$. *(Lessons 4-3, 4-4)*

33. Evaluate this expression when $T = 3$, $E = 2$, $F = 1$, and $S = 0$.   23

34. This expression has something to do with scoring in football. The letters T, E, F, and S have been chosen carefully. With these hints:
   a. What precisely do T, E, F, and S stand for?   See margin.
   b. What does the value of the expression tell you?   the total score

LESSON 4-5   Parentheses   **161**

NOTES ON QUESTIONS
Making Connections for Questions 30 and 31:
Encourage students to use trial and error to devise some sort of method for inserting trial parentheses. (*Trial and error* is a problem-solving strategy described in detail in Chapter 6.) For example, in **Question 31**, suggest that students first try parentheses around the first two terms, then around the next two, and finally around the last two terms. If none of these arrangements works, they may try parentheses around three terms at a time.

You may need to give the students some suggestions for analyzing the problem. For example, noticing that the answer, 14, is two less than 16 in **Question 31** can help a student focus on making the second part of the left-hand side subtract to equal 2.

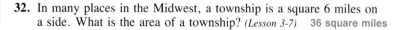

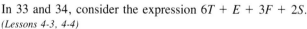

NAME _____

LESSON **MASTER   4–5**
QUESTIONS ON **SPUR** OBJECTIVES

■SKILLS   *Objectives B, C, and F (See pages 183–185 for objectives.)*

1. When you evaluate an expression such as $(2n)^3$, should parentheses or exponent be worked first?   parentheses

2. When you evaluate the following expression, what operation should be worked first? $2 + 1$
   $5(4 + 3(2 + 1))$

In 3–10, evaluate each expression.

3. $12 + 8(4 + 2)$ 60

4. $200 - (30 + .4(20 - 12))$ 166.8

5. $9 + 6(3 + 2)^3$ 759

6. $(6 + 12)(13 - (5 + 2 \cdot 3))$ 36

7. $3(2 \cdot x + 15) - 4$, when $x = 7$ 83

8. $5 + y(3 + y(1 + y))$, when $y = 10$ 1135

9. $(p + q)(5p + 3q)$, when $p = 3$ and $q = 4$ 189

10. $2(4 + a(a + 3) + 9)$, when $a = 5$ 106

11. *Multiple choice* Begin with a number m. Subtract 9 from it. Multiply the difference by 12. What number results?   d
   (a) $m - 9 + m \cdot 12$ (b) $m(12 - 9)$
   (c) $m - 9 \cdot 12$ (d) $12(m - 9)$

12. Insert parentheses to make the sentence true.
   $15 - 7 - 2 - 3 = 7$
   $15 - (7 - 2) - 3 = 7$

Transition Mathematics © Scott, Foresman and Company   **33**

NOTES ON QUESTIONS
Question 38c: This is an opportunity to note that two expressions are equal if they give the same values. The expression $36 - (17-n)$ happens to be equal to $n + 19$. Tell students that with algebra they will learn how to change one expression into others equal to it.

FOLLOW-UP

MORE PRACTICE
For more questions on SPUR Objectives, use *Lesson Master 4-5*, shown on page 161.

EXTENSIONS
Computer *Computer Master 6* gives practice solving problems similar to **Questions 30** and **31.**

Ask students to use parentheses (including nested parentheses) to show how the following equation could have at least three different solutions:
$36 \div 2 \times 3 + 24 \div 4 = n.$
samples: $(36 \div 2) \times (3 + (24 \div 4)) = 162$
$(36 \div (2 \times 3)) + (24 \div 4) = 12$
$((36 \div 2) \times 3) + (24 \div 4) = 60$

37. 4 or 5 parentheses are typical.

39. 20 INPUT Y
30 V=(Y+15)*(11-2*Y)

35. Three instances of a pattern are given. Describe the general pattern using one variable. *(Lesson 4-2)* $n^4 = n \cdot n \cdot n \cdot n$
$3^4 = 3 \cdot 3 \cdot 3 \cdot 3 \qquad 6^4 = 6 \cdot 6 \cdot 6 \cdot 6 \qquad 1^4 = 1 \cdot 1 \cdot 1 \cdot 1$

36. A person types a line in 5.7 seconds. Another person types it in one tenth of a second faster. What is the second person's time? *(Lesson 1-2)*   **5.6 seconds**

Exploration

37. Use the following exercise to find out how many nested parentheses with operations inside your calculator will allow. Key in $100 - (1 - (2 - (3 - (4 \ldots$ and so on. When your calculator shows an error message, the last number keyed is the calculator's limit. What is your calculator's limit? See margin.

38. This program finds values of the expression in Example 2 of this lesson.

```
10   PRINT "GIVE VALUE OF YOUR VARIABLE"
20   INPUT N
30   V = 36 − (17 − N)
40   PRINT "VALUE OF EXPRESSION IS", V
50   END
```

   a. Run the program when N = 4 to check that it gives the value of Example 2.   **V = 23**
   b. Run the program for at least five other values of N.   Answers will vary
   c. Without running this program, how can you predict what the value of the expression will be?   Add 19 to the value inputted.

39. Modify the program in Question 38 so that it evaluates the expression of Example 4 for any value of y. (Caution: Be careful to put the multiplication between the parentheses.) See margin.

LESSON 4-6

RESOURCES
■ Lesson Master 4-6
▱ Visual for Teaching Aid 21:
  Additional Examples
■ *Manipulative Activities
  Sourcebook,* Activity 5

OBJECTIVE

L Calculate the value of a variable, given the values of other variables in a formula.

TEACHING NOTES

Substitution into formulas is not an easy task for some students. It is helpful for students to follow the procedure in the **Example** on page 164, writing the formula on one line, the substitutions on the second, and the evaluation based on order of operations on the additional lines.

Making Connections
Although much is done in this lesson with the area of a rectangle, ready knowledge of the formula is not expected until Chapter 9.

The rectangle drawn here has length about 6.3 cm, width about 2.5 cm, and area about 15.75 cm^2.

6.3 cm

2.5 cm   Area 15.75 cm^2

The length, width, and area are related by a simple pattern.

$$\text{Area} = \text{length times width}$$

Using the variables A for area, ℓ for length, and w for width,

$$A = \ell w.$$

(Remember that multiplication signs are usually not written between variables.) The sentence $A = \ell w$ is a **formula** for the area of a rectangle **in terms of** its length and width.

Formulas are very useful. For instance, the formula $A = \ell w$ works for *any* rectangle. So suppose a rectangular field has a length of 110 ft and a width of 30 ft. Then its area can be calculated using the formula.

$$A = 110 \text{ ft} \cdot 30 \text{ ft}$$
$$= 3300 \text{ ft}^2$$

In formulas, the *units must be consistent*. If you measure the length of a rectangle in inches and the width in feet, the formula $A = \ell w$ will not work. For instance, suppose a rectangle has width 3 inches and length 4 feet. To calculate the area you would have to either change inches to feet or feet to inches. Also, you must remember that area is measured in square units.

LESSON 4-6 Formulas **163**

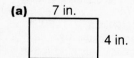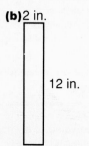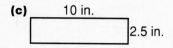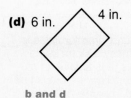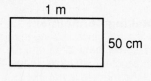
3 in.

4 ft

Area = 3 in. × 4 ft
     = 3 in. × 48 in.
     = 144 in.²

Letters in formulas are chosen carefully. Usually they are the first letter of what they represent. That is why we used A for area, ℓ for length, and w for width. But be careful. In formulas, capital and small letters often stand for *different* things.

■ ■ ■ ■ ■ ■ ■ ■ ■ ■ ■

Example The area A of the shaded region is $A = S^2 - s^2$. Find the area if $S = 1.75$ in. and $s = 1.25$ in.

Solution Substitute 1.75 in. for S and 1.25 in. for s in the formula. The unit of the answer is square inches.

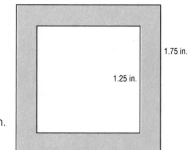

1.75 in.

1.25 in.

$A = S^2 - s^2$
$= (1.75 \text{ in.})^2 - (1.25 \text{ in.})^2$
$= 3.0625 \text{ sq. in.} - 1.5625 \text{ sq. in.}$
$= 1.5 \text{ sq. in.}$

Because capital and small letters can mean different things, in algebra you should not change capital letters to small letters, or vice versa. And you need to learn to write small letters differently from capitals, not just smaller. Do this by putting curves in the small letters. Here are the most confusing letters and one way to write them.

C F I J K L M P S U V W X Y Z

c f i j k l m p s u v w x y z

Questions

Covering the Reading

1. The formula $A = lw$ gives the ? of a rectangle in terms of its ? and ?. area, length, width

2. How do the letters in the formula of Question 1 make that question easier to answer? See margin.

164

3. What is the area of a rectangle that is 43 cm long and 0.1 cm wide? **4.3 cm²**

4. a. What is the area of a rectangle that is 3 in. long and 4 ft wide?
   b. What does part **a** tell you about units in formulas?
   a. 144 in.², or 1 ft²; b. They must be the same.

In 5–7, use the formula $A = S^2 - s^2$

5. Do S and s stand for the same thing? no

6. What do S and s stand for? See margin.

1.6 cm

0.6 cm

7. Give the area between the two squares drawn at left. **2.2 cm²**

8. In a formula, why should you not change a capital letter to a small letter? **Capital letters often stand for different things than small letters do.**

9. a. Write the alphabet from A to Z in capital letters.
   b. Write the alphabet in small letters. Make sure your small letters look different from (not just smaller than) the capital letters. **Answers will vary.**

In 10–13, use the formula $p = s - c$. This formula relates a store's cost c for an item, the selling price s, and the profit p for this item.

10. This formula gives profit in terms of __?__ and __?__.
   cost, selling price

11. Why are the letters p, s, and c used in this formula?
   They are the first letters of the quantities they represent.

12. Calculate p when $s = \$25$ and $c = \$15$. **$10**

13. Calculate p when s is $3 and c is 2¢. **$2.98**

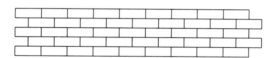

In 14 and 15, use the formula $N = 7LH$. This formula is used by some bricklayers. N is the number of bricks needed in a wall. L is the length of the wall in feet. H is the height of the wall in feet. According to this formula:

14. about how many bricks would a bricklayer need for a wall 10 feet high and 30 feet long? **2100 bricks**

15. are 1000 bricks enough for a wall $8\frac{1}{2}$ feet high and 20 feet long?
   No; about 1190 are needed.

NOTES ON QUESTIONS
Questions 1 and 10:
Point out the use of the phrase *in terms of*. Ask the students to use the phrase to describe the formulas in **Questions 5–7** and **Questions 14 and 15.**

Question 4: This stresses the need for using the same units in formulas. The students could solve this problem in two ways:
3 in. × 48 in. = 144 sq in.
or $\frac{1}{4}$ ft × 4 ft = 1 sq ft.

Question 9: This reinforces awareness of the need to distinguish between small and capital letters for use in formulas.

ADDITIONAL ANSWERS
2. The variables are the first letters of the words they represent.

6. S stands for length of a side of the big square; s stands for length of a side of the small square.

EXTENSION
Ask the students to choose a room at home "to be painted." Have everyone draw a diagram for each wall of his or her room, showing the overall dimensions of the room and the dimensions of any windows or doors. Have the students use the formula $A = lw$ to determine the area that will need paint. Explain that doors and windows are not to be painted. Students can then decide how many gallons of paint they will need, if 1 gallon covers 400 square feet.

17. inside parentheses, powers, multiplications or divisions from left to right, additions or subtractions from left to right

29. b. formula for the area of a rectangle; number of bricks required is 7 times the area of the wall in ft^2

16. A gardener wishes to surround her square garden by a walkway one meter wide. The garden is 5 meters on a side. How much ground will she have to clear?   **24 square meters**

Review

17. Put into the correct order of operations. *(Lessons 4-1, 4-5)*
multiplications or divisions from left to right
powers
inside parentheses
additions or subtractions from left to right
See margin.

In 18–21, evaluate each expression. *(Lessons 4-4, 4-5)*

18. $9 + 5(3 + 2 \cdot 7)$ 94   **19.** $3 + 4 \cdot 5^2$ 103

20. $12 - 4x$ when $x = .5$ **21.** $8/(8/(2 + 6))$
10   8

22. Convert 6 kilograms to grams. *(Lesson 3-3)*   **6000 grams**

23. One liter is how many cubic centimeters? *(Lesson 3-8)*
1000 cubic centimeters

In 24–27, put one of the symbols $>$, $=$, or $<$ in the blank.
(Lessons 1-6, 1-9, 2-2, 4-4)

24. $-5 \underline{\ ?\ } -5.1$ $>$ **25.** $4.09 \underline{\ ?\ } 4\frac{1}{11}$ $<$

26. $x + 14 \underline{\ ?\ } x - 14$ when $x = 20$. $>$

27. $a^3 \underline{\ ?\ } a^2$ when $a = 0.7$. $<$

28. Change $\frac{8}{4}$, $\frac{9}{4}$, $\frac{10}{4}$, $\frac{11}{4}$, and $\frac{12}{4}$ to decimals. *(Lesson 1-8)*   2; 2.25; 2.5;
2.75; 3

Exploration

29. a. According to the bricklayer's formula (Questions 14 and 15 above), how many bricks are needed for a square foot of wall?
7
b. The bricklayer's formula is related to one of the formulas given in this lesson. Which formula is that, and how are the formulas related?   See margin.

166

LESSON 4-7

Grouping Symbols

Parentheses are the most common **grouping symbols. Brackets** [ ] are grouping symbols sometimes used when there are nested parentheses. Brackets and parentheses mean exactly the same thing.

$5[x + 2y(3 + z)]$ and $5(x + 2y(3 + z))$ are identical.

Many people find brackets clearer than a second pair of parentheses. But some of today's calculators and computer languages do not allow brackets.

■ ■ ■ ■ ■ ■ ■ ■ ■ ■

Example 1   Simplify $2[4 + 6(3 \cdot 5 - 4)] - 3(30 - 3)$.

> **Solution** Work within the parentheses inside the brackets first.
> $= 2[4 + 6(15 - 4)] - 3(30 - 3)$
> $= 2[4 + 6 \cdot 11] - 3(30 - 3)$
> Now there are no nested grouping symbols.
> $= 2[4 + 66] - 3(27)$
> $= 2(70) - 3(27)$
> $= 140 - 81$
> $= 59$

Another important grouping symbol is the **fraction bar.** You may not have realized that the fraction bar is like parentheses. Here is how it works. Suppose you want to calculate the average of 10, 20, and 36. The average is given by the expression

$$\frac{10 + 20 + 36}{3}.$$

Now suppose you want to write this fraction using the slash /. If you write

$$10 + 20 + 36/3,$$

then, by order of operations, the division will be done first and only the 36 will be divided by 3. So you need to use parentheses.

$$\frac{10 + 20 + 36}{3} = (10 + 20 + 36)/3$$

LESSON 4-7 *Grouping Symbols*   **167**

LESSON 4-7

RESOURCES
■ Lesson Master 4-7
▆ Computer Master 7
■ Quiz on Lessons 4-5 Through 4-7
🗏 Visual for Teaching Aid 22: Summary of Rules for Order of Operations

OBJECTIVES

A Use order of operations to evaluate numerical expressions.
B Evaluate numerical expressions containing grouping symbols.
C Evaluate algebraic expressions given the values of all variables.
F Know the correct order of operations.

Once again students should carefully read and study the examples. Each example illustrates an important aspect of the study of order of operations. **Example 1** shows nested grouping symbols. **Example 2** is a simple fraction-bar problem. **Example 3** complicates the fraction bar with a variable and an order-of-operation issue to consider; Solution 2 demonstrates how complicated the example becomes using a calculator. **Example 4** puts all these aspects together in one long problem.

When discussing **Examples 2-4**, emphasize that the work must be done in the numerator and denominator separately before any division can be used to evaluate the fraction. In particular, caution against cancelling the variables or the 1s.

Computer You may wish to use *Computer Master 7* to provide practice in grouping and order of operations.

In this way the slash, /, and the fraction bar, —, are different. (Of course, with something as simple as $\frac{1}{2}$ or 1/2, there is no difference.) You should think of a fraction bar as always having unwritten parentheses. Because the fraction bar is a grouping symbol, you *must* work in the numerator and denominator of a fraction before dividing.

Example 2 Simplify $\dfrac{4 + 9}{2 + 3}$.

Solution Think $\dfrac{(4 + 9)}{(2 + 3)}$ and get $\dfrac{13}{5}$.

Example 3 Evaluate $\dfrac{4n + 1}{3n - 1}$ when $n = 11$.

Solution 1 Substitute. Then work first in the numerator and denominator.

$$\frac{4 \cdot 11 + 1}{3 \cdot 11 - 1} = \frac{44 + 1}{33 - 1} = \frac{45}{32}$$

Solution 2 Use a calculator to evaluate after substitution. Parentheses must be used to ensure that the entire numerator is divided by the entire denominator. They are emphasized in the key sequence shown here.

$\boxed{(}\ 4\ \boxed{\times}\ 11\ \boxed{+}\ 1\ \boxed{)}\ \boxed{\div}$

$\boxed{(}\ 3\ \boxed{\times}\ 11\ \boxed{-}\ 1\ \boxed{)}\ \boxed{=}$

You will get 1.40625, the decimal equivalent to $\frac{45}{32}$.

Example 4 Evaluate $x + \dfrac{100(4 + 2x) - 25}{200 - x}$ when $x = 50$.

Solution First substitute 50 for x whenever x appears.

$$50 + \frac{100(4 + 2 \cdot 50) - 25}{200 - 50}$$

Now work within the parentheses in the numerator.

$$= 50 + \frac{100(104) - 25}{200 - 50}$$

$$= 50 + \frac{10{,}400 - 25}{150}$$

$$= 50 + \frac{10{,}375}{150}$$

$$= 50 + 69.1\overline{6}$$

$$= 119.1\overline{6}$$

168

168

Summary of Rules for Order of Operations

1. First, do operations within parentheses or other grouping symbols.
   A. If there are nested grouping symbols, work within the innermost symbols first.
   B. Remember that fraction bars are grouping symbols and can be different from /.

2. Within grouping symbols or if there are no grouping symbols:
   A. First, do all powers.
   B. Second, do all multiplications or divisions in order, from left to right.
   C. Then do additions or subtractions in order, from left to right.

Questions

Covering the Reading

1. What are the symbols [ ] called?   **brackets**

2. *True or False* $2[x + 4]$ and $2(x + 4)$ mean the same thing.   **true**

3. When are the symbols [ ] usually used?
   when there are nested parentheses

4. Name three different grouping symbols.
   parentheses, brackets, fraction bars

5. When there are grouping symbols within grouping symbols, what should you do first?   **See margin.**

In 6–8, simplify.

6. $3[2 + 4(5 - 2)]$ **42**

7. $39 - [20 \div 4 + 2(3 + 6)]$ **16**

8. $[(3 - 1)^3 + (5 - 1)^4]^2$ **69,696**

9. Write the key sequence for evaluating the expression of Question 6 on your calculator.   **See margin.**

10. *Multiple Choice* Written on one line, $\dfrac{20 + 2 \cdot 30}{6 + 4} =$ **(d)**

    (a) $20 + 2 \cdot 30/6 + 4$ (b) $20 + 2 \cdot 30/(6 + 4)$
    (c) $(20 + 2 \cdot 30)/6 + 4$ (d) $(20 + 2 \cdot 30)/(6 + 4)$

In 11 and 12, simplify.

11. $\dfrac{50 + 40}{50 - 40}$ **9**

ADDITIONAL EXAMPLES
1. Evaluate.
a. $5[12 - 8(2.5 \cdot 2 - 4)] - 1.5(10 - 4)$ **11**

b. $\frac{1 + 4a}{2a - 3}$, when $a = 6$ $\frac{25}{9}$

c. $x^2 - 3x + 10$, when $x = 5$ **20**

2. Write the key sequence needed to evaluate $\frac{5 + 3 \cdot 7}{4 + 9}$ on your calculator.

ADDITIONAL ANSWERS
5. Work with the innermost grouping symbols first.

9. 3 × ((2 + 4 × (5 − 2))) =

Question 12: There are four possible answers: the fraction $\frac{560}{136.5}$; the simple fraction $\frac{1120}{273}$; the decimal approximation 4.102564..., which students may get as a result of evaluating the fraction (also see **Question 14**); and the repeating decimal 4.102564. We would accept all but the first of these as correct. A decimal in a numerator or denominator should be removed by multiplying both numerator and denominator by a power of 10, as shown in Lesson 2-7.

Questions 19-26: Discuss these carefully with students, because they provide applications of the content of the lesson. If necessary, work through **Questions 19, 20, and 24** with the class, and encourage the students to try the others on their own.

13. 560 ÷ (7 × (6 + 3 × 4.5)) =

31. samples: $2 = \frac{4}{4} + \frac{4}{4}$

$3 = \frac{4+4+4}{4}$

$4 = (4 - 4) \times 4 + 4$

$5 = \frac{4+4\times4}{4}$

$6 = \frac{4+4}{4} + 4$

$7 = 4 + 4 - \left(\frac{4}{4}\right)$

$8 = 4 + 4 + 4 - 4$

$9 = 4 + 4 + \left(\frac{4}{4}\right)$

$10 = \frac{44-4}{4}$

---

12. $\dfrac{560}{7(6 + 3 \cdot 4.5)}$ $\frac{1120}{273}$ or 4.102564 ...

13. Write a key sequence for evaluating Question 12 on your calculator.   **See margin.**

In 14 and 15, evaluate when $a = 5$ and $x = 4$.

14. $\dfrac{a + 3x}{a + x}$ $\frac{17}{9}$ or $1.\overline{8}$

15. $\dfrac{5x - 2}{(x - 1)(x - 2)}$ 3

The *average* of three numbers x, y, and z is $\dfrac{x + y + z}{3}$. Use this information in Questions 16–19.

16. Write an expression for the average of a, b, and c. $\frac{a + b + c}{3}$

17. A school district has three elementary schools with 236, 141, and 318 students in them. What is the average number of students per school? $231.\overline{6}$

18. A student scores 83, 91, and 89 on 3 tests. What is the average? $87.\overline{6}$

19. Grades can range from 0 to 100 on tests. A student scores 85 and 90 on the first two tests.
   a. What is the lowest the student can average for all 3 tests?
   b. What is the highest the student can average for the 3 tests?
   a. $58.\overline{3}$; b. $91.\overline{6}$

In 20–23, suppose a team wins W games and loses L games. Then its winning percentage is $\dfrac{W}{W + L}$. This number is always converted to a decimal. Then it is rounded to the nearest thousandth. Calculate the winning percentage for each team.

20. the 1990 Super Bowl Champion San Francisco 49ers, who had a regular season record of 14 wins and 2 losses   .875

21. the 1988 U.S. Olympic Women's basketball team, who won all 6 games they played   1.000

22. a volleyball team that wins 7 games and loses 7 games   .500

23. a team that wins 3 and loses 12 games   .200

In 24 and 25, use the formula $T \approx t - \dfrac{2f}{1000}$. This formula estimates the air temperature T at an altitude of f feet when the ground temperature is t. Suppose it is 75° at ground level.

24. Find the temperature at an altitude of 1000 ft.   73°

25. Find the temperature at an altitude of 3000 ft.   69°

170

26. *Multiple Choice* In a *Bill James Baseball Abstract*, the expression $\dfrac{2(HR \times SB)}{HR + SB}$ is called the Power/Speed number.

A newspaper writer once incorrectly wrote the expression as $2[HR \times SB]/HR + SB$.

What was wrong with the newspaper expression? (b)
(a) It had brackets instead of parentheses.
(b) It should have had parentheses around $HR + SB$.
(c) It had an $\times$ sign for multiplication.
(d) It was written on one line.
(e) It used HR and SB instead of single letters for variables.

Review

27. Arrange the numbers $7\frac{2}{3}$, $7\frac{3}{5}$, and 7.65 with the symbol $>$ between them. *(Lessons 1-6, 1-9)* $7\frac{2}{3} > 7.65 > 7\frac{3}{5}$

28. The U.S. budget deficit in 1989 is listed in *The 1990 Information Please Almanac* as $161,501 million. *(Lesson 1-1, 1-4, 2-3)*
a. Write this number as a decimal.   161,501,000,000
b. Round this number to the nearest billion.   162,000,000,000
c. Write the original number in scientific notation. 1.61501×10^{11}

29. Measure the length and width of a rectangular table to the nearest inch. What is the area of the table? *(Lessons 3-1, 4-6)*
Answers will vary, depending on the table.

30. Translate into mathematical symbols. *(Lesson 4-3)*
a. the sum of thirty and twenty $30 + 20$
b. three more than a number $3 + n$
c. a number decreased by one tenth $n - .1$

Exploration

31. The numerical expression $4 + \frac{4}{4} - 4$ uses four 4s and has a value of 1. Find numerical expressions using only four 4s that have the values of each integer from two to ten. You may use any operations and grouping symbols.   See margin.

32. This program will calculate the winning percentage using the formula given in Questions 20–23, if you complete Line 30 correctly. Do that and run your program with the values of W and L from Questions 20–23 to check.

```
10   PRINT "WINS"
15   INPUT W
20   PRINT "LOSSES"
25   INPUT L
30   PCT = __?__
40   PRINT "PCT = " PCT
50   END
```

a. Complete line 30 with the correct formula.   W/(W + L)
b. Run your program with the values of W and L from Question 20 to check. $11/(11 + 4) = .733\ldots$
c. Run your program with values of W and L from the record of a team you know.   Answers will vary.

LESSON 4-7   Grouping Symbols   **171**

FOLLOW-UP

MORE PRACTICE
For more questions on SPUR Objectives, use *Lesson Master 4-7*, shown below.

EXTENSION
After students have completed **Question 31**, you may want to ask who can represent the most integers between 0 and 101 using "four 4s." If your students plan to do this activity, make sure that the rules are clear to everyone. Decide in advance whether 44, square root signs, or decimal points (for example, $4/.4 + 4 - 4$ gives 10) are allowed.

EVALUATION
A quiz covering Lessons 4-5 through 4-7 is provided in the Teacher's Resource File on page 32.

NAME _____

LESSON **MASTER   4-7**
QUESTIONS ON **SPUR** OBJECTIVES

■ **SKILLS**   *Objective F (See Chapter Review, pages 183–185, for objectives.)*

1. Summarize the rules for order of operations into 4 general steps.
a. Do operations within parentheses.
b. Do all powers.
c. Do multiplications or divisions.
d. Do additions or subtractions.
2. Write $\frac{30 + 3 \cdot 7}{20 - 3}$ on one line. $(30 + 3 \cdot 7)/(20 - 3)$
3. Write a key sequence for evaluating $4[2^7 + 3(9 - 5)]$.
9 [−] 5 [=] [×] 3 + 2 [y^x] 3 [=] [×] 4

■ **SKILLS**   *Objectives A, B, and C*
In 4–8, evaluate each expression.

4. $[36 \div (3 \cdot 4)] + 2$ _____ 5
5. $19 - \frac{25 - 7}{5 + 4}$ _____ 17
6. $40 - \frac{16}{8} - 3$ _____ 35
7. $\frac{9^x}{3y}$ if $x = 3$ and $y = 2$ _____ 81
8. $14 + [a(b - 2)]$ if $a = 6$ and $b = 9$ _____ 56
9. Insert parentheses and brackets in the number sentence below to make it a true sentence.
$60 \div [(9 - 6) \cdot 5] + 7 = 11$
10. a. Write an expression for the sentence below.
b. Evaluate your expression when $r = 10$ and $s = 5$.
Divide the sum of r and s by the difference r minus s.
a. _____ $\frac{r + s}{r - s}$
b. _____ 3

LESSON 4-8

RESOURCES
■ Lesson Master 4-8

TEACHING NOTES

You might want to read this lesson aloud in class to get students thinking about unknowns in a positive way. Since solutions are done either by inspection or through multiple choice, the problems are not threatening. Students can look at the equation as a whole and think about a sensible solution, instead of following a series of mechanical steps for isolating the answer.

4-8

Open Sentences

A sentence with an equal sign $=$ is called an **equation.** Here are some examples of equations.

$$27 = 9(4 - 1) \qquad 1 + 1 = 3 \qquad x + 7 = 50$$

The left equation is true. The middle equation is false. The right equation may be true or false, depending on what you substitute for x. If you substitute 57, the equation is false, because

$$57 + 7 \text{ does not equal } 50.$$

If you substitute 43 for x, the equation is true.

$$43 + 7 = 50$$

The equation $x + 7 = 50$ is an example of an **open sentence.** An open sentence is a sentence with variables that can be true or false, depending on what you substitute for the variables. The **solution** to this open sentence is 43. A solution to an open sentence is a value of a variable that makes the sentence true.

Example 1 Mentally, find the solution to the open sentence $40 - A = 38$.

Solution Since $40 - 2 = 38$, the number 2 is the solution.

Example 2 *Multiple Choice* Which number is a solution to $30m = 6$?
(a) 24   (b) 0.5   (c) 5   (d) 0.2

Solution The answer is the value that works. Substitute to see which one works.
(a) $30 \cdot 24 = 720$, so 24 does not work.
(b) $30 \cdot 0.5 = 15$, so 0.5 does not work.
(c) $30 \cdot 5 = 150$, so 5 does not work.
(d) $30 \cdot 0.2 = 6$, so 0.2 is a solution.
Choice (d) is the correct choice.

One of the most important skills in algebra is finding solutions to open sentences. It is important because open sentences occur often in situations where decisions have to be made.

172

Example 3   A store is to have an area of 10,000 square feet. But it can only be 80 feet wide. Let ℓ be the length of the store. The value of ℓ is the solution to what open sentence?

Solution   Drawing a picture can help.
We know $A = \ell w$. The given information tells us that $A = 10,000$ and $w = 80$. Substituting in the formula, $10,000 = \ell \cdot 80$.

The solution to $10,000 = \ell \cdot 80$ is not obvious. The variable ℓ is called the **unknown.** Finding values of the unknown (or unknowns) that work is called **solving the sentence.** At this point, you are expected to be able to solve only very simple sentences. The solutions are either of the kind you can do in your head (as in Example 1) or you will be given choices (as in Example 2).

Questions

Covering the Reading

1. What is an equation?   a sentence with an equal sign

2. Give an example of an equation that is false.   Sample: 1 + 1 = 3.

3. What is an open sentence?   a sentence with variables

4. Give an example of an open sentence.   Sample: x + 7 = 50

5. Define: solution to an open sentence.
a value of the variable that makes the sentence true
6. What is meant by *solving* an open sentence?   See margin.

7. *Multiple choice*   The solution to $4x + 3 = 12$ is   (a)
(a) 2.25   (b) 0   (c) 2.5   (d) 1

In 8–11, give the solution to each sentence.
8. $18 + A = 19$ 1   **9.** $2B = 10$ 5

10. $C = 5 - .1$ 4.9   **11.** $4 = 3.5 + t$ .5

In 12 and 13, Rhee Taylor wants a store with an area of 1000 square meters. The store can only be 40 meters wide. Rhee wants to know how many meters long the store should be.

12. Solving what equation will give the length l of the store?
$40\ell = 1000$
13. Which of these lengths is the solution: 25 m, 960 m, 1040 m, or 4000 m?   25 m

LESSON 4-8   *Open Sentences*   **173**

ADDITIONAL EXAMPLES
1. Mentally, find the solution to each open sentence.
a. $12 + a = 12\frac{3}{4}$ $\frac{3}{4}$

b. $8 - 2.3 = b$ 5.7

c. $100 - c = 53$ 47

d. $\frac{d}{3} = 6$ 18

e. $2e + 6 = 6$ 0

2. *Multiple choice* Choose the solution to each open sentence.

a. $\frac{15}{a} = 30$ (ii)
(i) 2 (ii) $\frac{1}{2}$ (iii) 5 (iv) $\frac{1}{5}$
b. $100 = 2g - 6$ (iv)
(i) 50 (ii) 51 (iii) 52 (iv) 53
c. $\frac{25}{h} = 6.25$ (ii)
(i) 3 (ii) 4 (iii) 5 (iv) 6

ADDITIONAL ANSWERS
6. finding all values of the unknown that make the sentence true

Questions 15 and 19:
Each of these has more than one correct answer. These open sentences in English raise the question of whether multiple solutions are possible with algebraic sentences, anticipating inequalities in the next lesson.

Question 22: Although this looks complicated, it is a multiple-choice exercise like **Questions 7 and 13**. The students should substitute to see which value of *n* works.

Questions 24 and 25:
Emphasize that a variable that appears more than once in an expression must stand for the same number wherever it appears in that expression.

Question 35: A chart and a calculator will be useful in answering this question. First, ask the students which numbers can be multiplied to give 100. Since the numbers being multiplied, $(x + 1)$ and $(x + 2)$, are close in value, *x* must have a value close to 10. Help the students set up a chart like the one below to try out their proposed values. To determine the consecutive integers, tenths, and finally hundredths, students must compare their products of $(x + 1)(x + 2)$ with the required product of 100.

x	$x + 1$	$x + 2$	$(x + 1)(x + 2)$

Applying the Mathematics

In 14–17, give one solution to each of these nonmathematical open sentences.

14. __?__ is currently President of the United States.
In 1989, George Bush

15. In population, __?__ is a city bigger than Detroit.   See margin.

16. A trio has __?__ members.   three

17. An octet has __?__ members.   eight

In 18–21, give at least one solution.

18. There are *y* millimeters in a meter.   1000

19. *x* is a negative integer.   Sample: -9

20. You move the decimal point two places to the right when multiplying by *m*.   100

21. The number one million, written as a decimal, is a 1 followed by *z* zeros.   6

22. *Multiple choice*   Let *n* be the number of days a book is overdue. Let *F* be the fine. Suppose $F = .20 + .05n$ dollars, the situation described in Lesson 4-4. When the fine *F* is $1.00, what is the number of days overdue?   (c)
    (a) 20   (b) 15   (c) 16   (d) 25

23. Suppose $y = 2x + 3$. When $x = 4$, what value of *y* is a solution?   11

In 24–27, give a solution to each sentence.

24. $n + n = 16$ 8   25. $m \cdot m = 16$ 4

26. $z - 4 = 99$ 103   27. $y \cdot 25 = 25$ 1

174

28. In 1989, the world population reached 5.239 billion. *(Lessons 1-4, 2-1, 2-3)*
   a. Round this number to the nearest ten million.
   b. Write your answer to **a** in scientific notation.

a. 5,240,000,000; b. 5.24×10^9

In 29 and 30, put the three quantities into one sentence with two inequality signs. *(Lessons 1-6, 3-2, 3-3)*   See margin.

29. 5 km, 500 m, 50,000 mm   **30.** 2 miles, 5280 ft, 2000 yd

31. The sum of the integers from 1 to n is given by the expression $\frac{n(n + 1)}{2}$. *(Lessons 4-4, 4-5, 4-6)*
   a. Evaluate this expression for $n = 5$. $5(5 + 1)/2 = 15$
   b. Verify your answer to part **a** by adding the integers from 1 to 5.
   c. Find the sum of the integers from 1 to 100.

b. $1 + 2 + 3 + 4 + 5 = 15$; c. 5050

32. Evaluate $2x - (y + 3(y + 2))$ when $x = 5.5$ and $y = 0.5$. *(Lesson 4-5)*   3

33. Evaluate this rather complicated expression. *(Lesson 4-7)*
$$\frac{[6(2 + 4^3)^2 - 3^2]}{40 - 13 \cdot 3} \qquad 26{,}127$$

34. Write 0.009:
   a. in scientific notation; **b.** as a fraction. *(Lessons 2-7, 2-9)*
   9×10^{-3}; b. $\frac{9}{1000}$

35. Estimate a solution to $(x + 1)(x + 2) = 100$.
   a. between consecutive integers.   between 8 and 9
   b. between consecutive tenths.   between 8.5 and 8.6
   c. between consecutive hundredths   between 8.51 and 8.52

36. To find the average of the three numbers 83, 91, and 89 in Question 18, Laura typed the following into a computer: ?83 + 91 + 89/3. The answer came out higher than any of the numbers, so Laura knew something was wrong.
   a. What should Laura have typed?   ?(83 + 91 + 89)/3
   b. Check your answer by running the correct expression on a computer.   Sample output: 87.6666667

FOLLOW-UP

MORE PRACTICE
For more questions on SPUR Objectives, use *Lesson Master 4-8*, shown below.

15. samples: Los Angeles, London

29. 50,000 mm < 500 m < 5 km or 5 km > 500 m > 50,000 mm

30. 5280 ft < 2000 yd < 2 mi or 2 mi > 2000 yd > 5280 ft

NAME _____

■**SKILLS**   *Objective D (See Chapter Review, pages 183–185, for objectives.)*
In 1–6, choose the correct solution.

1. $4a + 3 = 25$	**b**		
(a) 5	(b) 5.5	(c) 18	(d) 22

2. $\frac{1}{5}x = 25$	**d**		
(a) 5	(b) 25	(c) 75	(d) 125

3. $30 + 5y - 3 = 57$	**c**		
(a) 18	(b) 8	(c) 6	(d) 4

4. $3 = .5n + .5$	**d**		
(a) .5	(b) 2.5	(c) 4	(d) 5

5. $12 + y = 24$	**c**		
(a) 2	(b) 32	(c) 12	(d) 22

6. $x - .05 = 6$	**b**		
(a) 5.95	(b) 6.05	(c) .11	(d) .65

In 7–17, write the solution to each sentence.

7. $9a = 54$ $a = 6$	8. $\frac{x}{5} = 20$ $x = 100$
9. $n + -5 = -15$ $n = -10$	10. $t + 5 = 27$ $t = 22$
11. $9t = 0$ $t = 0$	12. $m - 1 = 49$ $m = 50$

13. The alphabet has l letters. $l = 26$
14. There are d days in a week. $d = 7$
15. One mile equals f feet. $f = 5280$
16. An octopus has n legs. $n = 8$
17. A kilometer is x meters. $x = 1000$

LESSON

4-9

Inequalities

An **inequality** is a sentence with one of the following symbols.
$\neq$ is not equal to
$<$ is less than
$\leq$ is less than or equal to
$>$ is greater than
$\geq$ is greater than or equal to

$5 > -7$ is an inequality that is true. So is $5 \geq -7$.
An example of an inequality that is false is $3 < 2$.
The inequality $50\% \neq 0.5$ is also false.

The inequality $x + 2 < 30$ is an open sentence, neither true nor false. The number 20 is a solution, because $20 + 2 < 30$. The number 14 is also a solution, since $14 + 2 < 30$. However, 28 is not a solution, because $28 + 2 < 30$ is not true. Also, 554 is not a solution, because $554 + 2$ is not less than 30.

Inequalities that are open sentences usually have many solutions. The solutions are often easier to graph than to list.

Example 1   Graph all solutions to $y < 2$.

> **Solution**   Any number less than 2 is a solution. So there are infinitely many of them. Among the solutions are 0, 1, 1.5, -5, -4.3, and -2,000,000. Below is the graph. The shaded part covers the solutions. The open circle around the mark for 2 tells you that 2 is not a solution. It is not true that $2 < 2$.
>
> <-----|----|----|----|----|----|----|----|----|----|----○----|----|----|----|----|----|----->
>   -9   -8   -7   -6   -5   -4   -3   -2   -1   0   1   2   3   4   5   6   7   8

Remember that the inequality $2 > y$ means the same thing as $y < 2$. So the graph of all solutions to $2 > y$ would look identical to the graph in Example 1.

176

Example 2 Graph all solutions to $x \geq -1$.

Solution Any number greater than or equal to -1 is a solution. Some solutions are 0, $\frac{1}{2}$, 4, 43, $-\frac{1}{2}$, and 76.2. Below is the graph. The filled-in circle at -1 tells you that -1 is a solution.

Example 3 On some interstate highways, a car's speed must be from 45 mph to 55 mph. Graph all possible legal speeds s.

Solution

In Example 3, the legal speeds are the solutions to the inequality $45 \leq s \leq 55$. You may read this as "45 is less than or equal to s and s is less than or equal to 55" or "s ranges from 45 to 55." Another way to write this is with $\geq$ signs. $55 \geq s \geq 45$. Some solutions are 48, 50.3, 51, 55, 45, and 49.

Questions

Covering the Reading

1. What is an inequality? See margin.

In 2–5, give the meaning of the symbol.

2. $>$ is greater than

3. $\geq$ is greater than or equal to

4. $<$ is less than

5. $\leq$ is less than or equal to

6. Write an inequality that means the same thing as $y > 5$. $5 < y$

In 7 and 8, is the sentence an open sentence?

7. $3y \geq 90$ yes

8. $2 \leq 9$ no

In 9–12, *true or false?*

9. $-2 < 1$ true

10. $3 \leq \frac{6}{2}$ true

11. $-5 \geq 5$ false

12. $6 \neq 5 + 1$ false

LESSON 4-9 Inequalities **177**

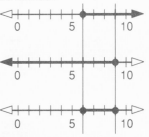
177

24.

25.

26.

27. a. $f > 55$
b. samples: 60, 57, 61
c.

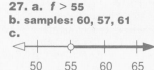

28. a. $0 \le d < 25{,}000$
b. samples: 5132; 4.32; 24,999
c.

29. a. $400 < A \le 500$
b. samples: 490, 439.36, 460
c.

0 400   440   480 500

In 13–16, name one solution to each sentence.

13. $A > 5000$ Sample: 5001   **14.** $n \le -5$ Sample: -13

15. $6\frac{1}{2} < d < 7\frac{1}{4}$ Sample: $6\frac{3}{4}$ **16.** $55 \ge s \ge 45$ Sample: 47

17. *Multiple choice*   The solutions to what sentence are graphed here?   (c)

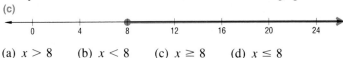

(a) $x > 8$ (b) $x < 8$ (c) $x \ge 8$ (d) $x \le 8$

In 18–21, match each sentence with the graph of its solutions.

18. $1 \le m \le 4$ (c)   **19.** $1 < m < 4$ (b)

20. $1 < m \le 4$ (d)   **21.** $1 \le m < 4$ (a)

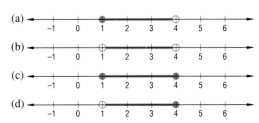

22. The legal speeds *s* on some interstate highways satisfy what inequality?   Samples: $55 \ge s \ge 45$ or $45 \le s \le 55$

23. *Multiple choice* $6 < a \le 9\frac{2}{3}$ has the same solutions as   (d)
   (a) $9\frac{2}{3} < a \le 6$.   (b) $9\frac{2}{3} > a \ge 6$.
   (c) $9\frac{2}{3} \le a < 6$.   (d) $9\frac{2}{3} \ge a > 6$.

In 24–26, graph all the solutions to each sentence.   See margin.
24. $w < \frac{40}{3}$ **25.** $-6 \le y$ **26.** $-2 < y < 3$

In 27–29: **a.** What inequality describes the situation? **b.** Give three solutions to the inequality. **c.** Graph all possible solutions.   See margin.

27. The speed limit is 55 mph. A person is driving *f* miles per hour and is speeding.

28. A person earns *d* dollars a year. The amount *d* is less than $25,000 a year.

29. The area is *A*. Rounded up to the nearest hundred, *A* is 500.

In 30–32, suppose it costs 30¢ for the first minute and 18¢ for each additional minute on a long-distance phone call. Then $c = .30 + .18(m - 1)$, where c is the total cost and m is the number of minutes talked. *(Lesson 4-8)*

30. Calculate c when $m = 6$. $1.20

31. What will it cost to talk for 10 minutes? $1.92

32. *Multiple choice* For $2.10, how long can you talk? (d)
(a) 7 minutes (b) 9 minutes
(c) 10 minutes (d) 11 minutes

33. Give three instances of this pattern: There are $6n$ legs on n insects. *(Lesson 4-2)* See Additional Answer, p. T53.

34. Three instances of a general pattern are given. Describe the pattern using two variables. *(Lesson 4-2)*

$$\frac{31.4}{2} \cdot \frac{2}{31.4} = 1 \qquad \frac{7}{8} \cdot \frac{8}{7} = 1 \qquad \frac{100}{11} \cdot \frac{11}{100} = 1 \qquad \frac{a}{b} \cdot \frac{b}{a} = 1$$

In 35 and 36, evaluate when $a = 3$, $b = 5$, and $c = 7$. *(Lessons 4-5, 4-7)*

35. $3(c + 10b - a^2)$ 144   **36.** $a[a + b(b + c)]$ 189

37. Scientific calculators often store more digits than they display.
a. Key in π. Record what you got. Then multiply by 100,000. Now subtract 314,159. Your calculator now displays some digits after those it displayed for π. What are these digits?
b. Key in $\frac{1}{17}$. Record what you get. Then multiply by 100,000. Now subtract 5882. Compare this result with what you recorded. What extra digits for $\frac{1}{17}$ were stored in the calculator?
c. Use a similar process to find the digits your calculator stores when you calculate $\frac{1}{13}$.
d. What is the repetend for $\frac{1}{13}$? See Additional Answers, p. T53.

38. Run this program with values of N that you pick.

```
10   PRINT "VALUE OF N"
15   INPUT N
20   IF N >= 8 THEN PRINT "TOO BIG"
25   IF N <= 6 THEN PRINT "TOO SMALL"
30   IF N <> 7 THEN PRINT "NOT CORRECT"
35   IF N = 7 THEN PRINT "JUST RIGHT"
40   END
```

a. What is the meaning of $>=$ in this program?
b. What is the meaning of $<=$ in this program?
c. What is the meaning of $<>$ in this program?

a. is greater than or equal to
b. is less than or equal to
c. is not equal to

LESSON 4-9 *Inequalities* **179**

FOLLOW-UP

MORE PRACTICE
For more questions on SPUR Objectives, use *Lesson Master 4-9*, shown below.

EVALUATION
Alternative Assessment
Call attention to **Questions 27 and 28**. Ask the students to name other situations where the concept of inequalities is used. (samples: ages for admission to movies, letter grades as assigned to numerical test scores)

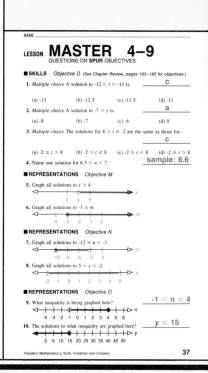

Summary

A variable is a symbol that can stand for any one of a set of numbers or other objects. Usually a variable is a single letter. Algebra is the study of variables and operations on them.

Introduced in this chapter are four uses of variables:
(1) Variables enable *patterns* to be described. For example, n people have $2n$ eyes. Descriptions with variables tend to be shorter and look like the instances of the pattern.
(2) Variables describe *properties* of numbers. For example, $a + b = b + a$.
(3) Variables are shorthand for quantities in *formulas*. For example, $A = lw$ is shorthand for area = length × width.

(4) Variables may be *unknowns*. For instance, suppose the area of a rectangle is 4 square meters and a length is 3 meters. Then the width w is the solution to the equation $4 = 3w$. The value of w can be found by solving this sentence.

Numerical and algebraic expressions may have a number of operations in them. To avoid confusion, rules for order of operations are used worldwide. To operate in a different order than given by these rules, parentheses and other grouping symbols are used.

Vocabulary

You should be able to give a general description and a specific example of each of the following ideas.

Lesson 4-1
symbols $+$, $-$, $\times$, $/$, and so on for operations
numerical expression
value of a numerical expression
evaluating an expression
order of operations

Lesson 4-2
pattern
instance
variable
symbol · for multiplication

Lesson 4-3
algebraic expression
sum, product

Lesson 4-4
value of a variable
value of an expression

Lesson 4-5
parentheses, ( ), nested parentheses

Lesson 4-6
formula
one variable in terms of others

Lesson 4-7
grouping symbols
brackets, [ ]
fraction bar, ——

Lesson 4-8
equation
open sentence
solution
unknown
solving an open sentence

Lesson 4-9
inequality
symbols $\leq$, $\geq$, $\neq$

180

Progress Self-Test

Take this test as you would take a test in class. You will need a ruler. Then check your work with the solutions in the Selected Answers section in the back of the book.

In 1–4, evaluate the expression.
1. $6 + 8 \cdot 7 + 9$ **71**
2. $(40 - 5) + (60 - 10)$ **85**
3. $75 - 50 - 3 - 1$ **21**
4. $5 + 3 \cdot 4^2$ **53**

5. Round to the nearest integer: $\dfrac{100 + 2 \cdot 5}{10 + 5}$. **7**

In 6–8, evaluate when $a = 3$, $b = 4$, $x = 10$, and $y = 100$.
6. $x + 3y$ **310**
7. $(a + b)(b - a)$ **7**
8. $y + 5[y + 4(y + 3)]$ **2660**

9. *Multiple choice* Which is a solution to $(4x)^2 = 64$? **(a)**
   (a) 2   (b) 4   (c) 8   (d) 16

In 10–12, three instances of a pattern are given. Describe the pattern using variables.
10. Use one variable. $10 \cdot a = 6 \cdot a + 4 \cdot a$
    $10 \cdot 5 = 6 \cdot 5 + 4 \cdot 5$
    $10 \cdot 8.2 = 6 \cdot 8.2 + 4 \cdot 8.2$
    $10 \cdot 0.04 = 6 \cdot 0.04 + 4 \cdot 0.04$
11. Use two variables. $a + b = b + a$
    $2 + 8 = 8 + 2$
    $3.7 + 7.3 = 7.3 + 3.7$
    $0 + 4 = 4 + 0$
12. Use one variable.
    In one year, we expect the town to grow by 200 people.
    In two years, we expect the town to grow by $2 \cdot 200$ people.
    In three years, we expect the town to grow by $3 \cdot 200$ people.
    In *p* years we expect the town to grow by *p* · 200 people.

In 13 and 14, the formula $c = 20n + 5$ gives the cost of first-class postage in 1988; c is the cost in cents; n is the weight in ounces of the mail, rounded up to the nearest ounce.
13. If $n = 5$, find c. **c = 105¢, or $1.05**
14. What is the cost of mailing a 9-ounce letter first class? Give your answer in dollars and cents. **c = $1.85**

In 15–18, translate into a numerical or algebraic expression or sentence.
15. the product of twelve and sixteen **12 × 16**
16. forty greater than forty-seven **47 + 40**
17. A number is less than zero. **n < 0**
18. a number divided into nine **9/a**
19. In the formula $p = s - c$, variable __?__ is in terms of __?__ and __?__. **p, s, and c**
20. In the formula $p = s - c$, calculate p if $s = \$45$ and $c = \$22.37$. **p = $22.63**

21. *Multiple choice* Written on one line, $\dfrac{W}{W + L}$ is equal to: **(b)**
    (a) $W/W + L$
    (b) $W/(W + L)$
    (c) $(W/W) + L$
    (d) $(W + L)/W$

22. *Multiple choice* Most of the symbols we now use for arithmetic operations were invented in the years **(c)**
    (a) before 1 A.D.
    (b) between 1 and 1000 A.D.
    (c) between 1000 and 1800 A.D.
    (d) since 1800 A.D.

PROGRESS SELF-TEST

For the development of mathematical competence, feedback and correction, along with the opportunity to practice are necessary. The Progress Self-Test provides the opportunity for feedback and correction; the Chapter Review provides additional opportunities for practice.

We cannot overemphasize the importance of these end-of-chapter materials. It is at this point that the material "gels" for many students, allowing them to solidify skills and understanding. In general, student performance should be markedly improved after these pages.

USING THE PROGRESS SELF TEST
Assign the Progress Self-Test as a one-night assignment. Worked-out *solutions* for all questions are in the Selected Answers section of the student book. Encourage students to take the Progress Self-Test honestly, grade themselves, and then be prepared to discuss the test in class.

Advise students to pay special attention to those Chapter Review questions (pages 183–185) which correspond to questions missed on the Progress Self-Test. A chart in the student text keys the Progress Self-Test questions to the lettered SPUR Objectives in the Chapter Review or to the Vocabulary. It also keys the questions to the corresponding lessons where the material is covered.

23. *Multiple choice* A sentence that means the same as $2 < y$ is **(b)**
  (a) $2 \leq y$
  (b) $y > 2$
  (c) $y \geq 2$
  (d) $y < 2$

In 24 and 25, find a solution to the given sentence.

24. $6x = 42$ 7

25. $-5 < y < -4$ **Samples:** -4.2, -4.9, $-4\frac{1}{2}$

26. Give an example to show why units in formulas must be consistent. **See margin.**

27. If $x = 7y$ and $y = 3$, what is the value of x

28. Graph all solutions to $x < 12$. **See margin.**

29. The solutions to what sentence are graphed here? $4.5 \leq y < 6$

In 30 and 31, give two instances of the pattern.

30. If your age is A years, your sister's age is $A - 5$ years. **See margin.**

31. $30c/5 = 6c$ **See margin.**

182

Chapter Review

Questions on **SPUR** Objectives

RESOURCES
- Chapter 4 Test, Form A
- Chapter 4 Test, Form B
- Chapter 4 Test, Cumulative Form

SPUR stands for **S**kills, **P**roperties, **U**ses, and **R**epresentations. The Chapter Review questions are grouped according to the SPUR Objectives for this chapter.

SKILLS deal with the procedures used to get answers.

Objective A: *Use order of operations to evaluate numerical expressions.* *(Lessons 4-1, 4-7)*

1. Evaluate $235 - 5 \times 4$. **215**
2. Evaluate $32 \div 16 \div 8 \times 12$. **3**
3. Evaluate $2 + 3^4$. **83**
4. Evaluate $4 \times 2^3 + \frac{28}{56}$. **32.5**
5. Evaluate $5 + 8 \times 3 + 2$. **31**
6. Evaluate $100 - \frac{80}{5} - 1$. **83**

Objective B: *Evaluate numerical expressions containing grouping symbols.* *(Lessons 4-5, 4-7)*

7. Evaluate $6 + 8(12 + 7)$. **158**
8. Evaluate $40 - 30/(20 - 10/2)$. **38**
9. Evaluate $1984 - (1947 - 1929)$. **1966**
10. Evaluate $(6 + 3)(6 - 4)$. **18**
11. Evaluate $3 + [2 + 4(6 - 3 \cdot 2)]$. **5**
12. Evaluate $4[7 - 2(2 + 1)]$. **4**
13. Evaluate $\dfrac{4 + 5 \cdot 2}{13 \cdot 5}$. $\frac{14}{65} = 0.215...$
14. Evaluate $\dfrac{3^3}{3^2}$. **3**

Objective C: *Evaluate algebraic expressions given the values of all variables.*
(Lessons 4-4, 4-5, 4-7)

15. If $x = 4$, then $6x = \underline{\ ?\ }$. **24**
16. If $m = 7$, evaluate $3m + (m + 2)$. **30**
17. Find the value of $2 + a + 11$ when $a = 5$.
18. Find the value of $3x^2$ when $x = 10$. **300**
19. Evaluate $2(a + b - c)$ when $a = 11$, $b = 10$, and $c = 9$. **24**

17. 18

20. Find the value of $x^3 + 2^y$ when $x = 5$ and $y = 5$. **157**
21. Evaluate $(3m + 5)(2m - 4)$ when $m = 6$.
22. Evaluate $(3m + 5) - (2m + 4)$ when **184** $m = 6$. **7**
23. Evaluate $\dfrac{3a + 2b}{2a + 4b}$ when $a = 1$ and $b = 2.5$. $\frac{8}{12} = .\overline{6}$
24. Find the value of $x + [1 + x(2 + x)]$ when $x = 7$. **71**

Objective D: *Given choices, pick the correct solution or solutions to an open sentence.* *(Lessons 4-8, 4-9)*

25. *Multiple choice* Which of these is a solution to $3x + 11 = 26$? **(b)**
   (a) 15   (b) 5   (c) 45   (d) 37
26. *Multiple choice* Which of these is a solution to $y > -5$? **(a)**
   (a) -4   (b) -5   (c) -6   (d) -7

Objective E: *Mentally find solutions to equations involving simple arithmetic.* *(Lesson 4-8)*

27. Find a solution to $3x = 12$. $x = 4$
28. Find a solution to $100 - t = 99$. $t = 1$
29. What is a solution to $y + 8 = 10$? $y = 2$
30. What value of m works in $20 = m \cdot 4$? $m = 5$

Objective F: *Know the correct order of operations.* *(Lessons 4-1, 4-5, 4-7)*

31. An expression contains only two operations, a powering and a multiplication. Which should you do first? **powering**

CHAPTER REVIEW

The main objectives for the chapter are organized here into sections corresponding to the four main types of understanding this book promotes: Skills, Properties, Uses, and Representations.

USING THE CHAPTER REVIEW
Whereas end-of-chapter material may be considered optional in some texts, in *Transition Mathematics* we have selected these objectives and questions with the expectation that they will be covered. Students should be able to answer these questions with about 85% accuracy after studying the chapter.

You may assign these questions over a single night to help students prepare for a test the next day, or you may assign the questions over a two-day period.

If you work the questions over two days, then we recommend assigning the *evens* for homework the first night so that students get feedback in class the next day, then assigning the *odds* the night before the test so the students can use the answers provided in the book.

32. *True or false*   If an expression contains nested parentheses, you should work the outside parentheses first.   **false**

33. *Multiple choice*   Written on one line,
$$\frac{30 + 5}{30 - 5} =$$ **(d)**
(a) 30 + 5/30 − 5   (b) (30 + 5)/30 − 5
(c) 30 + 5/(30 − 5)   (d) (30 + 5)/(30 − 5)

34. *Multiple choice*   Which of the following expressions would have the same value if the grouping symbols were removed?   **(b)**
(a) 10 − (7 − 2)   (b) (4 · 87 · 0) + 5
(c) 10/(5 − 2²)/2   (d) (9 · 3)²

PROPERTIES deal with the principles behind the mathematics.

■ **Objective G:** *Given instances of a pattern, write a description of the pattern using variables.* (Lesson 4-2)

35. Three instances of a pattern are given. Describe the general pattern using one variable.   **5 · x + 9 · x = 14 · x**
5 · 12 + 9 · 12 = 14 · 12
5 · 88 + 9 · 88 = 14 · 88
5 · π + 9 · π = 14 · π

36. Three instances of a pattern are given. Describe the general pattern using three variables.   **$a + b − c = a − c + b$**
6 + 7 − 8 = 6 − 8 + 7
10.2 + 0.5 − 0.22 = 10.2 − 0.22 + 0.5
30% + 10% − 20% = 30% − 20% + 10%

37. Three instances of a pattern are given. Describe the general pattern using two variables.
$$\frac{1}{9} + \frac{5}{9} = \frac{1 + 5}{9}; \qquad \frac{0}{9} + \frac{25}{9} = \frac{0 + 25}{9};$$
$$\frac{11}{9} + \frac{44}{9} = \frac{11 + 44}{9} \qquad \frac{a}{9} + \frac{b}{9} = \frac{a + b}{9}$$

■ **Objective H:** *Give instances of a pattern described with variables.* (Lesson 4-2)

38. Give two instances of the pattern
$5(x + y) = 5x + 5y$.

39. Give two instances of the pattern
$2 + A = 1 + A + 1$.

40. Give two instances of the pattern
$ab − c = ba − c$.
See margin.

USES deal with applications of mathematics in real situations.

■ **Objective I:** *Given instances of a real-world pattern, write a description of the pattern using variables.* (Lesson 4-2)

41. Three instances of a pattern are given. Describe the general pattern using variables.
If the weight is 5 ounces, the postage is 5¢ + 20 · 5¢.
If the weight is 3 ounces, the postage is 5¢ + 20 · 3¢.
If the weight is 1 ounce, the postage is 5¢ + 20 · 1¢.   See margin.

42. Three instances of a pattern are given. Describe the general pattern using variables.
One person has 10 fingers.
Two people have 2 · 10 fingers.
Seven people have 7 · 10 fingers.
p people have p · 10 fingers

■ **Objective J:** *Write a numerical expression for an English expression involving arithmetic operations.* (Lesson 4-3)

43. Translate into mathematical symbols: the sum of eighteen and twenty-seven.   **18 + 27**

44. Translate into mathematical symbols: fifteen less than one hundred thousand.

45. Translate into mathematical symbols: the product of four and twenty, decreased by one.   **4 × 20 − 1**

46. Translate into mathematical symbols: seven less six.   **7 − 6**

44. 100,000 − 15

184

Objective K: *Write an algebraic expression for an English expression involving arithmetic operations.* *(Lesson 4-3)*

47. Translate into an algebraic expression: seven more than twice a number. $2x + 7$

48. Translate into an algebraic expression: a number divided by six, the quotient decreased by three. $\frac{n}{6} - 3$

49. Translate into algebra: a number is less than five. $x < 5$

50. Translate into algebra: the product of thirty-nine and a number. $39n$

Objective L: *Calculate the value of a variable, given the values of other variables in a formula.* *(Lesson 4-6)*

51. The formula $I = 100m/c$ is sometimes used to measure a person's IQ. The IQ is I, mental age is m, and chronological age is c. What is I if $m = 7$ and $c = 5.5$? about 127

52. The formula $F = 1.8C + 32$ relates Fahrenheit (F) and Celsius (C) temperature. If C is 10, what is F? 50

53. The formula $A = bh$ gives the area A of a parallelogram in terms of its base b and height h. What is the area of a parallelogram with base 1 foot and height 6 inches? 72 in.² or .5 ft²

54. The formula $C = 0.6n + 4$ estimates the temperature C in degrees Celsius when n is the number of cricket chirps in 15 seconds. If a cricket chirps 25 times in 15 seconds, what is an estimate for the temperature? 19°

REPRESENTATIONS deal with pictures, graphs, or objects that illustrate concepts.

Objective M: *Graph the solutions to any inequality of the form $x < a$ and similar inequalities and identify such graphs.* *(Lesson 4-9)*

55. Graph all solutions to $x < 24$. See margin.

56. Graph all solutions to $y > 2$.

57. Graph all solutions to $-4 \geq t$.

58. Graph all solutions to $6 \leq d$.

59. The solutions to what sentence are graphed here? $y \geq 2$.

Objective N: *Graph the solutions to any inequality of the form $a < x < b$ and similar inequalities and identify such graphs.* *(Lesson 4-9)*

60. Graph all solutions to $3 < x < 7$. See margin.

61. Graph all solutions to $-1 > y \geq -2$.

62. The solutions to what sentence are graphed here? $0 < x \leq 3$

HISTORY

Objective O: *Give rough dates and names of people for key ideas in arithmetic and algebra notation.* *(Lessons 4-1, 4-2)*

63. Write two arithmetic symbols used by computers but not much elsewhere. sample: **, ↑

64. *Multiple choice* Who is sometimes considered the "father of algebra"? (c)
    (a) Jacques Cousteau
    (b) Albert Einstein
    (c) François Viète
    (d) Augustin-Louis Cauchy

CHAPTER 4 Chapter Review 185

CHAPTER 5 ■ PATTERNS LEADING TO ADDITION

DAILY PACING CHART ■ CHAPTER 5

Students in the Full Course should complete the entire text by the end of the year. Students in the Minimal Course spend more time when there are quizzes and more time on the Chapter Review. Therefore, these students may not complete all of the chapters in the text.

DAY	MINIMAL COURSE	FULL COURSE
1	5-1	5-1
2	5-2	5-2
3	5-3	5-3
4	5-4	5-4
5	Quiz (TRF); Start 5-5.	Quiz (TRF); 5-5
6	Finish 5-5.	5-6
7	5-6	5-7
8	5-7	Quiz (TRF); 5-8
9	Quiz (TRF); Start 5-8.	5-9
10	Finish 5-8.	5-10
11	5-9	Progress Self-Test
12	5-10	Chapter Review
13	Progress Self-Test	Chapter Test (TRF)
14	Chapter Review	
15	Chapter Test (TRF)	

TESTING OPTIONS

■ Quiz on Lessons 5-1 Through 5-4   ■ Chapter 5 Test, Form A   ■ Chapter 5 Test, Cumulative Form
■ Quiz on Lessons 5-5 Through 5-7   ■ Chapter 5 Test, Form B

A Quiz and Test Writer is available for generating additional questions, additional quizzes, or additional forms of the Chapter Test.

PROVIDING FOR INDIVIDUAL DIFFERENCES

The student text is written for the *average* student. The program, however, can be adapted for both less capable and more capable students.

A blackline master (in the Teacher's Resource File) is provided for each lesson for those students who need more practice. The Teacher's Edition frequently provides an Error Analysis feature to provide additional instructional strategies.

For students who require additional challenge, Extension activities are regularly provided in the Teacher's Edition.

OBJECTIVES ■ CHAPTER 5

Students should master the chapter objectives by the time they complete the chapter. To ensure objective mastery, there is continual review built into each set of lesson questions. After students complete the chapter lessons, they assess their mastery on the Progress Self-Test. Then they do the Chapter Review and pay special attention to those questions that match the objectives missed on the Progress Self-Test. Students can get extra practice on these objectives by using the master for each lesson in the Teacher's Resource File.

OBJECTIVES FOR CHAPTER 5 (Organized into the SPUR categories—Skills, Properties, Uses, and Representations)	Progress Self-Test Questions	Chapter Review Questions	Teacher's Resource File	
			Lesson Master*	Chapter Test Forms A and B
SKILLS				
A: Add any numbers written as decimals or fractions.	1, 2, 4, 12–15, 30	1–10	5-2, 5-3, 5-4, 5-5	1, 2, 3, 4, 9, 10 11, 12
B: Calculate absolute value.	5, 6, 8	11–14	5-5	7, 8
C: Apply properties of addition to simplify expressions.	3, 7	15–22	5-4	5, 6
D: Solve equations of the form $x + a = b$.	16, 25	23–30	5-8	17, 18, 19
E: Find the perimeter of a polygon.	9–11, 21	31–35	5-10	32
PROPERTIES				
F: Identify properties of addition.	17–19	36–39	5-4, 5-7	13, 14, 15, 16
G: Classify polygons.	20	40–42	5-9	28
H: Identify parts and give names of polygons.	34	43–46	5-9	29, 30, 31
USES				
I: Use the Putting-together Model for Addition to form sentences involving addition.	23	47–49	5-1, 5-2, 5-8	24, 25, 27
J: Apply the Putting-together Model to relate lengths.	26, 27	50–52	5-10	22
K: Use the Slide Model for Addition to form sentences involving addition.	24, 29	53–56	5-3, 5-8	26
REPRESENTATIONS				
L: Calculate magnitudes of turns given angle measures or revolutions.	31–33	57–60	5-6	20, 21
M: Picture addition of positive and negative numbers using arrows on a number line.	28	61–63	5-3	23

*The Lesson Masters are numbered to match the lessons.

OVERVIEW ■ CHAPTER 5

Chapter 5 introduces an approach that recurs with the other basic operations in later chapters of this text. We have gathered many different ideas about addition and put them all together in this chapter. We do the same with subtraction (Chapter 7), multiplication (Chapters 9 and 10), and with division (Chapter 11).

Chapter 5 is an excellent illustration of the SPUR concept. The *Skills* cover adding fractions (Lesson 5-2), adding positive and negative numbers (Lesson 5-5), and solving the simplest equations

(Lesson 5-8). The *Properties* include zero and opposites (Lesson 5-4), associativity and commutativity (Lesson 5-7) and those necessary for solving equations (Lesson 5-8). *Uses* are also important topics throughout the chapter. We introduce the Putting-together Model in Lesson 5-1; a special case, perimeter, in Lesson 5-10. The Slide Model is found in Lesson 5-3; a special case involving angles, in Lesson 5-6. *Representations* of addition appear with fraction pies (Lesson 5-2), on the number line (Lessons 5-3 and 5-5), and with

clockwise and counterclockwise turns (Lesson 5-6).

Topics develop from simple to more complex. Uses of addition appear first as motivation for the study of addition. Familiar situations such as putting-together are a good starting point. The uses lead to the necessary skills of adding fractions and integers. After the skills, the properties are examined. All of these ideas are finally applied to the solving of simple sentences (addition with variables), which for many students is a new topic.

PERSPECTIVES ■ CHAPTER 5

The Perspectives provide the rationale for the inclusion of topics or approaches, provide mathematical background, and make connections within UCSMP.

5-1

THE PUTTING-TOGETHER MODEL FOR ADDITION

One of the unique features of this book is the use of *models for operations*. We generalize many uses of an operation in a model. A model is like a property of uses and can be applied in many situations.

We use models for a number of reasons. First, they help to make sense out of applications. When students know all the models for an operation, they really know all its uses. Second, models help in choosing an operation. Third, models can be used to verify properties. (For example, someone might verify the Commutative and Associative Properties by explaining that piles of paper clips can be counted in any order without changing the sum.) Fourth, models can be used to teach an operation. Recall that in the earliest grades, addition almost always starts with putting-together activities.

When discussing the Putting-together Model, do not be concerned about whether the numbers are written as fractions or decimals

are written as fractions or decimals or in any other form. The model works regardless of the form; the expression $a + b$ seldom carries with it any knowledge of the way a and b look.

5-2

ADDING FRACTIONS

We introduce common denominators by making lists of equivalent fractions and then searching for a pair with the same denominator to add together. Our goal is simply to get students to realize that they need to have like denominators rather than have them concentrate on finding the denominators. If students do not already know this skill, it will come with experience.

If students own calculators that do operations with fractions, you can use them to check computations such as those in Questions 14-17.

5-3

THE SLIDE MODEL FOR ADDITION

The Putting-together Model would have to be distorted in order to ap-

ply to negative numbers. The Slide Model applies naturally. The remainder of the content in this lesson is standard: the introduction of addition with positive and negative numbers through applications and illustrations on the number line.

5-4

ZERO AND OPPOSITES

This lesson provides more practice on addition of positive and negative numbers. The three properties highlighted on pages 202–203 do not have names that are universally accepted. You may wish to use your own favorite, but be flexible enough to allow a student to use these.

5-5

ADDING POSITIVE AND NEGATIVE NUMBERS

This lesson, the third to deal with addition of positive and negative numbers, has two objectives. One is to introduce absolute value; the second is to use absolute value to give a definite rule for adding positive and negative numbers.

Note that many students will not need this rule. Do not force students to learn the rule if they do not need it—the rule is more complicated than the skill. The rule is there for those students who, even after all the slide-model situations, need a crutch.

5-6
TURNS

This lesson is very important for future work in geometry and trigonometry. In geometry, the Fundamental Property of Turns is called "angle addition." The idea is crucial to understanding relationships involving parallel lines and angle sums in polygons.

In trigonometry, students are expected to understand clockwise and counterclockwise turns immediately. If they have never seen such turns before, they can get very confused.

Turn is the simple name for *rotation*, one of the fundamental transformations that relate congruent figures. Although congruence is not mentioned in this lesson, there are hints of the concept. For example, the chairs in the Ferris wheel (Questions 21-23) are congruent to each other.

5-7
THE COMMUTATIVE AND ASSOCIATIVE PROPERTIES

Because the names for these properties are universal, students should memorize them.

Students frequently misspell the word *commutative*. Tell them to think of the word *commuter*, which has the same root. Commuters also switch order: they go from home to work, then from work to home.

Because addition is both commutative and associative, it is reasonable to say, "Add all those numbers," when more than two numbers are given. It is also cor-

rect to say, "Add *a* and *b*." Chapter 7 points out that because subtraction does not have these properties, it is not appropriate to say, "Subtract all those numbers"; it is also ambiguous to say, "Subtract *a* and *b* ."

In the deposit and withdrawal example in this lesson, and in many previous examples in this chapter, we are anticipating the later discussion of subtraction of positive and negative numbers. Here students are being taught to use addition $a + -b$. In Chapter 7, they will use $a - b$ for the same problem.

5-8
SOLVING *x* + *a* = *b*

This lesson presents a method for solving a type of equation. We have postponed this presentation to promote mental calculation where appropriate and to develop the ability to translate words into an equation. By now many students may have figured out all or part of this procedure on their own.

Throughout this book, we identify reasons for steps with names of properties. We do so to get the student ready for algebra. Even though we give the steps, it is not crucial at this point that a student know the reasons behind each step. However, students should know what it means to solve a sentence, how to check solutions, and how to translate real situations into sentences. The formal study of sentence solving should come in algebra courses.

A word of caution is in order. Once steps used in solving equations are introduced, many students proceed immediately with the mechanical steps of solving the equation. They do not first examine the equation to determine whether it can be solved mentally or whether it has an unusual feature that needs attention. Urge students to look closely at an equation *before* they begin the steps.

5-9
POLYGONS

A lesson on polygons is included at this time for four reasons. First, it is necessary for the discussion of perimeter that immediately follows. (Perimeter, or adding lengths, fits naturally in a chapter on addition.) Second, it provides a nice change of pace and a day for doing some terminology while at the same time continuing the practice of equation solving. Third, we use polygons quite a bit in Chapter 6 as vehicles for studying problem solving. And fourth, polygons are obviously an important topic in geometry.

The distinction between $\overleftrightarrow{AB}$ and $\overline{AB}$ is customary in most textbooks. However, this distinction is not always made by mathematicians, who usually use *AB* for both and rely on context to tell whether lines or segments are indicated.

Some people use the word *septagon* as the name for a 7-sided polygon. *Heptagon* is the more common name.

5-10
ADDING LENGTHS

Many students know perimeter from earlier courses. For those to whom it is new, this content is easy to learn.

In this lesson, students learn the fourth, and last, symbol using *AB* when *A* and *B* are points. $\overrightarrow{AB}$ was introduced in Lesson 3-5; $\overleftrightarrow{AB}$ and $\overline{AB}$ in Lesson 5-9. This symbol for length, *AB*, is the hardest to learn because it stands for a number, not a geometric figure. Furthermore, *AB* does not mean *A* times *B*.

Perimeter and area must be significantly numerically different to make the point that these are different ideas. To distinguish area from perimeter, consider a square whose side has a large numerical length, perhaps 125 feet. Its area then is 125^2, or 15,625 square feet. Its perimeter is 500 feet. That's enough of a difference to make the point.

CHAPTER 5

We suggest 13 to 15 days for this chapter: 10 to 12 days on the lessons, 1 day for the Progress Self-Test, 1 to 2 days for the Chapter Review, and 1 day for the exam.

CHAPTER 5

Patterns Leading to Addition

186

***U**rban* areas are cities and suburbs. Less-populated places outside the urban areas are called *rural* areas. The table below gives the 1970 populations of rural and urban areas in all of the regions in the United States. Some of the numbers in the table were calculated by adding other numbers.

Region	Urban	Rural	Total
New England (ME, NH, VT, MA, RI, CT)	9,043,517	2,798,146	11,847,186
Middle Atlantic (NY,NJ, PA)	30,406,301	6,792,739	37,203,339
East North Central (OH, IN, IL, MI, WI)	30,091,847	10,160,629	40,252,678
West North Central (MN, IA, MO, ND, SD, NB, KS)	10,388,913	5,930,274	16,324,389
South Atlantic (DE, MD, DC, VA, WV, NC, SC, GA, FL)	19,523,920	11,147,417	30,671,337
East South Central (KY, TN, AL, MS)	6,987,943	5,815,527	12,804,552
West South Central (AR, LA, OK, TX)	14,028,098	5,292,462	19,322,458
Mountain (MT, ID, WY, CO, NM, AZ, UT, NV)	6,054,979	2,226,583	8,283,585
Pacific (WA, OR, CA, AK, HI)	22,799,412	3,723,219	26,525,774
Totals	149,324,930	53,886,996	203,235,298

Every place in the United States is classified either as urban or rural. Knowing this, you can discover that the Census Bureau made errors in its tabulation. (The Bureau discovered the errors after tabulation.) Addition can help you locate the errors.

In this chapter, you will study many other uses of addition.

Direct student attention to the table showing the 1970 populations of rural and urban areas in the different regions of the United States. Ask students to analyze briefly the information given. (More people live in urban than in rural areas; in 1970, the population was greatest in the East North Central region.) Point out that population data of the type found in the table is collected only in years that end in "0".

On this page, we use the word "region" in its familiar, nontechnical sense. The official term used by the Bureau of the Census for what we call region is "division."

Students may wonder how big an area has to be before it is classified as urban. The Bureau of Census classifies urban areas as cities, suburbs, and towns with at least 2500 people. You might wish to ask students for examples of each type of area.

When you discuss Question 32 in Lesson 5-1, explain that the totals in the rightmost column are not the sums of the numbers in the urban and rural columns because the rural and urban figures are from the "initial tabulated count" of the 1970 Census, but the totals are from the "official count" of the 1970 Census. The total population in the initial tabulated count was 203,211,926. The total population in the official count was 203,235,298. The "errors" in the initial tabulation by the Census Bureau are normal and expected, and found in every census as large and as complex as the U.S. census.

RESOURCES
- Lesson Master 5-1
- Visual for Teaching Aid 24:
  Question 34

OBJECTIVE

■ Use the Putting-together Model for Addition to form sentences involving addition.

TEACHING NOTES

Two topics for discussion in this lesson are the purpose of models and the issue of overlaps in the Putting-together Model. Because students have little trouble deciding when to add in applications, and because most students have been taught to think of addition as putting-together, they may not appreciate the value of this particular model, and therefore of models in general. Mention that different models will be used in other lessons, and discuss some of the advantages of models (see Perspective for this lesson).

The questions will help you emphasize that, in order for the Putting-together Model to work, units must be the same, and there can be no overlap. When there is overlap, the overlapped portion must be subtracted. For example, if Team A has 16 members and Team B has 20 members, and if 5 students are on both teams, then $16 + 20 - 5$, or 31, students are on either one team or the other.

LESSON

5-1

The Putting-together Model for Addition

Addition is important because adding gives answers in many actual situations. It is impossible to list all the uses of addition. So we give a general pattern that includes many of the uses. We call this general pattern a model for the operation. In this book, we identify two models for addition: putting-together and slide. Here are five instances of the **Putting-together Model for Addition**.

1. You have 8 cassette tapes. A friend has 5. How many tapes are there in all?

2. Look at the table on the previous page. In 1970, the population of the New England region was 11,847,186 and the population of the Middle Atlantic region was 37,203,339. How many people lived in these regions combined?

3. Suppose a book is purchased for $2.95 and the tax is $0.18. What is the total cost?

4. Taken from my pay is 20% for taxes and 7% for social security. How much is taken altogether?

5. One package weighed $2\frac{1}{2}$ lb and the other weighed $2\frac{3}{4}$ lb. How much did they weigh altogether?

The general pattern is easy to describe using variables.

> **Putting-together Model for Addition:**
>
> A count or measure x is put together with a count or measure y with the same units. If there is no overlap, then the result has count or measure $x + y$.

188

The numbers in putting-together may be large or small. They may be written as decimals, percents, or fractions.

When the units are not the same, you must make them alike before the addition of the numbers will work. For instance:

6. 2 meters + 46 centimeters
   = 2 meters + 0.46 meter
   = 2.46 meters
7. 8 apples + 14 oranges
   = 8 pieces of fruit + 14 pieces of fruit
   = 22 pieces of fruit

Numbers to be added are called **addends**. If one addend is unknown, the putting-together model can still be used.

8. You weigh 50 kg and a friend weighs x kg. If you step on a scale together, the total weight is $(50 + x)$ kg.

The idea of Example 8 can be applied to weighing a cat that is too small to be weighed on an adult scale. Let c stand for the cat's weight.

9. Suppose a person steps on the scale and weighs 130.5 lb. Together the person and the cat weigh $(c + 130.5)$ lb. Now the person picks up the cat and steps on the scale again. Suppose the total weight is 136.25 lb. Then the cat's weight is the solution to the equation $c + 130.5 = 136.25$.

If you do not know how to solve an equation of this type, you will learn how to do so later in this chapter.

When there is overlap in the addends, simple addition will not give a correct answer. For example, imagine that 50 pages of a book have pictures and 110 pages have tables. You cannot conclude that 160 pages have either pictures or tables. Some pages might have both pictures and tables.

1. Write the addition example for each statement.
a. Myisha bought a skirt for $24.95 and a blouse for $19.95. How much did she spend?
$24.95 + $19.95
b. There were c children on the school bus. Five more got on at the next stop. How many children were on the bus then?
$c + 5$
c. Dora planted t tulip bulbs and d daffodil bulbs in her back yard. How many bulbs did she plant?
$t + d$

2. Write an equation that relates the three numbers mentioned.
a. Louis had m marbles, then got 25 more for his birthday. He now has 108 marbles.
$m + 25 = 108$
b. Mrs. Ruiz bought two packages of chicken for dinner. One package weighed 1.31 pounds; and the other, 1.42 pounds. Together the chicken packages weighed c pounds.
$1.31 + 1.42 = c$
c.

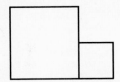

The area of the larger square is 100 square inches. The area of the small square is s^2. The total area is 125 square inches.
$100 + s^2 = 125$

189

NOTES ON QUESTIONS
Questions 4 and 5:
These require students to view the model from a different perspective. Students may want to share their examples with the class.

Questions 10 and 21:
There is *insufficient information* to answer these. Some students may spend a great deal of time trying to figure them out. Too often students assume that there is always enough information given to answer all questions.

ADDITIONAL ANSWERS
1. a general pattern including many uses of the operation

3. When a count or measure *x* is put together with a count or measure *y* with the same units and no overlap, the result is a count or measure *x* + *y*.

4. sample: If two letters weigh 15 g and 32 g, then their total weight is 47 g.

5. sample: If you bike $\frac{1}{4}$ mile and $\frac{1}{2}$ mile, then altogether you have biked $\frac{3}{4}$ miles.

7. Both are. If you change the units to pieces of fruit, then Carla is right. If you do not change the units, Peter is right.

9. 1. 13 pieces;
2. 49,050,525 people;
3. $3.13; 4. 27%;
5. 5.25 lb

10. not enough information to tell; also, there is overlap, so addition does not give the answer

Questions

Covering the Reading

1. What is a model for an operation? See margin.

2. What is an addend? a number to be added

3. What is the Putting-together Model for Addition? See margin.

In 4 and 5, give an example of the putting-together model when each addend:

4. has grams as its unit See margin.

5. is written using fractions See margin.

6. Mary gets on a scale and weighs *M* kg. Craig gets on a scale and it registers 60 kg. Together they get on the scale and the scale shows 108 kg. Write a sentence relating *M*, 60, and 108.
$M + 60 = 108$

7. Carla says you can add apples and oranges. Peter says you cannot. Who is right? See margin.

8. Write 3 meters + 4 centimeters as one quantity.
3.04 m, or 304 cm

9. Answer the questions given in instances 1-5 on page 188. (In instance 5, you may wish to change the fractions to decimals.)
See margin.

Applying the Mathematics

10. Together Dan and Diane have $20. Together Diane and Donna have $15. How much do the three of them have in total?
See margin.

In 11 and 12, give an equation relating the three numbers mentioned.

11. Rich owns 15 tapes. Ruth has *r* tapes. Together they have 43 tapes. $15 + r = 43$

12. Doris worked $23\frac{1}{2}$ hours last week at the grocery store. David worked 45 hours. Together they worked *T* hours. $23\frac{1}{2} + 45 = T$

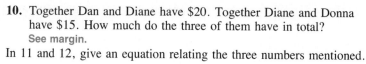

13. Give an inequality relating the three numbers mentioned. The chair will support at most 250 pounds. Mike weighs *M* pounds. Nina weighs 112 pounds. The chair will hold both of them.
$M + 112 \leq 250$

In 14–17, perform the addition.

14. 3 feet + 4 inches = __?__ inches 40

15. 6 pounds + 13 ounces = __?__ ounces 109

16. 4 meters + 351 millimeters = __?__ millimeters 4351

17. 100 grams + 2 kilograms = __?__ grams 2100

190

18. Jane has 2 brothers and 1 sister. Her sister Joan has 2 brothers and 1 sister. How many children are in the family?   **4**

19. Michelle has *b* brothers and *s* sisters. How many children are in the family?   **b + s + 1**

20. Of the 25 students in Ms. Jones's class, 9 are on a school team, 10 are in the band or chorus, and 7 are in some other school activity.
  a. Is this possible?   **Yes**
  b. Why or why not?   **Some students may be in more than one activity.**

21. In Springfield last year it rained or snowed on 140 days. The sun shone on *s* days. Can you determine *s* from this information?
  No, rain and sun could appear on the same day.

In 22–24, refer to the table on the page 187.

22. There are 30 numbers in the table. How many of these numbers are sums of other numbers in the table?   **12**

23. Which region has the smallest rural population?   **Mountain region**

24. Suppose there is an error in the number given for the South Atlantic urban population. If you correct this error, how many other numbers will you have to correct?   **3**

Review

25. Which are solutions to $0 \le x < 50$? *(Lesson 4-9)*
  (a) 35.2   (b) 0   (c) -4   (d) 1/100   (e) 50   (f) 60%
  (a), (b), (d), (f)

26. Round 99.3% to the nearest whole number. (Hint: Watch out!)
  (Lesson 2-5)   **1**

27. Mentally, find the solution to $4 + A = 7$. *(Lesson 4-8)*   **3**

28. How many degrees are there in: *(Lessons 3-5, 3-6)*
  a. a right angle?   **90°**
  b. half a circle?   **180°**
  c. an acute angle?   **less than 90°**

29. *True or false?* $-10 \le -8$ *(Lesson 1-5)*   **True**

LESSON 5-1   The Putting-together Model for Addition   **191**

FOLLOW-UP

MORE PRACTICE
For more questions on SPUR Objectives, use *Lesson Master 5-1*, shown below.

EXTENSION
There are many sizes and types of magic squares. A useful book on the topic is *Magic Squares and Cubes* by W. S. Andrews (Dover Publications). Students can do research on different types of magic squares. They can also try to find the pattern for constructing odd-numbered squares (3 × 3, 5 × 5, and so on).

NAME _____

LESSON MASTER 5-1
QUESTIONS ON **SPUR** OBJECTIVES

■**USES**   *Objective I (See Chapter Review, pages 237–239, for objectives.)*
In 1–4, write an equation relating the numbers mentioned.

1. Mark had 3 hits in last night's baseball game and Jeff had *h* hits. Together they had 7 hits. $3 + h = 7$

2. Gerry spent $105 at the grocery store, $18 on gas for the car, and $25 at a restaurant with friends. The total amount Gerry spent was $*M*. $105 + 18 + 25 = M$

3. The 130 eighth-graders in Pleasant School take 3 buses for a science field trip. There are *f* students in the first bus, *s* in the second, and *t* in the third bus. $f + s + t = 130$

4. In 1980, the population of the United States was 226,547,082. Of this number, *u* people lived in urban areas and *r* in rural areas. $u + r = 226{,}547{,}082$

5. Together Sam and Jan have 15 cousins. Together Dan and Jan have 21 cousins. How many cousins do Sam, Jan, and Dan have altogether?   **not enough information**

6. What needs to be done with this problem before performing the addition?
  15 roses + 5 carnations =   **The units must be the same, such as "flowers."**

In 7–12, perform the addition.

7. 1 mile + 3000 feet = ___**8280**___ feet

8. 3 pounds + 14 ounces = ___**62**___ ounces

9. 2 liters + 650 milliliters = ___**2.650**___ liters

10. 2 hours + 32 minutes = ___**152**___ minutes

11. 4 yards + 2 feet = ___**168**___ inches

12. 6.3 meters + 20 centimeters = ___**6.5**___ meters

32. Every number in the "total" column is not the sum of the urban and rural populations in its row except for the South Atlantic entry. From top to bottom, the sums would be 11,841,663; 37,199,040; 40,252,476; 16,319,187; 30,671,337 (already correct); 12,803,470; 19,320,560; 8,281,562; 26,522,631; 203,211,926.

33. There is overlap in the volumes of sugar and water when they are combined chemically.

34.

16	3	2	13
5	10	11	8
9	6	7	12
4	15	14	1

30. If climbing up 2 meters is represented by the number 2, what number will represent each event? *(Lesson 1-5)*
a. climbing down 6 meters   -6
b. staying at the same height   0

31. Which is larger, $\frac{3}{10}$ or $\frac{29}{97}$? *(Lesson 1-8)*   3/10

Exploration

32. Find an error in the table on the first page of this chapter.
See margin.

33. When 1 cup of sugar is added to 1 cup of water, the result is not 2 cups of the mixture. Why not?   See margin.

34. In the array of numbers shown here, the whole numbers from 1 to 9 are each used once. The numbers in each row, column, and diagonal add up to 15. The array is called a *magic square*.

2	9	4
7	5	3
6	1	8

Here is the start to a bigger magic square. Enough numbers are given to complete it. Find the missing numbers.   See margin.

		2	13
5		11	
	6		12
4	15	14	

192

5-2

Adding Fractions

OBJECTIVES

A Add positive fractions and mixed numbers.
I Use the Putting-together Model for Addition to form sentences involving addition of fractions.

Nanette put 1/3 cup of milk in a casserole. She forgot and then put in another 1/3 cup of milk. No, no, Nanette! Think of thirds as units. Then by the putting-together model for addition:

$$1 \text{ third} + 1 \text{ third} = 2 \text{ thirds (cups)}$$

$$\tfrac{1}{3} + \tfrac{1}{3} = \tfrac{2}{3} \text{ (cups)}$$

Milton runs to keep in shape. Today he ran 3/4 mile. Yesterday he ran 9/4 miles. Two days ago he ran 10/4 miles. My, my, Milton! The total amount he ran is:

$$3 \text{ fourths} + 9 \text{ fourths} + 10 \text{ fourths} = 22 \text{ fourths (miles)}$$

$$\tfrac{3}{4} + \tfrac{9}{4} + \tfrac{10}{4} = \tfrac{22}{4} \text{ (miles)}$$

The general pattern is easy to see. To add fractions with the same denominator, add the numerators and keep the denominator the same. Here is the pattern using variables:

Addition of fractions with the same denominator:

$$\frac{a}{c} + \frac{b}{c} = \frac{a + b}{c}$$

Example 1 Simplify $\frac{11}{8} + \frac{5}{8}$.

Solution $\frac{11}{8} + \frac{5}{8} = \frac{11 + 5}{8} = \frac{16}{8}$

Check Check by using decimals.
$\frac{11}{8} = 1.375$, $\frac{5}{8} = 0.625$, and $\frac{16}{8} = 2$.
Does $1.375 + 0.625 = 2$? Yes, so the answer checks.

Example 2 Simplify $\frac{3}{x} + \frac{5}{x}$.

Solution $\frac{3}{x} + \frac{5}{x} = \frac{3+5}{x} = \frac{8}{x}$

Check This should work for any value of x other than zero. So, to check, substitute some value for x. We pick 4, because fourths are terminating decimals.

Does $\frac{3}{4} + \frac{5}{4} = \frac{8}{4}$? Check by rewriting the fractions as decimals. Does $0.75 + 1.25 = 2$? Yes. Here is a picture of $3/4 + 5/4 = 2$.

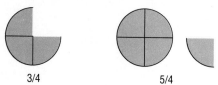

3/4   5/4

Bill ate 3 of 8 pieces of one pizza. He ate 2 of 6 pieces of another pizza of the same size. How much did he eat in all?

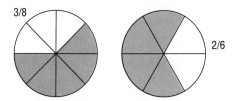

3/8   2/6

To figure this out requires adding $\frac{3}{8}$ and $\frac{2}{6}$, fractions with different denominators. Use the Equal Fractions Property to find equal fractions with the same denominator. Some fractions equal to 3/8 are 6/16, 9/24, 12/32, and so on. Some fractions equal to 2/6 are 4/12, 8/24, and so on. That's enough. Choose the fractions with denominator 24. The number 24 is a **common denominator.**

$$\frac{3}{8} + \frac{2}{6} = \frac{9}{24} + \frac{8}{24}$$
$$= \frac{17}{24}$$

Bill ate the equivalent of 17/24 of an entire pizza. Since $17/24 = 0.708... \approx 71\%$, we could say that Bill ate about 71% of a pizza.

Notice that the common denominator 24 is a multiple of both 8 and 6. In fact, it is the smallest common integer multiple of 8 and 6. For this reason, it is called the **least common multiple** of these numbers. If you use the least common multiple as the common denominator, the numbers will be smaller than if you use any other multiple. It is called the **least common denominator.** This is done in Example 3.

194

Example 3 Add $\frac{5}{6} + \frac{1}{2} + \frac{7}{3}$.

Solution The product of the denominators is 36, but that is much bigger than is needed. Since 6 is the least common multiple of the other denominators, 6 is the least common denominator.

$$= \frac{5}{6} + \frac{3}{6} + \frac{14}{6}$$
$$= \frac{22}{6}$$

In lowest terms, the answer is $\frac{11}{3}$.

All the examples can be checked by using decimals. For instance, to check Example 3:

$$5/6 \approx 0.83333$$
$$1/2 = 0.5$$
$$7/3 \approx 2.33333$$

So the sum of the fractions should equal about 3.66666. Since $11/3 = 3.66666...$, the answer checks.

When adding an integer and a fraction, use the denominator of the fraction as the common denominator.

Example 4 Write $2 + \frac{3}{5}$ as a simple fraction.

Solution Replace 2 by $\frac{2}{1}$. Then multiply the numerator and denominator of $\frac{2}{1}$ by 5.

$$= \frac{2}{1} + \frac{3}{5}$$
$$= \frac{10}{5} + \frac{3}{5}$$
$$= \frac{13}{5}$$

The sum $2 + \frac{3}{5}$ is often written as $2\frac{3}{5}$ without the + sign. To do Example 4, many people use a shortcut to find the numerator of the simple fraction: multiply 5 by 2, and then add 3.

LESSON 5-2 Adding Fractions   **195**

Covering the Reading

1. On Monday, Mary ran 7/4 kilometers. On Tuesday, she ran 9/4 km. What is the total number of kilometers Mary ran? **16/4 km, or 4 km**

2. Bill used 5/2 cups of flour in one recipe and 3/2 cups of flour in another. How much flour did he use altogether? **8/2 cups, or 4 cups**

3. Terri ate 1/3 of one pizza and 1/4 of another of the same size.
   a. What problem with fractions determines the total that Terri ate? **1/3 + 1/4**
   b. Name five fractions equal to 1/3. **See margin.**
   c. Name five fractions equal to 1/4. **See margin.**
   d. What is the total amount of pizza that Terri ate? **7/12**

4. a. To write $\frac{2}{7} + \frac{3}{5}$ as a single fraction, what number can be the denominator of the sum? **Sample: 35**
   b. Do the addition of part a. $\frac{31}{35}$

5. a. Write $\frac{4}{5} + \frac{3}{10}$ as a single fraction. $\frac{11}{10}$
   b. Check by using decimals. $.8 + .3 = 1.1 = \frac{11}{10}$

In 6–11, simplify.

6. $\frac{50}{11} + \frac{5}{11}$ $\frac{55}{11}$ or 5

7. $\frac{13}{x} + \frac{4}{x}$ $\frac{17}{x}$

8. $\frac{8}{9} + \frac{1}{15}$ $\frac{43}{45}$

9. $\frac{5}{8} + \frac{2}{5}$ $\frac{41}{40}$

10. $\frac{11}{7} + \frac{6}{7} + \frac{15}{7}$ $\frac{32}{7}$

11. $\frac{2}{3} + \frac{5}{3} + \frac{5}{6}$ $\frac{19}{6}$

12. a. Write $4 + \frac{2}{5}$ as a simple fraction. $\frac{22}{5}$
    b. How is $4 + \frac{2}{5}$ usually written? $4\frac{2}{5}$

Applying the Mathematics

13. Two stoplights are 2 km apart. The next stoplight is 1/2 km further. How far apart are the first and third lights? **5/2 km or 2 1/2 km**

In 14–17 write the sum as a simple fraction.

14. $4\frac{3}{8} + 2\frac{1}{5}$ $\frac{263}{40}$

15. $4\frac{3}{8} + 2\frac{2}{3}$ $\frac{169}{24}$

16. $\frac{6}{7} + 3\frac{7}{12}$ $\frac{373}{84}$

17. $9.75 + \frac{100}{11} + 3$ $\frac{961}{44}$

18. After a rainstorm, the water level in a swimming pool rose by $1\frac{1}{2}''$. The following day, after another storm, the water level rose $2\frac{1}{4}''$.
    a. What was the total change in the water level? $3\frac{3}{4}''$, or $\frac{15}{4}''$
    b. If the deep end of the pool was originally 9 ft deep, how deep was the water at the end of the second day? $9'3\frac{3}{4}''$, or $111\frac{3}{4}''$

196

19. The Venturi family ate 6 pieces of a 28-piece loaf of bread at breakfast. They used 12 pieces of the loaf in making sandwiches for lunch. One of them used 2 pieces for an after-school snack. How many pieces of the loaf were eaten altogether? *(Lesson 5-1)*
20 pieces

20. Minnie has 5 brothers and 2 sisters. Her brother Dennis has 4 brothers and 3 sisters. How many children are in the family? *(Lesson 5-1)*
8 children

21. A dinosaur known as Brontosaurus weighed about 60,000 pounds. Write this number in scientific notation. *(Lesson 2-3)* 6×10^4

22. Find the measure of angle FUD. *(Lesson 3-5)* **166°**

In 23 and 24. **a.** Name one solution to the sentence. **b.** Graph all solutions to the sentence. *(Lesson 4-9)*

23. $x < 3$ **a.** Samples: -3, 0, 1/2; **b.** See margin.

24. $-2 \leq y$ **a.** Samples: -1, .01, 5; **b.** See margin.

25. a. In music, two eighth notes take the same time as a quarter note. What addition of fractions explains this? **1/8 + 1/8 =**
  b. What amount of time is taken by a sixteenth note followed by another sixteenth note? **1/8**

two sixteenth notes

26. a. List all the factors of 28, 49, and of the least common multiple of 28 and 49.
  b. List all the factors of 30, 40, and of the least common multiple of 30 and 40.
  c. Suppose you know the factors of two numbers. Describe how to find the factors of the least common multiple of the numbers. **a. 28: 1, 2, 4, 7, 14, 28; 49: 1, 7, 49; 196: 1, 2, 4, 7, 14, 28, 49, 98, 196; b. 30: 1, 2, 3, 5, 6, 10, 15, 30; 40: 1, 2, 4, 5, 8, 10, 20, 40; 102: 1, 2, 3, 4, 5, 6, 8, 10, 12, 15, 20, 24, 30, 40, 60, 120; c. Divide the l.c.m. by each factor of each of the two numbers. The factors of the l.c.m. are all of these divisors and quotients.**

LESSON 5-2 Adding Fractions **197**

FOLLOW-UP

MORE PRACTICE
For more questions on SPUR Objectives, use *Lesson Master 5-2*, shown below.

EXTENSION
Have students investigate the sum of the infinite series below. (The sum approaches 1 but is always a little less than 1.) $\frac{1}{2} + \frac{1}{4} + \frac{1}{8} + \frac{1}{16} + \frac{1}{32} + \ldots$

EVALUATION
Alternative Assessment
Ask each student to write a problem similar to **Questions 1–3, 13,** or **18,** which use addition of fractions and/or mixed numbers. Some of the problems can be presented for class solution.

OBJECTIVES

A Add positive or negative numbers written as decimals or fractions.

K Use the Slide Model for Addition to form sentences involving addition.

M Picture addition of positive and negative numbers using arrows on a number line.

TEACHING NOTES

An important goal of this lesson is that a student be able to think of a situation requiring addition of positive and negative numbers. Then the student should use the situation to get the result to such an addition.

Students should learn how to add positive and negative numbers with and without the calculator. Emphasize that to use the calculator for simple additions is a waste of time. Also, since it is not so easy to enter negative numbers on a calculator, errors frequently occur. Students should always check their answers by thinking about a situation in which the numbers stand for something.

LESSON

5-3

The Slide Model for Addition

Recall that negative numbers are used when a situation has two opposite directions. Examples are deposits and withdrawals in a savings account, ups and downs of temperatures or weight, profits and losses in business, and gains and losses in football or other games. In these situations, you may need to add negative numbers. Here is a situation that leads to the addition problem $10 + -12$.

Example 1 Flood waters go up 10 feet and then go back 12 feet. What is the effect of all of this?

Solution The waters went down 2 feet. $10 + -12 = -2$

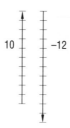

Example 1 is pictured above. Think of the waters sliding up and then sliding back down.

Example 2 Tony spends $4 for dinner and then earns $7 for baby-sitting. What is the net result of this?

Solution Tony has $3 more than he had before dinner.

Example 2 illustrates the addition problem -4 + 7. The -4 is for spending $4. The 7 is for earning $7. Ending up with $3 more is 3. So -4 + 7 = 3. You can picture this on a number line.

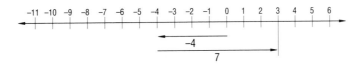

Start at 0. Think of -4 as a slide 4 units to the left. Draw the arrow pointing left. Think of 7 as an arrow going 7 units to the right but starting at -4. Where does the second arrow end? At 3, the sum.

In the **Slide Model for Addition,** positive numbers are shifts or changes or slides in one direction. Negative numbers are slides in the opposite direction. The + sign means "followed by." The sum indicates the net result.

Slide Model for Addition:

If a slide x is followed by a slide y, the result is a slide $x + y$.

Example 3 What is -3 + -2?

Solution Think of a slide 3 units to the left, followed by a slide 2 more units to the left. The result is a slide 5 units to the left. -3 + -2 = -5.

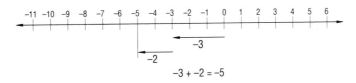

$$-3 + -2 = -5$$

The $\boxed{\pm}$ or $\boxed{+/-}$ key on a calculator changes a number to its opposite. The following key sequence can be used to add -3 and -2.

3 $\boxed{+/-}$ $\boxed{+}$ 2 $\boxed{+/-}$ $\boxed{=}$

There can be slides with positive numbers. If the temperature goes up 9° and then goes up 7° more, the result is an increase of 16°. Of course you know this. You have known some instances of the slide model for many years.

LESSON 5-3 The Slide Model for Addition **199**

1. Maria earns $12 shoveling snow but uses $8 to pay back money borrowed from her mother. What is the net result of this?
4; she has $4 left.

2. The hot-air balloon rose 25 feet to go over a tall building, then went down 45 feet so passengers could get a better view of the parade. What was the effect of all this?
-20; it went down 20 ft.

3. Write the key sequence to add on a calculator. Write the answer.
a. $-5 + -2$
5 $\boxed{\pm}$ $\boxed{+}$ 2 $\boxed{\pm}$ $\boxed{=}$; **-7**

b. $-10.3 + 90.42$
10.3 $\boxed{\pm}$ $\boxed{+}$ 90.42 $\boxed{=}$;
80.12

c. $\frac{1}{3} + -\frac{2}{3}$
1 $\boxed{\div}$ 3 $\boxed{+}$ 2 $\boxed{\pm}$ $\boxed{\div}$ 3 $\boxed{=}$;
-.3333333... or $-\frac{1}{3}$

4. Draw a picture using arrows and a number line.
a. $4 + -3 = ?$

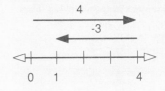

b. $-2.5 + -3.5 = ?$

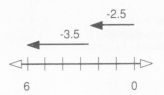

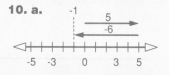
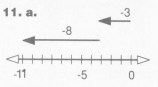

Questions

Covering the Reading

1. What is the Slide Model for Addition?   See margin.

In 2–5, what does each phrase mean in the slide model?

2. a positive number
   slide to the right or up

3. a negative number
   slide to the left or down

4. the + sign   followed by

5. the sum   the net result

In 6–9, the arrow below represents a slide of 5 on a number line. Using a number line with the same scale, draw an arrow for the given number.   See margin.

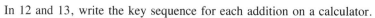

6. -5   7. 10   8. -10   9. 6

10. a. Draw a picture of 5 + -6 using arrows.   See margin.
    b. 5 + -6 =?   -1

11. a. Draw a picture of -3 + -8 using arrows.   See margin.
    b. -3 + -8 =?   -11

In 12 and 13, write the key sequence for each addition on a calculator.
   See margin.

12. 24 + -5 (the sum should be 19)

13. -1 + -8 (the sum should be -9)

In 14–18, **a.** what addition is suggested by each situation? **b.** What is the answer to that addition?

14. The temperature falls 5°, then falls 3° more.   a. -5 + -3; b. -8

15. A person gets a paycheck for $250, then buys a coat for $150.
    a. 250 + -150; b. 100

16. Flood waters gain 15 feet, then go back 17 feet.   a. 15 + -17; b. -2

Applying the Mathematics

17. A person withdraws $50, then withdraws $40.27.
    a. -50 + -40.27; b. -90.27

18. Pat gains 2.3 kg one month, loses 2.3 kg the next.
    a. 2.3 + -2.3; b. 0

19. Translate -7 + -5 into a real-life situation and do the addition.
    See margin.

20. Translate $\frac{3}{8}$ + -$\frac{2}{8}$ into a real-life situation and do the addition.
    See margin.

200

In 21–23, what is the result in each case?

21. A ship goes 40 km in one direction and then goes 60 km in the opposite direction. **It goes 20 km in the opposite direction.**

22. You walk north 300 feet and then walk south 50 feet.
You wind up 250 ft north.

23. The temperature is at -4° and then falls 3°. **The temperature is -7°.**

In 24–26, choose the answer from the following choices.
   (a) The sum is always positive.
   (b) The sum is always negative.
   (c) The sum is sometimes positive, sometimes negative.

24. Two negative numbers are added. **(b)**

25. Two positive numbers are added. **(a)**

26. A positive and a negative number are added. **(c)**

Review

27. In the Canadian province of Manitoba, 26% of the people belong to the United Church of Christ, 25% are Roman Catholic, 12% are Anglican, 7% Lutheran, 6% Mennonite, and 6% Ukrainian Catholic.
   a. Assuming no one belongs to two churches, what percent of Manitobans do not belong to any of these churches? **18%**
   b. The population of Manitoba is about 1,070,000. About how many people are Anglicans? *(Lesson 2-6)* **128,000 people**

28. The percent p of discount on an item can be calculated by using the formula $p = 100(1 - n/g)$. In this formula, g is the original price, and n is the new price. Find the percent of discount on an item reduced from: **a.** $2 to $1. **b.** $2.95 to $1.95. *(Lesson 4-6)*
a. 50%; b. 33.9%

29. Suppose $a = 3.2$ and $x = 1.5$. Evaluate $[40 - (4a - 10)]/(4x)$.
(Lesson 4-6) **6.2**

30. Simplify $\frac{11}{6} + \frac{2}{3}$. *(Lesson 5-2)* $\frac{15}{6}$, or $\frac{5}{2}$

31. Name two solutions to $-1 < t < 1$. *(Lesson 4-9)* **Samples: 0 or $\frac{1}{2}$**

32. Steve has h brothers and 4 sisters. There are c children in the family. Give a sentence relating these numbers. *(Lesson 5-1)*
$h + 4 + 1 = c$

33. **a.** 6 miles + 1000 feet = __?__ feet *(Lessons 3-2, 5-1)* **32,680**
   b. The sum of 6 miles and 1000 feet is __?__ miles. $6\frac{25}{132}$, or 6.189

Exploration

34. In this lesson, arrows were used to picture addition of negative numbers. Physicists use arrows called *vectors* to add forces. Find out how a physicist would add the two arrows pictured here.
See margin.

Zero and Opposites

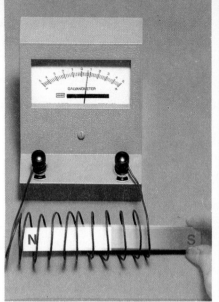

*Moving a magnet through the coils of the galvanometer from right to left has
generated an electric current of 0.7 milliampere. Moving from left to right at the
same speed generated a current in the opposite direction of -0.7 milliampere. If
the magnet is stationary, no current is generated, and the galvanometer reads 0.*

Suppose you have $25. If you get $4 from somewhere, then you
will have $25 + $4, or $29. If you spend $4, you will have
$25 − $4, or $21. If you do nothing, you will have $25 + $0,
or $25. When you add 0 to a number, the value of that num-
ber is kept. We say that adding 0 to a number keeps the identity
of that number. So 0 is called the **additive identity.**

Additive Identity Property of Zero:

For any number n: $n + 0 = n$.

For example, $-2.4 + 0 = -2.4$, $7777 + 0 = 7777$, and
$0 + -18 = -18$.

Remember that 5 and -5 are called *opposites*. This is because if
5 stands for gaining 5 pounds, then -5 stands for its opposite,
losing 5 pounds. Now suppose you gain 5 pounds and then lose
5 pounds. In the slide model, the result is found by adding 5 + -5.

But you know the result! If you gain 5 pounds and then lose
5 pounds, the result is no change in weight. This verifies that
5 + -5 = 0. The same thing works regardless of what number
you use. The sum of a number and its opposite is 0. In symbols,
-n is the opposite of n. The general pattern is called the Property
of Opposites.

202

Property of Opposites:

> For any number n: $n + -n = 0$.

The word "inverse" means opposite. Because of the property of opposites, the numbers n and $-n$ are called **additive inverses** of each other. For example, the additive inverse of 40 is -40. The additive inverse of -40 is 40. The additive inverse of -6.3 is 6.3. This can be written as $-(-6.3) = 6.3$. The parentheses are used so that it is clear that there are two dashes. Because $0 + 0 = 0$, the opposite of 0 is zero. That is, $-0 = 0$.

The opposite of the opposite of any number is the number itself. We call this the Op-op Property. Your class may wish to make up a different name.

Op-op Property:

> For any number n: $-(-n) = n$

To verify the Op-op Property: display any number; then press the $\boxed{+/-}$ key *twice*. After the first pressing, you will get the opposite of the number. After the second pressing, the original number will appear.

Questions

Covering the Reading

1. Why is zero called the additive identity?   See margin.

2. Add: $0 + 3 + 0 + 4$.   7   3. Add: $0 + -3 + 0 + -4$.   -7

4. Another name for additive inverse is __?__.   opposite

In 5–8, give the additive inverse of each number.

5. 70   -70   6. -13   13   7. $-\frac{1}{2}$ $\frac{1}{2}$ 8. $-x$ x

9. State the Property of Opposites.   For any number n, $n + -n = 0$.

10. Describe a real situation that illustrates $7 + -7 = 0$.   See margin.

11. State the Op-op Property.   For any number n, $-(-n) = n$.

In 12–15, an instance of what property is given?

12. $2 + -2 = 0$.
Prop. of Opposites

13. $-9.4 = 0 + -9.4$
Add. Identity Prop. of Zero

14. $7 = -(-7)$
Op-op Prop.

15. $0 = 1 + -1$
Prop. of Opposites

Applying the Mathematics

In 16–19, perform the additions.

16. $-51 + 51 + 2$ 2

17. $x + 0 + -x$ 0

18. $a + b + -b$ a

19. $-\frac{8}{3} + -\frac{2}{7} + 0 + \frac{2}{7} + \frac{8}{3} + \frac{14}{11}$ $\frac{14}{11}$

In 20 and 21: **a.** Translate the words into mathematical symbols. **b.** An instance of what property is given?

20. Withdraw $25, then make no other withdrawal or other deposit, and you have decreased the amount in your account by $25.
a. $-25 + 0 = -25$; b. Add. Identity Prop. of Zero

21. Walk 40 meters east, then 40 meters west, and you are back where you started.   a, $40 + -40 = 0$; b. Prop. of Opposites

In 22–25, simplify.

22. $-(-(-5))$ -5

23. $-(-(-(-6)))$ 6

24. $-(-(-x))$ -x

25. $-(-(-7 + 1))$ -6

26. Suppose you enter the number 5 on your calculator. After pressing the $\boxed{+/-}$ key 50 times, what number will be displayed?   5

27. If $x = -3$, then $-x = \underline{\ ?\ }$.   3

28. When $a = -4$ and $b = -5$, then $-(a + b) = \underline{\ ?\ }$.   9

Review

In 29 and 30: **a.** What is the result for each situation? **b.** What addition problem gets that result? *(Lesson 5-3)*

29. The temperature is $-11°$ and then goes up $2°$.
a. The temperature is $-9°$. b. $-11 + 2 = -9$

30. You are $150 in debt and take out another loan of $100.
a. You are $250 in debt. b. $-150 + -100 = -250$

In 31 and 32, give an equation or inequality relating the three numbers. *(Lesson 5-1)*

31. We were at an altitude of t meters. We went down 35 meters in altitude. Our altitude is now 60 meters below sea level.
$t + -35 = -60$

32. We need $50 to buy that gift for our parents. You have Y dollars. I have $14.50. Together we have more than enough. $Y + 14.50 > 50$

33. Put in order, from smallest to largest. *(Lessons 2-2, 2-8)*
$$3.2 \times 10^4 \qquad 9.7 \times 10^{-5} \qquad 5.1 \times 10^7$$
9.7 × 10⁻⁵; 3.2 × 10⁴; 5.1 × 10⁷

34. a. Evaluate $a + c/3 + b$ when $a = 20/3$, $b = 17/6$, and $c = -11$.
(Lesson 5-2) **35/6**
b. Write your answer to **a** in lowest terms. *(Lesson 1-10)* **35/6**

35. A rope d inches in diameter can lift a maximum of about
w pounds, where $w = 5000d(d + 1)$. *(Lesson 4-6)*
a. About how many pounds can a rope of diameter 1″ lift? **10,000 lb**
b. About how many pounds can a rope with a diameter of
one-half inch lift? **3750 lb**
c. A rope has diameter $\frac{9}{16}$ inch. Can it lift 5,000 pounds? **no**

Exploration

36. Opposites are common outside of mathematics. You know that
good and bad are opposites, and so are big and little. Find the
four pairs of opposites in the eight animal names given here.

moose	dove	hawk	mouse
tiger	shrimp	bear	bull

See below.

dove and hawk (war politics); bear and bull (stock market); moose and
shrimp (size); tiger and mouse (aggression)

FOLLOW-UP

MORE PRACTICE
For more questions on SPUR
Objectives, use *Lesson Master 5-4*, shown below.

EVALUATION
A quiz covering Lessons 5-1
through 5-4 is provided in the
Teacher's Resource File on
page 40.

LESSON 5-5

OBJECTIVES

A Add any numbers written as decimals or fractions.
B Calculate absolute value.

TEACHING NOTES

Absolute value is so easy to calculate that many students do not realize what they are doing. As a result, absolute values involving variables can be very confusing. It is very helpful to split the idea of absolute value into two parts: when the number is not negative; and when the number is negative.

Reading You may wish to have students read this lesson aloud in class. Ask students to explain absolute value in their own words after they read the explanation in the text. Do *not* let students say, "The absolute value is the number without its sign." Repeatedly stress that the absolute value of a negative number is the *opposite* of that number.

LESSON

5-5

Adding Positive and Negative Numbers

Suppose you want to add -50 and 30. In Lesson 5-2, you learned two ways of doing this. One way is to think of a slide model situation using the numbers -50 and 30.

> I lose $50 and I gain $30.
> How am I doing?

A second way is to draw a number line and arrows. This pictures the addition.

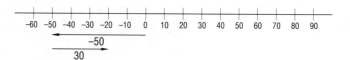

Either way, you should get the answer -20.

If the numbers are complicated, it isn't so easy to think of situations. And it takes a long time to draw a number line and arrows. So it helps to have a rule for adding positive and negative numbers. This rule is described using an idea called the **absolute value of a number.**

When a number is positive, it equals its absolute value. The absolute value of 5 is 5. The absolute value of 3.8 is 3.8. The absolute value of 4 million is 4 million.

The absolute value of a negative number is the opposite of that number. The absolute value of -2 equals 2. The absolute value of -4000 is 4000.

The symbol for absolute value is two vertical lines | |, one on each side of the number. For example $|5| = 5$; $|3.8| = 3.8$; $|4 \text{ million}| = 4$ million; $|-2| = 2$; and $|-4000| = 4000$.

The absolute value of a number tells how far the number is from 0 on the number line. It also is the length of the arrow that describes a number. The absolute value of 0 is defined to be zero.

Now it is possible to state rules for adding positive and negative numbers. If the numbers are both positive, no rule is needed. You have been adding positive numbers since first grade. For instance, $7 + 4 = 11$.

Suppose the numbers are both negative, as in $-7 + -4$. How are they added? First, you can add 7 and 4. (You have added the absolute values of the numbers.) Now put the negative sign on. (You have taken the opposite.)

> To add two negative numbers, add their absolute values and then take the opposite.

Adding two negative numbers is not very difficult. The big advantage of the idea of absolute value comes when one addend is positive and one is negative.

Consider $13 + -40$. You are 13 points ahead but you lose 40 points. How are you now doing? If you don't know the answer, arrows can help.

```
                                          _____→
                                             13
←_____
                    −40
```

Let's analyze this. The sum is certainly going to be negative. This is because the -40 has a larger absolute value than the 13.

How far negative? Just subtract 13 from 40. So the sum is -27.

> To add a positive and a negative number, take their absolute values. The sum is in the direction of the number with the larger absolute value. Subtract the smaller absolute value from the larger to find out how far the sum is in that direction.

▪ ▪ ▪ ▪ ▪ ▪ ▪ ▪

Example 1 Add 5 and -8.9 using the above rule.

Solution First take the absolute values. $|5| = 5$ and $|-8.9| = 8.9$. Since -8.9 has the larger absolute value, the sum is negative. Now subtract the absolute values. $8.9 - 5 = 3.9$. So the sum is -3.9.

LESSON 5-5 *Adding Positive and Negative Numbers* **207**

Alternate Approach/ Using Manipulatives
Allow students to use two-color counters to add positive and negative numbers. You may wish to relate the use of the counters to football. Suggest that one color represents a gain of one yard and the other color represents a loss of one yard. Ask what the net change in position would be if a team gained one yard and then lost one yard. (0) Have students conclude that a pair of counters—one of each color—represents zero.

To add 7 and -4, students would use 7 positive counters and 4 negative counters. After pairing the positive and negative counters, 3 positive counters are left. Hence, $7 + -4 = 3$. Repeat the procedure for other examples, and then allow students to work in groups to make up and solve their own addition problems.

ADDITIONAL EXAMPLES
1. Simplify.
a. $|\frac{3}{4}|$ $\frac{3}{4}$
b. $|-.5|$ **.5**
c. $|2| + |-3|$ **5**

2. Find each sum.
a. $8 + -10$ **-2**
b. $\frac{1}{2} + -\frac{3}{4}$ $-\frac{1}{4}$
c. $-.5 + -.05$ **-.55**

Error Analysis Students often have difficulty adding a positive and a negative number as in Additional Examples 2a and 2b. Suggest that students think about how they would represent the addition with arrows on the number line. Students may want to construct a number line from −10 to 10 and use it when completing addition problems with sums between −10 and 10. Instead of drawing the arrows, some students may benefit from tracing arrows with their fingers.

Example 2 $76 + {}^-5 = ?$

Solution   The absolute values of the addends are 76 and 5. Since 76 has the larger absolute value, the sum is positive. Now subtract the absolute values. $76 - 5 = 71$. So the sum is 71.

You may be able to find sums of positive and negative numbers without using the above rule. As long as you do not make errors, this is fine.

Questions

Covering the Reading

1. Which of (a) to (c) is **not** a way to find the sum of positive and negative numbers?   **(d)**
   (a) Think of a situation fitting the slide model for addition.
   (b) Use arrows and a number line.
   (c) Take absolute values and use a rule.
   (d) All of the above are valid ways.

In 2–5, give the absolute value of each number.

2. $^-58$ **58**   3. 4.01   **4.01**   4. 0   **0**   5. $^-11$ **11**

In 6–9, simplify.

6. $|12|$ **12**   7. $|^-20|$ **20**   8. $|0.0032|$ **0.0032**   9. $|0|$ **0**

In 10–13: **a.** Without adding, tell whether the sum is positive or negative. **b.** Add.

10. $^-40 + 41$
    a. positive; b. 1

11. $7.0 + ^-0.8$
    a. positive; b. 6.2

12. $^-4/9 + ^-4/9$
    a. negative; b. $^-8/9$

13. $6 + 7$
    a. positive; b. 13

In 14–19, *true or false?*

14. The sum of two positive numbers is always positive.   **True**

15. The sum of two negative numbers is always negative.   **True**

16. The sum of a negative number and a positive number is always negative.   **False**

17. The absolute value of a number is always positive.   **False**

18. The numbers 50 and $^-50$ have the same absolute value.   **True**

19. The absolute value of a negative number is the opposite of that number.   **True**

In 20–31, simplify.

20. $3 + -6$ -3 **21.** $-10 + -4$ -14 **22.** $-1.7 + .85$ -0.85

Applying the Mathematics

23. $-3 + 8 + -6$ -1 **24.** $\frac{2}{5} + -5 + \frac{3}{5}$ -4 **25.** $-\frac{112}{3} + \frac{1}{10}$ $-\frac{1117}{30}$

26. $-|-2|$ −2 **27.** $-|15/2|$ -15/2 **28.** $|-0.74|$ 0.74

29. $|3| + |-3|$ 6 **30.** $|3| - |-3|$ 0 **31.** $-|2.5| + |-6.8|$ 4.3

32. What is the value of $|x + y|$ when $x = -5$ and $y = 4$? 1

33. *True or false* When x is positive, $|x| = x$. True

34. *True or false* When x is negative, $|x| = x$. False

35. *True or false* When $x = 0$, $|x| = x$. True

Review

36. You are \$150 in debt and pay off \$50. **a.** What addition problem gets the result for this situation? **b.** What is that result? *(Lesson 5-3)*
a. -150 + 50; b. -100; You are \$100 in debt.

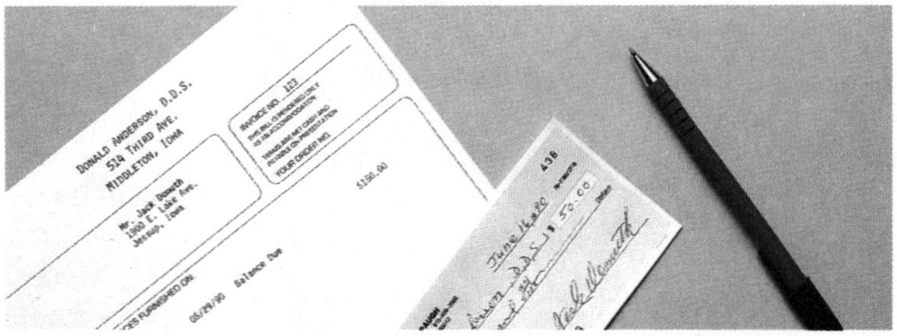

In 37–40, evaluate $-c + 13$ for the given value of c. *(Lessons 5-2, 5-4)*

37. $c = 13$ 0 **38.** $c = -2$ 15

39. $c = -51/6$ 129/6, or 21.5 **40.** $c = 0$ 13

41. Translate into mathematical symbols. The sum of a number and its additive inverse is the additive identity. *(Lessons 4-3, 5-4)* $n + -n = 0$

42. To the nearest degree, measure $\angle B$. *(Lesson 3-5)* 147°

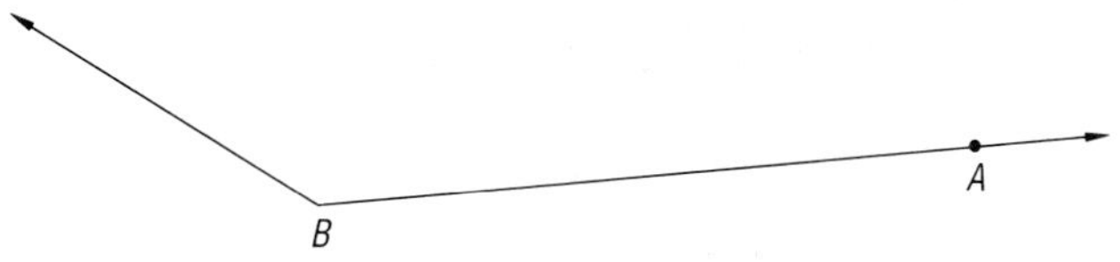

43. Measure the distance from A to B to the nearest 1/8 of an inch. *(Lesson 3-1)* $2\frac{1}{4}''$ or $2\frac{2}{8}''$

44. Simplify $\frac{(24 + 1)}{11} + \frac{4}{(3 + 5)}$. *(Lessons 4-1, 5-2)* $\frac{244}{88}$, or $\frac{61}{22}$

NOTES ON QUESTIONS
Question 39: You might ask students if they found this question easier to evaluate with mixed numbers or with fractions.

Making Connections for Question 42: Angle measure is reviewed in preparation for the work with turns in the next lesson.

NAME ________

LESSON **MASTER 5–5**
QUESTIONS ON **SPUR** OBJECTIVES

■ **SKILLS** *Objectives A and B (See pages 237–239 for objectives.)*
In 1–16, simplify.

1. $|-.05| =$ .05
2. $|1.25| =$ 1.25
3. $-|-9| =$ -9
4. $|12| - |-12| =$ 0
5. $-12 + 23 + -15 =$ -4
6. $-132 + 64 =$ -68
7. $|7| + |-9| =$ 16
8. $-|16| + |-68| =$ 52
9. $120 + -157 + -73 =$ -10
10. $-99 + -128 =$ -227
11. $|0| + |-2| =$ 2
12. $|3| + |-3| =$ 6
13. $-2.1 + -8.6 =$ -10.7
14. $-\frac{1}{2} + -\frac{3}{2} =$ -2
15. $3\frac{1}{3} + -1\frac{2}{3} =$ $1\frac{2}{3}$
16. $-9.06 + 2.1 + 0.38 =$ -6.58

In 17–20, complete.

17. What is the value of $|a + b|$ when $a = -41$ and $b = 14$? 27
18. What is the value of $|m + n|$ when $m = 41$ and $n = -14$? 27
19. *True or false* The absolute value of a negative number is the opposite of that number. True
20. *True or false* To add two negative numbers, add their absolute values and then take the opposite of that sum. True
21. What number has the same absolute value as 70? -70
22. What two numbers have an absolute value of 42? 42 and -42

42 *Transition Mathematics* © Scott, Foresman and Company

45. The quilt pattern below is made up of 16 small squares. How many bigger squares are in this pattern? **nine 2 by 2 squares, four 3 by 3, and one 4 by 4, a total of 14**

46. How many squares are in the pattern drawn below? (Hint: If you have done Question 45, it may be easier than you think.) **35**

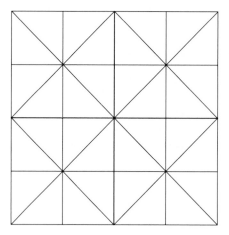

210

5-6

Turns

LESSON 5-6

RESOURCES
■ Lesson Master 5-6
▣ Computer Master 8
▣ Visual for Teaching Aid 27.
   Use with Teaching Notes.
▣ Visual for Teaching Aid 28:
   Questions 8–11 and
   21–23

OBJECTIVE

L Calculate magnitudes of turns given angle measures or revolutions.

A *full turn* around in a circle is called one **revolution** or a 360° turn. Pictured are two *quarter turns*. Each is 1/4 of a revolution or 90°.

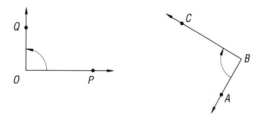

Notice that the turns are in different directions. Consider the turn at left above. Think of standing at point O (the center of the turn) and looking at point P. Then turn so that you are looking at point Q. You have turned *counterclockwise*, the opposite of the way clock hands usually move. Above at right, imagine yourself at point B. Look first at point A, then turn to look at point C. You have turned 90° *clockwise*.

In most of mathematics, the counterclockwise direction is considered positive and the clockwise direction is negative. The turn with center O above is a turn of 90°. The turn with center B is a turn of -90°.

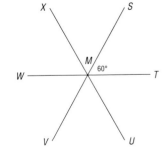

In the picture at left, the six small angles at M are drawn to have equal measures. Each angle has measure 60° because each is 1/6 of 360°. Think of standing at M and facing point S. If you now turn clockwise to face point U, you have turned -120°. If you turn from facing S to face point X, you have turned 60°. The quantities -120° and 60° are called the **magnitudes of the turns.**

LESSON 5-6 Turns **211**

After students read the lesson and discuss the diagram, you might work with them to draw a diagram showing turns with multiples of 45°. The diagram could illustrate turns of 45°, 90°, 180°, −45°, −90°, and −180°.

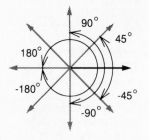

Such an activity relates turns to degree measure. It also develops intuition for later work in geometry and trigonometry.

Note that the physical turn is not exactly the same as the mathematical turn. Physical turns of magnitudes −120° and 240° are obviously different. Customarily, mathematical turns are concerned only with where a point "winds up," not with how it got there. As a result, the mathematical turns of −120° and 240° are considered identical. Adding or subtracting 360° from the magnitude of a mathematical turn does not change that turn.

For any clockwise turn, there is a counterclockwise turn that winds up in the same place. For instance, the -120° turn from *S* to *U* on page 211 can also be achieved by going 240° counterclockwise. So a turn of -120° is considered identical to a turn of 240°.

You can use protractors to help measure magnitudes of turns. But a protractor cannot tell you the direction of a turn.

Turns are discussed in this chapter because turns provide another use for addition. Pictured below is a 35° turn followed by a 90° turn. The result is a 125° turn. In general, if one turn is followed by another, the magnitude of the result is found by adding the magnitudes of the turns.

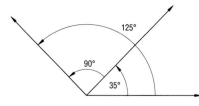

This addition property holds even if the turns are in opposite directions. Below a 60° turn is followed by a -90° turn. The result is a -30° turn (in other words, a turn of 30° clockwise).

$$60 + \text{-}90 = \text{-}30$$

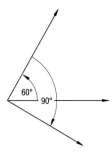

Fundamental Property of Turns:

If a turn of magnitude *x* is followed by a turn of magnitude *y*, the result is a turn of magnitude *x* + *y*.

Tops, figure skaters, gears, the Earth, pinwheels, and phonograph records turn. All of these objects may turn many revolutions. So it is possible to have turns with magnitudes over 360°. For example, a dancer who spins $1\frac{1}{2}$ times around has spun 540°, since it is the result of a full turn of 360° followed by a half turn of 180°.

212

Questions

In 1–4, give the number of degrees in:

1. a full turn   360°

2. one revolution   360°

3. a half turn   180°

4. a quarter turn   90°

5. On page 212, is the 35° turn clockwise or counterclockwise?
counterclockwise

6. __?__ turns have positive magnitudes.   counterclockwise

7. __?__ turns have negative magnitudes.   clockwise

In 8–11, all small angles at O have the same measure.
Think of turns around point O. Give the magnitude of:

8. the counterclockwise turn from D to B.   120°

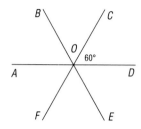

9. the counterclockwise turn from C to F.   180°

10. the clockwise turn from D to E.   -60°

11. the clockwise turn from A to F.   -300°

12. A turn of -80° winds up in the same place as a turn of what
positive magnitude?   280°

In 13–16, give the result of:

13. a 90° turn followed by a 35° turn.   125°

14. a 90° turn followed by a -35° turn.   55°

15. a -5° turn followed by a -6° turn.   -11°

16. a 1/4° turn followed by a 1/2° turn.   3/4°

ADDITIONAL EXAMPLES
1. You face the front of the room. You then turn 90° left (counterclockwise). In which direction are you facing? What other turns would leave you facing the same way?
Answer depends on the room; sample: two 45° turns

2. You face the back of the room. Then you turn −120°. In which direction are you facing? What other turns would leave you facing the same way?
Answer depends on the room; sample: a 240° turn

213

17. State the Fundamental Property of Turns. **See margin.**

18. An airplane pilot is at point *A* flying toward point *B*. Due to a change in plans, the pilot decides to turn the plane toward point *C*. What is the magnitude of the turn that is needed? (You need to use a protractor.) **-27°**

Applying the Mathematics

• *B*

A•

•*C*

In 19 and 20, the diagrams are pizzas that have been divided equally. What is the measure of an angle at the center of the pizza?

19. 120°

20. 72°

In 21– 23, a Ferris wheel is pictured. The spokes are equally spaced.

21. a. What magnitude turn will bring seat *J* to the position of seat *L*? **60° (or -300°)**
   b. Where will seat *B* wind up on this turn? **D**

22. a. What magnitude turn will bring seat *K* to the position of seat *G*? **240° (or -120°)**
   b. What magnitude turn will bring seat *K* back to its original position? **120° (or -240°)**

23. If seat *C* is moved to the position of seat *G*, what seat will be moved to the top? **I**

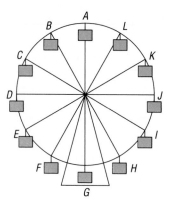

214

24. How many degrees does the *minute* hand of a watch turn in:
    a. an hour? **b.** 10 minutes? **a. -360°; b. -60°**

25. How many degrees does the *hour* hand of a watch turn in:
    a. an hour? **b.** 10 minutes? **a. -30°; b. -5°**

26. How many degrees are in 6 revolutions? **2160°**

Review

27. Consider this situation. It took Ralph 3 hours to do homework last night. He spent 45 minutes on math and *m* minutes on the rest. Give an open sentence that relates all the quantities in the situation. *(Lesson 5-1)*
    45 + m = 180 (in minutes), or m + 3/4 = 3 (in hours)

In 28–32, simplify. *(Lessons 4-1, 5-3, 5-4, 5-5)*

28. -74 + 9.8 **-64.2**

29. $(-\frac{2}{5} + \frac{2}{5}) + (-\frac{6}{7} + \frac{6}{7})$ **0**

30. -(-(2 + -4)) **-2**

31. (|7| + |-4|) · 5 **55**

32. 3 + 4 · 2 + -2 **9**

33. How many meters are in 6 kilometers? *(Lesson 3-3)* **6000 m**

34. Write 63.2 million: **a.** as a decimal; **b.** in scientific notation. *(Lessons 2-1, 2-3)* **a. 63,200,000; b. 6.32 × 10^7**

35. Three instances of a general pattern are given. Describe the general pattern using two variables. *(Lesson 4-2)*

    3 + 4 + 3 = 4 + (3 + 3)
    -2 + 9.1 + -2 = 9.1 + (-2 + -2)
    7 + 0 + 7 = 0 + (7 + 7)
    x + y + x = y + (x + x)

36. If *Y* stands for this year and time is measured in years, what stands for two years ago? *(Lesson 4-3)* **Y − 2**

Exploration

37. Phonograph records can be 33 rpm or 45 rpm.
    a. What does the abbreviation rpm mean?
    b. Name some other place where you can find the abbreviation rpm.
    a. revolutions per minute; b. Samples: car engine speeds; blender speeds; propeller speeds

FOLLOW-UP

MORE PRACTICE
For more questions on SPUR Objectives, use *Lesson Master 5-6*, shown below.

EXTENSION
Using Manipulatives
Have students use their protractors to draw a wheel with 10 equally-spaced spokes, labeling each spoke with a different capital letter. Then ask students to write five problems about their drawings. The problems could be similar to **Questions 21–23**. You may wish to have students exchange papers and solve the problems, or have students solve their own problems.

NAME _____

LESSON **MASTER 5-6**
QUESTIONS ON **SPUR** OBJECTIVES

■ **REPRESENTATIONS** *Objective L (See pages 237–239 for objectives.)*

1. A turn of 100° winds up in the same place as what clockwise turn?
   -260°

2. A wagon wheel is pictured here with the spokes spaced equally. What is the measure of each angle at the center of the wheel?
   30°

In 3–6, all small angles at *C* have the same measure. Think of turns around the point *C*.

3. What is the magnitude of the clockwise turn from *T* to *R*?
   -216°

4. What is the magnitude of the counterclockwise turn from *N* to *S*?
   72°

5. You are positioned at *R*. Turning 288° counterclockwise, at what position will you be?
   U

6. You are now positioned at *S* and turn 144° clockwise. At what position are you?
   R

In 7 and 8, give the number of degrees the **hour** hand of a clock turns in:

7. a half hour **15°**

8. 20 minutes **10°**

In 9 and 10, complete.

9. What is the result of a 90° turn followed by a -25° turn? **65° turn**

10. What is the result of a -15° turn followed by a -12° turn? **-27° turn**

Transition Mathematics © Scott, Foresman and Company **43**

The Commutative and Associative Properties

When two things have been put together, it does not make any difference which came first. Buying two items in different order will cost the same. Likewise, the order of slides or turns makes no difference. Gaining 3 pounds and then losing 4 pounds gives the same end result as first losing 4 pounds and then gaining 3.

$$3 + {}^-4 = {}^-4 + 3$$

The general pattern was first given a name by François Servois in 1814. He used the French word "commutatif," which means "switchable." The English name is the *commutative property*.

Commutative Property of Addition:

For any numbers a and b: $a + b = b + a$.

Think of spending $5, earning $14, and then spending $20. The end result is given by the addition $^-5 + 14 + {}^-20$. From order of operations, you know you should work from left to right. But does it matter in this case? Follow this experiment. By using parentheses, we can change which addition is to be done first.

Doing the left addition first is shown by:

$$({}^-5 + 14) + {}^-20$$
$$= \quad 9 \quad + {}^-20$$
$$= \quad\quad {}^-11.$$

Doing the right addition first is shown by:

$${}^-5 + (14 + {}^-20)$$
$$= {}^-5 + \quad {}^-6$$
$$= \quad {}^-11.$$

The sums are equal.

$$({}^-5 + 14) + {}^-20 = {}^-5 + (14 + {}^-20)$$

At left, the 14 is associated with the $^-5$ first. At right, the 14 is associated with the $^-20$. For this reason, in 1835, the Irish mathematician Sir William Rowan Hamilton called the general pattern the *associative property*.

216

Associative Property of Addition:

For any numbers *a*, *b*, and *c*: $(a + b) + c = a + (b + c)$

Both the commutative property and the associative property have to do with changing order. The commutative property says you can change the order of the *numbers* being added. The associative property says you can change the order of the *operations*.

Example 1   Which property is demonstrated by
3 + (18 + -12) = 3 + (-12 + 18)?

Solution   All that has been changed is the order of numbers within parentheses. So this is an instance of the Commutative Property of Addition.

Example 2   Below is an instance of which property of addition?
150 + -73 + -22 + 8 = 150 + (-73 + -22) + 8

Solution: The order of the numbers has not been changed. At left we would add the 150 and the -73 first. At right we would add the -73 to the -22 first. So the order of additions has been changed. This can be done because of the Associative Property of Addition.

Because addition is both commutative and associative, if an expression involves only addition:
    (1) addends can be put in any order before adding them;
    (2) parentheses can be removed or put in whenever you wish;
and (3) you can speak of adding three or more numbers.

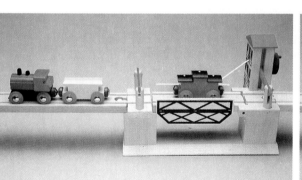 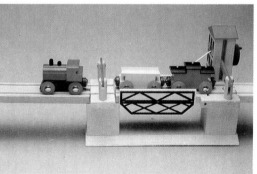

Reading   To create awareness of several critical details, you may want to read this lesson aloud with the students.

Use **Examples 1** and **2** to direct attention to the subtle distinction between the Commutative and Associative Properties. Use the paragraph before **Example 3** to stress the implications of both properties when taken together. Finally, emphasize that these properties make it possible to simplify additions containing several positive and negative numbers by first adding all the positives, then adding all the negatives, and finally combining the two sums. **Example 3** demonstrates the advantages of this method.

Students often confuse the Commutative and Associative Properties. Commutativity refers to switching the order of the numbers to be added; associativity refers to switching the order in which the additions take place. You may also want to mention the word *association*, a group, and point out that the Associative Property concerns the way that numbers are *associated*, or grouped, in order to add them.

■ ■ ■ ■ ■ ■ ■ ■ ■■

Example 3 Consider the following checking account, opened with $150 on October 24. How much is in the account after the deposit of November 6?

DATE	DEPOSIT	WITHDRAWAL (check)
10-24	$150.00	
10-27		$70.00
10-31	100.00	
11-01		40.00
11-03		60.00
11-06	50.00	

Solution In order, the deposits and withdrawals lead to the expression
$$150 + \text{-}70 + 100 + \text{-}40 + \text{-}60 + 50.$$
These numbers are all added, so they may be added in any order. It is usually best to group all deposits, then all withdrawals.
$$= (150 + 100 + 50) + (\text{-}70 + \text{-}40 + \text{-}60)$$
$$= \qquad 300 \qquad + \qquad \text{-}170$$
$$= \qquad\qquad 130$$

There is $130 in the account after the deposit of November 6.

Questions

Covering the Reading

1. Give an example of the Commutative Property of Addition.
   Sample: 3 + 2.4 = 2.4 + 3
2. Give an example of the Associative Property of Addition.
   Sample: (12 + 95) + 5 = 12 + (95 + 5)
3. In an expression involving only additions, you can change the order of the additions. Which property implies this?
   Associative Property of Addition

In 4–7, tell which property is illustrated.
(a) only the Commutative Property of Addition
(b) only the Associative Property of Addition
(c) both the commutative and associative properties
(d) neither the commutative nor the associative property

4. 2/3 + 3/4 = 3/4 + 2/3   (a)

5. 8 + (36 + -24) + -16 = (8 + 36) + (-24 + -16)   (b)

6. 3(4 + 9) = 3(9 + 4)   (a)

7. 1 + 2 + 3 = 3 + 2 + 1   (c)

8. In what century were the names commutative and associative first used? (Remember that the years 1901–2000 are the 20th century.)
19th century

9. Give a real-world situation that could lead someone to add many positive and negative numbers.   **Sample: gaining and losing weight**

10. On November 1, a person has $400 in a savings account. Here are the transactions for the next two weeks.

DATE	DEPOSIT	WITHDRAWAL
11-03	$102.00	
11-05		$35.00
11-08		75.00
11-11	40.00	
11-12		200.00

   a. What addition can you do to calculate the amount in the account at the end of the day on November 12?
   b. How much is in the account at that time?   **$232**
   a. 400 + 102 + -35 + -75 + 40 + -200

In 11 and 12, simplify.

11. $17 + -1 + -4$ **12**   **12.** $0 + -3 + -2 + 4 + -6 + 1$ **-6**

In 13 and 14, add the given numbers.

13. 99, -46, 12, -99, 46, -12   **0**

14. $-\frac{3}{8}, -\frac{3}{8}, \frac{40}{3}, -\frac{3}{8}, -\frac{3}{8}, \frac{40}{3}$ $\frac{604}{24}$, or $\frac{151}{6}$, or $25.1\overline{6}$

15. A family keeps a weekly budget. During a five-week period, they are $12.50 over, $6.30 under, $21 over, $7.05 under, and $9.90 under. How are they doing?   **They are $10.25 over budget.**

16. A robot turns 50°, -75°, 120°, -103°, and 17°. What is the total turn?   **9°**

17. The average of a, b, c, and d is $(a + b + c + d)/4$. Find the average of these daily low temperatures: -1°, 6°, 3°, -4°.   **1°**

In 18 and 19: **a.** Substitute numbers to show that the property is not always true. **b.** Tell what the property has to do with this lesson.

18. $a - b = b - a$.   **a. Sample: 5 − 3 ≠ 3 − 5; b. See margin.**

19. $(a - b) - c = a - (b - c)$.
   a. Sample: (9 − 6) − 2 ≠ 9 − (6 − 2); b. See margin.
In 20 and 21, follow the directions that were given for Questions 4–7 on page 218.

20. $4 + 3x = 3x + 4$ (a)

21. $8 + (-5 + 5) = 8 + -5 + 5$ (b)

Question 7: Have students consider the order in which addition takes place on each side of the equation to see how the Associative Property has been used. Explain that, because of order of operations, there is an implicit order $(1 + 2) + 3$ when the addition $1 + 2 + 3$ is written.

ADDITIONAL ANSWERS
18. b. Subtraction is not commutative.

19. b. Subtraction is not associative.

NAME _____

LESSON **MASTER   5–7**
QUESTIONS ON **SPUR** OBJECTIVES

■**PROPERTIES**   *Objective F (See pages 237–239 for objectives.)*
In 1–5, choose the property illustrated.

(a) only the Commutative Property of Addition
(b) only the Associative Property of Addition
(c) both the Commutative and Associative Properties
(d) neither the Commutative nor the Associative Property

1. $3 + (-12 + 8) = (3 + -12) + 8$	b
2. $6 + (-21 + -30) + 9 =$ $(6 + -21) + (-30 + 9)$	b
3. $(7.5 + 9.2) + -3.2 = 7.5 + (-3.2 + 9.2)$	c
4. $65 + 30\% = 65 + .3$	d
5. $\frac{3}{4} + -\frac{4}{9} = -\frac{4}{9} + \frac{3}{4}$	a

In 6–9, simplify.

6. $3 + -5 + -9 + 0 + -3 + 14 =$	0
7. $3 + -1.25 + -.5 =$	1.25
8. $-\frac{2}{3} + -\frac{2}{3} + \frac{11}{4} + -\frac{2}{3} + \frac{5}{6} =$	$2\frac{1}{12}$
9. $\$130 + \$70 + \$50 + \$40 + \$25 =$	$25

In 10–15, choose the property used to get to each step of the solution.
(a) Additive Identity Property of Zero
(b) Associative Property of Addition
(c) Commutative Property of Addition
(d) Op-op Property
(e) Property of Opposites

$(-3 + 8) + -(-3)$

10. $= (-3 + 8) + 3$	d
11. $= -3 + (8 + 3)$	b
12. $= -3 + (3 + 8)$	c
13. $= (-3 + 3) + 8$	b
14. $= 0 + 8$	e
15. $= 8$	a

44   *Transition Mathematics © Scott, Foresman and Company*

219

NOTES ON QUESTIONS

Question 33: The *mental computation* here is important. Once they have solved equations by a rule, many students forget that they can solve many of the same equations mentally.

FOLLOW-UP

MORE PRACTICE
For more questions on SPUR Objectives, use *Lesson Master 5-7*, shown on page 219.

EVALUATION
A quiz covering Lessons 5-5 through 5-7 is provided in the Teacher's Resource File on page 41.

30. not enough information for a single number answer; any number between 7 and 12

35. c. sample: −999 + −2 + 4046 with a sum of 3045

Review

In 22 and 23, the circles represent Gouda cheeses that have been divided equally.
  a. Find the measure of the smallest angle at the center of the cheese.
  b. Tell whether that angle is acute, obtuse, or right. *(Lessons 3-5, 3-6)*

22.

23.

a. 90°; b. right   a. 60°; b. acute

24. How many degrees are there in a half turn? *(Lesson 5-6)*   180°

25. How many degrees does the second hand of a watch turn in 10 seconds? *(Lesson 5-6)*   -60°

26. Refer to the picture of the Ferris wheel in Lesson 5-6. If seat *B* is turned to the position of seat *G*, what seat will be moved to the top? *(Lesson 5-6)*   H

In 27 and 28, perform the addition. *(Lesson 3-3)*

27. 8 kilograms + 453 grams   8453 grams, or 8.453 kg

28. 1 quart + 1 pint   3 pints, or 1.5 quarts

29. The temperature is $t°$ and goes down 3°. What is the end result? *(Lesson 5-3)* $(t − 3)$ degrees

30. Morrie and Lori together have 7 tickets to a concert. Corey and Lori together have 5 tickets. How many tickets do Corey, Lori, and Morrie have altogether? *(Lesson 5-1)*   See margin.

31. State the property of opposites. *(Lesson 5-4)*
  For any number a, $a + -a = 0$.
32. Another term for "additive inverse" is __?__. *(Lesson 5-4)*   opposite

33. Mentally solve the equation $x + 45 = 51$. *(Lesson 4-8)*   6

34. Simplify: $-5 + 6(3.7 + 1.3/2) − 4$. *(Lesson 4-5)*   17.1

Exploration

35. a. Add 203,275 + -89,635 + 265,164 on your calculator.   378804
  b. Turn your calculator 180°. What word does that display spell?   hOBB
  c. Find two negative numbers and a positive number whose sum on the calculator, when turned 180°, is ShOE.   See margin.

LESSON

5-8

Solving
$x + a = b$

LESSON 5-8

RESOURCES
■ Lesson Master 5-8
▣ Visual for Teaching Aid 29:
Questions 4 and **19**

| **OBJECTIVES** |

D Solve equations of the
form $x + a = b$.
I Use the Putting-together
Model for Addition to write
sentences of the form
$x + a = b$.
K Use the Slide Model for
Addition to form sentences
involving addition.

Children in second grade are expected to be able to fill in the
blank in

$$\_\_\_ + 3 = 4.$$

In algebra, usually the blank is replaced by a letter. If the
sentence involves simple numbers, you should be able to find
the solution mentally. For instance, in

$$x + 35 = 48$$

you should know that $x = 13$.

But some equations involve complicated numbers. Other
equations involve only variables and no specific numbers at all.
It helps to have a systematic way of solving these equations.
On one side of both $\_\_\_ + 3 = 4$ and $x + 35 = 48$, a number
is being added to an (unknown) variable. On the other side is a
single number. They are *equations of the form $x + a = b$*. Think
of x as the unknown. Think of a and b as known numbers.

One property of addition is particularly helpful in solving
equations. Here is an example. Begin with equal numbers.

$$\tfrac{1}{4} = 0.25$$

If the same number is added to both sides, then the sums will be
equal. For instance, if 3 is added to both sides:

$$3 + \tfrac{1}{4} = 3 + 0.25.$$

That is, $\quad 3\tfrac{1}{4} = 3.25.$

Of course, you could add any number to both sides. The sums
would still be equal. This property is a special form of the
Substitution Principle first mentioned in Lesson 2-6. It has its
own name.

To emphasize what "the form
$x + a = b$" means, suggest
that students think of a and b
as known numbers and x as
the unknown number. It may
be helpful to have volunteers
write a few equations of this
type on the board.

Encourage the students to
write successive sentences
with the equal signs underneath each other and to
check answers whenever
possible (which is virtually
always).

A goal of sentence solving is
to skip unnecessary steps.
However, for this lesson,
have students write in all
steps to indicate the care
with which equation solving is
done. Ultimately, students will
be able to omit the third and
fourth lines. But do not
quickly permit omitting the
second line; what is added to
both sides is critical.

Addition Property of Equality:

If $a = b$, then $a + c = b + c$.

The Addition Property of Equality says: If two numbers are
equal, then you can add anything you want to both numbers and
the sums will be equal. Here is how this property is used in
solving equations.

■ ■ ■ ■ ■ ■ ■ ■ ■

Example 1 Solve $x + \text{-}8 = 57$.

Solution Add 8 to both sides. (That can be done because of the
Addition Property of Equality.) Because addition is associative,
you do not have to worry about grouping.

$$x + \text{-}8 + 8 = 57 + 8$$

Now simplify. Since 8 and -8 are opposites, and 0 is the additive
identity,

$$x + 0 = 57 + 8$$
$$x = 65$$

Check Substitute 65 for x in the original equation.
Does $65 + \text{-}8 = 57$? Yes. So 65 is the solution.

The key thing is to know what number to add to both sides. In
Example 1, 8 was added to both sides. This caused the left side
to simplify to just x.

In Example 2, no equation is given. An equation has to be
figured out from the situation.

■ ■ ■ ■ ■ ■ ■ ■ ■

Example 2 The temperature was 4° this afternoon and now is -6°. By how
much has it changed?

Solution Let c be the change in temperature. (If c is positive, the
temperature has gone up. If c is negative, the temperature has
gone down.)
Then $\qquad\qquad\qquad 4 + c = \text{-}6$.
Since 4 is already added to c, we add -4 to both sides. This
ensures that c will wind up alone on its side of the equation.

$$\text{-}4 + 4 + c = \text{-}4 + \text{-}6$$
$$0 + c = \text{-}10$$
$$c = \text{-}10$$

So the change is -10°. To check, look at the original question.
If the temperature was 4° and changes -10°, will it be -6°?
Since the answer is yes, -10° is the correct solution.

222

You may be able to solve equations like these in your head. Still, you must learn the general strategy. More complicated problems require it.

In both Examples 1 and 2, after adding the same number to both sides, all you have to do is simplify the sides to find the solution. So there is only one step to remember.

> To solve an equation of the form $x + a = b$, add $-a$ to both sides and simplify.

In solving an equation, the unknown can be on either side. And since addition is commutative, the unknown may be first or second on that side. So all of these four equations have the same solution.

$$x + 43 = -18 \qquad 43 + x = -18 \qquad -18 = x + 43 \qquad -18 = 43 + x$$

When solving an equation, it is important to organize your work carefully. Write each step *underneath* the previous step. Some teachers like students to name properties. Here the equation $x + 43 = -18$ is solved with the properties named where they are used.

$x + 43 = -18$	(original equation)
$x + 43 + -43 = -18 + -43$	Addition Property of Equality
$x + 0 = -18 + -43$	Property of Opposites
$x = -18 + -43$	Additive Identity Property of Zero
$x = -61$	(arithmetic computation)

Check Substitute -61 for x in the original equation.
Does -61 + 43 = -18? Yes. So -61 is the solution.

Questions

Covering the Reading

1. Give the solution to 8 + ___ = 13. **5**

2. In algebra, the blank of Question 1 is usually replaced by what?
   a variable (a letter)

3. Begin with the equation $4/5 = 0.8$.
   a. Is it true that $6 + 4/5 = 6 + 0.8$? **Yes**
   b. Is it true that $-1 + 4/5 = -1 + 0.8$? **Yes**
   c. Is it true that $17.43 + 4/5 = 17.43 + 0.8$? **Yes**
   d. Parts **a** to **c** exemplify what property?
      Addition Property of Equality

ADDITIONAL EXAMPLES
1. Solve each equation.
a. $p + 5 = 3$ **-2**
b. $-8 + q = 10$ **18**
c. $3 = r + \frac{1}{2}$ **$2\frac{1}{2}$**
d. $10.6 = -5.2 + s$ **15.8**

2. William J. Cobb, who was a professional wrestler from Augusta, Georgia, lost 570 pounds over a period of $2\frac{1}{2}$ years. He weighed 232 pounds at the end of his diet.
a. Write an equation to find Cobb's original weight W.
$W + -570 = 232$
b. What was his original weight? **802 pounds**

4. Here are steps in the solution of the equation $3.28 = A + -5$. Give the reason for each step. **See margin.**
   a. $3.28 + 5 = A + -5 + 5$
   b. $3.28 + 5 = A + 0$
   c. $3.28 + 5 = A$
   d. $\qquad 8.28 = A$

In 5–8: **a.** To solve the equation, what number could you add to each side of the equation? **b.** Find the solution. **c.** Check your answer.

5. $x + 86 = 230$
   a. -86; b. 144

6. $-12 + y = 7$ **See margin**
   a. 12; b. 19 **for checks.**

7. $60 = z + \frac{22}{3}$
   a. -22/3; b. 158/3

8. $-5.9 = A + -3.2$.
   a. 3.2; b. -2.7

9. *Multiple choice* Which equation does not have the same solution as the others? **(b)**
   (a) $13 + x = -6$ (b) $-6 + x = 13$
   (c) $x + 13 = -6$ (d) $-6 = x + 13$

10. The temperature was -15° yesterday and is -20° today. Let c be the change in the temperature. **a.** What equation can be solved to find c? **b.** Solve that equation. **c.** Check your answer.
    a. -15 + c = -20 ; b. -5; c. -15 + -5 = -20

11. Suppose the temperature is two degrees below zero. By how much must it change to become three degrees above zero? **5°**

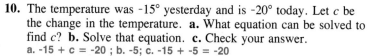
Applying the Mathematics

12. If $a = b$, the Addition Property of Equality says that $a + c = b + c$. But it is also true that $c + a = c + b$. Why?
    Commutative Property of Addition

In 13 and 14, you should simplify one side of the equation. Then solve and check.

13. $A + 43 + -5 = 120$ **82**   14. $-35 = 16 + d + 5$ **-56**

15. A family's income I satisfies the formula $I = F + M + C$, where F is the amount the father earns, M is the amount the mother earns, and C is the amount the children earn. If $I = 40,325$, $F = 18,800$, and $M = 20,500$, how much did the children earn? **$1025**

16. On Monday, Vito's savings account showed a balance of $103.52. He deposited $35 into the account Tuesday. Wednesday he withdrew $12.50. Thursday he asked the bank to tell him how much was in the account. They said that $130.05 was in the account. What happened is that the bank paid Vito some interest. How much interest? **$4.03**

17. George is G years old. Wilma is W years old.
    a. What will be George's age 10 years from now? **G + 10**
    b. What will be Wilma's age 10 years from now? **W + 10**
    c. If George and Wilma are the same age, how are G and W related? **G = W**
    d. Translate into mathematics: If George and Wilma are the same age now, then they will be the same age 10 years from now.
    e. Part **d** of this question is an instance of what property?
    d. If G = W, then G + 10 = W + 10; e. Addition Property of Equality

224

18. Solve for b: $a + b = c$.
   $b = c + \text{-}a$

Review

19. Which property is used in getting to each step? *(Lessons 5-4, 5-7)*
   $(5 + 7) + \text{-}5$ **See margin.**
   Step 1 $=$ $5 + (7 + \text{-}5)$
   Step 2 $=$ $5 + (\text{-}5 + 7)$
   Step 3 $=$ $(5 + \text{-}5) + 7$
   Step 4 $=$ $0 + 7$
   Step 5 $=$ 7

20. Simplify: $(4 \cdot 3 - 2 \cdot 1)(4 \cdot 3 + 2 \cdot 1)$. *(Lesson 4-5)*   **140**

21. Consider the inequality $x < \text{-}3$. **a.** Name a value of x that is a solution. **b.** Name a value of x that is not a solution. *(Lesson 4-9)*
   a. Sample: -4; b. Sample: 2

22. Graph $\text{-}3$, $\text{-}1$, and 2 on a vertical number line. *(Lesson 1-5)*
   See margin.

23. How many zeros follow the 1 in the decimal form of 10^{30}?
   (Lesson 2-2)   **30**

24. Approximate 7/16 to the nearest hundredth. *(Lessons 1-4, 1-8)*   **0.44**

25. Draw a picture of a 210° turn. *(Lesson 5-6)*   **See margin.**

26. If a $210\frac{1}{2}°$ turn is followed by a $150\frac{1}{8}°$ turn, what results? *(5-2, 5-6)*
   a 360 $\frac{5°}{8}$ turn, or a $\frac{5°}{8}$ turn

27. Draw a line segment with length 73 mm. *(Lessons 3-1, 3-3)*
   See margin.

In 28–30, translate into mathematics. *(Lesson 4-3)*

28. triple a number n **3n**   **29.** five less than a number t **t − 5**

30. a number B divided by twice a second number C **B/(2C) or $\frac{B}{2C}$**

In 31 and 32, translate into English. *(Lesson 3-5)*   **See margin.**

31. $\overrightarrow{AB}$ **32.** $m\angle LNP = 35°$

Exploration

33. We found this addition example in some scrap paper. Apparently a machine folded this paper funny. Four digits are missing, all in a line! What was the original problem?   **See margin.**

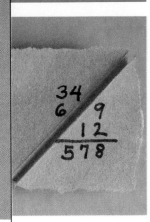

34. Run this program at least four times picking four different pairs of values for A and B.

```
10   PRINT "A"
15   INPUT A
20   PRINT "B"
25   INPUT B
30   X = A − B
40   PRINT "X = " X
50   END
```

  a. What does this program do?   **It subtracts B from A.**
  b. Does the program work when A and B are negative numbers?
  c. Does the program work when A and B are fractions?   **Yes**
  d. Modify the program so that it prints the average of A and B.
    b. Yes; d. Change line 30 to X = (A + B)/2

FOLLOW-UP

MORE PRACTICE
For more questions on SPUR Objectives, use *Lesson Master 5-8*, shown below.

EXTENSION
Some students may want to investigate solutions to equations of the form $|x| + a = b$. The students can answer the following questions: How many solutions do these equations generally have? (two) If $a = b$, how many solutions are there? (one) What happens if $b - a < 0$? (The equation has no solutions.)

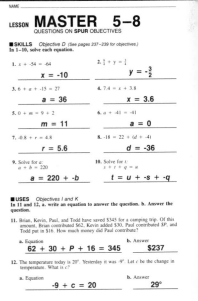

NAME _____

LESSON **MASTER** **5–8**
QUESTIONS ON SPUR OBJECTIVES

■ **SKILLS** *Objective D (See pages 237–239 for objectives.)*
In 1–10, solve each equation.

1. $x + \text{-}54 = \text{-}64$ 2. $\frac{3}{4} + y = \frac{1}{4}$
   x = -10   **y = -$\frac{3}{2}$**

3. $6 + a + \text{-}15 = 27$ 4. $7.4 = x + 3.8$
   a = 36   **x = 3.6**

5. $0 + m = 9 + 2$ 6. $a + \text{-}41 = \text{-}41$
   m = 11   **a = 0**

7. $\text{-}0.8 + r = 4.8$ 8. $\text{-}18 = 22 + (d + \text{-}4)$
   r = 5.6   **d = -36**

9. Solve for a: 10. Solve for t:
   $a + b = 220$ $s + t + q = u$
   a = 220 + -b   **t = u + -s + -q**

■ **USES** *Objectives I and K*
In 11 and 12, a. write an equation to answer the question. b. Answer the question.

11. Brian, Kevin, Paul, and Todd have saved $345 for a camping trip. Of this amount, Brian contributed $62, Kevin added $30, Paul contributed $P, and Todd put in $16. How much money did Paul contribute?

  a. Equation   b. Answer
  62 + 30 + P + 16 = 345   **$237**

12. The temperature today is 20°. Yesterday it was -9°. Let c be the change in temperature. What is c?

  a. Equation   b. Answer
  -9 + c = 20   **29°**

Transition Mathematics © Scott, Foresman and Company   **45**

LESSON

5-9

Polygons

Let A and B be any points. There is only one line containing both of them. The line goes on forever. So when it is *drawn*, arrows are put at both ends. This line is written $\overleftrightarrow{AB}$, with the two-sided arrow above the letters.

The points on $\overleftrightarrow{AB}$ that are between A and B, together with the points A and B themselves, make up a **line segment** or **segment**, written as $\overline{AB}$. A and B are the endpoints of $\overline{AB}$.

A **polygon** is a union of segments connected end to end. The segments are called the **sides** of the polygon. Two sides meet at a **vertex** of the polygon. (The plural of vertex is **vertices**.) The number of sides equals the number of vertices. Polygons are classified by that number.

226

Number of sides	Number of vertices	Type of polygon	Example
3	3	triangle	
4	4	quadrilateral	
5	5	pentagon	
6	6	hexagon	
7	7	heptagon	
8	8	octagon	
9	9	nonagon	
10	10	decagon	

Polygons with more than 10 sides do not always have special names. A polygon with 11 sides is called an 11-gon. A polygon with 42 sides is called a 42-gon. In general, a polygon with *n* sides is called an ***n*-gon.**

Polygons are named by giving their vertices in order around the figure. The boundary of the warehouse pictured at right is quadrilateral *WTUV*. You could also call it polygon *TUVW*, *WVUT*, or five other names. *WTVU* is not a correct name for this polygon because the vertices *W*, *T*, *V*, and *U* are not in order.

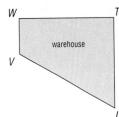

Extend two sides of a polygon drawn from a particular vertex to be rays with the vertex as the endpoint. These rays form an **angle of the polygon**. Every polygon has as many angles as it has sides or vertices. In warehouse polygon *WTUV*, angles *W* and *T* look like right angles. Angle *U* is acute. Angle *V* is obtuse.

TEACHING NOTES

Reading The students can read Lesson 5-9 independently. Although the importance of using appropriate notation for naming segments, lines, and polygons may need further discussion, most students easily understand the definitions in this lesson. Emphasize again the use of boldface type for important terms. Make certain that students understand the need to learn the polygon names in the chart on page 227.

ADDITIONAL EXAMPLES

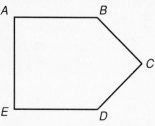

1. How many sides does the polygon have? How many vertices? **5, 5**

2. What name is given to a polygon with that number of sides? **pentagon**

3. Use the vertices to name the polygon.
sample: ABCDE

4. How many angles does the polygon have? **5**

Question

Covering the Reading

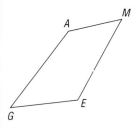

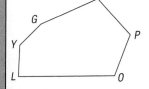

1. The line through points *A* and *B* is written __?__. $\overleftrightarrow{AB}$

2. The line segment with endpoints *C* and *D* consists of what points? See margin.

3. The line segment with endpoints *F* and *E* is written __?__. $\overline{FE}$ or $\overline{EF}$

4. Refer to the polygon pictured at left. See margin.
   a. Name this polygon. **b.** Name its sides. **c.** Name its vertices. **d.** Name its angles. **e.** What type of polygon is this?

In 5–16, what name is given to a polygon with the given number of sides?

5. 5   pentagon   **6.** 6   hexagon   **7.** 7   heptagon   **8.** 8   octagon

9. 9   nonagon   **10.** 10   decagon   **11.** 11   11-gon   **12.** *n*   *n*-gon

13. 3   triangle   **14.** 4   quadrilateral   **15.** 26   26-gon   **16.** 4302   4302-gon

17. How many angles does a 12-gon have?   12

18. A decagon has __?__ sides, __?__ angles, and __?__ vertices. 10, 10, 10

19. Refer to the figure at left.
    a. Give three possible names for this polygon.   See margin.
    b. What type of polygon is this?   hexagon

Applying the Mathematics

20. A square is what type of polygon mentioned in this lesson?   quadrilateral

21. Temples in the Baha'i religion have 9 sides. Suppose you view a Baha'i temple from directly overhead. The outline of the temple will have what shape?   nonagon

22. A famous building just outside Washington, D.C., is pictured below. A clue to its name is given by its shape. What is its name?   The Pentagon

A **diagonal** of a polygon is a segment that connects two vertices of the polygon but is not a side of the polygon. For example, $\overline{AC}$ and $\overline{BD}$ are the diagonals of quadrilateral ABCD drawn below. Use this information in Questions 23 and 24.

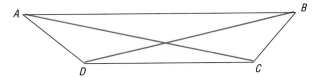

23. **a.** Draw a pentagon PQRST and name its diagonals. **b.** How many diagonals does it have?   a. $\overline{PR}$, $\overline{PS}$, $\overline{QT}$, $\overline{QS}$, $\overline{TR}$; b. 5

24. **a.** Draw a hexagon. **b.** How many diagonals does it have?
    a. See margin; b. 9

25. The triangle, quadrilateral, pentagon, and decagon pictured in the table in this lesson are **convex polygons**. The other polygons are not convex. Use this information to pick the correct description of convex polygon from this list. A convex polygon is: (c)
    (a) a polygon in which two sides are parallel.
    (b) a polygon in which there is a right angle.
    (c) a polygon in which no diagonals lie outside the polygon.
    (d) a polygon with a number of sides that is not a prime number.

Review

26. *Multiple choice*   Which equation does not have the same solution as the others? *(Lesson 5-8)*   (d)
    (a) $23 = 60 + y$ (b) $y + 60 = 23$
    (c) $23 = y + 60$ (d) $y + 23 = 60$

In 27 and 28, solve and check. *(Lesson 5-8)*

27. $x + 12 = -10$ -22   **28.** $300 = 172 + (45 + w)$ 83
    See margin for checks.

29. Given are steps in solving the general equation $a + x = b$ for x.
    Give the reason why each step is correct. *(Lessons 5-4, 5-8)*
    $$a + x = b$$
    Step 1 $-a + a + x = -a + b$
    Step 2 $0 + x = -a + b$ See margin.
    Step 3 $x = -a + b$

30. A sofa has length s inches. If the sofa were 3 inches longer, it would be 8 feet long. *(Lessons 4-3, 5-8)*
    a. Give an equation that involves the three quantities mentioned in the previous two sentences.
    b. Solve that equation for s.
    a. 8 ft = 96 in., so an equation is s + 3 = 96; b. 93 inches

Exploration

31. A triangle ABC can be named in 6 different ways using its vertices: ABC, ACB, BCA, BAC, CAB, and CBA.
    a. In how many different ways can a quadrilateral be named?
    b. In how many different ways can a pentagon be named?
    a. 8; b. 10

MORE PRACTICE
For more questions on SPUR Objectives, use *Lesson Master 5-9*, shown below.

EXTENSION
After the students have completed **Question 31**, you might ask them how many different names an *n*-gon can have (2*n*). You might also ask students to choose letters for the vertices of a quadrilateral so that the different names for the quadrilateral form words. (A good name is ITEM; MITE, TIME, and EMIT are also words.)

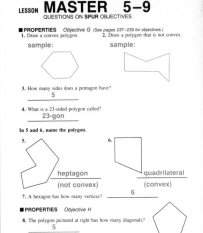

LESSON

5-10

Adding Lengths

In driving from Chicago to Louisville, the quickest way is to go through Indianapolis. It is 185 miles from Chicago to Indianapolis. It is 114 miles from Indianapolis to Louisville. How far is it from Chicago to Louisville?

Chicago

185

Indianapolis

114

Louisville

The answer is easy. Just add.

$$185 + 114 = 299$$

It is 299 driving miles from Chicago to Louisville.

The general pattern is easy. If you have two lengths x and y, the total length is $x + y$. This is another instance of the Putting-together Model for Addition.

x

y

total length = $x + y$

There are many situations in which more than two lengths are put together. Imagine walking around the building outlined below. You will have walked $40 + 40 + 50 + 10$ meters. This is the idea behind perimeter.

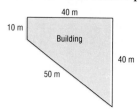

40 m

10 m

Building

40 m

50 m

The **perimeter** of a polygon is the sum of the lengths of the sides of the polygon.

Let the sides of a pentagon have lengths v, w, x, y, and z. If the perimeter is p, then $p = v + w + x + y + z$.

Now suppose $v = 12$, $w = 19$, $x = 15$, $z = 22$, and the perimeter $p = 82$. The situation is pictured below. What is the value of y? You can solve an equation to find out.

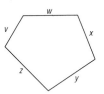 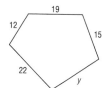

In general: $p = v + w + x + y + z$
In this case: $82 = 12 + 19 + 15 + y + 22$
Simplifying the right side: $82 = 68 + y$
Adding -68 to both sides
and simplifying: $14 = y$

Recall that if A and B are points, we use the following symbols.

$\overleftrightarrow{AB}$ line through A and B
$\overline{AB}$ segment with endpoints A and B
$\overrightarrow{AB}$ ray starting at A and containing B

There is one other related symbol. The **symbol AB** (with nothing over it) stands for the *length of the segment AB*. (It makes no sense to multiply points. So when A and B are points, putting the letters next to each other does not mean multiplication.) Here are some examples of this notation.

The perimeter of triangle PQR is $PQ + QR + RP$.

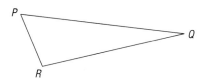

B is on $\overline{AC}$.
$AB + BC = AC$
$12 + 24 = AC$
$36 = AC$

ADDITIONAL EXAMPLES
1. Find the perimeter of each polygon.
a. a triangle with sides 3 ft, 4 ft, and 5 ft   **12 ft**
b. a triangle with sides x, y, and z.   **$x + y + z$**
c. a rectangle with length l and width w
$l + w + l + w$
d. a pentagon with sides $1\frac{1}{4}$ ft, 8 in., $1\frac{1}{2}$ ft, 1 ft, and 10 in.
63 in. or $5\frac{1}{4}$ ft

2. Use the drawing to write the correct symbol for each of the following:

a. all points on the ray starting with A and continuing through B $\overrightarrow{AB}$
b. all points on the line through A and B $\overleftrightarrow{AB}$
c. all points on the ray starting with B and continuing through A $\overrightarrow{BA}$
d. all points on both $\overrightarrow{AB}$ and $\overrightarrow{BA}$ $\overline{AB}$
e. the distance between A and B **AB**

3. Which of the above stands for a number?   **e**

Questions

Covering the Reading

1. Driving along the California coast, San Luis Obispo is between San Francisco and Los Angeles. A map shows that San Francisco is 241 miles from San Luis Obispo. Los Angeles is 195 miles from San Luis Obispo. By this route, how far is it from San Francisco to Los Angeles?   **436 miles**

2. The situation in Question 1 is an instance of what model for addition?   **the Putting-together Model**

In 3–6, *P* and *Q* are points. **a.** Give the meaning of each symbol.
b. Draw a picture (if possible) of the figure the symbol stands for.

3. $\overleftrightarrow{PQ}$ 4. $\overrightarrow{PQ}$ 5. $\overline{PQ}$ 6. *PQ*
See margin.

In 7–10, use the drawing. *B* is on $\overline{AC}$.

7. If *AB* = 5 and *BC* = 3, what is *AC*?   **8**

8. If *AB* = *x* and *BC* = *y*, what is *AC*?   **x + y**

9. If *AB* = *x* and *BC* = 3, what is *AC*?   **x + 3**

10. If *AB* = 14.3 cm, *BC* = *t* cm, and *AC* = *v* cm, how are 14.3, *t*, and *v* related?   **14.3 + t = v**

11. What is the perimeter of a polygon?
    the sum of the lengths of its sides

In 12 and 13, give the perimeter of the polygon.

12.

20 mm
11 mm
20 mm
21 mm
29 mm
101 mm

13.
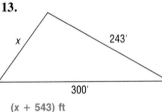
x
243'
300'
(x + 543) ft

14. In Question 13, suppose the perimeter of the triangle is 689 feet.
    a. What equation can you solve to find *x*? **b.** Solve the equation.
    a. x + 543 = 689; b. 146 feet

232

In 15 and 16: **a.** Write an equation that will help answer the question. **b.** Solve the equation.

15. Two sides of a pentagon have length 9 and two sides have length 5. The perimeter of the pentagon is 30. What is the length of the fifth side?   a. $9 + 9 + 5 + 5 + x = 30$; b. 2

16. A race is to be 10 km long. The organizers want the runners to run over a bicycle path that is 2800 meters long and a final leg that is 650 meters long. How much more of the course must be found?   a. $2800 + 650 + x = 10,000$; b. 6550 meters

17. Two sides of a triangle ABC have the same length, and $AB = 40$. The perimeter of triangle ABC is 100. What are the possible lengths for $\overline{BC}$ and $\overline{AC}$?   40 and 20; 30 and 30

18. Only one of these is not true. Which one is it?   (b)
    (a) $\overleftrightarrow{AB} = \overleftrightarrow{BA}$ (b) $\overrightarrow{AB} = \overrightarrow{BA}$
    (c) $\overline{AB} = \overline{BA}$ (d) $AB = BA$

19. A square has one side of length 5 m. **a.** Is this enough information to find its perimeter? **b.** If so, find it. If not, tell why there is not enough information.   a. yes; b. 20 m

20. Use the drawing below. B is on $\overline{AC}$. If $AC = 1$ ft and $BC = 1$ in., what is AB?   11 inches

21. Draw a polygon called *NICE* and put $\overrightarrow{CN}$ and $\overline{IE}$ on your drawing.
See margin.

22. Ernestine is E years old. Alfredo is A years old. *(Lesson 4-3)*
    a. How old was Ernestine 4 years ago? $E + -4$
    b. How old was Alfredo 4 years ago? $A + -4$
    c. Translate into mathematics: If Ernestine and Alfredo are the same age now, then they were the same age four years ago.
    d. Part **c** of this question is an instance of what property?
    c. If $E = A$, then $E + -4 = A + -4$; d. Addition Property of Equality

23. The temperature was $-22°$ yesterday and $10°$ today. Let t be the change in the temperature. **a.** What equation can be used to find t? **b.** Solve the equation. **c.** Check your answer. *(Lesson 5-8)*
    a. $-22 + t = 10$; b. 32; c. $-22 + 32 = 10$

24. Suppose the probability of rain is $\frac{1}{50}$. Then the probability of no rain is n, where $\frac{1}{50} + n = 1$. Solve this equation for n. *(Lesson 5-8)*
    $n = \frac{49}{50}$

25. Simplify: **a.** $-6 + -(-6)$; **b.** $-(-x) + -(-y)$. *(Lessons 5-4, 5-5)*
    a. 0; b. $x + y$

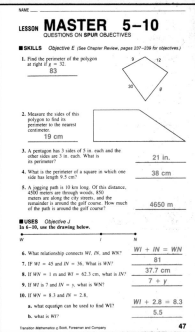
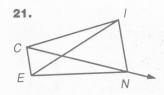

30.

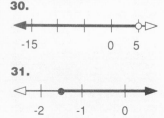

31.

In 26–29, use the drawing.

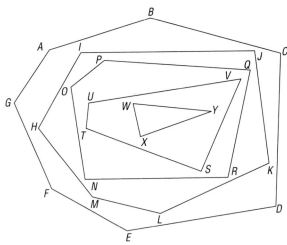

26. Measure the lengths to the nearest millimeter of all sides of the quadrilateral. *(Lesson 3-1)*
TS = 38 mm; *UT* = 7 mm; *UV* = 47 mm; *VS* = 30 mm

27. Which angles of the heptagon seem to be obtuse? *(Lessons 3-6, 5-9)*
all but ∠D

28. Which angles of the pentagon seem to be acute? *(Lessons 3-6, 5-9)*
∠Q

29. Measure angle *TSV*. *(Lesson 3-5)*   93°

In 30 and 31, graph the solutions to each inequality. *(Lesson 4-9)*

30. $x < 5$ **31.** $y \geq -3/2$ See margin.

32. Solve $-0.3 + A = 6.3$. *(Lesson 5-8)*   6.6

Exploration

33. Find the lengths of sides in all triangles satisfying *all* these conditions.
(a) The perimeter is 40.
(b) No side has length under 10.
(c) All sides have different lengths.
(d) The lengths of all sides are integers.
(Hint: Organize your work.)
33. 10, 11, 19   11, 12, 17   12, 13, 15
     10, 12, 18   11, 13, 16
     10, 13, 17   11, 14, 15
     10, 14, 16

Summary

A large variety of situations lead to addition. These situations are of two types: putting-together or slide. Some situations can be interpreted as either of these types.

In a putting-together situation, a count or measure x is put together with a count or measure y. If x and y have the same units and there is no overlap, the result has count or measure $x + y$. When the lengths of the sides of a polygon are put together, the result is the perimeter of the polygon. In a putting-together situation, x and y must be positive or zero.

In slide situations, a slide x is followed by a slide y. The result is a slide $x + y$. In slide situations, there may be changes forward or back, up or down, in or out, clockwise or counterclockwise. One direction is positive, the other negative. So in a slide situation, x and y can be positive, zero, or negative.

From these situations, you can see many properties of addition. Zero is the additive identity. Every number has an opposite or additive inverse. Addition is both commutative and associative.

Suppose you know one addend a and the sum b and would like to find the other addend. Then you are trying to find x in an equation $x + a = b$. This sentence can be solved using the Addition Property of Equality and the other properties of addition.

Vocabulary

You should be able to give a general description and a specific example of each of the following ideas.

Lesson 5-1
Putting-together Model for Addition
addend
Lesson 5-2
common denominator
least common multiple
least common denominator
Lesson 5-3
Slide Model for Addition
 or +/−

Lesson 5-4
additive identity
Additive Identity Property of Zero
additive inverse
Property of Opposites, Op-op Property
Lesson 5-5
absolute value, | |
Lesson 5-6
revolution, full turn, quarter turn
clockwise, counterclockwise

magnitude of turn
Fundamental Property of Turns
Lesson 5-7
Commutative Property of Addition
Associative Property of Addition
Lesson 5-8
Addition Property of Equality
situation of the form $x + a = b$
Lesson 5-9
line segment, segment, $\overline{AB}$
$\overleftrightarrow{AB}$
polygon, side, vertex (vertices), angle of polygon
quadrilateral, pentagon, hexagon, …, n-gon
diagonal of a polygon
convex polygon
Lesson 5-10
perimeter
AB

PROGRESS SELF-TEST

See Additional Answers on page T53 for answers not shown below.

Progress Self-Test

Take this test as you would take a test in class. Then check your work with the solutions in the Selected Answers section in the back of the book.

In 1–7, simplify.
1. $3 + -10$ -7
2. $-460 + -250$ -710
3. $-9.8 + -(-1)$ -8.8
4. $x + y + -x + 4$ $y + 4$
5. $|-8|$ 8
6. $|-2| + |1| + |0|$ 3
7. $-6 + 42 + -11 + 16 + -12$ 29
8. Evaluate $|-A + 8|$ when $A = -3$. 11

In 9–11, solve.
9. $x + 43 = 31$ $x = -12$
10. $-25 + y = 12$ $y = 37$
11. $8 = -2 + z + -5$ $z = 15$

In 12–15, write as a single fraction in lowest terms.
12. $\frac{53}{12} + \frac{11}{12}$ $\frac{16}{3}$
13. $\frac{5}{x} + \frac{10}{x}$ $\frac{15}{x}$
14. $\frac{17}{9} + \frac{8}{3}$ $\frac{41}{9}$
15. $\frac{1}{4} + \frac{3}{8} + \frac{2}{16}$ $\frac{3}{4}$

In 16 and 17, consider the equation $50 = W + -20$.
16. To solve this equation, what number should you add to both sides? 20
17. What property enables you to add the same number to both sides of an equation?
18. $(2 + 3) + 4 = 2 + (3 + 4)$ is an instance of what property? Assoc. Prop. of Addition
19. Give an instance of the Addition Property of Zero. Sample: 3 + 0 = 3
20. A polygon with 6 sides is called a __?__. hexagon
21. A pentagon has two sides of length 3 cm and three sides of length 4 cm. What is its perimeter? 18 cm
22. *Multiple choice* If L and K are points, which symbol stands for a number? (a)
    (a) LK (b) $\overline{LK}$ (c) $\overrightarrow{LK}$ (d) $\overleftrightarrow{LK}$

17. Addition Property of Equality

23. Ms. A's class has m students. Mr. B's class has n students. Together there are 50 students in the classes. How are m, n, and 50 related? $m + n = 50$

In 24 and 25, Sally was 20 points behind. Now she is 150 points ahead. Let c be the change in Sally's status.
24. What equation can be solved to find c?
25. Solve that equation. $c = 170$
    24. $-20 + c = 150$

In 26 and 27, use the figure below. A is on $\overline{MP}$.
26. If $MA = 16$ and $AP = 8$, what is MP? 24

M————————A————————P

27. If $MA = 2.3$ and $MP = 3$, what is PA? 0.7
28. Picture the addition problem $-3 + 2$ on a number line and give the sum.
29. An iron bar is 3 cm longer than 5 meters. In meters, how long is the bar? 5.03 m
30. Is $-5.498765432101 + 5.498765432102$ positive, negative, or zero? Positive

In 31 and 32, use the figure below. Assume all small angles with vertex O have the same measure.
31. What is m$\angle VOW$? 72°
32. If you are standing at O facing U and turn to X, what is the magnitude of your turn? -144°

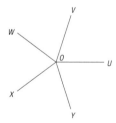

33. What is the result when a 50° clockwise turn is followed by a 250° counterclockwise turn?
34. *Multiple choice* Which is not a side of the polygon $WXYZ$? (a) $\overline{WX}$ (b) $\overline{WY}$ (c) $\overline{WZ}$ (d) Each of (a), (b), (c) is a side. (b)

33. a 200° counterclockwise turn

Chapter Review

Questions on **SPUR** Objectives

SPUR stands for **S**kills, **P**roperties, **U**ses, and **R**epresentations. The Chapter Review questions are grouped according to the SPUR Objectives for this chapter.

See margin for answers not shown below.

SKILLS deal with the procedures used to get answers.

Objective A: *Add any numbers written as decimals or fractions. (Lessons 5-2, 5-3, 5-5)*
In 1–9, add.

1. $-16 + 4$ -12
2. $-7 + -8 + -9$ -24
3. $7 + -2.4 + 5$ 9.6
4. $-31 + 32$ 1
5. $6/11 + 5/11$ 1
6. $\frac{12}{17} + -\frac{12}{17}$ 0
7. $6 + -\frac{8}{9}$ $\frac{46}{9}$
8. $2/3$ and $6/7$ 32/21
9. $1/2, 1/3,$ and $1/4$ 13/12
10. Write $\frac{40}{c} + \frac{-10}{c}$ as a single fraction. 30/c

Objective B: *Calculate absolute value. (Lesson 5-5)*

11. $|-12| = ?$ 12
12. $|4| = ?$ 4
13. $|0| + |3| + |-5| = ?$ 8
14. $-|7| + |4| = ?$ -3

Objective C: *Apply properties of addition to simplify expressions. (Lesson 5-4)*

15. $-(-(-17)) = ?$ -17
16. $-(-4) + 3 = ?$ 7
17. $-40 + 0 = ?$ -40
18. $(86 + -14) + (-86 + 14) = ?$ 0
19. $-(-(0 + \frac{2}{7})) = ?$ 2/7
20. $11/4 + y + -11/4 = ?$ y
21. When $a = -42$, then $-a + 6 = ?$ 48
22. If $b = 2$, then $b + -b = ?$ 0

Objective D: *Solve equations of the form $x + a = b$. (Lesson 5-8)*

23. Solve $x + -32 = -12$. 20
24. Solve $6.3 = t + 2.9$. 3.4
25. Solve $\frac{10}{3} + y = \frac{1}{3}$. -3
26. Solve $0 + a = 4 + 1$. 5
27. Solve $3 + c + -5 = 36$. 38
28. Solve $-8 = 14 + (d + -6)$. -16
29. Solve for x: $x + y = 180$. x = 180 + -y
30. Solve for c: $a + b + c = p$. c = p + -a + -b

Objective E: *Find the perimeter of a polygon. (Lesson 5–10)*

31. What is the perimeter of a square in which one side has length 3? 12
32. If $x = 23$, what is the perimeter of the polygon $ABCDE$? 80

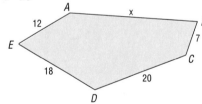

33. Measure the sides of polygon $GHIJ$ to find its perimeter to the nearest centimeter. 15 cm

34. An octagon has 3 sides of length 5 and 4 sides of length 6. What is its perimeter?
35. For polygon $ABCDE$ in Question 32, if the perimeter is 82, what equation can be solved to find x? 12 + 18 + 20 + 7 + x = 82

RESOURCES
- Chapter 5 Test, Form A
- Chapter 5 Test, Form B
- Chapter 5 Test, Cumulative Form

CHAPTER REVIEW

The main objectives for the chapter are organized here into sections corresponding to the four main types of understanding this book promotes: Skills, Properties, Uses, and Representations.

ADDITIONAL ANSWERS
34. Not enough information is given.

Whereas end-of-chapter material may be considered optional in some texts, in *Transition Mathematics* we have selected these objectives and questions in the Chapter Review with the expectation that they will be covered. Students should be able to answer these questions with about 85% accuracy after studying the chapter.

You may assign these questions over a single night to help students prepare for a test the next day, or you may assign the questions over a two-day period.

If you work the questions over two days, then we recommend assigning the *evens* for homework the first night so that students get feedback in class the next day, then assigning the *odds* the night before the test.

ADDITIONAL ANSWERS

36. Commutative Property of Addition

37. Addition Property of Equality

61.

62.
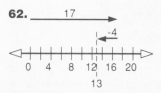

63.

PROPERTIES deal with the principles behind the mathematics.

■ **Objective F:** *Identify properties of addition.* (*Lessons 5-4, 5-7*)

In 36–39, an instance of what property of addition is given?

36. 3.53 meters + 6.74 meters
= 6.74 meters + 3.53 meters

37. Since 30% = 3/10, it is also true that
1/2 + 30% = 1/2 + 3/10.

38. -941 + 941 = 0   **Property of Opposites**

39. (1 + 2) + 3 = (2 + 1) + 3
Commutative Property of Addition

■ **Objective G:** *Classify polygons.* (*Lesson 5-9*)
In 40–42, classify the polygon and tell whether or not it is convex.

40.   quadrilateral, not convex
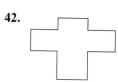

41.   pentagon, convex

42.   12-gon, not convex

■ **Objective H:** *Identify parts and give names of polygons.* (*Lesson 5-9*)

43. Which is not a correct name for the polygon below?
LAKE, LEAK, KALE, ELAK   **LEAK**

44. Name the two diagonals of the polygon below. $\overline{LK}$, $\overline{EA}$

45. The polygon below has __?__ vertices and __?__ sides.   4, 4

46. Name a side of the polygon *ABCDE*.
$\overline{AB}$, $\overline{BC}$, $\overline{CD}$, $\overline{DE}$, or $\overline{EA}$

USES deal with applications of mathematics in real situations.

■ **Objective I:** *Use the Putting-together Model for Addition to form sentences involving addition.* (*Lessons 5-1, 5-2, 5-8*)

47. Bob rode his bicycle a mile and a half to school. Then he rode 3/5 of a mile to his friend's house. Altogether he rode *M* miles. What relationship connects these distances? $1\frac{1}{2} + \frac{3}{5} = M$

48. You have read *x* books this year. A friend has read *y* books. Together you have read 16 books. What relationship connects *x*, *y*, and 16? $x + y = 16$

49. In the Johannson family, Dad earned *D* dollars last year. Mom earned *M* dollars. The children earned *C* dollars. The total family income was *T* dollars. What sentence relates *D*, *M*, *C*, and *T*?
$T = D + M + C$

■ **Objective J:** *Apply the putting-together model to relate lengths.* *(Lesson 5-10)*

In 50–52, use the figure at right. B is on $\overline{AC}$.

50. What relationship connects AB, BC, and AC? $AB + BC = AC$

51. If $AB = x$ and $BC = 3$, what is AC? $x + 3$

52. Let $AC = 10.4$ and $BC = 7.8$.
a. What equation can be used to find AB? **b.** What is AB?
a. $AB + 7.8 = 10.4$; b. 2.6

■ **Objective K:** *Use the slide model for addition to form sentences involving addition.*
(Lesson 5-3, 5-8)

53. Charyl's stock rose $\frac{3}{8}$ of a point on one day and fell $\frac{1}{4}$ point the next day.
a. What addition gives the total change in Charyl's stock? $\frac{3}{8} + \frac{-1}{4}$
b. What is the total change? $\frac{1}{8}$ point

54. Bernie gained 5 pounds one week, lost 7 the next, and lost 3 the next.
a. What addition gives the total change in Bernie's weight? $5 + \text{-}7 + \text{-}3$
b. What is the total change?   -5

55. A diving team was 250 feet below ground level and then came up 75 feet.
a. What addition tells where the team wound up? $\text{-}250 + 75$
b. Where did they wind up?
175 feet below the surface

56. The temperature was -3° and changed $c°$ to reach -10°. What is c?
-7, a 7° change downward

REPRESENTATIONS deal with pictures, graphs, or objects that illustrate concepts.

■ **Objective L:** *Calculate magnitudes of turns given angle measures or revolutions.* *(Lesson 5-6)*

In 57–59, all small angles at O have the same measure. Think of turns around the point O.

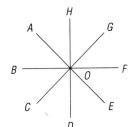

57. What is the magnitude of the turn from F to A?   135°

58. What is the magnitude of the turn from E to C?   -90°

59. If you are facing H and turn 315° clockwise, what point will you then be facing?   A

60. If you turn 90° counterclockwise, and then turn 40° clockwise, what is the result?
a 50° counterclockwise turn

■ **Objective M:** *Picture addition of positive and negative numbers using arrows on a number line.* *(Lesson 5-3)*

61. Picture the addition -5 + 8 on a number line and give the sum.

62. Picture the addition 17 + -4 on a number line and give the sum.

63. Picture the addition -3.5 + -6.5 on a number line and give the sum.

EVALUATION
Three tests are provided for this chapter in the Teacher's Resource File. Chapter 5 Test, Forms A and B cover just Chapter 5. The third test is Chapter 5 Test, Cumulative Form. About 50% of this test covers Chapter 5, 25% covers Chapter 4, and 25% covers earlier chapters. For information on grading, see *General Teaching Suggestions: Grading* on page T44 in the Teacher's Edition.

ASSIGNMENT RECOMMENDATION
We strongly recommend that you assign Lesson 6-1, both reading and some questions, for homework the evening of the test. It gives students work to do after they have completed the test and keeps the class moving.

CHAPTER 6 ■ PROBLEM-SOLVING STRATEGIES

DAILY PACING CHART 6

DAILY PACING CHART ■ CHAPTER 6

Students in the Full Course should complete the entire text by the end of the year. Students in the Minimal Course spend more time when there are quizzes and more time on the Chapter Review. Therefore, these students may not complete all of the chapters in the text.

DAY	MINIMAL COURSE	FULL COURSE
1	6-1	6-1
2	6-2	6-2
3	6-3	6-3
4	6-4	6-4
5	Quiz (TRF); 6-5	Quiz (TRF); 6-5
6	6-6	6-6
7	6-7	6-7
8	Progress Self-Test	Progress Self-Test
9	Chapter Review	Chapter Review
10	Chapter Review	Chapter Test (TRF)
11	Chapter Test (TRF)	Comprehensive Test (TRF)
12	Comprehensive Test (TRF)	

TESTING OPTIONS

TESTING OPTIONS

■ Quiz on Lessons 6-1 Through 6-4 ■ Chapter 6 Test, Form A ■ Chapter 6 Test, Cumulative Form
■ Chapter 6 Test, Form B ■ Comprehensive Test, Chapters 1-6

A Quiz and Test Writer is available for generating additional questions, additional quizzes, or additional forms of the Chapter Test.

PROVIDING FOR INDIVIDUAL DIFFERENCES

INDIVIDUAL DIFFERENCES

The student text is written for the *average* student. The program, however, can be adapted for both less capable and more capable students.

A blackline master (in the Teacher's Resource File) is provided for each lesson for those students who need more practice. The Teacher's Edition frequently provides an Error Analysis feature to provide additional instructional strategies.

For students who require additional challenge, Extension activities are regularly provided in the Teacher's Edition.

240A

OBJECTIVES ■ CHAPTER 6

Students should master the chapter objectives by the time they complete the chapter. To ensure objective mastery, there is continual review built into each set of lesson questions. After students complete the chapter lessons, they assess their mastery on the Progress Self-Test. Then they do the Chapter Review and pay special attention to those questions that match the objectives missed on the Progress Self-Test. Students can get extra practice on these objectives by using the master for each lesson in the Teacher's Resource File.

OBJECTIVES FOR CHAPTER 6 (Organized into the SPUR categories—Skills, Properties, Uses, and Representations)	Progress Self-Test Questions	Chapter Review Questions	Teacher's Resource File	
			Lesson Master*	Chapter Test Forms A and B
SKILLS				
A: Understand the methods followed by good problem solvers.	16	1–3	6-1	11
B: Determine solutions to sentences by trial and error.	4, 10	4–7	6-4	9
PROPERTIES				
C: Determine whether a number is prime or composite.	6	8–11	6-2	3
D: Find the meaning of unknown words.	1, 5	12, 13	6-2	1
E: Make a table to find patterns and make generalizations.	14, 15	14, 15	6-5	4
F: Work with a special case to determine whether a pattern is true.	13	16, 17	6-6	8
G: Use special cases to determine that a property is false or to give evidence that it is true.	7	18, 19	6-6	5
USES				
H: Use simpler numbers to answer a question requiring only one operation.	8	20, 21	6-7	7
I: Use drawings to solve real problems.	3	22–25	6-3	6
REPRESENTATIONS				
J: Draw a diagram to find the number of diagonals in a polygon.	2	26, 27	6-3	10
K: Draw a diagram to aid in solving geometric problems.	11, 12	28, 29	6-3	2

*The Lesson Masters are numbered to match the lessons.

OVERVIEW ■ CHAPTER 6

What is a problem? Today's generally accepted definition is that a problem is an unresolved question for which the potential solver does not have an algorithm. Under this definition, a standard word problem may or may not be a problem for a given student. Thus, in order to teach problem solving, one must use situations or questions students have not seen before.

All of *Transition Mathematics* works to develop problem-solving competence. We agree with the National Council of Supervisors of Mathematics and the National Council of Teachers of Mathematics that problem solving should be considered as a basic skill in mathematics programs. We devote a special chapter entirely to teaching the many processes involved in problem solving because it is important at times to focus on the strategies and not on a particular bit of mathematics. By bringing these lessons together, we heighten the importance of problem solving. The rest of the book, both before and after this chapter, applies the ideas found here.

This chapter discusses both general and specific problem-solving strategies. Lesson 6-1 contains the most general advice. Lessons 6-2 through 6-7 are each devoted to a particular general problem-solving strategy. Each strategy is applied to at least one typical kind of question a student should be able to answer. Each section also has examples of atypical problems utilizing that strategy.

Problem solving takes time and is not necessarily easy. Some students will not master the content in this chapter. You should expect to give credit for attempts, for partial answers, and for ingenuity.

Many students are so accustomed to single answers and rules that they do not know how to proceed when there are no rules. The goal is for students to experience the special delight of solving a problem unlike any they have seen before.

Many teachers have told us that this is their favorite chapter in the book.

PERSPECTIVES ■ CHAPTER 6

The Perspectives provide the rationale for the inclusion of topics or approaches, provide mathematical background, and make connections within UCSMP.

6-1

BEING A GOOD PROBLEM SOLVER

A full chapter is devoted to problem-solving strategies because knowledge of algorithms alone is not enough to solve problems. If there is an algorithm for a question, then the question can be (and today usually is) answered by computer or calculator. The important skill is to decide what to do when there is no algorithm or when you do not have one. The idea of this chapter is to teach students how to proceed when, in the past, they might have given up.

This lesson defines *problem* and gives advice about how to approach a problem. It is meant to provide background and to ease the students into problem solving.

6-2

READ CAREFULLY

Like Lesson 6-1, this lesson provides general advice about problem solving. It emphasizes reading for comprehension and reminds students to look up words they do not know. Having dictionaries, mathematics dictionaries, and several different mathematics texts readily available will encourage students to acquire the habit of using outside references.

Many students have never confronted a problem in which too much or too little information has been provided for finding a solution. In real-life circumstances, this situation is quite common. Thus, it is important to bring these considerations to the forefront before attacking problem solving directly.

6-3

DRAW A PICTURE

In spite of the adage "a picture is worth a thousand words," it is often difficult to get students to draw even the most obvious diagram. However, pictures or diagrams are helpful in devising a course of action and in avoiding careless mistakes in tricky problems. Devoting an entire lesson to this strategy will emphasize its usefulness. Giving partial credit for a drawing will encourage students to make liberal use of this problem-solving tool.

6-4

TRIAL AND ERROR

Trial and error has a long history of use outside the classroom as well as in it. Justice Louis Brandeis of the United States Supreme Court wrote in a 1932 decision: "...this court has often overruled its earlier decisions. The Court bows to the lessons of experience and the force of better reasoning, recognizing that the process of trial and error, so fruitful in the physical sciences, is appropriate also in the judicial function."

Although the discussion emphasizes testing an answer, in reality one often uses trial and error to select a strategy. That is, a person will try strategy 1, and if it does not work, go to strategy 2, and so on. This approach works well if there are only a few possible options.

Trial and error may be a particularly applicable strategy to use on a multiple-choice test, because it is no more than the simple logic of ruling out possibilities. The good multiple-choice test taker often rules out choices rather than doing the problem in a straightforward way. That person is making use of *all* the information given.

6-5

MAKE A TABLE

This lesson demonstrates how much easier it is to make generalizations from a table than from unorganized data. A table can reduce a complicated problem to one of describing patterns with variables, the focus of Lesson 4-2. Once described, the generalization can then be used to answer a specific question or sometimes other similar questions.

This lesson explains a fundamental way in which arithmetic leads to algebra: through patterns. We cannot overemphasize the importance of this idea.

6-6

WORKING WITH A SPECIAL CASE

A special case is simply an instance of a generalization used for a definite purpose. In this lesson, students learn how to work with a special case to test generalizations. Instances of generalizations were discussed in Chapter 4, so this content is not new. The only new idea is the way in which the instances are applied.

The variety in the four examples illustrates the power of this strategy. The first example uses special cases to see if a generalization is probably true; the second, to select the correct generalization from a few possibilities (a strategy for multiple-choice tests); the third, to aid recall; and the fourth, to show a generalization to be false.

6-7

TRY SIMPLER NUMBERS

Trying simpler numbers is similar to working with a special case, covered in Lesson 6-6. In that lesson, a generalization was given, and the procedure was to use a special case, or instance, to test the truth of the generalization. In this lesson, one instance is given. The idea is to use a simpler instance to figure out enough of the generalization so that you can work with the first instance.

For solving real problems, trying simpler numbers is an alternate strategy to using models for operations. Examples in this lesson could be done using the Rate Factor Model for Multiplication (Lesson 10-4). By trying simpler numbers, students can answer the questions by induction from the simpler cases rather than by deduction from a generalization.

CHAPTER 6

We suggest 10 to 11 days for this chapter: 1 day for each lesson, 1 day to review the Progress Test, 1 or 2 days for the Chapter Review, and 1 day for a Chapter Test. A test covering Chapters 1–6 is provided in the Teacher's Resource File. This Comprehensive Test can be used as a midyear exam.

USING PAGES 240–241
You may wish to ask students to explain what is funny (or not so funny, depending on the point of view) about the comic strip on page 241. Point out that asking for help or for a rule to follow is often an appropriate way to confront a problem. Tell the students that in this chapter, they will examine ways to approach problem solving without help from others.

CHAPTER 6

Problem-Solving Strategies

240

McGURK'S MOB

To solve a problem is to find a way where no way is known off-hand, to find a way out of a difficulty, to find a way around an obstacle, to attain a desired end that is not immediately attainable, by appropriate means.

—George Polya [1887–1985]

Solving problems is human nature itself.

—Polya

The person who makes no mistakes usually makes nothing.

—Anonymous

OBJECTIVE

A Understand the methods
followed by good
problem solvers.

TEACHING NOTES

Students can read this lesson
independently following the
test on Chapter 5. Yet you
will still need to emphasize
the strategies and steps on
page 243 to reinforce the
messages and help students
take this advice seriously.

Tell students that what is a
problem for someone else
may not be a problem for
them, and vice versa. They
may find some of the questions in this chapter quite
easy; some quite hard; the
level of difficulty depends
more on their experience
than on their ability. Stress
the need to make an honest
effort to answer the questions
in the chapter.

LESSON

6-1

Being a Good Problem Solver

In Chapter 5, you learned how to solve any equation of the form
$a + x = b$ for x. The method was to add $-a$ to each side and
then simplify. This method is an example of an algorithm. An
algorithm is a sequence of steps that leads to a desired result.

Not all algorithms are short. The algorithm called *long division*
can involve many steps.

$$
\begin{array}{r}
.75 \\
34\overline{)25.50} \\
\underline{23\ 8} \\
1\ 70 \\
\underline{1\ 70}
\end{array}
$$

You know another algorithm for dividing decimals. It is the
calculator algorithm. It is much easier to describe the algorithm
for division on a calculator than for long division. The key
sequence describes the algorithm.

Key sequence: 25.50   ÷   34   =
Display: (25.50) (25.50) (34) (0.75)

There is another way to think about algorithms. An algorithm is
something that a computer could be programmed to do.

An **exercise** is a question that you know how to answer. For
you, adding whole numbers is an exercise. You know an
algorithm for addition. A **problem** for you is a question you do
not know how to answer. It is a question for which you have
no algorithm. Many people think that if they do not have an
algorithm, then they cannot do a problem. But that isn't true.
By following some advice, almost anyone can become a better
problem solver.

242

In this chapter you will learn many strategies for solving problems. But you must do three things.

1. *Take your time.* Few people solve problems fast. (If a person solves a problem fast, then it may not have been a problem for that person!)

2. *Don't give up.* You will never solve a problem if you do not try. Do something! (In the cartoon on page 241, Rick and the man give up too soon.)

3. *Be flexible.* If at first you don't succeed, try another way. And if the second way does not work, try a third way.

George Polya was a mathematician at Stanford University who was famous for his writing about solving problems. He once wrote:

"Solving problems is a practical skill like, let us say, swimming. We acquire any practical skill by imitation and practice. Trying to swim, you imitate what other people do with their hands and feet to keep their heads above water, and, finally, you learn to swim by practicing swimming. Trying to solve problems, you have to observe and to imitate what other people do when solving problems and, finally, you learn to do problems by doing them."

In a famous book called *How to Solve It*, Polya described what good problem solvers do.

- They *read the problem carefully.* They try to understand every word. They make sure they know what is asked for. They reread. They make certain that they are using the correct information. They look up words they do not know.

- They *devise a plan.* Even guesses are planned. They arrange information in tables. They draw pictures. They compare the problem to other problems they know. They decide to try something.

- They *carry out the plan.* They attempt to solve. They work with care. They write things down so they can read them later. If the attempt does not work, they go back to read the problem again.

- They *check work.* In fact, they check their work at every step. They do not check by repeating what they did. They check by estimating, or by trying to find another way of doing the problem.

These are the kinds of strategies you will study in this chapter. You will also learn about some important problems and some fun problems.

1. How many different whole numbers can you make with the digits 1, 2, 3, and 4? Any number you make can have one to four digits in it. You cannot repeat a digit in any number you make. **24 with all 4 digits, 24 with 3 digits, 12 with 2 digits; 4 with 1 digit, for a total of 64 numbers.**

2. How many triangles are in this drawing?

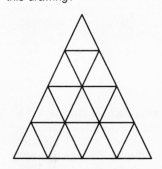

16 little ones; 7 four times as big; 3 nine times as big; 1 sixteen times as big; total 27

NOTES ON QUESTIONS
Small Group Work for
Questions 17 and 18:
It is more important that students try these problems than that they get the answers exactly right. You may want students in a group to compare their solution methods. Then have each group choose one of the methods to arrive at the correct answer.

Questions 19 and 20:
Each is a common type of counting question in which one must count everything from *a* to *b*, including the endpoints. The answer is one more than the length of the interval $b - a$.

Error Analysis for
Question 21: Some students may find this question confusing. Be sure they know the definition of *edge*. Then suggest that students *draw a picture* (the problem-solving strategy in Lesson 6-3). Students may need to number the edges in the drawing to keep track of them. Some students may need to examine a model of a cube.

Questions

Covering the Reading

1. What is an algorithm?
   See margin.
2. Give an example of an algorithm.
   Sample: long division
3. What is a problem?   a question you do not know how to answer

4. What is an exercise?   a question you know how to answer

In 5 and 6, refer to the algorithm pictured at right.

$$\begin{array}{r} 34.2 \\ 5.67 \\ \hline 2394 \\ 2052 \\ 1710 \\ \hline 193.914 \end{array}$$

5. What question does this algorithm answer?
   What is 34.2 x 5.67?
6. Write the calculator algorithm that answers the same question.   34.2 $\boxed{\times}$ 5.67 $\boxed{=}$

In 7–9, what problem-solving advice is suggested by each traffic sign?

7. Take your time.   8. Be flexible.   9. Don't give up.

10. Who was George Polya?   See margin.

11. What famous book did Polya write?   *How to Solve It*

In 12 and 13, tell what each person should have done.

12. Monty tried one way to do the problem. When that did not work, he tried the same way again.   He should have tried another way.

13. Priscilla said to herself: "I've never seen any problem like that before. I won't be able to do it."   She gave up instead of trying.

14. What four things do successful problem solvers do when solving a problem?   **See margin.**

15. Marjorie wants to devise a plan to solve a problem. What are some of the things she can do?   **See margin.**

16. Adam wrote down an answer very quickly and went on to the next problem. What did he do wrong?   **See margin.**

17. Consider the vowels A, E, I, O, U. Make two-letter monograms with these vowels, like AO, UE, II. How many two-letter monograms are there? (Hint: Make an organized list.)   **25**

18. You can buy stickers for digits from 0 through 9 at most hardware stores. They can be used for house addresses and room numbers. Suppose you buy stickers for all the digits in all the integers from 1 through 100.   **a.** What digit will be used most? **b.** What digit will be used least?   **a. 1; b. 0**

19. Trains leave Union Station every hour from 7 A.M. through 7 P.M. bound for Kroy. How many trains is that in a day?
13 trains

20. Suppose in Question 19, trains left every *half* hour, from 7 A.M. through 7 P.M. How many trains is that in a day?
25 trains

21. A cube has how many edges? *(Lesson 3-8)*   **12 edges**

22. What is the volume of a cube with an edge of length 5 centimeters? *(Lesson 3-8)*   **125 cubic centimeters**

23. Simplify: $\frac{2}{3} + \frac{5}{7} - \frac{1}{14}$. *(Lessons 5-2, 5-5)*   **55/42**

24. How many feet are in 5 miles? *(Lesson 3-2)*   **26,400 feet**

25. Find the value of $3 + 4a$ when $a = 2.5$. *(Lesson 4-4)*   **13**

26. Give the fraction in lowest terms equal to:
a. 10% $\frac{1}{10}$ **b.** 25% $\frac{1}{4}$ **c.** 75% $\frac{3}{4}$ **d.** $66\frac{2}{3}$% *(Lesson 2-5)* $\frac{2}{3}$

27. One-sixth is equal to __?__ percent. *(Lesson 2-7)*   **$16.\overline{6}$ or $16\frac{2}{3}$**

LESSON 6-1   Being a Good Problem Solver   **245**

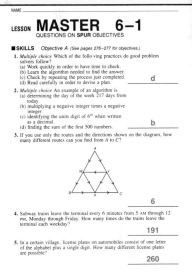

EXTENSION
Generalization, as discussed in Lesson 6-5, is an important problem-solving strategy. Students may want to make a generalization for **Question 17:** How many two-letter monograms can be made with *n* letters, if each letter can be used more than once? The students can consider two-letter monograms with two letters, three letters, four letters, and so on, until they see that n^2 two-letter monograms can be made with *n* letters.

EVALUATION
Alternative Assessment
Have students think of a non-mathematical problem they have had to solve, for example, losing their house key and finding themselves locked out. Ask the students to write down the problem and identify the steps they took to solve it. Compare non-mathematical problem solving with solving the kinds of problems in this book.

28. Here are changes in populations for the ten largest cities in the United States from 1980 to 1988. *(Lessons 1-5, 5-7)*

New York	280,700
Los Angeles	383,710
Chicago	−27,480
Houston	103,090
Philadelphia	−41,000
San Diego	194,230
Detroit	−167,180
Dallas	82,160
San Antonio	154,940
Phoenix	133,690

   a. Which cities lost in population from 1980 to 1988?
   b. What was the total change in population for the ten cities combined? **a. Chicago, Philadelphia, Detroit b. 1,096,860**

29. Of the 5.3 billion people on Earth in 1990, about 1% live in Egypt. How many people is this? *(Lessons 2-1, 2-6)* **about 53 million**

Exploration

30. Each letter stands for a different digit in this addition problem. The sum is 10440. Find the digits.

```
          U                Sample:      3
      C A N                          7 8 2
        D O                            4 5
      T H I S                        9 6 1 0
    ──────────                     ──────────
    1 0 4 4 0                      1 0 4 4 0
```

6-2

Read Carefully

To solve a problem, you must understand it. So, if the problem is written down, you must *read it carefully*. To read carefully, there are three things you must do.

1. Know the meaning of all words and symbols in the problem.
2. Sort out information that is not needed.
3. Determine if there is enough information to solve the problem.

Example 1 List the ten smallest positive composite integers.

Strategy To answer this question, you must know the meaning of "positive composite integer." In this book, we have already discussed the positive integers. So the new word here is "composite." Our dictionary has many definitions of "composite," but only one of "composite number." Here is that definition: "Any number exactly divisible by one or more numbers other than itself and 1; opposed to *prime number*." So a composite number is a positive integer that is not prime. Now the problem can be solved.

Solution The positive integers are 1, 2, 3, 4,.... Those that are prime are 2, 3, 5, 7, 11, 13, 17, and so on. The ten smallest composites are the others: 4, 6, 8, 9, 10, 12, 14, 15, 16, 18.

If you do not know the meaning of a word, look it up in a dictionary. Your school may even have a dictionary of mathematical words. Some mathematics books (including this one) have glossaries or indexes in the back that can help you locate words.

Some terms have more than one meaning even in mathematics. The word *divisor* can mean *the number divided by* in a division problem. (In $12 \div 3 = 4$, 3 is the divisor.). But *divisor* also means *a number that divides another number with a zero remainder*. For example, 7 is a divisor of 21. Then *divisor* has the same meaning as *factor*.

OBJECTIVES

C Determine whether a number is prime or composite.
D Find the meaning of unknown words.

TEACHING NOTES

Reading There are many sources for finding definitions. Many books, including this one, have an index and a glossary at the back. Have the students look carefully at both sections in their textbooks. If students cannot find a word in the Glossary or Index, suggest that they look in a regular or mathematical dictionary, an encyclopedia, or other mathematics books.

After this lesson, students should know the meanings of *prime*, *composite*, *divisor*, *factor*, and *natural number*. (In some books, the natural numbers include 0.) Although many students have learned these terms in previous classes, a review will be helpful.

Some symbols have more than one meaning. The dash "−" can mean subtraction. It can also mean "the opposite of." However, in phone numbers, like 555—1212, it has no meaning other than to separate the number to make it easier to remember. You must look at the situation to determine which meaning is correct in a given problem.

Here is an example of a problem with too much information. Can you tell what information is not needed?

Example 2   Last year the Williams family joined a reading club. Mrs. Williams read 20 books. Mr. Williams read 16 books. Their son Jed read 12 books. Their daughter Josie read 14 books and their daughter Julie read 7 books. How many books did these children of Mr. & Mrs. Williams read altogether?

Solution   Did you see that the problem asks only about the *children*? The information about the books read by Mr. and Mrs. Williams is not needed. The children read 12 + 14 + 7 books, for a total of 33 books.

Example 3   Read Example 2 again. How many children do the Williamses have?

Solution   Do you think 3? Reread the problem. Nowhere does it say that these are the only children. The Williamses have *at least* 3 children.

Questions

Covering the Reading

1. What three things should you do when you read a problem?
See margin.
2. Can a word have more than one mathematical meaning?   Yes
3. Give an example of a mathematical symbol that has more than one meaning.   Example: the dash −
4. Which number is not a composite integer?   6   7   8   9   10   7
5. Which number is not a prime number?   11   13   15   17   19   15
6. List the ten smallest positive prime numbers.
2, 3, 5, 7, 11, 13, 17, 19, 23, 29
7. Which number is a divisor of 91?   3   5   7   9   11   7

248

8. Which number is a factor of 91? 13 15 17 19 21   13

In 9–11, refer to Example 2.

9. How many books did Mr. & Mrs. Williams read altogether?   36

10. What word is a hint that the Williamses have more than three children?   "these" children

11. Of the three Williams children named, who is youngest?
Not enough information is given.

12. Name three places to look to find a definition of a mathematical term.   dictionary, glossary in back of book, encyclopedia

Applying the Mathematics

A **natural number** is one of the numbers 1, 2, 3, 4,.... Use this definition in Questions 13–15.

13. *Multiple choice*   Which of (a) to (c) is the same as natural number?   (c)
(a) whole number   (b) integer   (c) positive integer   (d) none

14. Name all natural numbers that are solutions to $10 > x > 7$.   8, 9

15. How many natural numbers are solutions of $v < 40$?   39

16. List all the divisors of 36.   1, 2, 3, 4, 6, 9, 12, 18, 36

17. In $\frac{24}{35}$ which number is the divisor?   35

18. Which of the following numbers are prime? 2; 57; 8^6; 5×10^4 2

In 19–21, give or draw an example of each item.   See margin.

19. a regular hexagon   20. a perfect number

21. a pair of twin primes

In 22 and 23, use the following information. The class in room 25 had 23 students last year and has 27 students this year. The class in room 24 had 25 students last year and has 26 students this year. There are 22 students this year and there were 28 students last year in room 23.

22. What was the total number of students in these classrooms last year?   76 students

23. In which year were there more students in these classrooms?
last year

In 24 and 25, use the following information. The class in room a had b students last year and has c students this year. The class in room d had e students last year and has f students this year. There are g students this year and there were h students last year in room i.

24. What was the total number of students in these classrooms last year? $b + e + h$ students

25. In which year were there more students in these classrooms?
See margin.

LESSON 6-2   Read Carefully   249

Review

26. What are Polya's four steps in problem solving? *(Lesson 6-1)*
See margin.

27. In a Scrabble® tournament, a person played six different people with the following results: won by 12, lost by 30, won by 65, won by 47, lost by 3, and lost by 91. What was the total point difference between this person and the other six people combined? *(Lesson 5-5)*   0 is the total difference

28. Simplify: $-(-(-(-y)))$. *(Lesson 5-5)*   y

29. Simplify: $5 + -(-(-3 + 4 \cdot 2))$. *(Lessons 4-5, 5-4)*   10

30. Solve for x: $x + 3 + y = y + 8$. *(Lesson 5-8)*   x = 5

31. Name two segments in the drawing that look perpendicular. *(Lesson 3-6)* $\overline{BC}$ and $\overline{CD}$

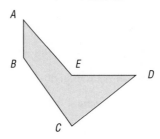

Exploration

32. List all even prime numbers.   2

6-3

Draw a Picture

LESSON 6-3

RESOURCES
■ Lesson Master 6-3
▣ Computer Master 11
■ Centimeter Cubes (from
*Transition Mathematics
Manipulative Kit*)

OBJECTIVES

I Use drawings to solve
real problems.
J Draw a diagram to find
the number of diagonals
in a polygon.
K Draw a diagram to aid
in solving geometric
problems.

You can understand every word in a problem yet still not be able
to solve it immediately. One way to devise a plan is to *draw a
picture*. Sometimes the picture is obvious, as in Example 1.

Example 1   How many diagonals does a heptagon have?

Strategy   The plan is obvious. Draw a heptagon and draw its
diagonals. Count the diagonals as you draw them.

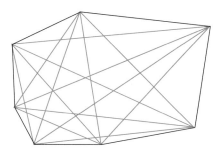

Solution   There are 14 diagonals. (Count them to check.)

Suppose you did not remember that a heptagon has 7 sides.
Then you could look back in Chapter 5. Or you could look in a
dictionary. The same is true if you forgot what a diagonal is.

TEACHING NOTES

There are three general kinds
of situations for which drawing a picture is appropriate.
The first is a geometric situation, as in **Example 1.** In
that instance, the need for a
picture is obvious.

Second are the situations
similar to **Example 2.** A
picture might not be obvious
at first. Once a student has
seen the connection,
however, he or she starts
thinking of solutions in terms
of diagrams.

A third kind of situation, exemplified by the ordering idea
in **Question 7,** does not
seem at first glance to
involve a picture. Nonethe-
less, a diagram helps solve
the problem.

MAG [I.]

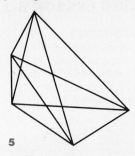
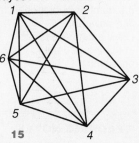
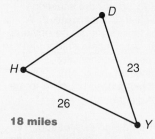
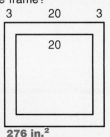
Sometimes a problem is not geometric. A drawing can still help.

Example 2   Seven teams are to play each other in a tournament. How many games are needed?

Solution   Name the teams *A*, *B*, *C*, *D*, *E*, *F*, and *G*. Use these letters to name points in a drawing. When *A* plays *D*, draw the segment *AD*. So each segment between two points represents a different game.

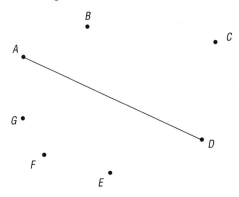

The number of games played is the number of segments that can be drawn. But the segments are the sides and diagonals of a heptagon. Since a heptagon has 7 sides and Example 1 showed that there are 14 diagonals in a heptagon, there are 21 segments altogether. Twenty-one games are needed for the tournament.

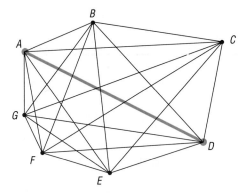

Drawing a picture is a very important problem-solving idea. You may never have thought of picturing teams as we did above. In newspapers and magazines you often see numbers pictured in bar graphs and circle graphs. Chapter 8 in this book is devoted to these kinds of displays.

252

Questions

Covering the Reading

1. How many diagonals does a heptagon have? **14 diagonals**

2. Seven teams are to play each other in a tournament. How many games are needed? **21 games**

3. How many diagonals does a quadrilateral have? **2 diagonals**

4. Four teams are to play each other in a tournament. How many games are needed? **6 games**

Applying the Mathematics

5. Eight teams are to play each other two times in a season. How many games are needed? **56 games**

In 6–9, the strategy of this lesson will help.

6. A square dog pen is 10 feet on a side. There is a post in each corner. There are posts every 2 feet on each side. How many posts are there in all? **20 posts**

7. Bill is older than Wanda and younger than Jill. Jill is older than Chris and younger than Pete. Chris is older than Wanda. Bill is younger than Pete. Chris is older than Bill. Who is youngest?
Wanda

8. Amy is driving along Interstate 55 in Illinois from Collinsville to Joliet. She will pass through Litchfield and then through Atlanta. The distance from Collinsville to Litchfield is half the distance from Litchfield to Atlanta. The distance from Atlanta to Joliet is three times the distance from Collinsville to Litchfield. The distance from Atlanta to Joliet is 114 miles. How far is it from Collinsville to Joliet? **228 miles**

9. The Sherman family has a pool 30 feet long and 25 feet wide. There is a walkway 4.5 feet wide around the pool.
   a. What is the perimeter of the pool? **110 ft**
   b. What is the perimeter of the outside of the walkway? **146 ft**

Review

10. Find the value of $6x^4$ when $x = 3$. *(Lesson 4-4)* **486**

11. List all the natural number factors of 40. *(Lesson 6-2)*
1, 2, 4, 5, 8, 10, 20, 40

12. Name three places to look if you do not know the meaning of a mathematical term. *(Lesson 6-2)* **glossary, dictionary, encyclopedia**

13. What number will you get if you follow this key sequence?

    $20 \boxed{y^x} 3 \boxed{\times} 2 \boxed{+} \boxed{(} 5 \boxed{+} 4 \boxed{)} \boxed{=}$ *(Lessons 1-7, 2-2)*

    16,009

14. List the natural numbers between 8.4 and 4.2. *(Lesson 6-2)*
5, 6, 7, 8

15. List all prime numbers between 40 and 50. *(Lesson 6-2)* **41, 43, 47**

NOTES ON QUESTIONS
Question 6: Students need to realize that the same "posts" work for both sides where the sides meet in each corner. A diagram makes this question easier.

Questions 7 and 8: Students who have difficulty with these problems will need to read back and forth from the beginning to the end of the question, evaluating each bit of information in terms of the other pieces of information as they draw their diagrams.

NAME _____

LESSON MASTER 6–3
QUESTIONS ON **SPUR** OBJECTIVES

■USES *Objective I (See Chapter Review, pages 276–277, for objectives.)*
In 1–8, draw a picture to help solve the problem.

1. Maureen is younger than Bridget and older than Peggy. Peggy is older than Jim. Tim is younger than Maureen and older than Jim. Peggy is older than Tim. Tim is younger than Bridget. Who is the middle child?   **Peggy**

2. A window in the Harringtons' kitchen measured 64 in. by 60 in., including the window frame. Kristin put a 3-in. border around the window.

   a. What is the perimeter of the window including the window frame?   **248 in.**

   b. What is the perimeter of the outside of the border?   **272 in.**

3. Ten teams are scheduled to play each other in a tournament. How many games are needed?   **45**

4. A weekly bowling league of six teams is organized so that each team bowls against each of the other teams twice. How many weeks of bowling are needed to complete the schedule?   **30**

■REPRESENTATIONS *Objective J*

5. How many diagonals does a pentagon have?   **5**

6. How many diagonals does a nonagon have?   **27**

■REPRESENTATIONS *Objective K*

7. In polygon *ABCDEF* all the diagonals from *D* are drawn. How many triangles are formed?   **4**

8. From any given point in the interior of a hexagon, a segment is drawn to each vertex. Into how many sections is the interior divided?   **6**

In 16 and 17, suppose that Sarah has S dollars and Dana has D dollars. Translate into English. *(Lesson 5-8)* **See margin.**

16. $S = D$

17. If $S = D$, then $S + 2 = D + 2$.

18. When $a = -3$ and $b = 6$, what is the value of $-(a + b)$? *(Lessons 4-5, 5-5)* **-3**

19. What is the absolute value of -30? *(Lesson 5-5)* **30**

20. Which is larger, 45 centimeters or 800 millimeters? *(Lesson 3-3)* **800 mm**

21. Round 56.831 to the nearest hundredth. *(Lesson 1-4)* **56.83**

22. Write .00000 0035 in scientific notation. *(Lesson 2-9)* **3.5×10^{-8}**

23. 10 kg is about how many pounds? *(Lesson 3-4)* **22 pounds**

24. Give three instances of the following pattern: $x + x + x = 3x$. *(Lesson 4-2)* **See margin.**

Exploration

25. 27 small cubes are arranged to form one big $3 \times 3 \times 3$ cube. Then the entire big cube is dipped in paint. How many small cubes will now be painted on exactly two sides? **12 cubes**

26. One local baseball league has 5 teams and another has 6 teams. Each team in the first league is to play each team in the second league. How many games are needed? (Hint: The drawing at left may be helpful.) **30 games**

6-4

Trial and Error

Trial and error is a problem-solving strategy everyone uses at one time or another. In trial and error, you try an answer. (The word "trial" comes from "try.") If the answer is in error, you try something else. You keep trying until you get a correct answer. This is a particularly good strategy if a question has only a few possible answers.

Example 1 Which of the numbers 4, 5, and 6 is a solution to $(n + 3)(n - 2) = 36$?

Strategy This type of equation is not discussed in this book. You probably do not know how to solve it. You have no algorithm. So it is a problem for you. However, since there are only three choices for a value of *n*, trial and error is a suitable strategy.

Solution Try the numbers one at a time.
Try 4.　Does $(4 + 3)(4 - 2) = 36$?　Does $7 \cdot 2 = 36$?　No.
Try 5.　Does $(5 + 3)(5 - 2) = 36$?　Does $8 \cdot 3 = 36$?　No.
Try 6.　Does $(6 + 3)(6 - 2) = 36$?　Does $9 \cdot 4 = 36$?　Yes.
So 6 is a solution.

Sometimes results of early trials can help in later ones. In Example 2, the first two trials are so easy that they encourage going on to try more complicated figures.

Example 2 A polygon has 9 diagonals. How many sides does the polygon have?

Strategy Combine two strategies. Draw pictures of various polygons with their diagonals. Keep trying until a polygon with 9 diagonals is found. Count the diagonals as you draw them.

Solution

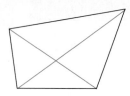

A triangle has 0 diagonals.

A quadrilateral has 2 diagonals.

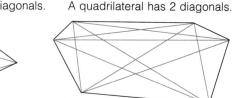

A pentagon has 5 diagonals.   A hexagon has 9 diagonals.

So the polygon with 9 diagonals has 6 sides.

Computers are able to try things very quickly. Even when there is a large number of possible solutions, a computer may use trial and error. In Example 2 we tested the polygons in order of number of sides. Likewise, a computer will search for solutions in an organized way. Trial and error is not a good procedure if the trials are not organized.

Questions

Covering the Reading

1. Describe the problem-solving strategy called "trial and error."   See margin.

2. When is trial and error a useful strategy?   See margin.

3. Which of the numbers 4, 5, or 6 is a solution to $(x + 3)(x - 2) = 24$?   5

4. Which of the numbers 4, 5, or 6 is a solution to $(x + 3)(x - 2) = 14$?   4

In 5–8, which of the numbers 1, 2, 3, 4, or 5 is a solution?

5. $(x + 7)(x + 2)(x + 3) = 300$ 3

6. $3y - 2 + 5y = 30$ 4

7. $1 + A/3 = 2$ 3

8. $11 - x = 7 + x$ 2

9. What polygon has 5 diagonals?   pentagon

10. A polygon has 14 diagonals. How many sides does it have?   7

11. Can a polygon have exactly 10 diagonals?   No

12. Do computers use trial and error?   Yes

256

In 13–17, trial and error is a useful strategy.

13. Choose one number from each row so that the sum of numbers is 300.

Row 1:	147	152	128	147
Row 2:	132	103	118	118
Row 3:	63	35	41	35

14. Joel was 13 years old in a year in the 1980s when he noticed that his age was a factor of the year. In what year was Joel born? **1976**

15. What two positive integers whose sum is 14 have the smallest product? **13 and 1**

16. Find all sets of three integers satisfying all of the following conditions: (1) The numbers are different. (2) The sum of the numbers is 0. (3) No number is greater than 4. (4) No number is less than -4. **See margin.**

17. Hidden inside the box are two two-digit numbers. The difference between the numbers is 54. The sum of the digits in each number is 10. What are the two numbers? **See margin.**

18. How many sides are in a dodecagon? *(Lesson 6-2)* **12**

19. Kenneth is older than Ali and Bill. Carla is younger than Ali and older than Bill. Don is older than Carla but younger than Kenneth. Don is Ali's older brother. If the ages of these people are 11, 12, 13, 14, and 15, who is the 13-year-old? *(Lesson 6-3)* **Ali**

20. List all composite numbers between 11 and 23. *(Lesson 6-2)* **12, 14, 15, 16, 18, 20, 21, 22**

21. What are the rules for order of operations? *(Lesson 4-7)* **See margin.**

22. Evaluate $2xy + x/z$ when $x = 3$, $y = 4$, and $z = 1.5$. *(Lesson 4-4)* **26**

23. Graph all solutions to $x \leq -2$. *(Lesson 4-9)* **See margin.**

24. Add: $\frac{1}{10} + \frac{-2}{7} + \frac{7}{18}$ *(Lessons 5-2, 5-3)* **64/315 or .2031746...**

25. Give an example of the Associative Property of Addition. *(Lesson 5-7)* **Sample: $(2 + 3) + 7 = 2 + (3 + 7)$**

26. Give an example of the Substitution Principle. *(Lessons 2-6, 5-8)* **Sample: $30\% \cdot 20 = .3 \cdot 20$**

27. To the nearest inch, how many inches are in 2.7 feet? *(Lesson 3-2)* **32 inches**

ADDITIONAL ANSWERS

1. Try an answer. If it doesn't work, try another one.

2. when there are only a few possible answers

16. -4, 0, 4; -4, 1, 3; -3, -1, 4; -3, 0, 3; -3, 1, 2; -2, -1, 3; -2, 0, 2; -1, 0, 1

17. three possible answers: 91 and 37, 82 and 28, or 73 and 19.

21. Work inside parentheses, then do powers, then multiplications or divisions from left to right, then additions or subtractions from left to right.

23.

28. Consider the number 5.843%. *(Lessons 1-2, 1-4, 2-5)*
    a. Convert this number to a decimal. 0.05843
    b. Round the number in **a** to the nearest thousandth. 0.058
    c. Between what two integers is this number? 0 and 1

29. Repeat Question 28 for the number $\frac{99}{70}$. *(Lessons 1-4, 1-8)*
    See margin.

Exploration

30. Put one of the digits 0, 1, 2, 3, 4, 5, 6, 7, 8, 9, in each circle. This will form two five-digit numbers. Make the sum as large as possible. (For example, 53,812 and 64,097 use all the digits, but their sum of 117,909 is easy to beat.) See margin.

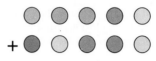

31. Computers are very good at trial and error. Try this program.

```
10   FOR N = 1 TO 100
20   IF (N+3) * (N−2) = 696 THEN PRINT N
30   NEXT N
40   END
```

    a. What does this program find?
    b. Modify the program so that it finds any integer solution between 1 and 50 to the equation x(x + 40) = 329.
    c. Modify the program so that it finds all integer solutions between -100 and 100 to n(n + 18) = 25(3n + 28)/n.
    See below.

a. integer solutions to (n + 3)(n − 2) = 696 between 1 and 100.
b. 10 FOR X = 1 TO 50
   20 IF X * (X + 40) = 329 THEN PRINT X
   (The rest of the program is unchanged.)
c. 10 FOR N = -100 TO 100
   20 IF N * (N + 18) = 25 * (3 * N + 28)/N
   rest unchanged

258

6-5

Make a Table

OBJECTIVE

E Make a table to find patterns and make generalizations.

Vadim thought he knew everything about diagonals and polygons. But this question had him stumped.

How many diagonals does a 13-gon have?

He read it carefully. It was easy to understand. He drew a picture of a 13-gon.

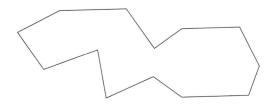

He started drawing diagonals and quickly gave up this approach. He thought about trial and error. He even thought about guessing. He had used all of the strategies of the last three lessons. What could he do?

Sometimes it helps to *make a table*. A table is an arrangement with rows and columns. Making a table is just one way of organizing what you know. Vadim's friend Rose recalled the following information from Lesson 6-2. She made a table with two columns.

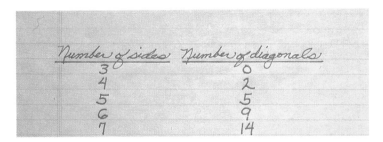

Number of sides	Number of diagonals
3	0
4	2
5	5
6	9
7	14

Discuss the tables and go over them carefully searching for patterns. Stress that making a table and looking for a pattern take time.

Francie's table, involving the cost of a phone call, displays a subtle strategy for coming up with an algebraic formula. Notice that Francie does all the arithmetic, finding the final result in each case. George does not do the calculations; instead, he looks immediately for a pattern in the original information. George does less work, but he winds up with a more effective table. **Questions 11** and **12** use the ideas developed in this example.

She noticed that the number of diagonals increases by 2, then 3, then 4, then 5. She thought if the pattern continued, then here would be the next three rows of the table.

8	20
9	27
10	35

She checked her work by drawing an octagon. It did have 20 diagonals. So she continued the pattern and answered Vadim's question. (You are asked to do this yourself in the questions following this lesson.)

In solving problems, there are three reasons for making a table.

First, a table organizes your thoughts.

Second, it helps to find patterns.

Third, it can help you to make a generalization.

A **generalization** is a statement that is true about many instances. The next story is about making a generalization.

Francie lives in Phoenix. She has a telephone in her room. She pays for all long-distance calls she makes. One Sunday she called her cousin Meg in San Diego. They got to talking and Francie forgot about the time. They had talked for at least an hour! She called her long-distance operator for rates and found that it cost $.25 for the first minute and $.18 for each additional minute. She had a problem.

What is the cost of a one-hour phone call, if the first minute costs $.25 and each additional minute costs $.18?

Francie began by making a table.

Number of minutes talked	Cost of phone call
1	$ .25
2	.43
3	.61
4	.79
5	.97

260

It wasn't working at all. Yet the pattern was simple. You add .18 to get the next cost. But she wanted to know the cost for 60 minutes. She did not want to add .18 all those times. She would probably make a mistake, even with a calculator.

George helped Francie by rewriting the costs to show a different pattern.

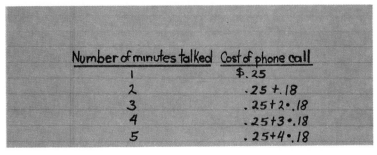

Number of minutes talked	Cost of phone call
1	$.25
2	.25 + .18
3	.25 + 2 · .18
4	.25 + 3 · .18
5	.25 + 4 · .18

"Look across the rows," he said. "See what stays the same and what changes. In the right column, the only number that changes is the number multiplied by .18. It is always one less than the number in the left column. So,

60	.25 + 59 · .18

now you can calculate the cost." Francie did the calculations.

$$.25 + 59 \cdot .18 = 10.87$$

The cost of her phone call was over $10.87! Francie then fainted.

She fainted before George could tell her something else about this. The table makes it possible to write a formula—a general pattern—for the cost.

m	$.25 + (m - 1) \cdot .18$

If Francie spoke for m minutes, it would cost $.25 + (m - 1) \cdot .18$ dollars, not including tax.

The formula enables you to find the cost for any number of minutes easily. It is a generalization made from the pattern the instances formed in the table.

LESSON 6-5   Make a Table   261

NOTES ON QUESTIONS

Question 10: Point out that making a table all the way to 50 is inefficient and misses the point of the lesson. Stress that the table should be used to find patterns and make generalizations. Once students make the generalization, it is no longer necessary to test 50 instances.

Question 15: Finding an intelligent process for narrowing possible solutions is more interesting than finding the answer. If $x \neq y$, there are initially 100 choices to try (10 bases each with 10 exponents). But the power, 343, is odd. Therefore, x must be odd. Neither x nor y can be 1, and 9 is unlikely because the answer would be too large. Also, $x \neq 5$ because the power does not end in a 5 or a 0. Thus, the only possibilities to test are powers of 3 and 7.

Question 21: This question leads to one of the properties of powering (sometimes called a *law of exponents*.)

ADDITIONAL ANSWERS

10.

Number of Sides	Number of Triangles
3	1
4	2
5	3
6	4
⋮	⋮
n	$n - 2$

if 50 sides, then 48 triangles

11.

Number of Minutes	Cost
1	$1.46
2	$1.46 + .82
3	$1.46 + 2 \cdot .82
4	$1.46 + 3 \cdot .82
5	$1.46 + 4 \cdot .82

19., 20., 21. See Additional Answers in the back of this book.

Questions

Covering the Reading

In 1–3, use information given in this lesson.

1. How many diagonals does a 10-gon have?   **35**

2. How many diagonals does an 11-gon have?   **44**

3. Answer the question Vadim could not answer.   **65 diagonals**

In 4–7, refer to the story about Francie in this lesson.

4. If Francie had only talked to her cousin Meg for 5 minutes, what would have been the cost of the phone call?   **97¢**

5. If Francie had talked to her cousin Meg for 30 minutes, what would have been the cost of the call?   **$5.47**

6. For a call to Meg that was m minutes long, it cost Francie how much?   **.25 + (m − 1) · .18 dollars**

7. For a two-hour phone call to Meg, what would it cost Francie?
$21.67

8. What is a generalization?
a statement that is true about many instances

9. In the story about Francie, what generalization is made?
The cost of an m-minute call for Francie is .25 + (m−1) · .18 dollars.

Applying the Mathematics

10. Make a table to help answer this question. In a 50-gon, all the diagonals from *one* particular vertex are drawn. How many triangles are formed?   **See margin.**

11. Inge wants to call her cousin Erich in Germany. The cost is $1.46 for the first minute and 82¢ for each additional minute.
    a. Make a table indicating the cost for calls of duration 1, 2, 3, 4, and 5 minutes.   **See margin.**
    b. What is the cost of a 25-minute call?   **$21.14**
    c. What is the cost of a call lasting m minutes?
    1.46 + (m − 1) · .82 dollars

12. In 1990, it cost 25¢ to mail a one-ounce first-class letter. It cost 20¢ for each additional ounce or part of an ounce up to 11 ounces.
    a. What was the cost to mail a letter weighing 4 ounces?   **85¢**
    b. What was the cost to mail a letter weighing 9.5 ounces?   **$2.05**
    c. What was the cost to mail a letter weighing w ounces, if w is a whole number?   **.25 + (w−1) · .20 dollars**

Review

13. Use trial and error. I am thinking of a number. When I add the number to 268, I get the same answer as if I had subtracted it from 354. What is the number? *(Lesson 6-4)*   **43**

14. One type of polygon is the *undecagon*. How many sides does an undecagon have? *(Lesson 6-2)*   **11 (look up in dictionary)**

262

15. $x^y = 343$ and x and y are integers between 1 and 10. Find x and y. *(Lessons 2-2, 6-4)*   **$x = 7$ and $y = 3$.**

16. List all the factors of 54. *(Lesson 1-8)*   **1, 2, 3, 6, 9, 18, 27, 54**

17. Mabel was 5 pounds overweight. Now she is 3 pounds underweight. If c is the change in her weight, what is c? *(Lesson 5-8)*
-8 pounds

18. Let k be the number of centimeters in one yard. *(Lessons 1-4, 3-4)*
   a. Give the exact value of k.   **91.44 cm**
   b. Round k to the nearest integer.   **91 cm**

Exploration

19. Here is a table of some positive integers and their squares.

Integer	Square	Integer	Square
1	1	11	121
2	4	12	144
3	9	13	169
4	16	14	196
5	25	15	225
6	36	16	256
7	49	17	289
8	64	18	324
9	81	19	361
10	100	20	400

   a. Find a pattern that determines the square of 21 without any multiplication or squaring.
   b. What is the units digit in the square of 43,847,217?
   c. Find some other pattern in the table.
   See margin.

20. The table on page 260 of this lesson can be printed by a computer using the following program.

```
10   PRINT "MINUTES", "COST"
20   FOR M = 1 TO 5
30   AMT = .25+(M − 1) ∗ .18
40   PRINT M, AMT
50   NEXT M
60   END
```

   a. Run a program which prints the number of minutes and the cost for from 1 to 10 minutes talking time.
   b. Modify this program to print the left two columns of the table in Question 19.   **See margin.**

21. Here is a table of some of the positive integer powers of 4.

exponent	1	2	3	4	5	6	7
power	4	16	64	256	1,024	4,096	16,384

See margin.
   a. Give the next three columns of the table.
   b. If you multiply two of the numbers in the power row, you can always find their product in that row. If you know the exponents for the two numbers, what is the exponent for their product?
   c. Make a corresponding table for powers of 5. Does the pattern you found in part **b** work for these numbers? **yes**
   d. Generalize what you have found in parts **b** and **c**.

LESSON 6-5   Make a Table   **263**

FOLLOW-UP

MORE PRACTICE
For more questions on *SPUR* Objectives, use *Lesson Master 6-5*, shown below.

NAME _____

LESSON **MASTER   6–5**
QUESTIONS ON **SPUR** OBJECTIVES

■**PROPERTIES**   *Objective E (See pages 276–277 for objectives.)*
In 1–3, make a table. Then answer the questions.

1. Christine is saving to buy a holiday gift for her favorite aunt. She has $6 now and adds $2.50 a week.
   a. How much will she have saved in 7 weeks?   **$23.50**
   b. How much will she have saved in w weeks?   **$6.00 + (w · 2.50)**

2. At Pizza Pete's, a 16" cheese pizza with one additional ingredient costs $10.60. Any other ingredients cost $1.15 each.
   a. How much will a supreme pizza with 9 additional ingredients cost?   **$19.80**
   b. How much will a pizza with n additional ingredients cost?   **$10.60 + (n − 1)(1.15)**

3. When Kyle entered high school, his father gave him an incentive to save money for college. His father agreed to add an amount equal to the money in Kyle's account at the end of each school year. (In other words, Kyle's account would double at the end of each year!) If Kyle saved $400 during each of his four years in high school and never withdrew any of that money, how much money would he have to begin college?   **$12,000**

52   *continued*   Transition Mathematics ©, Scott, Foresman and Company

NAME _____
Master 6–5 (page 2)

In 4 and 5, study each chart. Then answer the questions.

4.
	Rows	Dots
	2	3
	3	6
	4	10

   a. Continue the chart for at least 2 more rows.
   Rows 5   Dots 15
   Rows 6   Dots 21
   b. How many dots will there be after 8 rows?   **36**

5. Rates for the A-1 Fitness Center
Visits	Cost
1	$10
5	$35
9	$60
13	$85
17	$110
21	

   a. According to this table, after the initial visit the A-1 Fitness Center sells its visits in packages of ____   **4**
   b. How much would 21 visits cost?   **$135**

Transition Mathematics © Scott, Foresman and Company   53

Work with a Special Case

Elaine was not sure whether the generalization

$$x(y + z) = xy + xz$$

is true for all numbers x, y, and z. So she substituted 10 for x, 3 for y, and 2 for z. She asked:

$$\text{Does } 10(3 + 2) = 10 \cdot 3 + 10 \cdot 2 ?$$

Following rules for order of operations, she simplified. She asked:

$$\text{Does } 10(5) = 30 + 20 ?$$

The answer is yes. The question is true for this special case. A **special case** is an instance of a pattern used for some definite purpose. Elaine was using a strategy called **testing a special case**.

Special cases help to test whether a property or generalization is true.

■ ■ ■ ■ ■ ■ ■■

Example 1 Is it true that $-(a + b) = -a + -b$ for any numbers a and b?

Strategy Work with a special case. Let $a = 3$ and $b = 2$.
Does $-(3 + 2)$ = $-3 + -2$?
Does $-(5)$ = -5 ?   Yes.
This case may be *too* special. Both numbers are positive. So try another special case, this time substituting a negative number. Let $a = -4$ and $b = 7$. Now substitute.
Does $-(-4 + 7)$ = $-(-4) + -7$?
Does $-(3)$ = $4 + -7$?   Again, yes.
                                                    But it wasn't as
                                                    obvious this time.
You might want to try other special cases.

Solution We have evidence that the property is true. We still do not know for certain.

264

Suppose you know that only one of a small number of possibilities is true. Then working with a special case can help you decide which one.

Example 2 *Multiple choice* In an *n*-gon, how many diagonals from one vertex can be drawn?

(a) *n*   (b) *n* − 2   (c) *n* − 3   (d) *n*/2

Strategy Pick a special case. Let *n* be a small number that is easy to work with. We want a polygon with diagonals, so we need $n \geq 4$. Reword the question for the special case when *n* is 4.

Special case *Multiple choice* In a 4-gon, how many diagonals from one vertex can be drawn?

(a) 4   (b) 4 − 2   (c) 4 − 3   (d) 4/2

Draw a picture to answer the question for the special case.

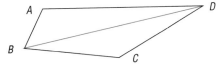

Solution There is only one diagonal from 1 vertex in a quadrilateral (a 4-gon). Choice (c) is correct for the quadrilateral. So choice (c) *n* − 3 is correct for an *n*-gon.

To check Example 2, try another special case, perhaps a pentagon. With a little knowledge, a special case can go a long way.

Example 3 Bob has forgotten how to divide a decimal by 100. He remembers that you can move the decimal point a certain number of places. But he has forgotten how many places. What can he do?

Strategy Work with a special case. Pick 400 as the decimal to be divided. (400 is picked because it is easy to divide by 100.)

$$400 \div 100 = 4$$

400 = 400. and 4 = 4., so the decimal point (in 400.) has been moved two places to the left (4.00), past the two zeros.

Solution To divide by 100, the general pattern is to move the decimal point two places to the left.

It is always a good idea to test more than one special case. In Example 3, you might want to use a calculator and try 123.456 divided by 100. The quotient is 1.23456. This verifies that the answer is correct.

1. Is it true that, regardless of the value of *m*, $m^3 \cdot m^2 = m^5$?
Special cases show that it appears true.

2. *Multiple choice* If *n* teams are to play each other in a tournament, how many games are needed?

(a) $n(n - 1)$

(b) $\dfrac{n(n - 1)}{2}$

(c) $n(n - 3)$

(d) $\dfrac{n(n - 3)}{2}$ **b**

3. Maria remembers it is all right to change the order of addends in addition because of the Commutative Property: $a + b = b + a$. She cannot remember whether or not there is a similar property in taking the power of a number:
Is $a^b = b^a$? What should she do?
Try special cases of a^b and b^a to see if the powers are equal.

4. Find a special case that demonstrates that |*x*| is not always positive. **0**

Caution:

Even if several special cases of a pattern are true, the pattern may not always be true.

■ ■ ■ ■ ■ ■ ■ ■

Example 4 Is x^2 always greater than or equal to x?

Strategy Try $x = 6$. $6^2 = 36$, which is bigger than 6. Test $x = 13$. $13^2 = 169$, which is greater than 13.

So you might think $x^2 \geq x$ is always true. But now try $x = 0.5$. $0.5^2 = 0.25$, which is less than 0.5.

Solution x^2 is *not* always greater than or equal to x.

Questions

Covering the Reading

1. What is a special case of a pattern?
   an instance of a pattern used for some definite purpose

In 2–4, consider the pattern $-(a + b) = -a + -b$.

2. Give an instance of this pattern. Sample: $-(4 + 3) = -4 + -3$

3. Let $a = -5$ and $b = -11$. Is this special case true? Yes

4. Let $a = 4.8$ and $b = 3.25$. Is this special case true? Yes

5. *True or false* If more than two special cases of a pattern are true, then the pattern is true. False

6. *True or false* When a special case of a pattern is not true, then the general pattern is not true. True

In 7–11, consider the following pattern: In an *n*-gon, there are $n - 3$ diagonals that can be drawn from one vertex.

7. **a.** When $n = 4$, to what kind of polygon does the pattern refer?
   b. Is the pattern true for that kind of polygon?
   a. quadrilateral; b. Yes

8. **a.** When $n = 7$, to what kind of polygon does the pattern refer?
   b. Is the pattern true for that kind of polygon?
   a. heptagon; b. Yes

9. **a.** What value of *n* refers to a hexagon? 6
   b. Is the pattern true for hexagons? Yes

266

10. a. What value of n refers to a triangle? **3**
  b. Is the pattern true for triangles?   **Yes**

11. Show, by a drawing, that this pattern is true for an octagon.
  See margin.

12. How should you move the decimal point in order to divide a
  decimal by 1000? (Test a special case if you are not sure of the
  answer.) **See margin.**

Which direction?

13. How should you move the decimal point in order to divide a
  decimal by .001? (Test a special case if you are not sure of the
  answer.) **See margin.**

14. Consider the pattern $x^2 \geq x$.
  a. Give two instances that are true.
  b. Give an instance that is false.
  c. What do parts **a** and **b** tell you about special cases?
    See margin.

Applying the Mathematics

15. Consider the pattern $x \cdot x - x = 0$.
  a. Is this pattern true for the special case $x = 0$? **Yes**
  b. Is this pattern true for the special case $x = 1$? **Yes**
  c. Is this pattern true for the special case $x = 2$? **No**
  d. From your answers to parts **a**, **b**, and **c**, do you think the
    pattern is true for every possible value of x? **No**

16. Consider the pattern $2a + 3b = 6ab$. Test at least two special
  cases with positive numbers. Decide whether the pattern is
  (a) possibly true, or   (b) definitely not always true.   **(b)**

17. Consider the pattern $-(-m + 9) = m + -9$. **See margin.**
  a. Test a special case with a positive number.
  b. Test the special case with a negative number.
  c. Decide whether the pattern is possibly true or definitely not
    always true.

Questions 18 and 19 are *multiple choice*. Use special cases to help you select.

18. The sum of all the whole numbers from 1 to *n* is   (c)
    (a) $n + 1$ (b) $n + 2$ (c) $n(n + 1)/2$ (d) n^2

19. The sum of the measures of the four angles of any quadrilateral is:
    (a) 180   (b) 360   (c) 540   (d) 720   (b)

Review

20. The number 17 is a divisor of *x* and $925 < x < 950$. Find *x*. *(Lesson 6-4)*   935

21. Five teams are to play each other in a tournament. How many games are needed? *(Lesson 6-3)*   10 games

22. Virginia's garden is in the shape of a triangle. Each side of the triangle is 12 feet long. There is a stake at each corner. There are stakes every 3 feet on each side. How many stakes are there in all? *(Lesson 6-4)*   12 stakes

23. A downtown parking lot charges $1.00 for the first hour and $.50 for each additional hour or part of an hour. *(Lesson 6-5)*
    a. What will it cost you to park from 9 A.M. to 4:45 P.M.? $4.50
    b. At this rate, what does it cost for *h* hours of parking?
    $1.00 + (h − 1).50

24. What is an algorithm? *(Lesson 6-1)*   See margin.

25. Write 1/3 as a decimal and as a percent. *(Lessons 1-8, 2-5)* $0.\overline{3}, 33\frac{1}{3}\%$

26. Solve for *x*: $14 + x = 14 + {-}438$. *(Lesson 5-8)*   ‑438

27. $AB + BC + CD + DA$ is called the ___?___ of polygon *ABCD*. *(Lesson 5-10)*   perimeter

28. Is ‑382,471.966638 + 382,471.966642 positive, negative, or zero? *(Lesson 5-5)*   positive

Exploration

29. What five integers between 1 and 101 have the most positive integer divisors?   60, 72, 84, 90, and 96 each has 12 divisors.

6-7

Try Simpler Numbers

Recall Polya's four main steps in solving a problem.

1. read carefully
2. devise a plan
3. carry out the plan
4. check work

You have learned a number of strategies to help with these steps. Drawing a picture can help you devise a plan and can be used to check work. Trial and error is a good way to solve many problems. Testing a special case is a way to check work.

A strategy called **try simpler numbers** can be used to devise a plan, to solve problems, and to check work. For this reason it is a powerful strategy. Here is an example of how it works.

■ ■ ■ ■ ■ ■ ■ ■

Example 1 In a delicatessen it costs $2.49 for a half pound of roast beef sliced. The person behind the counter slices .53 pound. What should it cost?

Strategy Try simpler numbers in place of those in the problem to help devise a plan for solving.
Suppose it cost $3.00 for 5 pounds of roast beef and the person sliced 2 pounds.
You could divide $3.00 by 5 to get the price per pound, $.60.
Then multiply by 2 to get the price for 2 pounds, $1.20.

Solution Replace the simpler numbers (chosen in the Strategy above) by the numbers in the problem.
Divide $2.49 by 0.5. (Half = 0.5.)
Then multiply the quotient by .53.
You will get $2.6394; so it should cost $2.64.

Check $2.64 is reasonable, since .53 pound is just over a half pound, and $2.64 is a little more than $2.49.

1. a. The area of a rectangle is 10.32 square inches. If its length is 4.3 in., what is its width?

If the area were 12 and the length 4, then the width would have to be $\frac{12}{4}$ = 3. Thus, $\frac{10.32}{4.3}$ = 2.4 in.

b. If the area of a rectangle is A and the length is ℓ, what is the width w?

$\frac{A}{\ell} = w$

2. In London, Juan bought British money (pounds). He got £43.35 for $75. How much is £1 worth in dollars?

If he had received £50 for $100, then each pound was worth $2, or $\frac{100 \text{ dollars}}{50 \text{ pounds}}$. This suggests dividing: $\frac{\$75}{\pounds 43.35} \approx \$1.73$

3. You have q quarters and d dimes. What is the value of the money you have?

With 5 quarters and 3 dimes, you would have 5 · .25 and 3 · .10 = $1.55. So q quarters and d dimes would be worth (q · .25) + (d · .10) = .25q + .10d.

4. If salad costs 18¢ an ounce and a plate (without salad) weighs 4 ounces, what is the cost if the scale reads 1.09 pounds?

Subtract 4 ounces from 1.09 pounds to get the weight of the salad. Then, convert pounds to ounces: multiply 1.09 × 16 = 17.44. Thus, the weight of the salad is 17.44 − 4 ounces, or 13.44 ounces. At 10¢ an ounce, salad would cost 10¢ · 2 for 2 ounces, so it costs 18¢ · 13.44 for 13.44 ounces; that is, a total cost of $2.4192, or $2.42.

In most situations, the same operations that you would use with simple numbers will work with more complicated ones. So, if you have complicated numbers, try simpler ones.

Example 2 Steve can bike one mile in 8 minutes. If he can keep up this rate, how far will he ride in 1 hour?

Strategy The numbers are complicated. There are minutes and hours—that makes things more difficult. Modify the problem so that the numbers are simpler and you can answer the question. Then look for a pattern.

> **Modified problem** Steve can bike one mile in <u>10</u> minutes. If he can keep up this rate, how far will he ride in 60 minutes (1 hour)?
>
> **Solution** The answer to this new problem is 6 miles. (Do you see why?)

Solution The answer 6 to the modified problem is 60 divided by 10. This suggests that the original problem can be solved by division. Dividing the corresponding numbers of the original problem, the number of miles is 60/8. Steve can go 7.5 miles in an hour.

Trying simpler numbers has a bonus. Suppose you can do a problem no matter how complicated the numbers are. This means you have found an algorithm for that type of problem. Then you can describe the answer even when the original information is given with variables. Examples 3 and 4 generalize Example 2.

Example 3 Alice can bike one mile in t minutes. At this rate, how far can she bike in an hour?

Strategy When t is 10, the answer was 60/10. When t is 8, the answer was 60/8.

Solution Therefore, in t minutes, Alice can ride 60/t miles.

Example 4   Therese can bike one mile in *t* minutes. At this rate, how far can she bike in *u* minutes?

Strategy   Example 3 has simpler numbers. When *u* was 60, the answer was 60/*t*.

Solution   Therese can ride *u*/*t* miles.

Questions

Covering the Reading

1. Suppose steak costs $5 a pound. You buy 2 pounds. How much should it cost you? $10

2. Suppose steak costs $4.49 a pound. The steaks you want weigh a total of 2.61 pounds. How much should it cost you? $11.72

3. How are Questions 1 and 2 the same? How are they different?
    See margin.

4. Consider this question. Turkey is $2.29 for a half pound. A shopper buys 1.87 pounds. How much should it cost the shopper?
    a. Change the problem so that it has simpler numbers.
    b. Answer the question for the simpler numbers.
    c. What operations did you use to get the answer to the simpler question?
    d. Use these operations to answer the original question.
       See margin.

5. What strategy is used in Question 4?   See margin.

ADDITIONAL ANSWERS
3. The same question is used; only the numbers differ.

4. a. sample: If turkey is $2.00 per half pound, what is the cost for 3 pounds?
b. $12; c. multiplied cost per half pound by 2, then by the number of pounds;
d. 2 × $2.29 × 1.87 ≈ $13.14

5. If you cannot do a problem with complicated numbers, try simpler numbers.

NOTES ON QUESTIONS
Question 10: 10 gallons is a simpler quantity.

Question 12: Students need to consider smaller combinations, say 3 boys and 2 girls, to find a pattern.

Question 24: Ask students to explain in words how to get the largest difference. (Make the minuend as large as possible and the subtrahend as small as possible, given that 0 cannot begin the number.)

6. a. sample: Buzz can bike 1 mile in 10 minutes. At this rate, how far can he bike in 60 minutes? **b.** 6 miles; **c.** divide 60 by 10; **d.** $\frac{60}{7} \approx 8.6$ miles

14. sample: Let $a = 2$, $b = -3$, $c = 4$. Then $a + -b + -c = 2 + -(-3) + -4 = 1$ and $-(b + -a + c) = -(-3 + -2 + 4) = 1$. Other special cases show the pattern as probably true all the time.

18. A problem is a question you do not know how to answer; an exercise is a question you do know how to answer.

6. Follow the directions of Question 4 on the following question:
Buzz can bike one mile in 7 minutes. At this rate, how far can he ride in an hour? See margin.

7. Kristin can bike one mile in M minutes. At this rate, how far can she bike in 30 minutes? 30/M miles

8. *True or false* A simpler number is always a smaller number. False

Applying the Mathematics

9. a. If tomatoes are 98¢ a kg, what will $2\frac{1}{2}$ kilograms cost? $2.45
b. If tomatoes are 98¢ per kg, what will k kilograms cost? 98k cents
c. If tomatoes cost c¢ per kg, what will k kilograms cost? ck cents

10. a. Judy drove 250 miles on 11.2 gallons of gas. How many miles per gallon is her car getting? about 22.3 mpg
b. Hank drove m miles on 11.2 gallons of gas. How many miles per gallon is his car getting? m/11.2 mpg
c. Louise drove m miles on g gallons of gas. How many miles per gallon is her car getting? m/g miles per gallon

In 11-13, if you cannot answer the question, try simpler numbers.

11. A roll of paper towels originally had R sheets. If Z sheets are used, how many sheets remain? (R − Z) sheets

12. There are 8 boys and 7 girls at a party. A photographer wants to take a picture of each boy with each girl. How many pictures are required? 56

13. A coat costs $49.95. You give the clerk G dollars. How much change should you receive? (G − 49.95) dollars

Review

14. Try at least two special cases with positive and negative numbers to decide whether the pattern is probably always true or definitely not true:
$a + -b + -c = -(b + -a + c)$. *(Lesson 6-6)* See margin.

272

15. How should you move the decimal point if you are dividing a decimal by 10^4? *(Lessons 2-4, 6-6)*   **4 places to the left**

16. An n-gon has exactly 77 diagonals. What is n? *(Lesson 6-5)*   **14**

17. $x + 5 \geq 2$, $x < 0$, x is an integer, and $-x$ is divisible by 2. Find x. *(Lesson 6-4)*   **-2**

18. When is a question a problem, and when is it an exercise? *(Lesson 6-1)*   **See margin.**

19. Write 350,000,000,000 in scientific notation. *(Lesson 2-3)*
    3.5×10^{11}
20. Write 0.9 in scientific notation. *(Lesson 2-9)*   **9×10^{-1}**

21. 4 kilograms + 25 grams + 43 milligrams equals how many grams? *(Lesson 5-1)*   **4025.043 grams**

22. Would an adult be more likely to weigh 10 kg, 70 kg, or 170 kg? *(Lesson 3-3)*   **70 kg**

23. Evaluate a^{b+c} when $a = 5$, $b = 2$, and $c = 4$. *(Lessons 2-2, 4-4)*
    15,625

Exploration

24. Put one of the digits 0, 1, 2, 3, 4, 5, 6, 7, 8, 9, in each circle. This will form two five-digit numbers. Make the difference as large as possible. (For example, 64097 and 53812 use all the digits, but their difference of 10285 is easy to beat.)

98765 − 10234 = 88531. (Make the minuend as large as possible and the subtrahend as small as possible.)

NAME _____

Summary

If you have an algorithm for answering a question, it is an exercise for you. If not, then the question is a problem for you. Problems are frustrating unless you know strategies that can help you approach them. This chapter discusses six general strategies. They are:

1. Read the problem carefully. Look up definitions for any unfamiliar words. Determine if enough information is given. Sort out information that is not needed.
2. Draw an accurate picture.
3. Use trial and error. Use earlier trials to help in choosing better later trials.
4. Make a table. Use the table to organize your thoughts. Use the table to find patterns. Use the table to make generalizations.
5. Use special cases to help decide whether a pattern is true.
6. Try simpler numbers. Generalize to more complicated numbers or variables.

These strategies can help in understanding a problem, in devising a plan, in solving, and in checking. Good problem solvers take their time. They do not give up. They are flexible. And they continually check their work.

Vocabulary

You should be able to give a general description and a specific example of each of the following ideas.

Lesson 6-1
algorithm, exercise, problem

Lesson 6-2
prime number, composite number
divisor, factor
natural number

Lesson 6-4
trial and error

Lesson 6-5
table
generalization

Lesson 6-6
special case
testing a special case

Lesson 6-7
simpler number

274

Progress Self-Test

See margin for answers not shown below.

Take this test as you would take a test in class. Then check your work with the solutions in the Selected Answers section in the back of the book.

1. Name two places to find the meaning of the term "trapezoid."

2. How many diagonals does an octagon have?

3. There are six players in a singles tennis tournament. Each player will compete with each of the others. How many games will be played?   **15**

4. What two positive integers whose product is 24 have the smallest sum?   **4 and 6**

5. *True or false* If you know an algorithm for multiplying fractions, then multiplying fractions is a problem for you.   **False**

6. List the prime numbers between 50 and 60.

7. Consider $|x| + |y| = |x + y|$. Find values of x and y that make this false.

8. How much will 1.62 pounds of hamburger cost if the price is $1.49 per pound?

9. *True or false* If a special case of a pattern is true, then the general pattern may still be false.   **True**

10. What integer between 5 and 10 is a solution to $(x - 3) + (x - 4) = 9$?   **8**

11. Donna has some disks numbered 1, 2, 3, 4, and so on. She arranges them in order in a circle, equally spaced. The last disk is the same space from the first disk. If disk 3 is directly across from disk 10, how many disks are in the circle?   **14**

12. When all the possible diagonals are drawn, an n-gon has $n+3$ diagonals. What is n?   **6**

13. How many decimal places and in which direction should you move a decimal point in order to divide by .01?   **two places to the right**

14. Phyllis was given $1000 by her parents to spend during her first year of college. She decided to spend $25 a week. Make a table to show how much she will have left after 1, 2, 3, and 4 weeks.

15. In the situation of Question 14, how much will Phyllis have after 31 weeks?   **$225**

16. Robert carefully read a problem, prepared a table to help solve the problem, and worked until he reached a conclusion. He wrote his answer and went on to the next problem. What step in good problem solving did Robert omit?   **Check your work.**

USING THE PROGRESS SELF-TEST
Assign the Progress Self-Test as a one-night assignment. Worked-out *solutions* for all questions are in the Selected Answers section of the student book. Encourage students to take the Progress Self-Test honestly, grade themselves, and then be prepared to discuss the test in class.

Advise students to pay special attention to those Chapter Review questions (pages 276–277) which correspond to questions missed on the Progress Self-Test. A chart in the Selected Answers section keys the Progress Self-Test questions to the lettered SPUR Objectives in the Chapter Review or to the Vocabulary. It also keys the questions to the corresponding lessons where the material is covered.

ADDITIONAL ANSWERS
1. dictionary, encyclopedia

2. 20

6. 53, 59

7. sample: $x = -5$, $y = 3$

8. $2.42 (rounded up)

14. weeks	amount left
1	$1000 - 25$
2	$1000 - 2 \cdot 25$
3	$1000 - 3 \cdot 25$
4	$1000 - 4 \cdot 25$

CHAPTER REVIEW

The main objectives for the chapter are organized here into sections corresponding to the main types of understanding this book promotes: Skills, Properties, Uses, and Representations.

USING THE CHAPTER REVIEW

Whereas end-of-chapter material may be considered optional in some texts, in *Transition Mathematics* we have selected these objectives and questions with the expectation that they will be covered. Students should be able to answer these questions with about 85% accuracy after studying the chapter.

You may assign these questions over a single night to help students prepare for a test the next day, or you may assign the questions over a two-day period.

If you work the questions over two days, then we recommend assigning the *evens* for homework the first night so that students get feedback in class the next day, then assigning the *odds* the night before the test so the students can use the answers provided in the book.

ADDITIONAL ANSWERS
3. sample: Divide answer by 1487 or 309.

12. a three-dimensional figure with four triangular faces

13. a number that equals the sum of its divisors

Chapter Review

Questions on **SPUR** Objectives

SPUR stands for **S**kills, **P**roperties, **U**ses, and **R**epresentations. The Chapter Review questions are grouped according to the SPUR Objectives for this chapter.

See margin for answers not shown below.

SKILLS deal with the procedures used to get answers.

Objective A: *Understand the methods followed by good problem solvers.* *(Lesson 6-1)*

1. *Multiple-choice* Which advice should be followed to become a better problem solver? **(b)**
   (a) Check work by answering the question the same way you did it.
   (b) Be flexible.
   (c) Skip over words you don't understand as long as you can write an equation.
   (d) none of (a) through (c)

2. If you can apply an algorithm to a problem, then the problem becomes an __?__. **exercise**

3. After Nancy multiplies 1487×309 on her calculator, what would be a good way to check her answer?

Objective B: *Determine solutions to sentences by trial and error.* *(Lesson 6-4)*

4. Which integer between 10 and 20 is a solution to $3x + 15 = 66$? **17**

5. *Multiple choice* Which number is *not* a solution to $n^2 \geq n$? **(b)**
   (a) 0 (b) 0.5 (c) 1 (d) 2

6. Choose one number from each row so that the sum of the numbers is 255.

88	84	9	**84**
69	79	76	**69**
108	104	102	**102**

7. What number between 1000 and 1050 has 37 as a factor? **1036**

PROPERTIES deal with the principles behind the mathematics.

Objective C: *Determine whether a number is prime or composite.* *(Lesson 6-2)*

8. Is 49 prime or composite? Explain your answer. **composite; 7 is a factor.**

9. Is 47 prime or composite? Explain your answer. **prime; only 1 and 47 are factors.**

10. List all composite numbers n with $20 < n < 30$. **21, 22, 24, 25, 26, 27, 28**

11. List all prime numbers between 30 and 40. **31, 37**

Objective D: *Find the meaning of unknown words.* *(Lesson 6-2)*

12. What is a tetrahedron?

13. What is a perfect number?

Objective E: *Make a table to find patterns and make generalizations.* *(Lesson 6-5)*

14. Mandy is saving to buy a present for her parents' anniversary. She has $10 now and adds $5 a week.
   a. How much will she save in 12 weeks?
   b. How much will she save in w weeks?

15. Consider 2, 4, 8, 16, 32, … (the powers of 2). Make a table listing all the factors of these numbers. How many factors does 256 have?

276

Objective F: *Work with a special case to determine whether a pattern is true. (Lesson 6-6)*

16. Is there any *n*-gon with $n+2$ diagonals?

17. To divide a decimal by 1 million, you can move the decimal point __?__ places to the __?__.   **6, left**

Objective G: *Use special cases to determine that a property is false or to give evidence that it is true. (Lesson 6-6)*

18. Let $a = 5$ and $b = -4$ to test whether $2a + b = a + (b + a)$. Is the property false or do you have more evidence that it is true?

19. Show that $5x + 5y$ is not always equal to $10xy$ by choosing a special case.

USES deal with applications of mathematics in real situations.

Objective H: *Use simpler numbers to answer a question requiring only one operation. (Lesson 6-7)*

20. If you fly 430 miles in 2.5 hours, how fast have you gone?   **172 mph**

21. If you buy 7.3 gallons of gas at a cost of $1.19 per gallon, what is your total cost (to the penny)?   **$8.69**

Objective I: *Use drawings to solve real problems. (Lesson 6-3)*

22. Nine teams are to play each other in a tournament. How many games are needed?

23. Five hockey teams are to play each other two times in a season. How many games are needed?   **20 games**

24. Bill is older than Becky. Becky is younger than Bob. Bob is older than Barbara. Barbara is older than Bill. Who is second oldest?   **Barbara**

25. Interstate 25 runs north and south through Wyoming and Colorado. Denver is 70 miles from Colorado Springs and 112 miles from Pueblo. Cheyenne is 171 miles from Colorado Springs and 101 miles from Denver. Pueblo is 42 miles from Colorado Springs. Cheyenne is north of Denver. Which of these four cities, all on Interstate 25, is farthest south?   **Pueblo**

REPRESENTATIONS deal with pictures, graphs or objects that illustrate concepts.

Objective J: *Draw a diagram to find the number of diagonals in a polygon. (Lesson 6-3)*

26. How many diagonals does a hexagon have?   **9**

27. How many diagonals does a decagon have?   **35**

Objective K: *Draw a diagram to aid in solving geometric problems. (Lesson 6-3)*

28. All the diagonals of a pentagon are drawn. Into how many sections is the interior divided?   **11 regions**

29. In polygon *ABCDEFGHI* all diagonals from *A* are drawn. How many triangles are formed?   **7 triangles**

CHAPTER 7 ■ PATTERNS LEADING TO SUBTRACTION

DAILY PACING CHART ■ CHAPTER 7

Students in the Full Course should complete the entire text by the end of the year. Students in the Minimal Course spend more time when there are quizzes and more time on the Chapter Review. Therefore, these students may not complete all of the chapters in the text.

DAY	MINIMAL COURSE	FULL COURSE
1	7-1	7-1
2	7-2	7-2
3	7-3	7-3
4	7-4	7-4
5	Quiz (TRF); 7-5	Quiz (TRF); 7-5
6	7-6	7-6
7	7-7	7-7
8	7-8	7-8
9	Quiz (TRF); Start 7-9.	Quiz (TRF); 7-9
10	Finish 7-9.	7-10
11	7-10	Progress Self-Test
12	Progress Self-Test	Chapter Review
13	Chapter Review	Chapter Test (TRF)
14	Chapter Review	
15	Chapter Test (TRF)	

TESTING OPTIONS
■ Quiz on Lessons 7-1 Through 7-4   ■ Chapter 7 Test, Form A   ■ Chapter 7 Test, Cumulative Form
■ Quiz on Lessons 7-5 Through 7-8   ■ Chapter 7 Test, Form B
A Quiz and Test Writer is available for generating additional questions, additional quizzes, or additional forms of the Chapter Test.

PROVIDING FOR INDIVIDUAL DIFFERENCES
The student text is written for the *average* student. The program, however, can be adapted for both less capable and more capable students.

A blackline master (in the Teacher's Resource File) is provided for each lesson for those students who need more practice. The Teacher's Edition occasionally provides Error Analysis and Alternate Approach features to provide additional instructional strategies.

For students who require additional challenge, Extension activities are regularly provided in the Teacher's Edition.

OBJECTIVES ■ CHAPTER 7

After students complete the chapter lessons, they assess their mastery on the Progress
Self-Test. Then they do the Chapter Review and pay special attention to those questions
that match the objectives missed on the Progress Self-Test. Students can get extra practice
on these objectives by using the master for each lesson in the Teacher's Resource File.

OBJECTIVES FOR CHAPTER 7 (Organized into the SPUR categories—Skills, Properties, Uses, and Representations)	Progress Self-Test Questions	Chapter Review Questions	Teacher's Resource File	
			Lesson Master*	Chapter Test Forms A and B
SKILLS				
A: Subtract any numbers written as decimals.	2, 3	1–4	7-2	1, 2, 3, 4
B: Solve sentences of the form $x - a = b$.	4, 6, 24	5–9	7-4	6, 7
C: Solve sentences of the form $a - x = b$.	5, 7	10–14	7-6	8, 9
D: Find measures of angles in figures with linear pairs, vertical angles, or perpendicular lines.	8, 9	15–18	7-7	15
E: Find measures of angles in figures with parallel lines and transversals.	10	19–22	7-8	16
F: Use the Triangle-Sum Property to find measures of angles.	14	23–26	7-10	17
G: Find measures of angles and sides in special quadrilaterals without measuring.	16	27–30	7-9	18
PROPERTIES				
H: Apply the properties of subtraction.	18	31, 32	7-2, 7-3	5
I: Distinguish equivalent from non-equivalent sentences and formulas.	19	33, 34	7-5	10
J: Know relationships among angles formed by intersecting lines.		35–37	7-7	14
K: Know relationships among angles formed by two parallel lines and a transversal.	11, 12, 15	38–41	7-8	19
L: Apply the definitions of parallelogram, rectangle, rhombus, and square to determine properties of these figures.	17	42–45	7-9	21
M: Explain the consequences of the Triangle-Sum Property.	13	46, 47	7-10	22
USES				
N: Use the Take-Away Model for Subtraction to form sentences involving subtraction.	21, 25	48–51	7-1, 7-4, 7-6	11
O: Use the Slide Model for Subtraction to form sentences involving subtraction.	23	52–54	7-2	13
P: Use the Comparison Model for Subtraction to form sentences involving subtraction.	20, 22	55–57	7-3	12
REPRESENTATIONS				
Q: Picture subtraction of positive and negative numbers on a number line.	1	58, 59	7-2	20

*The Lesson Masters are numbered to match the lessons.

OVERVIEW ■ CHAPTER 7

Lessons 7-1 through 7-3 present three models for subtraction: the Take-Away Model, the Slide Model, and the Comparison Model. Students have encountered examples of these since the early grades. New in this chapter are the names given to the models, the presence of all kinds of numbers (whole numbers, fractions, decimals, and percents), and the use of variables. The Slide Model is used for the relation $x - a = x + -a$ and the subtraction of positive and negative numbers.

Lessons 7-4 through 7-6 introduce sentence solving of the forms $x - a = b$ and $a - x = b$. Both forms deal with the operation of subtraction in equations. Lessons 7-7 through 7-9 discuss angles and lines. First, there is a look at linear pairs. The angles in a linear pair have measures x and $180° - x$; this relationship justifies the placement of this content in a chapter on subtraction. If we extend the lines, four angles are formed with one or the other of those measures. If we add a parallel line, eight angles are formed with those measures. A parallelogram is also formed; this development leads to an investigation of special quadrilaterals. Finally, in Lesson 7-10, we use the relationships to develop the Triangle-Sum Property.

PERSPECTIVES ■ CHAPTER 7

The Perspectives provide the rationale for the inclusion of topics or approaches, provide mathematical background, and make connections within UCSMP.

7-1

THE TAKE-AWAY MODEL FOR SUBTRACTION

It is logical to view *take-away* as a counterpart to *putting-together*, a model equivalent of the mathematical relationship of inverse operations.

Although the Take-Away Model itself is review, student use of it has often been limited to situations where the numbers are counts. The work in this lesson with length, angle measure, area, and variables is probably new. These applications are not difficult, however, especially when viewed as extensions of a familiar pattern.

7-2

THE SLIDE MODEL FOR SUBTRACTION

Some situations, such as bank account transactions, can be represented by either the Take-Away or the Slide Model for Subtraction. A withdrawal of funds decreases the total pool of money in the bank. A deposit increases the total pool.

The reality of the situation can be represented by a slide. But on paper, the situation seems to be taking-away and putting-together. Weight gain or loss is a similar type of model.

However, the temperature-change example is a pure slide subtraction that should not be construed as take-away. Temperatures differ from savings accounts or weights in that their values are scaled values. The 0° temperature does not mean absence of temperature; it is merely a convenient point on the scale. Therefore, you can decrease a 0° temperature, whereas you cannot take away from an amount of 0 dollars or a weight of 0 kg.

The Slide Model for Subtraction naturally yields situations that use what we call the Add-Opp Property of Subtraction. We believe that the "Add-Opp" name helps students understand the rule for subtracting positive and negative numbers.

We avoid any $+$ signs for positive numbers except when they appear in applications, as in the table on page 279. We also do not use the raised bar to denote negative numbers. We use parentheses around negative numbers only when taking the opposite of a negative number. Our rule is to use the notation that students will use later.

7-3

THE COMPARISON MODEL FOR SUBTRACTION

The answer in a subtraction problem is called a *remainder* or a *difference*. The former comes from the Take-Away Model; the latter from the Comparison Model. More subtraction problems may fit the Comparison Model than any of the other models.

Students have little trouble with comparison subtraction when the problems contain positive numbers. A problem involving negative numbers, however, can frequently cause confusion.

7-4

SOLVING $x - a = b$

This lesson combines ideas from two previous lessons: Lesson 5-8 (solving $x + a = b$) and Lesson 7-2 (the Add-Opp Property). Thus, students can easily change the equation $x - a = b$, a new concept, into the form $x + {-a} = b$, a familiar form introduced in Chapter 5, by applying the Add-Opp Property. Lessons 7-5 and 7-6 will continue with sentence solving and subtraction.

7-5

EQUIVALENT SENTENCES AND FORMULAS

This is an important lesson for several reasons. First, it discusses the vocabulary of sentence solving. This language is needed to discuss the more complicated sentences of Lesson 7-6.

Second, the idea of equivalent sentences provides an efficient way to check sentence solving. By substituting the final value for the variable in each of the intermediate equations used to solve the original equation, a student can quickly find any solution errors.

Third, the ability to rewrite formulas, that is, to solve for a different variable, is a basic skill in applying mathematics.

A fourth reason is more subtle. There is more than one way to solve an equation of the form $x - a = b$. When $x - a = b$, then it is always true that $x = b + a$. The idea of equivalent sentences justifies this way of looking at addition and subtraction.

7-6

SOLVING $a - x = b$

Several reasons make solving $a - x = b$ more difficult for students than solving $x - a = b$. First, students must either take the opposite of both sides, or add the variable for which they are solving to both sides—a new step in either case. Second, there are more steps. Third, students usually have had little experience in earlier grades solving corresponding arithmetic problems.

There are advantages to solving $50 - x = 36$ by adding x to both sides of the equation. The resulting equation, $50 = 36 + x$, can be solved using methods from Chapter 5, which students already know. This method helps prepare students to solve more complicated equations with variables on both sides (as in Chapter 12), or to solve inequalities (which they will encounter in Algebra).

The alternate method is to add -50 to both sides. This yields $-x = 36 + {-50}$, and, after simplifying, $-x = -14$. Taking the opposite of both sides results in $x = 14$. However, this method does not generalize easily to formulas, nor does it work on inequalities without additional explanations.

7-7

ANGLES AND LINES

Vocabulary is an important element of this lesson. However, new terms—straight angle, opposite rays, linear pair, vertical angles, supplementary angles, and perpendicular—are discussed in context and through doing new problems which require the terms to define and clarify a concept.

This lesson applies the ideas of previous lessons. If x is the measure of an angle, then $180° - x$ is its supplement. One might think of this as cutting off (taking away) an angle x from a straight angle of measure $180°$. The next two lessons apply these ideas to parallel lines and special quadrilaterals.

7-8

ANGLES AND PARALLEL LINES

There are several important reasons for this lesson, as well as for Lessons 7-7 and 7-9. First, the angle relationships discussed are an application of the subtraction concepts considered in this chapter.

Second, *Transition Mathematics* is designed to be both a pre-algebra and a pre-geometry book. By learning some definitions and notation now, students become familiar with basic geometric topics and can concentrate on higher-level concepts later in a formal geometry course.

Third, many students enjoy terminology and symbols. For these students, the lessons provide a nice respite from sentence-solving.

7-9

SPECIAL QUADRILATERALS

For most students, *rhombus* is the only new term in this lesson. However, the classification of special quadrilaterals is an important new idea.

Students should leave this lesson aware of the relationships between special quadrilaterals. Parallelograms include rectangles, rhombuses, and squares; rectangles and rhombuses include squares.

The popular name for a rhombus with horizontal and vertical diagonals is *diamond*. An alternate plural for rhombus is *rhombi*.

7-10

THE TRIANGLE-SUM PROPERTY

To complete the consideration of angle measures, this chapter concludes with the Triangle-Sum Property. This property is also an application of subtraction.

We recommend 13 to 15 days for this chapter: 10 to 11 days on the lessons, 1 day for the Progress Self-Test, 1 to 2 days for the Chapter Review, and 1 day for the exam.

USING PAGES 278–279
Call attention to the chart on page 279. Point out that the positive and negative signs help the reader quickly identify states that have had large population changes. Ask which states have gained large numbers of people (California, Florida, Texas), and which have lost large numbers of people (Illinois, New York, Michigan, Ohio). Ask why students think these states have gained or lost such large numbers.

Have students read the paragraphs below the chart. Then ask why subtraction is the appropriate operation to use to interpret the chart. (Students should suggest that subtraction is used to compare quantities.)

CHAPTER 7

Patterns Leading to Subtraction

278

The population figures below appeared in The United States Population Data Sheet, election year issue, August, 1988. Examine the numbers for your state.

Moving from state to state

Here is a state-by-state breakdown of the resident population, July 1, 1987, of each state and its gain or loss since 1980, through estimated net migration (moving, births, and deaths).

State	'87 population	gain (loss)	State	'87 population	gain (loss)
Alabama	4,083,000	+ 16,000	Montana	809,000	− 29,000
Alaska	523,000	+ 53,000	Nebraska	1,594,000	− 58,000
Arizona	3,386,000	+ 437,000	Nevada	1,007,000	+ 149,000
Arkansas	2,388,000	+ 15,000	New Hampshire	1,057,000	+ 90,000
California	27,663,000	+ 2,167,000	New Jersey	7,672,000	+ 75,000
Colorado	3,296,000	+ 160,000	New Mexico	1,500,000	+ 68,000
Connecticut	3,211,000	− 1,000	New York	17,825,000	− 324,000
Delaware	644,000	+ 19,000	North Carolina	6,413,000	+ 275,000
D.C.	622,000	− 36,000	North Dakota	672,000	− 27,000
Florida	12,023,000	+ 2,007,000	Ohio	10,784,000	− 478,000
Georgia	6,222,000	+ 424,000	Oklahoma	3,272,000	+ 67,000
Hawaii	1,083,000	+ 23,000	Oregon	2,724,000	− 39,000
Idaho	998,000	− 27,000	Pennsylvania	11,936,000	− 201,000
Illinois	11,582,000	− 420,000	Rhode Island	986,000	+ 15,000
Indiana	5,531,000	− 207,000	South Carolina	3,425,000	+ 121,000
Iowa	2,834,000	− 194,000	South Dakota	709,000	− 24,000
Kansas	2,476,000	− 20,000	Tennessee	4,855,000	+ 87,000
Kentucky	3,727,000	− 84,000	Texas	16,789,000	+ 1,245,000
Louisiana	4,461,000	− 74,000	Utah	1,680,000	− 2,000
Maine	1,187,000	+ 20,000	Vermont	548,000	+ 12,000
Maryland	4,535,000	+ 103,000	Virginia	5,904,000	+ 274,000
Massachusetts	5,855,000	− 49,000	Washington	4,538,000	+ 145,000
Michigan	9,200,000	− 503,000	West Virginia	1,897,000	− 99,000
Minnesota	4,246,000	− 70,000	Wisconsin	4,807,000	− 133,000
Mississippi	2,625,000	− 45,000	Wyoming	490,000	− 28,000
Missouri	5,103,000	− 7,000			

You can determine the population of your state in 1980 from this table. You must subtract the right number from the left number listed for your state. This subtraction involves both positive and negative numbers. It is one of many situations in which subtraction is the operation to use.

In this chapter, you will study many other situations that lead to subtraction. These naturally lead to equations and inequalities that involve subtraction.

7-1

The Take-Away Model for Subtraction

You walk into a store with $10 and spend $2.56. The amount
you have left is found by subtraction. $10 - $2.56 = $7.44.
Recall that a model for an operation is a general pattern that
includes many of the uses of the operation. This subtraction is
an instance of the **take-away model for subtraction.**

Take-Away Model for Subtraction:

> If a quantity y is taken away from an original quantity x
> with the same units, the quantity left is $x - y$.

Here are some examples of the many different situations that use
the take-away model.

Example 1   A dozen eggs were bought and 5 were used in a cake. How
many remain?

Solution   Units must be consistent in order for the subtraction to
work.
1 dozen eggs − 5 eggs = 12 eggs − 5 eggs = 7 eggs

Example 2   A piece 0.4 meters long is cut from a board of original length 3
meters. How long a piece remains?

Solution   Draw a picture.

3 − 0.4 = 2.6, so 2.6 meters of board remain.

280

In Example 2, if the original length was L meters, then there would be $L - 0.4$ meters left. If C meters were cut off, the remaining length would be $L - C$ meters.

Example 3 In the drawing below, what is the measure of $\angle ABC$?

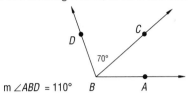

m $\angle ABD = 110°$

Solution Subtract the measure of $\angle CBD$ from the measure of $\angle ABD$. The difference is 40°.

Example 4 What is the area of the shaded region between the squares?

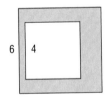

6   4

Solution The area of the larger square is 6^2 or 36. The area of the smaller square is 4^2 or 16. Think of cutting away the inner square from the outer. The amount left is $36 - 16$. The shaded area is 20 square units.

In a real situation, the shaded region might be a walkway around a house. The area would tell you how much concrete would be needed to pave the walkway. The shaded region could be a picture frame. The area would be the amount of material needed for the frame.

Questions

Covering the Reading

1. Hungry Heloise ate 8 of the dozen rolls her mother prepared for dinner. How many rolls are left for the others at the table?
   4 rolls
2. Hungry Heloise ate A of the dozen rolls her mother prepared for dinner. How many rolls are left for the others at the table?
   $12 - A$

1. If a sports store had one gross (144) of hockey sticks at the start of a sale and has 64 left after the first day, how many hockey sticks were sold that day?
80 sticks

2. A yard is cut off a meter stick. Approximately how long is the remaining piece?
3.37 in.

3. $\angle XYZ$ is a right angle. If m $\angle WYZ = 38°$, find m $\angle WYX$.
52°

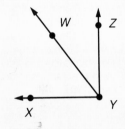

4. A square vegetable garden is 10 feet on a side. One corner, a square 5 feet on a side, will be planted with tomatoes. How many square feet will be left for other vegetables?
75

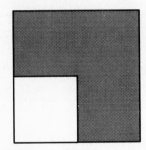

NOTES ON QUESTIONS
Questions 1 and 2, 3 and 4, 19 and 20: In these pairs of questions, the student works with a special case first, then generalizes.

3. There are 320 passenger seats in one wide-body jet plane. A flight attendant counts 4 vacant seats. How many passengers are on board?   **316 passengers**

4. There are S passenger seats in a wide-body jet plane. A flight attendant counts V vacant seats. How many passengers are on board?   **$S - V$**

5. Questions 1–4 are instances of what model for subtraction?
   the Take-Away Model

In 6–9, use the picture below.

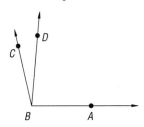

6. If m$\angle ABC = 100°$ and m$\angle DBA = 84°$, what is m$\angle DBC$?   **16°**

7. If m$\angle ABC = 103°$ and m$\angle DBC = 22°$, what is m$\angle DBA$?   **81°**

8. m$\angle ABC -$ m$\angle DBC =$ m$\angle \underline{\ ?\ }$ **m$\angle DBA$**

9. m$\angle ABC -$ m$\angle DBA =$ m$\angle \underline{\ ?\ }$ **m$\angle DBC$**

10. State the Take-Away Model for Subtraction.   **See margin.**

In 11–13, use the two squares pictured below.

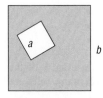

11. What is the area of the shaded region?   **$b^2 - a^2$**

12. Find the area of the shaded region if $a = 8$ and $b = 10$.
    36 square units.

13. Find the area of the shaded region if $a = 4\frac{1}{2}$ and $b = 6.7$.
    24.64 square units

282

In 14–17, use the picture below of towns *A*, *B*, *C*, and *D* along a highway.

A━━━━━━━B━━━━━━━C━━━━━━━D

14. Suppose *AD* = 10 km and *AC* = 6 km. **a.** What other distance can be found? **b.** What is that distance? **a. CD; b. 4 km**

15. If *DA* = 260 miles and *BD* = 147 miles, find all other lengths that are possible to determine. **AB = 113 miles**

16. **a.** *AD* − *CD* = __?__ **b.** *AD* − *AB* − *CD* = __?__ **a. AC; b. BC**

17. *CD* is 20% of the length of $\overline{AD}$. *AB* is 25% of the length of $\overline{AD}$. Then *BC* is what percent of the length of $\overline{AD}$? **55%**

18. According to the National Center for Health Statistics in 1987, on the average, of 100,000 people born in the years 1902–1907, 45,839 were still alive.
    a. How many had died? **54,161**
    b. How old were those that were still alive? **79 or 80 to 85 years**

19. Bill's savings account has $510.75 in it. How much will be left if:
    a. He withdraws $40? **b.** He withdraws *W* dollars?
    a. $470.75; b. 510.75 − W dollars

20. **a.** If the four corner squares of an 8-by-8 checkerboard are cut off, how many squares remain? **60**
    b. If *C* squares of an *n* by *n* checkerboard are cut off, how many squares remain? **n · n − C**

21. The weather forecast says there is a 60% chance of rain. What fraction represents the chance of rain? *(Lesson 2-5)* $\frac{3}{5}$

LESSON 7-1 The Take-Away Model for Subtraction **283**

ADDITIONAL ANSWERS
10. If a quantity *y* is taken away from a quantity *x* with the same units, the quantity left is *x* − *y*.

MORE PRACTICE
For more questions on SPUR
Objectives, use *Lesson Mas-
ter 7-1,* shown on page 283.

EXTENSION
A famous checkerboard problem is related to **Question
20**: If two opposite corner
squares are cut off from a
checkerboard, can the re-
maining 62 squares be covered with 31 dominoes (1 by
2 rectangles)? The answer is
no, based on the following
argument: The two opposite
corner squares are of the
same color, leaving 30
squares of one color and 32
of the other. Since each
domino covers 1 square of
each color, 31 dominoes
could not cover what re-
mains.

27. sample: Let $a = 5, b =$
-2. Then $-(a + b) = -(5 +$
-2) = -3 and $-b + -a =$
$-(-2) + -5 = -3.$

**29. sample: 3.00___, where
any digit except 0 can be
put in the blank.**

22. Give the additive inverse of: **a.** 5; **b.** -3.4; **c.** 0. *(Lesson 5-4)*
    a. -5; b. 3.4; c. 0
23. Evaluate $3p + q^4$ if $p = 4$ and $q = 5$. *(Lesson 2-2, 4-4)*   637
24. *True or false?* $\frac{5}{4} + \frac{5}{4} = \frac{10}{8}$ *(Lesson 5-2)*   **False**
25. How are milligrams and grams related? *(Lesson 3-3)*
    1 milligram = .001 gram (or 1000 mg = 1 g)
26. How are grams and pounds related? *(Lesson 3-4)*
    1000 grams ≈ 2.2 pounds
27. Try positive and negative numbers to see whether it is true that
    $-(a + b) = -b + -a$. *(Lesson 6-6)*   **See margin.**
28. Solve: $-5 + x = -5$. *(Lesson 5-8)*   **0**
29. Give a number that is between 3 and 3.01. *(Lesson 1-2)*
    See margin.
30. Select the largest number: π; $\frac{22}{7}$; 3.14. *(Lesson 1-2)* $\frac{22}{7}$

Exploration

31. If the same number is added to both numbers in a subtraction, the
    answer is not changed. For instance, if the question is

    $$\begin{array}{r} 4307 \\ -\ 2998 \end{array}$$

    you can add 2 to both numbers to get

    $$\begin{array}{r} 4309 \\ -\ 3000 \end{array}$$

    which is much easier. The answer to both questions is 1309. For
    each of the subtraction questions below, find a number to add to
    make the subtraction easier. Then do the subtraction.   See below.
    a. 136 **b.** 4905 **c.** 1117
       $-\ 97$ $-\ 1996$ $-\ 989$

a. Add 3.   b. Add 4.   c. Add 11.
   139   4909   1128
  −100   −2000   −1000
   39   2909   128

The Slide Model for Subtraction

LESSON 7-2

RESOURCES
- Lesson Master 7-2
- Visual for Teaching Aid 37: Use to demonstrate the Add-Opp Property.
- Two-Color Counters (from *Transition Mathematics Manipulative Kit*)
- Overhead Two-Color Counters (from *Transition Mathematics Teacher Kit*)
- *Manipulative Activities Sourcebook*, Activity 11

The temperature is 50° and goes down 12°. What temperature results? This situation can be pictured on a number line. Start at 50° and slide 12° to the left.

The resulting temperature is 38°.

The answer could also be found by subtracting $50 - 12$. This subtraction is not take-away, but a second model for subtraction called the **slide model.**

Slide Model for Subtraction:

If a quantity a is decreased by an amount b, the resulting quantity is $a - b$.

In slide situations, you usually can slide up or down. Results of sliding up are found by addition. Results of sliding down are either found by adding negative numbers or by subtracting.

	By subtraction	By addition	Answer
A person who weighs 60 kg loses 4 kg. What is the resulting weight?	60 kg − 4 kg	60 kg + -4 kg	56 kg
A temperature of -17° falls 20°. What is the resulting temperature?	-17° − 20°	-17° + -20°	-37°

These examples show a basic relationship between subtraction and addition. We call it the **Add-Opp Property of Subtraction.**

When discussing the Add-Opp Property, stress the advantage of addition over subtraction. Addition is commutative and associative; subtraction is neither. As a result, there are no order-of-operation worries with addition. **Example 5** illustrates this point.

Use the chart on page 279 to convince students that the Add-Opp Property works. Subtract the gain for your state from the 1987 population and you will get the population in 1980. Pick another state where the gain has the opposite sign and show that it works for that state also.

Using Manipulatives
You might provide students with two-color counters. Remind students how these are used to add integers and that one color represents negative numbers and the other color represents positive numbers. A pair of counters—one of each color—represents zero and so can be removed.

Ask students how they can use the Add-Opp Property of Subtraction to allow them to use the two-color counters to subtract. One possible explanation is to represent each number with counters, next flip over the counters representing the number to be subtracted, and then combine as they have done for addition.

Have students make up their own subtraction exercises and use two-color counters to find the answers.

Add-Opp Property of Subtraction:

For any numbers a and b
$$a - b = a + \text{-}b.$$
In words, subtracting b is the same as adding the opposite of b.

The Add-Opp Property allows any subtraction to be converted to an addition. This is helpful because you already know how to add both positive and negative numbers.

Example 1   Simplify: -5 − 2.

Solution 1   Use the slide model. Start at -5 and slide down 2. The result is -7.

Solution 2
Use the Add-Opp Property. $-5 - 2 = -5 + \text{-}2$
(Instead of subtracting 2, add -2.) $= \text{-}7$

Example 2   Simplify: 40 − 50.79.

Solution   Use the Add-Opp Property.
$40 - 50.79 = 40 + \text{-}50.79 = \text{-}10.79.$

Example 3   Simplify: -6 − -8.

Solution
Use the Add-Opp Property.
(Instead of subtracting -8, add its opposite, 8.)
$$-6 - \text{-}8 = \text{-}6 + 8$$
$$= 2$$

Example 4   Simplify: $x - \text{-}y$.

Solution   By the Add-Opp Property, $x - \text{-}y = x + y$.

Another reason for using the Add-Opp Property is that addition has the commutative and associative properties. You do not have to worry about order of additions. This is particularly nice if there are more than two numbers involved in the subtractions.

286

■ ■ ■ ■ ■ ■ ■ ■

Example 5 Simplify: -5 − -3 + 8 + -2 − 7 − 4.

Solution Remember order of operations. Proceed from left to right, converting subtractions to additions.

$$= -5 + 3 + 8 + -2 + -7 + -4$$

Now change order, putting all negatives together.

$$= -5 + -2 + -7 + -4 + 3 + 8$$
$$= \quad\quad -18 \quad\quad + \quad\quad 11$$
$$= \quad\quad\quad\quad -7$$

You have learned three uses of the − sign. Each use has a different English word.

where − sign is found	example	in English
between numbers or variables	2 − 5	2 *minus* 5
in front of a positive number	-3	*negative* 3
in front of a variable or	-x	*opposite of* x
negative number	-(-4)	*opposite of negative* 4

For example, 3 − -y is read "three minus the opposite of y."

Questions

Covering the Reading

1. To picture 3 − 4 on the number line, you can start at __?__ and draw an arrow __?__ units long pointing to the __?__.   **3, 4, left**

2. State the Slide Model for Subtraction.   **See margin.**

In 3–5: **a.** Give a subtraction problem that will answer the question. **b.** Give an addition problem that will answer the question. **c.** Answer the question.

3. The temperature is 74° F and is supposed to drop 20° by this evening. What is the expected temperature this evening?
a. 74 − 20; b. 74 + -20; c. 54° F

4. The temperature is -4° C and is supposed to drop 10° by morning. What is the expected morning temperature?
a. -4 − 10; b. -4 + -10; c. -14° C

LESSON 7-2   The Slide Model for Subtraction   **287**

ADDITIONAL EXAMPLES
1. Simplify:
a. −12 − −6
−6
b. 25 − 30.5
−5.5
c. −10 − 7
−17
d. −a − −b
−a + b
e. −8 − −2 + 5 − 8 − 2 + −4
−15

2. Read the expression.
a. −2
negative two
b. −(−3)
opposite of negative 3
c. a − b
a minus b
d. −c
opposite of c
e. 2 − −d
two minus the opposite of d

ADDITIONAL ANSWERS
2. If a quantity *a* is decreased by an amount *b*, the result is a quantity *a* − *b*.

**Error Analysis for
Question 23:** Students
may need help with the substitutions. Point out that only
the variable is replaced by a
number; the signs between
variables are operation signs
that must remain. After students make the substitutions
for *a*, *b*, *c*, and *d*, they
should convert subtractions
to additions using the Add-
Opp Property.

Question 24: Explain that
it is tricky to use calculators
for subtraction with negative
numbers. Therefore, it is important to be able to do such
problems without calculators.

**Making Connections for
Questions 25–28:** Point
out the suggested use of the
problem-solving strategy *trial
and error* from Chapter 6.

Question 35a: Careful
record keeping is crucial to
finding a solution. Students
need to record the numbers
tried and the results. **Question 35b** asks for a solution
that covers all possible years.

5. A person who weighs 72 kg loses 3 kg. What weight results?
   a. 72 − 3; b. 72 + -3; c. 69 kg

6. State the Add-Opp Property: **a.** in symbols; **b.** in words.
   See margin.

7. $5 - -8 = 5 + \underline{\ ?\ }$. **8**   8. $-x - -y = -x + \underline{\ ?\ }$. **y**

In 9–16, simplify.

9. $-8 - 45$ **-53**

10. $83 - 100$ **-17**

11. $1 - 5$ **-4**

12. $-22 - 8$ **-30**

13. $3 - -7$ **10**

14. $0 - -41$ **41**

15. $-9 - -6$ **-3**

16. $m - -2$ **m + 2**

17. Give two reasons why it is useful to be able to convert
    subtractions to additions. **See margin.**

18. Consider the expression $-43 - -x$. Which of the three dashes (left,
    center, or right) is read: **a.** minus; **b.** opposite of; **c.** negative?
    a. center; b. right; c. left

19. Translate into English: $-A - -4$.
    the opposite of A minus negative four

20. Simplify: $40 - 50 - 20$. **-30**

21. Evaluate $5 - y$:
    a. when $y = 2$;   **b.** when $y = 3$;   **c.** when $y = 4$;
    d. when $y = 5$;   **e.** when $y = 6$;   **f.** when $y = 7$.
    a. 3; b. 2; c. 1; d. 0; e. -1; f. -2

22. The formula $p = s - c$ connects profit p, selling price s, and cost c.
    a. Calculate p when $s = \$49.95$ and $c = \$30.27$. **$19.68**
    b. Calculate p when $s = \$49.95$ and $c = \$56.25$. **-$6.30**
    c. Your answer to part **b** should be a negative number. What does
    a negative profit indicate? **a loss**

23. Calculate $a - b + c - d$ when $a = -1$, $b = -2$, $c = -3$, and
    $d = -4$. **2**

24. **a.** On your calculator, give a key sequence that will do the
    subtraction $3 - -4$. **b.** Give a key sequence that will do the
    subtraction $-5 - -77$. **See margin.**

In 25–28, use trial and error, or test special cases.

25. *Multiple choice*   If $9 = 7 - x$, then $x =$ **(c)**
    (a) 2   (b) 16   (c) -2   (d) -16

26. *Multiple choice*   A person weighs 165 lb and goes on a diet,
    losing L lb. The resulting weight is R lb. Then $R =$ **(b)**
    (a) $L - 165$ (b) $165 - L$
    (c) $L - -165$ (d) $-165 - L$

288

27. *True or false?* **a.** When x is a positive number, $x - x = 0$.
b. When x is a negative number, $x - x = 0$. **a. True; b. True**

28. a. For all numbers x, y, and z, is it true that
$(x - y) - z = x - (y - z)$? **No**
b. Does subtraction have the associative property? **No**

29. a. What relationship among any numbers a and b would have to
be true in order for subtraction to be commutative?
b. Is subtraction commutative?
a. $a - b = b - a$ for all numbers a and b; b. no

Review

30. A symphony is 38 minutes long. If the orchestra has played for
t minutes, how many minutes remain? *(Lesson 7-1)* **38 − t minutes**

31. Let n be a number. What is the number that is four less than n?
(Lesson 4-3) **$n - 4$**

32. How many degrees does the minute hand of a watch turn in
1 minute? *(Lesson 5-6)* **6°**

33. What property justifies adding the same number to both sides of
an equation? *(Lesson 5-8)* **Addition Property of Equality**

34. In a single elimination tournament a team plays until it is beaten.
Eight teams are to play a single elimination tournament. How
many games must be played? *(Lesson 6-3)* **7**

Exploration

35. When $m = 3$ and $n = 7$,
$m^n - n^m = 3^7 - 7^3 = 2187 - 343 = 1844$.
a. Find integer values of m and n between 1 and 15 so that
$m^n - n^m = 1927$. **$2^{11} - 11^2$**
b. Find positive integer values of m and n so that the value of
$m^n - n^m$ is the current year on the calendar. **For the year 1990,
$1991^1 - 1^{1991}$; for the year k, $(k + 1)^1 - 1^{k+1} = k$.**

MORE PRACTICE
For more questions on SPUR
Objectives, use *Lesson Master 7-2*, shown below.

**6. a. For any numbers a
and b, $a - b = a + -b$.**
**b. Subtracting b is the
same as adding the opposite of b.**

**17. You already know how
to add positive and negative numbers; addition has
the Commutative and Associative properties.**

24. a. 3 ⊟ **4** ± **=**
b. 5 ± ⊟ **77** ± **=**

NAME _____

■**SKILLS** *Objective A (See Chapter Review, pages 330–333, for objectives.)*
In 1–4, simplify.

1. $16 - 120$ __**-104**__   **2.** $-31 - 7$ __**-38**__
3. $45 - 70$ __**-25**__   **4.** $-100 - -63$ __**-37**__

In 5 and 6, evaluate.

5. $-a - (-b) + -c$
when $a = 9$, $b = 34$, and $c = -16$ __**41**__

6. $-y - x$
when $y = -50$ and $x = -3$ __**53**__

■**PROPERTIES** *Objective H*
In 7 and 8, use the Add-Opp Property to rewrite each of the following.

7. $-9 - 2 = -9 +$ __**-2**__   **8.** $75 - 123 =$ __**75 + -123**__

9. Consider the expression $-92 - -y$.
Which of the three dashes (left, center, or right) is read:
a. minus __**center**__   **b.** opposite of __**right**__
c. negative __**left**__

■**USES** *Objective O*

10. On July 8, ozone levels in the Denver area
reached a dangerous high of 234 ppb (parts per
billion). By July 10th, the level had dropped by
57 ppb from the high. What was the ozone
reading in the Denver area on July 10th? __**177 ppb**__

11. Ray Bolger, dancer and actor best known as the
Scarecrow in *The Wizard of Oz*, died in 1987
at the age of 83. Based on this information,
in what two years might he have been born? __**1904 or 1903**__

■**REPRESENTATIONS** *Objective Q*
In 12 and 13, picture the subtraction on a number line and give the result.

12. $-9 - 4 =$ __**-13**__
13. $6 - 11 =$ __**-5**__

7-3

The Comparison Model for Subtraction

The first number in a subtraction problem is called the **minuend.**
The second number is the **subtrahend.** The answer is called the
difference.

$$
\begin{array}{r}
436.2 \quad \text{minuend} \\
- \ 98.5 \quad \text{subtrahend} \\
\hline
337.7 \quad \text{difference}
\end{array}
$$

The term ''difference'' comes from a third model of subtraction,
the *comparison* model. Here are two examples.

Example 1 Yvonne is 160 cm tall. Her boyfriend, Ulysses, is 184 cm tall.
How much taller is Ulysses than Yvonne?

Solution 184 cm − 160 cm, or 24 cm

Example 2 The highest point in California is the peak of Mount Whitney,
14,494 feet above sea level. The lowest point in California is in
Death Valley and is 282 feet below sea level. What is the
difference in the elevations of these two points?

Solution The elevation below sea level is represented by the
number -282.
14,494 − -282 = 14,494 + 282 = 14,776 feet

The general pattern is called the **comparison model for
subtraction.**

Comparison Model for Subtraction:

$x - y$ is how much more x is than y.

290

A special type of comparison is change. Suppose a school had 1200 students last year and 1150 this year. The change is 1150 − 1200, or -50 students. The negative answer signifies a loss. Notice that the later value comes first, the earlier value second.

---

change = later value − earlier value

Here is an example of change where the minuend and subtrahend are negative.

Example 3   The temperature was -3° earlier today. Now it is -17°. By how much has it changed?

   Solution $-17° − -3° = -17° + 3° = -14°$. The temperature has gone down 14°.

Another special type of comparison gives the amount of an error. Again, negative numbers may be involved.

---

error in estimate = estimated value − actual value

Example 4   Josie thought the girls' football team would lose their game by 10 points. Instead they won by 6. How far off was Josie?

   Solution   A loss by 10 is -10. A win by 6 is 6. The difference is $-10 − 6$, which equals $-10 + -6$, or -16. Josie was 16 points too low.

Think of $x − y$. When x is bigger than y, as in $5 − 2$, the difference is a positive number. When x is smaller than y, as in $2 − 5$, the difference is negative. This happens regardless of the numbers used. For instance, look again at Example 4. -10 is less than 6. So $-10 − 6$ is negative.

What happens if you subtract the numbers in reverse order?

$$6 − -10 = 6 + 10 = 16$$

The difference is now the opposite of -16. This pattern is always true.

Discuss all the examples with the students. **Examples 1 and 2** illustrate the general pattern for the Comparison Model. You may find a number line useful in picturing comparison subtraction. If x is greater than y, $x − y$ is the distance between x and y on the number line. If you do not know which of them is greater, then the distance is $|x − y|$, the formula often studied in geometry. **Examples 3 and 4** introduce special kinds of comparison: change and error in estimate.

Do not expect students to remember whether the estimated value or the actual value comes first in calculating error. Recommend that they use the strategy of *trying simpler numbers*.

The property that $x − y$ is the opposite of $y − x$ is usually not named but is very helpful in checking computation. You might call it the Subtraction Switch Property. You may want to put a chart of several instances on the board to reinforce the generalization.

$$1 − 2 = -1; \quad 2 − 1 = 1$$
$$-1 − 2 = -3; \quad 2 − -1 = 3$$
$$1 − -2 = 3; \quad -2 − 1 = -3$$
$$-1 − -2 = 1; \quad -2 − -1 = -1$$

Stress the use of this property in computing $a − b$ when $a < b$ and $a > 0$, $b > 0$.

ADDITIONAL EXAMPLES

1. In a high school track meet, Marla threw the discus 124 ft 9 in. The world record (as of 1987) is 244 ft 7 in. How much longer is the world record throw?
119 ft 10 in.

2. A submarine moved from 125 feet below sea level to 78 feet below sea level. How has its position changed?
47; the submarine has risen 47 feet.

3. Farmer Frank estimated he would get $2.35 per bushel of wheat, but he actually received $2.41 cents per bushel. How far off was his estimate?
–$0.06; it was 6 cents too low.

> **For all numbers x and y:**
>
> $x - y$ is the opposite of $y - x$.

This property can help in computation. Suppose you wish to calculate $432 - 999$. Just subtract in reverse order. Since $999 - 432 = 567$, so $432 - 999 = \text{-}567$.

Questions

Covering the Reading

In 1–3, consider the subtraction fact $12 - 8 = 4$. Identify the:

1. difference.   4   **2.** minuend.   12   **3.** subtrahend.   8

4. State the Comparison Model for Subtraction.
$x - y$ is how much more x is than y.

5. Jim weighs 150 pounds but wants to get his weight down to 144 pounds. How much does he need to lose?   6 lb

6. Nina has $240 saved for a stereo system that costs $395. How much more does she need? $155

7. The highest elevation in Louisiana is Driskill Mountain, at 535 feet above sea level. The lowest elevation is in New Orleans, at 5 feet below sea level. What is the difference in elevation between these two points?   540 ft

French Quarter, New Orleans

In 8 and 9, calculate the change in temperature from yesterday to today.

8. Yesterday, 27°; today, 13°.   -14°   **9.** Yesterday, -9°; today, -8°.   1°

Fred thinks that the Dallas Cowboys will win next Sunday's football game by 13 points. In 10 and 11, give the error in his guess if the Cowboys:

10. win by 20.   -7 points   **11.** lose by 4.   17 points

292

12. For all numbers x and y: $x - y$ is the opposite of ___?___. $y - x$

13. Since $835 - 467 = 368$, what is $467 - 835$?   -368

14. If $a - b = 40$, then $b - a = $ ___?___.   -40

In 15–20, without doing the subtraction, tell whether the difference is positive or negative.

15. $3.498764 - 2.99834657$ **16.** $7.08 - 12$
positive   negative

17. $-100 - -400$ positive   **18.** $65 - -430$ positive

19. $-2 - 1.00004$ negative   **20.** $-0.0094 - 0.0093$ negative

Applying the Mathematics

In 21 and 22, use special cases if you cannot first answer the question.

21. In 1990, the population of Arizona was estimated to be 1,034,000 more than in 1980. Suppose the 1990 population was x and the 1980 population was y. How are x, y, and 1,034,000 related?
$x - y = 1,034,000$

Arizona roadrunner

22. Last year the Peas Porridge Co. had a profit of D dollars. This year their profit was E dollars. What is the change in profit from last year to this? $E - D$ dollars

23. Here are census figures for Portland, Oregon.

1960	373,676
1970	379,967
1980	366,383
1990	420,920

   a. Calculate the change from each census to the next. You should get two positive numbers and one negative number.   See margin.
   b. Add the three numbers you got in part **a**. 47,244
   c. What does the sum in part **b** mean?   See margin.

24. The steps here show that $b - a$ and $a - b$ add to zero. This confirms that $b - a$ and $a - b$ are opposites. Give the property that tells why each step follows from the preceding one.   See margin.

	$(b - a) + (a - b)$
Step 1:	$= (b + {}^-a) + (a + {}^-b)$
Step 2:	$= b + ({}^-a + a) + {}^-b$
Step 3:	$= b + 0 + {}^-b$
Step 4:	$= b + {}^-b$
Step 5:	$= 0$

LESSON 7-3   The Comparison Model for Subtraction   **293**

NOTES ON QUESTIONS
Error Analysis for Questions 21 and 22:
Encourage students who find all the variables confusing to try simpler (positive) numbers to help set up the right subtraction problem.

Question 24: This is intended to increase readiness for proofs and analysis in later courses. Do not expect mastery at this time.

ADDITIONAL ANSWERS
23. a. from 1960 to 1970, 6,291; from 1970 to 1980, –13,584; from 1980 to 1990, 54,537; **c.** The population increased by 47,244 from 1960 to 1990.

24. Add-Opp Property, Associative Property of Addition, Property of Opposites, Additive Identity Property of Zero, Property of Opposites

25. The famous scientist, Marie Curie, was born in 1867 and died in 1934. From this information, how old was she when she died? (Watch out. There are two possible answers.) **66 or 67**

26. The Roman poet, Livy, was born in 59 B.C. and died in 17 A.D. From this information, how old was he when he died? (Watch out again. There was no year 0. The year 1 A.D. followed 1 B.C.) **74 or 75 years old**

27. Try simpler numbers if you cannot get the answer right away.
    a. How many integers are between 100 and 1000, not including 100 or 1000? **899**
    b. How many integers are between two integers *I* and *J*, not including *I* or *J*? **$J - I - 1$**

Review

3.5"

2.5"

28. Give a calculator sequence to do $-1 - -2 - -8$. *(Lessons 1-7, 7-2)*
    See margin.
29. Of 100,000 people born in the U.S. in the years 1967–1972, on the average, 98,536 were alive in 1987. **a.** How many had died? **b.** How old were those that were still alive? *(Lesson 7-1)*
    a. 1,464; b. 14–20
30. Solve $-a + y = b$ for *y*. *(Lesson 5-8)* **$y = a + b$**

31. Find the perimeter of the figure at left. *(Lesson 5-10)* **12 in**

32. Write $\frac{2}{5}$ as a percent. *(Lesson 2-7)* **40%**

Exploration

33. Ask five different people not in your class to estimate how many heads will turn up if you toss a penny ten times. Then toss the penny 10 times. Calculate the error for each person. (Remember that your answer should be negative if a guess was too low.)
    See margin.
34. Is $x - y$ the opposite of $y - x$ when *x* and *y* are complicated? Test this conjecture using the following computer program. Type in the following program.
```
NEW
10 PRINT "X"
15 INPUT X
20 PRINT "Y"
25 INPUT Y
30 PRINT "Y − X", "X − Y"
35 PRINT Y−X, X−Y
40 END
```
    a. Run the program inputting 5 for X and 3 for Y to test it. Record your results.
    b. What happens when you input 98.7 for X and -3.456 for Y?
    c. Try some numbers of your own choosing and record the results.
    See margin.

LESSON 7-4

Solving $x - a = b$

RESOURCES
- Lesson Master 7-4
- Quiz on Lessons 7-1 Through 7-4

The equation $x - 59 = 12$ is an equation of the form $x - a = b$. To solve this equation just convert the subtraction to addition using the Add-Opp Property. Then solve the resulting equation as you did in Chapter 5.

Example 1 Solve $x - 59 = 12$.

Solution
Convert to addition	$x + \text{-}59 = 12$
Add 59 to both sides.	$x + \text{-}59 + 59 = 12 + 59$
Simplify.	$x + 0 = 71$
	$x = 71$

Check Substitute 71 for x in the original sentence.
Does $71 - 59 = 12$? Yes. So 71 is the solution.

The equation $x - a = b$ can be used to model many real-life situations.

Example 2 From a large herd of cattle, cowhands drove away 230 cows. There were 575 cows left in the herd. How large was the original herd?

Solution Let C be the number of cows in the original herd. Then by the Take-Away Model of Subtraction, $C - 230 = 575$. Solve this equation.

Convert to addition.	$C + \text{-}230 = 575$
Add 230 to both sides.	$C + \text{-}230 + 230 = 575 + 230$
Simplify.	$C + 0 = 805$
	$C = 805$

So the herd started with 805 cattle.

Check If there were 805 cows in the original herd and 230 were driven away, would 575 remain? Yes.

TEACHING NOTES

Discuss each example with the students. Review the steps for solving an equation. Compare the solution of **Example 3** with that of **Example 1**, noting the corresponding steps. (**Examples 1, 2,** and **4** do not show associativity.) It may be helpful to write **Example 3** on the board, substituting numbers for the variables. Ask the students to justify each step of the solution.

Examples 1 and 2 tell *how* to solve a simple subtraction equation. The next example shows *why* the steps work.

Example 3 Solve $x - a = b$ for x, and give a reason why each step follows.

Solution

$$x + -a = b \qquad \text{(Add-Opp Property of Subtraction)}$$
$$(x + -a) + a = b + a \qquad \text{(Addition Property of Equality)}$$
$$x + (-a + a) = b + a \qquad \text{(Associative Property of Addition)}$$
$$x + 0 = b + a \qquad \text{(Property of Opposites)}$$
$$x = b + a \qquad \text{(Additive Identity Property of Zero)}$$

The next example shows an application of $x - a = b$ using the Slide Model for Subtraction.

Example 4 A group of divers paused on a natural plateau below the surface of the sea. After descending 20 meters more, they found themselves 83 meters below sea level. What was the elevation of the plateau?

Solution Let E be the elevation of the plateau (in meters). From the Slide Model for Subtraction, $E - 20 = -83$. Solve this equation.

Convert to addition. $E + -20 = -83$
Add 20 to both sides. $E + -20 + 20 = -83 + 20$
Simplify. $E + 0 = -63$
                                              $E = -63$

The plateau was 63 meters below sea level.

296

296

NOTES ON QUESTIONS
Questions 12 and 13:
Some students can undoubt-edly do these without writing an equation. However, the point of these questions is that equation solving works, not that students should use equations for easy questions. Encourage students to complete parts **a** and **b**.

Covering the Reading

1. What is the name of the property that enables $x - a$ to be replaced by $x + -a$? **Add-Opp Property of Subtraction**

2. What is the only difference between solving an equation of the form $x - a = b$ and solving an equation of the form $x + a = b$?
The subtraction is to be converted to addition.

In 3–6: **a.** Convert the sentence to one with only addition in it.
b. Solve.

3. $x - 14 = -2$
   a. x + -14 = -2; b. 12

4. $73 = y - 28$
   a. 73 = y + -28; b. 101

5. $a - 6 = 9$
   a. a + -6 = 9; b. a = 15

6. $c - 12.5 = 3$
   a. c + -12.5 = 3; b. c = 15.5

7. Is -42 the solution to $x - 13 = -29$? **no**

8. Is $y = -1$ the solution to $6 = y - -7$? **yes**

9. *Multiple choice* If $x - a = b$, then $x =$ **(c)**
   (a) $a - b$ (b) $b - a$ (c) $b + a$ (d) $b + -a$

In 10 and 11, solve and check.

10. $B - -5 = 6$ **1**

11. $3.01 = e - 9.2$ **12.21**

In 12 and 13: **a.** Write an equation involving subtraction describing the situation. **b.** Solve the equation. **c.** Answer the question.

12. After descending 75 feet, Monty Climber is at an elevation of 12,450 feet on the mountain. At what elevation was he originally?
See margin.

Applying the Mathematics

13. A volleyball team gives up 3 points and is now losing by 2 points. How was the team doing before they lost the points?
a. s − 3 = -2; b. 1; c. The team was ahead by one point.

14. The formula $p = s - c$ relates profit, selling price, and cost. Solve for the selling price s in terms of the profit and the cost.
s = p + c

15. A fish starts at a depth of d feet below the surface of a pond. While searching for food it ascends 4 feet, then descends 12 feet. Its final depth is 15 feet below the surface. What was the fish's initial depth? **-7 feet (7 feet below the surface)**

16. Solve for s: $s - \frac{1}{8} = \frac{1}{2}$. **0.625 or $\frac{5}{8}$**

Review

17. Calculate $2 - 3 - 10$. *(Lesson 7-2)* **-11**

18. Calculate $-8 - 9$. *(Lesson 7-2)* **-17**

19. The highest temperature ever recorded in the United States was 134°F, in Death Valley, California, on July 10, 1913. The lowest temperature ever recorded in the U.S. was -80°F, in Prospect Creek, Alaska, on January 23, 1971.
    a. To the nearest year, how many years separate the two dates?
    b. What is the difference between the temperatures? *(Lesson 7-3)*
       a. **58 years;** b. **214°**

20. A person was born in this century in the year B and died in the year D. What are the possible ages of this person at the time of death? (Use special cases if you cannot answer quickly.) *(Lessons 6-6, 7-3)* **$D - B$ or $D - B - 1$ years old**

21. An age guesser at a carnival gives a prize if your age is not guessed within (and including) five years. Let G be the guess. If a person is 26 years old, describe the values of G that will give that person a prize. *(Lessons 4-9, 7-3)* **$G < 21$ or $G > 31$**

22. Barry had $312 in his checking account and made out a check for $400. By how much was he overdrawn? *(Lessons 7-1, 7-2)* **overdrawn by $88**

23. On personal checks, dollar amounts must be written out in English. Write out $2305 as you would need to for a personal check. *(Lesson 1-1)* **See margin.**

24. If $-x = 17$, what is x? *(Lesson 5-4)* **-17**

25. B is on $\overline{AC}$. If $AC = 1$ meter and $AB = 30$ cm, what is BC? *(Lesson 7-1)* **70 cm or 0.7 m**

In 26–31, rewrite as a decimal.

26. $\frac{3}{4}$ *(Lesson 1-8)* **0.75**   27. 150% *(Lesson 2-5)* **1.5**

28. $\frac{6}{11}$ *(Lesson 1-8)* **$0.\overline{54}$**   29. 6.34×10^6 *(Lesson 2-3)* **6,340,000**

30. five trillion *(Lesson 2-1)* **5,000,000,000,000**

31. sixty-four millionths *(Lesson 1-2)* **.000064**

32. Measure $\angle V$ to the nearest degree. *(Lesson 3-5)* **10°**

Exploration

33. a. Replace each letter with a digit to make a true subtraction. Different letters stand for different digits. Each letter stands for the same digit wherever it occurs.
```
  T W O
- O N E
  O N E
```
    b. There is more than one solution. How many solutions are there? **See margin.**

7-5

Equivalent Sentences and Formulas

Stores use formulas to compute profit. See page 300.

LESSON 7-5

RESOURCES
■ Lesson Master 7-5
▣ Computer Master 13

OBJECTIVE

▌Distinguish equivalent from non-equivalent sentences and formulas.

Suppose you have to solve $30 + x = 52$. Using the techniques you have learned, you write down $x = 22$. You have written a sentence **equivalent** to the original. Two sentences are equivalent if they have exactly the same solutions.

■ ■ ■ ■ ■ ■ ■■

Example Which equation is *not* equivalent to the others?
$x + 3 = 8$ $2x = 10$ $-1 = 4 - x$ $x - 0.4 = 4.96$

Solution The first three equations have the single solution 5. The equation at the right has solution 5.36. It is not equivalent to the others.

Of all equations with solution 5, the simplest is $x = 5$.

> The idea in solving equations is to find a sentence of the form $x = \underline{\quad}$ that is equivalent to the original equation.

You can use equivalent sentences to locate an error in your work. A student wrote what is given here. Not all steps are shown because this student did some steps mentally. Lines are identified for future reference.

Line 1	$A - 35 - 12 = 40$
Line 2	$A - 23 \qquad = 40$
Line 3	$A + -23 \qquad = 40$
Line 4	$A \qquad = 40 + 23$
Line 5	$A \qquad = 63$

There must be an error because 63 does not work in the equation of Line 1.

$$63 - 35 - 12 \neq 40$$

But 63 does work on every other line. So all the other equations are equivalent. This says that the error must be in going from Line 1 to Line 2. Do you see the error? (Hint: It has to do with order of operations.)

TEACHING NOTES

Stress three main ideas concerning equivalent equations. First, discuss the definition and its relationship to the steps in writing out the solution of an equation. Each step should be equivalent to the previous one until the simplest equivalent form $x = \underline{\quad}$ is reached.

Second, point out that students can use equivalent equations to find the error in a solution. This is discussed following the **Example** on page 299.

Third, carefully explain the simple equivalent formulas of this lesson. Solving for one variable in a formula in terms of others is a difficult skill to learn for some students, but quite easy for others.

ADDITIONAL EXAMPLES

1. *Multiple choice* Which sentence is not equivalent to the others?

(a) $10 = \frac{1}{2}x$

(b) $\frac{x}{2} + 5 = 15$

(c) $x - .5 = 15$

(d) $75 = 4x - 5$

c

2. Find the step where the error occurs in this solution.
(1) $20 - x = 30$
(2) $20 + {-20} - x = 30 + {-20}$
(3) $0 - x = 10$
(4) $x = 10$
between (3) and (4)

3. In analyzing a runner's performance in a race, a coach often looks at a breakdown of times for parts of the race, called *splits*. If the split for the first half is f, the split for the second half is s, and the time for the whole race is r, then $f + s = r$. Give two equivalent formulas that involve a subtraction.
$r - s = f, r - f = s$

In applications it is important to know when you are dealing with **equivalent formulas.** Here is an example. You have seen the formula $p = s - c$. (Profit on an item equals its selling price minus the cost of producing it.) If the selling price is \$49.95 and the cost is \$30.27, then the profit is \$49.95 − \$30.27, or \$19.68.

Now solve the formula for s. You will get $s = c + p$. (Selling price equals cost plus profit.) The same three numbers work in the formula $s = c + p$.

$$p = s - c \qquad\qquad s = c + p$$
$$19.68 = 49.95 - 30.27 \qquad 49.95 = 30.27 + 19.68$$

The formulas $p = s - c$ and $s = c + p$ are equivalent because the same numbers work in both of them. When you take a formula and solve for a variable in it, you always get an equivalent formula.

Questions

Covering the Reading

1. When are two sentences equivalent?
if they have exactly the same solutions

2. What is the general idea in solving equations? *See margin.*

3. Sentences I, II, and III are equivalent.
I: $2 - x - 3 = 1$ II: $x + 5 = 3$ III: $x = -2$
a. Which sentence is the simplest? *III*
b. What is the solution to sentence I? *-2*

In 4–6, find the sentence that is not equivalent to the others.

4. $x = 5$ $5 - x = 10$ $x = -5$ $x = 5$

5. $y + 1 = 4$ $4 + 1 = y$ $1 + y = 4$ $4 + 1 = y$

6. $a + \frac{2}{3} = b$ $a - b = \frac{2}{3}$ $b - a = \frac{2}{3}$ $a - b = \frac{2}{3}$

In 7 and 8, an attempt was made to solve the sentence on Line 1. But an error was made. **a.** Find the one sentence that is not equivalent to the others. **b.** Between what lines was the error made? *See margin.*

7. Line 1: $-6 = y - 9$
Line 2: $-6 + 9 = y$
Line 3: $-15 = y$

8. Line 1: $A - 10 - 5 = 12$
Line 2: $A - 5 = 12$
Line 3: $A = 17$

9. When are formulas equivalent?
when the same numbers work in both (or all) of them

10. Which formula is not equivalent to the others? *$p = c - s$*
$s = p + c$ $p = s - c$ $p = c - s$

In 11–13, find the simplest sentence equivalent to the given sentence.

11. $x + 40 = 35$ $x = -5$

12. $\frac{6}{5} = \frac{2}{3} + A$ $\frac{8}{15} = A$, or $.5\overline{3} = A$

13. $y - 1.8 = 8.7$ $y = 10.5$

14. What *one word* could replace the directions to Questions 11–13?
Solve.

The three numbers 3, 4, and 7 are related in many ways. For example:
$$3 + 4 = 7; \qquad 7 - 4 = 3; \qquad \text{and} \qquad 7 - 3 = 4.$$
Because these sentences use the same numbers, they are called *related facts.* In 15–20, find a fact related to each given fact that does not use the same operation.

15. $80 + 14 = 94$ $80 = 94 - 14$ or $94 - 80 = 14$

16. $9 \cdot 79 = 711$ $9 = \frac{711}{79}$ or $79 = \frac{711}{9}$

17. $4 + -5 = -1$ $-1 - -5 = 4$ or $-5 = -1 - 4$

18. $.3 \cdot .5 = .15$ $.3 = \frac{.15}{.5}$ or $.5 = \frac{.15}{.3}$

19. $10 - 23 = -13$ $10 = -13 + 23$

20. $(\frac{2}{3})/(\frac{4}{5}) = \frac{5}{6}$ $(\frac{5}{6})(\frac{4}{5}) = \frac{2}{3}$

21. *Multiple choice* Which sentence is equivalent to $A = \ell w$? (Hint: If you do not know the answer quickly, test a special case.) (c)
(a) $A\ell = w$ (b) $Aw = \ell$
(c) $A/\ell = w$ (d) none of these

22. Solve $x - 11 = -11$. *(Lesson 7-4)*   0

23. Solve $8 = y - 40$. *(Lesson 7-4)* $y = 48$

24. Solve for d in terms of c: $c + d = 30$. *(Lesson 5-8)* $d = 30 - c$

25. Booker T. Washington was born in 1856 and died in 1915. How old was he when he died? *(Lesson 7-3)*   58 or 59 years old

Booker Taliaferro Washington (far left) and his two sons

LESSON 7-5 Equivalent Sentences and Formulas   **301**

MORE PRACTICE
For more questions on SPUR
Objectives, use *Lesson Mas-
ter 7-5*, shown on page 301.

EXTENSION
Divisibility by 9 is the topic in
Question 32. You might ask
students to list the divisibility
tests for 2, 5, 10, 3, and 6.
(2: the number ends in 0, 2,
4, 6, or 8. 5: the number
ends in 5 or 0. 10: the number ends in 0. 3: the sum of
the digits is divisible by 3. 6:
the number is divisible by 2
and 3.)

26. In Montreal, Quebec, the average normal high temperature in
January is -6°C. The average normal low temperature is -15°C.
What is the average range in the temperature on a January day in
Montreal? *(Lesson 7-3)* **9°C**

27. Evaluate $3 - x$ when: **a.** $x = 17$; **b.** $x = -85$. *(Lesson 7-2)*
a. -14; b. 88

28. Pick all of the following that are correct names for the angle
below. *(Lesson 3-5)* **(a), (c), (d)**
(a) $\angle O$ (b) $\angle OCW$
(c) $\angle COW$ (d) $\angle WOC$
(e) $\angle C$ (f) $\angle W$

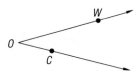

29. How many degrees are in a half turn? *(Lesson 5-6)* **180°**

30. Round 357.9124 up to the nearest thousandth. *(Lesson 1-3)* **357.913**

31. If n stands for a number, what stands for the number that is three
less than twice n? *(Lesson 4-3)* **2n − 3**

Exploration

32. Write down ten 3-digit numbers that are divisible by 9. Add up
the digits in each of these numbers. What pattern do you find?
**Samples: 810, 729, 648, 243, 108, 117, 126, 135, 144, 999;
the sum of the digits is always divisible by 9.**

302

Solving
$a - x = b$

An equation can be used to find how many tickets have been sold. See Example 2.

The equation $3 - x = 20$ is of the form $a - x = b$. To solve this equation, we can use the same strategy we used to solve $x - a = b$. Because the variable is subtracted, one more step is needed.

Example 1 Solve $3 - x = 20$.

Solution 1

First convert to addition.	$3 + \text{-}x = 20$
Now add -3 to both sides.	$\text{-}3 + 3 + \text{-}x = \text{-}3 + 20$
Simplify.	$\text{-}x = 17$

This equation is easy to solve. Just take the opposite of both sides.

	$\text{-}(\text{-}x) = \text{-}17$
Simplify.	$x = \text{-}17$

Check Substitute in the original sentence.
Does $3 - \text{-}17 = 20$? Yes.

Solution 2 Another way to solve $3 - x = 20$ is to add x to both sides.

First convert to addition	$3 + \text{-}x = 20$
Now add x to both sides.	$3 + \text{-}x + x = 20 + x$
Simplify.	$3 = 20 + x$

This is an equation you have solved many times before.

Add -20 to both sides.	$\text{-}20 + 3 = \text{-}20 + 20 + x$
Simplify.	$\text{-}17 = 0 + x$
	$\text{-}17 = x$

LESSON 7-6

RESOURCES
■ Lesson Master 7-6
▣ Computer Master 14
■ Protractors
▣ Visual for Teaching Aid 39:
Question 19.

OBJECTIVES

C Solve sentences of the form $a - x = b$.
N Use the Take-Away Model for Subtraction to form sentences involving subtraction.

TEACHING NOTES

Make certain the students recognize the difference between the forms $x - a = b$ and $a - x = b$. Since $x + a = b$ and $a + x = b$ are the same, many students fail to appreciate the problem created because there is no commutative property for subtraction.

There are two possible solution methods illustrated in **Example 1.** Students should understand that either is correct. In **Question 4,** the students are directed to use the strategy they like better.

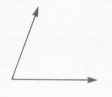

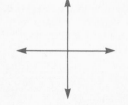
Look carefully at Solution 2. By adding x to both sides, the equation $3 - x = 20$ was converted to the equivalent equation $3 = 20 + x$. The equation $3 = 20 + x$ is one you know how to solve. This is the most important strategy in solving equations: Do things to both sides so that you wind up with a simpler equivalent equation.

Here is a situation that can lead to an equation of the form $a - x = b$.

Example 2 There were 3500 tickets available for a concert. Only 212 are left. How many tickets have been sold?

Solution This is an instance of the take-away model. Let S be the number of tickets sold. S is taken away from 3500, leaving 212.

$$3500 - S = 212$$

You are asked to solve this equation in the questions that follow.

Questions

Covering the Reading

1. Consider the equation $3 - x = 20$. To solve this equation, you can convert the subtraction to an addition. What sentence results?
$3 + -x = 20$

In 2–4, consider $-5 = 14 - t$.

2. To solve this equation using the strategy of Example 1, Solution 1, what should be added to both sides?   **-14**

3. To solve this equation using the strategy of Example 1, Solution 2, what should be added to both sides?   **t**

4. Solve the equation using the strategy you like better.   **19**

In 5–10, solve and check.

5. $300 - x = -2$ **302**   **6.** $61 = 180 - y$ **119**

7. $-45 = 45 - z$ **90**   **8.** $m - 3.3 = 1$ **4.3**

9. $A - 57 = -110$ **-53**   **10.** $\frac{2}{3} - B = \frac{88}{9}$ **$-\frac{82}{9}$**

11. a. Solve the equation of Example 2. **b.** Answer the question of Example 2.   **a. 3288; b. 3288 tickets have been sold.**

Applying the Mathematics

In 12 and 13, the question can lead to an equation of the form $a - x = b$. **a.** Give that equation. **b.** Solve the equation. **c.** Answer the question.

12. The temperature was 14° just 6 hours ago. Now it is 3° below zero. How much has it decreased?
a. $14 - d = -3$; b. $d = 17$; c. The temperature has decreased 17°.

304

13. The Himalayan mountain climbers pitched camp at 22,500 feet yesterday. Today they pitched camp at 20,250 feet. How far did they come down the mountain?
    a. 22,500 − d = 20,250; b. 2250 feet; c. They came down 2250 feet.

In 14–17, solve. You will have to simplify first.

14. $40 - x + 20 = 180$ **-120**   15. $-6 = -1 - y - 5$ **0**

16. $12 - \,-B = 6$ **-6**   17. $13 - 5 \cdot 2 = 9 - K$ **-7**   **13**

18. Solve for y: $x = 90 - y$.   **y = 90 − x**

19. Give a reason for each step in this detailed solution of $a - x = b$ for x.

Step 1:	$a + -x = b$	Add-Opp. Prop.
Step 2:	$(a + -x) + x = b + x$	Add. Prop. of Equality
Step 3:	$a + (-x + x) = b + x$	Assoc. Prop. of Add.
Step 4:	$a + 0 = b + x$	Prop. of Opposites
Step 5:	$a = b + x$	Add. Ident. Prop. of Zero
Step 6:	$-b + a = -b + (b + x)$	Add. Prop. of Equality
Step 7:	$-b + a = (-b + b) + x$	Assoc. Prop. of Add.
Step 8:	$-b + a = 0 + x$	Prop. of Opposites
Step 9:	$-b + a = x$	Add. Ident. Prop. of Zero

20. *Multiple choice* Which of (a) to (c) is not equal to $-b + a$?   **(c)**
    (a) $a + -b$ (b) $a - b$
    (c) $b + -a$ (d) All equal $-b + a$.

Review

21. What is a simple equation equivalent to $40 = A + 12$? *(Lesson 7-5)*
    A = 28
22. An event occurs half the time. What percent of the time is this? *(Lesson 2-6)*   **50%**

23. Draw an angle with a measure of $70°$. *(Lesson 3-5)*   **See margin.**

24. Draw an angle with a measure of $110°$. *(Lesson 3-5)*   **See margin.**

25. **a.** Draw two perpendicular lines. **b.** What kind of angles are formed? *(Lesson 3-6)*   **a. See margin. b. right angles**

In 26 and 27: **a.** Write an equation involving subtraction for the situation. **b.** Solve the equation. *(Lessons 7-1, 7-4)*

26. The hot air balloon fell 125 feet from its highest point. The new altitude was 630 ft. How high had it flown?
    a. h − 125 = 630; b. 755 ft
27. In the 1988 Summer Olympics, an American diver, Greg Louganis, defeated a Chinese diver, Xiong Ni, by one and fourteen-hundredths points. If Ni's total score was 637.47, what was Louganis's score?   **a. s − 1.14 = 637.47; b. 638.61**

NOTES ON QUESTIONS
Questions 5–10: These include equations of both forms $a - x = b$ and $x - a = b$, so that students do not get tied into one form.

Questions 14–17: You may want to help students simplify two of the equations. Then, have students complete these questions independently.

NAME _____

FOLLOW-UP

MORE PRACTICE
For more questions on SPUR Objectives, use *Lesson Master 7-6*, shown on page 305.

EXTENSION
Computer: Computer Master 14, provided in the Teacher's Resource File, extends the idea of **Question 30**.

28. **a.** Which of these famous English monarchs had the longest reign? *(Lesson 7-3)*   Queen Victoria
   King Henry II, who reigned from 1154 to 1189
   King Henry VIII, 1509-1547
   Queen Elizabeth I, 1558-1603
   Queen Victoria, 1837-1901
b. The present Queen of England, Elizabeth II, ascended to the throne in 1952. In what year could she become the longest-reigning queen? *(Lessons 7-1, 7-4)*   2017

29. Point O is on $\overline{AD}$. You are at O facing A. First you turn from A to B. Then you turn from B to C. Then you turn from C to D. What is the magnitude of the result of these three turns? *(Lesson 5-6)*
180°

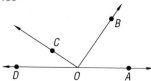

Exploration

30. Suppose $a = 5$, $b = 4$, $c = 3$, $d = 2$, and $e = 1$. Consider the expression $a - b - c - d - e$, in which all the dashes are for subtraction. Now put grouping symbols wherever you want. For instance, you could consider $(a - b) - (c - d) - e$; this gives the values $(5 - 4) - (3 - 2) - 1$, which simplifies to -1. Or consider $a - [b - (c - d)] - e$, which is $5 - [4 - (3 - 2)] - 1$, which simplifies to 1. How many different values of the expression are possible?
There are seven possible values: -5, -3, -1, 1, 3, 5, and 7.

306

LESSON 7-7

RESOURCES
■ Lesson Master 7-7
Visual for Teaching Aid 40:
Use to exemplify angle-line
relationships and with
Questions 17–21.
■ Protractors and Rulers or
Geometry Templates (from
*Transition Mathematics
Manipulative Kit*)

OBJECTIVES

D Find measures of angles
in figures with linear pairs,
vertical angles, or perpendicular lines.
J Know relationships among
angles formed by inter-
secting lines.

Suppose *B* is on $\overline{AC}$. Think of standing at *B*. If you turn from *C*
to *A*, you have turned half a revolution. The magnitude of this
turn is half of 360°, or 180°. For this reason, some mathematicians say that there is an angle *CBA* whose measure is 180°.
These mathematicians call $\angle CBA$ a **straight angle.** $\overrightarrow{BA}$ and $\overrightarrow{BC}$
are called **opposite rays** because they have the same endpoint
and together they form a line.

Now add a ray $\overrightarrow{BD}$ to the picture. Angles *DBC* and *DBA* are
formed.

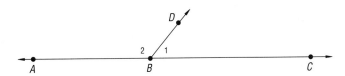

We name them 1 and 2 to make reading easier. These angles are
called a **linear pair** because they have a common side ($\overrightarrow{BD}$) and
their non-common sides ($\overrightarrow{BA}$ and $\overrightarrow{BC}$) are opposite rays. You
should measure these angles. Confirm that $m \angle 1 = 50°$ and
$m \angle 2 = 130°$. In fact, because of the Fundamental Property of
Turns, the sum of the measures of two angles in a linear pair
must be 180°.

If the line containing $\overrightarrow{BD}$ is drawn, angles 3 and 4 are formed.

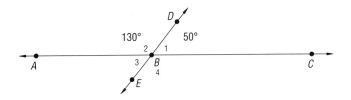

Stress that students must
learn the new terms describing rays, intersecting lines,
and angles formed by them.
Ask students to explain each
boldfaced term in their own
words, using diagrams if
needed.

Call on volunteers to explain
how to find the missing measure of one angle in a pair of
supplementary angles if the
other measure is known, and
how to find the three missing
measures for angles formed
by intersecting lines when the
fourth measure is given. Ask
different students to illustrate
these skills on the board during the discussion.

Point out the application of
angle measure to safety, as
explained on page 309: the
closer intersecting streets are
to perpendicularity, the easier
it is for drivers to see the
oncoming traffic in both
directions.

You may wish to use **Questions 8–12, 17–21, 23**,
and **25** for classwork and assign the remainder of the
problems for homework.

**Alternate Approach/
Using Manipulatives**
Have students use rulers and
protractors (or the Geometry
Template) to attempt to draw
pairs of intersecting lines for
each of these conditions:
• Angles of 100°, 80°, 100°,
  and 80° are formed.
• Angles of 60°, 40°, 60°, and
  40° are formed.
  (impossible)
• Four angles of 90° are
  formed.
• Two angles of 32° and two
  angles of some other measure are formed.
  (The other angles are each
  148°.)

Because angles 1 and 4 form a linear pair, $m\angle 4 = 130°$.
Because angles 2 and 3 form a linear pair, $m\angle 3 = 50°$.
You might want to measure angles 3 and 4 to check this.

Angles 1 and 3 are called **vertical angles.** Two angles are
vertical angles when they are formed by intersecting lines, but
are not a linear pair. Vertical angles always have the same
measure. Angles 2 and 4 are also vertical angles.

In summary, when two lines intersect, four angles are formed.
Two of these have one measure, call it x. The other two have
measure y. The sum of x and y is 180°. That is, $x + y = 180°$.

All of this is related to subtraction.
Solve the equation $x + y = 180$ for y.
$$-x + x + y = 180 + {-x}$$
$$0 + y = 180 + {-x}$$
$$y = 180 + {-x}$$
$$y = 180 - x$$

So if you know x, the measure of one angle when two lines
intersect, the measures of the other three angles are either
x or $180° - x$.
For instance, if $x = 110°$, then $y = 180° - x = 70°$.

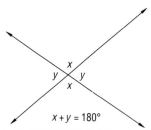

Two lines intersecting is a common situation. So angles whose
measures add to 180° appear often. Such angles are called
supplementary angles. Supplementary angles do not have to
form a linear pair. For instance, any two angles with measures
53° and 127° are supplementary because $53 + 127 = 180$, no
matter where the angles are located.

In this picture, two lines intersect to form right angles. Then all
four angles have measure 90°. Any two of the angles are
supplementary. Recall that the lines are called perpendicular.

308

308

Here is a sketch of part of a map of Chicago. Drexel and Ellis Avenues go north and south from 71st to 72nd streets. Then they bend so that they intersect South Chicago Avenue at right angles.

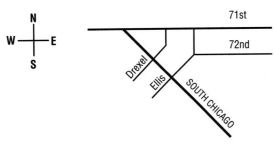

Suppose Drexel did not bend. Then the situation would be as pictured below. A driver going south on Drexel could easily see a car traveling northwest (from C_2 to C_1) on South Chicago. But the driver could not easily see a car going southeast (from C_1 to C_2) on South Chicago. By making the streets perpendicular, a driver can see both directions equally well. The intersection is safer.

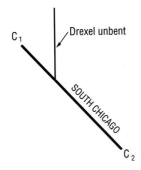

Questions

Covering the Reading

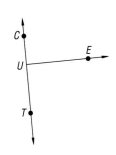

In 1–7, C, U, and T are points on the same line.

1. Angle CUT is sometimes called a __?__ angle.   straight

2. $\overrightarrow{UC}$ and $\overrightarrow{UT}$ are __?__ rays.   opposite

3. $\angle CUE$ and $\angle EUT$ form a __?__.   linear pair

4. $m\angle CUE + m\angle EUT = $ __?__ degrees.   180°

5. If $m\angle CUE = 88°$, then $m\angle EUT = $ __?__.   92°

6. If $m\angle CUE = 90°$, then $\overleftrightarrow{CT}$ and $\overrightarrow{UE}$ are __?__.   perpendicular

7. Angles CUE and EUT are __?__ angles.   supplementary

LESSON 7-7 Angles and Lines   **309**

ADDITIONAL EXAMPLES
1. Draw and label two intersecting lines on the board. Ask students to name the vertical angles, the supplementary angles, and two straight angles.

2. Have each student draw two intersecting lines and use a protractor to measure the four angles formed. Then have the students answer the following questions:
a. Do any of the four angles have the same measure?
There should be two pairs of equal angles.
b. Do the measures of any two angles form a sum of 180°?
There should be four pairs of supplementary angles.

In 8–12, $\overleftrightarrow{AB}$ and $\overleftrightarrow{CD}$ intersect at E.

8. Name all pairs of vertical angles.   See margin.

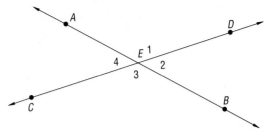

9. Name all linear pairs.   See margin.

10. Name all pairs of supplementary angles.   See margin.

11. If m∠1 = 125°, what are the measures of the other angles?
See margin.

12. Measure angles 1, 2, 3, and 4 (to the nearest degree) with a protractor.   m∠1 = m∠3 ≈ 135°; m∠2 = m∠4 ≈ 45°

In 13–15, find the unknown angle measures without using a protractor.

13. x = 135°

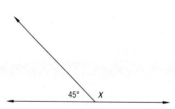

14. y = 16°

15. d = f = 90.5°, e = 89.5°

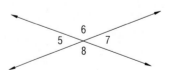

16. Two lines intersect below. If m∠5 = x, find the measure of
a. ∠6; **b.** ∠7; **c.** ∠8.   See margin.

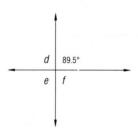

In 17–21, use the map below. Assume all the streets are two-way.

17. *True or false?* Drexel and South Chicago intersect at right angles.

True

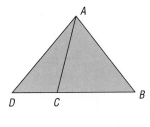

71st

72nd

Drexel

Ellis

SOUTH CHICAGO

18. *True or false?* Ellis and 71st intersect at right angles? **True**

19. How many street intersections are pictured on the map? **6**

20. At which intersection is the best visibility of oncoming traffic?
Ellis and 72nd

21. At which intersection is the worst visibility of oncoming traffic?
71st and South Chicago

22. Entrance ramps onto expressways usually form very small angles with the expressway. This is bad for visibility and is quite dangerous. Why aren't entrance ramps perpendicular to expressways? **See margin.**

In 23 and 24, name all linear pairs shown in the figure.

23. angles *DCA* and *ACB*   **24.** angles *NOM* and *POM*

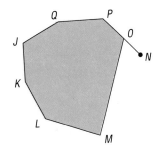

In 25–28, *true or false?*

25. If one angle of a linear pair is an acute angle, then the other angle is obtuse. **True**

26. If one of two vertical angles is acute, the other is obtuse. **False**

27. If two angles are both acute, they cannot be a linear pair. **True**

28. If two angles are supplementary, one must be acute, the other obtuse. **False**

---

22. If ramp is perpendicular to expressway, driver has to accelerate into fast-moving traffic while making 90° turn; if ramp is nearly parallel, acceleration is much easier.

NAME _____

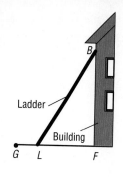

Ladder

Building

G L F

29. A firefighter places a ladder against a building so that m∠*BLF* = 58°. What is m∠*BLG*? **122°**

In 30 and 31, suppose x and y are measures of two angles. How are x and y related if:

30. The angles are vertical angles. **$x = y$**

31. The angles are supplementary. **$x + y = 180°$**

32. An angle has measure 40°. A supplement to this angle has what measure? **140°**

Review

In 33–36, solve.

33. $180 - x = 23$ *(Lesson 7-6)* **157**

34. $90 - y = 31$ *(Lesson 7-6)* **59**

35. $17 - (2 - 6) + A = 5 - 2(5 + 6)$ *(Lessons 5-8, 7-2)* **−38**

36. $4c = 12$ *(Lesson 4-8)* **3**

37. Suppose the sign in the cartoon is true. How much would you pay for a down jacket normally selling for $129.95? *(Lesson 2-6)* **$2.60**

HERMAN®

© 1984 Universal Press Syndicate 8-1

"Salesman of the week gets to go to Hawaii."

Exploration

38. In this lesson you learned about supplementary angles. What are **complementary** angles? **two angles whose measures add to 90°**

312

312

Angles and Parallel Lines

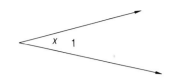

Begin with ∠1 that has measure x. Draw the lines t and m containing its sides. This forms four angles as pictured below. Angle 3, vertical to ∠1, has measure x, and the other angles have measure $180 - x$. For example, if $x = 25$, then the original angle has measure 25°. The other angles either measure 25° or $180° - 25°$, which is 155°.

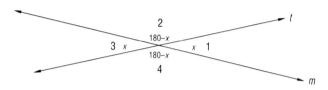

Two lines in a plane are **parallel** if they have no points in common. Now we draw a line n parallel to line m. It intersects line t and helps form angles 5, 6, 7, and 8. Because parallel lines go in the same direction, the measures of the four new angles equal the measures of the four angles that were already there.

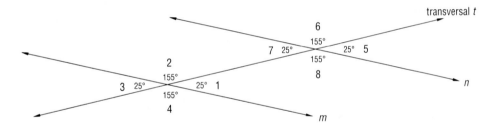

The line that is not parallel is called a **transversal.** The eight angles have names that tell how they are related to the two parallel lines and the transversal.

Name	Angles in above figure	Measures
Corresponding angles	1 and 5, 2 and 6 3 and 7, 4 and 8	equal
Interior angles	1, 2, 7, 8	
Alternate interior angles	2 and 8, 1 and 7	equal
Exterior angles	3, 4, 5, 6	

LESSON 7-8 Angles and Parallel Lines   **313**

LESSON 7-8

RESOURCES
- Lesson Master 7-8
- Quiz on Lessons 7-5 Through 7-8
- Visual for Teaching Aid 41: Angles and Parallel Lines
- Protractors and Rulers or Geometry Template (from *Transition Mathematics Manipulative Kit*)
- *Manipulative Activities Sourcebook*, Activity 12

OBJECTIVES

E Find measures of angles in figures with parallel lines and transversals.
K Know relationships among angles formed by two parallel lines and a transversal.

Reading To practice lis-
tening and visualizing and to
review some vocabulary, you
may wish to tell students to
keep their books closed, listen as you read the first
paragraph aloud, and sketch
the figure described. Then
have the students open their
books, reread the paragraph,
and compare their sketches
with the figure shown. Continue the lesson, carefully
discussing the vocabulary in
the chart on page 313.
Check that students can locate each type of angle in
the diagram.

Warn students not to learn
which angles are corresponding, vertical, and so on, by
using the numbers given to
them as clues. We change
the position of these numbers
to discourage this idea.

Point out that alternate interior, corresponding, interior,
and exterior angles exist
whenever two lines are inter-
sected by a transversal.
However, the relationships
among the angle measures
are as given only when the
two lines are parallel.

You may want to have stu-
dents complete the questions
without a protractor.

In work with angles, it helps to use special symbols to indicate
when angles have the same measure. Use a single arc when two
angles have the same measure. When two other angles are also
equal, use a double arc. And so on.

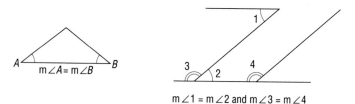

Arrows in the middle of two lines that look parallel mean that
they are parallel. The symbol $\parallel$ means *is parallel to*. If lines *m*
and *n* are parallel, you can write $m \parallel n$. Here is the drawing of
the previous page. The symbols for parallel lines and for angles
of equal measure are included. Also identified are the interior
and exterior angles.

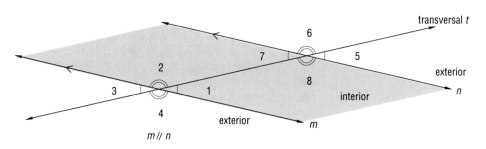

There are also symbols for perpendicularity. In a drawing, the
symbol ⌐ shows that lines or line segments are perpendicular. In
writing, $\perp$ means *is perpendicular to*.

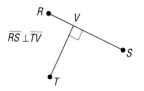

In drawings, put the ⌐ symbol
on only one of the angles at the
point of intersection.

314

Questions

In 1–6, $m \parallel n$. Give the measure of the indicated angle.

1. 1 118°

2. 2 118°

3. 3 62°

4. 4 118°

5. 5 118°

6. 6 62°

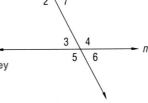

7. In the drawing of Questions 1–6, which line is the transversal? p

8. When are two lines parallel? when they have no points in common

In 9–18, use the drawing below. Lines r and s are parallel.

9. Name all pairs of corresponding angles.
   angles 1 and 6, 4 and 5, 2 and 8, 3 and 7

10. Name the exterior angles.
    angles 1, 4, 7, and 8

11. Name the interior angles.
    angles 2, 3, 5, and 6

12. Name the two pairs of alternate interior angles.
    angles 3 and 5, 2 and 6

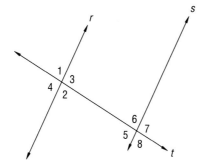

13. Do the corresponding angles 1 and 6 have the same measure?
    Yes

14. Do the alternate interior angles 3 and 5 have the same measure?
    Yes

15. If $m\angle 2 = 84°$, give the measure of all other angles. See margin.

16. If $m\angle 5 = x$, give the measure of all other angles. See margin.

17. If angle 6 is a right angle, which other angles are right angles?
    all of the angles 1 through 8

18. If angle 4 has measure t, which angles have measure $180 - t$?
    angles 1, 2, 6, and 8

LESSON 7-8 Angles and Parallel Lines **315**

Using Manipulatives
Remind students that they can draw two parallel lines by tracing along each edge of a ruler or by using the grid at the top of the Geometry Template. Have students draw a pair of parallel lines and a transversal for each of the conditions given below and then find the measures of all angles formed:
- two parallel lines and a transversal that forms a 50° angle with one of them (50°, 130°);
- two parallel lines and a transversal that is perpendicular to one of the parallel lines (90°);
- two parallel lines and a transversal that forms a 95° angle with one of them (95°, 85°).

Have students generalize their findings. (Students should conclude that alternate interior angles are congruent and corresponding angles are congruent. They also may conclude that if a transversal is perpendicular to one of two parallel lines, it is perpendicular to the other.)

ADDITIONAL EXAMPLES
1. On the board, draw two parallel lines cut by a transversal. Number the eight angles formed, and ask students to name:
a. corresponding angles
b. alternate interior angles
c. exterior angles

2. Give a measure for one of the angles. Ask the students to determine the measures of the other seven angles.

ADDITIONAL ANSWERS
15. $m\angle 1 = m\angle 6 = m\angle 8 = 84°$; $m\angle 3 = m\angle 4 = m\angle 5 = m\angle 7 = 96°$

16. $m\angle 1 = m\angle 2 = m\angle 6 = m\angle 8 = 180 - x$; $m\angle 3 = m\angle 4 = m\angle 5 = m\angle 7 = x$

316

19.

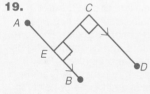

24.

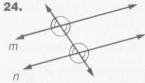

25. m∠1 = 90°, m∠2 = m∠4 = 40°, m∠3 = 140°

26. m∠1 = 105°, m∠3 = 110°, m∠4 = 75°, m∠5 = 35°, m∠6 = 70°

28.

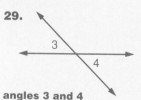

angles 1 and 2

29.

angles 3 and 4

30. sample:

In 19–23, use the drawing below. Consider segments that look perpendicular to be perpendicular. Segments that look parallel are parallel.

19. Copy the drawing and put in the symbols indicating parallel and perpendicular segments.   See margin.

20. What symbol completes the statement? $\overline{AB}$ __?__ $\overline{CE}$.   ⊥

21. What symbol completes the statement? $\overline{AB}$ __?__ $\overline{CD}$ ∥

22. m∠C = __?__ degrees   90°   **23.** m∠AEC = __?__ degrees   90°

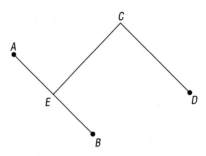

24. At right, $m \parallel n$. Copy the drawing and put in all symbols indicating equal angles.   See margin.

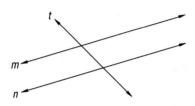

In 25 and 26, find the measure of each numbered angle.   See margin.

25.   **26.**

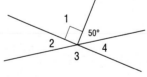   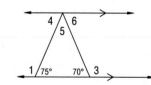

27. Find the sum of the measures of angles 1, 2, 3, and 4 in the drawing below.   360°

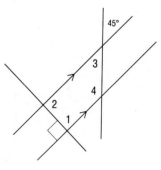

316

In 28–30, draw an accurate example and identify on your drawing:

28. a linear pair   See margin.

29. vertical angles   See margin.

30. supplementary angles that are not a linear pair. *(Lesson 7-7)*
See margin.

31. Three instances of a pattern are given. Describe the pattern using one variable. *(Lesson 4-2)*
$$73 \cdot 1 = 73 \qquad \frac{8}{7} \cdot 1 = \frac{8}{7} \qquad -4.02 \cdot 1 = -4.02$$
$a \cdot 1 = a$

32. Solve: $m - \frac{8}{3} = -3$. *(Lesson 7-4)* $-\frac{1}{3}$

33. Solve for c: $a + b + c = 180$. *(Lesson 5-8)* $c = 180 - a - b$

34. A savings account contains C dollars. Then $100 is withdrawn and $30.45 is deposited. How much is now in the account? *(Lesson 5-5)* $C - 69.55$ dollars

35. A savings account contains C dollars. Then W dollars are withdrawn and D dollars are deposited. How much is now in the account? *(Lesson 5-5)* $C - W + D$

36. Some students think that Question 34 is easier than Question 35. Some students think that Question 35 is easier.
a. Give your opinion. **b.** Give a reason defending your choice.
Answers will vary.

37. The photograph below pictures balusters (the parallel vertical supports) and a banister (the transversal) on stairs. Give two other places where it is common to find parallel lines and transversals.
See margin.

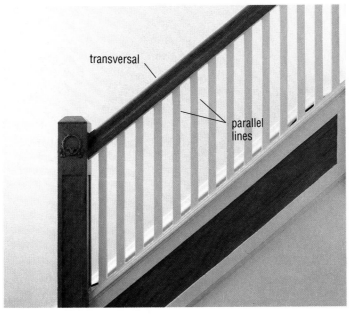

transversal

parallel lines

LESSON 7-8   Angles and Parallel Lines   **317**

FOLLOW-UP

MORE PRACTICE
For more questions on SPUR Objectives, use *Lesson Master 7-8*, shown below.

EVALUATION
A quiz covering Lessons 7-5 through 7-8 is provided in the Teacher's Resource File on page 57.

37. samples: windows, streets, parking lot stripes, guitar strings and the bridge

NAME _____

LESSON **MASTER   7–8**
QUESTIONS ON **SPUR** OBJECTIVES

■ **SKILLS**   *Objective E (See Chapter Review, pages 330–333, for objectives.)*
In 1–7, write the measure of each numbered angle in the figure at right.

1. $m\angle 1 =$ _124°_   2. $m\angle 2 =$ _56°_
3. $m\angle 3 =$ _124°_   4. $m\angle 4 =$ _56°_
5. $m\angle 5 =$ _124°_   6. $m\angle 6 =$ _56°_
7. $m\angle 7 =$ _124°_

8. Write the measure of each numbered angle in the diagram below.

   a. $m\angle 1 =$ _130°_
   b. $m\angle 2 =$ _55°_
   c. $m\angle 3 =$ _125°_
   d. $m\angle 4 =$ _55°_
   e. $m\angle 5 =$ _50°_

■ **PROPERTIES**   *Objective K*
In 9–14, fill in each blank. Refer to the figure at right.

9. According to the diagram, $\overrightarrow{PQ}$ and $\overleftrightarrow{MN}$ are ___parallel___.

10. State the idea in Question 9 using symbols: $\overrightarrow{PQ}$ __∥__ $\overleftrightarrow{MN}$.

11. $m\angle 4 =$ _90°_

12. What other angles have the same measure as $\angle 4$?
    ___all of them___

13. Angle 5 and ___angle 2___ are corresponding angles.

14. Name two pairs of alternate interior angles.
    ___angles 4 and 6; angles 3 and 5___

Transition Mathematics © Scott, Foresman and Company   **63**

LESSON 7-9

RESOURCES
■ Lesson Master 7-9
🖦 Visual for Teaching Aid 42:
   Question 23
■ Protractors and Rulers or
   Geometry Template (from
   *Transition Mathematics
   Manipulative Kit*)

OBJECTIVES

G Find measures of angles
and sides in special
quadrilaterals without
measuring.
L Apply the definitions of
parallelogram, rectangle,
rhombus, and square to
determine properties of
these figures.

LESSON

7-9

Special Quadrilaterals

Here is a drawing of two parallel lines *m* and *n* and a transversal *t*. The pattern of angle measures is shown.

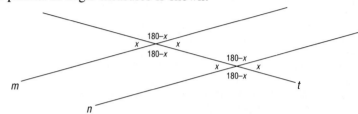

Now we add a fourth line *u* to the picture, parallel to *t*. This forms 8 new angles. Each angle either has measure *x* or 180 − *x*. Also formed is the quadrilateral known as a **parallelogram**. A parallelogram is a quadrilateral with two pairs of parallel sides.

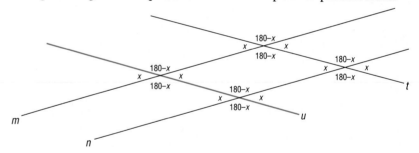

To see the parallelogram better, take it out of the picture. Call it *ABCD*.

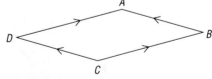

In this parallelogram, $\overline{AB}$ and $\overline{CD}$ are called *opposite sides*. $\overline{AD}$ and $\overline{BC}$ are also opposite sides. Angles *A* and *C* are *opposite angles*. So are angles *B* and *D*. From the parallel lines we know that m∠*A* = m∠*C* and m∠*B* = m∠*D*. So opposite angles have the same measure. Also, opposite sides have the same length. So *AB* = *CD* and *AD* = *BC*. This is true in any parallelogram.

318

In a parallelogram:

Opposite sides have the same length.
Opposite angles have the same measure.

For example, here is a parallelogram with side and angle measures indicated. The angle measures have been rounded to the nearest degree.

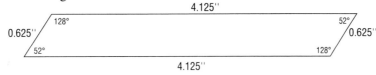

Many common figures are parallelograms. Among these are the rectangle, rhombus, and square. A **rectangle** is a parallelogram with a right angle. All angles of a rectangle have the same measure—they are all right angles. A **rhombus,** or *diamond*, is a parallelogram with all sides the same length. A **square** is a rectangle with the same length and width. Therefore, you can think of a square as a special type of rhombus.

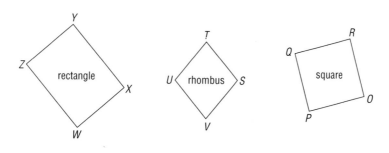

Questions

Covering the Reading

1. If two parallel lines intersect one other line, how many angles are then formed?   8

2. Suppose two parallel lines intersect two other parallel lines.
   a. How many angles are formed?   16
   b. If one of the angles has measure *x*, then all angles have either measure __?__ or __?__.   x, 180 − x
   c. If one of the angles has measure 30°, then all angles have either measure __?__ or __?__.   30° or 150°

In 3 and 4, refer to the quadrilaterals drawn above.
   a. Measure all sides to the nearest millimeter (tenth of a centimeter).
   b. Measure all angles to the nearest degree.   See margin.

3. rhombus *VUTS*   4. square *RQPO*

TEACHING NOTES

To help students understand relationships among special quadrilaterals, you may wish to draw a diagram showing the hierarchy:

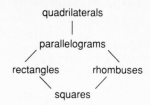

Explain that in this diagram, if a particular figure (such as a rhombus) has a property (such as all sides have equal length), then all figures connected to that figure and below it (squares) have that property. Point out that the reverse is not always true. A square has the properties of a rhombus, but a rhombus does not always have the properties of a square (such as all right angles).

ADDITIONAL EXAMPLES
Ask the students to identify everyday items shaped like quadrilaterals. If students cannot find or recall examples of the special quadrilaterals in this lesson, ask volunteers to draw those figures on the board. In each case, ask students to explain why the example is a particular figure.

ADDITIONAL ANSWERS
3. a. *TU = TS = SV = UV =* **15 mm;**
b. m∠U = m∠S ≈ 100°, m∠T = m∠V ≈ 80°

4. a. *OP = RO = QR =* **18 mm;**
b. All angles are right angles.

NOTES ON QUESTIONS
Question 10: Note that
more information is given
than is needed.

Questions 12–15:
These clarify the classification of quadrilaterals and can
form the basis for a discussion of the relationships
among these figures.

Making Connections for
Questions 20 and 21:
These use the problem-
solving strategy of *determin-*
ing whether there is enough
information before attempting
to find an answer. *Drawing a*
picture will also be helpful.
Both strategies were dis-
cussed in Chapter 6.

Question 22a: Many noncongruent figures can be
drawn. You can use this
question to provide insights
about similar figures by drawing several possibilties on
the board.

Error Analysis for
Question 23: Some students may not even try this
problem, since it looks complicated. Suggest that they
copy the drawing onto a
sheet of paper and then note
all the given information on
the drawing. They can write
an angle measure inside the
angle as soon as they know
it. Students should ask themselves why each piece of information is valuable in solving the problem.

Question 24: Relate this
to measures of supplemen-
tary angles.

22.

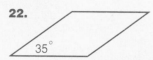

35°

31. a. from 1950 to 1960,
103,932; from 1960 to 1970,
-23,952; from 1970 to 1980,
-81,160; **b.** -1180; **c.** From
1950 to 1980, the population
decreased by 1180 people.

320

Applying the Mathematics

In 5–10, refer to parallelogram *MNPQ*.

5. Name a pair of opposite sides.
   $\overline{MN}$ and $\overline{QP}$, or $\overline{MQ}$ and $\overline{NP}$
6. Name a pair of opposite angles.
   ∠*M* and ∠*P*, or ∠*Q* and ∠*N*
7. ∠*N* and __?__ have the same measure.
   ∠*Q*
8. $\overline{PQ}$ and __?__ have the same length.
   $\overline{MN}$
9. If m∠*Q* = 70°, then m∠*M* = __?__.
   110°
10. If *PQ* = 5 and *PN* = 2.8, then *MN* = __?__.
    5

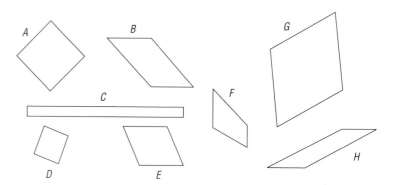

11. What must a parallelogram have in order to be a rhombus?
    all sides equal in length

In 12–15, consider the figures *A* through *H*.

12. Which seem to be rectangles? **A, C, D**

13. Which seem to be rhombuses? **A, D, E, G**

14. Which seem to be squares? **A, D**

15. Which seem to be parallelograms? **A, B, C, D, E, G, H**

In 16–19, consider quadrilaterals, parallelograms, rhombuses,
rectangles, and squares.

16. Which have all four sides equal in length?
    rhombuses and squares
17. Which have all four angles equal in measure?
    rectangles and squares
18. Which have both pairs of opposite angles equal in measure?
    parallelograms, rhombuses, rectangles, and squares
19. Which have both pairs of opposite sides equal in length?
    parallelograms, rhombuses, rectangles, and squares

In 20 and 21, give the perimeter of each figure.

20. a rhombus with one side having length 10   **40**

21. a parallelogram with one side having length 10
    not enough information

320

22. One angle of a rhombus has measure 35°.
   a. Draw such a rhombus. **See margin.**
   b. What are the measures of its other angles? **35° or 145°**

23. *ABCD* and *AEFG* are parallelograms and $\overline{AB}$ and $\overline{AE}$ are perpendicular. m∠*ABC* = 147°. *G*, *A*, *D*, and *H* are on the same line. Find the measure of: **a.** ∠*BAG*; **b.** ∠*GAE*; **c.** ∠*AGF*; **d.** ∠*CDH*.
a. 147°; b. 57°; c. 123°; d. 33°

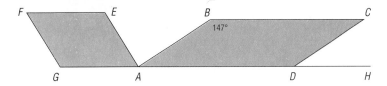

24. If *x* + *y* = 180, then *y* = __?__. *(Lesson 7-7)*   **180 − x**

In 25–29, use the figure at left. *(Lesson 7-7)*

25. Angles *CBG* and __?__ form a linear pair.   **ABG**

26. Angles *ABD* and __?__ are vertical angles.   **CBF**

27. If m∠*FBC* = 30°: **a.** What other angle measures can be found? **b.** Find them.   **m∠DBA = 30°; m∠CBD = m∠FBA = 150°**

28. If m∠*GBA* = 126°: **a.** What other angle measures can be found? **b.** Find them.   **m∠GBC = 54°**

29. If m∠*GBF* = 90°, then $\overline{BG}$ __?__ $\overline{DF}$.   **⊥**

30. Solve: **a.** *y* − 4 = 20; *(Lesson 7-4)* **b.** 4 − *x* = 20. *(Lesson 7-6)*
   24   **−16**

31. Here are census figures for Milwaukee, Wisconsin.

1950	637,392
1960	741,324
1970	717,372
1980	636,212
1990	599,380

   a. Calculate the change from each census to the next. You should get one positive and three negative numbers.
   b. Add the four changes you found in part **a.**
   c. What does the sum in part **b** mean? *(Lesson 7-3)* **See margin.**
a. from 1950 to 1960, 103,932; from 1960 to 1970, −23,952; from 1970 to 1980, −81,160; from 1980 to 1990, −36,832
b. −38,012
c. From 1950 to 1990, the population decreased by 38,012 people.

32. Rectangles are easy to find. Most windows, chalkboards, and doors are shaped like rectangles. Give an everyday example of something shaped like: **a.** a square; **b.** a parallelogram that is not a rectangle; **c.** a rhombus that is not a square. **See margin.**

Review

Exploration

FOLLOW-UP

MORE PRACTICE
For more questions on SPUR Objectives, use *Lesson Master 7-9*, shown below.

EXTENSION
Using Manipulatives
Have students draw a parallelogram, a rectangle, a rhombus, and a square. (Students may use the Geometry Template, if available.) Ask students to draw the diagonals of each figure and answer the following: Do the diagonals have equal lengths? Do they bisect each other? Are they perpendicular to each other? (parallelogram: diagonals bisect each other; rectangle: diagonals bisect each other and have equal lengths; rhombus: diagonals bisect each other and are perpendicular; square: diagonals bisect each other, have equal lengths, and are perpendicular to each other.)

32. samples: a. floor tiles; b. spaces in an expanding "baby gate"; c. diamond symbol in a deck of cards

LESSON

7-10

The Triangle-Sum Property

Kayo has been studying triangles too. Read this cartoon to see what he has discovered.

322

Since the three angles together formed a straight angle, Kayo can conclude that the sum of the three angles in a triangle is 180°. You can test this for yourself. Measure the angles of triangle *QUT* drawn below and calculate their sum. It should be very close to 180°.

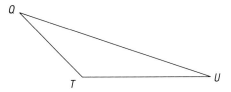

We call this famous property of triangles the **Triangle-Sum Property.**

Triangle-Sum Property:

In any triangle, the sum of the measures of the angles is 180°.

Example 1   Suppose two angles of a triangle have measures 57° and 85°. What is the measure of the third angle?

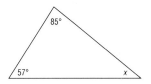

Solution   First draw a picture. Then let *x* be the measure of the third angle. Using the Triangle-Sum Property,

$$57° + 85° + x = 180°$$
$$142 \quad + x = 180$$

You know how to solve this equation.
$$-142 + 142 + x = -142 + 180$$
$$x = 38$$

So the third angle has measure 38°.

Check   Add the measures. Does 38 + 57 + 85 = 180? Yes.

You have now studied many different ways to find measures of angles. The next examples use some of these ways.

Students should actually measure the angles of at least one triangle. Some students can measure the triangle on page 323 (top); others can measure the four triangles formed by drawing diagonal $\overline{AQ}$ or $\overline{UD}$ in quadrilateral QUAD on page 327. Alternatively, each student can draw his or her own triangles.

Using Manipulatives
You may also want to do the experiment described in the Moon Mullins cartoon.

Many students will do one problem like **Example 1**, see the pattern, and not necessarily solve equations to do similar problems. They will just add the measures of the two given angles and then subtract the sum from 180°. There is nothing wrong with this strategy.

Consider **Example 3** in detail. Demonstrate how much easier the problem becomes if the figure is copied even if imperfectly and information is written on the picture as it is known.

1.

35°
55°
1

2.

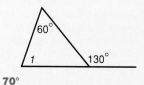

60°
1   130°
70°

3.

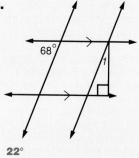

68°
1
22°

NOTES ON QUESTIONS
Question 10: Encourage students to find the angle measures in any order they wish, not necessarily the numerical order on the diagram.

Example 2 Find the measure of angle *EZY* in the drawing at right.

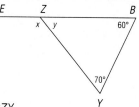

Solution Let *y* be the measure of ∠*BZY* and *x* be the measure of ∠*EZY*.
Using the Triangle-Sum Property,

$$60° + 70° + y = 180°.$$

Simplify. $130 + y = 180$
Solve for *y*. $-130 + 130 + y = -130 + 180$
So $y = 50$

Now notice that angles *EZY* and *BZY* form a linear pair.

This means that $x + y = 180°$
Substituting $x + 50 = 180$
Solve for *x*. $x = 130$

So m∠*EZY* = 130°.

Example 3 Use the information given in the drawing. Find m∠9.

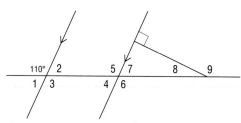

110° 2 5 7 8 9
1 3 4 6

Solution The drawing is complicated. Examine it carefully. You may wish to make an identical drawing and write in angle measures as they are found.

The arrows indicate that two of the lines are parallel. Angle 5 is a corresponding angle with the 110° angle. So m∠5 = 110°. ∠7 forms a linear pair with ∠5, so they are supplementary. Thus m∠7 = 70°.

The triangle has a 90° angle caused by the perpendicular lines. But it also has ∠7, a 70° angle. The Triangle-Sum Property says that the measures of the three angles add to 180°. This forces m∠8 to be 20°.

Finally, ∠9 is a linear pair with ∠8, so m∠9 = 160°.

324

Covering the Reading

1. The triangle drawn at the top of page 323 has m∠U = 18°, m∠T = 135°, and m∠Q = 27°. The sum of these measures is 180°.
   Multiple choice Which is true? **(b)**
   (a) In some but not all triangles the sum of the measures of the angles is 180°.
   (b) In all triangles the sum of the measures of the angles is 180°.
   (c) The sum of the measures of the angles of a triangle can be any number from 180° to 360°.

2. Why did the corners of the triangles in the cartoon fit together to make a straight line? **because of the Triangle-Sum Property**

3. What is the Triangle-Sum Property?
   In any triangle, the sum of the measures of the angles is 180°.

In 4–7, two angles of a triangle have the given measures. Find the measure of the third angle.

4. 30°, 60° **90°**

5. 117°, 62° **1°**

6. 1°, 2° **177°**

7. $x°$, $140° - x°$ **40°**

Applying the Mathematics

8. What is the sum of the measures of the four angles of a rectangle?
   360°

9. Explain why a triangle cannot have two obtuse angles.
   See margin.

10. Use the drawing below. Find the measures of angles 1 through 8.
    See margin.

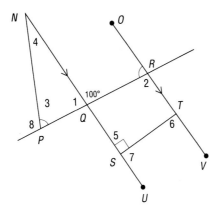

11. In a triangle with a right angle, what is the sum of the measures of the other two angles? **90°**

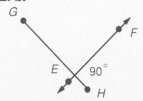

12. In the figure below, $\overline{BA} \perp \overline{AC}$. Angle *BAC* is bisected (split into two equal parts) by $\overline{AD}$. m∠*B* = 60°.
Find the measures of angles 1 and 2.   m∠1 = 75°, m∠2 = 105°

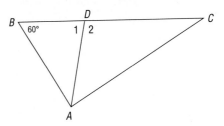

13. *Multiple choice*   Two angles of a triangle have measures *x* and *y*. The third angle must have what measure?   **(d)**
(a) $180 - x + y$ (b) $180 + x + y$
(c) $180 + x - y$ (d) $180 - x - y$

14. Find m∠*ABC*.   74° **15.** Find m∠*XYZ*.   146°

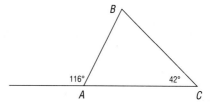 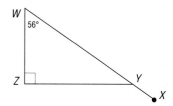

16. In the figure below, $\overline{EH}$ and $\overline{GI}$ intersect at *F*. Find the measure of as many angles as you can.   **See margin.**

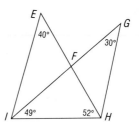

In 17–20, use the drawing at left. What is the meaning of each symbol? *(Lesson 7-8)*

17. the arrows on segments $\overline{AD}$ and $\overline{BC}$ $\overline{AD}$ and $\overline{BC}$ are parallel.

18. the sign that looks like an *L* by angle *A*
$\overline{AB}$ and $\overline{AD}$ are perpendicular.

19. the single arcs by points *B* and *C*   m∠*B* = m∠*BCD*

20. the double arcs by points *C* and *D*
The angles have the same measure.

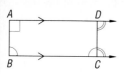

326

In 21 and 22: **a.** translate into English; **b.** draw a picture. *(Lesson 7-8)*

21. $\overline{AB} \parallel \overrightarrow{CD}$ a. Line segment *AB* is parallel to ray *CD*. b. See margin.

22. $\overleftrightarrow{EF} \perp \overline{GH}$
   a. Line *EF* is perpendicular to line segment *GH*. b. See margin.

23. a. *True or false?*   A square is a special type of rectangle.   **True**
   b. *True or false?*   A square is a special type of rhombus.
   (Lesson 7-9)   **True**

24. Four people went to a health club. Here are their weights on
   February 1 and March 1. **a.** How much did each person's
   weight change? **b.** Who gained the most? **c.** Who lost the most?
   (Lesson 7-3)   **a. See margin. b. Marlene and Daniel; c. Evelyn**

	February 1	**March 1**
Richard	65.3 kg	62.8 kg
Marlene	53.4 kg	54.3 kg
Evelyn	58.6 kg	55.1 kg
Daniel	71.1 kg	72.0 kg

25. Evaluate $a - b + c - d$ when $a = 0$, $b = $ -10, $c = $ -100, and
   $d = $ -1000. *(Lesson 7-2)*   **910**

26. Evaluate $a - b + c - d$ when $a = $ -43, $b = 2$, $c = 5$, and
   $d = 11$. *(Lesson 7-2)*   **-51**

27. Solve: -5 = 15.4 − *x*. *(Lesson 7-6)*   **20.4**

28. Solve: *x* − 3 = -3. *(Lesson 7-4)*   **0**

Exploration

29. Here is a quadrilateral that is not a parallelogram. **a.** Measure the
   four angles. **b.** What is the sum of the measures?
   See margin.

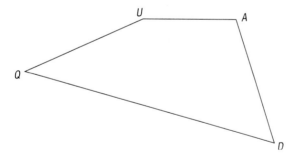

30. *Multiple choice*   The sum of the measures of the angles of an
   n-gon is: **(c)**
   (a) $180n$ (b) $180(n + 1)$
   (c) $180(n - 2)$ (d) $180(n + 3)$

FOLLOW-UP

MORE PRACTICE
For more questions on SPUR
Objectives, use *Lesson Mas-
ter 7-10*, shown below.

EXTENSION
You might want to outline the
proof of the Triangle-Sum
Property involving parallel
lines. Students have all the
required background except
the reason you can draw the
parallel line through *A* to
start the process.

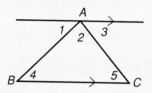

Step 1: m∠1 + m∠2 + m∠3
= 180°
(angle addition and linear
pair)
Step 2: m∠4 = m∠1 and
m∠5 = m∠3
(alternate interior angles)
Step 3: m∠4 + m∠2 + m∠5
= 180°
(substitution)

Summary

Subtraction arises from take-away, slide, or comparison situations. In take-away situations, $x - y$ stands for the amount left after y has been taken away from x. In the linear pair pictured here, $m \angle BDA$ can be thought of as the amount left after x has been taken from 180°. So $m \angle BDA = 180 - x$. Measures of linear pairs add to 180°.

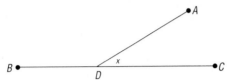

In slide situations, $x - y$ is the result after x has been decreased by y. Earlier this was described as an addition slide situation $x + -y$.
$x - y = x + -y$ always.

In comparison situations, $x - y$ is how much more x is than y. Special kinds of comparison are change and error. The word *difference* for the answer to a subtraction problem comes from this kind of subtraction.

All of these situations can lead to equations of the form $x - a = b$ or $a - x = b$.

By extending $\overline{AD}$ at left, vertical angles are formed. Then adding a line parallel to $\overline{BC}$ forms eight angles. Adding a line parallel to $\overline{AD}$ forms a parallelogram. All of the angles formed have measures x or $180 - x$. Special kinds of parallelograms are rectangles, rhombuses, and squares, so these ideas have many uses.

Vocabulary

You should be able to give a general description and a specific example for each of the following ideas.

Lesson 7-1
Take-Away Model for Subtraction

Lesson 7-2
Slide Model for Subtraction
Add-Opp Property of Subtraction

Lesson 7-3
minuend, subtrahend, difference
Comparison Model for Subtraction

Lesson 7-5
equivalent sentences
equivalent formulas

Lesson 7-7
straight angle, opposite rays
linear pair, vertical angles
supplementary angles

Lesson 7-8
parallel lines, transversal
corresponding angles
interior angles
alternate interior angles
exterior angles
$\parallel$, $\perp$
symbols in figures for parallel, perpendicular, and angles of equal measure

Lesson 7-9
parallelogram
rectangle, rhombus, square

Lesson 7-10
Triangle-Sum Property

328

Progress Self-Test

See margin for answers not shown below.

Take this test as you would take a test in class. Then check your work with the solutions in the selected Answers section in the back of the book.

1. Picture the subtraction $-6 - 22$ on a number line and give the result.

2. Simplify $45 - 110$. **-65**

3. Evaluate $5 - x + 2 - y$ when $x = 13$ and $y = -11$. **5**

4. Solve: $y - 14 = -24$ **y = -10**

5. Solve: $-50 = 37 - x$ **x = 87**

6. Solve: $g - 3.2 = -2$ **1.2**

7. Solve for a: $c - a = b$
c + -b = a

In 8 and 9, use the figure below. $m\angle ABD = 25°$.

8. $m\angle ABE = \underline{\ ?\ }°$
155

9. $m\angle CBD = \underline{\ ?\ }°$
65

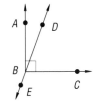

In 10–12, use the figure below. $m \parallel n$

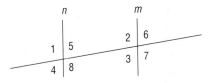

10. If $m\angle 5 = 74°$, then $m\angle 7 = \underline{\ ?\ }°$. **106**

11. Which angles have measures equal to the measure of angle 6? **angles 5, 3, and 4**

12. Which angles are supplementary to angle 5?

13. Why can't a triangle have three right angles?

14. Two angles of a triangle have measures 55° and 4°. What is the measure of the third angle? **121°**

15. What other angle in the figure below has the same measure as angle E? **∠CBE**

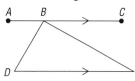

16. In parallelogram $WXYZ$ (not drawn), if $m\angle W = 50°$, what is $m\angle X$? **130°**

17. Of parallelograms, rectangles, rhombuses, and quadrilaterals, which have all sides equal in length? **rhombuses**

18. Convert all subtractions to additions:
$x - y - -5$. **x + -y + 5**

19. Which formula is not equivalent to the others? **(c)**
(a) $180 = x + y$ (b) $180 - y = x$
(c) $x - y = 180$ (d) $180 - x = y$

20. Valleyview H. S. scored V points against Newtown H. S. Newtown scored N points and lost by L points. How are V, N, and L related? **V − N = L, or N + L = V**

21. A piece 0.4 meters long was cut from a board 5 meters long. What was the length of the board that remained? **4.6 m**

22. Ray is Z inches tall. Fay is 67 inches tall. How much taller is Ray than Fay?
Z − 67 in.

After dropping 7°, the temperature is now -3°. Use this information in 23 and 24.

23. Solving what equation will tell what the temperature was? **x° − 7° = -3°**

24. Solve that equation. **x = 4°**

25. Below are two squares. The outer square is 8 meters on a side. The inner square is 4 meters on a side. Find the area of the shaded region.
48 square meters

PROGRESS SELF-TEST

The Progress Self-Test provides opportunity for feedback and correction; the Chapter Review provides additional opportunities for practice.

We cannot overemphasize the importance of these end-of-chapter materials. It is at this point that the material "gels" for many students, allowing them to solidify skills and understanding. In general, student performance should be markedly improved after these pages.

USING THE PROGRESS SELF-TEST
Assign the Progress Self-Test as a one-night assignment. Worked-out *solutions* for all questions are in the Selected Answers section of the student book. Encourage students to take the Progress Self-Test honestly, grade themselves, and then be prepared to discuss the test in class.

Advise students to pay special attention to those Chapter Review questions which correspond to questions missed on the Progress Self-Test. A chart in the student text keys the Progress Self-Test questions to the lettered SPUR Objectives in the Chapter Review or to the Vocabulary. It also keys the questions to the corresponding lessons where the material is covered.

ADDITIONAL ANSWERS
1. Students' number lines should show an answer of -28.

12. Angles 1, 8, 2, and 7

13. The sum of the measures of the angles would be more than 180°.

Chapter Review

Questions on **SPUR** Objectives

SPUR stands for Skills, Properties, Uses, and Representations. The Chapter Review questions are grouped according to the SPUR Objectives for this chapter.

SKILLS deal with the procedures used to get answers.

Objective A: *Subtract any numbers written as decimals. (Lesson 7-2)*

1. Simplify $40 - 360$.   -320
2. Simplify $-4 - -12$.   8
3. Evaluate $x - y - z$ when $x = 10.5$, $y = 3.8$, and $z = -7$.   13.7
4. Evaluate $a - (b - c)$ when $a = -2$, $b = -3$, and $c = 4$.   5

Objective B: *Solve sentences of the form $x - a = b$. (Lesson 7-4)*

5. Solve: $x - 64 = 8$.   72
6. Solve: $6 = y - \frac{1}{5}$.   6.2 or $6\frac{1}{5}$
7. Solve: $-4.2 = V - 3$.   -7.2
8. Solve: $2 + m - 5 = 4$.   7
9. Solve for c: $e = c - 45$.   c = e + 45

Objective C: *Solve sentences of the form $a - x = b$. (Lesson 7-6)*

10. Solve: $200 - b = 3$.   197
11. Solve: $-28 = 28 - z$.   56
12. Solve: $223 - x = 215$.   8
13. Solve: $\frac{4}{9} - y = \frac{5}{18}$. $\frac{1}{6}$
14. Solve for y: $180 - y = x$.   y = 180 − x

Objective D: *Find measures of angles in figures with linear pairs, vertical angles, or perpendicular lines. (Lesson 7-7)*

In 15–18, use the figure below to determine the measures.

15. $m\angle 1 = \underline{\ ?\ }$ degrees   90

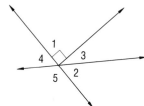

16. If $m\angle 2 = 60°$, then $m\angle 4 = \underline{\ ?\ }$.   60°
17. If $m\angle 4 = x°$, $m\angle 5 = \underline{\ ?\ }$.   180° − x°
18. If $m\angle 5 = 125°$, then $m\angle 3 = \underline{\ ?\ }$.   35°

Objective E: *Find measures of angles in figures with parallel lines and transversals. (Lesson 7-8)*

In 19–22, use the figure below.

19. Which angles have the same measure as $\angle 6$?   7, 1, and 3

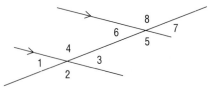

20. If $m\angle 3 = 43°$, then $m\angle 7 = \underline{\ ?\ }°$.   43
21. If $m\angle 2 = y°$, then $m\angle 7 = \underline{\ ?\ }°$.   180° − y°
22. If $m\angle 8 = 135°$, then $m\angle 1 = \underline{\ ?\ }°$.   45

Objective F: *Use the Triangle-Sum Property to find measures of angles. (Lesson 7-10)*

23. Two angles of a triangle have measures 118° and 24°. What is the measure of the third angle?   **38°**

24. Two angles of a triangle have measures $y°$ and $150° - y°$. What is the measure of the third angle?   **30°**

25. If $\overline{AB} \perp \overline{BC}$ and m∠ECF = 40°, find m∠A.   **50°**

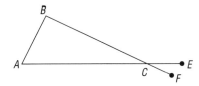

26. Use the figure for Question 25. If $\overline{AB} \perp \overline{BC}$ and m∠A = 72°, find m∠ECB.   **162°**

Objective G: *Find measures of angles and sides in special quadrilaterals without measuring. (Lesson 7-9)*

27. A rhombus has one side of length 2.5 cm. Is this enough to find its perimeter?

28. Each angle of a rectangle has measure __?__.   **90°**

29. In parallelogram ABCD, if DC = 4 and BC = 6, find AB.   **4**

30. In parallelogram ABCD, if m∠D = 105°, find m∠A.   **75°**

27. Yes, 10 cm.

PROPERTIES deal with the principles behind the mathematics.

Objective H: *Apply the properties of subtraction. (Lessons 7-2, 7-3)*

31. According to the Add-Opp Property, $7 - 3 = 7 +$ __?__ .   **-3**

32. If $967 - 432 = 535$, then $432 - 967 =$ __?__ .   **-535**

Objective I: *Distinguish equivalent from non-equivalent sentences and formulas. (Lesson 7-5)*

33. Which sentence is not equivalent to the others?   **a + c = b**
$a - c = b$ $a - b = c$ $a + c = b$
$b + c = a$

34. Which sentence is not equivalent to the others?   **3 − 8 = x**
$x - 8 = 3$ $3 - 8 = x$ $-x + 3 = -8$
$-8 + x = 3$

Objective J: *Know relationships among angles formed by intersecting lines. (Lesson 7-7)*

35. Angles 1 and 2 form a linear pair. If m∠1 = 40°, what is m∠2?   **140°**

36. Angles 1 and 2 are vertical angles. If m∠1 = 40°, what is m∠2?   **40°**

37. Angles 1 and 2 are supplementary. If m∠1 = $x°$, what is m∠2?   **180° − x°**

Objective K: *Know relationships among angles formed by two parallel lines and a transversal. (Lesson 7-8)*

In 38–41, use the figure below.

38. Angles 2 and __?__ are corresponding angles.   **4**

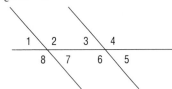

39. Name the exterior angles.   **1, 8, 4, and 5**

40. Angles 3 and __?__ are alternate interior angles.   **7**

41. Name four angles supplementary to angle 8.   **1, 7, 5, and 3**

58.

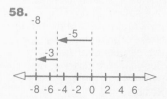

59.

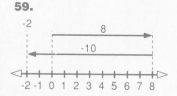

■ **Objective L:** *Apply the definitions of parallelogram, rectangle, rhombus, and square to determine properties of these figures. (Lesson 7-9)*

In 42–45, consider parallelograms, rectangles, rhombuses, and squares.

42. In which of these figures are all sides equal in length? **rhombuses and squares**

43. In which of these figures are all angles equal in measure? **rectangles and squares**

44. In which of these figures are both pairs of opposite sides equal in length? **all**

45. In which of these figures are both pairs of opposite angles equal in measure? **all**

■ **Objective M:** *Explain the consequences of the Triangle-Sum Property. (Lesson 7-10)*

46. Why can't a triangle have two 100° angles? **See margin.**

47. Can a triangle have three acute angles? Explain your answer. **See margin.**

USES deal with applications of mathematics in real situations.

■ **Objective N:** *Use the Take-Away Model for Subtraction to form sentences involving subtraction. (Lessons 7-1, 7-4, 7-6)*

48. A one-hour TV program allows $9\frac{1}{2}$ minutes for commercials. How much time is there for the program itself? **50.5 minutes**

49. A 2000 square-foot house was built on a lot of A square feet. Landscaping used the remaining 3500 square feet. How big was the original lot? **5500 square feet**

50. Anne must keep $100 in a bank account. The account had x dollars in it. Then Anne withdrew y dollars. There was just enough left in the account. How are x, y, and 100 related? **$x - y = 100$**

51. A, B, C, D, and E are points in order on a line. If $AE = 50$, $BC = 12$, and $CE = 17$, what is AB? **21**

■ **Objective O:** *Use the Slide Model for Subtraction to form sentences involving subtraction. (Lesson 7-2)*

52. O'Hare airport in Chicago is often 5°F colder than downtown Chicago. Suppose the record low for a day is -13°F and was recorded downtown. What was the possible temperature at O'Hare? **-18°F**

53. The famous actor Henry Fonda died in 1982 at the age of 77. Knowing only this information, in what two years might he have been born? **1905 or 1904**

54. *Multiple choice*   A person weighs 70 kg and goes on a diet, losing x kg. The resulting weight is y kg. Then $y =$
(a) $x - 70$ (b) $70 - x$ **(b)**
(c) $x - -70$ (d) $-70 - x$

Objective P: *Use the Comparison Model for Subtraction to form sentences involving subtraction.* *(Lesson 7-3)*

55. The average number of 16- to 19-year-olds working in 1960 was about 4.1 million. By 1987 the number had increased to about 6.6 million. About how many more teen-agers were working in 1987 than in 1960? **2.5 million**

56. Yvette believes that her team will win its next game by 12 points. But they lose by 1 point. How far off was Yvette?

57. An airline fare of *F* dollars is reduced by $*R*. The lower fare is *L* dollars. How are *F*, *R*, and *L* related? $F - R = L$

56. **13 points too high**

REPRESENTATIONS deal with pictures, graphs, or objects that illustrate concepts.

Objective Q: *Picture subtraction of positive and negative numbers on a number line.* *(Lesson 7-2)*

58. Picture the subtraction -5 − 3 on a number line and give the result. **-8**
See margin.

59. Picture the subtraction 8 − 10 on a number line and give the result. **-2**
See margin.

ASSIGNMENT RECOMMENDATION
We strongly recommend that you assign Lesson 8-1, both reading and some questions, for homework the evening of the test. It gives students work to do after they have completed the test and keeps the class moving.

CHAPTER 8 ■ DISPLAYS

DAILY PACING CHART ■ CHAPTER 8

Students in the Full Course should complete the entire text by the end of the year. Students in the Minimal Course spend more time when there are quizzes and more time on the Chapter Review. Therefore, these students may not complete all of the chapters in the text.

DAY	MINIMAL COURSE	FULL COURSE
1	8-1	8-1
2	8-2	8-2
3	8-3	8-3
4	Quiz (TRF); 8-4	Quiz (TRF); 8-4
5	8-5	8-5
6	8-6	8-6
7	Quiz (TRF); 8-7	Quiz (TRF); 8-7
8	8-8	8-8
9	Progress Self-Test	Progress Self-Test
10	Chapter Review	Chapter Review
11	Chapter Review	Chapter Test (TRF)
12	Chapter Test (TRF)	

TESTING OPTIONS
■ Quiz on Lessons 8-1 Through 8-3　■ Chapter 8 Test, Form A　■ Chapter 8 Test, Cumulative Form
■ Quiz on Lessons 8-4 Through 8-6　■ Chapter 8 Test, Form B

A Quiz and Test Writer is available for generating additional questions, additional quizzes, or additional forms of the Chapter Test.

PROVIDING FOR INDIVIDUAL DIFFERENCES
The student text is written for the *average* student. The program, however, can be adapted for both less capable and more capable students.

A blackline master (in the Teacher's Resource File) is provided for each lesson for those students who need more practice. The Teacher's Edition frequently provides an Error Analysis feature to provide additional instructional strategies.

For students who require additional challenge, Extension activities are regularly provided in the Teacher's Edition.

OBJECTIVES ■ CHAPTER 8

Students should master the chapter objectives by the time they complete the chapter. To ensure objective mastery, there is continual review built into each set of lesson questions. After students complete the chapter lessons, they assess their mastery on the Progress Self-Test. Then they do the Chapter Review and pay special attention to those questions that match the objectives missed on the Progress Self-Test. Students can get extra practice on these objectives by using the master for each lesson in the Teacher's Resource File.

OBJECTIVES FOR CHAPTER 8 (Organized into the SPUR categories—Skills, Properties, Uses, and Representations)	Progress Self-Test Questions	Chapter Review Questions	Teacher's Resource File	
			Lesson Master*	Chapter Test Forms A and B
SKILLS				
A: Draw the reflection image of a figure over a line.	15	1–4	8-6	11
B: Given a figure, identify its symmetry lines.	12, 13, 14	5–8	8-7	12, 13, 14, 15
C: Make a tessellation using a given figure as a fundamental region.	16	9, 10	8-8	21, 22
PROPERTIES				
D: Apply the relationships between a preimage, a reflecting line, and the reflection image.	18	11, 12	8-6	16
E: Apply the definition of congruence as it relates to translations, rotations, and reflections.	20	13, 14	8-5	20
USES				
F: Interpret bar graphs.	1, 2, 3	15–18	8-1	7
G: Display numerical information in a bar graph.	4	19–22	8-1	6
H: Interpret coordinate graphs.	11	23–26	8-2	2, 3, 4, 5
I: Display information in a coordinate graph.	17	27, 28	8-2	10
J: Know reasons for having graphs.	19	29	8-4	1
REPRESENTATIONS				
K: Plot and name points on a coordinate graph.	5, 6, 10	30–33	8-2	8, 18
L: Graph equations for lines of the form $x + y = k$ or $x - y = k$.	7, 9	34–37	8-3	9
M: Interpret reflections or translations on a coordinate graph.	8	38–41	8-5, 8-6	17, 19

*The Lesson Masters are numbered to match the lessons.

334B

OVERVIEW ■ CHAPTER 8

This chapter has two roughly equal themes. The first theme is the display of numerical information: bar graphs (Lesson 8-1), coordinates (Lesson 8-2), graphs of linear equations of the form $x + y = a$ or $x - y = a$ (Lesson 8-3), and the reasons for graphs (Lesson 8-4).

The second theme is that of transformations. We examine two types of transformations: translations (Lesson 8-5) and reflections (Lesson 8-6). Reflections are very much related to line symmetry (Lesson 8-7). Translations are inti-mately associated with tessellations, repeating patterns that cover the plane (Lesson 8-8).

The topics in this chapter are both important and timely. Some understanding of basic statistical ideas is required for intelligent citizenship and understanding of what is going on in the world. Bar graphs and coordinate graphs appear in daily newspapers and magazines. In mathematical terms, graphs of solutions to equations are fundamental in understanding relationships and underlie much of advanced mathematics. Transformations play a large part in computer graphics; symmetry and tessellations are common in both nature and art.

Students will need graph paper for work in this and the next three chapters. We have provided a Teaching Aid with blank grids if you wish to make copies for each student. However, we recommend that you remind students to bring their own graph paper to class and that you keep a supply of graph paper on hand.

PERSPECTIVES ■ CHAPTER 8

The Perspectives provide the rationale for the inclusion of topics or approaches, provide mathematical background, and make connections within UCSMP.

8-1

BAR GRAPHS

Most students find bar graphs easy to read but difficult to construct. Many students will make bars whose lengths bear little relation to any uniform scale. You may ask students to use a ruler or graph paper when making a bar graph.

Students should put enough information in the bar graph so that a reader would know what is being graphed. However, allow students some flexibility in their choice of the interval (distance between tick marks) on the scale. Notice the difference between the meaning of the words *interval* and *unit* as we use them. The unit of the bar graph on page 337 is 1 person; the interval is 100,000 people. Don't belabor the language, but it is helpful to students to be consistent.

The circle graph on page 335 illustrates one kind of display. Circle graphs are discussed as an application involving division and properties of circles in Chapter 13.

8-2

COORDINATE GRAPHS

Making and interpreting coordinate graphs can become quite natural for students, particularly if the graphs are introduced in a familiar context (such as the temperature idea used in this lesson). In fact, some science programs introduce coordinate graphs as early as second grade.

In this text, we view letters and ordered pairs as two different names for the same thing. To encourage flexibility, we speak of the point (2, 3) and write $A = (2, 3)$. In geometry, one uses letters to denote points; in algebra, coordinates.

8-3

GRAPHING EQUATIONS

The phrase *graphing an equation* is shorthand for "graphing all points whose coordinates satisfy the equation." This phrase is universally used in mathematical discourse.

In this lesson, all the lines graphed have equations equivalent to $x + y = k$ or $x - y = k$. If the scales on the axes are the same, then the graphs of these lines are all tilted 45° to the horizontal.

8-4

WHY GRAPH?

Lessons that tell students why they are studying things are as valuable as other lessons. If you know why something is important, you will probably want to learn more about it. This lesson is meant to encourage interest and provide perspective after three detailed lessons on types of graphs. It also allows time for a quiz.

8-5

TRANSLATIONS (SLIDES)

Four types of transformations result in congruent figures. In this book we study three of them: rotations or turns, already mentioned in Chapter 5; translations or slides in this lesson; and reflections in Lesson 8-6. (The fourth type of congruence transformation is the glide reflection.)

Translations reinforce an important point-plotting concept: the notion that the first coordinate determines the distance right or left, the second coordinate, up or down.

Translations also introduce the idea of graphing in geometry. Many students are surprised to see the connection between adding, translations, and congruence. This connection is an extension of the Slide Model for Addition, from the one-dimensional number line to a two-dimensional plane.

8-6

REFLECTIONS

Reflections are fundamental in the study of congruence; for example, the base angles of an isosceles triangle are reflection images of each other. Reflection images also provide the means by which symmetry can be defined; Lesson 8-7 deals with line symmetry.

The purpose of this lesson is to introduce the language of reflections and to afford students practice in making and analyzing reflection images. Notice the distinction in mathematics between *reflection* (the transformation) and *reflection image* (the result of applying the transformation). In everyday language, both expressions are called *reflections*, as when one says, "Look at your reflection in the water."

8-7

LINE SYMMETRY

Symmetry is an important idea in many areas other than mathematics. Since ancient times, symmetry has been used in art and architecture to create pleasing patterns. Concepts of symmetry are basic for the study of crystals in chemistry, the study of particle physics, and the study of geometry itself.

Generally, a figure is symmetric if there is a transformation under which the figure coincides with its image. Symmetries are categorized by the type of transformation; the figures studied in this lesson are called *reflection-symmetric*. Some other types of symmetry are covered in the questions and in Lesson 8-8.

8-8

TESSELLATIONS

The purposes of this lesson are to have fun, to introduce *regular polygons*, to give practice in putting together geometric shapes, and to review ideas from other parts of the chapter.

The underlying mathematics of *tessellations* is interesting. Any triangle or quadrilateral can be a fundamental region for a tessellation. The only regular polygons that tessellate are equilateral triangles, squares, and regular hexagons. There are *semi-regular tessellations* made up of more than one type of regular polygon. For example, if you try to tessellate regular octagons, you can fit small squares into the regions not covered by the octagons.

Of course, there are tessellations using wild fundamental regions, such as those created by M.C. Escher. However, what is surprising is that even the most complicated tessellations are based on rather simple tessellation designs.

Tessellation lore contains many interesting facts and puzzles. For example, in 1890, the Russian mathematician Fedorov proved that there are only 17 different symmetry patterns for tessellations in the plane. Some pentagons do not tessellate, but no one has ever been able to definitively list all pentagons that do tessellate.

CHAPTER 8

We recommend 11 to 12 days for this chapter. Plan to spend 1 day per lesson, 1 day on the Progress Self-Test, 1 to 2 days on the Chapter Review, and 1 day for the exam.

USING PAGES 334–335

A *display* is a presentation of information. The types of graphs shown on page 335 are important kinds of displays. Tables and prose are two other types of displays.

You may wish to tell students something of the history of the contents of this chapter. The ancient Greeks realized that numbers and operations could be represented geometrically. In the early 1600s, Pierre Fermât and René Descartes worked with coordinate graphs. In the 1790s, William Playfair, who was the first person to display information in circle graphs, also was probably the first to use bar graphs.

Transformations were used in the 1700s but were not systematized until the 1800s. In 1872, Felix Klein showed that all the geometries known at the time could be described in terms of transformations.

The work of Evariste Galois about 200 years ago led to recognition of the mathematical importance of symmetry. Galois demonstrated that the existence of formulas for solving polynomial equations is related to the existence of certain symmetry groups.

During the 1400s, the Moors used tessellations in tilings. However, the mathematical study of tessellations began only about one hundred years ago.

Displays

334

To *display* means to show. The most common ways of displaying numbers are in graphs and tables. Below, a day in the life of a high school freshman is displayed in three different ways. In this chapter, you will study various kinds of displays.

A Day in the Life of F. R. Eshman

Table

Sleep	8 hr.
Eat	1.5 hr
At School	7 hr
Going to/from school	1 hr
Homework	2 hr
School activity	2 hr
Relaxation time	2.5 hr

Circle Graph

Relaxation time (2.5 hr)
Homework (2 hr)
School activity (2 hr)
Eating (1.5 hr)
Going to/from school (1 hr)
At school (7 hr)
Sleep (8 hr)

Bar Graph

Number of hours

10
9
8
7
6
5
4
3
2
1
0

Sleep · School · School activity · Transportation · Eating · Homework · Relaxation

Activity

Bar Graphs

According to the preliminary figures of the 1990 U.S. Census, about 3.5 million people of Asian or Pacific Islander ancestry were living in the U.S. in 1990. This number includes 806,000 Chinese; 775,000 Filipinos; 701,000 Japanese; 355,000 Koreans; 262,000 Vietnamese; 260,000 Pacific Islanders; and 170,000 of other nationalities.

The preceding paragraph shows numerical information in **prose** writing. Prose allows a person to insert opinions and extra information. It is the usual way you are taught to write.

Numbers in paragraphs are not always easy to follow. Many people prefer to see numbers displayed. One common display is the **bar graph**.

Example 1 Display the above numerical information in a bar graph.

Solution Step 1: Every bar graph is based on a number line. Draw a number line with a *uniform scale*. A uniform scale is one where numbers that are equally spaced differ by the same amount. Below, the *interval* of the scale is 100,000 people. This interval is chosen so that all of the numbers will fit on the graph.

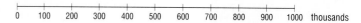

Step 2: Graph each of the numbers.

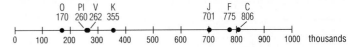

Step 3: Draw a segment from 0 to each number. Each segment is a *bar* of the bar graph. Then raise each bar above the number line.

336

Step 4: Identify the bars and put their length by them. Finally, label the entire graph so that someone else will know what you have graphed.

Number of people of Asian or Pacific Island ancestry in the U.S. in 1990

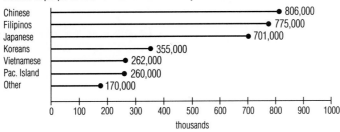

Chinese	806,000
Filipinos	775,000
Japanese	701,000
Koreans	355,000
Vietnamese	262,000
Pac. Island	260,000
Other	170,000

0 100 200 300 400 500 600 700 800 900 1000
thousands

The number line underneath the bar graph serves as a scale. It is not always drawn, but for now you should draw it.

A single bar graph takes up more space than prose. To save space, two related bar graphs can be combined into one.

Example 2 Display the information below in a double bar graph.

Seven Largest Cities in the United States in 1988

City	1970 Population	1988 Population
New York City	7,896,000	7,353,000
Los Angeles	2,812,000	3,533,000
Chicago	3,369,000	2,978,000
Houston	1,234,000	1,698,000
Philadelphia	1,950,000	1,648,000
San Diego	697,000	1,070,000
Detroit	1,514,000	1,036,000

Solution

Population of Seven Largest Cities in the U.S.

New York City	1988	
	1970	
Los Angeles	1988	
	1970	
Chicago	1988	
	1970	
Houston	1988	
	1970	
Philadelphia	1988	
	1970	
San Diego	1988	
	1970	
Detroit	1988	
	1970	

0   2   4   6   8
Millions of people

Independence Hall, Philadelphia

LESSON 8-1 Bar Graphs **337**

The bar graph below has several features to notice. The bars are vertical. There is no written scale, but horizontal lines are drawn for every four billion dollars. The bars are drawn in two directions because both positive and negative numbers are being graphed.

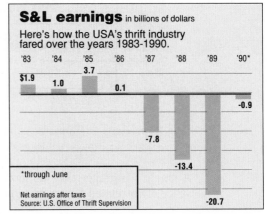

To make bar graphs, you must have several skills. Obviously you need to be able to use a ruler. You have to know subtraction and order of numbers well enough to construct a uniform scale. You must be able to estimate. And you have to be able to translate number words into decimals.

Questions

Covering the Reading

In 1–3, use the bar graph of F. R. Eshman's day, page 335.

1. What is the interval of the scale of the bar graph?   **1 hour**

2. Are the bars on this graph horizontal or vertical?   **vertical**

3. F. R. Eshman could spend more time on homework. Where could the time come from?   **Sample: relaxation time**

In 4–6, use the bar graph of Example 1.

4. What is the interval of the scale of the bar graph?   **100,000 people**

5. Are the bars on this graph horizontal or vertical?   **horizontal**

6. In 1990, were there more people of Filipino or Japanese ancestry living in the U.S.?   **Filipino**

In 7–9, use the bar graph of Example 2.

7. Which of the cities gained in population from 1970 to 1988?
   Los Angeles, Houston, San Diego
8. In which city did the population decrease the most from 1970 to 1988?   **New York City**

9. What is the interval of the scale of this bar graph?
   2 million people

338

In 10–12, use the bar graph of S & L earnings on page 338.

10. What is the interval of the scale?   **4 billion dollars**

11. a. Which year from 1983 to 1990 was the worst year for savings and loan associations?   **1989**
b. What were the earnings that year?   **$-20.7 billion**

12. a. Which year from 1983 to 1990 was the best year for savings and loan associations?   **1985**
b. What were the earnings that year?   **$3.7 billion**

13. On this graph, are the bars vertical or horizontal?   **vertical**

Applying the Mathematics

In 14–17: **a.** Is the scale uniform? **b.** If the scale is uniform, what is its interval? If the scale is not uniform, where is it not uniform?

14.
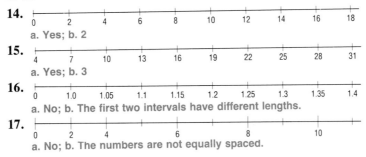
0 2 4 6 8 10 12 14 16 18
a. Yes; b. 2

15.
4 7 10 13 16 19 22 25 28 31
a. Yes; b. 3

16.
0 1.0 1.05 1.1 1.15 1.2 1.25 1.3 1.35 1.4
a. No; b. The first two intervals have different lengths.

17.
0 2 4 6 8 10
a. No; b. The numbers are not equally spaced.

In 18 and 19, suppose a bar graph had bars of lengths 3.39, 3.4, 3.391, and 3.294.

18. Which number will have the longest bar?   **3.4**

19. Which two bars will differ the most in length?   **3.4 and 3.294**

In 20 and 21, some information is given. To put the information into a bar graph, what might be a good interval to use?

20. Annual average unemployment rate in the United States: 1985, 7.2%; 1986, 7.0%; 1987, 6.2%; 1988, 5.5%; 1989, 5.3%
1% or 0.5%

21. Popular vote in the Presidential election of 1860: Abraham Lincoln, 1,866,352 votes; Stephen A. Douglas, 1,375,157 votes; John C. Breckinridge, 845,763 votes; John Bell, 589,581 votes.
100,000 or 200,000 votes

22. Here are the number of miles of coastline of those states bordering on the Gulf of Mexico: Alabama, 53; Florida, 770; Louisiana, 397; Mississippi, 44; Texas, 367. **a.** If you wanted to put this information into a bar graph, what might be a good interval to use?
b. Put this information into a bar graph.
a. 100 miles; b. See margin.

23. The record high and low Fahrenheit temperatures in selected states are: Alaska, 100° and -80°; California, 134° and -45°; Hawaii, 100° and 14°. Put this information into a double bar graph.
See margin.

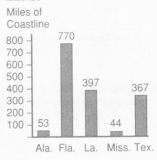

Miles of Coastline

All-time High and Low Temperatures In Alaska, California, and Hawaii

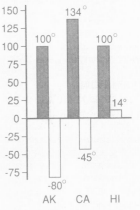

339

NOTES ON QUESTIONS

Question 31: Answers can vary according to the source examined. Sometimes populations given are not of the cities but of entire metropolitan areas.

Question 32: Many spreadsheet programs come with the ability to make bar graphs.

FOLLOW-UP

MORE PRACTICE

For more questions on SPUR Objectives, use *Lesson Master 8-1*, shown on page 339.

EXTENSION

Ask students to choose a bar graph from a magazine or newspaper and write a report about it. Students should give the source, tell something about the graph, and indicate if they think the graph is embellished or distorted in order to make some point.

30. b. sample: A triangle has two angles with measures 105° and 45°. What is the measure of the third angle?

31. a. yes; b. According to The 1988 Information Please Almanac: Bombay, India (8,248,000); Cairo, Egypt (12,560,000); Calcutta, India (9,194,000); Jakarta, Indonesia (7,636,000) Mexico City (12,900,000); Moscow (8,642,000); Peking (Beijing) (9,330,000); São Paulo, Brazil (12,600,000); Seoul, South Korea (9,600,000); Shanghai (11,940,000); Tianjin (Tientsin), China (7,850,000); Tokyo (8,386,000)

Review

24. Which of the states in Question 23 has the greatest difference between high and low temperatures? What is that difference? *(Lesson 7-3)* **Alaska, 180°**

25. The number -2.2 billion appears in a bar graph in this lesson. Write this number as a decimal. *(Lesson 2-1)* **-2,200,000,000**

26. Use the information of Question 20. If there were 100,000,000 people in the U.S. work force in 1985, how many people were unemployed? *(Lesson 2-6)* **7,200,000 people**

27. Round the numbers of Question 21 to the nearest hundred thousand. *(Lesson 1-4)* **1,900,000; 1,400,000; 800,000; 600,000**

28. How many degrees are in: **a.** half a circle; **b.** one third of a circle; **c.** one fifth of a circle? *(Lesson 3-5)* **a. 180°; b. 120°; c. 72°**

29. What is 40% of 360? *(Lesson 2-6)* **144**

30. **a.** Solve the equation $105 + 45 + x = 180$. **30**
    b. Write a problem about triangles that can lead to that equation. *(Lessons 5-8, 7-10)* **See margin.**

Exploration

31. As Example 2 shows, New York has the largest population of any city in the United States. **a.** Are there any cities in the world larger than New York? **b.** If so, make a list of these cities. If not, give the name and approximate population of the largest city in each of the following: Asia, Africa, Europe, Central or South America. **See margin.**

32. There is software that enables a computer to display a bar graph on a monitor. If you have access to a computer, find the name of such software. If the software is available, use it to draw the bar graph on page 335 of this chapter. **Answers will vary.**

340

8-2

Coordinate Graphs

The Art Institute, Chicago

Some patterns involve many *pairs* of numbers. A bar for each pair would take up too much space. **Coordinate graphs** are used instead.

Example 1 At left is a table of temperatures for a very cold January morning in Chicago. Put this information onto a coordinate graph.

Solution Here is the coordinate graph.

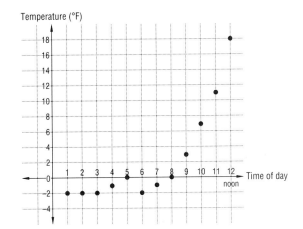

Time of day	Temperature (°F)
1 A.M.	-2
2 A.M.	-2
3 A.M.	-2
4 A.M.	-1
5 A.M.	0
6 A.M.	-2
7 A.M.	-1
8 A.M.	0
9 A.M.	3
10 A.M.	7
11 A.M.	11
12 noon	18

Examine the graph carefully. Notice that there are two number lines. The horizontal number line represents the time of day and goes from 1 to 12 (from 1 A.M. to 12 noon). The vertical number line represents temperature and goes from -4°F to 18°F. Its interval is chosen as 2° so that all the temperatures will fit on the graph. Each line of the table is a pair of numbers, and each pair of numbers corresponds to one point on the coordinate graph.

LESSON 8-2 Coordinate Graphs **341**

LESSON 8-2

RESOURCES
- Lesson Master 8-2
- Computer Master 16
- Visual for Teaching Aid 48: Graph Paper.
- Visual for Teaching Aid 49: Graph Paper (Four Quadrants)
- Overhead Coordinate Grid (*Transition Mathematics Teacher Kit*)

OBJECTIVES

H Interpret coordinate graphs.
I Display information in a coordinate graph.
K Plot and name points on a coordinate graph.

TEACHING NOTES

This lesson contains a great deal of terminology. Besides the vocabulary in the reading, students should learn the word "quadrant," which is introduced in the questions.

Use Teaching Aids 48 and 49, on the overhead projector. Discussing the examples will help students place the vocabulary in context, understand the importance of order, and learn to plot points.

The tasks of drawing coordinate axes, putting a uniform scale on them, and choosing an interval are very time consuming. For this reason, we encourage using graph paper or showing students scales made in advance, as is the case for **Questions 16–18.**

1. Janet made a list to show how much money she had at the end of each day last week. Just before she got her allowance on Friday, she had to borrow money. Put the information from her list onto a coordinate graph.

Monday	Day 1	$3
Tuesday	Day 2	$1.50
Wednesday	Day 3	$ .50
Thursday	Day 4	–$1
Friday	Day 5	$4
Saturday	Day 6	$2.50
Sunday	Day 7	$2.50

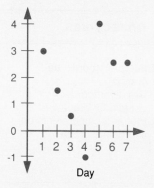

2. Give the coordinates of a point:
a. on the x-axis.
sample: (4, 0)
b. on the y-axis.
sample: (0, 4)
c. on both the x- and y-axis.
sample: (0, 0)

3. Give the coordinates of each point.

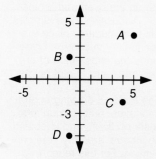

A = (5, 4); B = (–1, 2); C = (4, –2); D = (–1, –5)

The coordinate graph has advantages over the table. It pictures change. As the temperature rises, so do the points on the graph. Also, you can insert points between the times on the coordinate graph without making it larger.

When a pair of numbers is being graphed as a point, the numbers are put in parentheses with a comma between them. For instance, the left point on the graph in Example 1 is (1, -2). This means at 1:00 A.M. the temperature was -2°F. The next three points are (2, -2), (3, -2), and (4, -1). The point furthest to the right is (12, 18). So at 12:00 noon the temperature was 18°F.

The symbol (*a*, *b*) is called an **ordered pair.** *a* is called the **first coordinate** of the ordered pair; *b* is the **second coordinate.** *Order makes a difference.* In Example 1, the first coordinate is the number for the time of day and the second coordinate is the number for the temperature at that time. At 9 A.M. a temperature of 3° is graphed as the point (9, 3). This is not the same as a temperature of 9° at 3:00 A.M., which would be graphed as the point (3, 9).

Example 2   What are the coordinates of the points *A*, *B*, and *C* in the graph below?

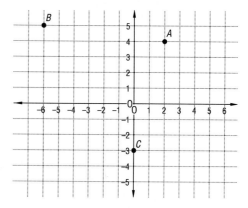

Solution   Find the first coordinate of *A* by looking at the horizontal number line. *A* is above the 2. The second coordinate is found by looking at the vertical number line. *A* is to the right of the 4. So *A* = (2, 4).

B is above the -6, so the first coordinate of *B* is -6. *B* is to the left of the 5, so the second coordinate of *B* is 5. *B* = (-6, 5).

C is below the 0 on the horizontal number line. *C* is at the -3 on the vertical number line. So *C* = (0, -3).

342

Example 3 Graph the points (-1, -3) and (7, 0) on a coordinate graph.

Solution To graph (-1, -3), go left to -1 on the horizontal number line. Then go down to -3. That point is *V* on the graph below.

To graph (7, 0), go right to 7 on the horizontal number line. Then stay there! The 0 tells you not to go up or down. This is point *T* on the graph.

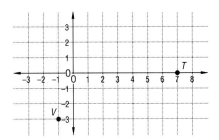

When variables stand for coordinates, it is customary to let *x* stand for the first coordinate and *y* stand for the second coordinate. For this reason, the first coordinate of a point is called the **x-coordinate**. The second coordinate is called the **y-coordinate**. For example, the point (-20, 4.5) has *x*-coordinate -20 and *y*-coordinate 4.5. The horizontal number line is called the **x-axis**. The vertical number line is the **y-axis**. The *x*-axis and the *y*-axis intersect at a point called the origin. The **origin** has coordinates (0, 0).

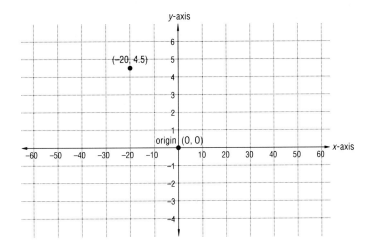

Covering the Reading

1. Trace the drawing below. Label the *x*-axis, *y*-axis, origin, and the point (2, 4). **See margin.**

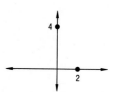

In 2–13, use the drawing below. The intervals on the graph are one unit. What letter names each point?

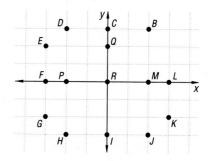

2. (2, 3) **B**   3. (-3, 2) **E**   4. (-2, 0) **P**   5. (0, 3) **C**

6. (0, -3) **I**   7. (-2, -3) **H**   8. (0, 0) **R**   9. (-3, 0) **F**

10. (3, -2) **K**   11. origin **R**   12. (3, 0) **L**   13. (2, -3) **J**

In 14 and 15, draw axes like those shown below. Plot the given points on your graph. Call the points *A*, *B*, *C*, and *D*.

14. (25, 10), (25, 5), (25, 0), (25, -5) **See margin.**

15. (-5, -5), (-10, -10), (-15, -15), (15, 15)
   See margin.

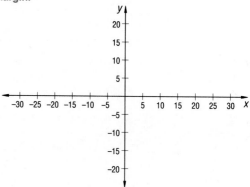

In 16 and 17, refer to Example 1.

16. **a.** From 3 A.M. to 5 A.M. in the table, did the temperature go up or down?   **up**
    b. How is this shown in the graph?   **The point for 5 A.M. is higher.**

17. Estimate the temperature at 11:30 A.M.   **14.5°**

18. Display the information given in the table on a graph like that below.   **See margin.**

Time of day	Temperature (°C)
1 A.M.	3
2 A.M.	-1
3 A.M.	-4
4 A.M.	-1
5 A.M.	0
6 A.M.	0
7 A.M.	2
8 A.M.	3
9 A.M.	5
10 A.M.	6
11 A.M.	8
12 noon	10

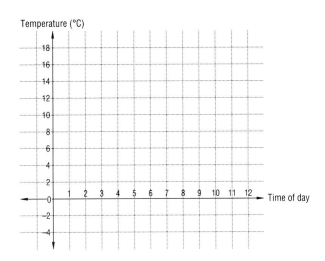

19. The x-coordinate of (-3, -1) is __?__.   **-3**

20. The point (0, 3) is on the __?__-axis.   **y**

21. The point (0, 0) is called the __?__.   **origin**

22. The second coordinate of a point is also called the __?__-coordinate.   **y**

23. The x-axis contains the point (-4, __?__).   **0**

24. The two coordinates of a point are always placed inside __?__ with a __?__ between them.   **parentheses, comma**

LESSON 8-2 Coordinate Graphs   **345**

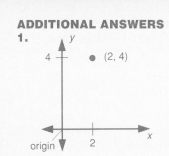
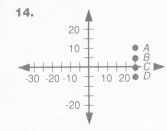
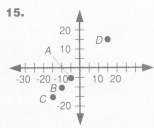
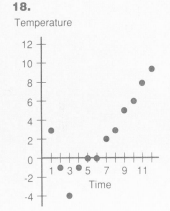

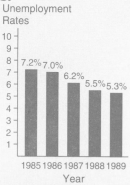

The four areas of a graph
determined by the axes are called
quadrants I, II, III, and IV,
as shown at right.

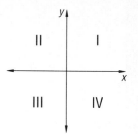

In 25–28, tell in which quadrant
the given point lies.

25. (-50, 400) II

26. (78, -78) IV

27. (-.005, -4) III

28. (14, 13) I

In 29–32, use the idea of Questions 25-28. Between which two
quadrants does the point lie?

29. (0, -4000) III and IV

30. (1 millionth, 0) I and IV

31. (-30.43, 0) II and III

32. (0, -989) III and IV

In 33–36, use the idea of Questions 25-28. In which quadrant is
the point (x, y) if:

33. x and y are both negative. III

34. x is positive and y is negative. IV

35. x is negative and y is positive. II

36. x and y are both positive. I

37. Convert this scale from miles to feet. *(Lesson 3-2)* See margin.

38. In Question 20 of the last lesson you picked an interval for a
graph of the average annual unemployment rate in the United
States. Put this information into a bar graph. 1985, 7.2%; 1986,
7.0%; 1987, 6.2%; 1988, 5.5%; 1989, 5.3%. *(Lesson 8-1)*
See margin.

346

39. Draw a picture of two parallel lines and a transversal. Label one pair of alternate interior angles. *(Lesson 7-8)* **See margin.**

40. If one of two vertical angles has measure 20°, what is the measure of the other angle? *(Lesson 7-7)* **20°**

41. Evaluate $y - x$ when $y = -\frac{13}{16}$ and $x = -\frac{17}{32}$. *(Lesson 7-2)* $-\frac{9}{32}$

42. If $a + b = 9$, find a when $b = 15$. *(Lesson 5-8)* **-6**

Exploration

43. Most business sections of newspapers contain coordinate graphs. Cut out an example of a coordinate graph either from a newspaper or a magazine.
  a. What information is graphed?
  b. Are the scales on the axes uniform?
  c. If so, what are their intervals?
  Answers will vary.

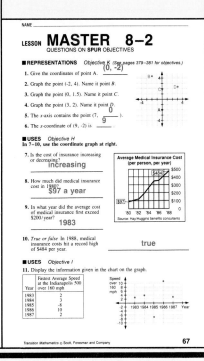

Graphing Equations

In a triangle, the sum of the measures of all three angles is 180°. In a *right triangle*, one angle has measure 90°. So the measures of the other two angles must add to 90°. Suppose these other angle measures are x and y. Seven pairs of possible values of x and y are in the table below. The ordered pairs are graphed below the table.

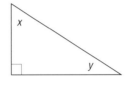

x	y
10	80
20	70
35	55
52	38
45	45
80	10
62.8	27.2

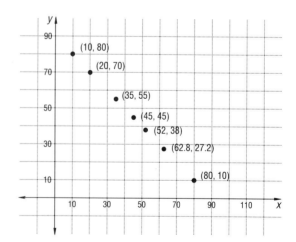

348

The *x*-coordinates and *y*-coordinates of all these points satisfy the equation $x + y = 90$. The seven points lie on a line. This line is the *graph of the solutions* to $x + y = 90$.

Of course there are many other pairs of numbers that work in $x + y = 90$. Some of them, like 110 and -20, involve negative numbers. Below, the entire line is graphed. The arrows on the line indicate that the line goes on forever in both directions.

Graph of *x* + *y* = 90

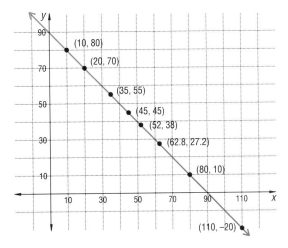

Every sentence with two variables has a graph. These graphs can be beautiful curves, but some of the simplest graphs are lines.

Example 1   Graph all solutions to the equation $x - y = 4$.

Solution   Find some pairs of numbers that work in the equation. Keep track of the numbers you find by putting them in a table.

If $x = 6$, then $6 - y = 4$. So $y = 2$.
If $x = 4$, then $4 - y = 4$. So $y = 0$.
If $x = -1$, then $-1 - y = 4$. Solving
    this equation, $y = -5$.

x	y
6	2
4	0
-1	-5

The graph is on the next page.

The use of two-color counters provides a way to generate ordered pairs to graph. Have students work in groups, and provide each group with exactly 20 two-color counters and grid paper. Students are to label each axis from 0 to 20. Tell students that one axis represents one color and the other axis represents the other color. The two-color counters are then randomly dropped on a table. Students note how many of each color there are, write that information in a table as an ordered pair of numbers, and graph the point associated with that pair of numbers. Repeat this procedure several times. Ask students to describe the results. (The points all lie on a line. The equation for the line is $x + y = 20$.)

ADDITIONAL EXAMPLES
1. Suppose that in Camelot, the evening temperatures (*y*) are always 10 degrees cooler than the daytime temperatures (*x*).
a. Write an equation that relates *x* and *y*.
$x - y = 10$
b. Graph the solutions to your equation.

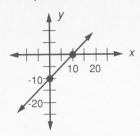

2. Does the point lie on the line of the following equation: $-x + y = -3$
a. $(-3, 0)$
no
b. $(0, -3)$
yes
c. $(1, -2)$
yes
d. $(-1, -2)$
no

Now graph the points (x, y) that you found. For the equations in this lesson, the graph is a line unless you are told otherwise. You should use at least three points in your table. Two points enable the line to be drawn. The third point is a check.

x	y
6	2
4	0
-1	-5

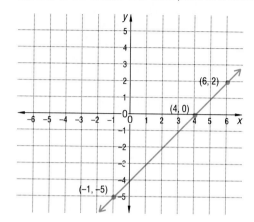

You may have to solve an equation to find a pair of numbers that works.

■ ■ ■ ■ ■ ■ ■ ■■

Example 2   Find a pair of numbers that works in the equation $-7 = -x - y$.

Solution   Pick a value for x, say 6. Substitute 6 for x and solve for y.

$$-7 = -6 - y$$
$$-7 + y = -6 + -y + y$$
$$-7 + y = -6$$
$$7 + -7 + y = 7 + -6$$
$$y = 1$$

So when $x = 6$, $y = 1$. Thus (6, 1) is one point on the graph of $-7 = -x - y$. Substituting other numbers for x and solving for y will give the coordinates of other points that work.

Questions

Covering the Reading

1. Name three pairs of numbers that work in $x + y = 90$.
   Samples: (10, 80), (2, 88), (45, 45)
2. When all pairs of numbers that work in $x + y = 90$ are graphed, they lie on a __?__.   line
3. Suppose x and y are measures of the two acute angles in a right triangle. How are x and y related? $x + y = 90$

350

4. Name three pairs of numbers that work in $x - y = 4$.
Samples: (6, 2), (-1, -5)
5. The graph of $x - y = 4$ is a ___?___ . line

6. If $x + y = 10$ and $x = 2$, then $y = $ ___?___ . 8

In 7 and 8, an equation and a value of x are given.
    a. Find the corresponding value of y.
    b. Tell what point these values determine on the line.

7. $x - y = 5; x = 3$
a. -2; b. (3, -2)

8. $x = 6 - y; x = 40$
a. -34; b. (40, -34)

In 9 and 10, graph all solutions to each equation.

9. $x + y = 10$ See margin. **10.** $x - y = 6$ See margin.

11. *Multiple choice* The point (2, 3) is not on which line? (c)
(a) $x - y = -1$ (b) $-5 = -x - y$
(c) $x - y = 1$ (d) $y - x = 1$

Applying the Mathematics

12. *Multiple choice* Which graph pictures the solutions to
$x + y = 10$? (c)

(a)
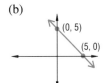

(b)
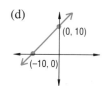

(c)
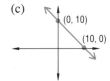

(d)

In 13 and 14: **a.** Write an equation that relates x and y.
b. Graph all pairs of values of x and y that work in the equation.

13. Margie had x dollars beginning the day. She spent y dollars. She wound up with $8. See margin.

14. There are 60 students, x of them in this classroom, y of them next door. See margin.

LESSON 8-3 Graphing Equations **351**

9.
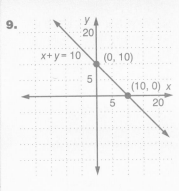

10.
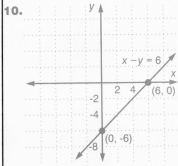

13.
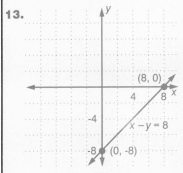

14.
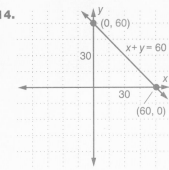

If you need to find many points in a graph, it is a good idea first to solve for one of the variables. In 15 and 16: **a.** Solve the equation for y. **b.** Use the solved equation to find three pairs of values of x and y that work in the equation.

15. $y + x = -7$ See margin.   16. $-x - y = 0$ See margin.

17. In which quadrant is the point $(-800, 403.28)$? *(Lesson 8-2)*   II

18. Between which two quadrants is the point $(-3, 0)$? *(Lesson 8-2)*
II and III

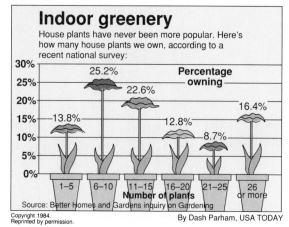

Indoor greenery
House plants have never been more popular. Here's how many house plants we own, according to a recent national survey:

Percentage owning

13.8%, 25.2%, 22.6%, 12.8%, 8.7%, 16.4%

Number of plants: 1–5, 6–10, 11–15, 16–20, 21–25, 26 or more

Source: Better Homes and Gardens inquiry on Gardening
Copyright 1984.
Reprinted by permission.   By Dash Parham, USA TODAY

19. According to the above graph:
    a. What percent of people own more than 20 house plants? 25.1%
    b. What percent of people have no house plants? *(Lesson 8-1)* 0.5%

20. Two angles of a triangle have measures 5° and 10°. What is the measure of the third angle of the triangle? *(Lesson 7-10)* 165°

21. Suppose a savings account gives 5.25% interest per year. How much interest a year should you expect on $200? *(Lesson 2-6)*
$10.50

22. How are quarts and liters related? *(Lesson 3-4)*
1 liter ≈ 1.06 quarts

23. An integer is a *palindrome* if it reads the same forward and backward. For example, 252, 12,321, and 18,466,481 are palindromes. How many palindromes are there between 10 and 1000? *(Lesson 6-1)* 99

24. In Question 14, $x + y = 60$. **a.** Name a pair of values of x and y that satisfy this equation but do not have meaning in the real situation. **b.** Describe all values of x which have meaning in the real situation.
    a. Samples: $(-10, 70)$, $(2.4, 57.6)$
    b. x must be an integer between 0 and 60 inclusive.

352

25. A table like that on page 348 in this lesson can be printed by a computer using the following program.   See below.

  a. Type and run this program, and describe the result.

```
10      PRINT "X", "Y"
20      FOR X = 10 TO 80
30      Y = 90 - X
40      PRINT X, Y
50      NEXT X
60      END
```

  b. Change line 20 as indicated here.

```
20      FOR X = 10 TO 80 STEP 10
```

    How does the change affect what the computer does and what is printed?

  c. Change the program so that it prints different tables of coordinates of points on the line. Record the changes you made and describe the tables printed.

---

25. a. The first two lines are

X	Y
1 0	8 0

Then the values of X increase by 1 and the values of Y decrease by 1. The last line is

8 0	1 0

b. The first two lines and last line are the same but now the values of X increase by 10 and the values of Y decrease by 10.

X	Y
1 0	8 0
2 0	7 0
3 0	6 0
4 0	5 0
5 0	4 0
6 0	3 0
7 0	2 0
8 0	1 0

c. Sample: Change line 20 to—FOR X = 10 TO 100 STEP 5
Then the first two lines are the same but now the third line is
15   75; the values of X increase by 5 and the values of Y decrease by 5. The last line is 100   -10.

MORE PRACTICE
For more questions on SPUR Objectives, use *Lesson Master 8-3*, shown below.

EVALUATION
A quiz covering Lessons 8-1 through 8-3 is provided in the Teacher's Resource File on page 64.

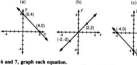

NAME _____

LESSON **MASTER** **8-3**
QUESTIONS ON **SPUR** OBJECTIVES

■ **REPRESENTATIONS**   *Objective L (See pages 379–381 for objectives.)*

1. The graph of $16 = x - y$ is a _____ line
2. Is the point $(30, -5)$ on the line $y = 25 - x$? yes
3. Is the point $(5, 4)$ on the line $x = 9 - y$? yes
4. If $x + y = 21$ and $x = -10$, then $y =$ 31
5. *Multiple choice* Which graph pictures the solutions to $x + y = -4$? C

    (a)   (b)   (c)

In 6 and 7, graph each equation.
6. $x - y = 6$ 7. $y = x + 4$

■ **USES**   *Objective I*
8. Of 50 glee club members, x are present and y are absent.
    a. Write an equation that relates x and y. $50 = x + y$
    b. Graph all pairs of values of x and y that work in the equation.

68   Transition Mathematics © Scott, Foresman and Company

LESSON 8-4

Why Graph?

In Lesson 8-3, you saw how a graph can picture relationships between numbers. For this reason, graphs are very important in mathematics. But graphs are used for other reasons.

You can find coordinate graphs in many newspapers. Here is a graph similar to one that may appear in your local newspaper. Before reading on, can you tell what the three broken lines represent?

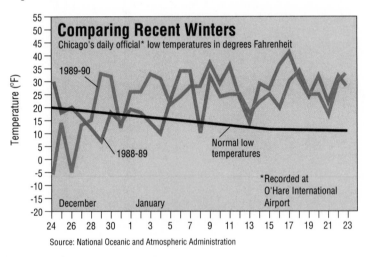

The line that starts near 20 on the vertical axis shows normal low temperatures for Chicago. The green broken line, starting at -6, shows temperatures for the winter of 1989-90. The red broken line, starting at 30, shows temperatures for the winter of 1988-89. This is much more information than could be put in a paragraph or table of the same size.

The above graph compares information and shows trends. Which winter was warmer, 1988-89 or 1989-90? How did each winter compare with the normal? Which month is usually colder—December or January? You can answer these questions just by looking at the graph.

354

In applications, as in the temperature graph, it is very important to select a useful scale on each axis. The scales may intersect at a point other than (0, 0). They may have different units. But in almost all simple graphs, each scale is uniform.

A barrel is pictured at right. Suppose you wanted to describe this picture to someone over the phone. You might use angle measures and segment lengths. But it is easier just to put the figure on a graph and tell someone the coordinates of the key points.

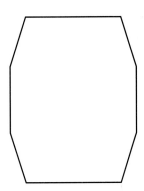

We put the origin at the center of the barrel because the barrel is symmetric.

Now, to describe the barrel over a phone, you can say that the barrel is pictured as a polygon with vertices (-4, -2), (-3, -5), (3, -5), and so on.

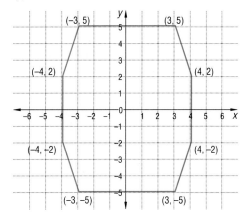

The same idea is used in many computer programs to store drawings or geometric figures in a computer.

You now have seen four reasons for using graphs.
Graphs can picture relationships between numbers.
Graphs can show a lot of information in a small space.
Graphs can show trends.
Graphs can describe drawings and geometric figures.

ADDITIONAL EXAMPLE
Using the coordinates of the vertices, describe how to reproduce this figure on another coordinate graph.

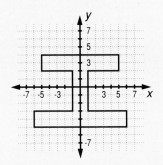

Graph the following points. Then join them in order with segments: (1, 2), (5, 2), (5, 4), (-5, 4), (-5, 2), (-1, 2), (-1, -3), (-6, -3), (-6, -5), (6, -5), (6, -3), (1, -3), (1, 2).

356

NOTES ON QUESTIONS

Question 9: Note that sometimes axes do not or cannot intersect at (0, 0). Ask students why this is the case in this question. (They cannot because there is no day 0 on the calendar.)

Error Analysis for Question 14: This is difficult for many students. Suggest that students try to reproduce the outline on graph paper. Begin with *A* at (0, 0), the origin, and *B*, 12 spaces up on the *y*-axis. Ask for the coordinates of *B* (0, 12). Next move to *C*. Ask which coordinate changes (*x*); graph *C*. Continue in this manner with the other points.

Question 15: We can translate the surface of the earth to a coordinate grid only because Europe is a relatively small part of the earth. Whereas in mathematics, the horizontal coordinate comes first, in geography, the latitude is given first.

Making Connections for Question 19: The idea here will be used in translations in Lesson 8-5.

Small Group Work for Question 20: Encourage groups to develop systematic ways of answering this. For example, students can count the lattice points in the first quadrant, multiply by 4, then count those on the positive part of the *x*-axis, and so on. An equation for the circle is $x^2 + y^2 = 25$, but few students will deduce this.

ADDITIONAL ANSWERS
10. Graphs can show a lot of information in a small space; graphs can also show trends.

11. Graphs can describe drawings and geometric figures.

12. by storing the coordinates of key points and the order in which points are to be joined

Questions

In 1–9, refer to the temperature graph on page 354.

1. Which December–January period was colder in Chicago, 1988–89 or 1989–90? **1988–89**

2. On January 18, give **a.** the normal low temperature, **b.** the low temperature in 1989, and **c.** the low temperature in 1990.
   a. 12° b. 34° c. 31°

3. Repeat Question 2 for January 4.
   a. 16° b. 10° c. 31°

4. Was either winter period warmer than the normal?
   Both winters were warmer than normal.

5. Which month is usually colder, December or January? **January**

6. On December 24, 1983, an all-time low temperature of -25° set a record for any day in Chicago. Which of the days listed came closest to that record? **December 24, 1989**

7. What is the interval of the scale on the horizontal axis? **1 day**

8. What is the interval of the scale on the vertical axis?
   5° Fahrenheit

9. At what point do the axes intersect? **(Dec 24, -20°)**

10. Which of the four reasons for graphs apply to the graph on page 354? **See margin.**

11. Which of the four reasons for graphs apply to the graph of the barrel? **See margin.**

12. How are drawings and geometric figures stored in many computers? **See margin.**

13. Graph the following 12 points. Then connect them *in order* by a smooth curve. What figure seems to be formed?
    (13, 0), (12, 5), (5, 12), (0, 13), (-5, 12), (-12, 5), (-13, 0), (-12, -5), (-5, -12), (0, -13), (5, -12), (12, -5), (13, 0)
    circle; see Additional Answers, p. T53.

14.

Outlined above is a miniature golf hole. All the angles are right angles. Lengths of sides are given. Suppose this outline were graphed with *A* at (0, 0) and *B* on the *y*-axis. **a.** Give the coordinates of points *B*, *C*, *D*, *E*, and *F*. **b.** Give the coordinates of the tee. **c.** Estimate the coordinates of the hole.
See Additional Answers, p. T53.

356

15. Given are the latitude and longitude of five European cities. Use these numbers as coordinates in graphing. Use axes like those at right, but make your drawing bigger. (If correct, your drawing will show how these cities are located relative to each other.) *See Additional Answers, p. T53.*

City	North Latitude	East Longitude
London	51°	0°
Paris	49°	2°
Berlin	53°	13°
Rome	42°	12°
Warsaw	52°	21°

Review

16. Refer to the barrel drawn in this lesson. **a.** What kind of polygon is this barrel? **b.** The angles of this polygon are all what kind of angle? **c.** If you drew the eight lines containing the sides of the polygon, how many pairs of parallel lines would you have? **d.** If you drew the eight lines containing the sides of the polygon, how many pairs of perpendicular lines would you have? *(Lessons 3-6, 5-9, 7-8)* **a. octagon; b. obtuse; c. four; d. four**

17. Graph all pairs of solutions to the equation $x - y = 3$. *(Lesson 8-3)* **some points on the line: (0, -3), (5, 2), (3, 0)**

18. The temperature x near the floor is 5° cooler than the temperature y near the ceiling.
    a. Find an equation that relates x and y. **Sample: $x = y - 5$**
    b. Graph five pairs of values of x and y that work in that equation. *(Lessons 4-3, 8-3)* **Sample points: (67, 72), (70, 75)**

19. A point is 2 units above (3, 6). What are the coordinates of the point? *(Lesson 8-2)* **(3, 8)**

Exploration

20. A *lattice point* is a point whose coordinates are both integers. Below a circle is graphed. **a.** How many lattice points are inside the circle? **b.** How many lattice points are on the circle?

a. 69; b. 12

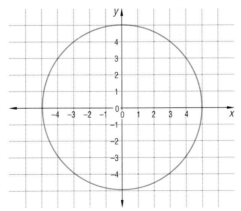

FOLLOW-UP

MORE PRACTICE
For more questions on SPUR Objectives, use *Lesson Master 8-4*, shown below.

EXTENSION
Students may want to draw a picture on a graph, and then try to copy it on another coordinate graph using coordinates of vertices as guides.

EVALUATION
Alternative Assessment
Ask students what kind of information they might want to show on a coordinate graph (for example, number of students in other classes or in club activities). Have students collect the data and display it in a coordinate graph.

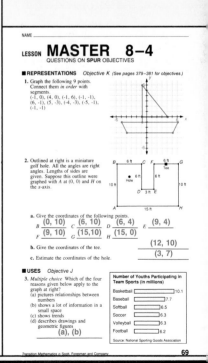

LESSON 8-5

Translations (Slides)

If you change coordinates of the points in a figure, the figure will be altered. Adding the same number to the coordinates yields a **translation image** or **slide image** of the original figure.

Imagine beginning with triangle *MNO*. Add 3 to each first coordinate. Then graph the new points. You get a triangle 3 units to the right of *MNO*. We call this $\triangle M'N'O'$ (read "triangle *M* prime, *N* prime, *O* prime").

This procedure replaces (0, 0) by (3, 0), (2, 4) by (5, 4) and (-4, 6) by (-1, 6). Each **image** point is 3 units to the right of the **preimage** point.

In general, if you add *h* to each first coordinate, you will get a slide image of the original figure that is *h* units to the right. (If *h* is negative, then you will go "negative right," which is left.)

This is a two-dimensional picture of the slide model for addition that you studied in Chapter 5.

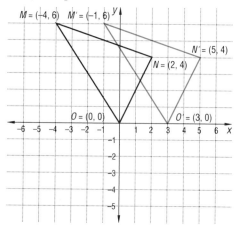

What happens if you add a particular number to the *second* coordinate? It's just what you might expect. The preimage slides up or down.

Below a third triangle is now on the graph. It is the image of △*M'N'O'* when -5 is added to the second coordinate. We call the image *M*N*O** (*M* star, *N* star, *O* star).

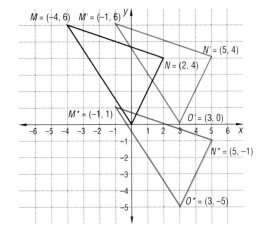

In general, if you add *k* to the second coordinate of all points in a figure, you will slide the figure *k* units up. (If *k* is negative, as it is here, then the slide is "negative up," which is down.)

Congruent figures are figures with the same size and shape. A translation image is always congruent to its preimage. The three triangles above are congruent.

Using Manipulatives If the *Transition Mathematics Teacher Kit* is available, the congruent triangles and coordinate grid allow slides to be easily demonstrated on the overhead projector. Students can also use the Geometry Template to help them illustrate slides.

ADDITIONAL EXAMPLES

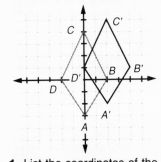

1. List the coordinates of the vertices of *ABCD*.
(0, −3), (2, 0), (0, 4), (−2, 0)

2. List the coordinates of the vertices of *A'B'C'D'*.
(2, −2), (4, 1), (2, 5), (0, 1)

3. Describe the translation.
2 units right, 1 unit up; or add 2 to the first coordinate, add 1 to the second coordinate.

Questions

Covering the Reading

In 1–4, what happens to the graph of a figure when:

1. 3 is added to the first coordinate of every point on it?
The figure is moved 3 units to the right.

2. 10 is added to the second coordinate of every point on it?
The figure is moved 10 units up.

3. -7 is added to the second coordinate of every point on it?
The figure is moved 7 units down.

4. 6 is subtracted from the first coordinate of every point on it?
The figure is moved 6 units to the left.

5. Another name for slide is ___?___.   translation

6. When you change the coordinates of points of a figure, the original figure is called the ___?___ and the resulting figure is called its ___?___.   preimage, image

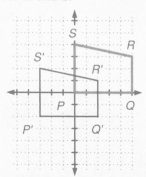
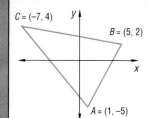

C = (−7, 4)   B = (5, 2)   A = (1, −5)

In 7 and 8, graph the triangle *ABC* shown at left. Then, on the same axes, graph its image under the translation that is described.

7. Add 2 to the first coordinate of each point.
Image triangle coordinates: (3, -5), (7, 2), (-5, 4)

8. Add -3 to the first coordinate and 5 to the second coordinate of each point.   Image triangle coordinates: (-2, 0), (2, 7), (-10, 9)

In 9 and 10, tell what happens to the graph of a figure when:

9. *k* is added to the second coordinate of each point and *k* is positive.
The graph is moved up *k* units.

10. *h* is added to the first coordinate of each point and *h* is negative.
The graph is moved *h* units to the left.

11. Congruent figures have the same __?__ and __?__.   size, shape

12. *True or false*   A figure and its slide image are always congruent.
True

13. a. Draw quadrilateral *PQRS* with *P* = (0, 0), *Q* = (5, 0), *R* = (5, 3), and *S* = (0, 4). **b.** On the same axes, draw its image when 3 is subtracted from each first coordinate and 2 is subtracted from each second coordinate. **c.** The preimage and image are __?__.
See margin.

14. Triangle *A′B′C′* is a slide image of triangle *ABC*. *A* = (0, 0), *B* = (3, 0), *C* = (0, -4), and *C′* = (-1, 5). What are the coordinates of *A′* and *B′*?   *A′* = (-1, 9), *B′* = (2, 9)

15. a. Give three instances of the following general pattern: Under a particular transformation, the image of (*x*, *y*) is (*x* + 4, *y* − 5). **b.** Draw the three points and their images.   See margin.

16.

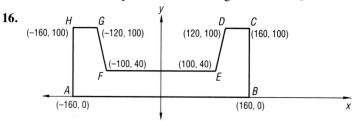

Polygon *ABCDEFGH* outlines a top view of a school building. The architect wishes to send this outline by computer to a builder. To avoid using negative numbers, the architect slides the graph so that the image of point *A* is at the origin. The image is drawn here.

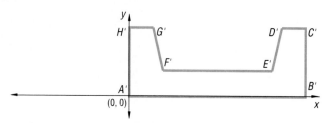

What will be the coordinates of *B′*, *C′*, *D′*, *E′*, *F′*, *G′*, and *H′*?
See margin.

361

17. Graph the line with equation $x + y = 0$. *(Lesson 8-3)*   Sample points: (2, -2), (-5, 5), (0, 0)

In 18 and 19, use the following information.

Year	Estimated World Population
1850	1.1 billion
1900	1.6 billion
1950	2.5 billion
2000	6.1 billion

18. Put this data into a vertical bar graph. *(Lesson 8-1)*   See margin.

19. a. Graph this data on a coordinate graph. **b.** What advantage does the coordinate graph have over the vertical bar graph? *(Lesson 8-2)*
a. See margin. b. It is easier to insert additional points.

20. The square below pictures a floor tile. A corner of the tile is shaded. Sixteen of these tiles are to be arranged to make a big 4 by 4 square. Create at least two nice patterns.   See margin.

21. An artist who used translations is M. C. Escher. Many libraries have books of his work. Find such a book and, from it, trace an example of a figure and its translation image.
Answers will vary. See page 373 for sample figure.

Self-portrait by Maurits Escher

MORE PRACTICE
For more questions on SPUR Objectives, use *Lesson Master 8-5*, shown below.

15. b.

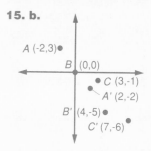

16. $B' = (320, 0)$, $C' = (320, 100)$, $D' = (280, 100)$, $E' = (260, 40)$, $F' = (60, 40)$, $G' = (40, 100)$, $H' = (0, 100)$

18., 19., 20. See Additional Answers in the back of this book.

NAME _____

LESSON **MASTER 8–5**
QUESTIONS ON **SPUR** OBJECTIVES

■ **PROPERTIES**   *Objective E (See pages 379–381 for objectives.)*

1. A translation is also called a _____ slide _____ .

2. The original figure of a translation is called the _____ preimage _____
and the resulting figure is called its _____ image _____ .

3. Congruent figures have the same _____ size _____ and _____ shape _____ .

4. What happens to the graph of a figure when 10 is subtracted from the second coordinate of every point on it?
It slides 10 units down.

5. Triangle *PQR* is slid 5 units to the right. Is it congruent to its image?   yes

■ **REPRESENTATIONS**   *Objective M*
6. A square with vertices (3, 2), (-1, 2), (-1, -2) and (3, -2) is slid 3 units down and 5 units to the left. What are the vertices of the image square?
(0, -3), (-4, -3), (-4, -7), (0, -7)

7. On the same axes, graph the image of quadrilateral *SLID* if -3 is added to each first coordinate and 2 is added to each second coordinate.

8. Triangle *P'E'A'* is a slide image of triangle *PEA*. If *P* = (0, 2), *E* = (4, -1), *A* = (-5, -2), and *E'* = (10, 7), what are the coordinates of *P'* and *A'*?
P' = _____ (6, 10) _____   *A'* = _____ (1, 6) _____

9. Under a translation, (3, 4) is the image of (4, 3). What is the image of (10, 5) under this translation?   (5, 10)

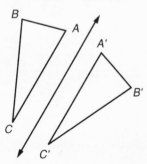
Reflections

*This view of the United Airlines connecting terminal at O'Hare Airport,
Chicago, suggests that each side is a reflection image of the other.*

Translating is not the only way to get an image of a figure. The
word "image" suggests a mirror. Mirrors are the idea behind
reflections. $\triangle ABC$ and $\triangle A'B'C'$, its **reflection image over the
line (or mirror) m,** are drawn below.

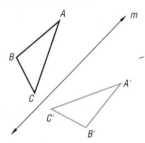

One way to draw the reflection image of a figure on paper is to
fold the paper on the reflecting line. Put the figure on the outside
of the fold. Hold the paper up to a light. Then trace the image.

You can find a reflection image without folding. To do this,
you need to find the images of some points. Examine the above
figure. If you drew $\overline{AA'}$, the line m would be perpendicular to
that segment. Also, the points A and A' are the same distance
from the line m. The same is true for B and B', and also for C
and C'. The segments perpendicular to m are drawn here.

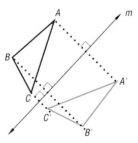

362

This suggests a way to draw the reflection image of a point over a line.

| Given point *P* and line *m*. | Draw the line perpendicular to *m* containing *P*. | Measure to find the image point on the other side of *m*. *P* and *P'* are the same distance from *m*. |

If the reflecting line is horizontal or vertical, then finding the image is easy. Here the reflecting line *m* is vertical.

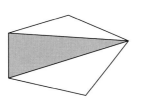 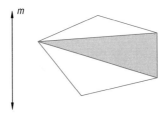

If a point is *on* the reflecting line, then it is its own image. We say that it *coincides* with (takes the same position as) its image. Below, the reflecting line is horizontal and the preimage intersects it. Point *E* coincides with its image.

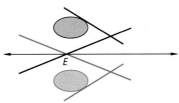

Coordinate graphs can also be reflected. In the exercises, you will learn how to do this over some special horizontal and vertical lines.

Figures and their reflection images have the same size and shape. They are congruent even though the reflection image may look reversed.

When you studied turns and their magnitudes in Chapter 5, you rotated points. Rotations, translations, and reflections are three ways that geometric figures can be changed or *transformed*. For this reason they are called **transformations**. You have seen computer-animated graphics. Animations are often done by beginning with a figure, then transforming it. (In fact, the above images were drawn by a computer.)

LESSON 8-6 Reflections **363**

The triangle will be on your right. This is a change in orientation.

You may wish to introduce the term *perpendicular bisector* to describe the line that is perpendicular to a segment and contains the midpoint of that segment. The term may be useful here because the reflecting line is the perpendicular bisector of the segment joining a preimage to its image.

Drawing reflection images can be tricky for students. Let students find images any way they can: with rulers, by folding, or with a translucent piece of plastic.

Using Manipulatives If the *Transition Mathematics Teachers Kit* is available, the congruent triangles and coordinate grid allow reflections to be easily demonstrated on the overhead projector. Students can also use the Geometry Template to help them illustrate reflections.

ADDITIONAL EXAMPLES
Draw the reflection image of each figure.

1.

2.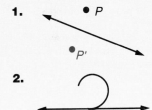

3.

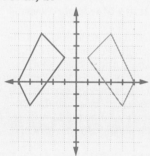
Questions

In 1–3, point P' is the reflection image of point P over the reflecting line m.

1. m is called the __?__.   **reflecting line or mirror**

2. $\overline{PP'}$ is __?__ to m.   **perpendicular**

3. P and P' are the same __?__ from m.   **distance**

4. If a point is on the reflecting line, then it __?__ with its image.
coincides

5. *True or false?*   A figure to be reflected cannot intersect the reflecting line.   **False**

6. *True or false?*   A figure and its reflection image are congruent.
True

7. Reflections, rotations, and translations are three types of __?__.
transformations

In 8–11, trace the drawing. Then draw the reflection image of the given figure over the given line.

8.

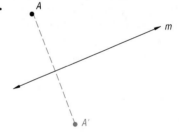

9.

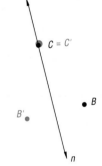

10.

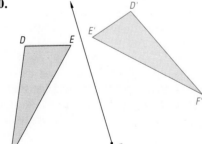

11.

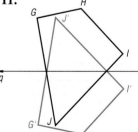

364

12. The point (2, 4) is reflected over the *x*-axis. What are the coordinates of its image? (Hint: Draw a picture.)   (2, -4)

13. a. Graph the quadrilateral with vertices (1, 2), (3, 4), (4, -2), and (5, 0). **b.** Change each first coordinate to its opposite and graph the quadrilateral with the new vertices. **c.** The preimage is reflected over what line?   See margin.

14. a. Give three instances of the following general pattern: Under a particular transformation, the image of (*x*, *y*) is (*y*, *x*).
b. Draw the three points and their images.   See margin.

In 15–18, trace the figure. What word results when the figure is reflected over the given line?

15.

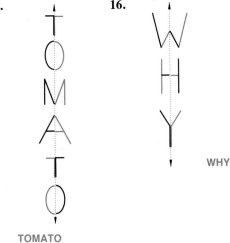

TOMATO

16.

WHY

17.

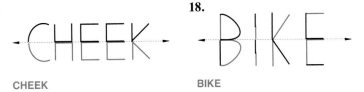

CHEEK

18.

BIKE

19. The picture of the letter L below is to be stored in a computer with point *A* having coordinates (0, 0) and point *B* on the *x*-axis. Give the coordinates of the other points. *(Lesson 8-4)*   See margin.

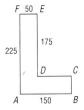

LESSON 8-6   Reflections   **365**

FOLLOW-UP

MORE PRACTICE
For more questions on SPUR Objectives, use *Lesson Master 8-6*, shown on page 365.

EXTENSION
Have students look in a mirror to observe and report what happens to their reflection image as they: get closer to the mirror; back away from the mirror; touch the mirror; turn left; and turn right. Explain that any point on the mirror appears equidistant from the corresponding point on the person looking into the mirror. Ask whether a mirror switches right and left. (No, it reverses orientation. The image of one's right hand has the same orientation as the left hand, but the image of the right hand is still on the right side.)

EVALUATION
A quiz covering Lessons 8-4 through 8-6 is provided in the Teacher's Resource File on page 65.

20. Graph the line with equation $x - y = 10$. *(Lesson 8-3)*
    Sample points: (0, -10), (10, 0), (5, -5)

21. Use this bar graph that appeared in *USA Today* on July 27, 1984.

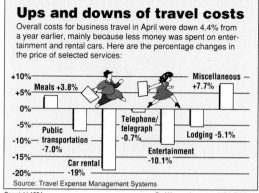

Ups and downs of travel costs
Overall costs for business travel in April were down 4.4% from a year earlier, mainly because less money was spent on entertainment and rental cars. Here are the percentage changes in the price of selected services:

Meals +3.8%
Miscellaneous — +7.7%
Public transportation —7.0%
Telephone/telegraph -0.7%
Lodging -5.1%
Entertainment -10.1%
Car rental -19%

Source: Travel Expense Management Systems
Copyright 1984.
Reprinted by permission.
By Warren Isensee, USA TODAY

a. What interval is used in the scale? **5%**
b. By how much more did car rentals decrease than public transportation? **12%**
c. Which travel cost area decreased the least? *(Lesson 8-1)*
   telephone/telegraph

Exploration

22. Make up some scrambled words like those in Questions 15-18.
    Answers will vary.

LESSON 8-7

Line Symmetry

Suppose triangle *ABC* is reflected over line *BD*. The image
of *A* is *C*. The image of *C* is *A*. And the image of *B* is *B* itself.
So the entire triangle coincides with its reflection image. We
say that the triangle is **symmetric with respect to line *BD*.**
It has **line symmetry**.

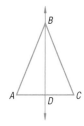

Symmetry lines do not have to be horizontal or vertical. Below at
left is a rhombus *PQRS*. This figure has two symmetry lines. You
can check this by folding the rhombus over either of these lines.

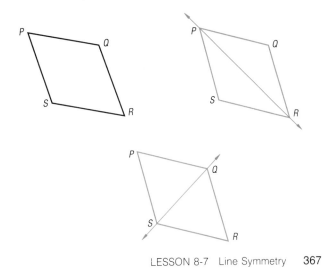

LESSON 8-7 Line Symmetry **367**

LESSON 8-7

RESOURCES
- Lesson Master 8-7
- Visual for Teaching Aid 49: Graph Paper
- *Manipulative Activities Sourcebook,* Activity 14

OBJECTIVE

B Given a figure, identify its symmetry lines.

TEACHING NOTES

The concept of symmetry is familiar to most students. They have either studied it in earlier courses or noticed it in designs and everyday occurrences.

You might want to have students draw all lines of symmetry on figures on the board: an equilateral triangle (there are three), a regular octagon (there are eight), an isosceles trapezoid (there is one), and a parallelogram that is not a rectangle or rhombus (there are none!).

Error Analysis Students sometimes find drawing oblique lines of symmetry (such as those in some of the Examples) tricky. Suggest that students trace rhombus *PQRS*, cut out the tracing, and actually fold along the proposed line of symmetry to determine if the line is indeed a line of symmetry.

367

Perhaps the line *m* shown below at left is another symmetry line
for *PQRS*. To test this, reflect *PQRS* over *m*. The image
P'Q'R'S' is shown in blue below at right.

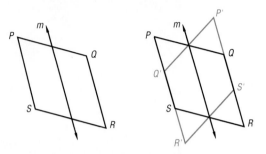

Since *P'Q'R'S'* does not coincide with the original rhombus,
m is not a symmetry line.

Line symmetry is found in many places. Here are some common
figures and their lines of symmetry.

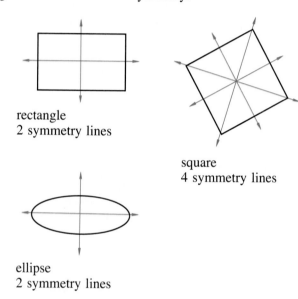

rectangle
2 symmetry lines

square
4 symmetry lines

ellipse
2 symmetry lines

Any line through the center of a circle is a line of symmetry. So
a circle has infinitely many symmetry lines.

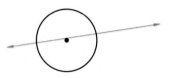

a circle with its center
and one of its symmetry lines

368

Questions

1. When does a figure have line symmetry?   See margin.

2. How many lines of symmetry does a rhombus have?   two

3. Draw a figure with no lines of symmetry.   See margin.

4. Draw a figure that has exactly one symmetry line.   See margin.

5. Draw a figure that has exactly two lines of symmetry.
See margin.

6. Draw a figure that has a symmetry line that is neither horizontal nor vertical.   See margin.

7. How many symmetry lines does a circle have?   infinitely many

Applying the Mathematics

In 8–10, examine these capital letters.

ABCDEFGHIJKLMNOPQRSTUVWXYZ

8. Which letters have a horizontal line of symmetry?
B, C, D, E, H, I, O, X

9. Which letters have a vertical line of symmetry?
A, H, I, M, O, T, U, V, W, X, Y

10. Which letters have a symmetry line that is neither horizontal nor vertical?   perhaps O and Q

Symmetry occurs often in nature. In 11 and 12, how many lines of symmetry does each of these pictures have?

11.

8

12.

6

In 13–16, draw all symmetry lines for these figures.

13.

14.

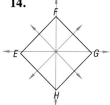

LESSON 8-7   Line Symmetry   **369**

ADDITIONAL ANSWERS
1. when it coincides with its reflection image over some line

3. sample:

4. sample

5. sample:

6. sample:

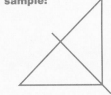

17.

18.

19.

20. sample:

21.

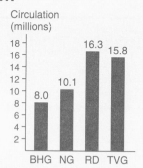

22.

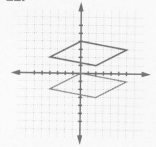

15.

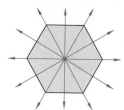

16.

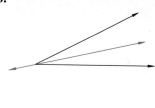

In 17 and 18, part of a symmetric figure is shown. All lines drawn are symmetry lines. Draw in the rest of the figure.

17.

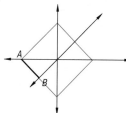

18. See margin.

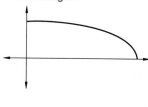

In 19 and 20, draw a hexagon with:

19. no lines of symmetry. See margin.

20. two lines of symmetry. See margin.

Review

21. Here are average circulations for the first six months of 1990 of four of the best-selling magazines in the United States. Draw a bar graph with this information. *(Lesson 8-1)* See margin.

Magazine	Circulation
Better Homes and Gardens	8,002,895
The National Geographic	10,182,911
Reader's Digest	16,343,599
TV Guide	15,837,064

22. a. Graph the quadrilateral with vertices (2, -3), (6, -1), (0, 0), and (-4, -2). **b.** Translate (slide) this quadrilateral up four units. *(Lessons 8-2, 8-5)* See margin.

23. Graph the line with equation $x + y = -4$. *(Lesson 8-3)*
Sample points: (-2, -2), (5, -9), (0, -4)

24. The point (-3, 8) is reflected over the x-axis. What is its image? *(Lesson 8-6)* (-3, -8)

25. Find the value of $a + 3(b + 4(c + 5))$ when $a = 1$, $b = 2$, and $c = 3$. *(Lesson 4-5)* 103

26. A figure has **rotation symmetry** if it coincides with an image under a rotation or turn. For instance, all parallelograms have rotation symmetry. Under a 180° rotation (half turn) about point O, $ABCD$ coincides with its image.

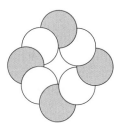

Tell whether the figure below has rotation symmetry. If so, give the magnitude of the smallest rotation under which the figure coincides with its image.   **Yes, 90°**

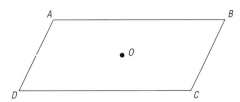

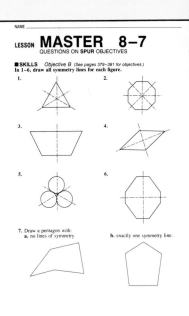

OBJECTIVE

C Make a tessellation using a given figure as a fundamental region.

TEACHING NOTES

DIscuss the Escher drawing on page 373 with the students. Ask them to describe how the pattern was formed by translation and reflection (light-colored birds by translation, dark-colored birds by reflection and translation).

Using Manipulatives
You may wish to do one or more of these activities to clarify the reading. Students may use a Geometry Template if it is available.
1. Try using a regular pentagon as a fundamental region in a tessellation. (It should not work.)
2. Make tessellations different from those on page 372 based on squares and equilateral triangles.
3. Demonstrate the four different types of symmetry (line, rotation, translation, and glide reflection) using a simple shape such as a rhombus.

LESSON

Tessellations

Pictured here are honey bees in their beehive. Each hexagon behind the bees is a cell in which the bees store honey. Bees are naturally talented at making such cells, so the pattern of hexagons is close to perfect. The pattern of hexagons is an example of a *tessellation*.

A **tessellation** is a filling up of a two-dimensional space by congruent copies of a figure that do not overlap. The figure is called the **fundamental region** or *fundamental shape* for the tessellation. Tessellations can be formed by combining translation, rotation, and reflection images of the fundamental region.

In the beehive the fundamental region is a *regular hexagon*. A **regular polygon** is a convex polygon whose sides all have the same length and whose angles all have the same measure. A regular polygon with six sides is a regular hexagon.

Only two other regular polygons tessellate. They are the square and the *equilateral triangle*. Pictured here are parts of tessellations using them. A fundamental region is shaded in each drawing.

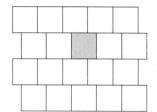

Variations of these regular polygons can also tessellate. If you modify one side of a regular fundamental region, and then modify the opposite side in the same way, the resulting figure will tessellate. (It is very much like balancing an equation as you solve it—always do the same thing to both sides.)

Example Modify a square to create a new tessellation.

> **Solution** Start with the square at left. Change one side. Then copy the change to the opposite side. At right is a picture of the new tessellation.

 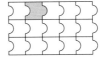

Many other shapes can be fundamental regions for tessellations. The Dutch artist, Maurits Escher, became famous for the unusual shapes he used in tessellations.
Here is a part of one of his drawings.

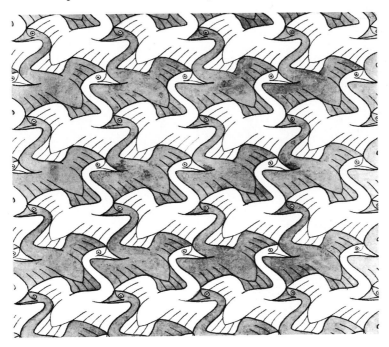

Some shapes do not tessellate. For instance, there can be no tessellation using only congruent regular *pentagons*. (You may want to try, but you will not succeed.)

LESSON 8-8 Tessellations **373**

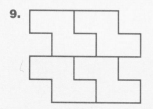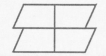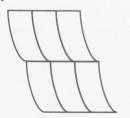
Questions

1. What is a tessellation?   **See margin.**

2. What is the fundamental region for a tessellation?
the figure whose copies fill up the space.

3. In a beehive, what figure is the fundamental region?
a regular hexagon

4. What is a regular polygon?   **See margin.**

5. Name three regular polygons that tessellate.
equilateral triangles, squares, regular hexagons

6. Can a polygon that is not a regular polygon tessellate?   **Yes**

7. If a figure is not a polygon, can it be a fundamental region for a tessellation?   **Yes**

8. Draw a tessellation with equilateral triangles.
Sample: see p. 372.

9. Draw a tessellation with a modified square different from the one pictured in the Example on page 373.   **See margin.**

In 10–13, trace the figure onto hard cardboard. Make a tessellation using the figure as a fundamental region. Figure 13 is from the drawings of Maurits Escher.

10.
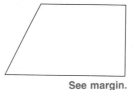
See margin.

11.
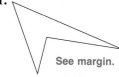
See margin.

12.

See margin.

13.

See margin.

14. **a.** Stop signs on highways are in the shape of what regular polygon? **b.** Can this shape be a fundamental shape for a tessellation?
a. octagon; b. No

15. Pictured here is a postage stamp from the Polynesian kingdom of Tonga.   **a.** Why are most postage stamps shaped like rectangles? **b.** Why do you think Tonga has stamps shaped like ellipses?   **See margin.**

16. How many degrees are in each angle of an equilateral triangle? (Hint: What is the sum of the measures of the angles?)   **60°**

17. Another name for *regular quadrilateral* is __?__.   **square**

18. Graph the line with equation $y = x + 5$. *(Lesson 8-3)*
  Sample points: (0, 5), (-2, 3), (-5, 0)
19. Draw the reflection image of triangle *ABC* over line *m*. *(Lesson 8-6)*.

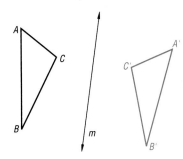

In 20 and 21, draw all symmetry lines for the given figure. *(Lesson 8-7)*

20.

21.

no symmetry lines

22. A quadrilateral is symmetric with respect to the *y*-axis. Two of the vertices of the quadrilateral are (4, 8) and (-2, 5). What are the other two vertices? *(Lessons 8-6, 8-7)*   (-4, 8), (2, 5)

23. Write 0.00000 002 in scientific notation. *(Lesson 2-9)* 2×10^{-8}

24. Solve for *C*: $A + B + C + D = 360$. *(Lesson 5-8)*
  $C = 360 - A - B - D$
25. *Multiple choice*   Which could be an expression for the measure of one angle of a regular *n*-gon? *(Lesson 6-6)*   (c)
  (a) $180n(n - 2)$ (b) $360/n$
  (c) $180(n - 2)/n$ (d) $180/n$

Exploration

26. Tiles on floors or ceilings usually form tessellations. Find at least two examples. Sketch the shape of the fundamental region in each.   Answers will vary.

27. If you visit the Alhambra you will see many examples of tessellations. **a.** Where is the Alhambra? **b.** What is it? **c.** Who built it? **d.** When was it built?
  a. Granada, Spain; b. a palace; c. Moorish kings; d. 1248-1354

ADDITIONAL ANSWERS
4.

Cost of a Thanksgiving Meal, 1988

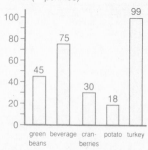

9.

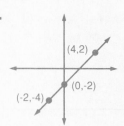

Summary

This chapter is concerned with two kinds of displays. The first kind is the display of numerical information. Bar graphs compare quantities by using segments or bars of lengths on a specific scale. The scale uses the idea of a number line.

Combining two number lines (usually one horizontal, one vertical), pairs of numbers can be pictured on a coordinate graph. These graphs enable a great amount of information to be pictured in a small space. They can show trends and relationships between numbers. Some simple relationships, such as those pairs of numbers satisfying $x + y = k$ or $x - y = k$, have graphs that are lines.

Relationships between geometric figures can also be displayed. A figure can be put on a coordinate graph. By changing the coordinates of points on the figure, an image of the figure can be drawn. By adding the same numbers to the coordinates, a slide or translation image results.

Coordinates are not necessary for figures and images. Any figure can be reflected over a line that acts like a mirror. The image is called a reflection image. If the figure coincides with its image, then it is said to be symmetric with respect to that line.

Reflections and translations are examples of transformations. So are the rotations you studied in an earlier chapter. Under these kinds of transformations, figures are congruent to their images. By taking a figure and congruent images, beautiful designs known as tessellations can be constructed.

Vocabulary

You should be able to give a general description and a specific example for each of the following ideas.

Lesson 8-1
bar graph
uniform scale, interval on scale

Lesson 8-2
coordinate graph
ordered pair, *x*-coordinate, *y*-coordinate
x-axis, *y*-axis, origin
quadrant

Lesson 8-5
translation image, slide image
preimage point, image point
congruent figures

Lesson 8-6
reflection image, reflecting line, mirror
coincide
transformation

Lesson 8-7
line symmetry, symmetry with respect to a line
symmetric figure

Lesson 8-8
tessellation
fundamental region
regular polygon

376

Progress Self-Test

See margin for answers not shown below.

Take this test as you would take a test in class. Then check your work with the solutions in the Selected Answers section in the back of the book.

In 1–3, use the graph below.

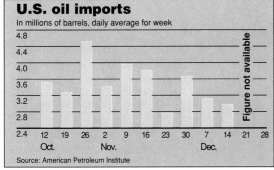

U.S. oil imports
In millions of barrels, daily average for week

Figure not available

Source: American Petroleum Institute

1. In which week of November were the most barrels of oil imported into the U.S.?   **Nov. 9**
2. About how many barrels of oil per day were imported into the U.S. during the week of December 14?   **about 3 million barrels**
3. What is the interval of the scale on the vertical axis of this graph?   **0.4 million barrels**
4. A Thanksgiving meal in 1988 cost the typical person about 45¢ for green beans, 75¢ for a beverage, 30¢ for cranberries, 18¢ for sweet potatoes, and 99¢ for turkey. Put this information into a bar graph.

In 5–7, use the graph below. The interval of each scale is 1 unit.

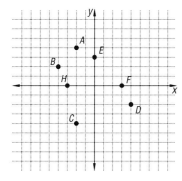

5. **a.** What letter names the point $(0, 3)$?   *E*
   b. What letter names the point $(-2, 4)$?   *A*
6. Which point or points are on the y-axis?   *E*
7. Which point or points are on the line $x + y = -2$?   *B*
8. Point Q has coordinates $(2, 5)$. What are the coordinates of the point that is ten units above Q?   **(2, 15)**
9. Graph the line with equation $x - y = 2$.

In 10 and 11, use the graph of the miniature golf hole at below left. All angles are right angles. The intervals on the axes are uniform.

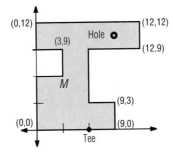

10. Give the coordinates of point M.   **M = (3, 6)**
11. Estimate the coordinates of the hole.   **(9, 10.5)**
12. Draw a quadrilateral with no lines of symmetry.
13. Draw a figure with exactly two lines of symmetry.
14. Draw all lines of symmetry of square $ABCD$.

CHAPTER 8 Progress Self-Test **377**

The Progress Self-Test provides the opportunity for feedback and correction; the Chapter Review provides additional opportunities for practice.

We cannot overemphasize the importance of these end-of-chapter materials. It is at this point that the material "gels" for many students, allowing them to solidify skills and understanding. In general, student performance should be markedly improved after these pages.

USING THE PROGRESS SELF-TEST
Assign the Progress Self-Test as a one-night assignment. Worked-out *solutions* for all questions are in the Selected Answers section of the student book. Encourage students to take the Progress Self-Test honestly, grade themselves, and then be prepared to discuss the test in class.

Advise students to pay special attention to those Chapter Review questions (pages 379–381) which correspond to questions missed on the Progress Self-Test. A chart in the student text keys the Progress Self-Test questions to the lettered SPUR Objectives in the Chapter Review or to the Vocabulary. It also keys the questions to the corresponding lessons where the material is covered.

ADDITIONAL ANSWERS
12. sample:

13. sample:

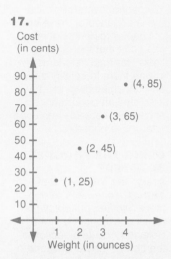
15. Trace triangle *GHI* and line *m*. Draw the reflection image of triangle *GHI* over line *m*.

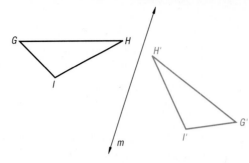

16. Draw part of a tessellation that uses triangle *GHI* as its fundamental region.

17. It costs 25¢ to mail a letter weighing 1 oz, 45¢ for a 2-oz letter, 65¢ for a 3-oz letter, and 85¢ for a 4-oz letter. Graph the ordered pairs suggested by this information.

18. *V* is the reflection image of *W* over line *l*. If m∠*UVW* = 72°, what is m∠*W*? **72°**

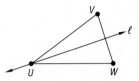

19. Give a reason for having graphs.

20. When are two figures congruent?
when they have the same size and shape

378

378

Chapter Review

Questions on **SPUR** Objectives

RESOURCES
■ Chapter 8 Test, Form A
■ Chapter 8 Test, Form B
■ Chapter 8 Test, Cumulative Form

See margin for answers not shown below.

SPUR stands for **S**kills, **P**roperties, **U**ses, and **R**epresentations.
The Chapter Review questions are grouped according to the SPUR Objectives for this chapter.

SKILLS deal with the procedures used to get answers.

■ **Objective A:** *Draw the reflection image of a figure over a line.* (Lesson 8-6)

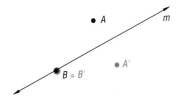

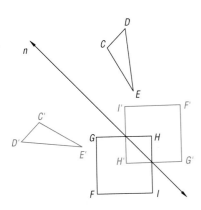

■ **Objective B:** *Given a figure, identify its symmetry lines.* (Lesson 8-7)

In 5–8, draw all symmetry lines for the given figure.

5.

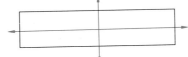

6.

There are no lines of symmetry.

7.   **8.**

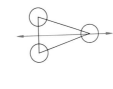

1. Draw the reflection image of point *A* over line *m*.

2. Draw the reflection image of point *B* over line *m*.

3. Draw the reflection image of triangle *CDE* over line *n*.

4. Draw the reflection image of square *FGHI* over line *n*.

■ **Objective C:** *Make a tessellation using a given figure as a fundamental region.* (Lesson 8-8)

9. Make a tessellation using the figure of Question 6 as a fundamental region.

10. Make a tessellation using △*ABC* as a fundamental region.

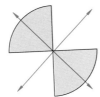

CHAPTER REVIEW

The main objectives for the chapter are organized here into sections corresponding to the main types of understanding this book promotes: Skills, Properties, Uses, and Representations.

USING THE CHAPTER REVIEW
Whereas end-of-chapter material may be considered optional in some texts, in *Transition Mathematics* we have selected these objectives and questions with the expectation that they will be covered. Students should be able to answer these questions with about 85% accuracy after studying the chapter.

You may assign these questions over a single night to help students prepare for a test the next day, or you may assign the questions over a two-day period.

If you work the questions over two days, then we recommend assigning the *evens* for homework the first night so that students get feedback in class the next day, then assigning the *odds* the night before the test so the students can use the answers provided in the book.

ADDITIONAL ANSWERS
9.

10.

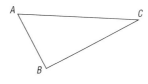

CHAPTER 8 Chapter Review   **379**

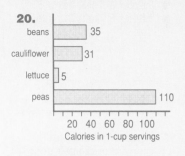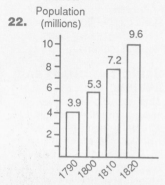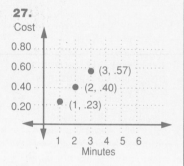
PROPERTIES deal with the principles behind the mathematics.

■ **Objective D:** *Apply the relationships between a preimage, a reflecting line, and the reflection image. (Lesson 8-6)*

In 11 and 12, use the figure below. P' is the reflection image of point P over line t. Answer with numbers.

11. $m\angle PQR = \underline{\ ?\ }$.　**90°**
12. If $PQ = 7$, then $PP' = \underline{\ ?\ }$.　**14**

■ **Objective E:** *Apply the definition of congruence as it relates to translations, rotations, and reflections. (Lessons 8-5, 8-6)*

13. Triangle ABC is a translation image of triangle DEF. Must the two triangles be congruent?　**Yes**

14. Can one of two congruent figures be the reflection image of the other?　**Yes**

USES deal with applications of mathematics in real situations.

■ **Objective F:** *Interpret bar graphs. (Lesson 8-1)*

In 15–18, use the graph below. It shows average heights of boys and girls for the ages 12-16.

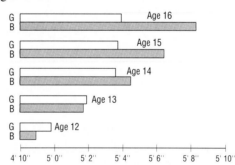

15. What is the interval of the horizontal scale of the graph?　**2″**

16. At which age do girls and boys most differ in height?　**16**

17. What is the average height of 12-year-old boys?　**4′11″**

18. Who grows more from age 12 to 13, girls or boys?　**boys**

■ **Objective G:** *Display numerical information in a bar graph. (Lesson 8-1)*

For 19 and 20, the calories in 1-cup servings of some vegetables are: green beans, 35; cauliflower, 31; lettuce, 5; peas, 110.

19. To put this information in a bar graph, what interval might you use on the scale?

20. Put this information into a bar graph.

For 21 and 22, use the population of the United States during the first four censuses: 1790, 3.9 million; 1800, 5.3 million; 1810, 7.2 million; 1820, 9.6 million.

21. To put this information in a bar graph, what interval might you use on the scale?

22. Put this information into a bar graph.

380

Objective H: *Interpret coordinate graphs.*
(Lesson 8-2)

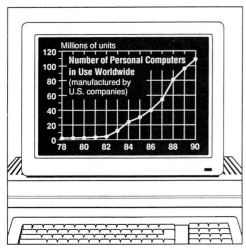

23. What major idea is shown in the graph above?

24. Name the first year there were more than ten million personal computers in use.
1983

25. In what year were about 30 million personal computers in use? **1985**

26. In what 2-year period did the number of personal computers in use increase the most? **1987–1989**

Objective I: *Display information in a coordinate graph. (Lesson 8-2)*

27. It costs 23¢ for a 1-minute call, 40¢ for a 2-minute call, and 57¢ for a 3-minute call. Graph three ordered pairs suggested by this information.

28. Graph the information of Questions 21-22 on a coordinate graph.

Objective J: *Know reasons for having graphs.*
(Lesson 8-4)

29. Give two reasons for having graphs. **Graphs show trends. Graphs can picture geometric figures.**

REPRESENTATIONS deal with pictures, graphs, or objects that illustrate concepts.

Objective K: *Plot and name points on a coordinate graph. (Lesson 8-2)*

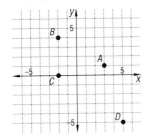

30. Give the coordinates of points *A* and *D*.

31. Give the coordinates of points *B* and *C*.

32. Graph the point (-4, -3).

33. Graph the point (2.5, 0).

Objective L: *Graph equations for lines of the form x + y = k or x − y = k. (Lesson 8-3)*

34. Graph the line with equation $x + y = -5$.

35. Graph the line with equation $x - y = 3$.

36. Graph the line with equation $y = x + 2$.

37. Which of the three lines of Questions 34-36 contains the point (-2, -5)?
$x - y = 3$

Objective M: *Interpret reflections or translations on a coordinate graph. (Lessons 8-5, 8-6)*

38. What are the coordinates of the point 5 units above (4, 0)? **(4, 5)**

39. If (2, -3) is reflected over the *y*-axis, what are the coordinates of its image? **(-2, -3)**

40. If (5, 6) is reflected over the *x*-axis, what are the coordinates of its image? **(5, -6)**

41. A triangle with vertices (2, 5), (0, 9), and (3, 7), is slid 2 units down and 7 units to the right. What are the coordinates of the vertices of the image triangle?

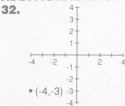
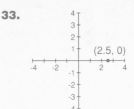
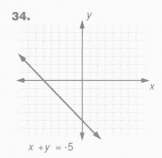

DAILY PACING CHART ■ CHAPTER 9

Students in the Full Course should complete the entire text by the end of the year. Students in the Minimal Course spend more time when there are quizzes and more time on the Chapter Review. Therefore, these students may not complete all of the chapters in the text.

DAY	MINIMAL COURSE	FULL COURSE
1	9-1	9-1
2	9-2	9-2
3	9-3	9-3
4	9-4	9-4
5	Quiz (TRF); Start 9-5.	Quiz (TRF); 9-5
6	Finish 9-5	9-6
7	9-6	9-7
8	9-7	Quiz (TRF); 9-8
9	Quiz (TRF); Start 9-8.	9-9
10	Finish 9-8.	Progress Self-Test
11	9-9	Chapter Review
12	Progress Self-Test	Chapter Test (TRF)
13	Chapter Review	Comprehensive Test (TRF)
14	Chapter Test (TRF)	
15	Comprehensive Test (TRF)	

TESTING OPTIONS

■ Quiz for Lessons 9-1 Through 9-4   ■ Chapter 9 Test, Form A   ■ Chapter 9 Test, Cumulative Form
■ Quiz for Lessons 9-5 Through 9-7   ■ Chapter 9 Test, Form B   ■ Comprehensive Test, Chapters 1–9

A Quiz and Test Writer is available for generating additional questions, additional quizzes, or additional forms of the Chapter Test.

PROVIDING FOR INDIVIDUAL DIFFERENCES

The student text is written for the *average* student. The program, however, can be adapted for both less capable and more capable students.

A blackline master (in the Teacher's Resource File) is provided for each lesson for those students who need more practice. The Teacher's Edition frequently provides Error Analysis and Alternate Approach features to provide additional instructional strategies.

For students who require additional challenge, Extension activities are regularly provided in the Teacher's Edition.

OBJECTIVES ■ CHAPTER 9

Students should master the chapter objectives by the time they complete the chapter. To ensure objective mastery, there is continual review built into each set of lesson questions. After students complete the chapter lessons, they assess their mastery on the Progress Self-Test. Then they do the Chapter Review and pay special attention to those questions that match the objectives missed on the Progress Self-Test. Students can get extra practice on these objectives by using the master for each lesson in the Teacher's Resource File.

OBJECTIVES FOR CHAPTER 9 (Organized into the SPUR categories—Skills, Properties, Uses, and Representations)	Progress Self-Test Questions	Chapter Review Questions	Teacher's Resource File	
			Lesson Master*	Chapter Test Forms A and B
SKILLS				
A: Multiply fractions.	1, 3, 4	1–6	9-8, 9-9	14, 16, 17
B: Find the area and perimeter of a rectangle, given its dimensions.	12, 24	7, 8	9-1	18
C: Find the surface area and volume of a rectangular solid, given its dimensions.	10	9, 10	9-2, 9-3	12
PROPERTIES				
D: Identify properties of multiplication.	5, 6, 13, 25	11–14	9-1, 9-3, 9-5, 9-8	1, 2, 8, 9, 10
E: Use properties to simplify expressions.	2	15–18	9-3	5, 13, 15
F: Use properties to check calculations.	14	19–21	9-1, 9-5, 9-9	7
USES				
G: Pick appropriate units in measurement situations.	11	22–24	9-1, 9-2, 9-3, 9-4	3, 4
H: Find areas of rectangles and numbers of elements in rectangular arrays in applied situations.	7, 8	25, 26	9-1	26
I: Find the surface area or volume of a rectangular solid in real contexts.	9	27–30	9-2, 9-3, 9-4	11
J: Apply the Size Change Model for Multiplication in real situations.	17, 20, 21	31–34	9-6, 9-7	19, 21, 22
K: Calculate probabilities of independent events.	22, 23	35, 36	9-8, 9-9	20
REPRESENTATIONS				
L: Picture multiplication using arrays or area.	15	37–40	9-1, 9-8, 9-9	27
M: Perform expansions or contractions on a coordinate graph.	16, 18	41–44	9-6, 9-7	6, 23, 24, 25

*The Lesson Masters are numbered to match the lessons.

OVERVIEW ■ CHAPTER 9

Multiplication is a much more diverse operation than addition or subtraction; two chapters are necessary to cover its applications and its connections with algebra and geometry. Chapter 9 has three main topics: the applications of multiplication to area and volume (Lessons 9-1 through 9-4), the Size Change Model for Multiplication (Lessons 9-6 and 9-7), and the multiplication of fractions (Lessons 9-8 and 9-9). This chapter contains more geometric topics than does Chapter 10, which deals with equations and multiplication with negative numbers.

Students study three models of multiplication in Chapter 9: area, size change, and repeated addition. In the Area Model, the two factors (length and width) play equal roles, so the Area Model is quite convenient for considering properties like commutativity. In the Size Change Model, the two factors (the size change factor and the quantity to which it is applied) play different roles. The Size Change Model is useful for considering multiplication by certain numbers.

The third model, Multiplication as Repeated Addition (Lesson 9-5)

has limited applicability. Any positive real number can be the length or the width of a rectangle, or can be involved in size changes. In Repeated Addition, however, one of the factors has to be a whole number. Thus, Repeated Addition does not help in interpreting, using, or understanding the multiplication of decimals, fractions, or negatives—and many applications of multiplication involve those sorts of numbers. Although Repeated Addition is the model with which students are most familiar from earlier courses, multiplication is much more than repeated addition.

PERSPECTIVES ■ CHAPTER 9

The Perspectives provide the rationale for the inclusion of topics or approaches, provide mathematical background, and make connections within UCSMP.

9-1

THE AREA MODEL FOR MULTIPLICATION

The area of squares was a topic in Chapter 3. Here students study areas of rectangles. In Chapter 13, we will discuss areas of right triangles, triangles, trapezoids, and circles.

Many students already know the formula for the area of a rectangle. What is new is the direct connection made with multiplication; that is, we take advantage of the formula to picture multiplication. Indeed, the area under a curve in calculus is a generalization of this particular idea. Also, this model helps verify the Commutative Property of Multiplication.

The ancient Greeks pictured multiplication with areas of rectangles. Because of that association, the word *square* applies both to the rectangle with equal dimensions and to the multiplication of a number by itself. You may need to point out that the area of a square ($A = s^2$) is a special case of the

area of a rectangle ($A = lw$); students often think of them as unrelated.

The reading in this lesson proceeds from area to array. Finding the number of elements in an array is the discrete form of finding area.

9-2

SURFACE AREA

Lesson 9-1 introduced the Area Model for Multiplication. Just as the area of a square was followed by the volume of a cube in Chapter 3, the area of a rectangle will be followed by the volume of a rectangular solid in Lesson 9-3. First, however, discuss the surface area of a rectangular solid.

We did not introduce surface area earlier because its computation is more involved than either area or volume. At this point in the course, students are more likely to understand the difference between surface area and volume and to complete successfully the multi-step calculation.

9-3

VOLUMES OF RECTANGULAR SOLIDS

This lesson deals with volumes of rectangular solids. The only other volume discussed in this book is that of spheres, in Chapter 13.

The Associative Property of Multiplication is sometimes written $a(bc) = (ab)c$. In this book, we add the third expression abc, because a key implication of the Associative Property is the removal of all grouping symbols when a collection of numbers is being multiplied. Technically, because of order of operations, $abc = (ab)c$.

Commutativity and associativity taken together allow numbers to be multiplied in any order. This is emphasized in both the examples and the questions of this lesson.

9-4

DIMENSIONS AND UNITS

This lesson focuses entirely on appropriate units of measure; no new skill is introduced.

By directing attention to the units of measure themselves, we hope to correct misconceptions early and avoid common mistakes later. A student should realize that two figures with the same volume can have quite different surface areas, and that two figures with the same surface areas can have quite different volumes.

Of all figures with the same perimeter, the circle has the greatest area. (Equivalently, of all figures with the same area, the circle has the least perimeter.) Of all figures with the same surface area, the sphere has the greatest volume. (Equivalently, of all figures with the same volume, the sphere has the least surface area.)

Also, students should realize the differences among conversions of length, area, and volume. For example, there are 12 inches in a foot, 144 square inches in a square foot, and 1728 cubic inches in a cubic foot. In the metric system, there are 100 centimeters in a meter, 10,000 square centimeters in a square meter, and 1,000,000 cubic centimeters in a cubic meter.

9-5

MORE PROPERTIES OF MULTIPLICATION

This lesson discusses three general properties. The Repeated Addition Model connects multiplication with addition. The model's key strength is in providing a means for simplifying certain long additions. For this reason, this model could more accurately be called *shortcut* rather than *repeated* addition.

Interestingly, repeated addition is conceived of as a way of turning multiplication into addition. In actual applications the reverse is often the case. An addition situation with equal addends is turned into a multiplication.

Students usually know the Multiplicative Identity Property of One by this time, although they may not have seen the generalization or the name.

Students will need to understand the Property of Reciprocals in order to use it properly in the equation solving of the next chapter.

9-6

SIZE CHANGES—EXPANSIONS

The Size Change Model for Multiplication (the model itself is stated in the next lesson) covers a huge number and variety of multiplication situations, including the familiar "times as many," "part of," and "percent of." The general idea is that there is a quantity multiplied by a scalar (a quantity with no unit). The answer is then a second quantity with the same unit:

$$\text{size change factor} \times \text{first quantity} = \text{second quantity}$$

When the size change factor is greater than 1, then the second quantity is greater than the first, and we say that an *expansion* has taken place. When the size change factor is less than 1, then a *contraction* has taken place. Examples of contractions are in Lesson 9-7.

Coordinates help to picture multiplication. For many people, the coordinate representations provide an effective way of thinking of multiplication. The idea of changing size is also fundamental in applications of geometry. Figures with different size but the same shape are *similar*. In fact, the size change transformation is as basic to the study of similarity as reflections, rotations, and translations are to congruence. Moreover, computers enlarge and contract figures by utilizing multiplications with coordinates analogous to those given here. Graphs of functions can be similarly modified.

9-7

SIZE CHANGES—CONTRACTIONS

Size changes are the topic in three lessons of this book: Lesson 9-6 (magnitudes greater than 1), Lesson 9-7 (magnitudes between 0 and 1), and Lesson 10-6 (magnitudes less than 0).

If the magnitude of a size change is 1, then each point coincides with its image. This transformation is called the *identity transformation*, because it keeps the identity of any figure. The analogy with the identity for multiplication is obvious.

If all coordinates are multiplied by 0, then the image of every point is (0, 0). This is sometimes considered a transformation; the result is an *annihilation* of the figure.

In summary, multiplication by *any* number can be pictured by the Size Change Model, unlike the situation with either the Area or Repeated Addition Models.

9-8

MULTIPLYING BY $\frac{1}{n}$

This is the first of two lessons devoted to multiplying fractions. The separation of $\frac{a}{b}$ into $a \cdot \frac{1}{b}$ and the multiplication of unit fractions in this lesson are fundamental for developing the general rule for multiplication of fractions in Lesson 9-9. We also introduce some important applications of multiplication of fractions, including applications to probability.

This lesson clearly illustrates the four-part SPUR approach to understanding. It includes the skill of multiplying fractions (in both arithmetic and algebraic contexts); the property that connects multiplication, reciprocals, and division; uses and applications to real situations; and the Area Model representation.

9-9

MULTIPLYING FRACTIONS

Most students have learned the rule for multiplying fractions, but they treat it as just another one of the many rules of mathematics. In this lesson, we try to justify that rule, to put the rule on firm ground, and to give students a way to get the answers to problems even if they should forget the rule.

We recommend that you plan to spend 12 to 14 days on Chapter 9: 1 day for each lesson, with a possible extra day to allow time for quizzes; 1 day for the Progress Self-Test, 1 day for the Review, and 1 day for the Chapter Test. An optional Comprehensive Test, Chapters 1–9, is also provided in the Teacher's Resource File.

USING PAGES 382–383
Before students open their books, ask them to suggest a problem that can be solved by multiplication. Write 2 or 3 student-suggested problems on the board. Then have the students read the first two sentences on page 383. As you discuss problems A through I with students, emphasize that there are many different kinds of multiplication applications. Call on students to classify the problems on the board as related to geometry, solving equations, or graphing.

CHAPTER 9

Patterns Leading to Multiplication

Finding the number of seats or the amount of sod needed for a football field are two tasks which use multiplication.

382

Multiplication is an important operation with connections to geometry, solving equations, and graphing. Each question below can be answered by multiplying 15 by 23.

A. How many seats are in an auditorium with 15 rows and 23 seats in each row?

B. What is the area of this rectangle?

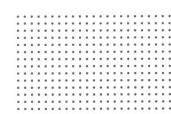

15 mm

23 mm

C. How many dots are in the above array?

D. If one can of fruit juice costs 23¢, what will 15 cans cost?

E. A leg on an insect is 23 mm long. How long will the leg be on a picture of the insect that is 15 times actual size?

F. How many segments are needed to connect each dot in the top row with each dot in the bottom row?

• • • • • • • • • • • • • •

• • • • • • • • • • • • • • • • • • • •

G. Perform these rather long additions.

23 + 23 + 23 + 23 + 23 + 23 + 23 + 23 + 23 + 23 + 23 + 23 + 23 + 23 + 23

15 + 15 + 15 + 15 + 15 + 15 + 15 + 15 + 15 + 15 + 15 + 15 + 15 + 15 + 15 + 15 + 15 + 15 + 15 + 15 + 15 + 15 + 15

H. If $x = 15$ and $y = 23$, what is the value of xy?

I. Solve for t: $15t = \frac{1}{23}$.

OBJECTIVES

B Find the area of a rectangle, given its dimensions.
D Identify the Commutative Property of Multiplication.
E Use the Commutative Property of Multiplication to simplify expressions.
F Use the Commutative Property of Multiplication to check calculations.
G Pick appropriate units in area situations.
H Find areas of rectangles and numbers of elements in rectangular arrays in applied situations.
L Picture multiplication using arrays or area.

9-1

The Area Model for Multiplication

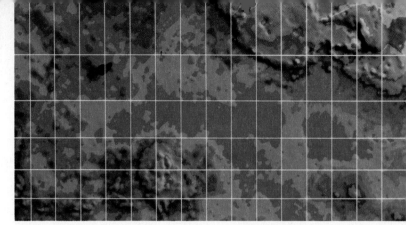

Topographic map of surface of Venus

Remember that the area of a plane figure tells you how much space is inside it. The area of any figure is measured in square units. The area of the square below is 1 square centimeter (actual size).

At left below the unit squares fit nicely inside the rectangle. So it is easy to find its area. You can count to get 12 square centimeters. But at right the unit squares do not fit so nicely. The area cannot be found just by counting.

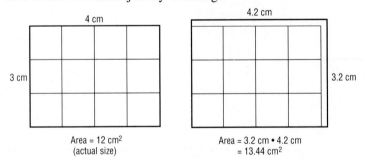

These examples are instances of a general pattern. The lengths of the sides of a rectangle are called its *dimensions*. Its area is the product of its dimensions. This pattern is a basic application of multiplication, the **area model for multiplication.**

Area model for multiplication:

The area of a rectangle with length ℓ and width w is $\ell \cdot w$ or ℓw.

384

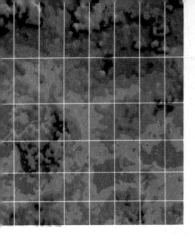

Put dots in the unit squares in the rectangle on page 384. The result looks like a box of cans seen from the top. The dots form a **rectangular array** with 3 rows and 4 columns. (*Rows* go across, *columns* go down.) The numbers 3 and 4 are the *dimensions of the array*. It is called a 3 by 4 array. The total number of dots is 12, the product of the dimensions of the array.

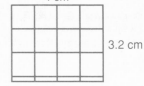

On page 383 is a 15 by 23 array, with 15 · 23, or 345 dots.

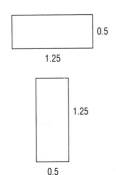

The two rectangles pictured at left have the same dimensions. You could say that the length and width have been switched. You could also think that one of the rectangles has been rotated 90°.

The two rectangles must have the same area. This means
$$1.25 \cdot 0.5 = 0.5 \cdot 1.25.$$

This happens no matter in what order the dimensions are; $\ell w = w\ell$. This pictures a fundamental property of multiplication.

Commutative Property of Multiplication:

> For any numbers a and b: $ab = ba$.

Questions

Covering the Reading

1. What is the area of a rectangle with dimensions 3 cm and 4 cm?
   12 cm²
2. Make an accurate drawing of rectangles to show that the product of 3.2 and 4 is greater than the product of 3 and 4. (Use 1 cm as the unit.)   See margin.

3. If the length and width of a rectangle are measured in centimeters, the area would probably be measured in what unit?   cm²

4. State the area model for multiplication.
   The area of a rectangle with length ℓ and width w is ℓw.

LESSON 9-1   The Area Model for Multiplication   **385**

In 5 and 6, give the area of the rectangle drawn.

5. **2 sq in.**

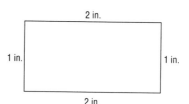

6. **24 square units**

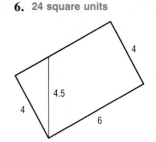

7. Use the array drawn here. **a.** How many rows are in this array? **b.** How many columns? **c.** How many dots are in the array?
a. 3; b. 20; c. 60

8. **a.** Draw a rectangular array of dots with 7 rows and 5 columns.
b. How many dots are in the array?
a. See margin. b. 35

9. State the Commutative Property of Multiplication.
For any numbers *a* and *b*, *ab* = *ba*.

10. How is the Commutative Property of Multiplication related to area? **See margin.**

11. Arrange 30 dots in two rectangular arrays with different dimensions. **See margin.**

12. Give the dimensions of two noncongruent rectangles each of whose area is 15 square inches. **Samples: 1 in. and 15 in., 2.5 in. and 6 in.**

13. A rectangular array of dots has *c* columns, *d* dots, and *r* rows. Write an equation relating *c*, *d*, and *r*. **cr = d**

14. Answer questions A and B on the first page of this chapter.
A: 345 seats; B: 345 mm²

15. *Multiple choice* Two stores are shaped like rectangles. Store 1 is 60 feet wide and 120 feet long. Store 2 is 90 feet wide and 90 feet long. Both stores are all on one floor. Then: **(b)**
(a) Store 1 has the greater floor space.
(b) Store 2 has the greater floor space.
(c) The two stores have equal floor space.
(d) Not enough information is given to decide which store has more floor space.

386

16. Find the area of the shaded region between rectangles *MNOP* and *RSTQ*. **1262.5 ft²**

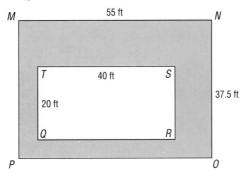

M   55 ft   N

T   40 ft   S

20 ft   37.5 ft

Q   R

P   O

17. *True or false?* If $x = 7.6092$, then $3(x + 4) = (x + 4) \cdot 3$.
True

18. Find the area of the rectangle with vertices (2, 4), (5, 4), (5, 10), and (2, 10). **18 square units**

19. Multiply the numbers in both orders. Are the products equal?
a. 357 and 246; **b.** 1/2 and 2/5 (convert to decimals);
c. 67.92 and 0.00043. **a. Yes; b. Yes; c. Yes**

Review

20. Solve the equation $x + \frac{22}{7} = -\frac{3}{2}$. *(Lesson 5-8)* **-65/14**

21. With your protractor, draw an angle with measure 40°. *(Lesson 3–5)*
See margin.

22. One kilogram equals approximately how many pounds? *(Lesson 3–4)*
2.2 lb

23. Evaluate $14 - 3(x + 3y)$ when $x = -2$ and $y = 5$. *(Lesson 4–5)*
-25

24. Consider 48.49:
a. Round to the nearest integer. *(Lesson 1–4)* **48**
b. Rewrite as a simple fraction. *(Lesson 2–7)* **4849/100**

25. The Northwest Ordinance of 1787 divided many areas of the central United States into square-shaped townships 6 miles on a side.
a. What is the perimeter of such a township? *(Lesson 5–10)*
b. What is the area? *(Lesson 3–7)*
  a. 24 miles; b. 36 square miles

26. There were about 2,673,000 high school graduates in the United States in 1988. Of these, about 59% went to a 2-year or 4-year college. How many college students is this? *(Lesson 2–6)*
about 1,577,000

11. Sample:

21. Check students' draw-ings.

Question 27: This provides another chance to talk about the power of powering. An increase of only one hundredth in the dimension of a cube increases the volume by over 27 hundredths.

Question 29a: You may want to have students organize the possible outcomes in a *tree diagram* as shown below.

H $\Big\langle$ H $\Big\langle$ H
    \ T
  \ T $\Big\langle$ H
         T

T $\Big\langle$ H $\Big\langle$ H
    \ T
  \ T $\Big\langle$ H
         T

FOLLOW-UP

MORE PRACTICE
For more questions on SPUR Objectives, use *Lesson Master 9-1,* shown on page 387.

27. How much bigger is the volume of a cube with edge 3.01 cm than the volume of a cube with edge 3 cm? *(Lesson 3–8)*   0.270901 cm³

Exploration

28. Rectangle *ABCD* is made up entirely of squares. The black square has a side of length 1 unit. What is the area of *ABCD*?
714 square units

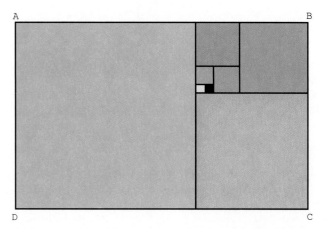

29. When a coin is tossed one time, the possible outcomes are H (heads) and T (tails). When a coin is tossed twice, the possible outcomes are HH, HT, TH, and TT. **a.** List the outcomes when a coin is tossed three times. **b.** Write a table indicating how many possible outcomes there are when a coin is tossed once, twice, and three times. **c.** Find a pattern which will enable you to determine the number of outcomes when a coin is tossed n times.
a. HHH, HHT, HTH, THH, HTT, THT, TTH, TTT

b.

Number of tosses of 1 coin	1	2	3
Number of possible outcomes	2 (or 2^1)	4 (or 2^2)	8 (or 2^3)

c. For n tosses, number of possible outcomes is 2^n.

Surface Area

LESSON 9-2

RESOURCES
■ Lesson Master 9-2
■ Empty cereal box
▤ Visual for Teaching Aid 59:
Use to demonstrate that a solid's surface area is the sum of the area of its faces.

The cereal box at the left is an example of a **rectangular solid.** The box has six sides, called *faces*. Each face is a rectangle. (In a drawing, you view some faces at an angle. So all of the faces don't seem to be rectangles.)

Rectangular solids like this cereal box are often constructed by cutting a pattern out of a flat piece of cardboard. This process is pictured below. The dotted segments show where folds are made. The folds become the edges of the box. (For a real box, the situation is a little more complicated. But the same idea is used.)

The flat pattern   After one fold

The **surface area** of a solid is the sum of the areas of its faces. For the cereal box, the surface area tells you how much cardboard is needed to make the box. The cereal box has six faces: top, bottom, right, left, front, and back. The flat pattern has six rectangles.

A typical cereal box is 24 cm high, 16 cm wide, and 5 cm deep. These are its dimensions.

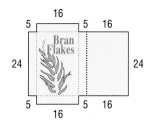

LESSON 9-2 Surface Area **389**

OBJECTIVES

C Find the surface area of a rectangular solid, given its dimensions.
G Pick appropriate units in surface area situations.
I Find the surface area of a rectangular solid in real contexts.

TEACHING NOTES

Using Manipulatives
Students often confuse surface area and volume. In teaching this lesson and the next, differentiate the two as often as possible: one is wrapping; the other, filling. A visual aid is helpful here. Bring in a cereal box, and unfold it into rectangles. (In advance, you may wish to cut off the overlapping parts of the top and bottom.) Once the box is flattened, there is no volume, and the idea of surface area is clear. Encourage students to make a chart like the one on the top of page 390 when calculating surface area.

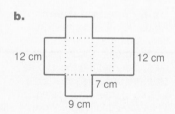
It may be easier to see the dimensions by separating the rectangles in the flat pattern. Adding the six areas gives the total surface area.

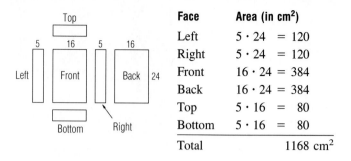

Face	Area (in cm^2)
Left	$5 \cdot 24 = 120$
Right	$5 \cdot 24 = 120$
Front	$16 \cdot 24 = 384$
Back	$16 \cdot 24 = 384$
Top	$5 \cdot 16 = 80$
Bottom	$5 \cdot 16 = 80$
Total	1168 cm^2

Example Find the surface area of a rectangular solid 10 in. high, 4 in. wide, and 3 in. deep.

Solution First, draw a picture. You may want to separate the faces as shown here.

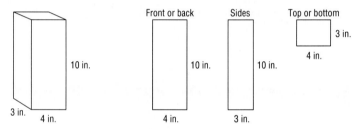

Now, just add the areas of the faces. The surface area is
$$10 \cdot 4 + 10 \cdot 4 + 10 \cdot 3 + 10 \cdot 3 + 4 \cdot 3 + 4 \cdot 3$$
$$= 40 + 40 + 30 + 30 + 12 + 12$$
$$= 164 \text{ square inches.}$$

Questions

Covering the Reading

1. A cereal box is an example of a figure called a __?__.
rectangular solid

2. Each face of a rectangular solid is a __?__. **rectangle**

3. How many faces does a rectangular solid have? **6**

4. What is the surface area of a solid?
the sum of the areas of its faces

In 5 and 6:
    a. Sketch a rectangular solid with the given dimensions.
    b. Draw a flat pattern out of which the solid could be made.
    c. Find the surface area of the solid.

390

5. dimensions 9 cm, 12 cm, and 7 cm
See margin. **c. 510 square centimeters**

6. dimensions 3″, 3″, and 3″   See margin. **c. 54 square inches**

7. Find the surface area of this rectangular solid.

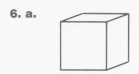

18 in.   3 in.

2 ft

1116 square inches

8. A rectangular solid has length ℓ, width w, and height h. What is its surface area?   **$2\ell w + 2\ell h + 2hw$**

9. A shirt to be given as a gift is put into a box . The dimensions of the box are 14″, 9″, and 2.5″. What is the least amount of wrapping paper needed to wrap the gift? (You are allowed to use a lot of tape.)   **367 square inches**

10. Pat Tern wanted to make a rectangular box out of cardboard. She drew the following flat pattern. Correct the error in this pattern by moving one rectangle.

Move one of the top rectangles to the bottom.

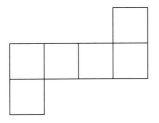

11. Using a sheet of notebook paper, a ruler, tape, and scissors, construct a box out of paper. You may pick whatever dimensions you wish.

12. Suppose that the Bran Flakes box mentioned in this lesson is made from a single rectangular sheet of cardboard. **a.** What are the smallest dimensions that sheet of cardboard could have? **b.** How much material will be wasted in making the box?
a. 34 cm by 42 cm; b. 260 cm²

13. Here is a flat pattern for a cube. All sides of the squares have length 5. What is the surface area of the cube?   **150 square units**

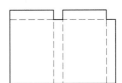

14. The bottom of a box has dimensions 24 cm and 20 cm. The box is 10 cm high and has no top. What is the surface area of the box?   **1360 cm²**

---

6. a.

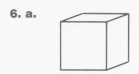

b. sample:

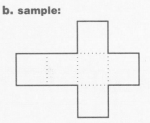

All sides are 3 inches long.

1.   10 cm

8 cm

5 cm

340 cm²

2.   6.2 yd   15 yd

4 yd

355.6 yd²

3. A box has length *l*, width *w*, and height *h*. Give its surface area.

2 (lw + lh + wh)

■**USES**   *Objective G*

4. The dimensions of a book are measured in centimeters. In what unit would its surface area most probably be measured?   **cm²**

■**USES**   *Objective I*

5. A box of paper clips is 11.2 cm long, 5.9 cm wide, and 3.1 cm high. Ignoring waste, at least how much cardboard was used to make the box?   **238.18 cm²**

6. The top of a square table is 3 ft on a side and is 2.5 ft high. How much material would be needed for a square table cloth that covers the top and sides?   **39 ft²**

NOTES ON QUESTIONS
Question 15: This can mislead students into thinking that the area of a parallelogram is the product of its sides. Emphasize that there are 4 rows with 13 in each row.

Questions 19 and 20: Note that if $x = 91$ and $y = 57$ in **Question 20,** the solving of $x - y = 34$ for y will give the related facts of **Question 19.**

Small Group Work for Question 24: Few students will come up with all the patterns. The joint effort will usually encourage students to attack this problem more vigorously.

FOLLOW-UP

MORE PRACTICE
For more questions on SPUR Objectives, use *Lesson Master 9-2* shown on page 391.

EXTENSION
Ask students to find a formula for the surface area of a cube with side s ($6s^2$).

Review

15. How many ellipses are pictured? *(Lesson 9–1)*   52

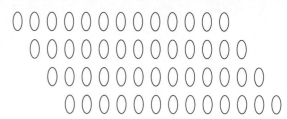

16. Simplify:
   a. $xy - xy$;   0
   b. $0.12 \cdot 3.4 + 3.4 \cdot 0.12 - 0.12 \cdot 3.4$. *(Lesson 9–1)*   0.408

17. What property guarantees that $x + 45$ equals $45 + x$? *(Lesson 5–7)*
   Commutative Property of Addition

18. Simplify: $\frac{1}{6} - \frac{3}{18} - \frac{2}{3} + \frac{5}{9}$. *(Lesson 7–2)*   -1/9

19. Give three true statements relating the numbers 57, 91, and 34.
   (Lesson 7–5) $34 + 57 = 91$; $91 - 57 = 34$; $91 - 34 = 57$

20. Solve for y: $x - y = 34$. *(Lesson 7–6)* $y = x - 34$

21. Let n be a number. Translate into mathematics:
   a. 2 less than a number. $n - 2$
   b. 2 is less than a number. $2 < n$
   c. 2 less a number. *(Lesson 4–3)* $2 - n$

22. What is the perimeter of a rectangle with length 40 and width 60? *(Lesson 5–10)*   **200 units**

23. What is the volume of the cube constructed in Question 13 above? *(Lesson 3–8)*   **125 cubic units**

Exploration

24. In Question 13 a pattern was given for a cube. Here is a different pattern. (Patterns are different if they are not congruent.)

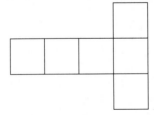

Draw all possible different patterns for a cube.   **See below.**

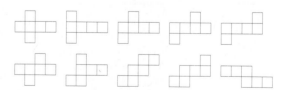

392

Volumes of Rectangular Solids

LESSON 9-3

RESOURCES
■ Lesson Master 9-3
■ Centimeter Cubes (from *Transition Mathematics Manipulative Kit*)

Whereas surface area measures the boundary of a solid, **volume** measures the space inside. Volume gives the capacity of containers ranging in size from atoms to objects even larger than the Earth. Knowing volume can help in finding weight, mass, pressure, and many other physical properties.

The volume of a rectangular solid can sometimes be calculated by counting. At other times a formula is needed.

Example 1 Find the volume of the rectangular solid pictured below. (The solid has been opened up to show the unit cube compartments.)

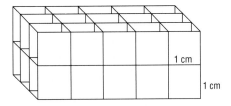

1 cm

1 cm

Solution 1 When the dimensions are integers, the unit cubes fit evenly into the solid. If the dimensions are small, you can count the cubes. There are 15 cubes on each level. The volume is therefore 30 cm³, 30 cubic centimeters.

Solution 2 This solid has height 2 cm, length 5 cm, and depth 3 cm. The volume is the product of these three dimensions.
$$\text{Volume} = 5 \text{ cm} \cdot 3 \text{ cm} \cdot 2 \text{ cm}$$
$$= 30 \text{ cm}^3$$

The volume of a rectangular solid is always the product of its three dimensions, even when the dimensions are not integers.

OBJECTIVES

C Find the volume of a rect-angular solid, given its dimensions.
D Identify the Associative Property of Multiplication.
E Use properties of multiplication to simplify expressions.
G Pick appropriate units in volume situations.
I Find the volume of a rectangular solid in real contexts.

TEACHING NOTES

Using Manipulatives
You may want to provide a large number of unit cubes and perform the following demonstration:
(1) Arrange them into a rect-angular solid, and ask how many cubes there are.
(2) Ask for the surface area.
(3) Rearrange the cubes, and ask the same two questions. (The volume will be the same, but the surface area can change.) Stress the dif-ference between surface area and volume.

To emphasize the importance of the Commutative and As-sociative Properties, remind students that problems involving only additions or only multiplications can be done in any order, but that this is not true for subtraction or division.

Example 2 Find the volume V of a rectangular solid 5.3 cm long, 2.7 cm high, and 3.1 cm deep.

Solution

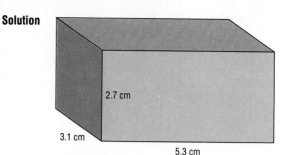

$V = 5.3 \text{ cm} \cdot 3.1 \text{ cm} \cdot 2.7 \text{ cm} = 44.361 \text{ cm}^3$

In Example 2, the product of 3.1 cm and 5.3 cm is the area of the bottom or *base* of the box. So the volume is the product of the area of the base and the height.

Let V be the volume of a rectangular solid with dimensions a, b, and c.
Then $V = abc$.
Or $V = Bh$,
where B is the area of the base and h is the height.

By flipping a rectangular solid over on its side, any two dimensions can become the length and width of the base.

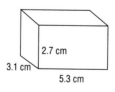
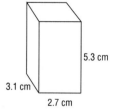

$V = \quad Bh$
$= (5.3 \text{ cm} \cdot 3.1 \text{ cm}) \cdot 2.7 \text{ cm}$
$= \quad 16.43 \text{ cm}^2 \quad \cdot 2.7 \text{ cm}$
$= \quad 44.361 \text{ cm}^3$

$V = \quad hB$
$= 5.3 \text{ cm} \cdot (3.1 \text{ cm} \cdot 2.7 \text{ cm})$
$= 5.3 \text{ cm} \cdot \quad 8.37 \text{ cm}^2$
$= \quad 44.361 \text{ cm}^3$

The volume is the same regardless what face is the base. This verifies that multiplication is associative.

394

NOTES ON QUESTIONS
Question 10: You might wish to show the steps using the properties:
$5 \cdot 437 \cdot 2 =$
$5 \cdot (437 \cdot 2) = 5 \cdot (2 \cdot 437) =$
$(5 \cdot 2) \cdot 437 = 10 \cdot 437$

ADDITIONAL ANSWERS
9. sample:
$3 \cdot (4 \cdot 0.5) = 3 \cdot 2 = 6$ **and**
$(3 \cdot 4) \cdot 0.5 = 12 \cdot 0.5 = 6$

Associative Property of Multiplication:

For any numbers a, b, and c: $a(bc) = (ab)c = abc$.

Because multiplication is both commutative and associative, numbers can be multiplied in any order without affecting the product. These properties can shorten multiplications.

Example 3 Multiply in your head: $35 \cdot 25 \cdot 4 \cdot 4 \cdot 25$.

Solution Notice that $4 \cdot 25 = 100$. Multiply these first.
Think:
$$35 \cdot 25 \cdot 4 \cdot 4 \cdot 25$$
$$= 35 \cdot (25 \cdot 4) \cdot (4 \cdot 25)$$
$$= 35 \cdot \quad 100 \quad \cdot \quad 100$$
$$= 350{,}000.$$

Questions

Covering the Reading

1. Name two ways of finding the volume of a rectangular solid.
   counting, using a formula

In 2–4, give the volume of a rectangular solid with the given dimensions.

2. height 6 cm, width 3 cm, and depth 4 cm **72 cm³**

3. width 12 in., height 6 in., and depth 2.25 in. **162 in.³**

4. height 10 meters, width w meters, and depth d meters
   10wd cubic meters

In 5–7, give the volume of a rectangular solid in which:

5. the area of the base is 40 square centimeters and the height is 4 cm. **160 cm³**

6. the base has one side of length 10 inches, another side 2 inches longer, and the height is 1.5 in. **180 in.³**

7. the base has area A and the height is h. **Ah**

8. State the Associative Property of Multiplication.
   For any numbers a, b, c: $a(bc) = (ab)c = abc$.

9. Give an instance of the Associative Property of Multiplication.
   See margin.

In 10–12, use the properties of multiplication to do these problems mentally. No calculator or pencil-and-paper figuring allowed.

10. $5 \cdot 437 \cdot 2$ **4370**

11. $6 \cdot 7 \cdot 8 \cdot 9 - 9 \cdot 8 \cdot 7 \cdot 6$ **0**

Applying the Mathematics

12. 50% of 67 times 2   67

13. The floor of a rectangularly shaped room is 9 feet by 12 feet. The ceiling is 8 feet high. How much air is in the room?   864 ft³

14. Give two possible sets of dimensions for a rectangular solid whose volume is 144 cubic units.   Samples: 12, 12, and 1; 12, 4, and 3

15. **a.** Draw a rectangular solid whose volume is 8 cm³ and has all dimensions the same. **b.** What is this rectangular solid called? **c.** Draw a second rectangular solid whose volume is 8 cm³ but whose dimensions are not equal.
a. See margin. b. cube; c. See margin.

16. Give **a.** the volume and **b.** the surface area of this box.
a. 1080 in.³; b. 762 in.²

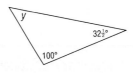
24''   9''   5''

Review

17. A computer has a display screen that can show up to 364 rows and 720 columns of dots. How many dots can be on that screen? *(Lesson 9-1)*   262,080 dots

18. A rectangular solid has width *W* centimeters, length *L* centimeters, and depth *D* centimeters. What is the surface area of the solid? *(Lesson 9-2)*   2WL + 2LD + 2WD

19. Solve the equation $83 - x = 110$. *(Lesson 7-6)*   -27

20. In the triangle below:

y $32\frac{1}{2}°$ $100°$

a. What is the value of *y*? *(Lesson 7-10)*   47 1/2°
b. How many angles are acute?   two
c. How many angles are obtuse? *(Lesson 3-6)*   one

21. **a.** Press the following keys on a calculator. *(Lesson 1-7)*
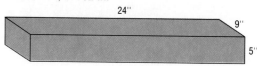
b. Press the following keys.
[5] [.] [6] [7] [×] [2] [3] [.] [4] [=]
c. Compare the displays you get for **a** and **b**. What property have you verified? *(Lesson 9-1)*   Both are 132.678; Commutative Property of Multiplication

396

In 22–24, put one of the signs $<$, $=$, or $>$ in the blank. *(Lesson 1-6)*

22. -4 − 4 _?_ -4 + 4 $<$

23. -7.352 _?_ -7.351 $<$

24. 2/3 _?_ .66666666 $>$

25. **a.** In which quadrant is the point (4, -1)?   **fourth**
  b. Give an equation for a line that goes through (4, -1).
    (Lessons 8-3, 6-1)   **Sample:** $y = x − 5$

26. If $n = 10$, what is the value of $(3n + 5)(2n − 3)$? *(Lesson 4-5)*
  595

27. 2.6 kilometers is how many meters? *(Lesson 3-3)*   **2600 meters**

28. What digit is in the thousandth place of 54,321.09876? *(Lesson 1-2)*
  8

29. To divide a decimal by .001, how many places should you move
the decimal point, and in what direction? *(Lesson 6-6)*
  three places to the right

Exploration

30. **a.** How many entries are needed to complete this multiplication
table?   **36**

×	3.0	3.2	3.4	3.6	3.8	4.0
7.0	21.0	22.4	23.8	25.2	26.6	28.0
7.2	21.6	23.04	24.48	25.92	27.36	28.8
7.4	22.2	23.68	25.16	26.64	28.12	29.6
7.6	22.8	24.32	25.84	27.36	28.88	30.4
7.8	23.4	24.96	26.52	28.08	29.64	31.2
8.0	24.0	25.6	27.2	28.8	30.4	32.0

  b. Fill in the table.   **See table above.**
  c. Find at least two patterns in the numbers you put into the table.
    **Possible answers: In any column, the difference between an ele-
    ment and the one just above it is constant. Every number ends in
    an even digit. Products increase as you go down or to the right.**

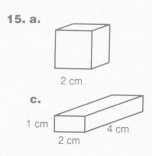
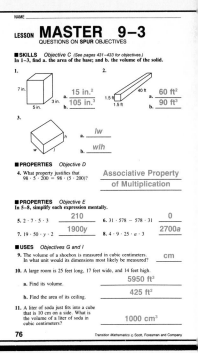

LESSON 9-4

Dimensions and Units

The size of a line segment is given by its length.

Rectangles and other polygons are two-dimensional. There are
two common ways of measuring these figures. Perimeter
measures the boundary (in black below). Area measures the
space inside the figure (shown below with hearts).

Area and perimeter are quite different. The perimeter of the
rectangle pictured below is 6 + 100 + 6 + 100, or 212 *feet.*
That's how far you have to go to walk around the rectangle.
Perimeter is measured in units of length.

100 ft

6 ft

Area measures how much space is taken up by the rectangle.
The area of the rectangle above is 600 *square feet.*

398

398

The area of the rectangle below is 6 cm · 3 cm, or 18 cm². Its perimeter is 6 cm + 3 cm + 6 cm + 3 cm, or 18 cm. Area and perimeter can never actually be equal because the units are different. In a situation like this one, the area and perimeter are called *numerically equal*.

In lakes, perimeter measures shoreline. Area measures fishing room. Lake Willy-Nilly does not have much fishing room despite a lot of shoreline. It has a small area compared to its perimeter.

Lake Willy-Nilly

There are three different ways to measure the size of a three-dimensional figure. Consider the shoebox below. We can measure the total length of its edges. Like perimeter, this is one-dimensional. We can measure its surface area. That is two-dimensional. Or we can measure its volume. That is three-dimensional.

The shoebox has edges of lengths 14 inches, 5 inches, and 7 inches. There are four edges of each length. (Some are hidden from view.) The total length of all edges is
$4 \cdot 5'' + 4 \cdot 7'' + 4 \cdot 14'' = 104$ *inches*.

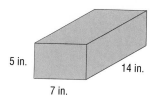

The surface area of this shoebox is found by adding the areas of the six rectangular faces. You should check that it is 406 *square inches*.

The volume of this box measures the space occupied by the box. It is 5 in. · 7 in. · 14 in., or 490 *cubic inches*.

Surface area and volume have different units. They measure different things, as the next example shows.

1. Find another rectangle that has the same area but less perimeter than the one shown.

2

10

sample: 4 × 5

2. Tell whether each would be measured in cm, cm², or cm³:
a. the surface of your desk **cm²**
b. a side of your desk **cm**
c. the air underneath your desk **cm³**

3. Suppose you are wrapping a present. Tell whether you need to measure edges, surface area, or volume to determine:
a. how much the box holds. **volume**
b. how much wrapping paper to use. **surface area**
c. how much ribbon to use. **edges**

Example The spaghetti box and teabag box have 750 cubic centimeters of volume each. Which box requires more cardboard?

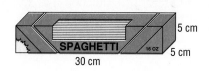

5 cm
5 cm
30 cm

10 cm
10 cm
7.5 cm

Solution The surface area of the spaghetti box is $30 \cdot 5 + 30 \cdot 5 + 30 \cdot 5 + 30 \cdot 5 + 5 \cdot 5 + 5 \cdot 5$, or 650 cm².

The surface area of the box of teabags is $10 \cdot 10 + 10 \cdot 10 + 10 \cdot 7.5 + 10 \cdot 7.5 + 10 \cdot 7.5 + 10 \cdot 7.5$, or 500 cm².

The spaghetti box needs more cardboard to hold the same volume as the teabag box. (This is because the spaghetti box is long and thin.)

To summarize: Length, perimeter, and edge length are 1-dimensional. Area and surface area are 2-dimensional, and usually measured in square units. Volume is 3-dimensional, and usually measured in cubic units.

Questions

Covering the Reading

In 1–4, suppose that length is measured in centimeters. In what unit would you expect each to be measured?

1. perimeter   cm

2. volume   cm³

3. area   cm²

4. surface area   cm²

5. __?__ measures the space inside a 2-dimensional figure.   Area

6. __?__ measures the space inside a 3-dimensional figure.   Volume

7. __?__ measures the distance around a 2-dimensional figure.
Perimeter

8. __?__ measures the surface of a 3-dimensional figure.
Surface area

9. Suppose the area of Lake Willy-Nilly is measured in square miles.
   a. In what unit would you expect its shoreline to be measured?   miles
   b. In what unit would you expect its fishing room to be measured?   square miles

400

10. Draw a lake that has lots of perimeter but very little area.
   See margin.

11. Each side of a square has length 4. *True or false:* The perimeter and area of the square are equal.
   False (they are only numerically equal).

12. Give an example of two rectangular solids with the same volume but with different surface areas.   **Sample: 24 by 2 by 1; 6 by 4 by 2**

13. Find the area of each face of the shoebox in this lesson.
   35 in.²; 98 in.²; 70 in.²

14. A small box has dimensions 11 mm, 12 mm, and 13 mm. Find:
   a. the total length of its edges; **b.** its surface area; **c.** its volume.
   a. 144 mm; b. 862 mm²; c. 1716 mm³

Applying the Mathematics

15. A box has dimensions ℓ, w, and h. What is the total length of its edges? $\ell + \ell + \ell + \ell + w + w + w + w + h + h + h + h$

16. A rectangle has a perimeter of over 100 inches. But its area is less than 1 square inch. **a.** Is this possible? **b.** If so, give dimensions of such a rectangle. If not, tell why it is not possible.
   a. Yes; b. Sample: 200 in. by 0.001 in.

In 17–19, tell whether the idea concerns surface area or volume.

17. the amount of wrapping paper needed for a gift   **surface area**

18. how many paper clips a small box can hold   **volume**

19. the weight of a rock   **volume**

20. An *acre* is a unit of area in the U.S. system. 640 acres = 1 square mile. A farm is measured in acres. *Multiple choice*   What is being measured about this farm?
   (a) its land area; (b) its perimeter; (c) its volume   **(a)**

21. Recall that a liter is a metric unit equal to 1000 cm³. *Multiple choice*   What does a liter measure?
   (a) length; (b) area; (c) volume   **(c)**

Review

22. Trace the drawing. Then reflect triangle *ABC* over the line *m*.
   (Lesson 8-6)   **See margin.**

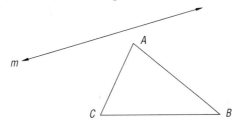

23. Find the area of the quadrilateral with vertices (4, -8), (-3, -8), (-3, 11), and (4, 11). *(Lessons 8-2, 9-1)*   **133 square units**

24. Graph the line with equation $y = x$. *(Lesson 8-3)*
   some points on the line: (3, 3), (0, 0), (-1.5, -1.5)

25. How many feet are in 3 miles? *(Lesson 3-2)*   **15,840 feet**

ADDITIONAL ANSWERS
10. sample:

22.

NAME _____

LESSON **MASTER   9–4**
QUESTIONS ON **SPUR** OBJECTIVES

■**USES**   *Objective G (See pages 431–433 for objectives.)*
1. What is the total edge length of the box pictured at right?
   $4(s + t + u)$

2. Sketch a figure that has a large perimeter but quite a small area.   **sample:**

3. Give dimensions for two rectangular solids that have the same volume but different surface areas.
   sample: 2 × 4 × 3   3 × 8 × 1

4. **a.** Length, perimeter and edge length are **one** -dimensional.
   b. Area and **surface** area are **two** -dimensional and are usually measured in **square** units.
   c. **Volume** is 3-dimensional and is measured in **cubic** units.

5. If the dimensions of a room are given in feet, in what unit would you measure the room's volume?   **ft³**

■**USES**   *Objective I*
6. Recall that a liter is a metric unit equal to 1000 cm³. A container has a base with area 60 square centimeters and a height of 18 cm.
   a. Can the container hold a liter of potato salad?   **yes**
   b. Explain your answer.
   It can hold 1080 cm³, and a liter is 1000 cm³.

7. **a.** Recall that 1 mile = 5280 ft. Use this information to find the number of square feet in a square mile.   **27,878,400**
   b. If 640 acre = 1 square mile, how many square feet are in an acre?   **43,560**

Transition Mathematics © Scott, Foresman and Company

MORE PRACTICE
For more questions on SPUR
Objectives, use *Lesson Mas-
ter 9-4*, shown on page 401.

EXTENSION
The square with area 25
square units has perimeter
20 units. Ask students to
draw a polygon with the
same perimeter whose area
is smaller. Then ask students
to draw a polygon with the
same area whose perimeter
is smaller, in numerical value,
than its area. (You may suggest that students work on
graph paper.)

samples:

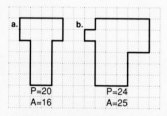

a. P=20 A=16	b. P=24 A=25

EVALUATION
A quiz covering Lessons 9-1
through 9-4 is provided in the
Teacher's Resource File on
page 75.

30. a.

(number line graph with open circle at 4, shaded to the right, showing 0 and 4)

31. a. A*B*C,
2*A*B + 2*B*C + 2*A*C
b. SIDES OF BOX
?2, 3, 4
VOLUME   SURFACE
                      AREA
      24   52
c. Sample: SIDES OF BOX
?10, 15, 7.5
VOLUME   SURFACE
                      AREA
    1125   675

---

26. In this figure, $\angle 2$ is a right angle and m$\angle 1 = 140°$. What is
m$\angle 3$? *(Lesson 7-8)*   130°

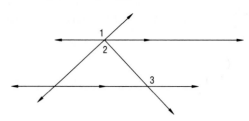

27. The point (8, -4) is translated 10 units down. What is its image?
(Lesson 8-5)   (8, -14)

28. a. Rewrite 3 trillion in scientific notation. 3×10^{12}
   b. Rewrite 3 trillionths in scientific notation. *(Lessons 2-3, 2-8)*
   3×10^{-12}
29. Rewrite each number as a percent. **a.** 1/3; **b.** 2/3; **c.** 4/5.
   (Lessons 1-8, 2-5)   a. 33.$\overline{3}$%, or $33\frac{1}{3}$%; b. 66.$\overline{6}$%, or $66\frac{2}{3}$%; c. 80%

30. Graph all solutions to the inequality $x > 4$. *(Lesson 4-9)*
   See margin.
31. In this program to calculate and print the surface area and volume
of a box, there are two incomplete lines.

```
10 PRINT "SIDES OF BOX"
15 INPUT A,B,C
20 PRINT "VOLUME", "SURFACE AREA"
30 VOL = ___
40 SA = ___
50 PRINT VOL,SA
60 END
```

   a. Fill in the blanks to make this program give correct values for
   VOL and SA.
   b. What will the computer print if A = 2, B = 3, and C = 4?
   c. Run the completed program with values of your own choosing
   to test it. *(Lessons 9-2, 9-3)*
   See margin.

Exploration

32. The "D" in 3-D movies is short for "dimensional." **a.** Are these
movies actually three dimensional? **b.** When you watch a 3-D
movie in a theater, you must wear special glasses. How do these
glasses work?   a. No; b. Each lens of the glasses is a different color
and blacks out part of the picture. Each eye sees a slightly different
image, so the brain thinks the viewer is seeing 3-D.

402

9-5

More Properties of Multiplication

OBJECTIVES

D Identify properties of multiplication.
F Use properties of multiplication to check calculations.

Even using a calculator, you may make a mistake in computation. So you should always learn ways to check problems. The worst way to check is to do a problem over the same way you did it the first time. You are likely to make the same mistake twice.

Properties of multiplication can help you check your work. For instance, to check the answer 2513 to the multiplication $7 \cdot 359$, you can use the commutative property and multiply in the reverse order. Doing $359 \cdot 7$, you should also get 2513.

When one factor in a multiplication problem is a small positive integer, you can check the answer using repeated addition. For example, you can check $7 \cdot 359 = 2513$ by doing the addition

$$359 + 359 + 359 + 359 + 359 + 359 + 359.$$

You should again get 2513. Obviously, if neither factor is a small positive integer, this check is too difficult. Repeated addition also does not work if both numbers are fractions or if both numbers are negative. You may have used repeated addition when you first learned to multiply. Many people continue to use repeated addition whenever they can.

Repeated addition model for multiplication:

If n is a positive integer, then
$$nx = \underbrace{x + x + \ldots + x}_{n \text{ addends}}$$

Specifically:
$1x = x$
$2x = x + x$
$3x = x + x + x$
$4x = x + x + x + x$
and so on.

Example 1   What is the perimeter of a square with side length *s*?

Solution   The perimeter is $s + s + s + s$.
By repeated addition, this equals $4s$.

Example 2   What is the perimeter of a rectangle with length ℓ and width *w*?

Solution: The perimeter $= \ell + w + \ell + w$.

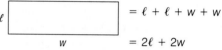

$= \ell + \ell + w + w$ (Commutative and Associative properties of Addition)

$= 2\ell + 2w$ (Repeated Addition Model for Multiplication)

From Examples 1 and 2 come the formulas $p = 4s$ for the perimeter of a square and $p = 2\ell + 2w$ for the perimeter of a rectangle.

Since $1x = 1 \cdot x = x \cdot 1 = x$, multiplying a number by 1 does not change its value. For this reason, the number 1 is called the *multiplicative identity*. It has the same role in multiplication that 0 has in addition.

Additive Identity Property of Zero:

For any number *n*: $n + 0 = 0 + n = n$.

Multiplicative Identity Property of One:

For any number *n*: $n \cdot 1 = 1 \cdot n = n$.

Recall that 4 and -4 are additive inverses or opposites because their sum is 0, the additive identity. Similarly, the numbers 3 and $\frac{1}{3}$ are called **multiplicative inverses** or **reciprocals**, because their product is 1, the multiplicative identity.

404

Property of Opposites:

For any number n: $n + -n = 0$.

Property of Reciprocals:

For any nonzero number n: $n \cdot \frac{1}{n} = 1$.

For example, the reciprocal of 6 is $\frac{1}{6}$, because $6 \cdot \frac{1}{6} = 1$. Notice that *the reciprocal of a number is 1 divided by that number*.

Example 3   Write the reciprocal of 12.5 as a decimal.

Solution   The reciprocal of 12.5 is $\dfrac{1}{12.5}$. A calculator shows that quotient to equal 0.08.

Check   Does $12.5 \cdot 0.08 = 1$? Yes.

Most scientific calculators have a reciprocal key $\boxed{1/n}$. Enter a number and then press this key. The reciprocal of the number you entered should be displayed.

Questions

Covering the Reading

1. Carlisle pressed the key sequence $3.00 \boxed{\times} 67.8 \boxed{=}$. **a.** Write two key sequences Carlisle could use to check his answer. **b.** Do your key sequences give the same answer?   a. See margin. b. yes

2. Heather presses $16 \boxed{1/n}$. **a.** What will the calculator do? **b.** How can she check her answer?   See margin.

3. Using repeated addition, check by hand whether $4 \cdot 953 = 3712$.
   $953 + 953 + 953 + 953 = 3812$; the answer does not check.

4. **a.** Name the multiplicative identity.   1
   b. Name the additive identity.   0

5. **a.** State the Multiplicative Identity Property of One.
   b. State the Additive Identity Property of Zero.
   See margin.

6. For the number 20, give: **a.** its reciprocal; **b.** its opposite;
   c. its additive inverse; and **d.** its multiplicative inverse.
   a. 1/20; b. -20; c. -20; d. 1/20

7. Repeat Question 6 for the number x.   a. 1/x; b. -x; c. -x; d. 1/x

In 8–10, simplify by using multiplication in place of the repeated addition.

8. $x + x + x$ 3x

9. $\ell + w + \ell + w$ 2ℓ + 2w

10. $25 + 20 + 20 + 25 + 20 + 20 + 25 + 20 + 25$
    $4 \cdot 25 + 5 \cdot 20 = 200$

LESSON 9-5   *More Properties of Multiplication*   **405**

ADDITIONAL EXAMPLES
1. A regular hexagon has sides of length h. What is its perimeter?
6h

2. A ticket to Saturday night's concert costs $7.50. If Todd wants to buy t tickets, how much money will he need?
$7.50t

3. Find the reciprocal of each number.
a. 5 $\frac{1}{5}$ or .2
b. -2 $-\frac{1}{2}$ or -.5
c. 0.3 $\frac{10}{3}$ or $3.\overline{3}$
d. -0.25   -4
e. 0.0001   **10,000**

4. What number has no reciprocal? Why? **0; there is no number by which you can multiply 0 and get 1.**

NOTES ON QUESTIONS
Question 6:   This provides a quick check on the four terms.

ADDITIONAL ANSWERS
1. a. $67.8 \boxed{X} 3.00 \boxed{=}$ or
$67.8 \boxed{+} 67.8 \boxed{+} 67.8 \boxed{=}$

2. a. The reciprocal of 16 is displayed. **b.** Multiply her answer by 16; she should get 1.

5. a. For any number n, $n \cdot 1 = 1 \cdot n = n$.
b. For any number n, $n + 0 = 0 + n = n$.

NOTES ON QUESTIONS

Making Connections for Questions 14 and 15: These, like all multiplications that fit the Repeated Addition Model for Multiplication, are special cases of rate factor multiplications to be studied in Chapter 10.

Error Analysis for Question 16: Many students get the answer 4. Check by substituting a value for *e*.

Question 25: The answers depend on whether you want to allow negative error. If not, the solutions are 1 point and |*w* − *z*| points, respectively.

Question 28: The property is $\frac{1}{\frac{1}{n}} = n$ and corresponds to the Op-op Property of Addition: -(-*n*) = *n*. In words, the reciprocal of the reciprocal of a number is the original number; you could call it the Rec-Rec Property.

11. What could the variables used in Question 9 represent?
    the length and width of a rectangle; the result is the perimeter.

In 12 and 13, change the multiplications to additions.

12. $6y$ $y + y + y + y + y + y$ 13. $2x + 4z$ $x + x + z + z + z + z$

Applying the Mathematics

14. Orange juice is \$1.19 per can in a grocery store. A shopper buys 6 cans. Name two ways the shopper can figure out the total cost.
    $6 \cdot \$1.19$ or $1.19 + 1.19 + 1.19 + 1.19 + 1.19 + 1.19$

15. Orange juice is \$1.19 per can in a grocery store. A shopper buys *c* cans. What is the total cost?   \$1.19c

16. Simplify: $4e - e$. (Hint: Change everything to additions.)   3e

17. *Multiple choice* Which does **not** equal the multiplicative identity?   (c)
    (a) $\frac{7}{7}$ (b) $.6 \cdot \frac{5}{3}$ (c) $x - x$ (d) $.3 + .7$

18. Which pairs of numbers are reciprocals?   (a), (b), (c), (d), (g)
    (a) 100 and 0.01   (b) 2 and 1/2
    (c) 2.5 and 2/5   (d) 7/4 and 4/7
    (e) 3.5 and 3/5   (f) 16 and -16
    (g) 1.5 and $0.\overline{6}$ (h) 3 and .3

19. Which of the pairs of numbers in Question 18 are opposites?   (f)

20. What simple sentence is being described? "The sum of the multiplicative identity and the additive identity is the multiplicative identity." $1 + 0 = 1$

21. Rewrite 12.5 and its reciprocal as simple fractions.   25/2, 2/25

Review

22. A rectangle with dimensions *a* and *b* is inside a rectangle with dimensions ℓ and *w*.
    a. What is the area of the shaded region?
    b. Suppose you tilt the smaller rectangle (as pictured at left). Does this change the area between the two rectangles?
    (Lessons 7-1, 9-1)   a. $\ell w - ab$; b. no

23. Name the general property. *(Lessons 5-7, 9-3, 7-2)*
    a. $a + (b + c) = (a + b) + c$ Assoc. Prop. of Addition
    b. $6.4 \cdot (3.7 \cdot 900) = (6.4 \cdot 3.7) \cdot 900$ Assoc. Prop. of Mult.
    c. $35 + {-}78 = 35 - 78$ Add-Opp Prop. of Subtraction

24. A box has dimensions 2′, 3′, and 4′. *(Lessons 9-2, 9-3)*
    a. Find the area and perimeter of the largest face of the box.
    b. Find the surface area and volume of the box.
    a. A = 12 ft²; p = 14 ft; b. S.A. = 52 ft²; V = 24 ft³

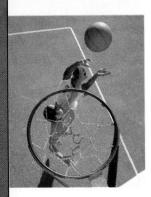

25. How far off is the person's estimate? *(Lesson 7-3)*
   a. A person estimates that a team will win by 4 points, but the team wins by 5.   **1 point**
   b. A person estimates that a team will win by w points, but the team wins by z points.   **$w - z$ points**

26. *True or false?* $1.005 \cdot 2.34567893456 > 2.34567893456$.
   (Lesson 4-9)   **true**

27. Find the measures of the numbered angles, given that $m \parallel n$.
   (Lesson 7-8)   **$m\angle 1 = m\angle 3 = m\angle 4 = 145°$; $m\angle 2 = 35°$**

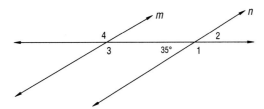

Exploration

28. Enter 5 on your calculator. Press the reciprocal key ⌊1/n⌋ twice.
   a. What number is displayed? **b.** What has happened? **c.** What will happen if you press the reciprocal key 75 times? **d.** Make a generalization.   **a. 5; b. The calculator has taken the reciprocal of the reciprocal of 5. c. You will get 0.2. d. If you press the reciprocal key an even number of times, you will get the original number. If you press the key an odd number of times, you will get its reciprocal.**

MORE PRACTICE
For more questions on SPUR Objectives, use *Lesson Master 9-5,* shown below.

LESSON 9-5   More Properties of Multiplication   **407**

LESSON

Size Changes — Expansions

As the zebra colt grows, its size expands.

Suppose the segment below has length *L*.

L ————

Place a copy next to it. The total length is $L + L$ or $2L$. Multiplying by 2 lengthens the segment. The new segment is twice the length of the original.

2L ————

Place another copy. The length is $2L + L$ or $3L$. Multiplying by 3 expands the segment even more.

3L ————

Example 1 Consider the segment above with length *L*. Draw a segment 2.5 times as long.

Solution Measure the segment with length *L*. Its length is 0.5″. Multiply 0.5 by 2.5.

$$2.5 \cdot 0.5 \text{ inches} = 1.25 \text{ inches}$$

The desired segment is 1.25 inches, or $1\frac{1}{4}$ inches long. Draw it.

2.5L ————

Check Notice that 2.5*L* should be halfway between 2*L* and 3*L*. It is.

These examples show that multiplying by a number can change the size of things. The number is called the **size change factor**. Above, the size change factors are 2, 3, and then 2.5.

408

With coordinates it is even easier to change the size of things. We begin with a quadrilateral (in black). Then multiply both coordinates of all vertices by 2. The image is in blue. It has the same shape as the preimage. But its sides are 2 times as long.

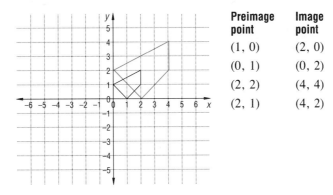

Preimage point	Image point
(1, 0)	(2, 0)
(0, 1)	(0, 2)
(2, 2)	(4, 4)
(2, 1)	(4, 2)

This transformation is called a *size change of magnitude 2*. The image of (x, y) is $(2x, 2y)$. Because the image figure is bigger, this size change is also called an **expansion** of magnitude 2.

Multiplying the coordinates by 3 results in a larger image. Still, each angle and its image have the same measure. Notice that corresponding sides of the preimage and image are parallel. This is a size change or expansion of magnitude 3. The number 3 is the size change factor.

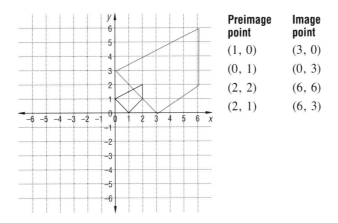

Preimage point	Image point
(1, 0)	(3, 0)
(0, 1)	(0, 3)
(2, 2)	(6, 6)
(2, 1)	(6, 3)

In general, under a size change of magnitude 3, the image of (x, y) is $(3x, 3y)$.

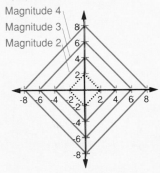

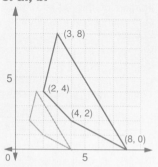
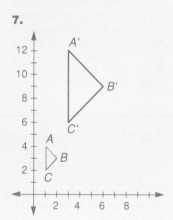
Pictured below is a size change of magnitude 2.25. Each coordinate of the preimage has been multiplied by 2.25.

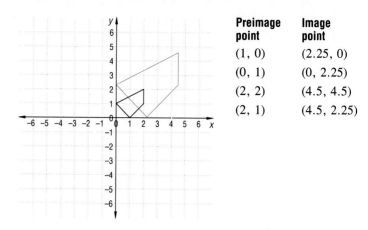

Preimage point	Image point
(1, 0)	(2.25, 0)
(0, 1)	(0, 2.25)
(2, 2)	(4.5, 4.5)
(2, 1)	(4.5, 2.25)

With a size change of magnitude 2.25, the image of (x, y) is $(2.25x, 2.25y)$.

In general, under a **size change of magnitude k,** the image of (x, y) is (kx, ky).

When two figures have the same shape, they are called **similar figures**. In a size change, the preimage and the image are always similar.

The idea of size change can involve quantities other than lengths.

Example 2
John weighed 6.3 pounds at birth. At age 1, his weight had tripled. How much did he weigh at age 1?

Solution "Tripled" means a size change of magnitude 3. Multiply his weight by 3. He weighed 3 · 6.3 pounds, or 18.9 pounds.

Example 3
Maureen works in a store for $5 an hour. She gets time-and-a-half for overtime. What does she make per hour when she works overtime?

Solution "Time-and-a-half" means to multiply by $1\frac{1}{2}$ or 1.5. Working overtime, she makes 1.5 · $5.00, or $7.50.

410

Covering the Reading

1. **a.** Copy this horizontal segment. ——————————— 4.4 cm
   b. If this segment has length L, draw a segment of length $2L$.
   c. Draw a segment of length $3L$.   **13.2 cm**
   d. Draw a segment of length $3.5L$.   **15.4 cm**
   b. 8.8 cm

2. Draw a line segment that is 1.5 times as long as the segment at left.   **(2.85 cm)**

3. **a.** Graph the quadrilateral with vertices (1.5, 4), (4, 0) (2, 1), and (1, 2). **b.** Find the image of this quadrilateral under an expansion of magnitude 2. **c.** How do lengths of the sides of the image compare with lengths of sides of the original quadrilateral? **d.** How do the measures of the angles in the preimage and image compare?
   See margin.

4. Figures with the same shape are called __?__ figures.   **similar**

5. Under a size change, a figure and its image are __?__.   **similar**

6. *True or false?*   Under a size change, a side of a preimage is parallel to the corresponding side of its image.   **True**

7. A triangle has vertices (1, 4), (2, 3), and (1, 2). Graph it and its image under a size change with magnitude 3.
   See margin.

8. Under a size change with magnitude k, the image of (x, y) is __?__.
   (kx, ky)

9. Suzanne saved $25.50. After doing three magic shows, she tripled this amount. **a.** What size change factor is meant by the word "tripled"? **b.** How much money does she have now?
   a. 3; b. $76.50

10. David gets $1.50 an hour for babysitting. After 10 P.M., he gets time-and-a-half for overtime. **a.** What does he make per hour after 10 P.M.? **b.** What will David earn for babysitting from 7 P.M. to 11 P.M.?   **a. $2.25; b. $6.75**

Applying the Mathematics

11. A microscope lens magnifies 150 times. Some human hair is about 0.1 mm thick. How thick would the hair appear under this microscope?   **15 mm**

12. The bookcase in the picture is 1/40 of the actual size. This means that the actual bookcase is 40 times as wide. Will the actual bookcase fit into a space 5 feet wide?   **No; it is more than 2 feet too long.**

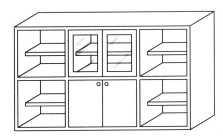

LESSON 9-6   Size Changes—Expansions   **411**

13. An object is 4 cm long. A picture of the object is 12 cm long. The image of the object is __?__ times actual size.   3

In 14–17, each word suggests an expansion of what magnitude?

14. doubled   2

15. quintupled   5

16. octupled   8

17. quadrupled   4

Review

18. Simplify mentally: $3.95 + $3.95 + $3.95 + $3.95 + $3.95 + $3.95 + $3.95 + $3.95 + $3.95 + $3.95 *(Lesson 9-5)* $39.50

19. The product of a number and its reciprocal is __?__. *(Lesson 9-5)*   1

20. The reciprocal of $\frac{1}{100}$ is __?__. *(Lesson 9-5)*   100

21. Suppose a city block is 200 meters long and 50 meters wide. **a.** If you walked around this block, how far would you have to walk? **b.** What is the perimeter of this block? **c.** What is its area? *(Lesson 9-4)*   a. 500 m; b. 500 m; c. 10,000 m²

22. A box is 9″ long, 10″ wide, and 15″ high. *(Lessons 9-2, 9-3)*
  a. What is its surface area?   750 in.²
  b. What is its volume?   1350 in.³

In 23–25, name the general property for the given instance. *(Lessons 9-3, 9-1, 1-10)*

23. 50% · (375 · 63) = (50% · 375) · 63   Associative Prop. of Mult.

24. 3(*ab*) = 3(*ba*)   Commutative Property of Multiplication

25. 7/13 = 28/52   Equal Fractions Property

26. Solve 3.8 = *E* − 0.09. *(Lesson 7-4)*   3.89

Exploration

27. What is the magnitude of a size change you might find in an electron microscope?   See margin.

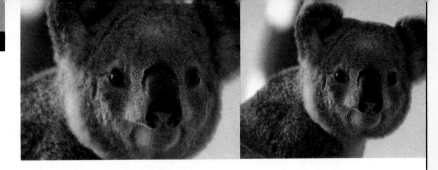
Size Changes— Contractions

LESSON 9-7

RESOURCES

■ Lesson Master 9-7
■ Quiz on Lessons 9-5 Through 9-7
▣ Computer Master 18
▧ Visual for Teaching Aid 61: Use to exemplify a contraction.
▧ Visual for Teaching Aid 62: Use with the Additional Examples.
■ Overhead Coordinate Grid and Similar Triangles (from *Transition Mathematics Teacher Kit*)
■ *Manipulative Activities Sourcebook,* Activity 16

In Lesson 9–6, all of the size change factors were numbers bigger than 1. This results in products with larger absolute value. In this lesson, we multiply by numbers between 0 and 1. This results in numbers with smaller absolute value. For instance, if 8 is multiplied by 0.35, the product is 2.8. The number 2.8 is smaller than 8.

This can be pictured. AB = 8 cm. CD = 0.35 · 8 cm = 2.8 cm. $\overline{CD}$ is shorter.

$$A \rule{6cm}{0.4pt} \overset{8 \text{ cm}}{} B$$

$$C \rule{2cm}{0.4pt} \overset{2.8 \text{ cm}}{} D \qquad 0.35 \cdot 8 = 2.8$$

Think of AB as having been reduced in size to 2.8 cm by a shrinking, or a **contraction**. A contraction is a size change with a magnitude whose absolute value is between 0 and 1. In the situation above, the *magnitude of the contraction* is 0.35.

Below is a two-dimensional picture of a contraction. The preimage is the black pentagon. We have multiplied the coordinates of all its vertices by 1/2. Since 1/2 is between 0 and 1, the resulting image is smaller than the original. Again the preimage and image are similar figures. In this case, sides of the image have 1/2 the length of sides of the preimage. Corresponding angles on the preimage and image have the same measure.

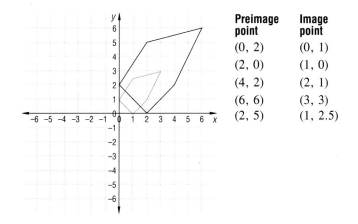

Preimage point	Image point
(0, 2)	(0, 1)
(2, 0)	(1, 0)
(4, 2)	(2, 1)
(6, 6)	(3, 3)
(2, 5)	(1, 2.5)

OBJECTIVES

J Apply the Size Change Model for Multiplication in real situations.
M Perform contractions on a coordinate graph.

TEACHING NOTES

Reading Before students begin this lesson, have them look at the reading section and determine what they think will be important. They should use visual clues such as italic and heavy type, as well as the material that has been boxed to make it stand out.
   We suggest you have students do this lesson on their own. Then ask for a brief summary of the reading, and spend the rest of the class discussion on troublesome questions.

LESSON 9-7 Size Changes—Contractions   413

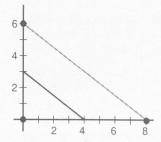
In general, under a size change of magnitude $\frac{1}{2}$, the image of (x, y) is $(\frac{1}{2}x, \frac{1}{2}y)$.

Expansions and contractions are types of size changes. The general idea is an important model for multiplication.

Size Change Model for Multiplication:

> If a quantity x is multiplied by a size change factor k, then the result is a quantity k times as big.

If k is bigger than 1, then the size change is an expansion. If k is between 0 and 1, the size change is a contraction.

Contractions also occur with quantities that are not lengths.

Example 1 A person buys an airplane ticket. Sometimes a spouse can travel for 2/3 the price and a child under 12 can travel for 1/2 price. On this plan, what will it cost a married couple and their 11-year-old child to fly if the normal price of a ticket is $150?

Solution   It will cost one of the adults $150.
It will cost the spouse 2/3 of $150. This can be calculated by using the decimal 0.6666666 for 2/3. Then, multiplying gives $99.99999, which rounds to $100.

It will cost the child 1/2 of $150. That is 0.5 · $150, or $75.
The total cost will be $150 + $100 + $75, or $325.

In Example 1, the size change factors are 2/3 and 1/2. Size change factors for contractions are often written as fractions or percents. You have seen the idea in Example 2 before. Now you can think of it as an example of size change multiplication.

Example 2 About 1.3% of the population of the United States is 85 or older. If the U.S. population is about 250,000,000, how many people are 85 or older?

Solution   The size change factor is 1.3%, or 0.013.
0.013 · 250,000,000 people = 3,250,000 people.

414

Covering the Reading

1. a. Measure the length of the segment below to the nearest half cm.   **3.5 cm**

t

b. If the segment has length *t*, draw a segment with length $0.3t$.
c. What is the magnitude of the contraction?   **0.3**   **b. 1.05 cm**

2. Any positive number between __?__ and __?__ can be the magnitude of a contraction.   **0, 1**

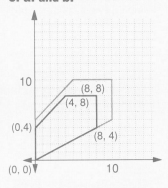

c. The lengths of the sides of the image are 0.8 times the lengths of the sides of the preimage.
d. The corresponding angles have the same measures.

7. If a quantity is multiplied by a size change factor k, the result is a quantity that is k times as big.

In 3–5, give the image of the point $(6, 4)$ under the contraction with the given magnitude.

3. 0.5   **(3, 2)**   **4.** 0.75   **(4.5, 3)**   **5.** $\frac{1}{4}$ **(1.5, 1)**

6. a. Graph the pentagon with vertices $(10, 10)$, $(10, 5)$, $(0, 0)$, $(0, 5)$, $(5, 10)$. **b.** Graph its image under a contraction with magnitude 0.8. **c.** How do the lengths of the corresponding sides of the preimage and image compare? **d.** How do the measures of corresponding angles in the preimage and image compare?
See margin.
7. State the Size Change Model for Multiplication.   **See margin.**

8. Repeat Example 1 if the cost of a ticket for an adult is $210.
$455
9. About 7.8% of the U.S. population is of Spanish origin. If the population is 250,000,000, about how many people in the U.S. are of Spanish origin?   **19,500,000**

10. In Question 9, what is the size change factor?   **7.8% or .078**

Applying the Mathematics

11. The actual damselfly is half the size of the damselfly pictured at left. How long is the actual damselfly?   **about 2.25 cm or .875 in.**

12. In doing Question 11, some students measure lengths of this insect in centimeters. Others measure in inches. If they measure accurately, will they get equal values for the length of the damselfly?   **They will get equal values.**

13. What is the image of $(12, 5)$ under a contraction with magnitude k?   **(12k, 5k)**

14. *Multiple choice*   A car was priced at $7000. The salesperson offered a discount of $350. What size change factor, applied to the original price, gives the discount?   **(b)**
(a) 0.02   (b) 0.05   (c) 0.20   (d) 0.245

LESSON 9-7   Size Changes—Contractions   **415**

NOTES ON QUESTIONS
Question 16: Making reasonable generalizations has been consistently emphasized in this course. In this case, drawing a picture may be helpful. You may wish to point out that this generalization connects graphing and reciprocals.

Question 31: You may want to suggest that students trace the stick figure onto a coordinate graph and use the idea of *expansions* to make the new drawing.

16. b. The magnitude of the size change is the reciprocal of the magnitude of the original size change.

15. *Multiple choice* A car was priced at $7000. The salesperson offered a discount of $350. What size change factor, applied to the original price, gives the offered price? **(d)**
    (a) 0.05   (b) 0.20   (c) 0.80   (d) 0.95

16. A size change of magnitude 1/2 was applied to a pentagon in this lesson. Suppose the preimage and image were switched.
    a. What magnitude size change would now be pictured?
    b. Generalize the idea of this question.   a. 2; b. See margin.

Review

In 17–19, use properties of multiplication to simplify in your head. *(Lessons 9-1, 9-5)*

17. $1000 \cdot m \cdot 0.01$ **10m**   18. $3 \cdot 20 \cdot \frac{1}{3} \cdot 5 \cdot 3$ **300**

19. $m + m + -m + m + 4m \cdot .25 + -m$ **2m**

In 20–24, find each number. *(Lessons 5-4, 9-5)*

20. the multiplicative inverse of 40   **1/40**

21. the additive inverse of 40   **-40**

22. the reciprocal of 40   **1/40**

23. the multiplicative identity   **1**

24. the product of 40 and its reciprocal   **1**

25. *Multiple choice* When $x + y = 180$, which is not equal to y?
    (Lesson 5-8) **(c)**
    (a) $180 - x$ (b) $180 + -x$ (c) $-180 + x$ (d) $-x + 180$

26. **a.** Simplify $-\frac{14}{5} - -\frac{3}{10} - \frac{2}{15} - -50$. $\frac{1421}{30}$, or 47.3$\overline{6}$
    b. State and name the property that enables all subtractions to be converted to additions. *(Lesson 7-2)*
    Add-Opp Property of Subtraction: $x - y = x + -y$

416

27. If the high temperature for the day was 20° and the low temperature was -2°, how much did the temperature drop? *(Lesson 7-3)*   22°

28. *R* is a positive number. Which is larger, *R* + 0.8 or 0.8*R*? *(Lesson 6-7)*   R + 0.8

29. Each edge of a cube has length 7 cm. **a.** Find its volume. **b.** Find its surface area. **c.** Find the total length of all its edges. *(Lessons 3-8, 9-2, 9-3)*   a. 343 cm³; b. 294 cm²; c. 84 cm

Exploration

30. A map (like a roadmap or a map of the United States) is a drawing of a contraction of the world. The *scale* of the map is the size change factor. For instance, if 1″ on the map is 1 mile on Earth, then the scale is 1″/1mi.
Now 1 mile = 5280 feet = 5280 · 12 inches = 63,360 inches. So the scale on such a map is 1/63,360. Find a map and determine its scale.   Answers will vary.

31. Below is a drawing. Make a drawing that is similar and 2.5 times the size.

Check by connecting the right hand and left foot on the drawing and the same on the image. The image connection should be 2.5 times as long.

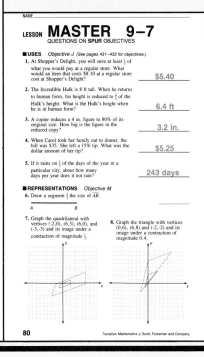

LESSON 9-8

RESOURCES
■ Lesson Master 9-8

OBJECTIVES

A Multiply fractions.
D Identify the Mult-Rec Property of Division and the Product of Reciprocals Property.
E Use properties to simplify expressions.
K Calculate probabilities of independent events.
L Picture multiplication of fractions using area.

TEACHING NOTES

Emphasize that a full understanding of multiplying fractions involves looking at the operation from many different points of view. You may wish to outline the content using the SPUR categories.
Skills: $\frac{3}{2} = 3 \cdot \frac{1}{2}$ or $\frac{1}{2} \cdot \frac{1}{3} = \frac{1}{6}$
Properties: The Mult-Rec Property of Division allows the first statement in the *Skills;* the Product of Reciprocals Property, the second.
Uses: Splitting problems (**Example 4**), and probability of independent events (**Example 5**) are two types of uses.
Representations:
Picture $3 \cdot \frac{1}{2}$

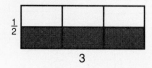

3

9-8

Multiplying by $\frac{1}{n}$

Suppose you make \$6.50 an hour but you work for only 1/2 hour. Do you divide \$6.50 by 2 to find out how much you make for that half hour? If so, then you are using a basic connection between multiplication, reciprocals, and division.

To multiply by $\frac{1}{2}$, you can divide by 2.

A pizza is to be split equally among 7 people. Each person will get 1/7 of the pizza. This is the same idea.

To divide by 7, you can multiply by $\frac{1}{7}$.

The general principle is called the **Mult-Rec Property of Division**. (Rec is for reciprocal.)

Mult-Rec Property of Division:

For any numbers a and b, when $b \neq 0$,

$$\frac{a}{b} = a \cdot \frac{1}{b}.$$

In words, dividing by b is the same as multiplying by the reciprocal of b.

As a simple instance, $\frac{5}{4} = 5 \cdot \frac{1}{4}$. And because of the Commutative Property of Multiplication, $\frac{5}{4}$ also equals $\frac{1}{4} \cdot 5$. Notice how the Mult-Rec Property is used in the next example.

■ ■ ■ ■ ■ ■ ■ ■

Example 1 A picture is to be reduced to 1/3 its original size. If an original length on the picture was 11 cm, what will be the new length?

Solution The new length will be $\frac{1}{3} \cdot 11$ cm.
Using the Mult-Rec Property, this equals $\frac{11}{3}$ cm, or $3.\overline{6}$ cm.

Remember that the area of a rectangle can picture products of numbers. To picture ab, draw a rectangle with length a and width b. The area is ab.

418

■ ■ ■ ■ ■ ■

Example 2   Picture 2 · 3.

Solution   Draw a rectangle with dimensions 2 and 3.

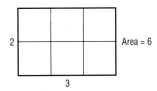

2   Area = 6

3

The area of this rectangle is 6, which is 2 · 3.

Using this same idea, multiplication by $\frac{1}{n}$ can be pictured.

■ ■ ■ ■ ■ ■ ■ ■

Example 3   Picture 2 · $\frac{1}{4}$.

Solution   Draw a rectangle with dimensions 2 and $\frac{1}{4}$. (A unit square split into 4 is drawn as a guide.) The area of this rectangle is 2 · $\frac{1}{4}$. You can see also that the area equals $\frac{2}{4}$ of the original unit square.

2

$\frac{1}{4}$

The fractions $\frac{1}{2}$, $\frac{1}{3}$, $\frac{1}{4}$, and so on, are **unit fractions.** A unit fraction is a fraction with 1 in its numerator and a natural number in its denominator. The Mult-Rec Property shows how to multiply any decimal by a unit fraction $\frac{1}{n}$. Here is a situation that requires multiplying two unit fractions together.

■ ■ ■ ■ ■ ■

Example 4   Five scouts have to stuff envelopes. They divide the job equally. But one of the scouts finds two other friends to help. These three divide their work equally. How much of the entire job did this scout do?

Solution   The scout originally had $\frac{1}{5}$ of the job to do. By dividing the job among three people, the problem is to calculate $\frac{1}{5}$ divided by 3.

By the Mult-Rec Property, this equals $\frac{1}{5} \cdot \frac{1}{3}$. Now let's figure that out.

LESSON 9-8   Multiplying by $\frac{1}{n}$ **419**

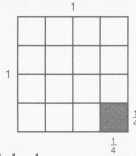

Again, draw a rectangle. This time one dimension should be $\frac{1}{5}$ and the other dimension $\frac{1}{3}$. The big square here is a unit square.

The area of the small outlined rectangle is $\frac{1}{5} \cdot \frac{1}{3}$. But the area is also $\frac{1}{15}$ of the unit square. (There are 15 congruent rectangles in the unit square.) So $\frac{1}{5} \cdot \frac{1}{3} = \frac{1}{15}$. The scout did $\frac{1}{15}$ of the work.

Here is the generalization of Example 4.

Product of Reciprocals Property:

If a and b are not zero, then $\dfrac{1}{a} \cdot \dfrac{1}{b} = \dfrac{1}{ab}$

From the Product of Reciprocals Property, we see that half of a third is a sixth. That is, $\frac{1}{2}$ times $\frac{1}{3}$ equals $\frac{1}{6}$. Also $\frac{1}{10}$ times $\frac{1}{10}$ equals $\frac{1}{100}$.

An important application of this property is in situations involving chance.

Example 5 Slips of paper with the 10 digits 0 through 9 are put in a hat. In another hat are slips for the 26 letters of the alphabet. One slip is taken from each hat. What are your chances of guessing *both* the digit and the letter?

Solution Your chances of guessing the digit are 1 in 10, or 1/10. Your chances of guessing the letter are 1 in 26, or 1/26. Since the guesses do not affect one another, your chances of guessing both is the product of 1/10 and 1/26.

$$\tfrac{1}{10} \cdot \tfrac{1}{26} = \tfrac{1}{260}$$

So the chances of guessing both are 1/260, or 1 in 260. (Most people think the chances are better than that.)

Check For each of the 10 numbers there are 26 letters to choose from. So there are $10 \cdot 26 = 260$ possible number-letter pairs. Only one of these pairs is correct. So the chances of guessing that pair are 1/260.

420

Covering the Reading

1. You can find half of a number by dividing that number by __?__.   2

2. You can find $\frac{1}{n}$ of a number by dividing that number by __?__.   n

In 3–6, simplify.

3. $2 \cdot \frac{1}{3}$ $\frac{2}{3}$ 4. $a \cdot \frac{1}{b}$ $\frac{a}{b}$ 5. $\frac{1}{8} \cdot 16$ 2   6. $\frac{1}{x} \cdot 5$ $\frac{5}{x}$

7. A picture of an elephant is 1/10 actual size. If the elephant is 5 meters tall, how tall is the picture of the elephant?   0.5 m

In 8–11, simplify.

8. $\frac{1}{3} \cdot \frac{1}{4}$ $\frac{1}{12}$ 9. $\frac{1}{5} \cdot \frac{1}{5}$ $\frac{1}{25}$ 10. $\frac{1}{40} \cdot \frac{1}{x}$ $\frac{1}{40x}$ 11. $\frac{1}{a} \cdot \frac{1}{b}$ $\frac{1}{ab}$

12. You are doing 1/4 of a job. You find a friend to help you do your part. You share your part equally with this friend. **a.** How much of the total job will your friend do? **b.** If the total job pays $100, how much should your friend receive?   a. 1/8; b. $12.50

13. One hat contains 50 pieces of paper. One of these pieces wins a prize. A second hat contains 75 pieces and one of those pieces wins a prize. Without looking, you pick a piece of paper from each hat. What are your chances of winning: **a.** the first prize? **b.** the second prize? **c.** both prizes?   a. 1/50; b. 1/75; c. 1/3750

14. What is a unit fraction?   a fraction with 1 in its numerator and a natural number in its denominator

Applying the Mathematics

15. A pie is divided into 6 pieces. Each piece is split into three congruent smaller pieces. Each smaller piece is what part of the whole pie?   1/18

16. Four shirts are in one drawer and five pair of slacks are on hangers. In the dark, you pick out a shirt and a pair of slacks. What are the chances of choosing the particular shirt and pair of slacks you want?   1/20

17. *D* shirts are in a drawer. *H* pair of slacks are on hangers. In the dark, you pick out one shirt and one pair of slacks. What are the chances of selecting both the particular shirt and the pair of slacks you want? $\frac{1}{DH}$

18. How much of a will does a person receive if the will is split into: **a.** 2 equal shares;   1/2   **b.** 6 equal shares;   1/6   **c.** *n* equal shares?   1/n

19. In a will, five people are left *W* dollars to share equally. How much should each person expect to receive?   *W*/5 dollars

20. *Multiple choice*   Which of (a) to (c) is not equal to $\frac{3}{8}$?   (c)
    (a) 3 divided by 8   (b) 3 times the reciprocal of 8
    (c) 8 times the reciprocal of 3   (d) All are equal to $\frac{3}{8}$.

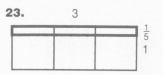
21. **a.** Give the fraction that is the product of 1/7 and 1/23.   **1/161**
    b. Convert your answer to a decimal.   **0.0062112**
    c. Multiply the decimal for 1/7 by the decimal for 1/23.   **0.0062112**
    d. Explain why the answers to parts **b** and **c** should be equal. **See margin.**

22. Use rectangles to picture the product $\frac{1}{3} \cdot \frac{1}{4} = \frac{1}{12}$. **See margin.**

23. Use rectangles to picture the product of 3 and $\frac{1}{5}$.   **See margin.**

24. Calculate: $\frac{1}{2} \cdot \frac{1}{3} \cdot \frac{1}{4}$. $\frac{1}{24}$

25. What is half of a half of a half of a half?   **1/16**

26. A contraction has magnitude $\frac{1}{4}$. You can divide lengths on the preimage by __?__ to get lengths on the image.   **4**

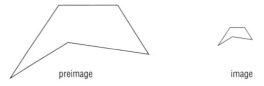

preimage   image

Review

27. **a.** Order from smallest to largest: $\frac{1}{3}$ $\frac{3}{8}$ $\frac{8}{30}$.
    b. Order from smallest to largest: $-\frac{1}{3}$ $-\frac{3}{8}$ $-\frac{8}{30}$. *(Lesson 1-8)*
    a. $\frac{8}{30}, \frac{1}{3}, \frac{3}{8}$; **b.** $-\frac{3}{8}, -\frac{1}{3}, -\frac{8}{30}$

In 28 and 29, simplify. *(Lesson 9-5)*.

28. $3a + a$ **4a**   29. $3a - a$ **2a**

30. A room is rectangularly shaped with length 5.1 meters and width 6.2 meters. To the nearest square meter, what is its floor area? *(Lesson 9-1)*   **32 square meters**

31. Which can be measured in yards: perimeter, area, volume, or surface area? *(Lesson 9-2)*   **perimeter**

32. Two figures with the same shape are called __?__. *(Lesson 9-6)*   **similar**

Exploration

33. The dimensions of a rectangular solid, *to the nearest cm*, are 9 cm, 15 cm, and 20 cm. These dimensions are rounded values. To the nearest cubic centimeter, give the smallest and largest volume the rectangular solid can have.

34. Ten slips of paper with the digits 0 through 9 are put in a hat. Two slips of paper are taken from the hat at the same time.
    a. What are your chances of correctly guessing both the numbers on the slips? **b.** Would your chances be better, worse, or the same if the first slip is returned to the hat before the second slip is taken? **a.** $\frac{1}{45}$ **b. worse; if returned, the chance of guessing both is** $\frac{1}{50}$

33. The smallest possible volume is 8.5 cm · 14.5 cm · 19.5 cm, or about 2403 cm³; the largest possible volume is 9.5 cm · 15.5 cm · 20.5 cm, or about 3019 cm³

LESSON

9-9

Multiplying Fractions

LESSON 9-9

RESOURCES
■ Lesson Master 9-9
■ *Manipulative Activities Sourcebook*, Activity 17

OBJECTIVES

A Multiply fractions.
F Use properties to check calculations.
K Calculate probabilities of independent events.
L Picture multiplication of fractions using arrays.

Suppose you feel you have a 9 in 10 chance of passing an English test. And you feel you have a 2 in 5 chance of getting an A on another test. The chances of having both of these come true are given by multiplying.

$$\frac{9}{10} \cdot \frac{2}{5}$$

You probably remember that you can multiply numerators and denominators to get the product.

$$\frac{9}{10} \cdot \frac{2}{5} = \frac{18}{50}$$

The general pattern is important to know.

Multiplication of Fractions Property:

$$\frac{a}{b} \cdot \frac{c}{d} = \frac{ac}{bd}$$

What if you forget this property? You can figure it out if you remember some of the other properties we have had. Again suppose the problem is to multiply.

$$\frac{9}{10} \cdot \frac{2}{5}$$

Break each fraction up using the Mult-Rec Property of Division.

$$= (9 \cdot \frac{1}{10}) \cdot (2 \cdot \frac{1}{5})$$

Now four numbers are multiplied. Because multiplication is commutative and associative, the multiplications can be done in any order.

$$= 9 \cdot 2 \cdot \frac{1}{10} \cdot \frac{1}{5}$$

Multiplying and using the Product of Reciprocals Property:

$$= 18 \cdot \frac{1}{50}$$

Again the Mult-Rec Property:

$$= \frac{18}{50}$$

Look back at the question that started this lesson. The chances are 18 in 50 that both things will come true.
Since 18/50 = 0.36, and 0.36 = 36%, there is a 36% chance that both things will come true.

LESSON 9-9 Multiplying Fractions   **423**

To focus on the mathematical rationales for the algorithm for the Multiplication of Fraction Property, you may want to copy the steps in multiplying $\frac{9}{10} \cdot \frac{2}{5}$ from the text and ask students to justify each. Note that the Mult-Rec Property of Division is used both ways: first to write a fraction as a multiplication and then to combine a multiplication into a fraction.

Point out the checks in **Examples 1-3**, where the fractions are replaced by decimals. This procedure will work for any fractions.

Simplifying fractions was covered in Lesson 1-10. Although the product in **Example 3** is reduced to lowest terms, you may wish to be flexible about requiring simplified answers in this lesson.

Example 1 Multiply $\frac{7}{3}$ by $\frac{5}{8}$.

Solution Using the multiplication of fractions property:

$$\frac{7}{3} \cdot \frac{5}{8} = \frac{7 \cdot 5}{3 \cdot 8} = \frac{35}{24}.$$

Check One way to check this is to approximate each fraction by a decimal. $\frac{7}{3} \approx 2.33$, $\frac{5}{8} \approx 0.63$, and $\frac{35}{24} \approx 1.46$.
Is $2.33 \cdot 0.63$ about equal to 1.46? Yes, since $2.33 \cdot 0.63 \approx 1.47$. You could do a more accurate check by using more decimal places.

Example 2 Layla bought a brush worth $8 on sale for 2/3 the price. How much did she pay?

Solution 2/3 of $8 can be found by simply multiplying 8 by $\frac{2}{3}$. Write 8 as the fraction $\frac{8}{1}$.

$$8 \cdot \frac{2}{3}$$
$$= \frac{8}{1} \cdot \frac{2}{3}$$
$$= \frac{8 \cdot 2}{1 \cdot 3}$$
$$= \frac{16}{3}$$

Since $\frac{16}{3} \approx 5.333333$, Layla spent $5.34.

Check Again change everything to decimals. $\frac{2}{3} \approx 0.666666$ and $\frac{16}{3} \approx 5.333333$. A calculator verifies that $8 \cdot 0.666666$ is about 5.333333.

Sometimes you can speed up the multiplication of fractions by using the Equal Fractions Property. Example 3 shows how this works.

Example 3 Multiply $\frac{9}{5}$ by $\frac{5}{8}$.

Solution By the Multiplication of Fractions Property,

$$\frac{9}{5} \cdot \frac{5}{8} = \frac{9 \cdot 5}{5 \cdot 8}$$

Now instead of multiplying out the numerator and denominator, remember that you can multiply both numerator and denominator by the same number.
Multiply both by 1/5.

$$\frac{9 \cdot 5 \cdot (1/5)}{5 \cdot 8 \cdot (1/5)} = \frac{9 \cdot 1}{8 \cdot 1} = \frac{9}{8}.$$

Check $\frac{9}{5} = 1.8$, $\frac{5}{8} = .625$, and $\frac{9}{8} = 1.125$.
Does $1.8 \cdot .625 = 1.125$? Yes.

424

Example 4 Multiply $\frac{4}{7}$ by $\frac{7}{4}$.

Solution $\frac{4}{7} \cdot \frac{7}{4} = \frac{4 \cdot 7}{7 \cdot 4} = \frac{28}{28} = 1$

Since their product is 1, the numbers $\frac{4}{7}$ and $\frac{7}{4}$ are reciprocals.

The general pattern of Example 4 is very easy to see.

The reciprocal of $\frac{a}{b}$ is $\frac{b}{a}$, where $a \neq 0$.

Questions

Covering the Reading

In 1–6, simplify.

1. $\frac{6}{5} \cdot \frac{2}{9}$ $\frac{12}{45}$, or $\frac{4}{15}$

2. $\frac{3}{5} \cdot \frac{5}{3}$ 1

3. $\frac{1}{9} \cdot \frac{9}{2}$ $\frac{1}{2}$

4. $(7 \cdot \frac{1}{12}) \cdot (3 \cdot \frac{1}{4})$ $\frac{21}{48}$, or $\frac{7}{16}$

5. $\frac{a}{b} \cdot \frac{c}{d}$ $\frac{ac}{bd}$

6. $12 \cdot \frac{3}{4}$ $\frac{36}{4} = 9$

7. Check your answer to Question 6 by rewriting the fraction as a decimal. $12 \cdot 0.75 = 9$

8. Check your answer to Question 1 by approximating the fractions by decimals. $1.2 \cdot .\overline{2} = .2\overline{6}$; $12/45 = .2\overline{6}$

9. What is the reciprocal of 5/6? 6/5

10. You feel you have a 3 in 4 chance of winning one contest and a 2 in 5 chance of winning another. What are your chances of winning both? 6 in 20 (or 3 in 10)

Applying the Mathematics

11. Verify that 5/8 is the reciprocal of 8/5 by converting both fractions to decimals and multiplying. $0.625 \cdot 1.6 = 1$

12. The days Monday through Friday are weekdays. Saturday and Sunday are on the weekend. A tornado hits a town.
  a. What are the chances that the tornado hit on a weekday?
  b. Years later a second tornado hits the town. What are the chances that both tornados hit on weekdays? a. 5/7; b. 25/49

ADDITIONAL EXAMPLES
1. Multiply.
a. $\frac{2}{7} \cdot \frac{2}{5}$ $\frac{4}{35}$
b. $\frac{8}{9} \cdot \frac{5}{4}$ $\frac{10}{9}$
c. $\frac{w}{x} \cdot \frac{y}{z}$ $\frac{wy}{xz}$
d. $\frac{m}{n} \cdot \frac{n}{m}$ 1

2. Steve gets paid by the pint when he picks strawberries. He needs to pick 100 pints to earn the money he needs. He plans to work two days but would like to finish $\frac{3}{5}$ of the job the first day. How many pints should he pick the first day?
60

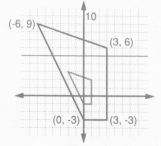
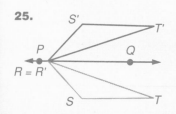
13. Verify that the scouts of Lesson 9-8 finished the job by showing that 4 scouts doing 1/5 of the job each, and 3 scouts doing 1/15 of the job each, altogether accomplish 1 job.
$4 \cdot 1/5 + 3 \cdot 1/15 = 4/5 + 1/5 = 1$

14. One hat contains 4 slips of paper with the digit 0 on them and 6 slips with the digit 1 on them. A second hat has slips with the 26 letters of the alphabet. You draw a 1 from the first hat and an R from the second hat. What are the chances someone else will guess what you drew? $6/10 \cdot 1/26 = 6/260$ (or 3/130)

15. A farm has a rectangular shape 4 miles long and 3/4 mile wide. What is the area of the farm? **3 square miles**

16. Multiplication of simple fractions can be pictured by arrays. Here is a picture of $\frac{3}{5} \cdot \frac{2}{7}$. **a.** Draw a picture of $\frac{4}{5} \cdot \frac{6}{7}$. **b.** What is the product? a. See margin. b. 24/35

17. **a.** Multiply $\frac{1}{2} \cdot \frac{1}{3} \cdot \frac{1}{4}$. $\frac{1}{24}$
    b. How do you know that the answer to part **a** must be a number less than 1, without doing any multiplication? See margin.

18. **a.** Multiply $\frac{3}{2} \cdot \frac{5}{4} \cdot \frac{7}{6}$. $\frac{35}{16}$, or $2\frac{3}{16}$
    b. How do you know that the answer to part **a** must be a number greater than 1, without doing any multiplication? See margin.

19. **a.** Multiply $3\frac{1}{2} \cdot 2\frac{3}{4}$. $\frac{77}{8}$, or $9\frac{5}{8}$
    b. How can you check your answer to part **a**? See margin.

Review

20. Simplify: $4 \cdot \frac{1}{3} \cdot 6$. *(Lesson 9-8)* 8

21. Using repeated addition, $1/4 + 1/4 + 1/4 = \underline{\quad?\quad}$ *(Lessons 9-5, 9-8)* 3/4

22. **a.** Graph the quadrilateral with vertices (1, 2), (-2, 3), (0, -1), and (1, -1).
    b. Graph the image of this quadrilateral under a size change of magnitude 3. *(Lesson 9-6)* See margin.

23. A size change has magnitude $\frac{5}{6}$. Is it a contraction or an expansion? *(Lessons 9-6, 9-7)*   **contraction**

In 24 and 25, given that $\overline{PQ} \parallel \overline{ST}$ and angle measures as shown on the figure:

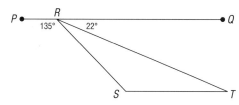

24. Find the measures of the three angles of triangle *RST*. *(Lessons 7-8, 7-10)* $m \angle SRT = 23°$; $m \angle S = 135°$; $m \angle T = 22°$

25. Trace the figure and draw the reflection image of $\triangle RST$ over the line containing $\overline{PQ}$. *(Lesson 8-6)*.   **See margin.**

26. Find **a.** the surface area and **b.** the volume of a rectangular box 50 cm high, 40 cm wide, and 36 cm deep. *(Lessons 9-2, 9-3)*
a. 10,480 square centimeters; b. 72,000 cubic centimeters

27. Make up a situation with a question that can be answered by multiplying the fractions $\frac{2}{3}$ and $\frac{1}{6}$.

28. A person tried to get dressed in the dark. Groping, the person picked a shirt from the four shirts in one drawer. The person also picked one pair of slacks from the three pairs in a closet. However, one of the shirts was stained and two pairs of slacks had holes. **a.** What are the chances that the person picked either a stained shirt or a pair of slacks with holes? (Hint: Arrange the possible shirt-slack combinations in an array.) **b.** What are the chances that the person picked both a stained shirt and a pair of slacks with holes? a. $\frac{9}{12}$ b. $\frac{2}{12}$

```
Shirts: A, B, C, D*          (* stains)
Slacks: X, Y#, Z#            (# holes)
Array:  AX   BX   CX   D*X
        AY#  BY#  CY#  D*Y#
        AZ#  BZ#  CZ#  D*Z#
```

27. Sample: Six people shared a pizza equally. Mary ate only 2/3 of her share. What part of the whole pizza did she eat?

NAME _____

LESSON **MASTER 9–9**
QUESTIONS ON **SPUR** OBJECTIVES

■**SKILLS** *Objective A (See pages 431–433 for objectives.)*
In 1–6, simplify.

1. $\frac{3}{5} \cdot \frac{8}{3}$ ___ $\frac{6}{5}$ 2. $\frac{7}{8} \cdot \frac{8}{7}$ ___ 1

3. $\frac{x}{y} \cdot \frac{z}{w}$ ___ $\frac{xz}{yw}$ 4. $(3 \cdot \frac{1}{10}) \cdot (5 \cdot \frac{1}{4})$ ___ $\frac{3}{8}$

■**PROPERTIES** *Objective F*
5. **a.** Multiply $\frac{7}{8} \cdot \frac{2}{5}$ using the Multiplication of Fractions Property. Show your work. $\frac{7}{8} \cdot \frac{2}{5} = \frac{7 \cdot 2}{8 \cdot 5} = \frac{14}{40} = \frac{7}{20}$

b. Multiply $\frac{7}{8} \cdot \frac{2}{5}$ rewriting each fraction as a decimal. Show your work. $\frac{7}{8} \cdot \frac{2}{5} = .875 \cdot .4 = .35$

■**USES** *Objective K*
6. In Neckoda Woods, the first day of the year over 70° usually occurs in early spring. What are the chances that the first day over 70° falls on a weekend two years in a row? $\frac{4}{49}$

7. A rectangular field is $\frac{2}{3}$ miles long and $\frac{2}{5}$ miles wide.
a. What is the area of the field? $\frac{4}{15}$ mi²
b. There are 640 acres in a square mile. The field is how many acres? $170\frac{2}{3}$ acres

■**REPRESENTATIONS** *Objective L*
8. What multiplication is pictured below? $\frac{2}{4} \cdot \frac{6}{7}$

9. Picture $\frac{2}{3} \cdot \frac{3}{4}$ using an array.

82   *Transition Mathematics* © Scott, Foresman and Company

427

Summary

Given the dimensions, multiplication helps to find the area of a rectangle, the number of elements in a rectangular array, and the volume of a rectangular solid. By adding six areas, the surface area of a rectangular solid can be found.

Multiplication arises also from size change situations. Multiplying by a number greater than 1 can be pictured by an expansion. Multiplying by a number less than 1 can be pictured by a contraction. In either case, the figure and its image are similar.

If the same number x is an addend n times, then the total sum is nx. In this way, multiplication arises from repeated addition. Instead of dividing by n, you can multiply by $1/n$. In this way, multiplication is related to division.

The properties of multiplication are like those for addition: Multiplication is commutative and associative. There is an identity (the number one) and every number but zero has an inverse (its reciprocal). From these properties, other properties show how to multiply fractions.

Vocabulary

You should be able to give a general description and a specific example for each of the following ideas.

Lesson 9–1
Area Model for Multiplication
rectangular array, row, column, dimensions
Commutative Property of Multiplication

Lesson 9–2
rectangular solid, faces
surface area

Lesson 9–3
volume
Associative Property of Multiplication

Lesson 9–5
Repeated Addition Model for Multiplication
perimeter of rectangle
Multiplicative Identity Property of One
multiplicative inverse, reciprocal
Property of Reciprocals

Lesson 9–6
size change factor
size change of magnitude k
expansion
similar figures

Lesson 9–7
contraction
Size Change Model for Multiplication

Lesson 9–8
Mult-Rec Property of Division
unit fraction
Product of Reciprocals Property

Lesson 9–9
Multiplication of Fractions Property

428

Progress Self-Test

See margin for answers not shown below.

Take this test as you would take a test in class. Then check your work with the solutions in the Selected Answers section in the back of the book.

In 1–4, simplify.

1. $\frac{3}{5} \cdot \frac{2}{5}$ $\frac{6}{25}$

2. $-y + y + y + 3 + y + y$ $3y + 3$

3. $4 \cdot \frac{1}{3} \cdot \frac{5}{4}$ $\frac{5}{3}$

4. $\frac{1}{x} \cdot \frac{7}{16}$ $\frac{7}{16x}$

In 5 and 6, name the general property.

5. $(12 \cdot 43) \cdot 225 = 12 \cdot (43 \cdot 225)$ Assoc. Prop. of Mult.

6. $m \cdot \frac{1}{m} = 1$ Property of Reciprocals

7. An auditorium has r rows and s seats in each row. Five seats are broken. How many seats are there to sit in? $rs - 5$

8. Give the area and perimeter of a rectangle with length 17.3 meters and width 6.8 meters. 117.64 m²; 48.2 m

9. How much cardboard is needed to make the closed carton pictured at right? 234 cm²

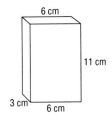
6 cm
11 cm
3 cm
6 cm

10. What is the volume of a rectangular solid with dimensions 3 feet, 4 feet, and 5 feet? 60 ft³

11. If the shoreline of a lake is measured in km, in what unit would you expect to measure the amount of room for fishing? sq. km

12. Give dimensions for two noncongruent rectangles whose area is 16.

13. Round the reciprocal of 38 to the nearest thousandth. 0.026

14. You buy 3 half gallons of milk at $1.29 a half gallon. Show two different ways of calculating the total cost. $3.87; see margin.

15. What multiplication of fractions is pictured below? $\frac{2}{3} \cdot \frac{2}{5} = \frac{4}{15}$

16. What is the image of (8, 2) under an expansion of magnitude 4? (32, 8)

17. Alta earns $5.80 per hour. She gets time-and-a-half for overtime. How much does she make per hour of overtime? $8.70

18. A parallelogram has vertices (2, 6), (6, 8), (8, 2), and (4, 0). Graph this parallelogram and its image under a size change of magnitude $\frac{1}{2}$.

19. In Question 18, the size change is called a ___?___. The image and preimage are said to be ___?___. contraction, similar

For the development of mathematical competence, feedback and correction, along with the opportunity to practice, are necessary. The Progress Self-Test provides the opportunity for feedback and correction; the Chapter Review provides additional opportunities for practice.

We cannot overemphasize the importance of these end-of-chapter materials. It is at this point that the material "gels" for many students, allowing them to solidify skills and understanding. In general, student performance should be markedly improved after these pages.

ADDITIONAL ANSWERS

12. samples: 8 and 2, 16 and 1, 1.6 and 10

14. $1.29 + $1.29 + $1.29 = 3 × $1.29 = $3.87

18. sample:

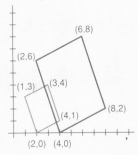

(6,8)
(2,6)
(1,3) (3,4)
(4,1) (8,2)
(2,0) (4,0)

CHAPTER 9 Progress Self-Test **429**

Assign the Progress Self-Test as a one-night assignment. Worked-out *solutions* for all questions are in the Selected Answers section of the student book. Encourage students to take the Progress Self-Test honestly, grade themselves, and then be prepared to discuss the test in class.

Advise students to pay special attention to those Chapter Review questions (pages 431–433) which correspond to questions missed on the Progress Self-Test. A chart in the Selected Answers section in the student text keys the Progress Self-Test questions to the lettered SPUR Objectives in the Chapter Review or to the Vocabulary. It also keys the questions to the corresponding lessons where the material is covered.

24. sample:

```
┌─────────────┐
│             │
└─────────────┘
```

20. 3/25 of Howdy High students are in the band. There are 850 students at Howdy High. How many students are in the band? **102 students**

21. Larry earned a scholarship which pays for 2/3 of his $8400 college tuition. How much is his scholarship? **$5600**

22. You have a one in ten chance of guessing a correct digit. What are your chances of correctly guessing three digits in a row? **1 in 1000**

23. You feel you have a 2 in 3 chance of getting an A on a history test, and a 2 in 5 chance of getting an A on your upcoming math test. What are your chances of doing both? **4 in 15**

24. Draw a rectangle with very little area for its perimeter. **See margin.**

25. *Multiple choice* Which number is the reciprocal of 1.25? **(c)**
(a) 0.125   (b) -1.25   (c) 0.8   (d) 0.75

Chapter Review

Questions on SPUR Objectives

See margin for answers not shown below.

SPUR stands for **S**kills, **P**roperties, **U**ses, and **R**epresentations. The Chapter Review questions are grouped according to the SPUR Objectives for this chapter.

SKILLS deal with the procedures used to get answers.

■ **Objective A:** *Multiply fractions. (Lessons 9-8, 9-9)*

1. Multiply 3 by 1/6 and write the answer in lowest terms.   1/2

2. Multiply 4/5 by 4/3 and write the answer in lowest terms.   16/15

3. Multiply $100 \cdot \frac{3}{8}$. $\frac{300}{8}$ or $\frac{75}{2}$

4. Multiply $\frac{2}{5} \cdot \frac{2}{5} \cdot \frac{2}{5}$. $\frac{8}{125}$

5. Multiply $10\frac{1}{8} \cdot 10$. $\frac{405}{4}$ or $101\frac{1}{4}$

6. Multiply $2\frac{1}{2} \cdot 3\frac{2}{3}$. $\frac{55}{6}$ or $9\frac{1}{6}$

■ **Objective B:** *Find the area and perimeter of a rectangle, given its dimensions. (Lesson 9-1)*

7. What are the area and perimeter of a rectangle with length 7 and width 3.5?

8. What are the area and perimeter of a rectangle with length 5 and width w?
   5w square units; 10 + 2w units

■ **Objective C:** *Find the surface area and volume of a rectangular solid, given its dimensions. (Lessons 9-2, 9-3)*

9. Give the surface area and volume of the rectangular solid pictured below.

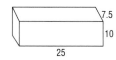

1025 sq. units; 1875 cu. units

10. Give the surface area and volume of the rectangular solid with dimensions x, y, and z.   **2xy + 2yz + 2xz; xyz**

PROPERTIES deal with the principles behind the mathematics.

■ **Objective D:** *Identify properties of multiplication. (Lessons 9-1, 9-3, 9-5, 9-8)*

11. Write in symbols: The product of a number and the multiplicative identity is that number. $n \cdot 1 = n$

12. What property justifies that $\frac{1}{5}$ divided by 2 equals $\frac{1}{5}$ times $\frac{1}{2}$?

13. What is the reciprocal of $\frac{2}{3}$?   3/2

14. What property justifies that $(78 \cdot 4) \cdot 25 = 78 \cdot (4 \cdot 25)$?
   Associative Property of Multiplication

■ **Objective E:** *Use properties to simplify expressions. (Lessons 9-1, 9-3, 9-5, 9-8)*

15. Simplify: $ab - ba$.   0

16. Simplify: $x + y + -x + 1$. $y + 1$

17. Simplify: $m + m + m + m + m + -m$.
   4m

18. Simplify: $\frac{1}{2} \cdot \frac{1}{5} \cdot 5 \cdot x$. $\frac{x}{2}$

RESOURCES
■ Chapter 9 Test, Form A
■ Chapter 9 Test, Form B
■ Chapter 9 Test, Cumulative Form
■ Comprehensive Test, Chapters 1-9

CHAPTER REVIEW

The main objectives for the chapter are organized here into sections corresponding to the four main types of understanding this book promotes: Skills, Properties, Uses, and Representations.

USING THE CHAPTER REVIEW

Whereas end-of-chapter material may be considered optional in some texts, in *Transition Mathematics* we have selected these objectives and questions with the expectation that they will be covered. Students should be able to answer these questions with about 85% accuracy after studying the chapter.

You may assign these questions over a single night to help students prepare for a test the next day, or you may assign the questions over a two-day period.

If you work the questions over two days, we suggest assigning the *evens* for homework the first night so that students get feedback in class the next day, then assigning the *odds* the night before the test so the students can use the answers provided in the book.

ADDITIONAL ANSWERS
7. 24.5 square units; 21 units

12. Mult-Rec Property of Division

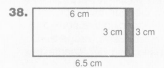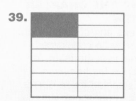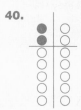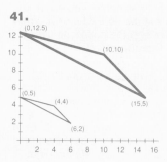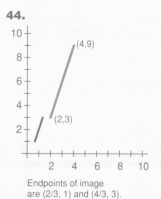
■ **Objective F:** *Use properties to check calculations. (Lessons 9-1, 9-5, 9-9)*

19. Using the commutative property, check whether $2.48 \cdot 6.54 = 16.1292$.

20. Check whether $5 \cdot $7.98 = 39.90 by using repeated addition.

21. Find the product of $\frac{1}{8}$ and $\frac{1}{5}$. Check by converting the fractions to decimals.

USES deal with applications of mathematics in real situations.

■ **Objective G:** *Pick appropriate units in measurement situations. (Lessons 9-1 through 9-4)*

22. The perimeter of a vegetable garden is measured in feet. In what unit would you expect to measure the amount of space you have for planting? **square feet**

23. If the dimensions of a rectangular solid are measured in inches, in what unit would the surface area most probably be measured? **square inches**

24. Name two units of volume.
Sample: cubic centimeters, liters, cubic feet

■ **Objective H:** *Find areas of rectangles and numbers of elements in rectangular arrays in applied situations. (Lesson 9-1)*

25. The flag of the United States has as many stars as states. How many states did the U.S. have when the flag below was in use? **48**

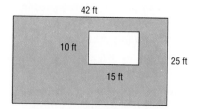

26. The smaller rectangle above is the space for a kitchen in a small restaurant. The larger rectangle is the space for the restaurant. The shaded region is space for seating. What is the area of the shaded region? **900 square feet**

■ **Objective I:** *Find the surface area or volume of a rectangular solid in real contexts.*
(Lessons 9-2, 9-3, 9-4)

27. A stick of margarine is approximately 11.5 cm long, 3 cm wide, and 3 cm high. To wrap the margarine in aluminum foil, at least what area of foil is needed?

28. What is the volume of the margarine in Question 27? **103.5 cubic centimeters**

29. The mattress of a water bed is 7′ long, 6′ wide, and 3/4′ high. Can a quilt with an area of 48 square feet cover the top and all sides of the mattress? **No**

30. A plastic container has a base with area 72 square centimeters and height 14 cm. Can it hold a liter of soup? **Yes**

432

Objective J: *Apply the Size Change Model for Multiplication in real situations.*
(Lessons 9-6, 9-7)

31. Mrs. Kennedy expects to save 1/4 of her weekly grocery bill of $150 a week by using coupons. How much money does she expect to save? **$37.50**

32. On the average, costs of items in the U.S. tripled from 1967 to 1985. If an item cost *x* dollars in 1967, what did it cost in 1985? **3x dollars**

33. If you make $3.50 an hour, what will you make per hour of overtime, if you are paid time-and-a-half? **$5.25**

34. Mr. Jones tithes. That is, he gives one-tenth of what he makes to charity. If he makes $500 a *week*, how much does he give every *year* to charity? **$2600**

Objective K: *Calculate probabilities of independent events. (Lessons 9-8, 9-9)*

35. On the TV show, "Let's Make a Deal," there are three doors with prizes. One door has a very valuable prize. What is the chance that a contestant picks the door with the valuable prize twice in a row? $\frac{1}{9}$

36. Five of seven days are weekdays. Resttown gets hit by a tornado about once every 25 years. What are the chances of Resttown being hit by a tornado next year on a weekday? **5/175 or 1/35**

REPRESENTATIONS deal with pictures, graphs, or objects that illustrate concepts.

Objective L: *Picture multiplication using arrays or area. (Lessons 9-1, 9-8, 9-9)*

37. Show that $5 \cdot 4 = 20$ using a rectangular array.

38. Show that $6.5 \cdot 3$ is larger than $6 \cdot 3$ using rectangles with accurate length and width. (Use centimeters as the unit.)

39. Picture the product of $\frac{1}{2}$ and $\frac{2}{7}$ using the area of rectangles.

40. Picture the product of $\frac{1}{2}$ and $\frac{2}{7}$ using arrays.

Objective M: *Perform expansions or contractions on a coordinate graph. (Lessons 9-6, 9-7)*

41. Graph the triangle with vertices $(0, 5)$, $(6, 2)$, and $(4, 4)$ and its image under an expansion of magnitude 2.5.

42. What is the image of (x, y) under an expansion of magnitude 1000? **(1000x, 1000y)**

43. Is a size change of magnitude $\frac{3}{7}$ an expansion or a contraction? **contraction**

44. Graph the segment with endpoints $(4, 9)$, and $(2, 3)$. Graph its image under a size change of magnitude $\frac{1}{3}$.

CHAPTER 10 MORE MULTIPLICATION PATTERNS

DAILY PACING CHART ■ CHAPTER 10

Students in the Full Course should complete the entire text by the end of the year. Students in the Minimal Course spend more time when there are quizzes and more time on the Chapter Review. Therefore, these students may not complete all of the chapters in the text.

DAY	MINIMAL COURSE	FULL COURSE
1	10-1	10-1
2	10-2	10-2
3	10-3	10-3
4	10-4	10-4
5	Quiz (TRF); Start 10-5.	Quiz (TRF); 10-5
6	Finish 10-5.	10-6
7	10-6	10-7
8	10-7	Quiz (TRF); 10-8
9	Quiz (TRF); 10-8	10-9
10	10-9	Progress Self-Test
11	Progress Self-Test	Chapter Review
12	Chapter Review	Chapter Test (TRF)
13	Chapter Review	
14	Chapter Test (TRF)	

TESTING OPTIONS

■ Quiz for Lessons 10-1 Through 10-4   ■ Chapter 10 Test, Form A   ■ Chapter 10 Test, Cumulative Form
■ Quiz for Lessons 10-5 Through 10-7   ■ Chapter 10 Test, Form B

A Quiz and Test Writer is available for generating additional questions, additional quizzes, or additional forms of the Chapter Test.

PROVIDING FOR INDIVIDUAL DIFFERENCES

The student text is written for the *average* student. The program, however, can be adapted for both less capable and more capable students.

A blackline master (in the Teacher's Resource File) is provided for each lesson for those students who need more practice. The Teacher's Edition frequently provides Error Analysis and Alternate Approach features to provide additional instructional strategies.

For students who require additional challenge, Extension activities are regularly provided in the Teacher's Edition.

OBJECTIVES ■ CHAPTER 10

Students should master the chapter objectives by the time they complete the chapter. To ensure objective mastery, there is continual review built into each set of lesson questions. After students complete the chapter lessons, they assess their mastery on the Progress Self-Test. Then they do the Chapter Review and pay special attention to those questions that match the objectives missed on the Progress Self-Test. Students can get extra practice on these objectives by using the master for each lesson in the Teacher's Resource File.

OBJECTIVES FOR CHAPTER 10 (Organized into the SPUR categories—Skills, Properties, Uses, and Representations)	Progress Self-Test Questions	Chapter Review Questions	Teacher's Resource File	
			Lesson Master*	Chapter Test Forms A and B
SKILLS				
A: Multiply positive and negative numbers.	9, 10, 11	1–4	10-5	11, 12, 13, 23
B: Solve and check equations of the form $ax = b$ mentally or by substitution.	1	5–10	10-1	29
C: Solve and check equations of the form $ax = b$ using the Multiplication Property of Equality.	20, 21, 22	11–16	10-2, 10-8	17, 18, 19
D: Solve and check equations of the form $ax + b = c$.	24, 25	17–20	10-9	20, 21
PROPERTIES				
E: Apply the Multiplication and Addition Properties of Equality.	6	21, 22	10-2, 10-9	4, 6
F: Apply the multiplication properties of 0 and –1.	12, 13, 14 17, 23	23–25	10-7	5, 14, 15, 16
G: Use the Related Facts Property of Multiplication and Division.	5	26–28	10-1	1, 2
USES				
H: Apply the Rate Factor Model for Multiplication.	7	29–33	10-4, 10-5	7, 8, 9, 10, 24, 27
I: Use conversion factors to convert from one unit to another.	18, 19	34–36	10-4	26, 28
J: Find unknowns in area, volume, or array situations involving multiplication.	3	37–39	10-2, 10-3	30
K: Find unknowns in size change situations involving multiplication.	4	40–44	10-3	25
REPRESENTATIONS				
L: Picture multiplication by negative numbers using size changes.	8, 15, 16	45–48	10-6	3, 22

*The Lesson Masters are numbered to match the lessons.

434B

OVERVIEW ■ CHAPTER 10

This chapter has two major themes: equations of the form $ax = b$; and multiplication with negative numbers. The interrelated nature of the topics makes for easy transition from one lesson to the next, and allows most students ample time for mastery.

Lesson 10-1 introduces the equation $ax = b$, to be solved either by substitution or by related facts. Lesson 10-2 demonstrates how the Multiplication Property of Equality can be employed to solve this equation, and Lesson 10-3 illustrates a number of uses for the equation. Thus skill, property, and use are all covered.

Lesson 10-4 describes the Rate Factor Model for Multiplication, which includes many uses of multiplication. This model also allows for and helps to explain multiplication by negative numbers, discussed in Lesson 10-5. The Size Change Model in Lesson 10-6 provides a second use for multiplication with negatives, and at the same time offers a way to picture multiplication with negative numbers. Lesson 10-7 discusses the special cases of multiplication by 0 and -1.

The last two lessons of the chapter combine both major themes. Lesson 10-8 deals with the solution of $ax = b$ when a is negative; Lesson 10-9 covers the solution of $ax + b = c$.

PERSPECTIVES ■ CHAPTER 10

The Perspectives provide the rationale for the inclusion of topics or approaches, provide mathematical background, and make connections within UCSMP.

10-1

SOLVING $ax = b$

Proficient equation solvers use three different methods for solving equations of the form $ax = b$. Some equations are solved mentally; for example, those involving basic facts (such as $6x = 24$) or an integer power of 10 (such as $35x = 3500$). We call this method *substitution* because the solver mentally substitutes for the variable a number that he or she thinks will work. *Trial and error*, combined with *substitution*, may work even when the answer is not quite so obvious.

Other equations are solved by *related facts*. Often these are equations in which both a and b are whole numbers. For instance, if $9x = 981$, then $x = \frac{981}{9}$; the solver may not think of "doing the same thing to both sides."

Finally, some equations are solved by using the Multiplication Property of Equality, that is, by multiplying both sides of the equation by the same number. This method is discussed in Lesson 10-2.

10-2

THE MULTIPLICATION PROPERTY OF EQUALITY

The development of a method for solving more complicated equations of the form $ax = b$ by using the Multiplication Property of Equality parallels the solving of equations of the form $a + x = b$ in Lesson 5-8, which emphasized the use of the Addition Property of Equality. Students may have balked at all that machinery developed just to solve an equation they could do in their heads, but one reason for using that property with addition was to make this lesson easier. In particular, an equation like $\frac{3}{5} \cdot A = \frac{1}{4}$, in which a and b are both fractions, is very difficult to solve either in one's head or by related facts; the Multiplication Property of Equality is particularly effective in solving this and similar equations.

10-3

USING $ax = b$

This lesson provides practice with problems that use the equation $ax = b$ in their solution. The list of applications that introduces the lesson reminds students of the different uses of multiplication that have been covered: area, arrays, volume, repeated addition, size change, and percents of. The students can apply the methods for solving $ax = b$, learned in Lessons 10-1 and 10-2, to a variety of problems.

10-4

THE RATE FACTOR MODEL FOR MULTIPLICATION

The unit in a rate is written with the fraction bar or slash because the calculation of rate is a fundamental use of division. For instance, if a person travels 200 miles in 5 hours, the rate is $\frac{200 \text{ miles}}{5 \text{ hours}} = 40$ miles/hour $= 40 \frac{\text{miles}}{\text{hour}}$. Lesson 11-1 discusses the corresponding Rate Model for Division.

The Rate Factor Model is the fourth and last multiplication model. Many instances or earlier models for multiplication can also be interpreted as rate factor multiplication, for example, arrays, repeated addition, and conversions. In Lesson 10-5, this model is used with applications of multiplication with negative numbers.

Note that we have included units in this lesson. Although putting units in an equation can sometimes be confusing, keeping track of units can also be a big help. By keeping track of units, students have one more way to check answers and to figure out which operation is reasonable. However, do not be rigid on this point. Units help some students more than others.

Although scientists use the word *cancel* with units, many mathematics teachers do not. In this lesson, we use the word *cancel* with units, but not with numbers.

10-5
MULTIPLICATION WITH NEGATIVE NUMBERS

The rules for multiplication with negative numbers are usually presented as in the four simple statements given on pages 455–456. We also encourage the *operator view* shown on these pages, which stresses that the sign of the answer is determined by what one factor does to the other.

This skill is easy, but students wonder why they need to learn it. The point of this lesson and the next is to give real-world situations that can be interpreted as multiplication with negative numbers.

10-6
PICTURING MULTIPLICATION WITH NEGATIVE NUMBERS

This lesson opens with a detailed review of material from Lesson 9-6. The new content, size changes of negative magnitude and a summary of characteristics of size change magnitude k, follows. Because of the logical, gradual progression of picturing transformations on the coordinate graph, this lesson is not difficult. Also, it serves to convince many students that multiplication by negative numbers is a useful idea.

10-7
MULTIPLICATION BY 0 AND -1

Although the properties discussed in this lesson are familiar, students should still consider the examples and questions carefully. The examples and questions discuss consequences of the properties that are not so obvious and that students may have missed or misunderstood. This lesson also provides time for students to work on ideas from earlier lessons.

10-8
SOLVING $ax = b$ WHEN a IS NEGATIVE

This lesson combines the two themes of the chapter: solving $ax = b$ and multiplication with negative numbers. Consequently, the lesson provides review even before the Progress Self-Test and Chapter Review. No new ideas are needed to answer the questions in this lesson.

10-9
SOLVING $ax + b = c$

The strategy of converting equations into simpler ones that can be more easily solved is the basic strategy in all sentence solving. The object in writing down steps when solving equations is to end up with a sentence whose solution is obvious. You may wish to review the idea of *equivalent sentences*, first introduced in Lesson 7-5. The goal in solving $ax + b = c$ for x is to end up with an equivalent sentence of the form $x = k$. This type of equation is frequently referred to as a two-step equation, since two operations are necessary to get to the form $x = k$.

Some students immediately see the general pattern in solving $ax + b = c$. They subtract b from c and divide by a. We see nothing wrong with this procedure; it's the mark of an excellent pattern finder.

More Multiplication Patterns

CHAPTER 10

CHAPTER 10

We recommend 12 to 14 days for this chapter: 9 to 10 days for the lessons, 1 day for the Progress Self-Test, 1 to 2 days for the Chapter Review, and 1 day for the exam. (See the Daily Pacing Chart on page 434A.) Keep in mind that each lesson includes Review questions to help students firm up content they have studied previously.

USING PAGES 434-435

Call attention to the figures graphed on page 435. Ask students to name or show two congruent figures (for example, 2A and -2A, 0.6A and -0.6A). Repeat the procedure, having students identify pairs of figures that are similar but not congruent (for example, 2A and A). You may want to review with students the difference between similarity and congruence.

434

Figure A below, with black lines, is the original. The figure named 2A is an expansion of A with magnitude 2. The figure 0.6A is a contraction of A with magnitude 0.6. The two figures called -2A and -0.6A are found by multiplying the coordinates of points on A by negative numbers. The multiplication by negatives reverses directions. As a result, the figures -2A and -0.6A look upside down. They are the figures 2A and 0.6A rotated 180° around the origin. In this chapter you will study this and other applications of multiplication.

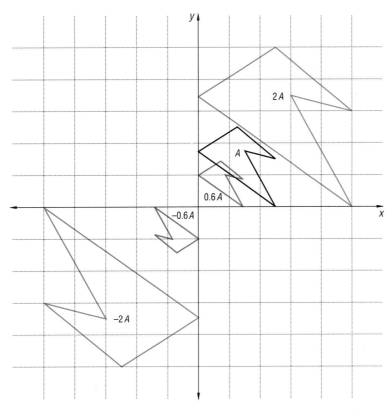

LESSON 10-1

Solving $ax = b$

Early pioneers in aviation used the trial and error method in their quest to learn more about aerodynamics.

In each equation shown below, a number is multiplied by an unknown number, x. The result is another number. These are **equations of the form $ax = b$,** where x is the unknown.

$$3x = 12 \qquad 405 = .38x \qquad \tfrac{3}{5} \cdot x = \tfrac{1}{2}$$

The letter x does not have to be used for the unknown. Here are equations of the form $ax = b$ where a different letter is the unknown.

$$862 = \tfrac{35}{71}m \qquad -6 = 2t \qquad \text{Solve for } v: \ uv = w.$$

Many common methods exist for solving these equations. Three methods are given here. A fourth method is in the next lesson.

Example 1 (Substitution) Is 8 a solution to $5 = 40m$?

Solution Substitute 8 for m. Since $5 \neq 40 \cdot 8$, 8 is not a solution.

Example 2 (Trial and error) Solve $3x = 12$.

Solution You know that $3 \cdot 4 = 12$. So 4 works. Since these equations almost always have only one solution, $x = 4$.

Trial and error works best on the simplest equations. Substitution is the best way to check the other methods.

In Example 2, we used the fact that $3 \cdot 4 = 12$. You also know that $12/4 = 3$ and $12/3 = 4$. These are *related facts*.

436

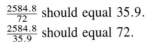

Numbers do not have to be simple to be involved in related facts. Suppose you multiply 72 by 35.9 and you get 2584.8 as the product. You can check this by using related facts. Divide 2584.8 by one of the factors. You should get the other factor. That is, if $72 \cdot 35.9 = 2584.8$, then:

$$\frac{2584.8}{72} \text{ should equal } 35.9.$$
$$\frac{2584.8}{35.9} \text{ should equal } 72.$$

The general property is very important to know. We let the letter P stand for the product. In this property, P cannot be zero.

Related Facts Property of Multiplication and Division:

If $xy = P$, then $\frac{P}{x} = y$ and $\frac{P}{y} = x$.

The method of related facts works well on equations involving decimals.

Example 3   (Related facts) Solve $2000 = 8y$.

Solution
Use the Related Facts Property of Multiplication and Division.
Since $8y = 2000$, 2000 divided by 8 equals y.
$$y = \frac{2000}{8}$$
Do the division.
$$y = 250$$

Check Substitute 250 for y in the original equation.
Does $2000 = 8 \cdot 250$? Yes.

Example 4   Solve $.38t = 405$ to the nearest tenth.

Solution Use related facts.
When $.38 \cdot t = 405$, then 405 divided by .38 equals t.
$$t = \frac{405}{.38}$$
$$\approx 1065.8 \quad \text{(Use a calculator for the division; then round.)}$$

Check Substitute 1065.8 for t in the original equation.
$.38 \cdot 1065.8 = 405.004$.
This is good enough since 1065.8 is only an estimate.

A situation is given in Lesson 10-3 that leads to the equation of Example 4.

LESSON 10-1 Solving $ax = b$ **437**

NOTES ON QUESTIONS
Questions 18 and 19:
Students can convert these into the $ax = b$ form by using the Repeated Addition Model for Multiplication (Lesson 9-5). They can also use *trial and error*.

Questions 21–25:
These set up the next lesson and should be discussed.

Error Analysis for Question 31: The difficulty here is with the units. Have students draw a picture to help them recall that one square foot equals 144 square inches. Then (from the Area Model),
1 inch $\cdot x = 144$ in.^{2},
$x = 144$ inches.

Covering the Reading

1. *Multiple choice* Which equation is not of the form $ax = b$? (a)
   (a) $5/x = 3$ (b) $3 = 5x$ (c) $5t = 3$ (d) $-5x = 3$

2. When is an equation in the form $ax = b$?   See margin.

3. Is 4 a solution to the equation? **a.** $7x = 28$; **b.** $7 = y \cdot 28$; **c.** $28t = 7$; **d.** $.28 = 0.7m$; **e.** $7 + x = 28$.
   a. Yes; b. No; c. No; d. No; e. No

In 4–6, solve mentally.

4. $36 = 18C$ 2   5. $.798x = .798$ 1   6. $3a = 150$ 50

7. What two division facts are related to $8 \cdot 9 = 72$?
   $72/9 = 8$; $72/8 = 9$

8. What two division facts are related to $37 \cdot 0.46 = 17.02$?
   $17.02/37 = 0.46$; $17.02/0.46 = 37$

9. State the Related Facts Property of Multiplication and Division.
   If $xy = P$, then $P/x = y$ and $P/y = x$.

10. **a.** What two division facts are related to $53t = 901$?
    b. Solve $53t = 901$ and check your answer.
    a. $901/t = 53$; $901/53 = t$ b. 17; $53 \cdot 17 = 901$

11. Solve $0.8n = 6$ by related facts and check your answer.
    7.5; $0.8 \cdot 7.5 = 6$

12. Solve $0.7n = 6$ to the nearest hundredth by related facts and check your answer. $n = 6/0.7 \approx 8.57$; $0.7 \cdot 8.57 = 5.999 \approx 6$

Applying the Mathematics

In 13–16, check whether the product is correct by doing a division involving related facts.

13. $684 \cdot 325 = 222,300$ Sample: $222,300/325 = 684$; correct

14. $0.4 \cdot 0.3 = 1.2$ Sample: $1.2/0.4 = 3$; not correct

15. 72% of $1600 = 1152$ Sample: $1152/.72 = 1600$; correct

16. $3/4 \cdot 12 = 9$ Sample: $9/12 = .75 = 3/4$; correct

17. **a.** Perform this key sequence on your calculator.

    $$4.2 \boxed{\div} 3.8 \boxed{=}$$

    What is shown in the display?   Sample: 1.1052632
    b. Round the display answer to the nearest hundredth.   1.11
    c. What equation of the form $ax = b$ does this key sequence solve? $3.8x = 4.2$

18. Solve $x + x + x = 801$.   **19.** Solve $t + t = 4.5$.   2.25
    267

Review

20. Why should you not check a problem by doing it the same way you did it the first time? *(Lesson 9-5)*
    You are likely to repeat any mistakes made.

21. What is the reciprocal of: **a.** 6; **b.** 5/12? *(Lesson 9-9)*   a. 1/6; b. 12/5

22. If x and y are reciprocals, what is the value of $3xy + 5$? *(Lesson 9-9)*   8

438

23. Simplify: $4 \cdot x \cdot \frac{1}{4}$. *(Lesson 9-9)*   **x**

24. a. To solve $\frac{31}{6} + m = -\frac{5}{8}$, what number can be added to both sides? $-\frac{31}{6}$
  b. Solve $\frac{31}{6} + m = -\frac{5}{8}$. *(Lesson 5-8)* $-\frac{139}{24}$

25. Which of these terms are synonyms (mean the same thing)? reciprocal; additive inverse; opposite; multiplicative inverse. *(Lessons 5-4, 9-5)*
reciprocal and multiplicative inverse; opposite and additive inverse

26. By the end of 1989, about 65% of households with TVs had VCRs. If a town has H households with TVs, about how many VCRs would there be? *(Lessons 6-7, 9-7)* **0.65 H**

27. A rectangle has length L feet and width 6 feet. **a.** What is its area? **b.** What is its perimeter? *(Lessons 9-1, 9-5)*
a. 6L square feet; b. 12 + 2L feet

28. With a protractor, measure $\angle ABC$ to the nearest degree. *(Lesson 3-5)*
157°

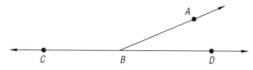

29. Simplify: $1 - 5 - 4$. *(Lesson 7-2)*   **-8**

30. Write one millionth **a.** as a decimal and **b.** as a power of 10.
(Lessons 1-2, 2-8)   **a. 0.000001; b. 10⁻⁶**

Exploration

31. A rectangle has a width of one inch and an area of one square foot. What is its length?   **12 ft., or 144 in.**

FOLLOW-UP

MORE PRACTICE
For more practice on SPUR Objectives, use *Lesson Master 10-1,* shown below.

ADDITIONAL ANSWER
2. when one number is multiplied by an unknown to get a second number

NAME

LESSON **MASTER 10–1**
QUESTIONS ON **SPUR** OBJECTIVES

■**SKILLS**   *Objective A (See pages 480–481 for objectives.)*
In 1–4, solve mentally.

1. $48 = 6y$ $y = 8$ 2. $7x = 7$ $x = 1$
3. $8a = 800$ $a = 100$ 4. $5t = 75$ $t = 15$

5. Is $\frac{1}{3}$ the solution to $\frac{3r}{4} = 4$?   **no**
6. Is .6 the solution to $15a = 9$?   **yes**

■**PROPERTIES**   *Objective G*

7. What two division facts are related to $1.9 \cdot 20 = 38$? $20 = \frac{38}{1.9}$ $1.9 = \frac{38}{20}$

8. What two division facts are related to $\frac{1}{2} \cdot 10 = 5$? $\frac{5}{10} = \frac{1}{2}$ $\frac{5}{\frac{1}{2}} = 10$

In 9 and 10, a. check whether the product is correct by using related facts. (Answer Yes or No.) b. Write the related fact you used in your check.

9. $.75 \cdot 1.25 = 93.75$
  a. **no**
  b. $.75 \neq \frac{93.75}{1.25}$

10. $12\frac{1}{2}\%$ of $7500 = 937$ 5
  a. **yes**
  b. $7500 = \frac{937.5}{.125}$

In 11–14, a. solve by related facts. b. Check each answer.

11. $29x = 1740$
  a. $x = \frac{1740}{29} = 60$
  b. $29 \cdot 60 = 1740$

12. $322 = 23w$
  a. $w = \frac{322}{23} = 14$
  b. $23 \cdot 14 = 322$

13. $4.1t = 217.3$
  a. $t = \frac{217.3}{4.1t} = 53$
  b. $4.1 \cdot 53 = 217.3$

14. 85% of $y = 8245$
  a. $y = \frac{8245}{.85} = 9700$
  b. $.85 \cdot 9700 = 8245$

Transition Mathematics © Scott, Foresman and Company

83

OBJECTIVES

C Solve and check equations of the form $ax = b$ using the Multiplication Property of Equality.
E Apply the Multiplication Property of Equality.
J Find unknowns in array situations involving multiplication.

TEACHING NOTES

After students have read the lesson, discuss the similarity between the Multiplication Property of Equality and the Addition Property of Equality from Lesson 5-8. Since students know how to use the latter, they already have a clue about how to apply this new property.

Each of the examples illustrates a use of the Multiplication Property of Equality. **Example 1** is a straightforward application with an explanation of each step. **Example 2** illustrates an equation that is difficult to solve by any of the methods described in Lesson 10-1. **Example 3** is the first percent problem in the book that is not a "percent of" question.

In discussing the examples, write out the steps you expect students to show on their papers: the original equation, a line showing what each side is multiplied by, and a line showing the solution. Also, stress the importance of the check.

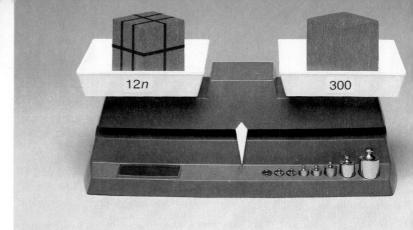

LESSON

10-2

The Multiplication Property of Equality

Equal numbers may not look equal. For instance:

$$50\% = \tfrac{1}{2}.$$

Now multiply both sides by 6. Are the products equal? Yes, because $\tfrac{1}{2}$ can always be substituted for 50%. The general idea working here is the substitution principle. You can verify the equality by doing the multiplication.

$$6 \cdot 50\% = 6 \cdot \tfrac{1}{2}$$
$$300\% = 3$$

It makes no difference what number you multiply by. The products will still be equal. This special use of the substitution principle is so important that it has its own name.

Multiplication Property of Equality:

If $x = y$, then $ax = ay$.

The most important application of this property is in solving equations.

■ ■ ■ ■ ■ ■ ■ ■

Example 1   Solve $12n = 300$ using the Multiplication Property of Equality.

Solution   First write down the equation. Leave room for work below it.

$$12n = 300$$

The Multiplication Property of Equality allows both sides of an equation to be changed without affecting the solutions. We pick a number that will leave n by itself on the left side. That number is $\tfrac{1}{12}$, the reciprocal of 12.

$$\tfrac{1}{12} \cdot (12n) = \tfrac{1}{12} \cdot 300$$

440

Because all numbers at the left are multiplied, there is no need to worry about parentheses. (That's the Associative Property of Multiplication.)

$$\frac{1}{12} \cdot 12n = \frac{1}{12} \cdot 300$$

The hard part is done. All that is left is to simplify. The names of the properties that are used are given at right. (You don't have to write the names down unless asked by your teacher.)

$$1 \cdot n = \frac{300}{12} \qquad \text{(Property of Reciprocals)}$$

$$n = 25 \qquad \text{(Multiplication Property of 1)}$$

Check Substitute 25 for n in the original equation $12n = 300$. It is true that $12 \cdot 25 = 300$.

The Multiplication Property of Equality is very much like the Addition Property of Equality. It can also be adapted to work with inequalities. For these reasons, many teachers prefer students to use the Multiplication Property of Equality rather than related facts in solving equations of the form $ax = b$.

The Multiplication Property of Equality is particularly effective in solving equations where there are fractions.

Example 2   Solve $\frac{3}{5} \cdot A = \frac{1}{4}$.

Solution   We want to multiply both sides by a number that will leave A by itself on the left side. That number is $\frac{5}{3}$, the reciprocal of $\frac{3}{5}$.

$$\frac{5}{3} \cdot (\frac{3}{5} \cdot A) = \frac{5}{3} \cdot \frac{1}{4} \qquad \text{(Multiplication Prop.of Equality)}$$

The only thing left is to simplify. Here are all the steps.

$$(\frac{5}{3} \cdot \frac{3}{5}) \cdot A = \frac{5}{3} \cdot \frac{1}{4} \qquad \text{(Associative Property of Mult.)}$$

$$1 \cdot A = \frac{5}{3} \cdot \frac{1}{4} \qquad \text{(Property of Reciprocals)}$$

Multiplying the fractions on the right side, and using $1 \cdot A = A$,

$$A = \frac{5}{12} \qquad \text{(Multiplication Property of 1 and Multiplication of Fractions Prop.)}$$

Check   Substitute $\frac{5}{12}$ for A in the original equation.
Does $\frac{3}{5} \cdot \frac{5}{12} = \frac{1}{4}$?

Multiplying the fractions, the left side is $\frac{3}{12}$. In lowest terms, this is $\frac{1}{4}$. So $\frac{5}{12}$ is the solution.

The equation in Example 2 looks hard. But with the Multiplication Property of Equality, it becomes easy to solve. On the next page is another question that seems hard. But it too is easy to answer by solving an equation.

LESSON 10-2   The Multiplication Property of Equality   **441**

■ ■ ■ ■ ■ ■ ■ ■ ■ ■

Example 3   Six percent of a number is 30. What is the number?

Solution   First translate into an equation. Let the number be n.

Six percent   of   a number   is   30.
$\downarrow$ $\downarrow$ $\downarrow$ $\downarrow$ $\downarrow$
.06   · n =   30

Here we solve using the Multiplication Property of Equality. Multiply both sides by the reciprocal of .06.

$$\frac{1}{.06} \cdot .06n = \frac{1}{.06} \cdot 30$$

Now simplify. $n = \frac{30}{.06}$

$$n = 500$$

Check   6% of 500 = .06 × 500 = 30

To use the Multiplication Property of Equality, you need to know how to find reciprocals, how to multiply fractions, and how to find equal fractions. Now you can see why these ideas were discussed in past chapters! But you should still wonder when these equations are solved outside of mathematics classes. That is the subject of the next lesson.

Questions

Covering the Reading

1. If $x = y$, then $6x = \underline{\quad?\quad}$.   **6y**

2. What property is needed to answer Question 1?
   Multiplication Property of Equality

3. **a.** To solve $5x = 80$ using the Multiplication Property of Equality, by what number should you multiply both sides? **b.** Solve $5x = 80$.
   a. 1/5; b. 16

4. **a.** To solve $\frac{6}{25} \cdot A = \frac{2}{9}$, it is most convenient to multiply both sides by what number? **b.** Solve this equation.
   a. 25/6; b. 50/54 or 25/27

5. **a.** To solve $3x = 0.12$ using the Multiplication Property of Equality, by what number should both sides be multiplied?
   b. Solve $3x = 0.12$ using the Multiplication Property of Equality.
   c. Solve $3x = 0.12$ using a related fact.
   a. 1/3; b. x = 0.12 · 1/3 = 0.04; c. x = 0.12/3 = 0.04

6. Delilah said the solution to $\frac{2}{3}x = 5$ is $\frac{15}{2}$. Is she correct?   **Yes**

7. Seven times a number is 413. What is the number?   **59**

8. Seven percent of a number is 84. What is the number?   **1200**

9. 40% of what number is 25?   **62.5**

10. Ten-thirds of a number is 30. What is the number?   **9**

442

11. Give the property telling why each step follows from the previous one. See margin.

$$\frac{7}{4} \cdot A = \frac{1}{5}$$

Step 1: $\frac{4}{7} \cdot (\frac{7}{4} \cdot A) = \frac{4}{7} \cdot \frac{1}{5}$

Step 2: $(\frac{4}{7} \cdot \frac{7}{4}) \cdot A = \frac{4}{7} \cdot \frac{1}{5}$

Step 3: $1 \cdot A = \frac{4}{7} \cdot \frac{1}{5}$

Step 4: $A = \frac{4}{35}$

ADDITIONAL ANSWER
11. Step 1: Multiplication Property of Equality; Step 2: Associative Property of Multiplication; Step 3: Property of Reciprocals; Step 4: multiplication of fractions, Multiplication Identity Property of 1

Applying the Mathematics

12. Consider the equation $x/6 = 4/25$. **a.** Rewrite this equation using the Mult-Rec Property of Division. **b.** Solve. **c.** Check.
a. $x \cdot \frac{1}{6} = \frac{4}{25}$; b. 24/25; c. 1/6 · 24/25 = 24/150 = 4/25

In 13–15, solve and check.

13. $16.56 = 7.2y$
2.3

14. $\frac{2}{3}k = 62\%$
93%

15. $3.2 + 4.8 = (3.6 + 2.4)x$
4/3 or 1.$\overline{3}$

16. *Multiple choice* Which equation does not have the same solution as the others? (c)
(a) $0.2x = 18$ (b) $\frac{1}{5}x = 18$ (c) $.2 = 18x$ (d) $18 = 20\%x$

Review

17. Seven less than a number is 50. What is the number? *(Lesson 7-4)*
57

18. Seven decreased by a number is 50. What is the number?
(Lesson 7-6) -43

19. Three sides of a pentagon have length H meters. The other two sides are each 10 meters long. What is the perimeter of the pentagon? *(Lesson 9-5)* 3H + 20 meters

20. Find the value of 1.08^n when $n = 1, 2, 3, 4,$ and 5. *(Lesson 2-2)*
1.08; 1.1664; 1.259712; 1.360489...; 1.469328...

21. Write 3.2×10^{11} as a decimal. *(Lesson 2-3)* 320,000,000,000

22. In October of 1990, some car dealers were offering 4.9% financing on a used car. What simple fraction is this? *(Lesson 2-7)* $\frac{49}{1000}$

23. A model airplane is 1/100 actual size. If an airplane wingspan is 80 meters long, how many centimeters long will the wingspan be on the model? *(Lessons 2-4, 9-7)* 80 cm

LESSON 10-2   The Multiplication Property of Equality   443

24. How many sides does a decagon have? *(Lesson 5-9)* 10

25. Estimate the product of 1.0123456789876 and 5.4321012345678 to the nearest thousandth. *(Lesson 1-4)* 5.499

Exploration

26. 144 seats can be arranged in a rectangular array with 6 rows and 24 seats in each row. What other rectangular arrays are possible for 144 seats? See below.

number of rows	number of seats in a row
1	144
2	72
3	48
4	36
6	24
8	18
9	16
12	12
16	9
18	8
24	6
36	4
48	3
72	2
144	1

444

10-3

Using $ax = b$

In this and earlier chapters you have learned a variety of applications of multiplication.

> areas of rectangles
> arrays
> volumes of rectangular solids
> repeated addition
> expansions (times as many)
> contractions (part of)
> percents of

Any of these types of applications can lead to an equation of the form $ax = b$. You have already done some problems of this kind. Here are some other examples.

Example 1 Claus' Clothes has 60 feet of frontage as shown in the diagram. The store must be split into selling space and storage space by a partition. Mrs. Claus wants 4200 square feet for selling space. Where should the partition be located?

60'

14'

Front view

Solution The selling space is a rectangle. One dimension of the rectangle is known to be 60'. The area is to be 4200 square feet. Now apply the formula (on the next page) for the area of a rectangle.

top view

storage

60'

selling space ℓ

w

front of store

You know that $A = \ell w$

Here $A = 4200$ square feet and $w = 60$ feet. Substitute for A and w.

$$4200 = \ell \cdot 60$$

Solve this equation either by related facts or by using the Multiplication Property of Equality. The solution is

$$\ell = \tfrac{4200}{60} \text{ feet.}$$

Divide. $\ell = 70$ feet

The partition should be 70 ft from the front of the store.

Check You should always check answers with the *original question*. If the depth (length) of the selling space is 70 feet, will there be 4200 square feet of selling space? Yes, because $60 \cdot 70 = 4200$.

The next example is of the size change type. Before you begin, read the question carefully to make certain you understand it. Without solving anything, you should know whether the answer will be greater than $12.60 or less than $12.60.

Example 2 A worker receives time-and-a-half for overtime. If a worker gets $12.60 for an overtime hour, what is the worker's normal hourly wage?

Solution Recall that time-and-a-half means the worker's normal wage is multiplied by $1\frac{1}{2}$ to calculate the overtime wage. Let W be the normal hourly wage. Then

$$1\tfrac{1}{2} \cdot W = \$12.60.$$

Now the job is to solve this equation. First change the fraction to a decimal.

$$1.5W = \$12.60$$

Solve. $W = \dfrac{\$12.60}{1.5}$

Do the arithmetic. $W = \$8.40$

Check Ask: If a worker makes $8.40 an hour, will that worker get $12.60 for overtime? Yes, because half of $8.40 is $4.20, and that half added to $8.40 equals $12.60.

446

In answering any of these questions, the steps are the same.

(1) Read carefully. Determine what is to be found and what is given.
(2) Let a variable equal the unknown quantity.
(3) Write an equation.
(4) Solve the equation.
(5) Check your answer back in the original question.

Example 3 In a small-town election, it was reported that Phineas Foghorn got 38% of the votes. It was also reported that he received 405 votes. How many people voted?

Solution Let v be the number of people who voted. Then 38% of v equals 405.

$$.38v = 405$$

This is the equation that was solved in Example 4 of Lesson 10-1, page 437. Only the letter v is different. So it has the same solution, $v \approx 1065.8$. There were approximately 1066 voters.

Check Ask: Is 38% of 1066 votes equal to 405 votes? Since 38% of 1066 is 405.08, the answer checks.

Example 4 Dollhouse models are often 1/12 actual size. A window that is 18 mm wide on the model is how wide in reality?

Solution Let w be the real width of the window. Then

$$\tfrac{1}{12}w = 18 \text{ mm.}$$

Multiplying both sides by 12, $w = 216$ mm.

The real width is 216 mm.

Check 1/12 of 216 is 18.

Error Analysis for Question 8: Students may have found the height of an adult giraffe correctly ($\frac{1}{3}h = 6$, $h = 18$; 18 ft) but answered the question incorrectly. (An additional calculation, $18 - 6 = 12$, is needed to answer the question.) Stress the importance of always returning to the original question to check an answer.

Making Connections for Question 16: Encourage students to do this using the Multiplication Property of Equality; that is, multiply both sides by 12. In Lesson 10-4, another method for converting is provided.

ADDITIONAL ANSWER
18.

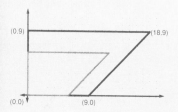

Questions

Covering the Reading

1. What is the first step you should do in solving a problem like those in this lesson?
   Read the question carefully to be sure you understand it.
2. You solve a problem using an equation. Why should you first check the equation's solution in the problem, not in the equation?
   You might have made an error when you set up the equation.
3. An artist living in a loft wants to split the loft into a living room and a working space. The loft is diagrammed below. The artist needs 330 square feet for working space. The working space is 22 feet wide. What should be the other dimension of the working space? **15 feet**

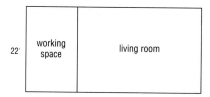

4. Some dollhouse furniture is 1/12 actual size. If a dollhouse table is 3.25 inches long, how long is the actual table? **39 inches**

5. Stacey gets paid time-and-a-half for each hour she babysits after midnight. She made $3.60 per hour after midnight on New Year's eve. How much did she make for each hour before midnight?
   $2.40
6. In the 1984 presidential election, Ronald Reagan got 51% of the votes in Massachusetts. He received 1,297,737 votes there. To the nearest ten thousand, how many people in Massachusetts voted?
   2,540,000 people

Applying the Mathematics

7. The tallest building in the world is the Sears Tower in Chicago. The gift shop at the top of the tower sells models of the tower that are 0.0002 times actual size. The height of the model is 11 cm.
   a. In centimeters, how tall is the tower? **55,000 cm**
   b. How many meters is this? **550 m**

8. A newborn giraffe is 1/3 the height of an adult giraffe. If the newborn is 6 feet tall, how much taller is the adult? (Be careful.)
   12 feet
9. The volume of a box needs to be 600 cubic centimeters. The base of the box has dimensions 8 cm and 10.5 cm. How high must the box be? **about 7.14 cm**

10. A sofa is on sale at 70% of the original price. The sale price is $489.95. What was the original price? **$699.93 (probably $700)**

11. A ballplayer earned three times as much this year as last year. This year the salary was $110,000. To the nearest thousand dollars, what was last year's salary? **$37,000**

12. If $x + x + x + x + x = 32$, what is x? **6.4**

13. An array has 3000 dots. If there are 75 rows, how many columns are in the array?   **40 columns**

14. In the election of Example 3, Wanda Fulperson received 41% of the vote. How many votes did she get?   **437 votes**

Review

15. Simplify $40 - 20 \cdot 3 + 200/5 + 5/1$. *(Lesson 4-1)*   **25**

16. Since 1 inch = 2.54 cm, 1 foot is how many centimeters?
(Lesson 3-4)   **30.48 cm**

17. Arrange these terms from most general to most specific: rectangle; square; parallelogram; polygon; quadrilateral. *(Lesson 7-9)*
polygon, quadrilateral, parallelogram, rectangle, square

18. a. Carefully graph the polygon with vertices (0, 6), (0, 0), (6, 0), and (12, 6).   **b.** Graph the image of this polygon under an expansion with magnitude $\frac{3}{2}$. *(Lesson 9-6)*   **See margin.**

19. The length of a rectangle is π cm and the width is 2 cm. Find its area to the nearest square centimeter. *(Lessons 1-2, 9-1)*   **6 cm²**

20. Pictured is one level of fruit in a crate. How many pieces are in this level? *(Lesson 9-1)*   **64 pieces**

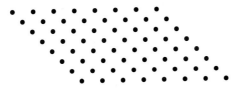

Exploration

21. If 4/3 of a number is 1200, what is 3/4 of that number?   **675**

22. The area of a rectangularly shaped farm is 240 acres, or 3/8 of a square mile. What might be the dimensions of the farm?
Sample: 1/2 mile by 3/4 mile.

NAME _____

OBJECTIVES

H Apply the Rate Factor
  Model for Multiplication.
I Use conversion factors to
  convert from one unit to
  another.

TEACHING NOTES

Before discussing the examples, you may want to ask
students what a *rate* is. Students are probably familiar
with some common, every-
day rates such as speeds.
They may not realize that
prices in the grocery store or
other quantities not associated with speeds can be
rates. **Examples 2, 3, and
5** show how the Rate Factor
Model provides an alternative
method for solving problems
students have seen before.

The other two examples are
more than alternative ap-
proaches, however, and
should be discussed care-
fully. When doing a problem
like **Example 1,** students
are often confused about
which operation(s) to use.
Here is an instance where
getting the units right helps to
get the problem right.

LESSON

10-4

The Rate Factor Model for Multiplication

Here are some examples of **rates.** Every rate has a **rate unit.**
The rate unit is in italics.

  55 *miles per hour* (speed limit)
  25.3 *students per class* (average class size)
  70 *centimeters* of snow *per year* (average snowfall in Chicago)
  $2\frac{1}{2}$ *pieces for each student* (result of splitting up a pizza)

A quantity is a rate when its unit contains the word "per" or
"for each" or some synonym. When used in an expression, the
slash / or horizontal bar — means "per." Notice how the above
rate units are written in fraction notation.

Using the slash	=	**Using the bar**
55 mi/hr	=	$55 \frac{mi}{hr}$
25.3 students/class	=	$25.3 \frac{students}{class}$
70 cm/yr	=	$70 \frac{cm}{yr}$
$2\frac{1}{2}$ pieces/student	=	$2\frac{1}{2} \frac{pieces}{student}$

Suppose a woman gains 2 pounds per month (perhaps during
pregnancy). Her rate of weight gain is then

$$2 \frac{pounds}{month}.$$

Suppose she keeps this rate up for 5 months. Multiplication gives
the total she gains.

$$5 \text{ months} \cdot 2 \frac{pounds}{month} = 10 \text{ pounds}$$

Look at the units in the above multiplication. They work as if
they were factors in fractions. The unit "months" at left cancels
the unit "month" in the denominator. The unit that remains is
pounds. You can see where the 10 comes from.

In the next example there are two rates that are multiplied.

450

Example 1 A secretary has 8 letters to type. Each letter is 4 pages long. Each page takes 6 minutes to type. About how long will it take to type the letters?

Solution Think rates. There are 4 pages per letter. There are 6 minutes per page.

$$8 \text{ letters} \cdot 4 \tfrac{\text{pages}}{\text{letter}} \cdot 6 \tfrac{\text{minutes}}{\text{page}}$$

$$= \quad 32 \text{ pages} \quad \cdot 6 \tfrac{\text{minutes}}{\text{page}}$$

$$= \quad\quad 192 \text{ minutes}$$

The general idea behind Example 1 is the **rate factor model for multiplication**.

Rate Factor Model for Multiplication:

When a rate is multiplied by another quantity, the unit of the product is the "product" of units multiplied like fractions. The product has meaning whenever its unit has meaning.

Some multiplications from earlier lessons can be thought of as rate factor multiplications.

Example 2 (Array) An auditorium contains 12 rows and 19 seats per row. How many seats are in the auditorium?

Solution $12 \text{ rows} \cdot 19 \tfrac{\text{seats}}{\text{row}} = 228 \text{ seats}$

Example 3 (Repeated addition) A person buys 7 cans of tuna at $1.39 per can. What is the total cost?

Solution Here is the way it looks with all units included.

$$7 \text{ cans} \cdot 1.39 \tfrac{\text{dollars}}{\text{can}} = 9.73 \text{ dollars}$$

Here is how it looks using the usual dollar signs and a slash.

$$7 \text{ cans} \cdot \$1.39/\text{can} = \$9.73$$

Making Connections
Example 4 is the opposite of the conversions that have been done up to this point. In Chapter 3, we used the equality 1 mile = 5280 feet and only converted miles to feet; here we convert feet to miles. The conversion factor $\frac{1 \text{ mile}}{5280 \text{ feet}}$ is chosen to make the units to be eliminated (feet) cancel and to leave the desired units (miles).

ADDITIONAL EXAMPLES
1. How many inches are in a mile?
$\frac{63,360 \text{ in.}}{\text{mi}}$

2. A calligrapher charges 5 cents a word to do fancy printing. If the middle school graduating class has 128 students and each student has a first, a middle, and a last name, how much will the calligrapher charge for writing the names on the diplomas?
$\frac{\$0.05}{\text{word}} \cdot \frac{3 \text{ words}}{\text{student}} \cdot \frac{128 \text{ students}}{\text{job}} = \frac{\$19.20}{\text{job}}$

3. A piece of notebook paper is about .004 in. thick. A ream of paper contains 500 sheets. How thick is a ream?
2.0 in. thick

4. There are 2.54 centimeters per inch. To the nearest ten-thousandth, how many inches are in a centimeter?
$\approx$ **.3937 in.**

A special kind of rate factor is the **conversion factor.** Start with a formula for converting from one unit to another. Here is an example.

$$1 \text{ mile} = 5280 \text{ feet}$$

Since the quantities are equal, dividing one by the other gives the number 1.

$$\frac{1 \text{ mile}}{5280 \text{ feet}} = 1 \qquad \text{and} \qquad \frac{5280 \text{ feet}}{1 \text{ mile}} = 1$$

You could say there is 1 mile for every 5280 feet or there are 5280 feet for every mile.

■ ■ ■ ■ ■ ■ ■ ■

Example 4 (Conversion) 40,000 feet equals how many miles?

Solution Multiply 40,000 feet by the conversion factor with miles in its numerator and feet in its denominator.

$$40,000 \text{ feet} \cdot \frac{1 \text{ mile}}{5280 \text{ feet}} = \frac{40,000}{5280} \text{ miles}$$
$$= 7.\overline{57} \text{ miles}$$

■ ■ ■ ■ ■ ■ ■ ■

Example 5 (Conversion) 26.2 miles (the approximate length of a marathon) is how many feet?

Solution Use the conversion factor with miles in its denominator.

$$26.2 \text{ miles} \cdot \frac{5280 \text{ feet}}{1 \text{ mile}} = 138,336 \text{ feet}$$

Questions

Covering the Reading

In 1 and 2: **a.** Copy the sentence and underline the rate.
b. Write the rate with its unit in fraction notation using the slash.
c. Write the rate with its unit in fraction notation using the fraction bar.

1. For the game only 4 tickets per student are available.   See margin.

2. The speed limit there is 45 miles per hour.   See margin.

In 3–6: **a.** Do the multiplication. **b.** Make up a question that leads to the multiplication.

3. $3 \text{ hours} \cdot 50 \frac{miles}{hr}$ a. 150 miles; b. See margin.

4. $8.2 \text{ pounds} \cdot \$2.29/\text{pound}$ a. $18.78; b. See margin.

5. $2 \frac{games}{week} \cdot 8 \frac{weeks}{season}$ a. $16 \frac{games}{season}$; b. See margin.

6. $30,000 \text{ ft.} \cdot \frac{1 \text{ mile}}{5280 \text{ ft}}$ a. ≈ 5.68 miles; b. Sample: Convert 30,000 feet to miles.

452

7. If an animal gains 1.5 kg a month for 7 months, how many kg will it have gained in all?   **10.5 kg**

8. A typist can type 40 words a minute. At this rate, how many words can be typed in 20 minutes?   **800 words**

9. An airplane flying 35,000 feet up is how many miles up?
about 6.63 miles

10. A section of a football stadium has 50 rows and has 20 seats in each row. How many people can be seated in this section?
1000 people

11. What is the Rate Factor Model for Multiplication?   **See margin.**

In 12 and 13, follow the directions of Questions 3-6.

Applying the Mathematics

12. 5 classes $\cdot$ 25 $\frac{\text{students}}{\text{class}}$ $\cdot$ 30 $\frac{\text{questions}}{\text{student}}$ **a. 3750 questions; b. See margin.**

13. $\frac{1.06 \text{ quarts}}{\text{liter}}$ $\cdot$ 6 liters   **a. 6.36 quarts; b. Convert 6 liters to quarts.**

14. Recall that 1 inch = 2.54 cm. Convert 10 cm to inches.
about 3.94 inches

15. If a heart beats 70 times a minute, how many times will it beat in a day?   **100,800 beats**

16. Solve for x: 4 hours $\cdot$ x = 120 miles.   **30 miles/hour**

17. When the twins went to France they found that 9 francs were worth 1 dollar. In Spain the next day they found that 1 franc was worth 8 pesetas. How many pesetas could they get for $10?
720 pesetas

18. A Chevrolet has a 14-gallon tank and can get about 25 miles per gallon. What do you get when you multiply these quantities?
350 miles, how far the Chevy can go on a tank of gas

Review

19. Seventy-four times a number is equal to forty-seven. To the nearest tenth, what is the number? *(Lesson 10-3)*   **0.6**

20. A 30% discount will save you $12 on that item. What was the original cost of the item? *(Lesson 10-3)*   **$40**

---

11. When a rate is multiplied by another quantity, the unit of the product is the "product" of units multiplied like fractions. The product has meaning whenever its unit has meaning.

12. b. sample: A teacher has 5 classes, each with 25 students. If each student takes a test with 30 questions, how many questions must the teacher grade?

NAME _____

LESSON **MASTER 10–4**
QUESTIONS ON **SPUR** OBJECTIVES

■**USES**   *Objective H (See pages 480–481 for objectives.)*

1. $\frac{3}{4}$ $\frac{\text{hours of homework}}{\text{class}}$ $\cdot$ 4 $\frac{\text{classes}}{\text{student}}$ = 3 $\frac{\text{hours of homework}}{\text{student}}$

2. Consider 17 $\frac{\text{miles}}{\text{gallon}}$ $\cdot$ 30 gallons.

   a. Do the multiplication.   **510 miles**

   b. Make up a question that leads to the multiplication.
   sample: Ann's car gets 17 miles per gallon of gas. If Ann used 30 gallons of gas on a trip, how far did she travel?

3. Mr. Colbert gained an average of three pounds per month when he was in training. How much had he gained at the end of nine months?   **27 pounds**

4. Luis runs 60 miles a month. At this rate, how many miles will he have run in a year?   **720 miles**

5. If you travel for 3.5 hours at 65 miles per hour, how far have you traveled?   **227.5 miles**

6. If Rochelle earns $7.50 an hour and works 25 hours a week, how much does she earn per year?   **$9750.00**

7. A restaurant has set up 32 tables for a banquet. There is seating for 8 people at each table. The dinner will cost $24.95 per person. How much will the restaurant collect at this banquet?   **$6387.20**

■**USES**   *Objective I*

8. Recall that 1 kg ≈ 2.2 lb. Convert 150 pounds to kilograms.   **≈68.2 kg**

9. Recall that 1 kilometer ≈ 0.62 miles. 600 miles equals how many kilometers?   **≈967.7 km**

10. 2500 minutes equals how many hours?   **$41\frac{2}{3}$ hr**

21. The length of this paper clip has been enlarged 1.6 times. Find the length of the actual clip to the nearest mm. *(Lesson 10-3)*
26 millimeters

22. Solve for t: $\frac{2}{5}t = 44$. *(Lesson 10-2)* **110**

23. What number is $\frac{2}{3}$ less than $-\frac{2}{3}$? *(Lesson 7-2)* $-\frac{4}{3}$

In 24–26, give an abbreviation for the unit. *(Lessons 3-2, 3-3)*

24. pound **lb**   25. kilogram **kg**   26. milliliter **mL**

27. How many feet must you go down to get from 25 feet above ground level to 30 feet below? *(Lesson 7-3)* **55 ft**

28. Evaluate $-|x + 5|$ when $x = -3$. *(Lesson 5-5)* **-2**

29. Graph the set of ordered pairs that satisfy $x = y + 4$. *(Lesson 8-3)*
Three points are (0, -4), (2, -2), and (4, 0).

30. If x stands for this year, what expression stands for: **a.** next year; **b.** last year; **c.** ten years ago? *(Lesson 4-3)*
a. $x + 1$; b. $x - 1$; c. $x - 10$

Exploration

31. Depending on the number of words it contains, a work of prose is often classified as a short story, a novelette, or a novel. For example, a short story is usually less than 10,000 words. To find the number of words per book, editors rarely count them all, but use a rate factor model.   **See margin.**
    a. Describe how you might estimate the number of words in a book.
    b. Estimate the number of words in this chapter.

454

454

Multiplication with Negative Numbers

Rates can be negative. Suppose a man loses 2 pounds per month on a diet. His rate of change in weight is then

$$-2 \ \frac{\text{pounds}}{\text{month}}.$$

If he keeps losing weight at this rate for 5 months, multiplying gives the total loss.

$$5 \text{ months} \cdot -2 \ \frac{\text{pounds}}{\text{month}} \ = -10 \text{ pounds}$$

Ignoring the units, a positive and a negative number are being multiplied. The product is negative.

$$5 \cdot -2 = -10$$

The number of months does not have to be a whole number. The rate does not have to be an integer. So this example verifies that when a positive number is multiplied by a negative number, the product is negative.

> positive · negative = negative

Multiplication is commutative. So the multiplication can be reversed.

> negative · positive = negative

You already know that the product of two positive numbers is positive.

> positive · positive = positive

OBJECTIVES

A Multiply positive and negative numbers.
H Apply the Rate Factor Model for Multiplication to negative factors.

TEACHING NOTES

Students can do this lesson independently, since the four rules and two generalizations are clear and straightforward. Students should be able to give the rules in class the following day along with some real-world situations to illustrate them.

Alternate Approach
Another way to introduce multiplication of positive and negative numbers is to use a pattern. Start with $5 \cdot 3 = 15$. Then reduce one of the factors by 1: $5 \cdot 2 = 10$; $5 \cdot 1 = 5$; $5 \cdot 0 = 0$. Continuing the pattern, ask what $5 \cdot -1$ should be. Then inquire about $5 \cdot -2$, and so on.
Question 17 provides practice with a similar pattern.

Putting these two things together, we have the following important property.

> When a number is multiplied by a positive number, its sign (positive or negative) is not affected.

The next example shows three different ways of finding the product of a positive and a negative number. Of course, all ways lead to the same answer.

Example 1 What is $5 \cdot -4.8$?

Solution 1 Think of this as a loss of 4.8 pounds per month for 5 months. The result is a loss. So the answer is negative. Since $5 \cdot 4.8 = 24$, $5 \cdot -4.8 = -24$.

Solution 2 -4.8 is multiplied by the positive number 5, so its sign is not affected. Since -4.8 is negative, the product is negative. Since $5 \cdot 4.8 = 24$, $5 \cdot -4.8 = -24$.

Solution 3 By repeated addition,
$5 \cdot -4.8 = -4.8 + -4.8 + -4.8 + -4.8 + -4.8 = -24$.

Example 2 What is $-7 \cdot 4$?

Solution Since -7 is multiplied by the positive number 4, the product is negative.
$-7 \cdot 4 = -28$

What happens if both numbers are negative? Again think of the weight-loss situation. A person loses 2 pounds a month. At this rate, 5 months *from now* the person will weigh 10 pounds less. You have already seen this multiplication.

5 months from now $\cdot -2 \frac{\text{pounds}}{\text{month}}$ = 10 pounds less = -10 pounds

Ignoring the units: $5 \cdot -2 = -10$

But also at this rate, 5 months *ago* the person weighed 10 pounds more. Going back is the negative direction for time. So here is the multiplication for this situation.

5 months ago $\cdot -2 \frac{\text{pounds}}{\text{month}}$ = 10 pounds more = 10 pounds

-5 months $\cdot -2 \frac{\text{pounds}}{\text{month}}$ = 10 pounds

Ignoring the units: $-5 \cdot -2 = 10$

456

negative · negative = positive

When a number is multiplied by a negative number, its sign (positive or negative) is changed.

Example 3   What is -4 · -1.5?

Solution 1   Think: Multiplication by a negative changes sign. Multiplying -1.5 by -4 changes its sign to positive. Since 4 · 1.5 = 6, -4 · -1.5 = 6.

Solution 2   Think: 4 months ago · 1.5 pound loss per month. The person weighed more 4 months ago, so the answer is positive. 4 · 1.5 = 6.

Questions

Covering the Reading

1. Copy the sentence and underline the negative rate in this sentence: A woman loses 3.8 pounds per month for 3 months.
loses 3.8 pounds/month

In 2–4: **a.** What multiplication problem involving negative numbers is suggested by the situation? **b.** What is the product and what does it mean?

2. A person loses 3 pounds a month for 2 months. How much will the person lose in all? See margin.

3. A person loses 5 pounds a month. How will the person's weight 4 months from now compare with the weight now? See margin.

4. A person has been losing 6 pounds a month. How does the person's weight 2 months ago compare with the weight now? See margin.

5. Multiplying by a negative number __?__ the sign of the other number. changes

6. Multiplying by a positive number __?__ the sign of the other number. keeps

In 7–12, simplify.

7. -4 · 8 -32

8. 73 · -45 -3285

9. -6 · -3 18

10. -1 · 2.9 -2.9

11. 8 · -8 -64

12. -5 · -100 500

LESSON 10-5 Multiplication with Negative Numbers   457

Question 17: The pattern in the answers gives additional evidence for the reasonableness of the rules for multiplying positive and negative numbers.

Question 22: This involves operations other than multiplication. Such questions give students an opportunity to review the operations with negative numbers that they have already learned. This question also requires that students pay attention to the signs that describe the situation, not just the numbers.

Making Connections for Question 31: Lesson 11-1 discusses many examples of rates, such as those that students may find in newspapers or magazines. Have students compare the ones they found with those in Lesson 11-1.

FOLLOW-UP

MORE PRACTICE
For more questions on SPUR Objectives, use *Lesson Master 10-5,* shown on page 457.

EXTENSION
Ask the students to answer the following questions and to explain their answers.

1. Is $(-x)$ $(-y)$ a positive number, a negative number, or zero? (The product could be any of those depending on the value of the unknowns.)

2. If $x \neq 0$, is x^2 always positive? (yes) What about x^3? (no, if $x < 0$)

27.

In 13–16, tell whether xy is positive or negative.

13. x is positive and y is positive.   positive

14. x is positive and y is negative.   negative

15. x is negative and y is positive.   negative

16. x is negative and y is negative.   positive

Applying the Mathematics

17. Find the value of $-5x$ when x is:
a. 2; **b.** 1; **c.** 0; **d.** -1; **e.** -2.
a. -10; b. -5; c. 0; d. 5; e. 10

18. Evaluate $3 + -7a + 2b$ when $a = -4$ and $b = -10$.   11

In 19–21, simplify.

19. $-3 \cdot 4 \cdot -5$ 60   **20.** $-6 \cdot -6 \cdot -6 \cdot -6$ 1296   **21.** $-\frac{2}{3} \cdot -\frac{9}{10}$ $\frac{3}{5}$

22. *Multiple choice*   Morry is now in debt for $2500 and has been spending money at the rate of $200/week. Which expression tells how he was doing 5 weeks ago?   (b)
(a) $2500 - 5 \cdot 200$ (b) $-2500 + -200 \cdot -5$ (c) $-2500 + 5 \cdot -200$

Review

23. Solve $2400x = 60$. *(Lesson 10-1)*   0.025, or $\frac{1}{40}$

24. Solve $\frac{1}{2}y = 54$. *(Lesson 10-2)*   108

25. Sliced roast beef is advertised in a store for $5.98/pound. How much should 0.45 pounds of roast beef cost? *(Lesson 10-3)* $2.69

26. Real estate agents in some places earn 3% of the sale value of a house for helping a person sell the house. This is called the *commission.* **a.** What is the commission on the sale of a house for $98,400, the median cost for an existing house in the United States in July, 1990? **b.** How much has to be sold in order for the agent to earn $25,000 from commissions? *(Lessons 2-6, 10-3)*
a. $2,952; b. about $833,333

27. Graph all solutions to $x > 5$ on a number line. *(Lesson 4-9)*
See margin.

28. Write these rates using fraction notation and abbreviations:
a. kilometers per second; **b.** grams per cubic centimeter.
(Lesson 10-4)   a. km/sec; b. g/cm³

29. Give an example of a positive number and a negative number whose sum is positive. *(Lesson 5-3)*   Sample: -2 + 3 = 1

30. What are supplementary angles? *(Lesson 7-7)*
two angles whose measures add to 180°

Exploration

31. Find an example of a rate in a newspaper or magazine.   Answers will vary.

LESSON

10-6

Picturing
Multiplication
with Negative
Numbers

LESSON 10-6

RESOURCES
■ Lesson Master 10-6
■ Computer Master 19
■ Visuals for Teaching Aids 63 and 64: Use to picture multiplication with negative numbers.
■ Visual for Teaching Aid 49 or graph paper: Use with **Questions 7** and **10.**
■ Overhead Coordinate Grid (*Transition Mathematics Teacher Kit*)

OBJECTIVES

L Picture multiplication by negative numbers using size changes.

Remember that multiplication can be pictured by expansions or contractions. In Chapter 9, the coordinates of preimage points were positive. Now that we have discussed multiplication with negative numbers, the coordinates can be any numbers. So the preimage can be anywhere. Here the preimage is a quadrilateral with a shaded region near one vertex.

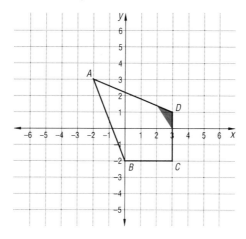

Preimage vertices

$A = (-2, 3)$
$B = (0, -2)$
$C = (3, -2)$
$D = (3, 1)$

TEACHING NOTES

Making Connections In Chapter 9, we considered two types of positive values of k : when $k > 1$, the size change is an expansion; when $0 < k < 1$, the size change is a contraction. Here we ask what happens when k is negative.

This lesson provides an opportunity to apply absolute value, because size changes of magnitudes k and $-k$ have much in common. In both cases, the length is multiplied by the absolute value of the magnitude k. For instance, a size change of magnitude 7 and one of magnitude -7 will both multiply lengths by 7.

Be sure to go over the characteristics of the size change of magnitude k on page 461.

First we multiply all coordinates by 2. You know what to expect.

1. The image is similar to the preimage.
2. The sides of the image are 2 times as long as the sides of the preimage.
3. The sides on the image are parallel to corresponding sides on the preimage.

ADDITIONAL EXAMPLES

1. Perform a size change of magnitude -2.5 on the triangle with coordinates $A = (0, 0)$, $B = (2, 0)$, and $C = (0, 2)$.

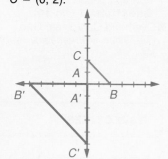

2. List 5 things that are true about the transformation.
samples: $\overline{BC} \parallel \overline{B'C'}$; $A = A'$; $\triangle ABC \sim \triangle A'B'C'$; $A'B' = 2.5$ AB; $\triangle A'B'C'$ is the image of $\triangle ABC$ under a size change of magnitude 2.5 followed by a rotation of 180°.

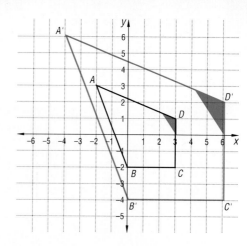

Expansion, magnitude 2

Preimage point
$A = (-2, 3)$
$B = (0, -2)$
$C = (3, -2)$
$D = (3, 1)$

Image point
$A' = (-4, 6)$
$B' = (0, -4)$
$C' = (6, -4)$
$D' = (6, 2)$

Notice also:

4. The line containing a preimage point and its image also contains $(0, 0)$.
5. Image points are 2 times as far from $(0, 0)$ as preimage points.

Now we find the image of the same quadrilateral under an expansion with the negative magnitude, -2. This is done by multiplying all coordinates by -2. We call the image $A''B''C''D''$. (Read this ''A double prime, B double prime,…'')

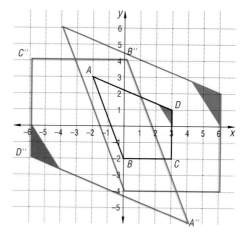

Expansion, magnitude -2

Preimage point
$A = (-2, 3)$
$B = (0, -2)$
$C = (3, -2)$
$D = (3, 1)$

Image point
$A'' = (4, -6)$
$B'' = (0, 4)$
$C'' = (-6, 4)$
$D'' = (-6, -2)$

Again

1. the preimage and image are similar.
2. The sides of $A''B''C''D''$ are 2 times the length of the sides of $ABCD$.
3. Preimage and image sides are parallel.
4. The line through a preimage and image point contains $(0, 0)$.
5. Image points are 2 times as far from $(0, 0)$ as preimage points.

460

But one new thing has happened.

6. The figure has been rotated 180°. It has been turned upside down. What was right is now left. What was up is now down.

Multiplication by a negative number reverses directions.

Multiplying the coordinates of all points on a figure by the number k yields the transformation known as a *size change of magnitude k*. The number k may be positive or negative. But in all cases:

1. The resulting figure (the image) will be similar to its preimage.
2. Lengths of sides of the resulting figure will be $|k|$ times lengths of sides of the preimage.
3. Corresponding sides will be parallel.
4. Preimage and image points will lie on a line that goes through the origin.
5. Image points will be $|k|$ times as far from the origin as preimage points.
6. If k is negative, the figure will be rotated 180°.

The examples have pictured what happens when $k = 2$ and when $k = -2$.

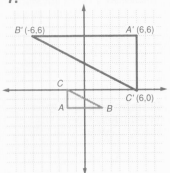

Questions

Covering the Reading

1. In a size change of magnitude -2, the image of (4, 5) is (_?_).
   (-8, -10)
2. In a size change of magnitude -5, the image of (-10, 7) is (_?_).
   (50, -35)
3. In any size change, a figure and its image are _?_.   similar

4. In a size change of magnitude -3, lengths on an image will be _?_ times the corresponding lengths on the preimage.   3

5. In any size change, a segment and its image are _?_.   parallel

6. What is the major difference between a size change of magnitude -3 and one of magnitude 3?
   For a size change of magnitude -3, the image is rotated 180°.
7. Let $A = (-2, -2)$, $B = (2, -2)$, and $C = (-2, 0)$. Graph $\triangle ABC$ and its image under an expansion of magnitude -3.
   See margin.
8. Multiplication by a negative number _?_ directions.   reverses

9. A size change of magnitude -2 is like one of magnitude 2 followed by a rotation of what magnitude?   180°

LESSON 10-6 Picturing Multiplication with Negative Numbers   461

10.

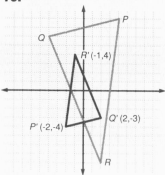

16.

10. A triangle has vertices $P = (4, 8)$, $Q = (-4, 6)$, and $R = (2, -8)$. Graph this triangle and its image under a contraction of magnitude $-\frac{1}{2}$. **See margin.**

11. Let $P = (3.45, -82)$. Suppose that P' is the image of P under a size change of magnitude -10.
True or false? $\overleftrightarrow{PP'}$ contains $(0, 0)$. **True**

12. **a.** Are the figures $A'B'C'D'$ and $A''B''C''D''$ on page 460 congruent? **Yes**
   b. If so, why? If not, why not?
   They are both 2 times the size of *ABCD*.

13. Recall that the four parts of the coordinate plane can be numbered from 1 to 4, as shown below. Consider a size change with magnitude -2.3. If a preimage is in quadrant 4, in what quadrant is its image? **2**

14. Translate each phrase into a numerical expression or equation:
   a. spending $50 a day; **-$50/day**
   b. 4 days from now; **4 days**
   c. 4 days ago; **-4 days**
   d. If you spend $50 a day for 4 days, you will have $200 less than you have now. **-$50/day · 4 days = -$200**
   e. If you have been spending $50 a day, 4 days ago you had $200 more than you have now. *(Lesson 10-5)*
   -$50/day · -4 days = $200

15. What is the area of a sheet of 8″ by 10.5″ notebook paper? Ignore the holes. *(Lesson 9-1)* **84 square inches**

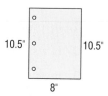

16. Drawn below is a square and one of its diagonals. Copy the figure and draw all of its lines of symmetry. *(Lesson 8-7)* **See margin.**

17. Find the value of $-5x + 6$ when $x = -9$. *(Lesson 4-4)* **51**

18. Find the value of $3a + 2a$ when $a = -7$. *(Lesson 4-4)* **-35**

462

19. Solve for y: $\frac{y}{7} = 30$. *(Lesson 10-2)*   **210**

20. Twelve hundred sixty is three-fourths of what number? *(Lesson 10-3)*
1680

21. Twelve hundred sixty is 75% of what number? *(Lesson 10-3)*   **1680**

22. One thousand two hundred sixty students were asked whether they thought Hardnox High would win its next football game. Seventy-five percent thought it would win. How many students is this? *(Lesson 2-6)*   **945**

23. Write 5^{10} as a decimal. *(Lesson 2-2)*   **9,765,625**

24. About 2/3 of the earth's surface is covered by water. (Some people think we should call our planet Water, not Earth.) If a meteor were to hit the earth, what are the chances it would hit on land on a Sunday? *(Lesson 9-9)*   **1/21**

25. Which is largest; -2/3, -0.6, or -0.66? *(Lesson 1-5)*   **-0.6**

26. Three instances of a pattern are given. Describe the pattern using one variable. *(Lesson 4-2)*
$$-3 \cdot 5 + 4 \cdot 5 = 5$$
$$-3 \cdot 7.8 + 4 \cdot 7.8 = 7.8$$
$$-3 \cdot -1 + 4 \cdot -1 = -1 \quad \textbf{-3n + 4n = n}$$

Exploration

27. Here are four true statements given in a particular order.
$4 \cdot -4 = -16$	**a.** $0 \cdot -4 = 0$
$3 \cdot -4 = -12$	$-1 \cdot -4 = 4$
$2 \cdot -4 = -8$	$-2 \cdot -4 = 8$
$1 \cdot -4 = -4$	$-3 \cdot -4 = 12$
	$-4 \cdot -4 = 16$

   a. Keeping the pattern going, what are the next five statements?
   b. Are your next five statements all true?   **Yes**

28. a. Verify the pattern of Question 27 using this computer program.

```
10 FOR X = 4 TO -10 STEP -1
20    PRINT X "TIMES -4 EQUALS", -4*X
30 NEXT X
40 END
```

   b. Modify the program to print different products of positive and negative numbers.   **See below.**

---

a. Output: 4 TIMES -4 EQUALS -16
3 TIMES -4 EQUALS -12
...
-10 TIMES -4 EQUALS 40

b. Sample: 10 FOR X = 10 TO -2 STEP -3
20   PRINT X "TIMES -5 EQUALS", -5*X
30 NEXT X
40 END

RUN
10 TIMES -5 EQUALS -50
7 TIMES -5 EQUALS -35
4 TIMES -5 EQUALS -20
1 TIMES -5 EQUALS -5
-2 TIMES -5 EQUALS 10

LESSON 10-7

RESOURCES
- Lesson Master 10-7
- Quiz on Lessons 10-5 Through 10-7
- Computer Master 20
- Visual for Teaching Aid 65: **Question 24**

OBJECTIVE

F Apply the multiplication properties of 0 and −1.

TEACHING NOTES

Discuss the examples with the students. Students often think all linear equations have exactly one solution because this is true of most of the linear equations they have seen. **Examples 1-3** demonstrate that this is not true. **Examples 4-6** deal with repeatedly applying the Multiplication Property of −1. **Example 4** provides a detailed analysis of what happens with two negative signs; **Examples 5** and **6** involve actual calculation.

LESSON

10-7

Multiplication by 0 and -1

Notice what happens when the number 5 is multiplied by positive numbers that get smaller and smaller.

$$5 \cdot 2 \qquad = 10$$
$$5 \cdot 0.43 \qquad = 2.15$$
$$5 \cdot 0.07 \qquad = 0.35$$
$$5 \cdot 0.000148 = 0.00074$$

The smaller the positive number, the closer the product is to zero. You know what happens when 5 is multiplied by 0. The product is 0.

$$5 \cdot 0 \qquad = 0$$

There is a similar pattern if you begin with a negative number. Multiply -7 by the same numbers as above.

$$-7 \cdot 2 \qquad = -14$$
$$-7 \cdot 0.43 \qquad = -3.01$$
$$-7 \cdot 0.07 \qquad = -0.49$$
$$-7 \cdot 0.000148 = -0.001036$$

The products are all negative. But again they get closer and closer to zero. You can check the following multiplication on your calculator.

$$-7 \cdot 0 \qquad = 0$$

These examples are instances of an important property of zero.

Multiplication Property of Zero:

For any number x, $x \cdot 0 = 0$.

Since multiplication is commutative, $0 \cdot x$ is also equal to zero. As a special case, $0 \cdot 0 = 0$. All of this makes it tricky to solve equations of the form $ax = b$ when a or b equals zero. Here are the three possibilities.

464

Example 1   Solve $0 \cdot A = 0$.

Solution   Every number works! So *any number* is a solution.

Example 2   Solve $0 \cdot B = 5$.

Solution   No number works. So there is *no solution*.

Example 3   Solve $3 \cdot B = 0$.

Solution   Multiplying both sides by $\frac{1}{3}$, we find $B = 0$. (You could also find that solution mentally.) So there is *one solution*, the number 0.

Some people confuse "no solution" with "0 is a solution." Notice the difference in the graphs of the solutions.

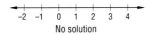
No solution

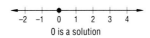
0 is a solution

You already know how to multiply by -1. Here are three instances of the general pattern.

$$-1 \cdot 53 = -53$$
$$-1 \cdot -4 = 4$$
$$-1 \cdot \tfrac{2}{3} = -\tfrac{2}{3}$$

In words, multiplication by -1 changes a number to its opposite. Here is a description with variables.

Multiplication Property of -1:

For any number x, $-1 \cdot x = -x$.

Using the multiplication property of -1, you can turn opposites into multiplications. This enables many expressions to be simplified.

■ ■ ■ ■ ■ ■ ■■

Example 4 Simplify: $-x \cdot -y$.

Solution

$$-x \cdot -y = (-1 \cdot x) \cdot (-1 \cdot y) \quad \text{Multiplication Property of -1}$$
$$= -1 \cdot x \cdot -1 \cdot y \quad \text{Multiplication is associative.}$$
$$= -1 \cdot -1 \cdot xy \quad \text{Multiplication is commutative.}$$
$$= 1 \cdot xy \quad \quad -1 \cdot -1 = 1$$
$$= xy \quad \quad \text{1 is the identity for multiplication.}$$

Example 4 shows that the product of two opposites equals the product of the original numbers. So an even number of opposites being multiplied will equal the product of the numbers without the opposites.

■ ■ ■ ■ ■ ■ ■■

Example 5 Is $-2 \cdot -5 \cdot 3 \cdot -4 \cdot 6 \cdot -2 \cdot -1 \cdot -3$ positive or negative?

Solution There are 6 negative numbers being multiplied. This is an even number; so the product is positive.

Caution: This kind of analysis should only be done when all numbers are multiplied.

Another way of thinking of Example 5 is that multiplication by a negative switches direction. So multiplication by two negatives switches back. An odd number of switches is just like one switch.

■ ■ ■ ■ ■ ■ ■■

Example 6 Tell whether $-1 \cdot -2 \cdot -3 \cdot -4 \cdot -5 \cdot -6 \cdot -7$ is positive or negative.

Solution The product is negative because there are 7 opposites. (Multiplication shows that the product is -5040.)

Questions

Covering the Reading

1. Describe the multiplication property of 0 using variables.
   For any number x, $x \cdot 0 = 0$.
2. Describe the multiplication property of -1 using variables.
   For any number x, $-1 \cdot x = -x$.

In 3–8, simplify.

3. $-1 \cdot -7$ 7   **4.** $8 \cdot -1$ -8   **5.** $-1 \cdot -1 \cdot -1$ -1

6. $0 \cdot -6$ 0   **7.** $0 \cdot -1$ 0   **8.** $-3 \cdot -2 \cdot -1 \cdot 0$ 0

466

9. Multiplication by __?__ changes a number to its opposite.   -1

In 10–12, simplify.

10. $-1 \cdot -y$ **y**   **11.** $-a \cdot -b$ **ab**   **12.** $-5 \cdot -x$ **5x**

In 13–15, tell how many solutions the equation has.

13. $10x = 0$ **14.** $0 = 0y$ **15.** $0z = 10$
one   infinitely many   none

16. Is $-1 \cdot -2 \cdot -3 \cdot -4 \cdot -5 \cdot -6 \cdot -7$ positive or negative?   **negative**

17. Is $-1 \cdot 1 \cdot -2 \cdot 2 \cdot -3 \cdot 3$ positive, negative, or zero?   **negative**

18. If you multiplied all the integers from -1 to -100 together, would the product be positive or negative? Explain your answer.
positive; you are multiplying an even number of negative numbers

19. Multiply all the integers from -5 to 5 together.   **0**

In 20–23, simplify.

20. $xy + -1 \cdot xy$ **21.** $-1 \cdot c + 0 \cdot c$ **22.** $1 \cdot -1 \cdot A$
0   -c   -A
23. $e + 0 \cdot e + 1 \cdot e + 2e + -e + -1 \cdot e$ **2e**

24. Copy the graph of $\triangle ABC$ as shown below.

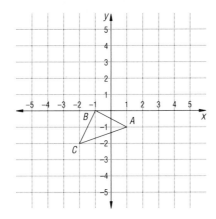

a. Apply a size change of magnitude -1 to $\triangle ABC$. Call the image $\triangle A'B'C'$.   **See margin.**
b. How do $\triangle ABC$ and $\triangle A'B'C'$ compare?   **See margin.**

25. In Europe, the number zero is sometimes called the *annihilator*. What is the reason for this name?   **See margin.**

26. a. Is it true that -1 is the reciprocal of -1? **b.** If so, why? If not, what number is the reciprocal of -1?   **a. Yes; b. $-1 \cdot -1 = 1$**

27. a. Is it true that 0 is the reciprocal of 0? **b.** If so, why? If not, why not?   **a. No; b. $0 \cdot 0 \neq 1$**

467

ADDITIONAL ANSWERS
24.

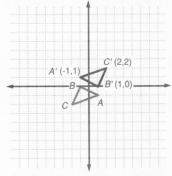

b. They are congruent; corresponding sides are parallel; $\triangle ABC$ has been rotated 180° to get $\triangle A'B'C'$.

25. If you could apply a size change with magnitude 0 to a figure, all image points would be (0, 0) and the original figure would be wiped out.

NAME _____

LESSON MASTER   10-7
QUESTIONS ON **SPUR** OBJECTIVES

■ **PROPERTIES**   *Objective F (See pages 480–481 for objectives.)*
In 1–8, solve.

1. $0x = 92$ 2. $-16y = 0$
   no solution   **$y = 0$**

3. $0z = 0$ 4. $-1 \cdot 57 = a$
   any number   **$a = -57$**

5. $-1n = 30$ 6. $41 \cdot m \cdot -1 = 0$
   $n = -30$ **$m = 0$**

7. $-1 + t = 0$ 8. $-1.3 + x = -1.5$
   $t = 1$ **$y = -.2$**

9. Is $-\frac{1}{2} \cdot -\frac{1}{3} \cdot -\frac{1}{4} \cdot -\frac{1}{5} \cdot -\frac{1}{6}$ positive or negative? Why?
   positive; even number of negative signs

In 10–14, simplify.
10. $1 \cdot t + 0 \cdot m + -1 \cdot -3p$ **$t + 3p$**

11. $-25(14 + -2 \cdot 5 \cdot 4)$ **0**

12. $-2 \cdot -1 \cdot 1 \cdot k$ **2k**

13. $-1 \cdot -1 + 0 \cdot 0 + -1 \cdot 0$ **1**

14. $(-1)^6$ **1**

Transition Mathematics © Scott, Foresman and Company   **89**

Review

28. Simplify $-1 + -2 + -3 + -4 + -5 + -6 + -7 + -8$. *(Lesson 7-2)*
-36

29. Simplify $-1 - -2 - -3 - -4 - -5 - -6 - -7 - -8$. *(Lesson 7-2)*
34

30. Evaluate $\frac{4}{9} - xy$ when $x = -\frac{2}{3}$ and $y = \frac{5}{4}$. *(Lesson 10-5)* 23/18

31. What is the Additive Identity Property of Zero? *(Lesson 5-4)*
For any number x, x + 0 = x.

32. What is the Multiplicative Identity Property of One? *(Lesson 9-5)*
For any number x, x · 1 = x.

33. Solve $57 - x = 4.6$. *(Lesson 7-6)* 52.4

34. If $C = 5(F - 32)/9$, find C when $F = 98.6$, normal body temperature. *(Lesson 4-6)* 37

35. How many diagonals does a regular heptagon have? *(Lesson 6-3)*
14

36. 4/7 of what number is 56? *(Lesson 10-2)* 98

37. A car on an unpaved highway travels 50 hours at an average speed of 25 miles per hour. How far has the car gone? *(Lesson 10-4)*
1250 miles

Exploration

38. This lesson started by finding out the values of $5x$ as x itself was chosen to be closer and closer to 0. The result was that $5x$ became closer to 0. Using your calculator, find the values of 5^x when x is 0.5, 0.4, 0.3, 0.2, 0.1, 0.01, 0.001, 0.0001, and 0.00001. What number are the values of 5^x getting closer to? What is the value of 5^0? **See below.**

x	5^x
0.5	2.2360680
0.4	1.9036539
0.3	1.6206566
0.2	1.3797297
0.1	1.1746189
0.01	1.0162246
0.001	1.0016107
0.0001	1.0001610
0.00001	1.0000161

The value of 5^x is getting closer to 1.
It seems that $5^0 = 1$.

468

10-8

Solving $ax = b$ when a Is Negative

Example 3 uses an equation of the form $ax = b$ to determine how many days it will take to use up the stack of paper.

The equation $-4x = 3$ is an equation of the form $ax = b$. In $-4x = 3$, a is negative. These equations can be solved using the Multiplication Property of Equality. But first you must be able to find the reciprocals of negative numbers.

The reciprocal of n is $\frac{1}{n}$, as you know. The reciprocal of $-n$ is $-\frac{1}{n}$, because the product of $-n$ and $-\frac{1}{n}$ is 1.

$$-n \cdot -\frac{1}{n} = 1$$

For example, the reciprocal of -4 is $-\frac{1}{4}$. The reciprocal of $-\frac{2}{3}$ is $-\frac{3}{2}$, or -1.5. The reciprocal of -18 is $-\frac{1}{18}$, or $-0.0555\ldots$ You should check these values using the $\boxed{1/n}$ key on your calculator.

Example 1   Solve $-4x = 3$.

Solution   As you did before, multiply both sides by the reciprocal of -4. Because of the Multiplication Property of Equality, this does not change the solution.

$$-\frac{1}{4} \cdot -4x = -\frac{1}{4} \cdot 3$$

Using the Associative Property, the left side simplifies to $1 \cdot x$, which equals x. The right side can be multiplied as usual. The result:

$$x = -\frac{3}{4}.$$

Check   As usual, substitute into the original equation.
$$\text{Does } -4 \cdot -\frac{3}{4} = 3?$$

The left side multiplies to $\frac{12}{4}$, which is 3, so the solution checks.

In solving equations with negatives, you should first decide whether the solution is positive or negative. Is it obvious in Example 1 that x is negative?

RESOURCES
■ Lesson Master 10-8

OBJECTIVE

C Solve and check equations of the form $ax = b$ when a is negative using the Multiplication Property of Equality.

TEACHING NOTES

Reading   You might have students read silently on their own, making a summary of the lesson or a list of important ideas as they go along. Since the new concept is really a combination of two previous ones, solving $ax = b$ and multiplication with negative numbers, students are likely to have a high level of comprehension. During class discussion, ask students to explain the solution to the examples in their own words.

In **Example 3,** it is possible to avoid negatives altogether: $\frac{3}{4}d = 12$ gives the same solution as $-\frac{3}{4}d = -12$. Either equation can be used.

ADDITIONAL EXAMPLES

1. Solve and check.

a. $-6q = 5$

$q = -\frac{5}{6}; -6 \cdot -\frac{5}{6} = 5$

b. $-8 = -\frac{2}{3}r$

$r = 12; -\frac{2}{3} \cdot 12 = -8$

c. $15 = -2.5s$

$s = -6; -2.5 \cdot -6 = 15$

2. Bill lost 6 lb during the first month of his diet. If he continues to lose weight at this rate, how long will it take him to lose 39 lb?

$6\frac{1}{2}$ **months**

Example 2   Solve $-4.5m = -27$.

Solution   Multiply both sides by $-\frac{1}{4.5}$, the reciprocal of -4.5.

$$-\tfrac{1}{4.5} \cdot -4.5m = -\tfrac{1}{4.5} \cdot -27$$

All that is left is to simplify both sides.

$$1 \cdot m = \tfrac{27}{4.5}$$
$$m = 6$$

Was it obvious from the beginning that m is positive?

The next example reviews many of the ideas you have studied in this chapter.

Example 3   If a computer uses 3/4 inch of a stack of paper each day of normal use, how long will it take to use up a one-foot high stack?

Solution   The stack gets lower by 3/4 inches a day. Let d be the number of days it will take for the stack to be reduced by 12 inches. Using the rate factor model for multiplication,

$$-\tfrac{3}{4} \tfrac{\text{inches}}{\text{day}} \cdot d \text{ days} = -12 \text{ inches.}$$

So the equation to solve is $-\frac{3}{4}d = -12$.

Multiply both sides by $-\frac{4}{3}$, the reciprocal of $-\frac{3}{4}$.

$$-\tfrac{4}{3} \cdot -\tfrac{3}{4}d = -\tfrac{4}{3} \cdot -12$$
$$d = \tfrac{48}{3}$$
$$d = 16$$

At this rate, the stack will be used up in 16 days.

Questions

Covering the Reading

In 1–6, give the reciprocal of each number.

1. -8 $-\frac{1}{8}$ or -0.125   **2.** $-\frac{1}{3}$ -3   **3.** $-\frac{9}{5}$ $-\frac{5}{9}$ or $-0.\overline{5}$

4. -1.2 $-0.8\overline{3}$ or $-\frac{5}{6}$ **5.** $-x$ $-\frac{1}{x}$ **6.** $-\frac{1}{x}$ $-x$

In 7–12, solve each equation. Check your solution.

7. $-4x = 8$ -2   **8.** $-4y = -52$ 13   **9.** $-1.2A = 84$ -70

10. $1.2 = -1.2B$ -1   **11.** $-\frac{2}{15} = -\frac{5}{3}t$ $\frac{2}{25}$ **12.** $1.2C = -0.3$ -0.25

470

13. What property enables both sides to be multiplied by the same number without the solutions being affected?
Multiplication Property of Equality

14. To solve $-ax = b$, by what number should you multiply both sides? $-\frac{1}{a}$

15. About 2/5 inch of a stack of paper is used each day. How long will it take to use 6 inches of the stack? about 15 days

NOTES ON QUESTIONS
Questions 15-17: These can be solved without using negative numbers. See the comments concerning **Example 3** in Teaching Notes on page 469.

Applying the Mathematics

16. A glacier is melting by 4.5 cm a year. At this rate how long will it take for the glacier to recede one meter? $-4.5x = -100$; 22.2 years

Error Analysis for Question 20: Some students confuse methods for solving addition and multiplication equations. You may also want to solve $-3x = -12$, discussing and comparing the procedures for both equations.

17. The Ragamuffin Bakery is now in debt $4500 and has been losing about $800 a month over the last year. About how long has the Bakery been in debt? $-800m = -4500$; about 5.6 months

18. Is the solution to $5.83146 = -24.987t$ positive or negative?
negative

19. Suppose $xy = z$ and both x and z are negative. What can be said about y? y is positive.

Review

20. Solve $-3 + x = -12$. *(Lesson 5-8)* -9

21. Simplify $a + 0 \cdot a - b + 1 \cdot b + -1 \cdot a - a$. *(Lesson 10-7)* -a

22. Evaluate $-7x + 2y - 3z$ when $x = -\frac{5}{3}$, $y = 4$, and $z = -2$.
(Lesson 10-5) $25\frac{2}{3}$ or 77/3

23. At Maple Jr. H. S. 30% of the 600 students are enrolled in a computer class. How many students is this? *(Lesson 2-6)*
180 students

24. At Elm Grove H. S. 600 students are on a team. This is 30% of all students. How many students are at Elm Grove High?
(Lesson 10-3) 2000 students

25. The probability that a sum of S will appear when two normal dice are thrown is $(6 - |S - 7|)/36$. (S must be an integer from 2 to 12 for the formula to work.) Use this formula to calculate the probability that a sum of 3 will appear. *(Lesson 4-6)* 1/18

LESSON 10-8 Solving $ax = b$ when a Is Negative   **471**

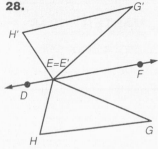

26. Find m$\angle DBC$ in terms of x. *(Lesson 7-7)* $180° - x$

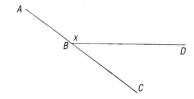

In 27 and 28, use the drawing below.

27. Find the measures of all angles of $\triangle EGH$. *(Lessons 7-8, 7-10)*
m$\angle HEG = 98°$; m$\angle H = 50°$; m$\angle G = 32°$

28. Trace the drawing and draw the reflection image of $\triangle EGH$ over
$\overleftrightarrow{DF}$. *(Lesson 8-6)* **See margin.**

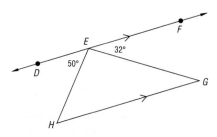

Exploration

29. What integer between -1111 and 1111 is the solution to the
following equation: $-11x - 111 = -11111$? **1000**

Solving
$ax + b = c$

LESSON 10-9

RESOURCES
■ Lesson Master 10-9
■ *Manipulative Activities Sourcebook*, Activity 19

OBJECTIVES

D Solve and check equations of the form $ax + b = c$.
E Apply the Addition and Multiplication Properties of Equality in solving the same equation.

TEACHING NOTES

Make sure students focus on the two-step nature of the process in **Example 1.** Ask what needs to be done to get x by itself on one side of the equation (add -35 and multiply by $\frac{1}{4}$) and which operation should be done first (add -35 to both sides). **Example 2** requires a simplification to get to the form $ax + b = c$, and **Example 3** illustrates how to handle a subtracted variable term. In discussing these examples, remind students to convert a sentence they cannot solve into one they can.

French fries have about 11 calories apiece. If you eat F french fries, you will have taken in about $11F$ calories. A plain 4-oz hamburger with a bun has about 500 calories. So together the hamburger and french fries have about $500 + 11F$ calories.

> How many french fries can you eat with this hamburger and bun for 800 total calories?

The answer is given by solving the following equation.

$$500 + 11F = 800$$

To solve this equation, first add -500 to both sides and simplify.

$$-500 + 500 + 11F = -500 + 800$$
$$0 + 11F = 300$$
$$11F = 300$$

You've solved many equations like this one. Multiply both sides by $\frac{1}{11}$ and simplify.

$$\frac{1}{11} \cdot 11F = \frac{1}{11} \cdot 300$$
$$F = \frac{300}{11} \approx 27$$

Approximately 27 french fries with the hamburger will give you 800 calories.

In the equation $500 + 11F = 800$, the unknown F is multiplied by a number. Then a second number is added. We call this an **equation of the form $ax + b = c$.** All equations of this type can be solved with two major steps. First add $-b$ to both sides. This step gets the term with the variable alone on one side. Then multiply both sides by $\frac{1}{a}$.

Solve and check.
1. $-20 = 15 + 7v$
$-5 = v$
Check: $15 + 7(-5)$
$= 15 + -35 = -20$

2. $10 + 8w - 4 = 14$
$w = 1$
Check: $10 + 8(1) - 4$
$= 10 + 8 - 4 = 14$

3. $25 - \frac{1}{2}y = 30$
$y = -10$
Check: $25 - \frac{1}{2}(-10)$
$= 25 + 5 = 30$

■ ■ ■ ■ ■ ■ ■ ■ ■

Example 1   Solve $4x + 35 = 91$.

Solution   Add -35 to both sides. This will leave $4x$ alone on one side.

$$4x + 35 = 91$$
$$4x + 35 + -35 = 91 + -35$$
$$4x + \quad 0 \quad = \quad 56$$
$$4x \quad = \quad 56$$

Multiply both sides by $\frac{1}{4}$.

$$\frac{1}{4} \cdot 4x = \frac{1}{4} \cdot 56$$
$$x = 14$$

Check   As usual, substitute 14 for x in the original sentence.
Does $4 \cdot 14 + 35 = 91$?
Yes, $4 \cdot 14 + 35 = 56 + 35 = 91$.

Look again at Example 1. By adding -35 to both sides, the equation that results is $4x = 56$. This is an equation of a type you have solved before. This illustrates a fundamental strategy true of all sentence-solving.

If you cannot solve a sentence, convert it into one you can solve.

Example 2 illustrates this strategy. The sentence may look complicated, but it is easy to change it to a sentence that can be solved.

■ ■ ■ ■ ■ ■ ■ ■ ■

Example 2   Solve $10 + 6h - 14 = 32$.

Solution   First simplify the left side. You may not need to write all the steps that are shown here.

$$10 + 6h - 14 = 32$$
$$10 + 6h + -14 = 32 \quad \text{(Add-Opp Property of Subtraction)}$$
$$10 + -14 + 6h = 32 \quad \text{(Assoc. and Comm. Properties of Addition)}$$
$$-4 + 6h = 32 \quad \text{(Simplify)}$$

This is an equation like the one solved in Example 1. Add 4 to both sides.

$$4 + -4 + 6h = 4 + 32 \quad \text{(Addition Property of Equality)}$$
$$6h \quad = 36 \quad \text{(Simplify)}$$

474

You can solve this equation in your head. If not, multiply both sides by $\frac{1}{6}$.

$$h = 6$$

Check Substitute: Does $10 + 6 \cdot 6 - 14 = 32$?

$$10 + 36 - 14 = 32?$$
$$46 - 14 = 32? \text{ Yes.}$$

Equations of the type $b - ax = c$, where the variable term is subtracted, can be solved with just one extra step.

Example 3 Solve $17 = 63 - 2t$.

Solution The extra step is to convert everything to addition using the Add-Opp Property of Subtraction.

$$17 = 63 - 2t$$
$$17 = 63 + \text{-}2t$$

Now add -63 to both sides. This leaves -2t alone.

$$\text{-}63 + 17 = \text{-}63 + 63 + \text{-}2t$$
$$\text{-}46 = 0 + \text{-}2t$$
$$\text{-}46 = \text{-}2t$$

Now solve as you have done before. Multiply both sides by $-\frac{1}{2}$.

$$-\frac{1}{2} \cdot \text{-}46 = -\frac{1}{2} \cdot \text{-}2t$$
$$23 = t$$

Check This solution checks because $17 = 63 - 2 \cdot 23$.

Questions

Covering the Reading

1. **a.** To solve the equation $4x + 25 = 85$, first add _?_ to both sides. **-25**
   b. Solve $4x + 25 = 85$. **15**

2. **a.** To solve the equation $3v - 8 = \text{-}50$, first add _?_ to both sides. **8**
   b. Solve $3v - 8 = \text{-}50$. **-14**

3. What fundamental strategy of sentence-solving is given in this lesson?
   If you cannot solve a sentence, convert it into one you can solve.

4. **a.** What should be the first step in solving $3 + 4x + 5 = 6$?
   b. Solve this sentence. **a. add 3 and 5; b. -1/2**

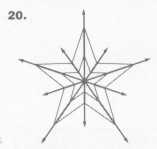
In 5–8, solve:

5. $2y + 7 = 41$ 17

6. $300 + 120t = -1500$ -15

7. $60 - 9x = 48$ 4/3

8. $17 + 60m + 3 = 100$ 4/3

In 9–13, use this information. A hamburger has about 80 calories per ounce. A bun has about 180 calories. A typical french fry has about 11 calories.

9. How many calories are in a plain 4-oz hamburger, bun, and 10 french fries?   **610 calories**

10. How many calories are in a plain 4-oz hamburger, bun, and F french fries?   **500 + 11F calories**

11. If you order a plain 4-oz hamburger with a bun, how many french fries can you eat for a total of 900 calories?   **about 36 french fries**

Applying the Mathematics

12. How many calories are in h ounces of hamburger without the bun and F french fries?   **80h + 11F**

13. Suppose you ate 20 french fries. How large a hamburger could you eat with a bun and have a total of 1000 calories?
7.5 ounce hamburger

14. a. To solve $mx + n = p$ for x, what could you add to both sides?   -n
b. Solve this equation. $x = \frac{p - n}{m}$

15. Is -17 the solution to $400 - 12x = 196$?   No

16. Solve and check: $2y + 1 = 0$.   -1/2

17. Solve and check: $\frac{3}{2} - 14z + \frac{7}{8} = 0$. $\frac{19}{112}$

18. Meticulous Matilda likes to put in every step in solving equations. Here is her solution to $5m + 7 = -3$. Give a reason for each step.
  a. $(5m + 7) + -7 = -3 + -7$ **e.** $\frac{1}{5} \cdot (5m) = \frac{1}{5} \cdot -10$
  b. $5m + (7 + -7) = -3 + -7$ **f.** $(\frac{1}{5} \cdot 5)m = \frac{1}{5} \cdot -10$
  c. $5m + 0 = -3 + -7$ **g.** $1 \cdot m = -2$
  d. $5m = -10$ **h.** $m = -2$
                                    See margin.

Review

19. Solve: $-\frac{2}{3}t = \frac{5}{4}$. *(Lesson 10-8)* $-\frac{15}{8}$

20. Trace the figure below and draw its lines of symmetry. *(Lesson 8-7)*
See margin.

21. 1 meter $\approx$ 39.37 inches. Then 25 inches is about how many meters? *(Lesson 10-4)*   .635 m

22. Simplify $-4(3 + -2 \cdot 6 - 1)$. *(Lesson 10-5)*   40

476

23. Simplify $1 \cdot x + 0 \cdot y + -1 \cdot -2z$. *(Lesson 10-7)* $x + 2z$

24. Zero times a certain number is one. What is the number? *(Lesson 10-7)* There is no such number.

25. In the Georgia primary of March, 1988, the Reverend Jesse Jackson received about 248,000 votes. This was about 39% of the total. In all, about how many people voted? *(Lesson 10-3)*
635,900 people

26. a. Simplify: $350 \frac{\text{words}}{\text{page}} \cdot 175 \frac{\text{pages}}{\text{book}}$ $61,250 \frac{\text{words}}{\text{book}}$

   b. Make up a problem that the multiplication of part **a** could answer. *(Lesson 10-4)* See margin.

27. On January 1 there were about 2500 deer in the White Forest. During the year, D deer died, B were born, and S were relocated. At the end of the year there were about 2300 deer in the forest. Give a relationship among all of these numbers and variables. *(Lessons 5-1, 7-1)* $2500 - D + B - S = 2300$

28. You wish to carpet a room that is 9' by 12'. The carpet you want costs $10.95 per square *yard*. How much will it cost for the carpet? *(Lessons 9-1, 10-4)* $131.40

29. First-class postage in 1990 cost 25¢ for the first ounce and 20¢ for each additional ounce. At these rates, give the cost of mailing a letter that weighs: **a.** 2 ounces; **b.** 3 ounces; **c.** 4 ounces; **d.** n ounces. *(Lesson 6-5)*
a. 45¢; b. 65¢; c. 85¢; d. $25 + 20(n - 1)$ cents

30. A projectile is shot upward from the ground at a velocity of 128 ft/sec. Ignoring air resistance (but not ignoring gravity), its velocity t seconds after being thrown will be $(-32t + 128)$ ft/sec. *(Lessons 10-5, 10-6)*

   a. What is its velocity 1 second after being thrown?

   b. What is its velocity 2 seconds after being thrown?

   c. Five seconds after being thrown, the projectile's velocity is negative. What does this mean?
   a. 96 ft/sec; b. 64 ft/sec; c. The projectile is falling.

Exploration

31. Look in a newspaper for the prices of stocks on the New York Stock Exchange. What fractions are used in describing these prices? positive and negative halves, quarters, and eighths

NAME _____

LESSON **MASTER 10-9**
QUESTIONS ON **SPUR** OBJECTIVES

■**SKILLS** *Objective D (See pages 480–481 for objectives.)*
In 1–8, a. solve each equation. b. Check your answer.

1. $2x - 9 = 13$
   a. ___ $x = 11$
   b. ___ $2 \cdot 11 - 9 = 13$

2. $4x + 21 = 5$
   a. ___ $x = -4$
   b. ___ $4(-4) + 21 = 5$

3. $\frac{1}{3}s + 9 = 12$
   a. ___ $s = 9$
   b. ___ $\frac{1}{3}(9) + 9 = 12$

4. $16 - 5p = -74$
   a. ___ $p = 18$
   b. ___ $16 - 5(18) = -74$

5. $\frac{2}{3}j - 8 = 14$
   a. ___ $j = 33$
   a. ___ $\frac{2}{3}(33) - 8 = 14$

6. $-9 + 3y + 11 = -6$
   a. ___ $y = -\frac{8}{3}$
   b. ___ $-9 + 3\left(-\frac{8}{3}\right) + 11 = -6$

7. $40x + 2000 = 3200$
   a. ___ $x = 30$
   b. ___ $40(30) + 2000 = 3200$

8. $-3.8 + 4.2n = 8.6$
   a. ___ $n \approx 3$
   b. ___ $-3.8 + 4.2(3) = 8.8 \approx 8.6$

■**PROPERTIES** *Objective E*

9. To solve $-75m + 25 = 100$, what would you add to both sides of the equation? -25

10. To solve $4y - 16 = 88$, what would you add to both sides of the equation? 16

11. In solving an equation of the type $ax + b = c$, which operation is done first? addition

Transition Mathematics © Scott, Foresman and Company   **91**

477

Summary

In Chapter 9, you learned that a size change can picture multiplication by a positive number. In this chapter, size changes picture multiplication by negative numbers. They show that multiplying by a negative changes direction as well as size. So negative · positive = negative, and negative · negative = positive.

Multiplying any number by 0 gives a product of 0. Multiplying by -1 changes a number to its opposite.

An important use of multiplication involves rate factors. Examples of rate factors are the quantities 600 miles/hour, $2.50 per bottle, 27.3 students per class, and -3 kg/month. When rate factors are multiplied by other quantities, the units are multiplied like fractions. Rate factors like 5280 feet/mile can be used to convert units.

These uses, and the area, volume, array, and repeated addition uses you learned in Chapter 9, often lead to equations to be solved. You may know one factor a and the product b, but not know the other factor. Then you have a situation of the type $ax = b$. There are at least three ways to solve these equations: substitution mentally, by related facts, and using the Multiplication Property of Equality. If $a \neq 0$, the solution to $ax = b$ is $x = \frac{b}{a}$.

Equations of the form $ax + b = c$ can be solved by first adding $-b$ to both sides. This gives an equation you already know how to solve.

Vocabulary

You should be able to give a general description
and a specific example for each
of the following ideas.

Lesson 10–1
equation of the form $ax = b$
Related Facts Property of Multiplication and
  Division

Lesson 10–2
Multiplication Property of Equality

Lesson 10–4
rate, rate unit, rate factor
Rate Factor Model for Multiplication
conversion factor

Lesson 10–7
Multiplication Property of Zero
Multiplication Property of -1

Lesson 10–9
equation of the form $ax + b = c$

478

Progress Self-Test

See margin for answers not shown below.

Take this test as you would take a test in class. Then check your work with the solutions in the Selected Answers section in the back of the book. Use graph paper and a ruler for Question 15.

1. The product of $\frac{3}{5}$ and another number is 15. Find the other number.   **25**

2. State the Multiplication Property of Equality.

3. The area of a rectangle is 5 square feet. Its length is 10 feet. What is its width?

4. A person made $2000 more this year than last. This increase is 8% of last year's income. What was last year's income?

5. Solve $13x = 1001$ by related facts.

6. Solve $13x = 1001$ using the Multiplication Property of Equality.

7. A person makes $8.50 an hour and works 37.5 hours a week. Multiply the two rates in this situation. What is the result?   **$318.75**

8. What multiplication with negative numbers is suggested by the following situation?
For four hours, the flood waters receded three centimeters an hour.

In 9–11, calculate:

9. $5 \cdot -9$ **-45**

10. $-3 \cdot -3 + -2 \cdot -2$ **13**

11. $2 \cdot -3 \cdot 4 \cdot -5 \cdot 6 \cdot -7$ **-5040**

12. Evaluate $6x - 3yz$ when $x = 0$, $y = -1$, and $z = 5$.   **15**

13. Simplify: $a + 1 \cdot a + b + 0 \cdot b + -1 \cdot c + c$.

14. If $de = f$, e is negative, and f is negative, what can you say about d?
d must be positive

In 15 and 16, a triangle has vertices (12, -24), (0, 6), and (-24, 24).

15. Graph this triangle and its image under an expansion of magnitude -2.5.

16. Name one thing that is the same about the preimage and image and one thing that is different.

17. Which expression does not equal the others, or are they all equal?   **all equal**
$a - b \qquad a + -1 \cdot b \qquad a + -b \qquad a - 1 \cdot b$

In 18 and 19, use the fact that 1 meter ≈ 39.37 inches.

18. What two conversion factors arise from this relationship? $\frac{39.37 \text{ in.}}{1 \text{ m}}, \frac{1 \text{ m}}{39.37 \text{ in.}}$

19. Use the appropriate conversion factor to convert 1200 inches to meters.
1200 in. · 1 m/39.37 in. ≈ 30.48 m

In 20–25, solve.

20. $-x = 4$ **$x = -4$**

21. $35.1 = -9t$ **$t = -3.9$**

22. $-\frac{2}{5}m = -\frac{3}{4}$ **$m = \frac{15}{8}$**

23. $0k = 0$ **k can be any number.**

24. $2 + 3A = 17$ **$A = 5$**

25. $12 - 4h - 15 = 10$ **$h = -13/4$**

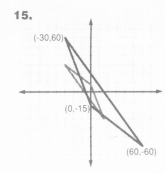

Chapter Review

See margin for answers not shown below.

Questions on **SPUR** Objectives

SPUR stands for **S**kills, **P**roperties, **U**ses, and **R**epresentations. The Chapter Review questions are grouped according to the SPUR Objectives for this chapter.

SKILLS deal with the procedures used to get answers.

■ **Objective A:** *Multiply positive and negative numbers. (Lesson 10-5)*

1. Simplify -8 · -2.   16
2. Simplify 3 + -10 · 4.   -37
3. Simplify 5 · -5 · 4 · -4.   400
4. If $x = -3$ and $y = -16$, what is the value of $5x - 2y$?   17

■ **Objective B:** *Solve and check equations of the form $ax = b$ mentally or by substitution. (Lesson 10-1)*

5. Solve $24 = 8h$ mentally.   3
6. Solve $-15z = 15$ mentally.   -1
7. Solve for x: $-x = 7$.   -7
8. Name all solutions to $10y = 0$.   0
9. Is the solution to $-2.6845 = -32.5m$ positive or negative?   positive
10. Is $\frac{1}{3}$ the solution to $\frac{3}{8}m = 8$?   No

■ **Objective C:** *Solve and check equations of the form $ax = b$ using the Multiplication Property of Equality. (Lessons 10-2, 10-8)*

In 11–16, solve and check.
11. $40t = 3000$ 75; 40 · 75 = 3000
12. $-22 = 4A$ -5.5; -22 = 4 · -5.5
13. $0.02v = 0.8$ 40; 0.02 · 40 = 0.8
14. $\frac{2}{3}x = 18$ 27; $\frac{2}{3}$ · 27 = 18
15. $-49 = -7y$ 7; -49 = -7 · 7
16. $2.4 + 3.6 = (5 - 0.2)x$ 1.25

■ **Objective D:** *Solve and check equations of the form $ax + b = c$. (Lesson 10-9)*

In 17–20, solve and check.
17. $8m + 2 = 18$ 2; 8 · 2 + 2 = 16 + 2 = 18
18. $-2.5 + .5y = 4.2$
19. $11 - 6u = -7$ 3; 11 - 6 · 3 = 11 - 18 = -7
20. $23 + 4x - 10 = -39$

PROPERTIES deal with the principles behind the mathematics.

■ **Objective E:** *Apply the Multiplication and Addition Properties of Equality. (Lessons 10-2, 10-9)*

21. To solve $\frac{11}{3}y = \frac{2}{9}$, by what number can you multiply both sides of the equation? $\frac{3}{11}$
22. To solve $-17r + 12 = 50$, what could you add to both sides of the equation?   -12

■ **Objective F:** *Apply the Multiplication Properties of 0 and -1. (Lesson 10-7)*

23. Simplify: $-1 \cdot -x$.   x

24. Simplify: $0 \cdot a + 1 \cdot b + -1 \cdot c$.   b − c, or b + -c
25. Solve: $0x = 3$.   no solutions

■ **Objective G:** *Use the Related Facts Property of Multiplication and Division. (Lesson 10-1)*

26. What two division facts are related to $16 = 6.4t$?   t = 16/6.4; 6.4 = 16/t
27. Check whether $48.4 \cdot 274 = 13,261.6$ by using related facts.
28. Solve $9x = 819$ by related facts. $x = \frac{819}{9} = 91$

USES deal with applications of mathematics in real situations.

Objective H: *Apply the Rate Factor Model for Multiplication. (Lessons 10-4, 10-5)*

In 29 and 30, **a.** do the multiplication, and **b.** make up a question that leads to this multiplication.

29. $2 \frac{\text{cookies}}{\text{day}} \cdot 365 \frac{\text{days}}{\text{year}}$

30. $5 \text{ hours} \cdot 25 \frac{\text{miles}}{\text{hour}}$

31. A person makes $10.50 an hour and works 37.5 hours a week. How much does the person earn per year?   **$20,475**

32. Fire laws say there is a maximum of 60 people per small conference room. There are 6 small conference rooms. Altogether, how many people can meet in them?

33. If Lois has been losing weight at the rate of 2.3 kg per month, how did her weight 4 months ago compare with her weight now?   **She weighed 9.2 kg more.**

Objective I: *Use conversion factors to convert from one unit to another. (Lesson 10-4)*

34. Name the two conversion factors from the equality 1 foot = 30.48 cm.

35. 500 cm equals about how many ft?   **about 16.4 ft**

36. 150 hours equals how many days?   **6.25 days**

Objective J: *Find unknowns in area, volume, or array situations involving multiplication. (Lesson 10-2, 10-3)*

37. A movie theater has 500 seats and 20 rows. There are the same number of seats in each row. How many seats are there per row?   **25 seats**

38. A store is in the shape of a rectangle. Find the depth of the store if the area of the store is 3500 sq ft and the width is 40 ft.

39. Find the height of this box if its volume is 2400 cubic centimeters.   **12 cm**

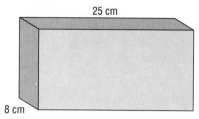

Objective K: *Find unknowns in size change situations involving multiplication. (Lesson 10-3)*

40. 6 times a number is 1/3. What is the number?   **1/18**

41. 12% of what number is 240?   **2000**

42. A sweater is on sale at 80% of the original price. The sale price is $40. What was the original price?   **$50**

43. When Jed works overtime at time-and-a-half, he makes $12 an hour. What is his usual hourly wage?   **$8/hr**

44. Seven-eighths of a number is 112. What is the number?   **128**

REPRESENTATIONS deal with pictures, graphs, or objects that illustrate concepts.

Objective L: *Picture multiplication by negative numbers using size changes. (Lesson 10-6)*

45. What is the image of (40, -80) under a size change of magnitude -0.2?   **(-8, 16)**

46. Under a size change of magnitude -5, how will a quadrilateral and its image be the same and how will they be different?

47. Let $A = (-4, 5)$, $B = (2, 0)$, and $C = (0, -3)$. Graph $\triangle ABC$ and its image under a size change of magnitude -2.

48. A size change of magnitude -12 is like a size change of magnitude 12 followed by a rotation of what magnitude?   **180°**

CHAPTER 10   Chapter Review   **481**

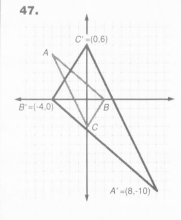

CHAPTER 11 ■ PATTERNS LEADING TO DIVISION

DAILY PACING CHART ■ CHAPTER 11

Students in the Full Course should complete the entire text by the end of the year. Students in the Minimal Course spend more time when there are quizzes and more time on the Chapter Review. Therefore, these students may not complete all of the chapters in the text.

DAY	MINIMAL COURSE	FULL COURSE
1	11-1	11-1
2	11-2	11-2
3	11-3	11-3
4	Quiz (TRF); Start 11-4.	Quiz (TRF); 11-4
5	Finish 11-4.	11-5
6	11-5	11-6
7	11-6	Quiz (TRF); 11-7
8	Quiz (TRF); Start 11-7.	11-8
9	Finish 11-7.	11-9
10	11-8	Progress Self Test
11	11-9	Chapter Review
12	Progress Self Test	Chapter Test (TRF)
13	Chapter Review	
14	Chapter Review	
15	Chapter Test (TRF)	

TESTING OPTIONS
■ Quiz for Lessons 11-1 Through 11-4   ■ Chapter 11 Test, Form A   ■ Chapter 11 Test, Cumulative Form
■ Quiz for Lessons 11-5 Through 11-7   ■ Chapter 11 Test, Form B

A Quiz and Test Writer is available for generating additional questions, additional quizzes, or additional forms of the Chapter Test.

PROVIDING FOR INDIVIDUAL DIFFERENCES
The student text is written for the *average* student. The program, however, can be adapted for both less capable and more capable students.

A blackline master (in the Teacher's Resource File) is provided for each lesson for those students who need more practice. The Teacher's Edition frequently provides an Error Analysis feature to provide additional instructional strategies.

For students who require additional challenge, Extension activities are regularly provided in the Teacher's Edition.

OBJECTIVES ■ CHAPTER 11

Students should master the chapter objectives by the time they complete the chapter. To ensure objective mastery, there is continual review built into each set of lesson questions. After students complete the chapter lessons, they assess their mastery on the Progress Self-Test. Then they do the Chapter Review and pay special attention to those questions that match the objectives missed on the Progress Self-Test. Students can get extra practice on these objectives by using the master for each lesson in the Teacher's Resource File.

OBJECTIVES FOR CHAPTER 11 (Organized into the SPUR categories—Skills, Properties, Uses, and Representations)	Progress Self-Test Questions	Chapter Review Questions	Teacher's Resource File	
			Lesson Master*	Chapter Test Forms A and B
SKILLS				
A: Divide fractions with numbers or variables.	3, 5	1–5	11-2	7
B: Divide positive and negative numbers.	4, 6	6–9	11-3	5, 8, 13
C: Solve proportions.	10, 11, 24, 25	10–12	11-6, 11-7, 11-9	11, 12
PROPERTIES				
D: Recognize the Means-Extremes Property and know why it works.	17, 18	13–15	11-7	3
E: Know the general properties for dividing positive and negative numbers.	8	16, 17	11-3	1
F: Apply the properties of probability.	22	18, 19	11-5	6
USES				
G: Use the Rate Model for Division.	1, 2	20–24	11-1, 11-2, 11-3	4
H: Find the mean of a set of numbers.	7	25, 26	11-3	17
I: Use the Ratio Comparison Model for Division.	12, 13, 14	27–30	11-4	9, 10, 15
J: Calculate probabilities in a situation with equally likely outcomes.	21	31–34	11-5	2
K: Recognize and solve problems involving proportions in real situations.	15, 16, 23	35–37	11-6, 11-7, 11-9	14, 16
L: Give situations that represent the division of negative numbers.	9	38, 39	11-3	20
REPRESENTATIONS				
M: Find missing lengths in similar figures.	19, 20	40–42	11-8	18, 19

*The Lesson Masters are numbered to match the lessons.

OVERVIEW ■ CHAPTER 11

Division, the last of the fundamental operations to be studied in this book, is by no means the least important. Rate and ratio comparison, the two principal uses of division, have applications throughout mathematics. Proportions, which arise from equal quotients, are also of fundamental significance.

Because hand calculation of answers to division problems is more difficult than for the other fundamental operations, most students have spent a great deal of time learning to divide. Often as a result, they have had very little work with applications of division. Thus, the applications tend to be unfamil-

iar, and intuition, particularly when the numbers are not small whole numbers, has never developed.

The chapter begins with the Rate Model. In Lesson 11-1, rates are calculated in which the divisor and dividend are either whole numbers or decimals. In Lessons 11-2 and 11-3, the model is used with fractions and with negative numbers.

Lesson 11-4 introduces the other major model, the Ratio Comparison Model. Ratio comparison leads to finding what percent one number is of another. Lesson 11-5 discusses probability, an important application of ratio comparison.

Lessons 11-6 through 11-9 constitute four lessons on proportions. In Lesson 11-6, students solve proportions using the techniques of equation solving learned earlier. Lesson 11-7 introduces a shortcut, the Means-Extremes Property. In Lessons 11-6 and 11-7, there are many applications of proportions, arising naturally from both rates and ratios. Lesson 11-8 discusses the important geometry application to similar figures. Finally, Lesson 11-9 is a summary lesson in which students are asked to think about solving or checking proportions mentally.

PERSPECTIVES ■ CHAPTER 11

The Perspectives provide the rationale for the inclusion of topics or approaches, provide mathematical background, and make connections within UCSMP.

11-1

THE RATE MODEL FOR DIVISION

The difference between ratio comparison (the focus of Lesson 11-4) and rate is simple. If the quantities being compared have the same units, as in comparing 5 miles to 8 miles, the use is classified as *ratio comparison*. If the quantities being related have different units, as in 4 miles and 10 hours, then the use is termed *rate*.

If we divide 4 miles by 10 hours, the result is the rate 0.4 miles per hour. If we divide 10 hours by 4 miles, the result is the rate 2.5 hours per mile. Division either way makes sense. The rates $0.4\frac{\text{mile}}{\text{hour}}$ and $2.5\frac{\text{hours}}{\text{mile}}$ are equal quantities. One must keep the rate units in mind for this idea to make any sense.

The word *per* is a key word in rates; it almost always signifies division. Scientists think of the units as having been divided in a rate; that is, they think of mi/hr as miles divided by hours. Do not discourage students from also thinking in this way.

11-2

DIVISION OF FRACTIONS

Most people believe that division of fractions seldom occurs. This is not the case, since rates (and ratios) can involve fractions. What happens is that people avoid division of fractions whenever possible.

Consider the following problem. In 2 seasons, the Yankees had won 64 games. At this rate, how many games did they win per season? The answer is $\frac{64 \text{ games}}{2 \text{ seasons}}$, or 32 games per season. Now replace the number 2 by the number $\frac{3}{4}$, and ask: In $\frac{3}{4}$ season, the Yankees had won 64 games. At this rate, how many would they win in the season? For this question, most people do not think of dividing, although dividing 64 games by $\frac{3}{4}$ season gives the correct answer.

The Mult-Rec Property of Division is called the *definition of division* in some books. However, to most students it is not a definition of division at all; they think of division as having the meaning "split-

ting up." Thus, at this level, we think it best to label it a property.

11-3

DIVISION WITH NEGATIVE NUMBERS

If students have learned the rules for multiplication of integers, division of negative numbers is not difficult. Two ways to justify the division are given in the solutions to **Example 1** on page 492: (1) through properties, namely the Mult-Rec Property; and (2) through uses, namely by using rate.

Some students will consider the rate examples in this lesson contrived. They are viewed that way only because many people do everything to keep from using negatives. For instance, we automatically think of weighing less some time ago as signifying an increase and forget that the words *less* and *time ago* could relate to negatives.

11-4

THE RATIO COMPARISON MODEL FOR DIVISION

Bill has $10, and Mary has $30. We can compare the quantities by saying that Bill has $\frac{1}{3}$ of Mary's amount or that Mary has 3 times what Bill has. This is a simple example of ratio comparison division.

We could also compare by subtraction. Since $10 - 30 = -20$, Bill has $20 less than Mary. Since $30 - 10 = 20$, Mary has $20 more than Bill. Just as numbers can be compared in either order using subtraction, numbers can be compared in either order with division.

In everyday usage, the words *rate* and *ratio* are often used synonymously. Sometimes the same quantity can be considered each way. For instance, a batting average can be thought of as either a rate or a ratio. As a rate, it is $\frac{\text{number of hits}}{\text{number of at-bats}}$; the unit is *hits per at-bat*. As a ratio, it is $\frac{\text{number of at-bats with a hit}}{\text{total number of at-bats}}$. We tend to think of a batting average as more a ratio than a rate because the average is never reported with a unit. Usually, if there are units in the quotient, it is a rate; if no units, it is a ratio.

11-5

PROPERTIES OF PROBABILITY

Some books use the terms *experimental probability* and *theoretical probability*. We call these concepts *relative frequency* and *probability* respectively. The difference is more than semantic. We want students to think of relative frequencies as values which come from statistical experiments and will *vary* with further experiments. We want students to think of *probabilities* as values taken as a result of assumptions or experiments, values that we either test or consider to be fixed.

11-6

PROPORTIONS

This lesson is the first of four lessons on proportions. Together with the end-of-chapter test and the reviews, at least a week will be spent on this important topic.

This lesson demonstrates the solving of proportions by multiplying both sides of the equation by the same number. We want students to realize that the usual equation-solving rules can be applied to solve proportions.

11-7

THE MEANS-EXTREMES PROPERTY

In the previous lesson, students solved proportions by applying the Multiplication Property of Equality. In this lesson, the Multiplication Property of Equality is used to formulate the Means-Extremes Property. The benefit is that the Means-Extren.es Property greatly simplifies the solving of proportions. The drawback is that many students forget how the property was derived and look for simple tricks for solving all equations, trying to avoid systematic procedures that take more than one step.

11-8

PROPORTIONS IN SIMILAR FIGURES

We have included a lesson on similar figures for three major reasons. First, the content and ideas are important in their own right. The understanding of similar figures is fundamental in geometry and provides a basis for trigonometry as well as for many applications.

Second, this content pictures the ideas of the preceding lessons. For some students, this mental picture of proportions will help them to understand what is going on.

Third, the topic of similar figures provides a different sort of application for the techniques of the previous lessons and is an interesting change of pace from the arithmetic and algebra that have dominated this chapter.

11-9

PROPORTIONAL THINKING

This is a review lesson, both for proportions and for problem solving. The idea is to encourage students to be flexible in solving problems. Many students think if they know one way to do a problem, there is no point in considering alternatives. But if a student knows more than one way to solve a problem, the second way can be used to check the first. Also, some problems may seem easier if a student considers them one way, whereas another problem looks more logical with a different method. It is useful to understand a variety of ways to think about a problem.

CHAPTER 11

We recommend 12 to 15 days for this chapter: 9 to 11 days for the lessons, 1 day to review the Progress Self-Test, 1 to 2 days for the Chapter Review, and 1 day for the exam. (See the Daily Pacing Chart on page 482A.) Keep in mind that each lesson includes Review questions to help students firm up content studied previously.

USING PAGES 482–483
You may wish to have students suggest original questions similar to some of the questions on page 483.

Ask students to identify those questions for which it would be more appropriate to have a fraction or decimal answer (all but D), and those for which it would be better to give a quotient and a remainder (D).

Patterns Leading to Division

482

Each of the eight questions on this page can be answered by dividing 20 by 7. This chapter is concerned with these and other situations that lead to division.

A. Solve for x. $7x = 20$

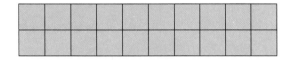

B. Above is pictured a subdivision of land for farming. Split it equally among 7 people. How much will each person get?

C. The distance from El Paso, Texas to Boston is about 2000 miles and from El Paso to Los Angeles is about 700 miles. How many times farther is it from El Paso to Boston than from El Paso to Los Angeles?

D. You expect 20 people at a dinner meeting. Seven can be seated around each of the tables you have. How many tables are needed?

E. Mr. & Mrs. Torrence have 3 daughters, 4 sons, and 20 grandchildren. On the average, how many children do each of their children have?

F. If $WX = 7$ cm, how long is $\overline{WZ}$?

G. If you run at a rate of 7 mi/hr, how long will it take you to run 20 miles?

H. What is the magnitude of the expansion that changed the smaller pentagon below into the larger pentagon?

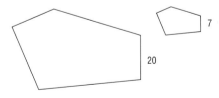

LESSON

11-1

The Rate Model for Division

Here are some examples of **rates**.

55 miles per hour   1.9 children per family $1.95 for each gallon

The **rate units** can be written as fractions.

$$\frac{\text{miles}}{\text{hour}} \qquad \frac{\text{children}}{\text{family}} \qquad \frac{\text{dollars}}{\text{gallon}}$$

In Chapter 10 you studied the Rate Factor Model for Multiplication. Then you were always given the rate. (You may not have realized this at the time.) You never had to calculate rates. The fraction in rate units suggests that rates can be calculated by dividing. This is exactly the case.

Example 1   A car is driven 250 miles in 5 hours. What is the average rate?

Solution $\dfrac{250 \text{ miles}}{5 \text{ hours}} = 50 \dfrac{\text{miles}}{\text{hour}}$

People do Example 1 so easily that sometimes they do not realize they divided to get the answer. Example 2 is of the same type. But the numbers are not so simple.

Example 2   A car goes 283.4 miles on 15.2 gallons of gas. How many miles per gallon is the car getting?

Solution $\dfrac{283.4 \text{ miles}}{15.2 \text{ gallons}} \approx 18.6 \dfrac{\text{miles}}{\text{gallon}}.$
The car is getting about 19 miles per gallon.

Do not let the numbers in rate problems scare you. If you get confused, try simpler numbers and examine how you got the answer.

Examples 1 and 2 are instances of the Rate Model for Division.

484

Rate Model for Division:

If *a* and *b* are quantities with different units, then *a/b* is the amount of quantity *a* per quantity *b*.

One of the most common examples of rate is **unit cost.**

Example 3   A 6-oz can of peaches sells for 89¢. An 8-oz can sells for $1.17. Which is the better buy?

Solution   Calculate the cost per ounce. To do this, divide the total cost by the number of ounces.

Cost per ounce for 6-oz can: $\dfrac{89¢}{6 \text{ oz}} = 14.83...$ cents per ounce

Cost per ounce for 8-oz can: $\dfrac{117¢}{8 \text{ oz}} = 14.625$ cents per ounce

The cost per ounce is called the *unit* cost. The 8-oz can has a slightly lower unit cost. So it is the better buy. But the unit costs do not differ by much. In this case, you should probably choose based on how much you need, not on the cost per can.

Example 4   Eleven people in the scout troop must deliver flyers to 325 households. If the job is split equally, how many flyers will each scout deliver? How many will be left over?

Solution   Think: flyers per scout. This means to divide the number of flyers by the number of scouts.

$$\dfrac{325 \text{ flyers}}{11 \text{ scouts}} = 29.54... \text{ flyers/scout}$$

Each scout will have to deliver 29 flyers. Since 29 · 11 = 319, this would mean that 6 flyers would still not be delivered. The job could be finished if six of the scouts delivered 30 flyers.

Notice in Example 4 that the unit is *flyers per scout*. The number of flyers is a whole number because flyers is a count. But the number of flyers per scout is a rate. Rates do not have to be whole numbers. As you will see in the next two lessons, rates may involve fractions or negative numbers.

Of course, rates can involve variables.

LESSON 11-1   The Rate Model for Division   485

Example 5 Hal typed W words in M minutes. What is his typing speed?

Solution The usual unit of typing speed is *words per minute.* So divide the total number of words by the number of minutes.

His typing speed is W/M words per minute.

Questions

Covering the Reading

In 1–4, calculate a rate suggested by each situation.

1. The family drove 400 miles in 8 hours.   50 miles/hour or 50 mph

2. The family drove 400 miles in 8.5 hours.   about 47.1 miles/hour

3. The family drove 600 kilometers in 9 hours.   about 66.7 km/hr

4. The animal traveled d meters in m minutes.
d/m meters per minute

In 5–7, calculate a rate suggested by each situation.

5. There were 28 boys and 14 girls at the party.   2 boys per girl

6. 150 students signed up for 7 geometry classes.
about 21 students/class

7. Six people live on 120 acres.   20 acres per person

8. State the rate model for division.   See margin.

9. The Smith family went to the grocery store. Boxes of cornflakes were being sold in two different sizes. A 12-oz box cost $1.29 and an 18-oz box cost $1.73.
   a. To the nearest tenth of a cent, give the unit cost of the 12-oz box.   10.8 cents per ounce
   b. To the nearest tenth of a cent, give the unit cost of the 18-oz box.   9.6 cents per ounce
   c. Based on unit cost, which box is the better buy?
   the 18-oz box

Applying the Mathematics

10. Nine nannies need to nail one hundred nineteen nails into a nook.
    a. If the job is split evenly, how many nails will each nanny nail?
    b. How many nails will be left over?   a. 13 nails; b. 2 nails

11. If in h hours you travel m miles, what is your rate in miles per hour? m/h miles per hour

12. A person earns $222 for working 34 hours. How much is the person earning per hour? (Answer to the nearest penny.)
$6.53 per hour

13. In one country a laborer may earn $20 for working 80 hours. How much is this person earning per hour? $0.25 per hour

486

14. According to the *1990 World Almanac,* Hawaii had 2,937 medical doctors and a population of 1,098,000 in 1988. California had 76,638 doctors for a population of 28,314,000. Which state had more doctors *per capita*? (The phrase *per capita* means per person. It comes from the Latin words meaning "per head.")
California

15. The school nurse used 140 bandages in 3 weeks. On the average, how many bandages were used per school day?
$9\frac{1}{3}$ **bandages per day**

16. Susannah calculated that she used an average of $8\frac{2}{5}$ sheets of paper per day. How many sheets of paper could she have used in how many days to get this rate?   **Sample: 84 sheets in 10 days**

Review

17. a. Convert $7\frac{1}{6}$ to a simple fraction. *(Lesson 5-2)* $\frac{43}{6}$
    b. Give its reciprocal. *(Lesson 9-9)* $\frac{6}{43}$

18. State the Mult-Rec Property of Division. *(Lesson 9-8)*
    For any numbers x and y, $\frac{x}{y} = x \cdot \frac{1}{y}$

19. Solve $-5 - 5m = 5$. *(Lesson 10-9)*   **m = -2**

20. If $a = -2$, $b = 5$, and $c = 1$, what is $|a - b + c| - |a|$?
    (Lessons 5-5, 7-2)   **4**

In 21–24, lines *m* and *n* are parallel. *(Lesson 7-8)*

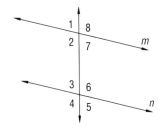

21. Name all pairs of alternate interior angles.
    angles 3 and 7; angles 2 and 6

22. Name all pairs of corresponding angles.
    angles 8 and 6; 1 and 3; 2 and 4; 7 and 5

23. If $m\angle 5 = 75°$, what is $m\angle 1$?   **75°**

24. If $m\angle 4 = x$, what is $m\angle 7$?   **180° − x**

25. An octagon has ? sides, ? angles, and ? diagonals.
    (Lessons 5-9, 6-3)   **8, 8, 20**

Exploration

26. Look in an almanac or other book to find at least one of these rates.
    a. the minimum number of grams of protein per day recommended in a diet for someone your age   **See margin.**
    b. the number of people per square mile in the United States
    c. the number of miles per gallon you should expect to get from a certain car   **Sample: a Toyota Tercel gets about 39 miles/gallon**
    d. the number of sunny days per year you can expect in El Paso, Texas (nicknamed the "Sun City")   **about 343 sunny days/year**
    b. about 69 people/square mile

FOLLOW-UP

MORE PRACTICE
For more questions on SPUR Objectives, use *Lesson Master 11-1,* shown below.

EXTENSION
Small Group Work   You may wish to allow students to work in small groups. Each group should use a daily newspaper and note the use of rates in different articles. The rate unit should be identified in each instance. A list can be made to see how many rates with different units can be found.

These different topics can then be used to make up rate problems. Then groups can exchange problems and solve them.

NAME _____

LESSON **MASTER   11-1**
QUESTIONS ON **SPUR** OBJECTIVES

■**USES**   *Objective G (See pages 527–529 for objectives.)*
In 1–8, calculate a rate suggested by each situation.

1. There were 105 people in 35 cars. How many people is this per car?	3
2. Fran earned $12.75 for 3 hours of work. How much does she earn per hour?	$4.25
3. In 5 minutes, a typist can type 375 words. How many words can the typist type in one minute?	75
4. Twelve children have 3 pizzas.	
a. What is the number of pizzas per child?	$\frac{1}{4}$
b. What is the number of children per pizza?	4
5. A student enrolled in 7 classes at Eastern High School is in class for 385 minutes each day. How many minutes per class is this?	55 minutes
6. A motorist drove 1200 km on 45 liters of gas. What kind of gas consumption is this?	$26\frac{2}{3}$ km per L
7. What is the hourly rate of a mechanic who charges $160 for 4 hours of labor?	$40 per hour
8. Bob pays $4.13 for 5 hours of parking. What is the hourly parking rate to the nearest cent?	83¢

In 9–12, identify the better buy.

9. an 18-ounce box of cereal at 79¢ or a 24-ounce box at $1.05	the 24-ounce box
10. a 195-gram box of detergent at 87¢ or a 295-gram box at $1.35	the 195-gram box
11. 4 pair for $5 or 3 pair for $4	4 pair
12. 6 for a dollar or 7 for a dollar	7 for a dollar

Division of Fractions

If quantities are given in fractions, then rate situations can lead to division of fractions.

Example 1   Suppose you make $8 for baby-sitting 1 hour 40 minutes. How many dollars have you made per hour?

Solution   40 minutes is $\frac{40}{60}$ or $\frac{2}{3}$ of an hour.
Change the 1 hour 40 minutes to $1\frac{2}{3}$ hours.
Then rewrite $1\frac{2}{3}$ as the simple fraction $\frac{5}{3}$.

Dollars per hour is a rate. Division gives the answer.
$$\text{salary per hour} = \frac{8 \text{ dollars}}{1 \text{ hour } 40 \text{ min}} = \frac{8 \text{ dollars}}{\frac{5}{3} \text{ hours}}$$

To divide 8 by $\frac{5}{3}$, use the Mult-Rec Property of Division:

x divided by $y = x$ times the reciprocal of y.
So, 8 divided by $\frac{5}{3} = 8$ times $\frac{3}{5}$

$$\frac{8}{\frac{5}{3}} = 8 \cdot \frac{3}{5}$$
$$= \frac{24}{5}$$
$$= 4.8$$

The wages per hour are $4.80.

The same idea can be used to divide one fraction by another.

Example 2   What is $\frac{6}{5}$ divided by $\frac{3}{4}$?

Solution   By the Mult-Rec Property of Division,
$\frac{6}{5}$ divided by $\frac{3}{4} = \frac{6}{5}$ times $\frac{4}{3}$.

$$\frac{\frac{6}{5}}{\frac{3}{4}} = \frac{6}{5} \cdot \frac{4}{3} = \frac{24}{15} = \frac{8}{5}$$

488

Check To check that $\frac{8}{5}$ is the answer, you can change the fractions to decimals. $\frac{6}{5} = 1.2$ and $\frac{3}{4} = 0.75$

$$\frac{\frac{6}{5}}{\frac{3}{4}} = \frac{1.2}{0.75} = 1.6$$

Since $\frac{8}{5} = 1.6$, the fraction answer checks.

- - - ■ ■ ■ ■ ■

Example 3 Simplify $\frac{2}{3}$ divided by 15.

Solution $\frac{2}{3}$ divided by $15 = \frac{2}{3} \cdot \frac{1}{15} = \frac{2}{45}$

The next example shows how powerful division of fractions can be.

- - - - ■ ■ ■ ■

Example 4 Three-fourths of the way through the season, the Yankees had won 64 games. At this rate, how many games would they win in the entire season?

Solution Games won per entire season $= \dfrac{64 \text{ games}}{\frac{3}{4} \text{ season}}$

$$= 64 \cdot \frac{4}{3} \frac{\text{games}}{\text{season}}$$

$$= \frac{256}{3} \frac{\text{games}}{\text{season}}$$

$$\approx 85.3 \frac{\text{games}}{\text{season}}$$

At this rate, they would win approximately 85 games in the season.

Questions

Covering the Reading

1. A person makes $12 for working two and a half hours. What is the person's wage per hour? **$4.80 per hour**

2. State the Mult-Rec Property of Division.
   For any numbers a and b, $\frac{a}{b} = a \cdot \frac{1}{b}$.

In 3–5, simplify.

3. $\dfrac{\frac{8}{9}}{\frac{4}{3}}$ **$\frac{2}{3}$**

4. $\dfrac{\frac{2}{5}}{7}$ **$\frac{2}{35}$**

5. $\dfrac{\frac{17}{6}}{\frac{2}{3}}$ **$\frac{17}{4}$ or $4\frac{1}{4}$**

6. Two-thirds of the way into the season, the Dodgers have won 66 games. At this rate, how many games will they win in the entire season? **99 games**

As you discuss **Examples 1–4,** ask the students to explain how the Mult-Rec Property is used in each one.

ADDITIONAL EXAMPLES
1. You read 35 pages of a novel in 90 minutes. At this rate, how many pages can you read in an hour?
$\approx 23\frac{1}{3}$ **pages**

2. Simplify.

a. $\dfrac{\frac{1}{2}}{\frac{1}{8}}$ **4**

b. Divide 10 by $\frac{2}{3}$.
15

c. $\frac{8}{15} \div \frac{2}{5}$
$\frac{4}{3}$

3. After painting $\frac{2}{3}$ of the school lockers, Lila was paid $75. At this rate, what would she earn for painting all the lockers?
$112.50

NOTES ON QUESTIONS
Question 1: Suggest that students do this question first with the fraction $\frac{5}{2}$ and then with the decimal 2.5. This also reinforces the Mult-Rec Property.

NOTES ON QUESTIONS
Questions 8 and 9:
Students already know how to divide simple fractions. Suggest that they change each mixed number to a fraction. Also discuss the *estimation* in parts **b;** the answers must make sense. Checking by decimals (parts **c**) further verifies the algorithm. Part **9d** focuses on an important advantage of fractions in some situations.

Question 25: Laying 1.5 eggs in 1.5 days is simply 1 egg per day (for 1.5 hens); so 3 hens could lay 2 eggs per day and two dozen hens could lay 8 times as many eggs, or 16 eggs per day. Thus in two dozen days, the hens would lay 24 · 16, or 384, eggs.

7. With one-fifth of the season gone, the Sox have lost 12 games. At this rate, how many games will they lose in the season?
60 games

8. **a.** Divide $4\frac{1}{4}$ by $3\frac{2}{5}$. $\frac{5}{4}$ or $1\frac{1}{4}$
   b. The answer you get to part **a** should be bigger than 1. How could you tell this before you did any division? $3\frac{2}{5}$ is smaller than $4\frac{1}{4}$.
   c. Check the answer you get to part **a** by changing each fraction to a decimal, dividing the decimals, and comparing the answers. $\frac{4.25}{3.4} = 1.25 = 1\frac{1}{4}$

9. **a.** Divide $1\frac{2}{3}$ by $5\frac{4}{7}$. $\frac{35}{117}$
   b. The answer you get to part **a** should be less than 1. How could you tell this before you did any division? $5\frac{4}{7}$ is greater than $1\frac{2}{3}$.
   c. Check the answer you get to part **a** by changing each fraction to a decimal, dividing the decimals, and comparing the answers. $\frac{1.6666667}{5.5714285} \approx 0.299145 \ldots \approx \frac{35}{117}$
   d. In this question, what advantage do the fractions have over the decimals?
   The decimals are infinite, so it is easier to work with the fractions.

10. Jay walked $\frac{1}{3}$ of a mile in 10 minutes. Ten minutes $= \frac{1}{6}$ hour.
    a. What is Jay's rate in miles per hour?
    b. At this rate, how far will Jay walk in an hour?
    a. 2 miles per hour; b. 2 miles

In 11 and 12, simplify.

11. $\dfrac{\frac{2}{x}}{\frac{1}{y}}$ $\frac{2y}{x}$

12. $\dfrac{\frac{a}{b}}{\frac{c}{d}}$ $\frac{ad}{bc}$

13. Seven and one-half times a number is 375. What is the number?
50

14. What is the hourly wage if you make $21.12 in 3.3 hours?
(Lesson 11-1) **$6.40/hour**

In 15–17, solve.

15. $-4 + G = -3$ *(Lesson 7-4)* **1**

16. $-4 - G = -3$ *(Lesson 7-6)* **-1**

17. $-4G = -3$ *(Lesson 10-8)* $\frac{3}{4}$

In 18–20, let $x = \frac{5}{4}$ and $y = \frac{1}{2}$. Write as a simple fraction.

18. $x + y$ *(Lesson 5-2)* $\frac{7}{4}$

19. $x - y$ *(Lesson 7-2)* $\frac{3}{4}$

20. $8xy$ *(Lesson 9-9)* **5**

21. Suppose the probability of a hole-in-one on a particular golf hole is 1 in 10,000. What would then be the probability of making two holes-in-one in a row? *(Lesson 9-8)* **1/100,000,000**

490

In 22–24, use the rectangular solid pictured below. Find the:

22. volume; *(Lesson 9-3)* **7350 cubic inches**

23. surface area; *(Lesson 9-2)* **2590 square inches**

24. perimeter of the largest face. *(Lessons 5-10, 9-4)* **112 inches**

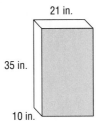

21 in.

35 in.

10 in.

Exploration

25. Here is a famous puzzler. If a hen and a half can lay an egg and a half in a day and a half, at this rate how many eggs can be laid by two dozen hens in two dozen days? **384 eggs**

LESSON

11-3

Division with Negative Numbers

Remember that any division can be converted to a multiplication. Instead of dividing by x, multiply by $\frac{1}{x}$. So, if you can multiply with negative numbers and find reciprocals of them, then you can divide with them.

Example 1 What is -10 divided by 2?

Solution 1 Dividing by 2 is the same as multiplying by $\frac{1}{2}$.

$$\frac{-10}{2} = -10 \cdot \frac{1}{2} = -5$$

Solution 2 Think of a negative rate. A gambler loses 10 dollars in 2 hours. What is the loss rate?

$$\frac{\text{loss of 10 dollars}}{2 \text{ hours}} = \text{loss of 5 dollars per hour}$$

Translate the loss into a negative number.

$$\frac{-10 \text{ dollars}}{2 \text{ hours}} = -5 \frac{\text{dollars}}{\text{hour}}$$

Either way the answer is -5.

In general, if a negative number is divided by a positive number, the quotient is negative. Another example is on the next page.

492

Example 2   On five consecutive days, the low temperature in a city was 3°, -4°, -6°, -2°, and 0°C. What was the mean low temperature for the five days?

Solution   The **mean** (or **average**) temperature is found by adding up the numbers and dividing by 5.

$$\frac{3 + {}^-4 + {}^-6 + {}^-2 + 0}{5} = \frac{{}^-9}{5} = {}^-1.8$$

The mean temperature was -1.8°C, or about -2°C. On the Celsius scale, that is a little below freezing.

In Example 3, a positive number is divided by a negative number. The quotient is again negative.

Example 3   What is 10 divided by -2?

Solution 1   Dividing by -2 is the same as multiplying by $-\frac{1}{2}$, the reciprocal of -2.

$$\frac{10}{{}^-2} = 10 \cdot {}^-\frac{1}{2} = {}^-5$$

Solution 2   Think of the gambler of Solution 2 in Example 1, but go back in time for the 2 hours. The gambler had $10 more 2 hours ago. What is the loss rate?

$$\frac{10 \text{ dollars more}}{2 \text{ hours ago}} = \frac{10 \text{ dollars}}{{}^-2 \text{ hours}} = {}^-5 \frac{\text{dollars}}{\text{hour}}$$

Here are two negatives. Is what will happen obvious?

Example 4   What is -150 divided by -7?

$$\frac{{}^-150}{{}^-7} = {}^-150 \cdot {}^-\frac{1}{7} \quad \text{(Now we know the answer will be positive.)}$$
$$= \frac{150}{7}$$
$$= 21\frac{3}{7}$$
$$\approx 21.43$$

LESSON 11-3   Division with Negative Numbers   **493**

TEACHING NOTES

The important information in this lesson is found in the examples and the concluding generalization. **Example 1** provides two rationales for the rules for dividing integers: the Mult-Rec Property of Division and a rate application. Make sure students recognize both. **Example 2** calculates a mean. Most students have done this before, but they may not have had a problem with negative numbers. **Example 3** provides the same two types of solutions as **Example 1,** but this time a positive is divided by a negative. **Example 4** repeats the process one more time with a negative divided by a negative.

ADDITIONAL EXAMPLES

1. Simplify.

a. 10 ÷ 2.5

4

b. 10 ÷ -2.5

-4

c. -10 ÷ 2.5

-4

d. -10 ÷ -2.5

4

2. Simplify.

a. -356 divided by 4

-89

b. -.35 ÷ -.7

.5

c. $\frac{2}{3} \div -\frac{1}{3}$

-2

3. *Multiple choice* Which number is not equal to the other numbers?

(a) $-\frac{3}{5}$ (b) $\frac{-3}{5}$

(c) $\frac{3}{-5}$ (d) $\frac{-3}{-5}$

d

Error Analysis

Emphasize that a fraction is a division problem. If the divisor or the dividend is negative, the quotient will be negative. Thus, only $\frac{-3}{-5}$ is positive and not equal to the others.

Division with two negative numbers can also be thought of using the rate model. Suppose you lift 14 kg more after 3.5 months' work. You have gained strength at the rate of 4 kg per month.

$$\frac{\text{14 kg more}}{\text{3.5 months later}} = \frac{\text{4 kg}}{\text{month}}\text{ gain}$$

Another way of looking at the situation is that 3.5 months ago you lifted 14 kg less.

$$\frac{\text{14 kg less}}{\text{3.5 months ago}} = \frac{\text{4 kg}}{\text{month}}\text{ gain}$$

Thus $$\frac{\text{14 kg more}}{\text{3.5 months later}} = \frac{\text{14 kg less}}{\text{3.5 months ago}}.$$

Ignoring the units but using negative numbers:

$$\frac{14}{3.5} = \frac{-14}{-3.5}$$

Changing the sign in both numerator and denominator of a fraction is like multiplying the fraction by $\frac{-1}{-1}$. This keeps the value of the fraction the same.

For instance, begin with $\frac{-10}{2}$. Multiplying both numerator and denominator by -1 yields the equal fraction $\frac{10}{-2}$.

Altogether, the rules for dividing with negative numbers are just like those for multiplying. If both divisor and dividend are negative, the quotient is positive. If one is positive and one is negative, the quotient will be negative. These properties can be stated with variables.

For all numbers *a* and *b*, except when *b* = 0:

$$\frac{a}{b} = \frac{-a}{-b}$$

$$\frac{-a}{b} = \frac{a}{-b} = -\frac{a}{b}$$

If you forget how to do operations with negative numbers, there are two things you can do. (1) Change subtractions to additions; change divisions to multiplications. (2) Think of a real situation using the negative numbers. Use the situation to help you find the answer.

Covering the Reading

In 1–4, simplify.

1. $\frac{-14}{7}$ **-2**

2. $\frac{-100}{300}$ **$-\frac{1}{3}$**

3. $\frac{-56}{-8}$ **7**

4. $\frac{60}{-2}$ **-30**

In 5–7, find the mean of each set of numbers.

5. 40, 60, 80, 100 **70**

6. -40, -60, -80, -100 **-70**

7. -11, 14, -17, -20, 6, -30 **-9.$\overline{6}$**

In 8–11, tell whether the number is positive or negative.

8. $\frac{-2.5}{6} \cdot$ -4 **positive**

9. $-\frac{-100}{300}$ **positive**

10. $-\frac{-54}{-81}$ **negative**

11. $\frac{53}{-2} \cdot \frac{55}{-2}$ **positive**

12. Separate the numbers given here into two collections of equal numbers. **See margin.**

$-\frac{1}{2}$ $\quad$ $\frac{-1}{2}$ $\quad$ $\frac{-1}{-2}$ $\quad$ $\frac{1}{-2}$ $\quad$ $-\frac{-1}{-2}$ $\quad$ $\frac{1}{2}$ $\quad$ $-\frac{-1}{2}$

13. Julie lost 4 pounds on a two-day crash diet.
   a. Calculate a rate from this information. **-2 pounds per day**
   b. What division problem with negative numbers gives this rate?
   c. Copy and complete: __?__ days ago, Julie weighed __?__ pounds __?__ than she does now. **2, 4, more**
   d. What division problem is suggested by part **c**? **See margin.**
   b. -4 pounds/2 days

14. In the twenty years from 1950 to 1970, California's population rose by 9,000,000.
   a. Calculate a rate from this information. **450,000 people per year**
   b. Copy and complete: __?__ years before 1970 California's population was nine million __?__ than it was in 1970. **20, less**
   c. What division problem is suggested by part **b**? What is the quotient? **See margin.**

15. What two things can you do if you forget how to calculate with negative numbers? **See margin.**

ADDITIONAL ANSWERS

12. $-\frac{1}{2} = \frac{-1}{2} = \frac{1}{-2} = -\frac{-1}{-2}$; $\frac{-1}{-2} = \frac{1}{2} = -\frac{-1}{2}$

13. d. $\frac{4 \text{ pounds more}}{2 \text{ days ago}} = \frac{4 \text{ pounds}}{-2 \text{ days}} = -2\frac{\text{pounds}}{\text{day}}$

14. c. $\frac{9,000,000 \text{ people less}}{20 \text{ years ago}} = \frac{-9,000,000 \text{ people}}{-20 \text{ years}} = 450,000\frac{\text{people}}{\text{year}}$

15. Change subtractions to additions and divisions to multiplications; think of a real situation using the numbers to help find the answer.

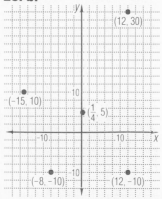
Applying the Mathematics

In 16–19, calculate $x + y$, $x - y$, xy, and $\frac{x}{y}$ for the given values of x and y.

16. $x = -10$ and $y = 5$ -5, -15, -50, -2

17. $x = -6$ and $y = -9$ -15, 3, 54, $\frac{2}{3}$

18. $x = 1$ and $y = -1$ 0, 2, -1, -1

19. $x = -12$ and $y = -12$ -24, 0, 144, 1

20. Use $C = 5(F - 32)/9$ to convert -40° Fahrenheit to Celsius.
-40°C; this is the one temperature at which $F = C$.

21. Multiply $\frac{15}{-8}$ by $\frac{2}{-3}$. $\frac{5}{4}$

22. Round $\frac{350}{-6}$ to the nearest integer.   -58

23. The *center of gravity* of a set of given points is the point whose first coordinate is the mean of the first coordinates of the given points and whose second coordinate is the mean of the second coordinates of the given points.
   a. Find the coordinates of the center of gravity of the four points given at left.
   b. Copy the drawing and graph the center of gravity on your drawing.   **See margin.**

Review

24. **a.** What simple fraction in lowest terms equals $\frac{10}{3}$ divided by $\frac{5}{6}$? $\frac{4}{1}$
   b. Check your answer by converting the fractions to decimals and dividing the decimals with a calculator. *(Lesson 11-2)*
   3.33.../0.833... ≈ 4.0000001

25. Begin at the point (14, 6). Move 20 units to the left and 3 units down. What are the coordinates of the image point? *(Lesson 8-5)*
(-6, 3)

26. In $3\frac{1}{2}$ days, the long-distance runner ran 100 miles. How many miles did the runner run per day? *(Lessons 11-1, 11-2)*
≈ 28.6 miles per day

27. **a.** Write 44% as a decimal. *(Lesson 5-2)*   0.44
   b. Write 44% as a simple fraction in lowest terms. *(Lesson 2-7)* $\frac{11}{25}$

28. What is 40% of 500? *(Lesson 2-6)*   200

29. 40% of a number is 500. What is the number? *(Lesson 10-3)*   1250

Exploration

30. **a.** Press 5 ÷ 0 on your calculator. What does the display show?
   b. Press 5 ÷ 0.001 on your calculator. What is displayed?
   c. Press 5 ÷ 0.001 ± on your calculator. What is displayed?
   d. Divide 5 by other numbers near zero. Record your results. Explain what happens.
   a. Sample: E, meaning error; b. 5000; c. -5000; d. See margin.

31. The *median* of a set of numbers is found by ordering the numbers and then picking the middle number in the set. (If there is an even number of numbers, then the **median** is the mean of the middle two numbers.) **a.** What is the median of the temperatures in Example 2? **b.** Make up a set of numbers whose mean is not close to its median. a. −2° b. sample: 110, 96, 87, 16, 11; median 87, mean 64

11-4

The Ratio Comparison Model for Division

OBJECTIVE

I Use the Ratio Comparison Model for Division.

TEACHING NOTES

Emphasize that rates and ratios are similar. Note that rates have units, whereas in a ratio the units have canceled in division. Point out in **Example 1** that the terms *rate* and *ratio* are not always used consistently. Stress in the discussion of **Example 2** that the numbers can be compared in either order.

Example 3 illustrates the third type of percent problem. Review all the types of percent problems together. You can use specific numbers: Find 5% of 40. (2) 5% of what number is 2? (40) 2 is what percent of 40? (5%) Another way to look at the pattern is to use the equation $ab = c$, where a is the *rate* or *ratio*, b is referred to as the *base*, and c is sometimes called the *percentage*. The three cases correspond to the three choices for the unknown.

In a certain city, it rained 70 of the 365 days last year. Dividing 70 by 365 indicates how often it rained.

$$\frac{70}{365} \approx .19$$

The answer is often converted to a percent. It rained about 19% of the time.

Notice what happens when the units are put into the numerator and denominator.

$$\frac{70 \text{ days}}{365 \text{ days}}$$

The units are the same. They cancel in the division, so the answer has no unit. Therefore, this is not an example of rate. The answer is called a **ratio.** Ratios have no units. Because the 70 days is being compared to the 365 days, this use of division is called **ratio comparison.**

Ratio Comparison Model for Division:

If a and b are quantities with the same units, then $\frac{a}{b}$ compares a to b.

Example 1 Suppose the tax is $0.42 on a $7.00 purchase. What is the tax rate? (It's called a tax rate even though it is technically a ratio.)

Solution Divide $0.42 by $7.00 to compare them.

$$\frac{\$0.42}{\$7.00} = \frac{0.42}{7.00} = .06$$

.06 = 6%, so the tax rate is 6%.

Check A tax of 6% is 6¢ for every dollar. So for $7, the tax should be 7 · 6¢, or 42¢.

LESSON 11-4   The Ratio Comparison Model for Division   **497**

Example 2   Compare the 1990 estimated populations of the United States (250,000,000 people) and Canada (27,000,000 people).

Solution   The units (people) are the same. Divide one of the numbers by the other to compare them.

$\frac{250,000,000}{27,000,000} \approx 9.3 \leftarrow$ The population of the U.S. is about 9.3 times that of Canada.

Dividing in the other order gives the reciprocal.

$\frac{27,000,000}{250,000,000} \approx .11 \leftarrow$ Canada has about 11% of the population of the U.S.

Either answer is correct. Comparisons can often be done in either order.

Example 3   5 is what percent of 40?

Solution   This problem asks you to compare 5 to 40. So divide, then convert to percent.
$$\frac{5}{40} = 0.125 = 12.5\%$$

Therefore, 5 is 12.5% of 40.

Check   Calculate 12.5% of 40.
12.5% of 40 = 0.125 · 40 = 5

Questions

Covering the Reading

1. In a city, it rained 12 of the 30 days in a month. What percent of the time is this?   **40%**

2. A store charges $0.64 tax on a $16.00 purchase. What is the tax rate?   **4%**

3. There is a tax of 35¢ on a purchase of $5.83.
a. What is the sales tax rate?   **6%**
b. 35 is what percent of 583?   **about 6%**

4. According to the ratio comparison model of division, what can you do to compare the numbers 6 and 25?
You can divide 6 by 25, or you can divide 25 by 6.

5. 6 is what percent of 25?   **24%**

6. What percent is 6 of 12?   **50%**

7. What percent is 6 of 6?   **100%**

8. 6 is what percent of 3?   **200%**

498

In 9 and 10, answer to the nearest whole number percent.

9. 41 is what percent of 300?   14%

10. 250 is what percent of 300?   83%

11. The population of Canton, Ohio (home of the pro football Hall of Fame) is 90 thousand. The population of Canton, China (from which we get the name Cantonese food) is about 3 million.
   a. Then Canton, Ohio has ___?___ percent the number of people of Canton, China.   3%
   b. Canton, China has ___?___ times as many people as Canton, Ohio.
   about 33
12. What is the difference between a rate and a ratio?   See margin.

Applying the Mathematics

13. 14 of the 25 students in the class are boys.
   a. What percent is this?   56%
   b. What percent are girls?   44%

14. What number is 12 percent of 90?   10.8

15. a. Banner H. S. has won 36 of its last 40 games. What percent is this?   90%
   b. What is 36 percent of 40?   14.4
   c. 40 is 36 percent of what number?   111.$\overline{1}$

16. If a $60 jacket is reduced $13.50, what is the percent of discount?
22.5%

17. If a population of 350,000 increases by 7000, what is the percent of increase?   2%

Review

18. What integer does -6 divided by -2 equal? *(Lesson 11-3)*   3

19. If $x = \frac{2}{5}$ and $y = \frac{-2}{15}$, write $\frac{x}{y}$ as a simple fraction.
(Lessons 11-2, 11-3) $\frac{-3}{1}$

20. A person traveled for 2.5 hours at 2.5 miles per hour. How long was the trip? *(Lesson 10-4)*   6.25 miles

NOTES ON QUESTIONS
Questions 5–10: Some people might answer these by solving proportions. We do not recommend the use of proportions with such simple division problems.

For example, consider **Question 5:** 6 is what percent of 25? Division yields 0.24. If the question had been "6 is what *part* of 25?", then 0.24 could well be the answer. Had the question been "6 is what *fraction* of 24?", then $\frac{6}{25}$, $\frac{12}{50}$, or $\frac{24}{100}$, or many other fractions could be the answer. But because the question calls for a percent, it is necessary to translate 0.24 into percent and conclude that 6 is 24% of 25. To use proportions only when percent is involved misleads students into thinking that percents are totally separate from what they already know.

Similarly, for **Question 15a,** no proportion is needed. Banner High has won 36 of 40 games, $\frac{36}{40}$ of their games, $\frac{9}{10}$ of their games, or 90% of their games.

NOTES ON QUESTIONS
**Making Connections for
Question 26:** This is a
preview of probability in
Lesson 11-5.

FOLLOW-UP

MORE PRACTICE
For more questions on SPUR
Objectives, use *Lesson Mas-
ter 11-4,* shown on page 499.

EXTENSION
Suggest that students find
percents in a newspaper or
some other source. Usually
these percents are calculated
by dividing one number by
another. Ask the students
how each percent was calculated, that is, which numbers
must have been compared.

EVALUATION
A quiz covering Lessons 11-1
through 11-4 is provided in
the Teacher's Resource File
on page 96.

21. Suppose a person earns time-and-three-quarters for overtime. If the overtime wage is $17.15 per hour, what is the person's normal hourly wage? *(Lesson 10-4)* $9.80

22. There are 12 members on the state math team. To send them to the state tournament, it will cost C dollars per team member. $200 has been collected. How much is left to collect? *(Lessons 4-3, 7-1)*
12C − 200 dollars

23. If $x = 43$, what does $90 - x$ equal? *(Lesson 4-4)*   47

24. What simple fraction equals $\frac{3}{5} + \frac{3}{4}$? *(Lesson 5-2)* $\frac{27}{20}$

25. Let $a = 10$, $b = 20$, $c = 30$, and $d = 40$. What is the value of $\frac{a - c}{b - d}$? *(Lessons 4-7, 7-2, 11-3)*   1

Exploration

26. The *relative frequency* of an event is the ratio

$$\frac{\text{number of times the event occurs}}{\text{number of times the event could occur}}$$

For instance, suppose it rains exactly 3 days in a week. Since it could rain 7 days in the week, the relative frequency of rain would be $\frac{3}{7}$.

a. Toss a coin 50 times. How many times does it land heads up?
b. What is the relative frequency of heads for your tosses?
c. Change your answer in **b** to a percent.   See below.

a. Sample: 24 heads
b. If answer to a is n heads, answer to b is $\frac{n}{50}$.
c. If answer a is n heads, answer to c is $2n\%$.

500

Properties of Probability

LESSON 11-5

RESOURCES
- Lesson Master 11-5
- Computer Master 22
- Thumbtacks
- Spinner (from *Transition Mathematics Teacher Kit*)
- *Manipulative Activity Sourcebook,* Activity 20

A **probability** is a number from 0 to 1 which tells you how likely something is to happen. A probability of 0 means that the event is *impossible*. A probability of $\frac{1}{5}$ means that you or someone else expects the event to happen 1 in 5 times in the long run. A probability of $\frac{2}{3}$ means that the event is expected to happen about 2 in 3 times. A probability of 1, the highest probability possible, means that the event *must* happen.

The closer a probability is to 1, the more likely the event. Because $\frac{2}{3}$ is greater than $\frac{1}{5}$, an event with a probability of $\frac{2}{3}$ is thought to be more likely than one with a probability of $\frac{1}{5}$. This can be pictured on a number line.

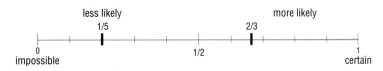

Probabilities can be written as fractions, decimals, or percents, or any way other numbers are written.

Example 1 The weather bureau says there is a 1 in 3 chance of rain tomorrow. It reports a 40% precipitation probability the day after tomorrow. On which day does the weather bureau think rain is more likely?

Solution The "1 in 3 chance of rain tomorrow" means a probability of $\frac{1}{3}$. To determine whether $\frac{1}{3}$ is larger than 40%, change both numbers to decimals. $\frac{1}{3} = 0.\overline{3}$ and 40% = 0.4, so 40% is larger. So rain is more likely the day after tomorrow.

If there is a $\frac{1}{3}$ probability of rain, then there is a $\frac{2}{3}$ probability that it will not rain. If there is a 40% chance of rain the day after tomorrow, then there is a 60% chance it will not rain.

OBJECTIVES

F Apply the properties of probability.
J Calculate probabilities in a situation with equally likely outcomes.

TEACHING NOTES

Ask students for a situation in which a probability is used; for instance, the probability that a school team will win its next game. Write the probability as a percent, a decimal, and a fraction, stressing that probabilities can be written in any of these forms.

Then ask how the probability was determined. One way is guessing; a second way is using past performance, that is, taking the result of an experiment—the relative frequency—as a probability. A third way is making an assumption—the teams are evenly matched or some such thing—and calculating the probability from that.

If the probability of an event is p, then the probability that the event will not occur is $1 - p$.

There are three common ways that people determine probabilities.

1. Guess. (This is not a great way, but sometimes it is the only thing you can do.)
2. Perform an experiment and take a probability close to the results of that experiment.
3. Assume that some events have certain probabilities and calculate other probabilities from these.

The weather bureau uses a combination of the second and third ways.

Example 2 Perform an experiment to determine the probability that a thumb-tack will land up when dropped.

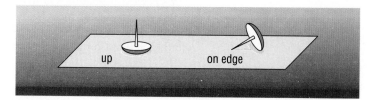

Solution One of the authors found 8 thumbtacks. The author de-cided to drop all of them 10 times, for a total of 80 dropped tacks. Here are the results.

experiment	1	2	3	4	5	6	7	8	9	10
up	5	3	3	4	5	7	1	5	5	4
on edge	3	5	5	4	3	1	7	3	3	4

Adding the numbers that landed up, a total of 42 tacks landed up. The tacks in the other 38 tosses landed on edge.

The *relative frequency* of a tack landing up was $\frac{42}{80}$. We might pick that number as the probability. However, $\frac{42}{80}$ = .525, which is rather close to .5. We might take the probability to be $\frac{1}{2}$.

In Example 2, suppose the experiment had stopped after 8 tacks were thrown. Then the relative frequency of landing up would have been $\frac{5}{8}$, or .625, quite a bit larger than .525. The more times an experiment is repeated, the surer you can be about a probability. But you can never be exactly sure.

502

Some situations involving probability are similar to the picking of pieces of paper out of a hat. If there are 25 pieces numbered 1 through 25, what is the probability of picking the piece numbered 8? It is reasonable to assume that there is the same probability for picking each of the pieces. Since the total probability is 1, each individual probability is $\frac{1}{25}$. So the probability of picking an 8 is $\frac{1}{25}$.

■ ■ ■ ■ ■ ■ ■ ■

Example 3   Suppose 25 pieces of paper in a hat are numbered 1 through 25. Assume the probability of picking each is equal. When a piece is picked, what is the probability that its number is prime?

Solution   The prime numbers less than 25 are 2, 3, 5, 7, 11, 13, 17, 19, and 23. There are 9 of them. So the probability of picking a prime number is $\frac{9}{25}$, or 0.36, or 36%.

Example 3 illustrates the following general principle.

> If a situation has n equally likely outcomes and an event includes s of these, then the probability of the event is $\frac{s}{n}$.

For instance, suppose you have 10 pairs of socks in a drawer and you pick one pair without looking. If the pairs are folded together, there are 10 possible outcomes. If 3 are red, then the event of picking a red pair has 3 of these outcomes. If each outcome is equally likely, the probability of picking a red pair is $\frac{3}{10}$.

Using Manipulatives
4. Using the spinner found in the *Transition Mathematics Teacher Kit,* allow students to experiment to find the relative frequency for each of the following:

a. An even number **about $\frac{1}{2}$**
b. a number divisible by 3 **about $\frac{1}{4}$**
c. a number less than 9 **1**
d. a number greater than 8 **0**

Questions

Covering the Reading

1. A probability can be no larger than __?__ and no smaller than __?__.
   1, 0

2. If an event is impossible, its probability is __?__.   **0**

3. What is the probability of a sure thing?   **1**

4. Suppose event A has a probability of $\frac{1}{2}$ and event B has a probability of $\frac{1}{3}$. Which event is more likely?   **A**

5. The weather bureau reports a 70% precipitation probability for tomorrow and a $\frac{3}{5}$ chance of thunderstorms the day after tomorrow. Which is more likely, precipitation tomorrow or thunderstorms the day after?   **Precipitation tomorrow**

LESSON 11-5   Properties of Probability   **503**

6. Suppose the probability that your teacher gives a test next Friday is 80%. What is the probability your teacher does not give a test next Friday?   **20%**

7. You listen to a radio station for an hour. You estimate that $\frac{1}{10}$ is the probability that your favorite song will be played. What is the probability that your favorite song will not be played? $\frac{9}{10}$

8. If the probability that an event occurs is x, what is the probability it does not occur?   **1 – x**

9. Identify two common ways in which people determine probabilities.   **See margin.**

10. According to the experiment in this lesson, what is a reasonable probability to assume for that thumbtack landing up? $\frac{1}{2}$

In 11 and 12, imagine a situation where fifty raffle tickets are put in a hat. Each ticket has the same probability of being selected.

11. If you have one of these tickets, what is the probability you will win the raffle? $\frac{1}{50}$

12. If you and two friends have one ticket apiece, what is the probability that one of you will win the raffle? $\frac{3}{50}$

13. A person says, "There is a negative probability that my uncle will leave me a million dollars." What is wrong with that statement?
A probability is never negative.

14. *Multiple choice* The probability that a coin will land heads up is often given as $\frac{1}{2}$. How is this number determined?   **(b)**
    (a) The coin was tossed 100 times and it came down heads 50 times.
    (b) The two sides of the coin are assumed to be equally likely.
    (c) A good guess is $\frac{1}{2}$.

15. A spinner in a game is pictured below. Assume all positions of the spinner are equally likely.

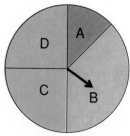

a. If the angle which forms region A has measure 45°, what is the probability that the spinner will land in region A? $\frac{45}{360}$, or $\frac{1}{8}$
b. Determine the probabilities of landing in the other regions. Assume radii that look perpendicular are.   B: $\frac{3}{8}$; C: $\frac{1}{4}$; D: $\frac{1}{4}$

504

16. Suppose in Example 2 that, in 60 of the 80 tosses, the thumbtack landed up. What number might be picked to be the probability that the tack lands up? $\frac{3}{4}$

17. An organization has a raffle and n people buy tickets. You buy 5 tickets. What is the probability that you will win the raffle? $\frac{5}{n}$

18. What way of determining probability is being used:
   a. in Question 16?   **b.** in Question 17?   **See margin.**

19. Slips of paper numbered from 1 to 100 are put into a hat. A slip is taken from the hat. What is the probability that the number is prime and ends in a 3? $\frac{7}{100}$

Review

20. Carla's Car Place had 50 used cars for sale a week ago. Today only 36 of these are left. How many cars have been sold per day? *(Lesson 11-1)*   **2 cars per day**

21. In the Maple Ridge School, 35 third-graders are boys and 47 are girls. What percent of the third-graders are boys? *(Lesson 11-4)*
   43%

22. **a.** What is 3% of 32? *(Lesson 2-6)*   **0.96**
   b. 3 is what percent of 32? *(Lesson 11-4)*   **9.375%**
   c. 3 is 32% of what number? *(Lesson 10-2)*   **9.375**

23. When $x = 5$ and $y = -3$, what is the value of $\frac{-9x}{y}(x + 2)$?
   (Lessons 4-1, 10-5, 11-3)   **105**

24. Write $2 \cdot 3^4$ as a decimal. *(Lesson 2-2)*   **162**

Exploration

25. Find a thumbtack or some other object that has more than one side on which it can land after dropped. Drop the object 50 times. Estimate the probability that the object will land on each of its possible sides.   **See margin.**

26. **a.** Pick a page of a local residential phone directory. Calculate the probability that the last digit of a phone number on that page is 0.
   b. Do part **a**, but use the yellow pages.
   c. Do commercial and residential phone numbers have about the same probability of having a last digit of zero?

Answers will vary, but the probability of commercial phone numbers ending in a 0 is greater than the probability of a residential number ending in 0. A yellow-pages customer representing a business or service often requests a phone number ending in one, two, or three 0s.

FOLLOW-UP

MORE PRACTICE
For more questions on SPUR Objectives, use *Lesson Master 11-5,* shown below.

EXTENSION
Odds are related to probabilities. When the probability of something happening is $\frac{1}{n}$, the odds of its happening are 1 to $n - 1$ and the odds against its happening are $n - 1$ to 1. Ask students to find examples of the odds of something happening or against something happening. Some almanacs give odds for card games.

NAME

LESSON **MASTER   11–5**
QUESTIONS ON **SPUR** OBJECTIVES

■ **PROPERTIES**   *Objective F (See pages 527–529 for objectives.)*

1. An impossible event has a probability of ____ **0** .

2. A probability of $\frac{7}{10}$ means that the event is expected to happen about
   ____ **7** in ____ **10** times.

3. If p is the probability that an event will occur,
   then what is the probability that the event will not occur?   **$1 - p$**

4. **a.** Which event is more likely: event A with a probability of $\frac{5}{7}$ or event B with a probability of $\frac{5}{8}$?   **a.** ____ **event B**

   b. Justify your answer.   **b.** ____ **$\frac{5}{7} > \frac{5}{8}$**

■ **USES**   *Objective J*

5. Maggie bought two tickets for the door prize at the Homecoming Dance at West State U. What is the probability of her winning the prize if the number on the tickets sold range from 000 to 999?   **$\frac{1}{500}$**

6. There are n tickets in a raffle for a personal computer. If Greg buys m tickets, what is the probability that he will win the computer?   **$\frac{m}{n}$**

7. You roll a number cube with a different digit from 1 to 6 on each face. What is the probability that you will roll an odd numbered face?   **$\frac{1}{2}$**

8. In a bag of marbles, there are 5 red, 2 green, 4 yellow and 4 orange marbles. You reach into the bag for a marble. What is the probability that you will pick an orange marble?   **$\frac{4}{15}$**

Proportions

Remember that the fraction $\frac{a}{b}$ is the result of dividing a by b. This means that every use of division gives rise to fractions. For instance, when 9 out of 12 students in a class ride a bus to school, then $\frac{9}{12}$ of the class ride the bus.

You know that $\frac{9}{12}$ is equal to $\frac{3}{4}$. In this case you could say that 3 of 4 students ride a bus to school. Equal fractions mean equal ratios.

Now consider a rate. A car goes 9 miles in 12 minutes. The fraction

$$\frac{9 \text{ miles}}{12 \text{ minutes}}$$

is the car's rate. This rate is $\frac{9}{12}$ miles per minute. Simplify the fraction.

$$\frac{9 \text{ miles}}{12 \text{ minutes}} = \frac{3 \text{ miles}}{4 \text{ minutes}}$$

Going 9 miles in 12 minutes is the same rate as going 3 miles in 4 minutes. Equal fractions mean equal rates.

A **proportion** is a statement that two fractions are equal. Here are three examples.

$$\frac{730}{365} = \frac{2}{1} \qquad \frac{12ab}{3b} = \frac{4ab}{b} \qquad \frac{3 \text{ miles}}{4 \text{ minutes}} = \frac{11 \text{ miles}}{y \text{ minutes}}$$

Some equations with fractions are not proportions. Examine these two equations.

$$\frac{x + 5}{8} = \frac{x}{2} \qquad\qquad \frac{x}{8} + \frac{5}{8} = \frac{x}{2}$$
$$\text{a proportion} \qquad\qquad \text{not a proportion}$$

The left equation is a proportion because on each side there is one fraction. The right equation is equivalent to the left equation. But it is not a proportion because its left side is not a single fraction.

Like other equations, proportions can be true or false.

$$\frac{30}{100} = \frac{1}{3} \qquad\qquad \frac{320}{100} = \frac{16}{5}$$
$$\text{False} \qquad\qquad\qquad \text{True}$$

When a proportion has variables in it, the question is often to **solve the proportion.** That means to find the values that make the proportion true. For example:

$$\frac{320}{100} = \frac{16}{x} \text{ has the solution } x = 5, \text{ because } \frac{320}{100} = \frac{16}{5}.$$

506

Solving a proportion is just like solving any other equation. No new properties are needed. But it may take more steps.

Example 1 Solve for m: $\dfrac{32}{m} = \dfrac{24}{25}$

Solution Multiply both sides by $25m$. This yields an equation with no fractions.

$$25m \cdot \frac{32}{m} = \frac{24}{25} \cdot 25m$$

We put in a step here that you may not need to write. It shows what is going on.

$$\frac{25m \cdot 32}{m} = \frac{24 \cdot 25m}{25}$$

Now simplify the fractions.

$$25 \cdot 32 = 24m$$
$$800 = 24m$$
$$\frac{800}{24} = m$$

Rewrite the fraction in lowest terms.
$$\frac{100}{3} = m$$

There are many ways to check the result of Example 1.

Check 1 The roughest check is to change $\frac{100}{3}$ to a decimal and substitute in the original sentence.

$$\frac{100}{3} = 33.3 \ldots$$

Does it look right? Does $\frac{32}{33.3}$ seem equal to $\frac{24}{25}$? It seems about right, because in each fraction the numerator is just slightly less than the denominator.

Check 2 A better check is to perform the divisions. $\frac{32}{33.3} \approx .961$, while $\frac{24}{25} = .96$. That's close enough, given the estimate for $\frac{100}{3}$.

Check 3 To do an exact check, substitute $\frac{100}{3}$ for m in the original proportion.

$$\text{Does } \frac{32}{\frac{100}{3}} = \frac{24}{25}?$$

Work out the division of fractions on the left side.

$$\frac{32}{\frac{100}{3}} = 32 \cdot \frac{3}{100} = \frac{96}{100}$$

Since $\frac{96}{100}$ simplifies to $\frac{24}{25}$ (the right side), the answer checks.

NOTES ON QUESTIONS
Question 2: This can be done by many students without solving an equation.
Question 10 is also of this type. Accept this *mental math* if it is accompanied by a check that shows a true proportion.

ADDITIONAL ANSWERS
6. d. sample: $\frac{40}{\frac{200}{7}} = 40 \cdot \frac{7}{200}$
$= \frac{280}{200} = \frac{7}{5}$; $\frac{21}{15} = \frac{7}{5}$ also.

Many real situations lead to having to solve proportions.

Example 2   If you can stuff 100 envelopes in 8 minutes, how many could you stuff in 30 minutes? Assume that you can keep up the same rate all this time.

Solution   Let N be the number of envelopes you can stuff in 30 minutes. Since the rates are equal,

100 envelopes in 8 minutes = N envelopes in 30 minutes.

$$\frac{100 \text{ envelopes}}{8 \text{ minutes}} = \frac{N \text{ envelopes}}{30 \text{ minutes}}$$

$$\frac{100}{8} = \frac{N}{30}$$

Multiply both sides by $30 \cdot 8$ to get rid of all fractions.

$$30 \cdot 8 \cdot \frac{100}{8} = \frac{N}{30} \cdot 30 \cdot 8$$
$$30 \cdot 100 = N \cdot 8$$
$$3000 = 8N$$
$$375 = N$$

Check $\frac{100}{8} = 12.5$, which equals $\frac{375}{30}$.
Thus at this rate, 375 envelopes can be stuffed in 30 minutes.

Questions

Covering the Reading

1. Suppose 20 out of 60 students in a class are boys. In lowest terms, __?__ out of __?__ students are boys.   **1, 3**

2. Suppose you type 300 words in 10 minutes. At this rate, you would type __?__ words in 20 minutes.   **600 words**

3. Define: proportion.
   A proportion is a statement that two fractions are equal.

4. *Multiple choice*   Which proportion is not true?   **(b)**
   (a) $\frac{100}{7} = \frac{50}{3.5}$ (b) $\frac{1}{3} = \frac{33}{100}$ (c) $\frac{24}{60} = \frac{14}{35}$

5. *Multiple choice*   Which equation is not a proportion?   **(c)**
   (a) $\frac{x}{5} = \frac{3}{4}$ (b) $\frac{1}{9} = \frac{15}{23}$ (c) $\frac{1}{2} + \frac{2}{2} = \frac{3}{2}$

6. Consider the equation $\frac{40}{t} = \frac{21}{15}$.
   a. By what can you multiply both sides to get rid of fractions?   **15t**
   b. What equation results after that multiplication?   **600 = 21t**
   c. Solve this equation. $t = \frac{200}{7}$
   d. Check your answer.   **See margin.**

508

In 7–9, solve.

7. $\frac{8}{7} = \frac{112}{Q}$ 98

8. $\frac{200}{8} = \frac{x}{22}$ 550

9. $\frac{L}{24} = \frac{0.5}{4}$ 3

10. Jennifer can assemble 3 cardboard boxes in 4 minutes. At this rate, how many boxes can she assemble in 24 minutes?   **18 boxes**

11. Victor can assemble 5 cardboard boxes in 6 minutes. At this rate, how many boxes can he assemble in 45 minutes?   **37.5 boxes**

Applying the Mathematics

12. In the book *Big Bucks for Kids,* the author says that a kid can earn $25 for singing 20 minutes at a wedding. At this rate, what should the fee be for singing 45 minutes?   **$56.25**

13. One car can travel 300 km on 40 liters of gas. To travel 450 km, will a tank of 50 liters be enough?   **No**

14. A recipe says to use $\frac{2}{3}$ of a teaspoon of salt for 6 people. In using this recipe for 25 people, how many teaspoonsful should be used? $2\frac{7}{9}$ **(almost 3) teaspoonsful**

15. At the end of the 1989-1990 season, hockey player Wayne Gretzky had scored 691 goals in 852 games in his career. At this rate, in what game would he score his 100th goal?   **in his 1,233rd game**

16. Mozart wrote 41 symphonies in a lifetime of only 35 years. At this rate, how many symphonies would he have written, had he lived to 70?   **82 symphonies**

Review

17. Pieces of paper numbered from 1 to 80 are put into a hat. A piece of paper is taken out. Assume each piece is equally likely. Mike's favorite number is 7. What is the probability that the number chosen has a 7 as one of its digits? *(Lesson 11-5)* $\frac{17}{80}$

18. What percent of 15 is 30? *(Lesson 11-4)*   **200%**

19. What percent of 30 is 15? *(Lesson 11-4)*   **50%**

LESSON 11-6   Proportions   **509**

FOLLOW-UP

MORE PRACTICE
For more questions on SPUR Objectives, use *Lesson Master 11-6,* shown on page 509.

EXTENSION
Ask the students to set up a proportion for the following situation: If Bill reads *p* pages in *m* minutes, how many minutes will it take him to read *g* pages?
$\left(\frac{p}{m} = \frac{g}{x}\right)$
Have the students solve for the unknown in terms of *g, p,* and *m.* $\left(x = \frac{gm}{p}\right)$

22. b. The area of the larger pizza is more than $1\frac{1}{2}$ times the area of the smaller pizza.

20. Felice and Felipe folded fancy napkins for a Friday feast. In $\frac{2}{3}$ of an hour Felice had folded 32 napkins. In 25 minutes Felipe folded 20 napkins. Who is folding faster? *(Lessons 11-1, 11-2)*
Neither. Both fold $\frac{4}{5}$ napkin per minute.

21. The amount of material needed to make a cubical box with edge of length *s* is $6s^2$. What is the amount of material needed for a cubical box where *s* = 30 cm? *(Lesson 4-1)*   5400 cm²

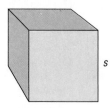

s

22. Suppose a 10″ pizza costs $5.

10″

15″

a. Using proportions, what should a 15″ pizza cost?
b. Most pizza places charge more for a large pizza than what would be calculated by proportions. Why must they charge more?
c. Find a menu from a place that sells pizza. Do the larger pizzas cost more per inch of diameter?
a. $7.50; b. See margin; c. Answers will vary.

510

LESSON 11-7

RESOURCES
■ Lesson Master 11-7
■ Quiz on Lessons 11-5 Through 11-7

In the Middle Ages, students used a shortcut called the Rule of Three to solve proportions. See Example 2.

OBJECTIVES

C Solve proportions using the Means-Extremes Property.
D Recognize the Means-Extremes Property and know why it works.
K Recognize and solve problems involving proportions in real situations.

Here is a true proportion. $\frac{4}{10} = \frac{6}{15}$

In some places in the world, this proportion is written

$$4:10 = 6:15.$$

In the United States, the colon sign means "ratio."
We say "the ratio of 4 to 10 equals the ratio of 6 to 15."
Or, we say "4 is to 10 as 6 is to 15."

Look again at $4:10 = 6:15$. The numbers 4 and 15 are on the outside and are called the **extremes** of the proportion. The numbers 10 and 6 are in the middle and are called the **means**. Notice that 4 times 15 equals 10 times 6. The product of the means equals the product of the extremes.

Here is another true proportion. The means are 23 and 3. The extremes are 34.5 and 2.

$$\frac{34.5}{23} \diagdown\!\!\!\!\diagup \frac{3}{2}$$

means   extremes

Again the product of the means equals the product of the extremes.

$$23 \cdot 3 = 34.5 \cdot 2$$

This happens because of the Multiplication Property of Equality. Suppose

$$\frac{a}{b} = \frac{c}{d}.$$

Now multiply both sides of the proportion by bd.

$$bd \cdot \frac{a}{b} = bd \cdot \frac{c}{d}$$
$$da = bc$$

LESSON 11-7 The Means-Extremes Property   **511**

Carefully explain the proof of the Means-Extremes Property, justifying each step. You may also want to do an arithmetic example next to the algebraic one to help students understand the application of the Multiplication Property of Equality and the reduction of the fraction. For example:

$$\frac{3}{x} = \frac{10}{21}$$

$$21 \cdot x \cdot \frac{3}{x} = \frac{10}{21} \cdot 21 \cdot x$$

$$\frac{21 \cdot x \cdot 3}{x} = \frac{10}{21} \cdot 21 \cdot x$$

$$21 \cdot 3 = 10 \cdot x$$

and

$$\frac{a}{b} = \frac{c}{d}$$

$$bd \cdot \frac{a}{b} = \frac{c}{d} \cdot bd$$

$$\frac{bda}{b} = \frac{cbd}{d}$$

$$da = bc$$

Many people write $ad = bc$ instead of $da = bc$. This is, of course, also correct. Emphasize that the property should be learned in words, not by the names of variables or in alphabetical order. Stress again that it is important to check answers, especially with a shortcut like the Means-Extremes Property.

On the right side of $da = bc$ is the product of the means. On the left side is the product of the extremes. This is an important property.

Means–Extremes Property:

In any proportion, the product of the means equals the product of the extremes.

The Means–Extremes Property can be used as a shortcut in solving proportions.

Example 1   Solve $\frac{2}{3} = \frac{12}{x}$.

Solution   You may be able to solve this equation in your head. But if you cannot, here is how to use the Means–Extremes Property.

The means are 3 and 12. The extremes are 2 and x. By the property:

$$3 \cdot 12 = 2 \cdot x.$$
$$36 = 2x$$

Solve this equation either mentally or by multiplying both sides by $\frac{1}{2}$.

$$18 = x$$

Check   Use substitution.
Does $\frac{2}{3} = \frac{12}{18}$? Yes, because the right fraction simplifies to the left.

In the Middle Ages, students who wanted to solve proportions used a shortcut called the Rule of Three. Here is a typical problem of that time.

Example 2   Suppose 6 bags of wheat cost 11 silver pieces. How much should 10 bags cost?

Solution 1   Clearly the answer involves the numbers 6, 11, and 10. Students were taught just to memorize: Multiply 10 by 11, then divide by 6. You get the right answer, $\frac{110}{6}$. But how do you remember which two numbers to multiply? Students were usually confused. A poem written in the late Middle Ages indicates the confusion.

> Multiplication is vexation,
> Division is as bad,
> The Rule of Three
> Does puzzle me
> And practice drives me mad. (Writer anonymous.)

512

Solution 2   Set up the two equal rates. $\dfrac{11 \text{ pieces}}{6 \text{ bags}} = \dfrac{p \text{ pieces}}{10 \text{ bags}}$

Now use the Means−Extremes Property.

$$6p = 110$$

Multiply both sides by $\frac{1}{6}$.

$$p = \frac{110}{6}$$
$$= 18\frac{2}{6}$$
$$= 18\frac{1}{3}$$

The 10 bags should cost a little more than 18 silver pieces.

Good problem solvers try to find shortcuts like the Means−Extremes Property, or even the Rule of Three. But they also try to understand why the shortcuts work. A shortcut in which you have to guess what to do is no good at all. And with shortcuts, it is essential to check answers.

Here is a check for Example 2. Does $\frac{11}{6} = \frac{18.\overline{3}}{10}$? Yes, each equals 1.8$\overline{3}$. Here is another check. Since 6 bags cost 11 pieces, 12 bags will cost twice as many, 22 pieces. Ten bags should cost something in between 11 and 22 pieces, which they do.

Questions

Covering the Reading

In 1–4, consider the proportion $\dfrac{15}{t} = \dfrac{250}{400}$.

1. Identify the means.   *t*, 250

2. Identify the extremes.   15, 400

3. According to the Means−Extremes Property, what equation will help you solve this proportion? $250t = 400 \cdot 15$

4. a. Solve this proportion for *t*. $t = 24$
   b. Check the answer you found in part **a**. $\frac{15}{24} = \frac{250}{400}$

5. Consider this situation. Eight cans of grapefruit juice cost \$1.79. You want to know how much ten cans might cost.
   a. Write a proportion that will help answer the question. $\frac{8}{\$1.79} = \frac{10}{c}$
   b. Solve the proportion using the Means−Extremes Property.
   c. Check the answer you found.   Does $\frac{8}{1.79} = \frac{10}{2.2375}$?   Yes
   b. c = \$2.2375 ≈ \$2.24

6. Write down how the proportion $2:3 = 6:9$ is read.
   2 is to 3 as 6 is to 9

7. Why did the Rule of Three puzzle students in the Middle Ages?
   It was difficult to remember which two numbers to multiply.

8. Cyril went to market and found that 5 bags of salt cost 12 silver pieces. How much should he pay for 8 bags? $19\frac{1}{5}$ silver pieces

9. What should you be sure to do when you use a shortcut to solve a proportion?   Check the answer.

LESSON 11-7   The Means-Extremes Property   **513**

NOTES ON QUESTIONS
Questions 10–13:
These combine the Commutative Property of Multiplication and the Means-Extremes Property. Since **Question 10** is true, **Question 13** must be true.

Question 15: This calls for an opinion, so a sample answer is provided. A solution to a proportion in a problem of this type will be accurate only for a constant rate. A proportion assumes the equality of rates, which is true only if the rate remains constant.

Applying the Mathematics

In 10–13, consider the proportion $\frac{a}{b} = \frac{c}{d}$. *True or false?*

10. $ad = bc$ True

11. $ab = cd$ False

12. $ac = bd$ False

13. $da = cb$ True

14. Lannie tried to solve the proportion of Question 1 by multiplying both sides by $400t$. Will this work? yes

15. On the first two days of the week-long hunting season, 47 deer were bagged. **a.** At this rate, how many deer will be killed during the week? **b.** Why might it be incorrect to assume the rate will stay the same all week?
    a. 164 or 165 deer; b. Sample: there could be more hunters on the weekend

16. If small cans of grapefruit juice are 5 for $1.69, how many cans can be bought for $10? 29 cans

17. Why won't the Means–Extremes Property work on the equation $x + \frac{2}{3} = \frac{4}{5}$? because the equation is not a proportion

Review

In 18–20, a television survey was done in a small town. Of 240 households called on the phone, 119 were watching television at the time.

18. To the nearest hundredth, what percent of households were watching television? *(Lesson 11-4)* about 49.58%

19. Of 25,000 households in this town, how many would you expect to have been watching TV? *(Lesson 11-6)* about 12,400 households

20. What number might you choose as the probability that someone in a household was watching television? *(Lesson 11-6)* $\frac{1}{2}$ or .5

In 21–24, simplify. *(Lessons 1-10, 11-3)*

21. $\frac{12}{18}$ $\frac{2}{3}$

22. $\frac{12}{-18}$ $-\frac{2}{3}$

23. $\frac{-12}{-18}$ $\frac{2}{3}$

24. $\frac{-12}{18}$ $-\frac{2}{3}$

25. Robert Wadlow of Alton, Illinois, was $5\frac{1}{3}$ feet tall at the age of 5 and $8\frac{2}{3}$ feet tall at the age of 21. On the average, how fast did he grow in these years? *(Lessons 11-1, 11-2)* $\frac{5}{24}$ feet/year or 2.5 inches/year

514

26. Simplify $\frac{7}{10} \div \frac{2}{7}$. *(Lesson 11-2)* $\frac{49}{20}$

27. Simplify $1\frac{4}{5} \div \frac{1}{15}$. *(Lesson 11-2)* 27

In 28–32, use the array of squares below. Assume each side of the little squares has length $\frac{1}{8}$ inch.

28. How many little squares are in the array? *(Lesson 9-1)* **169 squares**

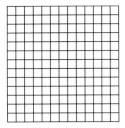

29. What is the area of a little square? *(Lessons 3-7, 9-9)*
$\frac{1}{64}$ **square inches**

30. What is the area of the entire figure? *(Lesson 9-1)*
$\frac{169}{64} \approx$ **2.64 square inches**

31. What is the perimeter of a little square? *(Lessons 5-2, 5-9)* $\frac{1}{2}$ **inch**

32. What is the total length of all the line segments in the figure?
(Lessons 9-5, 9-9) **45.5″**

Exploration

For 33 and 34, look again at the poem in this lesson.

33. What is the meaning of the word "vexation"? **annoyance**

34. Approximately when were the Middle Ages?
between about 500 and 1500 A.D.

LESSON 11-7   The Means-Extremes Property   515

MORE PRACTICE
For more questions on SPUR Objectives, use *Lesson Master 11-7*, shown below.

EXTENSION
Ask students to write as many proportions as they can that are equivalent to $\frac{a}{b} = \frac{c}{d}$, and use only those numbers.

$(\frac{b}{a} = \frac{d}{c}, \frac{c}{d} = \frac{a}{b}, \frac{d}{c} = \frac{b}{a}, \frac{a}{c} = \frac{b}{d},$
$\frac{b}{d} = \frac{a}{c}, \frac{d}{b} = \frac{c}{a}, \frac{c}{a} = \frac{d}{b})$

EVALUATION
A quiz covering Lessons 11-5 through 11-7 is provided in the Teacher's Resource File on page 97.

OBJECTIVE

M Find missing lengths in similar figures.

LESSON

11-8

Proportions in Similar Figures

Figure *B* below is the image of figure *A* under a contraction. Recall that these figures are called *similar*.

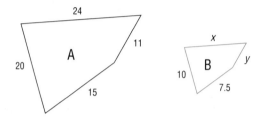

Look at the lengths of the sides in figures *B* and *A*. The sides of length 10 and 20 are **corresponding sides** in the figures and their ratio is $\frac{10}{20}$, or $\frac{1}{2}$. The ratio of 7.5 to 15 also equals $\frac{1}{2}$.

$$\frac{7.5}{15} = \frac{10}{20}$$

In similar figures, ratios of lengths of corresponding sides are always equal. For example, the ratio of the lengths of the top sides must also equal $\frac{10}{20}$.

$$\frac{x}{24} = \frac{10}{20}$$

The ratio of the lengths of the right sides in each figure must also equal $\frac{10}{20}$.

$$\frac{y}{11} = \frac{10}{20}$$

> In similar figures, ratios of lengths of corresponding sides are equal.

You may be able to figure out the values of *x* and *y* in your head. But if you can't, you could find their lengths by solving the above proportions.

$$x = 12 \text{ and } y = 5.5$$

Similar figures do not have to have their corresponding sides parallel. It still may be possible to find unknown lengths.

516

Example 1

Triangles *CAT* and *DOG* are similar. Corresponding sides are drawn with the same color. Name the corresponding sides.

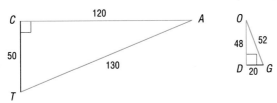

Solution $\overline{CA}$ and $\overline{DO}$ are corresponding sides. So are $\overline{AT}$ and $\overline{OG}$. So are $\overline{CT}$ and $\overline{DG}$. Notice that the ratios of these sides are equal. $\frac{50}{20} = \frac{130}{52} = \frac{120}{48}$

Example 2

The figures below are similar with corresponding sides parallel. Find *EF*.

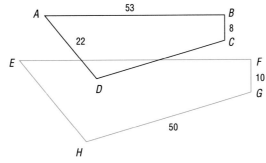

Solution $\overline{EF}$ corresponds to $\overline{AB}$. The only corresponding lengths given are *FG* and *BC*. Use them in the proportion.

$$\frac{AB}{EF} = \frac{BC}{FG}$$

Now substitute what is known. $FG = 10$; $BC = 8$; $AB = 53$.

$$\frac{53}{EF} = \frac{8}{10}$$

Solve as you would any other proportion. Use the Means–Extremes Property.

$$53 \cdot 10 = 8 \cdot EF$$

Multiply by $\frac{1}{8}$.

$$\frac{530}{8} = EF$$

$$EF = 66.25$$

Check For a rough check, look at the figure. Does a length of about 66 for *EF* seem correct? Yes, since *EF* should be larger than *AB*.

For an exact check, substitute in the proportion.

$$\frac{53}{66.25} = \frac{8}{10}$$

Division shows each side to equal 0.8.

After discussing figures *A* and *B* at the beginning of the lesson, you might ask what the dimensions of figure *C* would be if that figure were the image of figure *A* under an expansion of magnitude 3. (Its sides would be 3 times those of *A*: 72, 60, 45, 33.) Call on students to draw a diagram on the board, and show the equal ratios.

In **Example 1,** point out that students can check the lengths of corresponding sides by changing each ratio to a decimal: $\frac{120}{48} = \frac{50}{20} = \frac{130}{52} = 2.5$.

In **Example 2,** make certain that students understand the need to look first for a pair of corresponding sides with both lengths given in order to establish the ratio. Then that ratio is used in a proportion to find the missing sides.

Error Analysis Many students can solve these geometric problems only if the ratio of corresponding sides is an integer. This often occurs because students solve these problems by addition or multiplication rather than by proportions or ratios. When sides are not integers, suggest that after students identify corresponding sides, they set up a problem *using simpler numbers.* If the answer to this proportion is reasonable, they can use the same algorithm with the non-integers.

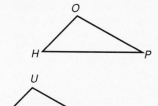
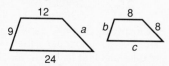
Begin with a real object. Take a photograph of it. Draw a picture of it. If it's very big, construct a scale model. If it's very small, magnify it. Any of these activities lead to similar figures in which you might want to find lengths of sides. For these reasons, proportions often arise involving similar figures.

Questions

Covering the Reading

1. In similar figures, what ratios are always equal?
ratios of lengths of corresponding sides

2. a. Polygon *HUGE* is an expansion image of polygon *TINY*. Name the equal ratios.   See margin.
  b. If *YN* = 16, *EG* = 24, and *TY* = 26, what is the value of *HE*?
  39

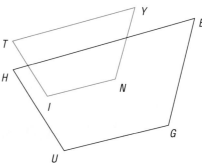

In 3 and 4, use the figure and given information of Example 2 on page 517.

3. Find *EH*.   **27.5**   **4.** Find *CD*.   **40**

5. Draw an example of similar figures that are not tilted the same way.   Answers will vary. See margin.

6. The figures below are similar. What is the value of *x*?   **7.5**

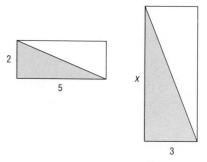

7. Name three places where similar figures can be found.
Samples: photographs, scale models, magnifications

518

8. A right triangle has sides with lengths 3, 4, and 5 centimeters. The smallest side of a similar right triangle has length 9.
   a. Draw an accurate picture of the original right triangle. See margin.
   b. Find the lengths of the other two sides of the similar right triangle. **12 cm, 15 cm**
   c. Draw an accurate picture of the similar right triangle. See margin.

9. A drawing is 20 cm long and 15 cm wide. It is put into a copy machine to be shrunk to 60% of its original size. **a.** What will the dimensions of the copy be? **b.** Are the ratios of corresponding sides of the drawing and its copy equal? **c.** Are the drawing and its copy similar? a. 12 cm long and 9 cm wide; b. Yes; c. Yes

10. Below is a map of the region around Santa Fe, New Mexico. The map is similar to the actual land. A distance of 11.7 mm on the map means an actual distance of 30 miles. The distance from Albuquerque to Santa Fe on the map is 26.5 mm. How far is this in actual miles? **about 68 miles**

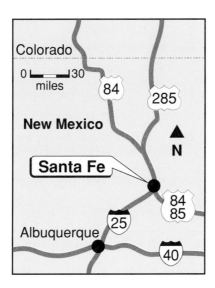

11. Solve for t: $\dfrac{t}{40} = \dfrac{5}{16}$. *(Lessons 11-6, 11-7)* **12.5**

12. A plane goes 300 miles in 36 minutes. At this rate, how far will it travel in an hour? *(Lesson 11-2)* **500 miles**

13. If $x = 60$ and $y = -10$, which of the following are negative?
   (a) $x + y$; (b) $x - y$; (c) $y - x$; (d) xy; (e) $\dfrac{x}{y}$; (f) $\dfrac{y}{x}$.
   (Lessons 5-5, 7-2, 10-5, 11-3) **(c), (d), (e), (f)**

14. Solve: $10A - 50 = 87$. *(Lesson 10-9)* **13.7**

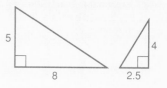
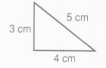

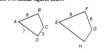

NOTES ON QUESTIONS
Question 25: This should
be discussed. Proportions
often occur within 3-
dimensional figures. For instance, in a pyramid, ratios of
lengths of corresponding
sides of parallel cross sections are equal. Using the
drawing for **Question 2,**
draw the lines $\overline{TH}$, $\overline{IU}$, $\overline{NG}$,
and $\overline{YE}$. These lines are con-
current; they have a point in
common. You can think of
the drawing as a 2-
dimensional picture of a pyramid whose base is HUGE,
with TINY as a cross section
and the vertex of the pyramid
as the point of concurrency.

FOLLOW-UP

MORE PRACTICE
For more questions on SPUR
Objectives, use Lesson Mas-
ter 11-8, shown on page 519.

EXTENSION
Using Manipulatives
Scale drawings use proportions. After the students have
carefully measured an object
or a room and chosen an appropriate scale, they can use
proportions to make a scale
drawing of their choice.

25.

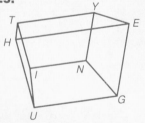

15. Consistent Constance always tips servers 15% of the bill for dinner. You see Constance leave a tip of $2.25. Estimate the dinner bill. *(Lesson 10-3)* $15

16. Merv knows that you can multiply both numerator and denomina-tor of a fraction by the same number without changing its value. He wonders what else you can do without changing the value.
   a. Can you add the same number to numerator and denominator?
   b. Can you subtract the same number from the numerator and de-nominator?
   c. Can you divide both numerator and denominator by the same number? *(Lessons 6-4, 6-6)*
   a. No; b. No; c. Yes

In 17–20, let $u = \frac{8}{5}$ and $v = \frac{7}{5}$. Evaluate:

17. $u + v$ *(Lesson 5-2)* 3

18. $u - v$ *(Lesson 7-2)* $\frac{1}{5}$

19. uv *(Lesson 9-9)* $\frac{56}{25}$

20. $\dfrac{u}{v}$ *(Lesson 11-2)* $\frac{8}{7}$

21. Write 3,800,000,000 in scientific notation. *(Lesson 2-3)* $3.8 \cdot 10^9$

22. Between what two whole numbers is $\frac{41}{8}$? *(Lesson 1-2)* 5 and 6

23. Write $\frac{41}{8}$ as a decimal and as a mixed number. *(Lessons 1-8, 2-7)*
   5.125, $5\frac{1}{8}$

24. Write $17\frac{2}{11}$ as a simple fraction and as a decimal. *(Lessons 1-9, 5-2)*
   $\frac{189}{11}$, $17.\overline{18}$

Exploration

25. Look again at the drawing for Question 2. Some people think that the drawing might be a picture of a 3-dimensional object. But some lines are missing. Trace the drawing and fill in these lines to picture such an object. See margin.

Proportional Thinking

RESOURCES
■ Lesson Master 11-9

Suppose 2 bags of peanuts cost 39¢. How much should 8 bags cost? You can answer this question by solving the following proportion.

$$\frac{2 \text{ bags}}{39¢} = \frac{8 \text{ bags}}{C}$$

But some people would say: 8 is 4 times 2. So the cost should be 4 times 39¢. These people have used **proportional thinking** to answer the question. Proportional thinking is the ability to get or estimate an answer to a proportion without solving an equation. Some people believe that proportional thinking is one of the most important kinds of thinking you can have in mathematics.

To work on proportional thinking, try first to estimate answers to questions involving proportions. Then try to get the exact answer.

Example 1 Traveling at 45 mph, how much time will it take to go 80 miles?

Solution 1 Estimate. At 45 mph, you can go 45 miles in 1 hour. You can go 90 miles in 2 hours. So it will take between 1 and 2 hours to go 80 miles. Since 80 is closer to 90 than 45, it will take closer to 2 hours.

Solution 2 Try simpler numbers. (This is a method from Chapter 6.) At 40 mph, it would take 2 hours. This answer is 80 divided by 40. This suggests that dividing 80 by 45 will get the answer.

$$\frac{80 \text{ miles}}{45 \frac{\text{miles}}{\text{hour}}} \approx 1.8 \text{ hours} = 1 \text{ hour } 48 \text{ minutes}$$

The answer seems right because it agrees with the estimate in Solution 1.

Solution 3 Set up a proportion: $\frac{45 \text{ miles}}{1 \text{ hour}} = \frac{80 \text{ miles}}{h \text{ hours}}$

Use the Means−Extremes Property or multiply both sides by h.

$$45h = 80$$
$$h = \frac{80}{45} \approx 1.8 \text{ hours}$$

OBJECTIVES

C Solve proportions.
K Recognize and solve problems involving proportions in real situations.

TEACHING NOTES

Although the solution methods used in **Examples 1** and **2** are important, the real point is flexibility. Ask students to identify advantages of knowing more than one way to solve a problem. (If you can't do it one way, maybe another will work; one way can check the other; one way might be easier for some problems.)

Solutions are categorized. **Example 1** is solved by estimating, dividing (after using simpler numbers), and proportions. **Example 2** uses estimating, the Rate Factor Model for Multiplication, and proportions.

ADDITIONAL EXAMPLES
Solve in at least two ways,
using one method to check
the other.

1. Find p: $\dfrac{\frac{2}{3}}{\frac{3}{4}} = \dfrac{8}{p}$

Solution 1: Estimate. $\frac{3}{4}$ is a
little greater than $\frac{2}{3}$, so p
must be somewhat greater
than 8.

Solution 2: Divide the fractions first.
$\frac{2}{3} \div \frac{3}{4} = \frac{8}{p}$, $\frac{2}{3} \cdot \frac{4}{3} = \frac{8}{p}$, $\frac{8}{9} = \frac{8}{p}$,
$p = 9$

Solution 3: Use the Means-Extremes Property.
$\frac{2}{3} \cdot p = \frac{24}{4} = 6$,
$\frac{3}{2} \cdot \frac{2}{3} p = \frac{3}{2} \cdot 6$, $p = \frac{18}{2} = 9$

2. A dozen pencils cost
$1.09. How much does one
pencil cost?
**Solution 1: Estimate. There
are 12 pencils in a dozen. If
each one costs 10¢, a
dozen will cost $1.20; so
each will cost a little less
than 10¢.**

Solution 2: Use a rate.
$\frac{\$1.09}{12 \text{ pencils}} \approx \frac{\$.09}{\text{pencil}}$

Solution 3: Use a proportion. $\frac{109}{12} = \frac{c}{1}$, $1 \cdot 109 =$
$12 \cdot c$, $109 = 12c$, $9 \approx c$.

The important thing here is flexibility. You do not have to know
every way there is of solving proportions. But you should have
at least *two* ways to do these questions. Use one way to check
the other.

Example 2 According to the *World Almanac*, about 715,194,000 acres of the
United States are forest. There are 640 acres in a square mile.
How many square miles of the U.S. are forest?

Solution 1 Estimate using proportional thinking. Since there are
640 acres in a square mile, there are 640 *million* acres in 1 *million*
square miles. 715,194,000 (or about 715 million) is more than 640
million, so more than 1 million square miles of the U.S. is forest.

Solution 2 The problem is to convert acres to square miles. Use
a method from Lesson 10-4.
$$715{,}194{,}000 \text{ acres} = 715{,}194{,}000 \text{ acres} \cdot \frac{1 \text{ square mile}}{640 \text{ acres}}$$
$$\approx 1{,}117{,}500 \text{ square miles}$$

Solution 3 Set up a proportion.
$$\frac{715{,}194{,}000 \text{ acres}}{F \text{ square miles}} = \frac{640 \text{ acres}}{1 \text{ square mile}}$$

Solve the proportion.
$$640F = 715{,}194{,}000$$
$$F = \frac{715{,}194{,}000}{640}$$
$$\approx 1{,}117{,}500$$

The entire land area of the United States is about 3,536,000
square miles. Dividing 1,117,500 by 3,536,000, we get about
0.32. So about 32% (almost 1/3) of the land of the United States
is forest.

522

Questions

NOTES ON QUESTIONS
Questions 11–13: List the different ways students use to get answers. You may want to list ways to estimate answers separately from ways to get exact answers.

Covering the Reading

1. What is proportional thinking? *getting or estimating an answer to a proportion without solving an equation*

2. Use proportional thinking to answer this question. If tuna is 2 cans for $2.50, how much will 6 cans cost?
Multiply by 3 to get $7.50

3. What proportion will answer the question of Question 2?
2 cans/$2.50 = 6 cans/$C

4. How many acres are in a square mile? *640 acres*

5. *True or false?* In a thousand square miles, there are more than 500,000 acres. *True*

6. The area of the state of Illinois is about 58,000 square miles. How many acres is this? *37,120,000 acres*

7. At 45 kph (kilometers per hour), it takes __?__ hours to travel 90 km. *2 hours*

8. At 45 kph, it takes __?__ hours to travel 450 km. *10 hours*

9. At 45 kph, it takes between __?__ and __?__ hours to go 200 km. *Sample: 4, 5*

10. At 45 kph, exactly how long does it take to go 200 km?
$4\frac{4}{9}$ hours (or 44.4 hr)

In 11–13, **a.** answer the question using any method you wish. Then **b.** check your answer using a different method.

11. At 55 mph, how long will it take to drive 120 miles?
$2.\overline{18}$ hr; b. See margin.

12. There are 12 eggs in a dozen. 100 eggs is how many dozen?
$8\frac{1}{3}$ dozens; See margin.

13. Suppose a forest fire burns 12,000 acres of timberland. How many square miles is this? *18.75 sq. mi; See margin.*

Applying the Mathematics

14. Speedy Spencer can type 30 words in 45 seconds. At this rate, how many words can he type in a minute? *40 words*

15. Jack can mow a lawn in 40 minutes. Jill can mow a lawn in 40 minutes. Working together, how long will it take Jack and Jill to mow two lawns? *40 minutes*

16. Beatrice used 100 stamps in 2 weeks. At this rate, how many stamps will she use up in 3 weeks? *150 stamps*

17. If it costs $500/month to feed a family of 4, how much should it cost to feed a family of 5? *$625/month*

ADDITIONAL ANSWERS
11. b. sample: Method 1:

$$\frac{55 \text{ mi}}{1 \text{ hr}} = \frac{120 \text{ mi}}{x \text{ hr}}$$
$$55x = 120$$
$$x = 2.\overline{18} \text{ hr}$$

12. b. sample:
$$\frac{12 \text{ eggs}}{1 \text{ doz}} = \frac{100 \text{ eggs}}{d \text{ doz}}$$
$$12d = 100$$
$$d = 8\frac{1}{3}$$

13. b. sample: There are 640 acres in a sq mi. Thus, 1200 acres is less than 2 sq mi, so 12,000 acres is less than 20 sq mi.

Review

In 18 and 19, triangles *ABC* and *DEF* are similar with corresponding sides parallel. *(Lesson 11-8)*

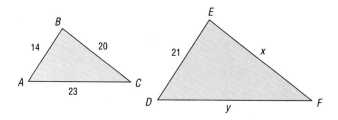

18. Find *x*.   x = 30   **19.** Find *y*.   y = 34.5

20. If 30% of a number is 51, what is 40% of that same number? *(Lessons 2-6, 10-3)*   68

21. If *x* = -4 and *y* = -2, what is -3*x* divided by 2*y*? *(Lessons 4-4, 10-5, 11-3)*   −3

22. What is 14% of 200? *(Lesson 2-6)*   28

23. 200 is 14% of what number? *(Lesson 10-3)*   about 1428.57

24. Answer Question E on page 483. *(Lesson 11-1)* $2\frac{6}{7}$ children/family

25. Answer Question G on page 483. *(Lesson 11-6)* $2\frac{6}{7}$ hours

Exploration

26. You often hear that the cost of living is going up. The government calculates a number called the "consumer price index" (CPI) to measure the cost of living. When the CPI doubles, it means that, on the average, prices have doubled. The CPI scale used in 1990 considers average prices in the years 1982-84 to be 100.
  a. In 1990, the CPI was 131.6. In 1970, the CPI was 38.8. Between 1970 and 1990, did prices more than triple or less than triple? more than tripled
  b. If a new car cost $11,630 in 1970, what would you expect a new car of the same type to cost in 1990? about $39,400

27. a. The following program prints the cost of peanuts if 2 bags cost $.39.

```
10   FOR N = 2 TO 20 STEP 2
20   PRINT N " BAGS OF PEANUTS COST $".39*N
30   NEXT N
40   END
```

Run the program and record its output.
  b. What could you do to print the costs for every whole number of bags from 1 to 20?
  c. Modify the program to print another similar table.
  See margin.

524

Summary

One basic use of division is to calculate rates. In a rate, the divisor and dividend have different units. The unit of the rate is written as a fraction. For example, if x words are divided by y minutes, the quotient is $\frac{x}{y}$ words per minute, written as

$$\frac{x}{y} \quad \frac{words}{minute}.$$

The numbers involved in rates can be fractions, or decimals, or negative numbers. So rates can help you learn how to divide these kinds of numbers.

To divide fractions, you can use the Mult-Rec Property of Division. Take the reciprocal of the divisor and multiply. To divide with negative numbers, follow the same rules for signs that work for multiplication.

Another basic use of division is in calculating ratios. In a ratio, both divisor and dividend have the same units. So the quotient has no unit. Ratios are numbers that compare two quantities. Percents are almost always ratios. Ratios may also be decimals, fractions, or integers.

If two fractions, rates, or ratios are equal, a proportion results. The form of a proportion is

$$\frac{a}{b} = \frac{c}{d}.$$

Proportional thinking is very important. You should be able to solve simple proportions mentally. In the above proportion, $ad = bc$. This is known as the Means–Extremes Property. You could also solve the proportion by multiplying both sides of the equation by bd. Proportions occur in geometry and all parts of mathematics. Proportions also occur in all sorts of daily experiences. So it helps to know more than one way to solve a proportion.

Vocabulary

You should be able to give a general description and a specific example for each of the following ideas.

Lesson 11-1
rate, rate unit
Rate Model for Division
unit cost

Lesson 11-3
mean, average
median

Lesson 11-4
ratio
ratio comparison model for division

Lesson 11-5
probability

Lesson 11-6
proportion
solving a proportion

Lesson 11-7
extremes, means
Means–Extremes Property

Lesson 11-8
corresponding sides

Lesson 11-9
proportional thinking

For the development of mathematical competence, feedback and correction, along with the opportunity to practice, are necessary. The Progress Self-Test provides the opportunity for feedback and correction; the Chapter Review provides additional opportunities for practice. In general, student performance should be markedly improved after these pages.

USING THE PROGRESS SELF-TEST
Assign the Progress Self-Test as a one-night assignment. Worked-out *solutions* for all questions are in the Selected Answers section of the student book. Encourage students to take the Progress Self-Test honestly, grade themselves, and then be prepared to discuss the test in class.

Advise students to pay special attention to those Chapter Review questions (pages 527–529) which correspond to questions missed on the Progress Self-Test. A chart in the student book keys the Progress Self-Test questions to the lettered SPUR Objectives in the Chapter Review. It also keys the questions to the corresponding lessons where the material is covered.

ADDITIONAL ANSWERS
1. 60 words per minute

2. $\frac{m}{h}$ kilometers per hour

9. sample: If you lose 8 kg in 2 months, what is the rate at which your weight has changed?

16. 6,400,000 acres

Progress Self-Test

See margin for answers not shown below.

Take this test as you would take a test in class. Then check your work with the solutions in the Selected Answers section in the back of the book.

1. What rate is suggested by this situation? A person types 300 words in 5 minutes.

2. If you travel m kilometers in h hours, what is your average speed in kilometers per hour?

3. Divide 4/9 by 1/3.   **4/3**

4. Simplify $\frac{-42}{-24}$.   **$\frac{7}{4}$**

5. Simplify $\frac{\frac{3}{5}}{\frac{6}{5}}$.   **$\frac{1}{2}$**

6. Give the value of $\frac{-2x}{8 + y}$ when $x = -5$ and $y = -9$.   **-10**

7. What is the mean of 7, -17, and 7?   **-1**

8. If a is negative and b is positive, which of the following are negative? $\frac{a}{b}$; $\frac{-a}{b}$; $\frac{-a}{-b}$ **$\frac{a}{b}$, $\frac{-a}{-b}$**

9. Give a rate question involving weight that could lead to dividing -8 by 2.

10. Solve $\frac{40}{x} = \frac{8}{5}$.   **x = 25**

11. Solve $\frac{5}{12} = \frac{p}{3}$.   **p = 1.25**

12. To the nearest percent, 14 is what percent of 150?   **about 9%**

13. If $0.30 is the tax on a $4 purchase, what percent tax rate is this?   **7.5%**

14. If 60% of a number is 30, what is the number?   **x = 50**

15. At 45 mph, how long does it take to travel 189 miles?   **4.2 hours**

16. There are 640 acres in a square mile. How many acres are in 10,000 square miles?

17. Name the means in the proportion of Question 18.   **b and c**

18. State the Means–Extremes Property as it applies to the proportion $\frac{a}{b} = \frac{c}{d}$.   **If $\frac{a}{b} = \frac{c}{d}$, then $ad = bc$.**

In 19 and 20, triangles ABC and DEF are similar with corresponding sides parallel.

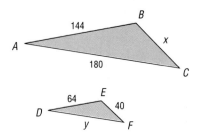

19. Find x.   **x = 90**
20. Find y.   **y = 80**

In 21 and 22, a box lands face up 12 of the first 15 times it is dropped.

21. At this rate, about how many times would it land face up if it were dropped 50 times?   **40**

22. From this experiment, what is the probability that the box lands face up?   **$\frac{4}{5}$**

23. A recipe for 4 people says to use $\frac{1}{3}$ tsp of pepper. How much should be used for 9 people?   **$\frac{3}{4}$ tsp.**

24. Solve $\frac{2}{3} = \frac{4}{A}$.   **A = 6**

25. Solve $\frac{3}{n} = 8$.   **$n = \frac{3}{8}$ or 0.375**

Chapter Review

See margin for answers
not shown below.

Questions on **SPUR** Objectives

SPUR stands for **S**kills, **P**roperties, **U**ses, and **R**epresentations.
The Chapter Review questions are grouped according to the
SPUR Objectives for this chapter.

RESOURCES
■ Chapter 11 Test, Form A
■ Chapter 11 Test, Form B
■ Chapter 11 Test,
  Cumulative Form

CHAPTER REVIEW

The main objectives for the chapter are organized here into sections corresponding to the four main types of understanding this book promotes—Skills, Properties, Uses, and Representations.

USING THE CHAPTER REVIEW
Whereas end-of-chapter material may be considered optional in some texts, in *Transition Mathematics* we have selected these objectives and questions with the expectation that they will be covered. Students should be able to answer these questions with about 85% accuracy after studying the chapter.

You may assign these questions over a single night to help students prepare for a test the next day, or you may assign the questions over a two-day period.

If you work the questions over two days, then we recommend assigning the *evens* for homework the first night so that students get feedback in class the next day, then assigning the *odds* the night before the test.

SKILLS deal with the procedures used to get answers.

Objective A: *Divide fractions with numbers or variables. (Lesson 11-2)*

1. What is 12 divided by $\frac{2}{3}$? **18**

In 2–4, simplify

2. $\dfrac{\frac{2}{3}}{\frac{4}{3}}$ $\frac{1}{2}$
3. $\dfrac{\frac{7}{6}}{\frac{14}{3}}$ $\frac{1}{4}$
4. $\dfrac{\frac{x}{y}}{\frac{a}{b}}$ $\frac{bx}{ay}$

5. Divide $3\frac{3}{4}$ by $2\frac{1}{7}$. $\frac{7}{4}$

Objective B: *Divide positive and negative numbers. (Lesson 11-3)*

6. $\frac{-10}{2} = ?$ **-5**

7. Is $-\frac{400}{-200}$ positive or negative? **positive**

8. Give the value of $\frac{2c}{d}$ when $c = 3$ and $d = -1$. **-6**

9. Give the value of -40 divided by -30. $\frac{4}{3}$

Objective C: *Solve proportions. (Lessons 11-6, 11-7, 11-9)*

10. Solve $\dfrac{40}{9} = \dfrac{12}{x}$. **2.7**

11. Solve $\dfrac{7}{G} = \dfrac{1}{3}$. **21**

12. In solving $\dfrac{7}{t} = \dfrac{168}{192}$, Jenny got $t = 24$. Is she correct? **No**

PROPERTIES deal with the principles behind the mathematics.

Objective D: *Recognize the Means–Extremes Property and know why it works. (Lesson 11-7)*

13. According to the Means–Extremes Property, if $\dfrac{a}{d} = \dfrac{b}{e}$, what is true? **bd = ae**

14. To get rid of fractions in the equation $\dfrac{3}{x} = \dfrac{5}{6}$, by what can you multiply both sides? **6x**

15. Why won't the Means–Extremes Property work on the equation $\frac{4}{5} + x = \frac{3}{4}$?
    The left side is not a single fraction.

Objective E: *Know the general properties for dividing positive and negative numbers. (Lesson 11-3)*

16. *Multiple choice* Which does *not* equal $\dfrac{-x}{y}$?

(a) $-\dfrac{x}{y}$ (b) $-x \cdot \dfrac{1}{y}$ (c) $\dfrac{x}{-y}$ (d) $\dfrac{-x}{-y}$

(d)

17. If $\dfrac{a}{b} = c$, a is negative, and c is positive, then is b positive or negative? **negative**

Objective F: *Apply the properties of probability. (Lesson 11-5)*

18. What is the largest value that a probability can have? **1**

19. If an experiment has 3 equally likely outcomes, what is the probability of each occurring? $\frac{1}{3}$

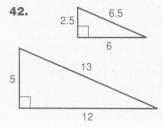
USES deal with applications of mathematics in real situations.

■ **Objective G:** *Use the Rate Model for Division.*
(Lessons 11-1, 11-2, 11-3)

20. A car travels 200 km in 4 hours. What is its average speed? **50 km/hr**

21. Sixteen hamburgers are made from 5 pounds of ground beef. How much beef is this per hamburger? $\frac{5}{16}$ **pound per hamburger**

22. On a diet, some people lose 10 pounds in 30 days. What rate is this?

23. In 1990, Boston had a population of about 578,000 people and an area of about 47 square miles. About how many people is this per square mile? **about 12,300**

24. Two-thirds of the way through the summer, Jeremy had earned $120 mowing lawns. At this rate, how much will he earn during the entire summer? **$180**

■ **Objective H:** *Find the mean of a set of numbers.*
(Lesson 11-3)

25. Find the mean of -3, 14, -22, -28, -26, and 2. **-10.5**

26. In Anchorage, Alaska, the following low temperatures were recorded for seven days in a week. -14°, -18°, -16°, -8°, -12°, -15°, -13°. To the nearest tenth, what was the mean low temperature? **about -13.7°**

■ **Objective I:** *Use the Ratio Comparison Model for Division. (Lesson 11-4)*

27. 8 is what percent of 40? **20%**

28. 10 is what percent of 5? **200%**

29. In Seattle, Washington, it rains 216 days a year on average. What percent of the days is this? (Answer to the nearest percent.) **59%**

30. In 1988, Ford Motor Company sold about 47,000 Lincoln Continentals. In 1989, the number of Continentals sold was about 9,000 more. So, in 1989 the company sold about __?__ times as many Continentals as in 1988. (Answer to the nearest tenth.) **1.2**

■ **Objective J:** *Calculate probabilities in a situation with equally likely outcomes.*
(Lesson 11-5)

31. A grab bag has 10 prizes. Two are calculators. If you choose a prize without looking, what is the probability you will select a calculator? $\frac{1}{5}$

32. A phone-in request show tells you your favorite song will be played in the next hour. What is the probability your song will be played in the next *m* minutes? $\frac{m}{60}$

33. A class has *b* boys and *g* girls. What is the probability the student first in alphabetical order is a boy? $b/(b + g)$

34. Fifty slips of paper numbered 1 to 50 are placed in a hat. A person picks a slip of paper out of the hat. What is the probability that the number on the slip ends in 4?

■ **Objective K:** *Recognize and solve problems involving proportions in real situations.*
(Lessons 11-6, 11-7, 11-9)

35. You have made 35 copies on a duplicating machine in 2.5 minutes. How long will it take the machine to make 500 copies?

36. A recipe for 6 people calls for $1\frac{1}{3}$ cups of sugar. How much sugar is needed for a similar recipe for 10 people? $\frac{20}{9}$ **cups**

37. You want to buy 5 cans. You see that 8 cans cost $3. At this rate, what will the 5 cans cost? **$1.88**

Objective L: *Give situations that represent the division of negative numbers.* *(Lesson 11-3)*

38. Betty spent $200 on a 4-day vacation. Use this information and make up a question involving division and negative numbers. Answer your question.

39. Three days ago, the repaving crew was 6 km down the road. Use this information and make up a question involving division and negative numbers. Answer your question.

EPRESENTATIONS deal with pictures, graphs, or objects that illustrate concepts.

Objective M: *Find missing lengths in similar figures.* *(Lesson 11-8)*

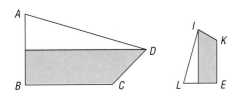

40. The above figures are similar. If $AB = 80$, $CD = 45$, and $EL = 56$, what is IK? **31.5**

In 41 and 42, a right triangle has sides with lengths 5, 12, and 13. The longest side of a similar right triangle has length 6.5.

41. Find the lengths of the other two sides of the similar right triangle. **2.5 and 6**

42. Draw accurate pictures of the two triangles using the same unit.

CHAPTER 12 ■ COMBINING OPERATIONS

DAILY PACING CHART ■ CHAPTER 12

Students in the Full Course should complete the entire text by the end of the year. Students in the Minimal Course spend more time when there are quizzes and more time on the Chapter Review. Therefore, these students may not complete all of the chapters in the text.

DAY	MINIMAL COURSE	FULL COURSE
1	12-1	12-1
2	12-2	12-2
3	12-3	12-3
4	Quiz (TRF); Start 12-4.	Quiz (TRF); 12-4
5	Finish 12-4.	12-5
6	Start 12-5.	12-6
7	Finish 12-5; Start 12-6.	Progress Self-Test
8	Finish 12-6.	Chapter Review
9	Progress Self-Test	Chapter Test (TRF)
10	Chapter Review	
11	Chapter Test (TRF)	

TESTING OPTIONS
■ Quiz for Lessons 12-1 Through 12-3 ■ Chapter 12 Test, Form B
■ Chapter 12 Test, Form A ■ Chapter 12 Test, Cumulative Form
A Quiz and Test Writer is available for generating additional questions, additional quizzes, or additional forms of the Chapter Test.

PROVIDING FOR INDIVIDUAL DIFFERENCES
The student text is written for the *average* student. The program, however, can be adapted for both less capable and more capable students.

A blackline master (in the Teacher's Resource File) is provided for each lesson for those students who need more practice. The Teacher's Edition frequently provides Error Analysis and Alternate Approach features to provide additional instructional strategies for those students.

For students who require additional challenge, Extension activities are regularly provided in the Teacher's Edition.

OBJECTIVES ■ CHAPTER 12

Students should master the chapter objectives by the time they complete the chapter. To ensure objective mastery, there is continual review built into each set of lesson questions. After students complete the chapter lessons, they assess their mastery on the Progress Self-Test. Then they do the Chapter Review and pay special attention to those questions that match the objectives missed on the Progress Self-Test. Students can get extra practice on these objectives by using the master for each lesson in the Teacher's Resource File.

OBJECTIVES FOR CHAPTER 12 (Organized into the SPUR categories—Skills, Properties, Uses, and Representations)	Progress Self-Test Questions	Chapter Review Questions	Teacher's Resource File	
			Lesson Master*	Chapter Test Forms A and B
SKILLS				
A: Simplify linear expressions when possible, using distributivity.	1–3	1–7	12-1, 12-3, 12-4	1, 4, 8, 9, 10, 11
B: Convert repeating decimals to fractions.	16, 17	8–11	12-2	3, 6, 7
C: Solve and check equations of the form $ax + b = cx + d$.	5–8	12–15	12-5	12, 13, 14
PROPERTIES				
D: Recognize and use the Distributive Property.	4, 18, 19	16–18	12-1, 12-4	22, 23
USES				
E: Translate real situations involving multiplication, addition, and subtraction into linear expressions and linear equations.	9, 10, 12	19–23	12-3, 12-4, 12-5	5, 15, 16, 17
REPRESENTATIONS				
F: Represent the Distributive Property by areas of rectangles.	11, 20	24 and 25	12-1, 12-4	24
G: Graph solutions to linear equations.	13–15	26–29	12-6	2, 18, 19, 20, 21

*The Lesson Masters are numbered to match the lessons.

OVERVIEW ■ CHAPTER 12

We could also have titled the chapter "Applications of Distributivity;" the fundamental idea running through this chapter is the Distributive Property, introduced in Lesson 12-1.

A major theme in the chapter is linear expressions. This theme begins with adding like terms $ax + bx$ in Lesson 12-1 and continues with the linear expression $ax + by$ in Lesson 12-3, solving equations of the form $ax + b = cx + d$ in Lesson 12-5, and graphing linear equations of the form $ax + by = c$ in Lesson 12-6.

The ideas of distributivity and fractions are combined in Lesson 12-2, which discusses fractions for infinite repeating decimals. Distributivity allows a different perspective on adding fractions. Fractions with like denominators can be treated as like terms, while fractions with different denominators are unlike terms. Problems combining fractions are found throughout the questions of the chapter.

The lessons dealing with linear expressions emphasize the algebra of distributivity. The lessons dealing with fractions stress arithmetic. Not until a later course is a student expected to become proficient in the algebra of rational expressions.

PERSPECTIVES ■ CHAPTER 12

The Perspectives provide the rationale for the inclusion of topics or approaches, provide mathematical background, and make connections within UCSMP.

12-1

THE DISTRIBUTIVE PROPERTY

There are two common forms of the Distributive Property:
$ax + bx = (a + b)x$; and
$a(b + c) = ab + ac$. In the first, one begins with an addition and converts it to a multiplication. In the second, one begins with a multiplication and converts it to an addition.

There are additional differences between the forms: the multiplier appears on a different side; different letters are commonly used to name the property; and there are different names given for the operations. Converting $ax + bx$ to $(a + b)x$ is called *adding like terms*. Converting $a(b + c)$ to $ab + ac$ is *multiplying the binomial by the monomial factor*.

Although the only mathematical difference between these forms is the Commutative Property of Multiplication, the differences in appearance cause students to consider these as two entirely different properties. In this lesson we discuss the easier form for students, $ax + bx = (a + b)x$. The other form is anticipated in the questions and is formally discussed in Lesson 12-4.

Notice that, just as the Distributive Property combines multiplication and addition, the rectangle display of the Distributive Property combines area, a model for multiplication, and putting together lengths, a model for addition.

12-2

FRACTIONS FOR REPEATING DECIMALS

Determining fractions for repeating decimals provides a new and unusual use of the Distributive Property. This topic offers important background for understanding the difference between a rational number, which has a terminating or a repeating decimal, and an irrational number, which has an infinite nonrepeating decimal. Rational and irrational numbers are discussed in Lesson 13-6.

Converting repeating decimals to fractions also provides symmetry and closure to the work with fractions. Students will be able to write any fraction as a decimal and any rational decimal as a fraction.

Students usually find the topic intriguing and are often surprised that the fraction can be found at all.

12-3

SITUATIONS LEADING TO LINEAR EXPRESSIONS

This lesson covers translation of an important group of situations from English to mathematics. The situations lead to *linear combinations* and are exceedingly common in business and statistics.

A *linear combination* is a sum of products of variables and constants, such as $3x + 4y$, or $0.5n + 3t + 8q$. Linear combinations arise when there are some items at one price, a second group of items at a different price, a third group at a third price, and so on. They can also occur when traveling a certain distance at one rate, another distance at a second rate, and so on.

The words *term*, *coefficient*, *like terms*, and *unlike terms* are introduced in this lesson.

12-4

MORE ON THE DISTRIBUTIVE PROPERTY

Lesson 12-1 first introduced the Distributive Property in the form $ax + bx = (a + b)x$. In this lesson, the multiplier is on the other side: $x(a + b) = xa + xb$. The difference can be justified by the Commutative Property of Multiplication. We refer to both forms as instances of the same general property.

12-5

SOLVING $ax + b = cx + d$

Equations of the form $ax + b = cx + d$ are the most complicated type solved systematically in *Transition Mathematics*. These can be difficult even if students can easily solve equations of the form $ax + b = c$. Stressing different pairs of like terms focuses attention on the use of the Distributive Property and can help students get started.

This lesson serves only to introduce equations of the form $ax + b = cx + d$. Many students will not achieve mastery of this material until a first-year algebra course.

12-6

GRAPHING LINES

In Chapter 8, students graphed equations of the form $x + y = k$ and $x - y = k$. Thus, this lesson really involves no new concepts.

The skill of graphing is covered in some detail in UCSMP *Algebra*, *Geometry*, and *Advanced Algebra*. At that time, students will learn about *slope*, *intercepts*, and *equations in standard form*. The goal of this lesson is simpler: merely to show that sentences have graphs. We introduce sentences arising from real-world situations, for example, postal rates, and other linear equations of the form $ax + by = c$.

Combining Operations

530

Each problem on this page involves both multiplication and addition. Each problem can be done in two ways. In one of these ways, you add before multiplying. In the other way, you do two multiplications before adding. Try to answer each question these two ways.

A. How many dots are there in all?   B. What is the total area?

C. $7 + 11 + 7 + 11 + 7 + 11 + 7 + 11 + 7 + 11 = ?$

D. How many segments will join a dot in the top row with a dot in one of the two bottom rows?

E. Pencils cost 5¢. If you buy 7 pencils one day and 11 the next, what is the total amount you have spent?

F. If $a = 5$, $b = 7$, and $c = 11$, what is the value of $ab + ac$?

Each of these questions leads to $5(7 + 11) = 5 \cdot 7 + 5 \cdot 11$, an instance of the **Distributive Property of Multiplication over Addition.** The Distributive Property is the basic property that combines multiplication with addition or subtraction. Such combinations of operations are useful in many situations.

OBJECTIVES

A Simplify linear expressions when possible, using distributivity.
D Recognize and use the Distributive Property.
F Represent the Distributive Property by areas of rectangles.

TEACHING NOTES

Because many students find distributivity difficult, discuss the reading and the examples in detail. You may wish to have students explain how the two situations at the beginning of the lesson are instances of the general pattern. The treatment of the rose problem not only sets up the Distributive Property, but also hints that one application of the property is in mental calculation. The Area Model provides a good visual interpretation of distributivity.

The examples illustrate the use of the Distributive Property when combining terms. **Example 1** is straightforward and an easy start. **Example 2** introduces the Distributive Property of Multiplication over Subtraction. **Example 3** combines three terms, and **Example 4** has unlike terms. The checks are also important, since they verify arithmetically that the Distributive Property works.

LESSON

12-1

The Distributive Property

Consider this question:

> Steve wants to buy his sister 21 long-stem roses for her 21st birthday. If the roses cost $2.50 apiece, what will be the total cost?

The answer can be found by a rate factor multiplication.

$$21 \text{ roses} \cdot \frac{\$2.50}{\text{rose}}$$

This multiplication can be done mentally. Ten roses cost $10 \cdot \$2.50$, which is $25. Another ten cost $25, making $50. The last rose costs $2.50, for a grand total of $52.50.

Suppose one rose cost x. Then the cost of 21 roses is $21x$. You could use the same idea to calculate the cost of 21 roses. The cost of 10 roses is $10x$. Another 10 cost another $10x$. The last rose costs x. So $21x = 10x + 10x + x$.

Here's another situation. Find the total area of these rectangles.

 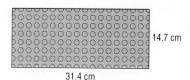

The obvious way is to multiply $6.9 \cdot 14.7$, then $31.4 \cdot 14.7$, and add the two products. But there is a way to do it with a simpler addition and only one multiplication.
Join the rectangles.

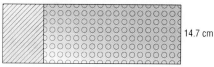

532

One dimension is still 14.7 cm. The other dimension is 6.9 cm + 31.4 cm, or 38.3 cm. Multiplying the two dimensions, 14.7 cm and 38.3 cm, gives the area. This shows

$$6.9 \cdot 14.7 + 31.4 \cdot 14.7 = (6.9 + 31.4) \cdot 4.7.$$

The general pattern is:

$$a \cdot x + b \cdot x = (a + b) \cdot x.$$

These two situations illustrate an important property connecting multiplication and addition.

The Distributive Property of Multiplication over Addition:

For any numbers a, b, and x: $ax + bx = (a + b)x$.

Example 1 Simplify $2m + 5m$.

Solution
Think: The cost of 2 roses + the cost of 5 roses
Write: $2m + 5m = (2 + 5)m = 7m$

Check Substitute some number for m, say 4.
Does $2 \cdot 4 + 5 \cdot 4 = 7 \cdot 4$? Remember to follow order of operations.
$$8 + 20 = 28, \text{ so the answer checks.}$$

Example 2 Simplify $4y - 3y$.

Solution Think: The cost of 4 roses minus the cost of 3 roses is the cost of one rose.
Putting in all steps, we write:
$$4y - 3y = 4y + \text{-}3y$$
$$= (4 + \text{-}3)y$$
$$= 1y$$
$$= y$$

There are too many steps in Example 2. It's easier to use a general property.

The Distributive Property of Multiplication over Subtraction:

For any numbers a, b, and x: $ax - bx = (a - b)x$.

LESSON 12-1 The Distributive Property 533

1. Use a diagram of rectangle areas to illustrate $ax + bx = (a + b)x$.
Begin with two rectangles.

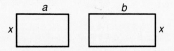

Sum of areas is $ax + bx$.
Put the rectangles together.

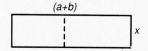

The total area is $(a + b)x$.

2. Simplify and check.
a. $5a + 2.4a$
$7.4a$; let $a = 3$: $5 \cdot 3 + 2.4 \cdot 3$
$= 15 + 7.2 = 22.2 = 7.4 \cdot 3$
b. $5a - 2.4a$
$2.6a$; let $a = 4$: $5 \cdot 4 - 2.4 \cdot 4$
$= 20 - 9.6 = 10.4 = 2.6 \cdot 4$
c. $6b - 4b + 8 - 2$
$2b + 6$; let $b = 2$:
$6 \cdot 2 - 4 \cdot 2 + 8 - 2 =$
$12 - 8 + 8 - 2 = 10$, and
$2 \cdot 2 + 6 = 4 + 6 = 10$

Example 3 Simplify $43.7x + 2x - 19.8x$.

Solution
$$43.7x + 2x - 19.8x$$
$$= (43.7 + 2)x - 19.8x$$
$$= 45.7x - 19.8x$$
$$= (45.7 - 19.8)x$$
$$= 25.9x$$

Check Again, substitute some number for *x*, say 10. You should find that $43.7 \cdot 10 + 2 \cdot 10 - 19.8 \cdot 10 = 25.9 \cdot 10$.

The name *distributive property* comes from the fact that the final multiplication (in Example 3, it is $25.9x$) was *distributed over* additions or subtractions. The names of these two properties are long, so we call them each just the **Distributive Property,** or even shorter, **distributivity.**

Example 4 Simplify $2t + 3t + 7$.

Solution Using distributivity,
$$2t + 3t + 7$$
$$= \quad 5t + 7$$

This cannot be simplified any more. Think of adding 7 dollars to the cost of 5 roses. There is no number being distributed over the additions.

You could think of Example 4 as coming from the cost of 2 roses at *t* dollars each, 3 more at *t* dollars each, and 7 dollars for a vase. The total is 5 roses at *t* dollars each plus the cost of the vase.

Questions

Covering the Reading

1. **a.** The cost of 21 roses equals the cost of 10 roses plus __?__.
   b. $21 \cdot 3.75 = 10 \cdot 3.75 + $ __?__. $10 \cdot 3.75 + 1 \cdot 3.75$
   c. $21x = 10x + $ __?__. $10x + x$
   a. the cost of 10 roses plus the cost of 1 rose
2. **a.** What is the total area of these rectangles? $70w$

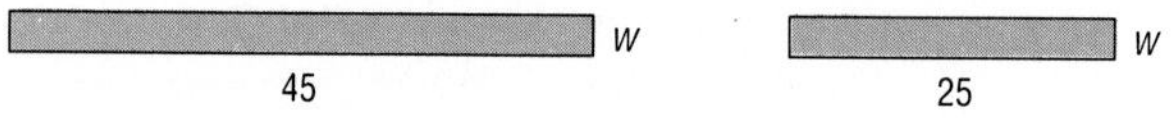

45 · *w*	25 · *w*

   b. How can you check your answer to part **a**?
   Substitute a number for *w*.

534

3. Draw a picture with rectangles to show that $3x + 5x = (3 + 5)x$.
See margin.

4. The equality of Question 3 is an instance of what property?
Distributive Property of Multiplication over Addition

5. Fred believes that $6m - m = 5m$. Nell believes that $6m - m = 6$. Who is correct and how can you tell? See margin.

In 6–13, simplify.

6. $3x + 5x$ 8x

7. $4y + 6y + 8$ 10y + 8

8. $2.4v + 3.5v + v$ 6.9v

9. $4b + 6b + 8$ 10b + 8

10. $v + v$ 2v

11. $9m - 7m + 3m$ 5m

12. $t + 6.34t - 2.12t$ 5.22t   **13.** $60h + 40 - 30h$ 30h + 40

14. Give an instance of the Distributive Property of Multiplication over Subtraction.   Sample: $15x - 3x = (15 - 3)x$

Applying the Mathematics

15. A hamburger costs x cents. Dave bought 3 hamburgers. Sue bought 2. How much did they spend altogether?
3x + 2x, or 5x cents

In 16 and 17, work mentally to simplify.

16. $994 \cdot 68 + 6 \cdot 68$ 68,000   **17.** $12 \cdot \$3.75 - 2 \cdot \$3.75$ $37.50

18. Suppose you buy 4 tapes at $7.99 each. You can figure out $7.99 \cdot 4$ by first multiplying $8 by 4 and then doing what?
subtracting $.01 · 4 or 4 cents

19. I don't know how many bushels of corn an acre of land will yield. So I'll call it B. Liz has 40 acres planted. Orville planted 15.5 acres. Nancy planted 24 acres. How many bushels of corn can the three expect to harvest altogether?   40B + 15.5B + 24B or 79.5B

20. Solve for x.
$2x + 3x = 600$ 120

21. Solve for y.
$7y - y = 12.6$ 2.1

22. a. On a calculator, how many presses of *operation* keys are needed to evaluate $ax + bx$?   3
b. How many presses of operation keys are needed to evaluate $(a + b)x$?   2
c. Which of these expressions would be more quickly evaluated by a computer?   (a + b)x

LESSON 12-1   The Distributive Property   **535**

ADDITIONAL ANSWERS
3.

The total area of the rectangles is $3x + 5x$. Put them together and the area is $(3+5)x$.

5. Fred is correct; $6m - m = 6 \cdot m - 1 \cdot m = (6 - 1)m = 5m$. You can check by substitution.

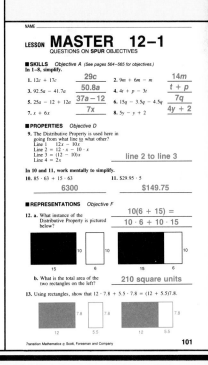

23. Try two special cases to check whether or not $a(b + c) = ab + ac$. *(Lesson 6-6)*
   Samples: $3(4 + 5) = 3 \cdot 4 + 3 \cdot 5$; $-2(8 + -8) = -2 \cdot 8 + -2 \cdot -8$

24. What is the measure of a supplement to an angle with a measure of 55°? *(Lesson 7-7)*   **125°**

25. a. Dividing by 3 is the same as multiplying by __?__. $\frac{1}{3}$
   b. Divide $\frac{12}{5}$ by 3. *(Lessons 9-8, 11-2)* $\frac{4}{5}$

26. $AB = 40$ and $BC = 25$. **a.** Draw a picture. **b.** What are the smallest and largest possible values of AC? *(Lessons 6-3, 6-6)*
   a. See margin. b. smallest 15, largest 65

In 27 and 28, rewrite in lowest terms. *(Lesson 1-10)*

27. $\frac{16}{56}$ $\frac{2}{7}$ **28.** $\frac{105}{235}$ $\frac{21}{47}$

29. Find a fraction equal to $\frac{3.14}{4}$ with whole numbers in its numerator and denominator. *(Lesson 2-7)*   In lowest terms: $\frac{157}{200}$

30. On the first page of this lesson, the Distributive Property of Multiplication over *Addition* was pictured by using areas of rectangles. Picture $35 \cdot 80 - 23 \cdot 80 = 12 \cdot 80$, an instance of the Distributive Property of Multiplication over *Subtraction*, by using rectangles.   See margin.

Decimals either stop or go on forever. Those that stop are called *terminating* or **finite decimals.**

$$2.3 \qquad 5.04 \qquad -0.00002187 \qquad 7890 \qquad 636.2$$

Recall that those that go on forever are called *infinite decimals*. Some infinite decimals repeat. Here are three examples of infinite repeating decimals.

$$0.\overline{142857} \qquad \text{(the entire decimal part repeats)}$$
$$0.5\overline{148} \qquad \text{(only the 148 repeats)}$$
$$34.\overline{54} \qquad \text{(only the 54 repeats)}$$

Every repeating decimal equals a simple fraction. You may remember that $0.\overline{142857}$ equals $\frac{1}{7}$. But how could you know that $0.5\overline{148} = \frac{139}{270}$? The way to find these fractions uses the Distributive Property in a surprising way.

■ ■ ■ ■ ■ ■ ■ ■ ■

Example 1 Find a simple fraction that equals $0.5\overline{148}$.

Solution
Step 1: Let $x = 0.5\overline{148}$. Write x with a few repetitions of the repetend.

$$x = 0.5148148148...$$

Step 2: The repetend has 3 digits, so multiply x by 1000. This moves the decimal point 3 digits to the right.

$$1000x = 514.8148148148...$$

Step 3: Rewrite $1000x$ with the repetend bar, starting the bar as in x. Subtract.

$$1000x - x = 514.8\overline{148} - 0.5\overline{148}$$

Step 4: Use the Distributive Property on the left. Subtract on the right.

$$(1000 - 1)x = 514.8\overline{148} - 0.5\overline{148}$$
$$999x = 514.3$$

Step 5: Solve the equation.

$$x = \frac{514.3}{999} = \frac{5143}{9990}$$

Dividing numerator and denominator by 37, this fraction equals $\frac{139}{270}$. Therefore,

$$0.5\overline{148} = \frac{139}{270}$$

Check Convert $\frac{139}{270}$ to a decimal using your calculator. It equals $0.5\overline{148}$.

LESSON 12-2 *Fractions for Repeating Decimals* **537**

LESSON 12-2

RESOURCES
■ Lesson Master 12-2
▣ Computer Master 24

OBJECTIVE

B Convert repeating decimals to fractions.

TEACHING NOTES

Because a number can be represented as a fraction in many ways, it is useful to identify the goal clearly: to represent a number as a *simple fraction*—that is, one with integers in the numerator and the denominator.

Because the process is not easy for some students, carefully go through the steps in **Examples 1-3.** Each one involves a repetend with a different number of digits. You may wish to present the general algorithm:

Step 1: Let x (or another variable) represent the repeating decimal. Write x with a few repetitions of the repetend.

Step 2: Determine the length of the repetend. Use that number as the power of 10 by which to multiply both sides of the equation. (Multiply by 10 for a single digit repetend, by 100 for a double digit repetend, and so on.)

Step 3: Subtract one equation (Step 1) from the other (Step 2).

Step 4: Simplify, using the Distributive Property.

Step 5: Solve for x. If necessary, rewrite the solution as a simple fraction.

Step 6: Check by division.

Example 2 Find a simple fraction equal to $5.0\overline{3}$.

Solution

Step 1: Let $\qquad x = 5.033333333...$

Step 2: The repetend has 1 digit, so multiply x by 10. This moves the decimal point one digit to the right.

$$10x = 50.33333333...$$

Step 3: Subtract. $10x - x = 50.3\overline{3} - 5.0\overline{3}$

Step 4: Simplify. $\qquad 9x = 45.3$

Step 5: Solve. $\qquad x = \dfrac{45.3}{9} = \dfrac{453}{90} = \dfrac{151}{30}$

Example 3 Cleo had just done a division on her calculator when she was distracted. When she returned to her work she realized she had forgotten which numbers she had divided! The display on the calculator read 187.54545.

What numbers might she have divided?

Solution The display is probably a rounding of the repeating decimal $187.\overline{54}$. To find out, use the method of this lesson.

Step 1: Let $\qquad x = 187.\overline{54}$

Step 2: Multiply by 100. $\qquad 100x = 18754.\overline{54}$

Step 3: Subtract. $\qquad 100x - x = 18754.\overline{54} - 187.\overline{54}$

Step 4: Simplify. $\qquad 99x = 18567$

Step 5: Solve. $\qquad x = \dfrac{18567}{99} = \dfrac{2063}{11}$

So Cleo may have divided 2063 by 11. Or, she divided any two numbers which make a fraction equal to 2063/11.

Check $2063 \boxed{\div} 11 \boxed{=}$ 187.54545

538

Questions

Covering the Reading

In 1–4, classify the decimal as repeating, terminating, or cannot tell.

1. 3.04444   *terminating*   **2.** 3.0$\overline{4}$ *repeating*

3. 3.040404…   *cannot tell*   **4.** 3.$\overline{04}$ *repeating*

5. Which of the decimals in Questions 1–4 are finite, which infinite?
   3.04444 is finite, the rest are infinite.

6. **a.** If $x = 0.\overline{24}$, then $100x = $? $24.\overline{24}$
   b. Find a simple fraction equal to $0.\overline{24}$. $\frac{24}{99}$ or $\frac{8}{33}$

7. Find a simple fraction equal to $5.\overline{24}$. $\frac{519}{99}$ or $\frac{173}{33}$

8. Name two numbers other than 2063 and 11 which could have
   given Cleo's calculator display in Example 3.
   Sample: 4126 and 22

Applying the Mathematics

9. Find a simple fraction equal to $0.\overline{810}$. $\frac{810}{999}$ or $\frac{30}{37}$

10. A hat contains less than 10 marbles. Some marbles are green and
    the rest are yellow. Without looking you are to reach into the hat
    and pull out a marble. You are told that the probability of getting
    a green marble is $0.\overline{2}$.
    a. Rewrite the probability of getting a green marble as a simple
    fraction. $\frac{2}{9}$
    b. Use your answer to part **a** to tell how many marbles are in the
    hat.   9
    c. How many of the marbles are green?   2

11. Convert $3.0\overline{405}$ to a fraction. $\frac{30,101}{9900}$

In 12 and 13, refer to this calculator display: `58.833333`

12. If the 3 repeats forever, name a division problem which would
    give this display.   *Sample: 353 ÷ 6*

13. If this display is the entire decimal, name a division problem
    which could have given it.   *Sample: 58,833,333/1,000,000*

14. Use the method of this section to show that $1 = 0.\overline{9}$.   *See margin.*

15. Write $99.\overline{4}\%$ as a simple fraction. $\frac{895}{900}$ or $\frac{179}{180}$

LESSON 12-2   Fractions for Repeating Decimals   **539**

NOTES ON QUESTIONS
Question 7: It is easier to add 5 to the answer to **Question 6** than to work from scratch.

Question 11: It may be easier to consider only the decimal part first and add the whole number 3 after finding the fraction.

Error Analysis for Question 15: Some students may forget the % and obtain $\frac{895}{9}$. Multiplying by $\frac{1}{100}$ leads to the correct answer.

ADDITIONAL ANSWERS
14.   Let $x = 0.\overline{9}$
       $10x = 9.\overline{9}$
       $10x - x = 9.\overline{9} - 0.\overline{9}$
       $9x = 9$
       $x = 1$
       So $x = 0.\overline{9} = 1$.

FOLLOW-UP

MORE PRACTICE
For more questions on SPUR Objectives, use *Lesson Master 12-2*, shown on page 539.

EXTENSION
Write the following decimal/fraction relationships on the board, and ask if the students can see a pattern.

$0.\overline{1} = \frac{1}{9}$ $0.\overline{6} = \frac{6}{9} = \frac{2}{3}$

$0.\overline{01} = \frac{1}{99}$ $0.\overline{54} = \frac{54}{99} = \frac{6}{11}$

$0.\overline{001} = \frac{1}{999}$ $0.\overline{203} = \frac{203}{999}$

(In each case, the repetend immediately follows the decimal point. The repetend becomes the numerator of the fraction; the denominator is 9, 99, 999, and so on, depending on the number of digits in the repetend.) Ask the students why this pattern works. (The final coefficient of x in the procedure to convert to fractions is 9, 99, 999, and so on. See **Example 3**.) Have the students use the pattern to convert additional decimals to simple fractions:
$.\overline{8}$ $\left(\frac{8}{9}\right)$, $.\overline{09}$ $\left(\frac{9}{99} = \frac{1}{11}\right)$, $.\overline{12}$ $\left(\frac{12}{99} = \frac{4}{33}\right)$, $.\overline{291}$ $\left(\frac{291}{999} = \frac{97}{333}\right)$, $.\overline{500}$ $\left(\frac{500}{999}\right)$, $.\overline{9009}$ $\left(\frac{9009}{9999} = \frac{91}{101}\right)$.

22.

Review

16. Simplify: $4x + 3y + 2x + y + 0x + -1y$. *(Lessons 10-7, 12-1)*
$6x + 3y$

17. Solve $10x - 1 = 30$. *(Lesson 10-9)*   3.1

18. To the nearest hundred, how many feet are in a mile?
(Lessons 3-2, 1-4)   **5300 feet**

In 19 and 20, use this drawing.

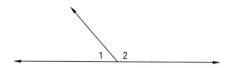

19. If the measure of angle 1 is $48\frac{2}{5}°$, what is the measure of angle 2?
(Lessons 5-5, 7-7) $131\frac{3}{5}°$

20. If angle 1 has measure x and angle 2 has measure $2x$, what is the value of x? *(Lessons 7-8, 12-1)*   **60°**

In 21 and 22, use the figure below.

21. How many lines of symmetry does the figure have? *(Lesson 8-7)*
none

22. Trace the figure and draw a tessellation using it as the fundamental region. *(Lesson 8-8)*   **See margin.**

Exploration

23. What fraction with 1 in its numerator and a two-digit integer in its denominator equals $0.\overline{012345679}$? $\frac{1}{81}$

24. a. What decimal is the sum of $0.\overline{12}$ and $0.\overline{345}$? $0.\overline{466557}$
   b. What simple fraction is the sum? $\frac{5127}{10,989} = \frac{1709}{3663}$

LESSON 12-3

Situations Leading to Linear Expressions

Finding the total cost of a store's stock is a situation leading to a linear expression.

An ounce of hamburger has about 80 calories. If you eat h ounces, you will take in about $80h$ calories. Here is the rate factor multiplication.

$$h \text{ ounces} \cdot 80 \, \frac{\text{calories}}{\text{ounce}} = 80h \text{ calories}$$

Now suppose you eat f french fries. Recall that a typical french fry may have about 11 calories. Using rate factor multiplication, you will take in about $11f$ calories. The total from the f french fries and h ounces of hamburger is

$$80h + 11f \text{ calories}.$$

The expression $80h + 11f$ involves four different numbers. Unlike $80h + 11h$, $80h + 11f$ *cannot be simplified* using the Distributive Property.

You can think of $80h$ as a multiple of h, and $11f$ as a multiple of f. Then $80h + 11f$ is a sum of multiples of different numbers. The expression $80h + 11f$ is a *linear expression*. A **linear expression** is one in which variables, numbers, or multiples of variables are added or subtracted. $3x - 5$ is a linear expression, but $8xy$ and $5t^2$ are not. Linear expressions arise from many everyday situations.

▪ ▪ ▪ ▪ ▪ ▪ ▪ ■

Example 1 A shoe store owner buys 120 pair of shoes at $11 a pair and 80 pair at $15/pair. What is the total cost to the owner?

Solution The total cost is

$$120 \text{ pair} \cdot 11 \, \frac{\text{dollars}}{\text{pair}} + 80 \text{ pair} \cdot 15 \, \frac{\text{dollars}}{\text{pair}}$$
$$= \quad \$1320 \quad + \quad \$1200$$
$$= \quad \$2520$$

LESSON 12-3 *Situations Leading to Linear Expressions*   **541**

LESSON 12-3

RESOURCES
■ Lesson Master 12-3
■ Quiz on Lessons 12-1 Through 12-3
▣ Visual for Teaching Aid 49: Use the graph paper with **Question 24.**

OBJECTIVES

A Simplify linear expressions when possible, using distributivity.
E Translate real situations involving multiplication, addition, and subtraction into linear expressions.

TEACHING NOTES

After the students have read the lesson, ask for examples of linear expressions. Point out that linear expressions do not include expresions such as $3xy + 2$, where variables are multiplied, or $4t^2$, where variables are raised to a power other than 1. Have students give the *terms* and *coefficients* in each example. Then ask for expressions with two like terms, three like terms, two unlike terms, and so on. Once the terminology is clear, check that students can write and simplify linear combinations as in **Examples 3** and **4** or examples you or the students make up. Note that in **Examples 3** and **4** we ask students to think of all terms as being added.

1. How many terms are in each expression?
a. $4 - 3b + \frac{c}{7}$
3
b. $10 + 2.5 - 8 + 2 + 3$
5

2. Name the coefficients in each expression.
a. $2x - 5y$
2, –5
b. $4t + r$
4, 1

3. Simplify as much as you can.
a. $4n + 6 - 8n$
–4n + 6, or 6 – 4n
b. $9r + 8s + 7s - 6r$
3r + 15s
c. $10k - 3$
already simplified
d. $2.5f + 3g - g + 1.5f - 4$
4f + 2g – 4

4. Card games provide the entertainment at a party. To play bridge, four people are required. Three people play each game of hearts. If there are three bridge games and five hearts games, how many people are at the party?
3 bridge games · $\frac{4 \text{ people}}{\text{bridge game}}$
+ 5 hearts · $\frac{3 \text{ people}}{\text{hearts}}$
= 12 people + 15 people
= 27 people
b. If there are b bridge games and h hearts games, how many people are at the party?
4b + 3h

Often you know how many things you want but you do not know the price. Then the arithmetic in Example 1 becomes the algebra of Example 2.

Example 2   A store owner buys 120 pair of shoes at x dollars a pair and 80 pair at y dollars a pair. What is the total cost to the store owner?

Solution   The total cost is now

$$120 \text{ pair} \cdot x \frac{\text{dollars}}{\text{pair}} + 80 \text{ pair} \cdot y \frac{\text{dollars}}{\text{pair}}$$
$$= \qquad \$120x \qquad + \qquad \$80y$$

The expression $120x + 80y$ cannot be simplified.

In the linear expression $120x + 80y$, $120x$ and $80y$ are called **terms**. Terms are numbers or expressions that are added or subtracted. The number 120 is called the **coefficient** of x. The number 80 is the coefficient of y.

The linear expression $6A + 4B - 5A$ has three terms. The terms $6A$ and $5A$ (or -5A, if you like to think of addition) are called **like terms** because they involve the same variable. $6A$ and $4B$ are called **unlike terms.** Like terms can be simplified using the Distributive Property. Unlike terms cannot be simplified.

Example 3   Name the coefficients of w, x, y, and z in $4w - 3x + y - z$.

Solution   In naming coefficients, think of all terms as being added. For instance, instead of subtracting $3x$, think of adding $-3x$. The expression becomes $4w + -3x + y + -z$. The coefficient of w is 4 and the coefficient of x is -3. Since $y = 1 \cdot y$, the coefficient of y is 1. Since $-z = -1 \cdot z$, the coefficient of z is -1.

Example 4   Simplify $3x + 2y - 5x + 6y + 40$.

Solution   Because there are some like terms, you can simplify. First, change subtractions mentally to adding the opposite $(3x + 2y + -5x + 6y + 40)$. Then reorder to have the like terms next to each other.

$$= 3x + -5x + 2y + 6y + 40$$
$$= (3 + -5)x + (2 + 6)y + 40$$
$$= \qquad -2x \quad + \quad 8y \quad + 40$$

Check Substitute one number for x and a different number for y in the original expression. We use $x = 7$ and $y = 8$. Then the value of the original expression is

$$3 \cdot 7 + 2 \cdot 8 - 5 \cdot 7 + 6 \cdot 8 + 40$$
$$= 21 + 16 - 35 + 48 + 40$$
$$= 90.$$

The value of the answer $(-2x + 8y + 40)$ is $-2 \cdot 7 + 8 \cdot 8 + 40$, which is $-14 + 64 + 40$, which is 90. The two values are the same, so the answer checks.

NOTES ON QUESTIONS
Questions 6-13: It is not necessary for students to write out the steps. They should realize that the Distributive Property justifies what is being done.

Questions

Covering the Reading

1. Steve went to the graduating class bake sale. He bought 5 cookies for 20¢ each and 4 brownies at 30¢ each. How much did he spend? **$2.20**

2. Ashley went to the same bake sale as Steve in Question 1. But she did not know how many she wanted. What would it cost her for c cookies and b brownies? **20c + 30b cents**

3. Give an example of a linear expression using m and n.
   Sample: 2m + 3n

4. Consider the expression $4r + 3s$.
   a. What is the coefficient of r? **4**
   b. What is the coefficient of s? **3**
   c. Simplify the expression. **It is already simplified.**

5. Consider the expression $5t - 4m + 2t + q$.
   a. How many terms are in this expression? **4**
   b. Name two like terms. **5t and 2t**
   c. Name two unlike terms. **Sample: -4m and q**
   d. What is the coefficient of m? **-4**
   e. What is the coefficient of q? **1**
   f. Simplify the expression. **7t - 4m + q**

In 6–9, simplify as much as you can. Check your answer.

6. $12a + 5a + 3b$
   17a + 3b

7. $-4x - y + y - 2$
   -4x - 2

8. $3t - 3a - a - t$
   2t - 4a

9. $-6 + 4v - 6 + -4v + v$
   v - 12

In 10–13, simplify if possible.

10. $3t + 6u + 9v$
    already simplified

11. $3t - 6t + 9$
    -3t + 9

12. $3 - 6t + 9$
    -6t + 12

13. $3t + 6u - 9u - 12t$
    -3u - 9t

Applying the Mathematics

14. A decagon has six sides of length L and all other sides of length M. What is its perimeter? **6L + 4M**

LESSON 12-3 Situations Leading to Linear Expressions **543**

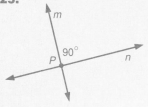

15. Use the information from this lesson. A hamburger bun has about 200 calories.
    a. If a person eats 4 oz of hamburger, a bun, and 20 french fries, how many calories will have been taken in?   **740 calories**
    b. If a person eats 4 oz of hamburger, a bun, and f french fries, how many calories will have been consumed?   **520 + 11f calories**

16. At many schools, a grade of C is worth 2 points, B is worth 3 points, and A 4 points.
    a. If you have 6 courses with Cs, 8 with Bs, and 5 with As, how many total points do you have?   **56 points**
    b. If you have c courses with Cs, b with Bs, and a with As, how many total points do you have?   **2c + 3b + 4a points**

17. Give the value of $3x + 4y$ to the nearest integer when $x = 1/2$ and $y = 1/3$.   **3**

18. Simplify: $(a + 2b) + (3a + 4b) + (5a + 6b)$.   **9$a$ + 12b**

19. Simplify: $(3a + 5a)x$.   **8ax**

Review

20. Solve $14x = \frac{2}{7}$. *(Lesson 10-2)* $\frac{1}{49}$

21. Write $0.2\overline{3}$ as a simple fraction. *(Lesson 12-2)* $\frac{7}{30}$

22. Add $\frac{a}{2} + \frac{b}{2}$. *(Lesson 5-2)* $\frac{a + b}{2}$

23. The box pictured below is open at the top. Find its surface area and volume. *(Lessons 9-2, 9-3)*   **surface area 13 ft², volume 3 ft³**

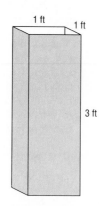

1 ft   1 ft

3 ft

24. Graph all solutions to $x + y = 7$. *(Lesson 8-3)*
    a line passing through (1, 6), (5, 2), (-3, 10)
25. A line m is perpendicular to the line n drawn here. Line m also contains point P. Trace n and P and draw m. *(Lesson 3-6)*
    See margin.

P n

544

26. Translate into mathematics:
   a. six less than a number *(Lesson 4-3)* $n - 6$
   b. Six is less than a number. *(Lesson 4-9)* $6 < n$

27. List the prime numbers between 60 and 70. *(Lesson 6-2)*   61, 67

28. Trace the triangle and draw part of a tessellation using your tracing as the fundamental region. *(Lesson 8-8)*   See margin.

29. Work mentally to simplify: $10.2 \cdot 4 - 0.2 \cdot 4$. *(Lesson 12-1)*   40

30. R is on $\overline{QS}$. If $QR = x$ and $RS = y$, what is QS in terms of x and y? *(Lesson 5-10)* $x + y$

Q   R   S

Exploration

31. Josie is building a staircase out of cubes for a doll house. The first three steps are pictured here. Each cube is 2.5 cm high. How many cubes will she need for a staircase that is 25 cm high?
   110 cubes

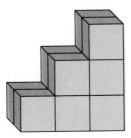

FOLLOW-UP

MORE PRACTICE
For more questions on SPUR Objectives, use *Lesson Master 12-3*, shown below.

EXTENSION
You could extend **Question 31.** Ask the students to look for shortcuts for other arithmetic series.
1. $1 + 2 + 3 + ... + 100$ (5050)
2. $5 + 10 + 15 + ... + 95 + 100$ (1050)
3. $10 + 20 + 30 + ... + 990 + 1000$ (50,500)
4. $1 + 2 + 3 + 4 + ... + n$ $\left(\frac{n}{2} \cdot (n + 1)\right)$

EVALUATION
A quiz covering Lessons 12-1 through 12-3 is provided in the Teacher's Resource File on page 104.

NAME _____

LESSON MASTER 12–3
Questions on **SPUR** Objectives

■ **SKILLS**   *Objective A (See pages 564–565 for objectives.)*
In 1–4, consider the following expression:
$$-6a + 2t - 7a + 9y.$$

1. How many terms are there?	4
2. Name two like terms.	$-6a, -7a$
3. Name the coefficients.	$-6a, -7a$
4. Simplify the expression.	$-13a + 2t + 9y$

In 5–10, simplify where possible. Otherwise write "already simplified."

5. $19t + 4y - 5t + 8$	$14t + 4y + 8$
6. $9a + 2b - 6c$	already simplified
7. $6y + 6 + y$	$7y + 6$
8. $-4.6x + 3y - 3.4x - 3y$	$-8x$
9. $9t - t - 12t$	$-4t$
10. $\frac{7}{8}n - \frac{3}{4}n + 4p$	$\frac{1}{8}n + 4p$

■ **USES**   *Objective E*

11. Allison's checking account charges were $3.00 per month plus $0.15 per check. If Allison wrote c checks in January, what was her charge for the month?	$.15c + 3.00$
12. A hexagon has 2 sides each of length L. The other sides are each A units long. What is the perimeter of the hexagon?	$2L + 4A$
13. Jonathan bought x pairs of shoes at $15.99 each and y shirts at $22 each. What is his total purchase before tax?	$15.99x + 22y$
14. C cars hold 4 passengers each and V vans hold 7 passengers each. How many passengers can be driven in all?	$4C + 7V$

Transition Mathematics © Scott, Foresman and Company

103

LESSON 12-4

More on the Distributive Property

Here are two rectangles with the same width but different lengths. What is the total area? Recall that there are two ways to solve this problem.

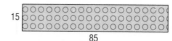

One way is to find the areas of the rectangles and add them.

$$\text{Total area} = 15 \cdot 85 + 15 \cdot 20$$

Another way to find the total area is to join the rectangles together.

$$\text{Total area} = 15(85 + 20)$$

This demonstrates that $15(85 + 20) = 15 \cdot 85 + 15 \cdot 20$. The multiplication of 15 times $85 + 20$ has been distributed over the addition. First 15 times 85, then 15 times 20. You can always put two rectangles with the same width together. The general pattern is another form of the Distributive Property of Multiplication over Addition.

Distributive Property of Multiplication over Addition (Alternate Form):

For any numbers x, a, and b: $x(a + b) = xa + xb$.

546

Example 1 Apply the Distributive Property to $3(v + 2)$.

Solution $3(v + 2) = 3 \cdot v + 3 \cdot 2$
$= 3v + 6$

Check Substitute some number for v. We substitute 5.
Then $3(v + 2) = 3(5 + 2) = 3 \cdot 7 = 21$.
Also, $3v + 6 = 3 \cdot 5 + 6 = 15 + 6 = 21$. The answer checks.

Example 2 A store owner bought 18 blouses for $10.50 each.
Mentally calculate the total cost to the store owner.

Solution Split the 10.50 into 10 and 0.50. Think of 0.50 as $\frac{1}{2}$.
Here are the mental steps.

$$18 \cdot 10.50 = 18(10 + 0.5)$$
$$= 18\left(10 + \frac{1}{2}\right)$$
$$= 18 \cdot 10 + 18 \cdot \frac{1}{2}$$
$$= \quad 180 \quad + \quad 9$$
$$= \qquad 189$$

It cost the store owner $189.

You met the Distributive Property in Lesson 12-1. At that time,
we wrote it as $ax + bx = (a + b)x$.
Now we are writing it as $x(a + b) = xa + xb$.
The only difference is that the multiplier x is on the left instead
of the right. The same answer results because multiplication is
commutative.

You have seen the Distributive Property of Multiplication over
Subtraction.
Before it was written as $ax - bx = (a - b)x$.
An alternative form is $x(a - b) = xa - xb$.

Example 3 Multiply 7 by 3.98 in your head.

Solution
First think of 3.98 as $4 - 0.02$. $\qquad 7 \cdot 3.98 = 7(4 - 0.02)$

Now apply the Distributive Property. $\qquad = 7 \cdot 4 - 7 \cdot 0.02$

These multiplications can be done mentally. $\quad = 28 - 0.14$

Think of taking 14¢ from 28 dollars. $\qquad = 27.86$

LESSON 12-4 More on the Distributive Property **547**

ADDITIONAL EXAMPLES
Rewrite the problem using
the Distributive Property so
that the calculation can be
done in your head. Then
solve the problem mentally.
1. $5 \cdot 4\frac{1}{2}$
$5(4 + \frac{1}{2})$, $22\frac{1}{2}$

2. $12 \cdot 6.02$
$12(6 + .02)$, 72.24

Multiply.
3. $7(a + b)$
$7a + 7b$

4. $\frac{1}{2}(12 + 6f - 9g)$
$6 + 3f - 4.5g$

5. $-5(3p - 4)$
$-15p + 20$

The distributive properties over addition and subtraction can be combined.

Example 4 Multiply $3(5x + y - 8)$.

Solution
Use the Distributive Property.

$$3(5x + y - 8)$$
$$= 3 \cdot (5x) + 3 \cdot y - 3 \cdot 8$$
$$= \quad 15x \quad + \quad 3y \quad - \quad 24$$

Check Substitute a different number for each variable. We use $x = 2$ and $y = 4$. The values for the given expression and the answer should be the same.

$$3(5x + y - 8) = 3(5 \cdot 2 + 4 - 8) = 3(10 + 4 - 8) = 3(6) = 18$$

$$15x + 3y - 24 = 15 \cdot 2 + 3 \cdot 4 - 24 = 30 + 12 - 24 = 18$$

Since we got the same value, the answer checks.

Questions

Covering the Reading

1. Verify that $3.29(853 + 268) = 3.29 \cdot 853 + 3.29 \cdot 268$ using a calculator. Write down the key sequence you use and the final display.   See margin.

2. **a.** What is the name of the general pattern found in Question 1?
   b. Describe the pattern of Question 1 with variables.
   a. Dist. Prop. b. $x(a + b) = xa + xb$

In 3–6, multiply and check.   See margin for checks.

3. $50(x + 4)$ $50x + 200$ 4. $2(6 + 7n)$ $12 + 14n$

5. $a(b + 2c)$ $ab + 2ac$ 6. $5(100 + t + u)$ $500 + 5t + 5u$

In 7 and 8, show how you can apply the Distributive Property of Multiplication over Subtraction to find the total cost in your head.

7. You buy three sweaters at $29.95 each.
   $3 \cdot \$29.95 = 3(\$30 - 5¢) = 3 \cdot \$30 - 3 \cdot 5¢ = \$90 - 15¢ = \$89.85$

8. You purchase 8 tapes at $8.99 each.
   $8 \cdot \$8.99 = 8(\$9 - 1¢) = 8 \cdot \$9 - 8 \cdot 1¢ = \$72 - 8¢ = \$71.92$

In 9 and 10, simplify.

9. $a(b - c)$ $ab - ac$ 10. $4(a - 5b)$ $4a - 20b$

In 11 and 12, use the picture.

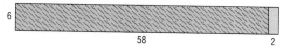

11. $6 \cdot 60 = 6 \cdot \underline{\ ?\ } + 6 \cdot \underline{\ ?\ }$
    58, 2

12. $6 \cdot 58 = 6 \cdot \underline{\ ?\ } - 6 \cdot \underline{\ ?\ }$
    60, 2

548

13. Multiply 732 by 999,999,999,999,999.   **731,999,999,999,999,268**

14. Betty bought three outfits. Each outfit consisted of a jacket costing $69.95, a skirt costing $40.75, and a blouse costing $15.50. How can she calculate the total cost with only one multiplication? What did she spend?   **3($69.95 + $40.75 + $15.50) = 3 · $126.20 = $378.60**

15. Phil, Gil, and Will each bought a turntable costing t dollars, an amplifier costing a dollars, and speakers costing s dollars. How much did they spend altogether?
    3($t + a + s$) or 3t + 3a + 3s dollars

16. Rosalie needs to paint three walls. Each wall is 8 feet high. The width of the first wall is 11 feet 3 inches. The width of the second wall is 7 feet 7 inches. The width of the third wall is 6 feet 2 inches. Altogether, how much area must be painted?
    200 square feet

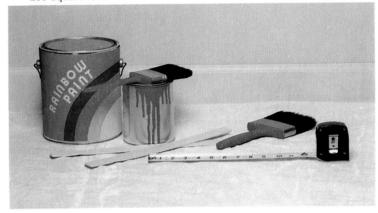

In 17 and 18, use the distributive property. Then simplify if possible.

17. $-2(3 + x) + 5(0.4x)$ **-6**

18. $\frac{1}{3}(3m + n) + \frac{1}{3}(3m - n)$ **2m**

19. $4x + 72 = 4(x + \underline{\ ?\ })$ **18**

20. $16x - 8y + 56 = 8(\underline{\ ?\ })$ **2x − y + 7**

21. Simplify $100m + 81m + 64$. *(Lesson 12-3)*   **181m + 64**

22. A pizza cost C dollars plus 50¢ for each additional ingredient. How much will a pizza with A additional ingredients cost?
    (Lessons 12-3, 6-5)   **C + .5A dollars**

In 23–26, name the quadrilateral. *(Lesson 7-9)*

23. It has all sides the same length and all angles the same measure.
    square

24. It has all sides the same length.   **rhombus**

25. All its angles are the same measure.   **rectangle**

26. It has two pairs of parallel sides.   **parallelogram**

LESSON 12-4   More on the Distributive Property   549

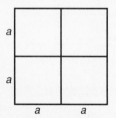
27. When Jean walks to school, she has two routes. She can either walk along roads or take a shortcut through a field. The choices are pictured below.

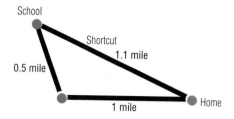

a. Walking along roads at 4 miles per hour, how long does it take her to get from home to school? *(Lesson 10-4)*   **22.5 minutes**
b. At this rate, how much time could she save by taking the shortcut? *(Lesson 7-3)*   **6 minutes**

28. A box with dimensions 20 cm, 15 cm, and 10 cm is filled with sand. 200 cubic centimeters of sand are removed.
a. What percent of the sand was removed? *(Lessons 9-3, 11-4)*
b. How much sand remains? *(Lesson 7-3)*
   a. about 6.7%; b. 2800 cm³

Exploration

29. Consider the pattern:

$1 - (2 - 3) = 2$
$1 - (2 - (3 - 4)) = -2$
$1 - (2 - (3 - (4 - 5))) = 3.$

Write the next two lines of this pattern.   **See margin.**

30. One way to express the area of this figure is $(a + b)(c + d)$. What is another expression for the area? $ac + ad + bc + bd$

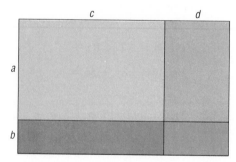

12-5

Solving
$ax + b = cx + d$

Finding Jamie's age is easy when you know how to solve an equation of the form $ax + b = cx + d$. See Example 3.

The Distributive Property can be applied to solve equations with the same variable on both sides.

Example 1   Solve $3x + 5 = 10x + 26$.

Solution   It takes only one step more to solve this equation than one of the form $ax + b = c$. That step is to add a quantity that will get rid of a variable on one side of the equation. Here we add $-10x$ to both sides. It will get rid of the variable on the right side.

$$-10x + 3x + 5 = -10x + 10x + 26$$

Simplify. $\quad -7x + 5 = 26$

Now add -5 to both sides. $\quad -7x + 5 + -5 = 26 + -5$

Simplify. $\quad -7x = 21$

Multiply both sides by $-\frac{1}{7}$. $\quad x = -3$

Check   Substitute -3 for x every place it occurs in the original equation. Does $3 \cdot -3 + 5 = 10 \cdot -3 + 26$? Yes, both sides equal -4.

The equation in Example 2 is not solved for L because there is an L on the right side. The method of Example 1 also works to solve equations of this type.

Example 2   Solve $L = 15 - 4L$.

Solution   First add $4L$ to both sides.
$$L + 4L = 15 - 4L + 4L$$
Simplify. $\quad 5L = 15$
Do in your head. $\quad L = 3$

Check   Does $3 = 15 - 4 \cdot 3$? Yes.

LESSON 12-5   Solving $ax + b = cx + d$ **551**

Do many examples in class together. The four lesson examples are a good start; each has a special point to make. **Example 1** sets the general pattern. **Example 2** has a coefficient of 1. **Example 3** translates a traditional word problem. **Example 4** requires the Distributive Property to solve the proportion.

Remind students that the check is also an integral part of the solution process.

Example 3   In 8 years, Benjamin's sister Jamie will be 3 times as old as she is now. How old is she now?

Solution   Let J = Jamie's age now. Then 8 years from now she will be $J + 8$.

So $$J + 8 = 3J$$

Solve this equation. First add $-J$ to both sides.
$$-J + J + 8 = -J + 3J$$
Simplify. $\qquad\qquad\qquad 8 = 2J$
Solve. $\qquad\qquad\qquad\quad 4 = J$

Benjamin's sister is 4 years old.

Check   If Jamie is 4 now, in 8 years she will be 12. That is 3 times her age now.

The next example combines a number of ideas from this and the last chapter.

Example 4   Solve: $$\frac{x - 2}{2} = \frac{x + 3}{4}.$$

Solution   First use the Means-Extremes Property.
$$4(x - 2) = 2(x + 3)$$

Now use the Distributive Property.
$$4x - 4 \cdot 2 = 2x + 2 \cdot 3$$
$$4x - 8 = 2x + 6$$

In this form the equation is easy to solve. Add $-2x$ to both sides.
$$-2x + 4x - 8 = -2x + 2x + 6$$
$$2x - 8 = 6$$

Add 8 to both sides and simplify.
$$2x = 14$$

Multiply both sides by $\frac{1}{2}$. $\qquad x = 7$

Check   Substitute. Does $\frac{7 - 2}{2} = \frac{7 + 3}{4}$?

Does $\qquad \frac{5}{2} = \frac{10}{4}$? Yes.

552

Questions

NOTES ON QUESTIONS
Question 9: Emphasize
the translation of the questions asked in **9a** and **9b**
into linear expressions. Many
students are surprised when
the question "When will they
be equal?" actually leads to
an equation to be solved.
You might extend the question and ask "When will more
money be paid in plan 1 than
in plan 2?" The result can be
found by solving an inequality. ($1000n + 200 > 750n +
250$)

Covering the reading

1. To solve $s = 18 - 35s$, first add __?__ to both sides. $35s$

2. **a.** To solve $3x + 2 = 9x + 5$, what could you add to both sides
   to get rid of the variable on one side of the equation? $-3x$ or $-9x$
   b. Solve the equation in part **a.** $-\frac{1}{2}$

3. In fourteen years Jamie's brother will be three times as old as he
   is now. How old is Jamie's brother?   7 years old

In 4–7, solve and check.   See margin for checks.

4. $4 - y = 6y - 8$ $y = \frac{12}{7}$ 5. $2(n - 4) = 3n$ $n = -8$

6. $\dfrac{t - 2}{4} = \dfrac{t - 6}{12}$ $t = 0$ 7. $0.6m + 5.4 = -1.3 + 2.6m$
   $m = 3.35$

Applying the Mathematics

8. Twice a number is 500 more than six times the
   number. What is the number? -125

9. Under rate plan 1 a new car costs $1000 down plus $200 per
   month. Under rate plan 2 the car costs $750 down and $250
   per month.
   a. Write an expression for the amount paid after n months under
   plan 1. $1000 + 200n$
   b. Write an expression for the amount paid after n months under
   plan 2. $750 + 250n$
   c. After how many months will the amount paid be the same for
   both plans?   5 months

In 10 and 11, solve and check.   See margin for checks.

10. $11p + 5(p - 1) = 9p - 12$ $p = -1$

11. $-n + 4 - 5n + 6 = 21 + 3n$ $n = -\frac{11}{9}$

12. In $\triangle PIN$, the measure of angle N is $4x + 36$. The measure of
    angle P is $10x$. If the measure of $\angle N$ equals the measure of $\angle P$,
    find the measures of all three angles in the triangle.
    $m\angle P = 60°$, $m\angle N = 60°$, $m\angle I = 60°$

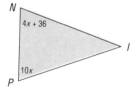

13. The formula for converting degrees Fahrenheit F to degrees
    Celsius C is $C = \frac{5}{9}(F - 32)$. Substitute an F for C in the formula
    and solve to find out what temperature reads the same in both
    systems. $-40°$

ADDITIONAL ANSWERS
4. Check:
Does $4 - \frac{12}{7} = 6 \cdot \frac{12}{7} - 8$?
Does $\frac{16}{7} = \frac{72}{7} - \frac{56}{7}$?
Yes, $\frac{16}{7} = \frac{16}{7}$

5. Check:
Does $2(-8 - 4) = 3 \cdot -8$?
Yes, $-24 = -24$.

6. Check: Does $\frac{0 - 2}{4} = \frac{0 - 6}{12}$?
Does $\frac{-2}{4} = \frac{-6}{12}$?
Yes, $-\frac{1}{2} = -\frac{1}{2}$.

7. Check:
Does $0.6 \cdot 3.35 + 5.4 = -1.3 + 2.6 \cdot 3.35$?
Yes, $7.41 = 7.41$.

10. Check: Does $11 \cdot -1 + 5(-1 - 1) = 9 \cdot -1 - 12$?
Does $-11 + 5 \cdot -2 = -9 - 12$?
Does $-11 + -10 = -21$?
Yes, $-21 = -21$.

11. Check: Does $-(-\frac{11}{9}) + 4 - 5(\frac{-11}{9}) + 6 = 21 + 3(\frac{-11}{9})$?
Does $10 + \frac{66}{9} = \frac{189}{9} - \frac{33}{9}$?
Yes, $\frac{156}{9} = \frac{156}{9}$.

553

14. Hasty Harry wrote the following solution to $5x - 1 = 2x + 8$. When he checked the answer, it didn't work.
   a. In which step did Harry make a mistake? Step 3
   b. What is the correct solution? 3

   Step 1: $-2x + 5x - 1 = -2x + 2x + 8$
   Step 2: $\qquad 3x - 1 = 0 + 8$
   Step 3: $\qquad\qquad 3x = 8 - 1$
   Step 4: $\qquad\qquad 3x = 7$
   Step 5: $\qquad\qquad\ x = \frac{7}{3}$

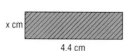
Review

15. Sixteen girls in the chorus each bought a blouse costing b dollars, a skirt costing s dollars, and a vest costing \$12. How much did they spend altogether? *(Lesson 12-4)*
   $16(b + s + 12)$ or $16b + 16s + 192$ dollars

16. What is the total area of these three rectangles? *(Lesson 12-1)*
   $9.1x$ cm²

In 17–19, rewrite as a simple fraction in lowest terms. *(Lessons 2-7, 12-2)*

17. 0.92 23/25   18. $4.\overline{3}$ 13/3   19. $6.\overline{36}$ 70/11

20. Draw a cube. *(Lesson 3-8)*   See margin.

21. Simplify: $1.3y + -4z - y - -2.7z + 8$. *(Lessons 7-2, 12-1)*
   $.3y - 1.3z + 8$

22. Graph all pairs of solutions to $x + y = 4$. *(Lesson 8-3)*
   Three points on the line: (2, 2), (-4, 8), (5, -1)

23. In 1988 there were approximately two million, one hundred sixty thousand farms in the United States. *(Lessons 1-1, 2-3)*
   a. Write this number as a decimal.   2,160,000
   b. Write this number in scientific notation. 2.16×10^6

24. Trace the figure below. What word results when the figure is reflected through the given line? *(Lesson 8-6)*   BOOK

25. In 1930 there were about 295% as many farms as in 1988 (refer back to Question 23). About how many farms were there in the U.S. in 1930? *(Lesson 2-6)* **6,372,000 farms**

Exploration

26. Paula wanted to solve $4x + 7 = 2x - 3$, but did not know the method of this lesson. She knew she wanted the value of the left side to equal the value of the right side. So she substituted a 2 for x to see what happened.

Left side	*Right side*
$4 \cdot 2 + 7 = 15$	$2 \cdot 2 - 3 = 1$

The left side was bigger than the right. Then Paula tried -10.

$$4 \cdot {-10} + 7 = -33 \qquad 2 \cdot {-10} - 3 = -23$$

Now the right side was bigger than the left. She figured that the solution must be some number between -10 and 2.
a. Find the value that makes the two sides of the equation equal.
b. Use Paula's method to solve $5x - 7 = 3x + 9$.
   a. -5; b. 8

FOLLOW-UP

MORE PRACTICE
For more questions on SPUR Objectives, use *Lesson Master 12-5*, shown below.

EVALUATION
Alternative Assessment
You may want to ask the students to solve the four equations below.

1. $3x - 2 = 7x - 4$
$(\frac{1}{2})$

2. $2(x - 2) = 12x + 1$
$(-\frac{1}{2})$

3. $2.4x + 3.8 = 6x - 3.4$
(2)

4. $\frac{x + 4}{8} = \frac{x + 6}{16}$
(-2)

NAME _____

LESSON MASTER 12-5
Questions on **SPUR** Objectives

■ **SKILLS** *Objective C (See pages 564–565 for objectives.)*
In 1–8, a. solve each equation. b. Check your answer.

1. $2y - 17 = 7y + 13$ $y = -6$

2. $35r - 75 = 24r + 24$ $r = 9$

3. $3a + 5 = -a$ $a = -\frac{5}{4}$

4. $m - 10 = -3m + 6 - 4m$ $m = 2$

5. $4w - 1 = 7(w + 2)$ $w = -5$

6. $5x + 2(1 - x) = 2(2x - 1)$ $x = 4$

7. $\frac{x - 4}{3} = \frac{2x}{2}$ $x = -2$

8. $\frac{16 - 2k}{6} = \frac{2k}{3}$ $k = -8$

■ **USES** *Objective E*

9. A twenty-one-year-old student teacher is 6 years younger than three times the average age of her students. What is the average age of the students?   **9 years old**

10. Six more than three times a number is 150 less than five times the number. What is the number?   **78**

11. In 3 years, Bernie will be 2.5 times as old as he is now. In 5 years, Bonnie will be 3 times as old as she is now.
a. Who is older at present, Bernie or Bonnie?   a. **Bonnie**
b. What is the difference in their current ages?   b. **6 months**

105

LESSON

12-6

Graphing Lines

The costs of mailing a first-class letter in 1990 are in the table below. At right, the pairs of numbers—the weight and cost—are graphed.

weight in ounces	cost in cents
1	25
2	45
3	65
4	85
5	105
6	125
7	145
8	165
9	185
10	205

Call the weight w and the cost c. The table shows a simple pattern connecting w and c. If you multiply w by 20 and add 5, you get c.

$$c = 20w + 5$$

You might say that it costs 5¢ to mail anything, and then add 20¢ for each ounce. For instance, suppose you want to mail some papers weighing 6.3 ounces. For the post office, the weight is 7 ounces. (Weights are rounded up to the next ounce.) So $w = 7$. Substituting in the formula:

$$c = 20 \cdot 7 + 5$$
$$c = 145.$$

This is in pennies. Dividing by 100 converts the pennies to dollars. The cost to mail these papers is $1.45. The table gives the same cost.

556

On page 556 are three ways to display postal rates: in a table, by a formula, and with a graph. The table is easiest to understand. The formula is shortest. The formula allows for values not in the table. Also, the formula can be used by a computer. The graph pictures the rates. It shows that they go up evenly. For a situation like this, the graph is not needed. But look at the graph below. The postal rates for 1965, 1975, and 1990 are compared. The picture displays the changes over time in a way that is easy to understand.

Postal rates
w = weight in ounces
c = cost in pennies

1965: $c = 5w$

1975: $c = 11w + 2$

1990: $c = 20w + 5$

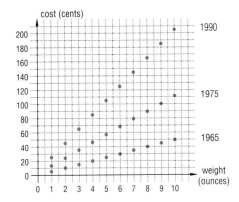

Each formula yields points on a line. The line $c = 5w$ is the lowest line. (The 1965 costs were lowest.)
The line $c = 11w + 2$ is in the middle.

In the equation for each line graphed above, w is multiplied by a number. This number indicates how fast the line goes up as you move one unit to the right. For instance, in $c = 11w + 2$, w is multiplied by 11. This causes the line to move up 11 units for every increase in w by one unit. This is because, in 1975, each additional ounce of weight increased the cost of mailing a letter by 11¢.

The equation $c = 11w + 2$ is a **linear equation.** The name *linear* arose because its graph is a line. On the next page is another example of a linear equation. Notice that you may have to solve equations to find points on the line.

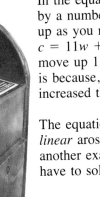

LESSON 12-6   Graphing Lines   557

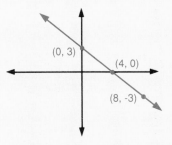

Using Manipulatives If the *Transition Mathematics Teacher Kit* is available, the coordinate grid and lines allow for the graphing of lines to be easily demonstrated on the overhead projector.

Small Group Work Have groups graph the equation $2x - 3y = 10$. Ask students to choose three pairs of numbers that fit the equation. Ask how many other ordered pairs could have been chosen (an infinite number).

ADDITIONAL EXAMPLES
1. Graph the line $3x + 4y = 12$ on graph paper.

Points shown on graph: $(0, 3)$, $(4, 0)$, $(8, -3)$

2. Name three points on the line with equation $x = 1 - 5y$.
samples: (1, 0), (2, –0.2), (–4, 1)

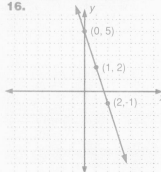
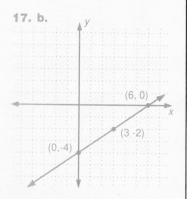
Example Graph the line with equation $2x - y = 8$.

Solution Pairs of values that work are needed.
When $x = 5$, then $2 \cdot 5 - y = 8$
Solve for y. $\qquad y = 2$
So (5, 2) is on the line.

When $x = 0$, then $2 \cdot 0 - y = 8$.
Solve for y. $\qquad y = -8$
So (0, -8) is on the line.

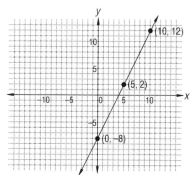

Graph of the line with equation $2x - y = 8$.

Two points determine the line. But find a third point to check.
When $x = 10$, $2 \cdot 10 - y = 8$.
Then $\qquad y = 12$.
So (10, 12) is on the line.

Some people like to solve equations of lines for the second variable y before graphing them. In the Example, since $2x - y = 8$, by adding y to both sides, $2x = y + 8$, and so $y = 2x + -8$. The numbers 2 and -8 in this equation both can be interpreted on the graph. The 2 means that the line goes up 2 units for every increase of one unit to the right. The -8 is the second coordinate of the point where the line intersects the y-axis.

Questions

Covering the Reading

In 1–4, use the first-class postal rates for 1990.

1. What formula relates the weight of a letter and the cost to mail it?
   $c = 20w + 5$

2. What is the cost of mailing a letter that weighs 6 ounces? **$1.20**

3. What is the cost of mailing a letter that weighs 2.4 ounces? **$.65**

4. What letters cost 45¢ to mail? **2 oz**

558

5. Convert 185¢ to dollars. $1.85

6. What is a general rule for converting cents to dollars?
divide by 100

7. What is an advantage of displaying postal rates in a table?
easy to find the rates, easy to understand

8. What is an advantage of having a formula for postal rates?   takes the least space, allows for any values, can be used by a computer

9. What is an advantage of graphing postal rates?
Graphing pictures the rates; shows changes over time.

In 10–14, use the first-class postal rates for 1965, 1975, and 1990.

10. What was the cost of mailing a 2-oz letter in 1965?   10¢

11. In 1965, what was the cost of mailing a letter weighing 9.2 oz?
50¢

12. You could mail a 3-oz letter in 1975 for what it cost to mail a   ? -oz letter in 1965.   7

13. What is the lowest cost for mailing a letter in:
   a. 1965; 5¢   b. 1975; 13¢   c. 1990 25¢

14. In 1975, by how much did the rate go up for each extra ounce of weight?   11¢

15. The line $2x - y = 8$ is graphed in this lesson. Give the coordinates of two points on this line that are not identified on the graph.   Samples: (4, 0), (2, -4)

Applying the Mathematics

16. Find three points on the line $y = -3x + 5$. Graph this line.
Sample points: (0, 5), (1, 2), (2, -1). See margin.

17. Consider the line with equation $2x - 3y = 12$.
   a. Find the coordinates of three points on this line.
   b. Graph this line.
   c. Imagine this line and the line graphed in the example on page 558 graphed on the same axes. Estimate the intersection.
   a. samples: (0,−4), (6,0), (3,−2); c. (3,−2) b. see margin.

18. *Multiple choice*   Which line could be the graph of $5x - y = 10$?

   (a)   (b)   (c)   (d)

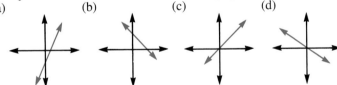

19. Today there are 400 packages of duplicating paper at the school. Each week about 12 packages are used.
   a. Make a table with two columns, "weeks from now" and "number of packages left."   See margin.
   b. Graph six pairs of numbers in the table. Let w, the number of weeks, be graphed on the x-axis. L, the number of packages left, should be graphed on the y-axis.   See margin.
   c. w and L are related by the equation $L = 400 - 12w$. Find the value of w when $L = 0$. $w = 33\frac{1}{3}$
   d. What does this value mean?
   In about 33 weeks the paper will be used up.

LESSON 12-6 *Graphing Lines*   559

Question 32: In this question students are asked to explore the solution to a *system of linear equations* by graphing. The graph of this system consists of two lines intersecting in one point, indicating there is one solution to the system. Graphs of other systems of two linear equations may consist of two parallel lines (indicating no solution) or two coincidental lines (indicating an infinite solution set).

20. b. sample: Change the program as follows:
20 FOR X = 1 TO 100
30 Y = -3*X + 5
21. Check:
Does 11 − 2(.6) = 8(.6) + 5?
Yes, 9.8 = 9.8.
22. Check:
Does 3(5 · $\frac{20}{3}$ + 22) =
5($\frac{20}{3}$) + 6 + 19($\frac{20}{3}$)?
Yes, 166 = 166.
23. Check: Does $\frac{35 - 9}{2}$ =
$\frac{35 + 4}{3}$?
Yes, 13 = 13.
30. d. e.

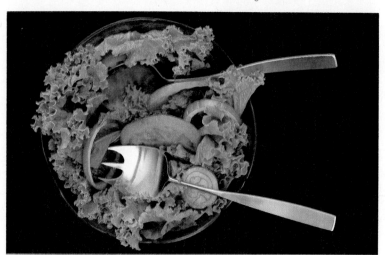

20. **a.** Coordinates of points on what line are found by this program?

$y = 11x + 2$

```
10 PRINT "X", "Y"
20 FOR X = 1 TO 10
30    Y = 11*X + 2
40    PRINT X, Y
50 NEXT X
60 END
```

b. Modify the program so that it will find 100 points on the line of Question 16.   See margin.

Review

In 21–23, solve and check. *(Lessons 12-4, 12-5)*   See margin for checks.

21. $11 − 2y = 8y + 5$ .6 or $\frac{3}{5}$

22. $3(5n + 22) = 5n + 6 + 19n$ $\frac{20}{3}$

23. $\dfrac{x − 9}{2} = \dfrac{x + 4}{3}$ 35

24. Alvin ate about $\frac{1}{4}$ of the tossed salad. Betty ate half of what was left. How much now remains? *(Lesson 9-8)* $\frac{3}{8}$ of the salad

25. Diana gave P plants $\frac{1}{2}$ cup water each and Q plants $\frac{3}{4}$ cup water each. How much water did she use altogether? *(Lesson 12-3)*
$\frac{1}{2}P + \frac{3}{4}Q$ cups

26. A salesperson keeps a record of miles traveled for business. A car was driven 18,000 miles last year and 65% of this was for business. The salesperson gets 22¢ per mile traveled back from the company. How much should the salesperson get back from the company? *(Lessons 2-6, 10-4)* $2574

27. Simplify: *(Lessons 5-5, 7-2, 10-5, 11-3)*
    a. -5 + -3   -8   **b.** -5 − -3   -2
    c. -5 · -3   15   **d.** $\frac{-5}{-3}$ $\frac{5}{3}$

28. Solve: $\dfrac{42}{5} = \dfrac{7x}{10}$. *(Lessons 11-5, 10-1)*   12

29. Use $\triangle BCD$. Find m$\angle BCD$. *(Lessons 7-7, 7-10)*   33°

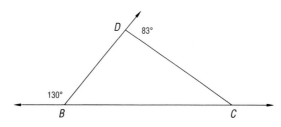

Exploration

30. Consider the equation $y = |x|$.
   a. When $x = 5$, $y = $ _?_.   5
   b. When $x = -2$, $y = $ _?_.   2
   c. When $x = 0$, $y = $ _?_.   0
   d. The answers to **a, b,** and **c** give three points on the graph of $y = |x|$. Graph these points.   graph (5, 5), (-2, 2), and (0, 0)
   e. Graph seven other points that satisfy $y = |x|$. Make sure you pick some negative values for x.   See margin.
   f. The points do not lie on the same line. What figure do they form?   a right angle

31. Are the current costs of mailing a first-class letter the same as the costs given in this lesson for 1990? If they are not, make a graph of the new rates similar to the graphs found on page 557.
Answers will vary.

32. The sum of two numbers is -9 and the difference of these numbers is 6. If x and y are the numbers, the given information says that $x + y = -9$ and $x - y = 6$. Graph these two lines and use the point of intersection to determine the two numbers.
x is $-1\frac{1}{2}$; y is $-7\frac{1}{2}$; see graph below.

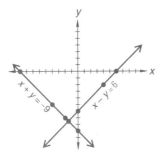

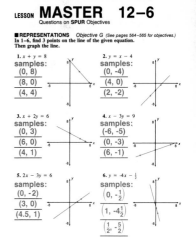

Summary

The main concern of this chapter is the Distributive Property and its applications. This property involves combining multiplication and addition (and subtraction). There are four main versions of the Distributive Property.

$$(a + b)x = ax + bx \qquad x(a + b) = xa + xb$$
$$(a - b)x = ax - bx \qquad x(a - b) = xa - xb$$

A repeating decimal x can be multiplied by a power of 10 so that the product has the same repetend. Then, when the two numbers are subtracted (using the distributive property), an equation of the form $ax = b$ results. Solving this equation for x gives the simple fraction for that repeating decimal.

The Distributive Property can be used to solve equations of the form $ax + b = cx + d$. After getting the variable terms all on one side of the equation, they can be combined. Then the equation is in a form you already know how to solve.

The linear expression $ax + by$ is a sum of multiples of different numbers. The points (x, y) that work in $ax + by = c$ lie on a line. These lines arise from the many situations that involve both addition and multiplication.

Vocabulary

You should be able to give a general description and a specific example for each of the following ideas.

Lesson 12-1
Distributive Property of Multiplication over Addition
Distributive Property of Multiplication over Subtraction
distributivity

Lesson 12-2
finite decimal, infinite decimal

Lesson 12-3
linear expression
terms, like terms, unlike terms
coefficient

Lesson 12-5
equation of the form $ax + b = cx + d$

Lesson 12-6
linear equation

562

Progress Self-Test

See margin for answers not shown below.

Take this test as you would take a test in class. Then check your work with the solutions in the Selected Answers section in the back of the book. You will need graph paper and ruler.

In 1–3, simplify.

1. $m - 3m$ **-2m**
2. $4x + 1 + 3x$ **7x + 1**
3. $7m - 2n - 4m + n$ **3m − n**
4. Write the Distributive Property of Multiplication over Addition.

In 5–8, solve.

5. $1 - 9x = 13 + 3x$ **-1 = x**
6. $2(y - 3) = 12y$ $y = -\frac{3}{5}$
7. $\dfrac{2t + 7}{4} = \dfrac{t - 8}{5}$ $t = -\frac{67}{6}$
8. $0.2m + 6 = -m + 2 + 0.4m$ **m = -5**
9. In 7 years Lee will be 1.5 times as old as he is now. How old is Lee?   **Lee is 14 years old.**

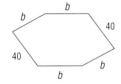

10. A bookstore sells T books at \$3.95, F books at \$4.95, and V books at \$5.95. How much money is taken in from these sales?
11. Write the perimeter of the hexagon below in simplest form.   **4b + 80**

12. A hamburger has about 80 calories per ounce. A bun has about 180 calories. A typical french fry has about 11 calories. If you eat H 4-oz hamburgers with buns, and F french fries, how many total calories will you have eaten?   **500 H + 11F calories**

13. A point is on the line $5x - 2y = 10$. The first coordinate of this point is 3. What is the second coordinate?   **2.5**

14. Find three points on the line $y = 3x - 2$.

15. Graph the line with equation $x + 3y = 6$.

16. Write $0.\overline{81}$ as a simple fraction.   **9/11**

17. Write $1.02\overline{8}$ as a simple fraction.   **463/450**

18. Explain how the Distributive Property can be used to calculate $49 \cdot 7$ mentally.

19. The Distributive Property is used here in going from what line to what line?
    Line 1 $ax + b = cx + d$
    Line 2 $-cx + ax + b = -cx + cx + d$
    Line 3 $-cx + ax + b = 0 + d$
    Line 4 $(-c + a)x + b = 0 + d$
    Line 5 $(-c + a)x + b = d$

20. Find the total area of these rectangles.

w(2.55) or 2.55w

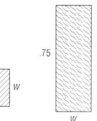

USING THE PROGRESS SELF-TEST
Assign the Progress Self-Test as a one-night assignment. Worked-out *solutions* for all questions are in the student book. Encourage students to take the Progress Self-Test honestly, grade themselves, and then be prepared to discuss the test in class.

Advise students to pay special attention to those Chapter Review questions (pages 527–529) which correspond to questions missed on the Progress Self-Test. A chart in the student text keys the Progress Self-Test questions to the lettered SPUR Objectives in the Chapter Review. It also keys the questions to the corresponding lessons where the material is covered.

ADDITIONAL ANSWERS
4. For any numbers a, b and x, $ax + bx = (a + b)x$.

10. $3.95T + $4.95F + $5.95V$

14. samples: (2, 4), (10, 28), (3, 7)

15.

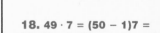

18. $49 \cdot 7 = (50 - 1)7 =$
$50 \cdot 7 - 1 \cdot 7 =$
$350 - 7 = 343$

19. from line 3 to line 4

CHAPTER REVIEW

The main objectives for the chapter are organized here into sections corresponding to the four main types of understanding this book promotes: Skills, Properties, Uses, and Representations.

USING THE CHAPTER REVIEW
Whereas end-of-chapter material may be considered optional in some texts, in *Transition Mathematics* we have selected these objectives and questions with the expectation that they will be covered. Students should be able to answer these questions with about 85% accuracy after studying the chapter.

You may assign these questions over a single night to help students prepare for a test the next day, or you may assign the questions over a two-day period.

If you work the questions over two days, then we recommend assigning the *evens* for homework the first night so that students get feedback in class the next day, then assigning the *odds* the night before the test so they can check their answers in the Selected Answers section of the book.

ADDITIONAL ANSWERS
4. $3m - 7$

5. $-5t - 14r + 7$

10. $\frac{72}{11}$

12. Check: Does $(15 \cdot 3) + 8 = (7 \cdot 3) + 32$? Yes, $53 = 53$.

Chapter Review

Questions on **SPUR** Objectives

See margin for answers not shown below.

SPUR stands for **S**kills, **P**roperties, **U**ses, and **R**epresentations. The Chapter Review questions are grouped according to the SPUR Objectives for this chapter.

SKILLS deal with the procedures used to get answers.

■ **Objective A:** *Simplify linear expressions when possible, using distributivity.*
(*Lessons 12-1, 12-3, 12-4*)

1. Simplify $2v + 8v$. **10v**
2. Simplify $5x - x - 2x$. **2x**
3. Simplify $13a + 4b + 7a$. **20a + 4b**
4. Simplify $-9 + 5m + 2 - 3m + m$.
5. Simplify $-6r + 3t - 8t + 7 - 8r$.
6. Simplify $m(1 + n) - m$. **mn**
7. Multiply $6(a - b + 2c)$. **6a − 6b + 12c**

■ **Objective B:** *Convert repeating decimals to fractions.* (*Lesson 12-2*)

8. Find a simple fraction equal to $5.\overline{7}$. **52/9**
9. Find a simple fraction equal to $0.89\overline{2}$.
   $\frac{803}{900}$

10. Find a simple fraction equal to $6.\overline{54}$.
11. Find a simple fraction equal to $0.\overline{393}$.
    $\frac{131}{333}$

■ **Objective C:** *Solve and check equations of the form $ax + b = cx + d$.* (*Lesson 12-5*)

12. Solve and check: $15x + 8 = 7x + 32$. **3**
13. Solve and check:
    $2 - 35m = 10m + 19 - 6m$. $-\frac{17}{39}$
14. Solve and check: $\dfrac{E - 9}{6} = \dfrac{3E + 5}{3}$. $-\frac{19}{5}$
15. Solve and check:
    $7(y - 3) = 2y + 9 + 6y$. **-30**
    See margin for checks.

PROPERTIES deal with the principles behind the mathematics.

■ **Objective D:** *Recognize and use the Distributive Property.* (*Lessons 12-1, 12-4*)

16. The Distributive Property is used here in going from what line to what other line?
    Line 1 $3x - x$
    Line 2 $= 3x - 1 \cdot x$
    Line 3 $= (3 - 1)x$
    Line 4 $= 2x$ **Line 2 to line 3**

17. Explain how the Distributive Property can be applied to calculate $\$19.95 \cdot 4$ mentally.
18. How can the Distributive Property be applied to simplify $5 \cdot 39 + 5 \cdot 39$?

564

USES deal with applications of mathematics in real situations.

▨ **Objective E:** *Translate real situations involving multiplication, addition, and subtraction into linear expressions and linear equations.* *(Lessons 12-3, 12-4, 12-5)*

19. A tablespoon of butter has about 100 calories. A piece of white bread has about 70 calories. How many calories are there in T tablespoons of butter and P pieces of white bread?   **100T + 70P**

20. Julie bought c cassettes at $7.99 each and a compact disc for $12.95. How much did she spend before tax?   **7.99c + 12.95 dollars**

21. E rows have 11 seats and T rows have 12 seats. How many seats are there altogether?   **11E + 12T**

22. In 21 years Elijah will be 2.5 times as old as he is now. How old is he?   **14 years**

23. 5 more than $\frac{2}{3}$ a number is 4 more than $\frac{3}{4}$ the number. What is the number?   **12**

REPRESENTATIONS deal with pictures, graphs, or objects that illustrate concepts.

▨ **Objective F:** *Represent the Distributive Property by areas of rectangles.* *(Lessons 12-1, 12-4)*

24. What instance of the Distributive Property is pictured here? $x \cdot 20 + x \cdot 5 = 25x$

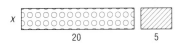

25. Using rectangles, show that $8.2 \cdot 13.6 + 9 \cdot 13.6 = (8.2 + 9)\ 13.6.$

▨ **Objective G:** *Graph solutions to linear equations.* *(Lesson 12-6)*

26. Find three points on the line with equation $y = 4x - 5.$ **Samples: (1, -1), (2, 3), (3, 7)**

27. Find three points on the line with equation $2x + 5y = 10.$ **Samples: (5, 0), (0, 2), (10, -2)**

28. Graph the line with equation $x - 2y = 11.$

29. Graph the line with equation $4x + 6y = 10.$

13. Check: Does $2 - 35(\frac{-17}{39})$ $= 10(\frac{-17}{39}) + 19?$
Yes, $\approx 17.25 = \approx 17.25.$

14. Check: Does $\dfrac{\frac{-19}{5} - 9}{6} =$ $\dfrac{(3 \cdot \frac{-19}{5}) + 5}{3}?$
Yes, $-2.1\overline{3} = -2.1\overline{3}.$

15. Check: Does $7(-30 - 3)$ $= (2 \cdot -30) + 9 + (6 \cdot -30)?$
Yes, $-231 = -231.$

17. $19.95 \cdot 4 = ($20.00 - $.05) \cdot 4 = $80.00 - $.20 = 79.80

18. $5 \cdot 39 + 5 \cdot 39 = (5 + 5) \cdot 39 = 10 \cdot 39 = 390$

25.
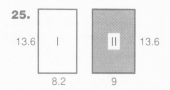
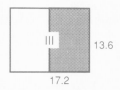

28., 29. See Additional Answers in the back of this book.

CHAPTER 13 ■ MEASUREMENT FORMULAS AND REAL NUMBERS

DAILY PACING CHART ■ CHAPTER 13

Students in the Full Course should complete the entire text by the end of the year.
Students in the Minimal Course spend more time when there are quizzes and more time on the Chapter Review. Therefore, these students may not complete all of the chapters in the text.

DAY	MINIMAL COURSE	FULL COURSE
1	13-1	13-1
2	13-2	13-2
3	13-3	13-3
4	Quiz (TRF); Start 13-4.	Quiz (TRF); 13-4
5	Finish 13-4.	13-5
6	13-5	13-6
7	13-6	Quiz (TRF); 13-7
8	Quiz (TRF); Start 13-7.	13-8
9	Finish 13-7.	13-9
10	13-8	Progress Self-Test
11	13-9	Chapter Review
12	Progress Self-Test	Chapter Test (TRF)
13	Chapter Review	
14	Chapter Review	
15	Chapter Test (TRF)	

TESTING OPTIONS
■ Quiz for Lessons 13-1 Through 13-3   ■ Chapter 13 Test, Form A   ■ Chapter 13 Test, Cumulative Form
■ Quiz for Lessons 13-4 Through 13-6   ■ Chapter 13 Test, Form B   ■ Comprehensive Test, Chapters 1–13
A Quiz and Test Writer is available for generating additional questions, additional quizzes, or additional forms of the Chapter Test.

PROVIDING FOR INDIVIDUAL DIFFERENCES
The student text is written for the *average* student. The program, however, can be adapted for both less capable and more capable students.

A blackline master (in the Teacher's Resource File) is provided for each lesson for those students who need more practice. The Teacher's Edition frequently provides Error Analysis and Alternate Approach features to provide additional instructional strategies.

For students who require additional challenge, Extension activities are regularly provided in the Teacher's Edition.

OBJECTIVES ■ CHAPTER 13

Students should master the chapter objectives by the time they complete the chapter. To ensure objective mastery, there is continual review built into each set of lesson questions. After students complete the chapter lessons, they assess their mastery on the Progress Self-Test. Then they do the Chapter Review and pay special attention to those questions that match the objectives missed on the Progress Self-Test. Students can get extra practice on these objectives by using the master for each lesson in the Teacher's Resource File.

OBJECTIVES FOR CHAPTER 13 (Organized into the SPUR categories—Skills, Properties, Uses, and Representations)	Progress Self-Test Questions	Chapter Review Questions	Teacher's Resource File	
			Lesson Master*	Chapter Test Forms A and B
SKILLS				
A: Find the area of any triangle.	8, 9, 12	1–4	13-1, 13-4	11, 12, 14, 21
B: Estimate square roots of a number without a calculator.	4	5–8	13-2	3, 4
C: Use the Pythagorean Theorem to find lengths of third sides in right triangles.	5, 6	9–12	13-3	8, 9, 20
D: Find the area of a trapezoid.	2, 10	13–16	13-5	10, 13
E: Find the circumference of a circle or sector, given its radius or diameter.	1, 15, 20	17–20	13-6, 13-7	6, 19
F: Find the surface area or volume of a sphere, given its radius or diameter.	18	21, 22	13-9	5
PROPERTIES				
G: Identify numbers as rational, irrational, or real.	7, 16	23–25	13-6	1, 2
USES				
H: Apply area formulas in real situations.	17	26–30	13-1, 13-4, 13-7, 13-9	16, 23
I: Apply formulas for the circumference of a circle and volume of a sphere in real situations.	14	31–34	13-6, 13-9	7, 15, 17
REPRESENTATIONS				
J: Know how square roots and geometric squares are related.	3	35–37	13-2	22
K: Read, make, and interpret circle graphs.	19	38–40	13-8	18

*The Lesson Masters are numbered to match the lessons.

566B

OVERVIEW ■ CHAPTER 13

With this chapter, *Transition Mathematics* comes full circle. Having started the year with two chapters on decimals followed by a chapter devoted to measurement, we end with a chapter that combines the two ideas.

The unifying concept of Chapter 13 is area. In Lesson 13-1, students use the relationship between rectangles and right triangles to derive the area formula for a right triangle. This formula, in an informal way, leads to the Pythagorean Theorem (Lesson 13-3) and the formula for the area of any triangle (Lesson 13-4). By putting triangular regions together, the students can calculate other areas. We concentrate on the formula for the area of

a trapezoid (Lesson 13-5). Later lessons in this chapter deal with π (Lesson 13-6) and some of the formulas that use π. We discuss the area of a circle and of sectors (Lesson 13-7), and the surface and volume of a sphere (Lesson 13-9).

Circle graphs (Lesson 13-8) round out the family of displays first introduced in Chapter 8. Though these graphs are probably the least functional of all the displays, they are used often in print media and provide a chance for students to practice using the properties of circles and sectors.

Understanding the area formulas requires a familiarity with the irrational numbers, the numbers represented by infinite, non-repeating

decimals. Lesson 13-2 introduces square roots just before the Pythagorean Theorem. Square roots of positive integers are either integers or irrational numbers. The number π, another irrational number, is the subject of Lesson 13-6, before the area of a circle is discussed. Both square roots and π are introduced via geometric ideas: square roots from the area of squares, and π from the circumference of a circle. With these lessons involving the most common irrational numbers, students have worked with all the major types of real numbers, that is, all the numbers that can be represented by decimals.

PERSPECTIVES ■ CHAPTER 13

The Perspectives provide the rationale for the inclusion of topics or approaches, provide mathematical background, and make connections within UCSMP.

13-1

AREA OF A RIGHT TRIANGLE
Since we consider right triangles first, the area formula is easily understood. It is derived by considering half a rectangle. The goals for this lesson are more subtle, however. First, students must realize that a right triangle may be tilted in any way. The lesson provides triangles in various orientations. Second, students will learn that the formula for the area of a right triangle can be used to find areas of more complicated figures. Not only will such figures appear in this lesson, but right triangles will also be used to give the area for any triangle in Lesson 13-4. Third, students will need the information from this lesson for the derivation of the Pythagorean Theorem in Lesson 13-3.

In mathematics, words such as *side*, *altitude*, or *radius* may refer either to a segment or to the length of that segment. The book speaks of *the length of the side*, and so on, so that students realize there is a difference between a segment and its length. However, do not penalize students for using the less precise, more common language that most mathematicians use.

13-2

SQUARE ROOTS
Most students know the term *square root* but do not know its origin. When the ancient Greeks thought of a number as the area of a square (that is, the number 36 would be represented by a square with area 36), they also thought of the side upon which the square rests as the *square root*. Why was the word *root* chosen? One interpretation is that a plant might be said to rest on its roots, and so may a square.

In the past, students learned a rather complicated algorithm to get a decimal approximation for a square root. With calculators, this is not necessary. Have students estimate square roots by guessing and then checking with calculator multiplication and by using the square root key. The experimentation will help them understand the relationship between squaring and taking the square root of a number.

13-3

THE PYTHAGOREAN THEOREM
The Pythagorean Theorem, one of the most important relationships in geometry, provides the basis for distances between points when graphing. It has many generalizations and more than 370 published proofs.

The lesson development on page 578 shows students how to find the length of the hypotenuse of a right triangle without the Pythagorean Theorem. This idea can be generalized to give a proof of the theorem. Although the student text does not develop a proof, one is offered as an Extension activity in this lesson.

Students may wonder how the Greeks ever discovered the Pythagorean Theorem. They appear to have generalized from a few specific cases, like the 3–4–5 triangle. We know that their proofs connected this theorem to areas. The ancient Chinese had also deduced the theorem. Some ancient Egyptians and Babylonians knew of special cases and may have known the general property.

13-4
AREA OF ANY TRIANGLE
Two different derivations of the formula $A = \frac{1}{2}hb$ are given in this lesson. First, using the Distributive Property, we derive the formula from the area formula for right triangles. Second, we show the area of the triangle as half the area of a rectangle with dimensions h and b.

13-5
AREAS OF POLYGONS
This lesson has two goals: to point out that the area of any polygon can be found by splitting it into triangles, a process called *triangulating the polygon*; and to use triangulation to derive a formula for the area of any trapezoid.

Our definition of *trapezoid*—a quadrilateral with *at least* one pair of parallel sides—differs from that given in some books. Some people prefer to restrict trapezoids to those figures which have *exactly* one pair of parallel sides. We see no reason for such a restriction. The area formula for trapezoids works for parallelograms. Moreover, it is efficient to have trapezoids include parallelograms just the way that parallelograms include rectangles and rhombuses, and each of these includes squares.

The formula for the area of a trapezoid is one of the more complicated area formulas. It is given here because it is standard content, it exemplifies the Distributive Property, and it provides good practice of many skills.

13-6
THE NUMBER π
The number π was introduced in Chapter 1 and should be familiar to students. One measure of its importance is the inclusion of a π key on scientific calculators.

Circumference in everyday language may refer to either a geometric object (the circle itself) or its length. Mathematicians tend to prefer only one meaning: circumference as a length. This meaning makes the use of *circumference* more like the use of *perimeter*. *Circumference* is the *perimeter* of a circle.

13-7
CIRCLES AND SECTORS
Most students find the formula for the area of a circle easy to apply. However, students need to be careful to use the radius, not the diameter, and to follow the correct order of operations.

The formula for the area of a sector looks more difficult than it really is. The important thing for students to realize is that the area of a sector is just a fractional part of the area of a circle. That fraction depends on the size of the sector; the fractional part is $\frac{m}{360}$, where m is the measure of the central angle of the sector.

13-8
CIRCLE GRAPHS
Circle graphs are included in this chapter for two reasons: (1) they are a good application of sectors, reinforcing the work of the previous lesson, and (2) they appear frequently in printed material.

Students need draw only one circle graph in this lesson and another one in the review of the next lesson. Constructing circle graphs takes a long time, and nowadays computers can easily draw any circle graphs.

13-9
SPHERES
Throughout this book, arithmetic, algebra, and geometry have been intertwined. The sphere is a perfect way to end. The formulas for the surface area and volume of spheres are algebraic formulas to describe geometric ideas and involve both rational and irrational numbers.

Measurement Formulas and Real Numbers

The figure below consists of a big circle, part of a smaller circle, and a right triangle. The bigger circle has center *B*. The smaller circle has center *M*. The portion of the smaller circle that is not part of the larger circle is called a *lune*. (It is the orange region.)

Which region has the greater perimeter, the lune or the triangle?

Which region has the greater area, the lune or the triangle?

These are hard questions. Even with an accurate drawing, you may not be able to answer them by just looking. In this chapter, you will learn how to calculate areas and perimeters of triangles, circles, and other figures. Along the way, you will meet some of the most famous numbers and formulas in all of mathematics.

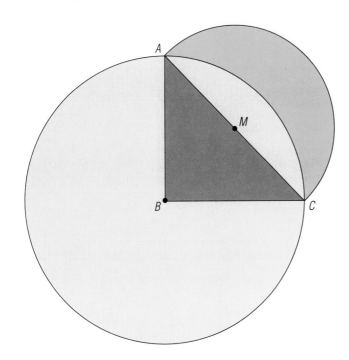

13-1

Area of a
Right Triangle

A triangle is made up of only the three segments you see. A
triangular region consists of a triangle and the space inside it.
To be precise, we should talk about the area of a triangular
region. But everyone talks about the area of a triangle.

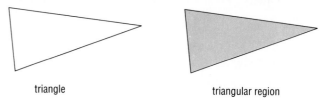

triangle   triangular region

In area, it is easy to see that every *right* triangle is half a
rectangle.

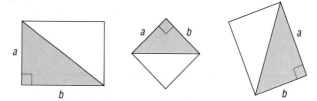

The two sides of a right triangle that help to form the right angle
are called the **legs** of the right triangle. The legs in each picture
above have lengths a and b. So the area of each rectangle is ab.
The area of each right triangle is half of that.

Area formula for a right triangle:

Let A be the area of a right triangle with legs of lengths
a and b. Then $A = \frac{1}{2} ab$.

The longest side of a right triangle is called its **hypotenuse.** In
each right triangle above, the hypotenuse is a diagonal of the
rectangle. You should ignore the hypotenuse when calculating
area.

568

Example 1 Find the area of a right triangle with sides of lengths 3 cm, 4 cm, and 5 cm.

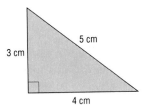

Solution The hypotenuse is the longest side. It has length 5 cm. So the legs have lengths 3 cm and 4 cm. Thus

$$A = \frac{1}{2}ab$$
$$= \frac{1}{2} \cdot 3 \text{ cm} \cdot 4 \text{ cm}$$
$$= 6 \text{ cm}^2.$$

By joining or cutting out right triangles, areas of more complicated figures can be found.

Example 2 A small garden is cut out of a larger garden as in the drawing. Both gardens are shaped like right triangles. What is the area of the shaded region that remains?

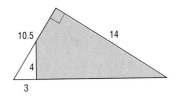

Solution The area of the large garden is $\frac{1}{2} \cdot 10.5 \cdot 14$, or 73.5.

The area of the small garden is 6, as found in Example 1. Take away the 6 from 73.5, and you have the area of the remaining region. The answer is 67.5.

In Example 2 no unit is named. You can assume then that the same unit applies to all lengths of sides. The area is still in square units. For instance, if the legs of the big garden are 10.5 feet and 14 feet, the area of the shaded region is 67.5 square feet. If the legs are 10.5 meters and 14 meters, the area of the shaded region is 67.5 square meters. Area is measured in square units even when the figures are not squares or rectangles.

LESSON 13-1 *Area of a Right Triangle* **569**

1. Find the area.

a.

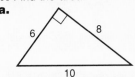

24 square units

b.

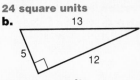

30 square units

2. Oprah wants to paint the door to her room like the school flag. The flag is a rectangle divided by a diagonal into two right triangles, one blue and one white. If the door is 3 feet wide and 7 feet tall, how many square inches will Oprah paint blue? **1512 in²**

3. Find the area of the shaded part of the big square.

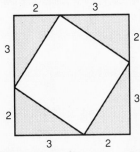

12 square units

Questions

1. What is the difference between a triangle and a triangular region? See margin.

2. Most precisely, people should talk about the area of a __?__. But people usually speak of the area of a __?__.
   triangular region, triangle

In 3–6, consider the right triangle with sides of lengths 9, 40, and 41.

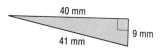

3. What are the lengths of the legs of this triangle? 40 mm, 9 mm

4. What is the length of its hypotenuse? 41 mm

5. What is its area? 180 square millimeters

6. What is its perimeter? 90 mm

7. Repeat Question 3–6 for the right triangle ABC.
   legs 8, 15; hypotenuse 17; area 60 square units; perimeter 40 units

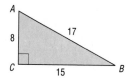
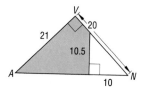

8. Find the area of the shaded region in the figure drawn above at right. 157.5 square units

9. What is the area of a right triangle with legs of lengths a and b?
   $\frac{1}{2} ab$

10. A tree is in the middle of a garden. Around the tree there is a square region where nothing will be planted. The dimensions of the garden are shown in the drawing below. How much area can be planted? 146.5 square feet

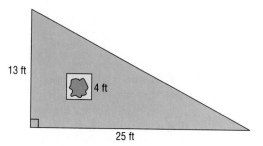

11. *RECT* is a rectangle with length 6 and height *h*.

    a. What is the area of triangle *ECT*?   **3h**
    b. What is the area of triangle *ERT*?   **3h**

In 12 and 13, use the drawing of the flag of the Caribbean island Bonaire.

12. The dimensions of a real flag are to be 20″ by 30″. The bottom right triangle of the flag is blue. What is the area of the blue part?
300 square inches

13. The small right triangle is yellow. The sides of this triangle are 2/5 the length and width of the whole flag. What is the area of the yellow part?   **48 square inches**

14. Find the area of △*RST*.   **40 square units**

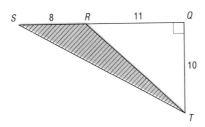

15. The area of a right triangle is 48 cm² and the length of one leg is 6 cm. What is the length of the other leg?   **16 cm**

16. a. Draw a right triangle with legs of length 1″ and 2″.   **See margin.**
    b. What is the area of this triangle?   **1 square inch**
    c. To the nearest eighth of an inch, measure the length of its hypotenuse. $2\frac{2}{8}''$ or $2\frac{1}{4}''$

17. Find the area of △*ELF*. *EA* = 8, *FA* = 6.4, *EL* = 6, and *EF* = 4.8.   **8.64 square units**

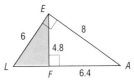

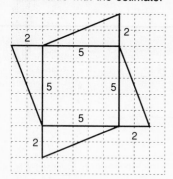

$(A = 5 + 5 + 5 + 5 + 25 = 45$ square units)

Review

18. Simplify $\frac{1}{3} \cdot \frac{1}{3}$. *(Lesson 9-8)* $\frac{1}{9}$

19. What is the volume of a cube with each edge of length 1/3 meter? *(Lessons 3-8, 9-8)* 1/27 cubic meter

20. What is the opposite of the reciprocal of 3/8? *(Lessons 1-5, 9-9)* -8/3

21. What simple fraction in lowest terms equals 0.41666666… (6 repeating)? *(Lesson 12-2)* $\frac{5}{12}$

22. *Multiple choice* A drawing is put in a copy machine. The machine reduces dimensions of figures by 1/5. A copy is made of the copy. How will the dimensions of the second copy compare with the original?
(a) They will be 1/25 the size of the original.
(b) They will be 60% of the size of the original.
(c) They will be 64% of the size of the original.
(d) They will be 80% of the size of the original.
(Lessons 2-7, 9-7, 9-8) (c)

23. Here are three instances of a pattern. Describe the general pattern using four variables. *(Lesson 4-2)*
$(40 + 13)(12 + 81) = 40 \cdot 12 + 40 \cdot 81 + 13 \cdot 12 + 13 \cdot 81$
$(6 + 3)(6 + -4) = 6 \cdot 6 + 6 \cdot -4 + 3 \cdot 6 + 3 \cdot -4$
$(30 + 5)(30 + 5) = 30 \cdot 30 + 30 \cdot 5 + 5 \cdot 30 + 5 \cdot 5$
$(a + b)(c + d) = ac + ad + bc + bd$

24. Solve $11 - 5x = 511$. *(Lesson 10-9)* -100

25. Evaluate $a^2 + b^2$ when $a = 7$ and $b = 10$. *(Lessons 2-2, 4-4)* 149

Exploration

26. The United States flag has 7 red stripes and 6 white ones. The stripes all have the same thickness. The upper left corner is blue with 50 white stars. Dimensions of a big flag are shown below.
a. What percent of the flag is red? 40%
b. What percent of the flag is made up of white stripes?
c. What percent of the flag is blue with white stars?
b. 93/260 ≈ 35.8%; c. 63/260 ≈ 24.2%

0.9 m

1.3 m

2 m

RESOURCES
- Lesson Master 13-2
- Visual for Teaching Aid 72: Use with **Questions 27–30.**

OBJECTIVES

B Estimate square roots of a number without a calculator.

J Know how square roots and geometric squares are related.

TEACHING NOTES

The $\boxed{\sqrt{x}}$ key on the calculator makes finding an approximation to a square root (or an exact value if the radicand is a perfect square) automatic, but it does not provide much sense of what is going on. Encourage the students to check their estimates on a calculator. Geometric interpretations also increase understanding.

There are two important details to stress that students often overlook. First, remind students that $\sqrt{5}$ is not *the* square root of 5, but rather the *positive* square root of 5. Second, emphasize order of operations. In Europe, people generally write $\sqrt{(a + b)}$ where we would write $\sqrt{a + b}$. This practice illustrates that the horizontal bar in our square root notation is actually the vinculum parentheses sign. Accordingly, one must work under that sign first.

Here are two squares and their areas.

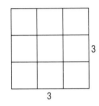

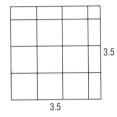

Area $= 3 \cdot 3 = 3^2 = 9$ Area $= 3.5 \cdot 3.5 = 3.5^2 = 12.25$

As you know, 9 is called the *square* of 3. We say that 3 is a **square root** of 9. Similarly, 12.25 is the square of 3.5 and we say that 3.5 is a square root of 12.25.

If $A = s^2$, then s is called a *square root* of A.

Since $-3 \cdot -3 = 9$, $(-3)^2 = 9$. So -3 and 3 are both square roots of 9. *Every positive number has two square roots.* The two square roots are opposites of each other. The symbol for the positive square root is $\sqrt{}$, called the **radical sign**. We write $\sqrt{9} = 3$. The negative square root of 9 is $-\sqrt{9}$, or -3.

All scientific calculators have a square root key $\boxed{\sqrt{}}$. This key gives or estimates the positive square root of a number. For instance, enter 12.25 into your calculator and then press the square root key. You should see 3.5 displayed. This tells you that the square roots of 12.25 are 3.5 and -3.5.

Notice what happens when you use a calculator to try to find $\sqrt{2}$.

Key sequence: 2 $\boxed{\sqrt{}}$

Display:

LESSON 13-2 *Square Roots*   573

ADDITIONAL EXAMPLES

1. a. Between which two
whole numbers is √75?

8 and 9

b. Estimate √75 to the
nearest tenth.

8.7

c. Approximate √75 using
your calculator.

8.660254

2. Without using the $\boxed{\sqrt{x}}$ key,
find:

a. √0̅

0

b. √484̅

22

c. √2500̅

50

d. √1369̅

37

3. Simplify √16̅ + 20.

6

The actual decimal for √2̅ is infinite and does not repeat. The number 1.4142136 is an estimate of √2̅. To check that 1.4142136 is a *good* estimate for √2̅, multiply it by itself. Our calculator shows that

$$1.4142136 \cdot 1.4142136 \approx 2.0000001$$

The negative square root of 2 is about -1.4142136.

It is easy to find a segment whose length is √2̅. The square below has area 2. (The four parts can be rearranged to fit 2 square units.) Let s be a side of this square. Then $s^2 = 2$. So $s = \sqrt{2}$.

Square roots of positive integers are either integers or infinite non-repeating decimals. If a square root is an integer, you should be able to find it without a calculator. If a square root is not an integer, then you should be able to estimate it without a calculator.

■ ■ ■ ■ ■ ■ ■ ■ ■

Example   Between what two whole numbers is √40̅?

Solution   Write down the squares of the whole numbers from 1 through 7.

$$1 \cdot 1 = 1$$
$$2 \cdot 2 = 4$$
$$3 \cdot 3 = 9$$
$$4 \cdot 4 = 16$$
$$5 \cdot 5 = 25$$
$$6 \cdot 6 = 36$$
$$7 \cdot 7 = 49$$

This indicates that √36̅ = 6 and √49̅ = 7. You know that √40̅ must be between √36̅ and √49̅. So √40̅ is between 6 and 7.

A better decimal approximation to √40̅ can be found without using a square root key. Beginning with 6.1, square the one-place decimals between 6 and 7. Stop as soon as you have a square greater than 40.

$$6.1 \cdot 6.1 = 37.21$$
$$6.2 \cdot 6.2 = 38.44$$
$$6.3 \cdot 6.3 = 39.69$$
$$6.4 \cdot 6.4 = 40.96$$

574

From this list, $\sqrt{39.69} = 6.3$ and $\sqrt{40.96} = 6.4$. So $\sqrt{40}$ must be between 6.3 and 6.4. By squaring decimals between 6.3 and 6.4 (not hard with a calculator), you can get a better decimal estimate to $\sqrt{40}$. However, anyone who needs to estimate square roots frequently should use a calculator with a $\sqrt{}$ key.

The idea of square root was known to the ancient Egyptians. The ancient Greeks discovered that square roots of many numbers cannot be simple fractions. The $\sqrt{}$ sign was invented in 1525 by the German mathematician Christoff Rudolff.

The bar of the radical sign is a grouping symbol. It is like parentheses. You must work under the bar before doing anything else. For example, to simplify

$$\sqrt{36 + 49},$$

you must add 36 and 49 first. Then take the square root.

$$\sqrt{36 + 49} = \sqrt{85} \approx 9.21954$$

Questions

Covering the Reading

1. Because $100 = 10 \cdot 10$, 10 is called a $\underline{\ ?\ }$ of 100.   square root

2. When $A = s^2$, A is called the $\underline{\ ?\ }$ of s and s is called a $\underline{\ ?\ }$ of A.
   square, square root

3. $6.25 = 2.5 \cdot 2.5$. Which number is a square root of the other?
   2.5 is a square root of 6.25

4. The two square roots of 9 are $\underline{\ ?\ }$ and $\underline{\ ?\ }$.   3, -3

In 5–7, calculators are not allowed. Give the square roots of each number.

5. 81   9, -9   6. 4   2, -2   7. 25   5, -5

8. The $\sqrt{}$ sign is called the $\underline{\ ?\ }$ sign.   radical

In 9–11, calculators are not allowed. Simplify.

9. $\sqrt{64}$ 8   10. $\sqrt{1}$ 1   11. $-\sqrt{49}$ -7

12. a. Approximate $\sqrt{300}$ using your calculator.   17.320508...
    b. How can you check that your approximation is correct?
    c. Round the approximation to the nearest hundredth.   17.32
       b. Multiply it by itself.

13. Approximate $\sqrt{2}$ to the nearest thousandth.   1.414

14. *Multiple choice* The decimal for $\sqrt{2}$ is:
    (a) finite
    (b) infinite and repeating
    (c) infinite and nonrepeating.   (c)

LESSON 13-2 Square Roots   575

15. The area of a square is 400 square meters.

Area 400 m²

   a. Give the length of a side of the square. **20 m**
   b. What is the positive square root of 400? **20**
   c. Simplify: $-\sqrt{400}$. **-20**

16. A square has area 8. To the nearest tenth, what is the length of a side of the square? **2.8**

In 17–22, simplify.

17. $\sqrt{25} + \sqrt{16}$ **9**
18. $\sqrt{25} - \sqrt{16}$ **1**
19. $\sqrt{25 + 16}$ $\sqrt{41} \approx 6.4031$
20. $\sqrt{25} \cdot \sqrt{25}$ **25**
21. $\sqrt{25 - 16}$ **3**
22. $\sqrt{5^2 + 4^2}$ $\sqrt{41} \approx 6.4031$

23. $\sqrt{50}$ is between what two whole numbers? **7 and 8**

Applying the Mathematics

24. A side of a square has length $\sqrt{10}$. What is the area of the square? **10 square units**

25. Which is larger, $\sqrt{2}$ or 239/169? $\sqrt{2}$

26. The length of each side of the little squares below is 1 unit.

   a. What is the area of the big tilted square? **8 square units**
   b. What is the length of a side of this square? $\sqrt{8}$ **units**

In 27–30, use the table of numbers and squares at right. Do not use a calculator. According to the table:

27. What is a square root of 268.96? **16.4**

28. $\sqrt{285.6}$ is about ___?___. **16.9**

29. $\sqrt{270}$ is between ___?___ and ___?___. **16.4, 16.5**

30. $\sqrt{250}$ is less than ___?___. **16**

Number	Square
16.0	256.00
16.1	259.21
16.2	262.44
16.3	265.69
16.4	268.96
16.5	272.25
16.6	275.56
16.7	278.89
16.8	282.24
16.9	285.61
17.0	289.00

576

31. A right triangle has sides of lengths 26 meters, 24 meters, and 10 meters. What is the area of the triangle? *(Lesson 13-1)*
120 square meters

32. Find the area of triangle *ABC*. *(Lesson 13-1)*   **140 square units**

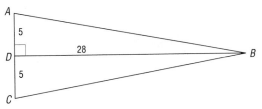

33. *Multiple choice* Which line could be the graph of $2x - y = 4$?
(Lesson 8-3) **(a)**

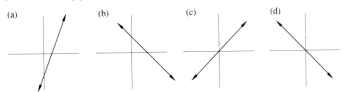

(a)   (b)   (c)   (d)

34. Simplify: $3x + 4y + 5x + 6y + 7x + 8y$. *(Lesson 12-1)*   **15x + 18y**

35. *Multiple choice* An item costs *C* dollars. The price is reduced by *R* dollars. You buy the item at the reduced price and pay *T* dollars tax. How many dollars must you pay for the item?
(a) $R - C + T$ (b) $C - R + T$
(c) $C - R - T$ (d) $R - C - T$ *(Lessons 5-3, 7-2)* **(b)**

36. a. Using your calculator, write down the square roots of the integers from 1 to 15. **See margin.**
   b. Verify that the product of $\sqrt{2}$ and $\sqrt{3}$ seems equal to $\sqrt{6}$.
   c. The product of $\sqrt{3}$ and $\sqrt{5}$ seems equal to what square root?
   d. Write the general pattern using variables. $\sqrt{a} \cdot \sqrt{b} = \sqrt{ab}$
   b. See margin. c. $\sqrt{15}$

37. To estimate $\sqrt{}$ with a computer, you can type in ?SQR( ).
   a. What does a computer print when ?SQR(150) is entered?
   b. You can do Question 36 with the help of the following program.

```
10 FOR N = 1 TO 15
20    PRINT N, SQR(N)
30 NEXT N
40 END
```
   Type and run this program. **See Additional Answers, p. T54.**
   c. If you have only one square root to calculate, a calculator is faster than a computer. If you have to calculate the square roots of whole numbers from 1 to 1000, using the above program and a computer would be faster. Assuming you have both a calculator and a computer, how many square roots would you think you would have to calculate before you would use the computer?   **a. Sample: 12.2474487 c. Answers will vary.**

LESSON 13-2 Square Roots   **577**

FOLLOW-UP

MORE PRACTICE
For more questions on SPUR Objectives, use *Lesson Master 13-2*, shown below.

EXTENSION
There are several related topics that students may wish to explore. One is the square roots of negatives. You might ask students to find out the meaning of $\sqrt{-25}$ and other square roots of negative numbers.

Besides square roots, there are cube roots, fourth roots, and other *n*th roots. Again, students can look in a reference book for the meanings of these terms.

A third related topic is that of fractional exponents: if $x \geq 0$, $\sqrt{x} = x^{\frac{1}{2}}$. Students may want to write other square roots using the fraction $\frac{1}{2}$ as an exponent.

The Pythagorean Theorem

The Pythagorean Theorem is a formula relating the lengths of the three sides of a right triangle. Here is the idea. Suppose a right triangle has legs of length 4 and 5. Such a triangle is pictured below. We want to find c, the length of the hypotenuse.

The idea is to form two squares by making copies of this triangle. Below the triangle is copied and rotated three times. This forms a large square with side 9 and a tilted square in the middle with side c.

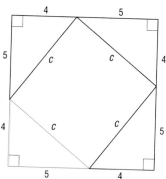

We find the length c by finding the area of the tilted square. The area of the big square is $9 \cdot 9$, or 81. The area of each corner right triangle is $1/2 \cdot 4 \cdot 5$, or 10. Cut off the four right triangles from the big square and you've cut off an area of 40. The remaining area, the area of the tilted square, is 41.

Since $c^2 = 41$, $c = \sqrt{41}$. The numbers 4, 5, and $\sqrt{41}$ are related in a simple but not obvious way.

$$4^2 + 5^2 = (\sqrt{41})^2$$

That is, add the squares of the two legs. The sum is the square of the hypotenuse. The Pythagorean Theorem is the general pattern. It is simple, surprising, and elegant.

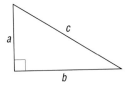

Pythagorean Theorem:

Let the legs of a right triangle have lengths a and b. Let the hypotenuse have length c. Then

$$a^2 + b^2 = c^2.$$

■ ■ ■ ■ ■ ■ ■ ■ ■

Example 1   What is the length of the hypotenuse of the right triangle drawn below?

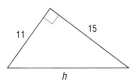

Solution   To answer this question, use the formula of the Pythagorean Theorem. From the formula,
$$11^2 + 15^2 = h^2$$
So $121 + 225 = h^2$
$$346 = h^2$$
$h = \sqrt{346}$ or $-\sqrt{346}$. But we know h is positive.
So $h = \sqrt{346}$. A calculator shows that $\sqrt{346} \approx 18.60$.

Check   Draw a right triangle with legs 11 and 15 units. Then measure the hypotenuse. It should be about 18.6 units.

When you know the lengths of *any* two sides of a right triangle, the Pythagorean Theorem can help get the length of the third side. Example 2 shows how to use this theorem to find lengths that cannot be measured.

Stress that the Pythagorean Theorem is a generalization which applies to *all* right triangles and that it cannot be *proved* by only examples. You might wish to note that many other statements in this book are theorems: the Triangle-Sum Property and the Means-Extremes Property are two examples. In each case, mathematicians use a logical argument to show that the property follows from other basic assumed properties.

Alternate Approach/ Using Manipulatives
Have the students construct a 3-4-5 right triangle on graph paper and then draw three squares such that one side of each square is also a side of the triangle. Tell the students to cut out the two smaller squares and fit them on the largest square. They will have to cut one of the smaller squares apart to make a fit. Another way of stating the Pythagorean Theorem is that the sum of the squares on the legs equals the square on the hypotenuse.

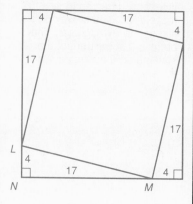
Example 2

The bottom of a 12-foot ladder is 3 feet
from a wall. How high up does the top
of the ladder touch the wall?

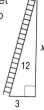

Solution First draw a picture.

According to the Pythagorean Theorem,
$$3^2 + x^2 = 12^2.$$

Now solve the equation.
First simplify. $9 + x^2 = 144$
Add -9 to both sides. $x^2 = 135$

Now, use the definition of square root.
$$x = \sqrt{135} \text{ or } -\sqrt{135}$$

But we know *x* cannot be negative. So
$$x = \sqrt{135}.$$

A calculator shows that $\sqrt{135} \approx 11.6$. This seems correct
because the ladder must be less than 12 feet up on the wall.

A *theorem* is a statement that follows logically from other statements known or assumed to be true. The Pythagorean Theorem
is the most famous theorem in all geometry. This theorem was
known to the ancient Chinese and ancient Egyptians. But it gets
its name from the Greek mathematician Pythagoras. Pythagoras
was born about 572 B.C. He and his followers may have been
the first people in the Western World to know that this amazing
theorem is true for any right triangle.

Caution:
The Pythagorean Theorem only works for right triangles.
It does not work for any other triangles.

Questions

Covering the Reading

1. What is a theorem?   a statement that follows logically from other
statements known (or assumed) to be true
2. *Multiple choice* Pythagoras was an ancient
   (a) Chinese   (b) Greek   (c) Egyptian   (d) Babylonian
   (b)
3. State the Pythagorean Theorem. See margin.

In 4 and 5, use the drawing below.

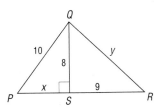

4. **a.** What relationship exists between 8, 9, and y? $8^2 + 9^2 = y^2$
   b. Find y. $\sqrt{145}$

5. **a.** What relationship exists between x, 8, and 10? $x^2 + 8^2 = 10^2$
   b. Find x. 6

6.

Lee had to find LM in the above triangle. She forgot the Pythagorean Theorem. Take Lee through steps which will lead her to find LM.
   a. Draw $\triangle LMN$. Then draw three copies of the triangle which will form a large square and a tilted square in the middle.
   b. Find the area of the large square. 441   a. See margin.
   c. Find the area of $\triangle LMN$. 34
   d. Find the area of the tilted square in the middle. 305
   e. Find LM. $\sqrt{305}$

7. The bottom of a 3-meter ladder is 1 meter away from a wall. How high up on the wall will the ladder reach? $\sqrt{8}$, or about 2.8 meters

8. A right triangle has legs with lengths 6″ and 7″. Find the length of its hypotenuse, to the nearest tenth. 9.2 inches

9. On what type of triangle can the Pythagorean Theorem be used?
   a right triangle

LESSON 13-3   The Pythagorean Theorem   581

10. *Multiple choice* On which of the following triangles can the Pythagorean Theorem be used? **(b)**

(a)   (b)   (c)

11. A farm is pictured below. It is 9 km long and 2 km wide. Danny wants to go from point *A* to point *B*.

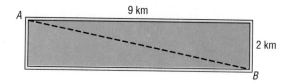

a. How long is the trip going along the roads that surround the farm?   **11 km**

b. How long is it by tractor directly through the farm?

c. How much shorter is it directly through the farm than going along the roads?

b. $\sqrt{85}$ or about 9.2 km; c. about 1.8 km

12. In the graph at left, point *C* has coordinates (1, 2). Point *D* has coordinates (3, 1). What is the distance between these points? (Hint: Use a right triangle with hypotenuse $\overline{CD}$.) $\sqrt{5}$

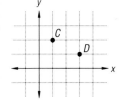

13. Typing paper is an 8.5″ by 11″ rectangle. Find the length of a diagonal of the rectangle:

a. by measuring with a ruler;   **about $13\frac{7}{8}$″ or 13.9″**

b. by using the Pythagorean Theorem. $\sqrt{193.25}$″ or about 13.9″

14. *Multiple choice* There was no year 0. What year is 2500 years after the estimated year of Pythagoras' birth?   **(b)**

(a) 1928   (b) 1929   (c) 1972   (d) 2072

15. Simplify: $\sqrt{225 - 144}$. *(Lesson 13-2)*   **9**

16. Simplify: $\sqrt{2^2 + 3^2}$. *(Lesson 13-2)* $\sqrt{13} \approx 3.6056$

17. *True or false?* $\sqrt{9} + \sqrt{16} = \sqrt{25}$. *(Lesson 13-2)*   **False**

18. a. The square of what number is 0?   **0**

b. Simplify: $\sqrt{0}$. *(Lesson 13-2)*   **0**

19. To the nearest integer, what is 2.5^7? *(Lesson 2-2)*   **610**

20. Solve: $5000 = 50 + x - 25$. *(Lessons 5-8, 7-2)*   **4975**

21. In the first 40 games of the baseball season, Homer had 31 hits. At this rate, how many hits will he have for the entire 125-game season? *(Lesson 11-2)*   **97**

582

22. *Multiple choice* $0 + (x + 1) = 0 + (1 + x)$ is an instance of what property? *(Lessons 5-4, 5-7)* (a)
   (a) Commutative Property of Addition
   (b) Associative Property of Addition
   (c) Addition Property of Zero
   (d) Addition Property of One

23. At 35 miles per hour, how long will it take to go 10 miles?
   (Lesson 11-5) 10/35 hours or about 17 minutes

Exploration

24. The Pythagoreans worshiped numbers and loved music. They discovered relationships between the lengths of strings and the musical tones they give.

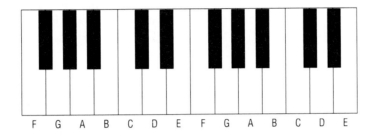

Look in an encyclopedia to find out one of the relationships discovered by the Pythagoreans. See below.

Sample: A string half as long as another sounds a note one octave higher than the other.

EXTENSION

Some students may be interested in the following proof of the Pythagorean Theorem. Let the legs of the right triangles be *a* and *b*, the hypotenuse *c*.

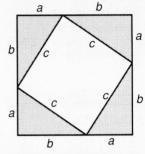

The area of the bigger square is $(a + b)^2$, or $(a + b)(a + b)$, which by the Distributive Property equals $(a + b)a + (a + b)b$, or $a^2 + 2ab + b^2$. But the area of the bigger square is also the sum of the areas of the 4 right triangles and the area of the tilted square, or $4(\frac{1}{2}ab) + c^2$, which simplifies to $2ab + c^2$. Thus, $a^2 + 2ab + b^2 = 2ab + c^2$. By subtracting $2ab$ from each side of the equation, the result is $a^2 + b^2 = c^2$, or the Pythagorean Theorem.

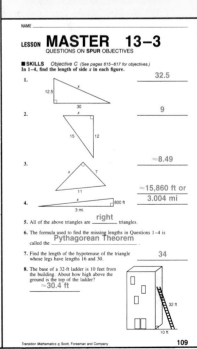

NAME _____

LESSON **MASTER 13-3**
QUESTIONS ON **SPUR** OBJECTIVES

■SKILLS   *Objective C (See pages 615–617 for objectives.)*
In 1–4, find the length of side *x* in each figure.

1.   32.5
   12.5
        30

2.   9
    15   12

3.   ≈8.49
      x   7
        11

4.   ≈15,860 ft or
      x   800 ft   3.004 mi
    3 mi.

5. All of the above triangles are ____right____ triangles.

6. The formula used to find the missing lengths in Questions 1–4 is called the ___Pythagorean Theorem___.

7. Find the length of the hypotenuse of the triangle whose legs have lengths 16 and 30.   34

8. The base of a 32-ft ladder is 10 feet from the building. About how high above the ground is the top of the ladder? ≈30.4 ft

Transition Mathematics © Scott, Foresman and Company   **109**

LESSON
13-4

Area of Any Triangle

If the proper information is given, you already know enough to get the area of any triangle.

Example 1   Find the area of △ABC.

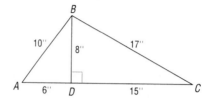

Solution   Separate △ABC into the two right triangles ABD and BDC.

Area of △ABD = $\frac{1}{2} \cdot 6 \cdot 8$ square in.

Area of △BDC = $\frac{1}{2} \cdot 8 \cdot 15$ square in.

Add the areas to get the area of the big triangle ABC.

$$\text{Area of } \triangle ABC = \tfrac{1}{2} \cdot 6 \cdot 8 + \tfrac{1}{2} \cdot 8 \cdot 15$$
$$= \quad 24 \quad + \quad 60$$
$$= 84 \text{ square inches}$$

(The 10″ and 17″ lengths are not needed here for the area.)

By using the Distributive Property, this idea can be generalized. The result is a formula for the area of any triangle. Start with any triangle ABC.

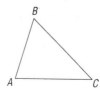

584

Draw the perpendicular segment from B to $\overline{AC}$. We call its length h, since it is the **height** of the triangle. This splits $\triangle ABC$ into two right triangles. It also splits $\overline{AC}$ into two segments with lengths we call x and y.

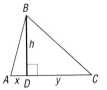

$$\text{Area of } \triangle ABC = \text{Area of } \triangle ABD + \text{Area of } \triangle BDC$$
$$= \tfrac{1}{2}hx + \tfrac{1}{2}hy$$

Now use the Distributive Property.

$$= \tfrac{1}{2}h(x + y)$$
$$= \tfrac{1}{2}h \cdot AC$$

Thus the area of this triangle is one-half times its height times the length of the side to which the height is drawn.

Every triangle has three heights. It depends to which side you draw the perpendicular. Below are three copies of $\triangle ABC$. The three heights are drawn with a heavy line. Also drawn are three rectangles. The area of the triangle is always one-half the area of the rectangle. That is, the area of the triangle is $\tfrac{1}{2}hb$.

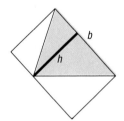
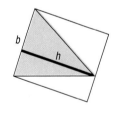

Another name for height is **altitude**. The side to which the altitude is drawn is called the **base** for that altitude. Using these words, the area of a triangle is half the product of any of its bases and the altitude to that base.

Area formula for any triangle:

Let b be the length of a side of a triangle with area A.
Let h be the length of the altitude drawn to that side.

Then $A = \tfrac{1}{2}hb$.

Have students draw several rectangles on graph paper and find the area of each. Then show students how to draw a triangle inside each rectangle where one side of the rectangle becomes the base of the triangle and the third vertex of the triangle lies on the opposite side of the rectangle, but not at a vertex. Have students count squares to estimate the area of the largest triangle. Ask what they notice about the relation of the area of each triangle to the area of the rectangle. (The area of the triangle is one-half the area of the rectangle.)

ADDITIONAL EXAMPLES
1. Find the area of this triangle.

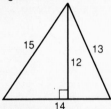

84 square units

2. Draw a large triangle with 3 acute angles. Then draw all the altitudes in your triangle.
sample:

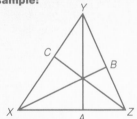

NOTES ON QUESTIONS
Question 7: This combines the Pythagorean Theorem and the area formula.

Error Analysis for Question 8: Some students will not know what to do, since they are finding an altitude, not an area. Tell them to write the formula first and then make substitutions. They will need to solve an equation of the form $ax = b$.

Question 10: The altitude of this triangle is outside the figure. Ask students why the altitude is placed outside the triangle. (Angle R is obtuse.)

ADDITIONAL ANSWERS
3.

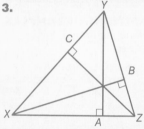

5. Let b be the length of a side of a triangle with area A, and let h be the length of the altitude drawn to that side; then $A = \frac{1}{2}hb$.

Example 2 $\overline{VY}$ is perpendicular to $\overline{XZ}$. Find the area of $\triangle XYZ$.

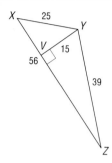

Solution Think of $\overline{XZ}$ as the base of the triangle. Then $\overline{VY}$ is the altitude to that base.

$$\text{Area} = \frac{1}{2} \cdot hb$$
$$= \frac{1}{2} \cdot VY \cdot XZ$$
$$= 0.5 \cdot 15 \cdot 56$$
$$= 420$$

Questions

Covering the Reading

1. Find the area of $\triangle DEF$.   468 square units

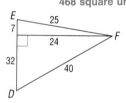

2. Find the area of $\triangle ABC$.   84 square units

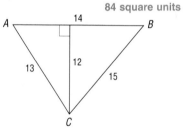

3. Trace $\triangle XYZ$.

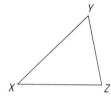

See margin.
a. Draw the altitude from Y to side $\overline{XZ}$. $\overline{YA}$
b. Draw the altitude from X to side $\overline{YZ}$. $\overline{XB}$
c. Draw the altitude from Z to side $\overline{XY}$. $\overline{ZC}$

4. Give another name for: **a.** altitude; **b.** the side of a triangle to which the altitude is perpendicular.   a. height; b. base

5. Give a formula for the area of a triangle.   See margin.

586

6. The squares in the grid below are 1 unit on a side. Find the area of △*MNP*.   **21 square units**

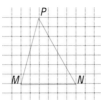

7. In an *equilateral* triangle, all sides have the same length. Drawn at left is equilateral triangle *ABC* with sides of length 8 cm.

  a. Find the length of the altitude $\overline{AD}$.   **√48 cm**
  b. Find the area of △*ABC*.   **4√48 cm²**

8. The triangle below has a base with length 40 cm and an area of 300 cm². What is the length of the altitude to that base?   **15 cm**

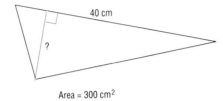

Area = 300 cm²

9. Below is a photograph of two of the great pyramids of Giza in Egypt. Each face of the largest pyramid has a base about 230 meters long. The height of each face is about 92 meters. What is the area of a face? **10,580 square meters**

10. Find the area of △*EAR* below.   **132 square units**

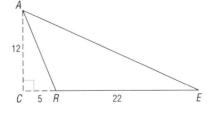

LESSON 13-4   Area of Any Triangle   **587**

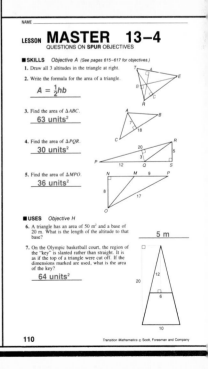

NOTES ON QUESTIONS

Question 11: The Distributive Property should be used to avoid more than one multiplication by 5.671.

Question 22: To find the area of a triangle in a real situation, one usually has to measure the lengths for the formula. There are three options, one for each altitude. The three sides have lengths about $3\frac{3}{8}$ in., $3\frac{5}{8}$ in., and $3\frac{3}{4}$ in. The corresponding altitudes have lengths about $3\frac{3}{8}$ in., 3 in., and 3 in. Regardless of the base and altitude used, the same approximate area 6 in.^{2} is found.

FOLLOW-UP

MORE PRACTICE
For more questions on SPUR Objectives, use *Lesson Master 13-4*, shown on page 587.

EVALUATION
Alternative Assessment
Draw a few triangles on the board, such as those below. Ask the students to find the area of each.

1.

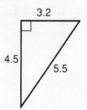

2.

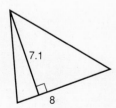

3.

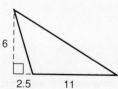

(7.2 square units; 28.4 square units; 33 square units)

Review

11. Evaluate $3x + 14x + 2x + x$ when $x = 5.671$. *(Lesson 12-1)*
113.42

12. Multiply $a(a + 2)$. *(Lesson 12-4)* $a^2 + 2a$

13. Solve: $x - 0.4 = 3.02$ *(Lesson 7-4)*   3.42

14. Round $\frac{440}{-6}$ to the nearest integer. *(Lessons 1-4, 11-3)*   -73

15. Order from smallest to largest: $\sqrt{3}$, 3%, $0.\overline{3}$, $\frac{3}{10}$.
(Lessons 1-8, 2-5, 13-2)   3%, $\frac{3}{10}$, $.\overline{3}$, $\sqrt{3}$

16. Add: $\frac{2}{5} + \frac{1}{3} + \frac{1}{4}$. *(Lesson 5-2)* $\frac{59}{60}$

17. What is the value of $-4m$ when $m = -4$? *(Lessons 4-4, 10-5)*   16

18. Translate into English: 345.29. *(Lesson 1-2)*
three hundred forty-five and twenty-nine hundredths

19. Ignoring air resistance, it takes about $0.25\sqrt{s}$ seconds for an object to fall s feet. A dime is dropped from the top of the Sears Tower, 1454 feet above the ground. To the nearest second, about how long will it take the dime to reach the ground? *(Lesson 13-2)*
10 seconds

20. How many two-digit numbers satisfy both of the following conditions?
(1) The first digit is 1, 3, 5, or 7.
(2) The second digit is 2, 4, or 6. *(Lessons 6-1, 9-1)*   12 numbers

21. Find the simple fraction in lowest terms equal to $\frac{0.46}{9.2}$. *(Lesson 1-10)*
$\frac{1}{20}$

Exploration

22. By drawing an altitude and measuring lengths, find the area of this triangle to the nearest square inch.   6 square inches

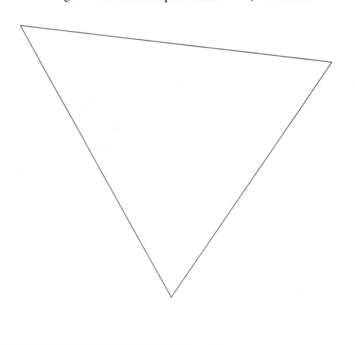

13-5

Areas of Polygons

Pentagon *ABCDE* is split into three triangles.

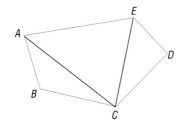

To find the area of *ABCDE*, you could add the areas of the triangles. This is one reason why you learned how to find the area of a triangle. *Any* polygon can be split into triangles.

If the triangles have the same altitude, then the areas can be added using the Distributive Property. A simple formula can be the result. Here is an example using a **trapezoid**. A trapezoid is a quadrilateral that has at least one pair of parallel sides.

Example   Find the area of trapezoid *TRAP*.

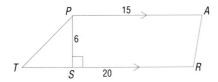

Solution   Draw the diagonal $\overline{PR}$. This splits the trapezoid into two triangles, *PAR* and *PRT*. Each triangle has altitude 6.

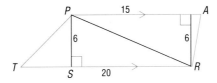

$$
\begin{aligned}
\text{Area of trapezoid } TRAP &= \text{Area of } \triangle PAR + \text{Area of } \triangle PRT \\
&= \tfrac{1}{2} \cdot 6 \cdot 15 \quad + \quad \tfrac{1}{2} \cdot 6 \cdot 20 \\
&= \quad 45 \quad + \quad 60 \\
&= \quad 105
\end{aligned}
$$

LESSON 13-5   *Areas of Polygons*   **589**

LESSON 13-5

RESOURCES
■ Lesson Master 13-5
▣ Computer Master 27

OBJECTIVE

D Find the area of a trapezoid.

TEACHING NOTES

When discussing the lesson, emphasize the derivation of the formula and the relationship of trapezoids to other quadrilaterals.

Because memorizing the formula for the area of a trapezoid is not recommended, students can focus on learning to divide the trapezoid into two triangles whose areas they can find. This process can be used for any polygon. Help students to follow the use of the Distributive Property in deriving the formula.

Stress that the definition of *trapezoid* includes any quadrilateral with at least one pair of parallel sides; there can be two pairs of parallel sides. One way to develop an appreciation of the implications is to show that the formula $A = \frac{1}{2}h(b + B)$ becomes $A = hb$ if the figure is a parallelogram ($b = B$), $A = \ell w$ if the figure is a rectangle ($h = \ell$, $b = B = w$), and $A = s^2$ if the figure is a square ($h = s$, $b = B = s$).

1.

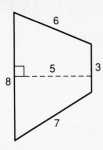

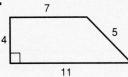

27.5 square units

2.

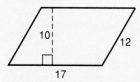

34 square units

3. (This figure is a parallelogram.)

170 square units
Using Manipulatives
4. If the Geometry Template is available, have students measure and find the area of each trapezoid on the Geometry Template. Remind students that squares, rectangles, rhombuses, and parallelograms are trapezoids because they have a pair of parallel sides.

The parallel sides of a trapezoid are called its **bases**. The distance between the bases is the **height** or **altitude** of the trapezoid. The example shows that you only need the lengths of the bases and the height to find the area of a trapezoid.

To find a general formula, replace the specific lengths with variables. Let the bases have lengths b and B. Let the height be h.

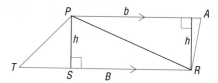

Area of trapezoid $TRAP$ = Area of $\triangle PAR$ + Area of $\triangle PRT$

$$= \tfrac{1}{2} \cdot h \cdot b + \tfrac{1}{2} \cdot h \cdot B$$

Now use the Distributive Property. The following formula is the result.

Area formula for a trapezoid:

> Let A be the area of a trapezoid with bases B and b and height h. Then
> $$A = \tfrac{1}{2} \cdot h(b + B).$$

Some people prefer the formula in words.

> The area of a trapezoid is one-half the product of its height and the sum of the lengths of its bases.

Trapezoids come in many different sizes and shapes. Here are some trapezoids with bases drawn darker. Heights are dotted. In the trapezoid at right, the trapezoid is quite slanted. So one base has to be extended to meet the height.

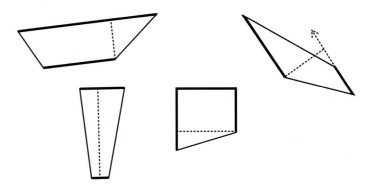

590

Rectangles, squares, rhombuses, and parallelograms have parallel sides. So they are trapezoids. This makes trapezoids important. Whatever is true for all trapezoids is true for all rectangles, squares, rhombuses, and parallelograms. The area formula for a trapezoid works for all these other figures also.

There is no general formula that works for the area of all polygons.

Questions

Covering the Reading

1. Why is the area formula for a triangle so important?   See margin.

2. How can you tell if a figure is a trapezoid?
   if it has at least one pair of parallel sides

In 3–7, *true or false*.

3. All quadrilaterals are trapezoids.   False

4. All squares are trapezoids.   True

5. All trapezoids are rectangles.   False

6. The formula for the area of a trapezoid can be used to find the area of a parallelogram.   True

7. There is a formula for the area of any polygon.   False

8. Use the trapezoid below.

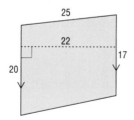

   a. Give the lengths of its bases.   20, 17
   b. Give its height.   22
   c. Give its area.   407 units²

9. a. Draw a trapezoid with bases of length 4 cm and 5 cm and a height of 2 cm.   See margin.
   b. Find the area of this trapezoid.   9 cm²

10. A trapezoid has bases b and B and height h. What is its area?
    $\frac{1}{2}h(b + B)$

11. In words, state the formula for the area of a trapezoid.
    See margin.

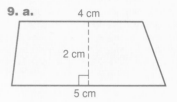

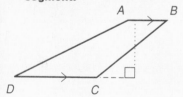
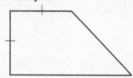
12. Draw a trapezoid with exactly two sides of equal length. See margin.

13. Find the area of the parallelogram drawn below. **320 square units**

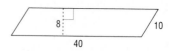

14. The shape of Egypt roughly approximates a trapezoid. The north edge of Egypt is about 900 km long, the south edge about 1100 km long, and the height is about 1100 km. What is the approximate area of Egypt? **1,100,000 square kilometers**

Cairo

15. A trapezoid has area 60 square meters. Its height is 10 meters. One of the bases has length 5 meters. What is the length of the other base? **7 meters**

16. Order these seven terms from most general to most specific.

polygon   square   trapezoid   figure
rectangle   quadrilateral   parallelogram   **See margin.**

17. Draw an altitude of trapezoid *ABCD*. **See margin.**

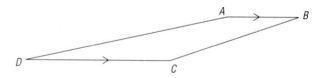

18. The diagonal of a rectangle is drawn. This splits the rectangle into two right triangles. *True or false:* The perimeter of each right triangle is one-half the perimeter of the rectangle. *(Lesson 5-10)*
False

19. Find the area of a right triangle with sides of lengths 12 ft, 16 ft, and 20 ft. *(Lesson 13-1)* **96 square feet**

20. Find the length of the hypotenuse of $\triangle ABC$ below. *(Lesson 13-3)*
1.3

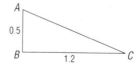

592

21. *True or false?* $\sqrt{\frac{1}{2}} > \frac{1}{2}$. *(Lesson 13-2)* True

22. Solve: $2t - 5 = 9 + 8t$. *(Lesson 12-5)* $-\frac{7}{3}$

23. Solve: $3(2u - 5) = 27$. *(Lessons 10-9, 12-5)* 7

24. To the nearest integer, what is the sum of the mixed numbers $2\frac{1}{3}$, $3\frac{1}{4}$, and $4\frac{1}{5}$? *(Lesson 5-2)* 10

25. Two-thirds of an amount of cloth was used. The starting amount was A. How much is left? *(Lesson 10-3)* $\frac{1}{3}A$ or $\frac{A}{3}$

26. Find the simple fraction equal to $8.\overline{2}$. *(Lesson 12-2)* $\frac{74}{9}$

Exploration

27. Words often have many meanings. Sometimes those meanings do not agree with each other. One of the meanings of trapezoid is "trapezium."
 a. Look in a dictionary to find another meaning of "trapezium."
 b. Draw a trapezium.
  a. Sample: a quadrilateral with no sides parallel; b. See margin.

FOLLOW-UP

MORE PRACTICE
For more questions on SPUR Objectives, use *Lesson Master 13-5*, shown below.

EXTENSION
Have each student draw a large quadrilateral on a sheet of paper. The quadrilateral should *not* have any parallel sides. Ask the students to find the areas of their figures by dividing them into triangles, measuring bases and altitudes, and adding the areas of the triangles.

27. b. sample:

NAME _____

■SKILLS *Objective D (See pages 615–617 for objectives.)*
In 1 and 2, draw an altitude of each trapezoid.

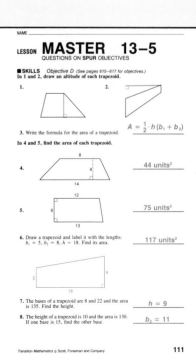

1.   **2.**

3. Write the formula for the area of a trapezoid. $A = \frac{1}{2} \cdot h\,(b_1 + b_2)$

In 4 and 5, find the area of each trapezoid.

4.   8 / 4 / 14   44 units²

5.   12 / 6 / 13   75 units²

6. Draw a trapezoid and label it with the lengths: $b_1 = 5$, $b_2 = 8$, $h = 18$. Find its area.   117 units²
 5 / 18 / 8

7. The bases of a trapezoid are 8 and 22 and the area is 135. Find the height. $h = 9$

8. The height of a trapezoid is 10 and the area is 130. If one base is 15, find the other base. $b_2 = 11$

111

LESSON 13-6

RESOURCES
- Lesson Master 13-6
- Quiz on Lessons 13-4 Through 13-6
- Visual for Teaching Aid 76: The Family of Real Numbers
- Visual for Teaching Aid 77: **Question 29**
- *Manipulative Activities Sourcebook,* Activity 24

OBJECTIVES

E Find the circumference of a circle or sector, given its radius or diameter.

G Identify numbers as rational, irrational, or real.

I Apply formulas for the circumference of a circle in real situations.

TEACHING NOTES

In this lesson, the two important ideas are the circumference of a circle and the introduction of irrational numbers. Students will need to memorize the formula for the circumference of a circle, since there is no convenient way to derive it. The chart on page 596 lists the types of numbers with which students should be familiar.

Point out to students that π can be left as part of a meaningful answer. It is not always necessary to write a decimal or fraction approximation. We tend to give an exact answer in terms of π to questions that do not refer to an application (Question 22 for example), and suggest approximations by decimals or fractions when there is a real world context (for example, Question 23).

The Number π

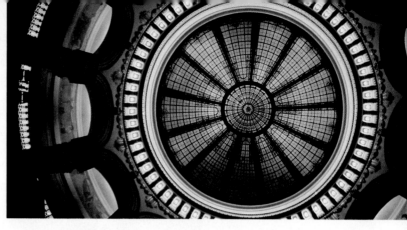

Suppose you put a tape measure around your waist. Then you can measure the perimeter of your waist. You can do this even though your waist is curved.

The same idea works for circles. The perimeter of a circle can be measured. It is the distance around the circle, the distance you would travel if you walked around the circle.

A **circle** is the set of points at a certain distance (its **radius**) from a certain point (its **center**). The distance across the circle is twice the length of its radius. That distance is the circle's **diameter**.

The plural of radius is *radii*. Both radii and diameters may be segments or distances. The circle at left below has center *C*. One radius of the circle is $\overline{CD}$. The radius of this circle is 5. One diameter of the circle is $\overline{DE}$. The diameter is 10.

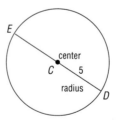

The top of the tin can pictured at right is a circle with diameter *s*. Think of the distance around this circle. (It is how far an electric can opener turns in opening the can.) The amount needed can be estimated by unraveling the circle. We draw the circle with different thicknesses so you can see the unraveling.

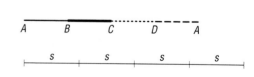

594

594

The unraveled circle is not 4 times the length of the diameter. It is just a little more than 3 times the diameter, as the picture shows. In fact, the unraveled length, called the **circumference** of the circle, is exactly 3.1415926535... times the diameter. You have seen this number before. It is called π (pi) and its decimal never repeats or ends.

The circumference of a circle is the circle's perimeter. Don't be fooled just because the word is long and different.

In a circle, the diameter d and circumference C are related by the formula $C = \pi d$.

Example To the nearest inch, what is the circumference of a tin can with a 4″ diameter?

4 in.

Solution $C = \pi \cdot 4 = 4\pi$ inches exactly.
To approximate C to the nearest inch, use 3.14 for π.
$C \approx 3.14 \cdot 4 = 12.56$ inches, so C is about 13″.

The number π is so important that scientific calculators almost always have a $\boxed{\pi}$ key. Pressing that key will give you many decimal places of π. Without a calculator, people use various approximations. For rough estimates, you can use 3.14 or $\frac{22}{7}$. Use more decimal places if you want more accuracy.

Because $C = \pi d$, $\pi = \frac{C}{d}$. That is, π is the ratio of the circumference of a circle to its diameter. $\frac{C}{d}$ looks like a simple fraction. However, the numbers C and d cannot both be whole numbers and still have the ratio equal π.

A number that *can* be written as a simple fraction is called a **rational number.** Finite decimals, repeating decimals, and mixed numbers all represent rational numbers. A number that *cannot* be written as a simple fraction is called an **irrational number.** Irrational numbers are exactly those numbers whose decimals are infinite and do not repeat. When the square root of a positive integer, like $\sqrt{2}$, is not an integer, then it is irrational.

LESSON 13-6   The Number π **595**

Irrational numbers are very important in many measurement formulas. Square roots often appear as lengths of sides of right triangles. With circles, all formulas for area and circumference involve π. As you study more mathematics, you will learn about many other irrational numbers.

A number that can be written as a decimal is called a **real number**. All of the numbers discussed in this book have been real numbers. (There are other numbers. You will learn about them in future mathematics courses.) Every real number is either rational or irrational. The chart shows how various kinds of numbers are related.

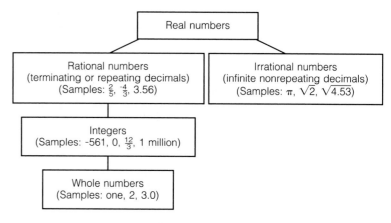

Real numbers

Rational numbers
(terminating or repeating decimals)
(Samples: $\frac{2}{5}$, $\frac{-4}{3}$, 3.56)

Irrational numbers
(infinite nonrepeating decimals)
(Samples: π, √2, √4.53)

Integers
(Samples: -561, 0, $\frac{12}{3}$, 1 million)

Whole numbers
(Samples: one, 2, 3.0)

Questions

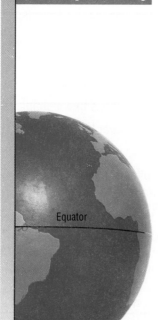

Equator

Covering the Reading

1. What is a circle?
   the set of points at a certain distance from a certain point

2. The distance across a circle at its center is called the __?__ of the circle.   diameter

3. The perimeter of a circle is called the __?__ of the circle.
   circumference

4. A circle has diameter 10 cm. To the nearest cm, what is its circumference?   31 cm

5. The circumference of a circle with diameter s is __?__.   πs

6. A simple fraction that is used as an approximation to π is __?__. $\frac{22}{7}$

7. A calculator shows π to be 3.141592654.
   a. Is this an exact value or an estimate?   estimate
   b. Round this number to the nearest hundredth.   3.14
   c. Round this number to the nearest hundred thousandth.   3.14159
   d. What does your calculator show for π?
   Sample: some calculators show 3.1415927

8. The equator of the earth is approximately a circle whose diameter is about 7920 miles. What is the distance around the earth at its equator?   about 24,900 miles

9. Name the two division facts related to $C = \pi d$. $\pi = \frac{C}{d}; d = \frac{C}{\pi}$

10. When is a number rational?
when it can be written as a simple fraction

11. When is a number irrational?
when it cannot be written as a simple fraction

In 12–17, tell whether the number is rational or irrational.

12. $\frac{2}{3}$ rational   **13.** π irrational   **14.** $6.\overline{87}$ rational

15. $\sqrt{5}$ irrational   **16.** $5\frac{1}{2}$ rational   **17.** 0.0004 rational

18. What is a real number? a number that can be written as a decimal

19. Which of the numbers of Questions 12–17 are real numbers?
all of them

20. Are there any numbers that are not real numbers? Yes

Applying the Mathematics

In 21–22, use the fact that the diameter of a circle is twice its radius.

21. The circle at left has radius 0.6″. What is its circumference?
1.2π inches $\approx 3.77″$

22. A circle has radius r. What is its exact circumference? $2r\pi$

23. To protect a city from attack, fortifications are built in the shape of a circle. The center of the circle is the center of the city. The radius of the circle is 12 miles. What is the length of the fortifications? 24π or about 75 miles

24. A plastic tube 50″ long is bent to make a hoop. To the nearest inch, what is the diameter of the hoop? 16″

25. Some bicycle wheels are 24″ in diameter. How far will the bike go if the wheels turn 10 revolutions? about 754 inches or 63 feet

26. The number $\frac{355}{113}$ is a good estimate for π. Which is a better approximation to π, $\frac{355}{113}$ or $\frac{22}{7}$? $\frac{355}{113}$

27. Which is larger, π or $\sqrt{10}$? $\sqrt{10}$

28. Approximate $\pi + 1$ to the nearest tenth. 4.1

LESSON 13-6 The Number π 597

29. Each side of polygon $ABCD$ has exactly one point in common with circle O. The radius of that circle to that point is perpendicular to the side. If the radius is 6, what is the area of $ABCD$? (Hint: Split the area into triangles OAB, OBC, OCD, ODA.)
162 square units

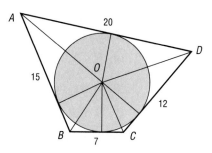

Review

30. What is the perimeter of the quadrilateral $ABCD$ of Question 29? *(Lesson 5-10)* 54

31. Simplify $\sqrt{841} - \sqrt{400}$. *(Lesson 13-2)* 9

32. Find the area of the trapezoid below. *(Lessons 13-3, 13-5)*
156 square units

33. Evaluate $5\sqrt{3}$ to the nearest integer. *(Lesson 13-2)* 9

34. Evaluate $|2 - n|$ when $n = 5$. *(Lesson 5-5)* 3

35. Evaluate $9x^3 - 7x^2 + 12$ when $x = 6$. *(Lesson 4-4)* 1704

36. Olivia biked m miles at 20 miles per hour. How many hours did it take her to do this? *(Lessons 6-7, 11-5)* $\frac{m}{20}$ hours

37. 6% of what number is 30? *(Lesson 10-3)* 500

38. 6 is what percent of 30? *(Lesson 11-4)* 20%

598

39. The Greek mathematician Archimedes knew that π was between $3\frac{1}{7}$ and $3\frac{10}{71}$. (Archimedes lived from about 287 B.C. to 212 B.C. and was one of the greatest mathematicians of all time.)
 a. Calculate the decimal equivalents of these mixed numbers.
 b. Why didn't Archimedes have a decimal equivalent for π?
 c. How old was Archimedes when he died?
 d. What were the sad circumstances that led to the death of this famous man? (Use references from your school library.)
 See below.

40. a. Run this program, putting a large number in the blank.

```
10 SUM = 0
20 FOR N = 1 TO ____
30    TERM = 1/(N*N)
40    SUM = SUM + TERM
50    NEARPI = SQR(6*SUM)
60    PRINT N, NEARPI
70 NEXT N
80 END
```

Write down the last line the computer prints.
 b. What does the program do?
 c. Try a larger number in the blank and see what happens.
 See margin.

39. a. 3.1428571, 3.1408451 b. Decimals had not been invented yet. c. 74 or 75 years old d. He was stabbed in the back by a soldier while drawing a diagram in sand.

LESSON 13-6   The Number π   599

FOLLOW-UP

MORE PRACTICE
For more questions on SPUR Objectives, use *Lesson Master 13-6*, shown below.

EVALUATION
A quiz covering Lessons 13-4 through 13-6 is provided in the Teacher's Resource File on page 112.

ADDITIONAL ANSWERS
**40. a. sample: If 100 is put in the blank, the last line is
100   3.13207653
b. It adds the reciprocals of the squares of integers from 1 to *n*, then takes the square root of 6 times this sum. As *n* gets larger and larger, the result gives a better and better approximation to π.
c. sample: If 1000 is put in the blank, the last line is
1000   3.14063806**

NAME ____

Circles and Sectors

All formulas for area or volume of circles and spheres involve the number π. The most famous of these is for the area of a circle.

At left are four little squares, each with side r. So their total area is $4r^2$. This shows that the area of the circle is less than $4r^2$. But it does not show the exact area of the circle. To figure that out requires more advanced mathematics. But it does seem that the area of the circle equals a little more than 3 of the 4 squares. In fact, the area equals 3.14159... of the squares.

Area formula for a circle:

> Let A be the area of a circle with radius r.
> Then $A = \pi r^2$.

Example 1 Find the area of a circle with a radius of 5 inches, to the nearest square inch.

Solution $A = \pi \cdot (5 \text{ in.})^2 = 25\pi \text{ in.}^2$
$\approx 25 \cdot 3.1416 \text{ in.}^2$
$\approx 78.54 \text{ in.}^2$
$\approx 79 \text{ in.}^2$

Check Notice that a square with side 10″ would cover the circle. The area of the square is 100 square inches. So an area of about 79 square inches for the circle seems about right.

10 inches

600

In the figure at left, angle *AOB* is called a *central angle* of circle *O*. A **central angle** is an angle with its vertex at the center. The part of the circle that looks like a slice of pie is called a **sector**.

The area of a sector depends on the size of the central angle.

■ ■ ■ ■ ■ ■ ■ ■

Example 2 Below a sector is pictured. Angle *VCR* is a right angle. *VC* = 8. Find the area of the sector.

Solution A right angle has measure 90°. This is $\frac{90}{360}$, or $\frac{1}{4}$ of a revolution. So the sector has $\frac{1}{4}$ the area of the circle.
$A = \frac{1}{4} \cdot \pi \cdot 8^2 = 16\pi$

Check Notice that $16\pi \approx 16 \cdot 3.14 \approx 50$. A square with sides $\overline{VC}$ and $\overline{CR}$ has area 64. This is larger than the area of the sector, as it should be.

■ ■ ■ ■ ■ ■ ■ ■

Example 3 Consider the figure below. *AG* = 1 cm. The measure of angle *BAG* is 45°. Find the area of sector *BAG*.

Solution 45 degrees is 45/360 = 1/8 of a revolution. The area of circle *A* is $\pi \cdot 1^2 = \pi$ cm². So the area of sector *BAG* is $\frac{1}{8}$ of π or approximately 0.4 cm².

The area of a sector of a circle is generalized in this formula.

Area formula for a sector:

Let *A* be the area of a sector of a circle with radius *r*. Let *m* be the measure of the central angle of the sector in degrees. Then $A = \frac{m}{360} \cdot \pi r^2$.

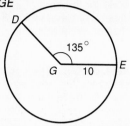

Questions

1. What is the area of a square with side length 8?   **64 square units**

2. What is the area of a circle with radius r?   **πr^2**

3. To the nearest integer, what is the area of a circle with radius 4?
   50 square units

4. Without calculating, how can you know that the answer to
   Question 3 must be less than the answer to Question 1?   **The square
   of Question 1 could completely cover the circle of Question 3.**

5. What is the area of one half of a circle with radius 6?
   18π square units

6. What is a central angle of a circle?
   an angle with its vertex at the center of the circle

In 7–10, use the figure at right.

7. What is the name of this figure?   **sector**

8. What is the measure of angle GHI?   **90°**

9. What part of a circle is pictured? $\frac{1}{4}$

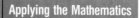

10. If $HI = 10$, what is the area of this figure?   **25π square units**

11. A quarter has radius 12.15 mm. What is the area of one of its
    faces?   **about 463.77 mm²**

12. What calculator key sequence will give you an estimate to the
    area of a circle with radius 50?   **See margin.**

13. A central angle of a sector has measure 50°. If the area of the
    circle is 180 square meters, what is the area of the sector?
    25 square meters

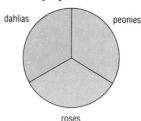

14. Assume that the smaller circle at left has radius 0.5 inches, and
    the larger circle has radius 0.75 inches.
    a. What is the area of the ring?
    b. Which has more area, the smaller circle or the shaded ring?
    a. 0.3125π or about 0.98 in²; b. the ring

15. Clyde decided to plant a circular flower garden. He wanted equal-
    sized plots of ground for each of three flower types. Below is his
    landscape plan.

    dahlias   peonies

    roses

    a. What is the measure of the central angle of each sector of
    Clyde's garden?   **120°**
    b. If the diameter of the garden is to be 14 feet, what is the area
    of each sector of the garden? $\frac{49\pi}{3} \approx 51.3$ sq. ft.

602

16. Lisa read that there were about 10 calories per square inch of a 12-inch diameter cheese pizza. If she ate $\frac{1}{8}$ of a pizza, about how many calories would she consume?   **141 calories**

17. A dog is on a leash tied to the corner of a building. This enables the dog to travel in a sector of the circle, as shown at left. If the leash is 9 meters long, what is the area of land on which the dog may roam?   **60.75π or about 191 square meters**

Review

18. To the nearest tenth of an inch, find the circumferences of the two circles in Question 14. *(Lesson 13-6)*   **3.1 inches, 4.7 inches**

19. The hypotenuse of a right triangle has length 50. One leg has length 14. What is the length of the other leg? *(Lesson 13-3)*   **48**

20. Find the area of △*NOW*. *(Lesson 13-4)*   **2400 square units**

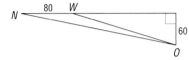

21. When does a decimal represent an irrational number? *(Lesson 13-6)*
    when it is infinite and does not repeat

22. A plant called the lichen grows 0.01 inch in a year. How many inches will it grow in a century? *(Lesson 10-4)*   **1 inch**

23. The triangles below are similar and tilted the same way. Find *PR*. *(Lesson 11-7)*   **36.36**

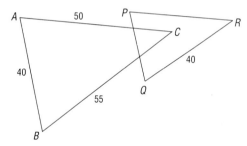

24. Simplify: $5(x - y + 12) + 6(y + x - 8)$. *(Lessons 12-3, 12-4)*
    11x + y + 12

Exploration

25. Take two pieces of string of equal length. Form the first string into a circle. Form the second string into a square.
    a. Which figure has the greater area?   **circle**
    b. Does the answer to part **a** depend on the length of the string?
       No

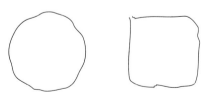

FOLLOW-UP

MORE PRACTICE
For more questions on SPUR Objectives, use *Lesson Master 13-7*, shown below.

EXTENSION
Ask the students to solve the following problems.

1. In the left figure, a square is inscribed in a circle with radius 6 cm. Find the area of the region between the circle and square, to the nearest cm.
$(36\pi - 72 \approx 41 \text{ cm}^2)$

2. In the right figure, a circle with radius 6 cm is inscribed in a square. Find the area of the shaded region, to the nearest cm.
$(12^2 - 36\pi \approx 31 \text{ cm}^2)$

NAME _____

LESSON **MASTER   13-7**
QUESTIONS ON **SPUR** OBJECTIVES

■**SKILLS**   *Objective E (See pages 615–617 for objectives.)*
1. Find the area and circumference of a circle whose radius is 8.
   area = ___**64π units²**___   circumference = ___**16π units**___

2. Find the area of a circle whose diameter is 13.   **42.25π units²**

3. Find the area of a circle whose circumference is 24π.   **144π units²**

In 4–6, find the area of each shaded sector.

4.   **π units²**

5.   **27π units²**

6.   **32π units²**

■**USES**   *Objective H*
In 7 and 8, the diagram at right represents a rectangular lawn with two sprinklers running. The sprinklers each spray a circular region with a 4 ft radius.

7. Find the total area of the part of the lawn that is watered.   **32π ≈ 100.48 ft²**

8. Find the area of the part of the lawn that is not watered.   **≈27.52 ft²**

113

13-8

Circle Graphs

Sectors of circles are commonly found in **pie** or **circle graphs**. A circle graph pictures a whole quantity that has been split up. For example, suppose 80 students were asked to choose one dessert at a carnival. At left this information is given in a table. At right the same information is displayed in a circle graph.

Choice	Number of Students Picking that Choice
Ice Cream	40
Popcorn	20
Fruit	15
None	5

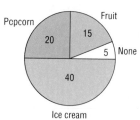

Here is how the circle graph is made.
$\frac{40}{80}$ of the students picked ice cream. This is $\frac{1}{2}$ of the students. So the sector for ice cream is half a circle, a **semicircle**.
Popcorn was picked by $\frac{20}{80}$ or $\frac{1}{4}$ of the students.
So the sector for popcorn is $\frac{1}{4}$ of the circle.
Fruit was picked by 15/80 of the students. Since a revolution is 360°, $\frac{15}{80} \cdot 360°$ is the measure of the central angle of the fruit sector. That turns out to be 67.5°.
No dessert was picked by $\frac{5}{80}$ of the students. The sector for "none" has a central angle of magnitude $\frac{5}{80} \cdot 360°$. That is 22.5°.

The choice most picked was ice cream. This is the *mode* of the choices. In a situation with many outcomes, the **mode** is the outcome that occurs most often.

604

Example The top six wheat producing countries in 1990 were the U.S.S.R., the U.S., China, India, Canada, and France. The chart below at left lists estimated production for each of these countries in millions of bushels. Make a circle graph to display this information.

Solution First find the total production. This is 328 million bushels. Now find what part of the total each country produced. Just divide 328 into the country's production. This is recorded in the table below at right in the column labeled $\frac{w}{328}$, where w stands for a country's wheat production (in millions of bushels).

1990 Leading wheat producers

China	87
U.S.S.R.	85
U.S.	57
India	46
France	27
Canada	26
Total	328

Country	$\frac{w}{328}$	$\frac{w}{328} \cdot 360°$
China	.27	95°
U.S.S.R.	.26	93°
U.S.	.17	63°
India	.14	50°
France	.08	30°
Canada	.08	29°

Finally, calculate the central angle of the sector for each country. This is simply the fraction in the second column times 360°. These results are recorded in the last column of the table on the right above.

The last step is to draw a circle and sectors with central angles equal to those calculated.

1990 Leading wheat producers

China, India, Canada, France, U.S.S.R., U.S.

Check There are two things you can do to check your work. First, add all the fractions in the $\frac{w}{328}$ column. The sum should be very near 1. Since .27 + .26 + .17 + .14 + .08 + .08 = 1.00, the sum checks.

Next, add all the central angles in the $\frac{w}{328} \cdot 360°$ column.

The sum should be 360°, the number of degrees in a revolution. 95° + 93° + 63° + 50° + 30° + 29° = 360°, so this checks too.

The first circle graphs were done by William Playfair in the late 1700s. Today circle graphs are found in many newspapers and magazines. There is software for most computers that will automatically construct circle graphs.

ADDITIONAL EXAMPLE
A family spends 17% of its income on taxes, 25% on housing, 20% on food, 10% on clothing and other necessities, 18% on entertainment and other nonnecessities, and saves 10%. Put this information into a circle graph.

The central angles are 90° for housing, 72° for food, 36° for clothing and for savings, 64.8° for entertainment, and 61.2° for taxes.

605

NOTES ON QUESTIONS

Question 13: Ask students why the graph is misleading. (The intervals of the age brackets are not consistent, and there appear to be no five-year-olds.)

Small Group Work for Question 14: You might suggest students work in pairs or small groups to complete the graph.

Questions

Covering the Reading

1. Who drew the first circle graphs, and when?
   William Playfair, late 1700s

2. What is another name for circle graph? pie graph

3. The central angle of a semicircle measures __?__. 180°

In 4 and 5, use the circle graph of dessert choices.

4. The total number of people choosing to have dessert is __?__.
   75 people

5. What fraction of people wanted popcorn? $\frac{1}{4}$

Applying the Mathematics

In 6 and 7, use the circle graph of wheat production.

6. Which country produced more wheat, Canada or India? India

7. What fraction of wheat was produced in the United States?
   $\frac{57}{328}$ or .17

8. *True or false* The sum of the central angles of all sectors in a circle graph could be 390°. False

In 9–12, use the circle graph at left. It shows how many days the Williams family spent on their recent vacation in four states.

9. **a.** What percent of the time did they spend in Utah? 20%
   b. What is the measure of the central angle for the Utah sector?
   72°

10. Give the measure of the central angle for the Colorado sector.
    108°

11. Give the measure of the central angle for the Wyoming sector.
    144°

12. *True or false* The Colorado sector has 3 times as much area as the Montana sector. True

13. From the circle graph below:
    a. Which age bracket has the fewest people? 60–64
    b. Which age bracket has the most people? 30–39
    c. Which age is missing? 5
    d. How many people are between the ages of 6 and 19? 49.4 million

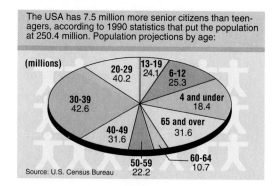

The USA has 7.5 million more senior citizens than teenagers, according to 1990 statistics that put the population at 250.4 million. Population projections by age:

(millions)
20-29 40.2
13-19 24.1
6-12 25.3
4 and under 18.4
30-39 42.6
65 and over 31.6
40-49 31.6
50-59 22.2
60-64 10.7

Source: U.S. Census Bureau

606

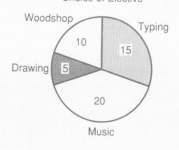

Choice of Elective

14. For their elective course, the students at Pumpkin Junction High School signed up as follows: 20 took Music, 10 took Woodshop, 5 took Drawing, and 15 took Typing.

a. What percent of students took Typing? **30%**
b. What is the fraction of students who took either Music or Drawing? $\frac{1}{2}$
c. Make a circle graph to display the given information.
d. Which choice is the mode? **music**   **See margin.**

Review

15. In the middle of a circular fountain 30 feet in diameter is a square structure supporting a statue. A side of the square is 3.5 feet. What is the surface area of the water around the structure?
(Lesson 13-7)   **about 695 square feet**

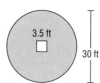

3.5 ft

30 ft

16. *Multiple choice* Which proportion is *not* true? *(Lessons 11-5, 12-5)*
(a) $\frac{2}{15} = \frac{6}{45}$ (b) $\frac{x-4}{2} = \frac{3x-12}{6}$ (c) $\frac{75}{8} = \frac{4}{.32}$ **(c)**

17. Solve $3.5x + 4 = 9x - 1$. *(Lesson 12-4)* $\frac{10}{11}$

In 18 and 19, use the figure below.

18. If $LB = .5''$ and $LI = 1''$, find IB. *(Lesson 13-3)* **about 1.1 inches**

19. If $LB = .5''$, $GL = .5''$ and $IL = 1.5''$, find the area of $\triangle GIB$.
(Lesson 13-4) **.5 square inches**

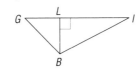

LESSON 13-8   Circle Graphs   **607**

NOTES ON QUESTIONS

Question 26: You might ask students to share the graphs they found and explain what each graph shows.

Question 27: Many spreadsheet programs come with the ability to make circle graphs.

FOLLOW-UP

MORE PRACTICE
For more questions on SPUR Objectives, use *Lesson Master 13-8,* shown on page 607.

EVALUATION
Alternative Assessment
Ask students to record how they spend their time over one week. First, each student must decide on categories of activities: sleeping; eating; school, chores or outside jobs; homework, television or other recreational activities; and so on. Then one must keep a careful record for the required number of days. Have each student show how he or she spends a typical day by creating a circle graph entitled "How I Spend My Time on a Typical Day." Averaging and some compromises will be necessary to show a "typical" day.

20. The distance from the earth to the moon averages about two hundred thirty-nine thousand miles. Write this number in scientific notation. *(Lessons 1-1, 2-3)* 2.39×10^5

In 21 and 22, simplify. *(Lessons 12-1, 12-4)*

21. $3(5m - 6t - 4)$ $15m - 18t - 12$

22. $8.7(4.2 - r) + r$ $36.54 - 7.7r$

23. What is the result of a -23° turn followed by a 14° turn? *(Lesson 5-5)*   a -9° turn

24. Approximate $4\pi(2)^2$ to the nearest tenth. *(Lesson 13-6)*   50.3

25. George Polya died in September of 1985. He was born in December of 1887.
    a. How old was he when he died? *(Lesson 7-1)*   97
    b. What are his four steps to successful problem solving?
    (Lesson 6-1)   1) Read the problem carefully. 2) Devise a plan.
    3) Carry out the plan. 4) Check work.

Exploration

26. Find a circle graph in a newspaper or magazine or make one up yourself. Bring the graph to class.   Answers will vary.

27. There is software that enables a computer to display a circle graph on a monitor. If you have access to a computer, find the name of such software. If the software is available, use it to draw the circle graph on the first page of this lesson.   See margin notes.

28. What is the meaning of the phrase *pie a la mode?* Does it have anything to do with the use of the word *mode* in this lesson?
    Sample: Pie *a la mode* means pie topped with ice cream. The phrase *a la mode* generally means stylish or fashionable; thus it is related to the use of the word *mode* as in the lesson, for the most common appearance of an event makes that event in a sense in fashion.

608

13-9

Spheres

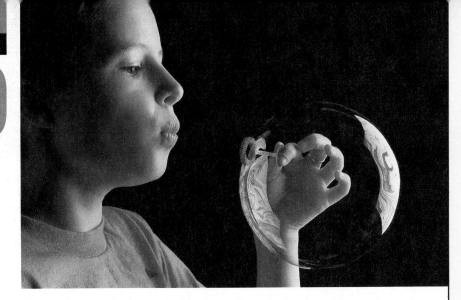

RESOURCES
- Lesson Master 13-9
- Model of a sphere, for instance, a basketball

OBJECTIVES

F Find the surface area or volume of a sphere, given its radius or diameter.

H Apply area formulas in real situations.

I Apply the formula for the volume of a sphere in real situations.

TEACHING NOTES

Using Manipulatives An example of a sphere is the best help in getting students to visualize the ideas of the lesson. A basketball works well because students can consider surface area as being the amount of material used to make the ball (ignoring its thickness) and volume as the amount of air inside.

Students do not need to memorize the formulas for the surface area and the volume of a sphere, but they should be able to tell which is which if given both. Area is measured in square units and requires r to be squared; volume is a cubic measure, and requires the variable to be cubed. In general, in area formulas, two dimensions are multiplied. In volume formulas, three dimensions are multiplied.

A **sphere** is the set of points *in space* at a given distance (its *radius*) from a given point (its *center*). Drawn below is a sphere with radius r. Planets and moons in space, baseballs, marbles, and many other objects are in the shape of spheres. In mathematics, a sphere is like a soap bubble. It doesn't include any points inside. Even the center C of a sphere is not a point on the sphere.

The formulas for the surface area and volume of a sphere were first discovered by Archimedes.

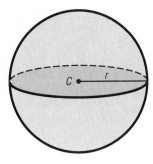

Surface area and volume formulas for a sphere:

In a sphere with radius r, surface area S, and volume V:
$$S = 4\pi r^2$$
$$\text{and} \quad V = \tfrac{4}{3}\pi r^3.$$

When computing surface areas and volumes of spheres, it helps to have a calculator.

LESSON 13-9 *Spheres* **609**

Example 1

The Earth is nearly a sphere with radius 3960 miles. What is its surface area?

Solution The formula for surface area is $S = 4\pi r^2$. Substitute 3960 for r. Here is a key sequence that will work on many calculators.

$$4 \; \boxed{\times} \; \boxed{\pi} \; \boxed{\times} \; 3960 \; \boxed{x^2} \; \boxed{=}$$

(By using the $\boxed{x^2}$ squaring key, 3960 does not have to be entered twice.)

The calculator should display a result close to 197,000,000 square miles.

Example 2

Find the volume of a sphere with radius 6.

Solution 1 Let V be the volume. $V = \frac{4}{3}\pi r^3 = \frac{4}{3}\pi \cdot 216 = 288\pi$

288π is the exact value. To get an approximate value, substitute an estimate for π, say 3.14. Then $V \approx 288 \cdot 3.14 \approx 904$.

Solution 2 Use a calculator to get an estimate. Here is a key sequence that usually will work.

$$4 \; \boxed{\div} \; 3 \; \boxed{\times} \; \boxed{\pi} \; \boxed{\times} \; 6 \; \boxed{y^x} \; 3 \; \boxed{=}$$

To the nearest hundredth, a calculator will give 904.78.
This differs from the answer of Solution 1 because a different estimate is used for π.

Remember that volume is measured in cubic units. Surface area is measured in square units (just as any other area). For instance, suppose the radius of a sphere is given in centimeters. Then the surface area is in square centimeters and the volume is in cubic centimeters.

The formulas for measuring spheres contain both rational and irrational numbers. They combine the three themes of this book: arithmetic, algebra, and geometry. We think it is nice to finish this book by discussing a topic that combines so much. But it is even nicer to finish with spheres, because the sphere is among the most beautiful of all figures.

610

Questions

Covering the Reading

1. What is a sphere?
   the set of points in space at a certain distance from a certain point

2. Give a formula for the surface area of a sphere.
   In a sphere of radius r and surface area S, $S = 4\pi r^2$.

3. Calculate the surface area of a sphere with radius 12 cm.
   576π or about 1810 cm^2

4. Give a formula for the volume of a sphere.
   In a sphere of radius r and volume V, $V = \frac{4}{3}\pi r^3$.

5. Calculate the volume of a sphere with radius 12 cm.
   2304π or about 7238 cm^3

6. Who discovered the formulas for the surface area and volume of a sphere?   **Archimedes**

7. What calculator sequence will yield the volume of a sphere with radius 7?   4 [÷] 3 [×] [π] [×] 7 [y^x] 3 [=]

Applying the Mathematics

In 8–11, tell whether the idea is more like surface area or volume.

8. how much land there is in the United States   **surface area**

9. how much material in a bowling ball   **volume**

10. how much material it takes to make a basketball   **surface area**

11. how much material in a marble   **volume**

For 12 and 13, a bowling ball is approximately 8.59 inches in diameter.

12. How much surface does a bowling ball have?
    about 232 square inches

13. How much material does it take to make a bowling ball? (Ignore the holes.)   **about 332 cubic inches**

14. The moon is approximately a sphere with radius 1080 miles.
    a. Estimate the surface area of the moon to the nearest million square miles.   **15 million square miles**
    b. How many times more surface area does the earth have than the moon?   **about 13 times**

15. A 12 cm diameter ball is put snugly into a box. What percent of the box is filled by the ball? (The answer surprises most people.)
    $\frac{\pi}{6} \approx 0.52 = 52\%$

Review

16. Make a circle graph from the information provided here.
    Of all adults: 22% sleep 6.5 hours or less
    26% sleep over 6.5 to 7.5 hours
    37% sleep over 7.5 to 8.5 hours
    9% sleep over 8.5 to 9.5 hours
    6% sleep 9.5 hours or more
    (Hint: Take percents of 360° to determine the number of degrees in each central angle.) *(Lesson 13-8)*   See margin.

LESSON 13-9   Spheres   **611**

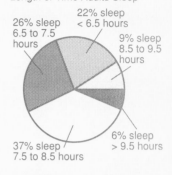

Length of Time Adults Sleep

26% sleep 6.5 to 7.5 hours
22% sleep < 6.5 hours
9% sleep 8.5 to 9.5 hours
6% sleep > 9.5 hours
37% sleep 7.5 to 8.5 hours

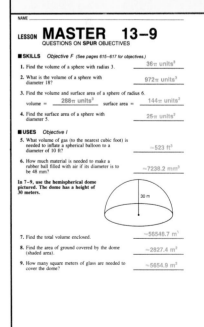

NAME _____

LESSON **MASTER 13–9**
QUESTIONS ON **SPUR** OBJECTIVES

■**SKILLS**   *Objective F (See pages 615–617 for objectives.)*

1. Find the volume of a sphere with radius 3. 36π units^3

2. What is the volume of a sphere with diameter 18? 972π units^3

3. Find the volume and surface area of a sphere of radius 6.
   volume = 288π units^3 surface area = 144π units^2

4. Find the surface area of a sphere with diameter 5. 25π units^2

■**USES**   *Objective I*

5. What volume of gas (to the nearest cubic foot) is needed to inflate a spherical balloon to a diameter of 10 ft?   ≈523 ft^3

6. How much material is needed to make a rubber ball filled with air if its diameter is to be 48 mm?   ≈7238.2 mm^3

In 7–9, use the hemispherical dome pictured. The dome has a height of 30 meters.   30 m

7. Find the total volume enclosed.   ≈56548.7 m^3

8. Find the area of ground covered by the dome (shaded area).   ≈2827.4 m^2

9. How many square meters of glass are needed to cover the dome?   ≈5654.9 m^2

Transition Mathematics © Scott, Foresman and Company   115

611

612

Question 18: The area of the United States is about 6% of the land area of the earth, and the population is less than 5% of the world's population. In contrast, the area of the Soviet Union is about 15% of the land area of the earth, and its population is about 5% of the world's population. China has just a little more area than the United States but about 23% of the world's population. Canada has a large area but not very many people compared to these other countries.

Question 19c: This answer was known to the ancient Greeks, who considered it disturbing that a figure bounded by arcs could have the same area as a polygon.

FOLLOW-UP

MORE PRACTICE
For more questions on SPUR Objectives, use *Lesson Master 13-9*, shown on page 611.

EVALUATION
Alternative Assessment
Quickly review the main measurement formulas of this chapter: the area of a triangle, a trapezoid, a circle, and a sector; the surface area and volume of a sphere. Ask the students where they might use this information. Can they think of situations at home, in a job, or at school (perhaps in science class) where these ideas might prove useful?

19. Let r be the radius of the circle.
a. $\frac{1}{2}r^2$
b. $\frac{1}{2}\pi(\frac{r\sqrt{2}}{2})^2 - (\frac{1}{4}\pi r^2 - \frac{1}{2}r^2)$
$= \frac{1}{2}r^2$
c. equal

17. From the top of a tall building, a person can see 15 miles away in any direction. How many square miles are then visible? *(Lesson 13-7)* 225π or about 707 square miles

18. The surface area of the world is given in this lesson. Only about 29.4% of the surface area is land.
   a. To the nearest million square miles, what is the total land area of the earth? *(Lesson 2-6)* 58 million square miles
   b. The area of the United States is approximately 3,540,000 square miles. What percent of the total land area of the earth is in the United States? *(Lesson 11-4)* about 6%

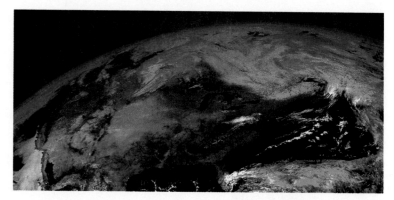

Exploration

   c. What three countries of the world have more land area than the United States? (Look in an almanac for this information, or look at a globe.) USSR, Canada, China

19. Consider the drawing at the beginning of this chapter.
   a. What is the area of triangle *ABC*?
   b. What is the area of the lune?
   c. Which area is larger, or are they equal?
   See margin.

Summary

This book began by discussing decimals. Numbers that can be represented as decimals are called *real numbers*. Real numbers are very important in measurement and are found in almost all measurement formulas. A formula is algebra, measurement is geometry, and numbers are arithmetic. So this chapter is about arithmetic, algebra, and geometry. It uses many of the ideas of earlier chapters and thus is a nice way to end this course.

The important arithmetic in this chapter is the use of irrational numbers. They are numbers with infinite decimals that do not repeat. If a square root of a positive integer is not an integer, the square root is irrational. So is π. Lengths, areas, and volumes may be rational or irrational.

The geometry of this chapter is concerned with length, area, and volume. Missing lengths of sides of a right triangle can be found using the Pythagorean theorem. From the area of a rectangle comes the area of a right triangle. Two right triangles can be combined to find the area of any triangle. Triangles may be combined to find areas of trapezoids and other polygons.

Formulas for the areas of these figures show the power of algebra. Other formulas give the circumference of a circle, the area of a circle, and the surface area and volume of a sphere. The area of a circle can be split up to make a circle graph display.

Vocabulary

You should be able to give a general description and a specific example for each of the following ideas.

Lesson 13-1
triangular region
legs, hypotenuse of a right triangle

Lesson 13-2
square root
radical sign, $\sqrt{\ }$

Lesson 13-3
Pythagorean Theorem, Pythagoras theorem

Lesson 13-4
height, altitude of a triangle
base of a triangle
equilateral triangle

Lesson 13-5
trapezoid
bases, height of a trapezoid

Lesson 13-6
circle
center, radius, diameter of circle
circumference
π, approximations to π
rational number, irrational number
real number

Lesson 13-7
central angle, sector

Lesson 13-8
pie graph, circle graph
semicircle
mode

Lesson 13-9
sphere
center, radius, diameter of sphere

CHAPTER 13 Summary and Vocabulary 613

SUMMARY

The Summary gives an overview of the chapter and provides an opportunity for students to consider the material as a whole. Thus, the Summary can be used to help students relate the concepts presented in the chapter.

VOCABULARY

Terms, symbols, and properties are listed by lesson to provide a checklist of concepts a student must know. Emphasize to students that they should read the vocabulary list carefully before starting the Progress Self-Test. If students do not understand the meaning of a term, they should refer back to the indicated lesson.

Definitions or descriptions of all terms in the vocabulary list may be found in the Glossary of the student book.

Progress Self-Test

See margin for answers not shown below.

Take this test as you would take a test in class. Then check your work with the solutions in the Selected Answers section in the back of the book.

1. A circle has radius $\frac{3''}{8}$. Find its circumference to the nearest tenth. **2.4 in.**

2. What is the area of a square if one side has length $\sqrt{3}$? **3**

3. If a square has area 10, what is the exact length of a side? **$\sqrt{10}$**

4. Estimate $\sqrt{30} + \sqrt{51}$ to the nearest integer.

5. Find x. **10**   6. Find the length of $\overline{AB}$.

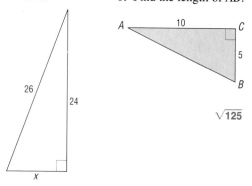

$\sqrt{125}$

7. Which number is rational?
$\sqrt{24}$ $\sqrt{25}$ $\sqrt{27}$ **$\sqrt{25}$ which is 5**

In 8–10, give the area of each figure.

8.   9.   10.

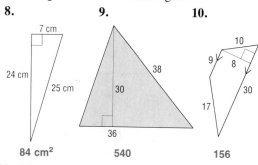

84 cm²   **540**   **156**

11. Name the hypotenuse and the two legs in the right triangle of Question 6.

12. The area of a triangle is 400 square inches. The height is 25 inches. What must be the length of the base? **32 in.**

13. Which is not always a trapezoid? quadrilateral; rectangle; square; parallelogram

14. To the nearest integer, what is the circumference of a 7" diameter record? **22 in.**

15. A circle has radius 16. What is its exact area? **256π**

16. When does a decimal represent an irrational number?

17. A basketball is hollow with a radius of about 12 cm. About how much material is needed to make it? **About 1810 cm²**

18. What is the volume of a sphere with radius 9, to the nearest cubic unit? **3054 units³**

19. The circle graph below tells about the number of players in a string orchestra. What percent of the orchestra are cellos (pictured below)? **about 20.8%**

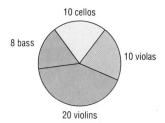

20. A circle has diameter 8 cm. What is the area of a sector of the circle having a central angle of 60°? **$\frac{8\pi}{3}$ cm²**

Chapter Review

Questions on **SPUR** Objectives

SPUR stands for **S**kills, **P**roperties, **U**ses, and **R**epresentations.
The Chapter Review questions are grouped according to the
SPUR Objectives for this chapter.

SKILLS deal with the procedures used to get answers.

Objective A: *Find the area of any triangle.*
(Lessons 13-1, 13-4)

1. Find the area of △*CAT*.   **150**

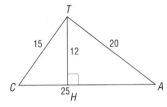

2. Find the area of △*NOW*.   **21,000 cm²**

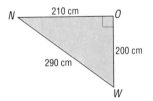

3. Find the area of △*BUI*.   **12**
4. Find the area of △*BIG*.   **48**

Objective B: *Estimate square roots of a number*
without a calculator. (Lesson 13-2)

5. Between what two integers is $\sqrt{80}$?   **8 and 9**
6. Between what two integers is $-\sqrt{3}$?   **-1 and -2**
7. Simplify $\sqrt{144 + 256}$.   **20**
8. Name the two square roots of 36.   **6 and -6**

Objective C: *Use the Pythagorean Theorem to*
find lengths of third sides in right triangles.
(Lesson 13-3)

9. Find *BI* in the figure for Questions
3 and 4. $\sqrt{73}$
10. Find *HA* in the figure for Question 1.   **16**
11. The legs of a right triangle have lengths
20 and 48. What is the length of the
hypotenuse of this triangle?   **52**
12. Find *y* in the figure below. $\sqrt{3}$

Objective D: *Find the area of a trapezoid.*
(Lesson 13-5)

13. If *ZY* = 350, find the area of *WXYZ*.   **24,600**
14. If *ZY* = 350, find the area of
parallelogram *WEYZ*.   **42,000**
15. If *ZD* = 110, find the area of *WXDZ*.
10,200

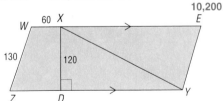

16. What is a formula for the area of a
trapezoid? $A = \frac{1}{2} \cdot h(b + B)$

CHAPTER 13   Chapter Review   **615**

RESOURCES
■ Chapter 13 Test, Form A
■ Chapter 13 Test, Form B
■ Chapter 13 Test,
   Cumulative Form
■ Comprehensive Test,
   Chapters 1–13

CHAPTER REVIEW

The main objectives for the
chapter are organized here
into sections corresponding
to the four main types of understanding this book promotes: Skills, Properties,
Uses, and Representations.

**USING THE CHAPTER
REVIEW**
Whereas end-of-chapter material may be considered
optional in some texts, in
Transition Mathematics we
have selected these objectives and questions with the
expectation that they will be
covered. Students should be
able to answer these questions with about 85%
accuracy after studying the
chapter.

You may assign these questions over a single night to
help students prepare for a
test the next day, or you may
assign the questions over a
two-day period.

If you work the questions
over two days, then we recommend assigning the *evens*
for homework the first night
so that students get feedback
in class the next day, then
assigning the *odds* the night
before the test.

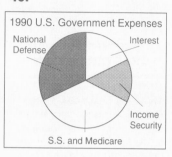
▧ **Objective E:** *Find the circumference or area of a circle or sector, given its radius or diameter.* *(Lessons 13-6, 13-7)*

17. Find the circumference and area of a circle with radius 10.   **20π; 100π**

18. To the nearest whole number, find the circumference and area of a circle with diameter 2 meters.   **6 m; 3 sq. m**

19. Give the area of a 90° sector of a circle with radius 10.   **25π**

20. Give the area of a 100° sector of a circle with radius 6, to the nearest square unit.

▧ **Objective F:** *Find the surface area or volume of a sphere, given its radius or diameter.* *(Lesson 13-9)*

21. A sphere has diameter 10. Give its exact surface area.   **100π**

22. To the nearest cubic inch, give the volume of a sphere with radius 4″.   **268 in.³**

PROPERTIES deal with the principles behind the mathematics.

▧ **Objective G:** *Identify numbers as rational, irrational, or real.* *(Lesson 13-6)*

23. Which of these numbers are rational?
   π   3.14 $\frac{22}{7}$ $3\frac{1}{7}$ **all but π**

24. Which of these numbers are irrational?
   $\sqrt{2}$ $\sqrt{3}$ $\sqrt{4}$ $\sqrt{5}$ **all but $\sqrt{4}$**

25. When does a decimal represent a real number?
   A decimal always represents a real number.

USES deal with applications of mathematics in real situations.

▧ **Objective H:** *Apply area formulas in real situations.* *(Lessons 13-1, 13-4, 13-7, 13-9)*

26. An 8″ by 10.5″ rectangular sheet of paper is cut in half at its diagonal. What is the area of each half?   **42 sq. in.**

27. A triangular sail (in gold below) is 3 meters high and 1.8 meters across. How much material does it take to make this sail?   **2.7 square meters**

28. A child is lost in a forest. Police decide to search every place within 2 miles of the place the child was last seen. To the nearest square mile, how much area must be searched?   **13 square miles**

29. What is the surface area of a ball 20 cm in diameter?   **about 1257 cm²**

30. Pearl is making a color wheel for school. She wants to put 12 equal-sized sectors on the wheel. What is the area of one of those sectors if the wheel is to be 18″ in diameter? $\frac{27\pi}{4}$ **or about 21.2 in.²**

▧ **Objective I:** *Apply formulas for the circumference of a circle and volume of a sphere in real situations.* *(Lessons 13-6, 13-9)*

31. To keep a famous statue from being touched, a rope is placed in a circle around the statue. Each point on the rope is 10 feet from the center of the statue. How long is the rope?   **20π or about 63 ft**

616

32. The Earth goes around the sun in an orbit that is almost a circle with radius 150,000,000 km. How far does Earth travel in one year in its orbit?

33. How much clay is needed to make a ball 4″ across? $\frac{32\pi}{3}$ or about 33.5 in.^{3}

34. To the nearest cubic centimeter, what is the volume of a soap bubble with a radius of 1.5 centimeters?   **14 cm^3**

32. 300,000,000π km

REPRESENTATIONS deal with pictures, graphs, or objects that illustrate concepts.

Objective J: *Know how square roots and geometric squares are related. (Lesson 13-2)*

35. A square has area 50. What is the exact length of a side? $\sqrt{50}$

36. A side of a square has length $\sqrt{4.9}$. What is the area of the square?   **4.9**

37. If the big square below has area 4, what is the length of a side of the tilted square?
   $\sqrt{2}$

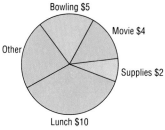

Objective K: *Read, make, and interpret circle graphs. (Lesson 13-8)*

In 38 and 39, the graph pictures the spending of $27.

Bowling $5
Movie $4
Other
Supplies $2
Lunch $10
Money Spent Last Week

38. How much was spent on "other" things? $6

39. How can you tell that more than 25% of the money spent was for lunch?
   See margin.

40. The table below gives approximations in billions of dollars of the top four areas of 1990 U.S. government expenses. Make a circle graph to display this information.

1990 U.S. Government Expenses

Income Security	137
National Defense	303
Interest on national debt	170
Social Security and Medicare	342

See margin.

EVALUATION
Four tests are provided for this chapter in the Teacher's Resource File. Chapter 13 Test, Forms A and B, cover just Chapter 13. The third test is Chapter 13 Test, Cumulative Form. About 50% of this test covers Chapter 13, 25% of it covers Chapter 12, and 25% of it covers earlier chapters. Finally Comprehensive Test, Chapters 1–13 gives roughly equal attention to all chapters. You may wish to use it as a final exam.

LESSON 1-1 (pp. 4–7)
11. 90 **13.** 8 **15.** 2 **17.** 6 **19.** No **25. a.** 50 **b.** stars
27. a. Appleton-Oshkosh, Wisconsin **b.** McAllen-Edinburg,
Texas **29.** 600,000,000 **31.** 506 **33.** 9999

LESSON 1-2 (pp. 8–13)
1. 21 and 22 **3.** 3 **5.** 3 **7.** 2 **9.** 6 **15.** largest, 0.033;
smallest, 0.015 **17.** largest, 0.98; smallest, 0.8 **19. a.** π
b. 14159 **21.** K **23.** S **27.** five and nine-tenths
29. twenty-four thousandths **31.** 2 **33.** $3.20 **35.** three
millionths, three thousandths, four thousandths **37.** faster
39. 31,068 **41.** Seattle **43.** count: 76; counting unit:
trombones

LESSON 1-3 (pp. 14–17)
5. 1800 **7.** 34¢ **9.** 0.012345 **11.** 0.97531246 **13. a.** 6000
b. 5000 **15. a.** $40 **b.** $30 **17.** high **19.** low **21.** 5.001,
5.01, 5.1 **23.** .086 **25.** Answers will vary. 5.9_, where
any digit except 0 can be put in the blank. **27. a.** Q **b.** R
c. Y

LESSON 1-4 (pp. 18–21)
1. a. 50 **b.** 40 **c.** 40 **3. a.** 88.89 **b.** 88.9 **c.** 89 **d.** 90
e. 100 **5.** $5.00 **7.** 200,000 miles per second **9.** 0.053 or
0.052 **11. a.** $89 **b.** $166 **c.** $101 **d.** $5324 **13.** 328
15. 12.53 **17. a.** 11 **b.** Sample: round to the nearest tenth
or hundredth **19.** $6 **21.** 5 **23.** Answers will vary. 3.2_ or
3.3_, where the blank can be filled by any digit but 0.
25. There are none. These numbers are equal. **27.** count:
12; counting unit: eggs. (Dozen is a collective, just like
hundred or score.) **29. a.** 1.01 **b.** 1.00 **31.** 7

LESSON 1-5 (pp. 22–25)
1. negative four, opposite of four **3.** behind **5.** below
7. See below. 9. Tomorrow is positive, yesterday was
negative, today is zero. **11.** . . . , -3, -2, -2, -1, 0, 1, 2,
3, . . . **15.** Samples: -1.5, -π, -2.36 **17. a.** 3 **b.** -10 **c.** 0
19. Q **21.** none **23.** -1, 0, $\frac{1}{2}$ **25.** -4 **27.** -1 **29.** 5.067,
5.60, 5.607, 5.67 **31.** 4 **33. a.** $29 **b.** $28 **c.** $28

7.

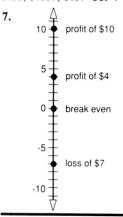

LESSON 1-6 (pp. 26–29)
5. 6 > -12 **7.** -2 < 0 < 2 or 2 > 0 > -2 **9.** 0 < 18
11. Negative three is less than three. **13.** Negative three is
greater than negative four and less than negative two.
15. 7'4" > 7'1" **19.** $8000 > -$2000 **21.** > **23.** >
25. < **27.** 0.621 < 6.21 < 62.1, or 62.1 > 6.21 > 0.621
29. 99.2 < 99.8 < 100.4, or 100.4 > 99.8 > 99.2
31. 0.07243, 0.07249, 0.0782 **33.** -3, -2, -1, 0, 1, 2 **35.** 77
37. 6.283

LESSON 1-7 (pp. 30–33)
3. On a scientific calculator, the blanks will be filled in with
8, 8, 7.2, 7.2, 10, 80. On a non-scientific calculator, the
blanks will be filled with 8, 8, 7.2, 15.2, 10, 152. **5.** If the
calculator displays 3.1415926 or 3.141592653, it truncates.
If it displays 3.1415927 or 3.141592654, it rounds to the
nearest. If it displays 3.14159265, you can't tell. **7.** On
many calculators the number of decimal places equals the
last digit in the display. **9.** 2.889 **11.** 206 **13.** Answer
depends on the calculator; sample: 99,999,999 or
9,999,999,999. **15.** usually the opposite of the answer to
Question 13: sample: -99,999,999. **17.** usually Ⓒ, CE , or
CE/C **19. a.** -2, -1.5, -1 **b.** -2 < -1.5 < -1, or -1 > -1.5 >
-2 **21.** > **23.** 54 seconds **25.** Answers will vary. -4.631_,
where the blank can be filled by any digit but 0. **27.** 5

LESSON 1-8 (pp. 34–38)
1. a. 15 **b.** 8 **c.** – **d.** $\frac{15}{8}$ **e.** No **f.** Yes **g.** 8 **h.** 15
i. 1.875 **7.** 1.15 **9.** $.\overline{571428}$ **11.** 27 **13.** 9.8777777777
15. -5.4444444444 **17.** $\frac{2}{5}$ or $\frac{4}{10}$ **19.** $\frac{1}{3}$ **21.** $\frac{7}{10}$ **23.** factor
25. 1, 2, 3, 5, 6, 10, 15, 30 **27.** .071 **29.** $\frac{2}{11}, \frac{2}{9}, \frac{2}{7}$
31. 34.0079 **33.** 99.6°

LESSON 1-9 (pp. 39–41)
1. a. 10 and 11 **b.** 10 **c.** 10.75 **d. See below. 3.** Fourths
are quarters, a term used in money. **5.** 7.4 **7.** 17.83
9. 12.1875 **11.** 20.5$\overline{3}$ **13.** $4.25 **15.** $2\frac{3}{5}, 3\frac{2}{5}, 5\frac{2}{3}$ **17.** 12.533
19. longer **21.** 1 **23.** 999,999 **25. a.** -4.3 **b.** Answers
will vary, -4.3_, where the blank can be filled in by any
digit but 0. **27.** 100 **29.** -9.99 < 9 < 9.99 **31.** 4
33. 1, 3, 13, 39

1. d.

LESSON 1-10 (pp. 42–46)
1. b **3.** All are equal. **5.** Sample: $\frac{42}{24}$ **7. a.** 1, 2, 3, 4, 6, 8,
12, 16, 24, 48 **b.** 1, 2, 3, 4, 5, 6, 10, 12, 15, 20, 30, 60
c. 1, 2, 3, 4, 6, 12 **d.** 12 **e.** $\frac{4}{5}$ **9. a.** 5 **b.** $\frac{3}{4}$ **11. a.** Sample: 24

b. $\frac{10}{3}$ **13.** Sample: $37\frac{6}{14}$ **15. See right. 17.** $\frac{24}{3}$
19. $\frac{75}{100} = \frac{3}{4}$ **21.** .01 **23.** Examples: $-\frac{1}{2}$, -.2, -.05
25. 4062 $\times$ .003 $\approx$ 12.2 **27.** 19.6 **29. a.** .4 **b.** .625
c. .75 **d.** $.\overline{3}$ **e.** $.8\overline{3}$ **31.** 1, 3, 17, 51

15.

CHAPTER 1 PROGRESS SELF-TEST (p. 48)

1. 700,000 **2.** 45.6 **3.** 0.25 **4.** $15\frac{13}{16} = 15 + \frac{13}{16} = 15 +$

0.8125 = 15.8125 **5.** 6 **6.** three thousandths
7. Remember that $.\overline{6}$ = .666 . . . , .66 = .660, and .6 =
.600. This indicates that $.\overline{6}$ is the largest. **8.** Change each

fraction to a decimal. $\frac{1}{2} = .5, \frac{2}{5} = .4, \frac{3}{10} = .3$ and $\frac{1}{3} =$

.333 . . . So $\frac{3}{10}$ is smallest. **9.** 98.7 **10.** 99 **11.** -80 ft >

-100 ft; the negative numbers are below sea level and the >
sign means "is higher than." **12.** Each tick mark to the

right of 0 is $\frac{1}{4}$. M is $\frac{2}{4}$ or $\frac{1}{2}$. **13.** Each tick mark to the left

of 0 is a decrease of 0.25. F corresponds to -1.25.
14. Rewrite the numbers as 16.50 and 16.60. Any decimal
beginning with 16.5 . . . is between. **15.** Rewrite the numbers as -2.3900 and -2.3910. Any decimal beginning with
-2.390 . . . is between. **16.** < **17.** =; Adding zeros to the
right of a number and the right of a decimal point does not

affect the value of the number. **18.** > **19.** $\frac{6}{10}$ or $\frac{3}{5}$

20. Any number other than 0, 1, 2, -2, etc. For example, $\frac{1}{2}$,

0.43, or 7.6. **21.** The store will round up. You will
pay 18¢. **22.** 3 + 9 = 12 **23.** 3.456 $\boxed{\times}$ 2.345 $\boxed{=}$

24. 6 $\boxed{\times}$ $\boxed{\pi}$ $\boxed{=}$ is a calculator sequence that will yield
18.8495 . . . Round to the nearest integer, the answer is 19.
25. 7 **26.** On the graph below each tick mark represents
0.1. **See below. 27. See below. 28.** Sample: the number of
people who watched a particular TV program **29.** Sample:
Twelve elephants marched in the circus parade. **30.** The
numbers are 0.1, 0.000001, 0.000000001, and .001. Of
these 0.1 is largest. **31.** 1, 2, 3, 6, 9, 18. **32.** Multiply the

numerator and denominator of $\frac{6}{1}$ by 5. This gives $\frac{30}{5}$.

33. 3 is a factor of both 12 and 21. So $\frac{12}{21} = \frac{4}{7}$. **34.** b,

around 800 A.D.

26.

7   7.7 8

27.

The chart below keys the **Progress Self-Test** questions to the objectives in the **Chapter Review** on pages 49–51 or to the **Vocabulary** (Voc.) on page 47. This will enable you to locate those **Chapter Review** questions that correspond to questions you missed on the **Progress Self-Test.** The lesson where the material is covered is also indicated in the chart.

Question	1	2	3	4	5	6	7–8	9	10	11
Objective	A	A	H	G	A	A	B	D	D	N
Lesson	1-1	1-2	1-8	1-9	1-1	1-2	1-8	1-3	1-4	1-6

Question	12	13	14	15	16–18	19	20	21	22	23
Objective	P	P	C	C	I	H	Voc.	L	E	Q
Lesson	1-2	1-5	1-2	1-5	1-6	1-8	1-5	1-4	1-4	1-7

Question	24	25	26	27	28	29	30	31–33	34
Objective	F	J	O	O	M	Voc.	B	K	R
Lesson	1-7	1-8	1-2	1-5	1-3	1-1	1-2	1-10	1-1

CHAPTER 1 REVIEW (pp. 49–51)

1. 4003 **3.** 120,000,000 **5.** five hundred thousand four
hundred **7.** 400,000,001 is largest; 0.4 is smallest

9. -586.363, -586.36, -586.34 **11.** $\frac{6}{10}$, 0.66, $\frac{2}{3}$ **13.** 4.33,

5.3, $5.\overline{3}$ **15.** -1.___, where anything other than 0 can be

put in the blank. **17.** Samples: 3.401, 3.402, 3.403
19. 5.84 **21.** 0.595959 **23.** 6.8 **25.** 62 **27.** 4402.912
29. 69.8584 **31.** $-5.\overline{3}$ **33.** 5.25 **35.** $0.\overline{6}$ **37.** $.1\overline{6}$ **39.** $\frac{1}{3}$
41. > **43.** $.6 < \frac{2}{3} < .667$ or $.667 > \frac{2}{3} > .6$ **45.** $468.5\overline{68}$
47. 1, 2, 3, 6, 7, 14, 21, 42 **49.** 29,000 **51.** 50¢

53. Example: number of minutes of travel time to school
55. -75,000 < 10,000 **57. See right. 59. See right.**

61. 46 **63.** $7\frac{1}{5}$ **65.** 77 $\boxed{\div}$ 8.2 $\boxed{=}$ **67.** c

57.

59.

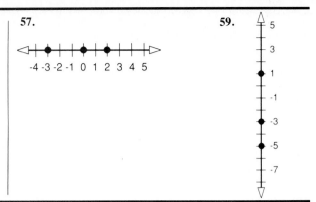

LESSON 2-1 (pp. 54–57)
1. 10 **3.** 24 **5.** 472.1 **7.** Move the decimal point two places to the right. **9.** 5 **11.** 630.1 **13.** Move the decimal point four places to the right. **15.** 32,000 **17.** 950 **25.** 1,350,000 **27.** Round 46.314 to 46 or 47. The answer should be between 46,000 and 47,000. **29.** 2.4 billion or 2.5 billion; 2,400,000,000 or 2,500,000,000 **31.** 4.4 billion or 4.5 billion; 4,400,000,000 or 4,500,000,000 **33.** 230 million **35.** 26.5 trillion **37. a.** 0.5 **b.** 0.1 **c.** G

LESSON 2-2 (pp. 58–61)
1. a. 4 **b.** 6 **c.** 4, 6, power **5.** 1,048,576; 400 **7.** 1.259712 **13.** 500 **17. a.** 4 **b.** 4^4, 4^3, 4^2, __ or 2^8, 2^6, 2^4, __. **19.** 3^2 **21.** seventh **23. a.** 96 or 7776 **b.** If the answer was 96, the calculator took the power first. If the answer was 7776, the calculator multiplied first.
25. Forty-three quintillion, two hundred fifty-two quadrillion, three trillion, two hundred seventy-four billion, four hundred eighty-nine million, eight hundred fifty-six thousand **27.** 3 × 7 **29.** $44.\overline{4}$ **31. a.** 1,000,000 **b.** 1,800,000 **c.** 8000

LESSON 2-3 (pp. 62–66)
1. 26,000,000,000,000 miles **5.** 8.04×10^2 **7.** 5.88×10^{21} **9.** $\$1.2 \times 10^{12}$ **11.** 7.654×10^2 **13.** $\boxed{4.9 \ 15}$ or equivalent **15.** $\boxed{3.8 \ 12}$ or equivalent
17. 31,536,000 **19.** 1×10^{10} **21.** 6 **23.** $14.6 = 14\frac{3}{5}$, $14.\overline{61}$, $14.\overline{6}$ **25. a.** q **b.** e **c.** s **d.** c **27. a.** 1,000,000,000 **b.** one billion

LESSON 2-4 (pp. 67–69)
5. Move the decimal point one place to the left. **7.** Move the decimal point two places to the left. **9.** 4.6 **11.** 4.6
13. .06 **15.** 7.7 **17.** .0052 **21.** $\frac{1}{10,000} \times 15.283 = 0.0015283$; $\frac{1}{100,000} \times 15.283 = 0.00015283$; $\frac{1}{1,000,000} \times 15.283 = 0.000015283$ **23.** Sample: 7 × 10 = 70 and 70 × .1 = 7 **25.** 9 pounds **27.** 9,690,000; 14,670,000; 12,500,000 **29. a.** 59 and 60 **b.** 59.45 **c.** $59.\overline{454545}$ **31.** 4.15×10^7 **33. a.** .2 **b.** .5 **c.** .6 **d.** $.8\overline{3}$

LESSON 2-5 (pp. 70–73)
5. .8 **7.** .05 **9.** .015 **11.** 3.00 **13.** 1.05 **15.** .085 **17.** .25; $\frac{1}{4}$ **19.** .2; $\frac{1}{5}$ **21.** $.\overline{3}$; $\frac{1}{3}$ **23.** .875; $\frac{7}{8}$ **25.** $\frac{2}{3}$ **27.** .5; 50%
29. .875; $87\frac{1}{2}$% **33.** $\frac{3}{2}$, $1\frac{1}{2}$, or 1.5; $\frac{34}{5}$, $6\frac{4}{5}$, or 6.8 **35.** b
37. 0 and 1 **39.** .04 = 4% **41. a.** 2300 **b.** 23 **c.** 23,000 **d.** .023 **e.** .00023 **43.** 9×10^4

LESSON 2-6 (pp. 74–78)
3. a. True **b.** True **c.** True **7.** 12 **9.** 45 **11.** $2.75
13. Let's split it equally, half for you, half for me.
15. 4,000,000 people **17.** store A **19.** half price **21.** $15
23. a. 29,028 feet **b.** 29,000 feet **c.** 29,000 feet **d.** 30,000 feet **25.** 0.7853 **27. a.** 25% **b.** $33\frac{1}{3}$% **c.** 125% **29.** $\frac{12}{25}$

LESSON 2-7 (pp. 79–82)
1. a. eight and twenty-seven hundredths **b.** $8\frac{27}{100}$
3. a. one thousandth **b.** $\frac{1}{1000}$ **5.** 72.4% **7.** $3\frac{14}{100}$ or $3\frac{7}{50}$ or $\frac{157}{50}$
9. 25% **11.** $\frac{105}{26}$ **13.** $\frac{675}{10,000}$ or $\frac{27}{400}$ **15.** $3\frac{1}{5}$; 320% **17.** $\frac{27}{100}$; 27%
19. $\frac{1}{3}$ off **21.** 32.34 **23.** one billion **25.** $\frac{1}{100}$; .011; $\frac{1}{10}$
27. 2.78784×10^7 **29.** $1.50 **31.** 240,000

LESSON 2-8 (pp. 83–86)
1. 7^3 **5.** $10^0 = 1$ **7. a.** positive **b.** positive **13.** .000345
15. .004 **17.** .000005 **19.** (f) **21.** .000001 **23.** 0, 10^{-5}, 1, 10^2 **25. a.** $12\frac{45}{100}$ or $12\frac{9}{20}$ **b.** 1245% **27.** They are the same price. **29. a.** .3 **b.** $\frac{3}{10}$ **31.** 9.3×10^7

LESSON 2-9 (pp. 87–90)
5. 6.008×10^{-5} **7.** 2.8×10^{-1} **11.** .00000 02 m
13. .009803; some calculators may put this small a number into scientific notation. **15.** .05 **17.** = **19. a.** 10^6 **b.** 10^{-6}
21. The team lost more often. **23.** .03 **25.** 1.50
27. a. $.001 **b.** $.0001 **c.** $.0111 **d.** $.01 **29.** low
31. $\frac{-2}{3}$, -.666, -.66, -.656, -.6

CHAPTER 2 PROGRESS SELF-TEST (p. 92)

1. Move the decimal point 8 places to the right. 2,351,864,000 **2.** 0.34 × 600 = 204 **3.** $32 \times 10^{-9} = 0.00000\ 0032$ **4.** Move the decimal point 5 places to the left. 0.0082459 **5.** 0.001 × 77 = 0.077 **6.** Move the decimal point 5 places to the right. 345,689,100

7. Move the decimal point 3 places to the left. 0.002816
8. 0.00000 01 **9.** 8% = 8 × .01 = .08 **10.** 216 **11.** base; exponent **12.** 125 $\boxed{y^x}$ 6 $\boxed{=}$ **13.** $\boxed{3.8146972 \ \ 12}$
14. 3,814,700,000,000 **15.** Start between the 2 and 1. You must move the decimal point 10 places to the right to get the given number. So the answer is 2.107×10^{10}. **16.** Start to the right of the 8. Move the decimal point 8 places to the

left to get the given number. So it equals 8×10^{-8}.
17. 4.5 $\boxed{EE}$ 13 **18.** First write in scientific notation:
1.23456 $\boxed{EE}$ 7 $\boxed{\pm}$. **19.** In the order given, the numbers
equal 256, 125, and 243. So from smallest to largest, they
are: 5^3, 3^5, 4^4. **20.** First change to a decimal. 40% = 0.40.
This number is between 0 and 1. **21. a.** $4.73 = \frac{4.73}{1} = \frac{473}{100}$;
b. $\frac{473}{100} = 473\%$ **22.** $\frac{1}{3}$ **23.** 30% × 150 = .3 × 150 = 45

24. You save $0.25 \times \$699 = \$174.75$. Subtract that from
\$699 to get the sale price, \$524.25. Rounded to the nearest
dollar, this is \$524. **25.** $0.8 \times 20 = 16$. This is the
number correct. So $20 - 16 = 4$ is the number missed.
26. 22.4 is not between 1 and 10. **27.** 6, since $10^6 =$
1,000,000 **28.** $\frac{3}{5} = 60\%$, $\frac{1}{10} = 10\%$, so fill the blanks with
60 and 10. **29.** 250 billion = 250,000,000,000 =
2.5×10^{11}

The chart below keys the **Progress Self-Test** questions to the objectives in the **Chapter Review** on pages 93–95 or to the **Vocabulary** (Voc.) on page 91. This will enable you to locate those **Chapter Review** questions that correspond to questions you missed on the **Progress Self-Test.** The lesson where the material is covered is also indicated in the chart.

Question	1	2	3	4–5	6	7	8	9	10	11	12–13	14	15
Objective	A	J	B	E	F	F	D	H	C	Voc.	P	C	G
Lesson	2-1	2-6	2-8	2-4	2-2	2-8	2-8	2-5	2-2	2-2	2-3	2-2	2-3

Question	16	17	18	19	20	21	22	23–25	26	27	28	29
Objective	G	P	P	C	H	K	I	N	M	D	L	O
Lesson	2-9	2-3	2-9	2-2	2-5	2-7	2-5	2-6	2-3	2-2	2-6	2-3

CHAPTER 2 REVIEW (pp. 93–95)

1. 320,000 **3.** 25,000 **5.** \$10,000,000,000 **7.** 64
9. 100,000 **11.** 0.0001 **13.** twelfth **15.** 0.00000 00273
17. 0.075 **19.** 30,000,000 **21.** 7.34 **23.** 4.8×10^5
25. 1.3×10^{-4} **27.** 0.15 **29.** 0.09 **31.** 50% **33.** $\frac{3}{10}$
35. 75 **37.** 6.2 **39.** Sample: $\frac{57}{10}$ **41.** 86% **43.** 42.8% or
42.9% (either answer is okay) **45.** If two numbers are equal,
one can be substituted for the other in any computation
without changing the results of the computation. **47.** $\frac{1}{2}$
and .5 **49.** 23 is not between 1 and 10. **51.** \$15.90
53. \$25,000 **55.** 5×10^{-3} **57.** 1 $\boxed{EE}$ 12 $\boxed{\pm}$ **59.** $\boxed{3.5184 \quad 13}$
61. 3.3516×10^{13} **63.** 3 $\boxed{EE}$ 21

LESSON 3-1 (pp. 98–103)

13. $2\frac{1}{8}$ in. **15.** $\frac{3}{4}$ in. **17. a.** 10.1 cm **b.** 4 in. **19.** Answers
will vary. **a.** may range from 25.1 cm to 25.3 cm; **b.** may
range from 19.5 cm to 20.1 cm **21.** The vertical segment at
right has length 3.5 in. **23.** If two numbers are equal, one
may be substituted for the other in any computation without
changing the results of the computation. **25. a.** improve
b. 156 **27.** 28,200,000 **29.** $\frac{7}{5}$

LESSON 3-2 (pp. 104–107)

13. 14,000 pounds **15.** 33.2 quarts **17.** 16.5 feet
19. 1,320 feet **21.** 80 **23.** A gallon is not a unit of length; it
is a unit of volume or capacity. **25. a.** 6 in. **b.** $6\frac{1}{4}$ in.
c. $6\frac{2}{8}$ in. or $6\frac{1}{4}$ in. **27. a.** 5.2 **b.** .0003446 **c.** 1.536
d. 6,400,000

LESSON 3-3 (pp. 108–112)

13. .345 liter **15.** 10,000 m **17.** .060 g **19. a.** Sample:
height of a doorknob **b.** Sample: 9 football fields
c. Sample: thickness of a dime **25.** b **27.** Yes
29. 57,000,000 tons **31. a.** \$.56 **b.** 1349¢ **c.** \$76,000
33. 0, 10^{-4}; $\frac{1}{100}$ **35. a.** < **b.** < **c.** < **d.** = **37.** 1.7 cm

LESSON 3-4 (pp. 113–116)

11. b. Sample: using 2.2 lb instead of 1 kg **13.** about

1.9 quarts **15.** 12.7 cm **17.** liter **19.** inch **21. a.** .3125
b. .8 cm or 8 mm **23.** about 10.2 miles **25.** 2
27. 36 inches **29.** 80 oz **31.** 80 mm **33.** 25

LESSON 3-5 (pp. 117–121)

1. $\overrightarrow{CB}$ (or $\overrightarrow{CA}$) and $\overrightarrow{CD}$ (or $\overrightarrow{CE}$) **3.** (a), (b), (c), (e), (g) **7.** B
9. 66° **11.** 151° **13.** 90° **17.** ∠JGH **19. See below.**
21. and 23. See below. 25. 93 miles **27.** .082 m **29.** quarts
or gallons **31.** $\frac{3}{4}$

19.   **21. and 23.**

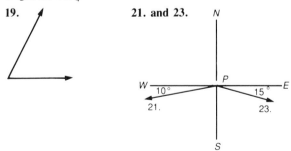

LESSON 3-6 (pp. 122–125)

7. acute **9.** right **11.** acute **13.** obtuse **15.** (c)
17. a. acute **b.** 87° **19. a.** right **b.** 90° **21. a.** acute
b. 60° **23. a.** See p. 622. **b.** See p. 622. **25. a.** .0004
inches **b.** 4×10^{-4} inches **27. a.** $3\frac{1}{2}$ in. **b.** $3\frac{1}{4}$ in.
29. a. > **b.** < **c.** < **d.** < **e.** = **f.** =

23. a. 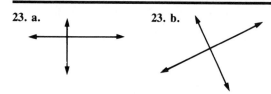 **23. b.**

15. a.

LESSON 3-7 (pp. 126–129)
5. Sample: a caution sign on a street **9.** 5625 ft²
11. 2.25 in.² **13.** 6 in.² **15. a. See right. b.** 9 ft²
17. a. square meters **b.** square feet **19.** 21,780 ft²
21. 1,074,000,000 **23. a.** 60 **b.** 120, 240, 420 (Do by multiplying by 2, 4, and 7 respectively.)

LESSON 3-8 (pp. 130–132)
9. 64 cubic inches **11.** 343 cubic yards
15. a. 34.328125 cubic feet **b.** 34.33 cubic feet
17. 241 **19.** 1000 g or 1 kg **21. a.** 411,800,000
b. 824,000,000 copies **c.** 8.24×10^8 **23. a.** .00034
b. $\frac{17}{50,000}$ **25.** 100 cm²

CHAPTER 3 PROGRESS SELF-TEST (p. 134)

1. $2\frac{5}{8}''$ **2. See below. 3.** 2.54 cm = 1 in.
4. kilogram **5.** $\frac{3}{4}$ mile = $\frac{3}{4} \times 5280$ feet = 0.75 ×
5280 ft. = 3960 ft **6.** 1 gallon = 4 quarts **7.** 1000 tons
8. 1103 mg = 1103 × .001 g = 1.103 g **9.** 5 cm =
5 × .01 m = .05 m **10.** 3.2 m ≈ 3.2 × 39.37 in. =
125.984 in. **11.** 4 km ≈ 4 × 0.62 mi = 2.48 mi **12.** 135°
13. 76° **14.** 0°; 90° **15.** a right angle **16. See below.**
17. Area = 4.5² square inches = 20.25 square inches
18. square centimeters **19.** 1000 cubic centimeters = 1 liter

20. Angles B and C are acute, angle A is obtuse, there are
no right angles. **21.** $V = (5 \text{ cm})^3 = 125 \text{ cm}^3$ **22.** 6 ft =
2 yd; (2 yd)² = 4 yd² **23.** 1 kilogram ≈ 2.2 pounds
24. 9 liters = 9 × 1 liter ≈ 9 × 1.06 quarts =
9.54 quarts. So 10 quarts is larger. **25.** England

2. _____

16.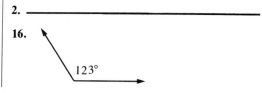
123°

The chart below keys the **Progress Self-Test** questions to the objectives in the **Chapter Review** on pages 135–137 or to the **Vocabulary** (Voc.) on page 133. This will enable you to locate those **Chapter Review** questions that correspond to questions you missed on the **Progress Self-Test.** The lesson where the material is covered is also indicated in the chart.

Question	1	2	3	4	5	6	7	8–9	10–11	12–13	14	15
Objective	A	P	H	J	K	F	G	L	M	B	Voc.	C
Lesson	3-1	3-1	3-4	3-3	3-2	3-2	3-3	3-3	3-4	3-5	3-6	3-6

Question	16	17	18	19	20	21	22	23	24	25
Objective	Q	D	Voc.	G	N	E	O	I	H	R
Lesson	3-5	3-7	3-7	3-8	3-6	3-8	3-7	3-4	3-4	3-1

CHAPTER 3 REVIEW (pp. 135–137)
1. 2 inches **3.** 7 cm **5.** 63° **7.** 36° **9.** obtuse **11.** 4 cm²
13. m² **15.** 53 in.³ **17.** 16 oz **19.** $\frac{1}{1000}$ or .001 **21.** 1000
23. 2.54 cm = 1 in. **25.** meter **27.** 1L ≈ 1.06 qt **29.** cm
31. gallons **33.** 29.2 qt **35.** 1980 ft **37.** 5000 m **39.** .06 g
41. about 540.64 mi **43.** about 220 lb **45.** ∠ABC, ∠BEA,
∠BCD, ∠DEC **47.** 1728 cm³ **49. See below. 51. See
below. 53. See below. 55.** It was the distance from the tip

of the nose of King Henry I of England to the tips of his
fingers.

49. _____

51.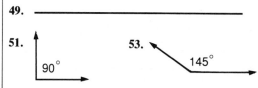
90°

53.
145°

LESSON 4-1 (pp. 140–144)
1. numerical **5.** division **7.** whichever is to the left **9.** 27
11. 10 **13.** 133 **23.** 15.2 **25.** 0.5 **27.** 14 **29.** 996 **31.** (c)
33. 87 + 12 − 3 **35.** 115° **37.** 6.543×10^{-12}
39. 125 cubic inches

LESSON 4-2 (pp. 145–148)
5. Samples: 5% = 5 × .01; 1.2% = 1.2 × .01; 300% =
300 × .01 **7.** Samples: 3 + 4 = 4 + 3; $\frac{1}{2} + \frac{3}{4} = \frac{3}{4} + \frac{1}{2}$;

0.8 + 6 = 6 + 0.8 **13.** Samples: 6 • 4 + 13 • 4 = 19 •
4; 6 • 9.7 + 13 • 9.7 = 19 • 9.7; 6 • 100 + 13 • 100 =
19 • 100 **15.** $a • 0 = 0$ (Any letter can be used.) **17.** in n
years we expect $n • 100$ more students and $n • 5$ more teach-
ers. **19.** $\frac{a}{3} + \frac{b}{3} = \frac{a + b}{3}$ **21.** 55 **23.** 74 **25.** 3 **27.** $\frac{50}{.0001}$;
500,000 **29.** 3 meters

LESSON 4-3 (pp. 149–153)

3. $n + 3$ or $3 + n$ **5.** $n - 5$ **7.** $n - 7$ **9.** $\frac{n}{9}$ **11.** $11 - n$

13. Sample: five times a number increased by six **15.** Samples: two minus a number; subtract a number from two; two decreased by a number **17.** It could mean $14 - 5 + 3$, with either the addition or the subtraction done first.
19. $6\% \cdot t$ or $.06 \cdot t$ **21. a.** $C + 50$ **b.** $C - 12$ **c.** $C \cdot 3$
23. a. $6 < n$ **b.** $n - 6$ **c.** $6 - n$ **25.** $2\frac{1}{2}$ or $2\frac{4}{8}$ inches
27. $\frac{a}{1} = a$ **29.** 688.2 miles **31.** Examples: **a.** See below.
b. See below. **c.** See below. **33. a.** .00001 **b.** .001%

31. a. **31. b.** **31. c.**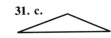

LESSON 4-4 (pp. 154–157)

1. (c) **3.** 3 **5.** 15 **9.** 50¢ **13.** 68 **15.** 5% **17.** 90
19. 254.469 **21. a.** 0 **b.** No, because $xy = yx$ for any numbers. **23. a.** $5n - 8$ **b.** 42 **25. a.** n^3 **b.** 1000
27. $1 \times b = b$ **29.** (a) **31.** (b) and (d)

LESSON 4-5 (pp. 158–162)

1. to change order of operations **3.** True **5.** False **7.** 52
9. 11 **11.** 0 **13.** $2 \times \boxed{(} 5 \boxed{+} 4 \times 8 \boxed{)} \boxed{=}$ **15.** 100
17. 50 **19. a.** $10 - 1$ **b.** 909 **21.** 163 **23.** No
25. $(a + 4)b + 3$ **27.** (d) **29.** 436 **31.** $16 - (8 - 4 - 2) = 14$ **33.** 23 **35.** $n^4 = n \cdot n \cdot n \cdot n$

LESSON 4-6 (pp. 163–166)

3. 4.3 cm² **5.** No **7.** 2.2 cm² **11.** They are the first letters of the quantities they represent. **13.** $2.98 **15.** No, about 1190 are needed. **17.** inside parentheses, then powers, then multiplications or divisions from left to right, then additions or subtractions from left to right **19.** 103 **21.** 8
23. 1000 cm³ **25.** < **27.** <

LESSON 4-7 (pp. 167–171)

7. 16 **9.** $3 \times \boxed{(} 2 \boxed{+} 4 \times \boxed{(} 5 \boxed{-} 2 \boxed{)} \boxed{)} \boxed{=}$ **11.** 9
13. 560  **15.** 3
17. $231.\overline{6}$ **19. a.** $58.\overline{3}$ **b.** $91.\overline{6}$ **21.** 1.000 **23.** .200 **25.** 69°
27. $7\frac{2}{3} > 7.65 > 7\frac{3}{5}$ **29.** Sample: depending on the table.

LESSON 4-8 (pp. 172–175)

7. (a) **9.** 5 **11.** .5 **13.** 25 m **15.** Samples: Los Angeles, London, Mexico City, Chicago **17.** eight **19.** Sample: -9
21. 6 **23.** 11 **25.** 4 **27.** 1 **29.** 50,000 mm < 500 m < 5 km, or 5 km > 500 m > 50,000 mm **31. a.** $\frac{5(5 + 1)}{2} = 15$ **b.** $1 + 2 + 3 + 4 + 5 = 15$ **c.** 5050 **33.** 26,127

LESSON 4-9 (pp. 176–179)

7. Yes **9.** True **11.** False **13.** Sample: 5001 **15.** Sample: $6\frac{3}{4}$ **17.** (c) **19.** (b) **21.** (a) **23.** (d) **25.** See below.
27. a. $f > 55$ **b.** Samples: 60, 57, 61 **c.** See below.
29. a. $400 < A \le 500$ **b.** Samples: 490, 421, 439.36
c. See below. **31.** $1.92 **33.** Sample: there are 6 · 3 legs on 3 insects; there are 6 · 108 legs on 108 insects; there are 6 million legs on 1 million insects **35.** 144

25.

27. c.

29. c.

CHAPTER 4 PROGRESS SELF-TEST (pp. 181–182)

1. $6 + 56 + 9 = 71$ **2.** $35 + 50 = 85$ **3.** 21; Do subtractions from left to right. **4.** $5 + 3 \cdot 16 = 5 + 48 = 53$
5. $\frac{100 + 10}{10 + 5} = \frac{110}{15} = 7.\overline{3} \approx 7$ **6.** $10 + 3 \cdot 100 = 10 + 300 = 310$ **7.** $(3 + 4)(4 - 3) = 7 \cdot 1 = 7$ **8.** $100 + 5[100 + 4(100 + 3)] = 100 + 5[100 + 4 \cdot 103] = 100 = 5[100 + 412] = 100 + 5 \cdot 512 = 100 + 2560 = 2660$ **9.** $(4x)^2 = 64$; $16x^2 = 64$; try 2: $16 \cdot 2^2 = 16 \cdot 4 = 64$. So 2 is a solution. 4, 8, and 16 do not work. The correct answer is (a). **10.** $10 \cdot a = 6 \cdot a + 4 \cdot a$ **11.** $a + b = b + a$ **12.** In p years, we expect the town to grow by $p \cdot 200$ people. **13.** $c = 20 + 5 = 105$¢, or $1.05 **14.** $c = 20 \cdot 9 + 5 = 185$¢, or $1.85 **15.** 12×16 **16.** $47 + 40$
17. $n < 0$ **18.** $\frac{9}{a}$ **19.** p, s, and c **20.** $p = \$45 - \$22.37 =$ $22.63 **21.** $\frac{W}{W + L} = \frac{W}{(W + L)}$; The correct answer is (b)
22. (c) **23.** (b) **24.** $6 \cdot 7 = 42$, so $x = 7$ **25.** Any number between -5 and -4 is a solution. Some are -4.2, -4.9, $-4\frac{1}{2}$.
26. If width is 3 inches and length is 4 feet, the area is not 12 of either unit, even though $A = lw$. **27.** $x = 7 \cdot 3 = 21$
28. See below. **29.** all numbers between 4.5 and 6, including 4.5 but not including 6. This is written as $4.5 \le y < 6$.
30. Samples: If you are 10 years old, your sister is $10 - 5$, or 5, years old. If you are 14 years old, your sister is $14 - 5$, or 9, years old. **31.** Samples: $30 \cdot \frac{2}{5} = 6 \cdot 2$; $30 \cdot \frac{8}{5} = 6 \cdot 8$. You can check that both of these are true.

28.

The chart below keys the **Progress Self-Test** questions to the objectives in the **Chapter Review** on pages 183–185 or to the **Vocabulary** (Voc.) on page 180. This will enable you to locate those **Chapter Review** questions that correspond to questions you missed on the **Progress Self-Test.** The lesson where the material is covered is also indicated in the chart.

Question	1	2	3–4	5	6	7	8	9	10–11	12
Objective	A	B	A	A	C	C	C	D	G	I
Lesson	4-1	4-7	4-1	4-7	4-4	4-5	4-7	4-8	4-2	4-2

Question	13–14	15–16	17–18	19	20	21	22	23	24–25	26
Objective	L	J	K	Voc.	L	F	O	Voc.	E	Voc.
Lesson	4-6	4-3	4-3	4-6	4-6	4-7	4-1	4-9	4-8	4-6

Question	27	28	29	30	31
Objective	C	M	N	H	H
Lesson	4-4	4-9	4-9	4-2	4-2

CHAPTER 4 REVIEW (pp. 183–185)

1. 215 **3.** 83 **5.** 31 **7.** 158 **9.** 1966 **11.** 5 **13.** $\frac{14}{65}$ = 0.215 . . . **15.** 24 **17.** 18 **19.** 24 **21.** 184 **23.** $\frac{8}{12}$ = $.\overline{6}$ **25.** (b) **27.** $x = 4$ **29.** $y = 2$ **31.** powering **33.** (d) **35.** $5 \cdot x + 9 \cdot x = 14 \cdot x$ **37.** $\frac{a}{9} + \frac{b}{9} + \frac{a+b}{9}$ **39.** Sample: $2 + 6 = 1 + 6 + 1$ **41.** If the weight is w ounces, the postage is $s + 20 \cdot w$ cents **43.** $18 + 27$ **45.** $4 \times 20 - 1$ **47.** $2x + 7$ **49.** $x < 5$ **51.** 127.27 **53.** 72 in.² or .5 ft²

55. See below. **57.** See below. **59.** $y \geq 2$ **61.** See below. **63.** **, ↑

55.

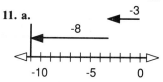
23   24   25

57.

-4   -2   0   2

61.

-3 -2 -1   0   1   2

LESSON 5-1 (pp. 188–192)

5. Sample: If you bike $\frac{1}{4}$ mile and $\frac{1}{2}$ mile, then altogether you have biked $\left(\frac{1}{4} + \frac{1}{2}\right)$ miles. **7.** Both are. If you change the units to pieces of fruit, then Carla is right. If you do not change the units, Peter is right. **9.** (1) 13 pieces (2) 49,050,525 people (3) $3.13 (4) 27% (5) 5.25 lb **11.** $15 + r = 43$ **13.** $M + 112 \leq 250$ **15.** 109 oz **17.** 2100 g **19.** $b + s + 1$ **21.** No, rain and sun could appear on the same day. **23.** Mountain region **25.** (a), (b), (d), (f) **27.** 3 **29.** True **31.** $\frac{3}{10}$

LESSON 5-2 (pp. 193–197)

1. $\frac{16}{4}$ km or 4 km **3. a.** $\frac{1}{3} + \frac{1}{4}$ **b.** Sample: $\frac{2}{6}, \frac{3}{9}, \frac{4}{12}, \frac{5}{15}, \frac{6}{18}$ **c.** Sample: $\frac{2}{8}, \frac{3}{12}, \frac{4}{16}, \frac{5}{20}, \frac{6}{24}$ **d.** $\frac{7}{12}$ **5. a.** $\frac{11}{10}$ **b.** $.8 + .3 = 1.1 = \frac{11}{10}$ **7.** $\frac{17}{x}$ **9.** $\frac{41}{40}$ **11.** $\frac{19}{6}$ **13.** $\frac{5}{2}$ km or $2\frac{1}{2}$ km **15.** $\frac{169}{24}$ **17.** $\frac{961}{44}$ **19.** 20 pieces **21.** 6×10^4 **23. a.** Sample: -3, 0, $\frac{1}{2}$ **b.** See below.

23. b.

1   2   3   4

LESSON 5-3 (pp. 198–201)

7. twice the length, pointed right **9.** $\frac{6}{5}$ of the length, a little longer than what is drawn, pointed right. **11. a.** See below. **b.** -11 **13.** 1 ± + 8 ± = **15. a.** 250 + -150 **b.** 100

17. a. -50 + -40.27 **b.** -90.27 **19.** Sample: Joe loses seven yards in football and then loses five more; the result is a loss of twelve yards, -12. **21.** It goes 20 km in the opposite direction. **23.** The temperature is -7°. **25.** (a) **27. a.** 18% **b.** 128,000 people **29.** 6.2 **31.** Sample: 0 or $\frac{1}{2}$ **33.** 32,680 feet **b.** 6.189 or $6\frac{25}{132}$

11. a.

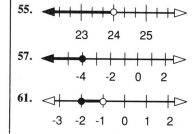
-10   -5   0

LESSON 5-4 (pp. 202–205)

3. -7 **5.** -70 **7.** $\frac{1}{2}$ **13.** Additive Identity Property of Zero **15.** Property of Opposites **17.** 0 **19.** $\frac{14}{11}$ **21. a.** $40 + -40 = 0$ **b.** Property of Opposites **23.** 6 **25.** -6 **27.** 3 **29. a.** The temperature is -9°. **b.** $-11 + 2 = -9$ **31.** $t + -35 = -60$ **33.** 9.7×10^{-5}; 3.2×10^4; 5.1×10^7 **35. a.** 10,000 lb **b.** 3750 lb **c.** No

LESSON 5-5 (pp. 206–210)

1. (d) **3.** 4.01 **5.** 11 **7.** 20 **9.** 0 **11. a.** positive **b.** 6.2 **13. a.** positive **b.** 13 **15.** True **17.** False **21.** -14 **23.** -1 **25.** $\frac{-1117}{30}$ **27.** $\frac{-15}{2}$ **29.** 6 **31.** 4.3 **33.** True **35.** True **37.** 0 **39.** $\frac{129}{6}$, or 21.5 **41.** $n + -n = 0$ **43.** $2\frac{1}{4}''$ or $2\frac{2}{8}''$

LESSON 5-6 (pp. 211–215)
3. 180° **5.** counterclockwise **9.** 180° **11.** -300° **13.** 125°
15. -11° **19.** 120° **21. a.** 60° (or -300°) **b.** D **23.** I
25. a. -30° **b.** -5° **27.** $45 + m = 180$ (in minutes), or
$m + \frac{3}{4} = 3$ (in hours) **29.** 0 **31.** 55 **33.** 6000 m
35. $x + y + x = y + (x + x)$

LESSON 5-7 (pp. 216–220)
1. Sample: $3 + 2.4 = 2.4 + 3$ **3.** Associative Property of
Addition **5.** (b) **7.** (c) **11.** 12 **13.** 0 **15.** They are $10.25
over budget. **17.** 1° **19. a.** Sample: $(9 - 6) - 2 \neq$
$9 - (6 - 2)$ **b.** Subtraction does not possess the
associative property. **21.** (b) **23. a.** 60° **b.** acute **25.** -60°
27. 8453 g or 8.453 kg **29.** $(t - 3)$ degrees **31.** For any
number a, $a + \text{-}a = 0$.

LESSON 5-8 (pp. 221–225)
1. 5 **3. a.** Yes **b.** Yes **c.** Yes **d.** Addition Property of
Equality **5. a.** -86 **b.** 144 **c.** $144 + 86 = 230$ **7. a.** $\frac{-22}{3}$
b. $\frac{158}{3}$ or $52\frac{2}{3}$ **c.** $60 = \frac{158}{3} + \frac{22}{3}$ **9.** (b) **11.** 5° **13.** 82;
$82 + 43 + \text{-}5 = 120$ **15.** $1025 **17. a.** $G + 10$
b. $W + 10$ **c.** $G = W$ **d.** If $G = W$, then $G + 10 =$
$W + 10$ **e.** Addition Property of Equality **19.** Step 1,
Associative Property of Addition; step 2, Commutative Property of Addition; step 3, Associative Property of Addition;
step 4, Property of Opposites; step 5, Additive Identity Property of Zero **21. a.** Sample: -4 **b.** Sample: 2 **23.** 30
25. See below. 27. 73 mm **29.** $t - 5$ **31.** the ray with
endpoint A containing B

25.

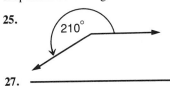

27. ────────────────────────

LESSON 5-9 (pp. 226–229)
3. $\overline{FE}$ or $\overline{EF}$ **15.** 26-gon **17.** 12 **19. a.** Sample:

POLYGON, LOPNGY, GNPOLY **b.** hexagon **21.** nonagon
23. a. $\overline{PR}$, $\overline{PS}$, $\overline{QT}$, $\overline{QS}$, $\overline{TR}$ **b.** 5; **See below. 25.** (c)
27. -22; $-22 + 12 = -10$ **29.** step 1, Addition Property of
Equality; step 2, Property of Opposites; step 3, Additive
Identity Property of Zero

23. b.

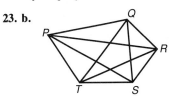

LESSON 5-10 (pp. 230–234)
1. 436 miles **3. a.** line through P and Q **b. See below.**
5. a. line segment from P to Q **b. See below. 7.** 8
9. $x + 3$ **13.** $(x + 543)$ft **15. a.** $9 + 9 + 5 + 5 +$
$x = 30$ **b.** 2 **17.** 40 and 20; 30 and 30 **19. a.** Yes
b. 20 **21. See below. 23. a.** $-22 + t = 10$ **b.** 32
c. $-22 + 32 = 10$ **25. a.** 0 **b.** $x + y$ **27.** All are obtuse.
29. 93° **31. See below.**

3. b. 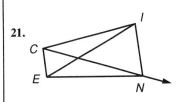   **5. b.**

21.

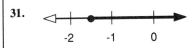

31.

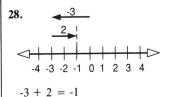

CHAPTER 5 PROGRESS SELF-TEST (p. 236)

1. -7 **2.** -710 **3.** $-9.8 + \text{-}(\text{-}1) = -9.8 + 1 = -8.8$
4. $x + y + \text{-}x + 4 = x + \text{-}x + y + 4 = 0 + y + 4 =$
$y + 4$ **5.** 8 **6.** $2 + 1 + 0 = 3$ **7.** $-29 + 58 = 29$
8. $|\text{-}(\text{-}3) + 8| = |3 + 8| = |11| = 11$ **9.** Add -43 to both
sides; $x = -12$ **10.** Add 25 to both sides; $y = 37$ **11.** $8 =$
$z + \text{-}7$; add 7 to both sides; $z = 15$ **12.** $\frac{53}{12} + \frac{11}{12} =$
$\frac{(53 + 11)}{12} = \frac{64}{12} = \frac{16}{3}$ **13.** $\frac{5}{x} + \frac{10}{x} = \frac{(5 + 10)}{x} = \frac{15}{x}$
14. 9 is the common denominator. So $\frac{8}{3} = \frac{24}{9}$ and $\frac{17}{9} + \frac{24}{9} =$
$\frac{41}{9}$. **15.** Notice that $\frac{2}{16} = \frac{1}{8}$. So 8 is a common denominator
and $\frac{2}{8} + \frac{3}{8} + \frac{1}{8} = \frac{6}{8} = \frac{3}{4}$. **16.** 20 **17.** Addition Property of
Equality **18.** Associative Property of Addition **19.** One
instance is $3 + 0 = 3$. There are many others. **20.** hexagon

21. $3\text{ cm} + 3\text{ cm} + 4\text{ cm} + 4\text{ cm} + 4\text{ cm} = 18\text{ cm}$
22. (a); (b) is a segment, (c) is a ray, and (d) is a line
23. $m + n = 50$ **24.** $-20 + c = 150$ **25.** Add 20 to both
sides; $c = 170$ **26.** $MP = MA + AP = 16 + 8 = 24$
27. $MA + PA = MP$, so $2.3 + PA = 3$. Add -2.3 to both
sides to get $PA = 0.7$. **28. See below. 29.** $5\text{ m} + 3\text{ cm} =$
$5\text{ m} + .03\text{ m} = 5.03\text{ m}$ **30.** Positive, since the absolute
value of the second addend is larger than the absolute value
of the first addend. **31.** $\frac{360°}{5} = 72°$ **32.** clockwise turn of
$72° + 72°$ has a magnitude of -144° **33.** $-50° + 250° =$
200° **34.** (b)

28.

$-3 + 2 = -1$

The chart below keys the **Progress Self-Test** questions to the objectives in the **Chapter Review** on pages 237–239 or to the **Vocabulary** (Voc.) on page 235. This will enable you to locate those **Chapter Review** questions that correspond to questions you missed on the **Progress Self-Test**. The lesson where the material is covered is also indicated in the chart.

Question	1	2	3	4	5–6	7	8	9–11	12–15	16	17	18
Objective	A	A	C	A	B	C	B	E	A	D	F	F
Lesson	5-5	5-3	5-4	5-3	5-5	5-4	5-5	5-10	5-2	5-8	5-8	5-7

Question	19	20	21	22	23	24	25	26–27	28	29	30	31–33	34
Objective	F	G	E	Voc.	I	K	D	J	M	K	A	L	H
Lesson	5-4	5-9	5-10	5-10	5-8	5-8	5-8	5-10	5-3	5-3	5-5	5-6	5-9

CHAPTER 5 REVIEW (pp. 237–239)

1. -12 **3.** 9.6 **5.** 1 **7.** $\frac{46}{9}$ **9.** $\frac{13}{12}$ **11.** 12 **13.** 8 **15.** -17 **17.** -40 **19.** $\frac{2}{7}$ **21.** 48 **23.** 20 **25.** -3 **27.** 38 **29.** $x = 180 + -y$ **31.** 12 **33.** 15 cm **35.** $12 + 18 + 20 + 7 + x = 82$ **37.** Addition Property of Equality **39.** Commutative Property of Addition **41.** pentagon, convex **43.** $\overline{LEAK}$ **45.** 4, 4 **47.** $1\frac{1}{2} + \frac{3}{5} = M$ **49.** $T = D + M + C$ **51.** $x + 3$ **53. a.** $\frac{3}{8} + -\frac{1}{4}$ **b.** $\frac{1}{8}$ point **55. a.** -250 + 75 **b.** 175 feet below the surface **57.** 135° **59.** A **61.** See below. **63.** See below.

61.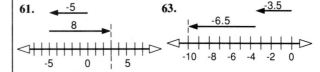

63.

LESSON 6-1 (pp. 242–246)

5. What is 34.2×5.67? **7.** Take your time. **9.** Don't give up. **13.** She gave up instead of trying. **17. 25.** Here is the list:

AA EA IA OA UA
AE EE IE OE UE
AI EI II OI UI
AO EO IO OO UO
AU EU IU OU UU

19. 13 trains **21.** 12 edges **23.** $\frac{55}{42}$ **25.** 13 **27.** $16.\overline{6}$ or $16\frac{2}{3}$ **29.** 53 million

LESSON 6-2 (pp. 247–250)

5. 15 **7.** 7 **9.** 36 **11.** Not enough information is given. **13.** (c) **15.** 39 **17.** 35 **19.** See below. Sides must have same length, angles same measure. **21.** two consecutive odd numbers that are both primes; sample: 29 and 31 **23.** last year **25.** Not enough information given. It depends on which is larger, $b + e + h$ or $c + f + g$. **27.** 0 is the total difference. **29.** 10 **31.** $\overline{BC}$ and $\overline{CD}$

19.

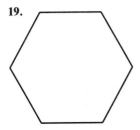

LESSON 6-3 (pp. 251–254)

3. 2 diagonals **5.** 56 games; **See right. 7.** Wanda is youngest. $W < B < J; C < J < P; W < C; B < P$ (known); $B < C$ **9. a.** 110 ft **b.** 146 ft; **See right. 11.** 1, 2, 4, 5, 8, 10, 20, 40 **13.** 16,009 **15.** 41, 43, 47 **17.** If Sarah and Dana have the same amount of money, then they will still have the same amount if each receives $2 more. **19.** 30 **21.** 56.83 **23.** 22 pounds

5.

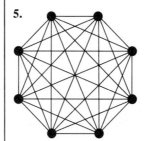

9. b.

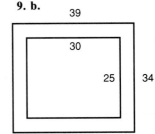

LESSON 6-4 (pp. 255–258)

3. 5 **5.** 3 **7.** 3 **11.** No **13.** 147, 118, 35 **15.** 13 and 1 **17.** three possible answers: 91 and 37, 82 and 28, or 73 and 19 **19.** Ali **21.** Work inside parentheses, then do powers, then multiplications or divisions from left to right, then additions or subtractions from left to right. **23. See below. 25.** Sample: $(2 + 3) + 7 = 2 + (3 + 7)$ **27.** 32 inches **29. a.** 1.4142857 **b.** 1.414 **c.** 1 and 2

23.

LESSON 6-5 (pp. 259–263)

3. 65 diagonals **5.** $5.47 **7.** $21.67 **9.** The cost of a m-minute call for Francie is $.25 + (m - 1) \cdot .18$ dollars. **11. a. See below. b.** $1.46 + 24 \cdot .82 = $21.14 **c.** $1.42 + (m - 1) \cdot .82 **13.** 43 **15.** $x = 7$ and $y = 3$ **17.** -8 pounds

11. a.

number of minutes	cost
1	$1.46
2	$1.46 + .82
3	$1.46 + 2 \cdot 82
4	$1.46 + 3 \cdot 82
5	$1.46 + 4 \cdot 82

LESSON 6-6 (pp. 264–268)

3. Yes **7. a.** quadrilateral **b.** Yes **9. a.** 6 **b.** Yes **11. See below.** Octagon = 8-gon; 8 − 3 diagonals from each vertex **13.** Move the decimal point 3 places to the right. **15. a.** Yes **b.** Yes **c.** No **d.** No **17. a.** Sample: if $m = 2$, $-(-2 + 9) = 2 + -9$, True **b.** Sample: if $m = -4$, $-(-(-4) + 9) = -4 + -9$, True **c.** possibly true **19.** (b) **21.** 10 games **23. a.** $4.50 **b.** $1.00 + (h − 1).50

25. $0.\overline{3}$, $33\frac{1}{3}\%$ **27.** perimeter

11.

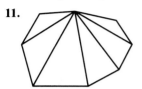

LESSON 6-7 (pp. 269–273)

1. $10 **3.** The same operation is used; only the numbers differ. **5.** If you cannot do a problem with complicated numbers, try simpler numbers. **7.** $\frac{30}{M}$ miles **9. a.** $2.45 **b.** 98$k$ cents **c.** ck cents **11.** $(R − Z)$ sheets **13.** $(G − 49.95)$ dollars **15.** 4 places to the left **17.** -2 **19.** 3.5×10^{11} **21.** 4025.043 grams **23.** 15,625

CHAPTER 6 PROGRESS SELF-TEST (p. 275)

1. any two of dictionary, glossary in a math book, encyclopedia **2.** An octagon has 20 diagonals. **See right.** **3.** Name the teams A, B, C, D, E and F. Draw all the segments connecting these points. The figure created is a hexagon. The number of games is equal to the number of diagonals plus the number of sides in the hexagon. That is $9 + 6 = 15$ games. **See right.** **4.** Use trial and error. The sums of each pair of factors of 24 are: $1 + 24 = 25$; $2 + 12 = 14$; $3 + 8 = 11$ and $4 + 6 = 10$. So 4 and 6 give the smallest sums. **5.** If you know an algorithm for an operation, you know how to answer the question. So multiplying fractions is only an exercise, not a problem. **6.** 53, 59 **7.** If one value is positive and one is negative, the pattern will be false. For instance, $|-5| + |3| = 5 + 3 = 8$, but $|-5 + 3| = |-2| = 2$. **8.** 2 pounds at $3 per pound cost $6, so multiplication gives the answer. $1.49 per pound • 1.62 pounds = $2.4138, which rounds up to $2.42. **9.** True **10.** By trial and error, $(8 − 3) + (8 − 4) = 5 + 4 = 9$, so 8 is the solution. **11.** Read carefully and draw a picture. There must be 6 more dots on the right side between 3 and 10, for a total of 14 dots. **See right.** **12.** Use trial and error. A 3-gon has 0 diagonals, a 4-gon has 2 diagonals, a 5-gon has 5 diagonals, a 6-gon has 9 diagonals. **13.** Use a special case. $\frac{.05}{.01} = 5$, which means that the decimal point is moved two places to the right. **14. See right.** **15.** After 31 weeks, Phyllis will have $1000 − 31 • 25$ dollars left. That computes to $225. **16.** After you find an answer, you should check your work.

2.

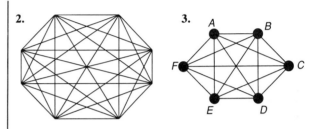

3.

11.

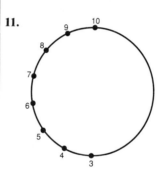

14.

weeks	amount left
1	$1000 − 25$
2	$1000 − 2 • 25$
3	$1000 − 3 • 25$
4	$1000 − 4 • 25$

The chart below keys the **Progress Self-Test** questions to the objectives in the **Chapter Review** on pages 276–277 or to the **Vocabulary** (Voc.) on page 274. This will enable you to locate those **Chapter Review** questions that correspond to questions you missed on the **Progress Self-Test.** The lesson where the material is covered is also indicated in the chart.

Question	1	2	3	4	5	6	7	8
Objective	D	J	I	B	D	C	G	H
Lesson	6-2	6-3	6-2	6-4	6-2	6-2	6-3	6-7

Question	9	10	11	12	13	14–15	16	
Objective	Voc.	B	K	K	F	E	A	
Lesson	6-6	6-4	6-3	6-3	6-6	6-5	6-1	

CHAPTER 6 REVIEW (pp. 276–277)

1. A good problem solver is flexible by trying different ways to solve a problem. **3.** There are several ways to check this answer. She could multiply 309×1487 on her calculator, or divide by 309 to see if she gets 1487. **5.** (b) **7.** 1036 **9.** prime; only 1 and 47 are factors. **11.** 31, 37 **13.** a number that equals the sum of all its divisors except itself **15.** 64, 128, and 256 are the next rows in the table below, so 256 has nine factors. **17.** 6, left **19.** If $x = 2$ and $y = 3$, then $5x + 5y = 5 \cdot 2 + 5 \cdot 3 = 25$, but $10xy = 10 \cdot 2 \cdot 3 = 60$ **21.** Simpler numbers indicate to multiply. Your cost is $8.69. **23.** Use a pentagon. 5 diagonals and 5 sides add to 10 games. Since they play twice it is 20 games for the season. **See right. 25.** A diagram helps. **See right.** Pueblo is the farthest south. **27.** The decagon has 35 diagonals. **See right. 29.** 7 triangles. **See right.**

15.
2	1, 2
4	1, 2, 4
8	1, 2, 4, 8
16	1, 2, 4, 8, 16
32	1, 2, 4, 8, 16, 32

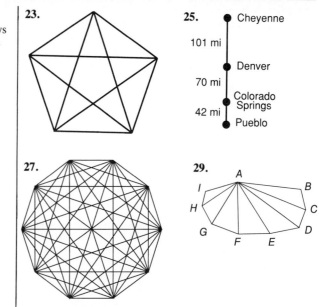

25.
- Cheyenne
- 101 mi
- Denver
- 70 mi
- Colorado Springs
- 42 mi
- Pueblo

LESSON 7-1 (pp. 280–284)

1. 4 rolls **3.** 316 passengers **5.** the take-away model **7.** 81° **9.** $m\angle DBC$ **11.** $b^2 - a^2$ **13.** 24.64 square units **15.** $AB = 113$ miles **17.** 55% **19. a.** $470.75

b. $510.75 - W$ dollars **21.** $\frac{3}{5}$ **23.** 637 **25.** 1 milligram = .001 gram (or 1000 mg = 1 g) **27.** Sample: let $a = 5$, $b = -2$. Then $-(a + b) = -(5 + -2) = -3$ and $-b + -a = -(-2) + -5 = -3$. It may be true always. **29.** Sample: $3.00\_$, where any digit except 0 can be put in the blank.

LESSON 7-2 (pp. 285–289)

1. 3, 4, left **3. a.** $74 - 20$ **b.** $74 + -20$ **c.** 54°F **5. a.** $72 - 3$ **b.** $72 + -3$ **c.** 69 kg **7.** 8 **9.** -53 **11.** -4 **13.** 10 **15.** -3 **19.** the opposite of A minus negative four **21. a.** 3 **b.** 2 **c.** 1 **d.** 0 **e.** -1 **f.** -2 **23.** 2 **25.** (c) **27. a.** True **b.** True **29. a.** $a - b = b - a$ for all numbers a and b **b.** No **31.** $n - 4$ **33.** Addition Property of Equality

LESSON 7-3 (pp. 290–294)

1. 4 **3.** 8 **5.** 6 lb **7.** 540 ft **9.** 1° **11.** 17 points (His guess was 17 points too high.) **13.** -368 **15.** positive **17.** positive **19.** negative **21.** $x - y = 1,034,000$ **23. a.** from 1960 to 1970, 6,291; from 1970 to 1980, -13,584; from 1980 to 1990, 54,537 **b.** 47,244 **c.** The population increased by 47,244 from 1960 to 1990. **25.** 66 or 67 **27. a.** 899 **b.** $J - I - 1$ **29. a.** 1464 people **b.** from 14 to 20 years old **31.** 12 in.

LESSON 7-4 (pp. 295–298)

3. a. $x + -14 = -2$ **b.** 12 **5. a.** $a + -6 = 9$ **b.** $a = 15$ **7.** No **9.** (c) **11.** 12.21; $3.01 = 12.21 - 9.2$ **13. a.** $s - 3 = -2$ **b.** 1 **c.** The team was ahead by one point. **15.** -7 feet (7 feet below the surface) **17.** -11 **19. a.** 58 years **b.** 214° **21.** $G < 21$ or $G > 31$ **23.** two thousand, three hundred five and 00/100 dollars **25.** 70 cm or 0.7 m **27.** 1.5 **29.** 6,340,000 **31.** .000064

LESSON 7-5 (pp. 299–302)

3. a. III **b.** -2 **5.** $4 + 1 = y$ **7. a.** $-15 = y$ **b.** between lines 2 and 3 **11.** $x = -5$ **13.** $y = 10.5$ **15.** $80 = 94 - 14$ or $94 - 80 = 14$ **17.** $-1 - -5 = 4$ or $-5 = -1 - 4$ **19.** $10 = -13 + 23$ **21.** (c) **23.** $y = 48$ **25.** 58 or 59 years old **27. a.** -14 **b.** 88 **29.** 180° **31.** $2n - 3$

LESSON 7-6 (pp. 303–306)

3. t **5.** 302; $300 - 302 = -2$ **7.** 90; $-45 = 45 - 90$ **9.** -53; $-53 - 57 = -110$ **11. a.** 3288 **b.** 3288 tickets have been sold. **13. a.** $22,500 - d = 20,250$ **b.** 2,250 feet **c.** They came down 2,250 feet. **15.** 0 **17.** 13 **19.** 1: Add-Opp Property; 2: Addition Property of Equality; 3: Assoc. Property of Addition; 4: Prop. of Opposites; 5: Additive Identity Property of Zero; 6: Addition Property of Equality; 7: Assoc. Property of Addition; 8: Property of Opposites; 9: Additive Identity Property of Zero **21.** $A = 28$ **23. See below. 25. a. See below. b.** right angles **27. a.** $s - 1.14 = 637.47$ **b.** 638.61 **29.** 180°

23. **25. a.**

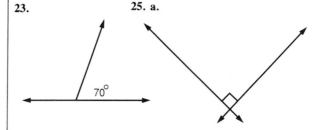

LESSON 7-7 (pp. 307–312)

1. straight **3.** linear pair **5.** 92° **7.** supplementary **9.** angles 1 and 4, 2 and 3, 3 and 4, 2 and 1 **11.** $m\angle 2 = 55°$, $m\angle 3 = 125°$, $m\angle 4 = 55°$ **13.** $x = 135°$ **15.** $d = f = 90.5°$, $e = 89.5°$ **17.** True **19.** 6 **21.** 71st and South Chicago **23.** angles DCA and ACB **25.** True **27.** True **29.** 122° **31.** $x + y = 180°$ **33.** 157 **35.** -38 **37.** $2.60

LESSON 7-8 (pp. 313–317)
1. 118° **3.** 62° **5.** 118° **7.** p **9.** angles 1 and 6, 4 and 5, 2 and 8, 3 and 7 **11.** angles 2, 3, 5, and 6 **13.** Yes
15. m∠1 = m∠6 = m∠8 = 84°, m∠3 = m∠4 = m∠5 = m∠7 = 96° **17.** all of the angles 1 through 8
19. See below. 21. // **23.** 90° **25.** m∠1 = 90°, m∠2 = m∠4 = 40°, m∠3 = 140° **27.** 360° **29.** angles 3 and 4;
See below. 31. $a \cdot 1 = a$ **33.** $c = 180 - a - b$
35. $C - W + D$

19. 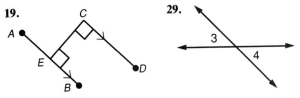 **29.**

LESSON 7-9 (pp. 318–321)
3. a. $TU = TS = SV = UV = 15$ mm **b.** m∠U = m∠S ≈ 100°, m∠T = m∠V ≈ 80° **5.** $\overline{MN}$ and $\overline{QP}$, or $\overline{MQ}$ and $\overline{NP}$ **7.** ∠Q **9.** 110° **11.** all sides equal in length

13. A, D, E, G **15.** A, B, C, D, E, G, H **17.** rectangles and squares **19.** parallelograms, rhombuses, rectangles, and squares **21.** not enough information **23. a.** 147° **b.** 57°
c. 123° **d.** 33° **25.** ABG **27.** m∠DBA = 30°; m∠CBD = m∠FBA = 150° **29.** ⊥ **31. a.** from 1950 to 1960, 103,932; from 1960 to 1970, -23,952; from 1970 to 1980, -81,160; from 1980 to 1990, -36,832 **b.** -38,012 **c.** from 1950 to 1990 the population decreased by 38,012 people

LESSON 7-10 (pp. 322–327)
5. 1° **7.** 40° **9.** If a triangle had two obtuse angles, the sum of their measures would be more than 180°. But the sum of the measures of all three angles is 180°. **11.** 90° **13.** (d)
15. 146° **17.** $\overline{AD}$ and $\overline{BC}$ are parallel. **19.** m∠B = m∠BCD **21. a.** Line segment AB is parallel to ray CD.
b. See below. 23. a. True **b.** True **25.** 910 **27.** 20.4

21. b.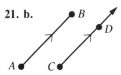

CHAPTER 7 PROGRESS SELF-TEST (p. 329)

1. -6 + -22 = -28 **See below. 2.** 45 + -110 = -65
3. 5 − 13 + 2 − -11 = 5 + -13 + 2 + 11 = 5
4. y + -14 = -24; add 14 to both sides; y = -10 **5.** Add x to both sides; x + -50 = 37; add 50 to both sides; x = 87
6. g + -3.2 = -2; add 3.2 to both sides; g = 1.2
7. c + -a = b; add a to both sides; c = b + a; add -b to both sides; c + -b = a **8.** Angles ABE and ABD are a linear pair, so their measures add to 180. So m∠ABE + 25 = 180, from which m∠ABE = 155. **9.** m∠CBD = 90 − m∠ABD = 90 − 25 = 65 **10.** ∠5 and ∠6 are corresponding angles, so have the same measure 74°. ∠7 forms a linear pair with ∠6, so 74 + m∠7 = 180, from which m∠7 = 106. **11.** ∠5, a corresponding angle; ∠3, a vertical angle; and ∠4, the vertical angle to ∠5 **12.** Angles 1 and 8 each form a linear pair with ∠5, so are supplementary. Angles 2 and 7, having the same measures as angles 1 and 8, are therefore also supplementary. **13.** The sum of

3 right angles would be 270°, which is greater than triangle-sum of 180°. **14.** 55 + 4 + x = 180; 59 + x = 180; x = 121 **15.** ∠CBE, an alternate interior angle
16. See below. 17. rhombuses, which are parallelograms with all sides of the same length **18.** x + -y + 5 **19.** (c); all others are facts related to x + y = 180 **20.** Use the comparison model. $V - N = L$, or $N + L = V$. **21.** Use the take-away model. 5 − 0.4 = 4.6 meters. **22.** Use the comparison model or try simpler numbers. $Z - 67$ inches **23.** Use the slide model. $x° - 7° = -3°$. **24.** Add 7 to both sides. $x = 4°$. **25.** Use the take-away model. Area of outer square = 8^2 square meters. Area of inner square = 4^2 square meters. $8^2 - 4^2 = 64 - 16 = 48$ square meters.

1.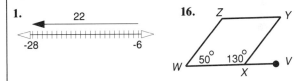

16.

The chart below keys the **Progress Self-Test** questions to the objectives in the **Chapter Review** on pages 330–333 or to the **Vocabulary** (Voc.) on page 328. This will enable you to locate those **Chapter Review** questions that correspond to questions you missed on the **Progress Self-Test.** The lesson where the material is covered is also indicated in the chart.

Question	1	2–3	4	5	6	7	8–9	10	11–12	13	14
Objective	Q	A	B	C	B	C	D	E	K	M	F
Lesson	7-2	7-2	7-4	7-6	7-4	7-6	7-7	7-8	7-8	7-10	7-10

Question	15	16	17	18	19	20	21	22	23	24	25
Objective	K	G	L	H	I	P	N	P	O	B	N
Lesson	7-8	7-9	7-9	7-3	7-5	7-3	7-1	7-3	7-2	7-3	7-1

CHAPTER 7 REVIEW (pp. 330–333)

1. -320 **3.** 13.7 **5.** 72 **7.** -7.2 **9.** $c = e + 45$ **11.** 56

13. $\frac{1}{6}$ **15.** 90° **17.** $180° - x°$ **19.** Angles 7, 1, and 3
21. $180° - y°$ **23.** 38° **25.** 50° **27.** Yes, 10 cm **29.** 4
31. -3 **33.** $a + c = b$ **35.** 140 **37.** $180° - x°$ **39.** 1, 8,

4, and 5 **41.** 1, 7, 5, and 3 **43.** rectangles and squares
45. all **47.** Yes, the angles could have measures 40°, 60°,
and 80°, which add to 180°. **49.** 5500 square feet **51.** 21
53. 1905 or 1904 **55.** 2.5 million **57.** $F - R = L$ **59.** See
below.

59.

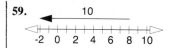

LESSON 8-1 (pp. 336–340)

1. 1 hour **3.** Sample: relaxation time **5.** horizontal **7.** Los
Angeles and Houston **9.** 2 million people **11. a.** 1981
b. -$4.9 billion **13.** vertical **15. a.** Yes **b.** 3 **17. a.** No
b. numbers are not equally spaced **19.** 3.4 and 3.294
21. 100,000 or 200,000 votes **23.** See below.
25. -2,200,000,000 **27.** Lincoln: 1,900,000; Douglas:
1,400,000; Breckinridge: 800,000; Bell: 600,000 **29.** 144

23.

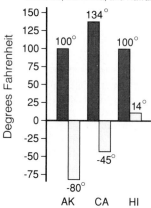

All-time High and Low Temperatures
in Alaska, California, and Hawaii

LESSON 8-2 (pp. 341–347)

1. See below. **3.** E **5.** C **7.** H **9.** F **11.** R **13.** J **15.** See
below. **17.** 14.5° **19.** -3 **23.** 0 **25.** II **27.** III **29.** III and
IV **31.** II and III **33.** III **35.** II **37.** Numbers on the scale
should be 0, 2640, 5280, 7920, 10,560, 13,200, 15,840,
18,480, and 21,120. **39.** See below. **41.** $-\frac{9}{32}$

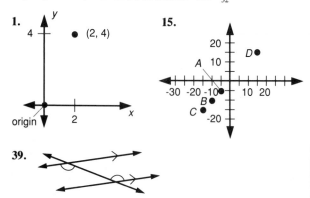

LESSON 8-3 (pp. 348–353)

7. a. -2 **b.** (3, -2) **9.** In these answers, to save space,
graphs of lines are not shown. Instead, some points are
given. Some points on this line: (0, 10), (5, 5), (8, 2)
11. c **13. a.** $x - y = 8$ **b.** some points on this line:
(0, -8), (8, 0), (10, 2) **15. a.** $y = -x - 7$ **b.** Samples:

(0, -7), (2, -9), (-10, 3) **17.** II **19. a.** 25.1% **b.** 0.5%
21. $10.50 **23.** 99

LESSON 8-4 (pp. 354–357)

1. 1988–89 **3. a.** 16° **b.** 10° **c.** 31° **5.** January **7.** 1 day
9. (Dec.24th, -20°) **11.** Graphs can describe drawings and
geometric figures. **13.** circle; See below. **15.** See below.
17. some points on the line: (0, -3), (5, 2), (3, 0) **19.** (3, 8)

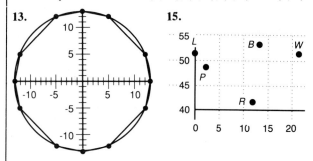

LESSON 8-5 (pp. 358–361)

3. The figure is moved 7 units down. **7.** The image is a triangle with vertices $A' = (3, -5)$, $B' = (7, 2)$, and $C' =$
(-5, 4). **9.** The graph is moved up k units. **13.** See below.
c. They are congruent. **15. a.** Samples: image of (0, 0) is
(4,-5), image of (3, -1) is (7, -6), image of (-2, 3) is (2, -2)
b. See below. **17.** some points on the line: (2, -2), (-5, 5),
(0, 0) **19. a.** See below. **b.** It is easier to insert additional
points.

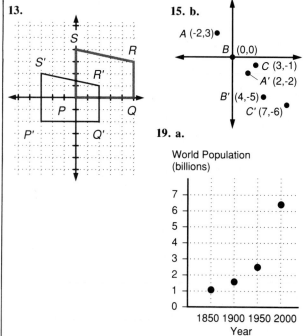

LESSON 8-6 (pp. 362–366)

9. See below. **11.** See below. **13. a.–b.** See below.
c. over the y-axis **15.** TOMATO **17.** CHEEK **19.** $B = (150, 0)$, $C = (150, 50)$, $D = (50, 50)$, $E = (50, 225)$, $F = (0, 225)$ **21. a.** 5% **b.** 12% **c.** $\frac{\text{telephone}}{\text{telegraph}}$

9.

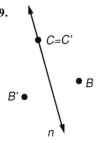

11.

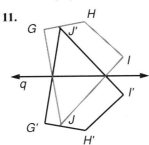

13. a.-b.

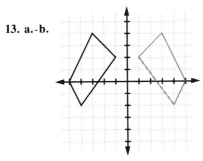

LESSON 8-7 (pp. 367–371)

9. A, H, I, M, O, T, U, V, W, X, Y **11.** 8 **13.** See below. **15.** See below. **17.** See below. **19.** Sample: See below. **21.** See below. **23.** some points on this line: (-2, -2), (5, -9), and (0, -4) **25.** 103

13.

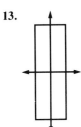

15.

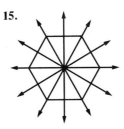

17.

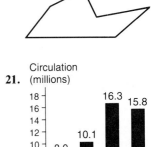

19.

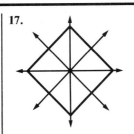

21.

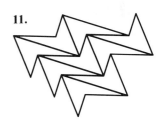

Circulation (millions)

	8.0	10.1	16.3	15.8
	BHG	NG	RD	TVG

LESSON 8-8 (pp. 372–375)

9. Sample: See below. **11.** Sample: See below. **13.** See below. **15. a.** A sheet of stamps is a tessellation; rectangles tessellate, so no paper is wasted. **17.** square **19.** See below. **21.** There are no symmetry lines. **23.** 2×10^{-8} **25.** (c)

9.

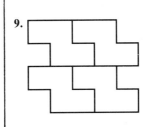

11.

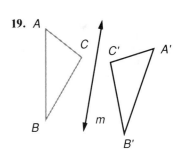

13.

19.

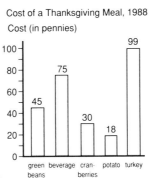

CHAPTER 8 PROGRESS SELF-TEST (p. 377)

1. the week of November 9 **2.** about 3 million barrels **3.** 0.4 million barrels **4.** See right. **5. a.** E **b.** A **6.** E **7.** B, since $-4 + 2 = -2$. **8.** Add 10 to the second coordinate to get (2, 15). **9.** See right. **10.** M is 3 units below (3, 9), so the first coordinate of M is 3 and the second coordinate $9 - 3$ or 6. $M = (3, 6)$. **11.** The hole is directly above (9, 3) so its first coordinate is 9. Its second coordinate is halfway between 9 and 12, so is 10.5. Hole = (9, 10.5) **12.** Sample: See p. 632. **13.** Sample: See p. 632. **14.** See p. 632. **15.** See p. 632. **16.** See p. 632. **17.** See p. 632. **18.** $m\angle V = m\angle W$; $m\angle W = 72°$ **19.** Sample: graphs can show a lot of information in a small place. Graphs can picture relationships. **20.** when they have the same size and shape

4.

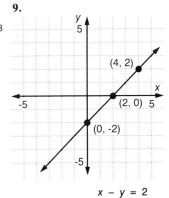

Cost of a Thanksgiving Meal, 1988

Cost (in pennies)

	45	75	30	18	99
	green beans	beverage	cranberries	potato	turkey

9.

$x - y = 2$

points: (4, 2), (2, 0), (0, -2)

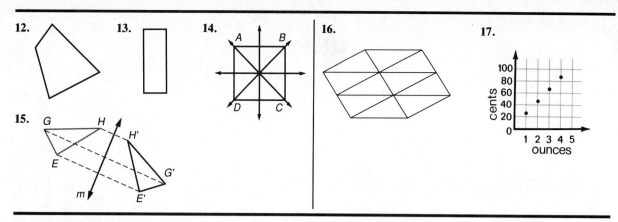

12. **13.** **14.** **16.** **17.**

15.

The chart below keys the **Progress Self-Test** questions to the objectives in the **Chapter Review** on pages 379–381 or to the **Vocabulary** (Voc.) on page 376. This will enable you to locate those **Chapter Review** questions that correspond to questions you missed on the **Progress Self-Test.** The lesson where the material is covered is also indicated in the chart.

Question	1–3	4	5–6	7	8	9	10	11	12–14	15
Objective	F	G	K	L	M	L	K	H	B	A
Lesson	8-1	8-1	8-2	8-3	8-5	8-3	8-2	8-2	8-7	8-6

Question	16	17	18	19	20
Objective	C	I	D	J	E
Lesson	8-8	8-2	8-6	8-4	8-5

CHAPTER 8 REVIEW (pp. 379–381)

1. See below. **3.** See below. **5.** See below. **7.** See right. **9.** See right. **11.** 90° **13.** Yes **15.** 2″ **17.** 4′11″ **19.** 10 calories **21.** 1 million **23.** The number of computer magazines published increased rapidly from 1982 through 1987. **25.** 1978 **27.** See right. **29.** Graphs show trends. Graphs can picture geometric figures. **31.** $B = (-2, 4)$; $C = (-2, 0)$ **33.** See right. **35.** See right. **37.** $x - y = 3$ **39.** (-2, -3) **41.** (9, 3); (7, 7); (10, 5)

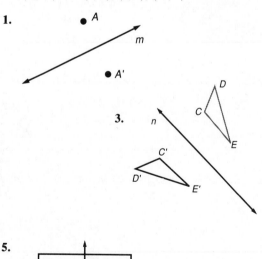

1.

3.

5.

7.

9.

27.

33.

35.

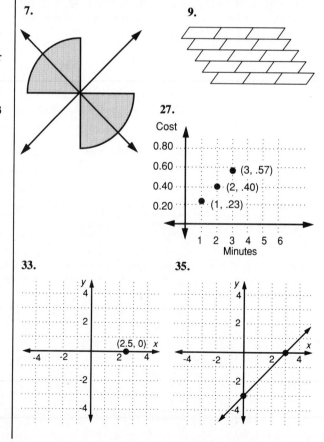

LESSON 9-1 (pp. 384–388)
5. 2 sq. in. **7. a.** 3 **b.** 20 **c.** 60 **11.** Sample: **See below.**
13. $cr = d$ **15.** b **17.** True **19. a.** Yes **b.** Yes **c.** Yes
21. See below. 23. -25 **25. a.** 24 miles **b.** 36 square miles
27. 0.270901 cm³

11.  **21.**

LESSON 9-2 (pp. 389–392)
5. a. See below. b. See below. c. 510 cm²
7. 1116 square inches, or 7.75 square feet **9.** 367 square
inches **11.** Construct a box. **13.** 150 square units **15.** 52
17. Commutative Property of Addition **19.** $34 + 57 = 91$;
$91 - 57 = 34$; $91 - 34 = 57$ **21. a.** $n - 2$ **b.** $2 < n$
c. $2 - n$ **23.** 125 cubic units

5. a. **5. b.**
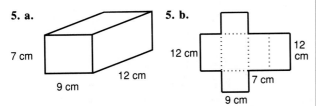

LESSON 9-3 (pp. 393–397)
3. 162 in.³ **5.** 160 cm³ **7.** Ah **9.** Sample: $3 \cdot (4 \cdot 0.5) =$
$3 \cdot 2 = 6$ and $(3 \cdot 4) \cdot 0.5 = 12 \cdot 0.5 = 6$ **11.** 0
13. 864 ft³ **15. a. See below. b.** cube **c. See below.**
17. 262,080 dots **19.** -27 **21. a.** 132.678 **b.** 132.678
c. Commutative Property of Multiplication **23.** $<$
25. a. fourth **b.** Sample: $y = x - 5$ **27.** 2600 meters
29. three places to the right

15. a. **15. c.**
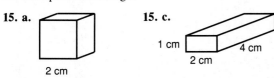

LESSON 9-4 (pp. 398–402)
1. cm **3.** cm² **7.** perimeter **9. a.** miles **b.** square miles
11. False (they are only numerically equal). **13.** 35 in.²;
98 in.²; 70 in.² **15.** $\ell + \ell + \ell + \ell + w + w + w +$
$w + h + h + h + h$ **17.** surface area **19.** volume **21.** c
23. 133 square units **25.** 15,840 feet **27.** (8, -14)
29. a. $33.\overline{3}\%$ or $33\frac{1}{3}\%$ **b.** $66.\overline{6}\%$ or $66\frac{2}{3}\%$ **c.** 80%

LESSON 9-5 (pp. 403–407)
1. a. Samples: 67.8 ⨯ 3.00 = or 67.8 + 67.8 + 67.8 =
b. Yes **3.** $953 + 953 + 953 + 953 = 3812$; the answer
does not check. **7. a.** $\frac{1}{x}$ **b.** -x **c.** -x **d.** $\frac{1}{x}$ **9.** $2\ell + 2w$
11. They can represent the length and width of a rectangle;
the result is the perimeter. **13.** $x + x + z + z + z + z$
15. $\$1.19c$ **17.** c **19.** f **21.** $\frac{25}{2}, \frac{2}{25}$ **23. a.** Associative
Property of Addition **b.** Associative Property of Multiplica-
tion **c.** Add-Opp Property of Subtraction **25. a.** 1 point
b. $w - z$ points **27.** m∠1 = m∠3 = m∠4 = 145°;
m∠2 = 35°

LESSON 9-6 (pp. 408–412)
1. a. 4.4 cm segment; **See below. b.** 8.8 cm segment.
c. 13.2 cm segment. **d.** 15.4 cm segment.
3. a.–b. See below. c. They are twice as long. **d.** They
are the same. **7. See below. 9. a.** 3 **b.** $76.50
11. 15 mm **13.** 3 **15.** 5 **17.** 4 **19.** 1 **21. a.** 500 m
b. 500 m **c.** 10,000 m² **23.** Associative Prop. of Mult.
25. Equal Fractions Property

1. a.

3. a.–b. **7.**
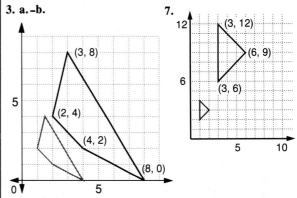

LESSON 9-7 (pp. 413–417)
1. a. 3.5 cm **b. See below.** 1.05 cm **c.** 0.3 **3.** (3, 2)
5. (1.5, 1) **9.** 19,500,000 **11.** about 2.25 cm or .875 in.
13. $(12k, 5k)$ **15.** (d) **17.** $10m$ **19.** $2m$ **21.** -40 **23.** 1
25. (c) **27.** 22° **29. a.** 343 cm³ **b.** 294 cm² **c.** 84 cm

1. b. ————

LESSON 9-8 (pp. 418–422)
3. $\frac{2}{3}$ **5.** 2 **7.** 0.5 m **9.** $\frac{1}{25}$ **11.** $\frac{1}{ab}$ **13. a.** $\frac{1}{50}$ **b.** $\frac{1}{75}$
c. $\frac{1}{3750}$ **15.** $\frac{1}{18}$ **17.** $\frac{1}{DH}$ **19.** $\frac{W}{5}$ dollars **21. a.** $\frac{1}{161}$
b. 0.0062112 **c.** $0.142857 \cdot 0.0434783 = 0.0062112$ **d.** A
number may be substituted for its equal without affecting the
answer (Substitution Principle). **23. See below.** $3 \cdot \frac{1}{5} = \frac{3}{5}$
25. $\frac{1}{16}$ **27. a.** $\frac{8}{30}, \frac{1}{3}, \frac{3}{8}$ **b.** $-\frac{3}{8}, -\frac{1}{3}, -\frac{8}{30}$ **29.** $2a$ **31.** perimeter

23.
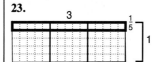

LESSON 9-9 (pp. 423–427)
1. $\frac{12}{45}$ (or $\frac{4}{15}$) **3.** $\frac{1}{2}$ **7.** $12 \cdot 0.75 = 9$ **9.** $\frac{6}{5}$ **11.** $0.625 \cdot 1.6 = 1$
13. $4 \cdot \frac{1}{5} + 3 \cdot \frac{1}{15} = \frac{4}{5} + \frac{1}{5} = 1$ **15.** 3 square miles
17. a. $\frac{1}{2} \cdot \frac{1}{3} \cdot \frac{1}{4} = \frac{1 \cdot 1 \cdot 1}{2 \cdot 3 \cdot 4} = \frac{1}{24}$ **b.** The magnitudes $\frac{1}{3}$ and $\frac{1}{4}$ are
each between zero and one, so they are contractions on $\frac{1}{2}$.
The answer must be less than $\frac{1}{2}$ and therefore less than 1.
21. $\frac{3}{4}$ **23.** contraction (the magnitude is between zero and
one) **25. See p. 634.**

25.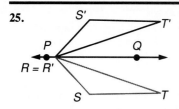

CHAPTER 9 PROGRESS SELF-TEST (pp. 429–430)

1. $\frac{6}{25}$ **2.** $3y + 3$ **3.** $\frac{5}{3}$ **4.** $\frac{7}{16x}$ **5.** Associative Property of Multiplication **6.** Property of Reciprocals **7.** There are rs seats broken or unbroken; there are $rs - 5$ seats to sit in. **8.** Area = 17.3 m • 6.8 m = 117.64 m²; perimeter = 2 • 17.3 m + 2 • 6.8 m = 34.6 m + 13.6 m = 48.2 m. **9.** 6 • 11 + 6 • 11 + 6 • 3 + 6 • 3 + 3 • 11 + 3 • 11 = 234 cm² **10.** 3 ft • 4 ft • 5 ft = 60 ft³ **11.** square kilometers, because area measures fishing room **12.** Sample: 8 and 2, 16 and 1, 10 and 1.6 **13.** The reciprocal is $\frac{1}{38}$ = 0.02631 . . . ≈ 0.026 **14.** $1.29 + $1.29 + $1.29 or 3 • $1.29 = $3.87 **15.** $\frac{2}{3} \cdot \frac{2}{5} = \frac{4}{15}$ **16.** (4 • 8, 4 • 2) = (32, 8) **17.** 1.5 • $5.80 = $8.70 **18. See below.** **19.** contraction (the magnitude is between zero and one), similar **20.** 0.12 • 850 = 102 students **21.** $\frac{2}{3}$ • $8400 = $5600 **22.** $\frac{1}{10} \cdot \frac{1}{10} \cdot \frac{1}{10} = \frac{1}{1000}$. Your chances are 1 in 1000.

23. $\frac{2}{3} \cdot \frac{2}{5} = \frac{4}{15}$. Your chances are 4 in 15. **24. See below.** Sample: Make the rectangle very thin as shown here. This rectangle has length 3 in. and width $\frac{1}{8}$ in. for a perimeter of 6.25 in. and an area of $\frac{3}{8}$ sq. in. **25.** $\frac{1}{1.25}$ = 0.8, choice (c).

18.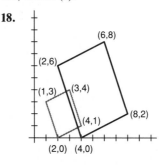

24.

The chart below keys the **Progress Self-Test** questions to the objectives in the **Chapter Review** on pages 431–433 or to the **Vocabulary** (Voc.) on page 428. This will enable you to locate those **Chapter Review** questions that correspond to questions you missed on the **Progress Self-Test.** The lesson where the material is covered is also indicated in the chart.

Question	1–4	2	3–4	5	6	7–8	9	10	11
Objective	A	E	A	D	D	H	I	C	G
Lesson	9-9	9-3	9-9	9-3	9-5	9-1	9-2	9-3	9-4

Question	12	13	14	15	16	17	18	19	20–21
Objective	B	D	F	L	M	J	M	Voc.	J
Lesson	9-1	9-8	9-5	9-9	9-6	9-6	9-7	9-7	9-7

Question	22	23	24	25
Objective	K	K	B	D
Lesson	9-8	9-9	9-1	9-8

CHAPTER 9 REVIEW (pp. 431–433)

1. $\frac{1}{2}$ **3.** $\frac{300}{8}$ or $\frac{75}{2}$ **5.** $\frac{405}{4}$ or $101\frac{1}{4}$ **7.** area = 24.5 square units; perimeter = 21 units **9.** surface area = 1025 square units; volume = 1875 cubic units **11.** For any number n, $n \cdot 1 = n$. **13.** $\frac{3}{2}$ **15.** 0 **17.** $4m$ **19.** Multiply in the reverse order. 6.54 • 2.48 ≠ 16.1292; it does not check. **21.** $\frac{1}{40}$; $\frac{1}{5}$ = 0.2, $\frac{1}{8}$ = 0.125; $\frac{1}{5} \cdot \frac{1}{8}$ = 0.2 • 0.125 = 0.025, which equals $\frac{1}{40}$ **23.** square inches **25.** 48 **27.** 156 square centimeters **29.** No **31.** $37.50 **33.** $5.25 **35.** $\frac{1}{9}$ **37. See below. 39. See below. 41. See p. 635. 43.** contraction

37.

39.

41.

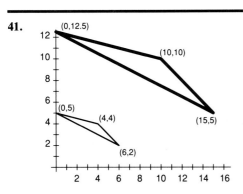

LESSON 10-1 (pp. 434–435)

1. (a) **3. a.** Yes **b.** No **c.** No **d.** No **e.** No **5.** 1 **7.** $\frac{72}{9}$ = 8; $\frac{72}{8}$ = 9 **11.** 7.5; 0.8 • 7.5 = 6 **13.** Sample: $\frac{222{,}300}{325}$ = 684; correct **15.** Sample: $\frac{1152}{.72}$ = 1600; correct **17. a.** Sample: 1.1052632 **b.** 1.11 **c.** 3.8x = 4.2 **19.** 2.25 **21. a.** $\frac{1}{6}$ **b.** $\frac{12}{5}$ **23.** x **25.** reciprocal and multiplicative inverse; opposite and additive inverse **27. a.** 6L square feet **b.** 12 + 2L feet **29.** -8

LESSON 10-2 (pp. 440–444)

1. 6y **3. a.** $\frac{1}{5}$ **b.** 16 **5. a.** $\frac{1}{3}$ **b.** x = 0.12 • $\frac{1}{3}$ = 0.04 **c.** x = $\frac{0.12}{3}$ = 0.04 **7.** 59 **9.** 62.5 **11.** step 1: Multiplication Prop. of Equality; step 2: Associative Prop. of Mult.; step 3: Prop. of Reciprocals; step 4: mult. of fractions and Mult. Identity Prop. of 1 **13.** 2.3; 7.2 • 2.3 = 16.56 **15.** $\frac{4}{3}$ or 1.$\overline{3}$; 3.2 + 4.8 = (3.6 + 2.4) • 1.$\overline{3}$ **17.** 57 **19.** 3H + 20 meters **21.** 320,000,000,000 **23.** 80 cm **25.** 5.499

LESSON 10-3 (pp. 445–449)

3. 15 feet **5.** $2.40 **7. a.** 55,000 cm **b.** 550 m **9.** about 7.14 cm **11.** $37,000 **13.** 40 columns **15.** 25 **17.** Polygon, quadrilateral, parallelogram, rectangle, square **19.** 6 cm²

LESSON 10-4 (pp. 450–454)

1. a. For the game only <u>4 tickets per student</u> are available. **b.** 4 tickets/student **c.** 4 $\frac{\text{tickets}}{\text{student}}$ **3. a.** 150 miles **b.** Sample: how far will a person travel driving at 50 miles per hour for 3 hours? **5. a.** 16 $\frac{\text{games}}{\text{season}}$ **b.** Sample: a team plays 2 games a week. There are 8 weeks in the season. How many games will the team play per season? **7.** 10.5 kg **9.** about 6.63 miles **11.** When a rate is multiplied by another quantity, the unit of the product is the ''product'' of the units, multiplied like fractions. The product has meaning whenever its unit has meaning. **13. a.** 6.36 quarts **b.** Convert 6 liters to quarts. **15.** 100,800 beats **17.** 720 pesetas **19.** 0.6 **21.** 26 millimeters **23.** -$\frac{4}{3}$ **25.** kg **27.** 55 ft **29.** Three points on the line are (0, -4), (2, -2), and (4, 0).

LESSON 10-5 (pp. 455–458)

1. -3.8 $\frac{\text{pounds}}{\text{month}}$, or loses 3.8 pounds per month **3. a.** -5 $\frac{\text{pounds}}{\text{month}}$ • 4 months **b.** -20 pounds; the person will be 20 pounds lighter. **5.** changes **7.** -32 **9.** 18 **11.** -64 **13.** positive **15.** negative **17. a.** -10 **b.** -5 **c.** 0 **d.** 5 **e.** 10 **19.** 60 **21.** $\frac{3}{5}$ **23.** 0.025 or $\frac{1}{40}$ **25.** $2.69 **27. See below. 29.** Sample: -2 + 3 = 1

27.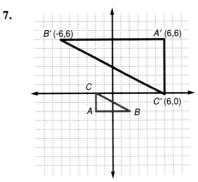

LESSON 10-6 (pp. 459–463)

1. (-8, -10) **7. See below. 9.** 180° **11.** True **13.** 2 **15.** 84 square inches **17.** 51 **19.** 210 **21.** 1680 **23.** 9,765,625 **25.** -0.6

7.

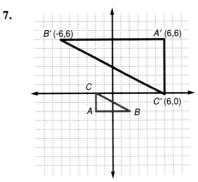

LESSON 10-7 (pp. 464–468)

3. 7 **5.** -1 **7.** 0 **11.** ab **13.** one **15.** none **17.** negative **19.** 0 **21.** -c **23.** 2e **27. a.** No **b.** 0 • 0 ≠ 1 **29.** 34 **31.** For any number x, x + 0 = x. **33.** 52.4 **35.** 14 **37.** 1250 miles

LESSON 10-8 (pp. 469–472)

1. -$\frac{1}{8}$ or -0.125 **3.** -$\frac{5}{9}$ or -0.$\overline{5}$ **5.** -$\frac{1}{x}$ **7.** -2; -4 • -2 = 8 **9.** -70; -1.2 • -70 = 84 **11.** $\frac{2}{25}$; Does -$\frac{2}{15}$ = -$\frac{5}{3}$ • $\frac{2}{25}$? Yes, since -$\frac{10}{75}$ = -$\frac{2}{15}$. **15.** about 15 days **17.** -800m = -4500; about 5.6 months **19.** y is positive **21.** -a

23. 180 students **25.** $\frac{1}{18}$ **27.** m$\angle HEG = 98°$; m$\angle H = 50°$; m$\angle G = 32°$

LESSON 10-9 (pp. 473–477)

1. a. -25 **b.** 15 **5.** 17 **7.** $\frac{4}{3}$ **9.** 610 calories **11.** about

36 French fries **13.** 7.5 ounce hamburger **15.** No **17.** $\frac{19}{112}$; $\frac{3}{2} - 14\left(\frac{19}{112}\right) + \frac{7}{8} = \frac{12}{8} - \frac{19}{8} + \frac{7}{8} = 0$ **19.** -$\frac{15}{8}$ **21.** .635 m **23.** $x + 2z$ **25.** 635,900 people **27.** $2500 - D + B - S = 2300$ **29. a.** 45¢ **b.** 65¢ **c.** 85¢ **d.** $25 + 20(n - 1)$ cents

CHAPTER 10 PROGRESS SELF-TEST (p. 479)

1. $\frac{3}{5}n = 15$; multiply both sides by $\frac{5}{3}$; $n = 25$. **2.** If $x = y$, then $ax = ay$. **3.** $10w = 5$; $w = \frac{1}{2}$ foot **4.** $2000 = .08L$; multiply both sides by $\frac{1}{.08}$; $L = \$25,000$
5. $x = \frac{1001}{13} = 77$ **6.** Multiply both sides by $\frac{1}{13}$; $x = \frac{1}{13} \cdot 1001 = 77$. **7.** 37.5 hours $\cdot \frac{\$8.50}{hr} = \$318.75$
8. 4 hours $\cdot -3 \frac{cm}{hr} = -12$ cm **9.** -45 **10.** $9 + 4 = 13$
11. There are three negatives, so the product is negative; $2 \cdot 3 \cdot 4 \cdot 5 \cdot 6 \cdot 7 = 5040$, so the answer is -5040.
12. $6 \cdot 0 - 3 \cdot -1 \cdot 5 = 0 - -15 = 0 + 15 = 15$
13. $a + a + b + 0 + -c + c = 2a + b$ **14.** $d \cdot$ negative = negative, so d must be positive. **15.** See right.
16. Samples: Things the same: Figures have same shape, same angle measures, corresponding sides parallel. Things different: lengths of sides of image are 2.5 times lengths on preimage; preimage is rotated 180° to get image. **17.** all equal **18.** $\frac{39.37 \text{ inches}}{1 \text{ meter}}$, $\frac{1 \text{ meter}}{39.37 \text{ inches}}$ **19.** 1200 inches $\cdot$

$\frac{1 \text{ meter}}{39.37 \text{ inches}} \approx 30.48$ meters **20.** Multiply both sides by -1; $x = -4$. **21.** Multiply both sides by -$\frac{1}{9}$; $t = -3.9$ **22.** Multiply both sides by -$\frac{5}{2}$; $m = \frac{15}{8}$. **23.** Since any number times 0 is 0, k can be any number. **24.** Add -2 to both sides; $3A = 15$. Multiply both sides by $\frac{1}{3}$; $A = 5$. **25.** Simplify the left side; $-4h - 3 = 10$. Add 3 to both sides; $-4h = 13$. Multiply both sides by -$\frac{1}{4}$; $h = -\frac{13}{4}$.

15.

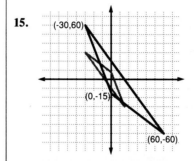

The chart below keys the **Progress Self-Test** questions to the objectives in the **Chapter Review** on pages 480–481 or to the **Vocabulary** (Voc.) on page 478. This will enable you to locate those **Chapter Review** questions that correspond to questions you missed on the **Progress Self-Test.** The lesson where the material is covered is also indicated in the chart.

Question	1	2	3	4	5	6	7	8
Objective	B	Voc.	J	K	G	E	H	L
Lesson	10-1	10-2	10-3	10-3	10-1	10-2	10-4	10-6

Question	9–11	12–14	15–16	17	18–19	20–22	23	24–25
Objective	A	F	L	F	I	C	F	D
Lesson	10-5	10-7	10-6	10-7	10-4	10-8	10-7	10-9

CHAPTER 10 REVIEW (pp. 480–481)

1. 16 **3.** 400 **5.** 3 **7.** -7 **9.** positive **11.** 75; $40 \cdot 75 = 3000$ **13.** 40; $0.02 \cdot 40 = 0.8$ **15.** 7; $-49 = -7 \cdot 7$ **17.** 2; $8 \cdot 2 + 2 = 16 + 2 = 18$ **19.** 3; $11 - 6 \cdot 3 = 11 - 18 = -7$ **21.** $\frac{3}{11}$ **23.** x **25.** no solutions **27.** Is $274 = \frac{13,261.6}{48.4}$? Yes **29. a.** 730 $\frac{\text{cookies}}{\text{year}}$ **b.** If an elf eats 2 cookies per day, how many will it eat in a year? **31.** \$20,475 **33.** She weighed 9.2 kg more. **35.** about 16.4 ft **37.** 25 seats **39.** 12 cm **41.** 2000 **43.** $\frac{\$8}{hr}$ **45.** (-8, 16)

47. See right.

47.

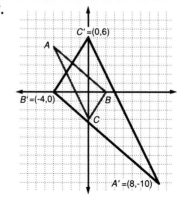

LESSON 11-1 (pp. 484–487)

1. $50 \frac{\text{mi}}{\text{hr}}$ or 50 mph **3.** about $66.7 \frac{\text{km}}{\text{hr}}$ **5.** 2 boys per girl **7.** 20 acres per person **9. a.** 10.8 cents per ounce **b.** 9.6 cents per ounce **c.** the 18-oz box **11.** $\frac{m}{h}$ miles per hour **13.** $0.25 per hour **15.** $9\frac{1}{3}$ bandages per day (5-day week) **17. a.** $\frac{43}{6}$ **b.** $\frac{6}{43}$ **19.** $m = $ -2 **21.** angles 3 and 7; angles 2 and 6 **23.** 75° **25.** 8, 8, 20

LESSON 11-2 (pp. 488–491)

1. $4.80 per hour **3.** $\frac{2}{3}$ **5.** $\frac{17}{4}$ or $4\frac{1}{4}$ **7.** 60 games **9. a.** $\frac{35}{117}$ **b.** $5\frac{4}{7}$ is greater than $1\frac{2}{3}$ **c.** $\frac{1.67}{5.57} \approx 0.3 \approx \frac{35}{117}$ **d.** The decimals are infinite, so it is easier to work with the fractions. **11.** $\frac{2y}{x}$ **13.** 50 **15.** 1 **17.** $\frac{3}{4}$ **19.** $\frac{3}{4}$ **21.** $\frac{1}{100,000,000}$ **23.** 2590 square inches

LESSON 11-3 (pp. 492–496)

1. -2 **3.** 7 **5.** 70 **7.** -9.6 **9.** positive **11.** positive **13. a.** -2 pounds per day **b.** $\frac{-4 \text{ pounds}}{2 \text{ days}}$ **c.** 2, 4, more **d.** $\frac{4 \text{ pounds more}}{2 \text{ days ago}} = \frac{4 \text{ pounds}}{-2 \text{ days}} = -2 \frac{\text{pounds}}{\text{day}}$ **17.** -15, 3, 54, $\frac{2}{3}$ **19.** -24, 0, 144, 1 **21.** $\frac{5}{4}$ **23. a.** $\left(\frac{1}{4}, 5\right)$ **b.** See below. **25.** (-6, 3) **27. a.** 0.44 **b.** $\frac{11}{25}$ **29.** 1250

23. b.

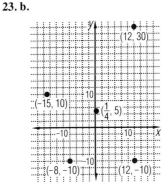

LESSON 11-4 (pp. 497–500)

1. 40% **3. a.** 6% **b.** about 6% **5.** 24% **7.** 100% **9.** 14% **11. a.** 3% **b.** $33.\overline{3}$ or $33\frac{1}{3}$ **13. a.** 56% **b.** 44% **15. a.** 90% **b.** 14.4 **c.** $111.\overline{1}$ **17.** 2% **19.** $\frac{-3}{1}$, or -3 **21.** $9.80 **23.** 47 **25.** 1

LESSON 11-5 (pp. 501–505)

1. 1, 0 **3.** 1 **5.** Precipitation tomorrow is more likely. **7.** $\frac{9}{10}$ **9.** One common way is to guess a probability; another

way is to calculate a probability based on assumptions made about the probability of an associated event. **11.** $\frac{1}{50}$ **13.** A probability cannot be a negative number; probability is a number from 0 to 1. **15. a.** $\frac{45}{360}$ or $\frac{1}{8}$ **b.** B: $\frac{3}{8}$; C: $\frac{1}{4}$; D: $\frac{1}{4}$ **17.** $\frac{5}{n}$ **19.** $\frac{7}{100}$ **21.** 43% **23.** 105

LESSON 11-6 (pp. 506–510)

1. 1, 3 **5.** (c) **7.** 98 **9.** 3 **11.** 37.5 boxes or 37 boxes **13.** No **15.** in his 1,233rd game **17.** $\frac{17}{80}$ **19.** 50% **21.** 5400 cm²

LESSON 11-7 (pp. 511–515)

1. t, 250 **3.** $250t = 400 \cdot 15$ **5. a.** $\frac{8}{\$1.79} = \frac{10}{c}$ **b.** $c = \$2.2375 \approx \$2.24$ **c.** Does $\frac{8}{1.79} = \frac{10}{2.2375}$? Yes **11.** False **13.** True **15. a.** 164 or 165 deer **17.** because the equation is not a proportion **19.** about 12,400 households **21.** $\frac{2}{3}$ **23.** $\frac{2}{3}$ **25.** $\frac{5}{24}$ feet/year or 2.5 inches/year **27.** 27 **29.** $\frac{1}{64}$ square inches **31.** $\frac{1}{2}$ inch

LESSON 11-8 (pp. 516–520)

3. 27.5 **5.** Answers will vary. Sample: **See below.** **7.** Answers will vary. Samples: photographs, scale models, magnifications **9. a.** 12 cm long and 9 cm wide **b.** Yes **c.** Yes **11.** 12.5 **13.** (c), (d), (e), (f) **15.** $15 **17.** 3 **19.** $\frac{56}{25}$ **21.** $3.8 \cdot 10^9$ **23.** 5.125; $5\frac{1}{8}$

5.

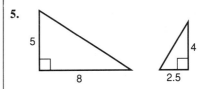

LESSON 11-9 (pp. 521–524)

3. $\frac{2 \text{ cans}}{\$2.50} = \frac{6 \text{ cans}}{\$C}$ **5.** True **7.** 2 hours **9.** 4, 5 **11. a.** $\frac{120 \text{ miles}}{55 \frac{\text{miles}}{\text{hour}}} = 2.\overline{18}$ **b.** At 55 mph, you go 110 miles in 2 hours, 165 miles in 3 hours, so the answer seems right. **13. a.** $12{,}000 \text{ acres} \cdot \frac{1 \text{ square mile}}{640 \text{ acres}} = 18.75$ square miles **b.** $\frac{640 \text{ acres}}{1 \text{ sq. mi}} = \frac{12{,}000 \text{ acres}}{x \text{ sq. mi}}$; from which $x = 18.75$ sq. mi **15.** 40 minutes **17.** $\frac{\$625}{\text{month}}$ **19.** $y = 34.5$ **21.** -3 **23.** about 1428.57 **25.** $2\frac{6}{7}$ hours

CHAPTER 11 PROGRESS SELF-TEST (p. 526)

1. $\frac{300 \text{ words}}{5 \text{ minutes}} = 60$ words per minute **2.** $\frac{m \text{ km}}{h \text{ hours}} = \frac{m}{h}$ kilometers per hour **3.** $\frac{4}{3}$ **4.** $\frac{7}{4}$ **5.** $\frac{3}{5} \cdot \frac{5}{6} = \frac{1}{2}$ **6.** $\frac{10}{-1} = -10$ **7.** Add them, then divide by 3. $\frac{(7 + -17 + 7)}{3} = \frac{-3}{3} = -1$

8. $\frac{a}{b}$ and $\frac{-a}{-b}$ **9.** Sample: If you lose 8 kilograms in 2 months, what is the rate at which your weight has changed? **10.** $8x = 200$, so $x = 25$ **11.** $12p = 15$, so $p = 1.25$ **12.** $\frac{14}{150} = 0.093 \ldots \approx 9\%$ **13.** $\frac{0.30}{4.00} = 0.075 = 7.5\%$ **14.** $.60x = 30$, so $x = 50$ **15.** $\frac{189 \text{ miles}}{45 \text{ mph}} = 4.2$ hours

16. 10,000 sq miles · $\frac{640 \text{ acres}}{1 \text{ sq mile}}$ = 6,400,000 acres

17. b and c **18.** If $\frac{a}{b} = \frac{c}{d}$, then $ad = bc$. **19.** $\frac{x}{40} = \frac{144}{64}$, so $64x = 5760$ and $x = 90$ **20.** $\frac{180}{y} = \frac{144}{64}$, so $144y = 11{,}520$ and $y = 80$ **21.** $\frac{12}{15} = \frac{n}{50}$, so $600 = 15n$ and

$n = 40$ **22.** $\frac{12}{15} = \frac{4}{5}$ **23.** $\frac{\frac{1}{3}}{4} = \frac{x}{9}$ gives $x = \frac{3}{4}$ tsp.

24. $A = 6$. (Do mentally.) **25.** Rewrite as $\frac{3}{n} = \frac{8}{1}$ if necessary. $8n = 3$, $n = \frac{3}{8}$ or 0.375

The chart below keys the **Progress Self-Test** questions to the objectives in the **Chapter Review** on pages 527–529 or to the **Vocabulary** (Voc.) on page 525. This will enable you to locate those **Chapter Review** questions that correspond to questions you missed on the **Progress Self-Test.** The lesson where the material is covered is also indicated in the chart.

Question	1–2	3	4	5	6	7	8	9	10–11
Objective	G	A	B	A	B	H	E	L	C
Lesson	11-1	11-2	11-3	11-2	11-3	11-3	11-3	11-3	11-6

Question	12–14	15–16	17–18	19–20	21	22	23	24	25
Objective	I	K	D	M	J	F	K	C	C
Lesson	11-4	11-7	11-7	11-8	11-5	11-5	11-9	11-6	11-7

CHAPTER 11 REVIEW (pp. 527–529)

1. 18 **3.** $\frac{1}{4}$ **5.** $\frac{7}{4}$ **7.** positive **9.** $\frac{4}{3}$ **11.** 21 **13.** $bd = ae$
15. The left side is not a single fraction. **17.** negative
19. $\frac{1}{3}$ **21.** $\frac{5}{16}$ pounds per hamburger **23.** about 12,300

25. -10.5 **27.** 20% **29.** 59% **31.** $\frac{1}{5}$ **33.** $\frac{b}{b + g}$ **35.** about 35.7 or 36 minutes **37.** \$1.88 **39.** How fast is the crew going up the road? Answer: $\frac{-6 \text{ km}}{-3 \text{ days}} = \frac{2 \text{ km}}{\text{day}}$.
41. 2.5 and 6

LESSON 12-1 (pp. 532–536)
3. The total area of the rectangles is $3x + 5x$. Put them together and the area is $(3 + 5)x$. **See below.** **5.** Fred is correct. $6m - m = 6 \cdot m - 1 \cdot m = (6 - 1)m = 5m$. You can check by substitution. **7.** $10y + 8$ **9.** $10b + 8$
11. $5m$ **13.** $30h + 40$ **15.** $3x + 2x$, or $5x$ cents
17. \$37.50 **19.** $40B + 15.5B + 24B$ or $79.5B$ **21.** 2.1
23. Samples: $3(4 + 5) = 3 \cdot 4 + 3 \cdot 5$; $-2(8 + -8) = -2 \cdot 8 + -2 \cdot -8$ **25. a.** $\frac{1}{3}$ **b.** $\frac{4}{5}$ **27.** $\frac{2}{7}$ **29.** In lowest terms: $\frac{157}{200}$

3.

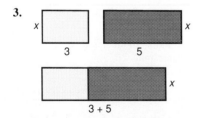

15. a. 740 calories **b.** $520 + 11f$ calories **17.** 3 **19.** $8ax$
21. $\frac{7}{30}$ **23.** surface area, 13 ft²; volume, 3 ft³
25. See below. **27.** 61, 67 **29.** 40

25.

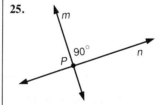

LESSON 12-4 (pp. 546–550)
1. $3.29 \boxed{\times} \boxed{(} 853 \boxed{+} 268 \boxed{)} \qquad \boxed{=}$
$\boxed{3.29} \quad \boxed{853} \quad \boxed{268} \boxed{1121} \quad \boxed{3688.09}$;
and $3.29 \boxed{\times} 853 \qquad \boxed{+} \qquad 3.29 \boxed{\times} 268 \qquad \boxed{=}$
$\boxed{3.29} \quad \boxed{853} \quad \boxed{2806.37} \quad \boxed{3.29} \quad \boxed{268} \quad \boxed{3688.09}$
3. $50x + 200$; Sample: let $x = 2$, then $50(2 + 4) = 50 \cdot 6 = 300$ and $50 \cdot 2 + 50 \cdot 4 = 100 + 200 = 300$
5. $ab + 2ac$; Sample: let $a = 5$, $b = 6$, $c = 10$, then $5(6 + 2 \cdot 10) = 5 (26) = 130$ and $5 \cdot 6 + 2 \cdot 5 \cdot 10 = 30 + 100 = 130$ **7.** $3(\$30 - 5¢) = 3 \cdot \$30 - 3 \cdot 5¢ = \$90 - 15¢ = \$89.85$ **9.** $ab - ac$ **11.** 58, 2
13. 731,999,999,999,999,268 **15.** $3(t + a + s)$ or $3t + 3a + 3s$ dollars **17.** -6 **19.** 18 **21.** $181m + 64$
23. square **25.** rectangle **27. a.** 22.5 minutes, or $\frac{3}{8}$ or .375 hr **b.** 6 minutes, or .1 hr

LESSON 12-2 (pp. 537–540)
1. terminating **3.** can't tell **5.** 3.04444 is finite, the rest are infinite. **7.** $\frac{519}{99}$ or $\frac{173}{33}$ **9.** $\frac{810}{999}$ or $\frac{30}{37}$ **11.** $\frac{30,101}{9900}$ **13.** Sample: $\frac{58,833,333}{1,000,000}$ **15.** $\frac{895}{900}$ or $\frac{179}{180}$ **17.** 3.1 or $\frac{31}{10}$ **19.** $131\frac{30}{5}$ **21.** none

LESSON 12-3 (pp. 541–545)
1. \$2.20 **3.** Sample: $2m + 3n$ **5. a.** 4 **b.** $5t$ and $2t$
c. Sample: $-4m$ and q **d.** -4 **e.** 1 **f.** $7t - 4m + q$
7. $-4x - 2$ **9.** $v - 12$ **11.** $-3t + 9$ **13.** $-3u - 9t$

LESSON 12-5 (pp. 551–555)
3. 7 years old **5.** -8; 2(-8 − 4) = 3(-8); -24 = -24
7. 3.35; .6(3.35) + 5.4 = -1.3 + 2.6(3.35); 2.01 +
5.4 = -1.3 + 8.71; 7.41 = 7.41 **9. a.** 1000 + 200n

b. 750 + 250n **c.** 5 months **11.** $-\frac{11}{9}$; $-\left(-\frac{11}{9}\right)$ + 4 −

$5\left(-\frac{11}{9}\right)$ + 6 = 21 + 3$\left(-\frac{11}{9}\right)$; 10 + $\frac{66}{9}$ = $\frac{189}{9}$ − $\frac{33}{9}$; $\frac{156}{9}$ =

$\frac{156}{9}$ **13.** -40° **15.** 16(b + s + 12) or 16b + 16s +

192 dollars **17.** $\frac{23}{25}$ **19.** $\frac{70}{11}$ **21.** .3y − 1.3z + 8

23. a. 2,160,000 **b.** 2.16 × 10⁶ **25.** 6,372,000 farms

LESSON 12-6 (pp. 556–561)
3. 65¢ **5.** $1.85 **11.** 50¢ **13. a.** 5¢ **b.** 13¢ **c.** 25¢
15. Samples: (4, 0), (2, -4) **17. a.** Sample points: (0, -4),
(6, 0), (3, -2); **b.** See right; **c.** (3, -2) **19. a.** See right
b. The pairs (1, 388), (2, 376), and so on lie on the same

line. **c.** 33$\frac{1}{3}$ **d.** In about 33 weeks the paper will be used

up. **21.** .6 or $\frac{3}{5}$ **23.** 35 **25.** $\frac{1}{2}P$ + $\frac{3}{4}Q$ cups **27. a.** -8 **b.** -2

c. 15 **d.** $\frac{5}{3}$ **29.** 33°

17. b.

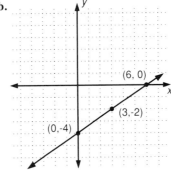

19. a.

weeks from now (w)	number of packages left (L)
1	388
2	376
3	364
4	352
5	340
6	328

CHAPTER 12 PROGRESS SELF-TEST (p. 563)

1. (1 − 3)m = -2m **2.** 4x + 3x + 1 = 7x + 1
3. 7m + -4m + n + -2n = (7 + -4)m + (1 + -2)n =
3m − n **4.** For any numbers a, b, and x, ax + bx =
(a + b)x. **5.** Add 9x to both sides; 1 = 13 + 12x. Add

-13 to both sides; -12 = 12x. Multiply both sides by $\frac{1}{12}$;

-1 = x. **6.** Distribute the 2; 2y − 6 = 12y. Add -2y to

both sides; -6 = 10y. Multiply both sides by $\frac{1}{10}$;

y = $\frac{-6}{10}$ = $\frac{-3}{5}$. **7.** Use the means-extremes property;

5(2t + 7) = 4(t − 8). Distribute; 10t + 35 = 4t − 32.
Add -4t to both sides; 6t + 35 = -32. Add -35 to both

sides; 6t = -67. Multiply both sides by $\frac{1}{6}$; t = -$\frac{67}{6}$.

8. Simplify; .2m + 6 = -.6m + 2. Add .6m to both sides;
.8m + 6 = 2. Add -6 to both sides; .8m = -4. Multiply

both sides by $\frac{1}{.8}$; m = -5. **9.** Let A = Lee's age now.

Then A + 7 = 1.5A. Add -A to both sides; 7 = .5A.

Multiply both sides by $\frac{1}{.5}$; 14 = A. Lee is 14 years old.

10. T books • $\frac{\$3.95}{\text{book}}$ + F books • $\frac{\$4.95}{\text{book}}$ + V books •

$\frac{\$5.95}{\text{book}}$ = 3.95T$ + 4.95F$ + 5.95V$ **11.** p = b + b +

40 + b + b + 40 = 4b + 80 **12.** The H 4-oz
hamburgers have 4H ounces and 80 • 4H = 320H calories.
The H buns have 180H calories. The F French fries have

11F calories. Together they have 320H + 180H + 11F =
500H + 11F calories. **13.** 5 • 3 − 2y = 10, 15 − 2y =
10. Add -15 to both sides; -2y = -5. Multiply both sides by

-$\frac{1}{2}$; y = $\frac{5}{2}$ = 2.5. So the second coordinate is 2.5.

14. Sample: when x = 2, y = 3 • 2 − 2 = 4, so (2, 4) is
on the line. When x = 10, y = 3 • 10 − 2 = 28, so
(10, 28) is on the line. Another point is (3, 7). **15. See
below. 16.** Let x = 0.$\overline{81}$. 100x = 81.$\overline{81}$. 100x − x =
81.$\overline{81}$ − 0.$\overline{81}$ = 81. 99x = 81. x = $\frac{81}{99}$ = $\frac{9}{11}$. **17.** Let

x = 1.02$\overline{8}$. 10x = 10.28$\overline{8}$. 10x − x = 10.28$\overline{8}$ −
1.02$\overline{8}$ = 9.26. 9x = 9.26. x = $\frac{9.26}{9}$ = $\frac{926}{900}$ = $\frac{463}{450}$.

18. 49 • 7 = 50 • 7 − 1 • 7 = 350 − 7 = 343 **19.** from
line 3 to line 4 **20.** w(1.5 + .75 + .3) = w(2.55)

15.

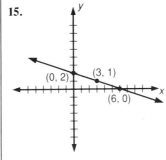

$x + 2y = 6$

The chart below keys the **Progress Self-Test** questions to the objectives in the **Chapter Review** on pages 564–565 or to the **Vocabulary** (Voc.) on page 562. This will enable you to locate those **Chapter Review** questions that correspond to questions you missed on the **Progress Self-Test.** The lesson where the material is covered is also indicated in the chart.

Question	1–3	4	5–8	9	10	11	12	13–15	16–17
Objective	A	D	C	E	E	F	E	G	B
Lesson	12-1	12-4	12-5	12-4	12-3	12-4	12-3	12-6	12-2

Question	18–19	20
Objective	D	F
Lesson	12-4	12-4

CHAPTER 12 REVIEW (pp. 564–565)

1. $10v$ **3.** $20a + 4b$ **5.** $-5t - 14r + 7$ **7.** $6a - 6b + 12c$
9. $\frac{803}{900}$ **11.** $\frac{131}{333}$ **13.** $-\frac{17}{39}$ **15.** -30 **17.** $19.95 • 4 =$
($20.00 - $0.5) • 4 = $80.00 - $.20 = $79.80
19. $100T + 70P$ **21.** $11E + 12T$ **23.** 12 **25. See below.**
27. Samples: (5, 0), (0, 2), (10, -2) **29. See right.**

25.

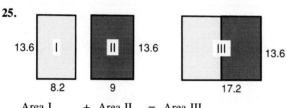

Area I   + Area II   = Area III
8.2 • 13.6 + 9 • 13.6 = (8.2 + 9) • 13.6

29.

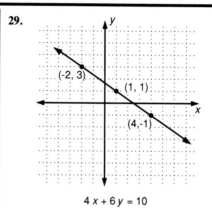

$4x + 6y = 10$

LESSON 13-1 (pp. 568–572)
3. 40 mm, 9 mm **5.** 180 square millimeters **7.** legs 8, 15; hypotenuse 17; area 60 square units; perimeter 40 units
9. $\frac{1}{2}ab$ **11. a.** $3h$ **b.** $3h$ **13.** 48 square inches **15.** 16 cm
17. 8.64 square units **19.** $\frac{1}{27}$ cubic meter **21.** $\frac{5}{12}$ **23.** $(a + b)$
$(c + d) = ac + ad + bc + bd$ **25.** 149

LESSON 13-2 (pp. 573–577)
1. square root **3.** 2.5 is the square root of 6.25 **5.** 9, -9
7. 5, -5 **9.** 8 **11.** -7 **13.** 1.414 **15. a.** 20 m **b.** 20 **c.** -20
17. 9 **19.** $\sqrt{41} \approx 6.4031$ **21.** 3 **23.** 7 and 8 **25.** $\sqrt{2}$
27. 16.4 **29.** 16.4, 16.5 **31.** 120 square meters **33.** (a)
35. (b)

LESSON 13-3 (pp. 578–583)
5. a. $x^2 + 8^2 = 10^2$ **b.** 6 **7.** $\sqrt{8}$ meters **11. a.** 11 km
b. $\sqrt{85}$ or about 9.2 km **c.** about 1.8 km **13. a.** about $13\frac{7}{8}''$
or 13.9″ **b.** $\sqrt{193.25}$″ or about 13.9″ **15.** 9 **17.** False
19. 610 **21.** 97 **23.** $\frac{10}{35}$ hour or about 17 minutes

LESSON 13-4 (pp. 584–588)
1. 468 square units **3. a.** $\overline{YA}$ **b.** $\overline{XB}$ **c.** $\overline{ZC}$ **See right.**
7. a. $\sqrt{48}$ cm **b.** $4\sqrt{48}$ cm² **9.** 10,580 square meters
11. 113.42 **13.** 3.42 **15.** 3%, $\frac{3}{10}$, $.\overline{3}$, $\sqrt{3}$ **17.** 16

19. 10 seconds **21.** $\frac{1}{20}$

3.

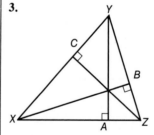

LESSON 13-5 (pp. 589–593)
3. False **5.** False **7.** False **9. a.** Sample: **See below.**
b. 9 cm² **13.** 320 square units **15.** 7 meters **17.** One example of an altitude is the dotted segment. **See p. 641.**
19. 96 square feet **21.** True **23.** 7 **25.** $\frac{1}{3}A$ or $\frac{A}{3}$

9. a. sample:

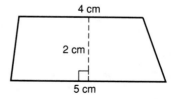

17.

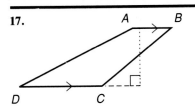

LESSON 13-6 (pp. 594–599)

5. πs **7. a.** estimate **b.** 3.14 **c.** 3.14159 **d.** Answers will vary. Some calculators show 3.1415927. **9.** $\pi = \dfrac{C}{d}$; $d = \dfrac{C}{\pi}$

13. irrational **15.** irrational **17.** rational **19.** all of them
21. 1.2π inches $\approx 3.77''$ **23.** 24π (or about 75) miles
25. about 754 inches or 63 feet **27.** $\sqrt{10}$ **29.** 162 square units **31.** 9 **33.** 9 **35.** 1704 **37.** 500

LESSON 13-7 (pp. 600–603)

1. 64 square units **3.** 50 square units **5.** 18π square units

7. sector **9.** $\frac{1}{4}$ **11.** about 463.77 mm² **13.** 25 square meters

15. a. 120° **b.** $\dfrac{49\pi}{3} \approx 51.3$ square feet **17.** 60.75π or about 191 square meters **19.** 48 **21.** when it is infinite and does not repeat **23.** 36.36

LESSON 13-8 (pp. 604–608)

3. 180° **7.** $\frac{57}{328}$ **9. a.** 20% **b.** 72° **11.** 144° **13. a.** 60–64
b. 30–39 **c.** 5 **d.** 49.4 million **15.** about 695 square feet
17. $\frac{10}{11}$ **19.** .5 square inches **21.** $15m - 18t - 12$ **23. a.** -9°
turn **25. a.** 97 **b.** 1) Read the problem carefully.
2) Devise a plan. 3) Carry out the plan. 4) Check work.

LESSON 13-9 (pp. 609–612)

3. 576π or about 1810 cm² **5.** 2304π or about 7238 cm³
7. 4 ÷ 3 × π × 7 y^x 3 = **9.** volume **11.** volume
13. about 332 cubic inches **15.** $\dfrac{\pi}{6} \approx 0.52 = 52\%$ **17.** 225π
or about 707 square miles

CHAPTER 13 PROGRESS SELF-TEST (p. 614)

1. $C = \pi d = \pi(2r)$. So $C = \pi\left(2 \cdot \frac{3}{8}\right) = \pi\left(\frac{3}{4}\right) \approx 2.4$ in.
2. $\sqrt{3} \cdot \sqrt{3} = 3$ **3.** $\sqrt{10}$ **4.** $5.48 + 7.14 \approx 12.62 \approx 13$
5. $x^2 + 24^2 = 26^2$, so $x^2 + 576 = 676$, so $x^2 = 100$,
$x = 10$ or -10. Since x is a length, $x = 10$ **6.** $AB^2 = 10^2 + 5^2 = 125$, so $AB = \sqrt{125}$ **7.** $\sqrt{25}$, which is 5
8. $A = \frac{1}{2} \cdot 24$ cm $\cdot 7$ cm $= 84$ cm² **9.** $A = \frac{1}{2} \cdot 30 \cdot 36 = 540$ **10.** $A = \frac{1}{2} \cdot 8 \cdot (30 + 9) = 156$ **11.** The legs are $\overline{AC}$ and $\overline{BC}$. The hypotenuse is $\overline{AB}$. **12.** Since $A = \frac{1}{2} \cdot bh$,

$400 = \frac{1}{2} \cdot b \cdot 25$, so $400 = 12.5b$, so $b = 32$ inches.
13. quadrilateral **14.** $7\pi \approx 22$ inches **15.** $A = \pi r^2 = \pi \cdot 16^2 = 256\pi$ **16.** when it is infinite and nonrepeating
17. $S = 4\pi r^2 = 4\pi \cdot 12^2 = 576\pi \approx 1810$ cm²
18. $V = \frac{4}{3}\pi r^3 = \frac{4}{3}\pi \cdot 9^3 = \frac{4}{3} \cdot \pi \cdot 729 = 972\pi \approx 3054$ cubic units **19.** The total number of players is 48.
$\frac{10}{48} = 0.208\overline{3} \approx 20.8\%$. **20.** 60° is $\frac{60}{360} = \frac{1}{6}$ of a circle.
The area of the circle is $\pi\left(\frac{8}{2}\right)^2 = \pi \cdot 4^2 = 16\pi$ cm². So
the area of the sector is $\frac{1}{6} \cdot 16\pi = \frac{8\pi}{3}$ cm²

The chart below keys the **Progress Self-Test** questions to the objectives in the **Chapter Review** on pages 615–617 or to the **Vocabulary** (Voc.) on page 613. This will enable you to locate those **Chapter Review** questions that correspond to questions you missed on the **Progress Self-Test.** The lesson where the material is covered is also indicated in the chart.

Question	1	2	3	4	5–6	7	8	9	10
Objective	E	D	J	B	C	G	A	A	D
Lesson	13-7	13-5	13-2	13-2	13-3	13-6	13-1	13-4	13-5

Question	11	12	13	14	15	16	17	18	19	20
Objective	Voc.	A	Voc.	I	E	G	H	F	K	E
Lesson	13-1	13-4	13-5	13-6	13-7	13-6	13-9	13-9	13-8	13-7

CHAPTER 13 REVIEW (pp. 615–617)

1. 150 **3.** 12 **5.** 8 and 9 **7.** 20 **9.** $\sqrt{73}$ **11.** 52 **13.** 24,600
15. 10,200 **17.** circumference 20π; area 100π **19.** 25π
21. 100π **23.** all but π **25.** Any decimal represents a real

number. **27.** 2.7 square meters **29.** about 1257 cm²
31. 20π or about 63 feet **33.** $\dfrac{32\pi}{3}$ or about 33.5 cubic inches
35. $\sqrt{50}$ **37.** $\sqrt{2}$ **39.** $25\% = \frac{1}{4}$, and the sector for lunch
has more than a quarter of the circle's area.

GLOSSARY

absolute value The absolute value of a positive number or zero is that number. The absolute value of a negative number is the opposite of that number. The absolute value of a number is the distance of a number from zero.

acute angle An angle whose measure is between $0°$ and $90°$.

addend A number to be added.

addition property of equality If $a = b$, then $a + c = b + c$.

additive identity The number 0.

Additive Identity Property of Zero For any number n: $n + 0 = n$.

additive inverse The number, which when added to a number, gives a sum of 0. The additive inverse of n is denoted $-n$. Also called *opposite*.

Add-opp Property of Subtraction For any numbers a and b: $a - b = a + -b$. In words, subtracting b is the same as adding the opposite of b.

algebraic expression An expression that contains a variable alone or with numbers and operation symbols.

algorithm A sequence of steps that leads to a desired result.

alternate interior angles Angles formed by two lines and a transversal that are between the two lines and on opposite sides of the transversal.

altitude of a triangle The perpendicular distance from any vertex of a triangle to the side opposite that vertex. Also called *height*.

angle The union of two rays with the same endpoint.

area Measure of the space inside a two-dimensional figure.

Area Model for Multiplication The area of a rectangle with length ℓ and width w is $\ell \cdot w$ *or* ℓw.

Associative Property of Addition For any numbers a, b, and c: $(a + b) + c = a + (b + c) = a + b + c$.

Associative Property of Multiplication For any numbers a, b, and c: $a(bc) = (ab)c = abc$.

average A number representing a set of other numbers determined by taking the sum of those numbers and dividing by the number of them. Also called *mean*.

bar graph A graph in which information is represented using bars of various lengths to show values of a particular category.

base In the power x^n, x is the base.

base of a triangle The side of a triangle to which an altitude is drawn.

bases of a trapezoid The parallel sides of a trapezoid.

billion A word name for 1,000,000,000 or 10^9.

billionth A word name for 0.000000001 or 10^{-9}.

brackets [ ] grouping symbols which serve the same role as parentheses.

center of a circle The given point from which the set of points of the circle are at a given distance.

center of a sphere The given point from which the set of points of the sphere are at a given distance.

centi- a prefix meaning $\frac{1}{100}$.

centimeter $\frac{1}{100}$ of a meter.

central angle of a circle An angle with its vertex at the center of the circle.

certain event An event with a probability of 1.

circle The set of points in a plane at a certain distance from a certain point.

circle graph A graph in which information is represented using a circle that is cut into sectors to show values of a particular category. Also called *pie graph*.

circumference A circle's perimeter.

clockwise The direction around a circle in which the hands of a clock usually move.

coefficient The number by which a certain variable in a term is multiplied.

coincide To occupy the same position.

column A vertical line of objects in a rectangular array.

common denominator A multiple of all the denominators in a problem.

Commutative Property of Addition For any numbers a and b: $a + b = b + a$.

Commutative Property of Multiplication For any numbers a and b: $ab = ba$.

Comparison Model for Subtraction $x - y$ is how much more x is than y.

composite number Any positive integer exactly divisible by one or more positive integers other than itself and 1.

congruent figures Figures with the same size and shape. Figures which are the image of each other under a reflection, rotation, or translation, or combination of these.

contraction A size change with a magnitude between 0 and 1.

conversion factor A factor by which one unit can be converted to another.

convex polygon A polygon in which no diagonals lie outside the polygon.

coordinate graph A graph displaying points as ordered pairs of numbers.

corresponding angles Any pair of angles in similar locations in relation to a transversal intersecting two lines.

corresponding sides Any pair of sides in the same relative positions in two similar figures.

count A number of particular things.

counterclockwise The direction around a circle opposite from that in which the hands of a clock move.

counting unit The name of the particular things being tallied in a count.

cube A three-dimensional figure with six faces, each face being a square.

cubic units Units for measuring volume.

decagon A ten-sided polygon.

decimal notation The notation in which numbers are written using ten digits and each place stands for a power of 10.

decimal system The system in which numbers are written in decimal notation.

degree A unit of measurement equal to $\frac{1}{360}$ of a complete revolution.

denominator The divisor in a fraction, b in the fraction $\frac{a}{b}$ or a/b.

diagonal of a polygon A segment that connects two vertices of the polygon but is not a side of the polygon.

diameter of a circle A segment connecting two points of a circle and containing its center. The length of that segment.

difference The answer to a subtraction problem.

digit One of the ten symbols, 0 1 2 3 4 5 6 7 8 9, used to write numbers from zero to nine.

dimensions The lengths of the sides of a rectangle. The number of rows and the number of columns in a rectangular array.

display The area on a calculator where numbers appear.

Distributive Property of Multiplication over Addition For any numbers a, b, and x:
$ax + bx = (a + b)x$ and $x(a + b) = xa + xb$.
Also called *distributivity*.

Distributive Property of Multiplication over Subtraction For any numbers a, b, and x:
$ax - bx = (a - b)x$ and $(a - b)x = ax - bx$.
Also called *distributivity*.

dividend The number in a quotient which is being divided. a is the dividend in $a \div b$ or $\frac{a}{b}$.

divisor (1) The number by which you divide in a quotient. b is the divisor in $a \div b$ or $\frac{a}{b}$. (2) A number that divides another number exactly. Also called *factor*.

endpoint of a ray The starting point of a ray.

Equal Fractions Property If the numerator and denominator of a fraction are both multiplied (or divided) by the same nonzero number, then the resulting fractions are equal.

equally likely outcomes Outcomes in a situation where each outcome is assumed to occur as often as every other outcome.

equation A sentence with an equal sign.

equation of the form $x + a = b$ An equation in which an unknown number x is added to a known number a, resulting in a known number b.

equation of the form $ax = b$ An equation in which the unknown number x is multiplied by a known number a, resulting in a known number b.

equation of the form $ax + b = c$ An equation in which an unknown number x is multiplied by a known number a, then added to a known number b, resulting in a known number c.

equation of the form $ax + b = cx + d$ An equation in which the same unknown number x is multiplied by numbers a and c and added to known numbers b and d, resulting in equal values.

equilateral triangle A triangle in which all the sides have the same length.

equivalent formulas Formulas in which the same numbers work.

equivalent sentences Sentences that have exactly the same solutions.

estimate A number which is near another number. Also called *approximation*.

Estimation Principle If two numbers are nearly equal, then when one is substituted for the other in a computation, the results of the computation will be nearly equal.

evaluating an expression Finding the value of an algebraic expression by substituting a value for the variable(s).

evaluating a numerical expression Working out the arithmetic in a numerical expression.

event A collection of possible outcomes of an experiment.

exercise A question which you know how to answer.

expansion A size change with magnitude greater than one.

exponent In the power x^n, n is the exponent.

exponential form The form a^b.

exterior angles Angles formed by two lines and a transversal that are not between the two lines.

extremes In the proportion $\frac{a}{b} = \frac{c}{d}$, the numbers a and d.

faces The sides of a solid.

factor A number that divides another number exactly. Also called *divisor*.

finite decimal A decimal that ends. Also called *terminating decimal*.

foot (ft) A unit of length in the U.S. system of measurement equal to 12 inches.

formula A sentence in which one variable is written in terms of other variables.

fraction A number written in the form $\frac{a}{b}$; b is nonzero.

fraction bar A grouping symbol separating the numerator and denominator of a fraction and standing for division.

full turn A turn of 360°. Also called *revolution*.

Fundamental Property of Turns If a turn of magnitude x is followed by a turn of magnitude y, the result is a turn of magnitude $x + y$.

fundamental region A figure which can be used to form a tessellation.

gallon (gal) A unit of capacity in the U.S. system of measurement equal to 4 quarts.

generalization A statement that is true about many instances.

gram A unit of mass in the metric system.

greatest common factor The largest positive integer which is a factor of two or more positive integers.

grouping symbols Symbols such as parentheses, brackets, and fraction bars that group numbers and/or variables together.

half turn A turn of 180°.

height of a trapezoid The distance between the bases of a trapezoid.

height of a triangle The perpendicular distance from any vertex of a triangle to the side opposite that vertex. Also called *altitude*.

heptagon A seven-sided polygon.

hexagon A six-sided polygon.

hundredth A word name for 0.01 or 10^{-2}.

hypotenuse of a right triangle The longest side of a right triangle.

image point A point resulting from applying a transformation.

impossible event An event with a probability of 0.

inch (in.) The base unit of length for the U.S. system of measurement.

inequality A sentence with one of the following symbols: $\neq$, $<$, $>$, $\leq$, $\geq$.

infinite decimal A decimal that goes on forever.

infinite repeating decimal A decimal in which a digit or group of digits to the right of the decimal point repeats forever.

instance An example of a pattern.

integer A number which is a positive whole number, a negative whole number, or zero.

interior angles Angles formed by two lines and a transversal that are between the two lines.

international system of measurement A system of measurement based on the decimal system. Also called *metric system*.

interval on a scale The constant difference between successive tick marks on the scale of a graph.

irrational number A number that cannot be written as a simple fraction. An infinite and nonrepeating decimal.

key in To press keys or enter information into a calculator.

key sequence A set of instructions for what to key in on a calculator to perform a certain operation.

kilo- A prefix meaning 1000.

least common multiple The smallest positive integer which is a common multiple of two or more positive integers.

least common denominator The least common multiple of two or more denominators.

legs of a right triangle The two sides of a right triangle that form the right angle.

like terms Terms that involve the same variables to the same powers.

linear combination A sum of multiples of different variables to the first power.

linear equation An equation in which the graph of the solutions is a line. An equation equivalent to $ax + b = cx + d$.

linear expression An expression in which the variables are to the first power and are not multiplied or divided.

linear pair Angles that have a common side, and whose non-common sides are opposite rays.

line segment The points A and B along with the points on $\overleftrightarrow{AB}$ between A and B. Also called *segment*.

line symmetry The property of a figure that coincides with its reflection image over a line. Also called *symmetry with respect to a line* or *reflection symmetry*.

liter A volume or capacity in the metric system equal to 1000 cubic centimeters.

lowest terms A fraction written with the smallest possible whole numbers.

mean A number representing a set of other numbers determined by taking the sum of those numbers and dividing by the number of them. Also called *average*.

means In the proportion $\frac{a}{b} = \frac{c}{d}$, the numbers b and c.

means-extremes property In any proportion, the product of the means equals the product of the extremes.

median The middle value of a set of numbers written in increasing order.

meter The basic unit of length in the metric system.

metric system of measurement A system of measurement based on the decimal system. Also called the *international system of measurement*.

mile (mi) A unit of length in the U.S. system of measurement equal to 5280 feet.

milli- A prefix meaning $\frac{1}{1000}$.

million A word name for 1,000,000.

millionth A word name for 0.000001 or 10^{-6}.

minuend The number a in $a - b$.

mirror A line over which a figure is reflected. Also called *reflecting line*.

mixed numeral A symbol consisting of a whole number with a fraction next to it denoting the sum of those numbers.

mixed number A number written as a mixed numeral.

mode The most frequently occurring value in a set of numbers.

Multiplication of Fractions Property For all numbers a, b, c, and d with $b \neq 0$ and $d \neq 0$:
$$\frac{a}{b} \cdot \frac{c}{d} = \frac{ac}{bd}.$$

Multiplication Property of Equality If $x = y$, then $ax = ay$.

Multiplication Property of -1 For any number x: $-1 \cdot x = -x$.

Multiplication Property of Zero For any number x: $x \cdot 0 = 0$.

Multiplicative Identity Property of One For any number n: $n \cdot 1 = 1 \cdot n = n$.

multiplicative inverse The number by which a given number can be multiplied resulting in a product equal to 1. Also called *reciprocal*.

Mult-Rec Property of Division For any numbers a and b, with $b \neq 0$: $\frac{a}{b} = a \cdot \frac{1}{b}$. In words, dividing by b is the same as multiplying by the reciprocal of b.

natural number Any one of the numbers 1, 2, 3, ... Also called *positive integer*. (Some people include 0 as a natural number.)

negative integer Any one of the numbers -1, -2, -3, ...

negative number A number which is the opposite of a positive number.

nested parentheses Parentheses which are inside parentheses.

n-gon A polygon with n sides.

nonagon A nine-sided polygon.

number line A line in which the points in order correspond to numbers in order.

numerator a in the fraction $\frac{a}{b}$.

numerical expression A symbol for a number.

obtuse angle An angle whose measure is between 90° and 180°.

octagon An eight-sided polygon.

open sentence A sentence with variables that can be true or false, depending on what is substituted for the variables.

Op-op Property For any number n: $-(-n) = n$.

opposite The number, which when added to a given number, yields a sum of 0. The opposite of a number n is denoted $-n$. Also called *additive inverse*.

opposite rays Rays that have the same endpoint and together form a line.

ordered pair A pair of numbers or objects (x, y) in which x is the first coordinate and y is the second coordinate.

order of operations Rules for evaluating an expression: work first within parentheses; then calculate all powers, from left to right; then do multiplications or divisions, from left to right; then do additions or subtractions, from left to right.

origin The point where the x- and y-axes intersect denoted by $(0, 0)$.

ounce (oz) A unit of weight in the U.S. system of measurement equal to $\frac{1}{16}$ of a pound.

parallel lines Two lines in a plane are parallel if they have no points in common or are identical.

parallelogram A quadrilateral with two pairs of parallel sides.

parentheses ( ) Grouping symbols which indicate the order of operations that should be followed in evaluating an expression; the work inside them should be done first.

pattern A general form for which there are many examples.

pentagon A five-sided polygon.

percent %, times $\frac{1}{100}$ or .01, one one-hundredth.

perimeter The sum of the lengths of the sides of a polygon.

perimeter of a rectangle $2\ell + 2w$ where ℓ is the length and w is the width of the rectangle.

perpendicular The name given to rays, segments, or lines that form right angles.

pi (π) The ratio of the circumference of a circle to its diameter: approximately $3.1415926535 \ldots$.

pie graph A graph in which information is represented using a circle that has been cut into sectors to show values of a particular category. Also called *circle graph*.

pint A unit of capacity in the U.S. system of measurement equal to one half quart.

place value The number that each digit stands for in a decimal.

polygon A union of segments connected end to end, such that each segment intersects exactly two others at its endpoints.

positive integer Any one of the numbers 1, 2, 3, ... Also called *natural number*.

pound (lb) A unit of weight in the U.S. system of measurement equal to 16 ounces.

power The answer to a problem a^b.

preimage point A point to which a transformation has been applied.

prime number A positive integer whose only positive integer divisors are itself and 1.

probability A number from 0 to 1 which indicates how likely something is to happen.

problem A question which you do not know how to answer.

product The result of doing a multiplication.

Product of Reciprocals Property If a and b are not zero, then $\frac{1}{a} \cdot \frac{1}{b} = \frac{1}{ab}$.

Property of Opposites For any number n: $n + -n = 0$.

Property of Reciprocals For any nonzero number n: $n \cdot \frac{1}{n} = 1$.

proportion A statement that two fractions are equal.

proportional thinking The ability to get or estimate an answer to a proportion without going through the equation-solving process.

protractor An instrument used for measuring angles.

Putting-together Model for Addition If a count or measure x is put together with another count or measure y in the same units, and there is no overlap, then the result has count or measure $x + y$.

Pythagorean theorem In a right triangle with legs a and b, and hypotenuse c, $a^2 + b^2 = c^2$.

quadrant One of the four parts into which the co-ordinate plane is divided by the x-axis and y-axis.

quadrilateral A four-sided polygon.

quadrillion A word name for 1,000,000,000,000,000.

quadrillionth A word name for 10^{-15}, or .00000 00000 00001 .

quart (qt) A unit of volume in the U.S. system of measurement equal to 2 pints.

quintillion A word name for 1,000,000,000,000,000,000.

quintillionth A word name for 10^{-18}, or .00000 00000 00000 001 .

quotient The result of dividing one number by another.

radius of a circle (plural radii) The distance from the center to any point on the circle.

radius of a sphere The distance from the center to any point on the sphere.

rate A quantity whose unit contains the word "per" or "for each" or some synonym.

rate factor A rate used in a multiplication.

Rate Model for Division If a and b are quantities with different units, then $\frac{a}{b}$ is the amount of quantity a per quantity b.

Rate Factor Model for Multiplication When a rate is multiplied by another quantity, the unit of the product is the "product" of units multiplied like fractions. The product has meaning whenever its units have meaning.

rate unit The unit of measurement in a rate.

ratio The quotient of two quantities with the same units.

Ratio Comparison Model for Division If a and b are quantities with the same units, then $\frac{a}{b}$ compares a to b.

rational number A number that can be written as a simple fraction. A terminating or repeating decimal.

ray A part of a line which begins at some point and goes forever in a particular direction.

real number A number that can be written as a decimal.

reciprocal A number which, when multiplied by a given number, yields the product 1. Also called *multiplicative inverse*.

rectangle A quadrilateral with four right angles.

rectangular array An arrangement of objects into rows and columns.

rectangular solid A box.

reflecting line The line over which a figure is reflected. Also called *mirror*.

reflection image The image of a figure reflected over a line.

regular polygon A convex polygon whose sides all have the same length and whose angles all have the same measure.

Related Facts Property of Multiplication and Division If $xy = P$, then $\frac{P}{x} = y$ and $\frac{P}{y} = x$.

Repeated Addition Model for Multiplication If n is a positive integer, then
$$nx = \underbrace{x + x + \ldots + x.}_{n \text{ addends}}$$

repetend The digits which repeat forever in an infinitely repeating decimal.

revolution A turn of 360°. Also called *full turn*.

rhombus A quadrilateral with all sides of the same length.

right angle An angle whose measure is 90°.

right triangle A triangle with a right angle.

rounding down Making an estimate that is smaller than the exact value.

rounding to the nearest Making an estimate to a particular decimal place by either rounding up or rounding down depending on which estimate the exact value is closest to.

rounding up Making an estimate that is bigger than the exact value.

row A horizontal line of objects in a rectangular array.

scientific calculator A calculator which writes very large or very small numbers in scientific notation and with the powering, factorial, square root, negative, and reciprocal keys.

scientific notation for large numbers A way of writing a large number in terms of a positive integer power of 10 multiplied by a number greater than or equal to 1 and less than 10.

scientific notation for small numbers A way of writing a small number in terms of a negative integer power of 10 multiplied by a number greater than or equal to 1 and less than 10.

sector A part of a circle bounded by two radii and the circle.

segment ($\overline{AB}$) The points A and B along with the points on $\overleftrightarrow{AB}$ between A and B. Also called *line segment*.

semicircle Half a circle.

short ton A unit of weight in the U.S. system of measurement equal to 2000 pounds.

side One of the segments which makes up a polygon. One of the rays of an angle. One of the faces of a solid.

similar figures Two figures that have the same shape, but not necessarily the same size.

simple fraction A fraction with an integer in the numerator and a nonzero integer in the denominator.

simpler number A number used to more easily solve problems with complicated numbers.

size change factor A number which multiplies other numbers to change their size.

size change of magnitude k A transformation in which the coordinates of the original figure have all been multiplied by k.

Size Change Model for Multiplication If a quantity x is multiplied by a size change factor k, then the result is a quantity k times as big.

slide image The result of adding the same number to the coordinates of the points in a figure. Also called *translation image*.

Slide Model for Addition If a slide x is followed by a slide y, the result is a slide $x + y$.

Slide Model for Subtraction If a quantity a is decreased by an amount b, the resulting quantity is $a - b$.

solution A value of a variable that makes an open sentence true.

solving an open sentence Finding values of the unknown(s) in an open sentence that make it true.

solving a proportion Finding the value of a variable that makes a proportion true.

special case An instance of a pattern used for some definite purpose.

sphere The set of points in space at a given distance from a given point.

square A four-sided figure with four right angles and four sides of equal length. A rectangle with the same length and width.

square root If $A = s^2$, then s is called a square root of A.

square units Units for measuring area.

straight angle An angle whose measure is 180°.

Substitution Principle If two numbers are equal, then one may be substituted for the other in any computation without changing the results of the computation.

subtrahend b in the subtraction $a - b$.

sum The result of an addition.

supplementary angles Two angles whose measures add to 180°.

surface area The sum of the areas of the faces of a solid.

symmetric figure A figure that is symmetric with respect to at least one line.

table An arrangement of data in rows and columns.

Take-away Model for Subtraction If a quantity y is taken away from an original quantity x with the same units, the quantity left is $x - y$.

tenth A word name for 10^{-1} or 0.1.

terminating decimal A decimal that ends. Also called *finite decimal*.

terms Numbers or expressions that are added or subtracted.

tessellation A filling up of a two-dimensional space by congruent copies of a figure that do not overlap.

transformation An operation on a geometric figure by which each point gives rise to a unique image.

translation image The result of adding the same numbers to the coordinates of the points in a figure. Also called *slide image*.

transversal A line that intersects two or more lines.

trapezoid A quadrilateral that has at least one pair of parallel sides.

trial and error A problem-solving strategy in which various solutions are tried until the correct solution is found.

Triangle-Sum Property In any triangle, the sum of the measures of the angles is $180°$.

triangular region A triangle and the space inside it.

trillion A word name for 1,000,000,000,000.

trillionth A word name for 10^{-12}, or .000000000001.

truncate To cut off a number at a particular decimal place.

uniform scale A scale in which numbers that are equally spaced differ by the same amount.

unit cost The cost per given unit of an object.

unit fraction A fraction with 1 in its numerator and a natural number in its denominator.

unknown A variable which is to be solved for in an equation.

unlike terms Terms that involve different variables or the same variable with different exponents.

U.S. system of measurement A measurement system in common use in the United States today, based on inches and pounds. Also called the *customary system of measurement*.

value of a numerical expression The number that is the result of evaluating a numerical expression.

value of an expression The number that is the result of evaluating an algebraic expression.

value of a variable A number that is substituted for a variable.

variable A symbol that can stand for any one of a set of numbers or other objects.

vertex (plural vertices) The point two sides of a polygon have in common. The point of intersection of the sides of an angle.

vertical angles Angles formed by two intersecting lines, but which are not a linear pair.

volume Measurement of the space inside a three-dimensional, or solid figure.

whole number Any of the numbers 0, 1, 2, 3, ...

x-axis The horizontal number line in a coordinate graph.

x-coordinate The first coordinate of an ordered pair.

y-axis The vertical number line in a coordinate graph.

y-coordinate the second coordinate of an ordered pair.

yard (yd) A unit of length in the U.S. system of measurement equal to 3 feet.

1 Overview of UCSMP

The Reasons for UCSMP

■ Recommendations for Change

The mathematics curriculum has undergone changes in every country of the world throughout this century, as a result of an increasing number of students staying in school longer, a greater number of technically competent workers and citizens being needed, and because of major advances in mathematics itself. In the last generation, these developments have been accelerated due to the widespread appearance of computers with their unprecedented abilities to handle and display information.

In the last 100 years, periodically there have been national groups examining the curriculum in light of these changes in society. (A study of these reports can be found in *A History of Mathematics Education in the United States and Canada*, the 30th Yearbook of the National Council of Teachers of Mathematics, 1970.) The most recent era of reports can be said to have begun in the years 1975–1980, with the publication of reports by various national mathematics organizations calling attention to serious problems in the education of our youth.

Beginning in 1980, these reports were joined by governmental and private reports on the state of American education with broad recommendations for school practice. Two of these are notable for their specific remarks about mathematics education.

1983: National Commission on Excellence in Education. *A Nation At Risk.*

"The teaching of mathematics in high school should equip graduates to: (a) understand geometric and algebraic concepts; (b) understand elementary probability and statistics; (c) apply mathematics in everyday situations; and (d) estimate, approximate, measure, and test the accuracy of their calculations. In addition to the traditional sequence of studies available for college-bound students, new, equally demanding mathematics curricula need to be developed for those who do not plan to continue their formal education immediately." (p. 25)

1983: College Board (Project EQuality). *Academic Preparation for College: What Students Need to Know and Be Able to Do.*

All students (college-bound or not) should have:
"The ability to apply mathematical techniques in the solution of real-life problems and to recognize when to apply those techniques.
Familiarity with the language, notation, and deductive nature of mathematics and the ability to express quantitative ideas with precision.
The ability to use computers and calculators.
Familiarity with the basic concepts of statistics and statistical reasoning.
Knowledge in considerable depth and detail of algebra, geometry, and functions." (p. 20)

The specific remarks about school mathematics in these documents for the most part mirror what appeared in the earlier reports. Thus, **given what seemed to be a broad consensus on the problems and desirable changes in pre-college mathematics instruction, it was decided at the outset of UCSMP, that UCSMP would not attempt to form its own set of recommendations, but undertake the task of translating the existing recommendations into the reality of classrooms and schools.**

At the secondary (7–12) level, these reports respond to two generally perceived problems pursuant to mathematics education.

GENERAL PROBLEM 1: Students do not learn enough mathematics by the time they leave school.

Specifically:

(A) Many students lack the mathematics background necessary to succeed in college, on the job, or in daily affairs.

(B) Even those students who possess mathematical skills are not introduced to enough applications of the mathematics they know.

(C) Students do not get enough experience with problems and questions that require some thought before answering.

(D) Many students terminate their study of mathematics too soon, not realizing the importance mathematics has in later schooling and in the marketplace.

(E) Students do not read mathematics books and, as a result, do not learn to become independent learners capable of acquiring mathematics outside of school when the need arises.

These situations lead us to want to
upgrade students' achievement.

GENERAL PROBLEM 2: The school mathematics curriculum has not kept up with changes in mathematics and the ways in which mathematics is used.

Specifically:

(A) Current mathematics curricula have not taken into account today's calculator and computer technology.

(B) Students who do succeed in secondary school mathematics are prepared for calculus, but are not equipped for the other mathematics they will encounter in college.

(C) Statistical ideas are found everywhere, from newspapers to research studies, but are not found in most secondary school mathematics curricula.

(D) The emergence of computer science has increased the importance of a background in discrete mathematics.

(E) Mathematics is now applied to areas outside the realm of the physical sciences, as much as within the field itself, but these applications are rarely taught and even more rarely tested.

(F) Estimation and approximation techniques are important in all of mathematics, from arithmetic on.

These existing situations lead us to a desire to
update the mathematics curriculum.

Since the inception of UCSMP, reports from national groups of mathematics educators have reiterated the above problems, and research has confirmed their existence. Three reports are of special significance to UCSMP.

Universities have for many years had to recognize that mathematics encompasses far more than algebra, geometry, and analysis. The term **mathematical sciences** is an umbrella designation which includes traditional mathematics as well as a number of other disciplines. The largest of these other disciplines today are statistics, computer science, and applied mathematics. In 1983, the Conference Board of the Mathematical Sciences produced a report, *The Mathematical Sciences Curriculum: What Is Still Fundamental and What Is Not*. THE UCSMP GRADES 7–12 CAN BE CONSIDERED TO BE THE FIRST MATHEMATICAL SCIENCES CURRICULUM.

The Second International Mathematics Study (SIMS) was conducted in 1981–82 and involved 23 populations in 21 countries. At the eighth-grade level, virtually all students attend school in all those countries. At the 12th-grade level, the population tested consisted of those who are in the normal college preparatory courses, which, in the United States, include precalculus and calculus classes.

The UCSMP grades 7–12 can be considered to be the first mathematical sciences curriculum.

At the eighth-grade level, our students scored at or below the international average on all five subtests: arithmetic, measurement, algebra, geometry, and statistics. We are far below the top: Japan looked at the test and decided it was too easy for their 8th-graders, and so gave it at 7th grade. Still, the median Japanese 7th-grader performed at the 95th percentile of United States 8th-graders. These kinds of results have been confirmed in other studies, comparing students at lower-grade levels.

At the twelfth-grade level, about 13% of our population is enrolled in precalculus or calculus; the mean among developed countries is about 16%. Thus, the United States no longer keeps more students in mathematics than other developed countries, yet our advanced placement students do not perform well when compared to their peers in other countries. SIMS found:

1987: Second International Mathematics Study (SIMS). *The Underachieving Curriculum.*

In the U.S., the achievement of the Calculus classes, the nation's **best** mathematics students, was at or near the average achievement of the advanced secondary school mathematics students in other countries. (In most countries, **all** advanced mathematics students take calculus. In the U.S., only about one-fifth do.) The achievement of the U.S. Precalculus students (the majority of twelfth grade college-preparatory students) was substantially below the international average. In some cases the U.S. ranked with the lower one-fourth of all countries in the Study, and was the lowest of the advanced industrialized countries. (*The Underachieving Curriculum, p. vii.*)

The situation is, of course, even worse for those who do not take precalculus mathematics in high school. Such students either have performed poorly in their last mathematics course, a situation which has caused them not to go on in mathematics, or they were performing poorly in junior high school and had to take remedial mathematics as 9th-graders. If these students go to college, they invariably take remedial mathematics, which is taught at a faster pace than in high school, and the failure rates in such courses often exceed 40%. If they do not go to college but join the job market, they lack the mathematics needed to understand today's technology. IT IS NO UNDERSTATEMENT TO SAY THAT UCSMP HAS RECEIVED ITS FUNDING FROM BUSINESS AND INDUSTRY BECAUSE THOSE WHO LEAVE SCHOOLING TO JOIN THE WORK FORCE ARE WOEFULLY WEAK IN THE MATHEMATICS THEY WILL NEED.

SIMS recommended steps to renew school mathematics in the United States. **The UCSMP secondary curriculum implements the curriculum recommendations of the Second International Mathematics Study.**

In 1986, the National Council of Teachers of Mathematics began an ambitious effort to detail the curriculum it would like to see in schools. The "NCTM Standards," as they have come to be called, involve both content and methodology. The *Standards* document is divided into four sections, K–4, 5–8, 9–12, and Evaluation. Space limits our discussion here to just a few quotes from the 5–8 and 9–12 standards.

It is no understatement to say that UCSMP has received its funding from business and industry because those who leave schooling to join the work force are woefully weak in the mathematics they will need.

1989: National Council of Teachers of Mathematics. *Curriculum and Evaluation Standards for School Mathematics*

"The 5–8 curriculum should include the following features:

■ Problem situations that establish the need for new ideas and motivate students should serve as the context for mathematics in grades 5–8. Although a specific idea might be forgotten, the context in which it is learned can be remembered and the idea can be re-created. In developing the problem situations, teachers should emphasize the application to real-world problems as well as to other settings relevant to middle school students.

■ Communication with and about mathematics and mathematical reasoning should permeate the 5–8 curriculum.

■ A broad range of topics should be taught, including number concepts, computation, estimation, functions, algebra, statistics, probability, geometry, and measurement. Although each of these areas is valid mathematics in its own right, they should be taught together as an integrated whole, not as isolated topics; the connections between them should be a prominent feature of the curriculum.

■ Technology, including calculators, computers, and videos, should be used when appropriate. These devices and formats free students from tedious computations and allow them to concentrate on problem solving and other important content. They also give them new means to explore content. As paper-and-pencil computation becomes less important, the skills and understanding required to make proficient use of calculators and computers become more important." (pp. 66–67)

"The standards for grades 9–12 are based on the following assumptions:

■ Students entering grade 9 will have experienced mathematics in the context of the broad, rich curriculum outlined in the K–8 standards.

The UCSMP secondary curriculum is the first full mathematics curriculum that is consistent with the recommendations of the NCTM Standards.

■ The level of computational proficiency suggested in the K–8 standards will be expected of all students; however, no student will be denied access to the study of mathematics in grades 9–12 because of a lack of computational facility.

■ Although arithmetic computation will not be a direct object of study in grades 9–12, conceptual and procedural understandings of number, numeration, and operations, and the ability to make estimations and approximations and to judge the reasonableness of results will be strengthened in the context of applications and problem solving, including those situations dealing with issues of scientific computation.

■ Scientific calculators with graphing capabilities will be available to all students at all times.

■ A computer will be available at all times in every classroom for demonstration purposes, and all students will have access to computers for individual and group work.

■ At least three years of mathematical study will be required of all secondary school students.

■ These three years of mathematical study will revolve around a core curriculum differentiated by the depth and breadth of the treatment of topics and by the nature of applications.

■ Four years of mathematical study will be required of all college-intending students.

■ These four years of mathematical study will revolve around a broadened curriculum that includes extensions of the core topics and for which calculus is no longer viewed as *the* capstone experience.

■ All students will study appropriate mathematics during their senior year." (pp. 124–125)

THE UCSMP SECONDARY CURRICULUM IS THE FIRST FULL MATHEMATICS CURRICULUM THAT IS CONSISTENT WITH THE RECOMMENDATIONS OF THE NCTM STANDARDS.

■ Accomplishing the Goals

We at UCSMP believe that the goals of the various reform groups since 1975 can be accomplished, but not without a substantial reworking of the curriculum. It is not enough simply to insert applications, a bit of statistics, and take students a few times a year to a computer. Currently the greatest amount of time in arithmetic is spent on calculation, in algebra on manipulating polynomials and rational expressions, in geometry on proof, in advanced algebra and later courses on functions. These topics—the core of the curriculum—are the most affected by technology.

It is also not enough to raise graduation requirements, although that is the simplest action to take. Increases in requirements characteristically lead to one of two situations. If the courses are kept the same, the result is typically a greater number of failures and even a greater number of dropouts. If the courses are eased, the result is lower performance for many students as they are brought through a weakened curriculum.

The fundamental problem, as SIMS noted, is the curriculum, and the fundamental problem in the curriculum is **time.** There is not enough time in the current 4-year algebra-geometry-algebra-precalculus curriculum to prepare students for calculus, and the recommendations are asking students to learn even more content.

Fortunately, there is time to be had, because the existing curriculum wastes time. It underestimates what students know when they enter the classroom and needlessly reviews what students have already learned. This needless review has been documented by Jim Flanders, a UCSMP staff member ("How Much of the Content in Mathematics Textbooks is New?" *Arithmetic Teacher,* September, 1987). Examining textbooks of the early 1980s, Flanders reports that at grade 2 there is little new. In grades 3–5, about half the pages have something new on them. But over half the pages in grades 6–8 are totally review.

And then in the 9th grade the axe falls. Flanders found that almost 90% of the pages of first-year algebra texts have content new to the student. The student, having sat for years in mathematics classes where little was new, is overwhelmed. Some people interpret the overwhelming as the student "not being ready" for algebra, but we interpret it as the student being swamped by the pace. When you have been in a classroom in which at most only 1 of 3 days is devoted to anything new, you are not ready for a new idea every day.

This amount of review in grades K–8, coupled with the magnitude of review in previous years, effectively decelerates students at least 1–2 years compared to students in other countries. It explains why almost all industrialized countries of the world, except the U.S. and Canada (and some French-speaking countries who do geometry before algebra), can begin concentrated study of algebra in the 7th or 8th grade.

Thus we believe that ALGEBRA SHOULD BE TAUGHT ONE YEAR EARLIER TO MOST STUDENTS THAN IS CURRENTLY THE CASE.

However, we do not believe students should take calculus one year earlier than they do presently. It seems that most students who take four years of college preparatory mathematics successfully in high schools do not begin college with calculus. As an example, consider the data reported by Bert Waits and Frank Demana in the *Mathematics Teacher* (January, 1988). Of students entering Ohio State University with exactly four years of college preparatory high-school mathematics, only 8% placed into calculus on the Ohio State mathematics placement test. The majority placed into pre-calculus, with 31% requiring one semester and 42% requiring two semesters of work. The remaining 19% placed into re-medial courses below precalculus.

Those students who take algebra in the 8th grade and are successful in calculus at the 12th grade are given quite a bit more than the normal four years of college preparatory mathematics in their "honors" or "advanced" courses. It is not stretching the point too much to say that they take five years of mathematics crammed into four years.

Thus, even with the current curriculum, four years are not enough to take a typical student from algebra to calculus. Given that the latest recommendations ask for students to learn more mathematics, **we believe five years of college preparatory mathematics** *beginning with algebra* **are necessary to provide the time for students to learn the mathematics they need for college in the 1990s.** The UCSMP secondary curriculum is designed with that in mind.

. . . algebra should be taught one year earlier to most students than is currently the case.

T23

The UCSMP Secondary Curriculum

The UCSMP curriculum for grades 7–12 consists of these six courses:

Transition Mathematics

Algebra

Geometry

Advanced Algebra

Functions, Statistics, and Trigonometry with Computers

Precalculus and Discrete Mathematics

EACH COURSE IS MEANT TO STAND ALONE. Each course has also been tested alone. HOWEVER, TO TAKE BEST ADVANTAGE OF THESE MATERIALS, AND TO HAVE THEM APPROPRIATE FOR THE GREATEST NUMBER OF STUDENTS, IT IS PREFERABLE TO USE THEM IN SEQUENCE.

Each course is meant to stand alone. . . . However, to take best advantage of these materials, and to have them appropriate for the greatest number of students, it is preferable to use them in sequence.

■ Content Features

Transition Mathematics: This text weaves three themes—applied arithmetic, pre-algebra and pre-geometry—by focusing on arithmetic operations in mathematics and the real world. Variables are used as pattern generalizers, abbreviations in formulas, and unknowns in problems, and are represented on the number line and graphed in the coordinate plane. Basic arithmetic and algebraic skills are connected to corresponding geometry topics.

Algebra: This text has a scope far wider than most other algebra texts. It uses statistics and geometry as settings for work with linear expressions and sentences. Probability provides a context for algebraic fractions, functions, and set ideas. There is much work with graphing. Applications motivate all topics, and include exponential growth and compound interest.

Geometry: This text presents coordinates, transformations, measurement formulas, and three-dimensional figures in the first half of the book. Concentrated work with proof-writing is delayed until midyear and later, following a carefully sequenced development of the logical and conceptual precursors to proof.

Advanced Algebra: This course emphasizes facility with algebraic expressions and forms, especially linear and quadratic forms, powers and roots, and functions based on these concepts. Students study logarithmic, trigonometric, polynomial, and other special functions both for their abstract properties and as tools for modeling real-world situations. A geometry course or its equivalent is a prerequisite, for geometric ideas are utilized throughout.

Functions, Statistics, and Trigonometry with Computers (FST): FST integrates statistical and algebraic concepts, and previews calculus in work with functions and intuitive notions of limits. Computers are assumed available for student use in plotting functions, analyzing data, and simulating experiments. Enough trigonometry is available to constitute a standard precalculus course in trigonometry and circular functions.

T24

Precalculus and Discrete Mathematics (PDM): PDM integrates the background students must have, to be successful in calculus, with the discrete mathematics helpful for computer study. The study of number systems, three-dimensional coordinate geometry, and some linear algebra is also included. Mathematical thinking, including specific attention to formal logic and proof, is a theme throughout.

■ General Features

Wider Scope: Geometry and discrete mathematics are present in all courses. Substantial amounts of statistics are integrated into the study of algebra and functions. The history of concepts and recent developments in mathematics and its applications are included as part of the lessons themselves.

Reality Orientation: Each mathematical idea is studied in detail for its applications to the understanding of real-world situations, or the solving of problems like those found in the real world. The reality orientation extends also to the approaches allowed the student in working out problems. Students are expected to use scientific calculators. Calculators are assumed throughout the series (and should be allowed on tests), because virtually all individuals who use mathematics today use calculators.

Problem Solving: Like skills, problem solving must be practiced. When practiced, problem solving becomes far less difficult. All lessons contain a variety of questions so that students do not blindly copy one question to do the next. Explorations are a feature of the first four years, and Projects are offered in the last two years. Some problem-solving techniques are so important that at times they (rather than the problems) are the focus of instruction.

Enhancing Performance: Each book's format is designed to maximize the acquisition of both skills and concepts, with lessons meant to take one day to cover. Within each lesson there is review of material from previous lessons from that chapter or from previous chapters. This gives the student more time to learn the material. The lessons themselves are sequenced into carefully constructed chapters. Progress Self-Test and Chapter Review questions, keyed to objectives in all the dimensions of understanding, are then used to solidify performance of skills and concepts from the chapter, so that they may be applied later with confidence. (See pages T35–T36 for more detail.)

Reading: Reading is emphasized throughout. Students can read; they must learn to read mathematics in order to become able to use mathematics outside of school. Every lesson has reading and contains questions covering that reading. (See page T37 for more detail.)

Understanding: Four dimensions of understanding are emphasized: skill in carrying out various algorithms; developing and using mathematical properties and relationships; applying mathematics in realistic situations; and representing or picturing mathematical concepts. We call this the SPUR approach: **S**kills, **P**roperties, **U**ses, **R**epresentations. On occasion, a fifth dimension of understanding, the historical dimension, is discussed. (See pages T38–T39 for more detail.)

Technology: Scientific calculators are recommended because they use an order of operations closer to that found in algebra and have numerous keys that are helpful in understanding concepts at this level. Work with computers is carefully sequenced within each year and between the years, with gradual gain in sophistication until FST, where computers are an essential element. In all courses, integrated computer exercises show how the computer can be used as a helpful tool in doing mathematics. Students are expected to run and modify programs, but are not taught programming. (See pages T40–T43 for more detail.)

■ Target Populations

We believe that all high-school graduates should take courses through *Advanced Algebra,* that all students planning to go to college should take courses through *Functions, Statistics, and Trigonometry with Computers*, and that students planning majors in technical areas should take all six UCSMP courses.

The fundamental principle in placing students into the first of these courses is that entry should not be based on age, but on mathematical knowledge. Our studies indicate that about 10% of students nationally are ready for *Transition Mathematics* at 6th grade, about another 40% at 7th grade, another 20% at 8th grade, and another 10–15% at 9th grade. We caution that these percentages are national, not local percentages, and the variability in our nation is enormous. We have tested the materials in school districts where few students are at grade level, where *Transition Mathematics* is appropriate for no more than the upper half of 8th-graders. We have tested also in school districts where as many as 90% of the students have successfully used *Transition Mathematics* in 7th grade.

However, the percentages are not automatic. Students who do not reach 7th-grade competence until the 9th-grade level often do not possess the study habits necessary for successful completion of these courses. At the 9th-grade level, *Transition Mathematics* has been substituted successfully either for a traditional pre-algebra course or for the first year of an algebra course spread out over two years. It does not work as a substitute for a general mathematics course in which there is no expectation that students will take algebra the following year.

On page T27 is a description of this curriculum and the populations for which it is intended. The percentiles are national percentiles on a 7th-grade standardized mathematics test using 7th-grade norms, and apply to students entering the program with *Transition Mathematics*. Some school districts have felt that students should also be reading at least at a 7th-grade reading level as well. See page T28 for advice when starting with a later course.

Top 10%: The top 10% nationally reach the 7th-grade level of competence a year early. They are ready for *Transition Mathematics* in 6th grade and take it then. They proceed through the entire curriculum by 11th grade and can take calculus in 12th grade. We recommend that these students be expected to do the Extensions suggested in this Teacher's Edition. Teachers may also wish to enrich courses for these students further with problems from mathematics contests.

50th–90th percentile: These students should be expected to take mathematics at least through the 11th grade, by which time they will have the mathematics needed for all college majors except those in the hard sciences and engineering. For that they need 12th-grade mathematics.

30th–70th percentile: These students begin *Transition Mathematics* one year later, in 8th grade. The college-bound student in this curriculum is more likely to take four years of mathematics because the last course is hands-on with computers and provides the kind of mathematics needed for any major.

15th–50th percentile: Students who do not reach the 7th-grade level in mathematics until 9th grade or later should not be tracked into courses that put them further behind. Rather, they should be put into this curriculum and counseled on study skills. The logic is simple: mathematics is too important to be ignored. If one is behind in one's mathematical knowledge, the need is to work more at it, not less.

Even if a student begins with *Transition Mathematics* at 9th grade, that student can finish *Advanced Algebra* by the time of graduation from high school. That would be enough mathematics to enable the student to get into most colleges.

UCSMP Target Populations in Grades 7–12

Each course is meant to stand alone. However, to take best advantage of these materials, and have them appropriate for the greatest number of students, it is preferable to use them in sequence. Although it is suggested that students begin with *Transition Mathematics,* students may enter the UCSMP curriculum at any point. Below is a brief description of the UCSMP curriculum and the populations for which it is intended.

The top 10% of students are ready for *Transition Mathematics* at 6th grade. These students can proceed through the entire curriculum by 11th grade and take calculus in the 12th grade.

Students in the 50th–90th percentile on a 7th-grade standardized mathematics test should be ready to take *Transition Mathematics* in 7th grade.

Students who do not reach the 7th-grade level in mathematics until the 8th grade **(in the 30th–70th percentile)** begin *Transition Mathematics* in 8th grade.

Students who don't reach the 7th-grade level in mathematics until the 9th grade **(in the 15th–50th percentile)** begin *Transition Mathematics* in the 9th grade.

Grade				
6	Transition Mathematics			
7	Algebra	Transition Mathematics		
8	Geometry	Algebra	Transition Mathematics	
9	Advanced Algebra	Geometry	Algebra	Transition Mathematics
10	Functions, Statistics, and Trigonometry	Advanced Algebra	Geometry	Algebra
11	Precalculus and Discrete Mathematics	Functions, Statistics, and Trigonometry	Advanced Algebra	Geometry
12	Calculus (Not part of UCSMP)	Precalculus and Discrete Mathematics	Functions, Statistics, and Trigonometry	Advanced Algebra

■ Starting in the Middle of the Series

From the beginning, every UCSMP course has been designed so that it could be used independently of other UCSMP courses. Accordingly, about half of the testing of UCSMP courses after *Transition Mathematics* has been with students who have not had any previous UCSMP courses. We have verified that any of the UCSMP courses can be taken successfully following the typical prerequisite courses in the standard curriculum.

ALGEBRA:
No additional prerequisites other than those needed for success in any algebra course are needed for success in UCSMP *Algebra*. Students who have studied *Transition Mathematics* tend to cover more of UCSMP *Algebra* than other students because they tend to know more algebra, because they are accustomed to the style of the book, and because they have been introduced to more of the applications of algebra.

UCSMP *Algebra* prepares students for any standard geometry course.

GEOMETRY:
No additional prerequisites other than those needed for success in any geometry course are needed for success in UCSMP *Geometry*. UCSMP *Geometry* can be used with faster, average, and slower students who have these prerequisites. Prior study of *Transition Mathematics* and UCSMP *Algebra* insures this background, but this content is also found in virtually all existing middle school or junior high school texts.

Classes of students who have studied UCSMP *Algebra* tend to cover more UCSMP *Geometry* than other classes because they know more geometry and are better at the algebra used in geometry.

Students who have studied UCSMP *Geometry* are ready for any second-year algebra text.

ADVANCED ALGEBRA:
UCSMP *Advanced Algebra* should not be taken before a geometry course but can be used following any standard geometry text. Students who have studied UCSMP *Advanced Algebra* are prepared for courses commonly found at the senior level, including trigonometry or precalculus courses.

FUNCTIONS, STATISTICS, AND TRIGONOMETRY:
FST assumes that students have completed a second-year algebra course. **No additional prerequisites other than those found in any second-year algebra text are needed for success in *FST*.**

PRECALCULUS AND DISCRETE MATHEMATICS:
PDM can be taken successfully by students who have had *FST*, by students who have had typical senior level courses that include study of trigonometry and functions, and by top students who have successfully completed full advanced algebra and trigonometry courses.

PDM provides the background necessary for any typical calculus course, either at the high school or college level, including advanced placement calculus courses.

Development Cycle for UCSMP Texts

The development of each text has been in four stages. First, the overall goals for each course are created by UCSMP in consultation with a national advisory board of distinguished professors, and through discussion with classroom teachers, school administrators, and district and state mathematics supervisors.

The Advisory Board for the Secondary Component at the time of this planning consisted of Arthur F. Coxford, Jr., University of Michigan; David Duncan, University of Northern Iowa; James Fey, University of Maryland; Glenda Lappan, Michigan State University; Anthony Ralston, State University of New York at Buffalo; and James Schultz, Ohio State University.

As part of this stage, UCSMP devoted an annual School Conference, whose participants were mathematics supervisors and teachers, to discuss major issues in a particular area of the curriculum. Past conferences have centered on the following issues:

1984   Changing the Curriculum in Grades 7 and 8

1985   Changing Standards in School Algebra

1986   Functions, Computers, and Statistics in Secondary Mathematics

1987   Pre-College Mathematics

1988   Mathematics Teacher Education for Grades 7–12

At the second stage, UCSMP selects authors who write first drafts of the courses. Half of all UCSMP authors currently teach mathematics in secondary schools, and all authors and editors for the first five courses have secondary school teaching experience. The textbook authors or their surrogates initially teach the first drafts of Secondary Component texts, so that revision may benefit from first-hand classroom experience.

After revision by the authors or editors, materials enter the third stage in the text development. Classes of teachers not connected with the project use the books, and independent evaluators closely study student achievement, attitudes, and issues related to implementation. For the first three years in the series, this stage involved a formative evaluation in six to ten schools, and all teachers who used the materials periodically met at the university to provide feedback to UCSMP staff for a second revision. For the last three years in the series, this stage has involved a second pilot.

The fourth stage consists of a wider comparative evaluation. For the first three books, this evaluation has involved approximately 40 classrooms and thousands of students per book in schools all over the country. For the last three books in the series, this stage has involved a careful formative evaluation. As a result of these studies, the books have been revised for commercial publication by Scott, Foresman and Company, into the edition you are now reading. (See pages T46–T50 for a summary of this research.)

T30

2 *Transition Mathematics*

Problems *TRANSITION MATHEMATICS* Is Trying to Address

This book is different from many other books for this level. The differences are due to its attempt to respond to six serious problems which cannot be treated by small changes in content or approach.

PROBLEM 1:
Large numbers of students are not able to apply the arithmetic they know.

Our response to this problem: Since the evidence is that students do have whole number arithmetic in hand, this is not reviewed again. Instead, from Chapter 1 on, the uses of numbers and operations are given very strong emphasis. These uses are the foundation upon which we build to provide motivation for studying algebra and geometry. There is a careful sequence. Numbers represent things. The models for the operations deal with these numbers. So, at first, there are simple uses. Our evidence is that by reviewing arithmetic in this way, with algebraic and geometric contexts emphasized, students gain considerable knowledge of algebra and geometry without loss of arithmetic skills and concepts.

PROBLEM 2:
The mathematics curriculum has been lagging behind today's widely available and inexpensive technology.

The *Transition Mathematics* response: There is unanimous sentiment in recent national reports on mathematics education in favor of the use of calculators in all mathematics courses. Scientific calculators are used starting in the first chapter. There are important reasons for using scientific calculators rather than simpler 4-function calculators. (See pages T40–T41). If a student is to buy a calculator, it should be one that will be useful for more than a single year of study. We strongly recommend using solar-powered scientific calculators to avoid problems with batteries.

The evidence from our evaluations of *Transition Mathematics* is that students gain considerably in arithmetic skills during the year. They are particularly able to do better than other students when allowed to use calculators. (The use of calculators is more and more a requirement in the outside world.) Teachers report that they are able to cover much more content because they do not have to waste time waiting for students to do complicated arithmetic that does not contribute to the ideas behind solving of problems.

PROBLEM 3:
Too many students fail algebra.

The *Transition Mathematics* response: It is too much to expect students to learn all of traditional first-year algebra in a single year. Students who have not had prior experience with algebra rarely master all the concepts of first-year algebra in a single year. *Transition Mathematics* students work not only on the transition into algebra, but also on the important concepts of algebra. The evidence from our studies is that students using *Transition Mathematics* knew much more algebra at the end of their year than students in comparison classes. Thus, although we expect students to do well in algebra even if they have not had *Transition Mathematics*, we expect much better performance from those who have had that kind of rich experience.

PROBLEM 4:
Even students who succeed in algebra often do poorly in geometry.

The *Transition Mathematics* response: The evidence is that the knowledge of geometry among American 8th-graders and among entering geometry students is quite poor. As with algebra, it is too much to expect students to learn all of geometry in a single year in high school. The best predictor of success with proof is a student's geometry knowledge at the beginning of a course. So, *Transition Mathematics* gives considerable attention to geometry, with particular attention paid to the numerical relationships involving lines, angles, and polygons.

The evidence from our studies of *Transition Mathematics* validates the UCSMP integration of geometry into these courses. In the *Transition Mathematics* summative evaluation, students in comparison classes showed no increase in geometry knowledge from September to June. However, students using *Transition Mathematics* knew as much at the end of the year as typical students entering a 10th-grade geometry class.

PROBLEM 5:
Students don't read.

The *Transition Mathematics* response: We have paid careful attention to the explanations, examples, and questions in each lesson. Students using traditional texts tell us they don't read because (1) the text is uninteresting, and (2) they don't have to read; the teacher explains it for them. But students *must* learn to read for future success in mathematics. So, every lesson of this book contains reading and questions covering the reading. *Transition Mathematics* is more than a resource for questions; it is a resource for information, for examples of how to do problems, for the history of major ideas, for applications of the ideas, for connections between ideas in one place in the book and in another, and for motivation.

First-time teachers of *Transition Mathematics* are often skeptical at first about the amount of reading in the book. As the year progresses, they tend to join those who have previously taught *Transition Mathematics* in viewing the reading as one of the strongest features of this series. Some teachers felt that *Transition Mathematics* was teaching reading comprehension; they all felt that the requirement to read helped develop thinkers who were more critical and aware.

PROBLEM 6:
*Students are not skillful enough,
regardless of what they are taught.*

The evidence is that students are rather skillful at routine problems but not with problems involving complicated numbers, different wordings, or new contexts. It is obvious that in order to obtain such skill, students must see problems with all sorts of numbers, a variety of wordings, and many different contexts. We also ask that students do certain problems mentally, which expands the level of competence expected of students.

Encountering such problems is not enough. *Transition Mathematics* employs a four-stage approach to develop skill.

■ **Stage 1** involves a concentrated introduction to the ideas surrounding the skill: why it is needed, how it is done, and the kinds of problems that can be solved with it. Most books are organized to include this stage, because teachers recognize that explanations of an idea require time. At the end of this stage, typically only the best students have the skill. But in *Transition Mathematics*, this is only the beginning.

■ **Stage 2** occupies the following lessons in the chapter and consists of questions designed to establish some competence in the skill. These are found in the daily Review questions. By the end of the lessons in the chapter, most students should have some competence in the skills, but some may not have enough.

■ **Stage 3** involves mastery learning. At the end of each chapter is a Progress Self-Test for students to take and judge how they are doing. Worked-out solutions are included to provide feedback and help to the student. This is followed by the Chapter Review to enable students to acquire those skills they didn't have when taking the Progress Self-Test. Teachers are expected to spend 1–3 days on these sections to give students time to reach mastery. By the end of this stage, students should have gained mastery at least at the level of typical students covering the content.

■ **Stage 4** continues the review through the daily Review sections in the *subsequent* chapters. Vital skills, such as measuring or working with percent, receive consistent emphasis throughout the book. The evidence is striking. *Transition Mathematics* students attain arithmetic skills virtually equivalent to those students who are learning only arithmetic all year. They attain algebra and geometry skills and concepts far above those reached by comparable students.

Goals of *TRANSITION MATHEMATICS*

It would be too easy and somewhat misleading to state that the goals of *Transition Mathematics* are to remove forever the problems detailed on pages T31–T33. Obviously we want to make headway on solving these. Nevertheless, it is more accurate to think of this book as an attempt to convey all the dimensions of the understanding of arithmetic: its skills, its properties, its uses, and its representations. In each, we want to update the curriculum and upgrade student achievement. It may be more accurate to think of this book as attempting to attack three areas—arithmetic, algebra, and geometry—simultaneously. Specifically, we want students to be better able to apply arithmetic, and to be more successful in future years in both algebra and geometry study. IF THERE WERE A SUBTITLE FOR THIS BOOK, IT WOULD BE *APPLIED ARITHMETIC, PRE-ALGEBRA, AND PRE-GEOMETRY.*

We have another, more lofty goal. *We want students to view their study of mathematics as worthwhile, as full of interesting and entertaining information, as related to almost every endeavor.* We want them to realize that mathematics is still growing and is changing fast. We want them to look for and recognize mathematics in places they haven't before, to use the library, to search through newspapers or almanacs, to get excited by knowledge.

If there were a subtitle for this book, it would be *Applied Arithmetic, Pre-Algebra, and Pre-Geometry.*

Who Should Take *TRANSITION MATHEMATICS?*

This book works with students who, *regardless of age,* enter the course knowing at least as much arithmetic as the typical student entering 7th grade nationally. Without a calculator, this student at a minimum

(1) is proficient at whole number arithmetic;
(2) can multiply fractions and can add or subtract fractions with the same denominator, but may not be so good at adding or subtracting with different denominators and with division of fractions;
(3) can add or subtract decimals when in columns, but may not be so good when they are on a horizontal line; can multiply decimals but cannot divide them with accuracy;
(4) has seen percentages, but only knows the simplest things about them.

We would like students to have measured lengths and be familiar with both customary and metric measures of length and weight, and know the names of common geometric figures. We would like students to be familiar with the idea of number line.

Older students—those in 9th grade or above—who are in a course where this book is used, have usually experienced years of frustration in courses where they have performed poorly, and years of boredom from encountering so little new material. These students should also be in a program where algebra is the next course, and they must be willing to work in this one.

Students who take *Transition Mathematics* should have the maturity to do homework every night and the expectation of studying algebra the next year, if successful in this course.

3 General Teaching Suggestions

The content and the approach of *Transition Mathematics* represent rather significant departures from standard practice. *A teacher should not expect to use this book to teach exactly the same material in exactly the same way he or she has been accustomed to teaching.*

The suggestions found on this and the following pages provide ideas which lead to success and discourage practices which do not lead to success. They should not be construed as rigid; students, teachers, classes, schools, and school systems vary greatly. But they should not be ignored. These suggestions come from users, from our extensive interviews with teachers of earlier versions of these materials, and from test results.

Optimizing Learning

■ Pace

Students adjust to the pace set by the teacher. It is especially important that Chapter 1 be taught at a one-day-per-lesson pace. At the end of this chapter, spend a few days on the Progress Self-Test and Chapter Review to cinch the major skills. We know from our studies that this pace produces the highest performance levels. Students need to be exposed to content in order to learn it.

There is a natural tendency, when using a new book, to go more slowly, to play it safe should one forget something. Teachers using these materials for the first time have almost invariably said that they would move more quickly the next year. Do not be afraid to move quickly.

Some classes in our studies of this book went very slowly; their teachers seemed reluctant to move to any new content. Where this happens, the students get into a rut. Better students are bored because they know the material. Slower students are frustrated because they are being asked to spend more time on the material they don't know. They all get discouraged and perform far lower than any other comparable students at the end of the year. We emphasize:

One day per lesson almost always,
two or three days at the end of each chapter
on the Progress Self-Test and Chapter Review,
and then a Chapter Test.

In classes with slower students, allow a half-day for each quiz. The Teacher's Edition provides a Daily Pacing Chart before each chapter, detailing two alternate ways to pace the chapter.

There are times when it will be difficult to maintain this pace. But be advised: a slow pace can make it too easy to lose perspective and relate ideas. A student needs to get to later content to realize why he or she was asked to learn earlier content. If necessary, spend more time on end-of-chapter activities. If you spend too much time in the lessons, you may find that your slowest students may have learned more by having gone through content slowly, but all the other students will have learned less. Try to strike a balance, going quickly enough to keep things interesting, but slowly enough to have time for explanations.

■ Review

Every lesson includes Review questions. These questions serve a variety of purposes. First, they develop competence in a topic. Because we do not expect students to master a topic on the day they are introduced to it, these questions, coming *after* the introduction of the topic, help to solidify the ideas. Second, they maintain competence from preceding chapters. This review is particularly effective with topics that have not been studied for some time.

At times, we are able to give harder questions in reviews than we could expect students to be able to do on the day they were introduced to the topic. Thus the reviews sometimes serve as questions which integrate ideas from previous lessons.

Finally, we occasionally review an idea that has not been discussed for some time, just before it is to surface again in a lesson. The Notes on Questions usually alert you to this circumstance.

Teachers in classes that perform the best, assign all the Review questions, give students the answers each day, and discuss them when needed. Those who do not assign all reviews tend to get poorer performance. *The Review questions must be assigned to insure optimum performance.*

■ Mastery

The mastery strategy used at the end of each chapter of *Transition Mathematics* is one that has been validated by a great deal of research. Its components are a Progress Self-Test (the literature on mastery learning may refer to this as the "formative test"), solutions to that test in the student textbook (the "feedback"), Chapter Review questions tied to the same objectives (the "correctives"), and finally a Chapter Test, again covering the same objectives.

To follow the strategy means assigning the Progress Self-Test as homework to be done *under simulated test conditions*. The next day should be devoted to answering student questions about the problems and doing some problems from the Chapter Review, if there is time. If a particular topic is causing a great deal of trouble, the corresponding Lesson Master (in the Teacher's Resource File) may be of help.

For most classes, as a second night's assignment, we suggest the *even-numbered* Chapter Review questions. Answers to the *even-numbered* questions are not in the student text, so students will have to work on their own. Discuss those Chapter Review questions in class the next day.

A Chapter Test (available in the Teacher's Resource File) should be given on the third day. The *odd-numbered* Chapter Review questions, for which answers are given in the student text, can be useful for studying for that test. In some classes, a third day before the test may be needed. If so, either the odd-numbered Chapter Review questions or selected Lesson Masters can be used as sources of problems.

We strongly recommend that teachers follow this strategy, except for classes of exceptionally talented students (where less review may be needed). THE EVIDENCE IS SUBSTANTIAL THAT USE OF THE CHAPTER END-MATTER MATERIALS PROMOTES HIGHER LEVELS OF PERFORMANCE.

The evidence is substantial that use of the chapter end-matter materials promotes higher levels of performance.

■ Reading

To become an independent learner of mathematics, a student must learn to learn mathematics from reading. You should expect students to read all lessons. At the beginning of the course, this may require oral reading in class. Do not expect overnight changes in behavior from students. Some will read immediately, others in a few days, others in a few weeks, and still others after a couple of months. Teachers of *Transition Mathematics* report that by the end of the year almost all their students are reading. Teachers of later UCSMP courses report that this behavior continues without the amount of prodding needed in this course. It is an effort well-spent.

In general, we should note that the typical student in this course can read English rather well, but cannot read mathematics well. Students may not be able to read numbers that are not simple fractions or three-digit whole numbers. They may have no vocabulary for symbols such as $+$, $-$, $\times$, $\div$, $=$, or $<$. (Many of us have trouble reading Greek letters such as μ or δ, because we have never had to say their names out loud.) For many students the same is true for common everyday mathematics symbols. Thus it is important to have students read out loud, as well as to give them assignments that involve reading.

The typical student of *Transition Mathematics* has not been asked to read mathematics. As a result, it is common for students to ask why they have to read.

Our response: You must read because you must learn to read for success in all future courses that use mathematics, not just in mathematics; because you must read to achieve success in life outside of school and on any job; because the reading will help you understand the uses of mathematics; because the reading contains interesting information; because the reading tells you how the material from one lesson is related to other material in the book; because there is not enough time in class to spend doing something that you can do in a study period or at home.

Teachers of *Transition Mathematics* have handled reading in a variety of ways. These methods differ depending on the backgrounds of the students, the difficulty of the particular lesson, and the personality of the teacher. Here are the two most common approaches:

(1) Consistently assign the reading for each lesson in advance without going over the content. In this approach the typical assignment is all the questions on that lesson. Accustom students to that pace. Expect students to correctly answer the questions Covering the Reading, but not necessarily the questions Applying the Mathematics. Spend most classes going over the problems in order. If the questions are gone through in order, all concepts will be developed and covered.

(2) Each day assign the reading and questions Covering the Reading from one lesson. Assign the questions Applying the Mathematics, the Review, and the Exploration from the previous lesson.

We strongly encourage teachers to present their own explanations and not to rely on the book for everything. We do, however, wish to discourage the practice of always doing these explanations *before* the students have had the opportunity to learn on their own. Particularly ineffective is to tell students that certain problems do not have to be tried ''because we have not yet explained them in class.''

Specific reading comprehension tips and strategies are provided in the Teacher's Edition margin notes for appropriate lessons.

Understanding— The SPUR Approach

"Understanding" is an easy goal to have, for who can be against it? Yet understanding means different things to different people. In UCSMP texts an approach is taken that we call the SPUR approach. It involves four different aspects, or dimensions, of understanding.

SKILLS: For many people, understanding mathematics means simply knowing *how* to get an answer to a problem with no help from any outside source. But in classrooms, when we speak of understanding how to use a calculator or a computer, we mean using a computer to do something for us. In UCSMP texts, these are both aspects of the same kind of understanding, the understanding of algorithms (procedures) for getting answers. This is the S of SPUR, the Skills dimension, and it ranges from the rote memorization of basic facts to the development of new algorithms for solving problems.

PROPERTIES: During the 1960s, understanding *why* became at least as important as understanding *how*. Mathematicians often view this kind of understanding as the ultimate goal. For instance, mathematics courses for prospective elementary school teachers assume these college students can do arithmetic and instead teach the properties and principles behind that arithmetic. This is the P of SPUR, the Properties dimension, and it ranges from the rote identification of properties to the discovery of new proofs.

USES: To the person who applies mathematics, neither knowing how to get an answer nor knowing the mathematical reasons behind the process is as important as being able to *use* the answer. For example, a person does not possess full understanding of linear equations until that person can apply them appropriately in real situations. This is the U of SPUR, the Uses dimension. It ranges from the rote application of ideas (for instance, when you encounter a take-away situation, subtract) to the discovery of new applications or models for mathematical ideas. *Transition Mathematics* is notable for its attention to this dimension of understanding.

REPRESENTATIONS: To some people, even having all three dimensions of understanding given above do not comprise full understanding. They require that students *represent* a concept and deal with the concept in that representation in some way. Ability to use concrete materials and models, or graphs and other pictorial representations, demonstrates this dimension of understanding. This is the R of SPUR, the Representations dimension, and it ranges from the rote manipulation of objects to the invention of new representations of concepts.

The four types of understanding have certain common qualities. For each there are people for whom that type of understanding is preeminent, and who believe that the other types do not convey the *real* understanding of mathematics. Each has aspects that can be memorized and the potential for the highest level of creative thinking. Each can be, and often is, learned in isolation from the others. We know there are students who have S and none of the others; in the 1960s some students learned P and none of the others; there are people on the street who have U and none of the others; and some people believe that children cannot really acquire any of the others without having R. There are continual arguments among educators as to which dimension should come first and which should be emphasized.

Because of this, IN UCSMP TEXTS WE HAVE ADOPTED THE VIEW THAT THE UNDERSTANDING OF MATHEMATICS IS A MULTI-DIMENSIONAL ENTITY. We believe each dimension is important, that each dimension has its easy aspects and its difficult ones. Some skills (for example, long division) take at least as long to learn as geometry proofs; some uses are as easy as putting together beads.

. . . in UCSMP texts we have adopted the view that the understanding of mathematics is a multi-dimensional entity.

For a specific example of what understanding means in these four dimensions, consider $\frac{2}{3} \cdot \frac{4}{5}$, and what would constitute evidence of that understanding.

Skills understanding means knowing a way to obtain a solution. (Obtain $\frac{8}{15}$ by some means.)

Properties understanding means knowing properties which you can apply. (Identify or justify the steps in obtaining $\frac{8}{15}$, such as the relationship of $\frac{a}{b}$ to division and the Associative Property of Multiplication.)

Uses understanding means knowing situations in which you could apply the solving of this equation. (Set up or interpret a solution: If $\frac{2}{3}$ of students would know how to set up this question, and $\frac{4}{5}$ of those could get the problem right, what portion of students would get the correct answer?)

Representations understanding means having a representation of the solving process, or a graphical way of interpreting the solution. (Consider an array of dots with 3 rows and 5 columns. Color 2 of the 3 rows red and 4 of the 5 columns blue. What portion of the points is colored both red and blue?)

We believe there are students who prefer one of these dimensions over the others when learning mathematics. Some students prefer applications, some would rather do manipulative skills, some most want to know the theory, and still others like the models and representations best. Thus the most effective teaching allows students opportunities in all these dimensions.

The SPUR approach is not a perfect sorter of knowledge; many ideas and many problems involve more than one dimension. For instance, the mathematics behind an algorithm may involve both S and P. And some understandings do not fit any of these dimensions. In *Transition Mathematics*, we sometimes add a fifth dimension H—the Historical dimension—for it provides still another way of looking at knowledge. (The fraction bar was used at least as early as 1050, by the Arabian mathematician al-Hassar; the slash as in a/b was first used by Manuel Valdes in 1784.)

In this book, you see the SPUR categorization at the end of each chapter in a set of Objectives and corresponding Chapter Review questions. The Progress Self-Test for each chapter and the Lesson Masters (in the Teacher's Resource File) are keyed to these objectives. We never ask students (or teachers) to categorize tasks into the various kinds of understanding; that is not a suitable goal. The categorization is meant only to be a convenient and efficient way to ensure that the book provides the opportunity for teachers to teach and for students to gain a broader and deeper understanding of mathematics than is normally the case.

You may wonder why the Chapter Review questions and the Lesson Masters are organized using the SPUR categorization. It is because we believe that practice is essential for mastery, but that blind practice, in which a student merely copies what was done in a previous problem to do a new one, does not help ultimate performance. The practice must be accompanied by understanding. The properties, uses, and representations enhance understanding and should be covered to obtain mastery, even of the skills.

The Lesson Masters are particularly appropriate for students who wish more practice; for helping students individually with problems they have not seen; after a chapter test has been completed, if you feel that students' performance was not high enough; and for in-class work on days when a normal class cannot be conducted. However, they should be used sparingly. *The Lesson Masters should not be part of the normal routine* and should seldom be used when they would delay moving on to the next lesson.

Using Technology

We use calculators and computers in UCSMP because they make important mathematical ideas accessible to students at an early age; they relieve the drudgery of calculation, particularly with numbers and equations encountered in realistic contexts; and they facilitate exploration and open-ended problem solving by making multiple instances easy to examine. Furthermore, as indicated in the section on Research and Development (pages T46–T50), our use of technology has resulted in no loss of paper-and-pencil skill in arithmetic, and has freed up time in the curriculum to spend on other topics that lead to overall better performance by UCSMP students.

■ Calculators

Hand-held calculators first appeared in 1971. Not until 1976 did the price of a four-function calculator come below $50 (equivalent to well over $100 today). Still, in 1975, a national commission recommended that hand-held calculators be used on all tests starting in eighth grade, and in 1980 the National Council of Teachers of Mathematics recommended that calculators be used in all grades of school from kindergarten on. It is reported that the Achievement section of the College Board exams will allow calculators beginning in 1990, and that the Advanced Placement exam will again allow calculators in the near future. Several standardized test batteries are being developed with calculators. And slowly but surely calculators are being expected on more and more licensing exams outside of school.

The business and mathematics education communities generally believe that paper-and-pencil algorithms are becoming obsolete. (The long division algorithm we use was born only in the late 1400s. Before that time, the abacus was used almost exclusively to get answers to problems. So mechanical means to do problems are really older than paper-and-pencil means.) Increasingly, businesses do not want their employees to use paper-and-pencil algorithms to get answers to arithmetic problems. Banks require that their tellers do all arithmetic using a calculator.

IT IS INEVITABLE THAT CALCULATORS WILL BE CONSIDERED AS NATURAL AS PENCILS FOR DOING MATHEMATICS. A century from now students will be amazed when they are told that some students as recent as the 1980s went to schools were calculators were not to be used.

It is wonderful to live in the age when calculators have been developed that quickly and efficiently do arithmetic. This frees us to use arithmetic more and, as teachers, to spend more time on mental arithmetic, estimation, and understanding algebra.

It is inevitable that calculators will be considered as natural as pencils for doing mathematics.

Section 3: General Teaching Suggestions

Transition Mathematics assumes the student has a scientific calculator. There are five basic reasons why 4-function nonscientific calculators do not suffice.

(1) Applications require the ability to deal with large and small numbers. On many 4-function calculators, a number as large as the population of the U.S. cannot be entered, and on all of them the national debt or the world population could not be entered. The calculator must have the ability to display numbers in scientific notation.

(2) 4-function calculators give error messages which do not distinguish between student error and calculator insufficiency. This restricts the kinds of problems one can assign.

(3) There are keys on scientific calculators that are very useful in algebra. The π, square root, power, scientific notation, and parentheses keys are all utilized in this book. These keys are not found on many 4-function calculators.

(4) Order of operations on a scientific calculator is the same as in algebra, so this kind of calculator motivates and reinforces algebra skills. In contrast, order of operations on a 4-function calculator is often different from that used in algebra and could confuse students.

(5) A scientific calculator can be used for later courses a student takes; it shows the student there is much more to learn about mathematics.

Students will overuse calculators. Part of learning to use any machine is to make mistakes: using it when you shouldn't, not using it when you should. Anyone who has a word processor has used it for short memos that could much more easily have been handwritten. Anyone who has a microwave has used it for food that could have been cooked either in a conventional oven or on top of the stove.

The overuse dies down, but it takes some months. In the meantime, stress that there are three ways to get answers to arithmetic problems: by paper and pencil, mentally, or by using some automatic means (a table, a calculator, a trusty friend, and so on). Some problems require more than one of these means, but the wise applier of arithmetic knows when to use each of these ways.

Generally this means that good arithmeticians do a lot of calculations mentally, either because they know basic facts (such as 3×5) or because they follow simple rules (such as $2/3 \times 4/5$, or 100×4.72). They may not use a calculator on these, because the likelihood of making an error entering or reading is greater than the likelihood of making a mental error. As a rule, we seldom say, "Do not use calculators here." We want students to learn for themselves when calculator use is appropriate and when not. However, you may feel the need to prod some students to avoid the calculator. An answer of 2.9999999 to $\sqrt{9}$ should be strongly discouraged.

Many lessons include questions to be done "in your head." These are designed to develop skill in mental arithmetic and show students situations in which mental calculation is an appropriate approach to calculation. You may wish to give quizzes on these kinds of problems and have a "no calculator" rule for these problems.

■ Computers

The computer is a powerful tool for you to use in your classroom to demonstrate the relationships, patterns, properties, and algorithms of arithmetic. From the very first chapter of this book, computer exercises appear. Do not ignore the computer questions even if you do not have computers available. THE GOAL IS NOT TO TEACH COMPUTER PROGRAMMING, BUT TO USE THE COMPUTER AS A TOOL. Students are not surprised that the computer can do difficult tasks, but many students are surprised that a computer can do easy things; for instance, act as a calculator.

Some questions ask students to use a computer. If students do not have access to a computer, exercise caution in your assigning such questions. As mathematical tools, a desirable computer has the ability to deal with a good amount of data and to display graphs with accuracy and precision.

The BASIC computer language was selected for use in this book, because it is packaged for the microcomputers which are most popular in American schools. The programs have been kept short so that students can type them relatively quickly. It is not necessary for every student to type and run the program. Most programs can be used as classroom demonstrations.

Computer educators have recommended that students be required to provide a block structure to programs; document their programs with abundant remarks; and declare variables. Since this is a mathematics course, not a programming course, you should emphasize the *computational* steps of a program. Can the students follow the steps of a program and tell what the output will be? Can the student modify a given program to solve an exercise with different values?

Programs which are printed in the text of this book follow several conventions.

1. Most programs start with a PRINT statement which serves a dual purpose: it is a title for the program LISTing and a title for the program output.

2. Extended remarks are offset from the body of the program. Brief comments appear as REM statements (remarks) in the program.

3. Indentation in program lines has been used to indicate blocking of lines, particularly in loops. This aid to program readability is not exploited on many computers. You will probably find that these spaces do not appear on your computer screen, and therefore need not be typed.

4. Variable names are kept short, sometimes only one character long. This reduces the amount of typing needed; is implementable on all computer forms of BASIC; and reflects the use of single letters for variables in algebra.

5. Tests for exceptional cases are frequently omitted unless the meaning of the topic is enhanced by the cases. In a program for solving $ax + b = c$, it is not really necessary for a student to write

$$\text{IF } a < > 0 \text{ THEN } \ldots$$

because he or she should recognize 0 will not work before using the computer. However, in a program to compute slope, a zero division is not as obvious to students, so the IF-THEN statement is included.

6. We do not type NEW, which students might have to type if they are not the first user of the day on the computer. We also do not type RUN, which students must do in order to execute their program. And we do not indicate that students must press the RETURN key after each line.

The goal is not to teach computer programming, but to use the computer as a tool.

Here are three examples of programs like those found in *Transition Mathematics*. If you understand these, you know enough about programs to be able to handle the programs in the book.

EXAMPLE 1
This program, from Chapter 4, gives a value of an expression for any inputted value of *x*.

```
10      PRINT "GIVE VALUE OF YOUR VARIABLE"
20      INPUT X
```
At this point the computer displays a question mark, waiting for the value of x to be inputted.
```
30      V = 30 * X - 12
```
The computer calculates v.
```
40      PRINT "VALUE OF EXPRESSION IS", V
```
The computer prints v.
```
50      END
```

EXAMPLE 2
This program, from Chapter 12, prints a table of values for the points on the line $y = 11x + 2$ with *x*-coordinates ranging from 1 to 10.

```
10      PRINT "X", "Y"
20      FOR X = 1 TO 10
30        Y = 11*X + 2
40        PRINT X, Y
50      NEXT X
60      END
```

EXAMPLE 3
This program prints the cost of peanuts for 2, 4, 6, 8, . . . 20 bags, if 2 bags cost $.39. It is from Chapter 11.

```
10      FOR N = 2 TO 20 STEP 2
20        PRINT N" BAGS OF PEANUTS COST",
          "$".39*N
30      NEXT N
40      END
```

Whether you are a novice or an expert in BASIC, we encourage you to try the programs we provide on your own system. Each version of BASIC and each computer has slightly different characteristics, and our generic programs may need to be modified slightly for your system.

Evaluating Learning

■ Grading

No problem seems more difficult than the question of grading. If a teacher has students who perform so well that they all deserve A's and the teacher gives them A's as a result, the teacher will probably not be given plaudits for being successful but will be accused of being too easy. This suggests that the grading scale ought to be based on a fixed level of performance, which is what we recommend.

Seldom in this book are there ten similar questions in a row. To teach the student to be flexible, questions have all sorts of wordings. The problems are varied because that's the way problems come in later courses and in life outside of school. We believe a student should be able to do each set of objectives at about the 85% mastery level. An 85% score on a test deserves no less than a high B, and probably an A. In the past, our tests have often led us to the following curve: 85–100, A; 72–84, B; 60–71, C; 50–59, D. Such a low curve may alarm some teachers, but as outlined on pages T46–T49, UCSMP students have performed well on standardized tests compared to students in other classes. STUDENTS IN UCSMP COURSES GENERALLY LEARN MORE MATHEMATICS OVERALL THAN STUDENTS IN COMPARISON CLASSES. We believe that the above grading policy rewards students fairly for work well done.

Some teachers use the grading scale 90–100, A; 80–89, B; 70–79, C; 60–69, D. One January a teacher of *Transition Mathematics* presented us with a problem. She had to make out grades for the fall semester. Her quandary was as follows: "I've never had a class that learned so much, but my grades are lower." Later she said, "I have students who are failing. But I can't switch them to another class [using another book at the same level] because they know too much." Her problem is not unusual. We advise such teachers to recall that a group of varied problems is inherently more difficult than a set of similar ones. We often make a basketball analogy. In *Transition Mathematics*, almost every question is a different shot (a problem), some close in, some from middle distance, a few from half-court. In a traditional course, most of the shots students try are done over and over again from the same court position close to the basket. ("Do the odd-numbered exercises from 1–49.") Since the variability of the shots in *Transition Mathematics* is much greater, it is unrealistic to expect percents of correct shots to be the same.

There are times, however, when you want to practice one specific shot to make it automatic. We suggest focusing in on a few topics for quizzes. The Teacher's Resource File contains at least one quiz for each chapter. If students perform well on quizzes and tests, it has a real effect on interest and motivation. We would like to see grading as a vehicle for breeding success as well as for rating students.

In light of all this, here are some general suggestions pertaining to grading:

(1) Let students know what they need to know in order to get good grades. All research on the subject indicates that telling students what they are supposed to learn increases the amount of material covered and tends to increase performance.

(2) Have confidence in your students. Do not arbitrarily consign some of them to low grades. Let them know that it is possible for all of them to get A's if they learn the material.

(3) Some teachers have found that because of the way that the Review questions maintain and improve performance, *cumulative tests* give students an opportunity to do well. For your convenience, the Teacher's Resource File has Chapter Tests in Cumulative Form (in addition to the regular Chapter Tests) for each chapter, beginning with Chapter 2. The Cumulative Tests allow students a chance to show what they have learned about a topic in the intervening weeks.

Students in UCSMP courses generally learn more mathematics overall than students in comparison classes.

■ Standardized Tests

At our first conference with school teachers and administrators early in the project, we were told in the strongest terms, "Be bold, but remember that you will be judged by old standardized tests."

In *Transition Mathematics*, we work in the four dimensions of understanding: Skills, Properties, Uses, and Representations. While it is thought that traditional standardized tests are almost entirely devoted to skills, this is not the case. *School-made placement tests* are most likely to be so distorted, because Properties seem out of favor these days and items for Uses and Representations are felt to be the most difficult to find. Standardized tests are usually more balanced. Traditional elementary school tests usually have a computation section and a concepts or application section.

We used a standardized test in our studies of *Transition Mathematics*, and we have data from a few school districts from standardized test batteries they have given. **It leads us to believe that *Transition Mathematics* students hold their own on paper-and-pencil skills while far exceeding other comparable students on concepts and applications.**

We have done an in-depth study of standardized tests students are likely to encounter later in their schooling. Our conclusions are as follows: Students studying UCSMP courses are likely to do better on the College Board SAT-M than other students. The SAT-M is a problem-solving test, and far more questions on the SAT-M cover content likely to be unfamiliar to other students than to UCSMP students. The ACT exams seem at least as favorable to our students as to students in other books. However, if the UCSMP idea is followed and more students take *Algebra* in the 8th grade, then there is no question that students in the UCSMP curriculum will far outscore comparable students who are a course behind.

Finally, a note about curriculum projects. Many people treat books from curriculum projects as "experimental." Few commercial textbooks, however, have been developed on the basis of large-scale testing. (See pages T46–T50 for details on the testing of this book.) Few have been produced as part of a coherent 7–12 curriculum design. This text has gone through extensive prepublication analysis and criticism. It has been revised on the basis of comments and evaluations of the pilot, formative and summative evaluation teachers. It is the intention of UCSMP to provide materials which are successful as well as teachable. SINCE *TRANSITION MATHEMATICS* HAS BEEN SUCCESSFULLY TESTED AND REVISED, IT SHOULD BE VIEWED AS A *NEW* TEXT, NOT AS AN EXPERIMENTAL TEXT.

Since *Transition Mathematics* has been successfully tested and revised, it should be viewed as a *new* text, not as an experimental text.

4 Research and Development of *Transition Mathematics*

Writing, Pilot, and Formative Evaluation

Ideas for *Transition Mathematics* originated as a result of two previous projects directed by Zalman Usiskin at the University of Chicago. The first was an NSF-sponsored project which developed a first-year algebra text entitled *Algebra Through Applications with Probability and Statistics*. The text was distributed by the National Council of Teachers of Mathematics in a two-volume paperback version from 1979–85. It is no longer available, but many of its ideas are

Transition Mathematics **students held their own on paper-and-pencil computation, gained three times as much as comparison classes in their knowledge of algebra, and even more than that in geometry.**

found in this book and in UCSMP *Algebra*. In developing that text, we found that one of the major reasons students had so much trouble applying algebra was that they did not know how to apply arithmetic beyond the arithmetic of adding and subtracting whole numbers.

In the years 1979–82, the Cognitive Development and Achievement in Secondary School Geometry project did much testing of senior high-school geometry students. It was found in these studies that the geometry knowledge of students entering a high-school geometry course was very low. Yet the best predictor of success in that course, be it with proof or with performance on a standardized test at the end of the year, was incoming geometry knowledge.

As a result, Dr. Usiskin planned a course to precede an algebra course that would incorporate the ideas of applying arithmetic and the geometry that students needed for success later. Plans were made for him to write and teach such a course in the 1983–84 school year. When in the summer of 1983 funding for UCSMP became assured, this course became the first course in the curriculum of the Secondary Component. It was piloted by Dr. Usiskin and one other teacher with 9th-grade students who would normally have been in a first course in algebra slowed down to take two years. The gut feeling then has been substantiated by research; this constitutes a more difficult population than either the 7th- or 8th-grade populations of students with the same knowledge.

The course began with a traditional look. In the middle of the year, dissatisfied with the performance of the students, the continual review strategy used in the elementary school curricula of many foreign countries was used. The SPUR mastery sequence also entered the course at that time. In the summer of 1984, four experienced secondary school teachers, Cathy Hynes, Lydia Polonsky, Susan Porter, and Steven Viktora revised the materials rather completely, so as to fit these new frameworks.

In 1984–85, a formative evaluation of a revised version of *Transition Mathematics* was conducted with 20 classes from 10 schools in the city of Chicago and suburbs. Classes at each of grades 7, 8, and 9 were represented. In addition, three 6th-grade classes, not part of the study, used the materials. The materials were spiral bound in four parts; teachers saw no more than a few chapters ahead of where they were teaching. Still, results were extremely encouraging. For example, calculators were rather easily implemented. Getting students to read was a problem at first, but tended to disappear as the year went on. TRANSITION MATHEMATICS STUDENTS HELD THEIR OWN ON PAPER-AND-PENCIL COMPUTATION, GAINED THREE TIMES AS MUCH AS COMPARISON CLASSES IN THEIR KNOWLEDGE OF ALGEBRA, AND EVEN MORE THAN THAT IN GEOMETRY. The results were so positive that the features of *Transition Mathematics* became incorporated into the UCSMP *Algebra* and *Advanced Algebra* texts, whose first drafts were written in the summer of 1985.

That summer, *Transition Mathematics* was revised for a second time, although most of the revisions were minor, befitting the success of the year.

Summative Evaluation and Test Results

In 1985–86, a carefully controlled study involving 1048 students in 41 *Transition Mathematics* classes and 976 students in 38 matched comparison classes was conducted. Fourteen of the *Transition Mathematics* classes were 7th grade, 17 were 8th grade, and 10 were composed of 9th-graders or older students. There was one less class at each level in the comparison group. Of the 35 schools involved, 7 were Chicago Public schools, 10 were in the metropolitan Chicago area, and the other 18 were from 9 states, coast to coast. Small town and rural areas were represented.

No teacher in this study taught both UCSMP and comparison classes. The sample was large so that evaluators could eliminate classes that did not match for any reason and still be left with enough pairs to judge overall results and enough students to conduct comparative item analyses. Information on obtaining the detailed results of this study is available by writing the UCSMP Evaluation Component, 5835 S. Kimbark Avenue, Chicago, IL 60637. Herein is a summary:

Several steps were taken to ensure that UCSMP and comparison students were comparable. First, students were pretested on arithmetic, geometry, and algebra readiness. This uncovered several pairs of classes that did not match. Second, if anything unusual happened to one class, such as changes in student composition, both classes of the pair were removed from the detailed analysis (though kept in the study for overall analysis). Third, when students were tested again in the late spring a few weeks before the end of the year, those students who were left in the classes had to have been well-matched at the beginning of the year. These matching criteria eliminated 20 of the 40 pairs. Of the 20 pairs that remained, 7 were 7th grade, 10 were 8th grade, and only 3 were 9th grade.

Three tests were given. First was a standardized test, the American Testronics *High School Subjects Test: General Mathematics* 40-question multiple-choice test (called HSST), chosen because it is representative of such tests, and was new and thus less likely to be familiar to any teacher. Students in all classes were tested for two other complete periods, during which they were given two additional tests: The 60-item Orleans-Hanna algebra readiness test (Orleans-Hanna) and a 19-item geometry readiness test (Geometry) used in an earlier study at the University of Chicago. It was felt that these tests would be fair to all students.

The HSST was given without calculators to three fourths of the students and with calculators to one fourth of the students. The purpose here was to see how well the *Transition Mathematics* students, accustomed to using calculators, performed in comparison to students accustomed to using paper-and-pencil. The results (for all grades) showed that when calculators were not allowed, the *Transition Mathematics* classes performed at about the same level as the comparison classes. However, when all students were allowed to use calculators on the test, the *Transition Mathematics* classes scored about 11.3% higher than the comparison classes. The results of the tests and an analysis are provided on pages T48–T49.

Test	UCSMP (7 classes)	Comparison (7 classes)	Difference (UCSMP— Comparison)
Means of class means in the sample of well-matched pairs, Grade 7			
HSST (without calculators)	24.71 (113 students)	25.56 (111 students)	-0.85
HSST (with calculators)	31.33 (49 students)	26.70 (37 students)	+4.63
Orleans-Hanna	41.36 (161 students)	38.91 (144 students)	+2.44
Geometry	9.93 (119 students)	9.17 (109 students)	+0.76
Means of class means in the sample of well-matched pairs, Grade 8			
HSST (without calculators)	24.25 (135 students)	24.97 (157 students)	-0.72
HSST (with calculators)	28.78 (58 students)	26.78 (62 students)	+2.00
Orleans-Hanna	37.24 (203 students)	35.94 (209 students)	+1.30
Geometry	10.18 (141 students)	9.12 (155 students)	+1.06
Means of class means in the sample of well-matched pairs, Grade 9			
HSST (without calculators)	19.89 (32 students)	17.77 (26 students)	+2.57
HSST (with calculators)	26.08 (13 students)	23.69 (13 students)	+2.39
Orleans-Hanna	35.76 (50 students)	34.19 (43 students)	+1.57
Geometry	7.42 (33 students)	4.82 (30 students)	+2.60
Means of class means in the sample of well-matched pairs, All Grades			
HSST (without calculators)	23.76 (280 students)	24.20 (294 students)	-0.44
HSST (with calculators)	29.27 (120 students)	26.29 (112 students)	+2.98
Orleans-Hanna	38.35 (414 students)	36.30 (396 students)	+2.05
Geometry	9.68 (293 students)	8.50 (30 students)	+1.18

■ Analysis of Test Results

The classes in the study included a very wide range of performance levels. For example, there were UCSMP and comparison classes with means over 55 (out of 70 items) on the Orleans-Hanna and other classes with means under 27 on that test. On virtually all tests, the *Transition Mathematics* classes outscored the comparison classes. These results hold for both high-performing and low-performing pairs, regardless of the year in school.

Here are the conclusions from the independent evaluators:

"THE *TRANSITION MATHEMATICS* STUDENTS OUTPERFORMED COMPARISON STUDENTS SIGNIFICANTLY IN GEOMETRY AND ALGEBRA READINESS, AND ALSO BECAME EFFECTIVE CALCULATOR USERS WITHOUT A DETERIORATION IN THEIR ARITHMETIC SKILLS."

Other results found, as given in the Summary of the report available from the Evaluation Component, are as follows: Student attitudes were not significantly different in the two groups. UCSMP students felt the real-life explanations were good, the text was challenging and interesting, and the problems difficult but fun. Reading was a problem early in the school year for teachers and students: students were unaccustomed to reading mathematics and considerable persuasion was required. Over time, reading became less problematic and teachers felt that the benefits outweighed the difficulties encountered at the beginning of the year.

Teachers also responded positively to the curriculum, and even when implementation difficulties were encountered, teachers still endorsed the ideas and intents of the curriculum. Ninth-grade teachers tended less to follow the suggestions of the project regarding pace and assignments. Only 24% of *Transition Mathematics* teachers frequently did arithmetic skill reviews, whereas 66% of the comparison teachers frequently did such reviews. Many *Transition Mathematics* teachers wanted to do more skill reviews (though studies, including this one, show that such reviews have little payoff). *Transition Mathematics* teachers liked the substantive aspects of the text, and many commented particularly on the value of the chapter on problem solving.

Despite the widespread belief that conditions favor newer materials in such studies, there is at least as much evidence that comparison classes have an advantage. In this study, teachers of comparison classes knew they were being tested from the first day of the year; we have evidence that comparison classes tested at the beginning of the year score higher on our spring tests than classes not tested at the beginning of the year. It is possible that some UCSMP and comparison classes covered a wider range of content than normal because their teachers knew what was in the other book and wanted to make sure their students had been exposed to it. UCSMP teachers have the advantage of the excitement of using materials for the first time. However, for the most part, the UCSMP teachers were using their texts for the first time and did not even have both parts of the text at the beginning of the school year. Some comparison teachers may have had the advantage of many years of teaching out of the books they used.

> "The *Transition Mathematics* students outperformed comparison students significantly in geometry and algebra readiness, and also became effective calculator users without a deterioration in their arithmetic skills."

T49

Continuing Research and Development

The summative evaluation convinced us that the approach is not only sound but quite effective and that no major changes should be made in the materials. However, many minor changes were made, based either on careful readings given to the materials by UCSMP and Scott, Foresman editors, on the test results reported on the preceding pages, or on remarks on detailed forms returned by the teachers in the summative evaluation. In particular, a lesson on probability was added to satisfy teacher requests. Also, computer exercises were integrated throughout the text.

The present version of *Transition Mathematics* also includes the appearance of four colors, of attractive pictures, and of many more supplements for teachers and students. Teachers, of course, will now have the benefit of having the full text at the beginning of the year. BECAUSE OF THE CHANGES MADE, WE EXPECT RESULTS FROM THE FORMATIVE EVALUATION TO EXTEND TO THE SCOTT, FORESMAN VERSION, FURTHER ENHANCING STUDENT PERFORMANCE.

Since November of 1985, UCSMP has sponsored an annual "User's Conference" at the University of Chicago, at which time users and prospective users of its materials can meet with each other and with authors. This conference now includes all components of the project. It provides a valuable opportunity for reports on UCSMP materials from those not involved in formal studies. We encourage users to attend this conference.

We desire to know of any studies school districts conduct using these materials. UCSMP will be happy to assist school districts by supplying a copy of the noncommercial tests we used in our summative evaluation and other information as needed.

Both Scott, Foresman and Company and UCSMP welcome comments on these materials. Please address comments either to Mathematics Product Manager, Scott, Foresman and Company, 1900 East Lake Avenue, Glenview, IL 60025, or to Zalman Usiskin, Director, UCSMP, 5835 S. Kimbark Avenue, Chicago, IL 60637.

Because of the changes made, we expect results from the formative evaluation to extend to the Scott, Foresman version, further enhancing student performance.

5 Bibliography

■ REFERENCES from Student Edition or Teacher's Edition

College Board. *Academic Preparation for College: What Students Need To Know and Be Able To Do.* New York: College Board, 1983.

Flanders, James. **"How Much of the Content in Mathematics Textbooks Is New?"** *Arithmetic Teacher,* September 1987, pp. 18–23.

Jones, Philip, and Coxford, A. *A History of Mathematics Education in the United States and Canada.* 30th Yearbook of the National Council of Teachers of Mathematics. Reston, VA: NCTM, 1970.

McKnight, Curtis, et al. *The Underachieving Curriculum: Assessing U.S. School Mathematics from an International Perspective.* Champaign, IL: Stipes Publishing Company, 1987.

National Commission on Excellence in Education. *A Nation at Risk: The Imperative for Educational Reform.* Washington, D.C.: U.S. Department of Education, 1983.

National Council of Teachers of Mathematics. *Curriculum and Evaluation Standards for School Mathematics.* Reston, VA: NCTM, 1989.

Polya, George. *How To Solve It.* Princeton, NJ: Princeton University Press, 1952.

Waits, Bert, and Demana, Franklin. **"Is Three Years Enough?"** *Mathematics Teacher,* January 1988, pp. 11–15.

■ ADDITIONAL GENERAL REFERENCES

Coxford, Arthur F., and Shulte, Albert P., editors. *The Ideas of Algebra, K–12.* Reston, VA: National Council of Teachers of Mathematics, 1988. This NCTM yearbook contains 34 articles on all aspects of the teaching of algebra.

Hanson, Viggo P., and Zweng, Marilyn J, editors. *Computers in Mathematics Education.* Reston, VA: NCTM, 1984. This NCTM yearbook provides practical suggestions about some computer activities that can be added to mathematics classes.

Hirsch, Christian R., and Zweng, Marilyn J., editors. *The Secondary School Mathematics Curriculum.* Reston, VA: NCTM, 1985. This forward-looking NCTM yearbook gives background for many of the ideas found in UCSMP texts.

Johnson, David R. *Every Minute Counts.* Palo Alto, CA: Dale Seymour Publications, 1982. *Making Minutes Count Even More.* Palo Alto, CA: Dale Seymour Publications, 1986. These booklets provide practical suggestions for using class time effectively. Comments on correcting homework, communicating in the classroom, and opening and closing activities are particularly good.

Lindquist, Mary Montgomery, and Shulte, Albert P., editors. *Learning and Teaching Geometry, K–12.* Reston, VA: NCTM, 1987. The development of geometry through all the grades is a theme throughout this yearbook, which contains many teaching ideas as well as general overviews on geometry in the curriculum.

The Mathematics Teacher. National Council of Teachers of Mathematics. 1906 Association Drive, Reston, VA 22091. This journal is an excellent source of information on all aspects of mathematics education. We believe that every secondary school mathematics teacher should join the NCTM and read this journal regularly.

Schoen, Harold L., and Zweng, Marilyn J., editors. *Estimation and Mental Computation*. Reston, VA: NCTM, 1986. This NCTM Yearbook contains as good a compilation on the subject of estimation as exists.

Usiskin, Zalman. **"Why Elementary Algebra Can, Should, and Must Be an Eighth-Grade Course for Average Students."** *Mathematics Teacher*, September 1987, pp. 428–438.

■ SOURCES for Additional Problems

The Diagram Group. *Comparisons*. New York. St. Martin's Press, 1980. This is an excellent source of visual and numerical data on such quantities as distance, area and volume, and time and speed.

Eves, Howard. *An Introduction to the History of Mathematics*. 5th ed. Philadelphia. Saunders College Publishing, 1983. This comprehensive history includes references to recent 20th-century mathematics, such as the proof of the four-color theorem. There is an outstanding collection of problems.

Hoffman, Mark, editor. *The World Almanac and Book of Facts, 1989*. New York: World Almanac, 1989.

Johnson, Otto, executive ed. *The 1989 Information Please Alamanac*. Boston: Houghton Mifflin Company, 1989. Almanacs are excellent sources of data for problems.

Joint Committee of the Mathematical Association of America and the National Council of Teachers of Mathematics. *A Sourcebook of Applications of School Mathematics*. Reston, VA: National Council of Teachers of Mathematics, 1980. This outstanding, comprehensive source of applied problems is organized in sections by mathematical content (advanced arithmetic through combinatorics and probability).

Kastner, Bernice. *Applications of Secondary School Mathematics*. Reston, VA: National Council of Teachers of Mathematics, 1978. This short paperback book provides interesting applications in physics, chemistry, biology, economics, and other fields. There is a chapter on mathematical modeling.

Sharron, Sidney, and Reys, Robert E., editors. *Applications in School Mathematics*. Reston, VA: NCTM, 1979. This NCTM yearbook is a collection of essays on applications, ways of including applications in the classroom, mathematical modeling, and other issues related to applications. There is an extensive bibliography on sources of applications.

U.S. Bureau of the Census. *Statistical Abstract of the United States: 1989*. 109th ed. Washington, D.C., 1988. This outstanding data source, published annually since 1878, summarizes statistics on the United States and provides reference to other statistical publications.

ADDITIONAL ANSWERS

CHAPTER 1 PROGRESS SELF TEST
(page 48)

26.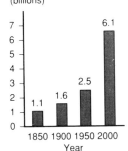
7   7.7 8

27.

29. sample: <u>Twelve</u> <u>elephants</u> marched in the circus parade.

LESSON 4-9 (pages 176–179)
33. sample: There are 6 • 3 legs on 3 insects. There are 6 • 108 legs on 108 insects. There are 6 million legs on 1 million insects. **37.** Answers vary. Samples:
a. 3.1415927, then 3.141592654; 654 not displayed; **b.** 0.0588235, then 0.058823529; 29 not displayed; **c.** 0.0769231, then 0.076923076; 076 not displayed; **d.** 076923;

CHAPTER 5 PROGRESS SELF TEST
(page 236)

28.

-4 -3 -2 -1 0 1 2 3 4

LESSON 6-5 (pages 259–263)
19.a. The difference of consecutive squares grows by 2; add 41 to 400 to get 21^2; **b.** 9; **c.** sample: The square of an even number is even, the square of an odd number is odd. **20. a.** Change line 20 to FOR M = 1 TO 10

Output:

MINUTES	COST
1	.25
2	.43
3	.61
4	.79
5	.97
6	1.15
7	1.33
8	1.51
9	1.69
10	1.87

---

b.
```
10   PRINT "INTEGER", "SQUARE"
20   FOR N = 1 TO 10
30        S = N*N
40        PRINT N, S
50   NEXT N
60   END
```

21. a.

8	9	10
63,536	262,144	1,048,576

b. the sum of the two exponents

c.

1	2	3	4	5	6	7
5	25	125	625	3,125	15,625	78,125

d. $x^a \cdot x^b = x^{(a+b)}$

LESSON 8-4 (pages 354–357)
13.

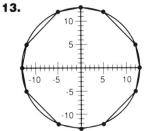

14. a. $B = (0, 12)$, $C = (8, 12)$, $D = (8, 2)$, $E = (24, 2)$, $F = (24, 0)$; **b.** $(24, 1)$; **c.** near $(4, 9)$

15.

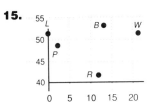

LESSON 8-5 (pages 358–361)
18. World Population (billions)

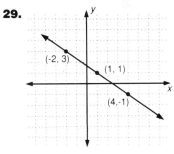

19. a. World Population (billions)

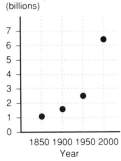

20. sample:

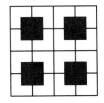

CHAPTER 12 REVIEW
(pages 564–565)

28.

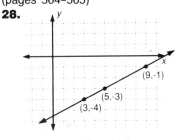

$x - 2y = 11$

29.

$4x + 6y = 10$

LESSON 13-2 (pages 573–577)
37. b. sample output:

1	1	9	3
2	1.41421356	10	3.16227766
3	1.7320501	11	3.31662479
4	2	12	3.46410162
5	2.23606798	13	3.60555128
6	2.44948974	14	3.74165739
7	2.64575131	15	3.87298335
8	2.82842713		

INDEX

international system of measurement *See* metric system of measurement.
intersecting lines, 308
interval, 8
inverse
   additive, 203
   multiplicative, 404
irrational number(s), 595–596

lattice point, 357
least common denominator, 194
least common multiple, 194, 197
legs of a right triangle, 568
Liebniz, Gottfried, 139
like terms, 542
line(s), 226
   intersecting, 308
   graphing, 556–558
   parallel, 313
   perpendicular, 122, 308
   reflecting, 362
line segment, 226
line symmetry, 367–368
linear equation(s), 556–558, 561
   graphing, 558
   intercept, 558
   slope, 557–558
   systems of, 561
linear expression, 541
linear pair, 307
list all possibilities *See* problem-solving strategies.
liter, 109, 131
long division
   algorithm, 242
   calculator key sequence, 242
lowest terms of a fraction, 43
lune, 567

magic square, 192
magnitude
   of size change, 409, 413, 460–461
   of turn, 211
make a graph *See* problem-solving strategies.
make a table *See* problem-solving strategies.
making connections
   See connections.
manipulative activities, 35, 78, 100, 113, 118, 126, 132, 202, 207, 215, 254, 286, 308, 315, 321, 323, 349, 359, 363, 372, 389, 393, 414, 460, 502, 503, 520, 550, 556, 579, 585, 590, 595, 609

mastery, T36
mathematics in other disciplines
(Applications and uses of mathematics in other disciplines are found throughout the text.)
   agriculture, 605
   art, 361, 373
   business, 22, 73, 165, 338, 445, 541
   consumer education, 15–65, 19–20, 50, 71, 73, 75, 76, 77, 144, 218, 260, 268, 269, 271, 272, 298, 424, 451, 458, 485, 497, 524, 560
   economics, 40, 41, 94, 112, 239, 605
   everyday life, 154, 165, 230, 270, 508, 556, 580
   health, 41, 86, 115, 468, 473
   language arts, 454
   music, 197, 583
   science, 9, 18, 62, 87, 201, 496
   social sciences, 6–7, 25, 78, 92, 95, 187, 279, 290, 306, 374, 512
   sports, 8, 12, 17, 103, 129, 153, 161, 170
mean, 493
means-extremes property, 512
means of a proportion, 511
measurement
   and accuracy, 100
   of angles, 118–119
   of area, 126–127, 398–400, 569
   customary system of, 104–105
   metric system of, 108–110
   of perimeter, 398–400
   of surface area, 399–400, 610
   of volume, 130–131, 399–400, 610
measuring
   numbers in, 8, 39
   three-dimensional figures, 398–400
   two-dimensional figures, 398–400
median, 496
mental math
   estimate by rounding, 19, 21
   look for special products, 395
   multiply by powers of ten, 61
   multiply using distributive property, 532, 547
   subtract using addition property of equality, 284
meter, 108
metric system of measurement, 98, 108–110
   area, 126–127
   capacity, 109
   length, 99–100, 108
   mass, 109
   prefixes, 108
   volume, 109, 130

mile, 104
minuend, 290
mirror, 362
mixed number, 39
   in decimal notation, 39–40
mode, 604, 608
model
   for addition
     putting-together, 188–189
     slide, 198–199
   for division
     rate, 484–486
     ratio comparison, 497–498
   for multiplication
     area, 384–385
     rate factor, 450–452
     repeated addition, 403
     size change, 414, 459
   for subtraction
     comparison, 290–293
     slide, 285–287
     take-away, 280–281
money system, 111, 112
multiplication
   of fractions, 418–420, 423–425
   of integers, 455–457, 465–466
   model
     area, 384–385
     rate factor, 450–452
     repeated addition, 403
     size change, 414, 459–461
   with negative numbers, 455–457, 459–461, 465–466
   by powers of ten, 54–55, 67–68, 84
   property(ies)
     associative, 395
     commutative, 385
     of equality, 440
     of one, 404
     of fractions, 423
     of negative one, 465
     related facts of multiplication and division, 437
     of zero, 464
   of rational numbers, 455–457
   using distributive property, 546–548
multiplication of fractions property, 423
multiplicative identity, 404
multiplicative identity property of one, 404
multiplicative inverse, 404
mult-rec property of division, 418

natural number, 23, 249
negative integers, 23
negative number(s), 22–23
   powers, 84, 87
   rules for addition with, 207

INDEX

use counterexamples *See* problem-solving strategies.

use a diagram/picture *See* problem-solving strategies.

use estimation *See* problem-solving strategies.

use a formula *See* problem-solving strategies.

use a graph *See* problem-solving strategies.

use logical reasoning *See* problem-solving strategies.

use a mathematical model *See* problem-solving strategies.

use physical models *See* problem-solving strategies.

use proportional thinking *See* problem-solving strategies.

use proportions *See* problem-solving strategies.

use ratios *See* problem-solving strategies.

use a table *See* problem-solving strategies.

use a theorem *See* problem-solving strategies.

U.S. system of measurement *See* customary system of measurement.

Valdes, Manuel Antonio, 34, 139 *See* history of mathematics.

value
of the expression, 140, 154
of the variable, 154

variable, 145

vectors, 201

vertex
of an angle, 117
of polygon, 226

vertical angles, 308

vertical number line, 22, 27

Viète, François, 146 *See* history of mathematics.

vinculum, 139

volume, 130–131, 393, 399–400
of a cube, 130
of rectangular solid, 393–395
of sphere, 609

whole numbers, 4, 596

Widman, Johann, 139 *See* history of mathematics.

write an equation *See* problem-solving strategies.

x-axis, 343

x-coordinate, 343

yard, 104

y-axis, 343

y-coordinate, 343

zero
absolute value of, 207
division by, 33
equations with, 465
as an integer, 23
multiplying by, 464
opposite of, 203
power, 83

$>$	is greater than	$\overleftrightarrow{AB}$	line through A and B
$<$	is less than	AB	length of segment from A to B
$=$	is equal to	$\overrightarrow{AB}$	ray starting at A and containing B
$\neq$	is not equal to	$\overline{AB}$	segment with endpoints A and B
$\leq$	is less than or equal to	$\angle ABC$	angle ABC
$\geq$	is greater than or equal to	$m\angle ABC$	measure of angle ABC
$\approx$	is approximately equal to	$\sqrt{n}$	positive square root of n
$+$	plus sign	π	Greek letter pi; $= 3.141592\ldots$ or $\approx \frac{22}{7}$.
$-$	minus sign		
$\times, \cdot$	multiplication signs	?	computer input or PRINT command
$\div, \overline{)}, /$	division signs	INT ( )	computer command rounding down to the nearest integer
$\%$	percent		
ft	abbreviation for foot	2*3	computer command for $2\cdot3$
yd	abbreviation for yard	4/3	computer command for $4\div3$
mi	abbreviation for mile	3^5	computer command for 3^5
in.	abbreviation for inch	$>=$	computer command for $\geq$
oz	abbreviation for ounce	$<=$	computer command for $\leq$
lb	abbreviation for pound	$<>$	computer command for not equal to
qt	abbreviation for quart	SQR (N)	computer command for $\sqrt{n}$
gal	abbreviation for gallon		
$n°$	n degrees	$\boxed{y^x}$ or $\boxed{x^y}$	calculator powering key
( )	parentheses	$\boxed{x!}$	calculator factorial key
[ ]	brackets	$\boxed{\sqrt{n}}$	calculator square root key
$\lvert x \rvert$	absolute value of x	$\boxed{\pm}$ or $\boxed{+/-}$	calculator negative key
$-x$	opposite of x	$\boxed{\pi}$	calculator pi key
$\perp$	is perpendicular to	$\boxed{1/x}$	calculator reciprocal key
$\parallel$	is parallel to	$\boxed{INV}, \boxed{2nd},$ or $\boxed{F}$	calculator second function key
$\rceil$	right angle symbol	$\boxed{EE}$ or $\boxed{EXP}$	calculator scientific notation key
(x, y)	ordered pair x, y		
A'	image of point A		